T0134747

Lecture Notes in Computer Science 11212

More information about this series at http://www.springer.com/series/7412

Vittorio Ferrari · Martial Hebert
Cristian Sminchisescu · Yair Weiss (Eds.)

Computer Vision – ECCV 2018

15th European Conference
Munich, Germany, September 8–14, 2018
Proceedings, Part VIII

Editors
Vittorio Ferrari
Google Research
Zurich
Switzerland

Cristian Sminchisescu
Google Research
Zurich
Switzerland

Martial Hebert
Carnegie Mellon University
Pittsburgh, PA
USA

Yair Weiss
Hebrew University of Jerusalem
Jerusalem
Israel

ISSN 0302-9743 ISSN 1611-3349 (electronic)
Lecture Notes in Computer Science
ISBN 978-3-030-01236-6 ISBN 978-3-030-01237-3 (eBook)
https://doi.org/10.1007/978-3-030-01237-3

Library of Congress Control Number: 2018955489

LNCS Sublibrary: SL6 – Image Processing, Computer Vision, Pattern Recognition, and Graphics

This Springer imprint is published by the registered company Springer Nature Switzerland AG
The registered company address is: Gewerbestrasse 11, 6330 Cham, Switzerland

Foreword

It was our great pleasure to host the European Conference on Computer Vision 2018 in Munich, Germany. This constituted by far the largest ECCV event ever. With close to 2,900 registered participants and another 600 on the waiting list one month before the conference, participation more than doubled since the last ECCV in Amsterdam. We believe that this is due to a dramatic growth of the computer vision community combined with the popularity of Munich as a major European hub of culture, science, and industry. The conference took place in the heart of Munich in the concert hall Gasteig with workshops and tutorials held at the downtown campus of the Technical University of Munich.

One of the major innovations for ECCV 2018 was the free perpetual availability of all conference and workshop papers, which is often referred to as open access. We note that this is not precisely the same use of the term as in the Budapest declaration. Since 2013, CVPR and ICCV have had their papers hosted by the Computer Vision Foundation (CVF), in parallel with the IEEE Xplore version. This has proved highly beneficial to the computer vision community.

We are delighted to announce that for ECCV 2018 a very similar arrangement was put in place with the cooperation of Springer. In particular, the author's final version will be freely available in perpetuity on a CVF page, while SpringerLink will continue to host a version with further improvements, such as activating reference links and including video. We believe that this will give readers the best of both worlds; researchers who are focused on the technical content will have a freely available version in an easily accessible place, while subscribers to SpringerLink will continue to have the additional benefits that this provides. We thank Alfred Hofmann from Springer for helping to negotiate this agreement, which we expect will continue for future versions of ECCV.

September 2018

Horst Bischof
Daniel Cremers
Bernt Schiele
Ramin Zabih

Preface

Welcome to the proceedings of the 2018 European Conference on Computer Vision (ECCV 2018) held in Munich, Germany. We are delighted to present this volume reflecting a strong and exciting program, the result of an extensive review process. In total, we received 2,439 valid paper submissions. Of these, 776 were accepted (31.8%): 717 as posters (29.4%) and 59 as oral presentations (2.4%). All oral presentations were presented as posters as well. The program selection process was complicated this year by the large increase in the number of submitted papers, +65% over ECCV 2016, and the use of CMT3 for the first time for a computer vision conference. The program selection process was supported by four program co-chairs (PCs), 126 area chairs (ACs), and 1,199 reviewers with reviews assigned.

We were primarily responsible for the design and execution of the review process. Beyond administrative rejections, we were involved in acceptance decisions only in the very few cases where the ACs were not able to agree on a decision. As PCs, and as is customary in the field, we were not allowed to co-author a submission. General co-chairs and other co-organizers who played no role in the review process were permitted to submit papers, and were treated as any other author is.

Acceptance decisions were made by two independent ACs. The ACs also made a joint recommendation for promoting papers to oral status. We decided on the final selection of oral presentations based on the ACs' recommendations. There were 126 ACs, selected according to their technical expertise, experience, and geographical diversity (63 from European, nine from Asian/Australian, and 54 from North American institutions). Indeed, 126 ACs is a substantial increase in the number of ACs due to the natural increase in the number of papers and to our desire to maintain the number of papers assigned to each AC to a manageable number so as to ensure quality. The ACs were aided by the 1,199 reviewers to whom papers were assigned for reviewing. The Program Committee was selected from committees of previous ECCV, ICCV, and CVPR conferences and was extended on the basis of suggestions from the ACs. Having a large pool of Program Committee members for reviewing allowed us to match expertise while reducing reviewer loads. No more than eight papers were assigned to a reviewer, maintaining the reviewers' load at the same level as ECCV 2016 despite the increase in the number of submitted papers.

Conflicts of interest between ACs, Program Committee members, and papers were identified based on the home institutions, and on previous collaborations of all researchers involved. To find institutional conflicts, all authors, Program Committee members, and ACs were asked to list the Internet domains of their current institutions. We assigned on average approximately 18 papers to each AC. The papers were assigned using the affinity scores from the Toronto Paper Matching System (TPMS) and additional data from the OpenReview system, managed by a UMass group. OpenReview used additional information from ACs' and authors' records to identify collaborations and to generate matches. OpenReview was invaluable in refining conflict definitions and in generating quality matches. The only glitch is that, once the matches were generated, a small percentage of papers were unassigned because of discrepancies between the OpenReview conflicts and the conflicts entered in CMT3. We manually assigned these papers. This glitch is revealing of the challenge of using multiple systems at once (CMT3 and OpenReview in this case), which needs to be addressed in future.

After assignment of papers to ACs, the ACs suggested seven reviewers per paper from the Program Committee pool. The selection and rank ordering were facilitated by the TPMS affinity scores visible to the ACs for each paper/reviewer pair. The final assignment of papers to reviewers was generated again through OpenReview in order to account for refined conflict definitions. This required new features in the OpenReview matching system to accommodate the ECCV workflow, in particular to incorporate selection ranking, and maximum reviewer load. Very few papers received fewer than three reviewers after matching and were handled through manual assignment. Reviewers were then asked to comment on the merit of each paper and to make an initial recommendation ranging from definitely reject to definitely accept, including a borderline rating. The reviewers were also asked to suggest explicit questions they wanted to see answered in the authors' rebuttal. The initial review period was five weeks. Because of the delay in getting all the reviews in, we had to delay the final release of the reviews by four days. However, because of the slack included at the tail end of the schedule, we were able to maintain the decision target date with sufficient time for all the phases. We reassigned over 100 reviews from 40 reviewers during the review period. Unfortunately, the main reason for these reassignments was reviewers declining to review, after having accepted to do so. Other reasons included technical relevance and occasional unidentified conflicts. We express our thanks to the emergency reviewers who generously accepted to perform these reviews under short notice. In addition, a substantial number of manual corrections had to do with reviewers using a different email address than the one that was used at the time of the reviewer invitation. This is revealing of a broader issue with identifying users by email addresses that change frequently enough to cause significant problems during the timespan of the conference process.

The authors were then given the opportunity to rebut the reviews, to identify factual errors, and to address the specific questions raised by the reviewers over a seven-day rebuttal period. The exact format of the rebuttal was the object of considerable debate among the organizers, as well as with prior organizers. At issue is to balance giving the author the opportunity to respond completely and precisely to the reviewers, e.g., by including graphs of experiments, while avoiding requests for completely new material or experimental results not included in the original paper. In the end, we decided on the two-page PDF document in conference format. Following this rebuttal period, reviewers and ACs discussed papers at length, after which reviewers finalized their evaluation and gave a final recommendation to the ACs. A significant percentage of the reviewers did enter their final recommendation if it did not differ from their initial recommendation. Given the tight schedule, we did not wait until all were entered.

After this discussion period, each paper was assigned to a second AC. The AC/paper matching was again run through OpenReview. Again, the OpenReview team worked quickly to implement the features specific to this process, in this case accounting for the existing AC assignment, as well as minimizing the fragmentation across ACs, so that each AC had on average only 5.5 buddy ACs to communicate with. The largest number was 11. Given the complexity of the conflicts, this was a very efficient set of assignments from OpenReview. Each paper was then evaluated by its assigned pair of ACs. For each paper, we required each of the two ACs assigned to certify both the final recommendation and the metareview (aka consolidation report). In all cases, after extensive discussions, the two ACs arrived at a common acceptance decision. We maintained these decisions, with the caveat that we did evaluate, sometimes going back to the ACs, a few papers for which the final acceptance decision substantially deviated from the consensus from the reviewers, amending three decisions in the process.

We want to thank everyone involved in making ECCV 2018 possible. The success of ECCV 2018 depended on the quality of papers submitted by the authors, and on the very hard work of the ACs and the Program Committee members. We are particularly grateful to the OpenReview team (Melisa Bok, Ari Kobren, Andrew McCallum, Michael Spector) for their support, in particular their willingness to implement new features, often on a tight schedule, to Laurent Charlin for the use of the Toronto Paper Matching System, to the CMT3 team, in particular in dealing with all the issues that arise when using a new system, to Friedrich Fraundorfer and Quirin Lohr for maintaining the online version of the program, and to the CMU staff (Keyla Cook, Lynnetta Miller, Ashley Song, Nora Kazour) for assisting with data entry/editing in CMT3. Finally, the preparation of these proceedings would not have been possible without the diligent effort of the publication chairs, Albert Ali Salah and Hamdi Dibeklioğlu, and of Anna Kramer and Alfred Hofmann from Springer.

September 2018

Vittorio Ferrari
Martial Hebert
Cristian Sminchisescu
Yair Weiss

Organization

General Chairs

Horst Bischof	Graz University of Technology, Austria
Daniel Cremers	Technical University of Munich, Germany
Bernt Schiele	Saarland University, Max Planck Institute for Informatics, Germany
Ramin Zabih	CornellNYCTech, USA

Program Committee Co-chairs

Vittorio Ferrari	University of Edinburgh, UK
Martial Hebert	Carnegie Mellon University, USA
Cristian Sminchisescu	Lund University, Sweden
Yair Weiss	Hebrew University, Israel

Local Arrangements Chairs

Björn Menze	Technical University of Munich, Germany
Matthias Niessner	Technical University of Munich, Germany

Workshop Chairs

Stefan Roth	TU Darmstadt, Germany
Laura Leal-Taixé	Technical University of Munich, Germany

Tutorial Chairs

Michael Bronstein	Università della Svizzera Italiana, Switzerland
Laura Leal-Taixé	Technical University of Munich, Germany

Website Chair

Friedrich Fraundorfer	Graz University of Technology, Austria

Demo Chairs

Federico Tombari	Technical University of Munich, Germany
Joerg Stueckler	Technical University of Munich, Germany

Publicity Chair

Giovanni Maria Farinella	University of Catania, Italy

Industrial Liaison Chairs

Florent Perronnin	Naver Labs, France
Yunchao Gong	Snap, USA
Helmut Grabner	Logitech, Switzerland

Finance Chair

Gerard Medioni	Amazon, University of Southern California, USA

Publication Chairs

Albert Ali Salah	Boğaziçi University, Turkey
Hamdi Dibeklioğlu	Bilkent University, Turkey

Area Chairs

Kalle Åström	Lund University, Sweden
Zeynep Akata	University of Amsterdam, The Netherlands
Joao Barreto	University of Coimbra, Portugal
Ronen Basri	Weizmann Institute of Science, Israel
Dhruv Batra	Georgia Tech and Facebook AI Research, USA
Serge Belongie	Cornell University, USA
Rodrigo Benenson	Google, Switzerland
Hakan Bilen	University of Edinburgh, UK
Matthew Blaschko	KU Leuven, Belgium
Edmond Boyer	Inria, France
Gabriel Brostow	University College London, UK
Thomas Brox	University of Freiburg, Germany
Marcus Brubaker	York University, Canada
Barbara Caputo	Politecnico di Torino and the Italian Institute of Technology, Italy
Tim Cootes	University of Manchester, UK
Trevor Darrell	University of California, Berkeley, USA
Larry Davis	University of Maryland at College Park, USA
Andrew Davison	Imperial College London, UK
Fernando de la Torre	Carnegie Mellon University, USA
Irfan Essa	GeorgiaTech, USA
Ali Farhadi	University of Washington, USA
Paolo Favaro	University of Bern, Switzerland
Michael Felsberg	Linköping University, Sweden

Sanja Fidler	University of Toronto, Canada
Andrew Fitzgibbon	Microsoft, Cambridge, UK
David Forsyth	University of Illinois at Urbana-Champaign, USA
Charless Fowlkes	University of California, Irvine, USA
Bill Freeman	MIT, USA
Mario Fritz	MPII, Germany
Jürgen Gall	University of Bonn, Germany
Dariu Gavrila	TU Delft, The Netherlands
Andreas Geiger	MPI-IS and University of Tübingen, Germany
Theo Gevers	University of Amsterdam, The Netherlands
Ross Girshick	Facebook AI Research, USA
Kristen Grauman	Facebook AI Research and UT Austin, USA
Abhinav Gupta	Carnegie Mellon University, USA
Kaiming He	Facebook AI Research, USA
Martial Hebert	Carnegie Mellon University, USA
Anders Heyden	Lund University, Sweden
Timothy Hospedales	University of Edinburgh, UK
Michal Irani	Weizmann Institute of Science, Israel
Phillip Isola	University of California, Berkeley, USA
Hervé Jégou	Facebook AI Research, France
David Jacobs	University of Maryland, College Park, USA
Allan Jepson	University of Toronto, Canada
Jiaya Jia	Chinese University of Hong Kong, SAR China
Fredrik Kahl	Chalmers University, USA
Hedvig Kjellström	KTH Royal Institute of Technology, Sweden
Iasonas Kokkinos	University College London and Facebook, UK
Vladlen Koltun	Intel Labs, USA
Philipp Krähenbühl	UT Austin, USA
M. Pawan Kumar	University of Oxford, UK
Kyros Kutulakos	University of Toronto, Canada
In Kweon	KAIST, South Korea
Ivan Laptev	Inria, France
Svetlana Lazebnik	University of Illinois at Urbana-Champaign, USA
Laura Leal-Taixé	Technical University of Munich, Germany
Erik Learned-Miller	University of Massachusetts, Amherst, USA
Kyoung Mu Lee	Seoul National University, South Korea
Bastian Leibe	RWTH Aachen University, Germany
Aleš Leonardis	University of Birmingham, UK
Vincent Lepetit	University of Bordeaux, France and Graz University of Technology, Austria
Fuxin Li	Oregon State University, USA
Dahua Lin	Chinese University of Hong Kong, SAR China
Jim Little	University of British Columbia, Canada
Ce Liu	Google, USA
Chen Change Loy	Nanyang Technological University, Singapore
Jiri Matas	Czech Technical University in Prague, Czechia

Yasuyuki Matsushita	Osaka University, Japan
Dimitris Metaxas	Rutgers University, USA
Greg Mori	Simon Fraser University, Canada
Vittorio Murino	Istituto Italiano di Tecnologia, Italy
Richard Newcombe	Oculus Research, USA
Minh Hoai Nguyen	Stony Brook University, USA
Sebastian Nowozin	Microsoft Research Cambridge, UK
Aude Oliva	MIT, USA
Bjorn Ommer	Heidelberg University, Germany
Tomas Pajdla	Czech Technical University in Prague, Czechia
Maja Pantic	Imperial College London and Samsung AI Research Centre Cambridge, UK
Caroline Pantofaru	Google, USA
Devi Parikh	Georgia Tech and Facebook AI Research, USA
Sylvain Paris	Adobe Research, USA
Vladimir Pavlovic	Rutgers University, USA
Marcello Pelillo	University of Venice, Italy
Patrick Pérez	Valeo, France
Robert Pless	George Washington University, USA
Thomas Pock	Graz University of Technology, Austria
Jean Ponce	Inria, France
Gerard Pons-Moll	MPII, Saarland Informatics Campus, Germany
Long Quan	Hong Kong University of Science and Technology, SAR China
Stefan Roth	TU Darmstadt, Germany
Carsten Rother	University of Heidelberg, Germany
Bryan Russell	Adobe Research, USA
Kate Saenko	Boston University, USA
Mathieu Salzmann	EPFL, Switzerland
Dimitris Samaras	Stony Brook University, USA
Yoichi Sato	University of Tokyo, Japan
Silvio Savarese	Stanford University, USA
Konrad Schindler	ETH Zurich, Switzerland
Cordelia Schmid	Inria, France and Google, France
Nicu Sebe	University of Trento, Italy
Fei Sha	University of Southern California, USA
Greg Shakhnarovich	TTI Chicago, USA
Jianbo Shi	University of Pennsylvania, USA
Abhinav Shrivastava	UMD and Google, USA
Yan Shuicheng	National University of Singapore, Singapore
Leonid Sigal	University of British Columbia, Canada
Josef Sivic	Czech Technical University in Prague, Czechia
Arnold Smeulders	University of Amsterdam, The Netherlands
Deqing Sun	NVIDIA, USA
Antonio Torralba	MIT, USA
Zhuowen Tu	University of California, San Diego, USA

Tinne Tuytelaars	KU Leuven, Belgium
Jasper Uijlings	Google, Switzerland
Joost van de Weijer	Computer Vision Center, Spain
Nuno Vasconcelos	University of California, San Diego, USA
Andrea Vedaldi	University of Oxford, UK
Olga Veksler	University of Western Ontario, Canada
Jakob Verbeek	Inria, France
Rene Vidal	Johns Hopkins University, USA
Daphna Weinshall	Hebrew University, Israel
Chris Williams	University of Edinburgh, UK
Lior Wolf	Tel Aviv University, Israel
Ming-Hsuan Yang	University of California at Merced, USA
Todd Zickler	Harvard University, USA
Andrew Zisserman	University of Oxford, UK

Technical Program Committee

Hassan Abu Alhaija
Radhakrishna Achanta
Hanno Ackermann
Ehsan Adeli
Lourdes Agapito
Aishwarya Agrawal
Antonio Agudo
Eirikur Agustsson
Karim Ahmed
Byeongjoo Ahn
Unaiza Ahsan
Emre Akbaş
Eren Aksoy
Yağız Aksoy
Alexandre Alahi
Jean-Baptiste Alayrac
Samuel Albanie
Cenek Albl
Saad Ali
Rahaf Aljundi
Jose M. Alvarez
Humam Alwassel
Toshiyuki Amano
Mitsuru Ambai
Mohamed Amer
Senjian An
Cosmin Ancuti
Peter Anderson
Juan Andrade-Cetto
Mykhaylo Andriluka
Anelia Angelova
Michel Antunes
Pablo Arbelaez
Vasileios Argyriou
Chetan Arora
Federica Arrigoni
Vassilis Athitsos
Mathieu Aubry
Shai Avidan
Yannis Avrithis
Samaneh Azadi
Hossein Azizpour
Artem Babenko
Timur Bagautdinov
Andrew Bagdanov
Hessam Bagherinezhad
Yuval Bahat
Min Bai
Qinxun Bai
Song Bai
Xiang Bai
Peter Bajcsy
Amr Bakry
Kavita Bala
Arunava Banerjee
Atsuhiko Banno
Aayush Bansal
Yingze Bao
Md Jawadul Bappy
Pierre Baqué
Dániel Baráth
Adrian Barbu
Kobus Barnard
Nick Barnes
Francisco Barranco
Adrien Bartoli
E. Bayro-Corrochano
Paul Beardlsey
Vasileios Belagiannis
Sean Bell
Ismail Ben
Boulbaba Ben Amor
Gil Ben-Artzi
Ohad Ben-Shahar
Abhijit Bendale
Rodrigo Benenson
Fabian Benitez-Quiroz
Fethallah Benmansour
Ryad Benosman
Filippo Bergamasco
David Bermudez

Jesus Bermudez-Cameo
Leonard Berrada
Gedas Bertasius
Ross Beveridge
Lucas Beyer
Bir Bhanu
S. Bhattacharya
Binod Bhattarai
Arnav Bhavsar
Simone Bianco
Adel Bibi
Pia Bideau
Josef Bigun
Arijit Biswas
Soma Biswas
Marten Bjoerkman
Volker Blanz
Vishnu Boddeti
Piotr Bojanowski
Terrance Boult
Yuri Boykov
Hakan Boyraz
Eric Brachmann
Samarth Brahmbhatt
Mathieu Bredif
Francois Bremond
Michael Brown
Luc Brun
Shyamal Buch
Pradeep Buddharaju
Aurelie Bugeau
Rudy Bunel
Xavier Burgos Artizzu
Darius Burschka
Andrei Bursuc
Zoya Bylinskii
Fabian Caba
Daniel Cabrini Hauagge
Cesar Cadena Lerma
Holger Caesar
Jianfei Cai
Junjie Cai
Zhaowei Cai
Simone Calderara
Neill Campbell
Octavia Camps
Xun Cao
Yanshuai Cao
Joao Carreira
Dan Casas
Daniel Castro
Jan Cech
M. Emre Celebi
Duygu Ceylan
Menglei Chai
Ayan Chakrabarti
Rudrasis Chakraborty
Shayok Chakraborty
Tat-Jen Cham
Antonin Chambolle
Antoni Chan
Sharat Chandran
Hyun Sung Chang
Ju Yong Chang
Xiaojun Chang
Soravit Changpinyo
Wei-Lun Chao
Yu-Wei Chao
Visesh Chari
Rizwan Chaudhry
Siddhartha Chaudhuri
Rama Chellappa
Chao Chen
Chen Chen
Cheng Chen
Chu-Song Chen
Guang Chen
Hsin-I Chen
Hwann-Tzong Chen
Kai Chen
Kan Chen
Kevin Chen
Liang-Chieh Chen
Lin Chen
Qifeng Chen
Ting Chen
Wei Chen
Xi Chen
Xilin Chen
Xinlei Chen
Yingcong Chen
Yixin Chen
Erkang Cheng
Jingchun Cheng
Ming-Ming Cheng
Wen-Huang Cheng
Yuan Cheng
Anoop Cherian
Liang-Tien Chia
Naoki Chiba
Shao-Yi Chien
Han-Pang Chiu
Wei-Chen Chiu
Nam Ik Cho
Sunghyun Cho
TaeEun Choe
Jongmoo Choi
Christopher Choy
Wen-Sheng Chu
Yung-Yu Chuang
Ondrej Chum
Joon Son Chung
Gökberk Cinbis
James Clark
Andrea Cohen
Forrester Cole
Toby Collins
John Collomosse
Camille Couprie
David Crandall
Marco Cristani
Canton Cristian
James Crowley
Yin Cui
Zhaopeng Cui
Bo Dai
Jifeng Dai
Qieyun Dai
Shengyang Dai
Yuchao Dai
Carlo Dal Mutto
Dima Damen
Zachary Daniels
Kostas Daniilidis
Donald Dansereau
Mohamed Daoudi
Abhishek Das
Samyak Datta

Achal Dave
Shalini De Mello
Teofilo deCampos
Joseph DeGol
Koichiro Deguchi
Alessio Del Bue
Stefanie Demirci
Jia Deng
Zhiwei Deng
Joachim Denzler
Konstantinos Derpanis
Aditya Deshpande
Alban Desmaison
Frédéric Devernay
Abhinav Dhall
Michel Dhome
Hamdi Dibeklioğlu
Mert Dikmen
Cosimo Distante
Ajay Divakaran
Mandar Dixit
Carl Doersch
Piotr Dollar
Bo Dong
Chao Dong
Huang Dong
Jian Dong
Jiangxin Dong
Weisheng Dong
Simon Donné
Gianfranco Doretto
Alexey Dosovitskiy
Matthijs Douze
Bruce Draper
Bertram Drost
Liang Du
Shichuan Du
Gregory Dudek
Zoran Duric
Pınar Duygulu
Hazım Ekenel
Tarek El-Gaaly
Ehsan Elhamifar
Mohamed Elhoseiny
Sabu Emmanuel
Ian Endres
Aykut Erdem
Erkut Erdem
Hugo Jair Escalante
Sergio Escalera
Victor Escorcia
Francisco Estrada
Davide Eynard
Bin Fan
Jialue Fan
Quanfu Fan
Chen Fang
Tian Fang
Yi Fang
Hany Farid
Giovanni Farinella
Ryan Farrell
Alireza Fathi
Christoph Feichtenhofer
Wenxin Feng
Martin Fergie
Cornelia Fermuller
Basura Fernando
Michael Firman
Bob Fisher
John Fisher
Mathew Fisher
Boris Flach
Matt Flagg
Francois Fleuret
David Fofi
Ruth Fong
Gian Luca Foresti
Per-Erik Forssén
David Fouhey
Katerina Fragkiadaki
Victor Fragoso
Jan-Michael Frahm
Jean-Sebastien Franco
Ohad Fried
Simone Frintrop
Huazhu Fu
Yun Fu
Olac Fuentes
Christopher Funk
Thomas Funkhouser
Brian Funt
Ryo Furukawa
Yasutaka Furukawa
Andrea Fusiello
Fatma Güney
Raghudeep Gadde
Silvano Galliani
Orazio Gallo
Chuang Gan
Bin-Bin Gao
Jin Gao
Junbin Gao
Ruohan Gao
Shenghua Gao
Animesh Garg
Ravi Garg
Erik Gartner
Simone Gasparin
Jochen Gast
Leon A. Gatys
Stratis Gavves
Liuhao Ge
Timnit Gebru
James Gee
Peter Gehler
Xin Geng
Guido Gerig
David Geronimo
Bernard Ghanem
Michael Gharbi
Golnaz Ghiasi
Spyros Gidaris
Andrew Gilbert
Rohit Girdhar
Ioannis Gkioulekas
Georgia Gkioxari
Guy Godin
Roland Goecke
Michael Goesele
Nuno Goncalves
Boqing Gong
Minglun Gong
Yunchao Gong
Abel Gonzalez-Garcia
Daniel Gordon
Paulo Gotardo
Stephen Gould

Venu Govindu
Helmut Grabner
Petr Gronat
Steve Gu
Josechu Guerrero
Anupam Guha
Jean-Yves Guillemaut
Alp Güler
Erhan Gündoğdu
Guodong Guo
Xinqing Guo
Ankush Gupta
Mohit Gupta
Saurabh Gupta
Tanmay Gupta
Abner Guzman Rivera
Timo Hackel
Sunil Hadap
Christian Haene
Ralf Haeusler
Levente Hajder
David Hall
Peter Hall
Stefan Haller
Ghassan Hamarneh
Fred Hamprecht
Onur Hamsici
Bohyung Han
Junwei Han
Xufeng Han
Yahong Han
Ankur Handa
Albert Haque
Tatsuya Harada
Mehrtash Harandi
Bharath Hariharan
Mahmudul Hasan
Tal Hassner
Kenji Hata
Soren Hauberg
Michal Havlena
Zeeshan Hayder
Junfeng He
Lei He
Varsha Hedau
Felix Heide
Wolfgang Heidrich
Janne Heikkila
Jared Heinly
Mattias Heinrich
Lisa Anne Hendricks
Dan Hendrycks
Stephane Herbin
Alexander Hermans
Luis Herranz
Aaron Hertzmann
Adrian Hilton
Michael Hirsch
Steven Hoi
Seunghoon Hong
Wei Hong
Anthony Hoogs
Radu Horaud
Yedid Hoshen
Omid Hosseini Jafari
Kuang-Jui Hsu
Winston Hsu
Yinlin Hu
Zhe Hu
Gang Hua
Chen Huang
De-An Huang
Dong Huang
Gary Huang
Heng Huang
Jia-Bin Huang
Qixing Huang
Rui Huang
Sheng Huang
Weilin Huang
Xiaolei Huang
Xinyu Huang
Zhiwu Huang
Tak-Wai Hui
Wei-Chih Hung
Junhwa Hur
Mohamed Hussein
Wonjun Hwang
Anders Hyden
Satoshi Ikehata
Nazlı Ikizler-Cinbis
Viorela Ila
Evren Imre
Eldar Insafutdinov
Go Irie
Hossam Isack
Ahmet Işcen
Daisuke Iwai
Hamid Izadinia
Nathan Jacobs
Suyog Jain
Varun Jampani
C. V. Jawahar
Dinesh Jayaraman
Sadeep Jayasumana
Laszlo Jeni
Hueihan Jhuang
Dinghuang Ji
Hui Ji
Qiang Ji
Fan Jia
Kui Jia
Xu Jia
Huaizu Jiang
Jiayan Jiang
Nianjuan Jiang
Tingting Jiang
Xiaoyi Jiang
Yu-Gang Jiang
Long Jin
Suo Jinli
Justin Johnson
Nebojsa Jojic
Michael Jones
Hanbyul Joo
Jungseock Joo
Ajjen Joshi
Amin Jourabloo
Frederic Jurie
Achuta Kadambi
Samuel Kadoury
Ioannis Kakadiaris
Zdenek Kalal
Yannis Kalantidis
Sinan Kalkan
Vicky Kalogeiton
Sunkavalli Kalyan
J.-K. Kamarainen

Martin Kampel
Kenichi Kanatani
Angjoo Kanazawa
Melih Kandemir
Sing Bing Kang
Zhuoliang Kang
Mohan Kankanhalli
Juho Kannala
Abhishek Kar
Amlan Kar
Svebor Karaman
Leonid Karlinsky
Zoltan Kato
Parneet Kaur
Hiroshi Kawasaki
Misha Kazhdan
Margret Keuper
Sameh Khamis
Naeemullah Khan
Salman Khan
Hadi Kiapour
Joe Kileel
Chanho Kim
Gunhee Kim
Hansung Kim
Junmo Kim
Junsik Kim
Kihwan Kim
Minyoung Kim
Tae Hyun Kim
Tae-Kyun Kim
Akisato Kimura
Zsolt Kira
Alexander Kirillov
Kris Kitani
Maria Klodt
Patrick Knöbelreiter
Jan Knopp
Reinhard Koch
Alexander Kolesnikov
Chen Kong
Naejin Kong
Shu Kong
Piotr Koniusz
Simon Korman
Andreas Koschan
Dimitrios Kosmopoulos
Satwik Kottur
Balazs Kovacs
Adarsh Kowdle
Mike Krainin
Gregory Kramida
Ranjay Krishna
Ravi Krishnan
Matej Kristan
Pavel Krsek
Volker Krueger
Alexander Krull
Hilde Kuehne
Andreas Kuhn
Arjan Kuijper
Zuzana Kukelova
Kuldeep Kulkarni
Shiro Kumano
Avinash Kumar
Vijay Kumar
Abhijit Kundu
Sebastian Kurtek
Junseok Kwon
Jan Kybic
Alexander Ladikos
Shang-Hong Lai
Wei-Sheng Lai
Jean-Francois Lalonde
John Lambert
Zhenzhong Lan
Charis Lanaras
Oswald Lanz
Dong Lao
Longin Jan Latecki
Justin Lazarow
Huu Le
Chen-Yu Lee
Gim Hee Lee
Honglak Lee
Hsin-Ying Lee
Joon-Young Lee
Seungyong Lee
Stefan Lee
Yong Jae Lee
Zhen Lei
Ido Leichter
Victor Lempitsky
Spyridon Leonardos
Marius Leordeanu
Matt Leotta
Thomas Leung
Stefan Leutenegger
Gil Levi
Aviad Levis
Jose Lezama
Ang Li
Dingzeyu Li
Dong Li
Haoxiang Li
Hongdong Li
Hongsheng Li
Hongyang Li
Jianguo Li
Kai Li
Ruiyu Li
Wei Li
Wen Li
Xi Li
Xiaoxiao Li
Xin Li
Xirong Li
Xuelong Li
Xueting Li
Yeqing Li
Yijun Li
Yin Li
Yingwei Li
Yining Li
Yongjie Li
Yu-Feng Li
Zechao Li
Zhengqi Li
Zhenyang Li
Zhizhong Li
Xiaodan Liang
Renjie Liao
Zicheng Liao
Bee Lim
Jongwoo Lim
Joseph Lim
Ser-Nam Lim
Chen-Hsuan Lin

Shih-Yao Lin
Tsung-Yi Lin
Weiyao Lin
Yen-Yu Lin
Haibin Ling
Or Litany
Roee Litman
Anan Liu
Changsong Liu
Chen Liu
Ding Liu
Dong Liu
Feng Liu
Guangcan Liu
Luoqi Liu
Miaomiao Liu
Nian Liu
Risheng Liu
Shu Liu
Shuaicheng Liu
Sifei Liu
Tyng-Luh Liu
Wanquan Liu
Weiwei Liu
Xialei Liu
Xiaoming Liu
Yebin Liu
Yiming Liu
Ziwei Liu
Zongyi Liu
Liliana Lo Presti
Edgar Lobaton
Chengjiang Long
Mingsheng Long
Roberto Lopez-Sastre
Amy Loufti
Brian Lovell
Canyi Lu
Cewu Lu
Feng Lu
Huchuan Lu
Jiajun Lu
Jiasen Lu
Jiwen Lu
Yang Lu
Yujuan Lu
Simon Lucey
Jian-Hao Luo
Jiebo Luo
Pablo Márquez-Neila
Matthias Müller
Chao Ma
Chih-Yao Ma
Lin Ma
Shugao Ma
Wei-Chiu Ma
Zhanyu Ma
Oisin Mac Aodha
Will Maddern
Ludovic Magerand
Marcus Magnor
Vijay Mahadevan
Mohammad Mahoor
Michael Maire
Subhransu Maji
Ameesh Makadia
Atsuto Maki
Yasushi Makihara
Mateusz Malinowski
Tomasz Malisiewicz
Arun Mallya
Roberto Manduchi
Junhua Mao
Dmitrii Marin
Joe Marino
Kenneth Marino
Elisabeta Marinoiu
Ricardo Martin
Aleix Martinez
Julieta Martinez
Aaron Maschinot
Jonathan Masci
Bogdan Matei
Diana Mateus
Stefan Mathe
Kevin Matzen
Bruce Maxwell
Steve Maybank
Walterio Mayol-Cuevas
Mason McGill
Stephen Mckenna
Roey Mechrez
Christopher Mei
Heydi Mendez-Vazquez
Deyu Meng
Thomas Mensink
Bjoern Menze
Domingo Mery
Qiguang Miao
Tomer Michaeli
Antoine Miech
Ondrej Miksik
Anton Milan
Gregor Miller
Cai Minjie
Majid Mirmehdi
Ishan Misra
Niloy Mitra
Anurag Mittal
Nirbhay Modhe
Davide Modolo
Pritish Mohapatra
Pascal Monasse
Mathew Monfort
Taesup Moon
Sandino Morales
Vlad Morariu
Philippos Mordohai
Francesc Moreno
Henrique Morimitsu
Yael Moses
Ben-Ezra Moshe
Roozbeh Mottaghi
Yadong Mu
Lopamudra Mukherjee
Mario Munich
Ana Murillo
Damien Muselet
Armin Mustafa
Siva Karthik Mustikovela
Moin Nabi
Sobhan Naderi
Hajime Nagahara
Varun Nagaraja
Tushar Nagarajan
Arsha Nagrani
Nikhil Naik
Atsushi Nakazawa

P. J. Narayanan
Charlie Nash
Lakshmanan Nataraj
Fabian Nater
Lukáš Neumann
Natalia Neverova
Alejandro Newell
Phuc Nguyen
Xiaohan Nie
David Nilsson
Ko Nishino
Zhenxing Niu
Shohei Nobuhara
Klas Nordberg
Mohammed Norouzi
David Novotny
Ifeoma Nwogu
Matthew O'Toole
Guillaume Obozinski
Jean-Marc Odobez
Eyal Ofek
Ferda Ofli
Tae-Hyun Oh
Iason Oikonomidis
Takeshi Oishi
Takahiro Okabe
Takayuki Okatani
Vlad Olaru
Michael Opitz
Jose Oramas
Vicente Ordonez
Ivan Oseledets
Aljosa Osep
Magnus Oskarsson
Martin R. Oswald
Wanli Ouyang
Andrew Owens
Mustafa Özuysal
Jinshan Pan
Xingang Pan
Rameswar Panda
Sharath Pankanti
Julien Pansiot
Nicolas Papadakis
George Papandreou
N. Papanikolopoulos
Hyun Soo Park
In Kyu Park
Jaesik Park
Omkar Parkhi
Alvaro Parra Bustos
C. Alejandro Parraga
Vishal Patel
Deepak Pathak
Ioannis Patras
Viorica Patraucean
Genevieve Patterson
Kim Pedersen
Robert Peharz
Selen Pehlivan
Xi Peng
Bojan Pepik
Talita Perciano
Federico Pernici
Adrian Peter
Stavros Petridis
Vladimir Petrovic
Henning Petzka
Tomas Pfister
Trung Pham
Justus Piater
Massimo Piccardi
Sudeep Pillai
Pedro Pinheiro
Lerrel Pinto
Bernardo Pires
Aleksis Pirinen
Fiora Pirri
Leonid Pischulin
Tobias Ploetz
Bryan Plummer
Yair Poleg
Jean Ponce
Gerard Pons-Moll
Jordi Pont-Tuset
Alin Popa
Fatih Porikli
Horst Possegger
Viraj Prabhu
Andrea Prati
Maria Priisalu
Véronique Prinet
Victor Prisacariu
Jan Prokaj
Nicolas Pugeault
Luis Puig
Ali Punjani
Senthil Purushwalkam
Guido Pusiol
Guo-Jun Qi
Xiaojuan Qi
Hongwei Qin
Shi Qiu
Faisal Qureshi
Matthias Rüther
Petia Radeva
Umer Rafi
Rahul Raguram
Swaminathan Rahul
Varun Ramakrishna
Kandan Ramakrishnan
Ravi Ramamoorthi
Vignesh Ramanathan
Vasili Ramanishka
R. Ramasamy Selvaraju
Rene Ranftl
Carolina Raposo
Nikhil Rasiwasia
Nalini Ratha
Sai Ravela
Avinash Ravichandran
Ramin Raziperchikolaei
Sylvestre-Alvise Rebuffi
Adria Recasens
Joe Redmon
Timo Rehfeld
Michal Reinstein
Konstantinos Rematas
Haibing Ren
Shaoqing Ren
Wenqi Ren
Zhile Ren
Hamid Rezatofighi
Nicholas Rhinehart
Helge Rhodin
Elisa Ricci
Eitan Richardson
Stephan Richter

Gernot Riegler
Hayko Riemenschneider
Tammy Riklin Raviv
Ergys Ristani
Tobias Ritschel
Mariano Rivera
Samuel Rivera
Antonio Robles-Kelly
Ignacio Rocco
Jason Rock
Emanuele Rodola
Mikel Rodriguez
Gregory Rogez
Marcus Rohrbach
Gemma Roig
Javier Romero
Olaf Ronneberger
Amir Rosenfeld
Bodo Rosenhahn
Guy Rosman
Arun Ross
Samuel Rota Bulò
Peter Roth
Constantin Rothkopf
Sebastien Roy
Amit Roy-Chowdhury
Ognjen Rudovic
Adria Ruiz
Javier Ruiz-del-Solar
Christian Rupprecht
Olga Russakovsky
Chris Russell
Alexandre Sablayrolles
Fereshteh Sadeghi
Ryusuke Sagawa
Hideo Saito
Elham Sakhaee
Albert Ali Salah
Conrad Sanderson
Koppal Sanjeev
Aswin Sankaranarayanan
Elham Saraee
Jason Saragih
Sudeep Sarkar
Imari Sato
Shin'ichi Satoh
Torsten Sattler
Bogdan Savchynskyy
Johannes Schönberger
Hanno Scharr
Walter Scheirer
Bernt Schiele
Frank Schmidt
Tanner Schmidt
Dirk Schnieders
Samuel Schulter
William Schwartz
Alexander Schwing
Ozan Sener
Soumyadip Sengupta
Laura Sevilla-Lara
Mubarak Shah
Shishir Shah
Fahad Shahbaz Khan
Amir Shahroudy
Jing Shao
Xiaowei Shao
Roman Shapovalov
Nataliya Shapovalova
Ali Sharif Razavian
Gaurav Sharma
Mohit Sharma
Pramod Sharma
Viktoriia Sharmanska
Eli Shechtman
Mark Sheinin
Evan Shelhamer
Chunhua Shen
Li Shen
Wei Shen
Xiaohui Shen
Xiaoyong Shen
Ziyi Shen
Lu Sheng
Baoguang Shi
Boxin Shi
Kevin Shih
Hyunjung Shim
Ilan Shimshoni
Young Min Shin
Koichi Shinoda
Matthew Shreve
Tianmin Shu
Zhixin Shu
Kaleem Siddiqi
Gunnar Sigurdsson
Nathan Silberman
Tomas Simon
Abhishek Singh
Gautam Singh
Maneesh Singh
Praveer Singh
Richa Singh
Saurabh Singh
Sudipta Sinha
Vladimir Smutny
Noah Snavely
Cees Snoek
Kihyuk Sohn
Eric Sommerlade
Sanghyun Son
Bi Song
Shiyu Song
Shuran Song
Xuan Song
Yale Song
Yang Song
Yibing Song
Lorenzo Sorgi
Humberto Sossa
Pratul Srinivasan
Michael Stark
Bjorn Stenger
Rainer Stiefelhagen
Joerg Stueckler
Jan Stuehmer
Hang Su
Hao Su
Shuochen Su
R. Subramanian
Yusuke Sugano
Akihiro Sugimoto
Baochen Sun
Chen Sun
Jian Sun
Jin Sun
Lin Sun
Min Sun

Qing Sun
Zhaohui Sun
David Suter
Eran Swears
Raza Syed Hussain
T. Syeda-Mahmood
Christian Szegedy
Duy-Nguyen Ta
Tolga Taşdizen
Hemant Tagare
Yuichi Taguchi
Ying Tai
Yu-Wing Tai
Jun Takamatsu
Hugues Talbot
Toru Tamak
Robert Tamburo
Chaowei Tan
Meng Tang
Peng Tang
Siyu Tang
Wei Tang
Junli Tao
Ran Tao
Xin Tao
Makarand Tapaswi
Jean-Philippe Tarel
Maxim Tatarchenko
Bugra Tekin
Demetri Terzopoulos
Christian Theobalt
Diego Thomas
Rajat Thomas
Qi Tian
Xinmei Tian
YingLi Tian
Yonghong Tian
Yonglong Tian
Joseph Tighe
Radu Timofte
Massimo Tistarelli
Sinisa Todorovic
Pavel Tokmakov
Giorgos Tolias
Federico Tombari
Tatiana Tommasi
Chetan Tonde
Xin Tong
Akihiko Torii
Andrea Torsello
Florian Trammer
Du Tran
Quoc-Huy Tran
Rudolph Triebel
Alejandro Troccoli
Leonardo Trujillo
Tomasz Trzcinski
Sam Tsai
Yi-Hsuan Tsai
Hung-Yu Tseng
Vagia Tsiminaki
Aggeliki Tsoli
Wei-Chih Tu
Shubham Tulsiani
Fred Tung
Tony Tung
Matt Turek
Oncel Tuzel
Georgios Tzimiropoulos
Ilkay Ulusoy
Osman Ulusoy
Dmitry Ulyanov
Paul Upchurch
Ben Usman
Evgeniya Ustinova
Himanshu Vajaria
Alexander Vakhitov
Jack Valmadre
Ernest Valveny
Jan van Gemert
Grant Van Horn
Jagannadan Varadarajan
Gul Varol
Sebastiano Vascon
Francisco Vasconcelos
Mayank Vatsa
Javier Vazquez-Corral
Ramakrishna Vedantam
Ashok Veeraraghavan
Andreas Veit
Raviteja Vemulapalli
Jonathan Ventura
Matthias Vestner
Minh Vo
Christoph Vogel
Michele Volpi
Carl Vondrick
Sven Wachsmuth
Toshikazu Wada
Michael Waechter
Catherine Wah
Jacob Walker
Jun Wan
Boyu Wang
Chen Wang
Chunyu Wang
De Wang
Fang Wang
Hongxing Wang
Hua Wang
Jiang Wang
Jingdong Wang
Jinglu Wang
Jue Wang
Le Wang
Lei Wang
Lezi Wang
Liang Wang
Lichao Wang
Lijun Wang
Limin Wang
Liwei Wang
Naiyan Wang
Oliver Wang
Qi Wang
Ruiping Wang
Shenlong Wang
Shu Wang
Song Wang
Tao Wang
Xiaofang Wang
Xiaolong Wang
Xinchao Wang
Xinggang Wang
Xintao Wang
Yang Wang
Yu-Chiang Frank Wang
Yu-Xiong Wang

Zhaowen Wang
Zhe Wang
Anne Wannenwetsch
Simon Warfield
Scott Wehrwein
Donglai Wei
Ping Wei
Shih-En Wei
Xiu-Shen Wei
Yichen Wei
Xie Weidi
Philippe Weinzaepfel
Longyin Wen
Eric Wengrowski
Tomas Werner
Michael Wilber
Rick Wildes
Olivia Wiles
Kyle Wilson
David Wipf
Kwan-Yee Wong
Daniel Worrall
John Wright
Baoyuan Wu
Chao-Yuan Wu
Jiajun Wu
Jianxin Wu
Tianfu Wu
Xiaodong Wu
Xiaohe Wu
Xinxiao Wu
Yang Wu
Yi Wu
Ying Wu
Yuxin Wu
Zheng Wu
Stefanie Wuhrer
Yin Xia
Tao Xiang
Yu Xiang
Lei Xiao
Tong Xiao
Yang Xiao
Cihang Xie
Dan Xie
Jianwen Xie
Jin Xie
Lingxi Xie
Pengtao Xie
Saining Xie
Wenxuan Xie
Yuchen Xie
Bo Xin
Junliang Xing
Peng Xingchao
Bo Xiong
Fei Xiong
Xuehan Xiong
Yuanjun Xiong
Chenliang Xu
Danfei Xu
Huijuan Xu
Jia Xu
Weipeng Xu
Xiangyu Xu
Yan Xu
Yuanlu Xu
Jia Xue
Tianfan Xue
Erdem Yörük
Abhay Yadav
Deshraj Yadav
Payman Yadollahpour
Yasushi Yagi
Toshihiko Yamasaki
Fei Yan
Hang Yan
Junchi Yan
Junjie Yan
Sijie Yan
Keiji Yanai
Bin Yang
Chih-Yuan Yang
Dong Yang
Herb Yang
Jianchao Yang
Jianwei Yang
Jiaolong Yang
Jie Yang
Jimei Yang
Jufeng Yang
Linjie Yang
Michael Ying Yang
Ming Yang
Ruiduo Yang
Ruigang Yang
Shuo Yang
Wei Yang
Xiaodong Yang
Yanchao Yang
Yi Yang
Angela Yao
Bangpeng Yao
Cong Yao
Jian Yao
Ting Yao
Julian Yarkony
Mark Yatskar
Jinwei Ye
Mao Ye
Mei-Chen Yeh
Raymond Yeh
Serena Yeung
Kwang Moo Yi
Shuai Yi
Alper Yılmaz
Lijun Yin
Xi Yin
Zhaozheng Yin
Xianghua Ying
Ryo Yonetani
Donghyun Yoo
Ju Hong Yoon
Kuk-Jin Yoon
Chong You
Shaodi You
Aron Yu
Fisher Yu
Gang Yu
Jingyi Yu
Ke Yu
Licheng Yu
Pei Yu
Qian Yu
Rong Yu
Shoou-I Yu
Stella Yu
Xiang Yu

Yang Yu
Zhiding Yu
Ganzhao Yuan
Jing Yuan
Junsong Yuan
Lu Yuan
Stefanos Zafeiriou
Sergey Zagoruyko
Amir Zamir
K. Zampogiannis
Andrei Zanfir
Mihai Zanfir
Pablo Zegers
Eyasu Zemene
Andy Zeng
Xingyu Zeng
Yun Zeng
De-Chuan Zhan
Cheng Zhang
Dong Zhang
Guofeng Zhang
Han Zhang
Hang Zhang
Hanwang Zhang
Jian Zhang
Jianguo Zhang
Jianming Zhang
Jiawei Zhang
Junping Zhang
Lei Zhang
Linguang Zhang
Ning Zhang
Qing Zhang
Quanshi Zhang
Richard Zhang
Runze Zhang
Shanshan Zhang
Shiliang Zhang
Shu Zhang
Ting Zhang
Xiangyu Zhang
Xiaofan Zhang
Xu Zhang
Yimin Zhang
Yinda Zhang
Yongqiang Zhang
Yuting Zhang
Zhanpeng Zhang
Ziyu Zhang
Bin Zhao
Chen Zhao
Hang Zhao
Hengshuang Zhao
Qijun Zhao
Rui Zhao
Yue Zhao
Enliang Zheng
Liang Zheng
Stephan Zheng
Wei-Shi Zheng
Wenming Zheng
Yin Zheng
Yinqiang Zheng
Yuanjie Zheng
Guangyu Zhong
Bolei Zhou
Guang-Tong Zhou
Huiyu Zhou
Jiahuan Zhou
S. Kevin Zhou
Tinghui Zhou
Wengang Zhou
Xiaowei Zhou
Xingyi Zhou
Yin Zhou
Zihan Zhou
Fan Zhu
Guangming Zhu
Ji Zhu
Jiejie Zhu
Jun-Yan Zhu
Shizhan Zhu
Siyu Zhu
Xiangxin Zhu
Xiatian Zhu
Yan Zhu
Yingying Zhu
Yixin Zhu
Yuke Zhu
Zhenyao Zhu
Liansheng Zhuang
Zeeshan Zia
Karel Zimmermann
Daniel Zoran
Danping Zou
Qi Zou
Silvia Zuffi
Wangmeng Zuo
Xinxin Zuo

Contents – Part VIII

Poster Session

Computational Photography

Stereo and Reconstruction

Poster Session

Learning 3D Keypoint Descriptors for Non-rigid Shape Matching

Hanyu Wang, Jianwei Guo, Dong-Ming Yan(✉), Weize Quan, and Xiaopeng Zhang

NLPR, Institute of Automation, Chinese Academy of Sciences, Beijing, China
jianwei.guo@nlpr.ia.ac.cn, yandongming@gmail.com, xiaopeng.zhang@ia.ac.cn

Abstract. In this paper, we present a novel deep learning framework that derives discriminative local descriptors for 3D surface shapes. In contrast to previous convolutional neural networks (CNNs) that rely on rendering multi-view images or extracting intrinsic shape properties, we parameterize the multi-scale localized neighborhoods of a keypoint into regular 2D grids, which are termed as 'geometry images'. The benefits of such geometry images include retaining sufficient geometric information, as well as allowing the usage of standard CNNs. Specifically, we leverage a triplet network to perform deep metric learning, which takes a set of triplets as input, and a newly designed triplet loss function is minimized to distinguish between similar and dissimilar pairs of keypoints. At the testing stage, given a geometry image of a point of interest, our network outputs a discriminative local descriptor for it. Experimental results for non-rigid shape matching on several benchmarks demonstrate the superior performance of our learned descriptors over traditional descriptors and the state-of-the-art learning-based alternatives.

Keywords: Local feature descriptor · Triplet CNNs
Non-rigid shapes

1 Introduction

Designing local descriptors for 3D surface points is within common interests in both computer vision and computer graphics communities. Typically, a local descriptor refers to an informative representation stored in a multi-dimensional vector that describes the local geometry of the shape around a keypoint. It plays a crucial role in a variety of vision tasks, such as shape correspondence [1,2], object recognition [3], shape matching [4,5], shape retrieval [6,7], and surface registration [8], to name a few.

H. Wang and J. Guo are joint first authors with equal contribution.

Electronic supplementary material The online version of this chapter (https://doi.org/10.1007/978-3-030-01237-3_1) contains supplementary material, which is available to authorized users.

V. Ferrari et al. (Eds.): ECCV 2018, LNCS 11212, pp. 3–20, 2018.
https://doi.org/10.1007/978-3-030-01237-3_1

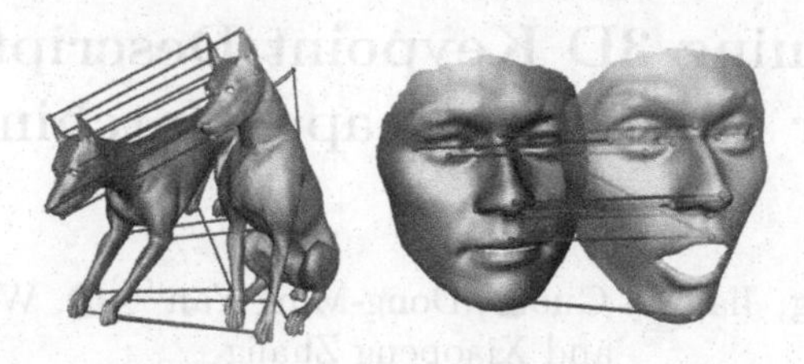

Fig. 1. Our non-rigid shape matching results using a set of landmark points (red and green spheres). The Dog shapes (21 correct matches from 22 keypoints) are from TOSCA [9] and Face shapes (13 correct matches from 15 keypoints) are from [10]. The incorrect correspondences are drawn using red lines. (Color figure online)

Over the last decades, a large number of local descriptors have been actively investigated by the research community. Despite the recent interests, however, designing discriminative and robust descriptors is still a non-trivial and challenging task. Early works focus on deriving shape descriptors based on hand-crafted features, including spin images [11], curvature features [12], heat kernel signatures [13], etc. Although these descriptors can represent the local behavior of the shape effectively, the performance of these methods is still largely limited by the representation power of the hand-tuned parameters.

Recently, convolutional neural networks (CNNs) have achieved a significant performance breakthrough in many image analysis tasks. Inspired by the remarkable success of applying deep learning in many fields, recent approaches have been proposed to learn local descriptors for 3D shapes in an either extrinsic or intrinsic manner. The former usually takes multi-view images [14] or volumetric representations [15] as input, but is suffers from strong requirements on view selection and low voxel resolutions. While the latter kind of methods generalizes the CNN paradigm to non-Euclidean manifolds [16], they are able to learn invariant shape signatures for non-rigid shape analysis. However, since these methods learn information relating to shape types and structures that vary from different datasets, their generalization ability is defective. As a result, these methods perform unstable on different domains.

In this paper, we propose another novel approach for local descriptors learning, that can capture the local geometric essence of a 3D shape. We draw inspiration from the recent work of [17] which used geometry images for learning global surface features for shape classification. Different from their work, we construct a small set of geometry images from multi-scale local patches around each keypoint on the surface. Then, the fundamental low-level geometric features can be encoded into the pixels of these regular geometry images, on which standard CNNs can be applied directly. More specifically, we train a well-known triplet network [18,19] with a pre-training phase and an improved triplet loss function. The objective is to learn a descriptor that minimizes the corresponding points distance while maximizes the non-corresponding points distance in descriptor space. In summary, our main contributions are the following:

- We develop a new 3D keypoint descriptor based on specially designed triplet networks, which is dedicated to processing local geometry images encoding very low-level geometric information.
- We design a novel triplet loss function that can control the dispersion of anchor-positive descriptor distance, thus improving the performance of our descriptor effectively.
- We show that the proposed concise framework has better generalization capability across different datasets than existing descriptors.

2 Related Work

A large variety of 3D local feature descriptors have been proposed in the literature. These approaches can be roughly classified into two categories: traditional hand-crafted descriptors and learned local descriptors.

Hand-Crafted Local Descriptors. Early works focus on deriving shape descriptors based on hand-crafted features [20,21]. A detailed survey is out of the scope of this paper, so we briefly review some representative techniques. For rigid shapes, some successful *extrinsic* descriptors have been proposed, for example, spin images (SI) [11], 3D shape context (3DSC) [22], MeshHOG descriptor [23], signature of histogram of orientations (SHOT) [24], rotational projection statistics (RoPS) [25]. Obviously, these approaches are invariant under rigid Euclidean transformations, but not under deformations. To deal with isometric deformations, there have been some *intrinsic* descriptors based on geodesic distances [26] or spectral geometry. Such descriptors include heat kernel signature (HKS) [13], wave kernel signatures (WKS) [27], intrinsic shape context (ISC) [28] and optimal spectral descriptors (OSD) [29]. However, both extrinsic and intrinsic descriptors rely on a limited predefined set of hand-tuned parameters, which are tailored for task-specific scenarios.

Deep-Learned Local Descriptors. Recently, deep learning based methods have attracted large attention because they tend to automatically learn features from raw input data, so as to avoid manually engineered features. Wei et al. [30] employe a CNN architecture to learn invariant descriptors in arbitrary complex poses and clothings, where their system is trained with a large dataset of depth maps. Zeng et al. [15] present another data-driven 3D keypoint descriptor for robustly matching local RGB-D data. Since they use 3D volumetric CNNs, this voxel-based approach is limited to low resolutions due to the high memory and computational cost. Qi et al. [31] propose a deep net framework, named PointNet, that can directly learn point features from unordered point sets to compute shape correspondences. Khoury et al. [32] present an approach to learn local compact geometric features (CGF) for unstructured point clouds, by mapping high-dimensional histograms into low-dimensional Euclidean spaces. Huang et al. [14] recently introduce a new local descriptor by taking multiple rendered views in multiple scales and processing them through a classic 2D CNN. While this method has been successfully used in many applications, it still suffers from strong requirements on view selection, as a result the 2D projection images are not geometrically informative. In addition, whether this approach can be used for non-rigid shape matching is somewhat elusive.

Another family of methods are based on the notion of *geometric deep learning* [33], where they generalize CNN to non-Euclidean manifolds. Various frameworks have been introduced to solve descriptor learning or correspondence learning problems, including localized spectral CNN (LSCNN) [34], geodesic CNN (GCNN) [35], Anisotropic CNN (ACNN) [36], mixture model networks (MoNet) [16], deep functional maps (FMNet) [37], and so on. Different from this kind of methods, our work utilizes geometry images to locally flatten the non-Euclidean patch to the 2D domain so that standard convolutional networks can be used.

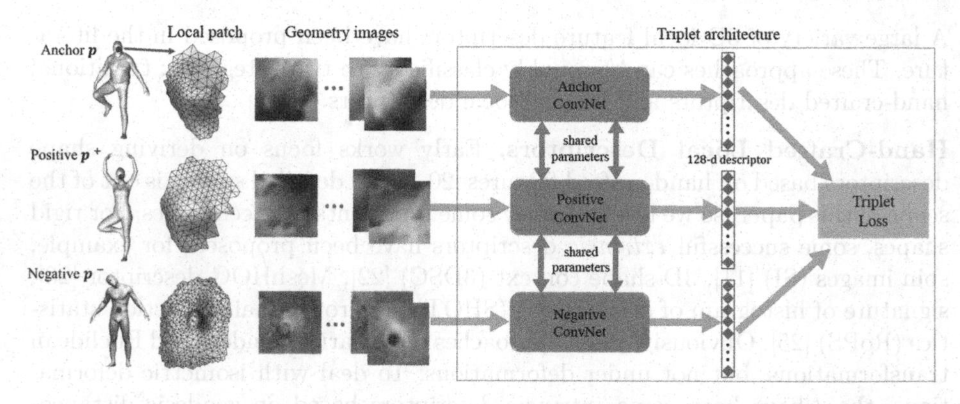

Fig. 2. Overview of our local descriptor training framework. We start with extracting local patches around the keypoints (shown in purple color), and generate geometry images for them. Then a triplet is formed and further processed through a triplet network, where we train this network using an objective function (triplet loss function). (Color figure online)

3 Methodology Overview

Given a keypoint (or any point of interest) $\mathbf{p}$ on a surface shape $\mathcal{S} \subset \mathbb{R}^3$, our goal is to learn a non-linear feature embedding function $f(\mathbf{p}) : \mathbb{R}^3 \rightarrow \mathbb{R}^d$ which outputs a d-dimensional descriptor $X_{\mathbf{p}} \in \mathbb{R}^d$ for that point. The embedding function is carefully designed such that the distance between descriptors of geometrically and semantically similar keypoints is as small as possible. In this paper, we use the L_2 Euclidean norm as the similarity metric between descriptors: $D(X_{\mathbf{p}_i}, X_{\mathbf{p}_j}) = ||X_{\mathbf{p}_i} - X_{\mathbf{p}_j}||_2$.

Geometry Image. Due to space limitations, here we just briefly review the concept of the *geometry image*, which is a new kind of mesh representation technique introduced by Gu et al. [38]. It represents an irregular mesh as a 2D image by parameterizing it onto a square domain. Using this parametrization, the geometric properties of the original mesh can be resampled and encoded into the pixels of an image. In order to parametrize arbitrary mesh onto a square, the mesh should be firstly cut into a topological disk.

Pipeline. The core part of our approach is a newly proposed learning framework as illustrated in Fig. 2. At off-line training phase, we propose to learn the descriptors by utilizing a triplet network, which are composed of three identical convolutional networks ("ConvNet" for simplicity) sharing the same architecture and parameters. We feed a set of triplets into the ConvNet branches to characterize the descriptor similarity relationship. Here, a triplet $t = (I(\mathbf{p}), I(\mathbf{p}^{+}), I(\mathbf{p}^{-}))$ contains an anchor point $\mathbf{p}$, a positive point $\mathbf{p}^{+}$, and a negative point $\mathbf{p}^{-}$, where $I(\mathbf{p})$ represents a geometry image encoding the local geometric context around $\mathbf{p}$. By "positive" we mean that $\mathbf{p}$ and $\mathbf{p}^{+}$ are correspondingly similar keypoints, and by "negative" we mean $\mathbf{p}^{-}$ is dissimilar to the anchor point $\mathbf{p}$. Based on the training data, we optimize the network parameters by using a minimized-deviation triplet loss function to enforce that, in the final descriptor space, the positive point should be much closer to the anchor point than any other negative points. Once trained, we could generate a 128-d local descriptor for a keypoint by applying the individual ConvNet on one input geometry image.

4 CNN Architecture and Training

In this section, we describe the details of our network architecture and how it can be trained automatically and efficiently to learn the embedding function.

4.1 Training Data Preparation

A rich and representative training dataset is the key to the success of CNN-based methods. For our non-rigid shape analysis purpose, a good local descriptor should be invariant with respect to noise, transformations, and non-isometric deformations. To meet above requirements, we choose the most recent and particularly challenging FAUST dataset [39], which contains noisy, realistically deforming meshes of different people in a variety of poses. Furthermore, full-body ground-truth correspondences between the shapes are known for all points.

However, note that our proposed approach is generalizable, that is to say, our network is trained on one dataset, but can be applied to other datasets. In Sect. 5, we will demonstrate the generalization ability of our method.

Keypoints Annotation. To detect the keypoints, we propose a semi-automatic approach. First, candidate keypoint locations can be determined by leveraging any 3D interest point detectors (e.g., 3D-Harris [40]). Then we manually adjust them by removing unsuitable candidates or adding some missing keypoints. Fortunately, since the ground-truth point-wise correspondence has already been defined in FAUST, the keypoint detection operation is only performed on one mesh, and each keypoint can easily be retrieved in all the other meshes. Thus it does not require too much manual effort. We finally annotate 48 keypoints on the FAUST dataset, as shown in Fig. 3.

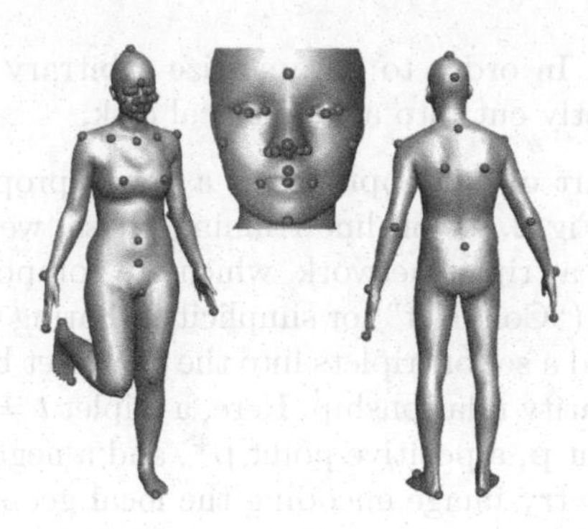

Fig. 3. Illustration of our annotated keypoints on two human models in dynamic poses in the FAUST dataset.

Local Geometry Images Generation. Partially motivated by [17], we use the geometry image representation to capture surface information, where surface signals are stored in simple 2D arrays. Unlike previous work converting the entire 3D shape into a single geometry image for shape classification, we generate a set of local geometry images for each keypoint.

We now generate local geometry images for each keypoint. A local patch mesh is first built by extracting the neighbor triangles around the keypoint. Then we map the local patch to a 2D square grid. Sinha et al. [17] have demonstrated that geometry images using authalic parameterization encode more information of the shape as compared to conformal geometry images, especially when the resolution of the geometry images is limited. In our approach, we perform an authalic and intrinsic parameterization method [41] which minimizes the intrinsic distortion, then the local patch is resampled to generate one geometry image using this parameterization. Nevertheless, other appropriate parameterization methods, such as the geodesic polar coordinates used in [35], could also be used. The resolution of a geometry image depends on specific applications, here we set its size to be 32×32 for all our experiments. Additionally, to be invariant to rotation, we rotate the local patch $K = 12$ times at $30°$ intervals around the average normal direction of faces, and align it with respect to the principal curvature direction as in [42]. For each rotation, we generate a corresponding geometry image. Furthermore, in order to capture multi-scale contexts around this keypoint, we extract the local patch at $L = 3$ scales, with neighbor radius $6r$, $9r$ and $12r$, respectively. Here r is computed as the average edge length of the entire mesh.

While geometry images can be encoded with any suitable feature of the surface mesh, we found that using only two fundamental low-level geometric features is sufficient in our approach: (1) vertex normal direction $\mathbf{n_v} = \{n_x, n_y, n_z\}$ at each vertex $\mathbf{v}$, which are calculated by weighted averaging face normals of its incident triangles; (2) two principal curvatures κ_{min} and κ_{max}, that measure the minimum and maximum bending in orthogonal directions of a surface point, respectively. Therefore, each geometry image is encoded with 15 feature chan-

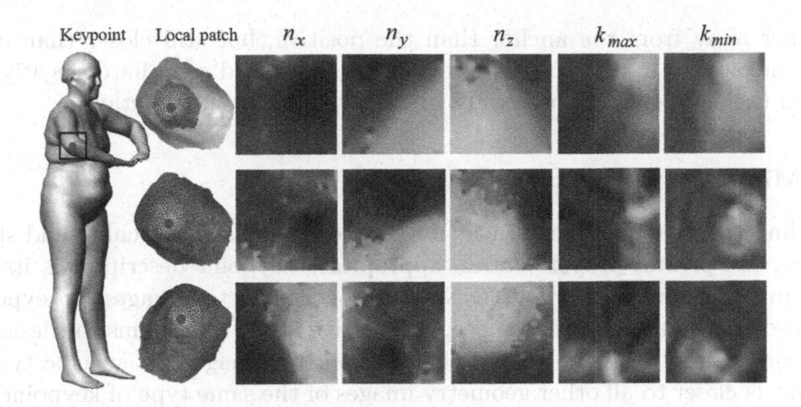

Fig. 4. Geometry images generated around a keypoint. From top to bottom are the geometry images of a smaller scale local patch, a larger scale local patch and a rotated larger scale local patch (rotation angle is 90° in clockwise). From left to right show the geometry images encoding normal $\{n_x, n_y, n_z\}$ and curvature $\{\kappa_{max}, \kappa_{min}\}$ features.

nels: $\{n_x^i, n_y^i, n_z^i, \kappa_{min}^i, \kappa_{max}^i\}_{i=1}^{L=3}$, where i represents each scale. Figure 4 shows some geometry image examples with different scales and rotations.

4.2 Triplet Sampling

For fast training convergence, it is important to select meaningful and discriminative triplets as input to the triplet network. The purpose of training is to learn a discriminative descriptor with the positive or negative points that are hard to be identified from the anchor point. That is to say, given an anchor point $\mathbf{p}$, we want to select a positive point $\mathbf{p}^+$ (*hard positive*) such that $argmax||f(\mathbf{p}_i) - f(\mathbf{p}_i^+)||_2$ and similarly a negative point $\mathbf{p}^-$ (*hard negative*) such that $argmin||f(\mathbf{p}) - f(\mathbf{p}^-)||_2$. Then, the question becomes: given an anchor point $\mathbf{p}$, how to select the hard positive and negative points? The most straightforward way is to pick samples by hard mining from all of the possible triplets across the whole training set. However, this global manner is time-consuming and may lead to poor training, because the noisy or poorly shaped local patches would cause great difficulties for defining good hard triplets. We use a stochastic gradient descent approach to generate the triplets within a mini-batch, similar to the approach used in [43] for 2D face recognition. Specifically, at each iteration of the training stage, we randomly select 16 keypoints out of 48 keypoints, then randomly select 8 geometry images out of $K \times M$ geometry images across the shapes for each keypoint, where $K = 12$ is the number of rotated geometry images of one keypoint on one shape, M is the number of shape models in training set. Totally, the batch size equals to 128. Then for all anchor-positive pairs within the batch, we select the semi-hard negatives instead of the hardest ones, because the hardest negatives can in practice lead to bad local minima early in training process. Here a semi-hard negative is a negative exemplar that is further away from the anchor than the positive, but still closer than other harder negatives. A rigorous definition of the hard and semi-hard negatives is given in the supplemental materials, or refer to [43] for more details.

4.3 Min-CV Triplet Loss

According to the requirements in real tasks such as shape matching and shape aligning, the pivotal property of an appropriate keypoint descriptor is its discriminability. Since we employ CNNs to embed geometry images of keypoints into a d-dimensional Euclidean space, an effective loss function must be designed. It encourages the CNNs to regard that a geometry image of a specific type of keypoint is closer to all other geometry images of the same type of keypoint and farther from geometry images of any other types of keypoint. To achieve this goal, we define the following classic triplet loss function [43]:

$$L = \sum_{i=1}^{N} \left[D_{pos}^{i} - D_{neg}^{i} + \alpha\right]_{+}, \tag{1}$$

$$D_{pos}^{i} = D\big(f(\mathbf{p}_i), f(\mathbf{p}_i^{+})\big),$$
$$D_{neg}^{i} = D\big(f(\mathbf{p}_i), f(\mathbf{p}_i^{-})\big),$$

where N is the batch size, α is the margin distance parameter that we expect between anchor-positive and anchor-negative pairs.

Combined with hard mining, such kinds of triplet loss functions are widely used in various metric learning tasks and perform well or at least acceptable. However, it suffers from some problems in our evaluation dataset. In particular, when training our model with this loss function, the average loss was continually decreasing, however, the single-triplet loss was oscillating violently. Besides, we noticed that for a large number of triplets, the distance between the anchor and the positive geometry images in descriptor space are still considerably large compared with the distance of anchor and negative. Only a few triplets resulted in almost zero loss that led to the decrease in average loss. This phenomenon indicated that our CNNs were failed to learn intrinsic local features but trapped into a local optimum.

To solve this problem, we propose a new triplet loss function, which minimizes the ratio of standard deviation to mean value (also called coefficient of variation-CV) of anchor-positive distance among one batch. This modification is inspired by the intuition that measured by distance in our descriptor space, one geometry image pair of a keypoint should be as similar (at least same order of magnitude) as other geometry image pairs of the same keypoint. By adding this part to the classic triplet loss, we get our minimized-CV (referred to as 'Min-CV') triplet loss:

$$L_{Min-CV} = \lambda \frac{\sigma(D_{pos})}{\mu(D_{pos})} + \sum_{i=1}^{N} \left[D_{pos}^{i} - D_{neg}^{i} + \alpha\right]_{+}, \tag{2}$$

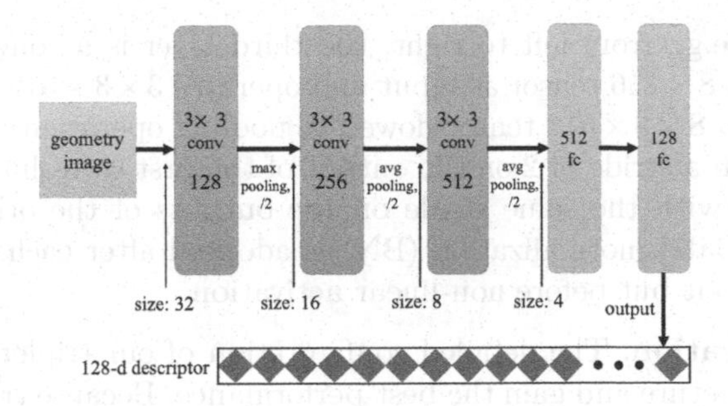

Fig. 5. Detailed network architecture of individual ConvNet shown in Fig. 2. (Color figure online)

where λ is a tunable non-negative parameter, $\sigma(\cdot)$ calculates the standard deviation among one batch, and $\mu(\cdot)$ calculates the empirical mean of one batch. Note that recent work [44,45] also introduced the mean value and variance/standard deviation into traditional triplet loss. Their loss functions (Kumar's [44] and Jan's [45]) are respectively defined as:

$$L_{Kumar's} = (\sigma^2(D_{pos}) + \sigma^2(D_{neg})) + \lambda max(0, \mu(D_{pos}) - \mu(D_{neg}) + \alpha), \quad (3)$$

$$L_{Jan's} = \sigma(D_{pos}) + \sigma(D_{neg}) + \mu(D_{pos}) + \lambda max(0, \alpha - \mu(D_{neg})), \quad (4)$$

where $\sigma^2(\cdot)$ calculates the variance among one batch. Different from these two approaches, we minimize the CV instead of the variance directly. The reason is that compared to the variance, the CV could measure the dispersion of D_{pos} without being influenced by the numerical scale of the descriptor distance (or the magnitude of the data), e.g., scaling down the descriptor distance will decrease the variance but not affect the CV. Thus, the CV better reflects the degree of data deviation. We make a comparison with these two loss functions in Sect. 5. Furthermore, extensive experiments show that our Min-CV triplet loss is able to help CNNs to learn significant features from one dataset and generalize well to other datasets.

4.4 CNN Architecture and Configuration

Considering the particularity and complexity of our task, we design a special CNN architecture dedicated to processing geometry images in our triplet structure, which is presented below.

Network Architecture. Figure 5 illustrates the architecture of our CNN model. In this figure, we have a compact stack of three convolutional layers ("conv", colored in blue), three pooling layers and two fully connected layers ("fc", colored in green). In particular, each convolutional layer is equipped with the size of convolution kernel shown above and the number of output feature maps shown below. For each fully connected layer, we show the number of units above. The "size" represents the length and the width of the tensor which is fed into next layer, e.g., from left to right, the third layer is a convolutional layer that takes an $8 \times 8 \times 256$ tensor as input and operates $3 \times 3 \times 512$ convolution on it, resulting in an $8 \times 8 \times 512$ tensor flowed to pooling operation. Next, we apply max pooling with a stride of 2 on the output of the first convolutional layer and average pooling with the same stride on the outputs of the other two convolutional layers. Batch normalization (BN) is adopted after each convolution or linear map of input but before non-linear activation.

CNN Configuration. The detailed configuration of our triplet CNN is set to adapt our architecture and gain the best performance. Because triplet loss is not as stable as other frequently-used loss functions, our old-version CNN with traditional ReLU activation often suffers from dying ReLU problem that may reduce the effective capacity of our CNN model and then lead to failure in generating meaningful descriptors. To avoid this defect, we employ leaky ReLU [46] with $slope = 0.1$ for negative input as our activation function. Experimental results demonstrate the effectiveness of this strategy. In addition, to speed up training, we first train a classification network with same architecture and training data of our triplet CNNs except the fully connected layers. The classification labels are the indices of the vertices of the mesh. When it is closed to convergence, its parameters can be used to initialize the convolutional layers of our triplet CNN. Besides, Xavier initialization [47] is adopted to initialize all layers of the classification network and the fully connected layers of our triplet CNNs. In training procedure, Adam algorithm [48] is employed to optimize the loss function. In all of our experiments, the learning rate starts with 0.01 and decreases by a factor of 10 every time when the validation loss begins to oscillate periodically. To avoid overfitting, L_2 regularization is also used with coefficient 0.005.

5 Experimental Results

In this section, we conduct a number of experiments on both real and synthetic datasets to demonstrate the efficacy of our learned local descriptors. We first give training details and evaluate the performance of our Min-CV triplet loss. Then we provide a complete comparison with state-of-the-art approaches with qualitative and quantitative experiments. The shown results are obtained on an Intel Core i7-3770 Processor with 3.4 GHz and 16 GB RAM. Offline training runs on an NVIDIA GeForce TITAN X Pascal (12 GB memory) GPU.

Datasets. In addition to FAUST, we further carry out experiments on four other public-domain datasets. The SCAPE dataset [49] contains 71 realistic registered meshes of a particular person in a variety of poses, while the TOSCA dataset [9] contains 80 synthetic models of animals and people with near-isometric deformations. The SPRING dataset [50] contains 3000 scanned body models which have also been placed in point to point correspondence. Finally, we test our method on the FACE models used in [10], where some facial expressions are provided.

Training Settings. We separate the FAUST dataset into training models (75%), validation models (10%), and testing models (15%). Any geometry image triplet is generated from one of above subsets depending on the stage it is used for, resulting in the triplet training set, validation set, and testing set, respectively. The training set contains, counted by combination, up to 8.1×10^{11} different triplets that could be fed into our triplet CNNs for training (due to imperfections on meshes, local patches of some keypoints on certain models may not able to be parameterized correctly and thus are discarded), while the triplet validation set and testing set contains up to 1.7×10^9 and 6.1×10^9 triplets, respectively. Our method is implemented based on TensorFlow [51]. Using our hardware configuration shown above, one full training takes about 8 h.

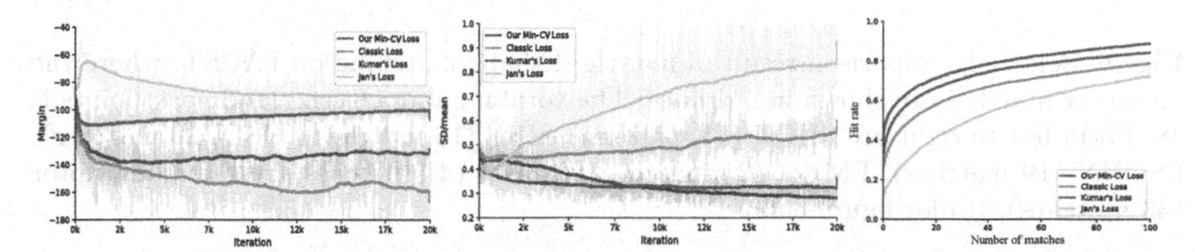

Fig. 6. Training behaviors using different triplet loss functions. Left: positive-negative margin curves. Middle: standard deviation mean ratio curves. Right: CMC curves.

Table 1. Numeric statistics of the CMC curve using different losses in the rightmost plots of Fig. 6.

Dataset	Method	$P_1\%$	$P_5\%$	$P_{10}\%$	$P_{20}\%$
FAUST	Ours	**40.42**	**55.94**	**64.76**	**71.29**
	Ours with Classic loss	25.93	42.37	49.66	57.82
	Ours with Kumar's loss	33.39	51.90	59.04	66.25
	Ours with Jan's loss	12.28	21.92	29.70	40.40

Next, we demonstrate the effectiveness of our proposed Min-CV triplet loss. In Fig. 6 we depict the training behaviors evaluated on validation dataset using classic triplet loss (Eq. 1), Kumar's loss [44] (Eq. 3), Jan's loss [45] (Eq. 4) and our Min-CV triplet loss (Eq. 2), where the margin distance parameter α is empirically set to a large number (e.g., 100 in this paper) and λ is set to 1.0. To be fair, we use the same network architecture and parameters proposed in this paper for different losses. The positive-negative margin curve shows the average distance between anchor-positive and anchor-negative pairs in each batch, and it is calculated by $\sum_{i=1}^{N}\left[D_{pos}^{i} - D_{neg}^{i}\right]_{+}$. The standard deviation mean ratio curve shows the average ratio $\frac{\sigma(D_{pos})}{\mu(D_{pos})}$ along the iterations. From the left two figures in Fig. 6, we see that Jan's loss performs worst in our task, and classic loss cannot control the degree of deviation of anchor-positive distance, while both Kumar's loss and our Min-CV loss significantly reduce it. Compared with Kumar's loss, the training behaviors of our loss are better in both figures, thus it effectively improves the robustness and generalization ability of our learned descriptor. Taking advantage of this, our descriptor performs stably on various datasets. From

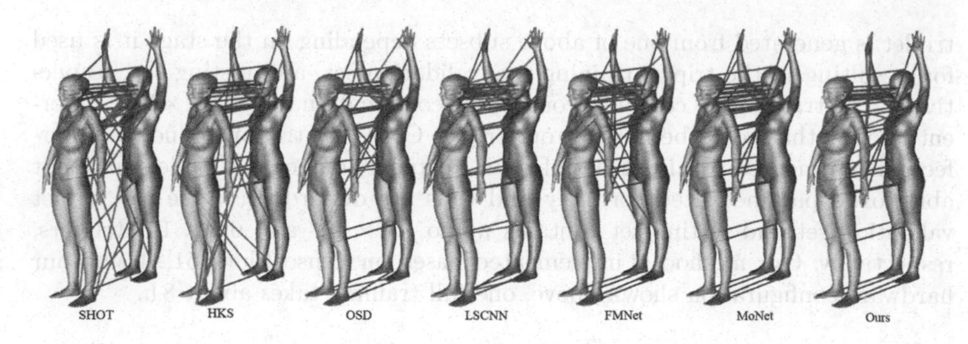

Fig. 7. Selected comparison result of non-rigid shape matching on FAUST, where the incorrect matches are shown in red lines. The total number of used landmark points is 48. From left to right are SHOT (11 matches), HKS (16 matches), OSD (20 matches), LSCNN (19 matches), FMNet (21 matches), MoNet (41 matches) and our descriptor (33 matches). (Color figure online)

the CMC curves (we will explain it below), our loss still outperforms Kumar's loss. A more thorough comparison is provided in Table 1.

Evaluation Metrics. Next, we thoroughly compare our method with several local descriptors of different types, including extrinsic hand-crafted features spin images (SI) [11], SHOT [24], and RoPS [25], intrinsic hand-crafted features HKS [13] and WKS [27], learning-based descriptor OSD [29], and the state-of-the-art deep-learned descriptors LSCNN [34], MoNet [16], FMNet [37]. All the learning-based methods are trained on our above FAUST train-test split. For fair comparison with others, FMNet is not post-processed with the correspondence refinement technique as used in their paper. We believe it makes sense because we focus on the performance of different descriptors, rather than the correspondence. The comparison contains two evaluation metrics that are commonly used in the literature. The first measure is the *cumulative match characteristic* (CMC) curve, which evaluates the probability of finding a correct correspondence among the k-nearest neighbors in the descriptor space. Another popular measure is the *precision-recall* (PR) curve with the average precision (i.e., area under PR curve, denoted by AP), that is based on two basic evaluation measures: recall and precision.

Comparison on FAUST Dataset. Figure 8 shows the CMC and PR plots for all the descriptors on the FAUST dataset. The numerical statistics about the curves are presented in Table 2. For a fair and unbiased comparison, we randomly select 200 pairs of shapes from the dataset. And for each pair of shapes, we generate 1000 feature points on them by using 3D-Harris detector [40]. Then the plots are drawn by averaging the calculation results of 200 pairs of shapes. From the curves, we observe that MoNet performs best. However, in fact MoNet does not learn a real descriptor, and it casts shape correspondence as a labelling problem. Thus, it cannot be directly generalized to other datasets once it is trained on FAUST, because the labelling spaces can be quite different.

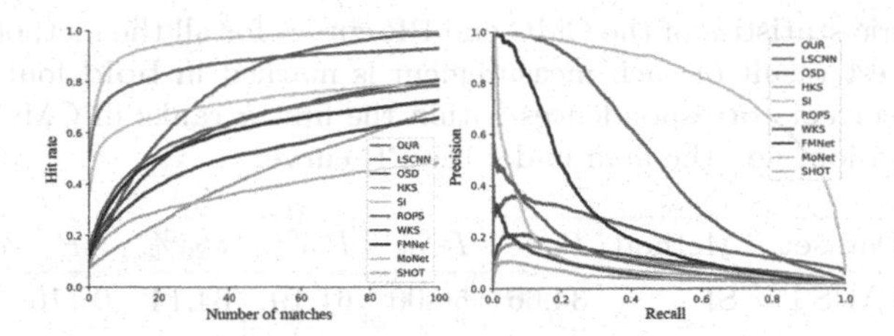

Fig. 8. Performance of different descriptors on FAUST dataset, measured using the CMC (left) and PR (right) plots.

Our learned descriptor performs better than all of the extrinsic and intrinsic hand-crafted features. Although our CMC curve converges a little slower than LSCNN, we have higher rank k CMC-percentage, i.e., more corresponding keypoints can be correctly matched in the top k ranks (see Table 2 for details). In addition, we show that our approach has better generalization capability than others in later experiments.

Next, as an application, we test the performance of different local descriptors for non-rigid shape matching, which is performed by computing the landmark correspondences. From the comparison in Fig. 7, we see that our learned local descriptor produces outstanding matching result.

Comparison on Other Datasets. In order to test our generalization ability, we perform a series of experiments on several other datasets. Here we only show the experimental results on the SPRING and FACE datasets. More exhaustive analysis and comparisons are provided in the supplemental materials. For all comparisons, the learned methods (OSD, LSCNN, FMNet and ours) are trained on FAUST dataset, then applied to other datasets. The evaluation curves are depicted in Fig. 9, and the numeric statistics are shown in Table 2. Note that for the 3D FACE dataset, we manually annotate 15 keypoints by considering the 2D facial point annotations [52] (see Fig. 1).

As it can be observed, hand-crafted features behave differently on different datasets, so their robustness is not strong. Another interesting phenomenon is that LSCNN performs similarly with OSD on the SPRING dataset, but it is the worst on the FACE dataset. The reason is that LSCNN uses a domain-dependent

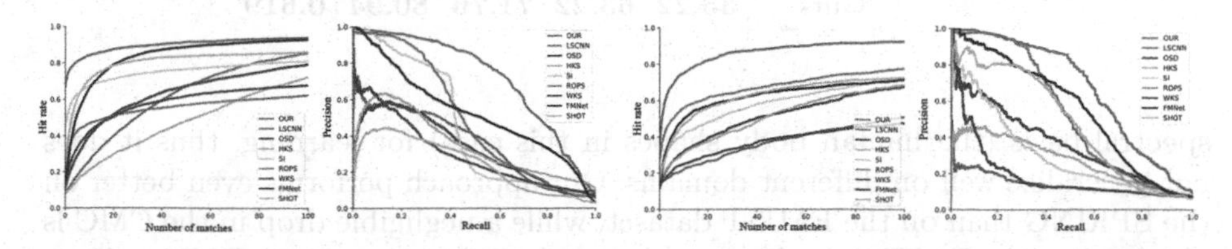

Fig. 9. Performance of different descriptors on SPRING and FACE dataset. The left two figures are the CMC and PR plots on SPRING respectively, while the right two figures are the CMC and PR plots on FACE.

Table 2. Numeric statistics of the CMC and PR curves for all the methods on different datasets. The best result of each measurement is marked in **bold** font. Here $P_k\%$ is the fraction of correct correspondences within the first k ranks in CMC curve; AP is the average precision, i.e., the area under the PR curve.

Dataset	Method	$P_1\%$	$P_5\%$	$P_{10}\%$	$P_{20}\%$	AP
FAUST	SI	34.66	56.00	61.19	64.14	0.116
	RoPS	14.04	29.95	40.64	51.85	0.128
	SHOT	8.77	17.94	23.36	29.07	0.045
	HKS	7.47	11.71	17.78	24.14	0.098
	WKS	11.26	21.24	28.55	38.98	0.071
	OSD	13.19	23.85	33.45	47.45	0.113
	LSCNN	11.97	22.02	38.12	58.61	0.210
	FMNet	12.43	27.12	38.10	49.59	0.508
	MoNet	**56.93**	**84.62**	**90.82**	**96.93**	**0.677**
	Ours	49.14	70.93	76.63	81.70	0.500
SPRING	SI	43.03	60.33	64.57	69.88	0.445
	RoPS	22.13	40.68	46.00	50.30	0.558
	SHOT	23.10	56.68	69.60	77.14	0.244
	HKS	8.58	14.83	19.75	28.73	0.348
	WKS	13.80	31.07	40.42	49.55	0.299
	OSD	10.52	26.60	37.95	50.58	0.327
	LSCNN	8.80	17.17	24.43	38.53	0.359
	FMNet	13.40	47.48	63.53	78.07	0.528
	Our	**63.30**	**77.71**	**81.70**	**85.99**	**0.631**
FACE	SI	19.33	34.03	40.13	47.23	0.304
	RoPS	26.93	47.27	55.17	60.77	0.629
	SHOT	16.50	35.53	45.93	55.20	0.479
	HKS	14.57	21.97	30.77	38.47	0.273
	WKS	12.67	19.57	24.63	25.43	0.193
	OSD	17.46	24.20	33.93	42.17	0.367
	LSCNN	15.53	18.47	20.83	23.70	0.140
	FMNet	12.00	36.89	48.30	56.67	0.558
	Ours	**35.22**	**63.22**	**71.76**	**80.94**	**0.619**

spectral basis (the human body shapes in this case) for learning, thus it does not generalize well on different domains. Our approach performs even better on the SPRING than on the FAUST dataset, while a negligible drop in the CMC is observed on the FACE data. Moreover, among all the descriptors, FMNet shows good generalization, but we still achieve the best performance on both datasets. It demonstrates that our approach has the best generalization ability.

6 Conclusion and Future Work

In this paper, we have proposed a new 3D keypoint descriptor based on end-to-end deep learning techniques. A triplet network is designed and efficiently trained, where we introduce a new triplet-based loss function to characterize the relative ordering of the corresponding and non-corresponding keypoint pairs. The significant advantage of our framework is that we can learn the descriptors using local geometry images, that encodes more surface information than rendered views or 3D voxels. Although many local descriptors exist, we have demonstrated better discriminability, robustness and generalization capability of our approach through a variety of experiments.

Though we only use low-level geometric information in this paper, any other extrinsic or intrinsic surface properties can also be encoded into the geometry images. In future work, we would like to extend our flexible approach to other data-driven 3D vision applications, e.g., shape segmentation, 3D saliency detection, etc.

Acknowledgments. We thank anonymous reviewer for their valuable comments and suggestions. This work is partially funded by the National Natural Science Foundation of China (No. 61620106003), Beijing Natural Science Foundation (4184102), National Natural Science Foundation of China (No. 61772523, 61761003, 61571439, 61702488).

References

1. Van Kaick, O., Zhang, H., Hamarneh, G., Cohen-Or, D.: A survey on shape correspondence. Comput. Graph. Forum **30**(6), 1681–1707 (2011)
2. Ovsjanikov, M., Ben-Chen, M., Solomon, J., Butscher, A., Guibas, L.: Functional maps: a flexible representation of maps between shapes. ACM Trans. Graph. (Proceedings of SIGGRAPH) **31**(4), 30 (2012)
3. Guo, Y., Bennamoun, M., Sohel, F., Lu, M., Wan, J.: 3D object recognition in cluttered scenes with local surface features: a survey. IEEE Trans. Pattern Anal. Mach. Intell. **36**(11), 2270–2287 (2014)
4. Corman, É., Ovsjanikov, M., Chambolle, A.: Supervised descriptor learning for non-rigid shape matching. In: Agapito, L., Bronstein, M.M., Rother, C. (eds.) ECCV 2014. LNCS, vol. 8928, pp. 283–298. Springer, Cham (2015). https://doi.org/10.1007/978-3-319-16220-1_20
5. Cosmo, L., Rodola, E., Masci, J., Torsello, A., Bronstein, M.M.: Matching deformable objects in clutter. In: Fourth International Conference on 3D Vision (3DV), pp. 1–10. IEEE (2016)
6. Bronstein, A.M., Bronstein, M.M., Guibas, L.J., Ovsjanikov, M.: Shape Google: geometric words and expressions for invariant shape retrieval. ACM Trans. Graph. **30**(1), 1 (2011)
7. Lian, Z., et al.: A comparison of methods for non-rigid 3D shape retrieval. Pattern Recognit. **46**(1), 449–461 (2013)
8. Shah, S.A.A., Bennamoun, M., Boussaid, F.: A novel 3D vorticity based approach for automatic registration of low resolution range images. Pattern Recognit. **48**(9), 2859–2871 (2015)

9. Bronstein, A.M., Bronstein, M.M., Kimmel, R.: Numerical Geometry of Non-rigid Shapes. Springer, New York (2008). https://doi.org/10.1007/978-0-387-73301-2
10. Sumner, R.W., Popović, J.: Deformation transfer for triangle meshes. ACM Trans. Graph. (Proceedings of SIGGRAPH) **23**(3), 399–405 (2004)
11. Johnson, A.E., Hebert, M.: Using spin images for efficient object recognition in cluttered 3D scenes. IEEE Trans. Pattern Anal. Mach. Intell. **21**(5), 433–449 (1999)
12. Gal, R., Cohen-Or, D.: Salient geometric features for partial shape matching and similarity. ACM Trans. Graph. **25**(1), 130–150 (2006)
13. Sun, J., Ovsjanikov, M., Guibas, L.: A concise and provably informative multi-scale signature based on heat diffusion. Comput. Graph. Forum (Proceedings of SGP) **28**(5), 1383–1392 (2009)
14. Huang, H., Kalogerakis, E., Chaudhuri, S., Ceylan, D., Kim, V., Yumer, E.: Learning local shape descriptors from part correspondences with multi-view convolutional networks. ACM Trans. Graph. **37**(1), 6:1–6:14 (2018)
15. Zeng, A., Song, S., Nießner, M., Fisher, M., Xiao, J., Funkhouser, T.: 3DMatch: learning local geometric descriptors from RGB-D reconstructions. In: IEEE Computer Vision and Pattern Recognition (CVPR), pp. 199–208 (2017)
16. Monti, F., Boscaini, D., Masci, J., Rodolà, E., Svoboda, J., Bronstein, M.M.: Geometric deep learning on graphs and manifolds using mixture model CNNs. In: IEEE Computer Vision and Pattern Recognition (CVPR), pp. 5425–5434 (2017)
17. Sinha, A., Bai, J., Ramani, K.: Deep learning 3D shape surfaces using geometry images. In: Leibe, B., Matas, J., Sebe, N., Welling, M. (eds.) ECCV 2016. LNCS, vol. 9910, pp. 223–240. Springer, Cham (2016). https://doi.org/10.1007/978-3-319-46466-4_14
18. Bromley, J., Guyon, I., LeCun, Y., Säckinger, E., Shah, R.: Signature verification using a "siamese" time delay neural network. In: Advances in Neural Information Processing Systems, pp. 737–744 (1994)
19. Wang, J., et al.: Learning fine-grained image similarity with deep ranking. In: IEEE Computer Vision and Pattern Recognition (CVPR), pp. 1386–1393 (2014)
20. Guo, Y., Bennamoun, M., Sohel, F., Lu, M., Wan, J., Kwok, N.M.: A comprehensive performance evaluation of 3D local feature descriptors. Int. J. Comput. Vis. **116**(1), 66–89 (2016)
21. Yang, J., Zhang, Q., Cao, Z.: The effect of spatial information characterization on 3D local feature descriptors: a quantitative evaluation. Pattern Recognit. **66**, 375–391 (2017)
22. Frome, A., Huber, D., Kolluri, R., Bülow, T., Malik, J.: Recognizing objects in range data using regional point descriptors. In: Pajdla, T., Matas, J. (eds.) ECCV 2004. LNCS, vol. 3023, pp. 224–237. Springer, Heidelberg (2004). https://doi.org/10.1007/978-3-540-24672-5_18
23. Zaharescu, A., Boyer, E., Varanasi, K., Horaud, R.: Surface feature detection and description with applications to mesh matching. In: IEEE Computer Vision and Pattern Recognition (CVPR), pp. 373–380 (2009)
24. Tombari, F., Salti, S., Di Stefano, L.: Unique signatures of histograms for local surface description. In: Daniilidis, K., Maragos, P., Paragios, N. (eds.) ECCV 2010. LNCS, vol. 6313, pp. 356–369. Springer, Heidelberg (2010). https://doi.org/10.1007/978-3-642-15558-1_26
25. Guo, Y., Sohel, F., Bennamoun, M., Lu, M., Wan, J.: Rotational projection statistics for 3D local surface description and object recognition. Int. J. Comput. Vis. **105**(1), 63–86 (2013)
26. Elad, A., Kimmel, R.: On bending invariant signatures for surfaces. IEEE Trans. Pattern Anal. Mach. Intell. **25**(10), 1285–1295 (2003)

27. Aubry, M., Schlickewei, U., Cremers, D.: The wave kernel signature: a quantum mechanical approach to shape analysis. In: IEEE International Conference on Computer Vision Workshops (ICCV Workshops), pp. 1626–1633 (2011)
28. Kokkinos, I., Bronstein, M.M., Litman, R., Bronstein, A.M.: Intrinsic shape context descriptors for deformable shapes. In: IEEE Computer Vision and Pattern Recognition (CVPR), pp. 159–166. IEEE (2012)
29. Litman, R., Bronstein, A.M.: Learning spectral descriptors for deformable shape correspondence. IEEE Trans. Pattern Anal. Mach. Intell. **36**(1), 171–180 (2014)
30. Wei, L., Huang, Q., Ceylan, D., Vouga, E., Li, H.: Dense human body correspondences using convolutional networks. In: IEEE Computer Vision and Pattern Recognition (CVPR), pp. 1544–1553 (2016)
31. Qi, C.R., Su, H., Mo, K., Guibas, L.J.: Pointnet: deep learning on point sets for 3D classification and segmentation. In: IEEE Computer Vision and Pattern Recognition (CVPR), pp. 77–85 (2017)
32. Khoury, M., Zhou, Q.Y., Koltun, V.: Learning compact geometric features. In: IEEE International Conference on Computer Vision (ICCV), pp. 153–161 (2017)
33. Bronstein, M.M., Bruna, J., LeCun, Y., Szlam, A., Vandergheynst, P.: Geometric deep learning: going beyond Euclidean data. IEEE Signal Process. Mag. **34**(4), 18–42 (2017)
34. Boscaini, D., Masci, J., Melzi, S., Bronstein, M.M., Castellani, U., Vandergheynst, P.: Learning class-specific descriptors for deformable shapes using localized spectral convolutional networks. Comput. Graph. Forum (Proceedings of SGP) **34**(5), 13–23 (2015)
35. Masci, J., Boscaini, D., Bronstein, M., Vandergheynst, P.: Geodesic convolutional neural networks on Riemannian manifolds. In: IEEE International Conference on Computer Vision Workshops (ICCV Workshops), pp. 37–45 (2015)
36. Boscaini, D., Masci, J., Rodolà, E., Bronstein, M.: Learning shape correspondence with anisotropic convolutional neural networks. In: Advances in Neural Information Processing (NIPS), pp. 3189–3197 (2016)
37. Litany, O., Remez, T., Rodola, E., Bronstein, A.M., Bronstein, M.M.: Deep functional maps: structured prediction for dense shape correspondence. In: IEEE International Conference on Computer Vision (ICCV), vol. 2, p. 8 (2017)
38. Gu, X., Gortler, S.J., Hoppe, H.: Geometry images. ACM Trans. Graph. (Proceedings of SIGGRAPH) **21**(3), 355–361 (2002)
39. Bogo, F., Romero, J., Loper, M., Black, M.J.: Faust: dataset and evaluation for 3D mesh registration. In: IEEE Computer Vision and Pattern Recognition (CVPR), pp. 3794–3801 (2014)
40. Sipiran, I., Bustos, B.: Harris 3D: a robust extension of the Harris operator for interest point detection on 3D meshes. Vis. Comput. **27**(11), 963–976 (2011)
41. Desbrun, M., Meyer, M., Alliez, P.: Intrinsic parameterizations of surface meshes. In: Computer Graphics Forum, vol. 21, pp. 209–218. Wiley Online Library (2002)
42. Boscaini, D., Masci, J., Rodolà, E., Bronstein, M.M., Cremers, D.: Anisotropic diffusion descriptors. Comput. Graph. Forum (Proceedings of EUROGRAPHICS) **35**(2), 431–441 (2016)
43. Schroff, F., Kalenichenko, D., Philbin, J.: Facenet: a unified embedding for face recognition and clustering. In: IEEE Computer Vision and Pattern Recognition (CVPR), pp. 815–823 (2015)
44. Kumar, B., Carneiro, G., Reid, I., et al.: Learning local image descriptors with deep Siamese and triplet convolutional networks by minimising global loss functions. In: IEEE Computer Vision and Pattern Recognition (CVPR), pp. 5385–5394 (2016)

45. Svoboda, J., Masci, J., Bronstein, M.M.: Palmprint recognition via discriminative index learning. In: 23rd International Conference on Pattern Recognition (ICPR), pp. 4232–4237. IEEE (2016)
46. Maas, A.L., Hannun, A.Y., Ng, A.Y.: Rectifier nonlinearities improve neural network acoustic models. In: Proceedings of ICML, vol. 30 (2013)
47. Glorot, X., Bengio, Y.: Understanding the difficulty of training deep feedforward neural networks. In: Proceedings of the Thirteenth International Conference on Artificial Intelligence and Statistics, pp. 249–256 (2010)
48. Kingma, D., Ba, J.: Adam: a method for stochastic optimization. arXiv preprint arXiv:1412.6980 (2014)
49. Anguelov, D., Srinivasan, P., Koller, D., Thrun, S., Rodgers, J., Davis, J.: SCAPE: shape completion and animation of people. ACM Trans. Graph. (Proceedings of SIGGRAPH) **24**(3), 408–416 (2005)
50. Yang, Y., Yu, Y., Zhou, Y., Du, S., Davis, J., Yang, R.: Semantic parametric reshaping of human body models. In: 2nd International Conference on 3D Vision (3DV), vol. 2, pp. 41–48. IEEE (2014)
51. Abadi, M., et al.: Tensorflow: large-scale machine learning on heterogeneous distributed systems (2015). https://www.tensorflow.org/
52. Sagonas, C., Antonakos, E., Tzimiropoulos, G., Zafeiriou, S., Pantic, M.: 300 faces in-the-wild challenge: database and results. Image Vis. Comput. **47**, 3–18 (2016)

A Trilateral Weighted Sparse Coding Scheme for Real-World Image Denoising

Jun Xu[1], Lei Zhang[1(✉)], and David Zhang[1,2]

[1] The Hong Kong Polytechnic University, Kowloon, Hong Kong SAR, China
{csjunxu,cslzhang,csdzhang}@comp.polyu.edu.hk
[2] School of Science and Engineering, The Chinese University of Hong Kong (Shenzhen), Shenzhen, China

Abstract. Most of existing image denoising methods assume the corrupted noise to be additive white Gaussian noise (AWGN). However, the realistic noise in real-world noisy images is much more complex than AWGN, and is hard to be modeled by simple analytical distributions. As a result, many state-of-the-art denoising methods in literature become much less effective when applied to real-world noisy images captured by CCD or CMOS cameras. In this paper, we develop a trilateral weighted sparse coding (TWSC) scheme for robust real-world image denoising. Specifically, we introduce three weight matrices into the data and regularization terms of the sparse coding framework to characterize the statistics of realistic noise and image priors. TWSC can be reformulated as a linear equality-constrained problem and can be solved by the alternating direction method of multipliers. The existence and uniqueness of the solution and convergence of the proposed algorithm are analyzed. Extensive experiments demonstrate that the proposed TWSC scheme outperforms state-of-the-art denoising methods on removing realistic noise.

Keywords: Real-world image denoising · Sparse coding

1 Introduction

Noise will be inevitably introduced in imaging systems and may severely damage the quality of acquired images. Removing noise from the acquired image is an essential step in photography and various computer vision tasks such as segmentation [1], HDR imaging [2], and recognition [3], etc. Image denoising aims to recover the clean image $\mathbf{x}$ from its noisy observation $\mathbf{y} = \mathbf{x} + \mathbf{n}$, where $\mathbf{n}$ is the corrupted noise. This problem has been extensively studied in literature, and numerous statistical image modeling and learning methods have been proposed in the past decades [4–26].

L. Zhang—This project is supported by Hong Kong RGC GRF project (PolyU 152124/15E).

V. Ferrari et al. (Eds.): ECCV 2018, LNCS 11212, pp. 21–38, 2018.
https://doi.org/10.1007/978-3-030-01237-3_2

Most of the existing methods [4–20] focus on additive white Gaussian noise (AWGN), and they can be categorized into dictionary learning based methods [4,5], nonlocal self-similarity based methods [6–14], sparsity based methods [4,5,7–11], low-rankness based methods [12,13], generative learning based methods [14–16], and discriminative learning based methods [17–20], etc. However, the realistic noise in real-world images captured by CCD or CMOS cameras is much more complex than AWGN [21–24,26–28], which can be signal dependent and vary with different cameras and camera settings (such as ISO, shutter speed, and aperture, etc.). In Fig. 1, we show a real-world noisy image from the Darmstadt Noise Dataset (DND) [29] and a synthetic AWGN image from the Kodak PhotoCD Dataset (http://r0k.us/graphics/kodak/). We can see that the different local patches in real-world noisy image show different noise statistics, e.g., the patches in black and blue boxes show different noise levels although they are from the same white object. In contrast, all the patches from the synthetic AWGN image show homogeneous noise patterns. Besides, the realistic noise varies in different channels as well as different local patches [22–24,26]. In Fig. 2, we show a real-world noisy image captured by a Nikon D800 camera with ISO = 6400, its "Ground Truth" (please refer to Sect. 4.3), and their differences in full color image as well as in each channel. The overall noise standard deviations (stds) in Red, Green, and Blue channels are 5.8, 4.4, and 5.5, respectively. Besides, the realistic noise is inhomogeneous. For example, the stds of noise in the three boxes plotted in Fig. 2(c) vary largely. Indeed, the noise in real-world noisy image is much more complex than AWGN noise. Though having shown promising performance on AWGN noise removal, many of the above mentioned methods [4–20] will become much less effective when dealing with the complex realistic noise as shown in Fig. 2.

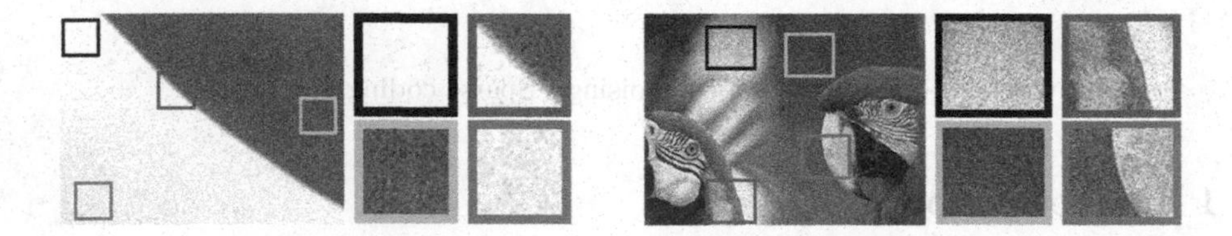

Fig. 1. Comparison of noisy image patches in real-world noisy image (left) and synthetic noisy image with additive white Gaussian noise (right). (Color figure online)

In the past decade, several denoising methods for real-world noisy images have been developed [21–26]. Liu et al. [21] proposed to estimate the noise via a "noise level function" and remove the noise for each channel of the real image. However, processing each channel separately would often achieve unsatisfactory performance and generate artifacts [5]. The methods [22,23] perform image denoising by concatenating the patches of RGB channels into a vector. However, the concatenation does not consider the different noise statistics among different channels. Besides, the method of [23] models complex noise via mixture

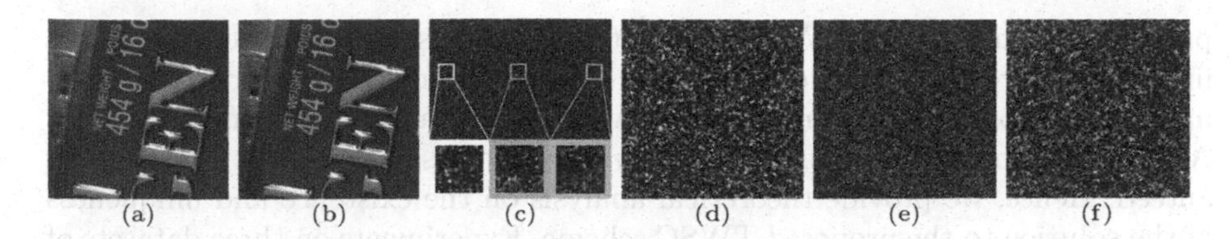

Fig. 2. An example of realistic noise. (a) A real-world noisy image captured by a Nikon D800 camera with ISO = 6400; (b) the "Ground Truth" image (please refer to Sect. 4.3) of (a); (c) difference between (a) and (b) (amplified for better illustration); (d)–(f) red, green, and blue channel of (c), respectively. The standard deviations (stds) of noise in the three boxes (white, pink, and green) plotted in (c) are 5.2, 6.5, and 3.3, respectively, while the stds of noise in each channel (d), (e), and (f) are 5.8, 4.4, and 5.5, respectively. (Color figure online)

of Gaussian distribution, which is time-consuming due to the use of variational Bayesian inference techniques. The method of [24] models the noise in a noisy image by a multivariate Gaussian and performs denoising by the Bayesian non-local means [30]. The commercial software Neat Image [25] estimates the global noise parameters from a flat region of the given noisy image and filters the noise accordingly. However, both the two methods [24,25] ignore the local statistical property of the noise which is signal dependent and varies with different pixels. The method [26] considers the different noise statistics in different channels, but ignores that the noise is signal dependent and has different levels in different local patches. By far, real-world image denoising is still a challenging problem in low level vision [29].

Sparse coding (SC) has been well studied in many computer vision and pattern recognition problems [31–33], including image denoising [4,5,10,11,14]. In general, given an input signal $\mathbf{y}$ and the dictionary $\mathbf{D}$ of coding atoms, the SC model can be formulated as

$$\min_{\mathbf{c}} \|\mathbf{y} - \mathbf{D}\mathbf{c}\|_2^2 + \lambda \|\mathbf{c}\|_q, \tag{1}$$

where $\mathbf{c}$ is the coding vector of the signal $\mathbf{y}$ over the dictionary $\mathbf{D}$, λ is the regularization parameter, and $q = 0$ or 1 to enforce sparse regularization on $\mathbf{c}$. Some representative SC based image denoising methods include K-SVD [4], LSSC [10], and NCSR [11]. Though being effective on dealing with AWGN, SC based denoising methods are essentially limited by the data-fidelity term described by ℓ_2 (or Frobenius) norm, which actually assumes white Gaussian noise and is not able to characterize the signal dependent and realistic noise.

In this paper, we propose to lift the SC model (1) to a robust denoiser for real-world noisy images by utilizing the channel-wise statistics and locally signal dependent property of the realistic noise, as demonstrated in Fig. 2. Specifically, we propose a trilateral weighted sparse coding (TWSC) scheme for real-world image denoising. Two weight matrices are introduced into the data-fidelity term of the SC model to characterize the realistic noise property, and another weight matrix is introduced into the regularization term to characterize the sparsity priors of natural images. We reformulate the proposed TWSC scheme into a linear equality-constrained optimization program, and solve it under the alternating direction method of multipliers (ADMM) [34] framework. One step of our ADMM is to solve a Sylvester equation, whose unique solution is not always guaranteed. Hence, we provide theoretical analysis on the existence and uniqueness of the solution to the proposed TWSC scheme. Experiments on three datasets of real-world noisy images demonstrate that the proposed TWSC scheme achieves much better performance than the state-of-the-art denoising methods.

2 The Proposed Real-World Image Denoising Algorithm

2.1 The Trilateral Weighted Sparse Coding Model

The real-world image denoising problem is to recover the clean image from its noisy observation. Current denoising methods [4–16] are mostly patch based. Given a noisy image, a local patch of size $p \times p \times 3$ is extracted from it and stretched to a vector, denoted by $\mathbf{y} = [\mathbf{y}_r^\top \ \mathbf{y}_g^\top \ \mathbf{y}_b^\top]^\top \in \mathbb{R}^{3p^2}$, where $\mathbf{y}_c \in \mathbb{R}^{p^2}$ is the corresponding patch in channel c, where $c \in \{r, g, b\}$ is the index of R, G, and B channels. For each local patch $\mathbf{y}$, we search the M most similar patches to it (including $\mathbf{y}$ itself) by Euclidean distance in a local window around it. By stacking the M similar patches column by column, we form a noisy patch matrix $\mathbf{Y} = \mathbf{X} + \mathbf{N} \in \mathbb{R}^{3p^2 \times M}$, where $\mathbf{X}$ and $\mathbf{N}$ are the corresponding clean and noise patch matrices, respectively. The noisy patch matrix can be written as $\mathbf{Y} = [\mathbf{Y}_r^\top \ \mathbf{Y}_g^\top \ \mathbf{Y}_b^\top]^\top$, where $\mathbf{Y}_c$ is the sub-matrix of channel c. Suppose that we have a dictionary $\mathbf{D} = [\mathbf{D}_r^\top \ \mathbf{D}_g^\top \ \mathbf{D}_b^\top]^\top$, where $\mathbf{D}_c$ is the sub-dictionary corresponding to channel c. In fact, the dictionary $\mathbf{D}$ can be learned from external natrual images, or from the input noisy patch matrix $\mathbf{Y}$.

Under the traditional sparse coding (SC) framework [35], the sparse coding matrix of $\mathbf{Y}$ over $\mathbf{D}$ can be obtained by

$$\hat{\mathbf{C}} = \arg\min_{\mathbf{C}} \|\mathbf{Y} - \mathbf{DC}\|_F^2 + \lambda \|\mathbf{C}\|_1, \tag{2}$$

where λ is the regularization parameter. Once $\hat{\mathbf{C}}$ is computed, the latent clean patch matrix $\hat{\mathbf{X}}$ can be estimated as $\hat{\mathbf{X}} = \mathbf{D}\hat{\mathbf{C}}$. Though having achieved promising performance on additive white Gaussian noise (AWGN), the traditional SC based denoising methods [4,5,10,11,14] are very limited in dealing with realistic noise in real-world images captured by CCD or CMOS cameras. The reason is that the realistic noise is non-Gaussian, varies locally and across channels, which cannot be characterized well by the Frobenius norm in the SC model (2) [21,24,29,36].

To account for the varying statistics of realistic noise in different channels and different patches, we introduce two weight matrices $\mathbf{W}_1 \in \mathbb{R}^{3p^2 \times 3p^2}$ and $\mathbf{W}_2 \in \mathbb{R}^{M \times M}$ to characterize the SC residual ($\mathbf{Y} - \mathbf{DC}$) in the data-fidelity term of Eq. (2). Besides, to better characterize the sparsity priors of the natural images, we introduce a third weight matrix $\mathbf{W}_3$, which is related to the distribution of the sparse coefficients matrix $\mathbf{C}$, into the regularization term of Eq. (2). For the dictionary $\mathbf{D}$, we learn it adaptively by applying the SVD [37] to the given data matrix $\mathbf{Y}$ as

$$\mathbf{Y} = \mathbf{D}\mathbf{S}\mathbf{V}^{\top}. \tag{3}$$

Note that in this paper, we are not aiming at proposing a new dictionary learning scheme as [4] did. Once obtained from SVD, the dictionary $\mathbf{D}$ is fixed and not updated iteratively. Finally, the proposed trilateral weighted sparse coding (TWSC) model is formulated as:

$$\min_{\mathbf{C}} \|\mathbf{W}_1(\mathbf{Y} - \mathbf{D}\mathbf{C})\mathbf{W}_2\|_F^2 + \|\mathbf{W}_3^{-1}\mathbf{C}\|_1. \tag{4}$$

Note that the parameter λ has been implicitly incorporated into the weight matrix $\mathbf{W}_3$.

2.2 The Setting of Weight Matrices

In this paper, we set the three weight matrices $\mathbf{W}_1$, $\mathbf{W}_2$, and $\mathbf{W}_3$ as diagonal matrices and grant clear physical meanings to them. $\mathbf{W}_1$ is a block diagonal matrix with three blocks, each of which has the same diagonal elements to describe the noise properties in the corresponding R, G, or B channel. Based on [29,36,38], the realistic noise in a local patch could be approximately modeled as Gaussian, and each diagonal element of $\mathbf{W}_2$ is used to describe the noise variance in the corresponding patch $\mathbf{y}$. Generally speaking, $\mathbf{W}_1$ is employed to regularize the row discrepancy of residual matrix $(\mathbf{Y} - \mathbf{D}\mathbf{C})$, while $\mathbf{W}_2$ is employed to regularize the column discrepancy of $(\mathbf{Y} - \mathbf{D}\mathbf{C})$. For matrix $\mathbf{W}_3$, each diagonal element is set based on the sparsity priors on $\mathbf{C}$.

We determine the three weight matrices $\mathbf{W}_1$, $\mathbf{W}_2$, and $\mathbf{W}_3$ by employing the *Maximum A-Posterior* (MAP) estimation technique:

$$\hat{\mathbf{C}} = \arg\max_{\mathbf{C}} \ln P(\mathbf{C}|\mathbf{Y}) = \arg\max_{\mathbf{C}}\{\ln P(\mathbf{Y}|\mathbf{C}) + \ln P(\mathbf{C})\}. \tag{5}$$

The log-likelihood term $\ln P(\mathbf{Y}|\mathbf{C})$ is characterized by the statistics of noise. According to [29,36,38], it can be assumed that the noise is independently and identically distributed (i.i.d.) in each channel and each patch with Gaussian distribution. Denote by $\mathbf{y}_{cm}$ and $\mathbf{c}_m$ the mth column of the matrices $\mathbf{Y}_c$ and $\mathbf{C}$, respectively, and denote by σ_{cm} the noise std of $\mathbf{y}_{cm}$. We have

$$P(\mathbf{Y}|\mathbf{C}) = \prod_{c\in\{r,g,b\}} \prod_{m=1}^{M} (\pi\sigma_{cm})^{-p^2} e^{-\sigma_{cm}^{-2}\|\mathbf{y}_{cm} - \mathbf{D}_c\mathbf{c}_m\|_2^2}. \tag{6}$$

From the perspective of statistics [39], the set of $\{\sigma_{cm}\}$ can be viewed as a $3 \times M$ contingency table created by two variables σ_c and σ_m, and their relationship could be modeled by a log-linear model $\sigma_{cm} = \sigma_c^{l_1}\sigma_m^{l_2}$, where $l_1 + l_2 = 1$. Here we consider $\{\sigma_c\}, \{\sigma_m\}$ of equal importance and empirically set $l_1 = l_2 = 1/2$. The estimation of $\{\sigma_{cm}\}$ can be transferred to the estimation of $\{\sigma_c\}$ and $\{\sigma_m\}$, which will be introduced in the experimental section (Sect. 4).

The sparsity prior is imposed on the coefficients matrix $\mathbf{C}$, we assume that each column $\mathbf{c}_m$ of $\mathbf{C}$ follows i.i.d. Laplacian distribution. Specifically, for each entry $\mathbf{c}_m^i$, which is the coding coefficient of the mth patch $\mathbf{y}_m$ over the ith atom of dictionary $\mathbf{D}$, we assume that it follows distribution of $(2S_i)^{-1}\exp(-\mathbf{S}_i^{-1}|\mathbf{c}_m^i|)$, where $\mathbf{S}_i$ is the ith diagonal element of the singular value matrix $\mathbf{S}$ in Eq. (3). Note that we set the scale factor of the distribution as the inverse of the ith singular value $\mathbf{S}_i$. This is because the larger the singular value $\mathbf{S}_i$ is, the more important the ith atom (i.e., singular vector) in $\mathbf{D}$ should be, and hence the distribution of the coding coefficients over this singular vector should have stronger regularization with weaker sparsity. The prior term in Eq. (5) becomes

$$P(\mathbf{C}) = \prod_{m=1}^{M}\prod_{i=1}^{3p^2}(2\mathbf{S}_i)^{-1}e^{-\mathbf{S}_i^{-1}|\mathbf{c}_m^i|}. \tag{7}$$

Put (7) and (6) into (5) and consider the log-linear model $\sigma_{cm} = \sigma_c^{1/2}\sigma_m^{1/2}$, we have

$$\begin{aligned}\hat{\mathbf{C}} &= \arg\min_{\mathbf{C}} \sum_{c\in\{r,g,b\}}\sum_{m=1}^{M}\sigma_{cm}^{-2}\|\mathbf{y}_{cm} - \mathbf{D}_c\mathbf{c}_m\|_2^2 + \sum_{m=1}^{M}\|\mathbf{S}^{-1}\mathbf{c}_m\|_1\\ &= \arg\min_{\mathbf{C}} \sum_{c\in\{r,g,b\}}\sigma_c^{-1}\|(\mathbf{Y}_c - \mathbf{D}_c\mathbf{C})\mathbf{W}_2\|_F^2 + \|\mathbf{S}^{-1}\mathbf{C}\|_1\\ &= \arg\min_{\mathbf{C}} \|\mathbf{W}_1(\mathbf{Y} - \mathbf{D}\mathbf{C})\mathbf{W}_2\|_F^2 + \|\mathbf{W}_3^{-1}\mathbf{C}\|_1,\end{aligned} \tag{8}$$

where

$$\begin{aligned}\mathbf{W}_1 &= \mathrm{diag}(\sigma_r^{-1/2}\mathbf{I}_{p^2}, \sigma_g^{-1/2}\mathbf{I}_{p^2}, \sigma_b^{-1/2}\mathbf{I}_{p^2}),\\ \mathbf{W}_2 &= \mathrm{diag}(\sigma_1^{-1/2}, ..., \sigma_M^{-1/2}), \mathbf{W}_3 = \mathbf{S},\end{aligned} \tag{9}$$

and $\mathbf{I}_{p^2}$ is the p^2 dimensional identity matrix. Note that the diagonal elements of $\mathbf{W}_1$ and $\mathbf{W}_2$ are determined by the noise standard deviations in the corresponding channels and patches, respectively. The stronger the noise in a channel and a patch, the less that channel and patch will contribute to the denoised output.

2.3 Model Optimization

Letting $\mathbf{C}^* = \mathbf{W}_3^{-1}\mathbf{C}$, we can transfer the weight matrix $\mathbf{W}_3$ into the data-fidelity term of (4). Thus, the TWSC scheme (4) is reformulated as

$$\min_{\mathbf{C}^*} \|\mathbf{W}_1(\mathbf{Y} - \mathbf{D}\mathbf{W}_3\mathbf{C}^*)\mathbf{W}_2\|_F^2 + \|\mathbf{C}^*\|_1. \tag{10}$$

To make the notation simple, we remove the superscript $*$ in $\mathbf{C}^*$ and still use $\mathbf{C}$ in the following development. We employ the variable splitting method [40] to solve the problem (10). By introducing an augmented variable $\mathbf{Z}$, the problem (10) is reformulated as a linear equality-constrained problem with two variables $\mathbf{C}$ and $\mathbf{Z}$:

$$\min_{\mathbf{C},\mathbf{Z}} \|\mathbf{W}_1(\mathbf{Y} - \mathbf{D}\mathbf{W}_3\mathbf{C})\mathbf{W}_2\|_F^2 + \|\mathbf{Z}\|_1 \text{ s.t. } \mathbf{C} = \mathbf{Z}. \tag{11}$$

Since the objective function is separable w.r.t. the two variables, the problem (11) can be solved under the alternating direction method of multipliers (ADMM) [34] framework. The augmented Lagrangian function of (11) is:

$$\mathcal{L}(\mathbf{C},\mathbf{Z},\mathbf{\Delta},\rho) = \|\mathbf{W}_1(\mathbf{Y}-\mathbf{D}\mathbf{W}_3\mathbf{C})\mathbf{W}_2\|_F^2 + \|\mathbf{Z}\|_1 + \langle \mathbf{\Delta}, \mathbf{C}-\mathbf{Z}\rangle + \frac{\rho}{2}\|\mathbf{C}-\mathbf{Z}\|_F^2, \tag{12}$$

where $\mathbf{\Delta}$ is the augmented Lagrangian multiplier and $\rho > 0$ is the penalty parameter. We initialize the matrix variables $\mathbf{C}_0$, $\mathbf{Z}_0$, and $\mathbf{\Delta}_0$ to be comfortable zero matrices and $\rho_0 > 0$. Denote by $(\mathbf{C}_k, \mathbf{Z}_k)$ and $\mathbf{\Delta}_k$ the optimization variables and Lagrange multiplier at iteration k ($k = 0, 1, 2, ...$), respectively. By taking derivatives of the Lagrangian function $\mathcal{L}$ w.r.t. $\mathbf{C}$ and $\mathbf{Z}$, and setting the derivatives to be zeros, we can alternatively update the variables as follows:

(1) **Update C by fixing Z and Δ:**

$$\mathbf{C}_{k+1} = \arg\min_{\mathbf{C}} \|\mathbf{W}_1(\mathbf{Y}-\mathbf{D}\mathbf{W}_3\mathbf{C})\mathbf{W}_2\|_F^2 + \frac{\rho_k}{2}\|\mathbf{C}-\mathbf{Z}_k + \rho_k^{-1}\mathbf{\Delta}_k\|_F^2. \tag{13}$$

This is a two-sided weighted least squares regression problem with the solution satisfying that

$$\mathbf{A}\mathbf{C}_{k+1} + \mathbf{C}_{k+1}\mathbf{B}_k = \mathbf{E}_k, \tag{14}$$

where

$$\begin{aligned} \mathbf{A} &= \mathbf{W}_3^\top \mathbf{D}^\top \mathbf{W}_1^\top \mathbf{W}_1 \mathbf{D} \mathbf{W}_3, \mathbf{B}_k = \frac{\rho_k}{2}(\mathbf{W}_2\mathbf{W}_2^\top)^{-1}, \\ \mathbf{E}_k &= \mathbf{W}_3^\top \mathbf{D}^\top \mathbf{W}_1^\top \mathbf{W}_1 \mathbf{Y} + (\frac{\rho_k}{2}\mathbf{Z}_k - \frac{1}{2}\mathbf{\Delta}_k)(\mathbf{W}_2\mathbf{W}_2^\top)^{-1}. \end{aligned} \tag{15}$$

Equation (14) is a standard Sylvester equation (SE) which has a unique solution if and only if $\sigma(\mathbf{A}) \cap \sigma(-\mathbf{B}_k) = \emptyset$, where $\sigma(\mathbf{F})$ denotes the spectrum, i.e., the set of eigenvalues, of the matrix $\mathbf{F}$ [41]. We can rewrite the SE (14) as

$$(\mathbf{I}_M \otimes \boldsymbol{A} + \mathbf{B}_k^\top \otimes \boldsymbol{I}_{3p^2})\text{vec}(\mathbf{C}_{k+1}) = \text{vec}(\mathbf{E}_k), \tag{16}$$

and the solution $\mathbf{C}_{k+1}$ (if existed) can be obtained via $\mathbf{C}_{k+1} = \text{vec}^{-1}(\text{vec}(\mathbf{C}_{k+1}))$, where $\text{vec}^{-1}(\bullet)$ is the inverse of the vec-operator $\text{vec}(\bullet)$. Detailed theoretical analysis on the existence of the unique solution is given in Sect. 3.1.

(2) **Update Z by fixing C and Δ:**

$$\mathbf{Z}_{k+1} = \arg\min_{\mathbf{Z}} \frac{\rho_k}{2}\|\mathbf{Z}-(\mathbf{C}_{k+1}+\rho_k^{-1}\mathbf{\Delta}_k)\|_F^2 + \|\mathbf{Z}\|_1. \tag{17}$$

This problem has a closed-form solution as

$$\mathbf{Z}_{k+1} = \mathcal{S}_{\rho_k^{-1}}(\mathbf{C}_{k+1} + \rho_k^{-1}\mathbf{\Delta}_k), \tag{18}$$

where $\mathcal{S}_\lambda(x) = \text{sign}(x)\cdot\max(x-\lambda, 0)$ is the soft-thresholding operator.

Algorithm 1: Solve the TWSC Model (4) via ADMM

Input: $\mathbf{Y}, \mathbf{W}_1, \mathbf{W}_2, \mathbf{W}_3, \mu$, Tol, K_1;

Initialization: $\mathbf{C}_0 = \mathbf{Z}_0 = \mathbf{\Delta}_0 = \mathbf{0}$, $\rho_0 > 0$, $k = 0$, T = False;

While (T == false) **do**

1. Update $\mathbf{C}_{k+1}$ by solving Eq. (13);
2. Update $\mathbf{Z}_{k+1}$ by soft thresholding (18);
3. Update $\mathbf{\Delta}_{k+1}$ by Eq. (19);
4. Update ρ_{k+1} by $\rho_{k+1} = \mu\rho_k$, where $\mu \geq 1$;
5. $k \leftarrow k + 1$;

 if (Converged) or ($k \geq K_1$)

6. T $\leftarrow$ True;

 end if

end while

Output: Matrices $\mathbf{C}$ and $\mathbf{Z}$.

---

(3) **Update $\mathbf{\Delta}$ by fixing X and Z:**

$$\mathbf{\Delta}_{k+1} = \mathbf{\Delta}_k + \rho_k(\mathbf{C}_{k+1} - \mathbf{Z}_{k+1}). \tag{19}$$

(4) **Update ρ:** $\rho_{k+1} = \mu\rho_k$, where $\mu \geq 1$.

The above alternative updating steps are repeated until the convergence condition is satisfied or the number of iterations exceeds a preset threshold K_1. The ADMM algorithm converges when $\|\mathbf{C}_{k+1} - \mathbf{Z}_{k+1}\|_F \leq$ Tol, $\|\mathbf{C}_{k+1} - \mathbf{C}_k\|_F \leq$ Tol, and $\|\mathbf{Z}_{k+1} - \mathbf{Z}_k\|_F \leq$ Tol are simultaneously satisfied, where Tol > 0 is a small tolerance number. We summarize the updating procedures in Algorithm 1.

Convergence Analysis. The convergence of Algorithm 1 can be guaranteed since the overall objective function (11) is convex with a global optimal solution. In Fig. 3, we can see that the maximal values in $|\mathbf{C}_{k+1} - \mathbf{Z}_{k+1}|$, $|\mathbf{C}_{k+1} - \mathbf{C}_k|$, $|\mathbf{Z}_{k+1} - \mathbf{Z}_k|$ approach to 0 simultaneously in 50 iterations.

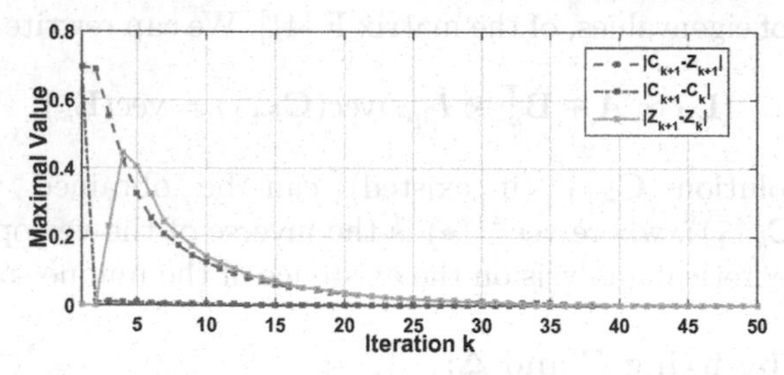

Fig. 3. The convergence curves of maximal values in entries of $|\mathbf{C}_{k+1} - \mathbf{Z}_{k+1}|$ (blue line), $|\mathbf{C}_{k+1} - \mathbf{C}_k|$ (red line), and $|\mathbf{Z}_{k+1} - \mathbf{Z}_k|$ (yellow line). The test image is the image in Fig. 2(a). (Color figure online)

2.4 The Denoising Algorithm

Given a noisy color image, suppose that we have extracted N local patches $\{\mathbf{y}_j\}_{j=1}^N$ and their similar patches. Then N noisy patch matrices $\{\mathbf{Y}_j\}_{j=1}^N$ can be formed to estimate the clean patch matrices $\{\mathbf{X}_j\}_{j=1}^N$. The patches in matrices $\{\mathbf{X}_j\}_{j=1}^N$ are aggregated to form the denoised image $\hat{\mathbf{x}}_c$. To obtain better denoising results, we perform the above denoising procedures for several (e.g., K_2) iterations. The proposed TWSC scheme based real-world image denoising algorithm is summarized in Algorithm 2.

Algorithm 2: Image Denoising by TWSC

Input: Noisy image $\mathbf{y}_c$, $\{\sigma_r, \sigma_g, \sigma_b\}$, K_2;
Initialization: $\hat{\mathbf{x}}_c^{(0)} = \mathbf{y}_c$, $\mathbf{y}_c^{(0)} = \mathbf{y}_c$;
for $k = 1 : K_2$ **do**
1. Set $\mathbf{y}_c^{(k)} = \hat{\mathbf{x}}_c^{(k-1)}$;
2. Extract local patches $\{\mathbf{y}_j\}_{j=1}^N$ from $\mathbf{y}_c^{(k)}$;
  for each patch $\mathbf{y}_j$ **do**
3. Search nonlocal similar patches $\mathbf{Y}_j$;
4. Apply the TWSC scheme (4) to $\mathbf{Y}_j$ and obtain the estimated $\mathbf{X}_j = \mathbf{DC}$;
  end for
5. Aggregate $\{\mathbf{X}_j\}_{j=1}^N$ to form the image $\hat{\mathbf{x}}_c^{(k)}$;
end for
Output: Denoised image $\hat{\mathbf{x}}_c^{(K_2)}$.

---

3 Existence and Faster Solution of Sylvester Equation

The solution of the Sylvester equation (SE) (14) does not always exist, though the solution is unique if it exists. Besides, solving SE (14) is usually computationally expensive in high dimensional cases. In this section, we provide a sufficient condition to guarantee the existence of the solution to SE (14), as well as a faster solution of (14) to save the computational cost of Algorithms 1 and 2.

3.1 Existence of the Unique Solution

Before we prove the existence of unique solution of SE (14), we first introduce the following theorem.

Theorem 1. *Assume that* $\mathbf{A} \in \mathbb{R}^{3p^2 \times 3p^2}$, $\mathbf{B} \in \mathbb{R}^{M \times M}$ *are both symmetric and positive semi-definite matrices. If at least one of* $\mathbf{A}, \mathbf{B}$ *is positive definite, the Sylvester equation* $\mathbf{AC} + \mathbf{CB} = \mathbf{E}$ *has a unique solution for* $\mathbf{C} \in \mathbb{R}^{3p^2 \times M}$.

The proof of Theorem 1 can be found in the supplementary file. Then we have the following corollary.

Corollary 1. *The SE (14) has a unique solution.*

Proof. Since $\mathbf{A}, \mathbf{B}_k$ in (14) are both symmetric and positive definite matrices, according to Theorem 1, the SE (14) has a unique solution.

3.2 Faster Solution

The solution of the SE (14) is typically obtained by the Bartels-Stewart algorithm [42]. This algorithm firstly employs a QR factorization [43], implemented via Gram-Schmidt process, to decompose the matrices $\mathbf{A}$ and $\mathbf{B}_k$ into Schur forms, and then solves the obtained triangular system by the back-substitution method [44]. However, since the matrices $\mathbf{I}_M \otimes \boldsymbol{A}$ and $\mathbf{B}_k^\top \otimes \boldsymbol{I}_{3p^2}$ are of $3p^2M \times 3p^2M$ dimensions, it is computationally expensive ($\mathcal{O}(p^6M^3)$) to calculate their QR factorization to obtain the Schur forms. By exploiting the specific properties of our problem, we provide a faster while exact solution for the SE (14).

Since the matrices $\mathbf{A}, \mathbf{B}_k$ in (14) are symmetric and positive definite, the matrix $\mathbf{A}$ can be eigen-decomposed as $\mathbf{A} = \mathbf{U_A \Sigma_A U_A^\top}$, with computational cost of $\mathcal{O}(p^6)$. Left multiply both sides of the SE (14) by $\mathbf{U_A^\top}$, we can get $\mathbf{\Sigma}_A \mathbf{U_A^\top C}_{k+1} + \mathbf{U_A^\top C}_{k+1}\mathbf{B}_k = \mathbf{U_A^\top E}_k$. This can be viewed as an SE w.r.t. the matrix $\mathbf{U_A^\top C}_{k+1}$, with a unique solution $\text{vec}(\mathbf{U_A^\top C}_{k+1}) = (\mathbf{I}_M \otimes \boldsymbol{\Sigma}_\mathbf{A} + \mathbf{B}_k^\top \otimes \boldsymbol{I}_{3p^2})^{-1}\text{vec}(\mathbf{U_A^\top E}_k)$. Since the matrix $(\mathbf{I}_M \otimes \boldsymbol{\Sigma}_\mathbf{A} + \mathbf{B}_k^\top \otimes \boldsymbol{I}_{3p^2})$ is diagonal and positive definite, its inverse can be calculated on each diagonal element of $(\mathbf{I}_M \otimes \boldsymbol{\Sigma}_\mathbf{A} + \mathbf{B}_k^\top \otimes \boldsymbol{I}_{3p^2})$. The computational cost for this step is $\mathcal{O}(p^2M)$. Finally, the solution $\mathbf{C}_{k+1}$ can be obtained via $\mathbf{C}_{k+1} = \mathbf{U_A}\text{vec}^{-1}(\text{vec}(\mathbf{U_A^\top C}_{k+1}))$. By this way, the complexity for solving the SE (14) is reduced from $\mathcal{O}(p^6M^3)$ to $\mathcal{O}(\max(p^6, p^2M))$, which is a huge computational saving.

4 Experiments

To validate the effectiveness of our proposed TWSC scheme, we apply it to both synthetic additive white Gaussian noise (AWGN) corrupted images and real-world noisy images captured by CCD or CMOS cameras. To better demonstrate the roles of the three weight matrices in our model, we compare with a baseline method, in which the weight matrices $\mathbf{W}_1, \mathbf{W}_2$ are set as comfortable identity matrices, while the matrix $\mathbf{W}_3$ is set as in (8). We call this baseline method the *Weighted Sparse Coding* (WSC).

4.1 Experimental Settings

Noise Level Estimation. For most image denoising algorithms, the standard deviation (std) of noise should be given as a parameter. In this work, we provide an exploratory approach to solve this problem. Specifically, the noise std σ_c of channel c can be estimated by some noise estimation methods [45–47]. In Algorithm 2, the noise std for the mth patch of $\mathbf{Y}$ can be initialized as

$$\sigma_m = \sigma \triangleq \sqrt{(\sigma_r^2 + \sigma_g^2 + \sigma_b^2)/3} \tag{20}$$

and updated in the following iterations as

$$\sigma_m = \sqrt{\max(0, \sigma^2 - \|\mathbf{y}_m - \mathbf{x}_m\|_2^2)}, \tag{21}$$

where $\mathbf{y}_m$ is the mth column in the patch matrix $\mathbf{Y}$, and $\mathbf{x}_m = \mathbf{Dc}_m$ is the mth patch recovered in previous iteration (please refer to Sect. 2.4).

Implementation Details. We empirically set the parameter $\rho_0 = 0.5$ and $\mu = 1.1$. The maximum number of iteration is set as $K_1 = 10$. The window size for similar patch searching is set as 60×60. For parameters p, M, K_2, we set $p = 7$, $M = 70$, $K_2 = 8$ for $0 < \sigma \leq 20$; $p = 8$, $M = 90$, $K_2 = 12$ for $20 < \sigma \leq 40$; $p = 8$, $M = 120$, $K_2 = 12$ for $40 < \sigma \leq 60$; $p = 9$, $M = 140$, $K_2 = 14$ for $60 < \sigma \leq 100$. All parameters are fixed in our experiments. We will release the code with the publication of this work.

Table 1. Average results of PSNR(dB) and SSIM of different denoising algorithms on 20 grayscale images corrupted by AWGN noise.

σ_n	Metric	BM3D-SAPCA	LSSC	NCSR	WNNM	TNRD	DnCNN	WSC	TWSC
15	PSNR	32.42	32.27	32.19	32.43	32.27	32.59	32.06	32.34
	SSIM	0.8860	0.8849	0.8814	0.8841	0.8815	0.8879	0.8673	0.8846
25	PSNR	30.02	29.84	29.76	30.05	29.87	30.22	29.57	29.98
	SSIM	0.8364	0.8329	0.8293	0.8365	0.8314	0.8415	0.8179	0.8372
35	PSNR	28.48	28.26	28.17	28.51	28.33	28.66	28.01	28.49
	SSIM	0.7969	0.7908	0.7855	0.7958	0.7907	0.8021	0.7765	0.7987
50	PSNR	26.85	26.64	26.55	26.92	26.75	27.08	26.35	26.93
	SSIM	0.7481	0.7405	0.7391	0.7499	0.7415	0.7563	0.7258	0.7530
75	PSNR	24.74	24.77	24.66	25.15	24.97	25.24	24.54	25.15
	SSIM	0.6649	0.6746	0.6793	0.6903	0.6801	0.6931	0.6612	0.6949

4.2 Results on AWGN Noise Removal

We first compare the proposed TWSC scheme with the leading AWGN denoising methods such as BM3D-SAPCA [9] (which usually performs better than BM3D [7]), LSSC [10], NCSR [11], WNNM [13], TNRD [19], and DnCNN [20] on 20 grayscale images commonly used in [7]. Note that TNRD and DnCNN are both discriminative learning based methods, and we use the models trained originally by the authors. Each noisy image is generated by adding the AWGN noise to the clean image, while the std of the noise is set as $\sigma \in \{15, 25, 35, 50, 75\}$ in this paper. Note that in this experiment we set the weight matrix $\mathbf{W}_1 = \sigma^{-1/2}\mathbf{I}_{p^2}$ since the input images are grayscale.

The averaged PSNR and SSIM [48] results are listed in Table 1. One can see that the proposed TWSC achieves comparable performance with WNNM, TNRD and DnCNN in most cases. It should be noted that TNRD and DnCNN are trained on clean and synthetic noisy image pairs, while TWSC only utilizes the tested noisy image. Besides, one can see that the proposed TWSC works much better than the baseline method WSC, which proves that the weight matrix $\mathbf{W}_2$ can characterize better the noise statistics in local image patches. Due to limited space, we leave the visual comparisons of different methods in the supplementary file.

4.3 Results on Realistic Noise Removal

We evaluate the proposed TWSC scheme on three publicly available real-world noisy image datasets [24, 29, 49].

Dataset 1 is provided in [49], which includes around 20 real-world noisy images collected under uncontrolled environment. Since there is no "ground truth" of the noisy images, we only compare the visual quality of the denoised images by different methods.

Dataset 2 is provided in [24], which includes noisy images of 11 static scenes captured by Canon 5D Mark 3, Nikon D600, and Nikon D800 cameras. The real-world noisy images were collected under controlled indoor environment. Each scene was shot 500 times under the same camera and camera setting. The mean image of the 500 shots is roughly taken as the "ground truth", with which the PSNR and SSIM [48] can be computed. 15 images of size 512×512 were cropped to evaluate different denoising methods. Recently, some other datasets such as [50] are also constructed by employing the strategies of this dataset.

Dataset 3 is called the Darmstadt Noise Dataset (DND) [29], which includes 50 different pairs of images of the same scenes captured by Sony A7R, Olympus E-M10, Sony RX100 IV, and Huawei Nexus 6P. The real-world noisy images are collected under higher ISO values with shorter exposure time, while the "ground truth" images are captured under lower ISO values with adjusted longer exposure times. Since the captured images are of megapixel-size, the authors cropped 20 bounding boxes of 512×512 pixels from each image in the dataset, yielding 1000 test crops in total. However, the "ground truth" images are not open access, and we can only submit the denoising results to the authors' Project Website and get the PSNR and SSIM [48] results.

Comparison Methods. We compare the proposed TWSC method with CBM3D [8], TNRD [19], DnCNN [20], the commercial software Neat Image (NI) [25], the state-of-the-art real image denoising methods "Noise Clinic" (NC) [22], CC [24], and MCWNNM [26]. We also compare with the baseline method WSC described in Sect. 4 as a baseline. The methods of CBM3D and DnCNN can directly deal with color images, and the input noise std is set by Eq. (20). For TNRD, MCWNNM, and TWSC, we use [46] to estimate the noise std σ_c ($c \in \{r, g, b\}$) for each channel. For blind mode DnCNN, we use its color version provided by the authors and there is no need to estimate the noise std. Since TNRD is designed for grayscale images, we applied them to each channel of real-world noisy images. TNRD achieves its best results when setting the noise std of the trained models at $\sigma_c = 10$ on these datasets.

Results on Dataset 1. Figure 4 shows the denoised images of "Dog" (the method CC [24] is not compared since its testing code is not available). One can see that CBM3D, TNRD, DnCNN, NI and NC generate some noise-caused color artifacts across the whole image, while MCWNNM and WSC tend to over-smooth a little the image. The proposed TWSC removes more clearly the noise without over-smoothing much the image details. These results demonstrate that the methods designed for AWGN are not effective for realistic noise

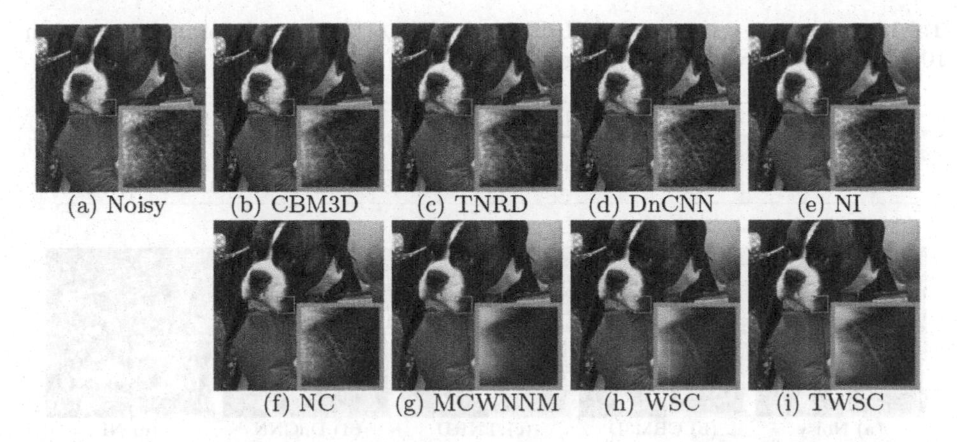

Fig. 4. Denoised images of the real noisy image *Dog* [49] by different methods. Note that the ground-truth clean image of the noisy input is not available.

removal. Though NC and NI methods are specifically developed for real-world noisy images, their performance is not satisfactory. In comparison, the proposed TWSC works much better in removing the noise while maintaining the details (see the zoom-in window in "Dog") than the other competing methods. More visual comparisons can be found in the supplementary file.

Results on Dataset 2. The average PSNR and SSIM results on the 15 cropped images by competing methods are listed in Table 2. One can see that the proposed TWSC is much better than other competing methods, including the baseline method WSC and the recently proposed CC, MCWNNM. Figure 5 shows the denoised images of a scene captured by Nikon D800 at ISO = 6400. One can see that the proposed TWSC method results in not only higher PSNR and SSIM measures, but also much better visual quality than other methods. Due to limited space, we do not show the results of baseline method WSC in visual quality comparison. More visual comparisons can be found in the supplementary file.

Table 2. Average results of PSNR(dB) and SSIM of different denoising methods on 15 cropped real-world noisy images used in [24].

	CBM3D	TNRD	DnCNN	NI	NC	CC	MCWNNM	WSC	TWSC
PSNR	35.19	36.61	33.86	35.49	36.43	36.88	37.70	37.36	**37.81**
SSIM	0.8580	0.9463	0.8635	0.9126	0.9364	0.9481	0.9542	0.9516	**0.9586**

Results on Dataset 3. In Table 3, we list the average PSNR and SSIM results of the competing methods on the 1000 cropped images in the DND dataset [29]. We can see again that the proposed TWSC achieves much better performance than the other competing methods. Note that the "ground truth" images of this dataset have not been published, but one can submit the denoised images to the project website and get the PSNR and SSIM results. More results can

Table 3. Average results of PSNR(dB) and SSIM of different denoising methods on 1000 cropped real-world noisy images in [29].

	CBM3D	TNRD	DnCNN	NI	NC	MCWNNM	WSC	TWSC
PSNR	32.14	34.15	32.41	35.11	36.07	37.38	36.81	**37.94**
SSIM	0.7773	0.8271	0.7897	0.8778	0.9013	0.9294	0.9165	**0.9403**

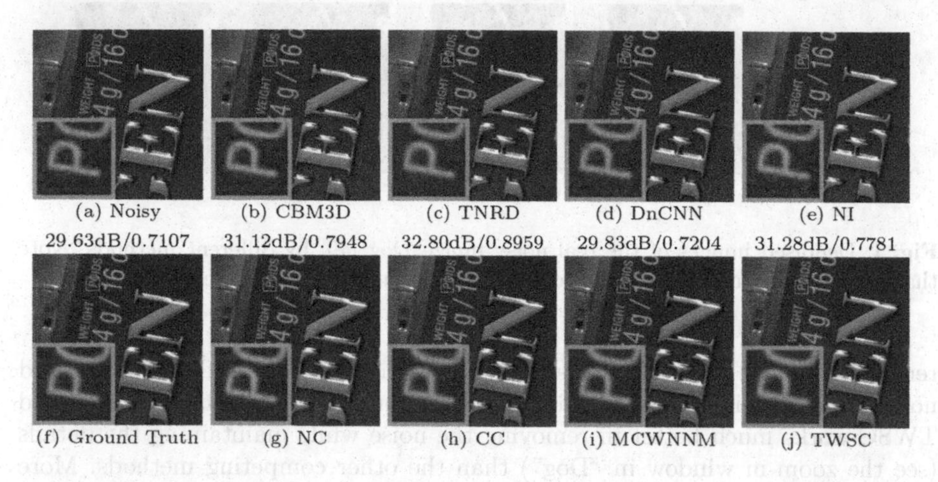

(a) Noisy 29.63dB/0.7107 (b) CBM3D 31.12dB/0.7948 (c) TNRD 32.80dB/0.8959 (d) DnCNN 29.83dB/0.7204 (e) NI 31.28dB/0.7781

(f) Ground Truth (g) NC (h) CC (i) MCWNNM (j) TWSC

Fig. 5. Denoised images of the real noisy image *Nikon D800 ISO 6400 1* [24] by different methods. This scene was shot 500 times under the same camera and camera setting. The mean image of the 500 shots is roughly taken as the "Ground Truth".

be found in the website of the DND dataset (https://noise.visinf.tu-darmstadt.de/benchmark/#results_srgb). Figure 6 shows the denoised images of a scene captured by a Nexus 6P camera. One can still see that the proposed TWSC method results better visual quality than the other denoising methods. More visual comparisons can be found in the supplementary file.

Comparison on Speed. We compare the average computational time (second) of different methods (except CC) to process one 512×512 image on the DND Dataset [29]. The results are shown in Table 4. All experiments are run under the Matlab2014b environment on a machine with Intel(R) Core(TM) i7-5930K CPU of 3.5 GHz and 32 GB RAM. The fastest speed is highlighted in bold. One can see that Neat Image (NI) is the fastest and it spends about 1.1 s to process an image, while the proposed TWSC needs about 195 s. Noted that Neat Image is a highly-optimized software with parallelization, CBM3D, TNRD, and NC are implemented with compiled C++ mex-function and with parallelization, while DnCNN, MCWNNM, and the proposed WSC and TWSC are implemented purely in Matlab.

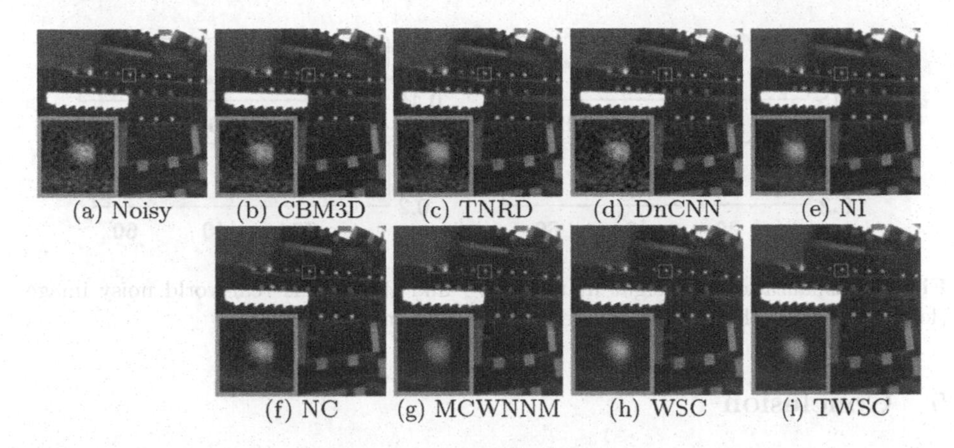

Fig. 6. Denoised images of the real noisy image "*0001_2*" captured by Nexus 6P [29] by different methods. Note that the ground-truth clean image of the noisy input is not publicly released yet.

Table 4. Average computational time (s) of different methods to process a 512 × 512 image in the DND dataset [29].

	CBM3D	TNRD	DnCNN	NI	NC	MCWNNM	WSC	TWSC
Time	6.9	5.2	79.5	**1.1**	15.6	208.1	188.6	195.2

4.4 Visualization of the Weight Matrices

The three diagonal weight matrices in the proposed TWSC model (4) have clear physical meanings, and it is interesting to analyze how the matrices actually relate to the input image by visualizing the resulting matrices. To this end, we applied TWSC to the real-world (estimated noise stds of R/G/B: 11.4/14.8/18.4) and synthetic AWGN (std of all channels: 25) noisy images shown in Fig. 1. The final diagonal weight matrices for two typical patch matrices ($\boldsymbol{Y}$) from the two images are visualized in Fig. 7. One can see that the matrix $\boldsymbol{W}_1$ reflects well the noise levels in the images. Though matrix $\boldsymbol{W}_2$ is initialized as an identity matrix, it is changed in iterations since noise in different patches are removed differently. For real-world noisy images, the noise levels of different patches in $\boldsymbol{Y}$ are different, hence the elements of $\boldsymbol{W}_2$ vary a lot. In contrast, the noise levels of patches in the synthetic noisy image are similar, thus the elements of $\boldsymbol{W}_2$ are similar. The weight matrix $\boldsymbol{W}_3$ is basically determined by the patch structure but not noise, and we do not plot it here.

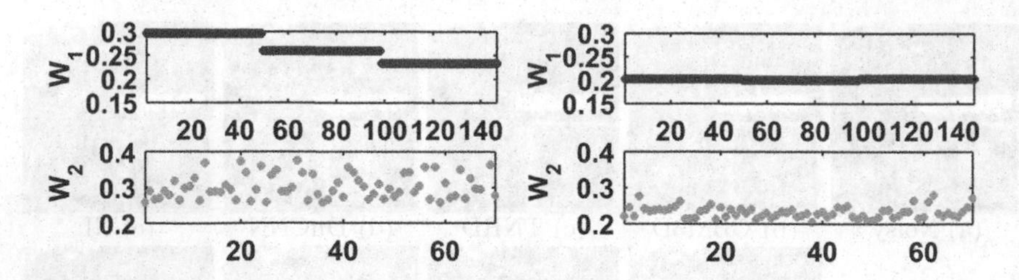

Fig. 7. Visualization of weight matrices $\boldsymbol{W}_1$ and $\boldsymbol{W}_2$ on the real-world noisy image (left) and the synthetic noisy image (right) shown in Fig. 1.

5 Conclusion

The realistic noise in real-world noisy images captured by CCD or CMOS cameras is very complex due to the various factors in digital camera pipelines, making the real-world image denoising problem much more challenging than additive white Gaussian noise removal. We proposed a novel trilateral weighted sparse coding (TWSC) scheme to exploit the noise properties across different channels and local patches. Specifically, we introduced two weight matrices into the data-fidelity term of the traditional sparse coding model to adaptively characterize the noise statistics in each patch of each channel, and another weight matrix into the regularization term to better exploit sparsity priors of natural images. The proposed TWSC scheme was solved under the ADMM framework and the solution to the Sylvester equation is guaranteed. Experiments demonstrated the superior performance of TWSC over existing state-of-the-art denoising methods, including those methods designed for realistic noise in real-world noisy images.

References

1. Zhu, L., Fu, C.W., Brown, M.S., Heng, P.A.: A non-local low-rank framework for ultrasound speckle reduction. In: CVPR, pp. 5650–5658 (2017)
2. Granados, M., Kim, K., Tompkin, J., Theobalt, C.: Automatic noise modeling for ghost-free hdr reconstruction. ACM Trans. Graph. **32**(6), 1–10 (2013)
3. Nguyen, A., Yosinski, J., Clune, J.: Deep neural networks are easily fooled: high confidence predictions for unrecognizable images. In: CVPR, pp. 427–436 (2015)
4. Elad, M., Aharon, M.: Image denoising via sparse and redundant representations over learned dictionaries. IEEE Trans. Image Process. **15**(12), 3736–3745 (2006)
5. Mairal, J., Elad, M., Sapiro, G.: Sparse representation for color image restoration. IEEE Trans. Image Process. **17**(1), 53–69 (2008)
6. Buades, A., Coll, B., Morel, J.M.: A non-local algorithm for image denoising. In: CVPR, pp. 60–65 (2005)
7. Dabov, K., Foi, A., Katkovnik, V., Egiazarian, K.: Image denoising by sparse 3-D transform-domain collaborative filtering. IEEE Trans. Image Process. **16**(8), 2080–2095 (2007)
8. Dabov, K., Foi, A., Katkovnik, V., Egiazarian, K.: Color image denoising via sparse 3D collaborative filtering with grouping constraint in luminance-chrominance space. In: ICIP, pp. 313–316. IEEE (2007)

9. Dabov, K., Foi, A., Katkovnik, V., Egiazarian, K.: BM3D image denoising with shape-adaptive principal component analysis. In: SPARS (2009)
10. Mairal, J., Bach, F., Ponce, J., Sapiro, G., Zisserman, A.: Non-local sparse models for image restoration. In: ICCV, pp. 2272–2279 (2009)
11. Dong, W., Zhang, L., Shi, G., Li, X.: Nonlocally centralized sparse representation for image restoration. IEEE Trans. Image Process. **22**(4), 1620–1630 (2013)
12. Dong, W., Shi, G., Li, X.: Nonlocal image restoration with bilateral variance estimation: a low-rank approach. IEEE Trans. Image Process. **22**(2), 700–711 (2013)
13. Gu, S., Zhang, L., Zuo, W., Feng, X.: Weighted nuclear norm minimization with application to image denoising. In: CVPR, pp. 2862–2869. IEEE (2014)
14. Xu, J., Zhang, L., Zuo, W., Zhang, D., Feng, X.: Patch group based nonlocal self-similarity prior learning for image denoising. In ICCV, pp. 244–252 (2015)
15. Roth, S., Black, M.J.: Fields of experts. Int. J. Comput. Vis. **82**(2), 205–229 (2009)
16. Zoran, D., Weiss, Y.: From learning models of natural image patches to whole image restoration. In: ICCV, pp. 479–486 (2011)
17. Burger, H.C., Schuler, C.J., Harmeling, S.: Image denoising: can plain neural networks compete with BM3D? In: CVPR, pp. 2392–2399 (2012)
18. Schmidt, U., Roth, S.: Shrinkage fields for effective image restoration. In: CVPR, pp. 2774–2781, June 2014
19. Chen, Y., Yu, W., Pock, T.: On learning optimized reaction diffusion processes for effective image restoration. In: CVPR, pp. 5261–5269 (2015)
20. Zhang, K., Zuo, W., Chen, Y., Meng, D., Zhang, L.: Beyond a Gaussian denoiser: residual learning of deep CNN for image denoising. IEEE Trans. Image Process. **26**, 3142–3155 (2017)
21. Liu, C., Szeliski, R., Kang, S.B., Zitnick, C.L., Freeman, W.T.: Automatic estimation and removal of noise from a single image. IEEE TPAMI **30**(2), 299–314 (2008)
22. Lebrun, M., Colom, M., Morel, J.M.: Multiscale image blind denoising. IEEE Trans. Image Process. **24**(10), 3149–3161 (2015)
23. Zhu, F., Chen, G., Heng, P.A.: From noise modeling to blind image denoising. In: CVPR, June 2016
24. Nam, S., Hwang, Y., Matsushita, Y., Kim, S.J.: A holistic approach to cross-channel image noise modeling and its application to image denoising. In: CVPR, pp. 1683–1691 (2016)
25. ABSoft, N.: Neat Image. https://ni.neatvideo.com/home
26. Xu, J., Zhang, L., Zhang, D., Feng, X.: Multi-channel weighted nuclear norm minimization for real color image denoising. In: ICCV (2017)
27. Xu, J., Ren, D., Zhang, L., Zhang, D.: Patch group based Bayesian learning for blind image denoising. In: Chen, C.-S., Lu, J., Ma, K.-K. (eds.) ACCV 2016. LNCS, vol. 10116, pp. 79–95. Springer, Cham (2017). https://doi.org/10.1007/978-3-319-54407-6_6
28. Xu, J., Zhang, L., Zhang, D.: External prior guided internal prior learning for real-world noisy image denoising. IEEE Trans. Image Process. **27**(6), 2996–3010 (2018)
29. Plötz, T., Roth, S.: Benchmarking denoising algorithms with real photographs. In: CVPR (2017)
30. Kervrann, C., Boulanger, J., Coupé, P.: Bayesian non-local means filter, image redundancy and adaptive dictionaries for noise removal. In: Sgallari, F., Murli, A., Paragios, N. (eds.) SSVM 2007. LNCS, vol. 4485, pp. 520–532. Springer, Heidelberg (2007). https://doi.org/10.1007/978-3-540-72823-8_45

31. Wright, J., Yang, A., Ganesh, A., Sastry, S., Ma, Y.: Robust face recognition via sparse representation. IEEE TPAMI **31**(2), 210–227 (2009)
32. Yang, J., Yu, K., Gong, Y., Huang, T.: Linear spatial pyramid matching using sparse coding for image classification. In: CVPR, pp. 1794–1801 (2009)
33. Yang, J., Wright, J., Huang, T., Ma, Y.: Image super-resolution via sparse representation. IEEE Trans. Image Process. **19**(11), 2861–2873 (2010)
34. Boyd, S., Parikh, N., Chu, E., Peleato, B., Eckstein, J.: Distributed optimization and statistical learning via the alternating direction method of multipliers. Found. Trends Mach. Learn. **3**(1), 1–122 (2011)
35. Tibshirani, R.: Regression shrinkage and selection via the lasso. J. R. Stat. Society. Ser. B (Methodol.) **58**, 267–288 (1996)
36. Khashabi, D., Nowozin, S., Jancsary, J., Fitzgibbon, A.W.: Joint demosaicing and denoising via learned nonparametric random fields. IEEE Trans. Image Process. **23**(12), 4968–4981 (2014)
37. Eckart, C., Young, G.: The approximation of one matrix by another of lower rank. Psychometrika **1**(3), 211–218 (1936)
38. Leung, B., Jeon, G., Dubois, E.: Least-squares luma-chroma demultiplexing algorithm for bayer demosaicking. IEEE Trans. Image Process. **20**(7), 1885–1894 (2011)
39. McCullagh, P.: Generalized linear models. Eur. J. Oper. Res. **16**(3), 285–292 (1984)
40. Eckstein, J., Bertsekas, D.P.: On the Douglas–Rachford splitting method and the proximal point algorithm for maximal monotone operators. Math. Program. **55**(1), 293–318 (1992)
41. Simoncini, V.: Computational methods for linear matrix equations. SIAM Rev. **58**(3), 377–441 (2016)
42. Bartels, R.H., Stewart, G.W.: Solution of the matrix equation AX + XB = C. Commun. ACM **15**(9), 820–826 (1972)
43. Golub, G., Van Loan, C.: Matrix Computations, 3rd edn. Johns Hopkins University Press, Baltimore (1996)
44. Bareiss, E.: Sylvesters identity and multistep integer-preserving Gaussian elimination. Math. Comput. **22**(103), 565–578 (1968)
45. Liu, X., Tanaka, M., Okutomi, M.: Single-image noise level estimation for blind denoising. IEEE Trans. Image Process. **22**(12), 5226–5237 (2013)
46. Chen, G., Zhu, F., Pheng, A.H.: An efficient statistical method for image noise level estimation. In: ICCV, December 2015
47. Sutour, C., Deledalle, C.A., Aujol, J.F.: Estimation of the noise level function based on a nonparametric detection of homogeneous image regions. SIAM J. Imaging Sci. **8**(4), 2622–2661 (2015)
48. Wang, Z., Bovik, A.C., Sheikh, H.R., Simoncelli, E.P.: Image quality assessment: from error visibility to structural similarity. IEEE Trans. Image Process. **13**(4), 600–612 (2004)
49. Lebrun, M., Colom, M., Morel, J.M.: The noise clinic: a blind image denoising algorithm. http://www.ipol.im/pub/art/2015/125/. Accessed 28 Jan 2015
50. Xu, J., Li, H., Liang, Z., Zhang, D., Zhang, L.: Real-world noisy image denoising: a new benchmark. CoRR abs/1804.02603 (2018)

NNEval: Neural Network Based Evaluation Metric for Image Captioning

Naeha Sharif[1(✉)], Lyndon White[1], Mohammed Bennamoun[1], and Syed Afaq Ali Shah[1,2]

[1] The University of Western Australia, 35 Stirling Highway, Crawley, WA, Australia
{naeha.sharif,lyndon.white}@research.uwa.edu.au,
mohammed.bennamoun@uwa.edu.au

[2] School of Engineering and Technology, Central Queensland University, Rockhampton, Australia
s.shah@cqu.edu.au

Abstract. The automatic evaluation of image descriptions is an intricate task, and it is highly important in the development and fine-grained analysis of captioning systems. Existing metrics to automatically evaluate image captioning systems fail to achieve a satisfactory level of correlation with human judgements at the sentence level. Moreover, these metrics, unlike humans, tend to focus on specific aspects of quality, such as the n-gram overlap or the semantic meaning. In this paper, we present the first learning-based metric to evaluate image captions. Our proposed framework enables us to incorporate both lexical and semantic information into a single learned metric. This results in an evaluator that takes into account various linguistic features to assess the caption quality. The experiments we performed to assess the proposed metric, show improvements upon the state of the art in terms of correlation with human judgements and demonstrate its superior robustness to distractions.

Keywords: Image captioning · Automatic evaluation metric
Neural networks · Correlation · Accuracy · Robustness

1 Introduction

With the rapid advancement in image captioning research [12,20,25,29,38–41], the need for reliable and efficient evaluation methods has become increasingly pressing. Describing images in natural language is an ability that comes naturally to humans. For humans, a brief glance is sufficient to understand the semantic meaning of a scene in order to describe the incredible amount of details and subtleties about its visual content [41]. While a reasonable amount of progress is made in the direction of replicating this human trait, it is still far from being solved [17,31]. Effective evaluation methodologies are necessary to facilitate the fine-grained analysis for system development, comparative analysis, and identification of areas for further improvement.

V. Ferrari et al. (Eds.): ECCV 2018, LNCS 11212, pp. 39–55, 2018.
https://doi.org/10.1007/978-3-030-01237-3_3

Evaluating image description is more complex than it is commonly perceived, mainly due to the diversity of acceptable solutions [18]. Human evaluations can serve as the most reliable assessments for caption quality. However, they are resource-intensive, subjective and hard to replicate. Automatic evaluation metrics on the other hand, are more efficient and cost effective. However, the automatic metrics currently in use for caption evaluation, fail to reach the desired level of agreement with human judgements at the sentence level [11,21]. According to the scores of some metrics, the best machine models outperform humans in the image captioning task[1] (Microsoft COCO challenge [8]), portraying an illusion that image captioning is close to being solved. *This reflects the need to develop more reliable automatic metrics which capture the set of criteria that humans use in judging the caption quality.*

Some of the automatic metrics which are commonly used to evaluate image descriptions, such as BLEU [33], METEOR [5] and ROUGE [27], were originally developed to assess *Machine Translation/Summarization* systems. Whereas, in the recent years CIDEr [37] and SPICE [4] were developed specifically for the image caption evaluation task and have shown more success as compared to the existing ones. All of these metrics output a certain score representing the similarity between the candidate and the reference captions. While there are a number of possible aspects to measure the quality of a candidate caption, all of the aforementioned metrics, rely on either lexical or semantic information to measure the similarity between the candidate and the reference sentences.

Our motivation to form a composite metric is driven by the fact that human judgement process involves assessment across various linguistic dimensions. We draw inspiration from the *Machine Translation* (MT) literature, where learning paradigms have been proposed to create successful composite metrics [6,7]. Learning-based approach is useful because it offers a systematic way to combine various informative features. However, it is also accompanied by the need of large training data. To avoid creating an expensive resource of human quality judgements, we make use of a training criteria as inspired by [9,24], which involves the classification of a caption as "human generated or machine generated". This enables us to utilize the available human generated and machine generated data for training (Sect. 4.1).

While it is hard to find a globally accepted definition of a "good caption", we hypothesize that the captions that are closer to human-generated descriptions can be categorized as acceptable/desirable. The better a captioning system, the more its output will resemble human generated descriptions. Moreover, the question of a caption being human or machine generated has the added advantage of being answered by the existing datasets containing human reference captions for corresponding images. Datasets such as MS COCO [8], Flickr30K [34], and Visual Genome [23] have multiple human generated captions that are associated with each image. These captions along with those generated by machine models can be used to train a network to distinguish between the two (human or

[1] http://cocodataset.org/#captions-leaderboard.

machine), thus overcoming the need of the labour intensive task of obtaining human judgements for a corpus.

In our proposed framework, we cast the problem of image description evaluation as a classification task. A multilayer neural network is trained with an objective to distinguish between human and machine generated captions, while using the scores of various metrics based on lexical/semantic information as features. In order to generate a score on a continuous scale of [0, 1], we use the confidence measure obtained through class probabilities, representing the believability of a caption being human-produced or otherwise. The proposed framework offers the flexibility to incorporate a variety of meaningful features that are helpful for evaluation. Moreover, with the evolution of image captioning systems, sensitive and more powerful features can be added in time. *To the best of our knowledge, this is the first "learning-based" metric designed specifically to evaluate image captioning systems.* Our main contributions are:

1. A novel learning-based metric, "NNEval", to evaluate image captioning systems.
2. A learning framework to unify various criteria to judge caption quality into a composite metric.
3. A detailed experimental analysis reflecting various aspects of NNEval, its ability to correlate better with human judgements at the sentence level and its robustness to various distractions.

2 Related Work

2.1 Automatic Evaluation Metrics

The significance of reliable automatic evaluation metrics is undeniable for the advancement of image captioning systems. While image captioning has drawn inspiration from MT domain for encoder-decoder based captioning networks [29,38–40,42], it has also benefited from the automatic metrics that were initially proposed to evaluate machine translations/text summaries, such as BLEU [33], METEOR [10] and ROUGE [27]. In order to evaluate the quality of candidate captions, these metrics measure the similarity between candidate and reference captions, which is reported as a score (higher score reflects better caption quality).

In recent years, two metrics CIDEr [37] and SPICE [4] have been developed specifically to evaluate image captioning systems. CIDEr measures the consensus between the candidate and reference captions, primarily using lexical information. SPICE on the other hand, uses semantic information in the form of a scene-graph to measure the similarity between candidate and reference sentences. Both SPICE and CIDEr have improved upon the commonly used metrics such as BLEU, ROUGE and METEOR in terms of mimicking human judgements. However, there is still a lot of room for improving the sentence-level correlation with human scores [21]. Authors in [28] showed that optimizing the captioning models for a *linear combination* of SPICE and CIDEr scores can lead to better captions. This *linear combination* of metrics was termed as SPIDEr (SPICE + CIDEr). However, SPIDEr was not assessed for its correlation with human judgements. Recently, [21] suggested the use of a distance measure known as "Word Mover's Distance" (WMD) [26] for image caption evaluation, highlighting various strengths of this metric against the existing ones. WMD, which was originally developed to measure distance between documents, uses the word2vec [30] embedding space to determine the dissimilarity between the two texts.

2.2 Deterministic vs Learned Metrics

The currently used automatic metrics for image captioning, judge the caption quality by making deterministic measurements of similarity between candidate and references captions. These metrics tend to focus on specific aspects of correspondence, such as common sequences of words or the semantic likeness (using scene graphs). Moreover, these deterministic metrics fail to achieve adequate levels of correlation with human judgements at the sentence level, which reflects the fact that they do not fully capture the set of criteria that humans use in evaluating caption quality. One way to capture more features for evaluation is to combine various indicators, each of which focuses on a specific aspect, to form a fused metric [28].

Machine learning offers a systematic way to combine stand-alone deterministic metrics (or features related to them) into a unified one. In the literature related to MT evaluation, various learning paradigms have been proposed and the existing learned metrics can broadly be categorized as, *Binary functions*, - "which classify the candidate translation as good or bad" [24], [15] and *Continuous functions*, - "which score the quality of translation on an absolute scale" [3]. It is also shown that machine learning can be used to successfully combine standalone metrics and/or linguistic features to create composite evaluation metrics, showing a higher correlation with human judgments compared to the individual metrics [3,7,15].

2.3 Features

The features used by the learning-based metrics can be scores of the stand-alone metrics (such as BLEU, NIST, METEOR, and TER) and/or other numerical measurements reflecting, the lexical, the syntactic or the semantic similarity between candidate and reference captions. Various combinations of features have been proposed for the above mentioned paradigms in MT [3,13,16]. Moreover, combining meaningful linguistic features has shown promising results in metric evaluation campaigns, such as WMT (Workshop on Machine Translation) [6,7]. Therefore, we hypothesize that a learning-based framework can be helpful in creating customized, reliable and efficient evaluators for captioning as well. We propose a neural network-based metric which combines the judgement of various existing metrics through a learning framework. Our work is more conceptually similar to the work in [24], which induces a *human-likeness* criteria. However, it differs in terms of the learning algorithm as well as the features used. In [24], a SVM classifier was trained with Gaussian Kernels to discriminate human and machine-like translations, using lexical features together with scores of individual metrics WER (Word Error Rate) and PER (Position-independent word Error Rate) [36]. In contrast, *we propose the first neural network-based framework to induce a metric for caption evaluation.* Our feature set consists of individual metric scores, some of which are from captioning specific metrics and others are from metrics used in MT. We also include newer state-of-the-art MT metric 'WMD' as a part of our feature set. We believe that the novel combination of metrics used as features will allow our learned composite metric to correlate well with the human judgements.

3 NNEval

In this section, we describe the proposed metric in detail. The overall architecture of NNEval is shown in Fig. 1.

3.1 Proposed Approach

To create a machine learning-based metric that is well aligned with human evaluations, we frame our learning problem as a classification task. We adopt a training criteria based on a simple question: "is the candidate caption human or machine generated?" The human generated captions are still easily distinguishable from the machine generated ones [17,31], as the former are of superior quality. Image captioning would be a solved problem, if outputs of image captioning systems were of such a high quality that they could not be distinguished from human generated captions. Exploiting this gap in quality, our trained classifier can set a boundary between human and machine produced captions. Furthermore, in order to obtain a continuous output score, instead of a class label, we use the class-probabilities. These probabilities represent the degree of confidence about a candidate belonging to one of the two classes. Thus the resulting evaluator's output can be considered as some "measure of believability" that the input caption was human produced.

Another possible way to create a learned metric could be to directly approximate human judgement scores as a function of some feature set which is generated over the input captions. However, this approach would require the availability of a large training corpora containing human-evaluated candidate captions and their reference counterparts. The development of such a resource can be very difficult, time consuming and even prohibitive [24]. Framing our learning problem as a classification task allows the creation of a training set from existing datasets containing human reference captions for given images [9]. The human generated captions paired with various machine generated ones, for the given images, can serve as the training examples for the metric. Thus, mitigating the need of obtaining expensive manual annotations. Moreover, such a dataset can be updated easily by including the outputs of more evolved models without incurring any additional cost.

We use a fully connected multilayer feed-forward neural network as our learning algorithm to build the proposed metric. We describe the details of NNEval's architecture and the learning task in Sect. 3.3, whereas the features used for NNEval in the following Section:

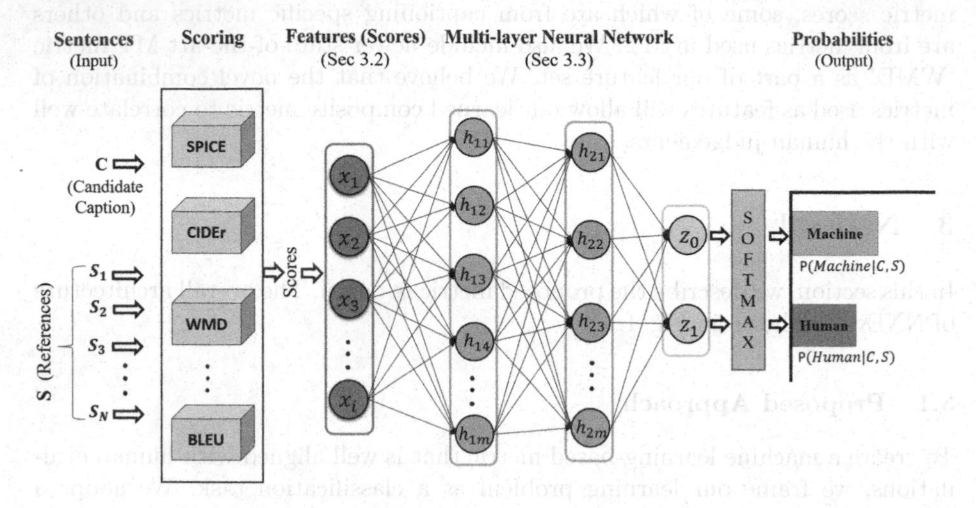

Fig. 1. Overall architecture of NNEval

3.2 NNEval Features

In our proposed framework, the candidate "C" and reference sentences "S" are not fed directly as an input to the neural network, instead, a set of numeric features are extracted from them as shown in Fig. 1. Only the feature vector is given as an input to the neural network, not allowing the network to directly analyse the candidate and reference sentences. Each entity in the feature vector corresponds to a quality score generated by an individual metric for the given candidate. Metrics that we use to generate our feature vector are found to be statistically different from each other [21] and complement each other in assessing the quality of the candidate captions. Our basic feature set consists of the scores of the following metrics:

SPICE [4] estimates the caption quality by first converting both candidate and reference texts to a semantic representation known as a "scene graph"; which encodes the objects, attributes and relationships found in the captions. Next, a set of logical tuples are formed by using possible combinations of the elements of the graphs. Finally, an F-score is computed based on the conjunction of candidate and reference caption tuples.

CIDEr [37] measures the consensus between candidate and reference captions using n-gram matching. N-grams that are common in all the captions are down-weighted by computing the *Term Frequency Inverse Document frequency* weighting. The mean cosine similarity between the n-grams of the reference and candidate captions is referred as $CIDEr_n$ score. The final CIDEr score is computed as the mean of $CIDEr_n$ scores, with $n = 1, 2, 3, 4$, which we use as a feature.

BLEU [33] evaluates the candidate captions by measuring the n-gram overlap between the candidate and reference texts. BLEU score is computed via geometric averaging of modified n-gram precisions scores multiplied by a brevity penalty factor to penalize short sentences. We use four variants of $BLEU$ i.e., $BLEU_1$, $BLEU_2$, $BLEU_3$ and $BLEU_4$ scores as our features.

METEOR [5] judgement is based on the unigram overlap between the candidate and reference captions. It matches unigrams based on their meanings, exact forms and stemmed forms. Whereas, the metric score is defined as the harmonic mean of unigram precision and n-gram recall.

WMD [26] measures the dissimilarity between two sentences as the minimum amount of distance that the embedded words of one sentence need to cover to reach the embedded words of the other sentence. More formally, each sentence is represented as a weighted point cloud of word embeddings $d \in R_N$, whereas the distance between two words i and j is set as the Euclidean distance between their corresponding word2vec embeddings [30]. To use it as feature, we convert this distance score to similarity by using a negative exponential.

We use the MS COCO evaluation code [8] to implement all of the above metrics except for WMD. To implement WMD, we use the Gensim library script [35]. We also map all the feature values (scores) in the range of $[-1, 1]$, using the min-max normalization.

3.3 Network Architecture and Learning Task

Given a candidate caption C and a list of references $S = \{S_1, S_2, S_3 ... S_N\}$, the goal is to classify the candidate caption as human or machine generated. We model this task using a feed-forward neural network, whose input is a fixed length feature vector $\boldsymbol{x} = \{x_1, x_2, x_3, ..x_i\}$, which we extract using the candidate caption and corresponding references (Sect. 3.2), and its output is the class probability, given as:

$$\boldsymbol{y_k} = \frac{e^{z_k}}{e^{z_0} + e^{z_1}}, k \in \{0, 1\} \tag{1}$$

Where z_k represents un-normalized class scores (z_0 and z_1 correspond to the machine and human class respectively). Our architecture has two hidden layers and the overall transformations in our network can be written as:

$$\boldsymbol{h_1} = \varphi(\boldsymbol{W_1 x} + \boldsymbol{b_1}) \tag{2}$$

$$\boldsymbol{h_2} = \varphi(\boldsymbol{W_2 h_1} + \boldsymbol{b_2}) \tag{3}$$

$$\boldsymbol{z_k} = \boldsymbol{W_3 h_2} + \boldsymbol{b_3} \tag{4}$$

$\boldsymbol{W_l}$ and $\boldsymbol{b_l}$, are the weights and the bias terms between the input, hidden and output layers respectively. Where, $\boldsymbol{W_l} \in R^{N_l \times M_l}$, $\boldsymbol{b_l} \in R^{M_l}$ given $l \in \{1, 2, 3\}$. Moreover, $\varphi(.) : R \rightarrow R$ is the non-linear activation function, given as:

$$\varphi(x) = max(x, 0) \tag{5}$$

We use $P(k = 1|\boldsymbol{x})$ as our metric score, which is the probability of an input candidate caption being human generated. It can be formulated as:

$$P(k = 1|\boldsymbol{x}) = \frac{e^{z_1}}{e^{z_0} + e^{z_1}} \tag{6}$$

The cross entropy loss for the training data with parameters, $\boldsymbol{\theta} = (\boldsymbol{W_1}, \boldsymbol{W_2}, \boldsymbol{W_3}, \boldsymbol{b_1}, \boldsymbol{b_2}, \boldsymbol{b_3})$ can be written as:

$$J_{\boldsymbol{\theta}} = -\frac{1}{p} \sum_{s=1}^{p} \log\left(\frac{e^{z^s_{\tilde{y}}}}{e^{z^s_0} + e^{z^s_1}}\right) + \beta L(\boldsymbol{\theta}) \tag{7}$$

In the above equation $z^s_{\tilde{y}}$ is the activation of the output layer node corresponding to the true class $\tilde{y}$, given the input $\boldsymbol{x}^s$. Where, $\beta L(\theta)$ is a regularization term, that is commonly used to reduce model over-fitting. For our network we use L_2 regularization [32].

3.4 Gameability

A common concern in the design of automatic evaluation metrics is that the system under evaluation might try to optimize for the metric score, leading to undesirable outcomes [4,37]. The resulting captions in such case might not be of good quality as per human judgement. However, by "gaming the metric", a captioning system can achieve a higher than deserving performance, which may lead to false assessments. For instance, a metric that only takes into account the lexical similarity between the candidate and reference captions, might be gamed to assign a higher than deserving score to a caption that just happens to have many n-gram matches against the reference captions. Since, NNEval itself is a composition of various metrics, it has a built-in resistance against systems which have gamed only one or few of the subset metrics. Having said that, the potential of a system gaming against all, or a subset of features is still plausible.

4 Experimental Settings

To train our metric, a dataset which contains both human and machine generated captions of each image is required. We create a training set by sourcing data from Flickr30k dataset [43]. Flickr30k dataset consists of 31,783 photos acquired from Flickr[2], each paired with 5 captions obtained through the Amazon Mechanical Turk (AMT). For each image in Flickr30k dataset we choose three amongst the

[2] https://www.flickr.com/.

five captions to use as human generated candidate captions. Whereas, we obtain machine generated captions of the same images, using three image captioning models, which achieved state-of-the-art performance when they were published [29,38,39]. In Sect. 4.1, we describe the training set-up for these image captioning models. In Sects. 4.2 and 4.3, we provide the details of the training and validation sets used for NNEval. The early stopping criteria and the network parameters for NNEval are discussed in Sects. 4.4 and 4.5 respectively.

Image (a)
Human Generated Captions (b)
1. "a man who is wearing the same colors as the bike is riding down the street"
2. "a cyclist dressed in blue is riding up a road"
3. "a bicycle racer is riding a bike on the street with people watching from the sidelines"
Machine Generated Captions (c)
1. "a man cycling on road and enjoying"
2. "a man riding a bike down a street"
3. "a group of people riding on the back of a horse"

Fig. 2. Shows, (a) an image from Flickr30k dataset, (b) human generated captions for the corresponding image, and (c) captions generated by machine models [29,38,39] for the given image.

4.1 Dataset for Image Captioning Models

The models that we use to obtain machine generated captions for our training set are: (**1**) Show and tell [38], (**2**) Show, attend and tell (soft-attention) [39], and (**3**) Adaptive attention [29]. We use publicly available official codes of these captioning models[3] and train them on MS COCO dataset [8], which is one of the largest image captioning datasets. The models that are trained on a large dataset tend to give a better performance when tested on an unseen dataset. MS COCO dataset consists of training, validation and testing set containing 82,783, 40,504 and 40,775 images respectively. Each image in these sets is associated with five or more captions (collected through AMT), except for the testing set. We combine the MS COCO training and validation sets and use this combined set for the training of captioning models, while reserving 10,000 image-caption pairs for validation and testing purposes. We train the image captioning models using the original experimental protocols to achieve close to their reported performances.

4.2 Training Set for NNEval

We use the trained image captioning models discussed above to generate captions for the images in Flickr30k dataset. For each image, we obtain three machine generated captions, one from each model. Moreover, we randomly choose three captions amongst the five human produced captions, which were originally paired with their respective image in Flickr30k, to use as human generated captions.

[3] We thank the authors of these captioning approaches for making their codes publicly available.

This provides us with an equal number of human and machine generated candidate captions per image. Figure 2 shows an example of human and machine produced candidate captions for a given image. In order to obtain reference captions for each candidate caption, we again utilize the human written descriptions of Flickr30k. For each machine-generated candidate caption, we randomly choose four out of five human written captions which were originally associated with each image. Whereas, for each human-generated candidate caption, we select the remaining four out of five original AMT captions.

We make sure that there is no overlap between each human candidate caption and its corresponding reference captions. In Fig. 3, a possible pairing scenario is shown to demonstrate the distribution of the candidate and reference captions. If we select S1 as the candidate human caption, we choose S2, S3, S4, S5 as its references. Whereas, when we select M1 as a candidate machine caption, we randomly choose any of the four amongst S1, S2, S3, S4, S5 as references. While different sorts of pairing strategies can be explored, we leave that to future work. Moreover, the reason why we select four references for each caption is to exploit the optimal performance of each metric. Most of these metrics have been tested and reported to give a better performance with a larger number of reference captions [4,10,33,37].

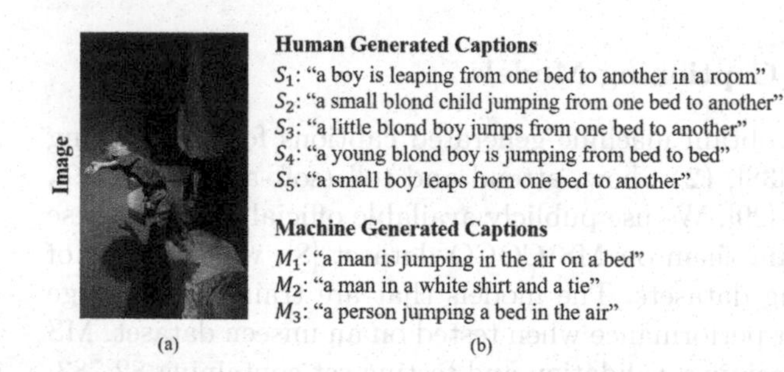

	Candidate Captions	References
1	M_1 (machine)	$\{S_1, S_2, S_3, S_4\}$
2	M_2 (machine)	$\{S_2, S_1, S_3, S_5\}$
3	M_3 (machine)	$\{S_1, S_4, S_5, S_2\}$
4	S_1 (human)	$\{S_2, S_3, S_4, S_5\}$
5	S_2 (human)	$\{S_1, S_3, S_5, S_4\}$
6	S_3 (human)	$\{S_1, S_2, S_4, S_5\}$

(c)

Fig. 3. Shows an image (a), its corresponding human and machine generated captions (b), and candidate (human and machine generated captions) and reference pairing for the given image in the training set (c).

4.3 Validation Set for NNEval

For our validation set we draw data from Flickr8k [43], which consists of 8,092 images, each annotated with five human generated captions. The images in this dataset mainly focus on people and animals performing some action. This dataset also contains human judgements for a subset of 5,822 captions corresponding to 1000 images in total. Each caption was evaluated by three expert judges on a scale of 1 (the caption is unrelated to the image) to 4 (the caption describes the image without any errors).

From our training set we remove the captions of images which overlap with the captions in the validation and test sets (discussed in Sect. 5), leaving us with a total of 132,984 non-overlapping captions for training the NNEval model.

4.4 Early Stopping

NNEval is optimized over the training set for a maximum of 500 epochs, and tested for classification accuracy on the validation set after each epoch. While the loss function is used during the training period to maximize the classification accuracy, we are primarily interested in maximizing the correlation with human judgements. As accuracy is not a perfect proxy for correlation [24], we use early stopping based on Kendall's τ (rank correlation), which is evaluated on the validation set after each epoch. We thus terminate (early-stop) the training when the correlation is maximized. Since each caption in the validation set is paired with three judgements, we use the mode value of these three judgements to evaluate the correlation coefficient.

4.5 Network Parameters

We use Adam optimizer [22] to train our network, with an initial learning rate of 0.25 and a mini-batch size of 75. We initialize the weights for our network by sampling values from a random uniform distribution [14]. Furthermore, we set the size of each of the hidden layers $\boldsymbol{h_1}$ and $\boldsymbol{h_2}$ (Sect. 3.3) to 72 nodes. The NNEval architecture is implemented using TensorFlow library [1].

5 Results and Discussion

To analyse the performance of our proposed metric, compared to the existing captioning metrics, we devise three sets of experiments, each judging a different aspect. *First* and foremost, we judge the metric's ability to correlate with human judgements (Sect. 5.1). *Second*, we observe how accurate it is in terms of distinguishing between two candidate captions given the human consensus over the pair (Sect. 5.2). *Third*, we observe the metric's ability to deal with various distractions introduced in the candidate sentences (Sect. 5.3). In the latter two experiments, we report the accuracy instead of the correlation.

5.1 Correlation with Human Judgements

The purpose of designing automatic metrics is to replace human judgements. Therefore, the most desirable characteristic of an automatic evaluation metric is its strong correlation with human scores [44]. A stronger correlation with human judgements indicates that a metric captures the features that humans look for, while assessing a candidate caption. In order to measure the sentence-level correlation of our proposed metric with human judgements we use the COMPOSITE dataset [2] which contains human judgements for 11,985 candidate captions and their image counterparts. The images in this dataset are obtained from MS COCO, Flickr8k and Flickr30k datasets, whereas, the associated captions consist of human generated captions (sourced from the aforementioned datasets) and machine generated captions (using two captioning models [2,19]). The candidate

Table 1. Caption-level correlation of evaluation metrics with human quality judgements. All p-values (not shown) are less than 0.001

Metric	Pearson	Spearman	Kendall
BLEU-1	0.373	0.366	0.269
BLEU-4	0.223	0.360	0.267
ROUGE-L	0.381	0.376	0.279
METEOR	0.448	0.451	0.337
CIDEr	0.440	0.479	0.359
SPICE	0.475	0.482	0.376
SPIDEr	0.467	0.495	0.381
NNEval	**0.532**	**0.524**	**0.404**

captions of images are scored for correctness on the scale of 1 (low relevance) to 5 (high relevance) by AMT workers. To ensure that the performance of NNEval is evaluated on unseen data, we remove the 771 image-caption pairs from this test set (which were overlapping with our validation set), leaving a total of 11,214 pairs for evaluation. Following the approach in [21], we report Pearson's r, Kendall's τ and Spearman's ρ correlation coefficients for commonly used caption evaluation metrics along with a newer metric SPIDEr (linear combination of SPICE and CIDEr) [28].

The results in Table 1 show that NNEval outperforms the existing automatic metrics for captioning by a decent margin in terms of linear (Pearson) and rank based (Spearman and Kendall) correlation coefficients. *This is an improvement in the current state of the art.*

Table 2. Comparative accuracy results on four kinds of caption pairs tested on PASCAL-50S

Metric	HC	HI	HM	MM	AVG
BLEU-1	53.5	95.6	91.1	57.3	74.4
BLEU-4	53.7	93.2	85.6	61.0	73.4
ROUGE-L	56.5	95.3	93.4	58.5	75.9
METEOR	**61.1**	97.6	**94.6**	62.0	78.8
CIDEr	57.8	98.0	88.8	68.2	78.2
SPICE	58.0	96.7	88.4	**71.6**	78.7
SPIDEr	56.7	98.5	91.0	69.1	78.8
NNEval	60.4	**99.0**	92.1	70.4	**80.5**

5.2 Accuracy

We follow the framework introduced in [37] to analyse the ability of a metric to discriminate between a pair of captions with reference to the ground truth caption. A metric is considered accurate if it assigns a higher score to the caption preferred by humans. For this experiment, we use PASCAL-50S [37], which contains human judgements for 4000 triplets of descriptions (one reference caption with two candidate captions). Based on the pairing, the triplets are grouped into four categories (comprising of 1000 triplets each) i.e., Human-Human Correct (HC), Human-Human Incorrect (HI), Human-Machine (HM), Machine-Machine (MM). The human judgements in PASCAL-50S were collected through AMT, where the workers were asked to identify the candidate sentence which is more similar to the given reference in the triplet. Unlike the previous study of [2], the AMT workers were not asked to score the candidate captions but to choose the best candidate. We follow the same original approach of [37] and use 5 reference captions per candidate to assess the accuracy of the metrics and report them in Table 2. The slight variation from the previously reported results [4,37] might be due to the randomness in the choice of references.

The results in Table 2 show that on average, NNEval is ahead of the existing metrics. In terms of individual categories, it achieves the best accuracy in differentiating between Human-Human Incorrect captions. We believe that the reason that has contributed to this improvement, is that our validation set had all human generated captions, which were scored by human judges for their relevance to the image. Moreover, by using early stopping (Sect. 4.2), we selected the model which achieved the best correlation with human judgements. Hence, our model was optimized for this specific case of Human-Human Incorrect scenario. As evident from the results in Table 2, *NNEval is the most consistently performing model, with the highest average accuracy.* Note that HC is the hardest category as all the metrics produced the lowest accuracy in this category. In HC category, NNEval comes in only marginally behind the best performing metric METEOR. NNEval outperforms the three captioning specific metrics (CIDEr, SPICE and SPIDEr) in three out of four categories, and is second only to SPICE in MM category with minor difference in the achieved accuracy.

Original Caption (b)
"a single man standing above the crowd at a busy bar"

Distracted Versions (c)

1. "a woman standing above the crowd at a busy bar"
2. "a single man standing above the crowd at a train station"
3. "a single man is wearing a life jacket in a small boat"
4. "a waitress offering cocktail at a busy bar"
5. "a single man"
6. "a busy bar"

Distraction Types (d)

Replace-Person
Replace-Scene
Share-Person
Share-Scene
Just-Person
Just-Scene

Fig. 4. Shows an image (a), corresponding correct caption (b), distracted versions of the correct caption (c), and type of distraction in each caption (d).

5.3 Robustness

The authors in [17] introduced recently a dataset to perform a focused evaluation of image captioning systems with a series of binary forced-choice tasks, each designed to judge a particular aspect of image captions. Each task contains an image paired with two candidate captions, one correct and the other incorrect (distracted version of correct caption). For our evaluation, a robust image captioning metric should mostly choose the correct over the distracted one, to show that it can capture semantically significant changes in words and can identify when a complete sentence description is better than a single Noun Phrase. In [21], the authors used this dataset to perform their robustness analysis of various image captioning metrics. Following their approach, we also use the same dataset. However, we report the performance on six different tasks instead of the four reported in [21], namely (**1**) Replace Person, (**2**) Replace Scene, (**3**) Share Person, (**4**) Share Scene, (**5**) Just Person and (**6**) Just Scene. An example of each of the six tasks is shown in Fig. 4. For the replace-scene and replace-person task, given a correct caption for an image, the incorrect sentences (distractors) were constructed by replacing the scene/person (first person) in the correct caption with different scene/people. For the share-person and share-scene tasks, the distractors share the same scene/task with the correct caption. However, the remaining part of the sentence is different. The just-scene and just-person distractors only consist of the scene/person of the correct caption.

We evaluate the metric scores for each correct and distracted version against the remaining correct captions that are available for an image in the dataset. The average accuracy scores for the caption evaluation metrics are reported in Table 3. The last row of Table 3 shows the numbers of instances tested for each category. It can be seen that NNEval outperforms the other metrics in three categories i.e., replace-person, share-person and share-scene task. Note that *NNEval is again the most consistent performer among all metrics. It has the best performance on average, and it also has the highest worst-case accuracy amongst all metrics.* Thus, we conclude that NNEval is overall the most robust metric.

Table 3. Comparative accuracy results on various distraction tasks

Metric	Replace Person	Replace Scene	Share Person	Share Scene	Just Person	Just Scene	AVG	Worst-case accuracy
BLEU-1	84.9	78.1	87.5	88.2	87.5	**98.4**	87.4	78.1
BLEU-4	85.9	75.2	83.5	82.4	54.9	67.7	72.1	54.9
ROUGE-L	83.3	71.1	86.8	86.8	83.4	94.1	84.1	71.1
METEOR	83.7	75.1	92.4	91.4	**91.9**	**98.4**	89.3	75.1
CIDEr	89.9	**95.0**	94.1	93.1	73.3	81.5	85.7	73.3
SPICE	84.0	76.0	88.5	88.8	78.1	92.0	83.6	76.0
SPIDEr	89.7	**95.0**	94.7	93.6	76.6	86.1	89.3	76.6
NNEval	**90.2**	91.8	**95.1**	**94.0**	85.8	94.7	**91.9**	**85.8**
#Instances	5816	2513	4594	2619	5811	2624	Total: 23977	

6 Conclusion and Future Work

We propose NNEval, a Neural-Network based Evaluation metric which measures the quality of a caption across various linguistic aspects. Our empirical results demonstrate that NNEval correlates with human judgements better than the existing metrics for caption evaluation. Moreover, our experiments show that it is also robust to the various distractions in the candidate sentences. Our proposed framework, facilitated the incorporation of various useful features that contributed to the successful performance of our metric. In order to further improve NNEval to mimic human score, we intend to carry out a detailed analysis on the impact of various features on correlation and robustness. We plan to release our code in the coming months and hope that it will lead to further development of learning-based evaluation metrics and contribute towards fine-grained assessment of captioning models.

Acknowledgements. We are grateful to Nvidia for providing Titan-Xp GPU, which was used for the experiments. We would also like to thank Somak Aditya and Ramakrishna Vedantam for sharing their COMPOSITE and PASCAL-50S dataset respectively. This work is supported by Australian Research Council, ARC DP150100294.

References

1. Abadi, M., et al.: Tensorflow: a system for large-scale machine learning. OSDI. **16**, 265–283 (2016)
2. Aditya, S., Yang, Y., Baral, C., Aloimonos, Y., Fermüller, C.: Image understanding using vision and reasoning through scene description graph. Comput. Vis. Image Underst. (2017)
3. Albrecht, J.S., Hwa, R.: Regression for machine translation evaluation at the sentence level. Mach. Transl. **22**(1–2), 1 (2008)
4. Anderson, P., Fernando, B., Johnson, M., Gould, S.: SPICE: semantic propositional image caption evaluation. In: Leibe, B., Matas, J., Sebe, N., Welling, M. (eds.) ECCV 2016. LNCS, vol. 9909, pp. 382–398. Springer, Cham (2016). https://doi.org/10.1007/978-3-319-46454-1_24
5. Banerjee, S., Lavie, A.: Meteor: an automatic metric for MT evaluation with improved correlation with human judgments. In: Proceedings of the ACL Workshop on Intrinsic and Extrinsic Evaluation Measures for Machine Translation and/or Summarization, pp. 65–72 (2005)
6. Bojar, O., Graham, Y., Kamran, A., Stanojević, M.: Results of the wmt16 metrics shared task. In: Proceedings of the First Conference on Machine Translation: Volume 2, Shared Task Papers. vol. 2, pp. 199–231 (2016)
7. Bojar, O., Helcl, J., Kocmi, T., Libovickỳ, J., Musil, T.: Results of the WMT17 neural MT training task. In: Proceedings of the Second Conference on Machine Translation, pp. 525–533 (2017)
8. Chen, X., et al.: Microsoft coco captions: Data collection and evaluation server. arXiv preprint arXiv:1504.00325 (2015)
9. Corston-Oliver, S., Gamon, M., Brockett, C.: A machine learning approach to the automatic evaluation of machine translation. In: Proceedings of the 39th Annual Meeting on Association for Computational Linguistics, pp. 148–155. Association for Computational Linguistics (2001)

10. Denkowski, M., Lavie, A.: Meteor universal: language specific translation evaluation for any target language. In: Proceedings of the Ninth Workshop on Statistical Machine Translation, pp. 376–380 (2014)
11. Elliott, D., Keller, F.: Comparing automatic evaluation measures for image description. In: Proceedings of the 52nd Annual Meeting of the Association for Computational Linguistics (Volume 2: Short Papers), vol. 2, pp. 452–457 (2014)
12. Fang, H., et al.: From captions to visual concepts and back (2015)
13. Giménez, J., Màrquez, L.: Linguistic features for automatic evaluation of heterogenous MT systems. In: Proceedings of the Second Workshop on Statistical Machine Translation, pp. 256–264. Association for Computational Linguistics (2007)
14. Glorot, X., Bengio, Y.: Understanding the difficulty of training deep feedforward neural networks. In: Proceedings of the Thirteenth International Conference on Artificial Intelligence and Statistics, pp. 249–256 (2010)
15. Guzmán, F., Joty, S., Màrquez, L., Nakov, P.: Pairwise neural machine translation evaluation. In: Proceedings of the 53rd Annual Meeting of the Association for Computational Linguistics and the 7th International Joint Conference on Natural Language Processing (Volume 1: Long Papers), vol. 1, pp. 805–814 (2015)
16. Guzmán, F., Joty, S., Màrquez, L., Nakov, P.: Machine translation evaluation with neural networks. Comput. Speech Lang. **45**, 180–200 (2017)
17. Hodosh, M., Hockenmaier, J.: Focused evaluation for image description with binary forced-choice tasks. In: Proceedings of the 5th Workshop on Vision and Language, pp. 19–28 (2016)
18. Hodosh, M., Young, P., Hockenmaier, J.: Framing image description as a ranking task: data, models and evaluation metrics. J. Artif. Intell. Res. **47**, 853–899 (2013)
19. Karpathy, A., Fei-Fei, L.: Deep visual-semantic alignments for generating image descriptions. In: Proceedings of the IEEE Conference on Computer Vision and Pattern Recognition, pp. 3128–3137 (2015)
20. Karpathy, A., Joulin, A., Fei-Fei, L.F.: Deep fragment embeddings for bidirectional image sentence mapping. In: Advances in Neural Information Processing Systems, pp. 1889–1897 (2014)
21. Kilickaya, M., Erdem, A., Ikizler-Cinbis, N., Erdem, E.: Re-evaluating automatic metrics for image captioning. arXiv preprint arXiv:1612.07600 (2016)
22. Kingma, D.P., Ba, J.: Adam: a method for stochastic optimization. arXiv preprint arXiv:1412.6980 (2014)
23. Krishna, R., et al.: Visual genome: connecting language and vision using crowdsourced dense image annotations. Int. J. Comput. Vis. **123**(1), 32–73 (2017)
24. Kulesza, A., Shieber, S.M.: A learning approach to improving sentence-level MT evaluation. In: Proceedings of the 10th International Conference on Theoretical and Methodological Issues in Machine Translation, pp. 75–84 (2004)
25. Kulkarni, G., et al.: Babytalk: understanding and generating simple image descriptions. IEEE Trans. Pattern Anal. Mach. Intell. **35**(12), 2891–2903 (2013)
26. Kusner, M., Sun, Y., Kolkin, N., Weinberger, K.: From word embeddings to document distances. In: International Conference on Machine Learning, pp. 957–966 (2015)
27. Lin, C.Y.: Rouge: A package for automatic evaluation of summaries. Text Summarization Branches Out (2004)
28. Liu, S., Zhu, Z., Ye, N., Guadarrama, S., Murphy, K.: Improved image captioning via policy gradient optimization of spider. arXiv preprint arXiv:1612.00370 (2016)
29. Lu, J., Xiong, C., Parikh, D., Socher, R.: Knowing when to look: Adaptive attention via a visual sentinel for image captioning. In: Proceedings of the IEEE Conference on Computer Vision and Pattern Recognition (CVPR), vol. 6 (2017)

30. Mikolov, T., Sutskever, I., Chen, K., Corrado, G.S., Dean, J.: Distributed representations of words and phrases and their compositionality. In: Advances in Neural Information Processing Systems, pp. 3111–3119 (2013)
31. van Miltenburg, E., Elliott, D.: Room for improvement in automatic image description: an error analysis. arXiv preprint arXiv:1704.04198 (2017)
32. Ng, A.Y.: Feature selection, l1 vs. l2 regularization, and rotational invariance. In: Proceedings of the Twenty-first International Conference on Machine Learning, ICML 2004, p. 78. ACM, New York (2004). https://doi.org/10.1145/1015330.1015435
33. Papineni, K., Roukos, S., Ward, T., Zhu, W.J.: Bleu: a method for automatic evaluation of machine translation. In: Proceedings of the 40th Annual Meeting on Association for Computational Linguistics, pp. 311–318. Association for Computational Linguistics (2002)
34. Plummer, B.A., Wang, L., Cervantes, C.M., Caicedo, J.C., Hockenmaier, J., Lazebnik, S.: Flickr30k entities: collecting region-to-phrase correspondences for richer image-to-sentence models. In: 2015 IEEE International Conference on Computer Vision (ICCV), pp. 2641–2649. IEEE (2015)
35. Řehůřek, R., Sojka, P.: Software framework for topic modelling with large corpora. In: Proceedings of the LREC 2010 Workshop on New Challenges for NLP Frameworks, ELRA, Valletta, Malta, pp. 45–50, May 2010. http://is.muni.cz/publication/884893/en
36. Tillmann, C., Vogel, S., Ney, H., Zubiaga, A., Sawaf, H.: Accelerated DP based search for statistical translation. In: Fifth European Conference on Speech Communication and Technology (1997)
37. Vedantam, R., Lawrence Zitnick, C., Parikh, D.: Cider: consensus-based image description evaluation. In: Proceedings of the IEEE Conference on Computer Vision and Pattern Recognition, pp. 4566–4575 (2015)
38. Vinyals, O., Toshev, A., Bengio, S., Erhan, D.: Show and tell: a neural image caption generator. In: 2015 IEEE Conference on Computer Vision and Pattern Recognition (CVPR), pp. 3156–3164. IEEE (2015)
39. Xu, K., et al.: Show, attend and tell: Neural image caption generation with visual attention. In: International Conference on Machine Learning, pp. 2048–2057 (2015)
40. Yao, T., Pan, Y., Li, Y., Qiu, Z., Mei, T.: Boosting image captioning with attributes. OpenReview **2**(5), 8 (2016)
41. You, Q., Jin, H., Luo, J.: Image captioning at will: A versatile scheme for effectively injecting sentiments into image descriptions. arXiv preprint arXiv:1801.10121 (2018)
42. You, Q., Jin, H., Wang, Z., Fang, C., Luo, J.: Image captioning with semantic attention. In: Proceedings of the IEEE Conference on Computer Vision and Pattern Recognition, pp. 4651–4659 (2016)
43. Young, P., Lai, A., Hodosh, M., Hockenmaier, J.: From image descriptions to visual denotations: new similarity metrics for semantic inference over event descriptions. Trans. Assoc. Comput. Linguist. **2**, 67–78 (2014)
44. Zhang, Y., Vogel, S.: Significance tests of automatic machine translation evaluation metrics. Mach. Transl. **24**(1), 51–65 (2010)

VideoMatch: Matching Based Video Object Segmentation

Yuan-Ting Hu[1(✉)], Jia-Bin Huang[2], and Alexander G. Schwing[1]

[1] University of Illinois at Urbana-Champaign, Champaign, USA
{ythu2,aschwing}@illinois.edu
[2] Virginia Tech, Blacksburg, USA
jbhuang@vt.edu

Abstract. Video object segmentation is challenging yet important in a wide variety of applications for video analysis. Recent works formulate video object segmentation as a prediction task using deep nets to achieve appealing state-of-the-art performance. Due to the formulation as a prediction task, most of these methods require fine-tuning during test time, such that the deep nets memorize the appearance of the objects of interest in the given video. However, fine-tuning is time-consuming and computationally expensive, hence the algorithms are far from real time. To address this issue, we develop a novel matching based algorithm for video object segmentation. In contrast to memorization based classification techniques, the proposed approach learns to match extracted features to a provided template without memorizing the appearance of the objects. We validate the effectiveness and the robustness of the proposed method on the challenging DAVIS-16, DAVIS-17, Youtube-Objects and JumpCut datasets. Extensive results show that our method achieves comparable performance without fine-tuning and is much more favorable in terms of computational time.

1 Introduction

Video segmentation plays a pivotal role in a wide variety of applications ranging from object identification, video editing to video compression. Despite the fact that delineation and tracking of objects are seemingly trivial for humans in many cases, video object segmentation remains challenging for algorithms due to occlusions, fast motion, motion blur, and significant appearance variation over time.

Research efforts developing effective techniques for video object segmentation continue to grow, partly because of the recent release of high-quality datasets, *e.g.*, the DAVIS dataset [40,42]. Two of the main setups for video object segmentation are the unsupervised and the semi-supervised setting [40,42]. Both

---

Electronic supplementary material The online version of this chapter (https://doi.org/10.1007/978-3-030-01237-3_4) contains supplementary material, which is available to authorized users.

V. Ferrari et al. (Eds.): ECCV 2018, LNCS 11212, pp. 56–73, 2018.
https://doi.org/10.1007/978-3-030-01237-3_4

cases are analogous in that the semantic class of the objects to be segmented during testing are not known ahead of time. Both cases differ in the supervisory signal that is available at test time. While no supervisory signal is available during testing in the unsupervised setting, the ground truth segmentation mask of the first frame is assumed to be known in the semi-supervised case. With video editing applications in mind, here, we focus on the *semi-supervised setting*, *i.e.*, our goal is to delineate in all frames of the video the object of interest which is specified in the first frame of the video.

Taking advantage of the provided groundtruth for the first frame, existing semi-supervised video object segmentation techniques follow deep learning based methods [4,5,25,26,47,48,53,59] and fine-tune a pre-trained classifier on the given ground truth in the first frame during online testing [4,5,23,25,26,53]. This online fine-tuning of a classifier during testing has been shown to improve accuracy significantly. However, fine-tuning during testing is necessary for each object of interest given in the first frame, takes a significant amount of time, and requires specialized hardware in the form of a very recent GPU due to the memory needs of back-propagation for fine-tuning.

In contrast, in this paper, we propose a novel end-to-end trainable approach for fast semi-supervised video object segmentation that does not require any fine-tuning. Our approach is based on the intuition that features of the foreground and background in any frame should match features of the foreground and background in the first frame. To ensure that the proposed approach can cope with appearance and geometry changes, we use a deep net to learn the features that should match and adapt the sets of features as inference progresses.

Our method yields competitive results while saving computational time and memory when compared to the current state-of-the-art approaches. On the recently released DAVIS-16 dataset [40], our algorithm achieves 81.03% in IoU (intersection over union) while reducing the running time by one order of magnitude compared to the state-of-the-art, requiring on average only 0.32 s per frame.

2 Related Work

Video object segmentation has been extensively studied in the past [5,15,22,25, 29–31,36,39,44,49,50,55]. In the following, we first discuss the related literature, (1) focusing on semi-supervised video object segmentation, and (2) discussing unsupervised video object segmentation. Subsequently, we examine the relationship of our work and the tracking and matching literature.

Semi-supervised Video Object Segmentation: Semi-supervised video object segmentation assumes that the groundtruth of the first frame is available during testing. Many approaches in this category employ fine-tuning during testing in order to achieve better performance [4,5,8,19,23,25,26,32,53]. It has been shown that fine-tuning on the first frame significantly improves accuracy. However, the fine-tuning step is computationally demanding, adding more than 700 s per video to test time [5].

Additional cues such as optical flow [8,25,26,32], semantic segmentation [4, 26] and re-identification modules [32] can be integrated into the framework to further improve the accuracy. Since fine-tuning is still required, those cues increase the computational needs.

Among the semi-supervised video object segmentation methods, the approach by Yoon *et al.* [59] is most related to our approach. Yoon *et al.* [59] also address video object segmentation by pixel matching. Their approach concatenates the features extracted from the template and the input images, and uses fully connected layers to simulate matching between the two images. Importantly, the approach still requires fine-tuning. In addition, the fully connected layers restrict the method to process frames at a specific, pre-defined spatial resolution.

Concurrent to our work, several recent methods (all developed independently) have been proposed to improve the speed of video object segmentation through part-based tracking [9], pixel-wise metric learning [7], or network modulation [38,56]. We refer the readers to these works for a more complete picture.

Unsupervised Video Object Segmentation: Neither groundtruth nor user annotation is available in the unsupervised video object segmentation setting. Therefore, the unsupervised setup requires algorithms to automatically discover the salient objects in video. Different methods such as motion analysis [39], trajectory clustering [37], and saliency-based spatio-temporal propagation [12, 20] have been proposed to identify the foreground objects. More recently, deep net based approaches have been discussed [22,47,48].

Object Tracking: Semi-supervised video object segmentation and object tracking [28,58] are related to our approach as they both keep track of the objects through the entire video. However, the two tasks differ in the format of the output. The output of video object segmentation is a pixel-level segmentation mask while the output of object tracking is a bounding box that delineates the position and scale of the object. From the tracking literature, work by Bertinetto *et al.* [3] is in a spirit similar to our proposed approach as they formulate tracking by matching. However, due to the difference in the output, Bertinetto *et al.* [3] calculated correlation by convolving the whole patch with the given template, while we propose a soft matching for pixel-wise segmentation.

Matching: Image matching [18,33] has been extensively studied over the last few decades. With the success of deep learning, research focus moved from matching using handcrafted features [35] to deep features [57]. Correlation between the extracted feature maps is typically computed to find correspondences [45], to estimate optical flow fields [10] and geometric transformations [46]. Since the objective of matching is to find point-to-point correspondences, the result will be noisy if the matching algorithm is directly applied to segmentation. To deal with the noisy prediction, we proposed a soft matching mechanism which estimates the similarity score between different segments as discussed next.

3 Matching Based Video Object Segmentation

In the following, we describe details of the proposed algorithm for video object segmentation. We first formally define the problem setting and provide an overview of our approach in Sect. 3.1. We then detail the new proposed soft matching mechanism in Sect. 3.2. Subsequently, we show in Sect. 3.3 how our model accommodates appearance changes of objects over time during online testing without the need for finetuning. Finally, we demonstrate how to easily extend our method to instance-level video object segmentation in Sect. 3.4.

3.1 Overview

Given a sequence of T video frames $\{I_1, \ldots, I_T\}$ and the groundtruth segmentation $y_1^* \in \{1, \ldots, N\}^{W \times H}$ of the first frame I_1, the task of semi-supervised video object segmentation is to predict the segmentation masks of the subsequent video frames $I_2, \ldots, I_T$, denoted as $y_2, \ldots, y_T \in \{1, \ldots, N\}^{W \times H}$. Hereby, N is the number of objects of interest in the given video. We denote width and height of the frames as W and H. We start by discussing the single instance case ($N = 1$) and explain how to extend the proposed method to $N > 1$ in Sect. 3.4. Importantly, we emphasize that semi-supervised video object segmentation requires object independent formulations since we do not know ahead of time the semantic class of the object to be segmented.

As the object category and appearance are unknown before test time, a network detecting objectness is usually trained offline. During test time a natural way is to use the given groundtruth for the first frame, *i.e.* y_1^*, as training data to fine-tune the pretrained objectness network [4,5,23,25,26,53]. Fine-tuning encourages the network to memorize appearance of the object of interest. In previous works on instance-level segmentation, memorization is achieved by fine-tuning a pretrained network N times, *i.e.*, to obtain one fine-tuned network for each object. As discussed before, although this fine-tuning step is the key to improving performance, it introduces a significant amount of processing time overhead and consumes more memory during testing even when there is only one object of interest in the video.

Our idea for efficient video object segmentation is to develop a network which is general enough such that the fine-tuning step can be omitted. To this end, we propose to match features obtained from the test frame I_t to features of the groundtruth foreground and background in the first frame I_1 (template). We designed an end-to-end trainable deep neural net, not only to extract features from video frames, but also to match two sets of features.

To achieve this goal, as shown in Fig. 1, we use a Siamese architecture that employs a convolutional neural network to compute the two feature maps. We use $\mathbf{x}_1 \in \mathbb{R}^{h \times w \times c}$ and $\mathbf{x}_t \in \mathbb{R}^{h \times w \times c}$ to refer to feature tensors extracted from the first frame (template) I_1 and the test frame I_t, respectively. The feature tensors $\mathbf{x}_1$ and $\mathbf{x}_t$ are of size $h \times w \times c$, where c is the number of the feature channels and w, h are the width and height of the feature maps, proportional to the $W \times H$

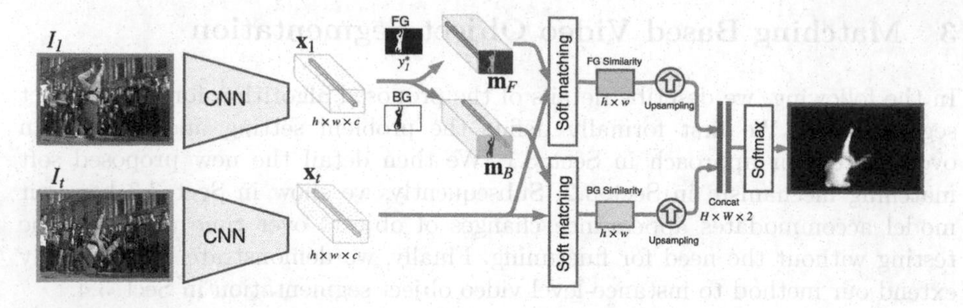

Fig. 1. Overview of the proposed video object segmentation algorithm. We use the provided ground truth mask of the first frame to obtain the set of foreground and background features ($\mathbf{m}_F$ and $\mathbf{m}_B$). After extracting the feature tensor $\mathbf{x}_t$ from the current frame, we use the proposed soft matching layer to produce FG and BG similarity. We then concatenates the two similarity scores and generate the final prediction via softmax.

sized video frame. The ratio between W and w depends on the downsampling rate of the convolutional neural net.

Next we define a set of features for the foreground and the background. We refer to those sets via $\mathbf{m}_F$ and $\mathbf{m}_B$ respectively. To formally define those sets of features, let $\mathbf{x}_t^i$ denote the c-dimensional vector representing the feature at pixel location i in the downsampled image. Given the groundtruth template y_1^* for the first frame, we collect the foreground features $\mathbf{m}_F$ and background features $\mathbf{m}_B$ for this first frame via

$$\mathbf{m}_F = \{\mathbf{x}_1^i : i \in g(y_1^*)\} \qquad \text{and} \qquad \mathbf{m}_B = \{\mathbf{x}_1^i : i \notin g(y_1^*)\}.$$

Hereby $g(y_1^*)$ is the set of pixels that belongs to foreground as indicated by the ground truth mask y_1^* downsampled to size $w \times h$.

After having extracted the foreground ($\mathbf{m}_F$) and background ($\mathbf{m}_B$) features from the template and after having computed features $\mathbf{x}_t \in \mathbb{R}^{h\times w\times c}$ from frame I_t using the same deep net, we match $\mathbf{x}_t^i$ $\forall i \in \{1, \ldots, wh\}$ to features collected in both sets $\mathbf{m}_F$ and $\mathbf{m}_B$ via a soft matching layer. The result of the soft matching layer for each pixel i is its foreground and background matching scores. Subsequently, the foreground and background matching scores are upsampled and normalized into a predicted foreground probability y_t via the softmax operation. We visualize this process in Fig. 1 and describe the proposed soft matching layer subsequently in greater detail.

3.2 Soft Matching Layer

A schematic illustrating the details of the proposed soft matching layer is given in Fig. 2. The developed soft matching layer, $\text{SML}(\mathbf{x}_t, \mathbf{m})$, takes two sets of features as inputs, *i.e.*, $\mathbf{x}_t$ and $\mathbf{m}$ ($\mathbf{m}$ refers to either $\mathbf{m}_F$ or $\mathbf{m}_B$) and computes a matching score matrix $S_t \in \mathbb{R}^{h\times w}$ which measures the compatibility of the frame

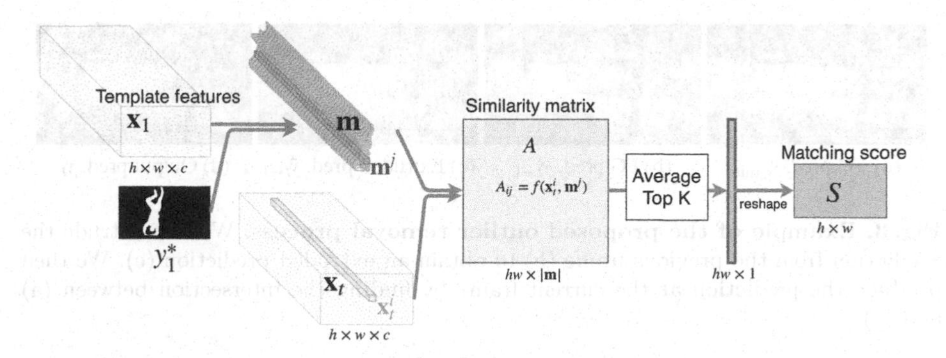

Fig. 2. Illustration of the proposed soft matching layer. We first take two sets of features and compute pairwise similarity between all pairs of features. We then produce the final matching score by computing the average of top K similarity scores.

I_t (represented by its features $\mathbf{x}_t$) with either foreground ($\mathbf{m}_F$) or background ($\mathbf{m}_B$) pixels of the template I_1 for every pixel $i \in \{1, \ldots, hw\}$. The entry S_t^i represents the similarity of the feature at pixel location i with respect to a subset of features in $\mathbf{m}$.

More formally, our developed soft matching layer first computes the pairwise similarity score matrix $A \in [-1, 1]^{(hw) \times |\mathbf{m}|}$ where the ij-th entry of A is calculated via

$$A_{ij} = f(\mathbf{x}_t^i, \mathbf{m}^j).$$

Hereby, f is a scoring function measuring the similarity between the two feature vectors $\mathbf{x}_t^i$ and $\mathbf{m}^j$. We use the cosine similarity, *i.e.*, $f(\mathbf{x}_t^i, \mathbf{m}^j) = \frac{\mathbf{x}_t^j \cdot \mathbf{m}^j}{\|\mathbf{x}_t^j\| \|\mathbf{m}^j\|}$, but any other distance metric is equally applicable once adequately normalized.

Given the similarity score matrix A, we compute the matching score matrix S_t of size $h \times w$, respectively its i-th entry ($i \in \{1, \ldots, hw\}$) via

$$S_t^i = \frac{1}{K} \sum_{j \in \mathrm{Top}(A_i, K)} A_{ij},$$

where the set $\mathrm{Top}(A_i, K)$ contains the indices with the top K similarity scores in the i-th row of the similarity score matrix A. K is set to 20 in all our experiments.

Intuitively, we use the average similarity of the top K matches because we assume a pixel to match to a number of pixels in a region as opposed to only one pixel, which will be too noisy, or to all pixels, which will be too strict in general as the foreground or background may be rather diverse. Consequently, we expect a particular pixel to match to one of the foreground or background regions rather than requiring a pixel only to match locally or to all regions. Again, an illustration of the soft matching layer, $\mathrm{SML}(\mathbf{x}_t, \mathbf{m})$, is presented in Fig. 2.

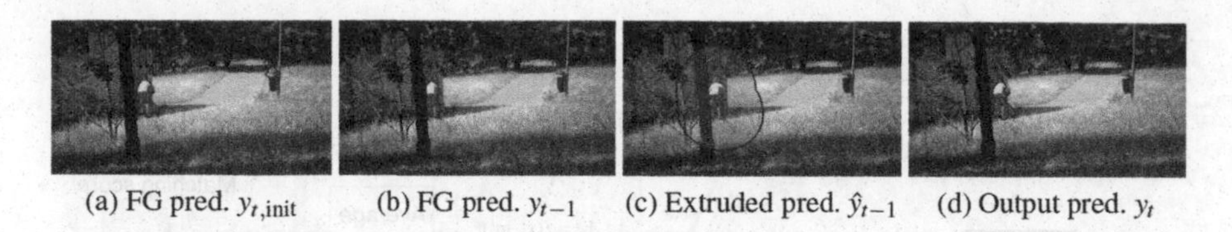

(a) FG pred. $y_{t,\text{init}}$ (b) FG pred. y_{t-1} (c) Extruded pred. $\hat{y}_{t-1}$ (d) Output pred. y_t

Fig. 3. Example of the proposed outlier removal process. We first extrude the prediction from the previous frame (b) to obtain an extruded prediction (c). We then produce the prediction at the current frame by finding the intersection between (a) and (c).

3.3 Outlier Removal and Online Update

Outlier Removal. To obtain the final prediction y_t for frame $t \in \{2, \ldots, T\}$ we convert the foreground and background matching score matrices into an initial foreground probability prediction $y_{t,\text{init}}$ via upsampling and via a subsequent weighted softmax operation. Finally, we obtain the prediction y_t by comparing the initial prediction $y_{t,\text{init}}$ with y_{t-1} to remove outliers. More specifically, we first extrude the prediction y_{t-1} of the previous frame to find pixels whose distance to the segmentation is less than a threshold d_c. We then compute y_t from $y_{t,\text{init}}$ by removing all initial foreground predictions that don't overlap with the extruded prediction $\hat{y}_{t-1}$. Note that the hat symbol '$\hat{\cdot}$' refers to the extrusion operation. This process assumes that the change of the object of interest is bounded from above. In Fig. 3, we visualize one example of the current foreground prediction $y_{t,\text{init}}$, previous foreground prediction y_{t-1}, the extruded prediction $\hat{y}_{t-1}$, and the final foreground prediction y_t.

Online Update. Obviously, we expect the appearance of the object of interest to change over time in a given video. In order to accommodate the appearance change, we repeatedly adjust the foreground and background model during testing. Inspired by [53], we update the foreground and background sets of features, *i.e.*, $\mathbf{m}_F$ and $\mathbf{m}_B$, by appending additional features after we predicted the segmentation for each frame. We find the additional features by comparing the initial prediction mask $y_{t,\text{init}}$ for $t \in \{2, \ldots, T\}$ with the extruded prediction $\hat{y}_{t-1}$ of the previous frame.

Specifically, we update the background model $\mathbf{m}_B$ at time t via

$$\mathbf{m}_B \leftarrow \mathbf{m}_B \cup \{\mathbf{x}_t^i : i \in \mathbf{b}_t\},$$

where the index set

$$\mathbf{b}_t = \{i : i \in g(y_{t,\text{init}}), i \notin g(\hat{y}_{t-1})\} = \{i : i \in g(y_{t,\text{init}}) \setminus g(y_t)\}$$

subsumes the set of pixels that are predicted as foreground initially, *i.e.*, in $y_{t,\text{init}}$, yet don't belong to the set of foreground pixels in the extruded previous prediction $\hat{y}_{t-1}$. Note that this is equivalent to the set of pixels which are predicted as foreground initially, *i.e.*, $y_{t,\text{init}}$, but are not part of the final prediction y_t.

Taking Fig. 3 as an example, $\mathbf{b}_t$ contains the indices of pixels being foreground in Fig. 3(a) but not in Fig. 3(b).

Intuitively, we find the possible outliers in the current predictions if a pixel is predicted as foreground at time t but does not appear to be foreground or is near to the foreground mask at time $t-1$.

Beyond adjusting the background model we also update the foreground model $\mathbf{m}_F$ via

$$\mathbf{m}_F \leftarrow \mathbf{m}_F \cup \{\mathbf{x}_t^i : i \in g(\breve{y}_t), y_t^i > c, i \notin \mathbf{b}_t\},$$

where $g(\breve{y}_t)$ is the set of foreground pixels in the eroded current segmentation prediction y_t and c is a constant threshold. Intuitively, we add the features of pixels that are not only predicted as foreground with high confidence (larger than c_1) but are also far from the boundary. In addition, we exclude those pixels in $\mathbf{b}_t$ to avoid conflicts between the foreground and background features.

Since our method just appends additional representations to the foreground and background features $\mathbf{m}_F$ and $\mathbf{m}_B$, the parameters of the employed network remain fixed, and the online update step is fast. Compared to [53], where each online update requires fine-tuning the network on the tested images, our approach is more efficient. Note that we designed a careful process to select features which are added in order to avoid the situation that the sizes of $\mathbf{m}_F$ and $\mathbf{m}_B$ grow intractably large, which will slow down the computation when computing the matching scores. It is obviously possible to keep track of how frequently features appear in the Top$-K$ set and remove those that don't contribute much. In practice, we didn't find this to be necessary for the employed datasets.

3.4 Instance-Level Video Object Segmentation

Next, we explain how the proposed method can be generalized for instance-level video object segmentation, where one or more objects of interest are presented in the first frame of the video. We consider the case where the ground truth segmentation mask contains a single or multiple objects, *i.e.*, $y_1^* \in \{1, \ldots, N\}^{H \times W}$, where $N \geq 1$. We construct the foreground and background features for every object, *i.e.*, we find the foreground features $\mathbf{m}_{F,k}$ and the background features $\mathbf{m}_{B,k}$ of the object $k \in \{1, \ldots, N\}$, where

$$\mathbf{m}_{F,k} = \{\mathbf{x}_1^i : i \in g(\delta(y_1^* = k))\} \quad \text{and} \quad \mathbf{m}_{B,k} = \{\mathbf{x}_1^i : i \notin g(\delta(y_1^* = k))\}.$$

Hereby, $\delta(\cdot) : \{1, \ldots, N\}^{H \times W} \rightarrow \{0, 1\}^{H \times W}$ is the indicator function which provides a binary output indicating the regions in y_1^* that belong to the k-th object. We then compute $y_{t,k}$, the foreground probability map of the frame t w.r.t. the k-th object by considering $\mathbf{x}_t$, $\mathbf{m}_{F,k}$ and $\mathbf{m}_{B,k}$ using the soft matching layer described above. After having computed k probability maps, we fuse them to obtain the final output prediction. The prediction y_t is computed by finding the index of the object that has maximum probability $y_{t,k}^i$ among all $k \in \{1, \ldots, N\}$ for all pixels i. If for all k, $y_{t,k}^i$ is less than a threshold c_2, the pixel i will be classified as background.

4 Experimental Results

In the following we first provide implementation details before evaluating the proposed approach on a variety of datasets using a variety of metrics.

4.1 Implementation Details, Training and Evaluation

To obtain the features $\mathbf{x}$, we found ResNet-101 [17] as the backbone with dilated convolutions [6] to perform well. More specifically, we use the representation from the top convolutional layer in the network as $\mathbf{x}_t$. The feature maps have spatial resolution 8 times smaller than the input image. In the experiments, we set $K = 20$, $d_c = 100$, $c_1 = 0.95$ and $c_2 = 0.4$. We initialized the parameters using the model pretrained on Pascal VOC [11,16] for semantic image segmentation. We trained the entire network end-to-end using the Adam optimizer [27]. We set the initial learning rate to 10^{-5} and gradually decreases over time. The weight decay factor is 0.0005.

To training our matching network, we use any two randomly chosen frames in a video sequence as training pairs. Importantly, the two frames are not required to be consecutive in time which provides an abundance of training data. We augmented the training data by random flipping, cropping and scaling between a factor of 0.5 to 1.5. We use Tensorflow to implement the algorithm. Training takes around 4 h for 1000 iterations on an Nvidia Titan X. At test time, a forward pass with an input image of size 480×854 takes around 0.17 s.

Training: We trained the proposed network using the 30 video sequences available in the DAVIS-16 training set [40] for 1000 iterations and evaluated on the DAVIS-16 validation set. Similarly, we used the 60 sequences in the DAVIS-17 training set [42] for training when testing on the DAVIS-17 validation set. Although the model is trained on DAVIS, we found it to generalize well to other datasets. Therefore, we use the model trained on the DAVIS-17 training set for evaluation on both the JumpCut [13] and the YouTube-Objects [43] datasets.

Evaluation: We validate the effectiveness of our method on the DAVIS-16 [40] validation, the DAVIS-17 [42] validation, the JumpCut [13] and the YouTube-Objects [43] datasets. For the YouTube-Objects dataset, we use the subset with groundtruth segmentation masks provided by [21], containing 126 video sequences. All of the datasets provide pixel-level groundtruth segmentation. More specifically, binary (foreground-background) ground truth is provided in the DAVIS-16, JumpCut, and YouTube-Objects datasets, while there is instance-level segmentation groundtruth available for the DAVIS-17 dataset. Challenges such as occlusion, fast motion, and appearance change are presented in the four datasets. Thus, these four datasets serve as a good test bed to evaluate different video object segmentation techniques.

4.2 Evaluation Metrics

Jaccard Index (mIoU): Jaccard index is a common evaluation metric to evaluate the segmentation quality. It is calculated as the intersection over union

(IoU) of the predicted and groundtruth masks. We compute the mean of the IoU across all the frames in a sequence and thus also refer to this metric as mIoU.

Contour Accuracy (F) [40]**:** To measure the quality of the predicted mask, we assess the contour accuracy by computing a bipartite matching between the contour points of the predicted segmentation and the contour points of the groundtruth segmentation. Based on the matching result we calculate the contour accuracy via the F-1 score.

Error Rate [13]**:** Following the evaluation protocol in [13], we compute the error rate on the JumpCut dataset. We select key frames $i = \{0, 16, ..., 96\}$ in each sequence and for the i-th keyframe, we compute the error in the predicted segmentation of the $i + d$-th frames, given the groundtruth segmentation mask of the i-th frame. Intuitively, we measure the transfer (or matching) error of methods with respect to a certain transfer distance d. The error is equal to the number of false positive and false negative pixels (the mislabeled pixels) divided by the number of all positive pixels (all foreground pixels) in the predicted segmentation of the $i + d$-th frame. We use $d = 16$ in the experiments and compute the average of the errors to obtain the error rate.

4.3 Quantitative Results

We carefully evaluated the proposed approach and compared the proposed method with a wide variety of video object segmentation methods *i.e.*, MSK [25], SFL [8], OSVOS [5], OnAVOS [53], PLM [59], MaskRNN [19], Lucid [26], SEA [1], HVS [15], JMP [13], FCP [41], BVS [34], OFL [50], CTN [24], VPN [23], SVC [54], JFS [36], LTV [37], HBT [14], AFS [51], SCF [21], RB [2] and DA [60]. Note that MSK, OSVOS, SFL, OnAVOS, PLM, MaskRNN, Lucid employ fine-tuning during testing.

We present the quantitative results on four datasets: DAVIS-16 [40], YouTube-Objects [43], JumpCut [13] and DAVIS-17 [42]. Our method outperforms state-of-the-art methods by 0.4% in mIoU and by 0.71 in error rate on Youtube-Objects and JumpCut datasets, respectively. On DAVIS-16 and DAVIS-17 datasets, our approach performs on par with state-of-the-art techniques while not using fine-tuning. The quantitative results are summarized in Tables 1, 2, 3, 4 and Fig. 4. The best method is highlighted in bold and the second-best method is underlined. Details are described in the following.

Evaluation on the DAVIS-16 Dataset: In Table 1, we compare our method with deep net baselines that do not require fine-tuning as well, such as VPN [23] and CTN [24]. We also compare to OSVOS [5], MSK [25], OnAVOS [53] and SFL [8], disabling their fine-tuning step. We use the super-script '$^-$' to denote methods with a disabled fine-tuning step. In Table 1, we report the mean IoU and the average running time per frame for each method tested on the DAVIS-16 dataset. Our method achieves the best mIoU, outperforming the baselines by more than 6% while running efficiently. Our method without the outlier

Table 1. Comparisons with deep net methods *without* fine-tuning (VPN and CTN) or with fine-tuning step disabled (denoted with $^-$) on DAVIS-16 validation set. OURS-NU: our method without online update and outlier removal.

	OURS	OURS-NU	OSVOS$^-$	MSK$^-$	OnAVOS$^-$	SFL$^-$	VPN	CTN
mIoU	**0.810**	0.792	0.525	0.699	0.736	0.674	0.702	0.735
Speed (s)	0.32	0.17	**0.12**	0.15	3.55	0.3	0.63	29.95

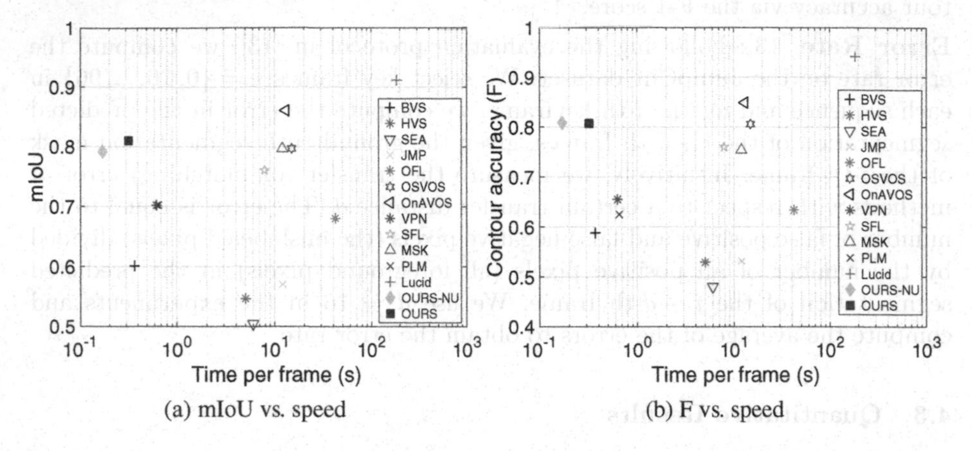

Fig. 4. Performance comparison on the DAVIS-16 validation set. The x axis denotes the average running time per frame in seconds (log scale) and the y axis is (a) mIoU (Jaccard index) and (b) F score (contour accuracy).

removal (denoted as OURS-NU in Table 1) runs 2 times faster while achieving competitive performance.

In Fig. 4, we compare our method which does not require fine-tuning with baselines that may or may not need fine-tuning. We report the mIoU vs average computational time per frame in Fig. 4(a) and the contour accuracy vs running time per frame in Fig. 4(b). Note that the average running time per frame also includes the fine-tuning step for those methods requiring fine-tuning. Since the network employed in our method is general enough to learn how to match we observe competitive performance at a fraction of the time required by other techniques. Note that the time axis scaling is logarithmic.

Evaluation on the YouTube-Objects Dataset: We present the evaluation results on the YouTube-Objects dataset [21,43] in Table 2. Our method outperforms the baselines despite the fact that our network is not fine-tuned, but other baselines such as OnAVOS and MSK and OSVOS are. Thus, our method is more favorable both in terms of computational time and in terms of accuracy.

Evaluation on the JumpCut Dataset: We present the evaluation results on the JumpCut dataset [13] in Table 3. We follow the evaluation in [13] and compute the error rates of different methods. The transfer distance d is equal to 16. In this experiment we don't apply the outlier removal described in Sect. 3.3 to

Table 2. Evaluation on the Youtube-Object dataset [21,43] using Jaccard index (mIoU).

Sequence	OURS	OnAVOS	MSK	OSVOS	OFL	JFS	BVS	SCF	AFS	FST	HBT	LTV
Fine-tuned?	-	Yes	Yes	Yes	-	-	-	-	-	-	-	-
Aeroplane	0.880	0.902	0.816	0.882	0.899	0.89	0.868	0.863	0.799	0.709	0.736	0.137
Bird	0.873	0.879	0.829	0.857	0.842	0.816	0.809	0.81	0.784	0.706	0.561	0.122
Boat	0.805	0.816	0.747	0.775	0.74	0.742	0.651	0.686	0.601	0.425	0.578	0.108
Car	0.779	0.738	0.670	0.796	0.809	0.709	0.687	0.694	0.644	0.652	0.339	0.237
Cat	0.788	0.759	0.696	0.708	0.683	0.677	0.559	0.589	0.504	0.521	0.305	0.186
Cow	0.771	0.787	0.750	0.778	0.798	0.791	0.699	0.686	0.657	0.445	0.418	0.163
Dog	0.803	0.809	0.752	0.813	0.766	0.703	0.685	0.618	0.542	0.653	0.368	0.18
Horse	0.688	0.742	0.649	0.728	0.726	0.678	0.589	0.54	0.508	0.535	0.443	0.115
Motorbike	0.774	0.663	0.498	0.735	0.737	0.615	0.605	0.609	0.583	0.442	0.489	0.106
Train	0.811	0.838	0.777	0.757	0.763	0.782	0.652	0.663	0.624	0.296	0.392	0.196
Average	**0.797**	0.793	0.718	0.783	0.776	0.74	0.68	0.676	0.625	0.538	0.463	0.155

Table 3. Error rates on the JumpCut dataset [13]. The transfer distance d is 16.

		RB	DA	SEA	JMP	SVC	PLM	OURS
	Fine-tuned?	-	-	-	-	-	Yes	-
ANIMAL	bear	4.58	4.48	4.21	4	**2.11**	3.45	5.14
	giraffe	22	11.2	17.4	**7.4**	9.67	17.4	11.96
	goat	13.1	13.3	8.22	**4.14**	4.97	15.2	4.73
	pig	9.22	9.85	10.3	3.43	**3.24**	5.15	5.12
	Avg.	12.23	9.71	10.03	**4.74**	5.00	10.30	6.74
HUMAN	couple	17.5	16	23.4	**5.13**	8.49	9.14	11.77
	park	11.8	6.54	6.91	5.39	**5.33**	10.2	11.42
	station	8.85	20.9	21.3	9.01	8.42	**4.68**	9.98
	Avg.	12.72	14.48	17.20	**6.51**	7.41	8.01	11.06
STATIC	car	**1.76**	5.93	5.08	2.26	2.57	2.18	1.86
	cup	5.45	12.9	9.31	**2.15**	2.4	6.04	5.38
	pot	2.43	5.03	2.98	2.95	**1.79**	2.66	5.55
	toy	**1.28**	3.19	2.16	1.3	1.49	2.25	2.81
	Avg.	2.73	6.76	4.88	2.17	**2.06**	3.28	3.90
SNAPCUT	animation	11.9	6.38	6.78	4.55	**3.35**	5.86	6.15
	fish	51.8	21.7	25.7	17.5	7.67	**7.42**	12.21
	horse	8.39	45.1	37.8	6.8	**4.84**	7.94	8.25
	Avg.	24.03	24.39	23.43	9.62	**5.29**	7.07	8.87
FAST	bball	18.4	8.47	8.89	**3.9**	4.16	8.04	6.19
	cheetah	31.5	16.6	7.68	8.16	**7.1**	11.8	7.61
	dance	56.1	50.8	43	18.7	26.5	**14.7**	17.31
	hiphop	67.5	51.1	33.7	14.2	21.9	13.6	**10.49**
	kongfu	40.2	40.8	17.9	8	**3.77**	6.25	4.05
	skater	38.7	40.8	29.6	22.8	21.4	**12.6**	13.57
	supertramp	129	60.5	57.4	42.9	27.1	**20.7**	22.12
	tricking	79.4	70.9	35.8	21.3	21.2	15.7	**8.32**
	Avg.	57.60	42.50	29.25	17.50	16.64	12.92	**11.21**
Average		28.68	23.75	18.89	9.82	9.07	9.23	**8.73**

restrict mask transfer between non-successive frames. Again, our method outperforms the baselines on this dataset with an average error rate that is 0.34 lower than the best competing baseline SVC [54].

Evaluation on the DAVIS-17 Dataset: We show the experiments on instance-level video object segmentation using the DAVIS-17 validation set. The results are shown in Table 4. Our method performs reasonably well when compared to methods without finetuning, *i.e.*, OSVOS$^-$, OnAVOS$^-$, MaskRNN$^-$ and OFL. We further finetune our method (denoted as OURS-FT), and the performance is competitive among the baselines while the computational time is much faster. Note that OnAVOS$^+$ [52] in Table 4 is OnAVOS with upsampling layers on top and model ensembles.

Table 4. Evaluation on the DAVIS-17 validation set.

	OURS	OFL	OSVOS$^-$	OnAVOS$^-$	MaskRNN$^-$	OSVOS	OnAVOS	MaskRNN	OnAVOS$^+$	OURS-FT
Fine-tuned?	-	-	-	-	-	Yes	Yes	Yes	Yes	Yes
mIoU	0.565	0.549	0.366	0.395	0.455	0.521	0.610	0.605	**0.645**	<u>0.614</u>
Speed (s)	<u>0.35</u>	130	**0.13**	3.78	0.6	5	13	9	30	2.62

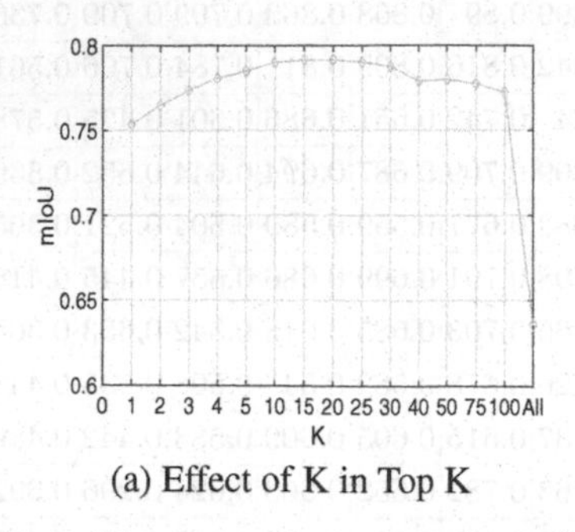

(a) Effect of K in Top K

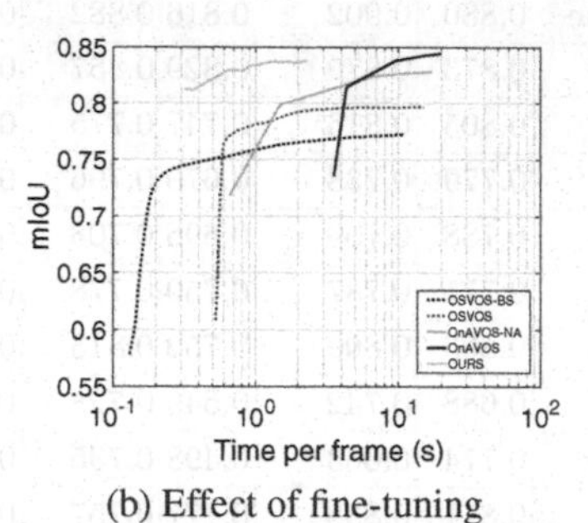

(b) Effect of fine-tuning

Fig. 5. Sensitivity analysis and finetuning. (a) The effect of K when computing the Top K similarity scores in the soft matching layer. (b) The effect of fine-tuning of our approach compared with other baselines. Both results are shown using the DAVIS-16 validation dataset.

4.4 Ablation Study

We study the important components of the proposed method. Subsequently, we discuss the effect of outlier removal and online update, the effect of K, the effect of foreground and background matching, the effect of fine-tuning and the memory consumption of the proposed approach.

Table 5. Ablation study of the three modules in our approach: (1) outlier removal, (2) online background update, and (3) online foreground update, assessed on the DAVIS-16 validation set.

Outlier removal	BG update	FG update	mIoU
-	-	-	0.792
✓	-	-	0.805
✓	✓	-	0.809
✓	✓	✓	0.810

Effect of K**:** We study the effect of K in the proposed soft matching layer where we compute the average similarity scores of top K matchings. We present the performance on DAVIS-16 with different settings of K in Fig. 5(a). We varied K to be between 1 and 100. The performance when K is equal to 1 ('hard matching') is 0.753 while the performance increases when K is larger than 1 ('soft matching') until K is equal to 20. When K is larger than 20, the performance keeps decreasing and the performance of computing the average similarity scores among all matchings is 0.636. Intuitively, a point is a good match to a region if the feature of the point is similar to a reasonable amount of pixels in that region, which motivates the proposed soft matching layer.

Outlier Removal and Online Update: In Table 5, we study the effects of outlier removal, online background feature update and foreground feature update. We found that our method with neither outlier removal nor online update performs competitively, achieving 0.792 on DAVIS-16. Removing of outliers improves the performance by 0.013. If we incorporate the online background feature update, the performance improves by 0.004 and having the foreground feature updated as well further improves the performance, achieving 0.810 in mIoU on the DAVIS-16 dataset.

Fig. 6. Visual results of our approach. Testing videos are from DAVIS-16 (1st row), Youtube-Objects (2nd row), JumpCut (3rd row), and DAVIS-17 datasets (4th row).

Fig. 7. Failure cases of our approach. For each case, we show the results of our approach at the beginning and toward the end of the video sequence.

Matching Foreground and Background: As shown in Fig. 1, we match the input image with not only the foreground region but also the background region in the template and thus we have two soft matching layers for computing the foreground similarity and the background similarity. We found that having both foreground and background models is important for good performance. Specifically, the performance of matching only the foreground, *i.e.*, only having one soft matching layer to compute foreground similarity, is only 0.527 in mIoU on DAVIS-16 while having both foreground and background similarity computed achieves 0.792.

Online Fine-Tuning: We would like to point out that the network in our method can be fune-tuned during testing when observing the groundtruth mask of the first frame. We show the trade-off between fine-tuning time and performance on DAVIS-16 in Fig. 5(b). Specifically, we show the average running time per frame taking the fine-tuning step into account, and compare with OSVOS, OSVOS-BS (OSVOS without the post-processing step), OnAVOS and OnAVOS-NA (OnAVOS without test time augmentation). We report the results of OnAVOS and OnAVOS-NA without a CRF as post-processing. Note that the time axis scaling is again logarithmic. The bottom left point of each curve denotes performance without fine-tuning. Clearly, the performance of our approach outperforms other baselines if fine-tuning is prohibited. After fine-tuning, our method can be further improved and still runs efficiently, taking 2.5 s per frame while other baselines require more than 10 s to achieve their peak performance. Note that we don't have any post-processing step to refine the segmentation mask in our method while still achieving competitive results.

4.5 Qualitative Results

In Fig. 6, we show visual results of our method on DAVIS-16 (1st row), Youtube-Objects (2nd row), JumpCut (3rd row), and DAVIS-17 datasets (4th row). We observe our method can accurately segment the foreground objects with challenges such as fast motion, cluttered background and appearance change. We also observe the proposed method produce accurate instance level segmentation on DAVIS-17 datasets.

We show the failure cases of our method in Fig. 7. Possible reasons for our method to fail include tiny objects and similar appearance of different instances.

5 Conclusion

We present an efficient video object segmentation algorithm base on a novel soft matching layer. The method generalizes well and does not require online fine-tuning while maintaining good accuracy. Our method achieves state-of-the-art on the Youtube-Objects and JumpCut datasets and is competitive on DAVIS-16 and DAVIS-17, while its computational time is at least one order of magnitude faster than current state-of-the-art.

Acknowledgments. This material is based upon work supported in part by the National Science Foundation under Grant No. 1718221, 1755785, Samsung, and 3M. We thank NVIDIA for providing the GPUs used for this research.

References

1. Avinash Ramakanth, S., Venkatesh Babu, R.: SeamSeg: video object segmentation using patch seams. In: Proceedings of CVPR (2014)
2. Bai, X., Wang, J., Simons, D., Sapiro, G.: Video snapcut: robust video object cutout using localized classifiers. In: SIGGRAPH (2009)
3. Bertinetto, L., Valmadre, J., Henriques, J.F., Vedaldi, A., Torr, P.H.: Fully-convolutional siamese networks for object tracking. In: Proceedings of CVPR (2017)
4. Caelles, S., Chen, Y., Pont-Tuset, J., Van Gool, L.: Semantically-guided video object segmentation (2017). arXiv preprint: arXiv:1704.01926
5. Caelles, S., Maninis, K.K., Pont-Tuset, J., Leal-Taixé, L., Cremers, D., Van Gool, L.: One-shot video object segmentation. In: Proceedings of CVPR (2017)
6. Chen, L.C., Papandreou, G., Kokkinos, I., Murphy, K., Yuille, A.L.: Deeplab: semantic image segmentation with deep convolutional nets, atrous convolution, and fully connected CRFs. PAMI **40**, 834–848 (2018)
7. Chen, Y., Pont-Tuset, J., Montes, A., Van Gool, L.: Blazingly fast video object segmentation with pixel-wise metric learning. In: Proceedings of CVPR (2018)
8. Cheng, J., Tsai, Y.H., Wang, S., Yang, M.H.: SegFlow: joint learning for video object segmentation and optical flow. In: Proceedings of ICCV (2017)
9. Cheng, J., Tsai, Y.H., Hung, W.C., Wang, S., Yang, M.H.: Fast and accurate online video object segmentation via tracking parts. In: Proceedings of CVPR (2018)
10. Dosovitskiy, A., et al.: Flownet: learning optical flow with convolutional networks. In: Proceedings of ICCV (2015)
11. Everingham, M., Eslami, S.A., Van Gool, L., Williams, C.K., Winn, J., Zisserman, A.: The PASCAL visual object classes challenge: a retrospective. IJCV **111**, 98–136 (2015)
12. Faktor, A., Irani, M.: Video segmentation by non-local consensus voting. In: BMVC (2014)
13. Fan, Q., Zhong, F., Lischinski, D., Cohen-Or, D., Chen, B.: JumpCut: non-successive mask transfer and interpolation for video cutout. In: SIGGRAPH (2015)
14. Godec, M., Roth, P.M., Bischof, H.: Hough-based tracking of non-rigid objects. In: Proceedings of ICCV (2011)
15. Grundmann, M., Kwatra, V., Han, M., Essa, I.: Efficient hierarchical graph-based video segmentation. In: Proceedings of CVPR (2010)
16. Hariharan, B., Arbeláez, P., Bourdev, L., Maji, S., Malik, J.: Semantic contours from inverse detectors. In: Proceedings of ICCV (2011)
17. He, K., Zhang, X., Ren, S., Sun, J.: Deep residual learning for image recognition. In: Proceedings of CVPR (2016)
18. Hu, Y.T., Lin, Y.Y., Chen, H.Y., Hsu, K.J., Chen, B.Y.: Matching images with multiple descriptors: an unsupervised approach for locally adaptive descriptor selection. TIP **24**, 5995–6010 (2015)
19. Hu, Y.T., Huang, J.B., Schwing, A.: MaskRNN: instance level video object segmentation. In: NIPS (2017)

20. Hu, Y.T., Huang, J.B., Schwing, A.: Unsupervised video object segmentation using motion saliency-guided spatio-temporal propagation. In: Ferrari, V., et al. (eds.) ECCV 2018, Part VIII. LNCS, vol. 11205, pp. 813–830. Springer, Cham (2018)
21. Jain, S.D., Grauman, K.: Supervoxel-consistent foreground propagation in video. In: Fleet, D., Pajdla, T., Schiele, B., Tuytelaars, T. (eds.) ECCV 2014, Part IV. LNCS, vol. 8692, pp. 656–671. Springer, Cham (2014). https://doi.org/10.1007/978-3-319-10593-2_43
22. Jain, S.D., Xiong, B., Grauman, K.: FusionSeg: learning to combine motion and appearance for fully automatic segmention of generic objects in videos. In: Proceedings of CVPR (2017)
23. Jampani, V., Gadde, R., Gehler, P.V.: Video propagation networks. In: Proceedings of CVPR (2017)
24. Jang, W.D., Kim, C.S.: Online video object segmentation via convolutional trident network. In: Proceedings of CVPR (2017)
25. Khoreva, A., Perazzi, F., Benenson, R., Schiele, B., Sorkine-Hornung, A.: Learning video object segmentation from static images. In: Proceedings of CVPR (2017)
26. Khoreva, A., Benenson, R., Ilg, E., Brox, T., Schiele, B.: Lucid data dreaming for object tracking (2017). arXiv preprint: arXiv:1703.09554
27. Kingma, D., Ba, J.: Adam: a method for stochastic optimization. In: International Conference on Learning Representations (2014)
28. Kristan, M., et al.: A novel performance evaluation methodology for single-target trackers. PAMI **38**, 2137–2155 (2016)
29. Lee, Y.J., Kim, J., Grauman, K.: Key-segments for video object segmentation. In: Proceedings of ICCV (2011)
30. Lezama, J., Alahari, K., Sivic, J., Laptev, I.: Track to the future: spatio-temporal video segmentation with long-range motion cues. In: Proceedings of CVPR (2011)
31. Li, F., Kim, T., Humayun, A., Tsai, D., Rehg, J.M.: Video segmentation by tracking many figure-ground segments. In: Proceedings of ICCV (2013)
32. Li, X., et al.: Video object segmentation with re-identification. In: The 2017 DAVIS Challenge on Video Object Segmentation - CVPR Workshops (2017)
33. Lowe, D.: Distinctive image features from scale-invariant keypoints. IJCV **60**, 91–110 (2004)
34. Maerki, N., Perazzi, F., Wang, O., Sorkine-Hornung, A.: Bilateral space video segmentation. In: Proceedings of CVPR (2016)
35. Mikolajczyk, K., Schmid, C.: A performance evaluation of local descriptors. IEEE Trans. Pattern Anal. Mach. Intell. **27**, 1615–1630 (2005)
36. Nagaraja, N., Schmidt, F., Brox, T.: Video segmentation with just a few strokes. In: Proceedings of ICCV (2015)
37. Ochs, P., Malik, J., Brox, T.: Segmentation of moving objects by long term video analysis. PAMI **36**, 1187–1200 (2014)
38. Oh, S.W., Lee, J.Y., Sunkavalli, K., Kim, S.J.: Fast video object segmentation by reference-guided mask propagation. In: Proceedings of CVPR (2018)
39. Papazoglou, A., Ferrari, V.: Fast object segmentation in unconstrained video. In: Proceedings of ICCV (2013)
40. Perazzi, F., Pont-Tuset, J., McWilliams, B., Gool, L.V., Gross, M., Sorkine-Hornung, A.: A benchmark dataset and evaluation methodology for video object segmentation. In: Proceedings of CVPR (2016)
41. Perazzi, F., Wang, O., Gross, M., Sorkine-Hornung, A.: Fully connected object proposals for video segmentation. In: Proceedings of ICCV (2015)

42. Pont-Tuset, J., Perazzi, F., Caelles, S., Arbeláez, P., Sorkine-Hornung, A., Van Gool, L.: The 2017 DAVIS challenge on video object segmentation (2017). arXiv preprint: arXiv:1704.00675
43. Prest, A., Leistner, C., Civera, J., Schmid, C., Ferrari, V.: Learning object class detectors from weakly annotated video. In: Proceedings of CVPR (2012)
44. Price, B.L., Morse, B.S., Cohen, S.: LIVEcut: learning-based interactive video segmentation by evaluation of multiple propagated cues. In: Proceedings of ICCV (2009)
45. Revaud, J., Weinzaepfel, P., Harchaoui, Z., Schmid, C.: Deepmatching: hierarchical deformable dense matching. IJCV **120**, 300–323 (2016)
46. Rocco, I., Arandjelovic, R., Sivic, J.: Convolutional neural network architecture for geometric matching. In: Proceedings of CVPR (2017)
47. Tokmakov, P., Alahari, K., Schmid, C.: Learning motion patterns in videos. In: Proceedings of CVPR (2017)
48. Tokmakov, P., Alahari, K., Schmid, C.: Learning video object segmentation with visual memory. In: Proceedings of ICCV (2017)
49. Tsai, D., Flagg, M., Rehg, J.: Motion coherent tracking with multi-label MRF optimization. In: Proceedings of BMVC (2010)
50. Tsai, Y.H., Yang, M.H., Black, M.J.: Video segmentation via object flow. In: Proceedings of CVPR (2016)
51. Vijayanarasimhan, S., Grauman, K.: Active frame selection for label propagation in videos. In: Fitzgibbon, A., Lazebnik, S., Perona, P., Sato, Y., Schmid, C. (eds.) ECCV 2012, Part V. LNCS, vol. 7576, pp. 496–509. Springer, Heidelberg (2012). https://doi.org/10.1007/978-3-642-33715-4_36
52. Voigtlaender, P., Leibe, B.: Online adaptation of convolutional neural networks for the 2017 DAVIS challenge on video object segmentation. In: The 2017 DAVIS Challenge on Video Object Segmentation - CVPR Workshops (2017)
53. Voigtlaender, P., Leibe, B.: Online adaptation of convolutional neural networks for video object segmentation. In: BMVC (2017)
54. Wang, W., Shen, J., Porikli, F.: Selective video object cutout. TIP **26**, 5645–5655 (2017)
55. Xiao, F., Lee, Y.J.: Track and segment: an iterative unsupervised approach for video object proposals. In: Proceedings of CVPR (2016)
56. Yang, L., Wang, Y., Xiong, X., Yang, J., Katsaggelos, A.K.: Efficient video object segmentation via network modulation. In: Proceedings of CVPR (2018)
57. Yang, T.Y., Hsu, J.H., Lin, Y.Y., Chuang, Y.Y.: DeepCD: learning deep complementary descriptors for patch representations. In: Proceedings of ICCV (2017)
58. Yilmaz, A., Javed, O., Shah, M.: Object tracking: a survey. ACM Comput. Surv. (CSUR) **38**, 13 (2006)
59. Yoon, J.S., Rameau, F., Kim, J., Lee, S., Shin, S., Kweon, I.S.: Pixel-level matching for video object segmentation using convolutional neural networks. In: Proceedings of ICCV (2017)
60. Zhong, F., Qin, X., Peng, Q., Meng, X.: Discontinuity-aware video object cutout. In: SIGGRAPH (2012)

Context Refinement for Object Detection

Zhe Chen(✉), Shaoli Huang, and Dacheng Tao

UBTECH Sydney AI Centre, SIT, FEIT, University of Sydney, Sydney, Australia
zche4307@uni.sydney.edu.au,
{shaoli.huang,dacheng.tao}@sydney.edu.au

Abstract. Current two-stage object detectors, which consists of a region proposal stage and a refinement stage, may produce unreliable results due to ill-localized proposed regions. To address this problem, we propose a context refinement algorithm that explores rich contextual information to better refine each proposed region. In particular, we first identify neighboring regions that may contain useful contexts and then perform refinement based on the extracted and unified contextual information. In practice, our method effectively improves the quality of the final detection results as well as region proposals. Empirical studies show that context refinement yields substantial and consistent improvements over different baseline detectors. Moreover, the proposed algorithm brings around 3% performance gain on PASCAL VOC benchmark and around 6% gain on MS COCO benchmark respectively.

Keywords: Object detection · Context analysis
Deep convolutional neural network

1 Introduction

Recent top-performing object detectors, such as Faster RCNN [29] and Mask RCNN [16], are mostly based on a two-stage paradigm which first generates a sparse set of object proposals and then refines the proposals by adjusting their coordinates and predicting their categories. Despite great success, these methods tend to produce inaccurate bounding boxes and false labels after the refinement because of the poor-quality proposals generated in the first stage. As illustrated in Fig. 1, if a proposed region has a partial overlap with a true object, existing methods would suffer refinement failures since this region does not contain sufficient information for holistic object perception. Although much effort such as [21] has been dedicated to enhance the quality of object proposals, it still cannot guarantee that the proposed regions can have a satisfactory overlap for each ground truth.

To tackle the aforementioned issue, we augment the representation for each proposed region by leveraging its surrounding regions. This is motivated by the fact that surrounding regions usually contain complementary information on object appearance and high-level characteristics, e.g., semantics and geometric

V. Ferrari et al. (Eds.): ECCV 2018, LNCS 11212, pp. 74–89, 2018.
https://doi.org/10.1007/978-3-030-01237-3_5

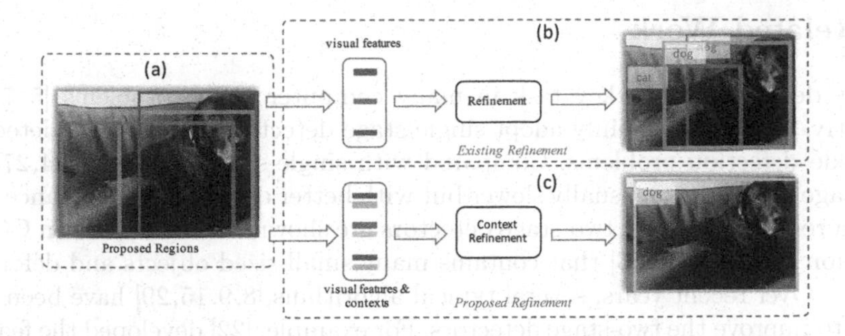

Fig. 1. Overview of the pipeline for the proposed context refinement algorithm comparing to existing refinement pipeline. Existing pipeline (b) refines each proposed region by performing classification and regression only based on visual features, while the proposed algorithm (c) can achieve a more reliable refinement by making use of both visual cues and contexts brought by surrounding regions.

relationships, for a proposed region. Different from related approaches [12,26,36,37] that mainly include additional visual features from manually picked regions to help refinement, our method is based on off-the-shelf proposals that are more natural and more reliable than hand-designed regions. Furthermore, by using a weighting strategy, our method can also take better advantage of contextual information comparing to other existing methods.

In this paper, we propose a learning-based context refinement algorithm to augment the existing refinement procedure. More specifically, our proposed method follows an iterative procedure which consists of three processing steps in each iteration. In the first processing step, we select a candidate region from the proposed regions and identify its surrounding regions. Next, we gather the contextual information from the surrounding regions and then aggregate these collected contexts into a unified contextual representation based on an adaptive weighting strategy. Lastly, we perform context refinement for the selected region based on both the visual features and the corresponding unified contextual representation. In practice, since the proposed method requires minor modification in detection pipeline, we can implement our algorithm by introducing additional small networks that can be directly embedded in existing two-stage detectors. With such simplicity of design and ease of implementation, our method can further improve the region proposal stage for two-stage detectors. Extensive experimental results show that the proposed method consistently boosts the performance for different baseline detectors, such as Faster RCNN [29], Deformable R-FCN [9], and Mask RCNN [16], with diversified backbone networks, such as VGG [32] and ResNet [17]. The proposed algorithm also achieves around 3% improvement on PASCAL VOC benchmark and around 6% improvement on MS COCO benchmark over baseline detectors.

2 Related Work

Object detection is the key task in many computer vision problems [5–7,18]. Recently, researchers mainly adopt single-stage detectors or two-stage detectors to tackle detection problems. Compared with single-stage detectors [24,27,30], two-stage detectors are usually slower but with better detection performance [20]. With a refinement stage, two-stage detectors are shown to be powerful on COCO detection benchmark [23] that contains many small-sized objects and deformed objects. Over recent years, several typical algorithms [8,9,15,29] have been proposed to improve the two-stage detectors. For example, [22] developed the feature pyramid network to address the challenge of small object detection. [16] proposes a novel feature warping method to improve the performance of the final refinement procedure. However, these methods are highly sensitive to the quality of object proposals and thereby may produce false labels and inaccurate bounding boxes on poor-quality object proposals.

To relieve this issue, post-processing methods have been widely used in two-stage detection systems. One of the most popular among them is the iterative bounding box refinement method [12,17,37]. This method repeatedly refines the proposed regions and performs a voting and suppressing procedure to obtain the final results. Meanwhile, rather than using a manually designed iterative refinement method, some studies [13,14] recursively perform regression to the proposed regions so that they can learn to gradually adapt the ground-truth boxes. Although better performance could be achieved with more iterations of processing, these methods are commonly computational costly. In addition, some other studies adopt a re-scoring strategy. For example, the paper [2] tends to progressively decrease the detection score of overlapped bounding boxes, lowering the risk of keeping false positive results rather than more reliable ones, while Hosang *et al.* [19] re-scores detection with a learning-based algorithm. However, the re-scoring methods do not consider contexts, thus only offering limited help in improving the performance.

More related studies refer visual contexts to improve object detection. Even without the powerful deep convolutional neural networks (DCNNs), the advantages of using contexts for object detection have already been demonstrated in [10,25,35]. In recent years, many studies [12,26,36,37] attempt to further incorporate contexts in DCNN. In general, they propose to utilize additional visual features from context windows to facilitate detection. A context window is commonly selected based on a slightly larger or smaller region comparing to the corresponding proposed regions. The visual features inside each context window will be extracted and used as contextual information for the final refinement of each region. However, since context windows are commonly selected by hand, the considered regions still have a limited range and surrounding contexts may not be fully exploited. Instead of using context windows, some studies [1,4,28] attempt to employ recurrent neural networks to encode contextual information. For example, the ION detector [1] attempts to collect contexts by introducing multi-directional recurrent neural network, but the resulting network becomes much more complicated and it requires careful initialization for stable training.

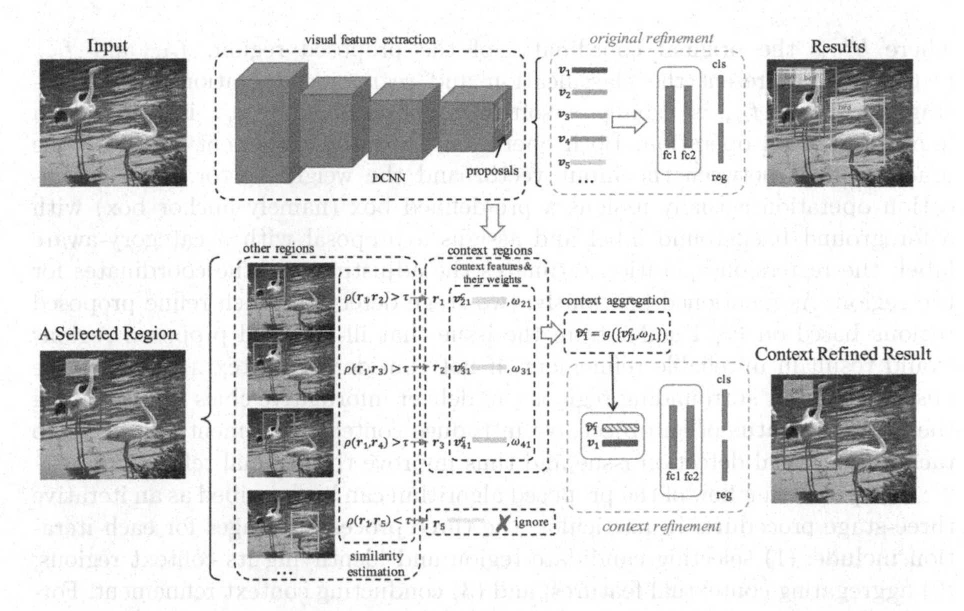

Fig. 2. The detailed working flow of the proposed context refinement algorithm for improving the original refinement (best view in color). Regarding each selected region, our algorithm first identifies its surrounding regions that may carry useful context based on a correlation estimation procedure. Afterwards, all the contextual information is aggregated to form a unified representation based on an adaptive weighting strategy. Using both the aggregated contexts and visual features extracted from DCNN, the proposed context refinement algorithm is able to improve the quality of detection results. The detailed definitions of the math symbols can be found in Sect. 3. (Color figure online)

Nevertheless, most of the prevailing context-aware object detectors only consider contextual features extracted from DCNNs, lacking the consideration of higher-level surrounding contexts such as semantic information and geometric relationship.

3 Context Refinement for Object Detection

Different from existing studies that mainly extract visual contexts from manually picked regions or RNNs, we propose to extensively incorporate contextual information brought by surrounding regions to improve the original refinement.

Mathematically, we define that the status of a region $\boldsymbol{r}$ is described by its four coordinates $\boldsymbol{b} = (x_1, y_1, x_2, y_2)$ and a confidence score s. Suppose $\boldsymbol{v}_i$ represents visual features extracted from the region $\boldsymbol{r}_i$ bounded by $\boldsymbol{b}_i$, then original refinement procedure of existing two-stage detectors commonly perform the following operations to refine the region $\boldsymbol{r}_i$:

$$\begin{cases} s_i = f_{cls}(\boldsymbol{v}_i) \\ \boldsymbol{b}_i = f_{reg}(\boldsymbol{b}_i^0, \boldsymbol{v}_i) \end{cases} \tag{1}$$

where $\boldsymbol{b}_i^0$ is the original coordinates of the proposed region, f_{cls} and f_{reg} respectively represent the classification and regression operations. In a two-stage detector, f_{cls} is usually a soft-max operation and f_{reg} is generally a linear regression operation. Both operations perform refinement based on the inner product between the input vector and the weight vector. The classification operation actually assigns a pre-defined box (namely anchor box) with a foreground/background label and assigns a proposal with a category-aware label; the regression operation estimates the adjustment of the coordinates for the region. As mentioned previously, two-stage detectors which refine proposed regions based on Eq. 1 suffer from the issue that ill-localized proposed regions would result in unreliable refinement, if not considering context. Based on the observation that surrounding regions can deliver informative clues for describing the accurate status of an object, we introduce context refinement algorithm to tackle the partial detection issue and thus improve the original refinement.

The processing flow of the proposed algorithm can be described as an iterative three-stage procedure. In particular, the three processing stages for each iteration include: (1) selecting candidate region and identifying its context regions; (2) aggregating contextual features; and (3) conducting context refinement. Formally, we make $\boldsymbol{r}_i$ represent the selected region in current iteration and further define the surrounding regions of $\boldsymbol{r}_i$ that may carry useful contexts as its context region. In the first stage, we select a candidate region $\boldsymbol{r}_i$ and then the context regions of $\boldsymbol{r}_i$ can be properly obtained by collecting other regions that are in the neighbourhood and closely related to the selected region. We use the symbol R_i^c to represent the set of the obtained context regions for $\boldsymbol{r}_i$. Afterwards, in the second stage, we extract contextual features from R_i^c and fuse these contexts into a unified representation, $\hat{\boldsymbol{v}}_i^c$, based on an adaptive weighting strategy. For the last stage, based on both $\boldsymbol{v}_i$ and $\hat{\boldsymbol{v}}_i^c$, we perform context refinement using the following operations:

$$\begin{cases} \boldsymbol{s}_i' = f_{cls}^c(\boldsymbol{s}_i, \boldsymbol{v}_i, \hat{\boldsymbol{v}}_i^c) \\ \boldsymbol{b}_i' = f_{reg}^c(\boldsymbol{b}_i, \boldsymbol{v}_i, \hat{\boldsymbol{v}}_i^c) \end{cases} \tag{2}$$

where $\boldsymbol{b}_i'$ and $\boldsymbol{s}_i'$ are the results of context refinement, and f_{cls}^c and f_{reg}^c are the context refinement functions for classification and regression respectively. The detailed workflow of context refinement for improving the detection is illustrated in Eq. 2.

3.1 Selecting Regions

In our proposed algorithm, the first step is to select a candidate region and identify its context regions for refinement. According to Eq. 2, we perform original refinement before the first step of our algorithm so that the regions can be first enriched with semantics and meaningful geometry information. This can also make the regions tend to cluster themselves around true objects and thus can convey helpful context.

After the original refinement, the estimated confidence score can indicate the quality of a region to some extents. In this study, we adopt a greedy strategy to select regions in each iteration, which means that regions of higher scores will be refined with contexts earlier. When a region is selected, we then identify its context regions for extracting contextual information. In our algorithm, the context regions represent closely related regions, considering that these regions could cover the same object with the selected region. In order to obtain an adequate set of context regions, we estimate the closeness between the selected region and the other regions. Therefore, the regions that are closer to the selected region can form an adequate set of context regions R_i^c.

We introduce the concept of correlation level to define the closeness between a selected region and other regions. The correlation level represents the strength of the relationship between any two regions. We use $\rho(\boldsymbol{r}_i, \boldsymbol{r}_j)$ to describe the correlation level between $\boldsymbol{r}_i$ and $\boldsymbol{r}_j$. Using this notation, we describe the set of context regions for $\boldsymbol{r}_i$ as:

$$R_i^c = \{\boldsymbol{r}_j | \rho(\boldsymbol{r}_i, \boldsymbol{r}_j) > \tau\} \tag{3}$$

where τ is a threshold. In our implementation, we measure the correlation level between two regions based on their Intersect-over-Union (IoU) score, thus $\rho(\boldsymbol{r}_i, \boldsymbol{r}_j) = IoU(\boldsymbol{b}_i, \boldsymbol{b}_j)$. The detailed setting for τ is defined in Sect. 5.

3.2 Fusing Context

Context extracted from R_i^c can provide complementary information that could be beneficial for rectifying the coordinates and improving the estimated class probabilities for the selected candidate regions. However, a major issue of using the collected contextual information is that the number of context regions is not fixed and can range from zero to hundreds. Using an arbitrary amount of contextual information, it will be difficult for an algorithm to conduct appropriate refinement for $\boldsymbol{r}_i$. To tackle this issue, we introduce the aggregation function g to fuse all the collected contextual information into a unified representation based on an adaptive weighting strategy, thus facilitating the context refinement.

We use $\boldsymbol{v}_{ji}^c$ to denote the contextual information carried by $\boldsymbol{r}_j$ w.r.t $\boldsymbol{r}_i$. Then we can build a set of contextual representation V_i^c by collecting all the $\boldsymbol{v}_{ji}^c$ from R_i^c:

$$V_i^c = \{\boldsymbol{v}_{ji}^c | \boldsymbol{v}_{ji}^c \text{ for } \boldsymbol{r}_j \in R_i^c\}. \tag{4}$$

Since the size of V_i^c will vary according to different selected regions, we attempt to aggregate all the contexts in V_i^c into a unified representation. In order to properly realize the aggregation operation, we propose that the more related context regions should make major contributions to the unified contextual representation. This can further reduce the risk of distracting the refinement if surrounding regions are scattered. In particular, we adopt the use of an adaptive weighting strategy to help define the aggregation function g.

Mathematically, we refer ω_{ji} as the weight of $\boldsymbol{v}_{ji}^c \in V_i^c$ that can be adaptively computed according to different selected regions. Since we are assigning larger weights to more related context regions, we attempt to estimate the relation score between $\boldsymbol{r}_j$ and $\boldsymbol{r}_i$ and make ω_{ji} depend on the estimated score. Considering that we are using semantics (i.e. classification results) and geometry information to define regions, it is appropriate to describe ω_{ji} as a combination of semantic relation score ω_{ji}^s and geometric relation score ω_{ji}^g:

$$\omega_{ji} = \omega_{ji}^s \cdot \omega_{ji}^g. \tag{5}$$

We instantiate the semantic relation score ω_{ji}^s and geometry relation score ω_{ji}^g using the following settings:

$$\begin{cases} \omega_{ji}^s = \mathbb{1}(l_j = l_i) \cdot s_j \\ \omega_{ji}^g = IoU(\boldsymbol{b}_i, \boldsymbol{b}_j) \end{cases} \tag{6}$$

where $\mathbb{1}(\cdot)$ is a bool function and l_i, l_j represent the predicted labels for corresponding regions. Using this setting, the context regions with lower confidence and lower overlap scores w.r.t the selected region will make minor contributions to the unified contextual representation.

By denoting Ω_i as the set of estimated ω_{ji} for $\boldsymbol{v}_{ji}^c \in V_i^c$, we introduce an averaging operation to consolidate all the weighted contextual information brought by a variable number of context regions. Recall that the unified contextual representation is $\hat{\boldsymbol{v}}_i^c$, we implement the aggregation operation g based on the following equation:

$$\hat{\boldsymbol{v}}_i^c = g(\{\boldsymbol{v}_{ji}^c, \omega_{ji} | \boldsymbol{v}_{ji}^c \in V_i^c, \ \omega_{ji} \in \Omega_i\}) \tag{7}$$

where:

$$g(\{\boldsymbol{v}_{ji}^c, \omega_{ji}\}) = \frac{\sum_j \omega_{ji} \cdot \boldsymbol{v}_{ji}^c}{\sum_j \omega_{ji}}. \tag{8}$$

3.3 Learning-Based Refinement

After $\hat{\boldsymbol{v}}_i^c$ is computed by Eq. 7, we are then able to perform context refinement for each selected regions based on Eq. 2. In this paper, we introduce a learning-based scheme to fulfill the context refinement. More specifically, we employ fully connected neural network layers to realize the functions f_{cls}^c and f_{reg}^c. By concatenating together the $\boldsymbol{v}_i$ and $\hat{\boldsymbol{v}}_i^c$, the employed fully connected layers will learn to estimate a context refined classification score s_i' and coordinates $\boldsymbol{b}_i'$. These fully connected layers can be trained together with original refinement network.

Overall, Algorithm 1 describes the detailed processing flow of the proposed context refinement algorithm over an original refinement procedure. The proposed algorithm is further visualized by Fig. 2.

Algorithm 1. Context Refinement

Require: A set of regions, $R = \{\boldsymbol{r}_i = (l_i, \boldsymbol{b}_i)\}$, that has been first refined by Eq. 1;
Ensure: A set of context refined regions $R' = \{\boldsymbol{r}'_i = (l'_i, \boldsymbol{b}'_i)\}$;
1: $R' \leftarrow \{\}$
2: **for** each selected originally refined region $\boldsymbol{r}_i \in R$ **do**
3: find the set of context regions R^c_i based on Eq. 3;
4: collect contextual representation V^c_i based on Eq. 4;
5: aggregate contexts and obtain the unified contextual representation $\hat{\boldsymbol{v}}^c_i$ based on Eq. 5 - Eq. 8;
6: perform learning-based context refinement for $\boldsymbol{r}_i$ based on Eq. 2, obtaining l'_i and $\boldsymbol{b}'_i$;
7: $R' \leftarrow R' \cup (l'_i, \boldsymbol{b}'_i)$;
8: **end for**
9: **return** R'

4 Embedded Architecture

Since the proposed method only alters refinement operations, such as classification and regression, of current two-stage detectors, it is straightforward to implement the proposed method by introducing an additional network that can be directly embedded into existing two-stage object detection pipelines. Such design is lightweight and can enable us to perform context refinement for both the final detection results and the region proposals because the proposals can be considered as the refined results of pre-defined anchor boxes.

As shown in Fig. 3, we can directly attach the context refinement module to both the proposal generation stage and final refinement stage compatibly. As mentioned previously, we attach networks for context refinement after the original refinement operations. It is especially necessary to perform original refinement prior to our context refinement for proposal generation stage because pre-defined anchor map does not contain semantic or geometric information that can indicate the existence of objects. Moreover, such embedding design does not revise the form of a detection result, which means that it is still possible to use post-processing algorithms.

5 Implementation Details and Discussions

To embed context refinement network in different phases of a two-stage object detector, we apply the following implementation. In the first stage that produces region proposals, we attach the network of context refinement to the top-6k proposals without performing NMS. We re-use original visual features as useful information and also include relative geometry information (i.e. coordinates offsets) and semantics to enrich the instance-level contextual information for context refinement. The resulting context feature vector then has a length of $(C + 4 + K)$ where C is the channel dimension of visual feature and K is the number of categories. The threshold for defining context regions for proposals is

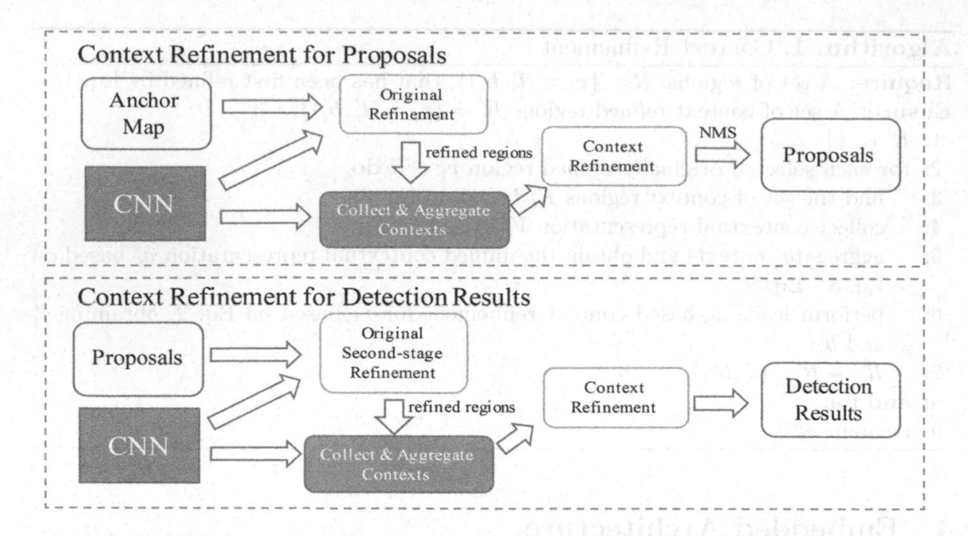

Fig. 3. Embedded architecture of the proposed algorithm. This design makes the context refinement algorithm compatible for both region proposal generation stage and final refinement stage in existing two-stage detection pipeline.

set as 0.5. In addition, f^c_{cls} and f^c_{reg} are conducted on the output of two consecutive fully connected layers with ReLU non-linear activation for the first layer. In the second refinement stage, we additionally involve the semantics estimated in the first context refinement stage. The f^c_{cls} and f^c_{reg} of this stage are performed with one fully connected layer. Other settings are kept the same. When training the context refinement network, since we are using an embedded architecture, it is possible to fix the weights of other parts of a detector to achieve much higher training speed, which would not sacrifice much accuracy. The loss functions used for training are cross entropy loss for classification and smooth L1 loss for regression. Except that in the second stage, we additionally penalize the redundant detection results following the strategy proposed by [19] and thus can relieve the impacts of unnecessary detection results.

Model Complexity. With the embedded design, the increase in model complexity brought by context refinement mainly comes from extracting and unifying contexts brought by context regions. Therefore, the required extra complexity would be at most $\mathcal{O}(M^2D)$ for using M candidate regions with the unified contextual feature of length D. In practice, our method will only use a small portion of proposals for context refinement. More specifically, based on Eq. 3, we can ignore a large number of proposals with a low correlation level when performing context refinement for each candidate region. In addition, we further conduct a thresholding procedure to eliminate the proposals with low confidence scores. As a result, our method only costs around 0.11 s extra processing time when processing 2000 proposals.

Context Refinement for Single-Stage Detectors. Although it is possible to realize context refinement for single-stage detectors, we find that these detectors (e.g. SSD [24]) usually perform refinement on a smaller number of regions, meaning that there would not be sufficient surrounding contexts to access considerable improvements.

Failure Cases. In general, our method brings limited improvements in two cases. The first one is that the context regions are inaccurate. In this case, the extracted contexts are not helping improve the performance. The second one is that the number of context regions is too small to provide sufficient contextual information for improvement.

6 Experiments

To evaluate the effectiveness of the proposed context refinement method for two-stage object detectors, we perform comprehensive evaluations on the well-known object detection benchmarks, including PASCAL VOC [11] and MS COCO [23]. We estimate the effects of our method on final detection results as well as region proposals, comparing to original refinement method and other state-of-the-art detection algorithms.

6.1 PASCAL VOC

PASCAL VOC benchmark [11] is a commonly used detection benchmark which contains 20 categories of objects for evaluating detectors. For all the following evaluation, we train models on both VOC 07 + 12 trainval datasets and perform the evaluation on VOC 07 test set, where mean Average Precision (mAP) will be majorly reported as detection performance.

In this section, we apply context refinement for both regional proposals and the second refinement stage in the Faster RCNN (FRCNN) detector [29]. Considering that this detector adopts region proposal network (RPN) to refine anchors, we abbreviate the context refined RPN as C-RPN. We further use C-FRCNN to represent the FRCNN whose RPN and the second refinement stage are both refined with contexts. We re-implement the FRCNN following the protocol of [3] and use † to represent this re-implemented FRCNN in following experiments.

Effects on Region Proposals. We first evaluate the effectiveness of the proposed algorithm for region proposal network (RPN). The improvements in recall rates w.r.t the ground-truth objects will illustrate the efficacy of our method. In this part, recall rates will be reported based on different IoU thresholds and different number of proposals. It is worth noting that our method is not a novel region proposal algorithm, thus we do not compare with SelectiveSearch [34] and EdgeBox [38]. We only report the performance gain with respect to the original refinement performed by region proposal network.

Using different IoU thresholds as the criteria, we report the recall rates by fixing the number of proposals in each plot, as illustrated in Fig. 4. From the

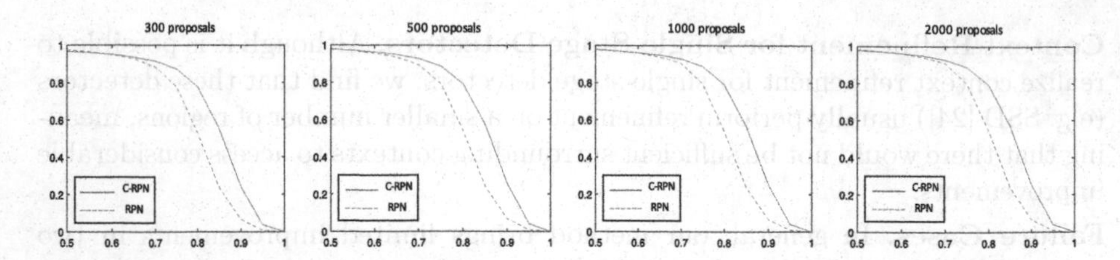

Fig. 4. Curves for the recall rates against IoU threshold on the PASCAL VOC07 test set for the original refined region proposal network and the context refined results. C-RPN refers to the region proposal network improved with contexts.

presented plots, we can find that although all the curves change slightly with the number of proposals increases, the proposed context refinement procedure can consistently boost recalls rates of original refinement. Especially, context refinement is able to improve the recall rates of original RPN with around 45% at an IoU threshold of 0.8 in each plot, which validates that the proposed algorithm is advantageous for improving the quality of region proposals.

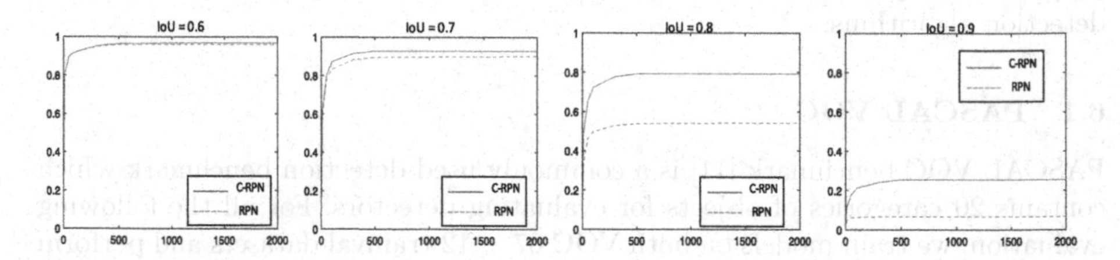

Fig. 5. Curves for the recall rates against the number of proposals on the PASCAL VOC07 test set for the original refined region proposal network and the context refined results. C-RPN refers to the region proposal network improved with contexts.

In addition, we report the recall rates for adopting different numbers of proposals in Fig. 5. In these plots, we can observe that the context refinement bring more improvements when using higher IoU thresholds as criteria. Starting from the IoU threshold of 0.8 for computing the recall rates, the improvements of the proposed method becomes obvious, out-performing the original refinement method in RPN with around 2 points for using more than 100 proposals. With a more strict IoU threshold (i.e. 0.9), the proposals refined with surrounding contexts can still capture 20% to 30% of ground-truth boxes, while original refinement only facilitates RPN to cover only around 7% ground-truth.

Effects on Detection. With the help of context refinement, we not only can boost recall rates of proposals but also can promisingly promote the final detection performance. Table 1 briefly shows the ablation results of the context refinement algorithm for improving performance in different refinement stages. In particular, by improving the recall rates of generated proposals, context refinement

Table 1. Ablation study on VOC 07 test set for using context refinement to improve different refinement stages in Faster RCNN (FRCNN) detector. "C-RPN" refers to the context refinement improved region proposal network (RPN). "C-FRCNN" means the FRCNN whose both refinement stages are improved with contexts. †: the FRCNN implemented following the protocol suggested by [3].

Method	AP@0.5	AP@0.7	AP@0.8
FRCNN† with RPN	0.796	0.633	0.442
FRCNN† with C-RPN	0.804	0.650	0.469
C-FRCNN†	**0.822**	**0.685**	**0.485**

Table 2. Performance of context refinement improved Faster RCNN (C-FRCNN) detector compared to other cutting-edge detectors on VOC 07 test set. †: the Faster RCNN implemented following the protocol suggested by [3].

Method	Network	aero	bike	bird	boat	bottle	bus	car	cat	chair	cow	table	dog	horse	motor	person	plant	sheep	sofa	train	tv	mAP
HyperNet [21]	VGG	84.2	78.5	73.6	55.6	53.7	78.7	79.8	87.7	49.6	74.9	52.1	86.0	81.7	83.3	81.8	48.6	73.5	59.4	79.9	65.7	71.4
ION [1]	VGG	79.2	83.1	77.6	65.6	54.9	85.4	85.1	87.0	54.4	80.6	73.8	85.3	82.2	82.2	74.4	47.1	75.8	72.7	84.2	80.4	75.6
CC [26]	BN-incep	80.9	84.8	83.0	75.9	**72.3**	**88.9**	88.4	**90.3**	66.2	87.6	74.0	89.5	89.3	83.6	79.6	55.2	83.4	81.0	**87.8**	80.7	81.1
R-FCN [8]	Res101	79.9	87.2	81.5	72.0	69.8	86.8	88.5	89.8	67.0	88.1	74.5	**89.8**	**90.6**	79.9	81.2	53.7	81.8	81.5	85.9	79.9	80.5
FRCNN† [3, 29]	VGG	76.1	82.5	75.3	65.3	65.6	84.8	87.5	87.5	57.7	82.4	67.7	83.3	85.3	77.1	78.4	44.1	76.9	70.1	82.6	77.0	75.3
C-FRCNN† (ours)	VGG	79.5	83.7	77.6	69.3	67.2	84.9	87.5	87.6	61.3	83.9	72.3	85.3	85.7	80.8	83.5	49.9	79.2	73.4	83.2	76.7	77.6
FRCNN† [3, 29]	Res101	83.1	86.0	79.7	74.2	68.3	87.7	88.0	88.4	62.3	86.8	70.4	88.5	87.3	82.9	82.9	52.8	81.0	77.7	84.5	79.3	79.6
C-FRCNN† (ours)	Res101	**84.7**	**88.2**	**83.1**	**76.2**	71.1	87.9	**88.7**	89.5	**68.7**	**88.6**	**78.2**	89.5	88.7	**84.8**	**86.2**	**55.4**	**84.7**	**82.0**	86.0	**81.7**	**82.2**

brings 0.8 point's gain in final mAP using 0.5 as IoU threshold. When further employing the proposed refinement to the final refinement stage of FRCNN, there is another 1.6 points' improvement using the same metric. The presented statistics reveal that the proposed context refinement is effective in improving detection performance, especially for the final refinement stage in two-stage detectors.

Moreover, by well-considering the contextual information carried with surrounding regions, the proposed method is supposed to greatly improve the detection results comparing to original detectors no matter what backbone network is used. To verify this, we evaluate the enhancement in detection performance of adopting the use of context refinement for using different backbone networks such as VGG and ResNet in FRCNN detector, comparing to other state-of-the-art two-stage detectors. All the other compared algorithms are processed as described in original papers, using VOC 07+12 dataset as training set.

Table 2 presents the detailed results of C-FRCNN based on different backbone networks, comparing to other state-of-the-art two-stage detectors based on similar backbone networks. According to the results, context refinement respectively achieves 2.3 points higher mAP for VGG-based FRCNN detector and 2.6 points higher mAP for ResNet101-based FRCNN detector. ResNet101-based C-FRCNN helps FRCNN surpass other state-of-the-art detectors, including the context-aware algorithms such as [1, 26].

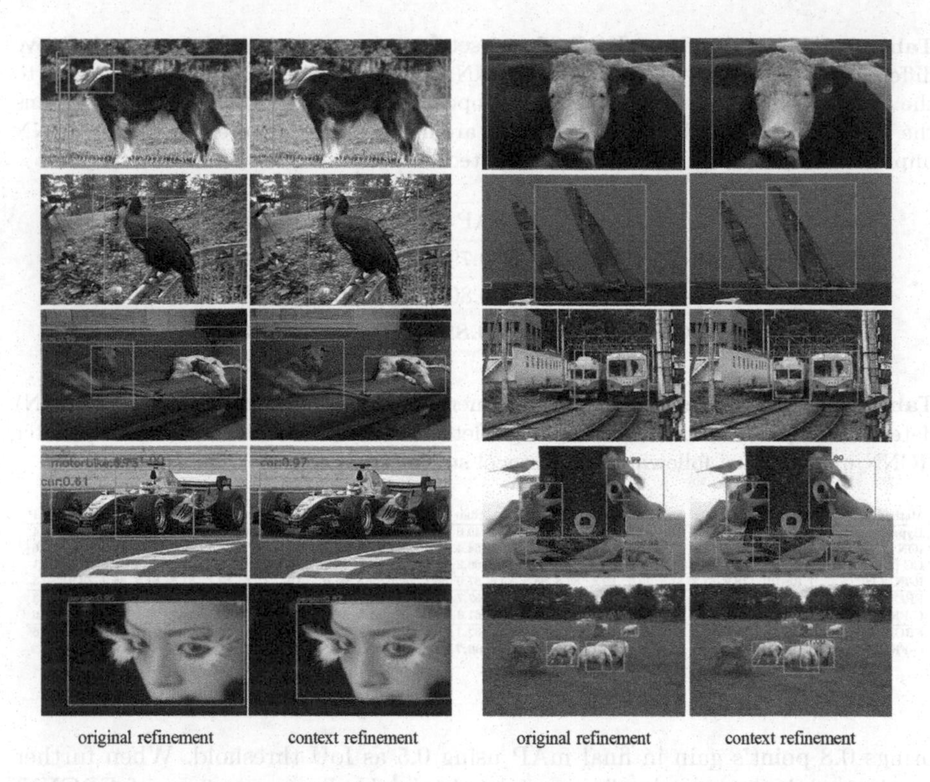

Fig. 6. Qualitative Results. Context refinement has shown to improve the coordinates as well as the labels of originally refined results. Best illustrated in color. (Color figure online)

6.2 MS COCO

We further evaluate our approach on MS COCO benchmark. The MS COCO benchmark contains 80 objects of various sizes and is more challenging than the PASCAL VOC benchmark. This dataset has 80k images as *train* set. We report the performance gain brought by context refinement on the *test-dev* set with 20k images. In this part, besides FRCNN detector, we also embed the context refinement module to the compelling deformable RFCN (DRFCN) detector and Mask RCNN detector and report enhancement in their detection performance. We use C-DRFCN and C-Mask RCNN to respectively represent the relating detectors refined by our algorithm.

Table 3 illustrates the detailed performance of AP in different conditions for the evaluated methods. From it, we can find that the context refinement generally brings 1.5 to 2.0 points improvement over original detectors. It shows that the performance for detecting objects of all the scales can be boosted to a better score using our algorithm, proving the effectiveness of the proposed method. Furthermore, the C-FRCNN and C-DRFCN detectors have outperformed FPN, by around 3 points. By improving the state-of-the-art detector, Mask RCNN, C-

Table 3. Performance of context refinement improved Faster RCNN (C-FRCNN), Deformable RFCN (C-DRFCN), and Mask RCNN (C-MaskRCNN) detectors compared to other cutting-edge detectors on MS COCO test-dev results. †: the FRCNN implemented following the protocol suggested by [3]. ∗: Mask RCNN trained with an end-to-end scheme.

Method	Network	AP	mAP@0.5	mAP@0.7	mAP (small)	mAP (medium)	mAP (large)
TDM [31]	Inception-ResNet-v2	36.8	57.7	39.2	16.2	39.8	52.1
GRMI [20]	Inception-ResNet-v2	34.8	55.5	36.7	13.5	38.1	52.0
FPN [22]	Res101	36.2	59.1	39.0	18.2	39.0	48.2
FRCNN† [3,29]	Res101	37.5	58.7	40.5	18.8	41.0	51.1
DRFCN [9]	Res101	37.1	58.9	39.8	17.1	40.3	51.3
Mask RCNN* [16]	Res101	40.2	62.0	43.9	22.8	43.0	51.1
C-FRCNN† (ours)	Res101	39.0	59.7	42.8	19.4	42.4	53.0
C-DRFCN (ours)	Res101	39.1	60.9	42.5	19.0	42.4	53.2
C-Mask RCNN* (ours) [16]	Res101	**42.0**	**62.9**	**46.4**	**23.4**	**44.7**	**53.8**

Mask RCNN detector achieves the highest AP among all the evaluated methods even compared to the models with a more powerful backbone network, i.e. InceptionResNetv2 [33]. This result also suggests that the proposed context refinement is insensitive to different two-stage detection pipelines.

6.3 Qualitative Evaluation

Figure 6 presents qualitative results of the proposed context refinement algorithm. The illustrated images show that our algorithm is effective in reducing the false positive predictions based on the contexts carried by surrounding regions. The context refined results also provide better coverage about the objects.

7 Conclusion

In this study, we investigate the effects of contextual information brought by surrounding regions to improve the refinement of a specific region. In order to properly exploit the informative surrounding context, we propose the context refinement algorithm which attempts to identify context regions, extract and fuse context based on adaptive weighting strategy, and perform refinement. We implement the proposed algorithm with an embedded architecture in both proposal generation stage and final refinement stage of the two-stage detectors. Experiments illustrate the effectiveness of the proposed method. Notably, the two-stage detectors improved by context refinement achieve compelling performance on well-known detection benchmarks against other state-of-the-art detectors.

Acknowledgement. This work was supported by Australian Research Council Projects FL-170100117, DP-180103424, and LP-150100671. We would like to thank Dr. Wanli Ouyang for his constructive suggestions on the response to review.

References

1. Bell, S., Lawrence Zitnick, C., Bala, K., Girshick, R.: Inside-outside net: detecting objects in context with skip pooling and recurrent neural networks. In: CVPR, pp. 2874–2883 (2016)
2. Bodla, N., Singh, B., Chellappa, R., Davis, L.S.: Soft-NMS-improving object detection with one line of code. In: ICCV (2017)
3. Chen, X., Gupta, A.: An implementation of faster RCNN with study for region sampling (2017). arXiv preprint: arXiv:1702.02138
4. Chen, X., Gupta, A.: Spatial memory for context reasoning in object detection. In: ICCV (2017)
5. Chen, Z., Chen, Z.: RBNet: a deep neural network for unified road and road boundary detection. In: Liu, D., Xie, S., Li, Y., Zhao, D., El-Alfy, E.S. (eds.) ICONIP 2017. LNCS, vol. 10634, pp. 677–687. Springer, Cham (2017). https://doi.org/10.1007/978-3-319-70087-8_70
6. Chen, Z., Hong, Z., Tao, D.: An experimental survey on correlation filter-based tracking (2015). arXiv preprint: arXiv:1509.05520
7. Chen, Z., You, X., Zhong, B., Li, J., Tao, D.: Dynamically modulated mask sparse tracking. IEEE Trans. Cybern. **47**(11), 3706–3718 (2017)
8. Dai, J., Li, Y., He, K., Sun, J.: R-FCN: object detection via region-based fully convolutional networks. In: NIPS, pp. 379–387 (2016)
9. Dai, J., et al.: Deformable convolutional networks (2017)
10. Divvala, S.K., Hoiem, D., Hays, J.H., Efros, A.A., Hebert, M.: An empirical study of context in object detection. In: CVPR, pp. 1271–1278. IEEE (2009)
11. Everingham, M., Van Gool, L., Williams, C.K., Winn, J., Zisserman, A.: The PASCAL visual object classes (VOC) challenge. IJCV **88**(2), 303–338 (2010)
12. Gidaris, S., Komodakis, N.: Object detection via a multi-region and semantic segmentation-aware CNN model. In: ICCV, pp. 1134–1142 (2015)
13. Gidaris, S., Komodakis, N.: Attend refine repeat: active box proposal generation via in-out localization. In: BMVC (2016)
14. Gidaris, S., Komodakis, N.: Locnet: improving localization accuracy for object detection. In: CVPR, pp. 789–798 (2016)
15. Girshick, R.: Fast R-CNN. In: ICCV, pp. 1440–1448 (2015)
16. He, K., Gkioxari, G., Dollár, P., Girshick, R.: Mask R-CNN. In: ICCV (2017)
17. He, K., Zhang, X., Ren, S., Sun, J.: Deep residual learning for image recognition. In: CVPR, pp. 770–778 (2016)
18. Hong, Z., Chen, Z., Wang, C., Mei, X., Prokhorov, D., Tao, D.: Multi-store tracker (muster): a cognitive psychology inspired approach to object tracking. In: CVPR, pp. 749–758 (2015)
19. Hosang, J., Benenson, R., Schiele, B.: Learning non-maximum suppression. In: CVPR (2017)
20. Huang, J., et al.: Speed/accuracy trade-offs for modern convolutional object detectors. In: CVPR (2017)
21. Kong, T., Yao, A., Chen, Y., Sun, F.: Hypernet: towards accurate region proposal generation and joint object detection. In: CVPR, pp. 845–853 (2016)

22. Lin, T.Y., Dollár, P., Girshick, R., He, K., Hariharan, B., Belongie, S.: Feature pyramid networks for object detection. In: CVPR (2017)
23. Lin, T.-Y., et al.: Microsoft COCO: common objects in context. In: Fleet, D., Pajdla, T., Schiele, B., Tuytelaars, T. (eds.) ECCV 2014, Part V. LNCS, vol. 8693, pp. 740–755. Springer, Cham (2014). https://doi.org/10.1007/978-3-319-10602-1_48
24. Liu, W., et al.: SSD: single shot multibox detector. In: Leibe, B., Matas, J., Sebe, N., Welling, M. (eds.) ECCV 2016, Part I. LNCS, vol. 9905, pp. 21–37. Springer, Cham (2016). https://doi.org/10.1007/978-3-319-46448-0_2
25. Mottaghi, R., et al.: The role of context for object detection and semantic segmentation in the wild. In: CVPR, pp. 891–898 (2014)
26. Ouyang, W., Wang, K., Zhu, X., Wang, X.: Learning chained deep features and classifiers for cascade in object detection. In: ICCV (2017)
27. Redmon, J., Divvala, S., Girshick, R., Farhadi, A.: You only look once: unified, real-time object detection. In: CVPR, pp. 779–788 (2016)
28. Ren, J., et al.: Accurate single stage detector using recurrent rolling convolution. In: CVPR (2017)
29. Ren, S., He, K., Girshick, R., Sun, J.: Faster R-CNN: towards real-time object detection with region proposal networks. In: NIPS, pp. 91–99 (2015)
30. Shen, Z., Liu, Z., Li, J., Jiang, Y.G., Chen, Y., Xue, X.: DSOD: learning deeply supervised object detectors from scratch. In: CVPR, pp. 1919–1927 (2017)
31. Shrivastava, A., Sukthankar, R., Malik, J., Gupta, A.: Beyond skip connections: top-down modulation for object detection (2016). arXiv preprint: arXiv:1612.06851
32. Simonyan, K., Zisserman, A.: Very deep convolutional networks for large-scale image recognition (2015)
33. Szegedy, C., Ioffe, S., Vanhoucke, V., Alemi, A.A.: Inception-v4, inception-resnet and the impact of residual connections on learning. In: AAAI, pp. 4278–4284 (2017)
34. Uijlings, J.R., Van De Sande, K.E., Gevers, T., Smeulders, A.W.: Selective search for object recognition. IJCV **104**(2), 154–171 (2013)
35. Yu, R.R., Chen, X.S., Morariu, V.I., Davis, L.S., Redmond, W.: The role of context selection in object detection. T-PAMI **32**(9), 1627–1645 (2010)
36. Zagoruyko, S., et al.: A multipath network for object detection (2016). arXiv preprint: arXiv:1604.02135
37. Zeng, X., et al.: Crafting GBD-net for object detection. T-PAMI **40**, 2109–2123 (2017)
38. Zitnick, C.L., Dollár, P.: Edge boxes: locating object proposals from edges. In: Fleet, D., Pajdla, T., Schiele, B., Tuytelaars, T. (eds.) ECCV 2014, Part V. LNCS, vol. 8693, pp. 391–405. Springer, Cham (2014). https://doi.org/10.1007/978-3-319-10602-1_26

SpiderCNN: Deep Learning on Point Sets with Parameterized Convolutional Filters

Yifan Xu[1,2], Tianqi Fan[2], Mingye Xu[2], Long Zeng[1], and Yu Qiao[2(✉)]

[1] Tsinghua University, Beijing, China
xuyf16@mails.tsinghua.edu.cn, zenglong@sz.tsinghua.edu.cn
[2] Guangdong Key Lab of Computer Vision and Virtual Reality, SIAT-SenseTime Joint Lab, Shenzhen Institutes of Advanced Technology, Chinese Academy of Sciences, Shenzhen, People's Republic of China
{tq.fan,my.xu,yu.qiao}@siat.ac.cn

Abstract. Deep neural networks have enjoyed remarkable success for various vision tasks, however it remains challenging to apply CNNs to domains lacking a regular underlying structures such as 3D point clouds. Towards this we propose a novel convolutional architecture, termed SpiderCNN, to efficiently extract geometric features from point clouds. SpiderCNN is comprised of units called SpiderConv, which extend convolutional operations from regular grids to irregular point sets that can be embedded in $\mathbb{R}^n$, by parametrizing a family of convolutional filters. We design the filter as a product of a simple step function that captures local geodesic information and a Taylor polynomial that ensures the expressiveness. SpiderCNN inherits the multi-scale hierarchical architecture from classical CNNs, which allows it to extract semantic deep features. Experiments on ModelNet40 demonstrate that SpiderCNN achieves state-of-the-art accuracy 92.4% on standard benchmarks, and shows competitive performance on segmentation task.

Keywords: Convolutional neural network
Parametrized convolutional filters · Point clouds

1 Introduction

Convolutional neural networks are powerful tools for analyzing data that can naturally be represented as signals on regular grids, such as audio and images [10]. Thanks to the translation invariance of lattices in $\mathbb{R}^n$, the number of parameters in a convolutional layer is independent of the input size. Composing convolution layers and activation functions results in a multi-scale hierarchical learning

---

Y. Xu and T. Fan contributed equally.
Work done during Yifan Xu's internship at SIAT.

Electronic supplementary material The online version of this chapter (https://doi.org/10.1007/978-3-030-01237-3_6) contains supplementary material, which is available to authorized users.

V. Ferrari et al. (Eds.): ECCV 2018, LNCS 11212, pp. 90–105, 2018.
https://doi.org/10.1007/978-3-030-01237-3_6

pattern, which is shown to be very effective for learning deep representations in practice.

With the recent proliferation of applications employing 3D depth sensors [23] such as autonomous navigation, robotics and virtual reality, there is an increasing demand for algorithms to efficiently analyze point clouds. However, point clouds are distributed irregularly in $\mathbb{R}^3$, lacking a canonical order and translation invariance, which prohibits using CNNs directly. One may circumvent this problem by converting point clouds to 3D voxels and apply 3D convolutions [13]. However, volumetric methods are computationally inefficient because point clouds are sparse in 3D as they usually represent 2D surfaces. Although there are studies that improve the computational complexity, it may come with a performance trade off [2,18]. Various studies are devoted to making convolution neural networks applicable for learning on non-Euclidean domains such as graphs or manifolds by trying to generalize the definition of convolution to functions on manifolds or graphs, enriching the emerging field of geometric deep learning [3]. However, it is challenging theoretically because convolution cannot be naturally defined when the space does not carry a group action, and when the input data consists of different shapes or graphs, it is difficult to make a choice for convolutional filters.[1]

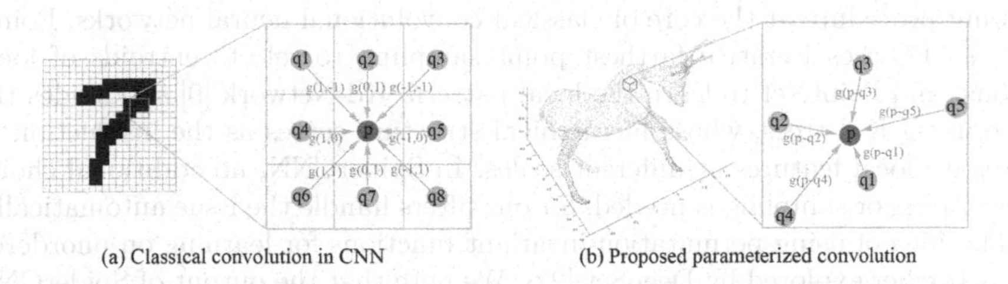

(a) Classical convolution in CNN (b) Proposed parameterized convolution

Fig. 1. The integral formula for convolution between a signal f and a filter g is $f * g(p) = \int_{q \in \mathbb{R}^n} f(q)g(p-q)dq$. Discretizing the integral formula on a set of points P in $\mathbb{R}^n$ gives $f * g(p) = \sum_{q \in P, \|p-q\| \leq r} f(q)g(p-q)$ if g is supported in a ball of radius r. **(a)** when P can be represented by regular grids, only 9 values of a filter g are needed to compute the convolution due to the translation invariance of the domain. **(b)** when the signal is on point clouds, we choose the filter g from a parameterized family of function on $\mathbb{R}^3$.

In light of the above challenges, we propose an alternative convolutional architecture, SpiderCNN, which is designed to directly extract features from point clouds. We validate its effectiveness on classification and segmentation benchmarks. By discretizing the integral formula of convolution as shown in Fig. 1, and using a special family of parametrized non-linear functions on $\mathbb{R}^3$ as filters, we introduce a novel convolutional layer, SpiderConv, for point clouds.

The family of filters is designed to be expressive while still being feasible to optimize. We combine simple step functions, which are used to capture the coarse

[1] There is no canonical choice of a domain for these filters.

geometry described by local geodesic distance, with order-3 Taylor expansions, which ensure the filters are complex enough to capture intricate local geometric variations. Experiments in Sect. 4 show that SpiderCNN with a relatively simple network architecture achieves the state-of-the-art performance for classification on ModelNet40 [4], and shows competitive performance for segmentation on ShapeNet-Part [4].

2 Related Work

First we discuss deep neural network based approaches that target point clouds data. Second, we give a partial overview of geometric deep learning.

Point Clouds as Input: PointNet [15] is a pioneering work in using deep networks to directly process point sets. A spatial encoding of each point is learned through a shared MLP, and then all individual point features aggregate to a global signature through max-pooling, which is a symmetric operation that doesn't depend on the order of input point sequence.

While PointNet works well to extract global features, its design limits its efficacy at encoding local structures. Various studies addressing this issue propose different grouping strategies of local features in order to mimic the hierarchical learning procedure at the core of classical convolutional neural networks. PointNet++ [17] uses iterative farthest point sampling to select centroids of local regions, and PointNet to learn the local pattern. Kd-Network [9] subdivides the space using K-d trees, whose hierarchical structure serves as the instruction to aggregate local features at different scales. In SpiderCNN, no additional choice for grouping or sampling is needed, for our filters handle the issue automatically.

The idea of using permutation-invariant functions for learning on unordered sets is further explored by DeepSet [22]. We note that the output of SpiderCNN does not depend on the input order by design.

Voxels as Input: VoxNet [13] and Voxception-ResNet [2] apply 3D convolution to a voxelization of point clouds. However, there is a high computational and memory cost associated with 3D convolutions. A variety of work [6,7,18] has aimed at exploiting the sparsity of voxelized point clouds to improve the computational and memory efficiency. OctNet [18] modified and implemented convolution operations to suit a hybrid grid-octree data structure. Vote3Deep [6] uses a feature-centric voting scheme so that the computational cost is proportional to the number of points with non-zero features. Sparse Submanifold CNN [7] computes the convolution only at activated points whose number does not increase when the convolution layers are stacked. In comparison, SpiderCNN can use point clouds as input directly and can handle very sparse input.

Convolution on Non-euclidean Domain: There are two main philosophically different approaches to define convolutions for non-Euclidean domains: one is spatial and the other is spectral. The recent work ECC [20] defines convolution-like operations on graphs where filter weights are conditioned on edge labels. Viewing point clouds as a graph, and taking the filters to be MLPs, SpiderCNN and ECC [20] result in similar convolution. However, we show that our proposed family of filters outperforms MLPs.

Spatial Methods: GeodesicCNN [12] is an early attempt at applying neural networks to shape analysis. The philosophy behind GeodesicCNN is that for a Riemannian manifold, the exponential map identifies a local neighborhood of a point to a ball in the tangent space centered at the origin. The tangent plane is isomorphic to $\mathbb{R}^d$ where we know how to define convolution.

Let M be a mesh surface, and let $F : M \to \mathbb{R}$ be a function, GeodesicCNN first uses the patch operator D to map a point p and its neighbors $N(p)$ to the lattice $\mathbb{Z}^2 \subseteq \mathbb{R}^2$, and applies Eq. 2. Explicitly, $F * g(p) = \sum_{j \in J} g_j(\sum_{q \in N(p)} w_j(u(p,q))F(q))$, where $u(p,q)$ represents the local polar coordinate system around p, $w_j(u)$ is a function to model the effect of the patch operator $D = \{D_j\}_{j \in J}$. By definition $D_j = \sum_{q \in N(p)} w_j(u(p,q))F(q)$. Later, AnisotropicCNN [1] and MoNet [14] further explore this framework by improving the choice for u and w_j. MoNet [14] can be understood as using mixtures of Gaussians as convolutional filters. We offer an alternative viewpoint. Instead of finding local parametrizations of the manifold, we view it as an embedded submanifold in $\mathbb{R}^n$ and design filters, which are more efficient for point clouds processing, in the ambient Euclidean space.

Spectral Methods: We know that Fourier transform takes convolutions to multiplications. Explicitly, If $f, g : \mathbb{R}^n \to \mathbb{C}$, then $\widehat{f * g} = \hat{f} \cdot \hat{g}$. Therefore, formally we have $f * g = (\hat{f} \cdot \hat{g})^{\vee}$,[2] which can be used as a definition for convolution on non-Euclidean domains where we know how to take Fourier transform.

Although we do not have Fourier theory on a general space without any equivariant structure, on Riemannian manifolds or graphs there are generalized notions of Laplacian operator. Taking Fourier transform in $\mathbb{R}^n$ could be formally viewed as finding the coefficients in the expansion of the eigenfunctions of the Laplacian operator. To be more precise, recall that

$$\hat{f}(\xi) = \int_{\mathbb{R}^n} f(x) \exp(-2\pi i x \cdot \xi) d\xi, \tag{1}$$

and $\{\exp(-2\pi i x \cdot \xi)\}_{\xi \in \mathbb{R}^n}$ are eigen-functions for the Laplacian operator $\Delta = \sum_{i=1}^n \frac{\partial}{\partial x_i}$. Therefore, if U is the matrix whose columns are eigenvectors of the graph Laplacian matrix and Λ is the vector of corresponding eigenvalues, for F, g two functions on the vertices of the graph, then $F * g = U(U^T F \odot U^T g)$, where U^T is the transpose of U and $\odot$ is the Hadamard product of two matrices. Since being compactly supported in the spatial domain translates into being smooth in the spectral domain, it is natural to choose $U^T g$ to be smooth functions in Λ. For instance, ChebNet [5] uses Chebyshev polynomials that reduces the complexity of filtering, and CayleyNet [11] uses Cayley polynomials which allows efficient computations for localized filters in restricted frequency bands of interest.

[2] If h is a function, then $\hat{h}$ is the Fourier transform, and $h^{\vee}$ is its inverse Fourier transform.

When analyzing different graphs or shapes, spectral methods lack abstract motivations, because different spectral domains cannot be canonically identified. SyncSpecCNN [21] proposes a weight sharing scheme to align spectral domains using functional maps. Viewing point clouds as data embedded in $\mathbb{R}^3$, SpiderCNN can learn representations that are robust to spatial rigid transformations with the aid of data augmentation.

3 SpiderConv

In this section, we describe SpiderConv, which is the fundamental building block for SpiderCNN. First, we discuss how to define a convolutional layer in neural network when the inputs are features on point sets in $\mathbb{R}^n$. Next we introduce a special family of convolutional filters. Finally, we give details for the implementation of SpiderConv with multiple channels and the approximations used for computational speedup.

3.1 Convolution on Point Sets in $\mathbb{R}^n$

An image is a function on regular grids $F : \mathbb{Z}^2 \to \mathbb{R}$. Let W be a $(2m+1) \times (2m+1)$ filter matrix, where m is a positive integer, the convolution in classical CNNs is

$$F * W(i,j) = \sum_{s=-m}^{m} \sum_{t=-m}^{m} F(i-s, j-t)W(s,t), \tag{2}$$

which is the discretization of the following integration

$$f * g(p) = \int_{\mathbb{R}^2} f(q)g(p-q)dq, \tag{3}$$

if $f, g : \mathbb{R}^2 \to \mathbb{R}$, such that $f(i,j) = F(i,j)$ for $(i,j) \in \mathbb{Z}^2$ and $g(s,t) = W(s,t)$ for $s,t \in \{-m, -m+1, ..., m-1, m\}$ and g is supported in $[-m, m] \times [-m, m]$.

Now suppose that F is a function on a set of points P in $\mathbb{R}^n$. Let $g : \mathbb{R}^n \to \mathbb{R}$ be a filter supported in a ball centered at the origin of radius r. It is natural to define SpiderConv with input F and filter g to be the following:

$$F * g(p) = \sum_{q \in P, \|q-p\| \leq r} F(q)g(p-q). \tag{4}$$

Note that when $P = \mathbb{Z}^2$ is a regular grid, Eq. 4 reduces to Eq. 3. Thus the classical convolution can be seen as a special case of SpiderConv. Please see Fig. 1 for an intuitive illustration.

In SpiderConv, the filters are chosen from a parametrized family $\{g_w\}$ (See Fig. 2 for a concrete example) which is piece-wise differentiable in w. During the training of SpiderCNN, the parameters $w \in \mathbb{R}^d$ are optimized through SGD algorithm, and the gradients are computed through the formula $\frac{\partial}{\partial w_i} F * g_w(p) = \sum_{q \in P, \|q-p\| \leq r} F(q) \frac{\partial}{\partial w_i} g_w(p-q)$, where w_i is the i-th component of w.

3.2 A Special Family of Filters $\{g_w\}$

A natural choice is to take g_w to be a multilayer perceptron (MLP) network, because theoretically an MLP with one hidden layer can approximate an arbitrary continuous function [8]. However, in practice we find that MLPs do not work well. One possible reason is that MLP fails to account for the geometric prior of 3D point clouds. Another possible reason is that to ensure sufficient expressiveness the number of parameters in a MLP needs to be sufficiently large, which makes the optimization problem difficult.

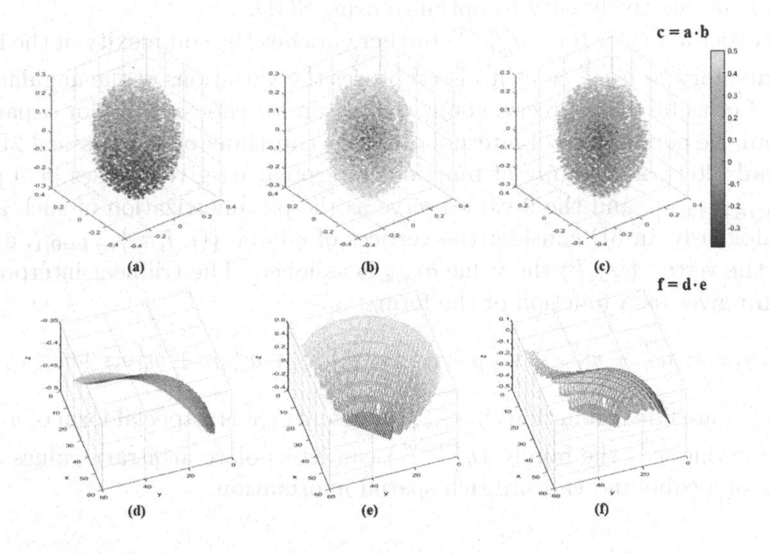

Fig. 2. Visualization of a filter in the family $\{g_w\}$. **(a)** is the scatter plot (color represents the value of the function) of $g^{Taylor}(x, y, z) = 1+x+y+z+xy+xz+yz+xyz$. **(b)** is the scatter plot of $g^{step}(x, y, z) = \frac{i+1}{8}$ if $\frac{i}{8} \leq \sqrt{x^2+y^2+z^2} < \frac{i+1}{8}$, when $i = 0, 1, ..., 7$. **(c)** is the scatter plot of the product $g = g^{Taylor} \cdot g^{step}$. In the second row, **(d) (e) (f)** are the graphs of g^{Taylor}, g^{step} and g respectively when restricting their domain to the plane $z = 0$ (the Z-axis represents the value of the function). (Color figure online)

To address the above issues, we propose the following family of filters $\{g_w\}$:

$$g_w(x, y, z) = g_{w^S}^{Step}(x, y, z) \cdot g_{w^T}^{Taylor}(x, y, z), \tag{5}$$

with $w = (w^S, w^T)$ is the concatenation of two vectors $w^S = (w_i^S)$ and $w^T = (w_i^T)$,[3] where

$$g_{w^S}^{Step}(x, y, z) = w_i^S \text{ if } r_i \leq \sqrt{x^2+y^2+z^2} < r_{i+1}, \tag{6}$$

[3] Here we use the notation $v = (v_i)$ to represent that $v_i \in \mathbb{R}$ is the i-th component of the vector v.

with $r_0 = 0 < r_1 < r_2... < r_N$, and

$$g_{w^T}^{Taylor}(x,y,z) = w_0^T + w_1^T x + w_2^T y + w_3^T z + w_4^T xy + w_5^T yz + w_6^T xz + w_7^T x^2 + w_8^T y^2 + w_9^T z^2 + w_{10}^T xy^2 + w_{11}^T x^2 y + w_{12}^T y^2 z + w_{13}^T yz^2 + w_{14}^T x^2 z + w_{15}^T xz^2 + w_{16}^T xyz + w_{17}^T x^3 + w_{18}^T y^3 + w_{19}^T z^3. \quad (7)$$

The first component $g_{w^S}^{Step}$ is a step function in the radius variable of the local polar coordinates around a point. It encodes the local geodesic information, which is a critical quantity to describe the coarse local shape. Moreover, step functions are relatively easy to optimize using SGD.

The order-3 Taylor term $g_{w^T}^{Taylor}$ further enriches the complexity of the filters, complementary to $g_{w^S}^{Step}$ since it also captures the variations of the angular component. Let us be more precise about the reason for choosing Taylor expansions here from the perspective of interpolation. We can think of the classical 2D convolutional filters as a family of functions interpolating given values at 9 points $\{(i,j)\}_{i,j\in\{-1,0,1\}}$, and the 9 values serve as the parametrization of such a family. Analogously, in 3D consider the vertices of a cube $\{(i,j,k)\}_{i,j,k=0,1}$, assume that at the vertex (i,j,k) the value $a_{i,j,k}$ is assigned. The trilinear interpolation algorithm gives us a function of the form

$$f_{w^T}(x,y,z) = w_0^T + w_1^T x + w_2^T y + w_3^T z + w_4^T xy + w_5^T yz + w_6^T xz + w_{16}^T xyz, \quad (8)$$

where w_i^T's are linear functions in c_{ijk}. Therefore f_{w^T} is a special form of $g_{w^T}^{Taylor}$, and by varying w^T, the family $\{g_{w^T}^{Taylor}\}$ can interpolate arbitrary values at the vertexes of a cube and capture rich spatial information.

3.3 Implementation

The following approximations are used based on the uniform sampling process constructing the point clouds:

1. K-nearest neighbors are used to measure the locality instead of the radius, so the summation in Eq. 4 is over the K-nearest neighbors of p.
2. The step function $g_{w^T}^{Step}$ is approximated by a permutation. Explicitly, let X be the $1 \times K$ matrix indexed by the K-nearest neighbors of p including p, and $X(1,i)$ is a feature at the i-th K-nearest neighbors of p. Then $F * g_{w^T}^{Step}(p)$ is approximated by Xw, where w is a $K \times 1$ matrix with $w(i,1)$ corresponds to w_i^T in Eq. 6.

Later in the article, we omit the parameters w, w^S and w^T, and just write $g = g^{Step} \cdot g^{Taylor}$ to simplify our notations.

The input to SpiderConv is a c_1-dimensional feature on a point cloud P, and is represented as $F = (F_1, F_2, ..., F_{c_1})$ where $F_v : P \to \mathbb{R}$. The output of a SpiderConv is a c_2-dimensional feature on the point cloud $\tilde{F} = (\tilde{F}_1, \tilde{F}_2, ..., \tilde{F}_{c_2})$ where $\tilde{F}_i : P \to \mathbb{R}$. Let p be a point in the point cloud, and $q_1, q_2, ..., q_K$ are its K-nearest neighbors in order. Assume $g_{i,v,t}^{Step}(p - q_j) = w_j^{(i,v,t)}$, where

$t = 1, 2, ..., b$ and $v = 1, 2, ..., c_1$ and $i = 1, 2, ...c_2$. Then a SpiderConv with c_1 in-channels, c_2 out-channels and b Taylor terms is defined via the formula: $\tilde{F}_i(p) = \sum_{v=1}^{c_1} \sum_{j=1}^{K} g_i(p - q_j) F_v(q_j)$, where $g_i(p - q_j) = \sum_{t=1}^{b} g_t^{Taylor}(p - q_j) w_j^{(i,v,t)}$, and g_t^{Taylor} is in the parameterized family $\{g_{w^T}^{Taylor}\}$ for $t = 1, 2, ..., b$.

4 Experiments

We analyze and evaluate SpiderCNN on 3D point clouds classification and segmentation. We empirically examine the key hyper-parameters of a 3-layer SpiderCNN, and compare our models with the state-of-the-art methods.

Implementation Details: All models are prototyped with Tensorflow 1.3 on 1080Ti GPU and trained using the Adam optimizer with a learning rate of 10^{-3}. A dropout rate of 0.5 is used with the fully connected layers. Batch normalization is used at the end of each SpiderConv with decay set to 0.5. On a GTX 1080Ti, the forward-pass time of a SpiderConv layer (batch size 8) with in-channel 64 and out-channel 64 is 7.50 ms. For the 4-layer SpiderCNN (batch size 8), the total forward-pass time is 71.68 ms.

4.1 Classification on ModelNet40

ModelNet40 [4] contains 12,311 CAD models which belong to 40 different categories with 9,843 used for training and 2,468 for testing. We use the source code for PointNet [15] to sample 1,024 points uniformly and compute the normal vectors from the mesh models. The same data augmentation strategy as [15] is applied: the point cloud is randomly rotated along the up-axis and the position of each point is jittered by a Gaussian noise with zero mean and 0.02 standard deviation. The batch size is 32 for all the experiments in Sect. 4.1. We use the (x, y, z)-coordinates and normal vectors of the 1,024 points as the input for SpiderCNN for the experiments on ModelNet40 unless otherwise specified.

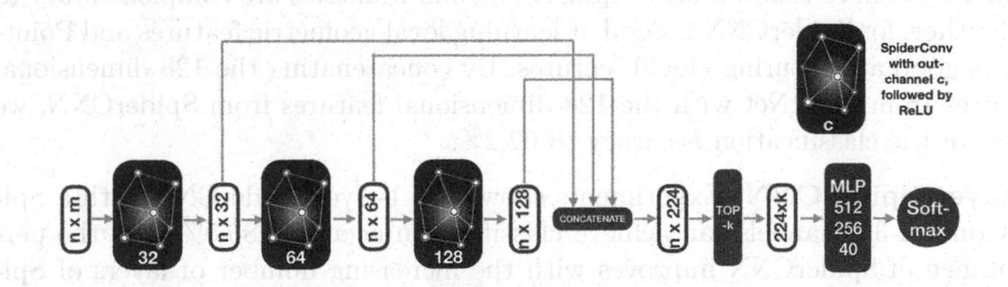

Fig. 3. The architecture of a 3-layer SpiderCNN used in ModelNet40 classification.

3-Layer SpiderCNN: Figure 3 illustrates a SpiderCNN with 3 layers of SpiderConvs each with 3 Taylor terms, and the respective out-channels for each layer being 32, 64, 128.[4] ReLU activation function is used here. The output features of the three SpiderConvs are concatenated in the end. Top-k pooling among all the points is used to extract global features.

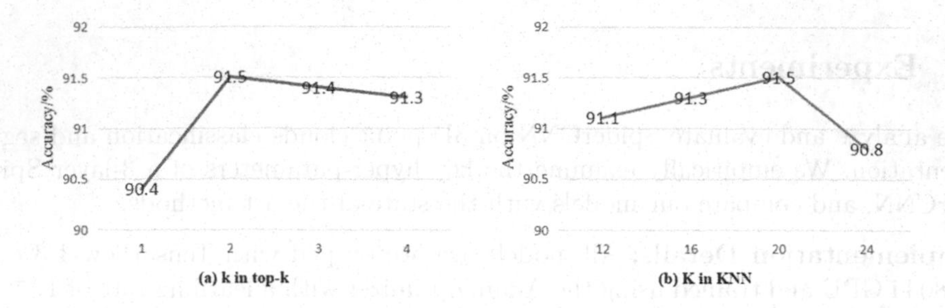

Fig. 4. On ModelNet40 **(a)** shows the effect of number of pooled features on the accuracy of 3-layer SpiderCNN with 20-nearest neighbors. **(b)** shows the effect of nearest neighbors in SpiderConv on the accuracy of 3-layer SpiderCNN with top-2 pooling.

Two important hyperparameters in SpiderCNN are studied: the number of nearest neighbors K chosen in SpiderConv, and the number of pooled features k after the concatenation. The results are summarized in Fig. 4. The number of nearest-neighbors K is analogous to size of the filter in the usual convolution. We see that 20 is the optimal choice among 12, 16, 20, and 24-nearest neighbors. In Fig. 5 we provide visualization for top-2 pooling. The points that contribute to the top-2 pooling features are plotted. We see that similar to PointNet, Spider CNN picks up representative critical points.

SpiderCNN + PointNet: We train a 3-layer SpiderCNN (top-2 pooling and 20-nearest neighbors) and PointNet with only (x, y, z)-coordinates as input to predict the classical robust local geometric descriptor FPFH [19] on point clouds in ModelNet40. The training loss of SpiderCNN is only $\frac{1}{4}$ that of PointNet's. As a result, we believe that a 3-layer SpiderCNN and PointNet are complementary to each other, for SpiderCNN is good at learning local geometric features and PointNet is good at capturing global features. By concatenating the 128 dimensional features from PointNet with the 128 dimensional features from SpiderCNN, we improve the classification accuracy to 92.2%.

4-Layer SpiderCNN: Experiments show that 1-layer SpiderCNN with a SpiderConv of 32 channels can achieve classification accuracy 85.5%, and the performance of SpiderCNN improves with the increasing number of layers of SpiderConv. A 4-layer SpiderCNN consists of SpiderConv with out-channels 32, 64, 128, and 258. Feature concatenation, 20-nearest neighbors and top-2 pooling are used. To prevent overfitting, while training we apply the data augmentation

[4] See Sect. 3.3 for the definition of a SpiderConv with c_1 in-channels, c_2 out-channels and b Taylor terms.

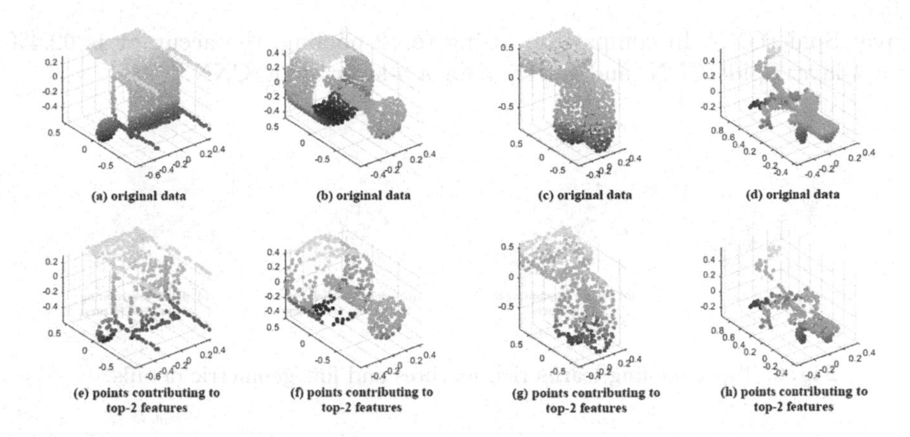

Fig. 5. Visualization of the effect of top-k pooling. Edge points and points with non-zero curvature are preserved after pooling. **(a)**, **(b)**, **(c)**, **(d)** are the original input point clouds. **(e)**, **(f)**, **(g)**, **(h)** are points contributing to features extracted via top-2 pooling.

method DP (random input dropout) introduced in [17]. Table 1 shows a comparison between SpiderCNN and other models. The 4-layer SpiderCNN achieves accuracy of 92.4% which improves over the best reported result of models with input 1024 points and normals. For 5 runs, the mean accuracy of a 4-layer SpiderCNN is 92.0%.

Table 1. Classification accuracy of SpiderCNN and other models on ModelNet40.

Method	Input	Accuracy
Subvolume [16]	Voxels	89.2
VRN Single [2]	Voxels	91.3
OctNet [18]	Hybrid grid octree	86.5
ECC [20]	GWe compute three intrinsicraphs	87.4
Kd-Network [9] (depth 15)	1024 points	91.8
PointNet [15]	1024 points	89.2
PointNet++ [17]	5000 points+normal	91.9
SpiderCNN + PointNet	1024 points+normal	92.2
SpiderCNN (4-layer)	1024 points+normal	**92.4**

Ablative Study: Compared to max-pooling, top-2 pooling enables the model to learn richer geometric information. For example, in Fig. 6, we see top-2 pooling preserves more points where the curvature is non-zero. Using max-pooling, the classification accuracy is 92.0% for a 4-layer SpiderCNN, and is 90.4% for a

3-layer SpiderCNN. In comparison, using top-2 pooling, the accuracy is 92.4% for a 4-layer SpiderCNN, and is 91.5% for a 3-layer SpiderCNN.

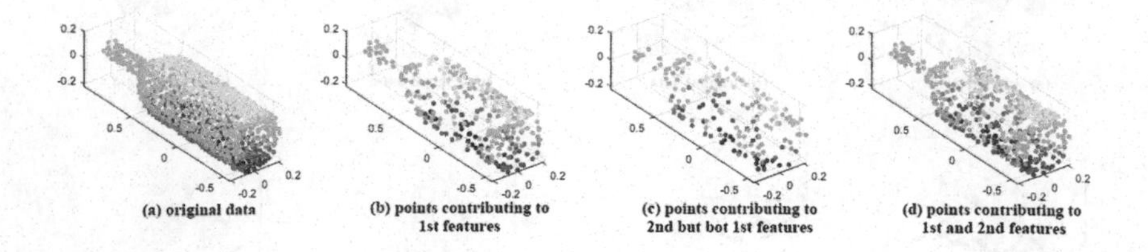

(a) original data
(b) points contributing to
1st features
(c) points contributing to
2nd but bot 1st features
(d) points contributing to
1st and 2nd features

Fig. 6. Top-2 pooling learns rich features and fine geometric details.

MLP filters do not perform as well in our setting. The accuracy of a 3-layer SpiderCNN is 71.3% with $g_w = \text{MLP}(16,1)$, and is 72.8% with $g_w = \text{MLP}(16,32,1)$.

Without normals, the accuracy of a 4-layer SpiderCNN using only the 1,024 points is 90.5%. Using normals extracted from the 1,024 input points via orthogonal distance regression, the accuracy of a 4-layer SpiderCNN is 91.8%.

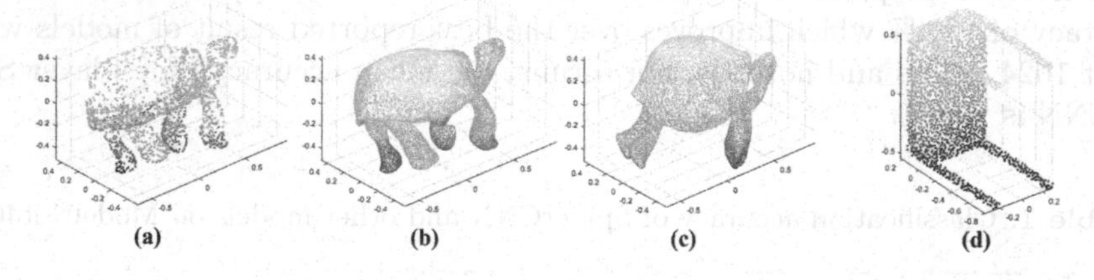

Fig. 7. **(b)** and **(c)** are shapes in SHREC15. **(d)** is a shape in ModelNet40. **(a)** is the point cloud sampled from **(b)**.

4.2 Classification on SHREC15

SHREC15 is a dataset for non-rigid 3D shape retrieval. It consists of 1,200 watertight triangle meshes divided in 50 categories. On average 10,000 vertices are stored in one mesh model. Comparing to ModelNet40, SHREC15 contains more complicated local geometry and non-rigid deformation of one object. See Fig. 7 for a comparison. 1,192 meshes are used with 895 for training and 297 for testing. We compute three intrinsic shape descriptors (Heat Kernel Signature, Wave Kernel Signature and Fast Point Feature Histograms) for deformable shape analysis from the mesh models. 1,024 points are sampled uniformly randomly from the vertices of a mesh model, and the (x, y, z)-coordinates are used as the input for SpiderCNN, PointNet and PointNet++. We use SVM with linear kernel when the inputs are classical shape descriptors. Table 2 summarizes the results. We see that SpiderCNN outperforms the other methods.

Table 2. Classification accuracy on SHEREC15.

Method	Input	Accuracy
SVM + HKS	Features	56.9
SVM + WKS	Features	87.5
SVM + FPFH	Features	80.8
PointNet	Points	69.4
PointNet++ [17]	Points	60.2
PointNet++ (our implementation)	Points	94.1
SpiderCNN (4-layer)	Points	**95.8**

4.3 Segmentation on ShapeNet Parts

ShapeNet Parts consists of 16,880 models from 16 shape categories and 50 different parts in total, with a 14,006 training and 2,874 testing split. Each part is annotated with 2 to 6 parts. The mIoU is used as the evaluation metric, computed by taking the average of all part classes. A 4-layer SpiderCNN whose architecture is shown in Fig. 8 is trained with batch of 16. We use points with their normal vectors as the input and assume that the category labels are known. The results are summarized in Table 3. For 4 runs, the mean of mean IoU of SpiderCNN is 85.24. We see that SpiderCNN achieves competitive results despite a relatively simple network architecture (Fig. 9).

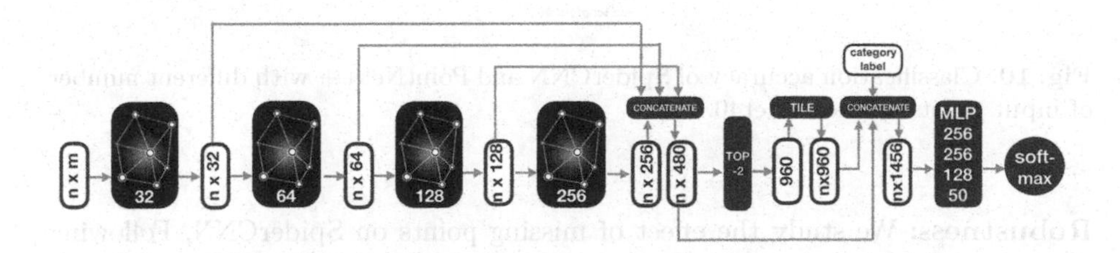

Fig. 8. The SpiderCNN architecture used in the ShapeNet Part segmentation task.

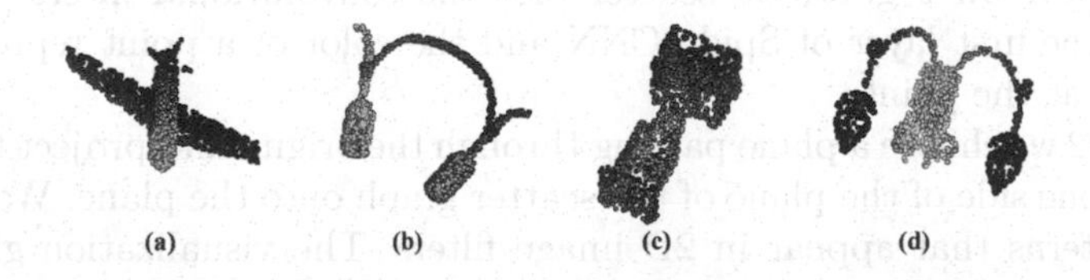

Fig. 9. Some examples of the segmentation results of SpiderCNN on ShapeNet Part.

Table 3. Segmentation results on ShapeNet Part dataset. Mean IoU and IoU for each categories are reported.

	Mean	Aero	Bag	Cap	Car	Chair	Ear ph	Guitar	Knife	Lamp	Laptop	Motor	Mug	Pistol	Rocket board	Skate	Table
PN [15]	83.7	83.4	78.7	82.5	74.9	89.6	73.0	91.5	85.9	80.8	95.3	65.2	93.0	81.2	57.9	72.8	80.6
PN++[17]	85.1	82.4	79.0	**87.7**	77.3	**90.8**	71.8	91.0	85.9	83.7	95.3	**71.6**	**94.1**	81.3	58.7	76.4	82.6
Kd-Net [9]	82.3	80.1	74.6	74.3	70.3	88.6	73.5	90.2	87.2	81.0	94.9	57.4	86.7	78.1	51.8	69.9	80.3
SSCNN [21]	84.7	81.6	**81.7**	81.9	75.2	90.2	74.9	**93.0**	86.1	**84.7**	95.6	66.7	92.7	81.6	**60.6**	**82.9**	82.1
SpiderCNN	**85.3**	**83.5**	81.0	87.2	**77.5**	90.7	**76.8**	91.1	**87.3**	83.3	**95.8**	70.2	93.5	**82.7**	59.7	75.8	**82.8**

5 Analysis

In this section, we conduct additional analysis and evaluations on the robustness of SpiderCNN, and provide visualization for some of the typical learned filters from the first layer of SpiderCNN.

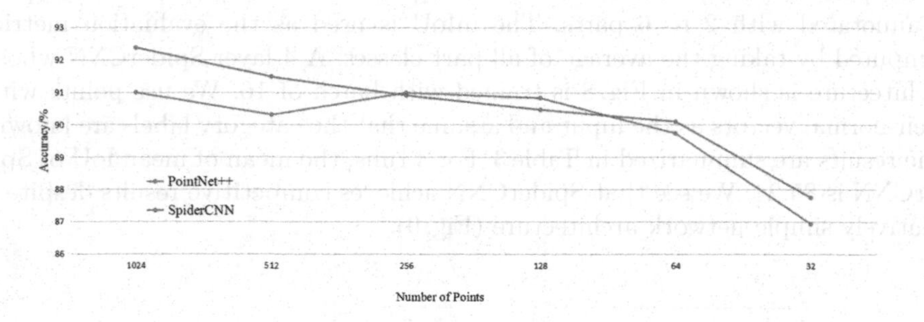

Fig. 10. Classification accuracy of SpiderCNN and PointNet++ with different number of input points on ModelNet40.

Robustness: We study the effect of missing points on SpiderCNN. Following the setting for experiments in Sect. 4.1, we train a 4-layer SpiderCNN and PointNet++ with 512, 248, 128, 64 and 32 points and their normals as input. The results are summarized in Fig. 10. We see that even with only 32 points, SpiderCNN obtains 87.7% accuracy.

Visualization: In Fig. 11, we scatter plot the convolutional filters $g_w(x, y, z)$ learned in the first layer of SpiderCNN and the color of a point represents the value of g_w at the point.

In Fig. 12 we choose a plane passing through the origin, and project the points that lie on one side of the plane of the scatter graph onto the plane. We see some similar patterns that appear in 2D image filters. The visualization gives some hints about the geometric features that the convolutional filters in SpiderCNN learn. For example, the first row in Fig. 12 corresponds to 2D image filters that can capture boundary information.

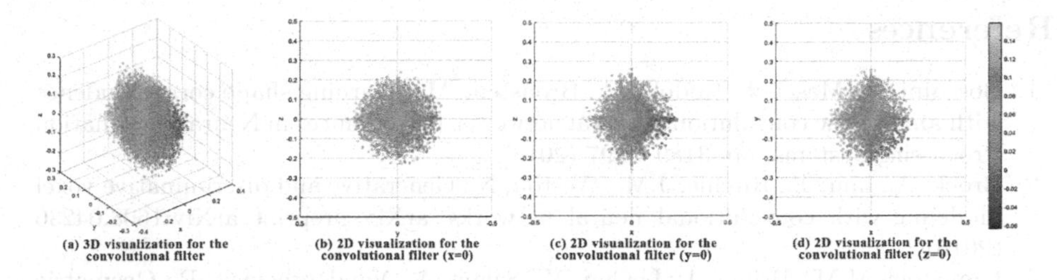

(a) 3D visualization for the convolutional filter (b) 2D visualization for the convolutional filter (x=0) (c) 2D visualization for the convolutional filter (y=0) (d) 2D visualization for the convolutional filter (z=0)

Fig. 11. Visualization of for the convolutional filters learned in the first layer of SpiderCNN.

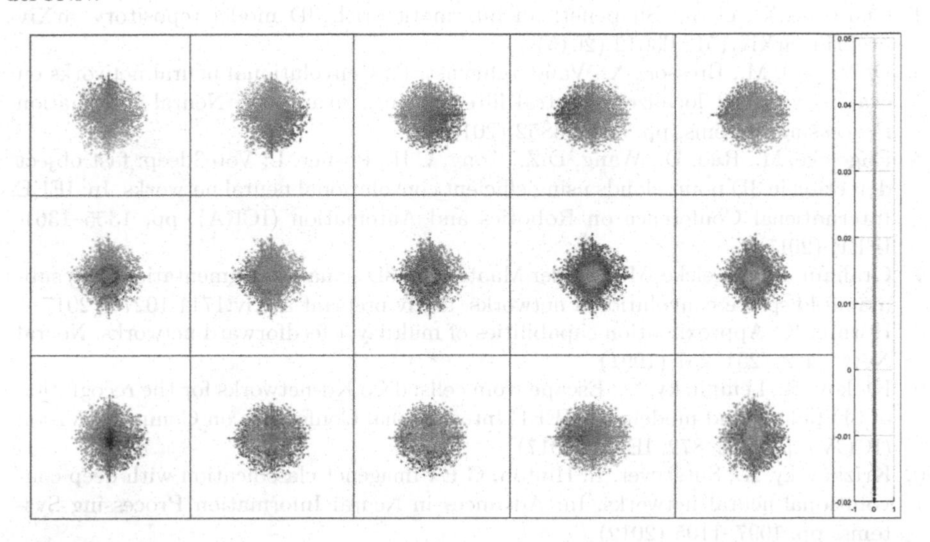

Fig. 12. Visualization for the convolutional filters learned in the first layer of SpiderCNN. The 3D filters are shown as scatter plots projected on to the planes $x = 0$ or $y = 0$ or $z = 0$.

6 Conclusions

A new convolutional neural network SpiderCNN that can directly process 3D point clouds with parameterized convolutional filters is proposed. More complex network architectures and more applications of SpiderCNN can be explored.

Acknowledgement. This work was supported by Shenzhen Basic Research Program (JCYJ201509251 63005055, JCYJ20170818164704758), National Natural Science Foundation of China (U1613211, 61633021, 61502263) and External Cooperation Program of BIC Chinese Academy of Sciences (172644KYSB20150019). We would like to thank Zhikai Dong for his technical assistance and helpful discussion.

References

1. Boscaini, D., Masci, J., Rodolà, E., Bronstein, M.: Learning shape correspondence with anisotropic convolutional neural networks. In: Advances in Neural Information Processing Systems, pp. 3189–3197 (2016)
2. Brock, A., Lim, T., Ritchie, J.M., Weston, N.: Generative and discriminative voxel modeling with convolutional neural networks. arXiv preprint arXiv:1608.04236 (2016)
3. Bronstein, M.M., Bruna, J., LeCun, Y., Szlam, A., Vandergheynst, P.: Geometric deep learning: going beyond Euclidean data. IEEE Signal Process. Mag. **34**(4), 18–42 (2017)
4. Chang, A.X., et al.: Shapenet: an information-rich 3D model repository. arXiv preprint arXiv:1512.03012 (2015)
5. Defferrard, M., Bresson, X., Vandergheynst, P.: Convolutional neural networks on graphs with fast localized spectral filtering. In: Advances in Neural Information Processing Systems, pp. 3844–3852 (2016)
6. Engelcke, M., Rao, D., Wang, D.Z., Tong, C.H., Posner, I.: Vote3deep: fast object detection in 3D point clouds using efficient convolutional neural networks. In: IEEE International Conference on Robotics and Automation (ICRA), pp. 1355–1361. IEEE (2017)
7. Graham, B., Engelcke, M., van der Maaten, L.: 3D semantic segmentation with submanifold sparse convolutional networks. arXiv preprint arXiv:1711.10275 (2017)
8. Hornik, K.: Approximation capabilities of multilayer feedforward networks. Neural Netw. **4**(2), 251–257 (1991)
9. Klokov, R., Lempitsky, V.: Escape from cells: deep Kd-networks for the recognition of 3D point cloud models. In: IEEE International Conference on Computer Vision (ICCV), pp. 863–872. IEEE (2017)
10. Krizhevsky, A., Sutskever, I., Hinton, G.E.: Imagenet classification with deep convolutional neural networks. In: Advances in Neural Information Processing Systems, pp. 1097–1105 (2012)
11. Levie, R., Monti, F., Bresson, X., Bronstein, M.M.: Cayleynets: graph convolutional neural networks with complex rational spectral filters. arXiv preprint arXiv:1705.07664 (2017)
12. Masci, J., Boscaini, D., Bronstein, M., Vandergheynst, P.: Geodesic convolutional neural networks on Riemannian manifolds. In: Proceedings of the IEEE International Conference on Computer Vision Workshops, pp. 37–45 (2015)
13. Maturana, D., Scherer, S.: Voxnet: a 3D convolutional neural network for real-time object recognition. In: IEEE/RSJ International Conference on Intelligent Robots and Systems (IROS), pp. 922–928. IEEE (2015)
14. Monti, F., Boscaini, D., Masci, J., Rodola, E., Svoboda, J., Bronstein, M.M.: Geometric deep learning on graphs and manifolds using mixture model CNNs. In: Proceedings of CVPR, vol. 1, p. 3 (2017)
15. Qi, C.R., Su, H., Mo, K., Guibas, L.J.: Pointnet: deep learning on point sets for 3D classification and segmentation. In: Proceedings of the Computer Vision and Pattern Recognition (CVPR), vol. 1, no. 2, p. 4. IEEE (2017)
16. Qi, C.R., Su, H., Nießner, M., Dai, A., Yan, M., Guibas, L.J.: Volumetric and multi-view CNNs for object classification on 3D data. In: Proceedings of the IEEE Conference on Computer Vision and Pattern Recognition, pp. 5648–5656 (2016)
17. Qi, C.R., Yi, L., Su, H., Guibas, L.J.: Pointnet++: deep hierarchical feature learning on point sets in a metric space. In: Advances in Neural Information Processing Systems, pp. 5105–5114 (2017)

18. Riegler, G., Ulusoy, A.O., Geiger, A.: Octnet: learning deep 3D representations at high resolutions. In: Proceedings of the IEEE Conference on Computer Vision and Pattern Recognition, vol. 3 (2017)
19. Rusu, R.B., Blodow, N., Beetz, M.: Fast point feature histograms (FPFH) for 3D registration. In: IEEE International Conference on Robotics and Automation, ICRA 2009, pp. 3212–3217. IEEE (2009)
20. Simonovsky, M., Komodakis, N.: Dynamic edge-conditioned filters in convolutional neural networks on graphs. In: Proceedings of CVPR (2017)
21. Yi, L., Su, H., Guo, X., Guibas, L.: Syncspeccnn: synchronized spectral CNN for 3D shape segmentation. In: Computer Vision and Pattern Recognition (CVPR) (2017)
22. Zaheer, M., Kottur, S., Ravanbakhsh, S., Poczos, B., Salakhutdinov, R.R., Smola, A.J.: Deep sets. In: Advances in Neural Information Processing Systems, pp. 3394–3404 (2017)
23. Zhang, Z.: Microsoft kinect sensor and its effect. IEEE Multimed. **19**(2), 4–10 (2012)

Modality Distillation with Multiple Stream Networks for Action Recognition

Nuno C. Garcia[1,2(✉)], Pietro Morerio[1], and Vittorio Murino[1,3]

[1] Istituto Italiano di Tecnologia, Genoa, Italy
{nuno.garcia,pietro.morerio,vittorio.murino}@iit.it
[2] Università degli Studi di Genova, Genoa, Italy
[3] Università di Verona, Verona, Italy

Abstract. Diverse input data modalities can provide complementary cues for several tasks, usually leading to more robust algorithms and better performance. However, while a (training) dataset could be accurately designed to include a variety of sensory inputs, it is often the case that not all modalities are available in real life (testing) scenarios, where a model has to be deployed. This raises the challenge of how to learn robust representations leveraging multimodal data in the training stage, while considering limitations at test time, such as noisy or missing modalities. This paper presents a new approach for multimodal video action recognition, developed within the unified frameworks of distillation and privileged information, named generalized distillation. Particularly, we consider the case of learning representations from depth and RGB videos, while relying on RGB data only at test time. We propose a new approach to train an hallucination network that learns to distill depth features through multiplicative connections of spatiotemporal representations, leveraging soft labels and hard labels, as well as distance between feature maps. We report state-of-the-art results on video action classification on the largest multimodal dataset available for this task, the NTU RGB+D, as well as on the UWA3DII and Northwestern-UCLA.

Keywords: Action recognition · Deep multimodal learning
Distillation · Privileged information

1 Introduction

Imagine you have a large multimodal dataset to train a deep learning model on, comprising for example RGB video sequences, depth maps, infrared, and skeleton joints data. However, at test time, the trained model may be deployed in scenarios where not all of these modalities are available. For example, most of the cameras capture RGB only, which is the most common and cheapest available data modality.

Electronic supplementary material The online version of this chapter (https://doi.org/10.1007/978-3-030-01237-3_7) contains supplementary material, which is available to authorized users.

V. Ferrari et al. (Eds.): ECCV 2018, LNCS 11212, pp. 106–121, 2018.
https://doi.org/10.1007/978-3-030-01237-3_7

Considering this limitation, we would like to answer the following: what is the best way of using all data available in order to learn robust representations to be exploited when there are missing modalities at test time? In other words, is there any added value in training a model by exploiting more data modalities, even if only one can be used at test time? Unsurprisingly, the simplest and most commonly adopted solution consists in training the model using only the modality in which it will be tested. However, a more interesting alternative is trying to exploit the potential of the available data and train the model using all modalities, realizing, however, that not all of them will be accessible at test time. This learning paradigm, i.e., when the model is trained using extra information, is generally known as *learning with privileged information* [30] or *learning with side information* [11].

In this work, we propose a multimodal stream framework that learns from different data modalities and can be deployed and tested on a subset of these. We design a model able to learn from RGB *and* depth video sequences, but due to its general structure, it can also be used to manage whatever combination of other modalities as well. To show its potential, we evaluate the performance on the task of video action recognition. In this context, we introduce a new learning paradigm, depicted in Fig. 1, to *distill* the information conveyed by depth into an *hallucination* network, which is meant to "mimic" the missing stream at test time. Distillation [1,10] refers to any training procedure where knowledge is transferred from a previously trained complex model to a simpler one. Our learning procedure introduces a new loss function which is inspired to the *generalized distillation* framework [15], that formally unifies distillation and privileged information learning theories.

Our model is inspired to the two-stream network introduced by Simonyan and Zisserman [25], which has been notably successful in the traditional setting for video action recognition task [2,5]. Differently from previous works, we use multimodal data, deploying one stream for each modality (RGB and depth in our case), and use it in the framework of privileged information. Another inspiring work for our framework is [11], which proposes an hallucination network to learn with side information. We build on this idea, extending it by devising a new mechanism to *learn* and *use* such hallucination stream through a more general loss function and inter-stream connections.

To summarize, the main contributions of this paper are the following:

- we propose a new multimodal stream network architecture able to exploit multiple data modalities at training while using only one at test time;
- we introduce a new paradigm to learn an hallucination network within a novel two-stream model;
- in this context, we have implemented an inter-stream connection mechanism to improve the learning process of the hallucination network, and designed a more general loss function, based on the generalized distillation framework;
- we report state-of-the-art results – in the privileged information scenario – on the largest multimodal dataset for video action recognition, the NTU RGB+D [23], and on two other smaller ones, the UWA3DII [21] and the Northwestern-UCLA [33].

The rest of the paper is organized as follows. Section 2 reviews similar approaches and discusses how they relate to the present work. Section 3 details the proposed architecture and the novel learning paradigm. Section 4 reports the results obtained on the various datasets, including a detailed ablation study performed on the NTU RGB+D dataset and a comparative performance with respect to the state of the art. Finally, we draw conclusions and future research directions in Sect. 5.

2 Related Work

Our work is at the intersection of three topics: privileged information [30], network distillation [1,10], and multimodal video action recognition. However, Lopez-Paz *et al.* [15] noted that privileged information and network distillation are instances of a the same more inclusive theory, called generalized distillation.

Generalized Distillation. Within the generalized distillation framework, our model is both related to the privileged information theory [30], considering that the extra modality (depth, in this case) is only used at training time, and, mostly, to the distillation framework. In fact, the core mechanism that our model uses to learn the hallucination network is derived from a distillation loss. More specifically, the supervision information provided by the teacher network (in this case, the network processing the depth data stream) is distilled into the hallucination network leveraging teacher's soft predictions and hard ground-truth labels in the loss function.

In this context, the closest works to our proposal are [11,16]. Luo *et al.* [16] addressed a similar problem to ours, where the model is first trained on several modalities (RGB, depth, joints and infrared), but tested only in one. The authors propose a graph-based distillation method that is able to distill information from all modalities at training time, while also passing through a validation phase on a subset of modalities. This showed to reach state-of-the-art results in action recognition and action detection tasks. Our work substantially differs from [16] since we benefit from an hallucination mechanism, consisting in an auxiliary network trained using the guidance distilled by the *teacher* network (that processes the depth data stream in our case). This mechanism allows the model to learn to emulate the presence of the missing modality at test time.

The work of Hoffman *et al.* [11] introduced a model to hallucinate depth features from RGB input for object detection task. While the idea of using an hallucination stream is similar to the one thereby presented, the mechanism used to learn it is different. In [11], the authors use an Euclidean loss between depth and hallucinated feature maps, that is part of the total loss along with more than ten classification and localization losses, which makes its effectiveness very dependent on hyperparameter tuning to balance the different values, as the model is trained jointly in one step by optimizing the aforementioned composite loss. Differently, we propose a loss inspired to the distillation framework, that not only uses the Euclidean distance between feature maps, and the one-hot labels, but also leverages soft predictions from the depth network. Moreover, we encourage the hallucination learning by design, by using cross-stream connections (see Sect. 3). This showed to largely improve the performance of our model with respect to the one-step learning process proposed in [11].

Multimodal Video Action Recognition. Video action recognition has a long and rich field of literature, spanning from classification methods using handcrafted features [3,13,31,32] to modern deep learning approaches [2,12,28,34], using either RGB-only or various multimodal data. Here, we focus on some of the more relevant works in multimodal video action recognition, including state-of-the-art methods considering the NTU RGB+D dataset, as well as architectures related to our proposed model.

The two-stream model introduced by Simonyan and Zisserman [25] is a landmark on video analysis, and since then has inspired a series of variants that achieved state-of-the-art performance on diverse datasets. This architecture is composed by an RGB and an optical flow stream, which are trained separately, and then fused at the prediction layer. The current state of the art in video action recognition [2] is inspired by such model, featuring 3D convolutions to deal with the temporal dimension, instead of the original 2D ones. In [5], a further variation of the two-stream approach is proposed, which models spatiotemporal features by injecting the motion stream's signal into the residual unit of the appearance stream. The idea of combining the two streams have also been explored previously by the same authors in [6].

Instead, in [24], the authors explore the complementary properties of RGB and depth data, taking the NTU RGB+D dataset as testbed. This work designed a deep autoencoder architecture and a structured sparsity learning machine, and showed to achieve state-of-the-art results for action recognition. Liu *et al.* [14] also use RGB and depth complementary information to devise a method for viewpoint invariant action recognition. Here, dense trajectories from RGB data are first extracted, which are then encoded in viewpoint invariant deep features. The RGB and depth features are then used as a dictionary to predict the test label.

All these previous methods exploited the rich information conveyed by the multimodal data to improve recognition. Our work, instead, proposes a fully convolutional model that exploits RGB and depth data at training time only, and uses exclusively RGB data as input at test time, reaching performance comparable to those utilizing the complete set of modalities in both stages.

3 Generalized Distillation with Multiple Stream Networks

This section describes our approach in terms of its architecture, the losses used to learn the different networks, and the training procedure.

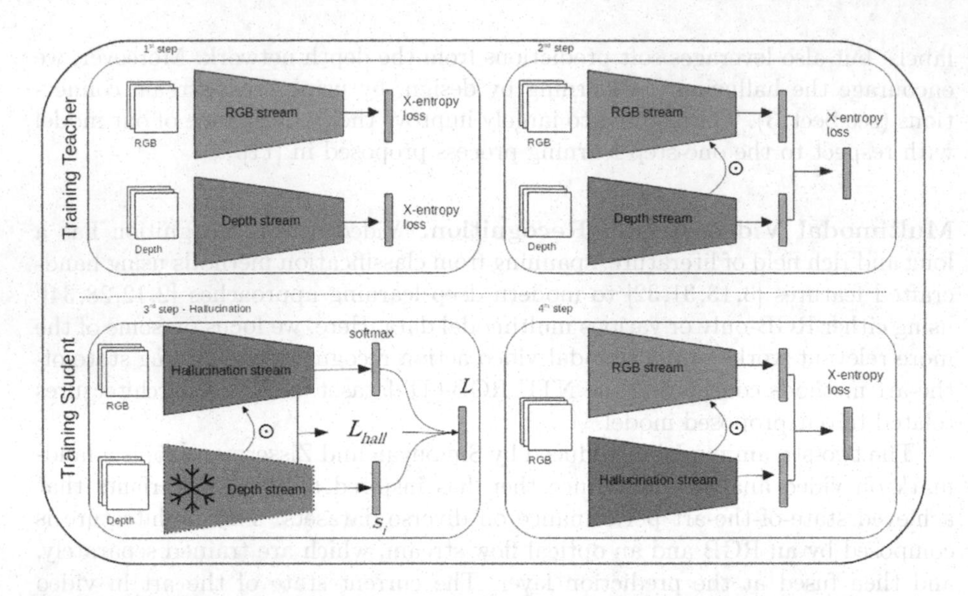

Fig. 1. Training procedure described in Sect. 3.3 (see also text therein). The 1st step refers to the separate (pre-)training of depth and RGB streams with standard cross entropy classification loss, with both streams initialized with ImageNet weights. The 2nd step represents the learning of the teacher network; both streams are initialized with the respective weights from step 1, and trained jointly with a cross entropy loss as a traditional two-stream model, using RGB and depth data. The 3rd step represents the learning of the student network: both streams are initialized with the depth stream weights from the previous step, but the actual depth stream is frozen; importantly, the input for the hallucination stream is RGB data; the model is trained using the loss proposed in Eq. 5. The 4th and last step refers to a fine-tuning step and also represents the test setup of our model; the hallucination stream is initialized from the respective weights from previous step, and the RGB stream with the respective weights from the 2nd step; this model is fine-tuned using a cross entropy loss, and importantly, using only RGB data as input for both streams.

3.1 Cross-Stream Multiplier Networks

Typically in two-stream architectures, the two streams are trained separately and the predictions are fused with a late fusion mechanism [5,25]. Such models use as input appearance (RGB) and motion (optical flow) data, which are fed separately into each stream, both in training and testing. Instead, in this paper we use RGB and depth frames as inputs for training, but only RGB at test time, as already discussed (Fig. 1).

We use the ResNet-50-based [8,9] model proposed in [5] as baseline architecture for each stream block of our model. In that paper, Feichtenhofer *et al.* proposed to connect the appearance and motion streams with multiplicative connections at several layers, as opposed to previous models which would only interact at the prediction layer. Such connections are depicted in Fig. 1 with the ⊙ symbol. Figure 2 illustrates this mechanism at a given layer of the multiple stream architecture, but, in our work, it is actually implemented at the four convolutional layers of the Resnet-50 model. The underlying intuition is that these connections enable the model to learn better spatiotemporal representations, and help to distinguish between identical actions that require the combination of appearance and motion features. Originally, the cross-stream connections consisted in the injection of the motion stream signal into the other stream's residual unit, without affecting the skip path. ResNet's residual units are formally expressed as:

$$\mathbf{x}_{l+1} = f(h(\mathbf{x}_l) + F(\mathbf{x}_l, \mathcal{W}_l)),$$

where $\mathbf{x}_l$ and $\mathbf{x}_{l+1}$ are l-th layer's input and output, respectively, F represents the residual convolutional layers defined by weights $\mathcal{W}_l$, $h(\mathbf{x}_l)$ is an identity mapping and f is a ReLU non-linearity. The cross-streams connections are then defined as

$$\mathbf{x}^a_{l+1} = f(\mathbf{x}^a_l) + F(\mathbf{x}^a_l \odot f(\mathbf{x}^m_l), \mathcal{W}_l),$$

where $\mathbf{x}^a$ and $\mathbf{x}^m$ are the appearance and motion streams, respectively, and $\odot$ is the element-wise multiplication operation. Such mechanism implies a spatial alignment between both feature maps, and therefore between both modalities. This alignment comes for free when using RGB and optical flow, since the latter is computed from the former in a way that spatial arrangement is preserved. However, this is an assumption we can not generally make. For instance, depth and RGB are often captured from different sensors, likely resulting in spatially misaligned frames. We cope with this alignment problem in the method's initialization phase (described in the supplementary material).

Temporal Convolutions. In order to augment the model temporal support, we implement 1D temporal convolutions in the second residual unit of each ResNet layer (as in [5]), as illustrated in Fig. 2. The weights $\mathcal{W}_l \in \mathbb{R}^{1\times1\times3\times C_l\times C_l}$ are convolutional filters initialized as identity mappings at feature level, and centered in time, and C_l is the number of channels in layer l.

Very recently in [29], the authors explored various network configurations using temporal convolutions, comparing several different combinations for the task of video classification. This work suggests that decoupling 3D convolutions into 2D (spatial) and 1D (temporal) filters is the best setup in action recognition tasks, producing best accuracies. The intuition for the latter setup is that factorizing spatial and temporal convolutions in two consecutive convolutional layers eases training of the spatial and temporal tasks (also in line with [27]).

3.2 Hallucination Stream

We also introduce and learn an hallucination network [11], using a new learning paradigm, loss function and interaction mechanism. The hallucination stream network has the same architecture as the appearance and depth stream models.

This network receives RGB as input, and is trained to "imitate" the depth stream at different levels, *i.e.* at feature and prediction layers. In this paper, we

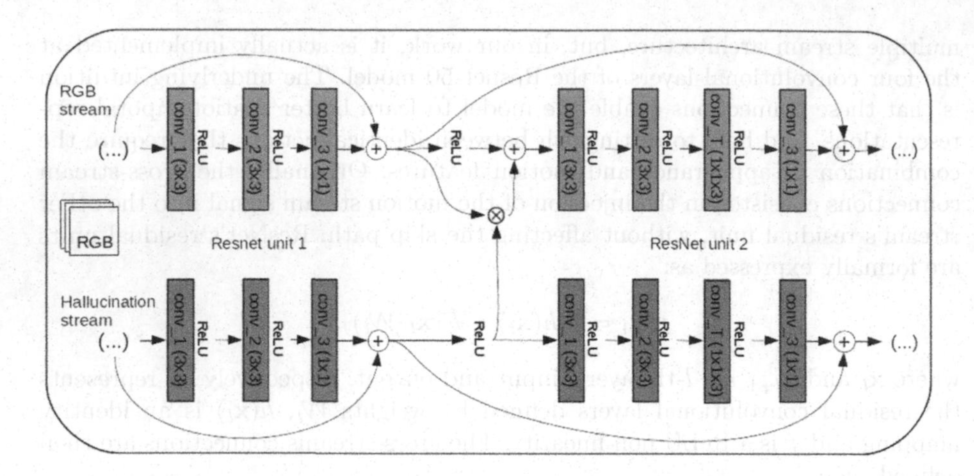

Fig. 2. Detail of the ResNet residual unit, showing the multiplicative connections and temporal convolutions [5]. In our architecture, the signal injection occurs before the 2nd residual unit of each of the four ResNet blocks.

explore several ways to implement such learning paradigm, including both the training procedure and the loss, and how they affect the overall performance of the model.

In [11] it is proposed a regression loss between the hallucination and depth feature maps, defined as:

$$L_{hall}(l) = \lambda_l \|\sigma(A_l^d) - \sigma(A_l^h)\|_2^2, \quad (1)$$

where σ is the sigmoid function, and A_l^d and A_l^h are the l-th layer activations of depth and hallucination network. This Euclidean loss forces both activation maps to be similar. In [11], this loss is weighted along with another ten classification and localization loss terms, making it hard to balance the total loss. One of the main motivations behind the proposed new staged learning paradigm, described in Sect. 3.3, is to avoid the inefficient, heuristic-based tweaking of so many loss weights, aka hyper-parameter tuning.

Instead, we adopt an approach inspired by the generalized distillation framework [15], in which a *student* model $f_s \in \mathcal{F}_s$ distills the representation $f_t \in \mathcal{F}_t$ learned by the *teacher* model. This is formalized as

$$f_s = \arg\min_{f \in \mathcal{F}_s} \frac{1}{n} \sum_{i=1}^{n} L_{GD}(i), n = 1, ..., N \quad (2)$$

where N is the number of examples in the dataset. The generalized distillation loss is so defined as:

$$L_{GD}(i) = (1 - \lambda)\ell(y_i, \varsigma(f(x_i))) + \lambda\ell(s_i, \varsigma(f(x_i))), \ \lambda \in [0, 1] \ f_s \in \mathcal{F}_s, \quad (3)$$

ς is the *softmax* operator and s_i is the soft prediction from the teacher network:

$$s_i = \varsigma(f_t(x_i)/T), \ T > 0. \quad (4)$$

The parameter λ in Eq. 3 allows to tune the loss by giving more importance either to imitating ground-truth hard or soft teacher targets, y_i and s_i, respectively. This mechanism indeed allows the transfer of information from the depth (teacher) to the hallucination (student) network. The temperature parameter T in Eq. 4 allows to smooth the probability vector predicted by the teacher network. The intuition is that such smoothing may expose relations between classes that would not be easily revealed in raw predictions, further facilitating the distillation by the student network f_s.

We suggest that both Euclidean and generalized distillation losses are indeed useful in the learning process. In fact, by encouraging the network to decrease the distance between hallucinated and true depth feature maps, it can help to distill depth information encoded in the generalized distillation loss. Thus, we formalize our final loss function as follows:

$$L = (1 - \alpha)L_{GD} + \alpha L_{hall}, \alpha \in [0, 1], \tag{5}$$

where α is a parameter balancing the contributions of the two loss terms during training. The parameters λ, α and T are estimated by utilizing a validation set. The details for their setting are provided in the supplementary material.

In summary, the generalized distillation framework proposes to use the student-teacher framework introduced in the distillation theory to extract knowledge from the privileged information source. We explore this idea by proposing a new learning paradigm to train an hallucination network using privileged information, which we will describe in the next section. In addition to the loss functions introduced above, we also allow the teacher network to share information with the student network by design, through the cross-stream multiplicative connections. We test how all these possibilities affect the model's performance in the experimental section through an extensive ablation study.

3.3 Training Paradigm

In general, the proposed training paradigm, illustrated in Fig. 1, is divided in two core parts: the first part (Step 1 and 2 in the figure) focuses on learning the teacher network f_t, leveraging RGB and depth data (the privileged information in this case); the second part (Step 3 and 4 in the figure) focuses on learning the hallucination network, referred to as student network f_s in the distillation framework, using the general hallucination loss defined in Eq. 5.

The *first training step* consists in training both streams separately, which is a common practice in two-stream architectures. Both depth and appearance streams are trained minimizing cross-entropy, after being initialized with a pre-trained ImageNet model for all experiments. Temporal kernels are initialized as $[0, 1, 0]$, *i.e.* only information on the central frame is used at the beginning - this eventually changes as the training continues. As in [4], depth frames are encoded into color images using a jet colormap.

The *second training step* is still focused on further training the teacher model. Since the model trained in this step has the architecture and capacity of the final one, and *has access to both modalities*, its performance represents an upper bound for the task we are addressing. This is one of the major differences between our approach and the one used in [11]: by decoupling the teacher learning phase with the hallucination learning, we are able to both learn a better teacher *and* a better student, as we will show in the experimental section.

In the *third training step*, we focus on learning the hallucination network from the teacher model, *i.e.*, the depth stream network just trained. Here, the weights of the depth network are frozen, while receiving in input depth data. Instead, the hallucination network, receiving in input RGB data, is trained with the loss defined in (5), while also receiving feedback from the cross-stream connections from the depth network. We found that this helps the learning process.

In the *fourth and last step*, we carry out fine tuning of the whole model, composed by the RGB and the hallucination streams. This step uses RGB only as input, and it also precisely resembles the setup used at test time. The cross-stream connections inject the hallucinated signal into the appearance RGB stream network, resulting in the multiplication of the hallucinated feature maps and the RGB feature maps. The intuition is that the hallucination network has learned to inform the RGB model where the action is taking place, similarly to what the depth model would do with real depth data.

4 Experiments

4.1 Datasets

We evaluate our method on three datasets, while the ablation study is performed only on the NTU RGB+D dataset. Our model is initialized with ImageNet pre-trained weights and trained and evaluated on the NTU RGB+D dataset. We later fine-tune this model on each of the two smaller datasets for the corresponding evaluation experiments.

NTU RGB+D [23]**.** This is the largest public dataset for multimodal video action recognition. It is composed by 56,880 videos, available in four modalities: RGB videos, depth sequences, infrared frames, and 3D skeleton data of 25 joints. It was acquired with a Kinect v2 sensor in 80 different viewpoints, and includes 40 subjects performing 60 distinct actions. We follow the two evaluation protocols originally proposed in [23], which are cross-subject and cross-view. As in the original paper, we use about 5% of the training data as validation set for both protocols, in order to select the parameters λ, α and T. In this work, we use only RGB and depth data. The masked depth maps are converted to a three channel map via a jet mapping, as in [4].

UWA3DII [21]**.** This dataset consists on 1075 samples of RGB, depth and skeleton sequences. It features 10 subjects performing 30 actions captured in 5 different views.

Northwestern-UCLA [33]**.** Similarly to the other datasets, it provides RGB, depth and skeleton sequences for 1475 samples. It features 10 subjects performing 10 actions captured in 3 different views.

4.2 Ablation Study

In this section we discuss the results of the experiments carried out to understand the contribution of each part of the model and of the training procedure. Table 1 reports performances at the several training steps, different losses and model configurations.

Table 1. Ablation study. A full set of experiments is provided for the NTU cross-subject evaluation protocol. For cross-view protocol, only the most important results are reported.

#	Method	Test modality	Loss	Cross-Subject	Cross-View
1	Ours - step 1, depth stream	Depth	x-entr	70.44%	75.16%
2	Ours - step 1, RGB stream	RGB	x-entr	66.52%	71.39%
3	Hoffman [11] w/o connections	RGB	Equation (1)	64.64%	–
4	Hoffman [11] w/o connections	RGB	Equation (3)	68.60%	–
5	Hoffman [11] w/o connections	RGB	Equation (5)	70.70%	–
6	Ours - step 2, depth stream	Depth	x-entr	71.09%	77.30%
7	Ours - step 2, RGB stream	RGB	x-entr	66.68%	56.26%
8	Ours - step 2	RGB & Depth	x-entr	**79.73%**	81.43%
9	Ours - step 2 w/o connections	RGB & Depth	x-entr	78.27%	**82.11%**
10	Ours - step 3 w/o connections	RGB (*hall*)	Equation (1)	69.93%	70.64%
11	Ours - step 3 w/ connections	RGB (*hall*)	Equation (1)	70.47%	–
12	Ours - step 3 w/ connections	RGB (*hall*)	Equation (3)	71.52%	–
13	Ours - step 3 w/ connections	RGB (*hall*)	Equation (5)	71.93%	74.10%
14	Ours - step 3 w/o connections	RGB (*hall*)	Equation (5)	71.10%	–
15	**Ours - step 4**	**RGB**	x-entr	**73.42%**	**77.21%**

Rows #1 and #2 refer to the first training step, where depth and RGB streams are trained separately. We note that the depth stream network provides better performance with respect to the RGB one, as expected.

The second part of the table (Rows #3–5) shows the results using Hoffman *et al.*'s method [11] - *i.e.*, adopting a model initialized with the pre-trained networks from the first training step, and the hallucination network initialized using the depth network. Row #3 refers to the original paper [11] (i.e., using the loss L_{hall}, Eq. 1), and rows #4 and #5 refer to the training using the proposed losses L_{GD} and L, in Eqs. 3 and 5, respectively. It can be noticed that the accuracies achieved using the proposed loss functions overcome that obtained in [11] by a significant margin (about 6% in the case of the total loss L).

The third part of the table (rows #6–9) reports performances after the training step 2. Rows #6 and #7 refer to the accuracy provided by depth and RGB stream networks belonging to the model of row #8, taken individually. The final model constitutes the upper bound for our hallucination model, since it uses RGB and depth for training and testing. Performances obtained by the model in row #8 and #9, with and without cross-stream connections, respectively, are the highest in absolute since using both modalities (around 78–79% for cross-subject and 81–82% for cross-view protocols, respectively), largely outperforming the accuracies obtained using only one modality (in rows #6 and #7).

The *fourth* part of the table (rows #10–14) shows results for our hallucination network after the several variations of learning processes, different losses and with and without cross-stream connections.

Finally, the last row, #15, reports results after the last fine-tuning step which further narrows the gap with the upper bound.

Contribution of the Cross-Stream Connections. We claim that the signal injection provided by the cross-stream connections helps the learning of a better hallucination network. Row #13 and #14 show the performances for the hallucination network learning process, starting from the same point and using the same loss. The hallucination network that is learned using multiplicative connections performs better than its counterpart, where depth and RGB frames are properly aligned. It is important to note though that this is not observed in the other two smaller datasets, due to the spatial misalignment of modalities, and consequently between feature maps.

Contributions of the Proposed Distillation Loss (Eq. 5). The distillation and Euclidean losses have complementary contributions to the learning of the hallucination network. This is observed by looking at the performances reported in rows #3, #4 and #5, and also #11, #12 and #13. In both the training procedure proposed by Hoffman *et al.* [11] and our staged training process, the distillation loss improves over the Euclidean loss, and the combination of both improves over the rest. This suggests that both Euclidean and distillation losses have its own share and act differently to align the hallucination (student) and depth (teacher) feature maps and outputs' distributions.

Contributions of the Proposed Training Procedure. The intuition behind the staged training procedure proposed in this work can be ascribed to the *divide et impera* (divide-and-conquer) strategy. In our case, it means breaking the problem in two parts: learning the actual task we aim to solve and learning the student network to face test-time limitations. Row #5 reports accuracy for the architecture proposed by Hoffman *et al.*, and rows #15 report the performance for our model with connections. Both use the same loss to learn the hallucination network, and both start from the same initialization. We observe that our method outperform the one in row #5, which justifies the proposed staged training procedure.

4.3 Inference with Noisy Depth

Suppose that in a real test scenario we can only access unreliable sensors which produce noisy depth data. The question we now address is: to which extent can we trust such noisy data? In other words, at which level of noise does it become favorable to hallucinate the depth modality with respect to using the full teacher model (step 2) with noisy depth data?

Table 2. Accuracy of the model tested with clean RGB and noisy depth data. Accuracy of the proposed hallucination model, i.e. with *no depth* at test time, is 77.21%.

σ^2	*no noise*	10^{-3}	10^{-2}	10^{-1}	10^{0}	10^{1}	*void*
Accuracy	81.43%	81.34%	81.12%	76.85%	62.47%	51.43%	14.24%

The depth sensor used in the NTU dataset (Kinect), is an IR emitter coupled with an IR camera, and has very complex noise characterization comprising at least 6 different sources [18]. It is beyond the scope of this work to investigate noise models affecting the depth channel, so, for our analysis we choose the most common one, i.e., the multiplicative speckle noise. Hence, we inject Gaussian noise in the depth images I in order to simulate speckle noise: $I = I * n, n \sim \mathcal{N}(1, \sigma)$. Table 2 shows how performances of the network degrade when depth is corrupted with such Gaussian noise with increasing variance (NTU cross-view protocol only). Results show that accuracy significantly decreases w.r.t. the one guaranteed by our hallucination model (77.21% - row #15 in Table 1), even with low noise variance. This means, in conclusion, that *training an hallucination network is an effective way not only to obviate to the problem of a missing modality, but also to deal with noise affecting the input data channel.*

4.4 Comparison with Other Methods

Table 3 compares performances of different methods on the various datasets. The standard performance measure used for this task and datasets is classification accuracy, estimated according to the protocols (training and testing splits) reported in the respective works we are comparing with.

The first part of the table (indicated by × symbol) refers to unsupervised methods, which achieve surprisingly high results even without relying on labels in learning representations.

The second part refers to supervised methods (indicated by △), divided according to the modalities used for training and testing. Here, we list the performance of the separate RGB and depth streams trained in step 1, as a reference. We expect our final model to perform better than the one trained on RGB only, whose accuracy constitutes a lower bound for our student network. The values reported for *our step 1* models for UWA3DII and NW-UCLA datasets refer to the fine-tuning of our NTU model. We have experimented training using pre-trained ImageNet weights, which led from 20% to 30% less accuracy. We also

Table 3. Classification accuracies and comparisons with the state of the art. Performances referred to the several steps of our approach (ours) are highlighted in bold. × refers to comparisons with unsupervised learning methods. △ refers to supervised methods: here train and test modalities coincide. □ refers to privileged information methods: here training exploits RGB+D data, while test relies on RGB data only. The 3rd column refers to cross-subject and the 4th to the cross-view evaluation protocols on the NTU dataset. The results reported on the other two datasets are for the cross-view protocol.

Method	Test mods.	NTU (p1)	NTU (p2)	UWA3DII	NW-UCLA	
Luo [17]	Depth	66.2%	–	–	–	×
Luo [17]	RGB	56.0%	–	–	–	
Rahmani [22]	RGB	–	–	67.4%	78.1%	
HOG-2 [19]	Depth	32.4%	22.3%	–	–	△
Action Tube [7]	RGB	–	–	37.0%	61.5%	
Ours - depth, step 1	**Depth**	**70.44%**	**75.16%**	**75.28%**	**72.38%**	
Ours - RGB, step 1	**RGB**	**66.52%**	**71.39%**	**63.67%**	**85.22%**	
Deep RNN [23]	Joints	56.3%	64.1%	–	–	
Deep LSTM [23]	Joints	60.7%	67.3%	–	–	
Sharoudy [23]	Joints	62.93%	70.27%	–	–	
Kim [26]	Joints	74.3%	83.1%	–	–	
Sharoudy [24]	RGB+D	74.86%	–	–	–	
Liu [14]	RGB+D	77.5%	84.5%	–	–	
Rahmani [20]	Depth+Joints	75.2	83.1	84.2%	–	
Ours - step 2	**RGB+D**	**79.73%**	**81.43%**	**79.66%**	**88.87%**	
Hoffman *et al.* [11]	RGB	64.64%	–	66.67%	83.30%	□
Ours - step 3	**RGB**	**71.93%**	**74.10%**	**71.54%**	**76.30%**	
Ours - step 4	**RGB**	**73.42%**	**77.21%**	**73.23%**	**86.72%**	

propose our baseline, consisting in the teacher model trained in step 2. Its accuracy represents an upper bound for the final model, which will not rely on depth data at test time.

The last part of the table (indicated by □) reports our model's performances at 2 different stages together with the other privileged information method [11]. For all datasets and protocols, we can see that our privileged information approach outperforms [11], which is the only fair *direct* comparison we can make (same training & test data). Besides, as expected, our final model performs better than "Ours - RGB model, step 1" since it exploits more data at training time, and worse than "Ours - step 2", since it exploits less data at test time. Other RGB+D methods perform better (which is comprehensible since they rely on RGB+D in both training and test) but not by a large margin.

4.5 Inverting Modalities - RGB Distillation

The results presented in Table 4 address the opposite case of what is studied in the rest of the paper, *i.e.*, the case when RGB data is missing. In this case, the hallucination stream distills knowledge from the RGB stream in step 3 (Fig. 1).

We observe that the performance of the final model degrades by almost 1%, 76.41% vs. 77.21% (cf. line 15 of Table 2 in the paper). A more consistent setting would be to modify the model, inverting the cross-stream connections in Step 3 and 4, thus having information flowing again from depth to RGB.

Table 4. RGB distillation (NTU RGB-D, cross-view protocol.)

#	Method	Test modality	Loss	Cross-View
13a	Ours - step 3	Depth (*hall*)	Equation 5	76.12%
15a	Ours - step 4	Depth	x-entr	76.41%

5 Conclusions and Future Work

In this paper, we address the task of video action recognition in the context of privileged information. We propose a new learning paradigm to teach an hallucination network to mimic the depth stream. Our model outperforms many of the supervised methods recently evaluated on the NTU RGB+D dataset, as well as the hallucination model proposed in [11]. We conducted an extensive ablation study to verify how the several parts composing our learning paradigm contribute to the model performance. As a future work, we would like to extend this approach to deal with additional modalities that may be available at training time, such as skeleton joints data or infrared sequences. Finally, the current model cannot be applied to still images due to the presence of temporal convolutions. In principle, we could remove them and apply our method to still images and other tasks such as object detection.

References

1. Ba, L.J., Caruana, R.: Do deep nets really need to be deep? In: Proceedings of Advances in Neural Information Processing Systems (NIPS) (2014)
2. Carreira, J., Zisserman, A.: Quo vadis, action recognition? A new model and the kinetics dataset. In: Proceedings of the IEEE Conference on Computer Vision and Pattern Recognition (2017)
3. Dalal, N., Triggs, B.: Histograms of oriented gradients for human detection. In: IEEE Computer Society Conference on Computer Vision and Pattern Recognition, CVPR 2005, vol. 1, pp. 886–893. IEEE (2005)
4. Eitel, A., Springenberg, J.T., Spinello, L., Riedmiller, M., Burgard, W.: Multimodal deep learning for robust RGB-D object recognition. In: IEEE/RSJ International Conference on Intelligent Robots and Systems (IROS), pp. 681–687. IEEE (2015)

5. Feichtenhofer, C., Pinz, A., Wildes, R.P.: Spatiotemporal multiplier networks for video action recognition. In: Proceedings of the IEEE Conference on Computer Vision and Pattern Recognition, pp. 4768–4777 (2017)
6. Feichtenhofer, C., Pinz, A., Zisserman, A.: Convolutional two-stream network fusion for video action recognition. In: Proceedings of the IEEE Conference on Computer Vision and Pattern Recognition, pp. 1933–1941 (2016)
7. Gkioxari, G., Malik, J.: Finding action tubes. In: IEEE Conference on Computer Vision and Pattern Recognition (CVPR), pp. 759–768. IEEE (2015)
8. He, K., Zhang, X., Ren, S., Sun, J.: Deep residual learning for image recognition. In: Proceedings of the IEEE Conference on Computer Vision and Pattern Recognition, pp. 770–778 (2016)
9. He, K., Zhang, X., Ren, S., Sun, J.: Identity mappings in deep residual networks. In: Leibe, B., Matas, J., Sebe, N., Welling, M. (eds.) ECCV 2016. LNCS, vol. 9908, pp. 630–645. Springer, Cham (2016). https://doi.org/10.1007/978-3-319-46493-0_38
10. Hinton, G., Vinyals, O., Dean, J.: Distilling the knowledge in a neural network. In: Deep Learning and Representation Learning Workshop: NIPS 2014 (2014)
11. Hoffman, J., Gupta, S., Darrell, T.: Learning with side information through modality hallucination. In: Proceedings of the IEEE Conference on Computer Vision and Pattern Recognition, pp. 826–834 (2016)
12. Karpathy, A., Toderici, G., Shetty, S., Leung, T., Sukthankar, R., Fei-Fei, L.: Large-scale video classification with convolutional neural networks. In: Proceedings of the IEEE Conference on Computer Vision and Pattern Recognition, pp. 1725–1732 (2014)
13. Laptev, I., Marszalek, M., Schmid, C., Rozenfeld, B.: Learning realistic human actions from movies. In: IEEE Conference on Computer Vision and Pattern Recognition, CVPR 2008, pp. 1–8. IEEE (2008)
14. Liu, J., Akhtar, N., Mian, A.: Viewpoint invariant action recognition using RGB-D videos. arXiv preprint arXiv:1709.05087 (2017)
15. Lopez-Paz, D., Bottou, L., Schölkopf, B., Vapnik, V.: Unifying distillation and privileged information. In: Proceedings of the International Conference on Learning Representations (ICLR) (2016)
16. Luo, Z., Jiang, L., Hsieh, J.T., Niebles, J.C., Fei-Fei, L.: Graph distillation for action detection with privileged information. arXiv preprint arXiv:1712.00108 (2017)
17. Luo, Z., Peng, B., Huang, D.A., Alahi, A., Fei-Fei, L.: Unsupervised learning of long-term motion dynamics for videos. In: IEEE Conference on Computer Vision and Pattern Recognition (CVPR). No. EPFL-CONF-230240 (2017)
18. Mallick, T., Das, P.P., Majumdar, A.K.: Characterizations of noise in kinect depth images: a review. IEEE Sens. J. **14**(6), 1731–1740 (2014). https://doi.org/10.1109/JSEN.2014.2309987
19. Ohn-Bar, E., Trivedi, M.M.: Joint angles similarities and HOG2 for action recognition. In: IEEE Conference on Computer Vision and Pattern Recognition Workshops (CVPRW), pp. 465–470. IEEE (2013)
20. Rahmani, H., Bennamoun, M.: Learning action recognition model from depth and skeleton videos. In: Proceedings of the IEEE Conference on Computer Vision and Pattern Recognition, pp. 5832–5841 (2017)
21. Rahmani, H., Mahmood, A., Huynh, D., Mian, A.: Histogram of oriented principal components for cross-view action recognition. IEEE Trans. Pattern Anal. Mach. Intell. **38**(12), 2430–2443 (2016)

22. Rahmani, H., Mian, A., Shah, M.: Learning a deep model for human action recognition from novel viewpoints. IEEE Trans. Pattern Anal. Mach. Intell. **40**(3), 667–681 (2018)
23. Shahroudy, A., Liu, J., Ng, T.T., Wang, G.: NTU RGB+D: A large scale dataset for 3D human activity analysis. In: Proceedings of the IEEE Conference on Computer Vision and Pattern Recognition, pp. 1010–1019 (2016)
24. Shahroudy, A., Ng, T.T., Gong, Y., Wang, G.: Deep multimodal feature analysis for action recognition in RGB+D videos. IEEE Trans. Pattern Anal. Mach. Intell. **40**(5), 1045–1058 (2018)
25. Simonyan, K., Zisserman, A.: Two-stream convolutional networks for action recognition in videos. In: Advances in Neural Information Processing Systems, pp. 568–576 (2014)
26. Soo Kim, T., Reiter, A.: Interpretable 3D human action analysis with temporal convolutional networks. In: Proceedings of the IEEE Conference on Computer Vision and Pattern Recognition Workshops, pp. 20–28 (2017)
27. Sun, L., Jia, K., Yeung, D.Y., Shi, B.E.: Human action recognition using factorized spatio-temporal convolutional networks. In: Proceedings of the IEEE International Conference on Computer Vision, pp. 4597–4605 (2015)
28. Tran, D., Bourdev, L., Fergus, R., Torresani, L., Paluri, M.: Learning spatiotemporal features with 3D convolutional networks. In: Proceedings of the IEEE International Conference on Computer Vision, pp. 4489–4497 (2015)
29. Tran, D., Wang, H., Torresani, L., Ray, J., LeCun, Y., Paluri, M.: A closer look at spatiotemporal convolutions for action recognition. In: Proceedings of the IEEE Conference on Computer Vision and Pattern Recognition, pp. 6450–6459 (2018)
30. Vapnik, V., Vashist, A.: A new learning paradigm: learning using privileged information. Neural Netw. **22**(5), 544–557 (2009)
31. Wang, H., Kläser, A., Schmid, C., Liu, C.L.: Action recognition by dense trajectories. In: IEEE Conference on Computer Vision and Pattern Recognition (CVPR), pp. 3169–3176. IEEE (2011)
32. Wang, H., Schmid, C.: Action recognition with improved trajectories. In: Proceedings of the IEEE International Conference on Computer Vision, pp. 3551–3558 (2013)
33. Wang, J., Nie, X., Xia, Y., Wu, Y., Zhu, S.C.: Cross-view action modeling, learning and recognition. In: Proceedings of the IEEE Conference on Computer Vision and Pattern Recognition, pp. 2649–2656 (2014)
34. Wang, X., Girshick, R., Gupta, A., He, K.: Non-local neural networks. arXiv preprint arXiv:1711.07971 (2017)

Interpretable Basis Decomposition for Visual Explanation

Bolei Zhou[1](✉), Yiyou Sun[2], David Bau[1], and Antonio Torralba[1]

[1] MIT CSAIL, Cambridge, USA
{bzhou,davidbau,torralba}@csail.mit.edu
[2] Harvard, Cambridge, USA
sunyiyou@seas.harvard.edu

Abstract. Explanations of the decisions made by a deep neural network are important for human end-users to be able to understand and diagnose the trustworthiness of the system. Current neural networks used for visual recognition are generally used as black boxes that do not provide any human interpretable justification for a prediction. In this work we propose a new framework called Interpretable Basis Decomposition for providing visual explanations for classification networks. By decomposing the neural activations of the input image into semantically interpretable components pre-trained from a large concept corpus, the proposed framework is able to disentangle the evidence encoded in the activation feature vector, and quantify the contribution of each piece of evidence to the final prediction. We apply our framework for providing explanations to several popular networks for visual recognition, and show it is able to explain the predictions given by the networks in a human-interpretable way. The human interpretability of the visual explanations provided by our framework and other recent explanation methods is evaluated through Amazon Mechanical Turk, showing that our framework generates more faithful and interpretable explanations (The code and data are available at https://github.com/CSAILVision/IBD).

1 Introduction

As deep networks continue to prove their capabilities on an expanding set of applications in visual recognition such as object classification [19], scene recognition [29], image captioning [24], and visual question answering [1], it is increasingly important not only for a network to make accurate predictions, but also to be able to explain why the network makes each prediction.

A good explanation of a deep network should play two roles: first, it should be a faithful representation of the operation of the network; and second, it should be simple and interpretable enough for a human to understand. There are two approaches for creating human-understandable explanations for the internals of a deep network. One is to identify the *evidence* that a network uses to make

B. Zhou, Y. Sun and D. Bau—Equally contributed.

V. Ferrari et al. (Eds.): ECCV 2018, LNCS 11212, pp. 122–138, 2018.
https://doi.org/10.1007/978-3-030-01237-3_8

a specific decision by creating a heatmap that indicates which portions of an input are most salient to the decision [2,20,28]. Such heatmaps can be created using a variety of techniques and can be applied to identify the most salient parts of images and training sets. A second approach is to identify the *purpose* of the internal representations of a network by identifying the concepts that each part of the network detects [3,7,27]. Such concept dictionaries can be created by matching network units to a broad concept data set, by generating or sampling example inputs that reveal the sensitivity of a unit, or by training parts of the network to solve interpretable subproblems.

In this paper we describe a framework called *Interpretable Basis Decomposition (IBD)*, for bringing these two approaches together to generate explanations for visual recognition. The framework is able to decompose the evidence for a prediction for image classification into semantically interpretable components, each with an identified purpose, a heatmap, and a ranked contribution, as shown in Fig. 1. In addition to showing where a network looks, we show which concepts a network is responding to at each part of the input image.

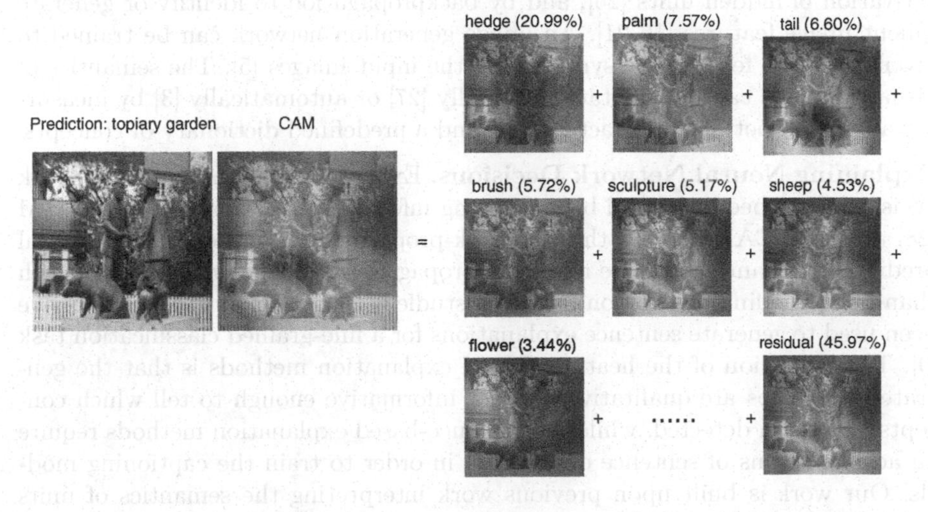

Fig. 1. Interpretable Basis Decomposition provides an explanation for a prediction by decomposing the decision into the components of interpretable basis. Top contributing components are shown with a label, contribution, and heatmap for each term.

Our framework is based on the insight that good explanations depend on context. For example, the concepts to explain what makes up a 'living room' are different from the concepts to explain an 'airport'. A overstuffed pillow is not an airliner, nor vice-versa. We formalize the idea of a salient set of concepts as a choice of a interpretable basis in the feature space, and describe how to construct a context-specific concept basis as the solution to a least-squares problem.

Each explanation we describe is both a visualization and a vector decomposition of a layer's internal state into interpretable components. As a vector decomposition, each explanation is faithful to the network, quantifying the contribution of each component and also quantifying any uninterpreted residual. The framework also provides explanations that are simple enough for a person to understand. We conduct human evaluations to show that the explanations give people accurate insights about the accuracy of a network.

We summarize our contributions as follows: (1) A new framework called Interpretable Basis Decomposition to provide semantic explanations with labels and heatmaps for neural decision making. (2) Application of the proposed framework on a wide range of network architectures, showing its general applicability. (3) Human evaluations to demonstrate that the explanations are understandable to people, outperforming previous heatmap and unit-based explanation methods.

1.1 Related Work

Visualizing Neural Networks. A number of techniques have been developed to visualize the internal representations of convolutional neural networks. The behavior of a CNN can be visualized by sampling image patches that maximize activation of hidden units [25], and by backpropagation to identify or generate salient image features [16,21]. An image generation network can be trained to invert the deep features by synthesizing the input images [5]. The semantics of visualized units can be annotated manually [27] or automatically [3] by measuring alignment between unit activations and a predefined dictionary of concepts.

Explaining Neural Network Decisions. Explanations of individual network decisions have been explored by generating informative heatmaps such as CAM [28] and grad-CAM [20], or through back-propagation conditioned on the final prediction [21] and layer-wise relevance propagation [2]. The attribution of each channel to the final prediction has been studied [18]. Captioning methods have been used to generate sentence explanations for a fine-grained classification task [9]. The limitation of the heatmap-based explanation methods is that the generated heatmaps are qualitative and not informative enough to tell which concepts have been detected, while the sentence-based explanation methods require an ad-hoc corpus of sentence description in order to train the captioning models. Our work is built upon previous work interpreting the semantics of units [3] and on heatmaps conditioned on the final prediction [20,28]. Rather than using the semantics of activated units to build explanations as in [26], we learn a set of interpretable vectors in the feature space and decompose the representation in terms of these vectors. We will show that the proposed method is able to generate faithful explanations which are more informative than the previous heatmap-based and unit-activation methods.

Component Analysis. Understanding an input signal by decomposing it into components is an old idea. Principal Component Analysis [12] and Independent Component Analysis [11] have been widely used to disentangle a low-dimensional basis from high-dimensional data. Other decomposition methods such as Bilinear models [23] and Isomap [22] are also used to discover meaningful subspaces and structure in the data. Our work is inspired by previous work on component decomposition. Rather than learning the components unsupervised, we learn the set of components from a fully annotated dataset so that we have a ground-truth label for each component. After projecting, the labeled components provide interpretations, forming human-understandable explanations.

Concurrent work [14] proposes examining the behavior of representations in the direction of a set of semantic concept vectors learned from a pre-defined dataset. Those Concept Activation Vectors play a similar role as our Interpretable Basis Vectors, but while that work focuses on using a single feature at a time for retrieval and scoring of samples, our work uses basis sets of vectors to create explanations and decomposed heatmaps for decisions.

2 Framework for Interpretable Basis Decomposition

The goal of Interpretable Basis Decomposition is to decode and explain every bit of information from the activation feature vector in a neural network's penultimate layer. Previous work has shown that it is possible to roughly invert a feature layer to recover an approximation to the original input image using a trained feature inversion network [5]. Instead of recovering the input image, our goal is to decode the meaningful nameable components from the feature vector so that we can build an explanation of the final prediction.

We will describe how we decompose feature vectors in three steps. We begin by describing a way to decompose an output class k into a set of interpretable components c. In our decomposition, both the class and the concepts are represented as vectors w_k and q_c that correspond to linear classifiers in the feature space, and the decomposition is expressed as an optimal choice of basis for w_k. The result of this step is a set of elementary concepts relevant to each class.

Next, we describe how to derive vectors q_c corresponding to a broad dictionary of elementary interpretable concepts c. Each q_c is learned by training a linear segmentation model to locate the concept within the feature space.

Finally, we describe how to create explanations of instance decisions. This is done by projecting the feature vector into the learned interpretable basis and measuring the contribution of each interpretable component. An explanation consists of a list of concepts that contribute most to the final score, together with a heatmap for each concept that shows where the contributions arise for the final prediction. The framework is illustrated in Fig. 2.

2.1 Defining an Interpretable Basis

Explaining a layer can be done by choosing an interpretable basis for the layer's input representation. To see why, set $f(x) \in \mathbb{R}^K$ as a deep net with K output dimensions, considered without the final softmax. We are interested in explaining properties of x which determine the score $f_k(x)$ for a particular class $k \leq K$: for example, we may wish to know if a concept c such as crowds of people tends to cause the input to be classified as an output class k such as airports.

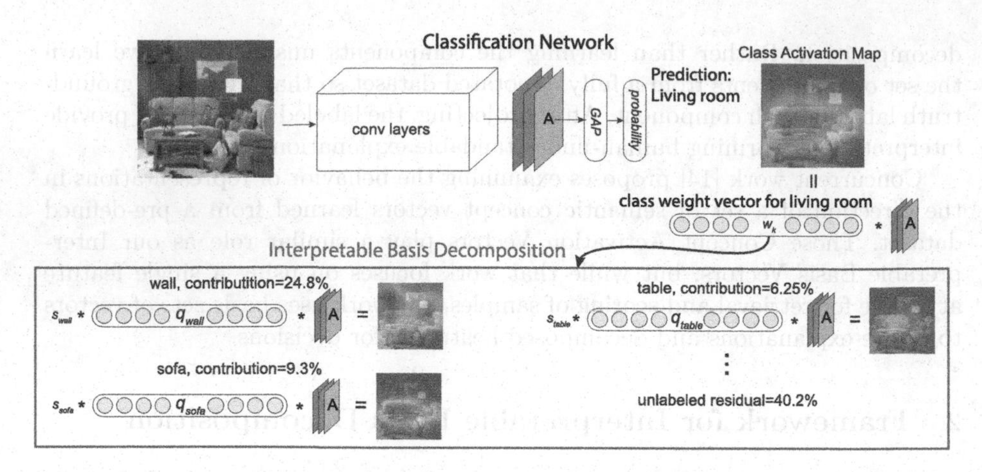

Fig. 2. Illustration of Interpretable Basis Decomposition. The class weight vector w_k is decomposed to a set of interpretable basis vectors $\sum s_{c_i} q_{c_i}$, each corresponding to a labeled concept c_i as well as a projection $q_{c_i}^T A$ that reveals a heatmap of the activations. An explanation of the prediction k consists of the concept labels c_i and the corresponding heatmaps for the most significant terms in the decomposition of $w_k^T a$. For this particular example, wall, sofa, table (and some others are not shown) are labels of the top contributing basis elements that make up the prediction of living room.

We can express our question in terms of an intermediate representation. Write $f(x) = h(g(x))$ where $h(a)$ is the top of the network and $a = g(x) \in \mathbb{R}^D$ is a point in the representation space of the layer of interest. Then to investigate the properties of x that determine $f_k(x)$, we can ask about the properties of the intermediate representation $a = g(x)$ that determine $h_k(a)$.

Let us focus on the simple case where $a = g(x)$ is the output of the second-to-last layer and $h(a)$ is a simple linear operation done by the last layer. Then h_k is a linear function that scores a according to the angle between a and $w_k \in R^D$:

$$h(a) \equiv W^{(h)} a + b^{(h)} \tag{1}$$

$$h_k(a) = w_k^T a + b_k \tag{2}$$

Not all directions in the representation space R^D are equally interpretable. Suppose we have a set of directions $q_{c_i} \in \mathbb{R}^D$ that each correspond to elementary interpretable concepts c_i that are relevant to class k but easier to understand than k itself. Then we can explain w_k by decomposing it into a weighted sum of interpretable components q_{c_i} as follows.

$$w_k \approx s_{c_1} q_{c_1} + \cdots + s_{c_n} q_{c_n} \tag{3}$$

Unless w_k lies exactly in the space spanned by the $\{q_{c_i}\}$, there will be some residual error in the decomposition. Gathering the q_{c_i} into columns of a matrix

C, we can recognize that minimizing this error is a familiar least-squares problem:

$$\text{Find } s_{c_i} \text{ to minimize } ||r|| \text{ where } w_k = s_{c_1}q_{c_1} + \cdots + s_{c_n}q_{c_n} + r \quad (4)$$
$$= Cs + r \quad (5)$$

The optimal s is given by $s = C^+ w_k$ where C^+ is the pseudoinverse of C.

When interpreting the decomposition of w_k, negations of concepts are not as understandable as positive concepts, so we seek decompositions for which each coefficient $s_{c_i} > 0$ is positive. Furthermore, we seek decompositions with a small number of concepts.

We build the basis q_{c_i} in a greedy fashion, as follows. Suppose we have already chosen a set of columns $C = [q_{c_1}| \cdots |q_{c_n}]$, and the residual error is in (4) is $\epsilon = ||w_k - Cs||$. Then we can reduce the residual by adding an $(n+1)$th concept to reduce error. The best such concept is the one that results in the minimum residual while keeping the coefficients positive:

$$\underset{c \in \mathcal{C}}{\text{argmin}} \min_{s, s_i > 0} ||w_k - [C|q_c]s|| \quad (6)$$

where $[C|q_c]$ indicates the matrix that adds the vector q_c for the candidate concept c to the columns of C.

2.2 Learning the Interpretable Basis from Annotations

For explaining an image classification task, we build the universe of candidate concepts $\mathcal{C}$ using the Broden dataset [3]. Broden includes pixel-level segmentations for a broad range of both high-level visual concepts such as objects and parts, as well as low-level concepts such as colors and materials. For each candidate concept c in Broden, we compute an embedding $q_c \in \mathcal{C} \subset \mathbb{R}^D$ as follows.

Since Broden provides pixel-level segmentations of every concept, we train a logistic binary classifier $h_c(a) = \text{sigmoid}(w_c^T a + b_c)$ to detect the presence of concept c. Training is done on a mix of images balancing c present or absent at the center, and hard negative mining is used to select informative negative examples during the training progress; the training procedure is detailed in Sect. 3.1. The learned w_c captures the features relevant to class c, but it is scaled in a way that is sensitive to the training conditions for c. To eliminate this arbitrary scaling, we standardize q_c as the normalized vector $q_c = (w_c - \overline{w}_c)/||w_c - \overline{w}_c||$.

2.3 Explaining a Prediction via Interpretable Basis Decomposition

The decomposition of any class weight vector w_k into interpretable components $C_k \subset \mathcal{C} \subset \mathbb{R}^D$ allows us to decompose the scoring of activations a into components of C_k in exactly the same way as we decompose w_k itself. This decomposition will provide an interpretable explanation of the classification.

Furthermore, if we include define a larger basis $C_k^* \supset C_k$ that adds the residual vector $r = w_k - C_k s$, we can say something stronger: projecting a into the basis of C_k^* captures the entire linear relationship described by the network's final layer score $h_k(a)$ for class k.

$$h_k(a) = w_k^T a + b_k \tag{7}$$

$$= (C_k^* s)^T a + b_k \tag{8}$$

$$= s_1 q_{c_1}^T a + \cdots + \underbrace{s_i q_{c_i}^T a}_{\text{contribution of concept } c_i} + \cdots + s_n q_{c_n}^T a + \underbrace{r^T a}_{\text{residual contribution}} + b_k \tag{9}$$

Thus we can decompose the score into contributions from each concept, and we can rank each concept according to its contribution. When the activation $a = \text{pool}(A)$ is derived by global average pooling of a convolutional layer A, we can commute the dot product inside the pooling operation to obtain a picture that localizes the contribution of concept c_i.

$$s_i q_{c_i}^T a = s_i q_{c_i}^T \text{pool}(A) \tag{10}$$

$$= \text{pool}(\underbrace{s_i\, q_{c_i}^T A}_{\text{heatmap for concept } c_i}) \tag{11}$$

The explanation we seek consists of the list of concepts c_i with the largest contributions to $h_k(a)$, along with the heatmaps $q_{c_i}^T A$ for each concept. The IBD heatmaps $q_{c_i}^T A$ are similar to the CAM heatmap $w_k^T A$ and can be used to reconstruct the CAM heatmap if they are all summed. However, instead of summarizing the locations contributing to a classification all at once, the interpretable basis decomposition separates the explanation into component heatmaps, each corresponding to a single concept that contributes to the decision.

Decomposing Gradients for GradCAM: Grad-CAM is an extension of CAM [28] to generate heatmap for networks with more than one final non-convolutional layers. Starting with the final convolutional featuremap $a = g(x)$, the Grad-CAM heatmap is formed by multiplying this activation by the pooled gradient of the higher layers $h(a)$ with respect class k.

$$w_k(a) = \frac{1}{Z} \sum_i \sum_j \nabla_a h_k(a) \tag{12}$$

Here the vector $w_k(a)$ plays the same role as the constant vector w_k in CAM: to create an interpretable basis decomposition, $w_k(a)$ can be decomposed as described in Eqs. 4–6 to create a componentwise decomposition of the Grad-CAM heatmap. Since $w_k(a)$ is a function of the input, each input will have its own interpretable basis.

3 Experiments

In this section, we describe how we learn an interpretable basis from an annotated dataset. Then we will show that the concepts of the interpretable basis that are associated with each prediction class of the networks sheds lights on the abstractions learned by each network. After that we use the interpretable basis decomposition to build explanations for the predictions given by the popular network architectures: AlexNet [15], VGG [13], ResNet (18 and 50 layers) [8], each trained scratch on ImageNet [4] and Places365 [29]. Finally we evaluate the fidelity of the explanations given by our method through Amazon Mechanical Turk and compare with other visual explanation generation methods.

3.1 Interpretable Basis Learned from Broden

We derive an interpretable basis from the fully annotated image dataset Broden [26]. Because our focus is to explain high-level features of the neural networks in terms of human interpretable concepts, we take a subset of the Broden dataset consisting of object and part concepts. The annotations of the objects and parts in Broden dataset originally come from the datasets ADE20K [30], Pascal Context [17], and Pascal Parts [6]. We filter out the concepts with fewer than 10 image samples, resulting to 660 concepts from 30K images used for training and testing.

For each concept in the Broden dataset, we learn a logistic binary classifier. The input of the classifier is a feature vector $a^{(i,j)} \in \mathbb{R}^D$ in activation $A \in \mathbb{R}^{D \times H \times W}$, and the output is the prediction of the probability of the concept appearing at $(i, j) \in (\text{range}(H), \text{range}(W))$. Our ground truth labels for the segmentations are obtained by downsampling the original concept masks to $H \times W$ size using nearest neighbor. Note that Broden provides multi-labeled segmentations, and there are often several concepts present in each downsampled pixel. Therefore it is appropriate for each concept classifier to be trained independent of each other. Because the number of positive samples and the number of negative samples for some concepts are highly unbalanced, we resample the training set to keep the ratio of positive and negative examples of each class fixed at 1:20 and use five rounds of hard negative mining.

We evaluate the accuracy of the deep features learned from several networks as shown in Table 1. All models are evaluated with mAP on a fixed validation set of Broden dataset.

Table 1. The mAP of the learned concept classifiers for the object and part concepts in the Broden dataset. The features used are the activations at the final convolutional layer of the network trained from scratch on Places365.

Model	AlexNet	VGG16	Resnet18	Resnet50
mAP	0.625	0.691	0.784	0.804

3.2 Explaining Classification Decision Boundaries

Interpretable Basis Decomposition assigns a basis of interpretable concepts for each output class. This basis can be seen as a set of *compositional rules* between the output classes and the elementary concepts in the Broden datasets. Different network learns a different set of such semantic rules for a prediction, thus by directly examining the interpretable basis decomposition of a network we can gain insight about the decision boundaries learned by each network for each class.

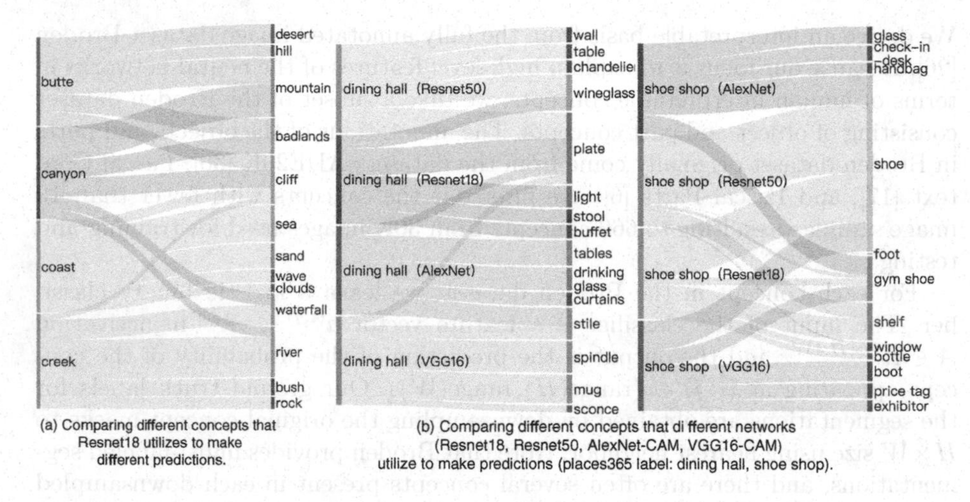

Fig. 3. Visualizing how different networks compose the final prediction classes using the Broden concepts. The left labels in each graph show the classes of Places365 and the right labels are the concepts of Broden. The thickness of each link between a class and a concept indicates the magnitude of the coefficient s_{c_i}.

Specifically, our method decomposes each weight vector w_k of class k in the last layer[1] as the sum $w_k = s_{c_1} q_{c_1} + \cdots + s_{c_n} q_{c_n} + r$, where q_{c_i} represents the embedding vector for concept c_i and s_{c_i} is the coefficient indicating its contribution to the overall class k. This decomposition indicates a relationship between the output class k and the concept c_i described by the coefficient s_{c_i}. In Fig. 3, we visualize a subset of Places365 classes k and how they are decomposed into Broden concepts c_i by different networks. The left column of the figure is the list of Places365 classes to be decomposed. The right column shows the related concepts from the Broden dataset. The thicknesses of the arcs between classes and concepts are drawn to show the magnitude of the coefficients s_{c_i}. The larger s_{c_i}, the more important concept c_i is to the prediction of class k.

[1] For this experiment, we replace the fc layers in AlexNet and VGG16 with a GAP layer and retrain them, similar to [28].

In Fig. 3(a), it can be seen how a single network composes concepts to constitute a variety of different prediction classes. Note that all the classes shown in (a) share the same concept "cliff" but differ in the importance given to this concept, which can be seen as different s_{c_i}. Figure 3(b), shows the different compositional rules that different networks use to make the same prediction for a class. For example, in the prediction class "shoe shop", all networks agree that "shoe" is a key element that contributes to this prediction, while they disagree on other elements. VGG16 treats "boot" and "price tag" as important indicators of a "shoe shop," while and AlexNet decomposes "shoe shop" into different concepts such as "glass" and "check-in-desk."

3.3 Explaining Image Predictions

Given the interpretable basis decomposition $w_k = s_{c_1} q_{c_1} + \cdots + s_{c_n} q_{c_n} + r$, the instance prediction result $w_k^T a$ is decomposed as $w_k^T a = s_{c_1} q_{c_1}^T a + \cdots + s_{c_n} q_{c_n}^T a + r^T a$ where each term $s_{c_i} q_{c_i}^T a$ can be regarded as the contribution of concept i to the final prediction. We rank the contribution scores and use the concept labels of the top contributed basis as an explanation for the prediction. Each term also corresponds to a contribution to the CAM or Grad-CAM salience heatmap.

Figure 4 shows qualitative results of visual explanations done by our method. For each sample, we show the input image, its prediction given by the network, the heatmaps generated by CAM [28] for Resnet18 and Resnet18, and the heatmaps generated by Grad-CAM heatmap [20] for AlexNet and VGG166, and the top 3 contributing interpretable basis components with their labels and numerical contribution.

In Fig. 4(a), we select three examples from Places365 in which VGG16 and ResNet18 make the same correct predictions. In two of the examples, the explanations provide evidence that VGG16 may be *right for the wrong reasons* in some cases: it matches the *airplane* concept to contribute to the *crosswalk* prediction, and it matches the sofa concept to contribute to its *market* prediction. In contrast, ResNet18 appears to be sensitive to more relevant concepts.

In Fig. 4(b), we show how our method can provide insight on an inconsistent prediction. ResNet18 classifies the image in last row as an *art school* because it sees features described as *hand* and *paper* and *drawing*, while VGG16 classifies the image as a *cafeteria* image because VGG16 it is sensitive to *table* and *chair* and *map* features. Both networks are incorrect because the table is covered with playing cards, not drawings or maps, and the correct label is *recreation room*.

In Fig. 4(c), we show the variations generated by different models for the same sample.

3.4 Human Evaluation of the Visual Explanations

To measure whether explanations provided by our method are reasonable and convincing to humans, we ask AMT raters to compare the quality of two different explanations for a prediction. We create explanations of decisions made by four different models (Resnet50, Resnet18, VGG16, and AlexNet, trained on

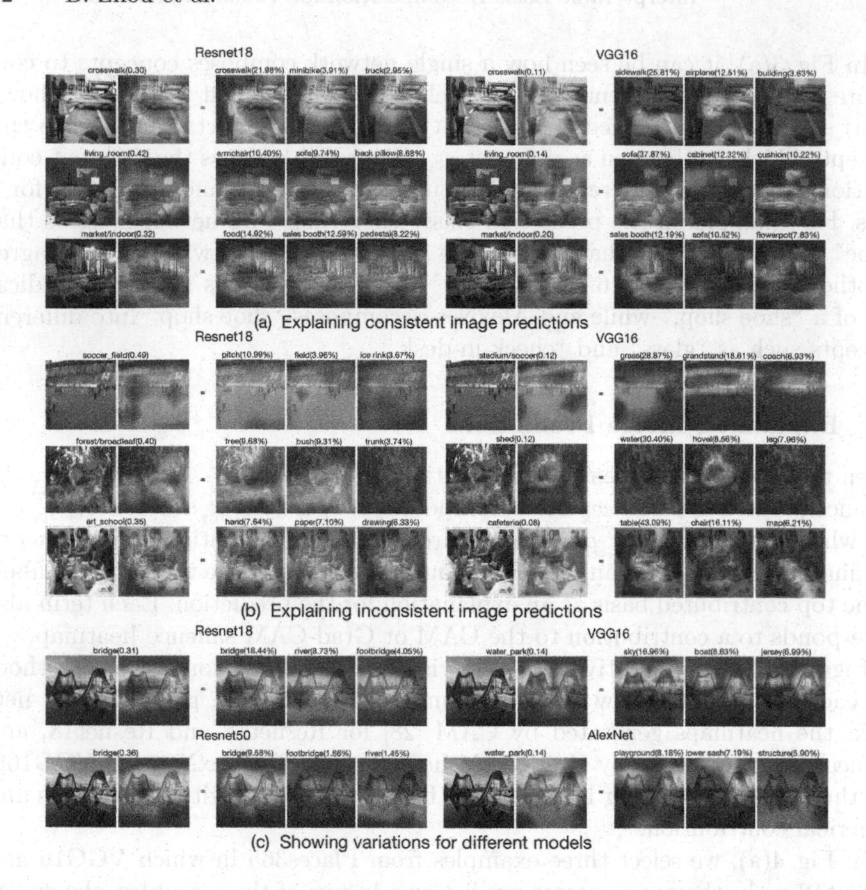

Fig. 4. Explaining specific predictions. The first image pair in each group contains original image (left) and single heatmap (right), with the predicted label and normalized prediction score in parentheses. Single heatmaps are CAM for ResNet and Grad-CAM for Alexnet and VGG. This is followed by three heatmaps corresponding to the three most significant terms in the interpretable basis decomposition for the prediction. The percentage contribution of each component to the score is shown. (a) Examples where two networks make the same prediction. (b) Explanations where two networks make different predictions. (c) Comparisons of different architectures.

Places365) using different explanation methods (Interpretable Basis Decomposition, Network Dissection, CAM and Grad-CAM).

The evaluation interface is shown in Fig. 5. In each comparison task, raters are shown two scene classification predictions with identical outcomes but with different explanations. One explanation is identified as Robot A and the other as Robot B, and raters are asked to decide which robot is more reasonable on a five-point Likert scale. Written comments about the difference are also collected. In the interface, heatmaps are represented as simple masks that highlight the top 20% of pixels in the heatmap; explanations are limited to four heatmaps; and each heatmap can be labeled with a named concept.

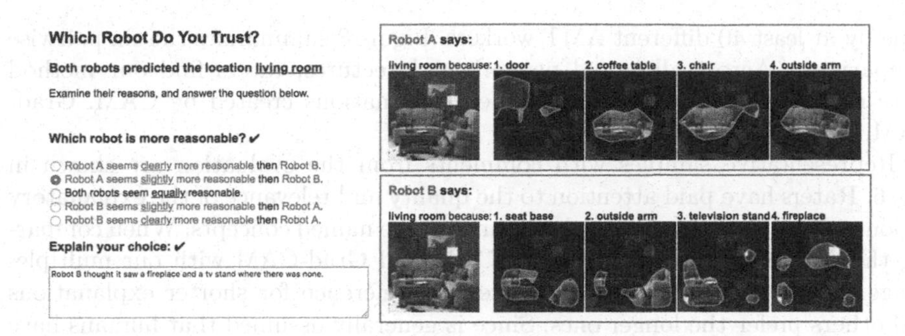

Fig. 5. Interface for human evaluations. Two different explanations of the same prediction are presented, and human raters are asked to evaluate which is more reasonable.

Baseline CAM, Grad-CAM, and Network Dissection Explanations. We compare our method to several simple baseline explanations. The first baselines are CAM [28] and Grad-CAM [20], which consist of a single salience heatmap for the image, showing the image regions that most contributed to the classification. Using the notation of Sect. 2.1, the CAM/Grad-CAM heatmap is given by weighting the pixels of the penultimate feature layer A according to the classification vector w_k, or to the pooled gradient $w_k(A)$:

$$\text{CAM}_k(A) \equiv w_k^T A \qquad \text{Grad-CAM}_k(A) \equiv w_k(A)^T A \tag{13}$$

The second baseline is a simple unit-wise decomposition of the heatmap as labeled by Network Dissection. In this baseline method, every heatmap corresponds to a single channel of the featuremap A that has an interpretation as given by Network Dissection [26]. This baseline explanation ranks channels according to the components i that contribute most to $w_k^T a = \sum_i w_{ki} a_i$. Using the notation of Sect. 2.1, this corresponds to choosing a fixed basis C where each concept vector is the unit vector in the ith dimension $q_{c_i} = e_i$, labeled according to Network Dissection. Heatmaps are given by:

$$\text{NetDissect}_{k,i}(A) \equiv e_i^T A, \quad \text{ranked by largest} w_{ki} a_i \tag{14}$$

CAM and the Network Dissection explanations can be thought of as extremal cases of Interpretable Basis Decomposition: CAM chooses no change in basis and visualizes the contributions from the activations directly; while Network Dissection always chooses the same unit-wise basis.

Comparing Explanation Methods Directly. In the first experiment, we compare explanations generated by our method head-to-head with explanations generated by Network Dissection [26] and CAM [28] and Grad-CAM [20]. In this experiment, both Robot A and Robot B are the same model making the same decision, but the decision is explained in two different ways. For each network and pair of explanation methods, 200 evaluations of pairs of explanations are done by at least 40 different AMT workers. Figure 8 summarizes the six pairwise comparisons. Across all tested network architectures, raters find our method more reasonable, on average, than then explanations created by CAM, Grad-CAM, and Network Dissection.

Representative samples with comments from the evaluation are shown in Fig. 6. Raters have paid attention to the quality and relevance of the explanatory regions as well as the quality and relevance of the named concepts. When comparing the single-image explanations of CAM and Grad-CAM with our multiple-image explanations, some raters express a preference for shorter explanations and others prefer the longer ones. Since is generally assumed that humans have a strong bias towards simpler explanations [10], it is interesting to find that, on average, human raters prefer our longer explanations. The second experiment, described next, controls for this bias by evaluating only comparisons where raters see the same type of explanation for both Robot A and Robot B.

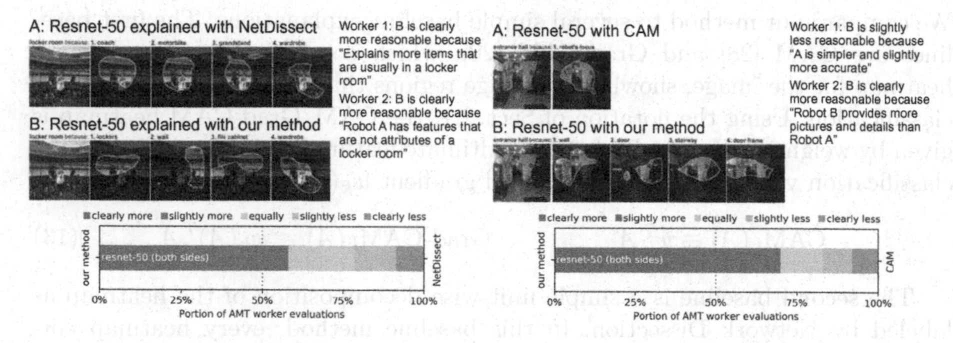

Fig. 6. Representative examples of human feedback in head-to-head comparisons of methods. For each image, one comparison is done. At left, explanations using Net Dissection and our method are compared on same ResNet50 decision. At right, explanations using CAM and our method are compared on another ResNet50 decision.

Comparing Evaluations of Model Trust. The second experiment evaluates the ability of users to evaluate trustworthiness of a model based on only a single pair of explanations. The ordinary way to evaluate the generalization ability of a model is to test its accuracy on a holdout set of many inputs. This experiment tests whether a human can compare two models based on a single comparison of explanations of identical decisions made by the models on one input image.

In this experiment, as shown in Fig. 7, explanations for both Robot A and Robot B are created using the same explanation method (either our method or CAM), but the underlying networks are different. One is always Resnet50, and the other is either AlexNet, VGG16, Resnet18, or a mirrored version of Resnet50 (resnet50*) where all the convolutions are horizontally flipped. Only explanations where both compared networks make the same decision are evaluated: as can be seen in the feedback, our explanation method allow raters to discern a quality

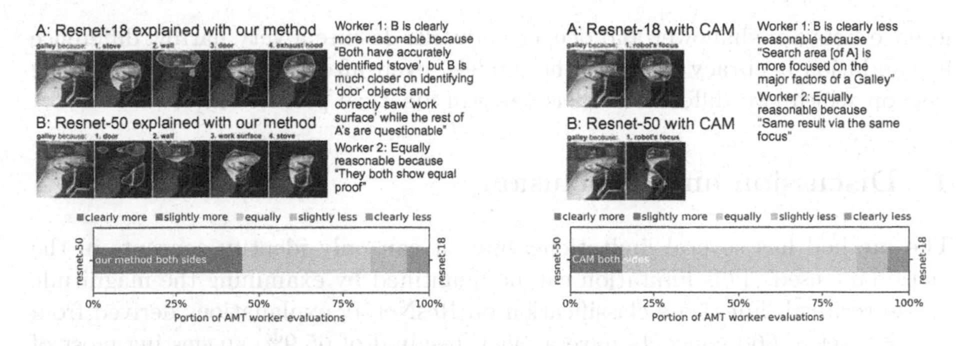

Fig. 7. Representative examples of human feedback in trust comparison. For each image, two independent comparisons are done. At left, a decision of ResNet50 and ResNet18 are compared using our method of explanation. At right, the same pair of decisions is compared using a CAM explanation.

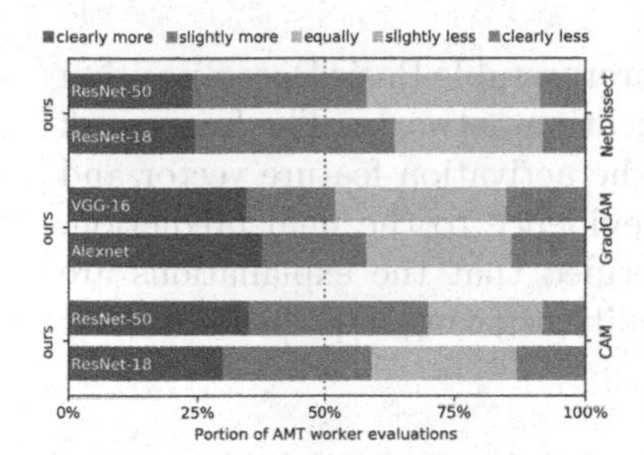

Fig. 8. Comparing different explanation methods side-by-side. Each bar keeps the network the same and compares our explanations to another method. Blue and green indicate ratings of explanations of our method that are clearly or slightly more reasonable, and yellow and orange indicate ratings for where our method is slightly or clearly less reasonable than a different explanation method. (Color figure online)

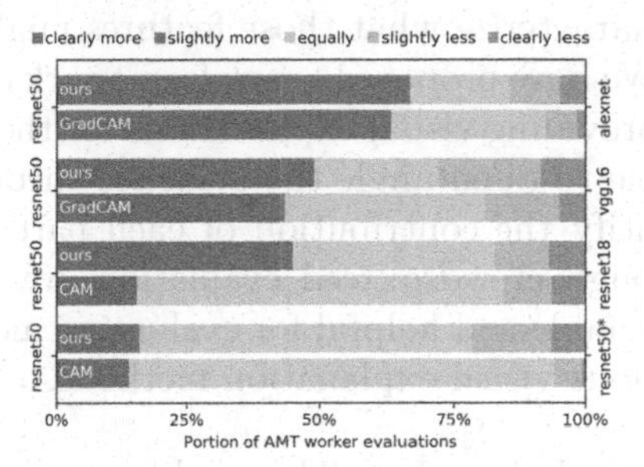

Fig. 9. Comparing ability of users to evaluate trust using different explanation methods. Each bar keeps the explanation method the same and compares ResNet50 to another model. Blue and green indicate evaluations where ResNet50 explanations are rated clearly and slightly more reasonable, and yellow and orange indicate explanations where ResNet50 is slightly and clearly less reasonable. (Color figure online)

difference between deeper and shallower methods, while the single-image CAM heatmap makes the two networks seem less different.

Figure 9 summarizes results across several different network architectures. With our explanation method, raters can identify that Resnet50 is more trustworthy than Alexnet, VGG16 and Resnet18; the performance is similar to or marginally better than Grad-CAM, and it outperforms CAM. Comparisons of two Resnet50 with each other are evaluated as mostly equivalent, as expected, under both methods. It is interesting to see that it is possible to discern the difference between shallower and deeper networks despite a very narrow difference in validation accuracy between the models, even after observing only a single case on which two different models perform identical predictions.

4 Discussion and Conclusion

The method has several limitations: first, it can only identify concepts in the dictionary used. This limitation can be quantified by examining the magnitude of the residual. For scene classification on ResNet50, explanations derived from our dataset of 660 concepts have a mean residual of 65.9%, suggesting most of the behavior of the network remains orthogonal to the explained concepts. A second limitation is that the residual is not guaranteed to approach zero even if the concept dictionary were vast: decisions may depend on visual features that do not correspond to *any* natural human concepts. New methods may be needed to characterize what those features might be.

We have proposed a new framework called Interpretable Basis Decomposition for providing visual explanations for the classification networks. The framework is able to disentangle the evidence encoded in the activation feature vector and quantify the contribution of each part of the evidence to the final prediction. Through crowdsourced evaluation, we have verified that the explanations are reasonable and helpful for evaluating model quality, showing improvements over previous visual explanation methods.

Acknowledgement. The work was partially funded by DARPA XAI program FA8750-18-C0004, the National Science Foundation under Grants No. 1524817, and the MIT-IBM Watson AI Lab. B. Zhou is supported by a Facebook Fellowship.

References

1. Antol, S., et al.: VQA: visual question answering. In: Proceedings of CVPR (2015)
2. Bach, S., Binder, A., Montavon, G., Klauschen, F., Müller, K.R., Samek, W.: On pixel-wise explanations for non-linear classifier decisions by layer-wise relevance propagation. PLoS ONE **10**(7), e0130140 (2015)
3. Bau, D., Zhou, B., Khosla, A., Oliva, A., Torralba, A.: Network dissection: quantifying interpretability of deep visual representations. In: Proceedings of CVPR (2017)
4. Deng, J., Dong, W., Socher, R., Li, L.J., Li, K., Fei-Fei, L.: ImageNet: a large-scale hierarchical image database. In: CVPR 2009 (2009)
5. Dosovitskiy, A., Brox, T.: Generating images with perceptual similarity metrics based on deep networks. In: Advances in Neural Information Processing Systems, pp. 658–666 (2016)
6. Everingham, M., Eslami, S.M.A., Van Gool, L., Williams, C.K.I., Winn, J., Zisserman, A.: The pascal visual object classes challenge: a retrospective. Int. J. Comput. Vis. **111**(1), 98–136 (2015)
7. Gonzalez-Garcia, A., Modolo, D., Ferrari, V.: Do semantic parts emerge in convolutional neural networks? Int. J. Comput. Vis. 1–19 (2017)

8. He, K., Zhang, X., Ren, S., Sun, J.: Deep residual learning for image recognition. arXiv preprint arXiv:1512.03385 (2015)
9. Hendricks, L.A., Akata, Z., Rohrbach, M., Donahue, J., Schiele, B., Darrell, T.: Generating visual explanations. In: Leibe, B., Matas, J., Sebe, N., Welling, M. (eds.) ECCV 2016. LNCS, vol. 9908, pp. 3–19. Springer, Cham (2016). https://doi.org/10.1007/978-3-319-46493-0_1
10. Herman, B.: The promise and peril of human evaluation for model interpretability. arXiv preprint arXiv:1711.07414 (2017)
11. Hyvärinen, A., Oja, E.: Independent component analysis: algorithms and applications. Neural Netw. **13**(4–5), 411–430 (2000)
12. Jolliffe, I.T.: Principal component analysis and factor analysis. In: Jolliffe, I.T. (ed.) Principal component analysis, pp. 115–128. Springer, New York (1986). https://doi.org/10.1007/978-1-4757-1904-8_7
13. K. Simonyan, A.Z.: Very deep convolutional networks for large-scale image recognition (2014)
14. Kim, B., Wattenberg, M., Gilmer, J., Cai, C., Wexler, J., Viegas, F., et al.: Interpretability beyond feature attribution: quantitative testing with concept activation vectors (TCAV). In: International Conference on Machine Learning (2018)
15. Krizhevsky, A., Sutskever, I., Hinton, G.E.: Imagenet classification with deep convolutional neural networks. In: Pereira, F., Burges, C.J.C., Bottou, L., Weinberger, K.Q. (eds.) Advances in Neural Information Processing Systems, vol. 25, pp. 1097–1105. Curran Associates, Inc. (2012). http://papers.nips.cc/paper/4824-imagenet-classification-with-deep-convolutional-neural-networks.pdf
16. Mahendran, A., Vedaldi, A.: Understanding deep image representations by inverting them. In: Proceedings of CVPR (2015)
17. Mottaghi, R., et al.: The role of context for object detection and semantic segmentation in the wild. In: IEEE Conference on Computer Vision and Pattern Recognition (CVPR) (2014)
18. Olah, C., et al.: The building blocks of interpretability. Distill (2018). https://doi.org/10.23915/distill.00010. https://distill.pub/2018/building-blocks
19. Russakovsky, O.: Imagenet large scale visual recognition challenge. Int. J. Comput. Vis. **115**, 211–252 (2015)
20. Selvaraju, R.R., Das, A., Vedantam, R., Cogswell, M., Parikh, D., Batra, D.: Grad-CAM: why did you say that? arXiv preprint arXiv:1611.07450 (2016)
21. Simonyan, K., Vedaldi, A., Zisserman, A.: Deep inside convolutional networks: visualising image classification models and saliency maps. In: International Conference on Learning Representations Workshop (2014)
22. Tenenbaum, J.B., De Silva, V., Langford, J.C.: A global geometric framework for nonlinear dimensionality reduction. Science **290**(5500), 2319–2323 (2000)
23. Tenenbaum, J.B., Freeman, W.T.: Separating style and content. In: Advances in Neural Information Processing Systems, pp. 662–668 (1997)
24. Vinyals, O., Toshev, A., Bengio, S., Erhan, D.: Show and tell: a neural image caption generator. In: Proceedings of CVPR. IEEE (2015)
25. Zeiler, M.D., Fergus, R.: Visualizing and understanding convolutional networks. In: Fleet, D., Pajdla, T., Schiele, B., Tuytelaars, T. (eds.) ECCV 2014. LNCS, vol. 8689, pp. 818–833. Springer, Cham (2014). https://doi.org/10.1007/978-3-319-10590-1_53
26. Zhou, B., Bau, D., Oliva, A., Torralba, A.: Interpreting deep visual representations via network dissection. IEEE Trans. Pattern Anal. Mach. Intell. (2018)

27. Zhou, B., Khosla, A., Lapedriza, A., Oliva, A., Torralba, A.: Object detectors emerge in deep scene CNNs. In: International Conference on Learning Representations (2015)
28. Zhou, B., Khosla, A., Lapedriza, A., Oliva, A., Torralba, A.: Learning deep features for discriminative localization. In: IEEE Conference on Computer Vision and Pattern Recognition (CVPR), pp. 2921–2929. IEEE (2016)
29. Zhou, B., Lapedriza, A., Xiao, J., Torralba, A., Oliva, A.: Learning deep features for scene recognition using places database. In: Advances in Neural Information Processing Systems (2014)
30. Zhou, B., Zhao, H., Puig, X., Fidler, S., Barriuso, A., Torralba, A.: Scene parsing through ADE20K dataset. In: Proceedings of the IEEE Conference on Computer Vision and Pattern Recognition (2017)

Partial Adversarial Domain Adaptation

Zhangjie Cao[1,2], Lijia Ma[1,2], Mingsheng Long[1,2(✉)], and Jianmin Wang[1,2]

[1] School of Software, Tsinghua University, Beijing, China
caozhangjie14@gmail.com, malijia15@gmail.com,
{mingsheng,jimwang}@tsinghua.edu.cn

[2] National Engineering Laboratory for Big Data Software, Beijing National Research Center for Information Science and Technology, Beijing, China

Abstract. Domain adversarial learning aligns the feature distributions across the source and target domains in a two-player minimax game. Existing domain adversarial networks generally assume identical label space across different domains. In the presence of big data, there is strong motivation of transferring deep models from existing big domains to unknown small domains. This paper introduces partial domain adaptation as a new domain adaptation scenario, which relaxes the fully shared label space assumption to that the source label space subsumes the target label space. Previous methods typically match the whole source domain to the target domain, which are vulnerable to negative transfer for the partial domain adaptation problem due to the large mismatch between label spaces. We present Partial Adversarial Domain Adaptation (PADA), which simultaneously alleviates negative transfer by down-weighing the data of outlier source classes for training both source classifier and domain adversary, and promotes positive transfer by matching the feature distributions in the shared label space. Experiments show that PADA exceeds state-of-the-art results for partial domain adaptation tasks on several datasets.

1 Introduction

Deep neural networks have made significant advances to a variety of machine learning problems and applications. However, the significant advances attribute to the availability of large-scale labeled data. Since manually labeling sufficient training data for various applications is often prohibitive, for problems short of labeled data, there is strong incentive to designing versatile algorithms to reduce the labeling consumption. Domain adaptation methods [1] enable the ability to leverage labeled data from a different but related source domain. At the core of these methods is the shift in data distributions across different domains, which hinders the generalization of predictive models to new target tasks [2].

Existing domain adaptation methods generally assume that the source and the target domains share identical label space but follow different distributions. These methods close the large gap between different domains by learning domain-invariant feature representations using both domain data but without using target labels, and apply the classifier trained on the source domain to the target

V. Ferrari et al. (Eds.): ECCV 2018, LNCS 11212, pp. 139–155, 2018.
https://doi.org/10.1007/978-3-030-01237-3_9

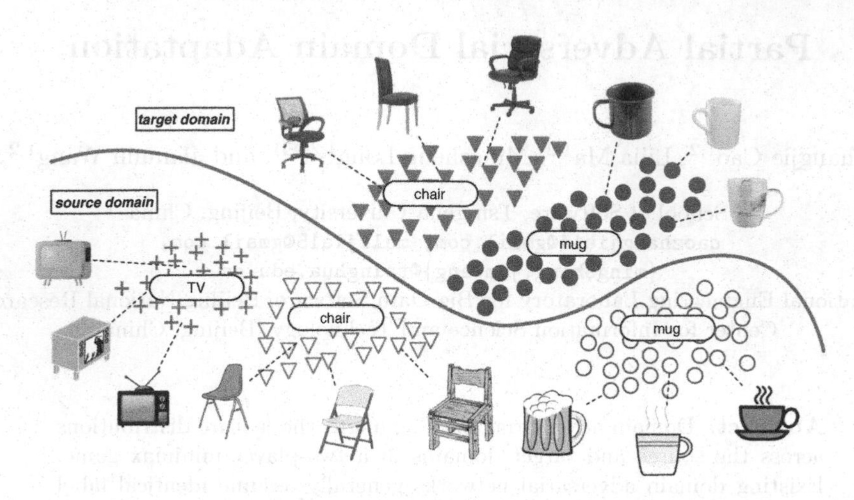

Fig. 1. The partial domain adaptation scenario introduced in this paper, where source label space ('TV', 'chair', 'mug') is a superset of target label space ('chair', 'mug'). This scenario is difficult as the source domain may have some outlier classes not appearing in the target domain, e.g. the 'TV' class. These outlier source classes will make the well-known negative transfer bottleneck more prominent. Another technical difficulty is that it is nontrivial to identify which classes are outlier source classes since the target classes are unknown during training. In this paper, we will tackle these challenges in an end-to-end deep learning framework, Partial Adversarial Domain Adaptation (PADA).

domain. Recent research has shown that deep networks can disentangle explanatory factors of variations underlying domains to learn more transferable features for domain adaptation [3–5]. Along this line, domain adaptation modules such as moment matching [6–9] and adversarial adaptation [10–12] have been embedded in deep networks to learn domain-transferable representations.

However, in real applications, it is usually not easy to find a source domain with identical label space as the target domain of interest. Thus, previous domain adaptation methods can hardly fit into proper datasets to train a domain-invariant model. Also, it is really cumbersome to seek for new source domains for emerging target domains. Thanks to the big data evolution, large-scale datasets with rich supervised information such as ImageNet-1K become accessible. As a common practice, ImageNet-1K is used as a universal repository to train deep models that are later fine-tuned to a variety of significantly different tasks. However, until now we can only reuse the learned features. And a natural ambition is to further transfer the classification layers of deep networks from a large dataset with supervision e.g. ImageNet, to a small target dataset without supervision e.g. Caltech-256. Since the large dataset is required to be big enough, it is reasonable to assume that its label space subsumes that of our target dataset.

Towards the aforementioned ambition, we introduce a novel *partial domain adaptation* problem, which assumes that the target label space is a subspace of the source label space. As shown in Fig. 1, this novel scenario is more general and challenging than standard domain adaptation, since the *outlier* source classes ('TV') will trigger negative transfer when discriminating the target classes ('chairs' and 'mug'). Negative transfer is the worst case that an adapted learner performs even worse than a supervised classifier trained solely on the source domain, which is the key bottleneck of domain adaptation to be widely adopted by practical applications [1]. Thus, matching the whole source and target domains as previous methods is not an effective solution to this new problem.

In this paper, we present Partial Adversarial Domain Adaptation (PADA), an end-to-end framework that largely extends the ability of domain adversarial adaptation approaches [10–12] to address the new partial domain adaptation scenario. PADA aligns the feature distributions of the source and target data in the shared label space and more importantly, identifies the irrelevant source data belonging to the outlier source classes and down-weighs their importance automatically. The key improvement over previous methods is the capability to simultaneously promote positive transfer of relevant source data and alleviate negative transfer of irrelevant source data. Experiments show that our models exceed state-of-the-art results for partial domain adaptation on public datasets.

2 Related Work

Domain adaptation [1] bridges different domains following different distributions to mitigate the burden of manual labeling for machine learning [13–16], computer vision [17–19] and natural language processing [20]. Supervised domain adaptation [11,21–23] exploits a few labeled data in the target domain. While supervised domain adaptation achieves significant performance, unsupervised domain adaptation [6–10,12] is more practical since no labeled data is required. We focus on unsupervised domain adaptation in this paper.

Deep networks disentangle different explanatory factors of variations in the learned representations [24] and manifest invariant factors underlying different populations that transfer well across similar tasks [5]. Therefore, we mainly focus on deep domain adaptation methods, which enables domain adaptation by reducing the distribution discrepancy of deep features across different domains and have been proved to yield state-of-the-art performance on several domain adaptation tasks. Maximum Mean Discrepancy (MMD) based methods [6,7,9] transfers deep convolutional networks (CNNs) by adding adaptation layers through which the kernel embeddings of distributions are matched by minimizing MMD. Residual transfer network [8] improves the MMD-based methods by adding a shortcut path and adopting entropy minimization criterion.

Driven by the popularity of generative adversarial networks (GANs), several methods [10,12] add a subnetwork as a domain discriminator on the last feature layers to discriminate features of different domains, while the deep features are learned to deceive the domain discriminator in a two-player game. Label Efficient Learning [25] addresses different label spaces by extending the entropy minimization criterion [8] over the pairwise similarity of a target image with each source image, enforcing each target image to be similar to only a few source images.

These methods may be restricted by the assumption that the source and target domains share the same label space, which does not hold in partial domain adaptation. Adaptive Deep Learning [26], somehow reduces the negative transfer of outlier classes by localizing the image regions more responsible for the domain shift as well as the regions that are shared among domains to guide the attention of the classifier. But for images with no regions related to the target domain, the attention mechanism may fail by wrongly localizing related regions.

3 Partial Adversarial Domain Adaptation

This paper introduces *partial domain adaptation*, a novel domain adaptation scenario where the source domain label space $\mathcal{C}_t$ is a superset of the target domain label space $\mathcal{C}_s$ i.e. $\mathcal{C}_t \subset \mathcal{C}_s$. This scenario generalizes standard domain adaptation with identical label spaces, and can be widely applied to real applications, since with the availability of big data, it is not difficult to find a large-scale dataset (e.g. ImageNet) and adapt our model trained on that dataset to any small-scale dataset of interest (e.g. Caltech-256), given the partial assumption holds. By this means, we can avoid burdensome work to provide supervised information for the target dataset.

Similar to standard domain adaptation, in partial domain adaptation we are also provided with a *source* domain $\mathcal{D}_s = \{(\mathbf{x}_i^s, y_i^s)\}_{i=1}^{n_s}$ of n_s labeled examples associated with $|\mathcal{C}_s|$ classes and a *target* domain $\mathcal{D}_t = \{\mathbf{x}_i^t\}_{i=1}^{n_t}$ of n_t unlabeled examples associated with $|\mathcal{C}_t|$ classes, but differently, we have $|\mathcal{C}_s| > |\mathcal{C}_t|$ in partial domain adaptation. The source and target domains are sampled from distributions p and q respectively. While in standard domain adaptation we have $p \neq q$, in partial domain adaptation, we further have $p_{\mathcal{C}_t} \neq q$, where $p_{\mathcal{C}_t}$ denotes the distribution of the source domain labeled data belonging to label space $\mathcal{C}_t$. The goal of this paper is to design a deep neural network that enables learning of transferable features $\mathbf{f} = G_f(\mathbf{x})$ and adaptive classifier $y = G_y(\mathbf{f})$ to close the domain gap, such that the target risk $\Pr_{(\mathbf{x},y)\sim q}[G_y(G_f(\mathbf{x})) \neq y]$ can be bounded by minimizing the source domain risk and the cross-domain discrepancy.

In standard domain adaptation, one of the main difficulties is that the target domain has no labeled data and thus the source classifier G_y trained on source domain $\mathcal{D}_s$ cannot be directly applied to target domain $\mathcal{D}_t$, due to the distribution discrepancy of $p \neq q$. In partial domain adaptation, another more difficult challenge is that we even do not know which part of the source domain label space $\mathcal{C}_s$ is shared with the target domain label space $\mathcal{C}_t$, because $\mathcal{C}_t$ is not known during training. This results in two technical difficulties. On one hand, the source domain labeled data belonging to *outlier* label space $\mathcal{C}_s \backslash \mathcal{C}_t$ will cause **negative transfer** effect to the overall performance. Existing deep domain adaptation methods [7,8,10,11] generally assume source domain and target domain have the same label space and match the whole distributions p and q, which are prone to negative transfer since the source and target label spaces are different and thus the outlier classes should not be matched. Thus, how to undo or at least decay the influence of the source labeled data in outlier label space $\mathcal{C}_s \backslash \mathcal{C}_t$ is the key to mitigating negative transfer. On the other hand, reducing the distribution discrepancy between $p_{\mathcal{C}_t}$ and q is crucial to enabling **positive transfer** in the shared label space $\mathcal{C}_t$. These two interleaving challenges should be tackled jointly through filtering out the negative influence of unrelated part of source domain and meanwhile enabling effective domain adaptation between related part of source domain and target domain.

In summary, we should tackle two challenges to enabling partial domain adaptation. **(1)** Mitigate negative transfer by filtering out unrelated source labeled data belonging to the outlier label space $\mathcal{C}_s \backslash \mathcal{C}_t$. **(2)** Promote positive transfer by maximally matching the data distributions $p_{\mathcal{C}_t}$ and q in the shared label space $\mathcal{C}_t$. We propose a partial domain adversarial network to address both challenges.

3.1 Domain Adversarial Neural Network

Domain adaptation is usually reduced to matching the feature distributions of the source and target domains. In the deep learning regime, this can be done by learning new feature representations such that the source and target domains are not distinguishable by a domain discriminator. This idea leads to the a series of domain adversarial neural networks (DANN) [10,11], achieving strong performance in standard domain adaptation with shared label space across domains. More formally, DANN is a two-player minimax game, where the first player is a domain discriminator G_d trained to distinguish the source domain from the target domain, and the second player is a feature extractor G_f simultaneously trained to confuse the domain discriminator.

In order to extract domain-transferable features $\mathbf{f}$, the parameters θ_f of the feature extractor G_f are learned by maximizing the loss of domain discriminator G_d, while the parameters θ_d of domain discriminator G_d are learned by minimizing the loss of the domain discriminator. In addition, the loss of source classifier G_y is also minimized to guarantee lower source domain classification error. The overall objective of the Domain Adversarial Neural Network (DANN) [10] is

$$
\begin{aligned}
C_0\left(\theta_f, \theta_y, \theta_d\right) = & \frac{1}{n_s} \sum_{\mathbf{x}_i \in \mathcal{D}_s} L_y\left(G_y\left(G_f\left(\mathbf{x}_i\right)\right), y_i\right) \\
& - \frac{\lambda}{n_s + n_t} \sum_{\mathbf{x}_i \in \mathcal{D}_s \cup \mathcal{D}_t} L_d\left(G_d\left(G_f\left(\mathbf{x}_i\right)\right), d_i\right)
\end{aligned}
\tag{1}
$$

where d_i is the domain label of $\mathbf{x}_i$, and λ is a hyper-parameter to trade off the two objectives L_y and L_d. After training convergence, the learned parameters $\hat{\theta}_f$, $\hat{\theta}_y$, $\hat{\theta}_d$ will deliver a saddle point of functional (1) in the minimax optimization:

$$
\begin{aligned}
(\hat{\theta}_f, \hat{\theta}_y) &= \arg\min_{\theta_f, \theta_y} C_0\left(\theta_f, \theta_y, \theta_d\right), \\
(\hat{\theta}_d) &= \arg\max_{\theta_d} C_0\left(\theta_f, \theta_y, \theta_d\right).
\end{aligned}
\tag{2}
$$

Domain adversarial neural network has been widely applied to standard domain adaptation where the source domain label space and target domain label space are exactly the same, $\mathcal{C}_s = \mathcal{C}_t$, proving powerful for computer vision problems.

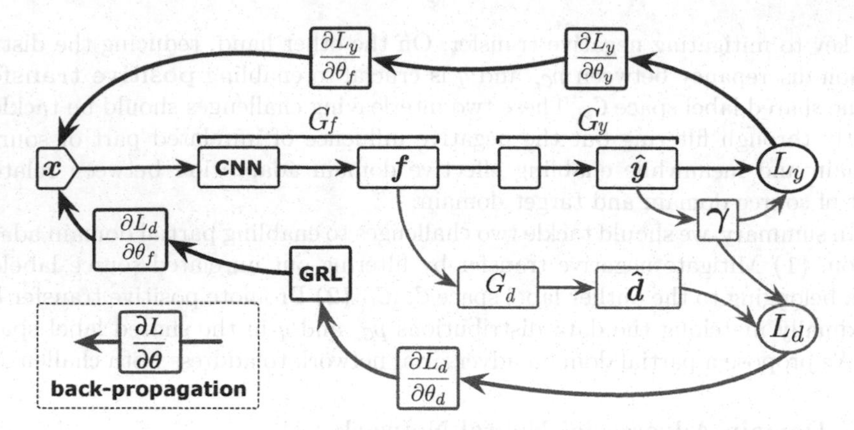

Fig. 2. The architecture of Partial Adversarial Domain Adaptation (PADA), where **f** is the extracted deep features, $\hat{\mathbf{y}}$ is the data label prediction (softmax probability), and $\hat{\mathbf{d}}$ is the domain label prediction; G_f is the feature extractor, G_y and L_y are the source classifier and its loss, G_d and L_d are the domain discriminator and its loss; γ is the class weights averaged over the label predictions of target data. GRL stands for Gradient Reversal Layer. The blue part shows the partial adversarial domain discriminator with weighting mechanism newly designed in this paper. *Best viewed in color*. (Color figure online)

3.2 Partial Adversarial Domain Adaptation

In partial domain adaptation, the target domain label space is a subspace of the source domain label space, $\mathcal{C}_t \subset \mathcal{C}_s$. Thus, aligning the whole source domain distribution p and target domain distribution q will cause negative transfer since the target domain is also forced to match the *outlier* label space $\mathcal{C}_s \backslash \mathcal{C}_t$ in the source domain. And the larger the outlier label space $\mathcal{C}_s \backslash \mathcal{C}_t$ compared to the target label space $\mathcal{C}_t$, the severer the negative transfer will be. Note that $|\mathcal{C}_t| \ll |\mathcal{C}_s \backslash \mathcal{C}_t|$ is a natural scenario of partial domain adaptation in real world applications because we usually need to transfer from very large-scale source dataset (e.g. ImageNet) to relatively small target dataset. Thus, when performing adversarial domain adaptation to mitigate **negative transfer**, we should reduce or even eliminate the negative influence of the outlier source classes as well as the associated source labeled data in $\mathcal{C}_s \backslash \mathcal{C}_t$.

In this paper, we propose a novel approach, Partial Adversarial Domain Adaptation (**PADA**), to address the aforementioned challenges. The key idea is to down-weigh the contribution of the source data within the outlier source label space $\mathcal{C}_s \backslash \mathcal{C}_t$ to the training of both the source classifier and the domain adversarial network. This idea is implemented in a novel architecture shown in Fig. 2. For now the technical problem is reduced to finding some metrics that have large difference between the source outlier classes and the target classes, in order to discriminate the source data belonging to the outlier label space and the target label space. Fortunately, we observe that the output of the source classifier $\hat{\mathbf{y}}_i = G_y(\mathbf{x}_i)$ to each data point $\mathbf{x}_i$ gives a probability distribution over the source label space $\mathcal{C}_s$. This distribution well characterizes the probability of assigning $\mathbf{x}_i$ to each of the $|\mathcal{C}_s|$ classes. Since the source outlier label space and target label space are disjoint, the target data should be significantly dissimilar to the source data in the outlier label space. Hence, the probabilities of assigning the target data to the source outlier classes, i.e. $y_i^k, \mathbf{x}_i \in \mathcal{D}_t, k \in \mathcal{C}_s \backslash \mathcal{C}_t$, should be sufficiently small. It is possible that the source classifier can make a few mistakes on some target data and assign large probabilities to false classes or even to outlier classes. To eliminate the influence of such few mistakes, we propose to average the label predictions $\hat{\mathbf{y}}_i$ on all target data. Hence, the weight indicating the contribution of each source class to the training can be calculated as follows

$$\boldsymbol{\gamma} = \frac{1}{n_t} \sum_{i=1}^{n_t} \hat{\mathbf{y}}_i, \tag{3}$$

where $\boldsymbol{\gamma}$ is a $|\mathcal{C}_s|$-dimensional weight vector quantifying the contribution of each source class. Specifically, since the target data are not belonging to the source outlier label space, the corresponding weight for source outlier labels $\gamma_k, k \in \mathcal{C}_s \backslash \mathcal{C}_t$ will be significantly smaller than the weight for target labels $\gamma_k, k \in \mathcal{C}_t$. In practice, it is possible that some of the weights are very small, since by definition, $\sum_{k=1}^{|\mathcal{C}_s|} \gamma_k = 1$. Thus, we normalize the weight $\boldsymbol{\gamma}$ by dividing its largest element, i.e. $\boldsymbol{\gamma} \leftarrow \boldsymbol{\gamma} / \max(\boldsymbol{\gamma})$.

We enable partial adversarial domain adaptation by down-weighing the contributions of all source data belonging to the outlier source label space $\mathcal{C}_s \backslash \mathcal{C}_t$. This is achieved by applying the class weight vector $\boldsymbol{\gamma}$ to both the source label classifier and the partial adversarial domain discriminator over the source domain data. The objective of the Partial Adversarial Domain Adaptation (**PADA**) is

$$\begin{aligned} C(\theta_f, \theta_y, \theta_d) = & \frac{1}{n_s} \sum_{\mathbf{x}_i \in \mathcal{D}_s} \gamma_{y_i} L_y (G_y (G_f (\mathbf{x}_i)), y_i) \\ & - \frac{\lambda}{n_s} \sum_{\mathbf{x}_i \in \mathcal{D}_s} \gamma_{y_i} L_d (G_d (G_f (\mathbf{x}_i)), d_i) \\ & - \frac{\lambda}{n_t} \sum_{\mathbf{x}_i \in \mathcal{D}_t} L_d (G_d (G_f (\mathbf{x}_i)), d_i) \end{aligned} \tag{4}$$

where y_i is the ground truth label of source point $\mathbf{x}_i$ while γ_{y_i} is the corresponding class weight, and λ is a hyper-parameter that trade-offs the source label classifier and the partial adversarial domain discriminator in the optimization problem.

The optimization problem finds the optimal parameters $\hat{\theta}_f$, $\hat{\theta}_y$ and $\hat{\theta}_d$ by

$$\begin{aligned} (\hat{\theta}_f, \hat{\theta}_y) &= \arg\min_{\theta_f, \theta_y} C(\theta_f, \theta_y, \theta_d), \\ (\hat{\theta}_d) &= \arg\max_{\theta_d} C(\theta_f, \theta_y, \theta_d). \end{aligned} \tag{5}$$

Note that the proposed PADA approach as in Eq. (5) successfully enables partial domain adaptation, which simultaneously mitigates negative transfer by filtering out outlier source classes $\mathcal{C}_s \backslash \mathcal{C}_t$, and promotes positive transfer by maximally matching the data distributions $p_{\mathcal{C}_t}$ and q in the shared label space $\mathcal{C}_t$.

4 Experiments

We conduct experiments on three datasets to evaluate our partial adversarial domain adaptation approach against several state-of-the-art deep transfer learning methods. Codes and datasets is available at https://github.com/thuml/PADA.

4.1 Setup

The evaluation is conducted on three standard domain adaptation datasets: Office-31, Office-Home and ImageNet-Caltech.

Office-31 [17] is a most widely-used dataset for visual domain adaptation, with 4,652 images and 31 categories from three distinct domains: *Amazon* (**A**), which contains images downloaded from amazon.com, *Webcam* (**W**) and *DSLR* (**D**), which contain images respectively taken by web camera and digital SLR camera. We denote the three domains as **A**, **W** and **D**. We use the ten categories shared by *Office-31* and *Caltech-256* and select images of these ten categories in each domain of *Office-31* as target domains. We evaluate all methods across six partial domain adaptation tasks $\mathbf{A} \rightarrow \mathbf{W}$, $\mathbf{D} \rightarrow \mathbf{W}$, $\mathbf{W} \rightarrow \mathbf{D}$, $\mathbf{A} \rightarrow \mathbf{D}$, $\mathbf{D} \rightarrow \mathbf{A}$ and $\mathbf{W} \rightarrow \mathbf{A}$. Note that each source domain here contains 31 categories and each target domain here contains 10 categories.

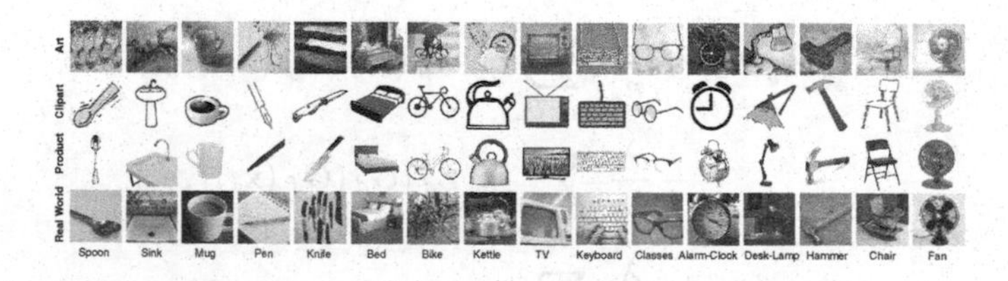

Fig. 3. Example images of the Office-Home dataset.

Office-Home [27] was released recently as a more challenging domain adaptation dataset, crawled through several search engines and online image directories, as shown in Fig. 3. It consists of 4 different domains: Artistic images (**Ar**), Clipart images (**Cl**), Product images (**Pr**) and Real-World images (**Rw**). For each domain, the dataset contains images from 65 object categories. In each transfer task, when a domain is used as source domain, we use the images from all 65 categories; when a domain is used as target domain, we choose (in alphabetic order) the first 25 categories as target categories and select all images of these 25 categories as target domain. Denoting the four domains as **Ar**, **Cl**, **Pr**, **Rw**, we can build twelve partial domain adaptation tasks: $\mathbf{Ar} \rightarrow \mathbf{Cl}$, $\mathbf{Ar} \rightarrow \mathbf{Pr}$,

Ar $\rightarrow$ **Rw**, **Cl** $\rightarrow$ **Ar**, **Cl** $\rightarrow$ **Pr**, **Cl** $\rightarrow$ **Rw**, **Pr** $\rightarrow$ **Ar**, **Pr** $\rightarrow$ **Cl**, **Pr** $\rightarrow$ **Rw**, **Rw** $\rightarrow$ **Ar**, **Rw** $\rightarrow$ **Cl** and **Rw** $\rightarrow$ **Pr**. The transfer tasks from this dataset can test the performance of our method on more visually-dissimilar domains.

ImageNet-Caltech is constructed from *ImageNet-1K* [28] and *Caltech-256*. They share 84 common classes, and thus we form two partial domain adaptation tasks: **ImageNet-1K** $\rightarrow$ **Caltech-84** and **Caltech-256** $\rightarrow$ **ImageNet-84**. To prevent the effect of the pre-trained model on ImageNet, we adopt the validation set when ImageNet is used as target domain and adopt the training set when ImageNet is used as source domain. This setting represents the performance on partial domain adaptation tasks with large number of classes.

VisDA2017 has two domains where one consists of synthetic 2D renderings of 3D models and the other consists of photo-realistic images or real images. They have 12 classes in common. We choose (in alphabetic order) the first 6 categories as target categories and select all images of these 6 categories as target domain and construct two domain adaptation tasks: **Real-12** $\rightarrow$ **Synthetic-6** and **Synthetic-12** $\rightarrow$ **Real-6**. In this dataset, both domains have large number of images, which validates the efficiency of PADA on large-scale dataset.

We compare the performance of **PADA** with state-of-the-art transfer learning and deep learning methods: **ResNet-50** [29], Deep Adaptation Network (**DAN**) [7], Residual Transfer Networks (**RTN**) [8], Domain Adversarial Neural Network (**DANN**) [10], Adversarial Discriminative Domain Adaptation (**ADDA**) [12] and Joint Adaptation Network (**JAN**) [9]. In order to go deeper with the efficacy of the proposed partial adversarial mechanism, we perform ablation study by evaluating two variants of **PADA**: (1) **PADA-classifier** is the variant without the weight on the source classifier; (2) **PADA-adversarial** is the variant without the weight on the partial adversarial domain discriminator.

We follow standard evaluation protocols and use all labeled source data and all unlabeled target data for unsupervised domain adaptation [7,17]. We compare the average classification accuracy of each partial domain adaptation task using three random experiments. For MMD-based methods (DAN and RTN), we use Gaussian kernel with bandwidth set to median pairwise squared distances on training data, i.e. the median heuristic [30]. For all methods, we use importance-weighted cross-validation [31] on labeled source data and unlabeled target data to select their hyper-parameters.

We implement all deep methods in **PyTorch**, and fine-tune from PyTorch-provided models of ResNet-50 [32] pre-trained on ImageNet. We add a bottleneck layer between the $res5c$ and fc layers as DANN [10] except for the transfer task **ImageNet (1000 classes)** $\rightarrow$ **Caltech (84 classes)**, since the pre-trained model is trained on ImageNet dataset and it can fully exploit the advantage of pre-trained model with the original network parameters. For PADA, we fine-tune all the feature layers and train the bottleneck layer, the classifier layer and the partial adversarial domain discriminator though back-propagation. Since these new layers are trained from scratch, we set their learning rate to be 10 times that of the other layers. We use mini-batch stochastic gradient descent (SGD) with momentum of 0.9 and the learning rate strategy implemented in DANN [10]: the learning rate is adjusted during SGD using $\eta_p = \frac{\eta_0}{(1+\alpha p)^\gamma}$, where p is the training progress changing from 0 to 1, η_0, while α and γ are optimized with importance-weighted cross-validation [31] on one task of a dataset and fixed for all the other tasks of this dataset. As **PADA** works stably across different tasks, the penalty of adversarial networks is increased progressively from 0 to 1 as DANN [10].

4.2 Results

The classification accuracy results of partial domain adaptation on the twelve tasks of *Office-Home*, the six tasks of *Office-31*, and the two tasks of *ImageNet-Caltech* are shown in Tables 1, 2, and 3, respectively. PADA outperforms all comparison methods on all the tasks. In particular, PADA substantially improves the average accuracy by huge margins on *Office-31* of small domain gaps, e.g. **Amazon → Webcam**, and on *Office-Home* of large domain gaps, e.g. **Clipart → Real World**. It is inspiring that PADA achieves considerable accuracy gains on **ImageNet → Caltech** with large-scale source domain and target domain. These consistent results suggest that PADA can learn transferable features and classifiers for partial domain adaptation on all the partial domain adaptation tasks, varying by the sizes of the source and target domains and the gaps between the source and target domains.

Previous deep domain adaptation methods, including those based on adversarial networks (e.g. DANN) and those based on MMD (e.g. DAN), perform worse than standard ResNet on most of the tasks, showing the undesirable influence of the **negative transfer** effect. Adversarial-network based methods try to learn deep features that deceive the domain discriminator, while MMD based methods align the source and target feature distributions. Both mechanisms will mix up the whole source and target domains in the feature space, since they aim to match all classes of source domain to target domain. But there are classes in the source domain that do not exist in the target domain, a.k.a. outlier source classes. This explains their weak performance for partial domain adaptation. Not surprisingly, PADA outperforms all the comparison methods by large margins, indicating that PADA can effectively avoid negative transfer by eliminating the influence of outlier source classes irrelevant to the target domain.

Methods based on domain-adversarial networks perform worse than MMD-based methods. Since adversarial-network based methods try to confuse a nonlinear domain discriminator, it has more power to match source and target domains and is more vulnerable to the outlier source classes than MMD based methods. Although PADA is also based on adversarial networks, it establishes a partial adversarial domain discriminator, which down-weighs the source data in the outlier source classes to eliminate the negative influence of the outlier source classes and meanwhile enhances the positive influence of shared classes, successfully boosting the performance of partial domain adaptation.

Among previous deep domain adaptation methods, RTN is the only approach that generally performs better than ResNet-50. The remedy of RTN is to introduce entropy minimization criterion which can increase the contributions of target data and thus implicitly avoid the impact of outlier source data to some

Table 1. Accuracy of partial domain adaptation tasks on *Office-Home* (ResNet-50)

Method	Office-Home												
	Ar→Cl	**Ar→Pr**	**Ar→Rw**	**Cl→Ar**	**Cl→Pr**	**Cl→Rw**	**Pr→Ar**	**Pr→Cl**	**Pr→Rw**	**Rw→Ar**	**Rw→Cl**	**Rw→Pr**	Avg
ResNet [32]	38.57	60.78	75.21	39.94	48.12	52.90	49.68	30.91	70.79	65.38	41.79	70.42	53.71
DAN [7]	44.36	61.79	74.49	41.78	45.21	54.11	46.92	38.14	68.42	64.37	45.37	68.85	54.48
DANN [10]	44.89	54.06	68.97	36.27	34.34	45.22	44.08	38.03	68.69	52.98	34.68	46.50	47.39
RTN [8]	49.37	64.33	76.19	47.56	51.74	57.67	50.38	41.45	75.53	70.17	51.82	74.78	59.25
PADA-classifier	47.45	58.15	74.32	43.62	37.93	51.91	48.21	41.67	71.62	67.13	52.98	71.60	55.55
PADA-adversarial	47.10	47.54	67.53	41.32	39.72	52.70	43.07	35.94	70.51	61.80	48.24	70.08	52.13
PADA	**51.95**	**67**	**78.74**	**52.16**	**53.78**	**59.03**	**52.61**	**43.22**	**78.79**	**73.73**	**56.6**	**77.09**	**62.06**

Table 2. Accuracy of partial domain adaptation tasks on *Office-31* (ResNet-50)

Method	Office-31						
	A → W	D → W	W → D	A → D	D → A	W → A	Avg
ResNet [32]	54.52	94.57	94.27	65.61	73.17	71.71	75.64
DAN [7]	46.44	53.56	58.60	42.68	65.66	65.34	55.38
DANN [10]	41.35	46.78	38.85	41.36	41.34	44.68	42.39
ADDA [12]	43.65	46.48	40.12	43.66	42.76	45.95	43.77
RTN [8]	75.25	97.12	98.32	66.88	85.59	85.70	84.81
JAN [9]	43.39	53.56	41.40	35.67	51.04	51.57	46.11
LEL [25]	73.22	93.90	96.82	76.43	83.62	84.76	84.79
PADA-classifier	83.12	99.32	100	80.16	90.13	92.34	90.85
PADA-adversarial	65.76	97.29	97.45	77.07	87.27	87.37	85.37
PADA	**86.54**	**99.32**	**100**	**82.17**	**92.69**	**95.41**	**92.69**

Table 3. Classification accuracy on *ImageNet-Caltech* and *VisDA2017* (ResNet-50)

Method	ImageNet-Caltech			VisDA2017		
	ImageNet → Caltech	Caltech → ImageNet	Avg	Real → Synthetic	Synthetic → Real	Avg
ResNet [32]	71.65	66.14	68.90	64.28	45.26	54.77
DAN [7]	71.57	66.48	69.03	68.35	47.60	57.98
DANN [10]	68.67	52.97	60.82	73.84	51.01	62.43
RTN [8]	72.24	68.33	70.29	72.93	50.04	61.49
PADA	**75.03**	**70.48**	**72.76**	76.50	53.53	65.01

degree. Unlike RTN, PADA does not use the entropy minimization criterion. But we observe that PADA outperforms RTN in all the partial domain adaptation tasks, proving that RTN also suffers from the negative transfer effect and even the residual branch of RTN, originally designed for large domain gap, cannot bridge the large discrepancy between source and target caused by different label spaces. These results validate that our partial adversarial mechanism is versatile enough to jointly promote positive transfer from relevant source domain data (belonging to target label space) and circumvent negative transfer from irrelevant source domain data (belonging to outlier source label space).

We perform ablation study of PADA by comparing the PADA variants in Tables 1 and 2. We can make some insightful observations from the results. **(1)** PADA outperforms PADA-classifier, proving that using weighting mechanism on the source classifier can reduce the influence of the source data in the outlier classes and focus the source classifier more on the source data belonging to the target label space. **(2)** PADA outperforms PADA-adversarial with large margin, which proves that our weighting mechanism on the domain adversarial network can assign small weight on the outlier classes and down-weigh the source data of the outlier classes. In this way, PADA is able to avoid matching the whole source domain and target domain and boost performance of partial domain adaptation.

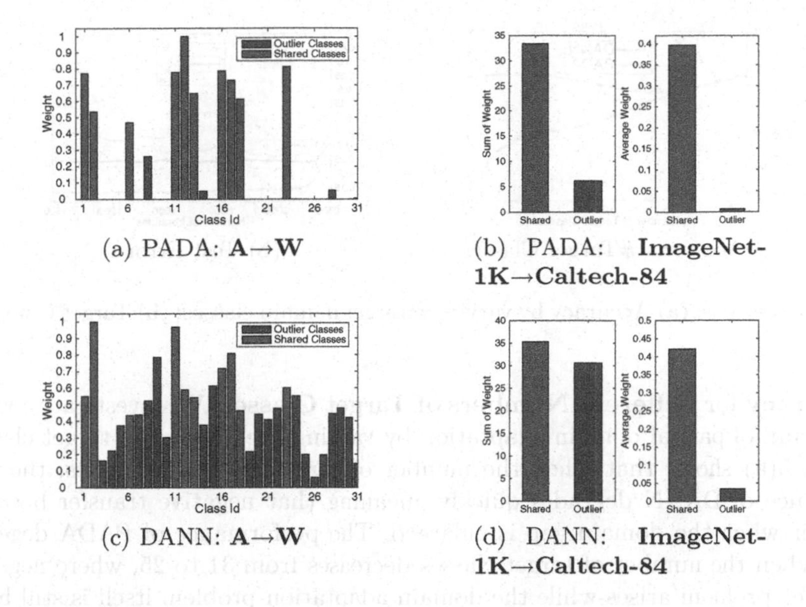

(a) PADA: **A**→**W**

(b) PADA: **ImageNet-1K**→**Caltech-84**

(c) DANN: **A**→**W**

(d) DANN: **ImageNet-1K**→**Caltech-84**

Fig. 4. Histograms of class weights learned by PADA and DANN on two typical tasks.

4.3 Empirical Analysis

Statistics of Class Weights: We illustrate the learned class weight for each class in our weighting mechanism on the task **A** (31 classes) → **W** (10 classes) in Fig. 4(a). Since it is difficult to visualize all the 1000 weights in one plot, we visualize the sum and average of the weights of all classes on the task **ImageNet-1K** → **Caltech-84** in Fig. 4(b). As shown in Fig. 4(a), our partial adversarial mechanism assigns much larger weights to the shared classes than to the outlier classes. It is inspiring that and some outlier classes even have nearly zero weights, by carefully observing the plot for task **A** → **W**. Not only for task with small number of classes, our partial adversarial mechanism also works well on dataset with large number of classes, as shown in Fig. 4(b). In task **ImageNet-1K** → **Caltech-84**, the average weights of the shared classes are significantly larger than those of the outlier classes. Note that even though the number of the outlier classes is much larger than that of the shared classes, the sum of the weights for shared classes is still larger than the sum of the weights for outlier classes. These results prove that PADA can automatically discriminate the shared and outlier classes and down-weigh the outlier classes data.

We also show the corresponding class weights learned by DANN on task **A** (31 classes) → **W** (10 classes) in Fig. 4(c), and task **ImageNet-1K** → **Caltech-84** in Fig. 4(d). The results clearly demonstrate that the weights for outlier source classes are still substantially large, which cannot down-weigh these harmful outlier classes in the domain adversarial learning procedure. As a result, these outlier source classes will cause severe negative transfer, as shown in Tables 1 and 2.

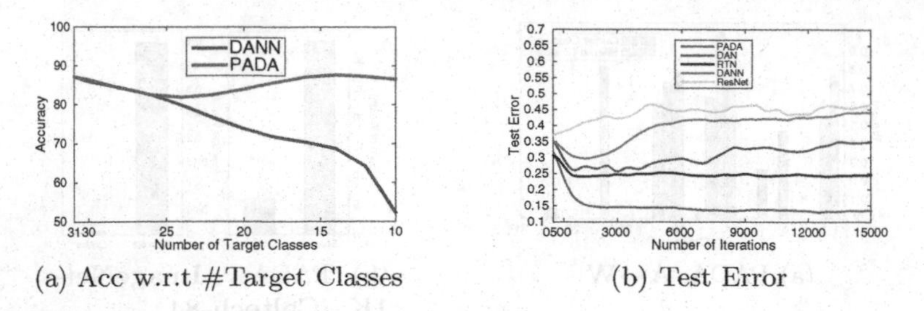

(a) Acc w.r.t #Target Classes (b) Test Error

Fig. 5. Analysis: (a) Accuracy by varying #target domain classes; (b) Target test error.

Accuracy for Different Numbers of Target Classes: We investigate a wider spectrum of partial domain adaptation by varying the number of target classes. Figure 5(a) shows that when the number of target classes decreases, the performance of DANN degrades quickly, meaning that negative transfer becomes severer when the domain gap is enlarged. The performance of PADA degenerates when the number of target classes decreases from 31 to 25, where negative transfer problem arises while the domain adaptation problem itself is still hard; but it increases when the number of target classes decreases from 25 to 10, where the domain adaptation problem itself becomes easier. The margin that PADA outperforms DANN becomes larger when the number of target classes decreases. Note that PADA performs comparably to DANN in standard domain adaptation when the number of target classes is 31, meaning that the weighting mechanism will not wrongly filter out classes when there are no outlier classes.

Convergence Performance: We examine the convergence of PADA by studying the test error through training process. As shown in Fig. 5(b), the test errors of ResNet, DAN and DANN are increasing due to negative transfer. Their test errors are not stable as well, attributed to the possibility that the target domain is falsely matched to different parts of the source domain during the training process. RTN converges very fast depending on the entropy minimization criterion, but it converges to a higher test error. PADA converges fast and stably to the lowest test error, implying that it can be trained efficiently and stably to tackle partial domain adaptation problems.

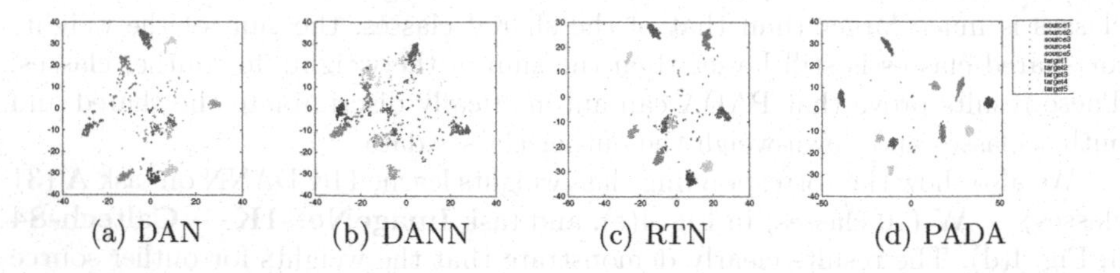

(a) DAN (b) DANN (c) RTN (d) PADA

Fig. 6. The t-SNE visualization of DAN, DANN, RTN, and PADA with class info.

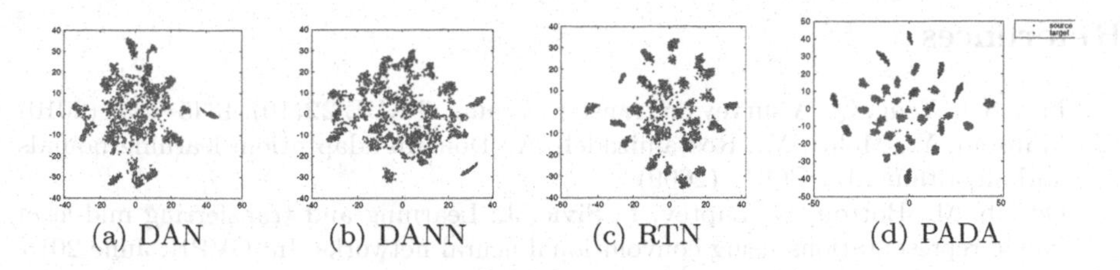

Fig. 7. The t-SNE visualization of DAN, DANN, RTN, and PADA with domain info.

Feature Visualization: We visualize the t-SNE embeddings [4] of the bottleneck representations by DAN, DANN, RTN and PADA on the partial domain adaptation task **A** (31 classes) → **W** (10 classes) in Fig. 6(a)–(d) (with class information) and Fig. 7(a)–(d) (with domain information). We randomly select five classes in the source domain not shared with target domain and five classes shared with target domain. **(1)** Fig. 6(a), (b) show that the bottleneck features are mixed all together, meaning that DAN and DANN cannot discriminate both source and target classes very well; Fig. 7(a)–(b) show that the target data are aligned to all source classes including those outlier ones, which triggers negative transfer. **(2)** Fig. 6(b), (c) show that RTN discriminates the source domain well but the features of most target data are very close to the source data even to the wrong source classes; Fig. 7(c) further indicates that RTN tends to draw target data close to all source classes even to those not existing in target domain. Thus, their performance on target data degenerates due to negative transfer. **(3)** Figs. 6(d) and 7(d) show that PADA can discriminate different classes in both source and target while the target data are close to the right source classes, while the outlier source classes cannot influence the target classes. These in-depth results show the versatility of the weighting mechanism.

5 Conclusion

This paper presented a novel approach to partial domain adaptation. Unlike previous adversarial domain adaptation methods that match the whole source and target domains based on the shared label space assumption, the proposed approach simultaneously circumvents negative transfer by down-weighing the outlier source classes and promotes positive transfer by maximally matching the data distributions in the shared label space. Our approach successfully tackles partial domain adaptation problem where source label space subsumes target label space, testified by extensive experiments on various benchmark datasets.

Acknowledgements. This work is supported by National Key R&D Program of China (2016YFB1000701), and National Natural Science Foundation of China (61772299, 61672313, 71690231).

References

1. Pan, S.J., Yang, Q.: A survey on transfer learning. TKDE **22**(10), 1345–1359 (2010)
2. Mansour, Y., Mohri, M., Rostamizadeh, A.: Domain adaptation: learning bounds and algorithms. In: COLT (2009)
3. Oquab, M., Bottou, L., Laptev, I., Sivic, J.: Learning and transferring mid-level image representations using convolutional neural networks. In: CVPR, June 2013
4. Donahue, J., et al.: DeCAF: a deep convolutional activation feature for generic visual recognition. In: ICML (2014)
5. Yosinski, J., Clune, J., Bengio, Y., Lipson, H.: How transferable are features in deep neural networks? In: NIPS (2014)
6. Tzeng, E., Hoffman, J., Zhang, N., Saenko, K., Darrell, T.: Deep domain confusion: maximizing for domain invariance (2014)
7. Long, M., Cao, Y., Wang, J., Jordan, M.I.: Learning transferable features with deep adaptation networks. In: ICML (2015)
8. Long, M., Zhu, H., Wang, J., Jordan, M.I.: Unsupervised domain adaptation with residual transfer networks. In: NIPS, pp. 136–144 (2016)
9. Long, M., Zhu, H., Wang, J., Jordan, M.I.: Deep transfer learning with joint adaptation networks. In: ICML, pp. 2208–2217 (2017)
10. Ganin, Y., Lempitsky, V.: Unsupervised domain adaptation by backpropagation. In: ICML (2015)
11. Tzeng, E., Hoffman, J., Zhang, N., Saenko, K., Darrell, T.: Simultaneous deep transfer across domains and tasks. In: ICCV (2015)
12. Hoffman, J., Tzeng, E., Darrell, T., Saenko, K.: Simultaneous deep transfer across domains and tasks. In: Csurka, G. (ed.) Domain Adaptation in Computer Vision Applications. ACVPR, pp. 173–187. Springer, Cham (2017). https://doi.org/10.1007/978-3-319-58347-1_9
13. Pan, S.J., Tsang, I.W., Kwok, J.T., Yang, Q.: Domain adaptation via transfer component analysis. TNNLS **22**(2), 199–210 (2011)
14. Duan, L., Tsang, I.W., Xu, D.: Domain transfer multiple kernel learning. TPAMI **34**(3), 465–479 (2012)
15. Zhang, K., Schölkopf, B., Muandet, K., Wang, Z.: Domain adaptation under target and conditional shift. In: ICML (2013)
16. Wang, X., Schneider, J.: Flexible transfer learning under support and model shift. In: NIPS (2014)
17. Saenko, K., Kulis, B., Fritz, M., Darrell, T.: Adapting visual category models to new domains. In: Daniilidis, K., Maragos, P., Paragios, N. (eds.) ECCV 2010, Part IV. LNCS, vol. 6314, pp. 213–226. Springer, Heidelberg (2010). https://doi.org/10.1007/978-3-642-15561-1_16
18. Gong, B., Shi, Y., Sha, F., Grauman, K.: Geodesic flow kernel for unsupervised domain adaptation. In: CVPR (2012)
19. Hoffman, J., et al.: LSDA: Large scale detection through adaptation. In: NIPS (2014)
20. Collobert, R., Weston, J., Bottou, L., Karlen, M., Kavukcuoglu, K., Kuksa, P.: Natural language processing (almost) from scratch. JMLR **12**, 2493–2537 (2011)
21. Koniusz, P., Tas, Y., Porikli, F.: Domain adaptation by mixture of alignments of second- or higher-order scatter tensors. In: CVPR, July 2017
22. Motiian, S., Piccirilli, M., Adjeroh, D.A., Doretto, G.: Unified deep supervised domain adaptation and generalization. In: ICCV, October 2017
23. Motiian, S., et al., (eds.): NIPS. Curran Associates, Inc., pp. 6670–6680 (2017)

24. Bengio, Y., Courville, A., Vincent, P.: Representation learning: a review and new perspectives. TPAMI **35**(8), 1798–1828 (2013)
25. Luo, Z., Zou, Y., Hoffman, J., Fei-Fei, L.F.: Label efficient learning of transferable representations acrosss domains and tasks. In: Guyon, I. (eds.) NIPS. Curran Associates, Inc., pp. 165–177 (2017)
26. Angeletti, G., Caputo, B., Tommasi, T.: Adaptive deep learning through visual domain localization. CoRR abs/1802.08833 (2018)
27. Venkateswara, H., Eusebio, J., Chakraborty, S., Panchanathan, S.: Deep hashing network for unsupervised domain adaptation. In: CVPR (2017)
28. Russakovsky, O., et al.: ImageNet large scale visual recognition challenge. IJCV **115**(3), 211–252 (2015)
29. He, K., Zhang, X., Ren, S., Sun, J.: Deep residual learning for image recognition. In: CVPR (2016)
30. Gretton, A., et al.: Optimal kernel choice for large-scale two-sample tests. In: NIPS (2012)
31. Sugiyama, M., Krauledat, M., Muller, K.R.: Covariate shift adaptation by importance weighted cross validation. JMLR **8**(May), 985–1005 (2007)
32. Krizhevsky, A., Sutskever, I., Hinton, G.E.: Imagenet classification with deep convolutional neural networks. In: NIPS (2012)

How Local Is the Local Diversity? Reinforcing Sequential Determinantal Point Processes with Dynamic Ground Sets for Supervised Video Summarization

Yandong Li[1,2](✉), Liqiang Wang[1], Tianbao Yang[3], and Boqing Gong[4]

[1] University of Central Florida, Orlando, FL, USA
lyndon.leeseu@outlook.com
[2] Jiulong Lake Campus, Southeast University, Nanjing 211189, Jiangsu Province, P.R. China
[3] University of Iowa, Iowa City, IA, USA
[4] Tencent AI Lab, Seattle, WA, USA

Abstract. The large volume of video content and high viewing frequency demand automatic video summarization algorithms, of which a key property is the capability of modeling diversity. If videos are lengthy like hours-long egocentric videos, it is necessary to track the temporal structures of the videos and enforce local diversity. The local diversity refers to that the shots selected from a short time duration are diverse but visually similar shots are allowed to co-exist in the summary if they appear far apart in the video. In this paper, we propose a novel probabilistic model, built upon SeqDPP, to dynamically control the time span of a video segment upon which the local diversity is imposed. In particular, we enable SeqDPP to learn to automatically infer *how local the local diversity is supposed to be* from the input video. The resulting model is extremely involved to train by the hallmark maximum likelihood estimation (MLE), which further suffers from the exposure bias and non-differentiable evaluation metrics. To tackle these problems, we instead devise a reinforcement learning algorithm for training the proposed model. Extensive experiments verify the advantages of our model and the new learning algorithm over MLE-based methods.

1 Introduction

The Internet age has come to such a new phase that high-definition videos are both ubiquitous and dominant in the IP traffic featured by the boom of video sharing websites, online movies and television shows, and the emerging live video streaming services. Some statistics indicate that about 300 h of video are uploaded to YouTube per minute and more than 500 million hours of video are watched on YouTube daily. Such a large volume of video content and high viewing frequency demand automatic video summarization algorithms. By distilling important events from the original video and condensing them to a short

V. Ferrari et al. (Eds.): ECCV 2018, LNCS 11212, pp. 156–174, 2018.
https://doi.org/10.1007/978-3-030-01237-3_10

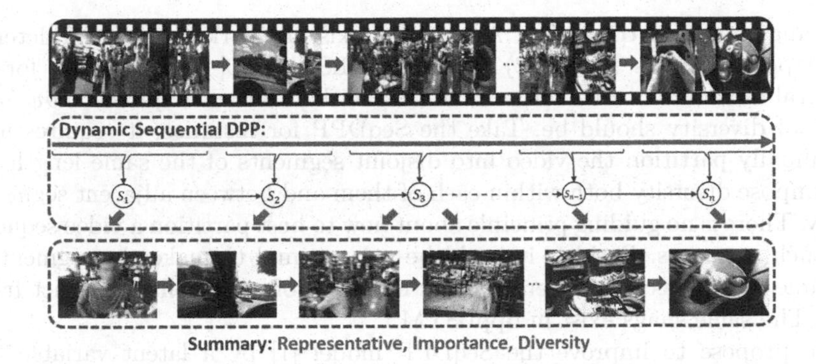

Fig. 1. Dynamic Sequential DPP (DySeqDPP) for video summarization

video clip (or a story board, text description, etc.), video summarization has a great potential in many real-world applications.

Video summarization has been one of the basic research areas in the fields of computer vision and multimedia for decades [2]. A variety of techniques have been proposed for different scenarios of video summarization. In general, a good video summary is supposed to describe main events [3–5] happened in the video and meanwhile remove the video shots that are redundant [6,7] and/or unimportant [8,9].

We consider video summarization as a *diverse* subset selection problem: given a video that can be seen a collection of shots, the goal is to select a subset from the collection to summarize the whole video. This view opens the door for supervised learning approaches to video summarization [1,10–13] that fit subset selection models to the video summaries annotated by users. Unlike the conventional unsupervised video summarization methods [3–5,7–9,14,15], the supervised ones implicitly infer users' intentions and summarization criteria as opposed to domain experts' handcrafting.

In the supervised video summarization models, a key factor they are supposed to encompass is the diversity of the selected subset of video shots. This is often imposed by submodularity [10,16] and determinant [1,11,17]. When a video sequence is short, **global diversity** over the whole sequence seems like a natural choice [10,11].

However, if the videos are lengthy like the egocentric videos that are often hours long, it is necessary to track the temporal structures of the videos and enforce **local diversity** instead [1,18]. The local diversity refers to that the shots selected from a short time duration are diverse but visually similar shots are allowed to co-exist in the summary if they appear far apart in the video. Consider a video sequence that is about "leaving home for shopping in the morning and then coming back home to have lunch". Although the video shots of the "home" scene in the morning may be similar to those at noon, the summary should contain some shots of both in order to make the summary a complete story carried by the video.

In this paper, we are mainly interested in summarizing extremely lengthy (e.g., egocentric) videos and, accordingly, models that are capable of observing the **local diversity**. Among the existing works, sequential determinantal point process (SeqDPP) [1] and dppLSTM [19] both account for the temporal dynamics of the videos. However, neither of them explores *"how local"* the local diversity should be. Take the SeqDPP for instance, it requires users to manually partition the video into disjoint segments of the same length and then impose diversity both within each of them and between adjacent segments, locally. There is no guiding principle about how to best partition a video sequence into such segments. Besides, it could be sub-optimal to make the segments of the same length because different types of events often unroll at distinct frame rates. The same snags exist in dppLSTM.

We propose to improve the SeqDPP model [1] by a latent variable that dynamically controls the time span of a segment upon which the local diversity is then defined in the form of a conditional DPP. In other words, we enable SeqDPP to learn to automatically infer *how local the local diversity is* in the input video. Figure 1 illustrates our main idea. Given an input video shown on the top panel, our dynamic SeqDPP seeks the appropriate and possibly different lengths of the segments (cf. the middle panel) from which it selects video shots (the bottom panel) and places them on a story board or links them into a short video clip as the summary of the video.

Another contribution of this paper is a novel reinforcement learning algorithm for the proposed dynamic SeqDPP (DySeqDPP). While DySeqDPP seems like a straightforward extension to the vanilla SeqDPP, it is less obvious how to efficiently train the model. The DPPs [20] and its variants (e.g., SeqDPP [1], dppLSTM [19], and SH-DPP [17]) are almost all trained by the hallmark maximum likelihood estimation (MLE) except for the large-margin DPP [21] and Bayesian DPP [22]. However, it is often difficult to maximize the likelihood of a sequential model with latent variables; gradient ascent fails to track the statistical structure, and the EM algorithm [23] becomes involved and inefficient unless one assumes special compositions of a sequential model [24].

In light of these challenges, we instead provide a reinforcement learning perspective for understanding SeqDPPs. The proposed DySeqDPP is used as a policy by an agent to interact with the environment—the input video. Accordingly, we train this DySeqDPP model by policy gradient descent [25]. Not only we do not have to explicitly deal with the latent variables, but also we benefit from the flexible reward functions in policy gradient descent—we can bridge the training and validation phases of the summarizer by defining the reward function as some evaluation metric(s).

We evaluate this dynamic SeqDPP model on standard video summarization datasets. Extensive results show that it significantly outperforms competing baselines especially the vanilla SeqDPP, verifying the necessity of dynamically determining how local the local diversity is. The rest of the paper is organized as follows. Section 2 discusses some related existing video summarization works. After that, we describe our dynamic SeqDPP and the reinforcement learning algorithm in Sect. 4. We report empirical results in Sect. 5 and then conclude the paper by Sect. 6.

2 Related Work

2.1 Video Summarization

Different algorithms for automatic video summarization are generally designed by the same principles. Those informative guidelines contain three main factors: (1) individual interestingness or relevance [8,9], which means selecting frames/shots that are important in the video; (2) representativeness [3–5], which means the summary should contain the main event of the videos; (3) collective diversity or coverage [6,7], which is to reduce redundant frames/shots without losing much information. These factors are used in most of the existing works. Next, we review the representative approaches in two common classes, unsupervised and supervised video summarization.

Unsupervised Video Summarization: A variety of prior works is designed based on basic visual quality like low-level appearance and motion cues [3–9,14,15, 26]. Graph models are utilized for event detection in some approaches [5,26]. In general, the criteria applied in those methods for making decisions about including or excluding shots are devised by the system developers empirically. Besides, some approaches leverage Web images for video summarization based on the assumption that the static Web pictures tend to contain information of interest to people, so the Web images reveal user-oriented importance selecting video shots/frames [4,27–29].

Supervised Video Summarization: Recently, several explorations on supervised video summarization have been exerted for various goals [1,8–13,17–19,30]. They achieve superior performance over the traditional unsupervised clustering algorithms. Among them, Gygli *et al.* try to add some supervised flavor to optimize mixture objectives with learning each criterion's weight [10,12]. A hierarchical model has been proposed to learn with few labels, and it is optimized to generate video summary containing interesting objects [30]. Egocentric videos [31] can be compacted with importance of people and objects [8]; on the other hand, Zheng *et al.* explicitly consider how one sub-event leads to another in order to provide a better sense of story for those kinds of videos [9]. Meanwhile, Yao *et al.* propose a pairwise deep ranking model to highlight video segments of first-person videos [32]. In conclusion, supervised methods are capable of utilizing the intentions of users about what a qualified video summary is rather than designing the systems only relying on the experts' own perspective.

Besides, as a powerful diverse subset selection model, the determinantal point process (DPP) has been widely used for video summarization. For instance, Gong *et al.* propose the first supervised video summarization method [1] (SeqDPP) as far as we know, it models local diversity to capture the temporal information of videos rather than modeling global diversity. Combining long short-term memory (LSTM) with DPPs has been studied in [19] to model the variable-range temporal dependency and diversity among video frames at the same time. Effort has been spent to study transferring summary structures from annotated videos to unseen test videos in [11]. Sharghi *et al.* explore the query-focused video summarization in [17,18]. Large margin separation principle has been leveraged for DPPs to estimate parameters in [13].

We will provide more details of DPPs and SeqDPP in Sects. 3.1 and 3.2.

Reinforcement learning (RL) provides a unified solution to both problems above. The REINFORCE algorithm [38] is utilized to train recurrent neural network [33]. Rennie *et al.* borrow ideas from [33] in the image captioning task and obtain very promising results [39]. We note that the use of RL in those contexts is icing on the case in the sense that, while RL boosts the results to some degree, the MLE is still applicable. For our DySeqDPP model, however, RL becomes a necessary choice because it is highly involved to handle the latent variables in DySeqDPP by MLE.

3 Background: DPP and SeqDPP

We briefly review the determinantal point process (DPP) and the sequential DPP (SeqDPP) in this section. It will become clear soon how the former promotes diversity in the selected subsets and the latter enables local diversity.

3.1 DPPs

A discrete DPP defines a distribution over the subsets of a ground set and assigns high probability to a subset if its items are diverse from each other. The notion of diversity is induced by a kernel matrix whose entries can be understood as pairwise similarities between the items. The more similar two items are, the less likely they co-occur in a subset sampled from the DPP.

More concretely, given a ground set $\mathcal{Y} = \{1, 2, \ldots, \mathsf{N}\}$ of N items, let $\boldsymbol{K} \in \mathbb{R}^{\mathsf{N}\times\mathsf{N}}$ be a symmetric positive semidefinite matrix, called the kernel of DPP. It measures pairwise similarities between the N items. A distribution over a random subset $Y \subseteq \mathcal{Y}$ is a DPP, if for every $\boldsymbol{y} \subseteq \mathcal{Y}$ we have

$$P_{dpp}(\boldsymbol{y} \subseteq Y; \boldsymbol{K}) = \det(\boldsymbol{K}_{\boldsymbol{y}}), \tag{1}$$

where $P_{dpp}(\cdot)$ is the probability of an event, $\boldsymbol{K}_{\boldsymbol{y}}$ denotes a squared submatrix of $\boldsymbol{K}$ with rows and columns indexed by $\boldsymbol{y}$, and $\det(\cdot)$ is the determinant of a matrix. All the eigenvalues of the kernel matrix $\boldsymbol{K}$ are between 0 and 1. Since $P(i, j \in Y; \boldsymbol{K}) = K_{ii}K_{jj} - K_{ij}^2$, *i.e.*, the probability of any two items i, j co-existing in the random subset Y is discounted by their similarity K_{ij}. In other words, the subsets whose items are less similar to each other are assigned higher probabilities than the other subsets.

L-Ensemble. In practice, it is often more convenient to use the so-called L-ensemble DPP that directly assigns atomic probabilities to all the possible subsets of the ground set. Let $\boldsymbol{L}$ denote a symmetric positive semidefinite matrix in $\mathbb{R}^{\mathsf{N}\times\mathsf{N}}$. The L-ensemble DPP draws a subset $\boldsymbol{y} \subseteq \mathcal{Y}$ with probability

$$P_L(Y = \boldsymbol{y}; \boldsymbol{L}) = \det(\boldsymbol{L}_{\boldsymbol{y}})/\det(\boldsymbol{L} + \boldsymbol{I}), \tag{2}$$

where $\boldsymbol{I}$ is an identity matrix. The corresponding marginal kernel that defines the marginal probability in (1) is given by $\boldsymbol{K} = \boldsymbol{L}(\boldsymbol{L} + \boldsymbol{I})^{-1}$.

Conditional DPP. One of the appealing properties of DPP is that there exists an analytic form of its conditional distribution. For any $\boldsymbol{y}_1 \subseteq \mathcal{Y}$ and $\boldsymbol{y}_0 \subseteq \mathcal{Y}$, $\boldsymbol{y}_1 \cap \boldsymbol{y}_0 = \emptyset$,

$$P_L(Y = \boldsymbol{y}_1 \cup \boldsymbol{y}_0 | \boldsymbol{y}_0 \subseteq Y; \boldsymbol{L}) = \det(\boldsymbol{L}_{\boldsymbol{y}_1 \cup \boldsymbol{y}_0}) / \det(\boldsymbol{L} + \boldsymbol{I}_{\mathcal{Y} \setminus \boldsymbol{y}_0}), \tag{3}$$

where $\boldsymbol{I}_{\mathcal{Y} \setminus \boldsymbol{y}_0}$ is a matrix with ones in the diagonal entries indexed by $\mathcal{Y} \setminus \boldsymbol{y}_0$ and zeros everywhere else. Kulesza and Taskar have written an excellent tutorial about DPPs [40].

3.2 Sequential DPPs

A sequential DPP (SeqDPP) [1] was proposed for supervised video summarization. It adheres to the inherent temporal structure in video sequences, thus overcoming the deficiency of DPPs which treat video frames/shots as randomly permutable items. The main technique is to use the conditional DPPs to construct a Markov chain.

Given a long video sequence $\mathcal{V}$, we partition it into T disjoint yet consecutive short segments $\bigcup_{t=1}^{\mathsf{T}} \mathcal{V}_t = \mathcal{V}$. At the t-th time step, SeqDPP selects a diverse subset of items (e.g., frames or shots), by a variable $X_t \subseteq \mathcal{V}_t$, from the corresponding segment conditioning on the items $\boldsymbol{x}_{t-1} \subseteq \mathcal{V}_{t-1}$ selected from the immediate past segment. This subset selection variable X_t follows a distribution given by the conditional DPP,

$$P_{seq}(X_t = \boldsymbol{x}_t | X_{t-1} = \boldsymbol{x}_{t-1}, \mathcal{V}_t) := P_L(Y_t = \boldsymbol{x}_t \cup \boldsymbol{x}_{t-1} | \boldsymbol{x}_{t-1} \subseteq Y_t; \boldsymbol{L}^t) \tag{4}$$

$$= \det(\boldsymbol{L}^t_{\boldsymbol{x}_t \cup \boldsymbol{x}_{t-1}}) / \det(\boldsymbol{L}^t + \boldsymbol{I}^t_{\mathcal{V}_t}), \tag{5}$$

where $P_L(Y_t; \boldsymbol{L}^t)$ is an L-ensemble with the ground set $\boldsymbol{x}_{t-1} \cup \mathcal{V}_t$. Denote by $\boldsymbol{x}_0 = \emptyset$. The SeqDPP over all the subset selection variables is factorized as

$$P_{seq}(\{X_t = \boldsymbol{x}_t\}_{t=1}^{\mathsf{T}}, \mathcal{V}) = \prod_{t=1}^{\mathsf{T}} P_{seq}(X_t = \boldsymbol{x}_t | X_{t-1} = \boldsymbol{x}_{t-1}, \mathcal{V}_t). \tag{6}$$

Figure 2 illustrates SeqDPP and compares it to the vanilla DPP and Markov DPP [41]. Unlike the vanilla or Markov DPPs which considers the video frames/shots as orderless items, SeqDPP maintains the temporal order among the segments and yet ignores it among the frames/shots within an individual segment, locally. Furthermore, it retains the diversity property for adjacent video segments but not for those that are far apart. Indeed, users may want to keep visually similar video clips in the summary if they are far apart in a lengthy video in order to tell a complete story of the video.

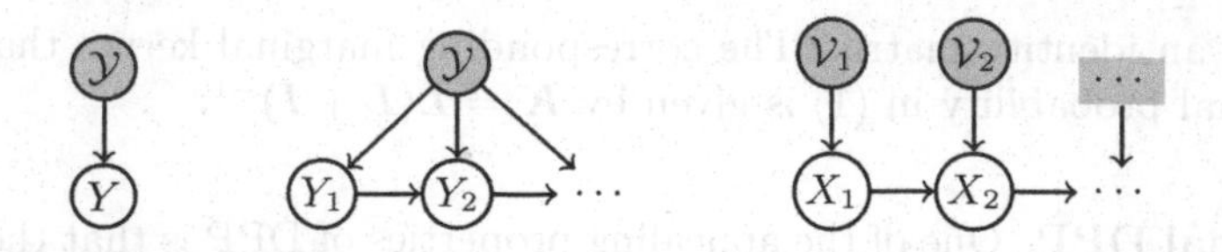

Fig. 2. From left to right: Determinantal point process (DPP) [40], Markov DPP [41], and sequential DPP (SeqDPP) [1]. The ground sets are denoted by the shaded nodes.

3.3 Reinforcement Learning

Consider an agent that takes actions according to some policy to interact with the environment. Following the popular Markov decision process (MDP) formalism, we describe the problem by $(\mathcal{S}, \mathcal{A}, P, R, \gamma)$, where $\mathcal{S}$ and $\mathcal{A}$ are the state (s) space and action (a) space, respectively, $P(s_{t+1}|s_t, a_t)$ is a state transition distribution, $R(s_{t+1}; s_t, a_t)$ is a reward the agent receives if it takes action a_t at state s_t and results in state s_{t+1}, and $\gamma \in (0, 1)$ is a discount factor. A policy is denoted by $\pi : \mathcal{S} \mapsto \mathcal{A}$, which is essentially a conditional distribution $\pi(a_t|s_t)$ over the actions given any state. Reinforcement learning aims to find the agent a policy that maximizes the expected total discounted reward $\mathbb{E}_\pi \sum_{i=0}^{\infty} \gamma^i R_{t+i}$ starting from time step t.

4 Reinforcing Dynamic SeqDPPs

We are now ready to present our dynamic SeqDPP (DySeqDPP) along with a reinforcement learning algorithm for estimating the model parameters.

4.1 DySeqDPP

We describe the DySeqDPP model using the MDP formalism $(\mathcal{S}, \mathcal{A}, P, R, \gamma)$ so that the corresponding learning algorithm follows naturally. We note that, in addition to the new DySeqDPP, another contribution of this section is the reinforcement learning perspective for understanding SeqDPPs. Under this framework, SeqDPP and DySeqDPP can be seen as two types of stochastic policies.

State s_t at time step t: An information state is about the history of an agent's observations (and rewards) about the environment. It is used to determine what happens next upon an action taken by the agent. In our context, the state $s_t = \{\bigcup_{t'=1}^{t-1} \boldsymbol{x}_{t'}, \mathcal{V}_t\}$ comprises the dynamic partition of the video $\mathcal{V}_t$ at time step t and the generated video summary $\bigcup_{t'=1}^{t-1} \boldsymbol{x}_{t'}$ right before the current step t. One may wonder to alternatively treat all the video segments $\mathcal{V}_1, \cdots, \mathcal{V}_t$ until step t as the state. We contend that it is oppressive and unnecessary to carry them along over time. Instead, the summary of the past conveys similar amount of information by design.

Action a_t at time step t: In DySeqDPP, the agent takes actions (1) to select a subset X_t from the video segment $\mathcal{V}_t$ and (2) to propose the length L_t of the next segment $\mathcal{V}_{t+1}$. The subset selection variable $X_t \subseteq \mathcal{V}_t$ and the partition proposal variable $L_t \in \mathcal{L}$ jointly define the action space. In other words, an action takes the form of $A_t = (X_t, L_t)$ whose realization is denote by $a_t = (\boldsymbol{x}_t, l_t)$. We limit the search of the segment's length to the range of $\mathcal{L} = \{5, 6, \cdots, 15\}$ shots.

Policy π: We let the agent take a stochastic policy in the following manner,

$$\pi(a_t|s_t) = P(\boldsymbol{x}_t, l_t|s_t) = P(\boldsymbol{x}_t|s_t)P(l_t|\boldsymbol{x}_t, s_t), \tag{7}$$

where $P(\boldsymbol{x}_t|s_t)$ is a conditional DPP used to build SeqDPP [1], *i.e.*,

$$P(\boldsymbol{x}_t|s_t) = P(\boldsymbol{x}_t| \cup_{t'=1}^{t-1} \boldsymbol{x}_{t'}, \mathcal{V}_t) := P_L(Y_t = \boldsymbol{x}_t \cup \boldsymbol{x}_{t-1}|\boldsymbol{x}_{t-1} \subseteq Y_t; \boldsymbol{L}^t) \tag{8}$$

and $P(l_t|\boldsymbol{x}_t, s_t)$ is defined as a softmax function,

$$P(l_t|\boldsymbol{x}_t, s_t) = P(l_t| \cup_{t'=1}^{t} \boldsymbol{x}_{t'}, \mathcal{V}_t) := \texttt{softmax}(\boldsymbol{w}_{l_t}^T \phi(\cup_{t'=1}^{t} \boldsymbol{x}_{t'}, \mathcal{V}_t)). \tag{9}$$

There are several points in the above worth clarifying and discussing. First of all, Eq. (7–9) describe the main body of our DySeqDPP model. It improves SeqDPP by the partition proposal variable L_t. It is a latent variable because users annotate summaries of videos without explicitly knowing the boundaries of the local diversities they have in their minds. Secondly, we condition the DPP in Eq. (8) on its immediate past time step $(\boldsymbol{x}_{t-1})$ only instead of the whole history of summaries included in the state s_t. This is due to the same modeling intuition as SeqDPP, *i.e.*, in order to maintain local diversity in the summaries. Thirdly, $\phi(\cdot)$ in Eq. (9) extracts features by max-pooling the representations of all the video shots in the current state s_t as well as the new summary $\boldsymbol{x}_t$ selected according to Eq. (8). This ensures that sufficient information about both the whole past history and the current of the video is supplied to the `softmax` for the agent to predict the appropriate length of the next segment. Last but not the least, $\{\boldsymbol{w}_l, l \in \mathcal{L}\}$ are the model parameters to be learned from the user-annotated summaries. It is important to note that the parameters are not bound to any particular environments/videos at all, so the policy can be generalized to unseen videos, too. We postpone the parameterization of the L-ensemble DPP's kernel L to Sect. 4.2.

State-action value function: Our goal is to learn a policy to maximize the expected total discounted reward the agent receives, called the state-action value function,

$$Q^{\pi}(s_0, a_0) := \mathbb{E}_{\pi}\Big[\sum_{t=0}^{T} g(\gamma, t)R_t|S_0 = s_0, A_0 = a_0\Big], \tag{10}$$

where $g(\gamma, t) \in [0, 1]$ is a discount function and the reward $R_t = R(s_{t+1}; s_t, a_t)$ is a function of the state and action. For video summarization, the reward can be evaluation metrics like precision, recall, or F-score computed between the video shots $\cup_{t'=1}^{t} \boldsymbol{x}_{t'}$ selected by the agent and the user summaries of the video (until the current segment $\mathcal{V}_t$). The total number of time steps the agent can take is T, which satisfies $\sum_{t=0}^{T-1} l_t < |\mathcal{V}|$ and $\sum_{t=0}^{T} l_t \geq |\mathcal{V}|$.

It is import to note that our goal is to maximize the state-action value function at the initial state and action (s_0, a_0) which are fixed to $s_0 = \emptyset$ and $a_0 = (\boldsymbol{x}_0 = \emptyset, l_0 = 10)$ in our experiments. In contrast to conventional setups in reinforcement learning, we do not care about the state-action values at other states because only the initial state gives rise to a whole summary of the video, which is our interest. This insight also suggests a special design of the discount function $g(\gamma, t)$. Instead of using the common practice γ^t, we let it be $g(\gamma, t) = \gamma^{|\mathcal{V}-t|}, \gamma \in (0, 1)$, monotonically increasing with respect to t in order to weigh the reward of the whole summary more than the incomplete summaries at any other time steps.

Those differences highlight the fact that video summarization actually lacks some characteristics of reinforcement learning (e.g., delayed feedback). Hence, we have to customize the MDP formalism in order to match it with the goal of interest. Nonetheless, by casting DySeqDPP as a policy, we can conveniently learn its model parameters by algorithms in reinforcement learning—we employ gradient descent in this paper.

4.2 Policy Gradient Descent for Learning DySeqDPP

We review the model parameters in DySeqDPP before deriving the learning algorithm. We parameterize two conditional distributions in DySeqDPP for the purpose of out-of-sample extension, so that one can readily apply the learned model to unseen test videos. The first is the partition proposal distribution (Eq. (9)) and the second is the conditional DPP (Eq. (8)) at each time step t, whose L-ensemble kernel is constructed as follows,

$$[\boldsymbol{L}^t]_{ij} = \boldsymbol{z}_i^T \boldsymbol{W}^T \boldsymbol{W} \boldsymbol{z}_j, \qquad \boldsymbol{z}_i = \texttt{ReLU}(\boldsymbol{U}\,\texttt{ReLU}(\boldsymbol{V} \boldsymbol{f}_i)) \tag{11}$$

where $\boldsymbol{f}_i$ is the feature representation of video shot i in the ground set $\boldsymbol{x}_{t-1} \cup \mathcal{V}_t$ of the time step t. This feature vector goes through a feedforward network with ReLU activations. Denote by θ the union of the weights of the network $(\boldsymbol{W}, \boldsymbol{U}, \boldsymbol{V})$ and the unknowns $\{\boldsymbol{w}_l, l \in \mathcal{L}\}$ in Eq. (8). We next derive a learning algorithm using the policy gradient descent [42] to estimate the model parameters θ.

Recall that our goal is to maximize the state-action value function at the initial state and action. Denoting by $J \triangleq -Q^{\pi}(s_0, a_0)$, we can minimize it by gradient descent,

$$\nabla_\theta J|_{\theta=\theta_{\text{old}}} = -\mathbb{E}_{\boldsymbol{\tau} \sim \pi(\theta_{\text{old}})} \Big[\sum_{t=1}^{T} g(\gamma, t) R_t \nabla_\theta \log p(\boldsymbol{\tau}; \theta)|_{\theta=\theta_{\text{old}}} \Big] \tag{12}$$

$$\approx -\frac{1}{K} \sum_{k=1}^{K} \Big[\sum_{t=1}^{T_k} g(\gamma, t)\, r_{tk}\, \nabla_\theta \log p(\boldsymbol{\tau}_k; \theta)|_{\theta=\theta_{\text{old}}} \Big] \tag{13}$$

where the last equation is obtained by sampling K trajectories $\{\tau_k\}$ from the policy instantiated by the old parameter θ_{old}, r_{tk} is the reward that the agent receives at time step t of the k-th trajectory, and the first equation is due to the following fact,

$$\nabla_\theta \mathbb{E}_{x\sim\theta}[f(x)]|_{\theta=\theta_{\text{old}}} = \mathbb{E}_{x\sim\theta_{\text{old}}}\Big[\nabla_\theta \log p(x;\theta)|_{\theta=\theta_{\text{old}}} f(x)\Big]. \quad (14)$$

We still need to work out $\nabla_\theta \log p(\boldsymbol{\tau};\theta)$ in Eq. (13). The key is that the state-transition distribution $p(s_{t+1}|s_t, a_t)$ is actually deterministic under our context laid out in Sect. 4 (because the action a_t fully determines the summary $\boldsymbol{x}_t$ and the next segment $\mathcal{V}_{t+1}$, and hence the next state). Therefore, for a trajectory $s_0, a_0, s_1, a_1, \cdots$, we have

$$\nabla_\theta \log p(\boldsymbol{\tau};\theta) = \nabla_\theta \log\Big[p(s_0, a_0)\prod_{t=1}^{T} p(s_t|s_{t-1}, a_{t-1})\pi(a_t|s_t;\theta)\Big] \quad (15)$$

$$= \nabla_\theta \sum_{t=1}^{T} \log \pi(a_t|s_t;\theta) = \sum_{t=1}^{T}\Big[\nabla_\theta \log P(\boldsymbol{x}_t|s_t) + \nabla_\theta \log P(l_t|\boldsymbol{x}_t, s_t)\Big] \quad (16)$$

where the first summand of the last equation is the gradient with respect to the parameters of conditional DPP and the second is of the `softmax` (Eq. (9)).

Implementation: Instead of computing the gradients explicitly, one may use the "autodiff" feature of many existing deep learning tools to obtain the gradients. Take PYTORCH (http://pytorch.org) for instance. We may program the following for a trajectory,

$$J(\boldsymbol{\tau};\theta) = -\sum_{t=1}^{T} g(\gamma, t)\, r_t \Big[\log P(\boldsymbol{x}_t|s_t;\theta) + \log P(l_t|\boldsymbol{x}_t, s_t;\theta)\Big],$$

and then use the `backward()` function to automatically compute the gradients followed by calling the `step()` function to do a one-step gradient descent. After that, we sample another trajectory and repeat the procedure until the termination condition.

5 Experiments

We run experiments on three datasets, UTE [8], SumMe [12], and TVSum [43], and compare our approach to several competing baselines.

5.1 The UT Egocentric (UTE) Dataset

Data and Features. UTE [8] contains four egocentric videos, each of which lasts between three and five hours long. It captures daily activities such as shopping in a grocery store, having lunch, working, chatting with friends, meeting with colleagues, etc. In addition to the big variety of content, the videos are also quite challenging due to ego motions—as a result, the views change frequently. The motion blur is more frequent and severe than "third-person" videos. In general, the video shots of an activity are placed in between of blurred frames and nuisance views. Following the experiment protocol of [18], we run four rounds of experiments. In each round, we use two videos for training, one for validation, and the last for testing. We uniformly divide the videos to 5-second shots. From each video frame, we extract 4,096D deep CNN features as the activation of the last fully connected layer of the VGG19 network [44] pretrained on ImageNet [45]. After that, we use PCA to reduce the feature dimension from 4,096D to 512D, followed by max-pooling within each shot in order to have a shot-level feature representation (*i.e.*, $\boldsymbol{f}_i$ in Eq. (11)).

Competing Methods. We mainly compare our approach (DySeqDPP) to the following methods and their variations which, like ours, locally promote diversity in video summaries: SeqDPP [1,9], dppLSTM [19], and uniform sampling (Uniform). We let the methods automatically work out the lengths of the summaries except for the uniform sampling, to which we supply the lengths of the oracles. For SeqDPP, however, the length of each segment has to be manually set. In addition to the 10-shot segments suggested in the original work [1], we also include the results of segments of 5 shots and 12 shots. Finally, we include another comparison by improving the original SeqDPP with our reinforcement learning algorithm. This is implemented by fixing the partition proposal distribution $P(L_t|\boldsymbol{x}_t, s_t)$ as a Dirac delta function $\delta(L_t = l)$, where $l = 10$ is independent of the time steps. Besides, we learn using the reward of the whole summary by setting $g(\gamma, t) = 0$ for $t < T$ and $g(\gamma, T) = 1$, unless specified otherwise.

Evaluation. In the literature, system-generated summaries have been evaluated in a variety of manners including but not limited to user studies [46], percentage of frames overlapped with user summaries [19], bipartite matching based on distances of low-level visual features [18], etc. Arguably, user study is the "gold" standard, but it is extremely time-consuming. In this paper, we instead use the bipartite matching based on a "semantic distance"—pairwise Hamming distance between video shots computed upon the concepts annotated for each shot. This imitates user studies in the sense that the "semantic distance" is strongly correlated with users' perceptions about the difference between a system-generated summary and an actual user's summary. The concepts per video shot are borrowed from an earlier work by Sharghi et al. [18], in which the authors asked users to choose from 54 concepts the ones relevant to a given video shot.

Given two summaries (*i.e.*, a system-generated one and a user summary), we construct a bipartite graph between them with the shots as nodes. A node in one part is connected to all the nodes in the other part with edge weights as the (negative) Hamming distance computed from the per-shot concepts [18]. After that, we find the size of the maximum bipartite matching and divide it by the length of the user (system) summary to obtain the recall (precision).

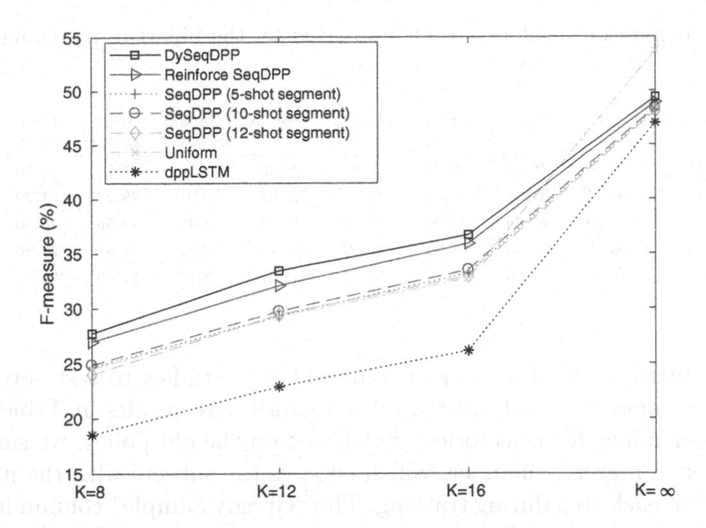

Fig. 3. Comparison results in terms of average F1-score (the higher, the better) for 4 videos in UTE dataset where horizon axis means different K used in local bipartite matching.

Additionally, we improve this metric by removing the edges between the video shots that are more than K time steps away from each other. In other words, if two shots are far away from each other for more than $5K$ seconds, there is no edge between them in the improved evaluation metric.

Comparison Results. Figure 3 reports the results using the above evaluation scheme at $K = 8, 12, 16, \infty$. Each system-generated summary is compared against three user summaries and the corresponding precision, recall, and F-measure scores are averaged to reduce user bias. We can see that the proposed DySeqDPP outperforms the competing methods by a large margin. The SeqDPP trained by our reinforcement learning algorithm ranks the second. These results verify the benefit of understanding the SeqDPPs from the novel reinforcement learning perspective. Moreover, the latent variable for dynamically partitioning the videos into segments also helps. It not only removes the need of handcrafting the segments but also gives rise to superior performance over the equally paced segments.

Another intriguing observation is that there is no significant difference among the results of SeqDPP when we change the sizes of the segments (*i.e.*, 5, 10, and 12 shots). It indicates that one can hardly find an "optimal" length for the equally placing segments of SeqDPP, signifying the need of dynamically partitioning the videos to segments of variable lengths as our DySeqDPP does.

It is a little surprising to see that dppLSTM underperforms uniform sampling. Upon examining the existing works [18,47] carefully, we find that uniform sampling is actually a very competitive baseline partially because it receives unfair information at inference—length of the oracle summary. Another possible reason is that we did not pre-train the dppLSTM using any additional datasets as done in [19].

Table 1. Comparison results on UTE evaluated by the bipartite matching F1-score ($K = 12$)

Method	$\gamma = 1e^{-20}$	Full $\gamma = 0.2$	Full $\gamma = 0.5$	Full $\gamma = 0.9$	Partial $\gamma = 0.2$	Partial $\gamma = 0.5$	Partial $\gamma = 0.9$	Greedy sample	Pool seg	Pool video
Video 1	29.53	28.96	28.03	29.27	28.83	28.33	28.23	27.76	29.19	30.33
Video 2	31.17	30.67	31.61	30.80	32.53	32.07	30.91	29.24	31.20	31.90
Video 3	46.38	45.79	45.88	42.04	45.20	45.23	44.42	43.56	40.40	43.68
Video 4	26.72	26.93	26.35	26.51	26.07	26.41	27.51	23.81	24.56	24.91
Avg.	33.45	33.08	32.96	32.16	33.15	33.01	32.77	31.09	31.33	32.71

Ablation Study. Besides, we run some ablation studies to test several variations to our approach and illustrate the quantitative results in Table 1. First, instead of sampling K trajectories $\{\boldsymbol{\tau}_k\}$ based on the old policy, we sample the trajectory $\boldsymbol{\tau}$ in a greedy manner, which chooses the subsets with the maximum probability at each step during training. The "Greedy Sample" column in Table 1 indicates that greedy sampling produces worse video summarization results. The reason is that the system can not explore the real environment (video) thoroughly under the greedy sampling strategy.

We also study how the hyper-parameter γ ($\gamma = 1e^{-20}, 0.2, 0.5, 0.9$) influences the model. Specifically, larger γ means we give higher weight to the incomplete summaries at early time steps. Meanwhile $\gamma = 1e^{-20}$ means we just consider the whole video summary at the final time step. The experimental results in Table 1 verify our intuitive assumption that weighing more on the reward of the whole summary is better than on the incomplete summaries at other time steps. In addition, we notice a problem that it is unreasonable to calculate the reward of each time step by comparing the incomplete summary up to the current step with the full user summary (shown in the columns titled "Full $\gamma = 0.2/0.5/0.9$"). To address this problem, we compute the reward by comparing the current system summary with the user summary until this time step, as shown in the column titled "Partial $\gamma = 0.2/0.5/0.9$". The experimental results verify that the latter kind of reward calculation is more reasonable.

Finally, we also study what features work better for predicting l_t. Recall that, for $\phi(\cup_{t'=1}^{t} \boldsymbol{x}_{t'}, \mathcal{V}_t)$, we concatenate the features of the generated video summary until the current time step and the features of the current segment. We test two alternatives. One is pooling the features of this segment only (PoolSeg) and the other is pooling the features of the whole video sequence up to the current segment (PoolVideo). PoolSeg gives rise to worse results than PoolVideo since it lacks the larger context than the current segment only. PoolVideo is a little worse than and certainly incurs more computation cost than $\phi(\cup_{t'=1}^{t} \boldsymbol{x}_{t'}, \mathcal{V}_t)$ because pooling over the video encounters redundant information.

5.2 The SumMe and TVSum Datasets

Experiment Setup. In addition to the egocentric videos, we also test our approach on two other popular datasets for video summarization: **SumMe** [12]

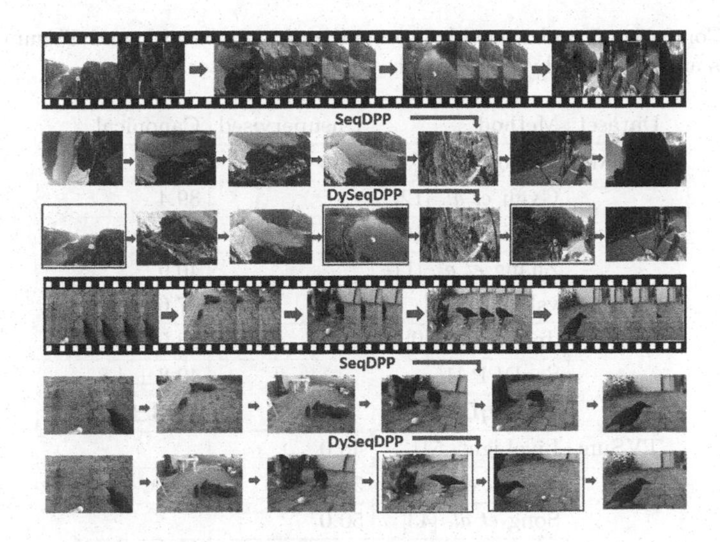

Fig. 4. Generated video summary examples with SeqDPP and DySeqDPP

and **TVSum** [43]. They are both "third-person" video datasets. SumMe consists of 25 consumer videos covering holidays, events, and sports. The lengths of the videos range from about one to six minutes. TVSum contains 50 videos of 10 categories downloaded from YouTube. The videos are one to five minutes in length.

We follow the same experimental setup as dppLSTM [19] in this work. We extract the output (1,024D) of the penultimate layer (pool 5) of GoogLeNet [48] for each video frame. Followed by max-pooling within each shot (15 frames), we get the shot-level feature representation. In our experiments, we train the model with 60% videos of SumMe (TVSum), validate on 20% of the dataset, and test on the remaining 20% videos. We run 10 rounds of experiments with different random splits of the dataset and report both the mean F1-scores and standard errors.

Evaluation. We evaluate the results again by F1-score. However, the precisions and recalls for computing the F1-score are calculated in a different way from the bipartite graph matching earlier. Following by the practice in dppLSTM [19], we first split a video into a set of disjoint temporal scenes (which are usually longer and contain more visual information than the segments and shots used in the UTE dataset) using the KTS approach [49]. We train the model with shot-level feature representations and then use it to obtain shot-level importance scores. Specifically, the importance score of each frame is equal to the score of shots they belong to. We compute the scene-level scores by averaging the scores of frames within each scene and then rank the scenes in the descending order by their scores. In order to generate a video summary, we select the scenes with a duration below a certain threshold (*e.g.*, using the knapsack algorithm as in [43]).

Table 2. Comparison results on video summarization on SumMe and TVsum dataset. The results are evaluated by F1-score, the higher the better.

Dataset	Method	Unsupervised	Canonical
SumMe	Video-MMR [50]	26.6	
	Gygli *et al.* [12]		39.4
	Gygli *et al.* [10]		39.7
	Zhang *et al.* [11]		40.9
	vsLSTM [19]		37.6 ± 0.8
	dppLSTM [19]		38.6 ± 0.8
	SeqDPP [1]		40.8 ± 4.8
	DySeqDPP		$\mathbf{44.3 \pm 2.8}$
TVSum	LiveLight [51]	46.0	
	Khosla *et al.* [4]	36.0	
	Song *et al.* [43]	50.0	
	vsLSTM [19]		54.2 ± 0.7
	dppLSTM [19]		54.7 ± 0.7
	SeqDPP [1]		57.4 ± 2.0
	DySeqDPP		$\mathbf{58.4 \pm 2.5}$

Finally, we calculate the precision, recall, and F1-score according to the temporal overlap between the generated summary and the user summaries.

In order to account for the above evaluation scheme, we make some changes to our reinforcement learning algorithm on these two datasets. For training process, firstly we sample the partition proposal l_t with oracle summary based on the old policy on each time step. Thus we can utilize the diagonal values of $\boldsymbol{L}^t$ as shot-level scores and then generate the video summary using the approach described above. Consequently, we can get the reward (F1-score) with the generated video summary. Note that the trajectory $\boldsymbol{\tau}$ here is the oracle summary. Therefore, we can optimize the dynamic SeqDPP with reinforcement learning.

Comparison Results. Table 2 shows the comparison results between our DySeqDPP and several baselines. Note that some of the baseline methods are unsupervised so they are tuned to achieve the best results on the test set. Nonetheless, the supervised ones in general perform better than them. Both SeqDPP and DySeqDPP significantly outperform the others and DySeqDPP ranks to the first by a big margin on SumMe.

Qualitative Results. Figure 4 demonstrates some exemplar video summaries generated by SeqDPP and our DySeqDPP, respectively. It is interesting to see that DySeqDPP captures some shots that are key for the story flow and are yet missed by SeqDPP. Take the first video for instance. The sky diver shows up only at the end of SeqDPP's summary while s/he is kept at both the beginning and the end of DySeqDPP's summary. The second is an amusing video recording how a bird saves a ball from a dog's mouth. However, SeqDPP fails to select the key shot in which the dog bites the ball.

6 Conclusion

In this paper, we study *"how local"* the local diversity should be for video summarization and utilize it as a guideline to devise a sequential model to tackle the dynamic diverse subset selection problem. Furthermore, we apply reinforcement inference [25] in the dynamic seqDPP model to solve the problem of *exposure bias* [33] as well as the issue of non-differentiable metrics existing in SeqDPP [1]. The proposed DySeqDPP can not only seek the appropriate and possibly different lengths of segments dynamically, but also bridge the training and validation phases. Experimental results on video summarization demonstrate the effectiveness of our approach.

Acknowledgements. This work was supported in part by NSF IIS 1741431 & 1566511, gifts from Adobe, and gift GPUs from NVIDIA. B.G. would like to thank Trevor Darrell, Charless Fowlkes, Alexander Ihler, Dequan Wang, and Huazhe Xu for the insightful discussions on SeqDPP which inspired this work.

References

1. Gong, B., Chao, W., Grauman, K., Sha, F.: Diverse sequential subset selection for supervised video summarization. In: Advances in Neural Information Processing Systems (NIPS), pp. 2069–2077 (2014)
2. Money, A.G., Agius, H.: Video summarisation: a conceptual framework and survey of the state of the art. J. Vis. Commun. Image Represent. **19**(2), 121–143 (2008)
3. Hong, R., Tang, J., Tan, H.K., Yan, S., Ngo, C., Chua, T.S.: Event driven summarization for web videos. In: The First SIGMM Workshop on Social Media, pp. 43-48. ACM (2009)
4. Khosla, A., Hamid, R., Lin, C.J., Sundaresan, N.: Large-scale video summarization using web-image priors. In: Proceedings of the IEEE Conference on Computer Vision and Pattern Recognition, pp. 2698–2705 (2013)
5. Ngo, C.W., Ma, Y.F., Zhang, H.J.: Automatic video summarization by graph modeling. In: IEEE The Ninth International Conference on Computer Vision (ICCV), pp. 104–109 (2003)
6. Liu, T., Kender, J.R.: Optimization algorithms for the selection of key frame sequences of variable length. In: Heyden, A., Sparr, G., Nielsen, M., Johansen, P. (eds.) ECCV 2002, Part IV. LNCS, vol. 2353, pp. 403–417. Springer, Heidelberg (2002). https://doi.org/10.1007/3-540-47979-1_27
7. Zhang, H.J., Wu, J., Zhong, D., Smoliar, S.W.: An integrated system for content-based video retrieval and browsing. Pattern Recognit. **30**(4), 643–658 (1997)
8. Lee, Y.J., Ghosh, J., Grauman, K.: Discovering important people and objects for egocentric video summarization. In: 2012 IEEE Conference on Computer Vision and Pattern Recognition (CVPR), pp. 1346–1353. IEEE (2012)

9. Lu, Z., Grauman, K.: Story-driven summarization for egocentric video. In: Proceedings of the IEEE Conference on Computer Vision and Pattern Recognition, pp. 2714–2721 (2013)
10. Gygli, M., Grabner, H., Van Gool, L.: Video summarization by learning submodular mixtures of objectives. In: Proceedings of the IEEE Conference on Computer Vision and Pattern Recognition, pp. 3090–3098 (2015)
11. Zhang, K., Chao, W.L., Sha, F., Grauman, K.: Summary transfer: exemplar-based subset selection for video summarization. In: Proceedings of the IEEE Conference on Computer Vision and Pattern Recognition, pp. 1059–1067 (2016)
12. Gygli, M., Grabner, H., Riemenschneider, H., Van Gool, L.: Creating summaries from user videos. In: Fleet, D., Pajdla, T., Schiele, B., Tuytelaars, T. (eds.) ECCV 2014, Part VII. LNCS, vol. 8695, pp. 505–520. Springer, Cham (2014). https://doi.org/10.1007/978-3-319-10584-0_33
13. Chao, W., Gong, B., Grauman, K., Sha, F.: Large-margin determinantal point processes. In: Proceedings of the Thirty-First Conference on Uncertainty in Artificial Intelligence (UAI), pp. 191–200 (2015)
14. Kang, H.W., Chen, X.Q.: Space-time video montage. In: 2006 IEEE Computer Society Conference on Computer Vision and Pattern Recognition, Volume 2, pp. 1331–1338. IEEE (2006)
15. Ma, Y.F., Lu, L., Zhang, H.J., Li, M.: A user attention model for video summarization. In: The tenth ACM International Conference on Multimedia, pp. 533–542. ACM (2002)
16. Xu, J., Mukherjee, L., Li, Y., Warner, J., Rehg, J.M., Singh, V.: Gaze-enabled egocentric video summarization via constrained submodular maximization. In: Proceedings of the IEEE Conference on Computer Vision and Pattern Recognition, pp. 2235–2244 (2015)
17. Sharghi, A., Gong, B., Shah, M.: Query-focused extractive video summarization. In: Leibe, B., Matas, J., Sebe, N., Welling, M. (eds.) ECCV 2016, Part VIII. LNCS, vol. 9912, pp. 3–19. Springer, Cham (2016). https://doi.org/10.1007/978-3-319-46484-8_1
18. Sharghi, A., Laurel, J.S., Gong, B.: Query-focused video summarization: dataset, evaluation, and a memory network based approach. In: 2017 IEEE Conference on Computer Vision and Pattern Recognition (CVPR), pp. 2127–2136. IEEE (2017)
19. Zhang, K., Chao, W.-L., Sha, F., Grauman, K.: Video summarization with long short-term memory. In: Leibe, B., Matas, J., Sebe, N., Welling, M. (eds.) ECCV 2016, Part VII. LNCS, vol. 9911, pp. 766–782. Springer, Cham (2016). https://doi.org/10.1007/978-3-319-46478-7_47
20. Kulesza, A., Taskar, B.: Learning determinantal point processes. In: Proceedings of 27th Conference on Uncertainty in Artificial Intelligence (UAI), pp. 419–427 (2011)
21. Chao, W.L., Gong, B., Grauman, K., Sha, F.: Large-margin determinantal point processes. In: UAI (2015)
22. Affandi, R.H., Fox, E.B., Adams, R.P., Taskar, B.: Learning the parameters of determinantal point process kernels. In: ICML, pp. 1224–1232 (2014)
23. Dempster, A.P., Laird, N.M., Rubin, D.B.: Maximum likelihood from incomplete data via the EM algorithm. J. R. Stat. Soc. Series B **39**, 1–38 (1977)
24. Welch, L.R.: Hidden markov models and the Baum-Welch algorithm. IEEE Inf. Theory Soc. Newsl. **53**(4), 10–13 (2003)
25. Sutton, R.S., Barto, A.G.: Reinforcement learning: An introduction, vol. 1. MIT press, Cambridge (1998)

26. Kwon, J., Lee, K.M.: A unified framework for event summarization and rare event detection from multiple views. IEEE Trans. Pattern Anal. Mach. Intell. **37**(9), 1737–1750 (2015)
27. Kim, G., Sigal, L., Xing, E.P.: Joint summarization of large-scale collections of web images and videos for storyline reconstruction. In: Proceedings of the IEEE Conference on Computer Vision and Pattern Recognition, pp. 4225–4232 (2014)
28. Xiong, B., Grauman, K.: Detecting snap points in egocentric video with a web photo prior. In: Fleet, D., Pajdla, T., Schiele, B., Tuytelaars, T. (eds.) ECCV 2014, Part V. LNCS, vol. 8693, pp. 282–298. Springer, Cham (2014). https://doi.org/10.1007/978-3-319-10602-1_19
29. Chu, W.S., Song, Y., Jaimes, A.: Video co-summarization: video summarization by visual co-occurrence. In: Proceedings of the IEEE Conference on Computer Vision and Pattern Recognition, pp. 3584–3592 (2015)
30. Liu, D., Hua, G., Chen, T.: A hierarchical visual model for video object summarization. IEEE Trans. Pattern Anal. Mach. Intell. **32**(12), 2178–2190 (2010)
31. del Molino, A.G., Tan, C., Lim, J.H., Tan, A.H.: Summarization of egocentric videos: a comprehensive survey. IEEE Trans. Hum.-Mach. Syst. **47**(1), 65–76 (2017)
32. Yao, T., Mei, T., Rui, Y.: Highlight detection with pairwise deep ranking for first-person video summarization. In: Proceedings of the IEEE Conference on Computer Vision and Pattern Recognition, pp. 982–990 (2016)
33. Ranzato, M., Chopra, S., Auli, M., Zaremba, W.: Sequence level training with recurrent neural networks. arXiv preprint arXiv:1511.06732 (2015)
34. Papineni, K., Roukos, S., Ward, T., Zhu, W.J.: BLEU: a method for automatic evaluation of machine translation. In: Proceedings of the 40th Annual Meeting on Association for Computational Linguistics, pp. 311–318 (2002)
35. Lin, C.Y.: Rouge: A package for automatic evaluation of summaries. In: Proceedings of the ACL 2004 Workshop on Text summarization Branches Out, vol. 8, Barcelona, Spain (2004)
36. Banerjee, S., Lavie, A.: Meteor: an automatic metric for MT evaluation with improved correlation with human judgments. In: The ACL Workshop on Intrinsic and Extrinsic Evaluation Measures for Machine Translation and/or Summarization. vol. 29, pp. 65–72 (2005)
37. Vedantam, R., Lawrence Zitnick, C., Parikh, D.: Cider: consensus-based image description evaluation. In: Proceedings of the IEEE Conference on Computer Vision and Pattern Recognition, pp. 4566–4575 (2015)
38. Williams, R.J.: Simple statistical gradient-following algorithms for connectionist reinforcement learning. Mach. Learn. **8**(3–4), 229–256 (1992)
39. Rennie, S.J., Marcheret, E., Mroueh, Y., Ross, J., Goel, V.: Self-critical sequence training for image captioning. arXiv preprint arXiv:1612.00563 (2016)
40. Kulesza, A., Taskar, B. Determinantal point processes for machine learning. Found. Trends® Mach. Learn. **5**(2–3), 123–286 (2012)
41. Affandi, R.H., Kulesza, A., Fox, E.B.: Markov determinantal point processes. arXiv preprint arXiv:1210.4850 (2012)
42. Sutton, R., Barto, A.: Reinforcement Learning. MIT Press, Cambridge (1998)
43. Song, Y., Vallmitjana, J., Stent, A., Jaimes, A.: TVSUM: summarizing web videos using titles. In: Proceedings of the IEEE Conference on Computer Vision and Pattern Recognition, pp. 5179–5187 (2015)
44. Simonyan, K., Zisserman, A.: Very deep convolutional networks for large-scale image recognition. arXiv preprint arXiv:1409.1556 (2014)

45. Jia Deng, Wei Dong, R.S.L.J.L.K.L., Fei-Fei, L.: ImageNet: a large-scale hierarchical image database. In: Proceedings of the IEEE Annual Conference on Computer Vision and Pattern Recognition (CVPR) (2009)
46. Lee, Y.J., Grauman, K.: Predicting important objects for egocentric video summarization. Int. J. Comput. Vis. **114**(1), 38–55 (2015)
47. Sharghi, A., Gong, B., Shah, M.: Query-focused extractive video summarization. In: European Conference on Computer Vision (2016)
48. Szegedy, C., et al.: Going deeper with convolutions. In: The IEEE Conference on Computer Vision and Pattern Recognition (CVPR), June 2015
49. Potapov, D., Douze, M., Harchaoui, Z., Schmid, C.: Category-specific video summarization. In: Fleet, D., Pajdla, T., Schiele, B., Tuytelaars, T. (eds.) ECCV 2014, Part VI. LNCS, vol. 8694, pp. 540–555. Springer, Cham (2014). https://doi.org/10.1007/978-3-319-10599-4_35
50. Li, Y., Merialdo, B.: Multi-video summarization based on video-MMR. In: 2010 11th International Workshop on Image Analysis for Multimedia Interactive Services (WIAMIS), pp. 1–4. IEEE (2010)
51. Zhao, B., Xing, E.P.: Quasi real-time summarization for consumer videos. In: Proceedings of the IEEE Conference on Computer Vision and Pattern Recognition, pp. 2513–2520 (2014)

Toward Scale-Invariance and Position-Sensitive Region Proposal Networks

Hsueh-Fu Lu, Xiaofei Du(✉), and Ping-Lin Chang

Umbo Computer Vision, London, UK
{topper.lu,xiaofei.du,ping-lin.chang}@umbocv.com,
https://umbocv.ai

Abstract. Accurately localising object proposals is an important precondition for high detection rate for the state-of-the-art object detection frameworks. The accuracy of an object detection method has been shown highly related to the average recall (AR) of the proposals. In this work, we propose an advanced object proposal network in favour of translation-invariance for objectness classification, translation-variance for bounding box regression, large effective receptive fields for capturing global context and scale-invariance for dealing with a range of object sizes from extremely small to large. The design of the network architecture aims to be simple while being effective and with real-time performance. Without bells and whistles the proposed object proposal network significantly improves the AR at 1,000 proposals by 35% and 45% on PASCAL VOC and COCO dataset respectively and has a fast inference time of 44.8 ms for input image size of 640^2. Empirical studies have also shown that the proposed method is class-agnostic to be generalised for general object proposal.

Keywords: Object detection · Region proposal networks
Position-sensitive anchors

1 Introduction

Object detection has been a challenging task in computer vision [6,17]. Significant progress has been achieved in the last decade from traditional sliding-window paradigms [7,28] to recent top-performance proposal-based [27] detection frameworks [9–11]. A proposal algorithm plays a crucial role in an object detection pipeline. On one hand, it speeds up the detection process by considerably reducing the search space for image regions to be subsequently classified. On the other hand, the average recall (AR) of the object proposal method has

Electronic supplementary material The online version of this chapter (https://doi.org/10.1007/978-3-030-01237-3_11) contains supplementary material, which is available to authorized users.

V. Ferrari et al. (Eds.): ECCV 2018, LNCS 11212, pp. 175–190, 2018.
https://doi.org/10.1007/978-3-030-01237-3_11

been shown notably correlating with the precision of final detection, in which AR essentially reveals how accurate the detected bounding boxes are localised comparing with the ground truth [13].

Instead of using low-level image features to heuristically generate the proposals [27,30], trendy methods extract high-level features by using deep convolutional neural networks (ConvNets) [12,26,29] to train a class-agnostic classifier with a large number of annotated objects [15,21,23]. For general objectness detection, such supervised learning approaches make an important assumption that given enough number of different object categories, an objectness classifier can be sufficiently generalised to unseen categories. It has been shown that learning-based methods indeed tend to be unbiased to the dataset categories and learn the union of features in the annotated object regions [4,13,15,20]. Despite their good performance [5,12,23], there is still much room to improve the recall especially for small objects and accuracy for the bounding box localisation [2,14,16,20].

To tackle object detection using ConvNets at various scales and for more accurate localisation, prior works adopted an encoder-decoder architecture with skip-connections [24] for exploiting low-resolution strong semantic and high-resolution weak semantic features [16], used position sensitive score maps for enhancing translation variance and invariance respectively for localisation and classification [5], and used a global convolutional network (GCN) component for enlarging valid receptive field (VRF) particularly for capturing larger image context [19].

In this paper, we devise an advanced object proposal network which is capable of handling a large range of object scales and accurately localising proposed bounding boxes. The proposed network architecture embraces fully convolutional networks (FCNs) [18] without using fully-connected and pooling layers to preserve spatial information as much as possible. The design takes simplicity into account, in which the features extracted by ConvNets are entirely shared with a light-weight network head as shown in Fig. 2.

Ablation studies have been conducted to show the effectiveness of each designed component. We have empirically found that GCN and position-sensitivity structure can each individually improves the AR at 1,000 proposals. As shown in Tables 2 and 3, evaluating the baseline model on PASCAL VOC and COCO dataset, GCN brings performance gains from 0.48 and 0.42 to 0.59 (22%) and to 0.54 (29%) respectively, and, the use of position-sensitivity to 0.61 (26%) and to 0.45 (6%) respectively. Using them together can furthermore boost the scores to 0.65 (35%) and to 0.61 (44%) respectively. Together the proposed framework achieves the state of the art and has a real-time performance.

2 Related Works

Traditional object proposal methods take low-level image features to heuristically propose regions containing objectness. Methods such as Selective Search [27], CPMC [3] and MCG [1] adopt grouping of multiple hierarchical segmentations to produce the final proposals. Edge boxes [30] on the other hand takes an assumption that objectness is supposed to have clearer contours. Hosang et al. [13] have comprehensively evaluated different proposal methods. Learning-based proposal approaches have gained more attentions recently. DeepBox [15] uses convolutional neural network to re-rank object proposals based on other bottom-up non-learning proposal methods. Faster R-CNN [23] trains a region proposal network (RPN) on a large number of annotated ground truth bounding boxes to obtain high-quality box proposals for object detection. Region-based fully-convolutional network (R-FCN) [5] introduces position-sensitive score maps to improve localisation of the bounding boxes at detection stage. Feature pyramid network (FPN) [16] takes multi-scale feature maps into account to exploit scale-invariant features for both object proposal and detection stages. Instead of using feature pyramids and learning from ground truth bounding boxes, DeepMask [20] and SharpMask [21] use feed-forward ConvNets trained by ground truth masks and exploit multi-scale input images to perform mask proposals to achieve state-of-the-art performances.

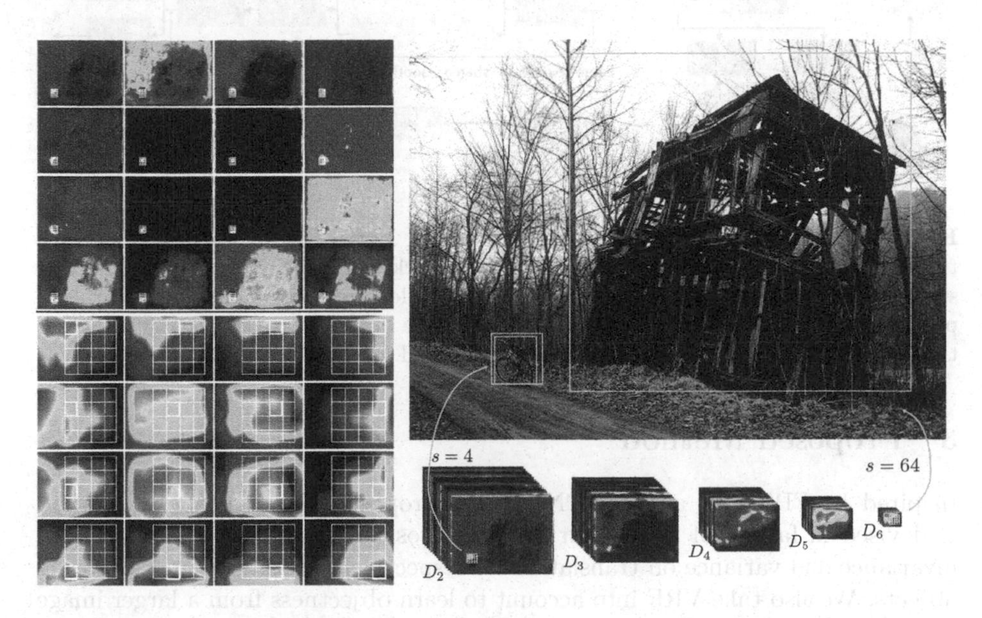

Fig. 1. The proposed method. **Left:** The position-sensitive score maps and windows with k^2 grids ($k = 4$) in yellow at D_2 and D_6 shown at the top and bottom respectively. One can see the D_2 activates on small objects while D_6 activates on extreme large ones. Note that D_6 is enlarged for visualisation, in which the window size is in fact identical to the one shown in D_2. **Right:** The windows are mapped into anchors in cyan in the input image with sizes of the multiple of layer stride s. **Both:** The bounding box in orange is the only labeled ground truth (in `bike` category) on this image from PASCAL VOC 2007. The large object on the right has no ground truth but the proposed class-agnostic method can still be generalised to extract its objectness features as shown in the visualised D_6 feature maps.

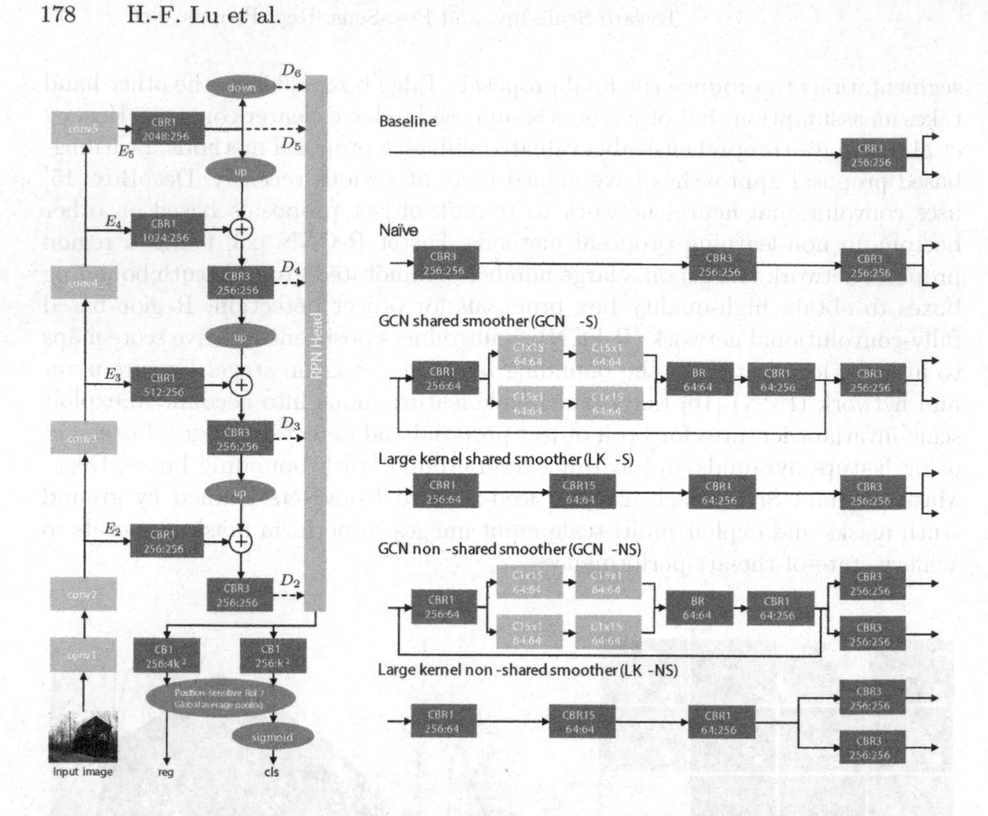

Fig. 2. The overall proposed system architecture. **Left:** The ResNet together with the feature pyramid structure form the general backbone of RPN heads. **Right:** The structures of different RPN heads. **Both:** Rectangles are components with learnable parameters to train and ellipses are parameter-free operations. Dash arrow indicates that the RPN head is shared by all feature pyramid levels.

3 Proposed Method

Inspired by FPN [16] and R-FCN [5], the proposed object proposal method is devised in favour of scale-invariance and position-sensitivity to retain both invariance and variance on translation for respectively classifying and localising objects. We also take VRF into account to learn objectness from a larger image spatial context [19]. In addition, instead of regressing and classifying a set of anchors using default profile (i.e., scale and aspect ratio) by a fixed (3×3) convolutional kernel in certain layers [16,23], we propose directly mapping anchors from sliding windows in each decoding layer together with sharing the position-sensitive score maps. The overall ConvNets takes an input image with arbitrary size to bottom-up encode and top-down decode features with skip connections to preserve object locality [24]. Scale-invariance as one of the important traits of the proposed method is thus achieved by extracting multi-scale features from the input image. These semantically weak to strong features are then feed into a series of decoding layers being shared by a RPN head. Anchors are generated by a dense sliding window fashion shared by a bank of position sensitive score maps. In the end, the network regresses the anchors to localise objects (*reg* for short) and classifies the objectness with scores (*cls* for short).

3.1 Encoder

The encoder is a feed-forward ConvNet as the backbone feature extractor, which scales down by a factor of 2 several times. Although the proposed method can be equipped with any popular ConvNet architectures [26,29] for the backbone, ResNet [12] is adopted particularly for its FCN structure being able to retain the local information as much as possible. ResNets are structured with residual *blocks* each consisting of a subset of ConvNets. We note the conv2, conv3, conv4 and conv5 blocks from the original paper [12] as $\{E_2, E_3, E_4, E_5\}$ with the corresponding dense sliding window strides $s = \{4, 8, 16, 32\}$ in regard to the input image.

3.2 Decoder

The decoder recovers the feature resolution for the strongest semantic feature maps from low to high with skip connections in between the corresponding encoder and decoder layers. The skip connection is substantial for the accuracy of bounding box proposal as it propagates detail-preserving and position-accurate features from the encoding process to the decoded features which are later shared by the RPN head.

Specifically with ResNet, the decoding process starts from $E5$ using 1×1 convolution and 256 output channels for feature selection followed by batch normalisation (BN) and rectified linear unit (ReLU) layers, which together we brief as CBR$\{\cdot\}$ where $\cdot$ is the kernel size. Likewise, each skip connection at a layer takes a CBR1 with 256 output channels. The bottom-up decoding process is therefore done by using bilinear upsampling followed by element-wise addition with the CBR1 selected features from the encoding layers. A CBR3 block is inserted in each decoding layer right after the addition for the purpose of de-aliasing. We note the decoding layers as $\{D_2, D_3, D_4, D_5\}$ corresponding to $\{E_2, E_3, E_4, E_5\}$ in the encoding layers. An extra D_6 is added by directly down sampling D_5 for gaining an even larger stride $s = 64$, which is in favor of extremely large objectness detection.

3.3 RPN Heads

A RPN head is in charge of learning features across a range of scales for *reg* and *cls*. The learnable parameters in the RPN head share all features in the decoding layers to capture different levels of semantics for various object sizes. We will show that the design of a RPN head has a significant impact on the final proposal accuracy in Sect. 4. We show a number of different RPN head designs in Fig. 2. Each head takes 256 channel feature map as input and outputs two sibling CB1 blocks for *reg* and *cls* with $4 \times k^2$ and k^2 channels respectively, where k^2 is the number of regular grids for position-sensitive score maps described in Sect. 3.4. We regard the state-of-the-art RPN used in FPN [16] as a *Baseline* method, in which a CBR3 block is adopted for fusing multi-scale features. Our *Baseline* implementation, which is a bit different from [16], uses BN and ReLU which have been found helpful in converging the end-to-end training.

Inspired by GCN within residual structure [19], we hypothesise that enlarging VRF to learn from larger image context can improve the overall object proposal performance. For the *GCN shared smoother* (GCN-S) and *Large kernel shared smoother* (LK-S), a larger convolution kernel (15×15) is inserted before the CBR3 smoothing. Additionally their non-shared smoother counterpart (GCN-NS and LK-NS) are also compared.

To study the effect of model capacity and the increased number of parameters, a *Naïve* head is taken into account, which is simply added with more CBR3 blocks to approximately match the number of learnable parameters compared with other RPN heads. Table 1 lists the number of parameters of all RPN heads. Compared with the *Baseline*, the numbers of parameter ratio of the other models are within a 0.015 standard deviation.

3.4 Position-Sensitive Anchors

We argue that using a default set of scales and aspect ratios to map anchors from a constant-size convolution kernel can potentially undermine the accuracy of *reg* and *cls*. This could be due to the mismatch of the receptive field of network and the mapped anchors. Prior works have used such strategy [5,16,23] with little exploration of other varieties. To improve the fidelity of relationship between features and anchors with respect to the receptive field of ConvNets, in the proposed method, at each layer, the size of an anchor is calculated by $(w \cdot s) \times (h \cdot s)$ where w and h are the width and height of the sliding window.

Since the anchor and the sliding window are now naturally mapped, position-sensitive score maps can be further exploited for improving the accuracy of localisation. Fig. 1 illustrates the stack of score maps for k^2 regular grids in the sliding window. Each grid in the window takes average of its coverage on the corresponding score map (i.e., average pooling). All k^2 grids then undergo a global average pooling to output 4-channel t and 1-channel o for the final *reg* and *cls* result respectively. We further feed o to an activation function *sigmoid* for evaluating the objectness score. Details of position-sensitive pooling can be found in [5]. In this paper we use $k = 4$ for illustration as well as for all experiments.

3.5 Implementation Details

In this paper, all the experiments were conducted with ResNet-50 with the removal of average pooling, fully-connected and softmax layers in the end of the original model. We do not use conv1 in the pyramid due to the high memory footage and too low-level features which contribute very little for semantically representing objectness. The architecture is illustrated in Fig. 2. A set of window sizes $w : h = \{8 : 8, 4 : 8, 8 : 4, 3 : 9, 9 : 3\}$ are used for the dense sliding windows at each layer for generating anchors. At the most top D_6 and bottom D_2 layer, additional window sizes $\{12 : 12, 6 : 12, 12 : 6, 12 : 4, 4 : 12\}$ and $\{4 : 4, 2 : 4, 4 : 2\}$ are respectively used for discovering extremely large and small objectness.

The proposed position-sensitive anchors mapped from the windows are all inside the input image, but the bounding boxes regressed from anchors can possibly exceed the image boundary. We simply discard those bounding boxes exceeding the image boundary. In addition, the number of total anchors depends on the size of input image and the used anchor profile. The effect of anchor number is discussed in the supplementary material.

Training. In each image, a large amount of anchors are generated across all decoding layers to be further assigned positive and negative labels. An anchor having intersection-over-union (IoU) with any ground truth bounding box greater than 0.7 is assigned a positive label p and less than 0.3 a negative label n. For each ground truth bounding box, the anchor with the highest IoU is also assigned to a positive label, only if the IoU is greater than 0.3. This policy is similar to [23] but with the additional lower bound for avoiding distraction of outliers. N_A anchors (half positive and half negative anchors) are selected for each training iteration. The model can be trained end-to-end with N_B mini-batch images together with the sampled anchors using a defined loss:

$$L = \frac{1}{N_B \cdot N_A} \sum_{i=1}^{N_B} \left[\sum_{j=1}^{N_A} \left[L_{reg}(t_{i,j}^p, t_{i,j}^*) + L_{cls}(o_{i,j}^p) \right] + \sum_{j=1}^{N_A} L_{cls}(o_{i,j}^n) \right], \quad (1)$$

where t is the regressed bounding box with t^* as its ground truth correspondent, and o is the objectness score. L_{reg} is the smooth L_1 loss taking the difference between normalised bounding box coordinates with the ground truth as defined in [9], and L_{cls} the cross-entropy loss. We use stochastic gradient descent (SGD) with momentum of 0.9, weight decay of 10^{-4} and exponential decay learning rate $l_e = l_0 b^{-\lambda e}$, in which the e is the epoch number and we set $l_0 = 0.1$ and $\lambda = 0.1$ for the base $b = 10$.

4 Empirical Studies

We have conducted comprehensive experiments for comparing different RPN heads as well as ablation studies to show the impact of position-sensitive score maps. The experiment platform is equipped with an Intel(R) Xeon(R) CPU E5-2650 v4@2.20GHz CPU and Nvidia Titan X (Pascal) GPUs with 12 GB memory. Such hardware spec allowed us to train the models with batch size N_B listed in Table 1. Note that we particularly focus on conducting ablation studies on different components. In all experiments we therefore did not exploit additional tricks for boosting the performance such as using multi-scale input images for training [11] and testing [12], iterative regression [8], hard example mining [25], etc.

Table 1. The number of parameters in the different models and the corresponding inference time T in *ms* averaged on the number of all testing images

	w/o position-sensitive				w/ position-sensitive			
	# params	N_B	$T_{\texttt{07test}}$	$T_{\texttt{minival}}$	# params	N_B	$T_{\texttt{07test}}$	$T_{\texttt{minival}}$
Baseline	26,858,334	28	26.6	58.2	26,875,104	18	35.7	79.5
Naïve	28,039,006	18	32.2	-	28,055,776	14	41.5	-
GCN-S	27,137,630	18	34.3	76.3	27,154,400	14	44.1	96.1
LK-S	27,81,3470	18	45.2	-	27,830,240	14	55.1	-
GCN-NS	27,727,966	16	35.9	83.5	27,744,736	12	44.8	103.6
LK-NS	28,403,806	16	48.8	-	28,420,576	12	57.5	-

Baseline Model. The implementation of our *Baseline* model, with or without using position-sensitive score maps, differ from the original FPN [16] in the use of BN and ReLU in the RPN head, as well as the de-aliasing CBR3 block in each layer. In addition, the evaluation in their paper was conducted with rescaling image short side to 800 pixels. The rest of setting such as anchor generation, the number of pyramid layers, etc. are remained the same. Note that such discrepancy do not affect the ablation studies here to compare the baseline architecture. The main purpose is to assess performance gains when adding other network components.

Evaluation Protocol. All models are evaluated on PASCAL VOC [6] and COCO [17]. For Pascal VOC we used all train and validation dataset in 2007 and 2012 (denoted as `07+12`), which has in total 16,551 images with 40,058 objects, and report test result on the 2007 test dataset (denoted as `07test`) consisting of 4,952 images with 12,032 objects. For COCO we employed the union of train and a subset of validation set for in total 109,172 images and 654,212 objects (denoted as `trainval35k`), and report test results on the rest of validation set for 4,589 images and 27,436 objects (denoted as `minival`). Our evaluation is consistent with the official COCO evaluation protocol, in which areas marked as "crowds" are ignored and do not affect detector's scores [17].

In order to perform mini-batch training, we rescaled images in `07+12` with the long side fixed and zero-pad along the rescaled short side to 640 × 640 for batching, and for images in `trainval35k`, the short side were fixed to 768 with random crop along the rescaled long side to 768 × 768. For testing, images in `07test` and `minival` are padded to have width and height being the closest multiple of the maximum stride (i.e., $s = 64$), to avoid rounding errors. All models were trained for 40 epochs which roughly take 30 and 90 h for PASCAL VOC `07+12` and COCO `trainval35k` respectively.

Following [4,13,17], we evaluated models at AR with different proposal numbers of 10, 100 and 1,000 $\{\text{AR}^{10}, \text{AR}^{100}, \text{AR}^{1k}\}$ and the area under the curve (AUC) of recall across all proposal numbers. Besides, we also evaluated models at AR for different object area a: small ($a < 32^2$), medium ($32^2 < a < 96^2$) and large ($a > 96^2$) with 1,000 proposals $\{\text{AR}_s^{1k}, \text{AR}_m^{1k}, \text{AR}_l^{1k}\}$. It is worth noting that COCO has more complex scenes with diverse and many more small objects than PASCAL VOC does [17,22]. We therefore evaluated all models with PASCAL VOC while selected the top-performance GCN-S and GCN-NS models for COCO evaluation. In the tables, numbers with underline indicate the highest score of a metric among models with different RPN heads, and numbers in bold indicate the highest score of a metric among models with or without using position-sensitivity.

4.1 Impact of Using GCN

The results of Tables 2 and 3 reveal that by adding GCN in the RPN head, the overall AR can be remarkably improved regardless the number of considered proposals or if the position-sensitivity is employed. This can be also observed in Fig. 3 in which GCN-S and GCN-NS curves are always on the top of others.

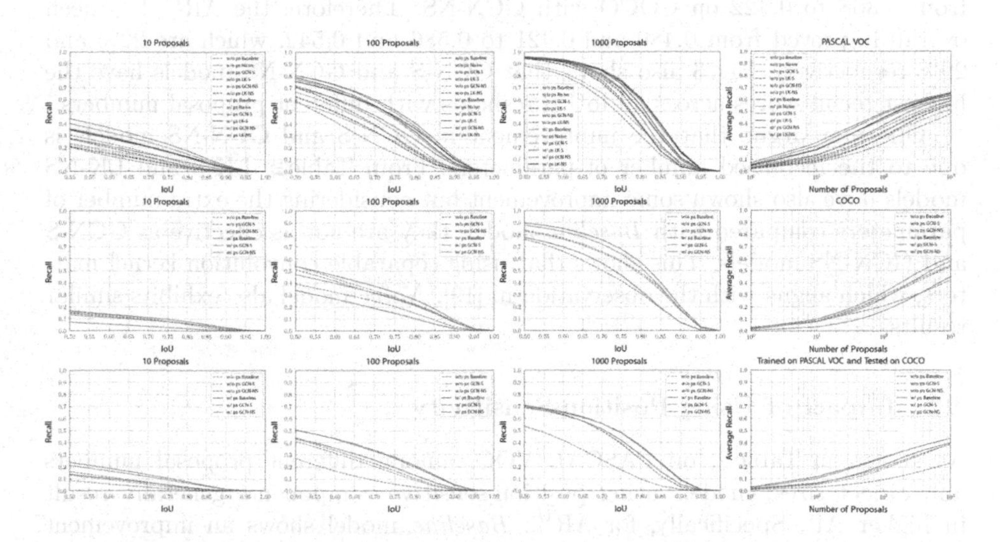

Fig. 3. Recall against IoU with different proposal numbers of 10, 100 and 1,000 and average recall against the number of proposals of all models: The results of PASCAL VOC `07test` using models trained on PASCAL VOC `07+12` (**Row 1**). The results of COCO `minival` using models trained on COCO `trainval35k` (**Row 2**) and models trained on PASCAL VOC `07+12` (**Row 3**).

Table 2. Object proposal results of all models trained on PASCAL VOC 07+12 and evaluated on 07test

	w/o position-sensitive							w/ position-sensitive						
	AR^{10}	AR^{100}	AR^{1k}	AUC	AR_s^{1k}	AR_m^{1k}	AR_l^{1k}	AR^{10}	AR^{100}	AR^{1k}	AUC	AR_s^{1k}	AR_m^{1k}	AR_l^{1k}
Baseline	.074	.234	.480	.272	.254	.414	.566	.131	.385	.605	.399	.423	.583	.655
Naïve	.094	.286	.515	.313	.410	.418	.596	.182	.434	.613	.435	.466	.593	.655
GCN-S	.103	.325	.584	.356	**.471**	.558	.623	.212	.479	.644	.471	.445	.603	.709
LK-S	.113	.333	.562	.356	.441	.547	.595	.178	.447	.630	.446	.463	**.613**	.674
GCN-NS	.136	.365	.586	.383	.445	.569	.625	**.238**	**.490**	**.653**	**.484**	.453	.593	**.730**
LK-NS	.084	.290	.551	.326	.420	.553	.575	.179	.447	.645	.450	.429	.582	.728

Table 3. Object proposal results of all models trained on COCO trainval35k and evaluated on minival

	w/o position-sensitive							w/ position-sensitive						
	AR^{10}	AR^{100}	AR^{1k}	AUC	AR_s^{1k}	AR_m^{1k}	AR_l^{1k}	AR^{10}	AR^{100}	AR^{1k}	AUC	AR_s^{1k}	AR_m^{1k}	AR_l^{1k}
Baseline	.083	.208	.421	.242	.308	.562	.392	.034	.165	.448	.219	.385	.411	.566
GCN-S	.082	.294	.542	.322	.414	.558	.680	.075	.270	.579	.321	.485	.592	.677
GCN-NS	.079	.277	.532	.310	.422	.552	.643	**.096**	**.316**	**.607**	**.358**	**.493**	**.623**	**.726**

AR_s^{1k} in particular benefits from learning the global image context. One can observe that compared to *Baseline* model, the scores have been boosted by 85% from 0.254 to 0.471 on PASCAL VOC with GCN-S model, and by 37% from 0.308 to 0.422 on COCO with GCN-NS. Therefore, the AR^{1k} has been overall improved from 0.480 and 0.421 to 0.586 and 0.542, which are 22% and 29% respectively. Fig. 3 also shows that GCN-S and GCN-NS models have the highest recall scores across all IoU thresholds with different proposal numbers.

One may argue that the improvement in GCN-S and GCN-NS models is due to the increased number of parameters. From Table 2, LK-S and LK-NS models have also shown some improvement but considering the extra number of parameters compared with *Baseline* model, they are not as effective as GCN-S and GCN-NS models. This shows that using separable convolution kernel matters, which aligns with the observation in [19]. *Naïve* model also exhibits similar results.

4.2 Impact of Using Position-Sensitivity

As shown in Table 2, on PASCAL VOC, among different proposal numbers and object sizes, models using position-sensitive components generally result in higher AR. Specifically, for AR^{1k}, *Baseline* model shows an improvement from 0.480 to 0.605 (26%) and GCN-NS from 0.586 to 0.653 (11%). As shown in Table 3, the experiment on COCO shows similar results, in which *Baseline* model has an improvement from 0.421 to 0.448 (6%) and GCN-NS model from 0.532 to 0.607 (14%). To investigate on the small object proposals, AR_s^{1k} reveal that training on a large number of annotated small objects in COCO indeed helps in higher AR_s^{1k} scores, compared with the results of PASCAL VOC counterpart.

GCN-NS has achieved much higher AR_s^{1k} (0.493) score, which is a 17% improvement compared to the counterpart. Fig. 4 visualises the distribution heatmap and hit-and-miss of top 1,000 proposals using GCN-NS models with and without taking position-sensitivity into account, in which the hits are with a threshold 0.7 for the ground truth IoU. One can qualitatively tell that by using the position-sensitivity, models can generate proposals closer to objects and thus result in more hits, especially for objects with extremely large or small sizes.

4.3 Inference Time

Introducing both GCN structure and position-sensitive score maps in the RPN head brings in more learnable parameters resulting in more computation. Beside the input image size which has a directly impact on the overall inference time, the number of anchors, the kernel size of GCN and the grid number k of position-sensitive score maps are also key factors. Table 1 lists the models' inference times averaged on all input images in both `07test` and `minival`, in which *Baseline* model shows a performance of 26.6/58.2 (denoted for `07test/minival`) ms. Adding the position-sensitive score maps (with grid size $k = 4$) takes extra 9.1/21.3 ms, 9.8/19.8 ms and 8.9/20.1 ms for *Baseline*, GCN-S and GCN-NS model respectively, which show a comparable time difference. In contrast, introducing the GCN structure in the *Baseline* model adds 7.7/18.1 ms for GCN-S model while additional 9.3/25.3 ms for GCN-NS model. This reveals that using non-shared smoother generally takes more times than using shared smoother does. GCN-NS with position-sensitivity, as the best performance model, has a running time 44.8 ms ($\sim$22 fps) for `07+12` and 103.6 ms ($\sim$10 fps) for `minival`.

4.4 Model Generalisation

To evaluate the generalisation ability of the proposed method, the models trained on PASCAL VOC `07+12` are used to evaluate on COCO `minival`. Note that compared to COCO (80 categories), PASCAL VOC is a much smaller dataset with limited object categories (20 categories) and almost all categories in PASCAL VOC are included in COCO. We separate the categories of COCO into two sets: *common* and *non-common*. Common categories are ones in PASCAL VOC, while non-common are unseen categories. In addition, image scenes in PASCAL VOC are relatively simple with less small objects annotations. It is therefore more challenging for a model learned from PASCAL VOC to performance object proposal on COCO images. The results are shown in Table 4 and Fig. 3 (**Row 3**). Surprisingly, the AR^{1k} of the best performance models, GCN-S and GCN-NS with position-sensitivity, trained with PASCAL VOC `07+12` can still outperform *Baseline* model trained with COCO `trainval35k` (i.e., 0.438 vs. 0.421). It is expected that the model will not work well on small objects since PASCAL VOC does not contain many small objects, but nevertheless the model still shows decent performance on large objects in which the AR_l^{1k} is up to 0.693 as shown in Table 4. The score is comparable to the other models trained on COCO `trainval35k` as shown in Table 3. Delving into the details, we

Fig. 4. The impact of position-sensitivity: visualisation on the distribution heatmap and hit-and-miss of the top 1,000 proposals by GCN-NS models for a number of selected PASCAL VOC `07test` (**Row 1–2**) and COCO `minival` (**Row 3–5**) images. For each pair of images, model without position-sensitivity is on the left and the one with position-sensitivity is on the right. **Col 1–2:** The heatmaps are plotted by stacking the proposal boxes. **Col 3–4:** The bounding boxes in orange are ground truth boxes with their corresponding hit proposals in cyan, in which the IoU threshold is set to 0.7, and the bounding boxes in red are missed cases. **Row 6–7:** All models tend to fail in images with complex scenes and diverse object aspect ratios. Nonetheless, note that models with position-sensitivity generally have higher hit rate. Sect. 4.2 for detailed discussions.

show the breakdown results of the model generalisation experiment for common and non-common categories are shown in Table 5. All models have better performance on common categories overall. However, compared to the *Baseline* model, the proposed components significantly improved the performance on both common and non-common categories. The per-category AUC performance in Fig. 5 shows that non-common categories do not necessarily have worse performance than common categories (e.g., bear, zebra, and toilet). This indicates that the proposed object proposal networks are able to generalise proposals from a smaller to a larger and more complex dataset, from common to non-common categories, and that the proposed architecture can further improve the generalisation for all categories. Fig. 6 qualitatively demonstrates the generalisation ability of the proposed method. Although the model trained on PASCAL VOC 07+12 fails at detecting small objectness, it still exhibits a certain degree of generalisation to unseen categories (e.g., elephant, teddy bear, or fire hydrant).

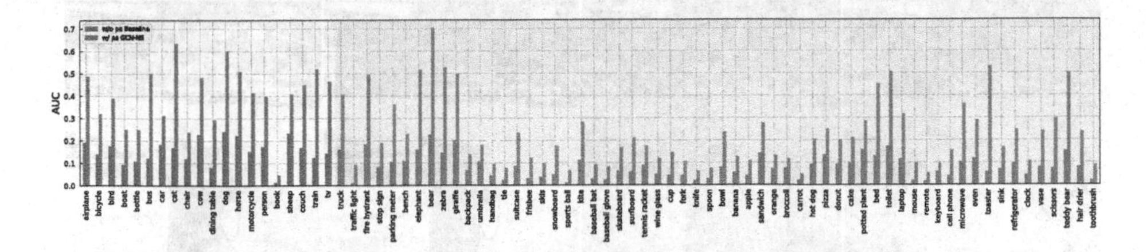

Fig. 5. Per-category AUC performance of models trained on PASCAL VOC 07+12 and evaluated on COCO `minival`. Common and non-common categories are split in the white and green region respectively.

Table 4. Object proposal results of all models trained on PASCAL VOC 07+12 and evaluated on COCO `minival`

	w/o position-sensitive							w/ position-sensitive						
	AR^{10}	AR^{100}	AR^{1k}	AUC	AR_s^{1k}	AR_m^{1k}	AR_l^{1k}	AR^{10}	AR^{100}	AR^{1k}	AUC	AR_s^{1k}	AR_m^{1k}	AR_l^{1k}
Baseline	.031	.097	.234	.122	.114	.234	.382	.061	.218	.400	.240	.224	.401	.614
GCN-S	.053	.185	.390	.217	**.240**	.430	.524	.104	.277	**.438**	.288	.227	**.463**	.665
GCN-NS	.066	.200	.390	.228	.239	.420	.538	**.118**	**.282**	**.438**	**.292**	.235	.432	**.693**

Table 5. Object proposal results of all models trained on PASCAL VOC 07+12 and evaluated on COCO `minival` for *common* and *non-common* categories. Note that *(*non) denotes models evaluated on *non-common* categories

	w/o position-sensitive							w/ position-sensitive						
	AR^{10}	AR^{100}	AR^{1k}	AUC	AR_s^{1k}	AR_m^{1k}	AR_l^{1k}	AR^{10}	AR^{100}	AR^{1k}	AUC	AR_s^{1k}	AR_m^{1k}	AR_l^{1k}
Baseline	.046	.129	.285	.156	.180	.316	.369	.076	.271	.483	.294	.329	.506	.629
Baseline (*non*)	.013	.055	.170	.079	.035	.139	.402	.043	.151	.295	.171	.099	.280	.590
GCN-S	.061	.217	.447	.252	.329	.499	.524	.128	.344	.520	.351	.327	**.564**	.687
GCN-S (*non*)	.042	.144	.317	.172	.134	.349	.525	.073	.192	.334	.207	.107	.346	.632
GCN-NS	.078	.240	.451	.269	.323	.493	.549	**.149**	**.353**	**.524**	**.360**	**.335**	.540	**.716**
GCN-NS (*non*)	.050	.150	.312	.175	.138	.334	.522	.078	.192	.328	.206	.114	.305	.658

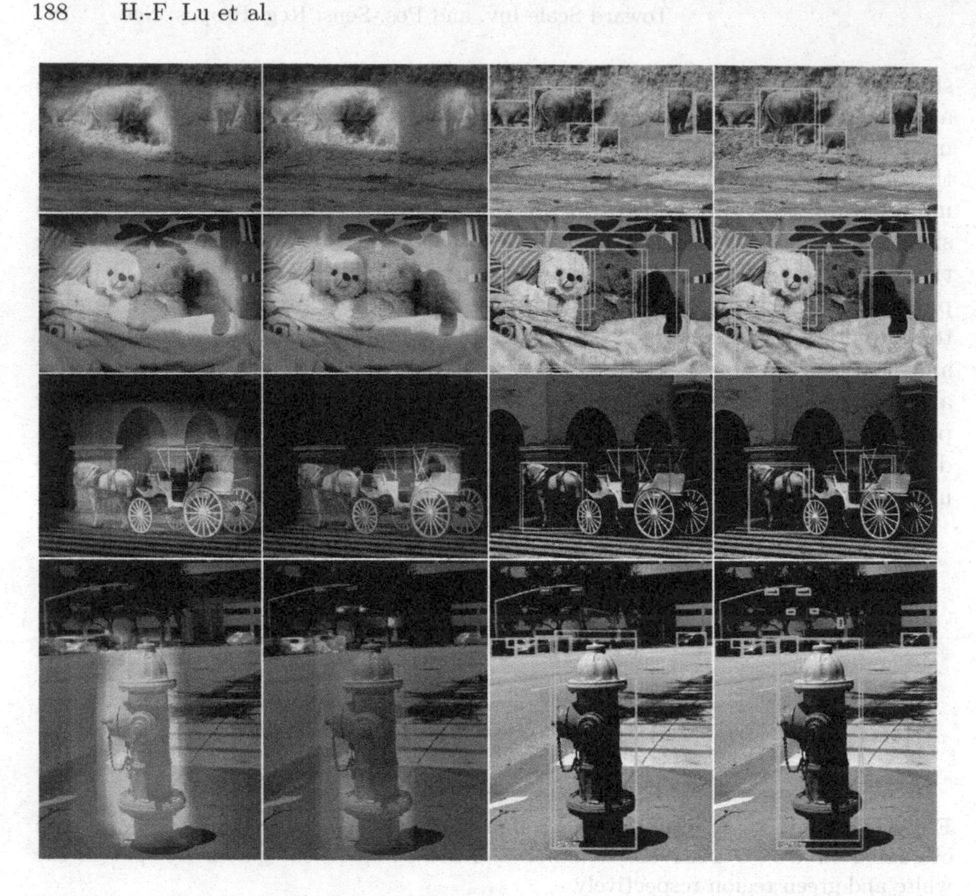

Fig. 6. The results of model generalisation experiments visualised in the distribution heatmap and hit-and-miss of the top 1,000 proposals by GCN-NS models for a number of selected COCO `minival`. For each pair of COCO `minival` images, result of model trained on PASCAL VOC is on the left and the one of model trained on COCO is on the right. See Sect. 4.4 for detailed discussions.

5 Conclusions

In this paper, we have proposed object proposal networks based on the observation that accurate detection relies on translation-invariance for objectness classification, translation-variance for localisation as regression and scale-invariance for various object sizes. Thorough experiments on PASCAL VOC and COCO datasets have shown that the adoption of global convolutional network (GCN) and position-sensitivity components can significantly improve object proposal performance while keeping the network lightweight to achieve real-time performance.

References

1. Arbeláez, P., Pont-Tuset, J., Barron, J.T., Marques, F., Malik, J.: Multiscale combinatorial grouping. In: CVPR (2014)
2. Bell, S., Lawrence Zitnick, C., Bala, K., Girshick, R.: Inside-outside net: detecting objects in context with skip pooling and recurrent neural networks. In: CVPR (2016)
3. Carreira, J., Sminchisescu, C.: CPMC: automatic object segmentation using constrained parametric min-cuts. In: TPAMI (2012)
4. Chavali, N., Agrawal, H., Mahendru, A., Batra, D.: Object-proposal evaluation protocol is 'gameable'. In: CVPR (2016)
5. Dai, J., Li, Y., He, K., Sun, J.: R-FCN: object detection via region-based fully convolutional networks. In: NIPS (2016)
6. Everingham, M., Van Gool, L., Williams, C.K., Winn, J., Zisserman, A.: The PASCAL visual object classes (VOC) challenge. IJCV **88**, 303–338 (2010)
7. Felzenszwalb, P.F., Girshick, R.B., McAllester, D., Ramanan, D.: Object detection with discriminatively trained part-based models. TPAMI **32**, 1627–1645 (2010)
8. Gidaris, S., Komodakis, N.: Object detection via a multi-region and semantic segmentation-aware CNN model. In: ICCV (2015)
9. Girshick, R.: Fast R-CNN. In: ICCV (2015)
10. Girshick, R., Donahue, J., Darrell, T., Malik, J.: Rich feature hierarchies for accurate object detection and semantic segmentation. In: CVPR (2014)
11. He, K., Zhang, X., Ren, S., Sun, J.: Spatial pyramid pooling in deep convolutional networks for visual recognition. In: Fleet, D., Pajdla, T., Schiele, B., Tuytelaars, T. (eds.) ECCV 2014. LNCS, vol. 8691, pp. 346–361. Springer, Cham (2014). https://doi.org/10.1007/978-3-319-10578-9_23
12. He, K., Zhang, X., Ren, S., Sun, J.: Deep residual learning for image recognition. In: CVPR (2016)
13. Hosang, J., Benenson, R., Dollár, P., Schiele, B.: What makes for effective detection proposals? TPAMI **38**, 814–830 (2016)
14. Kong, T., Yao, A., Chen, Y., Sun, F.: Hypernet: towards accurate region proposal generation and joint object detection. In: CVPR (2016)
15. Kuo, W., Hariharan, B., Malik, J.: DeepBox: Learning objectness with convolutional networks. In: ICCV (2015)
16. Lin, T.Y., Dollár, P., Girshick, R., He, K., Hariharan, B., Belongie, S.: Feature pyramid networks for object detection. In: CVPR (2017)
17. Lin, T.-Y., et al.: Microsoft COCO: common objects in context. In: Fleet, D., Pajdla, T., Schiele, B., Tuytelaars, T. (eds.) ECCV 2014. LNCS, vol. 8693, pp. 740–755. Springer, Cham (2014). https://doi.org/10.1007/978-3-319-10602-1_48
18. Long, J., Shelhamer, E., Darrell, T.: Fully convolutional networks for semantic segmentation. In: CVPR (2015)
19. Peng, C., Zhang, X., Yu, G., Luo, G., Sun, J.: Large kernel matters-improve semantic segmentation by global convolutional network. In: CVPR (2017)
20. Pinheiro, P.O., Collobert, R., Dollár, P.: Learning to segment object candidates. In: NIPS (2015)
21. Pinheiro, P.O., Lin, T.-Y., Collobert, R., Dollár, P.: Learning to refine object segments. In: Leibe, B., Matas, J., Sebe, N., Welling, M. (eds.) ECCV 2016. LNCS, vol. 9905, pp. 75–91. Springer, Cham (2016). https://doi.org/10.1007/978-3-319-46448-0_5

22. Pont-Tuset, J., Van Gool, L.: Boosting object proposals: from pascal to COCO. In: ICCV (2015)
23. Ren, S., He, K., Girshick, R., Sun, J.: Faster R-CNN: towards real-time object detection with region proposal networks. In: Advances in neural information processing systems (2015)
24. Ronneberger, O., Fischer, P., Brox, T.: U-Net: convolutional networks for biomedical image segmentation. In: Navab, N., Hornegger, J., Wells, W.M., Frangi, A.F. (eds.) MICCAI 2015. LNCS, vol. 9351, pp. 234–241. Springer, Cham (2015). https://doi.org/10.1007/978-3-319-24574-4_28
25. Shrivastava, A., Gupta, A., Girshick, R.: Training region-based object detectors with online hard example mining. In: CVPR (2016)
26. Simonyan, K., Zisserman, A.: Very deep convolutional networks for large-scale image recognition. In: ICLR (2014)
27. Uijlings, J.R., Van De Sande, K.E., Gevers, T., Smeulders, A.W.: Selective search for object recognition. IJCV **104**, 154–171 (2013)
28. Viola, P., Jones, M.J.: Robust real-time face detection. IJCV **57**, 137–154 (2004)
29. Zeiler, M.D., Fergus, R.: Visualizing and understanding convolutional networks. In: Fleet, D., Pajdla, T., Schiele, B., Tuytelaars, T. (eds.) ECCV 2014. LNCS, vol. 8689, pp. 818–833. Springer, Cham (2014). https://doi.org/10.1007/978-3-319-10590-1_53
30. Zitnick, C.L., Dollár, P.: Edge boxes: locating object proposals from edges. In: Fleet, D., Pajdla, T., Schiele, B., Tuytelaars, T. (eds.) ECCV 2014. LNCS, vol. 8693, pp. 391–405. Springer, Cham (2014). https://doi.org/10.1007/978-3-319-10602-1_26

A Systematic DNN Weight Pruning Framework Using Alternating Direction Method of Multipliers

Tianyun Zhang[1](✉), Shaokai Ye[1], Kaiqi Zhang[1], Jian Tang[1], Wujie Wen[2], Makan Fardad[1], and Yanzhi Wang[3]

[1] Syracuse University, Syracuse, NY 13244, USA
{tzhan120,sye106,kzhang17,jtang02,makan}@syr.edu
[2] Florida International University, Miami, FL 33199, USA
[3] Northeastern University, Boston, MA 02115, USA

Abstract. Weight pruning methods for deep neural networks (DNNs) have been investigated recently, but prior work in this area is mainly heuristic, iterative pruning, thereby lacking guarantees on the weight reduction ratio and convergence time. To mitigate these limitations, we present a systematic weight pruning framework of DNNs using the alternating direction method of multipliers (ADMM). We first formulate the weight pruning problem of DNNs as a nonconvex optimization problem with combinatorial constraints specifying the sparsity requirements, and then adopt the ADMM framework for systematic weight pruning. By using ADMM, the original nonconvex optimization problem is decomposed into two subproblems that are solved iteratively. One of these subproblems can be solved using stochastic gradient descent, the other can be solved analytically. Besides, our method achieves a fast convergence rate.

The weight pruning results are very promising and consistently outperform the prior work. On the LeNet-5 model for the MNIST data set, we achieve 71.2× weight reduction without accuracy loss. On the AlexNet model for the ImageNet data set, we achieve 21× weight reduction without accuracy loss. When we focus on the convolutional layer pruning for computation reductions, we can reduce the total computation by five times compared with the prior work (achieving a total of 13.4× weight reduction in convolutional layers). Our models and codes are released at https://github.com/KaiqiZhang/admm-pruning.

Keywords: Systematic weight pruning
Deep neural networks (DNNs)
Alternating direction method of multipliers (ADMM)

T. Zhang and S. Ye—Equal contribution.

V. Ferrari et al. (Eds.): ECCV 2018, LNCS 11212, pp. 191–207, 2018.
https://doi.org/10.1007/978-3-030-01237-3_12

1 Introduction

Large-scale deep neural networks or DNNs have made breakthroughs in many fields, such as image recognition [12,16,17], speech recognition [4,13], game playing [24], and driver-less cars [23]. Despite the huge success, their large model size and computational requirements will add significant burden to state-of-the-art computing systems [10,16,27], especially for embedded and IoT systems. As a result, a number of prior works are dedicated to *model compression* in order to simultaneously reduce the computation and model storage requirements of DNNs, with minor effect on the overall accuracy. These model compression techniques include *weight pruning* [5,9–11,21,25,29,31], sparsity regularization [19,30,32], weight clustering [3,10,26], and low rank approximation [6,7], etc.

A simple but effective weight pruning method has been proposed in [11], which prunes the relatively less important weights and performs retraining for maintaining accuracy in an iterative manner. It can achieve 9× weight reduction ratio on the AlexNet model with virtually no accuracy degradation. This method has been extended and generalized in multiple directions, including energy efficiency-aware pruning [31], structure-preserved pruning using regularization methods [30], and employing more powerful (and time-consuming) heuristics such as evolutionary algorithms [5]. While existing pruning methods achieve good model compression ratios, they are heuristic (and therefore cannot achieve optimal compression ratio), lack theoretical guarantees on compression performance, and require time-consuming iterative retraining processes.

To mitigate these shortcomings, we present a systematic framework of weight pruning and model compression, by (i) formulating the weight pruning problem as a constrained nonconvex optimization problem with combinatorial constraints, which employs the cardinality function to induce sparsity of the weights, and (ii) adopting the *alternating direction method of multipliers* (ADMM) [2] for systematically solving this optimization problem. By using ADMM, the original nonconvex optimization problem is decomposed into two subproblems that are solved iteratively. In the weight pruning problem, one of these subproblems can be solved using stochastic gradient descent, and the other can be solved analytically. Upon convergence of ADMM, we remove the weights which are (close to) zero and retrain the network.

Our extensive numerical experiments indicate that ADMM works very well in weight pruning. The weight pruning results consistently outperform the prior work. On the LeNet-5 model for the MNIST data set, we achieve 71.2× weight reduction without accuracy loss, which is 5.9 times compared with [11]. On the AlexNet model for the ImageNet data set, we achieve 21× weight reduction without accuracy loss, which is 2.3 times compared with [11]. Moreover, when we focus on the convolutional layer pruning for computation reductions, we can reduce the total computation by five times compared with the prior work (achieving a total of 13.4× weight reduction in convolutional layers). Our models and codes are released at https://github.com/KaiqiZhang/admm-pruning.

2 Related Work on Weight Reduction/Model Compression

Mathematical investigations have demonstrated a significant margin for weight reduction in DNNs due to the redundancy across filters and channels, and a number of prior works leverage this property to reduce weight storage. The techniques can be classified into two categories: *(1) Low rank approximation* methods [6,7] such as Singular Value Decomposition (SVD), which are typically difficult to achieve zero accuracy degradation with compression, especially for very large DNNs; *(2) Weight pruning* methods which aim to remove the redundant or less important weights, thereby achieving model compression with negligible accuracy loss.

A prior work [11] serves as a pioneering work for weight pruning. It uses a heuristic method of iteratively pruning the unimportant weights (weights with small magnitudes) and retraining the DNN. It can achieve a good weight reduction ratio, e.g., 9× for AlexNet, with virtually zero accuracy degradation, and can be combined with other model compression techniques such as weight clustering [3,10]. It has been extended in several works. For instance, the *energy efficiency-aware pruning* method [31] has been proposed to facilitate energy-efficient hardware implementations, allowing for certain accuracy degradation. The *structured sparsity learning* technique has been proposed to partially overcome the limitation in [11] of irregular network structure after pruning. However, neither technique can outperform the original method [11] in terms of compression ratio under the same accuracy. There is recent work [5] that employs an evolutionary algorithm for weight pruning, which incorporates randomness in both pruning and growing of weights, following certain probabilistic rules. Despite the higher compression ratio it achieves, it suffers from a prohibitively long retraining phase. For example, it needs to start with an already-compressed model for further pruning on the ImageNet data set, instead of the original AlexNet or VGG models.

In summary, the prior weight pruning methods are highly heuristic and suffer from a long retraining phase. On the other hand, our proposed method is a systematic framework, achieves higher compression ratio, exhibits faster convergence rate, and is also general for structured pruning and weight clustering.

3 Background of ADMM

ADMM was first introduced in the 1970s, and theoretical results in the following decades have been collected in [2]. It is a powerful method for solving regularized convex optimization problems, especially for problems in applied statistics and machine learning. Moreover, recent works [18,28] demonstrate that ADMM is also a good tool for solving nonconvex problems, potentially with combinatorial constraints, since it can converge to a solution that may not be globally optimal but is sufficiently good for many applications.

For some problems which are difficult to solve directly, we can use variable splitting first, and then employ ADMM to decompose the problem into two subproblems that can be solved separately and efficiently. For example, the optimization problem

$$\underset{\mathbf{x}}{\text{minimize}} \quad f(\mathbf{x}) + g(\mathbf{x}), \tag{1}$$

assumes that $f(\cdot)$ is differentiable and $g(\cdot)$ is non-differentiable but has exploitable structure properties. Common instances of g are the ℓ_1 norm and the indicator function of a constraint set. To make it suitable for the application of ADMM, we use variable splitting to rewrite the problem as

$$\underset{\mathbf{x},\ \mathbf{z}}{\text{minimize}} \quad f(\mathbf{x}) + g(\mathbf{z}),$$

$$\text{subject to} \quad \mathbf{x} = \mathbf{z}.$$

Next, via the introduction of the augmented Lagrangian, the above optimization problem can be decomposed into two subproblems in $\mathbf{x}$ and $\mathbf{z}$ [2]. The first subproblem is $\underset{\mathbf{x}}{\text{minimize}}\ f(\mathbf{x}) + q_1(\mathbf{x})$, where $q_1(\cdot)$ is a quadratic function of its argument. Since f and q_1 are differentiable, the first subproblem can be solved by gradient descent. The second subproblem is $\underset{\mathbf{z}}{\text{minimize}}\ g(\mathbf{z}) + q_2(\mathbf{z})$, where $q_2(\cdot)$ is a quadratic function of its argument. In problems where g has some special structure, for instance if it is a regularizer in (1), exploiting the properties of g may allow this problem to be solved analytically. More details regarding the application of ADMM to the weight pruning problem will be demonstrated in Sect. 4.2.

4 Problem Formulation and Proposed Framework

4.1 Problem Formulation of Weight Pruning

Consider an N-layer DNN, where the collection of weights in the i-th (convolutional or fully-connected) layer is denoted by $\mathbf{W}_i$ and the collection of biases in the i-th layer is denoted by $\mathbf{b}_i$. In a convolutional layer the weights are organized in a four-dimensional tensor and in a fully-connected layer they are organized in a two-dimensional matrix [18].

Assume that the input to the (fully-connected) DNN is $\mathbf{x}$. Every column of $\mathbf{x}$ corresponds to a training image, and the number t of columns determines the number of training images in the input batch. The input $\mathbf{x}$ will enter the first layer and the output of the first layer is calculated by

$$\mathbf{h}_1 = \sigma(\mathbf{W}_1\mathbf{x} + \mathbf{b}_1),$$

where $\mathbf{h}_1$ and $\mathbf{b}_1$ have t columns, and $\mathbf{b}_1$ is a matrix with identical columns. The non-linear activation function $\sigma(\cdot)$ acts entry-wise on its argument, and is typically chosen to be the ReLU function [22] in state-of-the-art DNNs. Since the output of one layer is the input of the next, the output of the i-th layer for $i = 2, \dots, N-1$ is given by

$$\mathbf{h}_i = \sigma(\mathbf{W}_i \mathbf{h}_{i-1} + \mathbf{b}_i).$$

The output of the DNN corresponding to a batch of images is

$$\mathbf{s} = \mathbf{W}_N \mathbf{h}_{N-1} + \mathbf{b}_N.$$

In this case $\mathbf{s}$ is a $k \times t$ matrix, where k is the number of classes in the classification, and t is the number of training images in the batch. The element $\mathbf{s}_{ij}$ in matrix $\mathbf{s}$ is the score of the j-th training image corresponding to the i-th class. The total loss of the DNN is calculated as

$$f(\{\mathbf{W}_1, \dots, \mathbf{W}_N\}, \{\mathbf{b}_1, \dots, \mathbf{b}_N\}) = -\frac{1}{t} \sum_{j=1}^{t} \log \frac{e^{\mathbf{s}_{y_j j}}}{\sum_{i=1}^{k} e^{\mathbf{s}_{ij}}} + \lambda \sum_{i=1}^{N} \|\mathbf{W}_i\|_F^2,$$

where $\|\cdot\|_F^2$ denotes the Frobenius norm, the first term is cross-entropy loss, y_j is the correct class of the j-th image, and the second term is L_2 weight regularization.

Hereafter, for simplicity of notation we write $\{\mathbf{W}_i\}_{i=1}^N$, or simply $\{\mathbf{W}_i\}$, instead of $\{\mathbf{W}_1, \dots, \mathbf{W}_N\}$. The same notational convention applies to writing $\{\mathbf{b}_i\}$ instead of $\{\mathbf{b}_1, \dots, \mathbf{b}_N\}$. The training of a DNN is a process of minimizing the loss by updating weights and biases. If we use the gradient descent method, the update at every step is

$$\mathbf{W}_i = \mathbf{W}_i - \alpha \frac{\partial f(\{\mathbf{W}_i\}, \{\mathbf{b}_i\})}{\partial \mathbf{W}_i},$$

$$\mathbf{b}_i = \mathbf{b}_i - \alpha \frac{\partial f(\{\mathbf{W}_i\}, \{\mathbf{b}_i\})}{\partial \mathbf{b}_i},$$

for $i = 1, \dots, N$, where α is the learning rate.

Our objective is to prune the weights of the DNN, and therefore we minimize the loss function subject to constraints on the cardinality of weights in each layer. More specifically, our training process solves

$$\begin{array}{ll} \underset{\{\mathbf{W}_i\}, \{\mathbf{b}_i\}}{\text{minimize}} & f(\{\mathbf{W}_i\}, \{\mathbf{b}_i\}), \\ \text{subject to} & \text{card}(\mathbf{W}_i) \le l_i, \; i = 1, \dots, N, \end{array}$$

where $\text{card}(\cdot)$ returns the number of nonzero elements of its matrix argument and l_i is the desired number of weights in the i-th layer of the DNN[1]. A prior work [15] uses ADMM for DNN training with regularization in the objective function, which can result in sparsity as well. On the other hand, our method directly targets at sparsity with incorporating hard constraints on the weights, thereby resulting in a higher degree of sparsity.

[1] Our framework is also compatible with the constraint of l total number of weights for the whole DNN.

4.2 Systematic Weight Pruning Framework Using ADMM

We can rewrite the above weight pruning optimization problem as

$$\begin{aligned} &\underset{\{\mathbf{W}_i\},\{\mathbf{b}_i\}}{\text{minimize}} && f\big(\{\mathbf{W}_i\},\{\mathbf{b}_i\}\big),\\ &\text{subject to} && \mathbf{W}_i \in \mathbf{S}_i,\ i=1,\ldots,N, \end{aligned}$$

where $\mathbf{S}_i = \{\mathbf{W}_i \mid \text{card}(\mathbf{W}_i) \leq l_i\}, i = 1,\ldots,N$. It is clear that $\mathbf{S}_1,\ldots,\mathbf{S}_N$ are nonconvex sets, and it is in general difficult to solve optimization problems with nonconvex constraints. The problem can be equivalently rewritten in a form without constraint, which is

$$\underset{\{\mathbf{W}_i\},\{\mathbf{b}_i\}}{\text{minimize}} \quad f\big(\{\mathbf{W}_i\},\{\mathbf{b}_i\}\big) + \sum_{i=1}^{N} g_i(\mathbf{W}_i), \tag{2}$$

where $g_i(\cdot)$ is the indicator function of $\mathbf{S}_i$, i.e.,

$$g_i(\mathbf{W}_i) = \begin{cases} 0 & \text{if } \text{card}(\mathbf{W}_i) \leq l_i,\\ +\infty & \text{otherwise.} \end{cases}$$

The first term of problem (2) is the loss function of a DNN, while the second term is non-differentiable. This problem cannot be solved analytically or by stochastic gradient descent. A recent paper [2], however, demonstrates that such problems lend themselves well to the application of ADMM, via a special decomposition into simpler subproblems. We begin by equivalently rewriting the above problem in ADMM form as

$$\begin{aligned} &\underset{\{\mathbf{W}_i\},\{\mathbf{b}_i\}}{\text{minimize}} && f\big(\{\mathbf{W}_i\},\{\mathbf{b}_i\}\big) + \sum_{i=1}^{N} g_i(\mathbf{Z}_i),\\ &\text{subject to} && \mathbf{W}_i = \mathbf{Z}_i,\ i=1,\ldots,N. \end{aligned}$$

The augmented Lagrangian [2] of the above optimization problem is given by

$$\begin{aligned} L_\rho\big(\{\mathbf{W}_i\},\{\mathbf{b}_i\},\{\mathbf{Z}_i\},\{\mathbf{\Lambda}_i\}\big) &= f\big(\{\mathbf{W}_i\},\{\mathbf{b}_i\}\big) + \sum_{i=1}^{N} g_i(\mathbf{Z}_i)\\ &\quad + \sum_{i=1}^{N} \text{tr}[\mathbf{\Lambda}_i^T(\mathbf{W}_i - \mathbf{Z}_i)] + \sum_{i=1}^{N} \frac{\rho_i}{2}\|\mathbf{W}_i - \mathbf{Z}_i\|_F^2, \end{aligned}$$

where $\mathbf{\Lambda}_i$ has the same dimension as $\mathbf{W}_i$ and is the Lagrange multiplier (also known as the dual variable) corresponding to the constraint $\mathbf{W}_i = \mathbf{Z}_i$, the positive scalars $\{\rho_1,\ldots,\rho_N\}$ are penalty parameters, $\text{tr}(\cdot)$ denotes the trace, and $\|\cdot\|_F^2$ denotes the Frobenius norm. Defining the scaled dual variable $\mathbf{U}_i = (1/\rho_i)\mathbf{\Lambda}_i$, the augmented Lagrangian can be equivalently expressed as

$$L_\rho(\{\mathbf{W}_i\},\{\mathbf{b}_i\},\{\mathbf{Z}_i\},\{\mathbf{\Lambda}_i\}) = f(\{\mathbf{W}_i\},\{\mathbf{b}_i\}) + \sum_{i=1}^N g_i(\mathbf{Z}_i)$$
$$+\sum_{i=1}^N \frac{\rho_i}{2}\|\mathbf{W}_i - \mathbf{Z}_i + \mathbf{U}_i\|_F^2 - \sum_{i=1}^N \frac{\rho_i}{2}\|\mathbf{U}_i\|_F^2.$$

The ADMM algorithm proceeds by repeating, for $k = 0, 1, \ldots$, the following steps [2,20]:

$$\{\mathbf{W}_i^{k+1}, \mathbf{b}_i^{k+1}\} := \underset{\{\mathbf{W}_i\},\{\mathbf{b}_i\}}{\arg\min} \quad L_\rho(\{\mathbf{W}_i\},\{\mathbf{b}_i\},\{\mathbf{Z}_i^k\},\{\mathbf{U}_i^k\}) \tag{3}$$

$$\{\mathbf{Z}_i^{k+1}\} := \underset{\{\mathbf{Z}_i\}}{\arg\min} \quad L_\rho(\{\mathbf{W}_i^{k+1}\},\{\mathbf{b}_i^{k+1}\},\{\mathbf{Z}_i\},\{\mathbf{U}_i^k\}) \tag{4}$$

$$\mathbf{U}_i^{k+1} := \mathbf{U}_i^k + \mathbf{W}_i^{k+1} - \mathbf{Z}_i^{k+1}, \tag{5}$$

until both of the following conditions are satisfied

$$\|\mathbf{W}_i^{k+1} - \mathbf{Z}_i^{k+1}\|_F^2 \le \epsilon_i, \quad \|\mathbf{Z}_i^{k+1} - \mathbf{Z}_i^k\|_F^2 \le \epsilon_i. \tag{6}$$

In order to solve the overall pruning problem, we need to solve subproblems (3) and (4). More specifically, problem (3) can be formulated as

$$\underset{\{\mathbf{W}_i\},\{\mathbf{b}_i\}}{\text{minimize}} \quad f(\{\mathbf{W}_i\},\{\mathbf{b}_i\}) + \sum_{i=1}^N \frac{\rho_i}{2}\|\mathbf{W}_i - \mathbf{Z}_i^k + \mathbf{U}_i^k\|_F^2, \tag{7}$$

where the first term is the loss function of the DNN, and the second term can be considered as a special L_2 regularizer. Since the regularizer is a differentiable quadratic norm, and the loss function of the DNN is differentiable, problem (7) can be solved by stochastic gradient descent. More specifically, the gradients of the augmented Lagrangian with respect to $\mathbf{W}_i$ and $\mathbf{b}_i$ are given by

$$\frac{\partial L_\rho(\{\mathbf{W}_i\},\{\mathbf{b}_i\},\{\mathbf{Z}_i^k\},\{\mathbf{U}_i^k\})}{\partial \mathbf{W}_i} = \frac{\partial f(\{\mathbf{W}_i\},\{\mathbf{b}_i\})}{\partial \mathbf{W}_i} + \rho_i(\mathbf{W}_i - \mathbf{Z}_i^k + \mathbf{U}_i^k),$$
$$\frac{\partial L_\rho(\{\mathbf{W}_i\},\{\mathbf{b}_i\},\{\mathbf{Z}_i^k\},\{\mathbf{U}_i^k\})}{\partial \mathbf{b}_i} = \frac{\partial f(\{\mathbf{W}_i\},\{\mathbf{b}_i\})}{\partial \mathbf{b}_i}.$$

Note that we cannot prove optimality of the solution to subproblem (3), just as we can not prove optimality of the solution to the original DNN training problem due to the nonconvexity of the loss function of DNN.

On the other hand, problem (4) can be formulated as

$$\underset{\{\mathbf{Z}_i\}}{\text{minimize}} \quad \sum_{i=1}^N g_i(\mathbf{Z}_i) + \sum_{i=1}^N \frac{\rho_i}{2}\|\mathbf{W}_i^{k+1} - \mathbf{Z}_i + \mathbf{U}_i^k\|_F^2.$$

Since $g_i(\cdot)$ is the indicator function of the set $\mathbf{S}_i$, the globally optimal solution of this problem can be explicitly derived as [2]:

$$\mathbf{Z}_i^{k+1} = \mathbf{\Pi}_{\mathbf{S}_i}(\mathbf{W}_i^{k+1} + \mathbf{U}_i^k), \tag{8}$$

where $\mathbf{\Pi}_{\mathbf{S}_i}(\cdot)$ denotes the Euclidean projection onto the set $\mathbf{S}_i$. Note that $\mathbf{S}_i$ is a nonconvex set, and computing the projection onto a nonconvex set is a difficult problem in general. However, the special structure of $\mathbf{S}_i = \{\mathbf{W} \mid \text{card}(\mathbf{W}) \leq l_i\}$ allows us to express this Euclidean projection analytically. Namely, the solution of (4) is to keep the l_i elements of $\mathbf{W}_i^{k+1} + \mathbf{U}_i^k$ with the largest magnitudes and set the rest to zero [2]. Finally, we update the dual variable $\mathbf{U}_i$ according to (5). This concludes one iteration of the ADMM algorithm.

We observe that the proposed systematic framework exhibits multiple major advantages in comparison with the heuristic weight pruning method in [11]. Our proposed method achieves a higher compression ratio with a higher convergence rate compared with the iterative pruning and retraining method in [11]. For example, we achieve 15× compression ratio on AlexNet with only 10 iterations of ADMM. Additionally, subproblem (3) can be solved in a fraction of the number of iterations needed for training the original network when we use warm start initialization, i.e., when we initialize subproblem (3) with $\{\mathbf{W}_i^k, \mathbf{b}_i^k\}$ in order to find $\{\mathbf{W}_i^{k+1}, \mathbf{b}_i^{k+1}\}$. For example, when training on the AlexNet model using the ImageNet data set, convergence is achieved in approximately $\frac{1}{10}$ of the total iterations required for the original DNN training. Also, problems (4) and (5) are straightforward to carry out, thus their computational time can be ignored. As a synergy of the above effects, the total computational time of 10 iterations of ADMM will be similar to (or at least in the same order of) the training time of the original DNN. Furthermore, we achieve 21× compression ratio on AlexNet without accuracy loss when we use 40 iterations of ADMM.

4.3 The Final Retraining Step

For very small values of ϵ_i in (6), ADMM needs a large number of iterations to converge. However, in many applications, such as the weight pruning problem considered here, a slight increase in the value of ϵ_i can result in a significant speedup in convergence. On the other hand, when ADMM stops early, the weights to be pruned may not be identically zero, in the sense that there will be small nonzero elements contained in $\mathbf{W}_i$. To deal with this issue, we keep the l_i elements with the largest magnitude in $\mathbf{W}_i$, set the rest to zero and no longer involve these elements in training (i.e., we prune these weights). Then, we *retrain the DNN*. Note that we only need a single retraining step and the convergence is much faster than training the original DNN, since the starting point of the retraining is already close to the point which can achieve the original test/validation accuracy.

4.4 Overall Illustration of Our Proposed Framework

We take the weight distribution of every (convolutional or fully connected) layer on LeNet-5 as an example to illustrate our systematic weight pruning method. The weight distributions at different stages are shown in Fig. 1. The subfigures in the left column show the weight distributions of the pretrained model, which serves as our starting point. The subfigures in the middle column show that

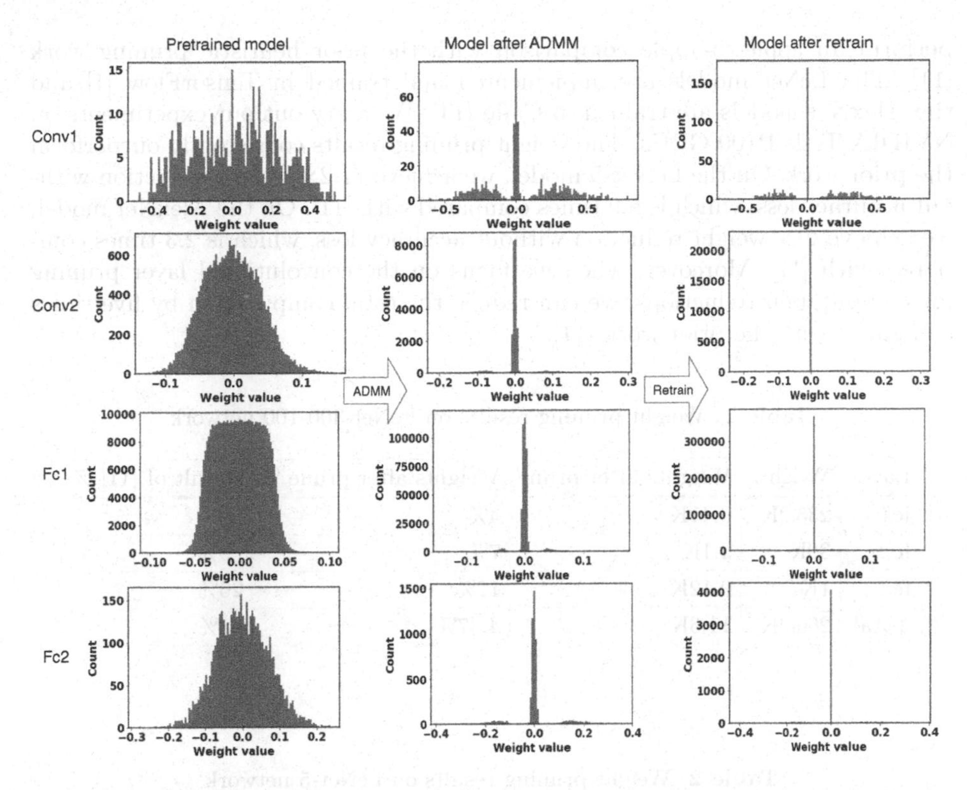

Fig. 1. Weight distribution of every (convolutional or fully connected) layer on LeNet-5. The subfigures in the left column are the weight distributions of the pretrained DNN model (serving as our starting point); the subfigures of the middle column are the weight distributions after the ADMM procedure; the subfigures of the right column are the weight distributions after our final retraining step. Note that the subfigures in the last column include a small number of nonzero weights that are not clearly visible due to the large number of zero weights.

after the convergence of ADMM for moderate values of ϵ_i, we observe a clear separation between weights whose values are close to zero and the remaining weights. To prune the weights rigorously, we set the values of the close-to-zero weights exactly to zero and retrain the DNN without updating these values. The subfigures in the right column show the weight distributions after our final retraining step. We observe that most of the weights are zero in every layer. This concludes our weight pruning procedure.

5 Experimental Results

We have tested the proposed systematic weight pruning framework on the MNIST benchmark using the LeNet-300-100 and LeNet-5 models [17] and the ImageNet ILSVRC-2012 benchmark on the AlexNet model [16], in order to perform an apple-to-apple comparison with the prior heuristic pruning work [11]. The LeNet models are implemented and trained in TensorFlow [1] and the AlexNet models are trained in Caffe [14]. We carry out our experiments on NVIDIA Tesla P100 GPUs. The weight pruning results consistently outperform the prior work. On the LeNet-5 model, we achieve 71.2× weight reduction without accuracy loss, which is 5.9 times compared with [11]. On the AlexNet model, we achieve 21× weight reduction without accuracy loss, which is 2.3 times compared with [11]. Moreover, when we focus on the convolutional layer pruning for computation reductions, we can reduce the total computation by five times compared with the prior work [11].

Table 1. Weight pruning results on LeNet-300-100 network

Layer	Weights	Weights after prune	Weights after prune %	Result of [11] %
fc1	235.2K	9.41K	4%	8%
fc2	30K	2.1K	7%	9%
fc3	1K	0.12K	12%	26%
Total	266.2K	11.6K	4.37%	8%

Table 2. Weight pruning results on LeNet-5 network

Layer	Weights	Weights after prune	Weights after prune %	Result of [11] %
conv1	0.5K	0.1K	20%	66%
conv2	25K	2K	8%	12%
fc1	400K	3.6K	0.9%	8%
fc2	5K	0.35K	7%	19%
Total	430.5K	6.05K	1.4%	8%

5.1 Testing Results on LeNet Models on MNIST Data Set

Table 1 shows our per-layer pruning results on the LeNet-300-100 model. LeNet-300-100 is a fully connected network with 300 and 100 neurons on the two hidden layers, respectively, and achieves 98.4% test accuracy on the MNIST benchmark. Table 2 shows our per-layer pruning results on the LeNet-5 model. LeNet-5 contains two convolutional layers, two pooling layers and two fully connected layers, and can achieve 99.2% test accuracy on the MNIST benchmark.

Our pruning framework does not incur accuracy loss and can achieve a much higher compression ratio on these networks compared with the prior iterative pruning heuristic [11], which reduces the number of parameters by 12× on both

LeNet-300-100 and LeNet-5. On the LeNet-300-100 model, our pruning method reduces the number of weights by 22.9×, which is 90% higher than [11]. Also, our pruning method reduces the number of weights by 71.2× on the LeNet-5 model, which is 5.9 times compared with [11].

5.2 Testing Results on AlexNet Model Using ImageNet Benchmark

We implement our systematic weight pruning method using the BAIR/BVLC AlexNet model[2] on the ImageNet ILSVRC-2012 benchmark. The implementation is on the Caffe tool because it is faster than TensorFlow. The original BAIR/BVLC AlexNet model can achieve a top-5 accuracy 80.2% on the validation set. AlexNet contains 5 convolutional (and pooling) layers and 3 fully connected layers with a total of 60.9M parameters, with the detailed network structure shown in deploy.prototxt text on the website indicated in footnote 5.

Our first set of experiments only target model size reductions for AlexNet, and the results are shown in Table 3. It can be observed that our pruning method can reduce the number of weights by 21× on AlexNet, which is more than twice compared with the prior iterative pruning heuristic. We achieve a top-5 accuracy of 80.2% on the validation set of ImageNet ILSVRC-2012. Layer-wise comparison results are also shown in Table 3, while comparisons with some other model compression methods are shown in Table 5. These results clearly demonstrate the advantage of the proposed systematic weight pruning framework using ADMM.

Table 3. Weight pruning results on AlexNet network (purely focusing on weight reductions) without accuracy loss

Layer	Weights	Weights after prune	Weights after prune%	Result of [11]
conv1	34.8K	28.19K	81%	84%
conv2	307.2K	61.44K	20%	38%
conv3	884.7K	168.09K	19%	35%
conv4	663.5K	132.7K	20%	37%
conv5	442.4K	88.48K	20%	37%
fc1	37.7M	1.06M	2.8%	9%
fc2	16.8M	0.99M	5.9%	9%
fc3	4.1M	0.38M	9.3%	25%
Total	60.9M	2.9M	4.76%	11%

Our second set of experiments target computation reduction besides weight reduction. Because the major computation in state-of-the-art DNNs is in the convolutional layers, we mainly target weight pruning in these layers. Although on AlexNet, the number of weights in convolutional layers is less than that

[2] https://github.com/BVLC/caffe/tree/master/models/bvlc_alexnet.

Table 4. Weight pruning results on AlexNet network (focusing on computation reductions) without accuracy loss

Layer	Weights	Weights after prune	Weights after prune%	Result of [11]
conv1	34.8K	21.92K	63%	84%
conv2	307.2K	21.5K	7%	38%
conv3	884.7K	53.08K	6%	35%
conv4	663.5K	46.45K	7%	37%
conv5	442.4K	30.97K	7%	37%
fc1	37.7M	3.39M	9%	9%
fc2	16.8M	1.51M	9%	9%
fc3	4.1M	1.03M	25%	25%
Total of conv1-5	2332.6K	173.92k	7.46%	37.1%

in fully connected layers, the computation on AlexNet is dominated by its 5 convolutional layers. In our experiments, we conduct experiments which keep the same portion of weights as [11] in fully connected layers but prune more weights in convolutional layers. For AlexNet, Table 4 shows that we can reduce the number of weights by 13.4× in convolutional layers, which is five times compared with 2.7× in [11]. This indicates our pruning method can reduce much more computation compared with the prior work [11]. Layer-wise comparison results are also shown in Table 4. Still, it is difficult to prune weights in the first convolutional layer because they are needed to directly extract features from the raw inputs. Our major gain is because (i) we can achieve significant weight reduction in conv2 through conv5 layers, and (ii) the first convolutional layer is relatively small and less computational intensive.

Several extensions [30,31] of the original weight pruning work have improved in various directions such as energy efficiency for hardware implementation and regularity, but they cannot strictly outperform the original work [11] in terms of compression ratio under the same accuracy. The very recent work [5] employs an evolutionary algorithm for weight pruning, which incorporates randomness in both pruning and growing of weights following certain probability rules. It can achieve a comparable model size with our work. However, it suffers from a prohibitively long retraining phase. For example, it needs to start with an already-compressed model with 8.4M parameters for further pruning on ImageNet, instead of the original AlexNet model. By using an already-compressed model, it can reduce the number of neurons per layer as well, while such reduction is not considered in our proposed framework.

Table 5. Weight reduction ratio comparisons using different model compression techniques on the AlexNet model

Network	Top-5 Error	Parameters	Weight reduction ratio
Baseline AlexNet [16]	19.8%	60.9M	1.0×
SVD [7]	20.6%	11.9M	5.1×
Layer-wise pruning [8]	20.0%	6.7M	9.1×
Network pruning [11]	19.7%	6.7M	9.1×
Our result (10 iterations of ADMM)	19.8%	4.06M	15×
NeST [5]	19.7%	3.9M	15.7×
Dynamic surgery [9]	20.0%	3.45M	17.7×
Our result (25 iterations of ADMM)	19.8%	3.24M	18.8×
Our result (40 iterations of ADMM)	19.8%	2.9M	21×

6 Discussion

6.1 Parameters and Initialization of ADMM

For nonconvex problems in general, there is no guarantee that ADMM will converge to an optimal point. ADMM can converge to different points for different choices of initial values $\{\mathbf{Z}_1^0, \ldots, \mathbf{Z}_N^0\}$ and $\{\mathbf{U}_1^0, \ldots, \mathbf{U}_N^0\}$ and penalty parameters $\{\rho_1, \ldots, \rho_N\}$ [2]. To resolve this limitation, we set the pretrained model $\{\mathbf{W}_i^p, \mathbf{b}_i^p\}$, a good solution of $\underset{\{\mathbf{W}_i\},\{\mathbf{b}_i\}}{\text{minimize}}\ f\big(\{\mathbf{W}_i\}, \{\mathbf{b}_i\}\big)$, to be the starting point when we use stochastic gradient descent to solve problem (7). We initialize $\mathbf{Z}_i^0$ by keeping the l_i elements of $\mathbf{W}_i^p$ with the largest magnitude and set the rest to be zero. We set $\mathbf{U}_1^0 = \cdots = \mathbf{U}_N^0 = 0$. For problem (7), if the penalty parameters $\{\rho_1, \ldots, \rho_N\}$ are too small, the solution will be close to the minimum of $f(\cdot)$ but fail to regularize the weights, and the ADMM procedure may converge slowly or not converge at all. If the penalty parameters are too large, the solution may regularize the weights well but fail to minimize $f(\cdot)$, and therefore the accuracy of the DNN will be degradated. In actual experiments, we find that $\rho_1 = \cdots = \rho_N = 10^{-4}$ is an appropriate choice for LeNet-5 and LeNet-300-100, and that $\rho_1 = \cdots = \rho_N = 1.5 \times 10^{-3}$ works well for AlexNet.

6.2 Parameters of the Desired Number of Weights in Each Layer

We initialize l_i based on existing results in the literature, then we implement our weight pruning method on the DNN and test its accuracy. If there is no accuracy loss on the DNN, we decrease l_i in every layer proportionally. We use binary search to find the smallest l_i that will not result in accuracy loss.

6.3 Convergence Behavior of ADMM and Loss Value Progression on AlexNet

Convergence behavior of ADMM (5 CONV layers in AlexNet) is shown in Fig. 2 (left sub-figure). The loss value progression of AlexNet is shown in Fig. 2 (right sub-figure). We start from an existing DNN model without pruning. After the convergence of ADMM, we remove the weights which are (close to) zero, which results in an increase in the loss value. We then retrain the DNN and the loss decreases to the same level as it was before pruning.

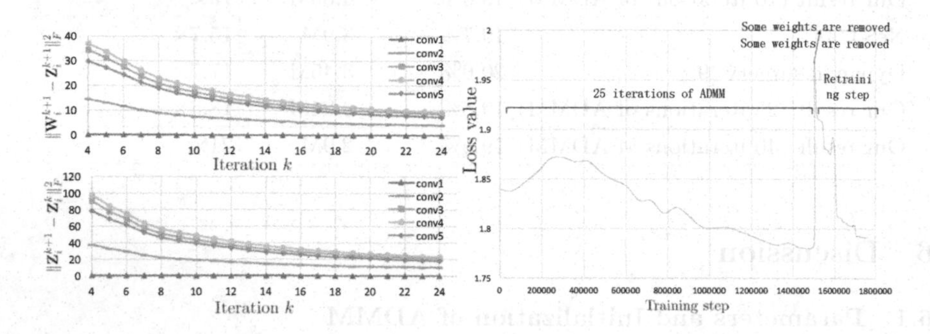

Fig. 2. Convergence behavior of ADMM and loss value progression of AlexNet

6.4 Discussion on Our Proposed Framework

The cardinality function is nonconvex and nondifferentiable, which complicates the use of standard gradient algorithms. ADMM circumvents the issue of differentiability systematically, and does so without introducing additional numerical complexity. Furthermore, although ADMM achieves global optimality for convex problems, it has been shown in the optimization literature that it performs extremely well for large classes of nonconvex problems. In fact, ADMM-based pruning can be perceived as a smart regularization technique in which the regularization target will be dynamically updated in each iteration. The limitation is that we need to tune the parameters l_i. However, *some* parameter tuning is generally inevitable; even a soft regularization parameter requires fine-tuning in order to achieve the desired solution structure. On the positive side, the freedom in setting l_i allows the user to obtain the exact desired level of sparsity.

7 Conclusions and Future Work

In this paper, we presented a systematic DNN weight pruning framework using ADMM. We formulate the weight pruning problem of DNNs as a nonconvex optimization problem with combinatorial constraints specifying the sparsity requirements. By using ADMM, the nonconvex optimization problem is decomposed into two subproblems that are solved iteratively, one using stochastic gradient descent and the other analytically. We reduced the number of weights by 22.9× on LeNet-300-100 and 71.2× on LeNet-5 without accuracy loss. For AlexNet, we reduced the number of weights by 21× without accuracy loss. When we focued on computation reduction, we reduced the number of weights in convolutional layers by 13.4× on AlexNet, which is five times compared with the prior work.

In future work, we will extend the proposed weight pruning method to incorporate structure and regularity in the weight pruning procedure, and develop a unified framework of weight pruning, activation reduction, and weight clustering.

Acknowledgments. Financial support from the National Science Foundation under awards CNS-1840813, CNS-1704662 and ECCS-1609916 is gratefully acknowledged.

References

1. Abadi, M., Agarwal, A., Barham, P., et al.: Tensorflow: large-scale machine learning on heterogeneous distributed systems. arXiv preprint arXiv:1603.04467 (2016)
2. Boyd, S., Parikh, N., Chu, E., Peleato, B., Eckstein, J.: Distributed optimization and statistical learning via the alternating direction method of multipliers. Found. Trends® Mach. Learn. **3**(1), 1–122 (2011)
3. Chen, W., Wilson, J., Tyree, S., Weinberger, K., Chen, Y.: Compressing neural networks with the hashing trick. In: International Conference on Machine Learning, pp. 2285–2294 (2015)
4. Dahl, G.E., Yu, D., Deng, L., Acero, A.: Context-dependent pre-trained deep neural networks for large-vocabulary speech recognition. IEEE Trans. Audio Speech Lang. Process. **20**(1), 30–42 (2012)
5. Dai, X., Yin, H., Jha, N.K.: Nest: a neural network synthesis tool based on a grow-and-prune paradigm. arXiv preprint arXiv:1711.02017 (2017)
6. Denil, M., Shakibi, B., Dinh, L., De Freitas, N., et al.: Predicting parameters in deep learning. In: Advances in neural information processing systems, pp. 2148–2156 (2013)
7. Denton, E.L., Zaremba, W., Bruna, J., LeCun, Y., Fergus, R.: Exploiting linear structure within convolutional networks for efficient evaluation. In: Advances in neural information processing systems, pp. 1269–1277 (2014)
8. Dong, X., Chen, S., Pan, S.: Learning to prune deep neural networks via layer-wise optimal brain surgeon. In: Advances in Neural Information Processing Systems, pp. 4860–4874 (2017)
9. Guo, Y., Yao, A., Chen, Y.: Dynamic network surgery for efficient DNNs. In: Advances in Neural Information Processing Systems, pp. 1379–1387 (2016)
10. Han, S., Mao, H., Dally, W.J.: Deep compression: compressing deep neural networks with pruning, trained quantization and huffman coding. In: International Conference on Learning Representations (ICLR) (2016)
11. Han, S., Pool, J., Tran, J., Dally, W.: Learning both weights and connections for efficient neural network. In: Advances in Neural Information Processing Systems (NIPS), pp. 1135–1143 (2015)
12. He, K., Zhang, X., Ren, S., Sun, J.: Deep residual learning for image recognition. In: Proceedings of the IEEE Conference on Computer Vision and Pattern Recognition, pp. 770–778 (2016)

13. Hinton, G., et al.: Deep neural networks for acoustic modeling in speech recognition: the shared views of four research groups. IEEE Signal Process. Mag. **29**(6), 82–97 (2012)
14. Jia, Y., et al.: Caffe: convolutional architecture for fast feature embedding. In: Proceedings of the 22nd ACM International Conference on Multimedia, pp. 675–678. ACM (2014)
15. Kiaee, F., Gagné, C., Abbasi, M.: Alternating direction method of multipliers for sparse convolutional neural networks. arXiv preprint arXiv:1611.01590 (2016)
16. Krizhevsky, A., Sutskever, I., Hinton, G.E.: Imagenet classification with deep convolutional neural networks. In: Advances in Neural Information Processing Systems, pp. 1097–1105 (2012)
17. LeCun, Y., Bottou, L., Bengio, Y., Haffner, P.: Gradient-based learning applied to document recognition. Proc. IEEE **86**(11), 2278–2324 (1998)
18. Leng, C., Li, H., Zhu, S., Jin, R.: Extremely low bit neural network: squeeze the last bit out with ADMM. arXiv preprint arXiv:1707.09870 (2017)
19. Liu, B., Wang, M., Foroosh, H., Tappen, M., Pensky, M.: Sparse convolutional neural networks. In: Proceedings of the IEEE Conference on Computer Vision and Pattern Recognition, pp. 806–814 (2015)
20. Liu, S., Fardad, M., Masazade, E., Varshney, P.K.: On optimal periodic sensor scheduling for field estimation in wireless sensor networks. In: Global Conference on Signal and Information Processing (GlobalSIP), pp. 137–140. IEEE (2013)
21. Luo, J.H., Wu, J., Lin, W.: ThiNet: a filter level pruning method for deep neural network compression. In: 2017 IEEE International Conference on Computer Vision (ICCV), pp. 5068–5076. IEEE (2017)
22. Maas, A.L., Hannun, A.Y., Ng, A.Y.: Rectifier nonlinearities improve neural network acoustic models. In: Proceedings of ICML, vol. 30, p. 3 (2013)
23. Makantasis, K., Karantzalos, K., Doulamis, A., Doulamis, N.: Deep supervised learning for hyperspectral data classification through convolutional neural networks. In: 2015 IEEE International Geoscience and Remote Sensing Symposium (IGARSS), pp. 4959–4962. IEEE (2015)
24. Mnih, V., et al.: Playing atari with deep reinforcement learning. arXiv preprint arXiv:1312.5602 (2013)
25. Molchanov, D., Ashukha, A., Vetrov, D.: Variational dropout sparsifies deep neural networks. In: International Conference on Machine Learning, pp. 2498–2507 (2017)
26. Park, E., Ahn, J., Yoo, S.: Weighted-entropy-based quantization for deep neural networks. In: IEEE Conference on Computer Vision and Pattern Recognition (CVPR) (2017)
27. Simonyan, K., Zisserman, A.: Very deep convolutional networks for large-scale image recognition. arXiv preprint arXiv:1409.1556 (2014)
28. Takapoui, R., Moehle, N., Boyd, S., Bemporad, A.: A simple effective heuristic for embedded mixed-integer quadratic programming. Int. J. Control. 1–11 (2017)
29. Tung, F., Muralidharan, S., Mori, G.: Fine-pruning: joint fine-tuning and compression of a convolutional network with Bayesian optimization. arXiv preprint arXiv:1707.09102 (2017)
30. Wen, W., Wu, C., Wang, Y., Chen, Y., Li, H.: Learning structured sparsity in deep neural networks. In: Advances in Neural Information Processing Systems, pp. 2074–2082 (2016)

31. Yang, T.J., Chen, Y.H., Sze, V.: Designing energy-efficient convolutional neural networks using energy-aware pruning. arXiv preprint arXiv:1611.05128 (2016)
32. Zhou, H., Alvarez, J.M., Porikli, F.: Less Is more: towards compact CNNs. In: Leibe, B., Matas, J., Sebe, N., Welling, M. (eds.) ECCV 2016. LNCS, vol. 9908, pp. 662–677. Springer, Cham (2016). https://doi.org/10.1007/978-3-319-46493-0_40

Multi-object Tracking with Neural Gating Using Bilinear LSTM

Chanho Kim[1(✉)], Fuxin Li[2], and James M. Rehg[1]

[1] Center for Behavioral Imaging, Georgia Institute of Technology, Atlanta, GA, USA
{chkim,rehg}@gatech.edu
[2] Oregon State University, Corvallis, OR, USA
lif@oregonstate.edu

Abstract. In recent deep online and near-online multi-object tracking approaches, a difficulty has been to incorporate long-term appearance models to efficiently score object tracks under severe occlusion and multiple missing detections. In this paper, we propose a novel recurrent network model, the Bilinear LSTM, in order to improve the learning of long-term appearance models via a recurrent network. Based on intuitions drawn from recursive least squares, Bilinear LSTM stores building blocks of a linear predictor in its memory, which is then coupled with the input in a multiplicative manner, instead of the additive coupling in conventional LSTM approaches. Such coupling resembles an online learned classifier/regressor at each time step, which we have found to improve performances in using LSTM for appearance modeling. We also propose novel data augmentation approaches to efficiently train recurrent models that score object tracks on both appearance and motion. We train an LSTM that can score object tracks based on both appearance and motion and utilize it in a multiple hypothesis tracking framework. In experiments, we show that with our novel LSTM model, we achieved state-of-the-art performance on near-online multiple object tracking on the MOT 2016 and MOT 2017 benchmarks.

1 Introduction

With the improvement in deep learning based detectors [16,35] and the stimulation of the MOT challenges [32], tracking-by-detection approaches for multi-object tracking have improved significantly in the past few years. Multi-object tracking approaches can be classified into three types depending on the number of lookahead frames: online methods that generate tracking results immediately after processing an input frame [1,22,33], near-online methods that look ahead a fixed number of frames before consolidating the decisions [7,24], and batch methods that consider the entire sequence before generating the decisions [38,39]. For tracking multiple people, a recent state-of-the-art batch approach [38] relies upon person re-identification techniques which leverage a deep CNN network that can recognize a person that has left the scene and re-entered. Such

V. Ferrari et al. (Eds.): ECCV 2018, LNCS 11212, pp. 208–224, 2018.
https://doi.org/10.1007/978-3-030-01237-3_13

an approach is able to thread together long tracks in which a person is not visible for dozens of frames, whereas the margin for missing frames in online and near-online approaches is usually much shorter.

A key challenge in online and near-online tracking is the development of deep appearance models that can automatically adapt to the diverse appearance changes of targets over multiple video frames. A few approaches based on Recurrent Neural Networks (RNNs) [1,33] have been proposed in the context of multi-object tracking. [33] focuses on building a non-linear motion model and a data association solver using RNNs. [1] successfully adopted Long Short-Term Memory (LSTM) [21] to integrate appearance, motion, and interaction cues, but Fig. 7. (b) in [1] reports results for sequences (tracks) of maximum length 10. In practice, object tracks are much longer than 10 frames, and it is unclear whether the method is equally effective for longer tracks.

Our own experience, coupled with the reported literature, suggests that it is difficult to use LSTMs to model object appearance over long sequences. It is therefore worthwhile to investigate the fundamental issues in utilizing LSTM for tracking, such as what is being stored in their internal memory and what factors result in them being either able or unable to learn good appearance models. Leveraging intuition from classical recursive least squares regression, we propose a new type of LSTM that is suitable for learning sequential appearance models. Whereas in a conventional LSTM, the memory and the input have a linear relationship, in our *Bilinear LSTM*, the LSTM memory serves as the building blocks of a *predictor* (classifier/regressor), which leads to the output being based on a multiplicative relationship between the memory and the input appearance. Based on this novel LSTM formulation, we are able to build a recurrent network for scoring object tracks that combines long-term appearance and motion information. This new track scorer is then utilized in conjunction with an established near-online multi-object tracking approach, multiple hypothesis tracking, which reasons over multiple track proposals (hypotheses). Our approach combines the benefits of deep feature learning with the practical utility of a near-online tracker.

Our second contribution is a training methodology for generating sequential training examples from multi-object tracking datasets that accounts for the cases where detections could be noisy or missing for many frames. We have developed systematic data augmentation methods that allow our near-online approach to take advantage of long training sequences and survive scenarios with detection noise and dozens of frames of consecutive missing detections.

With these two improvements, we are able to generate state-of-the-art multi-target tracking results for near-online approaches in the MOT challenge. In the future, our proposed Bilinear LSTM could be used in other scenarios where a long-term online predictor is needed.

2 Related Work

There is a vast literature on multi-target tracking. Top-performing tracking algorithms that do not train a deep network include [7,24,29]. These methods usually utilize long-term appearance models as well as structural cues and motion cues. A review of earlier tracking papers can be found in [28].

The prior work that is closest to ours uses RNNs as a track proposal classifier in the Markov Decision Process (MDP) framework [1]. Three different RNNs that handle appearance, motion, and social information are trained separately for track proposal classification and then combined for joint reasoning over multiple cues to achieve the best performance. Our method is different from this approach both in terms of the network architecture and training sequence generation from ground truth tracks. Also, we present the first incorporation of deep learned track model into an MHT framework.

Other recent approaches [26,37] adopt siamese networks that learn the matching function for a pair of images. The network is trained for the binary classification problem where the binary output represents whether or not the image pair comes from the same object. The matching function can be utilized in a tracking framework to replace any previous matching function. Approaches in this category are limited to only modeling the information between a pair of the detections, whereas our approach can model the interaction between a track and a detection, thereby exploiting long-term appearance and motion information.

Milan et al. [33] presented a deep learning framework that solves the multi-object tracking problem in an end-to-end trainable network. Unlike our approach, they attempted to solve state estimation and data association jointly in one framework. While this was highly innovative, an advantage of MHT is the ability to use highly optimized combinatoric solvers.

RNN has been applied in single-object tracking [18,41], however multi-target tracking is a more challenging problem due to the amount of occlusion and problem of ID switches, which is much more likely to happen in a multi-object setting.

3 Overview of MHT

In tracking-by-detection, multi-object tracking is solved through data association, which generates a set of tracks by assigning a track label to each detection. MHT solves the data association problem by explicitly generating multiple track proposals and then selecting the most promising ones. Let $T_l(t) = \{d^l_1, d^l_2, ..., d^l_{t-1}, d^l_t\}$ denote the lth track proposal at frame t and let d^l_t be a detection selected by the lth track proposal at frame t. The selected detection d^l_t can be either an actual detection generated by an object detector or a dummy detection that represents a missing detection.

The track proposals for each object are stored in a track tree in which each tree node corresponds to one detection. For example, the root node represents the first detection of the object and the child nodes represent the detections in subsequent frames (i.e. tree nodes at the same depth represent detections in the same frame). Thus, multiple paths from the root to the leaf nodes correspond to multiple track proposals for a single object. The proposals are scored, and the task of finding the best set of proposals can be formulated as a Maximum Weighted Independent Set (MWIS) problem [34], with the score for each proposal being the weight of it. Once the best set of proposals is found, proposal pruning is performed. Only the surviving proposals are kept and updated in the next frame. More details about MHT can be found in [24,34].

3.1 Gating in MHT

In MHT, track proposals are updated by extending existing track proposals with new detections. In order to keep the number of proposals manageable, existing track proposals are not updated with all of the new detections, but rather with a few selected detections. The selection process is called *gating*. Previous gating approaches rely on hand-designed track score functions [5,9,24,34]. Typically, the proposal score $S(T_l(t))$ is defined recursively as:

$$S(T_l(t)) = S(T_l(t-1)) + \Delta S(T_l(t)) \tag{1}$$

Gating is done by thresholding the score increment $\Delta S(T_l(t))$. New track proposals with score increments below a certain threshold are pruned instantly. Usually the proposal score includes an appearance term, which could be learned by recursive least squares, as well as a motion term which could be learned with Kalman filtering.

3.2 Recursive Least Squares as an Appearance Model

An important advantage of our previous MHT-DAM approach [24] is the use of long-term appearance models that leverage all prior appearance samples from a given track and train a discriminative model to predict whether each bounding box belongs to each given track. Because we would like to be able to perform a similar task in our LSTM framework, we briefly review the recursive least squares appearance model used in [24]. Given all the n_t detections at frame t, one can extract appearance features (e.g. CNN fully-connected layer) for them and store them in an $n_t \times d$ matrix $\mathbf{X}_t$, where d is the feature dimensionality. Then, suppose that we are tracking k object tracks, an output vector can be created for each track as, e.g. the spatial overlap between the bounding box of each detection and each track (represented by one detection in the frame), with the set of output vectors denoted as an $n_t \times k$ matrix $\mathbf{Y}_t$. Then a regressor for each target can be found by least squares regression:

$$\min_{\mathbf{W}} \sum_{t=1}^{T} \|\mathbf{X}_t \mathbf{W} - \mathbf{Y}_t\|_F^2 + \lambda \|\mathbf{W}\|_F^2 \tag{2}$$

where $\|\cdot\|_F^2$ is a squared Frobenius norm and λ is the regularization parameter. As is well-known, the solution can be written as:

$$\mathbf{W} = \left(\sum_{t=1}^{T} \mathbf{X}_t^\top \mathbf{X}_t + \lambda \mathbf{I} \right)^{-1} \left(\sum_{t=1}^{T} \mathbf{X}_t^\top \mathbf{Y}_t \right) \tag{3}$$

where $\mathbf{I}$ is the identity matrix. Notably, one can store $\mathbf{Q}_t = \sum_{i=1}^{t} (\mathbf{X}_i^\top \mathbf{X}_i)$ and $\mathbf{C}_t = \sum_{i=1}^{t} (\mathbf{X}_i^\top \mathbf{Y}_i)$ and update them online at frame $t+1$, by adding $\mathbf{X}_{t+1}^\top \mathbf{X}_{t+1}$ and $\mathbf{X}_{t+1}^\top \mathbf{Y}_{t+1}$ to $\mathbf{Q}_t$ and $\mathbf{C}_t$ respectively, while maintaining the optimality of the solution for $\mathbf{W}$. Moreover, the computation of $\mathbf{W}$ is only linear in the number of tracks k. The resulting model can train on all the positive examples (past detections in each track) and negative examples (past detections in other tracks not overlapping with a given track) and generate a regressor with good discriminative power. The computational efficiency of this approach and its optimality are the two keys to the success of the MHT-DAM framework.

4 RNN as a Gating Network

We use the term *gating network* to denote a neural network that performs gating. We utilize recurrent neural networks (RNNs) for training gating networks since track proposals constitute sequential data whose data size is not fixed. In this work, we adopt Long Short-Term Memory (LSTM) as a recurrent layer due to its success in modeling long sequences on various tasks [17].

We formulate the problem of gating as a sequence labeling problem. The gating network takes track proposals as inputs and performs gating by generating a binary output for every detection in the track proposal. In this section, we describe network inputs and outputs and its utilization within the MHT framework. More details about the network architecture can be found in Sect. 4.2.

Input. Track proposals contain both motion and appearance information. We use the bounding box coordinates (x, y, w, h) over time as motion inputs to the network. The coordinates are normalized with respect to the frame resolution $(\frac{x}{\text{image width}}, \frac{y}{\text{image height}}, \frac{w}{\text{image width}}, \frac{h}{\text{image height}})$ to make the range of the input values fixed regardless of the frame resolution. We also calculate sample mean and standard deviation from track proposals (see Sect. 5 for more details on how to generate track proposals from multi-object tracking datasets) and perform another normalization in order to make the input data zero-centered and normalized across different dimensions.

We use object images cropped to detection bounding boxes as appearance inputs to the network. RGB cropped images are first converted to convolutional features by Convolutional Neural Networks (CNN) before the gating networks process them. We use the ImageNet pretrained ResNet-50 [19] as our CNN.

Output. Given a current detection, the network makes a binary decision about whether or not it belongs to the proposal based on its compatibility with the appearance and motion of the other detections assigned to the proposal. Thus, the gating networks solve a binary classification task using cross-entropy loss. Note that we have multiple binary labels for each track sequence since gating is done on every frame.

Track Scorer in MHT. We use the softmax probability p of the positive output (i.e. current detection belongs to the same object in the proposal) for calculating the score increment $\Delta S(T_l(t))$ as shown in Eq. (4). A higher score increment implies a higher matching quality between the track proposal $T_l(t-1)$ and the detection d_t^l.

$$\Delta S(T_l(t)) = p(d_t^l \in T_l(t-1) | T_l(t-1)) \tag{4}$$

This is a simple aggregation scheme that combines the per-frame predictions from the gating network in order to score tracks. Our assumption is that proposals that generate higher per-frame matching scores are more likely to be correct than proposals with lower per-frame matching scores. New track proposals with score increment below a threshold are pruned instantly by gating. In MHT, every track proposal in the track trees has a unique detection sequence, which is represented as a unique LSTM memory state in the gating network. The memory state for surviving proposals is stored for further gating and scoring in the next frame. The weights of the gating network are shared across all track proposals.

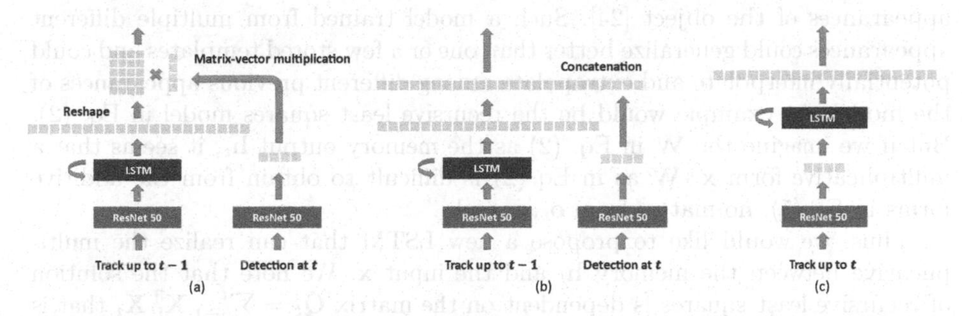

Fig. 1. Motion gating network and appearance gating network are trained separately before training the full model. We evaluate multiple network architectures for each module. (a) The Bilinear LSTM network with a multiplicative relationship between the memory and the input CNN features. The LSTM memory is reshaped into a matrix and multiplied with the input appearance feature vector; (b) Input appearance is concatenated with the LSTM memory output before a fully-connected layer; (c) A conventional LSTM architecture.

4.1 Bilinear LSTM

Our experience suggests that conventional LSTMs are far more effective at modeling motion than appearance. This led us to ask, "what information about object appearance is being stored in the internal memory of a standard LSTM, and what would be an ideal memory representation for this task?".

Conventional LSTMs utilizes the following update rule:

$$\begin{aligned} \mathbf{c}_t &= \mathbf{f}_t \circ \mathbf{c}_{t-1} + \mathbf{i}_t \circ \mathbf{g}_t, & \mathbf{h}_t &= \mathbf{o}_t \circ \tanh(\mathbf{c}_t) \\ \mathbf{f}_t &= \sigma(\mathbf{W}_f[\mathbf{h}_{t-1}, \mathbf{x}_t]), & \mathbf{i}_t &= \sigma(\mathbf{W}_i[\mathbf{h}_{t-1}, \mathbf{x}_t]), \\ \mathbf{g}_t &= \sigma(\mathbf{W}_g[\mathbf{h}_{t-1}, \mathbf{x}_t]), & \mathbf{o}_t &= \tanh(\mathbf{W}_o[\mathbf{h}_{t-1}, \mathbf{x}_t]) \end{aligned} \tag{5}$$

where $\circ$ represents the Hadamard product. $\mathbf{x}_t$ is the current input. $\mathbf{f}_t$, $\mathbf{i}_t$, and $\mathbf{o}_t$ are the forget gate, the input gate, and the output gate. $\mathbf{c}_t$ and $\mathbf{h}_t$ are the cell state and the hidden state that are repeatedly updated throughout the sequence. $\mathbf{g}_t$ is the new update values for the cell state.

When building an appearance model for multi-object tracking (i.e. data association), $\mathbf{x}_t$ represents the current appearance of an object candidate. For LSTM to solve the tracking task, one intuition is that $\mathbf{h}_t$ may represent some information about the acceptance/rejection of an object candidate. $\mathbf{c}_t$ can roughly be thought of as representing a stored template of the object appearance, and then the output gate $\mathbf{o}_t$ compares the previous stored appearance $\mathbf{c}_{t-1}$ and the new appearance $\mathbf{x}_t$ in order to decide the current output $\mathbf{h}_t$. Experiments in [1] where LSTM performance seems to saturate with a sequence length of $2-4$ frames, seems to suggest that the aforementioned intuition might be partially correct.

However, the main appeal of a long-term appearance model in previous work is the capability of using a classifier/regressor that learns from *all* the previous appearances of the object [24]. Such a model trained from multiple different appearances could generalize better than one or a few stored templates and could potentially interpolate and extrapolate among different previous appearances of the model. An example would be the recursive least squares model in Eq. (2). But if we imagine the $\mathbf{W}$ in Eq. (2) as the memory output $\mathbf{h}_t$, it seems that a multiplicative form $\mathbf{x}^\top\mathbf{W}$ as in Eq. (2) is difficult to obtain from the additive forms in Eq. (5), no matter from $\mathbf{o}_t, \mathbf{c}_t$ or $\mathbf{h}_t$.

Thus, we would like to propose a new LSTM that can realize the multiplicative between the memory $\mathbf{h}_t$ and the input $\mathbf{x}$. We note that the solution of recursive least squares is dependent on the matrix $\mathbf{Q}_t = \sum_{i=1}^{t} \mathbf{X}_i^\top\mathbf{X}_i$ that is updated at each time linearly. It is difficult for LSTM to store a positive-definite matrix as memory, but a common approach to simplify such a positive-definite matrix is to use a low-rank approximation, e.g. assuming $\mathbf{Q}_t^{-1} = \sum_{i=1}^{r} \mathbf{q}_{ti}\mathbf{q}_{ti}^\top$. With this assumption and considering Eq. (3), the regressor output becomes:

$$\mathbf{w}^\top\mathbf{x} = \mathbf{C}_t^\top\mathbf{Q}_t^{-1}\mathbf{x} = \sum_{i=1}^{r} \mathbf{C}_t^\top\mathbf{q}_{ti}\mathbf{q}_{ti}^\top\mathbf{x} \tag{6}$$

Note that when there is only 1 track, $\mathbf{C}_t$ is of the dimensionality $d \times 1$, and hence $\mu_i = \mathbf{C}_t^\top\mathbf{q}_i$ is a scalar. We have:

$$\mathbf{w}^\top\mathbf{x} = \sum_{i=1}^{r} \mu_i\mathbf{q}_{ti}^\top\mathbf{x} \tag{7}$$

Here μ_i is dependent on both $\mathbf{y}$ and $\mathbf{q}$, hence without loss of generality it could be a standalone variable that is separately estimated. With this derivation, it seems that the approach to emulate a linear regressor is to have several vectors $\mathbf{h}_{ti}$ to be learnable and gradually changing with time (in other words, serve as the memory in the LSTM), and a layer of learnable μ_i on top of a multiplicative relationship between $\mathbf{h}_{ti}$ and $\mathbf{x}$.

In this spirit, we propose the Bilinear LSTM (bLSTM) which utilizes the following forward pass that enables the multiplicative interaction between the input and the memory:

$$\begin{aligned} \mathbf{h}_{t-1} &= [\mathbf{h}_{t-1,1}^\top|\mathbf{h}_{t-1,2}^\top|...|\mathbf{h}_{t-1,r}^\top]^\top = \mathbf{o}_{t-1} \circ \tanh(\mathbf{c}_{t-1}) \\ \mathbf{H}_{t-1}^{\text{reshaped}} &= [\mathbf{h}_{t-1,1}|\mathbf{h}_{t-1,2}|...|\mathbf{h}_{t-1,r}]^\top, \quad \mathbf{m}_t = f(\mathbf{H}_{t-1}^{\text{reshaped}}\mathbf{x}_t) \end{aligned} \tag{8}$$

where $f(\cdot)$ is a non-linear activation function and $\mathbf{m}_t$ is the new hidden state for bLSTM. $\mathbf{x}_t$ denotes the features from a box at frame t. Basically, we utilize a long vector as the LSTM memory which contains the concatenation of all the $\mathbf{h}_{t-1,i}$s. When it comes to the time to multiply $\mathbf{h}_{t-1,i}$ with $\mathbf{x}_t$, the rd dimensional vector $\mathbf{h}_{t-1}$ is reshaped into the $r \times d$ matrix $\mathbf{H}_{t-1}^{\text{reshaped}}$ so that we could utilize matrix-vector multiplication between $\mathbf{h}_{t-1}$ and $\mathbf{x}_t$.

The new hidden state $\mathbf{m}_t$ can then be used as input to other fully-connected layers (resembling the μ_i in Eq. (7)) to generate the final prediction. Note that in online recursive least squares μ_i should be trained for each tracked object separately, however in our network the fully-connected layers after bLSTM are trained globally and fixed during testing time. Implementing a dynamic μ_i which is dependent on each object track did not result in significant improvement in performance. We believe that since the system is trained end-to-end, the LSTM updates of $\mathbf{h}$ should be able to encompass the potential changes in μ_i, hence we can keep the fully-connected layers fixed without additional issues.

Intuitively, by saving a matrix-valued memory that resembles a low-rank decomposition of the matrix, at least r templates (as well as combinations of the r templates) can be used for the prediction. Hence bLSTM can store longer-term appearance models than traditional LSTMs and improve on maintaining track identity over many frames.

4.2 Network Architecture

We have three types of gating networks based on the network input: Motion, Appearance, and Motion + Appearance. We test three different architectures in Fig. 1 for the motion gating and appearance gating networks. We select the best architecture for each type of input among the three and combine them for motion+appearance gating networks. Experimental results that we used for selecting the architecture are included in Sect. 6.3.

Motion Gating. For motion gating, the vanila version of LSTM Eq. (5) works the best. Thus, we adopt LSTM as a sequence labeler where LSTM reads motion input recursively and store the sequence information in its hidden state. The FC layers are built on top of the hidden state to produce the final output. Architectures that we used for the comparison are shown in Table 1.

Appearance Gating. We propose to use Bilinear LSTM as appearance gating network where LSTM's hidden state becomes a weight vector for the appearance model of the current object. Details about the network architecture and other two baseline architectures are shown in Table 2.

Table 1. Different experimented architectures for motion gating. (a) Bilinear LSTM (b) LSTM as a feature extractor for the previous track (c) Vanila LSTM (LSTM as a sequence labeler)

(a)

Soft-max			
Matrix-vector Multiplication-tanh 4			
Reshape	4×64	Reshape	64×1
LSTM	256		
FC-relu	64	FC-relu	64
Input at $t-1$	4	Input at t	4

(b)

Soft-max			
FC-tanh 64			
Concatenation $64 + 64$			
LSTM	64		
FC-relu	64	FC-relu	64
Input at $t-1$	4	Input at t	4

(c)

Soft-max	
FC-tanh	8
LSTM	64
FC-relu	64
Input at t	4

Table 2. Different experimented architectures for appearance gating: (a) Bilinear LSTM (b) LSTM as a feature extractor for the previous track (c) Vanila LSTM

(a)

Soft-max			
Matrix-vector Multiplication-relu 8			
Reshape	8×256	Reshape	256×1
LSTM	2048		
FC-relu	256	FC-relu	256
ResNet-50	2048	ResNet50	2048
Input at $t-1$	$128 \times 64 \times 3$	Input at t	$128 \times 64 \times 3$

(b)

Soft-max			
FC-relu 512			
Concatenation $2048 + 256$			
LSTM	2048		
FC-relu	256	FC-relu	256
ResNet-50	2048	ResNet50	2048
Input at $t-1$	$128 \times 64 \times 3$	Input at t	$128 \times 64 \times 3$

(c)

Soft-max	
FC-relu	512
LSTM	2048
FC-relu	256
ResNet-50	2048
Input at t	$128 \times 64 \times 3$

Motion + Appearance Gating. In order to enable a joint reasoning over both motion and appearance for object tracking, we construct a motion+gating network based on our analysis of different baseline architectures. We use Bilinear LSTM to process appearance data and vanila LSTM to process motion data. Then motion and appearance representations (i.e. outputs before soft-max) from both gating networks are concatenated after L2 normalization is applied to each representation separately. Prediction layers are built upon the concatenated features. We first train motion gating and appearance gating networks separately. Then we load all the pretrained layers before the concatenation layer from both gating networks and fine-tune them jointly.

4.3 Handling Missing Detections

In tracking-by-detection, it is important to handle missing detections while keeping the correct track identity over time. In traditional Kalman filter-based motion tracking, the diagonal of the noise covariance matrix keeps increasing over time in the case of missing detections, resulting in accepting more detections from gating with a gradually larger gating area.

In the case of recurrent gating networks, the occurrences of missing detections should also modulate the gating network. For instance, one can imagine a gating network applying a stricter gating policy when all the detections are available for the current object than the case where detections are missing in recent frames. In order to encode such information inside the LSTM hidden states, we propose to input to the recurrent network all-zero input vectors in the case of missing detections. By doing so, the LSTM internal (both cell and hidden) states will be updated solely based on its previous states, which is different from normal LSTM updates where both the input data and the previous state are utilized. The gating network does not need to make any prediction for the missing detection but only need to update the LSTM internal memory. In Sect. 6.3, we show the effectiveness of such explicit missing detection handling for the motion gating networks.

5 Generating Training Sequences

Artificial track proposals are generated from ground truth track annotations as training data for training our LSTM network. First, we randomly pick one ground truth track annotation from which we sample track proposals. The starting frame and the ending frame are randomly selected. Due to the memory limit of GPUs, we select them in a way that the length of the track proposal does not exceed $N_{\max}$. Let N be the selected length $(2 \leq N \leq N_{\max})$ of the proposal. Then we collect first $N-1$ bounding boxes of the selected object and pick the last N^{th} detection from a different object. Positive labels are assigned for the first $N-1$ detections representing the correct object and a negative label is assigned for the Nth detection representing a different object. Thus, each proposal is associated with a binary label vector where only the last element is a negative label as presented in Fig. 2. The maximum length $N_{\max}$ needs to be large enough so that the network learns the gating mechanism regardless of its input length. We show experimental results with different $N_{\max}$ values in Sect. 6.3.

Data Augmentation. If ground truth tracks are used without any augmentation to generate track proposals, each track proposal will consist of bounding boxes perfectly aligned with the object in consecutive frames, which may poorly

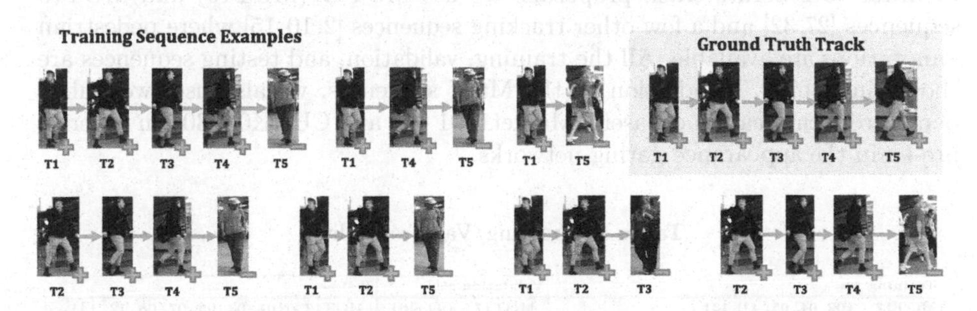

Fig. 2. Training sequences are generated from the public MOT dataset. Each training sequence has detections from the same object throughout the track and one detection from different object at the end. Training sequences are generated in the manner that they reflect actual track proposals that MHT generates during tracking.

represent actual track proposals consisting of noisy detections. Thus, it is important to perform proper data augmentation so that the track proposals reflect actual detection noise. There are two types of detection errors which need to be considered: localization error and missing detections.

In order to reflect the localization noise, we jitter the bounding boxes in the training track proposals using a noise model estimated from the training data. For estimating this noise model, given a set of detections and ground truth annotations, we first assign each detection to its closest ground truth bounding box, and then calculate localization error from each detection to its assigned ground truth bounding box. We then fit a normal distribution to these localization errors for all true positive detections. Since the MOT Challenge Benchmark [32] provides three public detectors (DPM [13], FRCNN [40], SDP [35]) which have different accuracy and noise levels, we estimate a different normal distribution for each public detector. Thus, before the training data generator samples random localization errors for the proposal, it first chooses a normal distribution based on the detector. Then for each bounding box in each track proposal, a different localization error is sampled from the estimated normal distribution.

In order to simulate missing detections, for 50% of the tracks, we randomly pick a missing detection rate $p_{\text{miss}}(0.0 \sim 0.5)$ and drop the bounding boxes in the track proposal according to the selected missing rate except for the first bounding box (current object) and the last bounding box (different object). Example track proposals with this missing detection augmentation are shown in Fig. 1. The other 50% of the tracks are retained without missing detections.

6 Experiments

We report all our experimental results on the validation set except for the final benchmark result which was evaluated on MOT 16/17 test sequences.

6.1 Training Data

In order to generate track proposals, we use MOT17 (MOT16) and MOT15 sequences [27,32] and a few other tracking sequences [2,10,15] where pedestrian annotations are available. All the training, validation, and testing sequences are shown in Table 3. In addition to the MOT sequences, we also use two public person re-identification datasets, Market1501 [42] and CUHK03 [30], in order to pre-train the appearance gating networks.

Table 3. Training/Val/Test Splits

Training set	Validation set	Test set
MOT17 - {02, 04, 05, 11, 13},	MOT17 - {09, 10}	MOT17 - {01, 03, 06, 07, 08, 12, 14}
MOT15 - {01, 02, 03, 04, 05, 06, 07},		
ETH - {Jelmoli, Seq01}, KITTI - {16, 19},		
PETS09-S2L2, TUD-Crossing, AVG-TownCentre		

6.2 Pre-training on Person Re-identification

In the person re-identification task, a pair of images is given to the learner and the learner decides whether two images come from the same person or not. One can treat the pair of two images as a track proposal with a temporal length 2. Such training examples can be also generated from multi-object tracking dataset. Thus, we utilize a person re-identification dataset in addition to the training set shown in Table 3 to pre-train our appearance gating network for person re-identification. Similar pre-training was also done in [1,38]. Table 5 shows the effect of pre-training for person re-identification on the performance of gating networks.

6.3 Ablation Study

We conduct an ablation study for different network architectures and training settings on our validation sequences (MOT17-09 and MOT17-10). The MOT17 Benchmark provides three different public detectors. We used the Faster R-CNN detector for the experimental results in this section.

Metrics. Among many different tracking metrics, we choose the Multiple Object Tracking Accuracy (MOTA) [4], identity switches (IDS), and IDF1 [36] for this study. MOTA is calculated by object detection mistakes (false positive and false negative) and tracking mistakes (identity switches). MOTA is often dominated by object detection mistakes since the number of false positive/negative is typically much higher than IDS. IDS counts the number of track ID changes for all the objects. IDF1 is a tracking metric which measures how often objects are correctly identified by the same track ID.

Network Architectures. We test the three deep architectures shown in Fig. 1 for MHT gating. The results in Table 4 are generated by MHT with different appearance gating networks. Motion gating results for different architectures can be found in the supplementary material. The left table in Table 4 shows the tracking performance of different deep architectures as gating networks. Bilinear LSTM works best as the appearance gating network. In terms of the network sizes (LSTM state dimensions), 2048 state dimension is a good choice for Bilinear LSTM as an appearance gating network.

Training Settings. We also try differerent training settings such as different maximum sequence lengths, missing detection augmentations, and network pre-training. The results are included in Tables 4, 5 and 6. We used the (M)+(A) model (in Table 6 (Middle)) which balances well between IDF1 and IDS as our final model for the comparison with MHT and the MOT benchmark in Sect. 6.4.

We used the Adam optimizer [25] for training motion gating networks and set the initial learning rate to 0.01 with the batch size of 64. We used the stochastic gradient optimizer for training appearance and motion+appearance gating networks and set the initial learning rate to 0.005 with the batch size of 16. In all cases, we let the learning rate decrease every 5000 iterations by exponential decay with the decay rate 0.9 until we observe a decrease in performance on the validation set.

Table 4. Ablation Study for Appearance Gating Networks. Baseline1 and Baseline2 are the networks shown in Table 2(b) and (c) respectively. **(Left)** State dim. = 2048, N_{max} = 40 **(Middle)** LSTM: Bilinear, N_{max} = 40, **(Right)** LSTM: Bilinear, State dim. = 2048

LSTM	MOTA	IDF1	IDS
Bilinear	**52.33**	**59.07**	**233**
Baseline1	50.43	51.28	412
Baseline2	50.97	51.49	462

State dim.	MOTA	IDF1	IDS
512	52.14	56.66	283
1024	52.36	55.85	**222**
2048	52.33	**59.07**	233

N_{max}	MOTA	IDF1	IDS
10	51.96	54.36	271
20	52.27	58.38	228
40	52.33	**59.07**	233
80	52.32	57.21	239
160	52.41	55.19	**222**

Table 5. Pre-training vs Random initialization **(Left)** LSTM: Bilinear, State dim. = 2048, N_{max} = 40 **(Right)** LSTM: Baseline2 (Motion) + Bilinear (Appearance), State dim. = 64 (Motion), 2048 (Appearance), N_{max} = 40

Input type	MOTA	IDF1	IDS
(A) Random	52.00	57.46	268
(A) Pre-training	52.33	**59.07**	**233**

Pre-training	MOTA	IDF1	IDS
(M)+(A) Random	50.31	50.39	499
(M)+(A) Pre-training	**52.63**	**58.08**	**197**

Table 6. (Left) Missing Detection Augmentation On/Off. N_{max} = 40. We update LSTM states with zero input vectors (as described in Sect. 4.3) for the models which are trained with the missing detection augmentation. The results in this table show that such LSTM state update is beneficial for the motion gating network, but not for the appearance gating network. Thus, we utilize the missing detection handling only for the motion gating network and the motion part in the motion+appearance gating network. **(Middle and Right)** Different input types with different maximum lengths of training sequences (Middle) N_{max} = 40 (Right) N_{max} = 80.

Missing Det.	MOTA	IDF1	IDS
(M) Yes	52.47	**50.22**	229
(M) No	52.58	47.71	**203**
(A) Yes	52.29	41.37	244
(A) No	52.33	**59.07**	**233**

Input type	MOTA	IDF1	IDS
Motion (M)	52.47	50.22	229
Appearance (A)	52.33	**59.07**	233
(M) + (A)	52.63	58.08	**197**

Input type	MOTA	IDF1	IDS
Motion (M)	52.30	51.14	255
Appearance (A)	52.32	**57.21**	239
(M) + (A)	52.69	54.63	**208**

6.4 MOT Challenge Benchmark

In this section, we report the performance comparison with MHT-DAM and our tracking results on the MOT Challenge 17/16 Benchmark.

Comparison with MHT-DAM. In order to see whether our trained models work well with MHT, we first compare the tracking performance with MHT-DAM [24] on the validation split. Unlike bLSTM, [24] does not benefit from any off-line training using multi-object tracking datasets. It rather builds appearance models for multiple objects in an online manner. Table 7 shows the comparison in results. Our new MHT with bLSTM works well when Faster RCNN and SDP provide input detections. However, for the case of DPM, MOTA score is

Table 7. Comparison with MHT-DAM on our val split (MOT17-02 and MOT17-11). $N_{\max} = 80$. Tracks are interpolated through smoothing. **(Left)** DPM **(Middle)** Faster R-CNN **(Right)** SDP.

Method	MOTA	IDF1	IDS
MHT-DAM	**47.6**	48.2	**72**
Ours	43.8	**52.9**	91

Method	MOTA	IDF1	IDS
MHT-DAM	53.7	54.8	**136**
Ours	**54.8**	**60.5**	140

Method	MOTA	IDF1	IDS
MHT-DAM	**69.4**	62.7	**128**
Ours	**69.7**	**68.6**	137

lower compared to MHT-DAM, although our new method still shows stronger performance on IDF1. We believe that this is because DPM produces quite noisy detections while we use ground truth tracks to generate training sequences for our model. Thus, there could be still some gap between our training data (even after the data augmentation) and track proposals constructed from DPM.

MOT16/17 Challenge Benchmarks. We used the same model and setting as shown in Table 7 as our final method for evaluating on the MOT test sequences. The results are included in Table 8. we grouped previous methods that are closely related to our method separately in order to see the performance difference among these methods.

Table 8. Results from MOT 2017/2016 Challenge (accessed on 7/26/2018)

Method	MOTA	IDF1	IDS	Hz
JCC [23]	**51.2**	**54.5**	**1,802**	1.8
MOTDT17* [31]	50.9	52.7	2,474	**18.3**
PHD-GSDL17 [14]	48.0	49.6	3,998	6.7
FWT* [20]	**51.3**	47.6	2,648	0.2
MHT Methods				
EDMT17* [6]	50.0	51.3	2,264	0.6
MHT-DAM [24]	**50.7**	47.2	2,314	0.9
MHT-bLSTM*	47.5	**51.9**	**2,069**	**1.9**

* indicates the use of additional training data

Method	MOTA	IDF1	IDS	Hz
NOMT [7]	46.4	**53.3**	**359**	2.6
MCjoint [23]	47.1	52.3	370	0.6
LMP* [38]	**48.8**	51.3	481	0.5
STAM16 [8]	46.0	50.0	473	0.2
RAR16pub [12]	45.9	48.8	648	0.9
NLLMPa [29]	47.6	47.3	629	**8.3**
JMC [40]	46.3	46.3	657	0.8
LINF1 [11]	41.0	45.7	430	4.2
CDA-DDALv2* [3]	43.9	45.1	676	0.5
MHT and LSTM-based Methods				
EDMT* [6]	45.3	**47.9**	639	**1.8**
AMIR* [1]	**47.2**	46.3	774	1.0
MHT-DAM [24]	45.8	46.1	**590**	0.8
MHT-bLSTM*	42.1	**47.8**	735	**1.8**

7 Conclusion

In this paper, we proposed using an LSTM network to score track proposals in a near-online multiple hypothesis tracking framework. In order to properly take into account multiple past appearances, we proposed a Bilinear LSTM algorithm that slices the LSTM memory into several vectors and uses a matrix vector multiplication between the memory output and the appearance input to simulate a discriminatively trained predictor model. Such an algorithm is shown to be significantly better than traditional LSTM in modeling the appearance of each track, especially in terms of maintaining track identities. Jointly using appearance and motion LSTM gating networks in an MHT framework, we have achieved state-of-the-art performances in the MOT challenges for near-online methods. We believe the proposed Bilinear LSTM is general and could be applicable in many other problems that require learning an online sequential discriminative model using an end-to-end approach and will explore those as future work.

Acknowledgments. This work was supported in part by NIH award 1R24OD020174-01A1. Fuxin Li was partially supported by NSF award 1751402, and DARPA under contract N66001-17-2-4030.

References

1. A. Sadeghian, A. Alahi, S.S.: Tracking the untrackable: learning to track multiple cues with long-term dependencies. In: ICCV (2017)
2. Andriluka, M., Roth, S., Schiele, B.: People-tracking-by-detection and people-detection-by-tracking. In: CVPR (2008)
3. Bae, S.H., Yoon, K.J.: Confidence-based data association and discriminative deep appearance learning for robust online multi-object tracking. IEEE Trans. Pattern Anal. Mach. Intell. **40**, 595–610 (2018)
4. Bernardin, K., Stiefelhagen, R.: Evaluating multiple object tracking performance the CLEAR MOT metrics. Image Video Process. **2008**, 246309 (2008)
5. Blackman, S.: Multiple hypothesis tracking for multiple target tracking. Aerosp. Electron. Syst. Mag. **19**(1), 5–18 (2004)
6. Chen, J., Sheng, H., Zhang, Y., Xiong, Z.: Enhancing detection model for multiple hypothesis tracking. In: CVPR Workshops (2017)
7. Choi, W.: Near-online multi-target tracking with aggregated local flow descriptor. In: ICCV (2015)
8. Chu, Q., Ouyang, W., Li, H., Wang, X., Liu, B., Yu, N.: Online multi-object tracking using CNN-based single object tracker with spatial-temporal attention mechanism. In: ICCV (2017)
9. Cox, I.J., Hingorani, S.L.: An efficient implementation of Reid's multiple hypothesis tracking algorithm and its evaluation for the purpose of visual tracking. IEEE Trans. Pattern Anal. Mach. Intell. **18**, 138–150 (1996)
10. Ess, A., Leibe, B., Schindler, K., van Gool, L.: A mobile vision system for robust multi-person tracking. In: CVPR (2008)
11. Fagot-Bouquet, L., Audigier, R., Dhome, Y., Lerasle, F.: Improving multi-frame data association with sparse representations for robust near-online multi-object tracking. In: Leibe, B., Matas, J., Sebe, N., Welling, M. (eds.) ECCV 2016. LNCS, vol. 9912, pp. 774–790. Springer, Cham (2016). https://doi.org/10.1007/978-3-319-46484-8_47
12. Fang, K., Xiang, Y., Li, X., Savarese, S.: Recurrent autoregressive networks for online multi-object tracking. In: WACV (2018)
13. Felzenszwalb, P.F., Girshick, R.B., McAllester, D., Ramanan, D.: Object detection with discriminatively trained part based models. IEEE Trans. Pattern Anal. Mach. Intell. **32**(9), 1627–1645 (2010)

14. Fu, Z., Feng, P., Angelini, F., Chambers, J.A., Naqvi, S.M.: Particle phd filter based multiple human tracking using online group-structured dictionary learning. IEEE Access **6**, 14764–14778 (2018)
15. Geiger, A., Lenz, P., Urtasun, R.: Are we ready for autonomous driving? the KITTI vision benchmark suite. In: CVPR (2012)
16. Girshick, R., Donahue, J., Darrell, T., Malik, J.: Rich feature hierarchies for accurate object detection and semantic segmentation. In: CVPR (2014)
17. Goodfellow, I., Bengio, Y., Courville, A., Bengio, Y.: Deep Learning, vol. 1. MIT Press, Cambridge (2016)
18. Gordon, D., Farhadi, A., Fox, D.: Re3: Real-time recurrent regression networks for visual tracking of generic objects. IEEE Robot. Autom. Lett. **3**(2), 788–795 (2018)
19. He, K., Zhang, X., Ren, S., Sun, J.: Deep residual learning for image recognition. In: CVPR (2016)
20. Henschel, R., Leal-Taixé, L., Cremers, D., Rosenhahn, B.: Fusion of head and full-body detectors for multi-object tracking. In: CVPR Workshops (2018)
21. Hochreiter, S., Schmidhuber, J.: Long short-term memory. Neural Comput. **9**, 1735–1780 (1997)
22. Hong Yoon, J., Lee, C.R., Yang, M.H., Yoon, K.J.: Online multi-object tracking via structural constraint event aggregation. In: CVPR. pp. 1392–1400 (2016)
23. Keuper, M., Tang, S., Yu, Z., Andres, B., Brox, T., Schiele, B.: A multi-cut formulation for joint segmentation and tracking of multiple objects. arXiv:1607.06317 (2016)
24. Kim, C., Li, F., Ciptadi, A., Rehg, J.: Multiple hypothesis tracking revisited. In: ICCV (2015)
25. Kingma, D.P., Ba, J.: Adam: a method for stochastic optimization. In: ICLR (2015)
26. Leal-Taixé, L., Canton-Ferrer, C., Schindler, K.: Learning by tracking: siamese CNN for robust target association. In: CVPR Workshops (2016)
27. Leal-Taixé, L., Milan, A., Reid, I., Roth, S., Schindler, K.: MOTChallenge 2015: Towards a benchmark for multi-target tracking. arXiv:1504.01942 (2015)
28. Leal-Taixe, L., Milan, A., Schindler, K., Cremers, D., Reid, I., Roth, S.: Tracking the trackers: an analysis of the state of the art in multiple object tracking. arXiv:1704.02781 (2017)
29. Levinkov, E., et al.: Joint graph decomposition & node labeling: problem, algorithms, applications. In: CVPR (2017)
30. Li, W., Zhao, R., Xiao, T., Wang, X.: DeeReID: deep filter pairing neural network for person re-identification. In: CVPR (2014)
31. Long, C., Haizhou, A., Zijie, Z., Chong, S.: Real-time multiple people tracking with deeply learned candidate selection and person re-identification. In: ICME (2018)
32. Milan, A., Leal-Taixé, L., Reid, I., Roth, S., Schindler, K.: MOT16: A benchmark for multi-object tracking. arXiv:1603.00831 (2016)
33. Milan, A., Rezatofighi, S.H., Dick, A., Reid, I., Schindler, K.: Online multi-target tracking using recurrent neural networks. In: AAAI (2017)
34. Papageorgiou, D.J., Salpukas, M.R.: The maximum weight independent set problem for data association in multiple hypothesis tracking. In: Hirsch, M.J., Commander, C.W., Pardalos, P.M., Murphey, R. (eds.) Optimization and Cooperative Control Strategies. LNCIS, vol. 381, pp. 235–255. Springer, Heidelberg (2009)
35. Ren, S., He, K., Girshick, R., Sun, J.: Faster R-CNN: towards real-time object detection with region proposal networks. In: NIPS (2015)

36. Ristani, E., Solera, F., Zou, R., Cucchiara, R., Tomasi, C.: Performance measures and a data set for multi-target, multi-camera tracking. In: Hua, G., Jégou, H. (eds.) ECCV 2016. LNCS, vol. 9914, pp. 17–35. Springer, Cham (2016). https://doi.org/10.1007/978-3-319-48881-3_2
37. Son, J., Baek, M., Cho, M., Han, B.: Multi-object tracking with quadruplet convolutional neural networks. In: CVPR (2017)
38. Tang, S., Andriluka, M., Andres, B., Schiele, B.: Multiple people tracking with lifted multicut and person re-identification. In: CVPR (2017)
39. Tang, S., Andres, B., Andriluka, M., Schiele, B.: Multi-person Tracking by multicut and deep matching. In: Hua, G., Jégou, H. (eds.) ECCV 2016. LNCS, vol. 9914, pp. 100–111. Springer, Cham (2016). https://doi.org/10.1007/978-3-319-48881-3_8
40. Yang, F., Choi, W., Lin, Y.: Exploit all the layers: Fast and accurate CNN object detector with scale dependent pooling and cascaded rejection classifiers. In: CVPR (2016)
41. Yang, T., Chan, A.B.: Recurrent filter learning for visual tracking. arXiv:1708.03874 (2017)
42. Zheng, L., Shen, L., Tian, L., Wang, S., Wang, J., Tian, Q.: Scalable person reidentification: a benchmark. In: ICCV (2015)

Clustering Convolutional Kernels to Compress Deep Neural Networks

Sanghyun Son, Seungjun Nah, and Kyoung Mu Lee(✉)

Department of ECE, ASRI, Seoul National University, Seoul 08826, Korea
{thstkdgus35,kyoungmu}@snu.ac.kr,
seungjun.nah@gmail.com

Abstract. In this paper, we propose a novel method to compress CNNs by reconstructing the network from a small set of spatial convolution kernels. Starting from a pre-trained model, we extract representative 2D kernel centroids using k-means clustering. Each centroid replaces the corresponding kernels of the same cluster, and we use indexed representations instead of saving whole kernels. Kernels in the same cluster share their weights, and we fine-tune the model while keeping the compressed state. Furthermore, we also suggest an efficient way of removing redundant calculations in the compressed convolutional layers. We experimentally show that our technique works well without harming the accuracy of widely-used CNNs. Also, our ResNet-18 even outperforms its uncompressed counterpart at ILSVRC2012 classification task with over 10x compression ratio.

Keywords: CNNs · Compression · Quantization · Weight sharing
Clustering

1 Introduction

The recent era of computer vision witnessed remarkable advances from deep learning. The analysis presented in [35] shows that CNNs not only figure out the scene types but also well recognizes spatial patterns. Therefore, state-of-the-art convolutional neural networks [15,16,31] and their variants apply to a broad range of problems such as image classification, object detection, segmentation, image restoration, etc. However, most of the CNNs are designed to be executed on high-end GPUs with substantial memory and computational power. In mobile or embedded environments where computational resources are limited, those networks need to be compressed for practical applications [12,34].

Most of the studies on network compression have investigated to figure out redundancies of weights [6] and unnecessary parameters [14,24]. Then, those parameters can be removed while preserving the original performance of the model. In [7,20], the weight matrices and tensors were factorized and approximated to low-rank for efficient computation. Pruning became popular in recent works [10,13,26,27] since it directly saves storage and computations. On the

V. Ferrari et al. (Eds.): ECCV 2018, LNCS 11212, pp. 225–240, 2018.
https://doi.org/10.1007/978-3-030-01237-3_14

other side, the quantization based approaches have also become common. Extensive studies on binary and ternary networks [4,5,12,17,25,29,39] proved that even 1 or 2 bits parameters can make CNNs work. Other works tried to quantize adjacent elements of a weight tensor as a form of vector quantization [9,34]. Those methods utilize k-means clustering so that we can express the compressed model in the form of codebook and indices. Especially, [34] extracted a sub-vector from the weight tensor in channel dimension to exploit product quantization.

In this paper, we propose a more structured quantization method that is built upon 2D convolution kernels. As the convolution itself is inherently *spatial*, we opt to use a spatial slice of weight tensors as a unit to be compressed. Unless mentioned otherwise, we denote these 2D slices as kernels. Under our expression, a weight tensor of a single convolutional layer is composed of $C_{\text{out}} \times C_{\text{in}}$ number of kernels where C_{out} and C_{out} denote the output and input channels, respectively. For example, widely used VGG-16 [31] and ResNets [15] consist of more than a million 3×3 kernels.

Similarly to the vector quantization methods [9,34], we perform clustering on 3×3 kernels and replace the redundant kernels with their centroids. Therefore, we represent the compressed model with a set of centroids and a corresponding cluster index per each kernel. Thus, kernels that have the same index share their weights. While maintaining the compressed state, we train our model through the weight-sharing. We also present methods to accelerate the convolution when the same centroid repeatedly appears in a single layer.

Our compression method brings following contributions and benefits. First, we propose a new method to compress and accelerate the CNN by applying k-means clustering to 2D kernels. To the best of our knowledge, this is the first approach on network compression that considers the redundant spatial patterns of kernels. Second, our transform invariant clustering method extends the valid number of kernel centroids with geometric transforms. Our improved experimental results imply the transform invariance imposes regularization effect. Lastly, our extensive experiments show that our method is generally applicable to various CNN architectures and datasets. In particular, our compressed ResNet [15] achieves higher accuracy on ILSVRC12 image classification than the original model at over 10x compression ratio.

2 Related Works

Network quantization is one of the typical approaches to compress deep neural networks. It focuses on reducing the number of bits to represent each parameter. Earlier works utilized the weight sharing and indexed representation of the parameters to save the storage. Han et al. [12] first demonstrated that 2^5 distinctive weights are enough for a single convolutional layer, and proposed 5-bit quantization of CNN. To save more storages, HashedNets [1] utilized a hash function to reduce the overhead from storing index terms. Those methods do not restrict the precision, but the diversity of each parameter by sharing a full-precision weight between similar values. Although their implementations can be tricky, we can train those models with the traditional gradient descent.

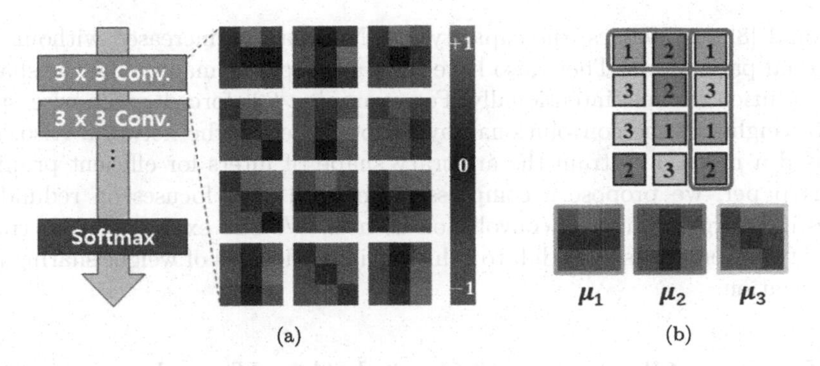

Fig. 1. We compress convolutional layers (a) of given CNN as (b). We apply k-means clustering to the kernels and use indexed representations with a codebook $\mathcal{M} = \{\mu_i | i = 1, \cdots, k\}$. We also accelerate the CNN by removing redundant computations from overlapping kernels in red and **blue** boxes. Note that we handle all convolutional layers simultaneously, rather than compress each layer individually. (Color figure online)

On the other side of network quantization, there have been attempts to limit the precision of parameters. It is already proven that binary [4] and ternary [25, 39] weights work well on challenging ImageNet [30] classification task. These methods can even accelerate the CNNs by redefining the convolution in more efficient ways. Recently, [37] proposed a method to represent each weight as a power of two that can utilize high-speed bit-shift operations. Since the major goal of the quantization is resource-efficient neural networks, intermediate features [5, 29] and gradients [11,17,38] can also be quantized, too.

While the above methods mainly focus on reducing the bit-width of each parameter, vector quantization directly quantizes a weight vector and maps it to an index. Although intrinsic high-dimensionality makes it more challenging than the scalar quantization, product quantization works well on compressing fully-connected [9] and convolutional layers [34]. Our work is a particular case of weight sharing and vector quantization, as we assign the same index to multiple kernels and share their weights. However, unlike weight or sub-vector quantization, we quantize 2D kernels which have geometrical meanings in the CNNs.

Network pruning [14,24] aims to remove unnecessary connections from the networks. Usually, small weights are removed from the network by iterative optimization steps [12,13]. However, weight-wise pruning has several limitations in practice due to their irregular structures. Therefore, structured pruning [26,27] methods for the convolutional neural networks are getting popular. As they prune unnecessary convolution kernels of CNNs, they would be much suitable for the practical case. Our algorithm is not directly related to pruning itself. However, we will show that the proposed method can benefit from the pruning as [12] mentioned.

There are several works which utilize the geometric shapes of convolution kernels for efficient CNNs. By exploiting translational [36], reflectance [3], and rotational [8] symmetries, the capacity of CNNs can be increased without any additional parameters. There also have been attempts to manipulate the shapes of convolution kernels intentionally. For example, [23] forced group-wise sparsity to weights of the convolutional layers to accelerate the network. Also, [33] proposed a method to train the arbitrary shape of filters for efficient pruning. In this paper, we propose a compression method that focuses on redundant shapes in a large number of convolution kernels. We also explore various transforms of the kernels as [3,8] did, to achieve higher degrees of weight sharing and regularization.

3 K-means Clustering of Convolution Kernels

Before going into the details, we define the terms to be used in the following descriptions. We will assume that there are total N many kernels in our target CNN and all of them have the same spatial sizes. Then, a weight tensor of m-th convolution layer can be denoted as $\mathbf{w}^m \in \mathbb{R}^{C_{\text{out}} \times C_{\text{in}} \times h \times w}$ whose input $\mathbf{x}$ and output $\mathbf{y}$ have C_{in} and C_{out} channels, respectively. Here, we will omit the term m when we describe the convolutional layer. $\mathbf{x}_i$ refers to a i-th input channel of $\mathbf{x}$, and $\mathbf{y}_j$ is a j-th output channel of $\mathbf{y}$. A kernel $\mathbf{w}_{ij}$ is applied to $\mathbf{x}_i$ and the responses are accumulated to compute $\mathbf{y}_j$ as Eq. (1).

$$\mathbf{y}_j = \sum_{i=1}^{C_{\text{in}}} \mathbf{w}_{ij} * \mathbf{x}_i. \tag{1}$$

In the following subsections, we explain our compression algorithm and its computational benefits. In Sect. 3.1, We formulate our algorithm with a concept of k-means clustering. In Sect. 3.2, we describe a method to train our model. In Sect. 3.3, we demonstrate that the proposed method can accelerate the convolutions. Lastly, in Sect. 3.4, we propose an advanced clustering method that can act as a strong regularization.

3.1 Compact Representation of the Kernels

In general, a CNN is trained without any structural restrictions on the shapes of its weight tensors. Therefore, there may exist N distinctive kernels in the network. Our main strategy is to represent those kernels more compactly with k-means clustering. After grouping the kernels into k many clusters, we replace each kernel $\mathbf{w}_{ij}^m$ in a cluster $\mathcal{W}_n$ to its corresponding centroid $\mu_n = \mathbb{E}_{\mathbf{w}_{ij}^m \in \mathcal{W}_n}\left[\mathbf{w}_{ij}^m\right]$. Then, we apply weight-sharing to the all kernels that belong to $\mathcal{W}_n$ and represent them with their cluster index n. Considering that a single-precision 3×3 kernel requires 36-byte storage, the indexed representation can reduce the model size a lot.

One possible problem is that the distribution of kernel weights can vary across different convolutional layers. In that case, our approach may not derive meaningful representations as k-means clustering cannot find representative centroids.

Therefore, we utilize the basic concept of convolution and normalize all kernels to handle this problem. To put it concretely, we handle the kernels that have similar shapes but different norms together because they show similar behaviors in filtering. Thus, rather than compute the distances between kernels directly from their raw values, we use normalized kernels. Consequently, the k-means clustering objective becomes

$$\underset{\mathcal{M}}{\operatorname{argmin}} \sum_{n=1}^{k} \sum_{\hat{\mathbf{w}}_{ij}^m \in \mathcal{W}_n} \|\hat{\mathbf{w}}_{ij}^m - \mu_n\|^2, \tag{2}$$

where $\hat{\mathbf{w}}_{ij}^m = \mathbf{w}_{ij}^m / s_{ij}^m$ and $s_{ij}^m = sign(\mathbf{w}_{ij*}^m)\|\mathbf{w}_{ij}^m\|^2$. Here, $\mathbf{w}_{ij*}^m$ is a center pixel of a kernel. By defining s_{ij}^m in this manner, we also cluster the kernels that have similar structures but opposite signs together. A compressed representation of each kernel includes a cluster index l_{ij}^m such that $\hat{\mathbf{w}}_{ij}^m \in \mathcal{W}_{l_{ij}^m}$, and its scale s_{ij}^m. From the viewpoint of compression, storing those scale parameters requires additional storage and lowers the compression ratio. However, it enables our method to learn fine-grained centroids and increases the representation power as we disentangle the kernel shapes and norms. Also, we will demonstrate that those scale parameters sometimes can be ignored in Sects. 4.6 and 4.7

3.2 Training Method

After clustering, we fine-tune the compressed model while maintaining the cluster assignment of each kernel. To do so, we replace a convolution in Eq. (1) with Eq. (3). In other words, we use a centroid $\mu_{l_{ij}}$ with a scale instead of the original kernel $\mathbf{w}_{ij}$. Therefore, our method has two trainable parameter sets: centroids and scales. We can use a standard back-propagation algorithm to train those parameters because Eq. (3) is fully differentiable. Note that a centroid $\mu_{l_{ij}}$ appear at different layers through the network, and therefore a single centroid can take gradients from various layers. We efficiently implemented this algorithm with PyTorch [28] framework, which automatically differentiates the variables through the computational graph.

$$\mathbf{y}_j = \sum_{i=1}^{C_{\text{in}}} s_{ij}\mu_{l_{ij}} * \mathbf{x}_i. \tag{3}$$

3.3 Accelerating Convolution via Shared Kernel Representations

Although our primary interest is network compression, we can also accelerate a CNN by reducing the duplicated computations from shared kernel representations. To be specific, there can be two types of redundancy in a convolutional layer. One is duplication among the kernels generating the same output channel from different input channels. The other is a duplication of kernels generating multiple output channels from a single input channel. In both cases, we can compute the 2D convolution only once per each unique centroid.

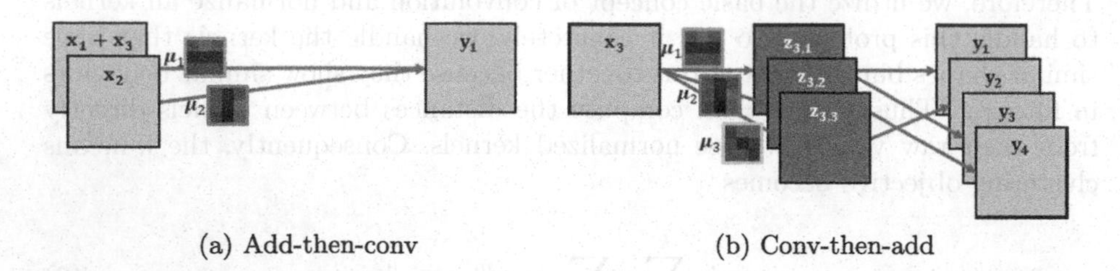

(a) Add-then-conv (b) Conv-then-add

Fig. 2. A compressed convolutional layer with $C_{\text{in}} = 3$ and $C_{\text{out}} = 4$ from Fig. 1(b) can be accelerate by two ways. (a) We calculate $\mathbf{x}_1 + \mathbf{x}_3$ first and then apply a shared kernel μ_1. (b) We compute intermediate features $\mathbf{z}_k$ first and accumulate them to $\mathbf{y}_j$. For example, $\mathbf{z}_{3,1}$ is accumulated to $\mathbf{y}_1$ and $\mathbf{y}_3$.

In Fig. 2(a), we add the input channels before convolution to avoid the computations between a single kernel and multiple input features. We provide a detailed explanation of this procedure in Eq. (4). Since we do not need to calculate the convolution when $n \neq l_{ij}$ for $\forall i$, the proposed method requires less computation than the traditional convolution. We call it 'Add-then-conv'.

$$\begin{aligned}
\mathbf{y}_j &= \sum_{i=1}^{C_{\text{in}}} \mu_{l_{ij}} * (s_{ij}\mathbf{x}_i) (\text{associative law}) \\
&= \sum_{i=1}^{C_{\text{in}}} \left(\sum_{n=1}^{k} \mu_n \delta\left[n = l_{ij}\right] \right) * (s_{ij}\mathbf{x}_i) (\text{marginalization}) \\
&= \sum_{n=1}^{k} \mu_n * \left(\sum_{i=1}^{C_{\text{in}}} \delta\left[n = l_{ij}\right] s_{ij}\mathbf{x}_i \right) (\text{associative law}).
\end{aligned} \tag{4}$$

In Fig. 2(b), the responses of all output channels from a single input channel are computed simultaneously. An input channel $\mathbf{x}_i$ responds to multiple centroids and generate $\mathcal{Z}_i = \{\mathbf{z}_{i,l_{ij}} = \mu_{l_{ij}} * \mathbf{x}_i | j = 1, 2, \cdots, C_{\text{out}}\}$. Then, we can compute $\mathbf{y}_j$ as a weighted sum of $\mathbf{z}$ such that

$$\mathbf{y}_j = \sum_{i=1}^{C_{\text{in}}} s_{ij}\mathbf{z}_{i,l_{ij}}. \tag{5}$$

Similarly to above, we call it 'Conv-then-add'. Once the clustering is done, we choose and apply the faster method by comparing the number of computations.

3.4 Transform Invariant Clustering

Since 3×3 kernels have relatively simple structures, many of them are flipped and rotated version of each other. Inspired by this idea, we newly propose the transform invariant clustering (TIC) for the convolutional kernels. The basic idea of TIC is to allow a centroid to represent its transformed shapes, too. Therefore,

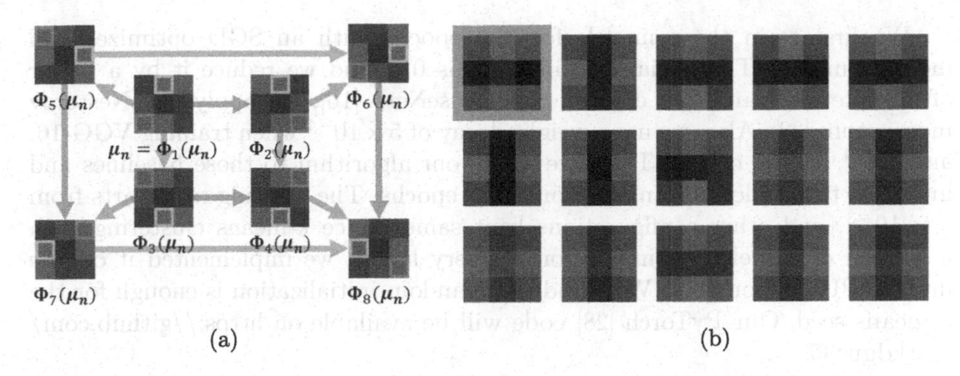

Fig. 3. (a) We combine horizontal, vertical flips and 90° **rotation** to represent various kernels using one centroid. Weights that are marked with same colors (cyan, magenta) share their values. (b) We visualize how TIC actually works. We mark the centroid with green, and the other kernels belong to the same cluster even they have different orientations. (Color figure online)

when m distinct transforms are allowed, k centroids can represent mk shapes. In this paper, we use a maximum of eight different transforms as shown in Fig. 3(a).

With TIC, we use Eqs. (6) and (7) instead of Eqs. (2) and (3). Here, $\mathbf{\Phi}_{t_{ij}^m}(\cdot)$ represents the transformations that are demonstrated in Fig. 3(a). Equation(6) can be optimized like traditional k-means clustering, where a centroid of $\mathcal{W}_n$ is defined as $\mu_n = \mathbb{E}_{\mathbf{w}_{ij}^m \in \mathcal{W}_n}\left[\mathbf{\Phi}_{t_{ij}}^{-1}\left(\mathbf{w}_{ij}^m\right)\right]$. TIC does not further compress and accelerate our model since we require additional bits to store $\mathcal{T}$ which is a set of all t_{ij}^m. However, in Sect. 4.3, we will demonstrate that TIC allows very compact representation of a CNN and acts as a strong regularization term.

$$\underset{\mathcal{M},\mathcal{T}}{\operatorname{argmin}} \sum_{n=1}^{k} \sum_{\hat{\mathbf{w}}_{ij}^m \in \mathcal{W}_n} \left\| \hat{\mathbf{w}}_{ij}^m - \mathbf{\Phi}_{t_{ij}^m}(\mu_n) \right\|_2^2, \tag{6}$$

$$\mathbf{y}_j = \sum_{i=1}^{C_{\text{in}}} \mathbf{\Phi}_{t_{ij}}\left(s_{ij}\mu_{l_{ij}}\right) * \mathbf{x}_i. \tag{7}$$

4 Experiments

We apply the proposed method to recent popular CNN architectures for image classification task: VGG [31], ResNets [15], and DenseNets [16]. We use CIFAR-10 [21] dataset to evaluate the performance of the compressed models. Our training and test dataset contain 50,000 and 10,000 test images, respectively. We normalize all images using channel-wise means and standard deviations of the training set. During the training, we apply random flip and translation augmentation to input images as previous works [15,16,31] did.

We first train those models for 300 epochs with an SGD optimizer and momentum 0.9. The initial learning rate is 0.1, and we reduce it by a factor of 10 after 150 and 225 epochs. For DenseNets [16], we apply the Nesterov momentum [32]. Also, we use a weight decay of 5×10^{-4} when training VGG-16, and 10^{-4} for the others. Then, we apply our algorithm to those baselines and fine-tune the models for an additional 300 epochs. The learning rate starts from 5×10^{-3}, and other configurations kept same. Since k-means clustering with a million of kernels is computationally very heavy, we implemented it on the multi-GPU environment. We found that random initialization is enough for the k-means seed. Our PyTorch [28] code will be available on https://github.com/thstkdgus35.

4.1 Clustering Kernels from Various Models

We apply our method to a VGG-16 [31] variant first. The original VGG-16 has 13 convolution layers, and three fully-connected layers follow. In our implementation, there is one fully-connected layer after the last pooling. Also, batch normalizations [19] follow after all convolutions. The modified architecture contains 1,634,496 many 3×3 kernels which account over 99.9% of the total parameters. We also compress more recent architectures, ResNets [15] and DenseNets [16]. Although some of their configurations contain the bottleneck structure that comes with many 1×1 convolutions, we use the models without the bottleneck. The baseline ResNet-56 and DenseNet-12-40 have 94,256 and 101,160 kernels, respectively. Similar to VGG-16, 3×3 kernels are also dominant in those models.

We demonstrate the results in Table 1 with varying the number of clusters k. Since previous works on network compression do not provide unified comparisons, we only show our results here. As we expected, using more centroids results in lower error rates. However, we found that the model performances are reasonable when we use only 128 centroids. Notably, the results from VGG-16 is impressive because the original model contains more than 1.6×10^6 kernels. In other words, over 10,000 kernels of the CNN are sharing their shapes together while maintaining the classification accuracy.

4.2 Analyzing Compression and Acceleration Ratio

In this section, we analyze how our method can compress and accelerate the CNN. We only count the weights from 3×3 kernels, as they compose the most

Table 1. We compress various CNN architectures on CIFAR10 and report the classification error rates (%). C'k' denote the proposed method with k centroids.

Model	C128	C256	C512	C1024	Baseline
VGG-16 [31]	6.24	6.23	6.16	6.01	5.98
ResNet-56 [15]	6.76	6.54	6.61	6.30	6.28
DenseNet-12-40 [16]	5.44	5.49	5.39	5.38	5.26

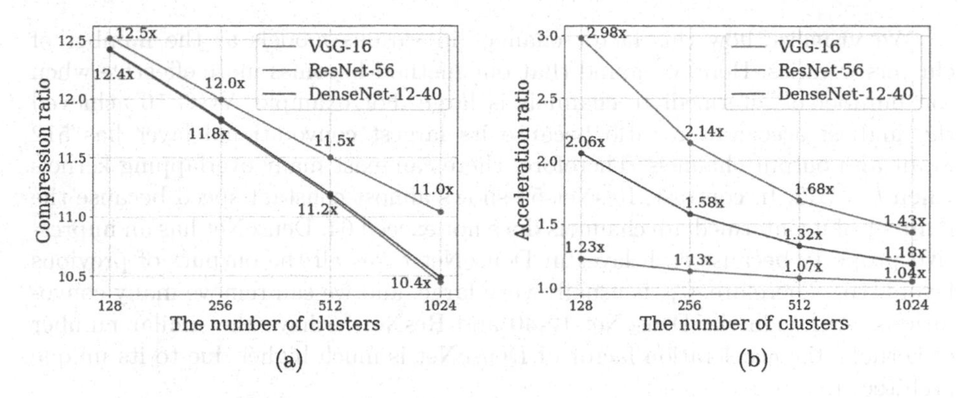

Fig. 4. Compression(a) and acceleration(b) ratios of various architecture and different k values. Those factors tend to decrease as the number of clusters increases.

parts of our baselines. Also, we assume that the original CNNs requires $b_{\mathbf{w}} = 32$ bits to represent each weight. Our method store an index l_{ij}^{m} and a scale parameter s_{ij}^{m} per each kernel $\mathbf{w}_{ij}^{m}$. After clustering, our centroid representation requires $log_2 k$ and $b_{\mathbf{s}}$ bits for each index and scale parameter, respectively. We assign 16-bit for each s_i for simplicity. We also store a codebook with k centroids which occupy total $kb_{\mathbf{w}}hw$ bits. This codebook can be ignored in many cases as N is much larger than k in usual. To sum up, we calculate the compression ratio r_{comp} as Eq. (8). For the experiments in Table 1, we plot compression ratios with respect to various k values in Fig. 4(a).

$$r_{\text{comp}} = \frac{N b_{\mathbf{w}} hw}{N\left(\log_2 k + b_{\mathbf{s}}\right) + k b_{\mathbf{w}} hw} \simeq \frac{b_{\mathbf{w}} hw}{\log_2 k + b_{\mathbf{s}}}. \tag{8}$$

We also analyze the way to accelerate the CNNs with our method. Here, we ignore the scale parameters without losing generality since their computations are negligible. For the 'Add-then-conv,' let us define λ_j as the number of distinctive centroids that contribute to the computation of $\mathbf{y}_j$. In the case of Fig. 1(b), λ_1 is equal to 2 since only μ_1 and μ_3 are used to compute $\mathbf{y}_1$. As we explained in Sec. 3.3, we first add all input features that share the same kernels and then compute convolutions. Therefore, we can reduce the number of convolutions from C_{in} to λ_j for each output channels.

For the 'Conv-then-add,' we define another variable ν_i that indicates the number of distinctive centroids that are convolved with $\mathbf{x}_i$. In Fig. 1(b), ν_1 is equal to 3 because the long blue box contains three centroids. Therefore, we only compute ν_i many convolutions instead of C_{out} for each $\mathbf{x}_i$. Finally, we calculate the theoretical acceleration factor r_{accel} of each convolutional layer by simply choosing the method which has the fewer FLOPs as illustrated in Eq. (9).

$$r_{\text{accel}} \simeq \frac{C_{\text{in}} C_{\text{out}}}{\min\left(\sum_{j=1}^{C_{\text{out}}} \lambda_j, \sum_{i=1}^{C_{\text{in}}} \nu_i\right)} \tag{9}$$

We visualize how this factor changes in various models as the number of clusters k varies. Here, we found that our method becomes more effective when the number of intermediate channels is large. For example, VGG-16 achieved the highest acceleration ratio because its largest convolutional layer has 512 input and output channels. Therefore, there can exist many overlapping kernels when $k < 512$. In contrast, ResNet-56 shows almost constant speed because the number of its intermediate channels does not exceed 64. DenseNet has an impressive property because each layer in DenseNet takes all the outputs of previous layers [16]. Therefore, C_{in} is usually very large, and we can remove many convolutions. Although the DenseNet-12-40 and ResNet-56 have the similar number of kernels, the acceleration factor of DenseNet is much higher due to its unique architecture.

In this paper, we only report the theoretical FLOPs because the proposed method has some compatibility issues with cuDNN [2]. However, our algorithm can be implemented using group convolution.

4.3 Transform Invariant Clustering for Compact Representation

We apply transform invariant clustering on VGG-16 to see how the proposed method can benefit from higher degrees of weight sharing. We first allow vertical flips, and then horizontal flips to take four types of transforms into account during clustering. Finally, we also consider the rotational transform [3,8] in the clustering to acquire very compact centroid representation. Note that the valid number of representative kernels are 256 in all three configurations in the experimental results shown in Table 2.

Since transform indication bits are additionally required to include transforms, the gains in compression ratio are trivial. For example, our 'T' models in Table 2 consume similar amounts of storage with a VGG-16-C256 model in Fig. 4, having compression ratio of 11.99. However, we observed that TIC has a strong regularization effect on redundant kernel shapes. When we exploited the vertical symmetry of the kernels, VGG-16-C128-TIC2 achieves lower classification errors compared to the baseline. Note that the performance has dropped a little bit when we include the horizontal transforms (TIC4) because the number of centroids is limited to 64. However, it has a compatible performance compared to VGG-16-C256 in Table 1, while having much more compact representations. TIC8 suffers a slight performance drop, but it is surprising that only 32 centroids are necessary to represent the VGG-16 with reasonable accuracy.

4.4 Multi Clustering

The proposed method performs better as the number of clusters k increases. However, it is not desirable to set k boundlessly large regarding compression and acceleration ratio. Therefore, we handle this trade-off by dividing the given kernels to $n \geq 2$ sets and applying our method individually. By doing so, we find $\mathcal{M}_1, \cdots, \mathcal{M}_n$ instead of computing a single set of centroids $\mathcal{M}$. If we keep k same for all sets, the number of effective centroids will be nk while we still

Table 2. Our method allows various design choices. 'M' refers to the multi clustering, and the number of groups follows. After TIC, the number of allowed transformations follows. We report the error rates on CIFAR-10 dataset. We also report the compression and acceleration ratios with respect to the baseline.

Model	Error (%)	Sizes (MB)	FLOPs (M)
VGG-16-baseline	5.98	58.8	313
VGG-16-C32	6.78	4.29 (13.7x)	42 (7.63x)
VGG-16-C64	6.44	4.49 (13.1x)	68 (4.60x)
VGG-16-C64-M2	6.27	4.50 (13.0x)	75 (4.17x)
VGG-16-C64-M13	6.21	4.51 (13.0x)	78 (4.01x)
VGG-16-C256-M2	6.16	4.91 (12.0x)	159 (1.97x)
VGG-16-C256-M13	6.10	4.96 (11.8x)	166 (1.89x)
VGG-16-C128-TIC2	**5.92**	4.91 (12.0x)	145 (2.16x)
VGG-16-C64-TIC4	6.25	4.91 (12.0x)	145 (2.16x)
VGG-16-C32-TIC8	6.51	4.91 (12.0x)	145 (2.16x)

require log_2k bits to represent each index. Therefore, we can efficiently increase the network capacity without enlarging the model.

We evaluate the multi clustering method using our VGG-16 [31] variant. It has 13 convolutional layers, so we try two simple dividing strategies because finding an optimal partition is challenging. In the M2 configuration, we apply k-means clustering to the first ten and the last three layers separately, so that both groups contain the similar amount of kernels. Our M13 configuration treats all layers individually. Because the first convolutional layer only contains 192 kernels, we allocate $\min(k, 192)$ clusters for this layer. Although we keep k the same for the other layers, it is possible to assign different k to each group for more elaborate tuning. We provide the results in Table 2. We first compressed VGG-16 with only 64 clusters and observed a slight performance drop, since 25,000 kernels are sharing their weights on average. With the multi clustering, however, the performances get better without any noticeable decrease in the compression ratio. Although the acceleration factors slightly decrease with the multi clustering, we observed meaningful performance gain as the number of effective centroids increases.

4.5 Clustering with Pruning

Prior works on network pruning [10,12,13,26,27] showed that it is possible to remove a large number of unnecessary weights from CNNs without accuracy loss. In this section, we analyze how our method can benefit from pruning. As [12] mentioned, k centroids will provide a better approximation of the network if the number of whole kernels decreases with pruning.

Table 3. We combine our method with pruning and report the error rates on the CIFAR-10 dataset. Here, 'P' denotes the simple pruning strategy we mentioned.

Model	Error (%)	Size (MB)	FLOPs (M)
VGG-16-P	6.08	28.7 (2.05x)	223 (1.41x)
VGG-16-Filter-pruning [26]	5.91	21.0 (2.80x)	206 (1.52x)
VGG-16-C512	6.16	5.11 (11.5x)	186 (1.68x)
VGG-16-PC512	6.13	3.19 (23.5x)	151 (2.07x)
VGG-16-Filter-pruning [26]-C512	5.99	2.35 (31.8x)	149 (2.10x)

Here, we try two pruning strategies to VGG-16 before applying our method. The first method is simple thresholding which removing 50% of the spatial kernels from each layer based on their L_1 norms. For the advanced method, we focus on filter-level pruning [26,27] instead of weight-wise pruning [10,12,13] because we treat the individual kernel for a basic unit of CNNs. We adopt a method from [26] that performs structured pruning [27] to reduce the number of intermediate channels with kernels. Then, we apply the proposed method to pruned models. We found that the pruning works as expected, regardless of the specific strategies. We report the results in Table 3.

4.6 Bottleneck Architectures and Clustering

The bottleneck structure demonstrated its power in recent deep architectures [15, 16,18]. It utilizes 1×1 convolutions before 3×3 convolutions to build more efficient CNNs. Although our method is less efficient with 1×1 convolutions, we demonstrate that kernels in the bottleneck architectures are heavily redundant. We selected 100-layer DenseNet-BC ($k = 12$) [16] as our baseline. It contains 27,720 spatial kernels which comprise only 34% of the total parameters. All the other parameters construct 1×1 convolutional layers. In this section, we only compress the 3×3 kernels and report the results in Table 4.

Interestingly, our method works well and even exceeds the baseline without s_i. In other words, we do not normalize the kernels and share them across different layers. When we consider dominant 1×1 kernels, the compression ratio is quite low. However, it is surprising that our method requires only $576 = 64 \times 3 \times 3$ trainable parameters for 3×3 convolutions in C64N configuration. We also applied pruning to DenseNet-BC and successfully removed over 98% of the parameters from 3×3 convolutional layers.

4.7 Experients on ImageNet Dataset

We also evaluate our method on more challenging ILSVRC12 dataset [30] using ResNet-18 [15] in which 3×3 convolutions are dominant and 1×1 kernels are in shortcut connections only. There exist 7×7 convolutions in the first layer, but they are also negligible. To handle the various kernel sizes, we use

Table 4. We apply the proposed method to DenseNet-BC and evaluate those models on the CIFAR-10 dataset. 'N' denotes the model without any scale parameters ($s_i \equiv 1$).

Model	Error (%)	Size (KB) 3 × 3 / Total	FLOPs (M) 3 × 3 / Total
DenseNet-BC [16]	4.50	998 / 2967	112 / 288
DenseNet-BC-C64	4.50	77 (13.0x) / 2046 (1.45x)	54 (2.09x) / 230 (1.25x)
DenseNet-BC-C128	4.51	82 (12.2x) / 2051 (1.45x)	66 (1.71x) / 242 (1.19x)
DenseNet-BC-C64N	4.60	22 (45.5x) / 1991 (1.49x)	43 (2.59x) / 219 (1.32x)
DenseNet-BC-C128N	**4.44**	27 (37.5x) / 1996 (1.49x)	57 (1.96x) / 233 (1.24x)
DenseNet-BC-PC128N	4.57	14 (61.7x) / 1983 (1.50x)	36 (3.11x) / 212 (1.36x)

Table 5. Error rates of compressed ResNet-18 on the ILSVRC12 validation set. INQ [37] does not report the acceleration performance explicitly in the paper.

Model	Top-1 / Top-5 Error (%)	Compression ratio	Acceleration ratio*
ResNet-18 [15] from torchvision [28]	30.2 / 10.9	-	-
BWN [29]	39.2 / 17.0	32.0x	2.00x
TWN [25]	34.7 / 13.8	16.0x	2.00x
TTQ [39]	33.4 / 12.8	16.0x	2.00x
INQ (3-bit) [37]	31.9 / 11.6	10.7x	-
INQ (5-bit) [37]	31.0 / 10.9	6.40x	-
C256 (Proposed)	30.5 / 11.0	11.1x	1.68x
C1024 (Proposed)	**30.1** / **10.7**	10.3x	1.27x
C1024N (Proposed)	32.3 / 12.2	23.6x	1.35x

multi clustering method from Sect. 4.4. Kernels of equal sizes belong to the same group, and we ignore 1 × 1 convolutions here. We use $k = 64$ clusters for 7 × 7 kernels to keep as much information as possible from the inputs and preserve the variety of the large kernels. Here, our primary interest is to compress 1,220,608 many 3 × 3 kernels. We compare the proposed method with extreme weight quantizations [25,29,37,39] that perform well on challenging dataset. Results are reported in Table 5.

An impressive property of our method is that we allow various design choices. For example, we can ignore the scale parameters and achieve 23.6x compression ratio or enhance the model accuracy by sacrificing compactness. INQ [37] also has a design parameter to control the size-performance trade-off, but our method outperforms other methods at given accuracy or compression ratio. However, it is difficult to compare the computational gain of the proposed method and previous works directly since different compression methods take advantage of the different hardware designs. For example, our method can utilize the fastest convolution algorithm [22] since we do not modify the convolution itself. On the other hand, INQ [37] redefines the convolution with shift operations, which can be implemented very efficiently on the custom hardware. Although we report the acceleration ratio of each method in Table 5, we cannot say which way is the fastest in general. The more detailed analysis is beyond our scope.

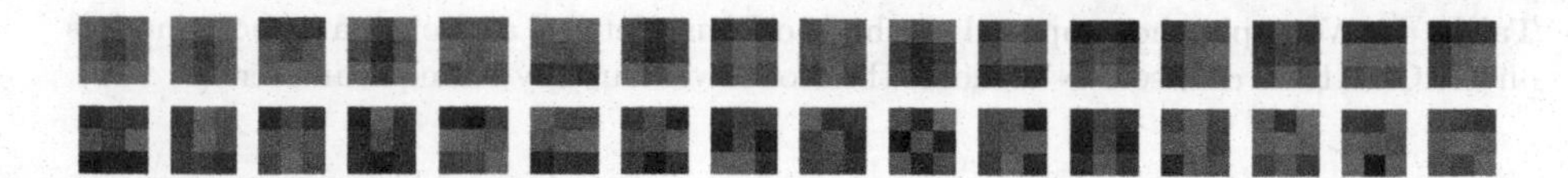

Fig. 5. The 16 most(Top)/least(Bottom) frequent centroids from ResNet-18-C256. They occupy 19% and 2% of the total kernels, respectively.

5 Conclusion

In this paper, we compress CNNs by applying k-means clustering to their convolution kernels. Our primary interest is to remove redundancies in convolutional layers by sharing weights between similar kernels. We reduce the size and required computations of modern CNNs while keeping their performances. Various experiments about TIC and multi clustering show that the proposed method has multiple design choices for compression. Combined with pruning, our compressed VGG-16 achieved over 30x compression ratio with only 0.01% accuracy drop on the CIFAR-10 dataset. The proposed method also fits for the challenging ImageNet task and even enhances the accuracy of ResNet-18. Although our method is not fully optimized for bottleneck architectures yet, we will handle them in our future works. Also, we will further enhance our method based on Fig. 5 as frequently appearing centroids are often low-frequency and low-rank.

Acknowledgement. This work was partially supported by the National Research Foundation of Korea(NRF) grant funded by the Korea Government(MSIT). (No. NRF-2017R1A2B2011862)

References

1. Chen, W., Wilson, J., Tyree, S., Weinberger, K., Chen, Y.: Compressing neural networks with the hashing trick. In: 32nd International Conference on Machine Learning, pp. 2285–2294 (2015)
2. Chetlur, S., et al.: cuDNN: Efficient primitives for deep learning. arXiv preprint arXiv:1410.0759 (2014)
3. Cohen, T., Welling, M.: Group equivariant convolutional networks. In: 33rd International Conference on Machine Learning, pp. 2990–2999 (2016)
4. Courbariaux, M., Bengio, Y., David, J.P.: Binaryconnect: training deep neural networks with binary weights during propagations. In: Advances in Neural Information Processing Systems, pp. 3123–3131 (2015)
5. Courbariaux, M., Hubara, I., Soudry, D., El-Yaniv, R., Bengio, Y.: Binarized neural networks: Training deep neural networks with weights and activations constrained to+ 1 or −1. arXiv preprint arXiv:1602.02830 (2016)
6. Denil, M., Shakibi, B., Dinh, L., De Freitas, N., et al.: Predicting parameters in deep learning. In: Advances in Neural Information Processing Systems, pp. 2148–2156 (2013)
7. Denton, E.L., Zaremba, W., Bruna, J., LeCun, Y., Fergus, R.: Exploiting linear structure within convolutional networks for efficient evaluation. In: Advances in Neural Information Processing Systems, pp. 1269–1277 (2014)

8. Dieleman, S., De Fauw, J., Kavukcuoglu, K.: Exploiting cyclic symmetry in convolutional neural networks. In: 33rd International Conference on Machine Learning, pp. 1889–1898 (2016)
9. Gong, Y., Liu, L., Yang, M., Bourdev, L.: Compressing deep convolutional networks using vector quantization. arXiv preprint arXiv:1412.6115 (2014)
10. Guo, Y., Yao, A., Chen, Y.: Dynamic network surgery for efficient DNNs. In: Advances in Neural Information Processing Systems, pp. 1379–1387 (2016)
11. Gupta, S., Agrawal, A., Gopalakrishnan, K., Narayanan, P.: Deep learning with limited numerical precision. In: 32nd International Conference on Machine Learning, pp. 1737–1746 (2015)
12. Han, S., Mao, H., Dally, W.J.: Deep compression: compressing deep neural networks with pruning, trained quantization and huffman coding. In: International Conference on Learning Representations (2016)
13. Han, S., Pool, J., Tran, J., Dally, W.: Learning both weights and connections for efficient neural network. In: Advances in Neural Information Processing Systems, pp. 1135–1143 (2015)
14. Hassibi, B., Stork, D.G.: Second order derivatives for network pruning: optimal brain surgeon. In: Advances in Neural Information Processing Systems, pp. 164–171 (1993)
15. He, K., Zhang, X., Ren, S., Sun, J.: Deep residual learning for image recognition. In: Proceedings of the IEEE Conference on Computer Vision and Pattern Recognition, pp. 770–778 (2016)
16. Huang, G., Liu, Z., Weinberger, K.Q., van der Maaten, L.: Densely connected convolutional networks. In: Proceedings of the IEEE Conference on Computer Vision and Pattern Recognition (2017)
17. Hubara, I., Courbariaux, M., Soudry, D., El-Yaniv, R., Bengio, Y.: Quantized neural networks: training neural networks with low precision weights and activations. J. Mach. Learn. Res. **18**(187), 1–30 (2018)
18. Iandola, F.N., Han, S., Moskewicz, M.W., Ashraf, K., Dally, W.J., Keutzer, K.: Squeezenet: Alexnet-level accuracy with 50x fewer parameters and <0.5 mb model size. arXiv preprint arXiv:1602.07360 (2016)
19. Ioffe, S., Szegedy, C.: Batch normalization: accelerating deep network training by reducing internal covariate shift. In: 32nd International Conference on Machine Learning, pp. 448–456 (2015)
20. Jaderberg, M., Vedaldi, A., Zisserman, A.: Speeding up convolutional neural networks with low rank expansions. arXiv preprint arXiv:1405.3866 (2014)
21. Krizhevsky, A., Hinton, G.: Learning multiple layers of features from tiny images (2009)
22. Lavin, A., Gray, S.: Fast algorithms for convolutional neural networks. In: Proceedings of the IEEE Conference on Computer Vision and Pattern Recognition, pp. 4013–4021 (2016)
23. Lebedev, V., Lempitsky, V.: Fast convnets using group-wise brain damage. In: Proceedings of the IEEE Conference on Computer Vision and Pattern Recognition, pp. 2554–2564 (2016)
24. LeCun, Y., Denker, J.S., Solla, S.A.: Optimal brain damage. In: Advances in Neural Information Processing Systems, pp. 598–605 (1990)
25. Li, F., Zhang, B., Liu, B.: Ternary weight networks. arXiv preprint arXiv:1605.04711 (2016)
26. Li, H., Kadav, A., Durdanovic, I., Samet, H., Graf, H.P.: Pruning filters for efficient convnets. In: International Conference on Learning Representations (2017)

27. Luo, J.H., Wu, J., Lin, W.: ThiNet: A filter level pruning method for deep neural network compression (2017)
28. Paszke, A., et al.: Automatic differentiation in PyTorch (2017)
29. Rastegari, M., Ordonez, V., Redmon, J., Farhadi, A.: XNOR-Net: ImageNet classification using binary convolutional neural networks. In: Leibe, B., Matas, J., Sebe, N., Welling, M. (eds.) ECCV 2016. LNCS, vol. 9908, pp. 525–542. Springer, Cham (2016). https://doi.org/10.1007/978-3-319-46493-0_32
30. Russakovsky, O., et al.: ImageNet large scale visual recognition challenge. Int. J. Comput. Vis. **115**(3), 211–252 (2015)
31. Simonyan, K., Zisserman, A.: Very deep convolutional networks for large-scale image recognition. arXiv preprint arXiv:1409.1556 (2014)
32. Sutskever, I., Martens, J., Dahl, G., Hinton, G.: On the importance of initialization and momentum in deep learning. In: 30th International Conference on Machine Learning, pp. 1139–1147 (2013)
33. Wen, W., Wu, C., Wang, Y., Chen, Y., Li, H.: Learning structured sparsity in deep neural networks. In: Advances in Neural Information Processing Systems, pp. 2074–2082 (2016)
34. Wu, J., Leng, C., Wang, Y., Hu, Q., Cheng, J.: Quantized convolutional neural networks for mobile devices. In: Proceedings of the IEEE Conference on Computer Vision and Pattern Recognition, pp. 4820–4828 (2016)
35. Zeiler, M.D., Fergus, R.: Visualizing and understanding convolutional networks. In: Fleet, D., Pajdla, T., Schiele, B., Tuytelaars, T. (eds.) ECCV 2014. LNCS, vol. 8689, pp. 818–833. Springer, Cham (2014). https://doi.org/10.1007/978-3-319-10590-1_53
36. Zhai, S., Cheng, Y., Zhang, Z.M., Lu, W.: Doubly convolutional neural networks. In: Advances in Neural Information Processing Systems, pp. 1082–1090 (2016)
37. Zhou, A., Yao, A., Guo, Y., Xu, L., Chen, Y.: Incremental network quantization: Towards lossless CNNs with low-precision weights. In: International Conference on Learning Representations (2017)
38. Zhou, S., Wu, Y., Ni, Z., Zhou, X., Wen, H., Zou, Y.: DoReFa-Net: training low bitwidth convolutional neural networks with low bitwidth gradients. arXiv preprint arXiv:1606.06160 (2016)
39. Zhu, C., Han, S., Mao, H., Dally, W.J.: Trained ternary quantization. In: International Conference on Learning Representations (2017)

Fine-Grained Visual Categorization Using Meta-learning Optimization with Sample Selection of Auxiliary Data

Yabin Zhang, Hui Tang, and Kui Jia(✉)

School of Electronic and Information Engineering,
South China University of Technology, Guangzhou, China
{zhang.yabin,eehuitang}@mail.scut.edu.cn,
kuijia@scut.edu.cn

Abstract. Fine-grained visual categorization (FGVC) is challenging due in part to the fact that it is often difficult to acquire an enough number of training samples. To employ large models for FGVC without suffering from overfitting, existing methods usually adopt a strategy of pre-training the models using a rich set of auxiliary data, followed by fine-tuning on the target FGVC task. However, the objective of pre-training does not take the target task into account, and consequently such obtained models are suboptimal for fine-tuning. To address this issue, we propose in this paper a new deep FGVC model termed MetaFGNet. Training of MetaFGNet is based on a novel regularized meta-learning objective, which aims to guide the learning of network parameters so that they are optimal for adapting to the target FGVC task. Based on MetaFGNet, we also propose a simple yet effective scheme for selecting more useful samples from the auxiliary data. Experiments on benchmark FGVC datasets show the efficacy of our proposed method.

Keywords: Fine-Grained Visual Categorization · Meta-learning
Sample selection

1 Introduction

Fine-grained visual categorization (FGVC) aims to classify images of subordinate object categories that belong to a same entry-level category, e.g., different species of birds [3,26,27] or dogs [9]. The visual distinction between different subordinate categories is often subtle and regional, and such nuance is further obscured by variations caused by arbitrary poses, viewpoint change, and/or occlusion. Subordinate categories are leaf nodes of a taxonomic tree, whose samples are often difficult to collect. Annotating such samples also requires professional expertise, resulting in very few training samples per category in existing FGVC datasets [9,26]. FGVC thus bears problem characteristics of few-shot learning.

Most of existing FGVC methods spend efforts on mining global and/or regional discriminative information from training data themselves. For example, state-of-the-art methods learn to identify discriminative parts from images

V. Ferrari et al. (Eds.): ECCV 2018, LNCS 11212, pp. 241–256, 2018.
https://doi.org/10.1007/978-3-030-01237-3_15

of fine-grained categories either in a supervised [32,33] or in a weakly supervised manner [6,17,29,35–37]. However, such methods are approaching a fundamental limit since only very few training samples are available for each category. In order to break the limit, possible solutions include identifying auxiliary data that are more useful for (e.g., more related to) the FGVC task of interest, and also better leveraging these auxiliary data. These solutions fall in the realm of domain adaptation or transfer learning [15].

A standard way of applying transfer learning to FGVC is to fine-tune on the target dataset a model that has been pre-trained on a rich set of auxiliary data (e.g., the ImageNet [22]). Such a pre-trained model learns to encode (generic) semantic knowledge from the auxiliary data, and the combined strategy of pre-training followed by fine-tuning alleviates the issue of overfitting. However, the objective of pre-training does not take the target FGVC task of interest into account, and consequently such obtained models are suboptimal for transfer.

Inspired by recent meta-learning methods [5,19,25] for few-shot learning, we propose in this paper a new deep learning method for fine-grained classification. Our proposed method is based on a novel *regularized meta-learning objective* for training a deep network: the regularizer aims to learn network parameters such that they can encode generic or semantically related knowledge from auxiliary data; the meta-learning objective is designed to guide the process of learning, so that the learned network parameters are optimal for adapting to the target FGVC task. We term our proposed FGVC method as MetaFGNet for its use of the meta-learning objective. Figure 1 gives an illustration. Our method can effectively alleviate the issue of overfitting, as explained in Sect. 3.

An important issue to achieve good transfer learning is that data in source and target tasks should share similar feature distributions [15]. If this is not the case, transfer learning methods usually learn feature mappings to alleviate this issue. Alternatively, one may directly identify source data/tasks that are more related to the target one. In this work, we take the later approach and propose a simple yet very effective scheme to select more useful samples from the auxiliary data. Our scheme is naturally admitted by MetaFGNet, and only requires a forward computation through a trained MetaFGNet for each auxiliary sample, which contrasts with a recent computationally expensive scheme used in [7]. In this work, we investigate ImageNet [22], a subset of ImageNet and a subset of L-Bird [11] as the sets of auxiliary data. For the L-Bird subset, for example, our scheme can successfully remove noisy, semantically irrelevant images. Experiments on the benchmark FGVC datasets of CUB-200-2011 [26] and Stanford Dogs [9] show the efficacy of our proposed MetaFGNet with sample selection of auxiliary data. Our contributions are summarized as follows.

- We propose a new deep learning model, termed MetaFGNet, for fine-grained classification. Training of MetaFGNet is based on a novel *regularized meta-learning objective*, which aims to guide the learning of network parameters so that they are optimal for adapting to the target FGVC task (cf. Sect. 3).
- Our proposed MetaFGNet admits a natural scheme to perform sample selection from auxiliary data. Given a trained MetaFGNet, the proposed scheme

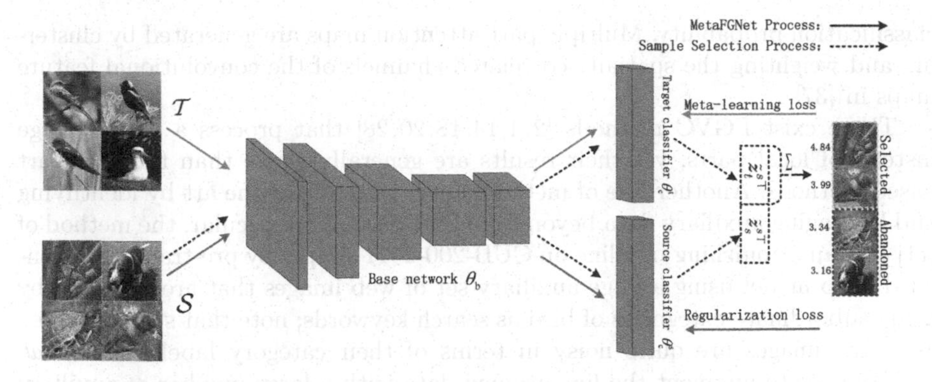

Fig. 1. Illustrations of MetaFGNet with regularized meta-learning objective (solid line) and the process of sample selection from auxiliary data (dashed line).

only requires a forward computation through the network to produce a score for each auxiliary sample (cf. Sect. 4). Such scores can be used to effectively select semantically related auxiliary samples (or remove noisy, semantically irrelevant ones).

- We present intensive comparative studies on different ways of leveraging auxiliary data for the target FGVC task. Experiments on the benchmark CUB-200-2011 [26] and Stanford Dogs [9] datasets also show the efficacy of our proposed method. In particular, our result on Stanford Dogs is better than all existing ones with a large margin. Based on a better auxiliary dataset, our result on CUB-200-2011 is better than those of all existing methods even when they use ground-truth part annotations (cf. Sect. 5).

2 Related Works

In this section, we briefly review recent fine-grained classification methods, in particular those aiming for better leveraging auxiliary data, and also meta learning methods for the related problem of few-shot learning. We present brief summaries of these methods and discuss their relations and differences with our proposed one.

Fine-Grained Visual Categorization. State-of-the-art FGVC methods usually follow the pipeline that first discovers discriminative local parts from images of fine-grained categories, and then utilizes the discovered parts for classification. For example, Lam *et al.* [13] search for discriminative parts by iteratively evaluating and generating bounding box proposals with or without the supervision of ground-truth part annotations. Based on off-the-shelf object proposals [24], part detectors are learned in [35] by clustering subregions of object proposals. In [6], a hierarchical three-level region attention mechanism is proposed that is able to attend to discriminative regions, where region discrimination is measured by classification probability. Multiple part attention maps are generated by clustering and weighting the spatially-correlated channels of the convolutional feature maps in [37].

There exist FGVC methods [2,4,14,18,20,28] that process a whole image instead of local parts, yet their results are generally worse than those of part based methods. Another line of methods push the state of the art by identifying and leveraging auxiliary data beyond the ImageNet. In particular, the method of [11] sets an astonishing baseline on CUB-200-2011 simply by pre-training a standard deep model using a huge auxiliary set of web images that are obtained by using subordinate categories of bird as search keywords; note that such obtained auxiliary images are quite noisy in terms of their category labels. Xie *et al.* [30] propose to augment the fine-grained data with a large number of auxiliary images labeled by hyper-classes; these hyper-classes are some attributes that can be annotated more easily than the fine-grained category labels, so that a large number of images labeled with attributes can be easily acquired; by joint training the model for hyper-class classification and FGVC, the performance of FGVC gets improved. Instead of searching for more semantically relevant auxiliary data from the Internet, Ge and Yu [7] propose to refine the ImageNet images by comparing them with those in the training set of the target FGVC task, using low-level features (e.g., the Gabor filter responses); such a refined ImageNet is then used to jointly train a model with training images of the FGVC task.

All the above methods use auxiliary data either to pre-train a model, or to jointly train a model with training images of the target FGVC task. In contrast, our proposed MetaFGNet uses a regularized meta-learning objective that can make full use of the auxiliary data, while at the same time making the obtained model optimal for a further adaptation to the target FGVC task. We also compare our training objective with that of joint training technically in Sect. 3 and empirically in Sect. 5.

Few-Shot Learning via Meta Learning. Meta learning aims to learn experience from history and adapt to new tasks with the help of history knowledge. Few-shot learning is one of its applications. [10] trains a siamese neural network for the task of verification, which is to identify whether input pairs belong to the same class; once the verification model is trained, it can be used for few- or one-shot learning by calculating the similarity between the test image and the labelled images. [25] realizes few-shot learning with a neural network which is augmented with external memories; it uses two embeddings to map the images to feature space and the classification is obtained by measuring the cosine distance in the feature space; the embedding of the test images can be modified by the whole support set through a LSTM attention module, which makes the model utilize the support set more reasonably and effectively. In [19], SGD is replaced by a meta-LSTM that can learn an update rule for training networks. Finn *et al.* [5] propose a meta learning method termed MAML, which trains a meta model in a multi-task fashion. Different from the problem setting of MAML, which learns meta models from a set of training tasks that are independent of the target task, our proposed MetaFGNet involves directly the target task into the training objective.

3 The Proposed MetaFGNet

For a target FGVC of interest, suppose we have training data $\mathcal{T} = \{(\mathbf{x}_i^t, \mathbf{y}_i^t)\}_{i=1}^{|\mathcal{T}|}$, where each pair of $\mathbf{x}_i^t$ and $\mathbf{y}_i^t$ represents an input image and its one-hot vector representation of class label. We also assume that a set of auxiliary data (e.g., the ImageNet) is available that contains images different from (but possibly semantically related to) the target data $\mathcal{T}$. Denote the auxiliary data as $\mathcal{S} = \{(\mathbf{x}_i^s, \mathbf{y}_i^s)\}_{i=1}^{|\mathcal{S}|}$. As illustrated in Fig. 1, our proposed MetaFGNet is based on a deep neural network consisting of two parallel classifiers of fully-connected (FC) layers that share a common base network. The two classifiers are respectively used for $\mathcal{T}$ and $\mathcal{S}$. We correspondingly denote parameters of the two classifiers as θ_c^s and θ_c^t, and denote those of the base network collectively as θ_b, which contains parameters of layer weights and bias. For ease of subsequent notations, we also denote the parameters of target and source model as $\theta^t = (\theta_b, \theta_c^t)$ and $\theta^s = (\theta_b, \theta_c^s)$ respectively.

In machine learning, $\mathcal{T}$ is usually sampled i.i.d. from an underlying (unknown) distribution $\mathcal{D}$. To learn a deep model θ^t, one may choose an appropriate loss function $L(\mathbf{x}^t, \mathbf{y}^t; \theta^t)$, and minimize the following expected loss over $\mathcal{D}$

$$\min_{\theta^t} \mathbf{E}_{(\mathbf{x}^t,\mathbf{y}^t)\sim\mathcal{D}} \left[L(\mathbf{x}^t, \mathbf{y}^t; \theta^t)\right]. \quad (1)$$

In practice, however, minimizing the above objective is infeasible since the underlying distribution $\mathcal{D}$ is unknown. As an alternative, one chooses to minimize the following empirical loss to learn θ^t

$$\min_{\theta^t} \frac{1}{|\mathcal{T}|} L\left(\mathcal{T}; \theta^t\right) = \frac{1}{|\mathcal{T}|} \sum_{i=1}^{|\mathcal{T}|} L\left(\mathbf{x}_i^t, \mathbf{y}_i^t; \theta^t\right). \quad (2)$$

As discussed in Sect. 1, fine-grained classification bears problem characteristics of few-shot learning, and its training set $\mathcal{T}$ is usually too small to well represent the underlying distribution $\mathcal{D}$. Thus directly minimizing the empirical loss (2) causes severe overfitting. In the literature of fine-grained classification, this issue is usually addressed by pre-training the model θ^t using an auxiliary set of data $\mathcal{S}$ (e.g., the ImageNet), and then fine-tuning it using $\mathcal{T}$. Note that this strategy alleviates overfitting in two aspects: (1) pre-training gives the model a good initialization that has learned (generic) semantic knowledge from $\mathcal{S}$; and (2) fine-tuning itself reduces overfitting via early stop of training. In other words, one may understand the strategy of fine-tuning as imposing *implicit regularization* on the learning of θ^t. Alternatively, one may apply *explicit regularization* to (2), resulting in the following general form of regularized loss minimization

$$\min_{\theta^t} \frac{1}{|\mathcal{T}|} L\left(\mathcal{T}; \theta^t\right) + R(\theta^t). \quad (3)$$

The auxiliary set $\mathcal{S}$ can be used as an instantiation of the regularizer, giving rise to the following *joint training method*

$$\min_{\theta_b,\theta_c^t,\theta_c^s} \frac{1}{|\mathcal{T}|} L\left(\mathcal{T};\theta_b,\theta_c^t\right) + \frac{1}{|\mathcal{S}|} R\left(\mathcal{S};\theta_b,\theta_c^s\right), \tag{4}$$

where regularization is only imposed on parameters θ_b of the base network. By leveraging $\mathcal{S}$, the joint training method (4) could be advantageous over fine-tuning since network training has a chance to converge to a more mature, but not overfitted, solution. Based on a similar deep architecture as in Fig. 1, the joint training method (4) is used in a recent work of fine-grained classification [7]. The choice of the auxiliary set $\mathcal{S}$ also matters in (4). Established knowledge from the literature of transfer learning [15] suggests that $\mathcal{S}$ should ideally have similar distribution of feature statistics as that of $\mathcal{T}$, suggesting that a refinement of $\mathcal{S}$ could be useful for better regularization.

3.1 A Meta-Learning Objective for MetaFGNet

Inspired by recent meta learning methods [5,19,25] that learn a meta model from a set of training few-shot learning tasks, we propose in this paper a meta-learning objective for the target fine-grained classification task $\mathcal{T}$. Instead of using the loss $L(\mathcal{T};\theta^t)$ directly as in (3), the meta-learning objective is to *guide the optimization of* θ^t so that the obtained θ^t can fast adapt to the target task via a second process of fine-tuning. Suppose the fine-tuning process achieves

$$\theta^t \leftarrow \theta^t + \triangle(\theta^t), \tag{5}$$

where $\triangle(\theta^t)$ denotes the amount of parameter update. The problem nature of few-shot learning suggests that fine-tuning should be a fast process: a small number of (stochastic) gradient descent steps may be enough to learn effectively from $\mathcal{T}$, and taking too many steps may result in overfitting. One-step gradient descent can be written as

$$\triangle(\theta^t) = -\eta \frac{1}{|\mathcal{T}|} \nabla_{\theta^t} L(\mathcal{T};\theta^t), \tag{6}$$

where η denotes the step size. Based on (6), we write our proposed *regularized meta-learning objective* for fine-grained classification as

$$\min_{\theta_b,\theta_c^t,\theta_c^s} \frac{1}{|\mathcal{T}|} L\left(\mathcal{T};\theta^t - \eta \frac{1}{|\mathcal{T}|} \nabla_{\theta^t} L(\mathcal{T};\theta^t)\right) + \frac{1}{|\mathcal{S}|} R\left(\mathcal{S};\theta^s\right). \tag{7}$$

Our proposed meta-learning objective can also be explained from the perspective of reducing effective model capacity, and can thus achieve additional alleviation of overfitting apart from the effect of the regularizer $R(\mathcal{S};\theta_b,\theta_c^s)$, in which the regularization is achieved by base parameters updating from auxiliary data.

Remarks. Both our proposed MetaFGNet and the meta-learning methods [5,19] contain loss terms of meta-learning, which guide the trained model to be able to fast adapt to a target task. We note that our method is for a problem setting different from those of [5,19], and consequently is the objective (7): they learn meta models from a set of training tasks and subsequently use the learned meta model for a new target task; here training set $\mathcal{T}$ of the target task is directly involved in the main learning objective.

3.2 Training Algorithm

Solving the proposed objective (7) via stochastic gradient descent (SGD) involves computing gradient of a gradient for the first term, which can be derived as

$$\nabla_{\theta^{t'}} \frac{1}{|\mathcal{T}_j|} L\left(\mathcal{T}_j; \theta^{t'}\right) \left[\mathbf{I} - \eta \frac{1}{|\mathcal{T}_i|} \left(\frac{\partial^2 L(\mathcal{T}_i; \theta^t)}{\partial (\theta^t)^2}\right)\right], \tag{8}$$

where $\mathcal{T}_i$ and $\mathcal{T}_j$ denote mini-batches of $\mathcal{T}$, and $\theta^{t'} = \theta^t - \eta \frac{1}{|\mathcal{T}_i|} \nabla_{\theta^t} L(\mathcal{T}_i; \theta^t)$. Hessian matrix is involved in (8), computation of which is supported by modern deep learning libraries [1,16]. In this work, we adopt the Pytorch [16] to implement (8), whose empirical computation time is about 0.64s per iteration (batchsize = 32) when training MetaFGNet on a GeForce GTX 1080 Ti GPU. Training of MetaFGNet is given in Algorithm 1.

Algorithm 1. Training algorithm for MetaFGNet

Require: $\mathcal{T}$: target train data; $\mathcal{S}$: auxiliary train data
Require: η, α: hyperparameters of step size
1: initialize θ_b, θ_c^t, θ_c^s
2: **while** not done **do**
3: Sample mini-batches $\mathcal{T}_i$, $\mathcal{S}_i$ from $\mathcal{T}$, $\mathcal{S}$
4: Evaluate:
$[\triangle(\theta_b; \mathcal{S}_i), \triangle(\theta_c^s; \mathcal{S}_i)] = \frac{1}{|\mathcal{S}_i|} \nabla_{\theta^s} R(\mathcal{S}_i; \theta^s)$
$[\triangle(\theta_b; \mathcal{T}_i), \triangle(\theta_c^t; \mathcal{T}_i)] = \frac{1}{|\mathcal{T}_i|} \nabla_{\theta^t} L(\mathcal{T}_i; \theta^t)$
5: Compute adapted parameters with SGD:
$\theta^{t'} = \theta^t - \eta \frac{1}{|\mathcal{T}_i|} \nabla_{\theta^t} L(\mathcal{T}_i; \theta^t)$
6: Sample another mini-batch $\mathcal{T}_j$ from $\mathcal{T}$
7: Evaluate:
$[\triangle(\theta_b; \mathcal{T}_j), \triangle(\theta_c^t; \mathcal{T}_j)] = \nabla_{\theta^{t'}} \frac{1}{|\mathcal{T}_j|} L\left(\mathcal{T}_j; \theta^{t'}\right) \left[\mathbf{I} - \eta \frac{1}{|\mathcal{T}_i|} \left(\frac{\partial^2 L(\mathcal{T}_i; \theta^t)}{\partial (\theta^t)^2}\right)\right]$
8: Update:
$\theta_b \leftarrow \theta_b - \alpha[\triangle(\theta_b; \mathcal{S}_i) + \triangle(\theta_b; \mathcal{T}_j)]$
$\theta_c^t \leftarrow \theta_c^t - \alpha \triangle(\theta_c^t; \mathcal{T}_j)$
$\theta_c^s \leftarrow \theta_c^s - \alpha \triangle(\theta_c^s; \mathcal{S}_i)$
9: **end while**

4 Sample Selection of Auxiliary Data Using the Proposed MetaFGNet

Established knowledge from domain adaptation suggests that the auxiliary set $\mathcal{S}$ should ideally have a similar distribution of feature statistics as that of the target set $\mathcal{T}$. This can be achieved either via transfer learning [15], or via selecting/refining samples of $\mathcal{S}$. In this work, we take the second approach and propose a simple sample selection scheme that is naturally supported by our proposed MetaFGNet (and in fact by any deep models with a two-head architecture as in Fig. 1).

Given a trained MetaFGNet, for each auxiliary sample $\mathbf{x}^s$ from $\mathcal{S}$, we compute through the network to get two *prediction vectors* $\mathbf{z}_s^s$ and $\mathbf{z}_t^s$, which are respectively the output vectors of the two classifiers (before the softmax operation) for the source and target tasks. Length of $\mathbf{z}_s^s$ (or $\mathbf{z}_t^s$) is essentially equal to category number of the source task (or that of the target task). To achieve sample selection from the auxiliary set $\mathcal{S}$, we take the approach of assigning a score to each $\mathbf{x}^s$ and then ranking scores of all auxiliary samples. The score of $\mathbf{x}^s$ is computed as follows: we first set negative values in $\mathbf{z}_s^s$ and $\mathbf{z}_t^s$ as zero; we then concatenate the resulting vectors and apply L2 normalization, producing $\tilde{\mathbf{z}}^s = [\tilde{\mathbf{z}}_s^{s\top}, \tilde{\mathbf{z}}_t^{s\top}]^\top$; we finally compute the score for $\mathbf{x}^s$ as

$$O^s = \tilde{\mathbf{z}}_t^{s\top} \cdot \mathbf{1}, \tag{9}$$

where $\mathbf{1}$ represents a vector with all entry values of 1. A specified ratio of top samples can be selected from $\mathcal{S}$ and form a new set of auxiliary data. Rationale of the above scheme lies in that auxiliary samples that are more semantically related to the target task would have higher responses in the target classifier, and consequently would have higher values in $\tilde{\mathbf{z}}_t^{s\top}$.

Experiments in Sect. 5 show that such a sample selection scheme is effective to select images that are semantically more related to the target task and improve performance of fine-grained classification. Some high-scored and low-scored samples in the auxiliary data are also visualized in Fig. 3.

5 Experiments

5.1 Datasets and Implementation Details

CUB-200-2011. The CUB-200-2011 dataset [26] contains 11,788 bird images. There are altogether 200 bird species and the number of images per class is about 60. The significant variations in pose, viewpoint, and illumination inside each class make this task very challenging. We adopt the publicly available split [26], which uses nearly half of the dataset for training and the other half for testing.

Stanford Dogs. The Stanford Dogs dataset [9] contains 120 categories of dogs. There are 12,000 images for training and 8,580 images for testing. This dataset is also challenging due to small inter-class variation, large intra-class variation, and cluttered background.

ImageNet Subset. The ImageNet Subset contains all categories of the original ImageNet [22] except the 59 categories of bird species, providing more realistic auxiliary data for CUB-200-2011 [26]. Note that almost all existing methods on CUB-200-2011 use the whole ImageNet dataset as the auxiliary set.

L-Bird Subset. The original L-Bird dataset [11] contains nearly 4.8 million images which are obtained by searching images of a total of 10,982 bird species from the Internet. The dataset provides urls of these images, and by the time of our downloading the dataset, we only manage to get 3.3 million images from effective urls. To build the dataset of L-Bird Subset, we first choose bird species/classes out of the total 10,982 ones whose numbers of samples are beyond 100; we then remove all the 200 bird classes that are already used in CUB-200-2011, since the L-Bird Subset will be used as an auxiliary set for CUB-200-2011; we finally hold out 1% of the resulting bird images as a validation set, following the work of [11]. The final auxiliary L-Bird Subset contains 3.2 million images.

Remarks on the Used Datasets. We use the ImageNet Subset, the ImageNet ILSVRC 2012 training set [22], or the L-Bird Subset as the set of auxiliary data for CUB-200-2011, and use the ImageNet ILSVRC 2012 training set as the set of auxiliary data for Stanford Dogs.

Implementation Details. Many existing convolutional neural networks (CNNs), such as AlexNet [12], VGGNet [23], or ResNet [8], can be used as backbone of our MetaFGNet. In this work, we use the pre-activation version of the 34-layer ResNet [8] in our experiments, *which can achieve almost identical performance on ImageNet with a batch normalization powered VGG16.* To adapt any of them for MetaFGNet, we remove its last fully-connected (FC) layer and keep the remaining ones as the base network of MetaFGNet, which are shared by the auxiliary and target data as illustrated in Fig. 1. Two parallel FC layers of classifiers are added on top of the base network which are respectively used for the meta-learning objective of the target task and the regularization loss of the auxiliary task. The MetaFGNet adapted from the 34-layer ResNet is used for both the ablation studies and the comparison with the state of the art. For a fair comparison with existing FGVC methods, base network is pre-trained on ImageNet for all experiments reported in this paper. When using ImageNet Subset or ImageNet as the auxiliary data, we start from the 60th epoch pre-trained model, mainly for a quick comparison with baseline methods. When using L-Bird Subset as the auxiliary data, we employ the released pre-trained model from [8]. The architectural design of our MetaFGNet is straightforward and simple; in contrast, most of existing FGVC methods [6,13,32] adopt more complicated network architectures in order to exploit discrimination of local parts with or without use of ground-truth part annotations.

During each iteration of SGD training, we sample one mini-batch of auxiliary data for the regularization loss, and two mini-batches of target data for the meta-learning loss (cf. Algorithm 1 for respective use of the two mini-batches). Each mini-batch includes 256 images. We do data augmentation on these images according to [8]. In experiments using ImageNet Subset or ImageNet as the auxiliary data, the learning rate (α in Algorithm 1) starts from 0.1 and is divided by 10 after every 10 epochs; we set momentum as 0.9 and weight decay as 0.0001; the meta learning rate (η in Algorithm 1) starts from 0.01 and is divided by 10 after every 10 epochs, in order to synchronize with the learning rate; the experiments end after 30 training epochs, which gives a total of the same 90 epochs as that of a pre-trained model. When using L-Bird Subset as the auxiliary data, the experiments firstly fine-tune an ImageNet pre-trained model on L-Bird Subset for 32 epochs, and then train our MetaFGNet for 8 epochs starting from the 24th epoch fine-tuned model; the learning rate and meta learning rate are divided by 10 respectively after 4 and 6 epochs; other settings are the same as in experiments using ImageNet or ImageNet Subset as the auxiliary data. Given parameters of such trained MetaFGNets and re-initialized target classifiers, we fine-tune (θ_b, θ_c^t) of them on the target data for another 160 epochs, which is the same for all comparative methods. We do sample selection from the auxiliary data as the way described in Sect. 4, *using the trained MetaFGNets before fine-tuning*. For the auxiliary sets of ImageNet Subset, ImageNet and L-Bird Subset, we respectively use 50%, 6%, and 80% of their samples as the selected top samples. Note that such ratios are empirically set and are suboptimal. After sample selection, we use the remained auxiliary samples to form a new auxiliary set, and train and fine-tune a MetaFGNet again from the MetaFGNet that have been trained using the original auxiliary datasets.

5.2 Comparison with Alternative Baselines

The first baseline method (referred as "Fine-tuning" in tables reported in this subsection) simply fine-tunes on the target dataset a model that has been pre-trained on the ImageNet Subset or ImageNet, of which the latter is typically used in existing FGVC methods. The second baseline (referred as"Joint training" in tables reported in this subsection) uses a joint training approach of the objective (4). The third baseline (referred as "Fine-tuning L-Bird Subset" in tables reported in this subsection) firstly fine-tunes the ImageNet pre-trained 34-layer ResNet model on L-bird Subset, and then fine-tunes the resulting model on CUB-200-2011. Experiments in this subsection are based on a MetaFGNet adapted from the 34-layer ResNet, for which we refer to it as"MetaFGNet". The baselines of Fine-tuning and Fine-tuning L-Bird Subset use half of the MetaFGNet that contains parameters of (θ_b, θ_c^t). The baseline of Joint training uses the same MetaFGNet structure as our method does.

Tables 1 and 2 report these controlled experiments on the CUB-200-2011 dataset [26]. Using ImageNet Subset or ImageNet as the set of auxiliary data, Fine-tuning gives baseline classification accuracies of 73.5% and 76.8% respectively; the result of Joint training is better than that of Fine-tuning, suggesting the usefulness of the objective (4) for FGVC tasks - note that a recent method [7] is essentially based on this objective. Our proposed MetaFGNet with regularized meta-learning objective (7) achieves a result better than that of Joint training. Our proposed sample selection scheme further improves the results to 75.3% and 80.3% respectively, thus justifying the efficacy of our proposed method. When using L-Bird Subset as the auxiliary set, our method without sample selection improves the result to 87.2%, showing that a better auxiliary set is essential to achieve good performance on FGVC tasks. Note that L-Bird Subset does not contain the 200 bird species of the CUB-200-2011 dataset. Our method with sample selection further improves the result to 87.6%, confirming the effectiveness of our proposed scheme. Samples of the selected images and abandoned images from three auxiliary datasets are also shown in Sect. 5.5.

Table 1. Comparative studies of different methods on the CUB-200-2011 dataset [26], using ImageNet Subset as the auxiliary set. Experiments are based on networks adapted from a 34-layer ResNet.

Methods	Auxiliary set	Accuracy (%)
Fine-tuning	ImageNet Subset	73.5
Joint training w/o sample selection	ImageNet Subset	74.5
Joint training with sample selection	ImageNet Subset	75.0
MetaFGNet w/o sample selection	ImageNet Subset	75.0
MetaFGNet with sample selection	ImageNet Subset	75.3

Table 2. Comparative studies of different methods on the CUB-200-2011 dataset [26], using ImageNet [22] or L-Bird Subset as the auxiliary set.

Methods	Auxiliary set	Accuracy (%)
Fine-tuning	ImageNet	76.8
Joint training w/o sample selection	ImageNet	78.8
Joint training with sample selection	ImageNet	79.4
MetaFGNet w/o sample selection	ImageNet	79.5
MetaFGNet with sample selection	ImageNet	80.3
Fine-tuning L-Bird Subset	L-Bird Subset	86.2
MetaFGNet w/o sample selection	L-Bird Subset	87.2
MetaFGNet with sample selection	L-Bird Subset	87.6

In Fig. 2, we also plot the training loss curves, using both the ImageNet auxiliary data and the target CUB-200-2011 data, of our method and Joint training, and also their fine-tuning loss curves on the target data. Figure 2 shows that our MetaFGNet converges to a better solution that supports a better fine-tuning than Joint training does.

5.3 Results on the CUB-200-2011

We use the MetaFGNet adapted from a 34-layer ResNet to compare with existing methods on CUB-200-2011 [26]. The most interesting comparison is with the methods [2,4,11,14,18,20,28] that focus on learning from the whole bird images. In contrast, part based methods [6,13,31–35,37] enjoy a clear advantage by exploiting discrimination of local parts either in a weakly supervised manner, or

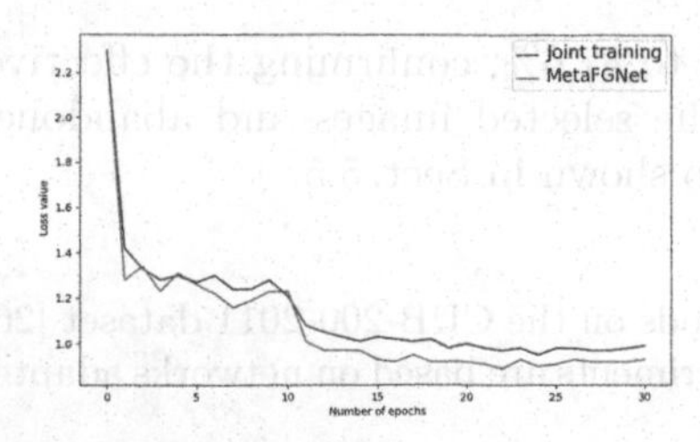

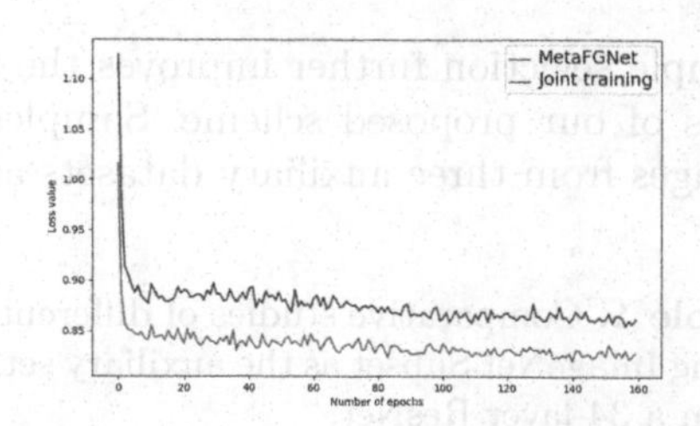

Fig. 2. Left: training loss curves of MetaFGNet and Joint training. Right: fine-tuning loss curves of MetaFGNet and Joint training. The auxiliary and target datasets are ImageNet and CUB-200-2011 respectively. MetaFGNet and Joint training models are adapted from the 34-layer ResNet.

in a supervised manner using ground-truth part annotations. Table 3 also shows that our method with L-Bird Subset as auxiliary data outperforms all existing methods even when they use ground-truth part annotations. We also construct our MetaFGNet based on the popular VGGNet. Using L-Bird Subset as the auxiliary set, our MetaFGNet with sample selection gives an accuracy of 87.5%, which also confirms the efficacy of our proposed method.

5.4 Results on the Stanford Dogs

We apply the MetaFGNet to the Stanford Dogs dataset [9], using ImageNet as the auxiliary data. The used MetaFGNet is adapted from a 152-layer ResNet [8], which is the same as the one used in the state-of-the-art method [7]. Table 4 shows the comparative results. Our method outperforms all exiting methods with a large margin. *We note that previous methods use ImageNet as the auxiliary data for the Stanford Dogs task, however, it is inappropriate because the dataset of Stanford Dogs is a subset of ImageNet.* Thus, we remove all the 120 categories of dog images from ImageNet to introduce an appropriate auxiliary dataset for the Stanford Dogs dataset [9]. Based on a 34-layer ResNet [8], simple fine-tuning after pre-training on the resulting ImageNet images gives an accuracy of 69.3%; our MetaFGNet with sample selection improves it to 73.2%.

5.5 Analysis of Selected and Abandoned Auxiliary Images

In Fig. 3, we qualitatively visualize the selected top-ranked images from ImageNet [22], ImageNet Subset, and L-Bird Subset, and also the abandoned bottom-ranked images respectively from the three auxiliary sets, when using CUB-200-2011 [26] as the target data. It can be observed that for ImageNet and ImageNet Subset, images that are semantically related to the target CUB-200-2011 task are ranked top and selected by our proposed scheme; for L-Bird Subset, noisy images that are irrelevant to the target task are ranked bottom and removed. Quantitatively, when using ImageNet as the auxiliary dataset, 65.3% of the selected auxiliary images belong to the basic-level category of "bird".

Table 3. Comparison of different methods on the CUB-200-2011 dataset [26]. Methods of 'part supervised' use ground-truth part annotations of bird images. Methods of 'part aware' detect discriminative local parts in a weakly supervised manner. Result of [11] is based on own implementation using the currently available L-Bird Subset. *The method* [14] *generates high-dimensional, second-order features via bilinear pooling, and the result of* [28] *is from a multi-scale ensemble model; both of the methods make contributions to image based FGVC complementary to our proposed MetaFGNet.*

Methods	Auxiliary set	Part supervision	Acc. (%)
CNNaug-SVM [20]	ImageNet	n/a	61.8
Deep optimized [2]	ImageNet	n/a	67.1
MsML [18]	ImageNet	n/a	67.9
Deep metric [4]	ImageNet + Web	n/a	80.7
Bilinear [14]	ImageNet	n/a	84.1
Deep image [28]	ImageNet	n/a	84.9
Rich data [11]	L-Bird Subset	n/a	**86.2**
MetaFGNet with sample selection	ImageNet	n/a	80.3
MetaFGNet with sample selection	L-Bird Subset	n/a	**87.6**
Weakly sup. [35]	ImageNet	Part-aware	80.4
PDFS [34]	ImageNet	Part-aware	84.5
RA-CNN [6]	ImageNet	Part-aware	85.3
MA-CNN [37]	ImageNet	Part-aware	86.5
Part R-CNN [33]	ImageNet	Part supervised	73.9
SPDA-CNN [32]	ImageNet	Part supervised	81.0
Webly-sup. [31]	ImageNet + Web	Part supervised	84.6
Hsnet [13]	ImageNet	Part supervised	87.5

Table 4. Comparison of different methods on the Stanford Dogs dataset [9].

Methods	Auxiliary set	Part supervision	Acc. (%)
Weakly sup. [35]	ImageNet	Part-aware	80.4
DVAN [36]	ImageNet	Part-aware	81.5
MsML [18]	ImageNet	n/a	70.3
MagNet [21]	ImageNet	n/a	75.1
Selective joint training [7]	ImageNet	n/a	90.3
MetaFGNet with sample selection	ImageNet	n/a	**96.7**

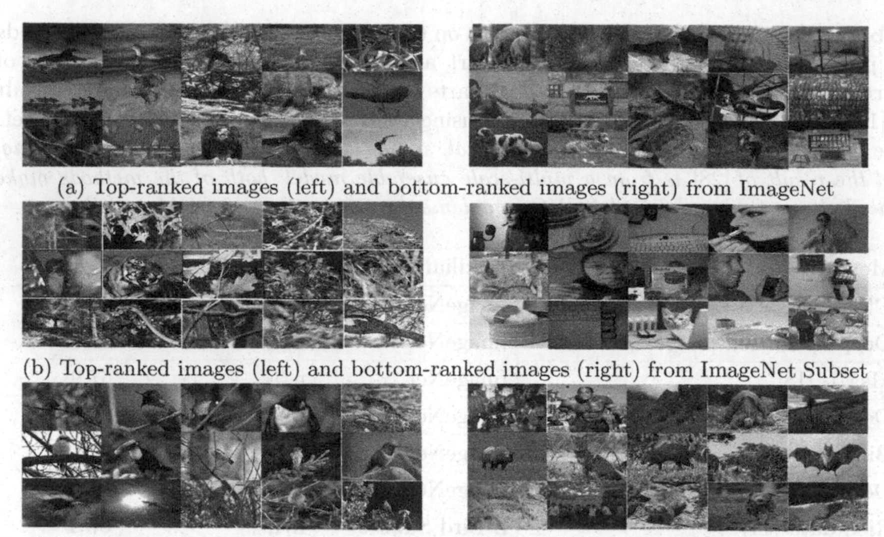

(a) Top-ranked images (left) and bottom-ranked images (right) from ImageNet

(b) Top-ranked images (left) and bottom-ranked images (right) from ImageNet Subset

(c) Top-ranked images (left) and bottom-ranked images (right) from L-Bird Subset

Fig. 3. (a) Top-ranked images and bottom-ranked images from ImageNet. (b) Top-ranked images and bottom-ranked images from ImageNet Subset. (c) Top-ranked images and bottom-ranked images from L-Bird Subset. Results are obtained by using MetaFGNet and our sample selection scheme on the CUB-200-2011 dataset [26].

6 Conclusion

In this paper, we propose a new deep learning model termed MetaFGNet, which is based on a novel regularized meta-learning objective that aims to guide the learning of network parameters so that they are optimal for adapting to a target FGVC task. Based on MetaFGNet, we also propose a simple yet effective scheme for sample selection from auxiliary data. Experiments on the benchmark CUB-200-2011 and Stanford Dogs datasets show the efficacy of our proposed method.

Acknowledgment. This work is supported in part by the Program for Guangdong Introducing Innovative and Enterpreneurial Teams (Grant No.: 2017ZT07X183), and the National Natural Science Foundation of China (Grant No.: 61771201).

References

1. Abadi, M., et al.: Tensorflow: a system for large-scale machine learning. In: 12th USENIX Symposium on Operating Systems Design and Implementation (OSDI 16), pp. 265–283 (2016). https://www.usenix.org/system/files/conference/osdi16/osdi16-abadi.pdf
2. Azizpour, H., Razavian, A.S., Sullivan, J., Maki, A., Carlsson, S.: From generic to specific deep representations for visual recognition. In: CVPRW DeepVision Workshop, IEEE Conference Proceedings, 11 June 2015, Boston, MA, USA (2015)

3. Berg, T., Liu, J., Woo Lee, S., Alexander, M.L., Jacobs, D.W., Belhumeur, P.N.: Birdsnap: large-scale fine-grained visual categorization of birds. In: Proceedings of the IEEE Conference on Computer Vision and Pattern Recognition, pp. 2011–2018 (2014)
4. Cui, Y., Zhou, F., Lin, Y., Belongie, S.: Fine-grained categorization and dataset bootstrapping using deep metric learning with humans in the loop. In: Proceedings of the IEEE Conference on Computer Vision and Pattern Recognition, pp. 1153–1162 (2016)
5. Finn, C., Abbeel, P., Levine, S.: Model-agnostic meta-learning for fast adaptation of deep networks. arXiv preprint arXiv:1703.03400 (2017)
6. Fu, J., Zheng, H., Mei, T.: Look closer to see better: recurrent attention convolutional neural network for fine-grained image recognition. In: IEEE Conference on Computer Vision and Pattern Recognition (CVPR) (2017)
7. Ge, W., Yu, Y.: Borrowing treasures from the wealthy: deep transfer learning through selective joint fine-tuning. In: Proceedings of the IEEE Conference on Computer Vision and Pattern Recognition, Honolulu, HI, vol. 6 (2017)
8. He, K., Zhang, X., Ren, S., Sun, J.: Deep residual learning for image recognition. In: Proceedings of the IEEE Conference on Computer Vision and Pattern Recognition, pp. 770–778 (2016)
9. Khosla, A., Jayadevaprakash, N., Yao, B., Li, F.F.: Novel dataset for fine-grained image categorization: Stanford dogs. In: Proceedings of CVPR Workshop on Fine-Grained Visual Categorization (FGVC), vol. 2 (2011)
10. Koch, G., Zemel, R., Salakhutdinov, R.: Siamese neural networks for one-shot image recognition. In: ICML Deep Learning Workshop, vol. 2 (2015)
11. Krause, J., et al.: The unreasonable effectiveness of noisy data for fine-grained recognition. In: Leibe, B., Matas, J., Sebe, N., Welling, M. (eds.) ECCV 2016. LNCS, vol. 9907, pp. 301–320. Springer, Cham (2016). https://doi.org/10.1007/978-3-319-46487-9_19
12. Krizhevsky, A., Sutskever, I., Hinton, G.E.: ImageNet classification with deep convolutional neural networks. In: Advances in Nneural Information Processing Systems, pp. 1097–1105 (2012)
13. Lam, M., Mahasseni, B., Todorovic, S.: Fine-grained recognition as HSnet search for informative image parts. In: Proceedings of the IEEE Conference on Computer Vision and Pattern Recognition, pp. 2520–2529 (2017)
14. Lin, T.Y., RoyChowdhury, A., Maji, S.: Bilinear CNN models for fine-grained visual recognition. In: Proceedings of the IEEE International Conference on Computer Vision, pp. 1449–1457 (2015)
15. Pan, S.J., Yang, Q.: A survey on transfer learning. IEEE Trans. Knowl. Data Eng. **22**(10), 1345–1359 (2010)
16. Paszke, A., et al.: Automatic differentiation in PyTorch (2017)
17. Peng, Y., He, X., Zhao, J.: Object-part attention model for fine-grained image classification. IEEE Trans. Image Process. **27**(3), 1487–1500 (2018)
18. Qian, Q., Jin, R., Zhu, S., Lin, Y.: Fine-grained visual categorization via multi-stage metric learning. In: Proceedings of the IEEE Conference on Computer Vision and Pattern Recognition, pp. 3716–3724 (2015)
19. Ravi, S., Larochelle, H.: Optimization as a model for few-shot learning (2016)
20. Razavian, A.S., Azizpour, H., Sullivan, J., Carlsson, S.: CNN features off-the-shelf: an astounding baseline for recognition. In: 2014 IEEE Conference on Computer Vision and Pattern Recognition Workshops (CVPRW), pp. 512–519. IEEE (2014)
21. Rippel, O., Paluri, M., Dollar, P., Bourdev, L.: Metric learning with adaptive density discrimination. arXiv preprint arXiv:1511.05939 (2015)

22. Russakovsky, O.: ImageNet large scale visual recognition challenge. Int. J. Comput. Vis. **115**(3), 211–252 (2015)
23. Simonyan, K., Zisserman, A.: Very deep convolutional networks for large-scale image recognition. arXiv preprint arXiv:1409.1556 (2014)
24. Uijlings, J.R., Van De Sande, K.E., Gevers, T., Smeulders, A.W.: Selective search for object recognition. Int. J. Comput. Vis. **104**(2), 154–171 (2013)
25. Vinyals, O., Blundell, C., Lillicrap, T., Wierstra, D., et al.: Matching networks for one shot learning. In: Advances in Neural Information Processing Systems, pp. 3630–3638 (2016)
26. Wah, C., Branson, S., Welinder, P., Perona, P., Belongie, S.: The caltech-USCD birds-200-2011 dataset (2011)
27. Welinder, P., et al.: Caltech-USCD birds 200 (2010)
28. Wu, R., Yan, S., Shan, Y., Dang, Q., Sun, G.: Deep image: Scaling up image recognition. arXiv preprint arXiv:1501.02876 7(8) (2015)
29. Xiao, T., Xu, Y., Yang, K., Zhang, J., Peng, Y., Zhang, Z.: The application of two-level attention models in deep convolutional neural network for fine-grained image classification. In: Proceedings of the IEEE Conference on Computer Vision and Pattern Recognition, pp. 842–850 (2015)
30. Xie, S., Yang, T., Wang, X., Lin, Y.: Hyper-class augmented and regularized deep learning for fine-grained image classification. In: Proceedings of the IEEE Conference on Computer Vision and Pattern Recognition, pp. 2645–2654 (2015)
31. Xu, Z., Huang, S., Zhang, Y., Tao, D.: Webly-supervised fine-grained visual categorization via deep domain adaptation. IEEE Trans. Pattern Anal. Mach. Intell. **40**, 1100–1113 (2016)
32. Zhang, H., et al.: SPDA-CNN: unifying semantic part detection and abstraction for fine-grained recognition. In: Proceedings of the IEEE Conference on Computer Vision and Pattern Recognition, pp. 1143–1152 (2016)
33. Zhang, N., Donahue, J., Girshick, R., Darrell, T.: Part-based R-CNNs for fine-grained category detection. In: Fleet, D., Pajdla, T., Schiele, B., Tuytelaars, T. (eds.) ECCV 2014. LNCS, vol. 8689, pp. 834–849. Springer, Cham (2014). https://doi.org/10.1007/978-3-319-10590-1_54
34. Zhang, X., Xiong, H., Zhou, W., Lin, W., Tian, Q.: Picking deep filter responses for fine-grained image recognition. In: Proceedings of the IEEE Conference on Computer Vision and Pattern Recognition, pp. 1134–1142 (2016)
35. Zhang, Y., et al.: Weakly supervised fine-grained categorization with part-based image representation. IEEE Trans. Image Process. **25**(4), 1713–1725 (2016)
36. Zhao, B., Wu, X., Feng, J., Peng, Q., Yan, S.: Diversified visual attention networks for fine-grained object classification. arXiv preprint arXiv:1606.08572 (2016)
37. Zheng, H., Fu, J., Mei, T., Luo, J.: Learning multi-attention convolutional neural network for fine-grained image recognition. In: International Conference on Computer Vision, vol. 6 (2017)

Verisimilar Image Synthesis for Accurate Detection and Recognition of Texts in Scenes

Fangneng Zhan(✉), Shijian Lu(✉), and Chuhui Xue(✉)

School of Computer Science and Engineering, Nanyang Technological University, Singapore, Singapore
{fnzhan,shijiian.lu}@ntu.edu.sg, xuec0003@e.ntu.edu.sg

Abstract. The requirement of large amounts of annotated images has become one grand challenge while training deep neural network models for various visual detection and recognition tasks. This paper presents a novel image synthesis technique that aims to generate a large amount of annotated scene text images for training accurate and robust scene text detection and recognition models. The proposed technique consists of three innovative designs. First, it realizes "semantic coherent" synthesis by embedding texts at semantically sensible regions within the background image, where the semantic coherence is achieved by leveraging the semantic annotations of objects and image regions that have been created in the prior semantic segmentation research. Second, it exploits visual saliency to determine the embedding locations within each semantic sensible region, which coincides with the fact that texts are often placed around homogeneous regions for better visibility in scenes. Third, it designs an adaptive text appearance model that determines the color and brightness of embedded texts by learning from the feature of real scene text images adaptively. The proposed technique has been evaluated over five public datasets and the experiments show its superior performance in training accurate and robust scene text detection and recognition models.

Keywords: Image synthesis · Data augmentation
Scene text detection · Scene text recognition

1 Introduction

The capability of obtaining large amounts of annotated training images has become the bottleneck for effective and efficient development and deployment of deep neural networks (DNN) in various computer vision tasks. The current practice relies heavily on manual annotations, ranging from in-house annotation of small amounts of images to crowdsourcing based annotation of large amounts of images. On the other hand, the manual annotation approach is usually expensive, time-consuming, prone to human errors and difficult to scale while data are collected under different conditions or within different environments.

V. Ferrari et al. (Eds.): ECCV 2018, LNCS 11212, pp. 257–273, 2018.
https://doi.org/10.1007/978-3-030-01237-3_16

Three approaches have been investigated to cope with the image annotation challenge in DNN training to the best of our knowledge. The first approach is probably the easiest and most widely adopted which augments training images by various label-preserving geometric transformations such as translation, rotation and flipping, as well as different intensity alternation operations such as blurring and histogram equalization [48]. The second approach is machine learning based which employs various semi-supervised and unsupervised learning techniques to create more annotated training images. For example, bootstrapping has been studied which combines the traditional self-training and co-training with the recent DNN training to search for more training samples from a large number of unannotated images [34,45]. In recent years, unsupervised DNN models such as Generative Adversarial Networks (GAN) [6] have also been exploited to generate more annotated training images for DNN training [42].

The third approach is image synthesis based which has been widely investigated in the area of computer graphics for the purpose of education, design simulation, advertising, entertainment, etc. [9]. It creates new images by modelling the physical behaviors of light and energy in combination of different rendering techniques such as embedding objects of interest (OOI) into a set of "background images". To make the synthesized images useful for DNN training, the OOI should be embedded in the way that it looks as natural as possible. At the same time, sufficient variations should be included to ensure that the learned representation is broad enough to capture most possible OOI appearances in real scenes.

We propose a novel image synthesis technique that aims to create a large amount of annotated scene text images for training accurate and robust scene text detection and recognition models. The proposed technique consists of three innovative designs as listed:

1. It enables "semantic coherent" image synthesis by embedding texts at semantically sensible regions within the background image as illustrated in Fig. 1, e.g. scene texts tend to appear over the wall or table surface instead of the food or plant leaves. We achieve the semantic coherence by leveraging the semantic annotations objects and image regions that have been created and are readily available in the semantic segmentation research, more details to be described in Sect. 3.1.
2. It exploits visual saliency to determine the embedding locations within each semantic coherent region as illustrated in Fig. 1. Specifically, texts are usually placed at homogeneous regions in scenes for better visibility and this can be perfectly captured using visual saliency. The exploitation of saliency guidance helps to synthesize more natural-looking scene text images, more details to be discussed in Sect. 3.2.
3. It designs a novel scene text appearance model that determines the color and brightness of source texts by learning from the feature of real scene text images adaptively. This is achieved by leveraging the similarity between the neighboring background of texts in scene images and the embedding locations within the background images, more details to be discussed in Sect. 3.3.

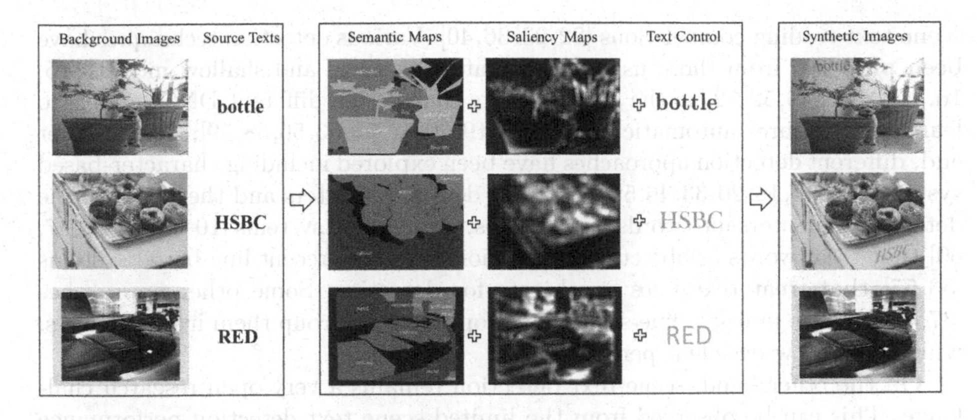

Fig. 1. The proposed scene text image synthesis technique: Given background images and source texts to be embedded into the background images as shown in the left-side box, a semantic map and a saliency map are first determined which are then combined to identify semantically sensible and apt locations for text embedding. The color, brightness, and orientation of the source texts are further determined adaptively according to the color, brightness, and contextual structures around the embedding locations within the background image. Pictures in the right-side box show scene text images synthesized by the proposed technique. (Color figure online)

2 Related Work

Image Synthesis. Photorealistically inserting objects into images has been studied extensively as one mean of image synthesis in the computer graphics research [4]. The target is to achieve insertion verisimilitude, i.e., the true likeness of the synthesized images by controlling object size, object perspective (or orientation), environmental lighting, etc. For example, Karsch et al. [24] develop a semi-automatic technique that inserts objects into legacy photographs with photorealistic lighting and perspective.

In recent years, image synthesis has been investigated as a data augmentation approach for training accurate and robust DNN models when only a limited number of annotated images are available. For example, Jaderberg et al. [17] create a word generator and use the synthetic images to train text recognition networks. Dosovitskiy et al. [5] use synthetic floating chair images to train optical flow networks. Aldrian et al. [1] propose an inverse rendering approach for synthesizing a 3D structure of faces. Yildirim et al. [55] use the CNN features trained on synthetic faces to regress face pose parameters. Gupta el al. [10] develop a fast and scalable engine to generate synthetic images of texts in scenes. On the other hand, most existing works do not fully consider semantic coherence, apt embedding locations and appearance of embedded objects which are critically important while applying the synthesized images to train DNN models.

Scene Text Detection. Scene text detection has been studied for years and it has attracted increasing interests in recent years as observed by a number of scene text reading competitions [22,23,36,40]. Various detection techniques have been proposed from those using hand-crafted features and shallow models [15, 16,21,28,32,46,52,52] to the recent efforts that design different DNN models to learn text features automatically [10,13,19,20,47,53,53,56,58,59]. At the other end, different detection approaches have been explored including character-based systems [13,15,16,20,33,46,59] that first detect characters and then link up the detected characters into words or text lines, word-based systems [10–12,19,26,27, 60] that treat words as objects for detection, and very recent line-based systems [53,57] that treat text lines as objects for detection. Some other approaches [37,47] localize multiple fine-scale text proposals and group them into text lines, which also show excellent performances.

On the other hand, scene text detection remains a very open research challenge. This can be observed from the limited scene text detection performance over those large-scale benchmarking datasets such as coco-text [49] and RCTW-17 dataset [40], where the scene text detection performance is less affected by overfitting. One important factor that impedes the advance of the recent scene text detection research is very limited training data. In particular, the captured scene texts involve a tremendous amount of variation as texts may be printed in different fonts, colors and sizes and captured under different lightings, viewpoints, occlusion, background clutters, etc. A large amount of annotated scene text images are required to learn a comprehensive representation that captures the very different appearance of texts in scenes.

Scene Text Recognition. Scene text recognition has attracted increasing interests in recent years due to its numerous practical applications. Most existing systems aim to develop powerful character classifiers and some of them incorporate a language model, leading to state-of-the-art performance [2,3,7,17,18,30,35,50,54]. These systems perform character-level segmentation followed by character classification, and their performance is severely degraded by the character segmentation errors. Inspired by the great success of recurrent neural network (RNN) in handwriting recognition [8], RNN has been studied for scene text recognition which learns continuous sequential features from words or text lines without requiring character segmentation [38,39,43,44]. On the other hand, most scene text image datasets such as ICDAR2013 [23] and ICDAR2015 [22] contain a few hundred/thousand training images only, which are too small to cover the very different text appearance in scenes.

3 Scene Text Image Synthesis

The proposed scene text image synthesis technique starts with two types of inputs including "Background Images" and "Source Texts" as illustrated in column 1 and 2 in Fig. 1. Given background images, the regions for text embedding can be determined by combining their "Semantic Maps" and "Saliency Maps" as illustrated in columns 3–4 in Fig. 1, where the "Semantic Maps" are available as ground truth in the semantic image segmentation research and the "Saliency

Maps" can be determined using existing saliency models. The color and brightness of source texts can then be estimated adaptively according to the color and brightness of the determined text embedding regions as illustrated in column 5 in Fig. 1. Finally, "Synthesized Images" are produced by placing the rendered texts at the embedding locations as illustrated in column 6 in Fig. 1.

3.1 Semantic Coherence

Semantic coherence (SC) refers to the target that texts should be embedded at semantically sensible regions within the background images. For example, texts should be placed over the fence boards instead of sky or sheep head where texts are rarely spotted in real scenes as illustrated in Fig. 2. The SC thus helps to create more semantically sensible foreground-background pairing which is very important to the visual representations as well as object detection and recognition models that are learned/trained by using the synthesized images. To the best of our knowledge, SC is largely neglected in earlier works that synthesize images for better deep network model training, e.g. the recent work [10] that deals with a similar scene text image synthesis problem.

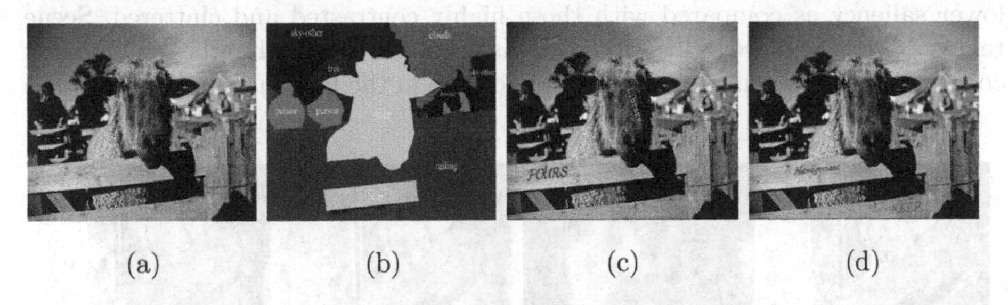

Fig. 2. Without semantic coherence (SC) as illustrated in (b), texts may be embedded at arbitrary regions such as sky and the head of sheep which are rarely spotted in scenes as illustrated in (c). SC helps to embed texts at semantically sensible regions as illustrated in (d).

We achieve the semantic coherence by exploiting a large amount of semantic annotations objects and image regions that have been created in the semantic image segmentation research. In particular, a number of semantic image segmentation datasets [14] have been created each of which comes with a set of "ground truth" images that have been "semantically" annotated. The ground truth annotation divides an image into a number of objects or regions at the pixel level where each object or region has a specific semantic annotation such as "cloud", "tree", "person", "sheep", etc. as illustrated in Fig. 2.

To exploit SC for semantically sensible image synthesis, all available semantic annotations within the semantic segmentation datasets [14] are first classified into two lists where one list consists of objects or image regions that are semantically sensible for text embedding and the other consists of objects or image regions not semantically sensible for text embedding. Given some source texts for embedding and background images with region semantics, the image regions that are suitable for text embedding can thus be determined by checking through the pre-defined list of region semantics.

3.2 Saliency Guidance

Not every location within the semantically coherent objects or image regions are suitable for scene text embedding. For example, it's more suitable to embed scene texts over the surface of the yellow-color machine instead of across the two neighboring surfaces as illustrated in Figs. 3c and 3d. Certain mechanisms are needed to further determine the exact scene text embedding locations within semantically coherent objects or image regions.

We exploit the human visual attention and scene text placement principle to determine the exact scene text embedding locations. To attract the human attention and eye balls, scene texts are usually placed around homogeneous regions such as signboards to create good contrast and visibility. With such observations, we make use of visual saliency as a guidance to determine the exact scene text embedding locations. In particular, homogeneous regions usually have lower saliency as compared with those highly contrasted and cluttered. Scene texts can thus be place at locations that have low saliency within the semantically coherent objects or image regions as described in the last subsection.

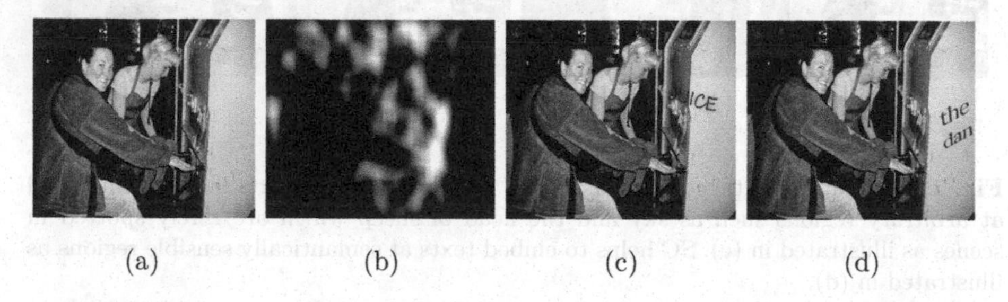

Fig. 3. Without saliency guidance (SG) as illustrated in (b), texts may be embedded across the object boundary as illustrated in (c) which are rarely spotted in scenes. SG thus helps to embed texts at right locations within the semantically sensible regions as illustrated in (d)

Quite a number of saliency models have been reported in the literature [41]. We adopt the saliency model in [29] due to its good capture of local and global contrast. Given an image, the saliency model computes a saliency map as illustrated in Fig. 3, where homogeneous image regions usually have lower saliency. The locations that are suitable for text embedding can thus be determined by thresholding the computed saliency map. In our implemented system, a global threshold is used which is simply estimated by the mean of the computed saliency map. As Fig. 3 shows, the saliency guidance helps to embed texts at right locations within the semantically sensible regions. The use of saliency guidance further helps to improve the verisimilitude of the synthesized images as well as the learned visual representation of detection and recognition models.

3.3 Adaptive Text Appearance

Visual contrast as observed by low-level edges and corners is crucial feature while training object detection and recognition models. Texts in scenes are usually presented by linear strokes of different sizes and orientations which are rich in contrast-induced edges and corners. Effective control of the contrast between source texts and background images is thus very important to the usefulness of the synthesized images while applying them to train scene text detection and recognition models.

We design an adaptive contrast technique that controls the color and brightness of source texts according to what they look like in real scenes. The idea is to search for scene text image patches (readily available in a large amount of scene text annotations within existing datasets) whose background has similar color and brightness to the determined background regions as described in Sects. 3.1 and 3.2. The color and brightness of the source texts can then be determined by referring to the color and brightness of text pixels within the searched scene text image patches.

The scene text image patches are derived from the scene text annotations as readily available in existing datasets such as ICDAR2013 [23]. For each text annotation, a HoG (histogram of oriented gradient) feature H_b is first built by using the background region surrounding the text annotation under study. The mean and standard deviation of the color and brightness of the text pixels within the annotation box are also determined in the Lab color space, as denoted by (μ_L, σ_L), (μ_a, σ_a) and (μ_b, σ_b). The background HoG H_b and the text color and brightness statistics (μ_L, σ_L), (μ_a, σ_a) and (μ_b, σ_b) of a large amount of scene text patches thus form a list of pairs as follows:

$$P = \{H_{b_1} : (\mu_{L_1}, \sigma_{L_1}, \mu_{a_1}, \sigma_{a_1}, \mu_{b_1}, \sigma_{b_1}), \cdots H_{b_i} : (\mu_{L_i}, \sigma_{L_i}, \mu_{a_i}, \sigma_{a_i}, \mu_{b_i}, \sigma_{b_i}), \cdots\} \quad (1)$$

The H_b in Eq. 1 will be used as the index of the annotated scene text image patch, and (μ_L, σ_L), (μ_a, σ_a) and (μ_b, σ_b) will be used as a guidance to set the color and brightness of the source text. For each determined background patch (suitable for text embedding) as illustrated in Fig. 4, its HoG feature H_s can be extracted and the scene text image patch that has the most similar background can thus be determined based on the similarity between H_s and H_b. The color and brightness of the source text can thus be determined by taking the corresponding (μ_L, μ_a, μ_b) plus random variations around $(\sigma_L, \sigma_a, \sigma_b)$.

The proposed technique also controls the orientation of the source texts adaptively according to certain contextual structures lying around the embedding locations within the background image. In particular, certain major structures (such as the table borders and the boundary between two connected wall surfaces as illustrated in Fig. 4) as well as their orientation can be estimated from the image gradient. The orientation of the source texts can then be determined by aligning with the major structures detected around the scene text embedding locations as illustrated in Fig. 4. Beyond the text alignment, the proposed technique also controls the font of the source texts by randomly selecting from a pre-defined font list as illustrated in Fig. 4.

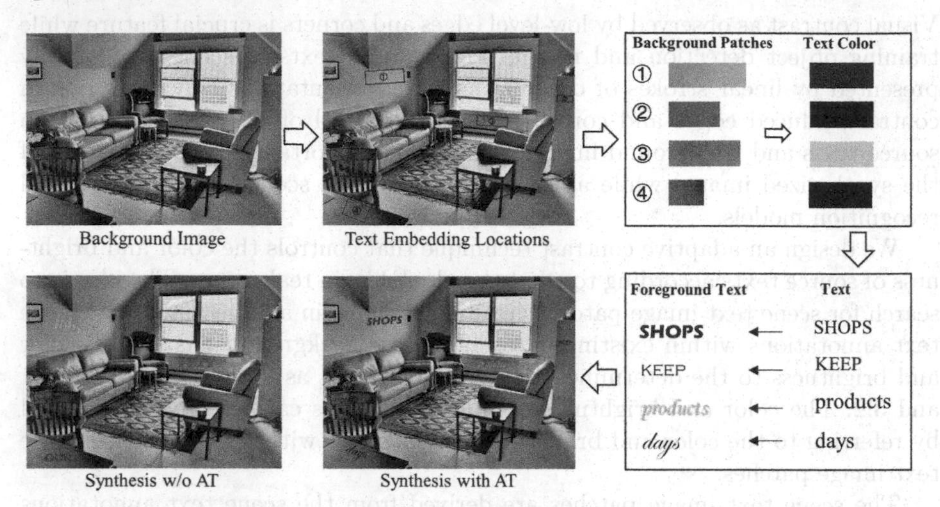

Fig. 4. Adaptive text appearance (ATA): The color and brightness of source texts are determined adaptively according to the color and brightness of the background image around the embedding locations as illustrated. The orientations of source texts are also adaptively determined according to the orientation of the contextual structures around the embedding locations. The ATA thus helps to produce more verisimilar text appearance as compared random setting of text color, brightness, and orientation. (Color figure online)

4 Implementations

4.1 Scene Text Detection

We use an adapted version of EAST [60] to train all scene text detection models to be discussed in Sect. 5.2. EAST is a simple but powerful detection model that yields fast and accurate scene text detection in scene images. The model directly predicts words or text lines of arbitrary orientations and quadrilateral shapes in the images. It utilizes the fully convolutional network (FCN) model that directly produces words or text-line level predictions, excluding unnecessary and redundant intermediate steps. Since the implementation of the original EAST is not available, we adopt an adapted implementation that uses ResNet-152 instead of PVANET [25] as the backbone network.

4.2 Scene Text Recognition

For the scene text recognition, we use the CRNN model [38] to train all scene text recognition models to be described in Sect. 5.3. The CRNN model consists of the convolutional layers, the recurrent layers and a transcription layer which integrates feature extraction, sequence modelling and transcription into a unified framework. Different from most existing recognition models, the architecture in CRNN is end-to-end trainable and can handles sequences in arbitrary lengths, involving no character segmentation. Moreover, it is not confined to any predefined lexicon and can reach superior recognition performances in both lexicon-free and lexicon-based scene text recognition tasks.

5 Experiments

We evaluate the effectiveness of the proposed image synthesis technique on a scene text detection task and a scene text recognition task. The evaluations are performed over 5 public datasets to be discussed in the following subsections.

5.1 Datasets and Evaluation Metrics

The proposed technique is evaluated over five public datasets including ICDAR 2013 [23], ICDAR 2015 [22], MSRA-TD500 [52], IIIT5K [31] and SVT [50].

ICDAR 2013 dataset is obtained from the Robust Reading Challenges 2013. It consists of 229 training images and 233 test images that capture text on sign boards, posters, etc. with word-level annotations. For recognition task, there are 848 word images for training recognition models and 1095 word images for recognition model evaluation. We use this dataset for both scene text detection and scene text recognition evaluations.

ICDAR 2015 is a dataset of incidental scene text and consists of 1,670 images (17,548 annotated text regions) acquired using the Google Glass. Incidental scene text refers to text that appears in the scene without the user taking any prior action in capturing. We use this dataset for the scene text detection evaluation.

MSRA-TD500 dataset consists of 500 natural images (300 for training, 200 for test), which are taken from indoor and outdoor scenes using a pocket camera. The indoor images mainly capture signs, doorplates and caution plates while the outdoor images mostly capture guide boards and billboards with complex background. We use this dataset for the scene text detection evaluation.

IIIT5K dataset consists of 2000 training images and 3000 test images that are cropped from scene texts and born-digital images. For each image, there is a 50-word lexicon and a 1000-word lexicon. All lexicons consist of a ground truth word and some randomly picked words. We use this dataset for scene text recognition evaluation only.

SVT dataset consists of 249 street view images from which 647 words images are cropped. Each word image has a 50 word lexicon. We use this dataset for scene text recognition evaluation only.

Table 1. Scene text detection recall (R), precision (P) and f-score (F) on the ICDAR2013, ICDAR2015 and MSRA-TD500 datasets, where "*EAST*" denotes the adapted EAST model as described in Sect. 4.1, "Real" denotes the original training images within the respective datasets, "Synth 1K" and "Synth 10K" denote 1K and 10K synthesized images by our method.

Methods	ICDAR2013			ICDAR2015			MSRA-TD500		
	R	P	F	R	P	F	R	P	F
I2R NUS FAR [23]	73.0	66.0	69.0	-	-	-	-	-	-
TD-ICDAR [52]	-	-	-	-	-	-	52.0	53.0	50.0
NJU [22]	-	-	-	36.3	70.4	47.9	-	-	-
Kang et al. [21]	-	-	-	-	-	-	62.0	71.0	66.0
Yin et al. [56]	65.1	84.0	73.4	-	-	-	63.0	81.0	71.0
Jaderberg et al. [19]	68.0	86.7	76.2	-	-	-	-	-	-
Zhang et al. [58]	78.0	88.0	83.0	43.1	70.8	53.6	67.0	83.0	74.0
Tian et al. [47]	83.0	93.0	88.0	51.6	74.2	60.9	-	-	-
Yao et al. [53]	80.2	88.9	84.3	58.7	72.3	64.8	**76.5**	75.3	75.9
Gupta et al. [10]	76.4	**93.8**	84.2	-	-	-	-	-	-
Zhou et al. [60]	82.7	92.6	87.4	**78.3**	83.3	80.7	67.4	**87.3**	76.1
EAST (Real)	80.5	85.6	83.0	75.8	84.1	79.7	69.2	78.1	73.4
EAST (Real+Synth 1K)	83.5	89.3	86.3	76.2	85.4	80.5	70.6	80.9	75.4
EAST (Real+Synth 10K)	**85.0**	91.7	**88.3**	77.2	**87.1**	**81.9**	72.7	85.7	**78.6**

For the scene text detection task, we use the evaluation algorithm by Wolf et al. [51]. For the scene text recognition task, we perform evaluations based on the correctly recognized words (CRW) which can be calculated according to the ground truth transcription.

5.2 Scene Text Detection

For the scene text detection task, the proposed image synthesis technique is evaluated over three public datasets ICDAR2013, ICDAR2015 and MSRA-TD500. We synthesize images by catering to specific characteristics of training images within each dataset in term of text transcripts, text languages, text annotation methods, etc. Take the ICDAR2013 dataset as an example. The source texts are all in English and the embedding is at word level because almost all texts in the ICDAR2013 are in English and annotated at word level. For the MSRA-TD500, the source texts are instead in a mixture of English and Chinese and the embedding is at text line level because MSRA-TD500 contains both English and Chinese texts with text line level annotations. In addition, the source texts are a mixture of texts from the respective training images and publicly available corpses. The number of embedded words or text lines is limited at the maximum

Table 2. Scene text detection performance on the ICDAR2013 dataset by using the adapted EAST model as described in Sect. 4.1, where "Synth" and "Gupta" denote images synthesized by our method and Gupta et al. [10] respectively, "1K" and "10K" denote the number of synthetic images used, "Random" means embedding texts at random locations, SC, SG and ATA refer to semantic coherence, saliency guidance, and adaptive text appearance.

Training Data	Recall	Precision	F-measure
ICDAR2013 (Baseline)	80.49	85.56	82.95
ICDAR2013 + 1k Synth (Random)	81.66	84.49	83.08
ICDAR2013 + 1k Synth (SC)	82.15	86.34	84.19
ICDAR2013 + 1k Synth (SG)	82.26	87.33	84.72
ICDAR2013 + 1k Synth (ATA)	81.90	84.95	83.40
ICDAR2013 + 1k Synth (SC+SG)	82.74	89.39	85.94
ICDAR2013 + 1k Synth (SC+ATA)	82.79	87.54	85.10
ICDAR2013 + 1k Synth (SG+ATA)	82.70	88.95	85.72
ICDAR2013 + 1k Synth (SC+SG+ATA)	83.46	89.34	86.29
ICDAR2013 + 10k Synth (SC+SG+ATA)	85.02	91.74	88.25
ICDAR2013 + 1k Gupta [10]	82.81	89.01	85.80
ICDAR2013 + 10k Gupta [10]	84.93	90.74	87.74

of 5 for each background image since we have sufficient background images with semantic segmentation.

Table 1 shows experimental results by using the adapted EAST (denoted by *EAST*) model as described in Sect. 4.1. For each dataset, we train a baseline model "*EAST* (Real)" by using the original training images only as well as two augmented models "*EAST* (Real+Synth 1K)" and "*EAST* (Real+Synth 10K)" that further include 1K and 10K our synthesized images in training, respectively. As Table 1 shows, the scene text detection performance is improved consistently for all three datasets when synthesized images are included in training. In addition, the performance improvements become more significant when the number of synthesis images increases from 1K to 10K. In fact, the trained models outperform most state-of-the-art models when 10K synthesis images are used, and we can foresee further performance improvements when a larger amount of synthesis images are included in training. Furthermore, we observe that the performance improvements for the ICDAR2015 dataset are not as significant as the other two datasets. The major reason is that the ICDAR2015 images are videos frames as captured by Google glass cameras many of which suffer from motion and/or out-of-focus blur, whereas our image synthesis pipeline does not include image blurring function. We conjecture that the scene text detection models will perform better for the ICDAR2015 dataset if we incorporate the image blurring into the image synthesis pipeline.

In particular, a f-score of 83.0 is obtained for the ICDAR2013 dataset when the model is trained using the original training images. The f-score is improved to 86.2 when 1K synthetic images are included, and further to 88.3 when 10K synthetic images are included in training. Similar improvements are observed for the ICDAR2015 dataset, where the f-score is improved from the baseline 79.7 to 80.5 and 81.9 when 1K and 10K synthetic images are included in training. For the MSRA-TD500, a f-score of 73.4 is obtained when only the original 300 training images are used in model training. The f-score is improved to 75.4 and 78.6 respectively, when 1K and 10K synthetic images are included in training. This further verifies the effectiveness of the synthesized scene text images that are produced by our proposed technique.

We also perform ablation study of the three proposed image synthesis designs including semantic coherence (SC), saliency guidance (SG) and adaptive text appearance (ATA). Table 2 shows the experimental results over the ICDAR2013 dataset. As Table 2 shows, the inclusion of synthesized images (including random embedding in "ICDAR2013 + 1k Synth (Random)") consistently improves the scene text detection performance as compared with the baseline model "ICDAR2013 (Baseline)" that is trained by using the original training images only. In addition, the inclusion of either one of our three designs help to improve the scene text detection performance beyond the random embedding, where SG improves the most as followed by SC and AC. When all three designs are included, the f-score reaches 86.26 which is much higher than 83.09 by random embedding. Furthermore, the f-score reaches 88.25 when 10K synthesized images are included in training. We also compared our synthesized images with those created by Gupta et al. [10] as shown in Table 2, where the scene text detection models using our synthesized training images show superior performance consistently.

5.3 Scene Text Recognition

For the scene text recognition task, the proposed image synthesis technique is evaluated over three public datasets ICDAR2013, IIIT5K and SVT as shown in Table 3 where the CRNN is used as the recognition model as described in Sect. 4.2. The baseline model "CRNN (Real)" is trained by combining all annotated word images within the training images of the three datasets. As Table 3 shows, the baseline recognition accuracy is very low because the three datasets contain around 3100 word images only. As a comparison, the recognition model "CRNN (Real+Ours 5M)" achieves state-of-the-art performance, where the 5 million word images are directly cropped from our synthesized scene text images as described in the last subsection. The significant recognition accuracy improvement demonstrates the effectiveness of the proposed scene text image synthesis technique.

In particular, the correctly recognized words (CRW) increases to 87.1% for the ICDAR2013 dataset (without using lexicon) when 5 million synthetic images (synthesized by our proposed method) are included in training. This CRW is significantly higher than the baseline 31.2% when only the original 3100 word

Table 3. Scene text recognition performance over the ICDAR2013, IIIT5K and SVT datasets, where "50" and "1K" in the second row denote the lexicon size and "None" means no lexicon used. CRNN denotes the model as described in Sect. 4.2, "Real" denote the original training images, "Ours 5M", "Jaderberg 5M" and "Gupta 5M" denote the 5 million images synthesized by our method, Jaderberg et al. [17] and Gupta et al. [10] respectively.

Methods	ICDAR2013		IIIT5K		SVT	
	None	50	1k	None	50	None
ABBYY [50]	-	24.3	-	-	35.0	-
Mishra et al. [30]	-	64.1	57.5	-	73.2	-
Rodrguez-Serrano et al. [35]	-	76.1	57.4	-	70.0	-
Yao et al. [54]	-	80.2	69.3	-	75.9	-
Almazan et al. [2]	-	91.2	82.1	-	74.3	-
Gordo [7]	-	93.3	86.6	-	91.8	-
Jaderberg et al. [18]	81.8	95.5	89.6	-	93.2	71.7
Shi et al. [38]	86.7	97.6	94.4	78.2	96.4	80.8
Bissacco et al. [3]	87.6	-	-	-	90.4	78.0
Shi et al. [39]	**88.6**	96.2	93.8	**81.9**	95.5	**81.9**
CRNN (Real)	31.2	64.4	54.4	38.7	62.1	35.5
CRNN (Real+Jaderberg 5M [17])	85.6	97.1	93.2	77.1	95.6	79.9
CRNN (Real+Gupta 5M [10])	86.4	96.7	92.4	76.0	95.3	79.2
CRNN (Real+Ours 5M)	87.1	**98.1**	**95.3**	79.3	**96.7**	81.5

images are used in training. For the IIIT5K, the CRW is increased to 79.3% (no lexicon) when the same 5 million word images are included in training. The CRW is further improved to 95.3% and 98.1%, respectively, when the lexicon size is 1K and 50. Similar CRW improvements are also observed on the SVT dataset as shown in Table 3.

We also benchmark our synthesized images with those created by Jaderberg et al. [17] and Gupta et al. [10]. In particular, we take the same amounts of synthesized images (5 million) and train the scene text recognition model "CRNN (Real+Jaderberg 5M [17])" and "CRNN (Real+Gupta 5M [10])" by using the same CRNN network. As Table 3 shows, the model trained by using our synthesized images outperforms the models trained by using the "Jaderberg 5M" and "Gupta 5M" across all three datasets. Note that the model by Shi et al. [38] achieves similar accuracy as the "CRNN (Real+Ours 5M)", but it uses 8 million synthesized images as created by Jaderberg et al. [17].

The superior scene text recognition accuracy as well as the significant improvement in the scene text detection task as described in the last subsection is largely due to the three novel image synthesis designs which help to generate verisimilar scene text images as illustrated in Fig. 5. As Fig. 5 shows, the proposed scene text image synthesis technique is capable of embedding source texts at semantically sensible and apt locations within the background image. At the same time, it is also capable of setting the color, brightness and orientation of the embedded texts adaptively according to the color, brightness, and contextual structures around the embedding locations within the background image.

Fig. 5. Several sample images from our synthesis dataset that show how the pro-posed semantic coherence, saliency guidance and adaptive text appearance work together for verisimilar text embedding in scene images automatically.

6 Conclusions

This paper presents a scene text image synthesis technique that aims to train accurate and robust scene text detection and recognition models. The proposed technique achieves verisimilar scene text image synthesis by combining three novel designs including semantic coherence, visual attention, and adaptive text appearance. Experiments over 5 public benchmarking datasets show that the proposed image synthesis technique helps to achieve state-of-the-art scene text detection and recognition performance.

A possible extension to our work is to further improve the appearance of source texts. We currently make use of the color and brightness statistics of real scene texts to guide the color and brightness of the embedded texts. The generated text appearance still has a gap as compared with the real scene texts because the color and brightness statistics do not capture the spatial distribution information. One possible improvement is to directly learn the text appearance of the dataset under study and use the learned model to determine the appearance of the source texts automatically.

Acknowledgement. This work is funded by the Ministry of Education, Singapore, under the project "A semi-supervised learning approach for accurate and robust detection of texts in scenes" (RG128/17 (S)).

References

1. Aldrian, O., Smith, W.A.: Inverse rendering of faces with a 3D morphable model. IEEE Trans. Pattern Anal. Mach. Intell. **35**(5), 1080–1093 (2013)
2. Almazan, J., Gordo, A., Fornes, A., Valveny, E.: Word spotting and recognition with embedded attributes. PAMI **36**(12), 2552–2566 (2014)
3. Bissacco, A., Cummins, M., Netzer, Y., Neven, H.: Photoocr: reading text in uncontrolled conditions. In: ICCV (2013)
4. Debevec, P.: Rendering synthetic objects into real scenes: bridging traditional and image-based graphics with global illumination and high dynamic range photography. In: Proceedings of the 25th Annual Conference Proceeding SIGGRAPH 1998, pp. 189–198 (1998)
5. Dosovitskiy, A., et al.: FlowNet: learning optical flow with convolutional networks. In: Proceedings of ICCV (2015)
6. Goodfellow, J., et al.: Generative adversarial networks. arXiv:1406.2661 (2014)
7. Gordo, A.: Supervised mid-level features for word image representation. In: CVPR (2015)
8. Graves, A., Liwicki, M., Fernndez, S.: A novel connectionist system for unconstrained handwriting recognition. IEEE Trans. Pattern Anal. Mach. Intell. (TPAMI) **31**, 855–868 (2009)
9. Greenberg, D.P., et al.: A framework for realistic image synthesis. Commun. ACM (8), 42–53 (1999)
10. Gupta., A., Vedaldi., A., Zisserman, A.: Synthetic data for text localisation in natural images. In: IEEE Conference on Computer Vision and Pattern Recognition (2016)
11. He, P., Huang, W., He, T., Zhu, Q., Qiao, Y., Li, X.: Single shot text detector with regional attention. arXiv:1709.00138 (2017)
12. He, T., Huang, W., Qiao, Y., Yao, J.: Accurate text localization in natural image with cascaded convolutional text network. arXiv:1603.09423 (2016)
13. He, T., Huang, W., Qiao, Y., Yao, J.: Text-attentional convolutional neural network for scene text detection. IEEE Trans. Image Process. **6**, 2529–2541 (2016)
14. http://cocodataset.org/
15. Huang, W., Lin, Z., Yang, J., Wang, J.: Text localization in natural images using stroke feature transform and text covariance descriptors. In: Proceedings of the IEEE International Conference on Computer Vision, pp. 1241–1248 (2013)
16. Huang, W., Qiao, Y., Tang, X.: Robust scene text detection with convolution neural network induced MSER trees. In: Fleet, D., Pajdla, T., Schiele, B., Tuytelaars, T. (eds.) ECCV 2014. LNCS, vol. 8692, pp. 497–511. Springer, Cham (2014). https://doi.org/10.1007/978-3-319-10593-2_33
17. Jaderberg, M., Simonyan, K., Vedaldi, A., Zisserman, A.: Synthetic data and artificial neural networks for natural scene text recognition. arXiv preprint arXiv:1406.2227 (2014)
18. Jaderberg, M., Simonyan, K., Vedaldi, A., Zisserman, A.: Deep structured output learning for unconstrained text recognition. In: ICLR (2015)
19. Jaderberg, M., Simonyan, K., Vedaldi, A., Zisserman, A.: Reading text in the wild with convolutional neural networks. Int. J. Comput. Vis. **116**(1), 1–20 (2016)

20. Jaderberg, M., Vedaldi, A., Zisserman, A.: Deep features for text spotting. In: Fleet, D., Pajdla, T., Schiele, B., Tuytelaars, T. (eds.) ECCV 2014. LNCS, vol. 8692, pp. 512–528. Springer, Cham (2014). https://doi.org/10.1007/978-3-319-10593-2_34
21. Kang, L., Li, Y., Doermann, D.: Orientation robust textline detection in natural images. In: Proceedings of CVPR (2014)
22. Karatzas, D., et al.: ICDAR 2015 competition on robust reading. In: Document Analysis and Recognition (ICDAR), pp. 1156–1160 (2015)
23. Karatzas, D., et al.: ICDAR 2013 robust reading competition. In: Proceedings of ICDAR, pp. 1484–1493 (2013)
24. Karsch, K., Hedau, V., Forsyth, D., Hoiem, D.: Rendering synthetic objects into legacy photographs. ACM Trans. Graph. **30**(6), 157:1–157:12 (2011)
25. Kim, K., Hong, S., Roh, B., Cheon, Y., Park, M.: PVANET: deep but lightweight neural networks for real-time object detection. arXiv:1608.08021 (2016)
26. Liao, M., Shi, B., Bai, X., Wang, X., Liu, W.: Textboxes: a fast text detector with a single deep neural network. In: AAAI, pp. 4161–4167 (2017)
27. Liu, Y., Jin, L.: Deep matching prior network: toward tighter multi-oriented text detection. In: CVPR (2017)
28. Lu, S., Chen, T., Tian, S., Lim, J.H., Tan, C.L.: Scene text extraction based on edges and support vector regression. Int. J. Doc. Anal. Recognit. **2**, 125–135 (2015)
29. Lu, S., Tan, C., Lim, J.H.: Robust and efficient saliency modeling from image co-occurrence histograms. IEEE Trans. Pattern Anal. Mach. Intell. **36**(1), 195–201 (2014)
30. Mishra, A., Alahari, K., Jawahar, C.V.: Scene text recognition using higher order language priors. In: BMVC (2012)
31. Mishra, A.: Iiit 5k-word. http://tc11.cvc.uab.es/datasets/IIIT5K-Word
32. Neumann, L., Matas, J.: Real-time scene text localization and recognition. In: Computer Vision and Pattern Recognition (CVPR), pp. 3538–3545 (2012)
33. Neumann, L., Matas, J.: Real-time lexicon-free scene text localization and recognition. IEEE Trans. Pattern Anal. Mach. Intell. **9**, 1872–1885 (2016)
34. Papandreou, G., Chen, L.C., Murphy, K.P., Yuille., A.L.: Weakly-and semi-supervised learning of a deep convolutional network for semantic image segmentation. In: International Conference on Computer Vision (ICCV), pp. 1742–1750 (2015)
35. Rodrguez-Serrano, J.A., Gordo, A., Perronnin, F.: Label embedding: a frugal baseline for text recognition. IJCV **113**, 193–2017 (2015)
36. Shahab, A., Shafait, F., Dengel, A.: ICDAR 2011 robust reading competition challenge 2: reading text in scene images. In: 2011 International Conference on Document Analysis and Recognition (ICDAR), pp. 1491–1496 (2011)
37. Shi, B., Bai, X., Belongie, S.: Detecting oriented text in natural images by linking segments. In: CVPR (2017)
38. Shi, B., Bai, X., Yao, C.: An end-to-end trainable neural network for image-based sequence recognition and its application to scene text recognition. IEEE Trans. Pattern Anal. Mach. Intell. **39**(11), 2298–2304 (2017)
39. Shi, B., Wang, X., Lyu, P., Yao, C., Bai, X.: Robust scene text recognition with automatic rectification. arXiv:1603.03915 (2016)
40. Shi, B., et al.: ICDAR 2017 competition on reading chinese text in the wild (RCTW-17). In: 2017 14th IAPR International Conference on Document Analysis and Recognition (ICDAR), vol. 1, pp. 1429–1434 (2017)
41. Simonyan, K., Vedaldi, A., Zisserman, A.: Deep inside convolutional networks: visualising image classification models and saliency maps. arXiv:1312.6034 (2013)

42. Sixt, L., Wild, B., Landgraf, T.: Rendergan: generating realistic labeled data. arXiv:1611.01331 (2017)
43. Su, B., Lu, S.: Accurate scene text recognition based on recurrent neural network. In: Cremers, D., Reid, I., Saito, H., Yang, M.-H. (eds.) ACCV 2014. LNCS, vol. 9003, pp. 35–48. Springer, Cham (2015). https://doi.org/10.1007/978-3-319-16865-4_3
44. Su, B., Lu, S.: Accurate recognition of words in scenes without character segmentation using recurrent neural network. Pattern Recognit. **63**, 397–405 (2017)
45. Tian, S., Lu, S.: WeText: scene text detection underweak supervision. In: IEEE International Conference on Computer Vision, pp. 1492–1550 (2017)
46. Tian, S., Pan, Y., Huang, C., Lu, S., Yu, K., Tan, C.L.: Text flow: a unified text detection system in natural scene images. In: Proceedings of the IEEE International Conference on Computer Vision, pp. 4651–4659 (2015)
47. Tian, Z., Huang, W., He, T., He, P., Qiao, Y.: Detecting text in natural image with connectionist text proposal network. In: Leibe, B., Matas, J., Sebe, N., Welling, M. (eds.) ECCV 2016. LNCS, vol. 9912, pp. 56–72. Springer, Cham (2016). https://doi.org/10.1007/978-3-319-46484-8_4
48. Timofte, R., Rothe, R., Gool, L.V.: Seven ways to improve example-based single image super resolution. In: CVPR (2016)
49. Veit, A., Matera, T., Neumann, L., Matas, J., Belongie, S.: COCO-text: dataset and benchmark for text detection and recognition in natural images. arXiv:1601.07140 (2016)
50. Wang, K., Babenko, B., Belongie, S.: End-to-end scene text recognition. In: ICCV (2011)
51. Wolf, C., Jolion, J.M.: Object count/area graphs for the evaluation of object detection and segmentation algorithms. Int. J. Doc. Anal. **8**(4), 280–296 (2006)
52. Yao, C., Bai, X., Liu, W., Ma, Y., Tu, Z.: Detecting texts of arbitrary orientations in natural images. In: Computer Vision and Pattern Recognition (CVPR), pp. 1083–1090 (2012)
53. Yao, C., Bai, X., Sang, N., Zhou, X., Zhou, S., Cao, Z.: Scene text detection via holistic, multi-channel prediction. arXiv:1606.09002 (2016)
54. Yao, C., Bai, X., Shi, B., Liu, W.: Strokelets: a learned multi-scale representation for scene text recognition. In: IEEE Computer Vision and Pattern Recognition (CVPR) (2014)
55. Yildirim, I., Kulkarni, T.D., Freiwald, W.A., Tenenbaum, J.B.: Efficient and robust analysis-by-synthesis in vision: a computational framework, behavioral tests, and modeling neuronal representations. In: Annual Conference of the Cognitive Science Society (2015)
56. Yin, X.C., Pei, W.Y., Zhang, J., Hao, H.W.: Multiorientation scene text detection with adaptive clustering. IEEE Trans. PAMI **37**(9), 1930–1937 (2015)
57. Zhang, Z., Shen, W., Yao, C., Bai, X.: Symmetry-based text line detection in natural scenes. In: Proceedings of the IEEE Conference on Computer Vision and Pattern Recognition, pp. 2558–2567 (2015)
58. Zhang, Z., Zhang, C., Shen, W., Yao, C., Liu, W., Bai, X.: Multi-oriented text detection with fully convolutional networks. In: Proceedings of CVPR (2015)
59. Zhang, Z., Zhang, C., Shen, W., Yao, C., Liu, W., Bai, X.: Multi-oriented text detection with fully convolutional networks. In: Proceedings of the IEEE Conference on Computer Vision and Pattern Recognition, pp. 4159–4167 (2016)
60. Zhou, X., et al.: East: an efficient and accurate scene text detector. arXiv:1704.03155 (2017)

Quantization Mimic: Towards Very Tiny CNN for Object Detection

Yi Wei[1(✉)], Xinyu Pan[2], Hongwei Qin[3], Wanli Ouyang[4], and Junjie Yan[3]

[1] Tsinghua University, Beijing, China
wei-y15@mails.tsinghua.edu.cn

[2] The Chinese University of Hong Kong, Hong Kong, China
THUSEpxy@gmail.com

[3] SenseTime, Beijing, China
{qinhongwei,yanjunjie}@sensetime.com

[4] The University of Sydney, SenseTime Computer Vision Research Group, Sydney, New South Wales, Australia
wanli.ouyang@sydney.edu.au

Abstract. In this paper, we propose a simple and general framework for training very tiny CNNs (*e.g.* VGG with the number of channels reduced to $\frac{1}{32}$) for object detection. Due to limited representation ability, it is challenging to train very tiny networks for complicated tasks like detection. To the best of our knowledge, our method, called Quantization Mimic, is the first one focusing on very tiny networks. We utilize two types of acceleration methods: mimic and quantization. Mimic improves the performance of a student network by transfering knowledge from a teacher network. Quantization converts a full-precision network to a quantized one without large degradation of performance. If the teacher network is quantized, the search scope of the student network will be smaller. Using this feature of the quantization, we propose Quantization Mimic. It first quantizes the large network, then mimic a quantized small network. The quantization operation can help student network to better match the feature maps from teacher network. To evaluate our approach, we carry out experiments on various popular CNNs including VGG and Resnet, as well as different detection frameworks including Faster R-CNN and R-FCN. Experiments on Pascal VOC and WIDER FACE verify that our Quantization Mimic algorithm can be applied on various settings and outperforms state-of-the-art model acceleration methods given limited computing resouces.

Keywords: Model acceleration · Model compression
Quantization · Mimic · Object detection

1 Introduction

In recent years, CNN achieved great success on various computer vision tasks. However, due to their huge model size and computation complexity, many CNN

Y. Wei and X. Pan—The work was done during an internship at SenseTime

V. Ferrari et al. (Eds.): ECCV 2018, LNCS 11212, pp. 274–290, 2018.
https://doi.org/10.1007/978-3-030-01237-3_17

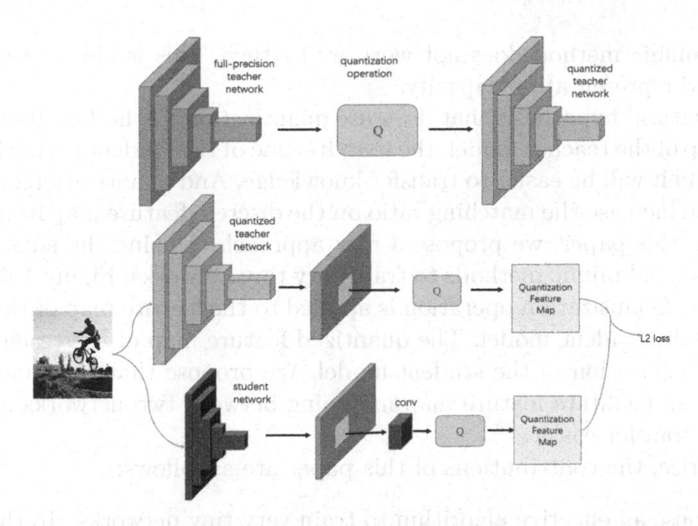

Fig. 1. The pipeline of our method. First we train a full-precision teacher network. Then we operate quantization on the feature map of full-precision teacher network and we get a quantized network. Finally we use this quantized network as teacher model to teach a quantized student network. We emphasize that we do both quantization operation on feature maps of student and teacher networks in training stages.

models cannot be applied on real world devices directly. Many previous works focus on how to accelerate CNNs. They can be roughly divided to four categories: quantization (*e.g.* BinaryNet [1]), group convolution based method (*e.g.* MobileNet [2]), pruning (*e.g.* channel pruning [3]) and mimic (*e.g.* Li *et al.* [4]).

Although most of these works can accelerate models without degradation of performance, their speed-up ratios are limited (*e.g.* compress VGG to VGG-1-4[1]). Few methods are experimented on very tiny models (*e.g.* compress VGG to VGG-1-16). "Very tiny" is a relative concept and we define it as a model whose channel numbers of every layer is less than or equal to $\frac{1}{16}$ compared with original model. Our experiments show that our method outperform other approaches for very tiny models.

As two kinds of model acceleration methods, quantization and mimic are widely used to compress model. Quantization methods can transfer a full-precision model to a quantized model[2] while maintaining similar accuracy. However, using quantization method to directly speed up models usually need extra specific implementation (*e.g.* FPGA) and specific instruction set. Mimic methods can be used on different frameworks and easy to implement. The essence of these methods is knowledge transfer in which student networks learn the high-level representations from teacher networks. However, when applied on very tiny

[1] In this paper *-1-n* network means a network whose channel numbers of every layer is reduced to $\frac{1}{n}$ compared with original network.

[2] The quantized network in this paper means a network whose output feature map is quantized but not means parameter is quantized

networks, mimic method does not work well either. This is also caused by the very limited representation capacity.

It is a natural hypothesis that if we use quantization method to discretize the feature map of the teacher model, the search scope of the student network will get shrinked and it will be easier to transfer knowledge. And quantization on student network can increase the matching ratio on the discrete feature map from teacher network. In this paper, we propose a new approach utilizing the advantages of quantization and mimic methods to train very tiny networks. Figure 1 illustrates the pipeline. Quantization operation is applied to the feature map of the teacher model and the student model. The quantized feature map of the teacher model is used as supervision of the student model. We propose that this quantization operation can facilitate feature map matching between two networks and make knowledge transfer easier.
To summarize, the contributions of this paper are as follows:

- We propose an effective algorithm to train very tiny networks. To the best of our knowledge, this is the first work focusing on very tiny networks.
- We utilize quantized feature maps to facilitate knowledge distilling, *i.e.* quantization and mimic.
- We use a complicated task object detection instead of image classification to verify our method. Sufficient experiments on various CNNs, frameworks and datasets validate our approach effective.
- The method is easy to implement and has no special limitation during training and inference.

2 Related Work

2.1 Object Detections

The target of object detection [5–10] is to locate and classify the objects in images. Before the success of convolutional neural network, some traditional pattern recognition algorithms (HOG [11], DPM [12] *et al.*) are used on this task. Recently, R-CNN [13] and its variants become the popular method for object detection task. The SPP-Net [14] and Fast R-CNN [15] reuse feature maps to speed up R-CNN framework. Beyond the pipeline of Fast R-CNN, Faster R-CNN add region proposal networks and use joint-train method during training. R-FCN utilize position-sensitive score maps to reduce more computation. YOLO [16] and SSD [17] are the typical algorithms of region-free methods. Although the frameworks used in this paper are from region proposal solutions family, Quantization Mimic can easily transform to YOLO and SSD methods.

2.2 Model Compression and Acceleration

Group Convolution Based Methods: The main point of this kind of methods is to use group convolution for acceleration. Mobilenet [2] and Googlenet Xception [18] utilize Depthwise Convolution to extract features and Pointwise

Convolution to merge features. Beyond these works, Zhang *et al.* [19] propose a general group convolution algorithm and show that Xception is the special case of their method. Group operation will block the information flow between different group convolutions and most recently, Shufflenet [20] introduces channel shuffle approach to solve this problem.

Quantization: Quantization methods [21,22] can reduce the size of models efficiently and speed up for special implementation. BinaryConnect [23], binarized neural network (BNN) [1] and LBCNN [24] replace floating convolutional filter with binary filter. Furthermore, INQ [25] introduce a training method to quantize model whose weights are constrained to be either powers of two or zero without a decrease on performance. Despite these advantages, quantization models can only be used to speed up on special devices.

Pruning and Sparse Connection: [26,27] set sparse constraint during training for pruning. [28,29] focus on the importance of different filter weights and do pruning operation according to weights' importance. And these methods are training-based, which are more costly. Recently He *et al.* [3] propose an inference-time pruning method, using LASSO regression and least square construction to select channels in classification and detection task. Furthermore, Molchanov *et al.* [30] combine transfer learning and greedy criteria-based pruning. We use He *et al.* [3] and Molchanov *et al.* [30] for comparing our alogrithm and we will show that it is difficult for them to prune a large network (such as VGG) to a very tiny network (such as VGG-1-32). Sparse connection [31–34] can be considered as parameter-wise pruning method, eliminating connection between neurons.

Mimic: The principle of mimic is Knowledge Transfer. As a pioneering work, Knowledge Distillation (KD) [35] defines soft targets as outputs of the teacher network. Compared with labels, soft targets provide extra information about inter-class similarities. FitNet [36] develops Knowledge Transfer as whole feature map mimic learning to compress wide and shallow networks to thin and deep networks. Li *et al.* [4] extend mimic techniques for object detection task. We use their joint-train version as our baseline.

3 Our Approach

In this section, we first introduce the quantization method and mimic method we use separately, then combine them and propose the pipeline of Quanzition Mimic algorithm. In Sect. 3.4 we show the theoretical analysis of our approach.

3.1 Quantization

[21–23] use quantization method to compress models directly. Unlike them, we use quantization to limit the range and help mimic learning. In details, the

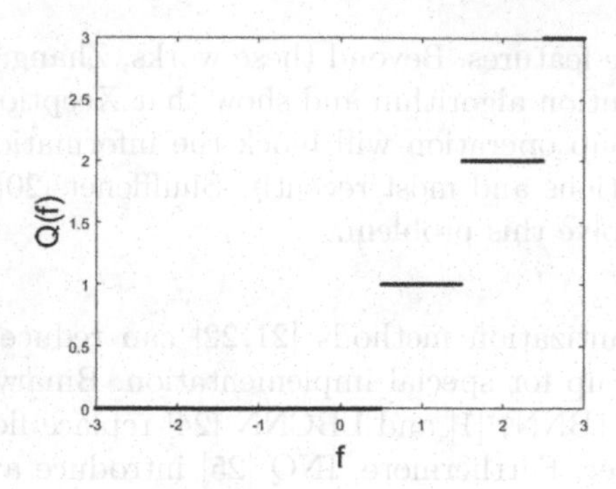

Fig. 2. Quantized ReLU function. The new activation function is defined as $\widetilde{f} = Q(f)$, where f is the original activation function.

quantization for teacher network is to discretize its output and in the meanwhile we can guarantee the accuracy of teacher network when doing quantization. And quantizing the output of student network can help it match the discrete output of teacher network, which is the goal of mimic learning. In our work, we do quantization operation on the last activation layer of the teacher network.

INQ [25] constrains the output to be either zero or power of two. Different from them, we use uniform quantization for the following reason. R-FCN [37] and Faster R-CNN [38] use RoI pooling operation which is a kind of max pooling operation. The output of RoI pooling layer is determined by the max response of every block in RoIs. So it is important to describe strong response of feature maps more accurately. Uniform quantization can better describe large value than power of two quantization. We define the element-wise quantization function Q as:

$$Q(f) = \beta \quad \text{if} \ \frac{\alpha + \beta}{2} < f \leq \frac{\gamma + \beta}{2} \tag{1}$$

where α,β and γ are the adjacent entries in the code dictionary D:

$$D = \{0, s, 2s, 3s..\} \tag{2}$$

where s is the stride of uniform quantization. We use function Q to convert full-precision feature maps to quantized feature maps:

$$\widetilde{f} = Q(f) \tag{3}$$

where f is the feature map. Figure 2 illustrates quantized ReLU function. As for backward propagation, inspired by BNN [1], we use the full-precision gradient. We find that quantized gradient will cause the student network difficult to converge.

3.2 Mimic

In popular CNN detectors, the feature map from feature extractors (*e.g.* VGG, Resnet) will affect both localization and classification accuracy. We use L2 regression to let student networks learn the feature map from the teacher networks and utilize Li *et al.* [4] joint-train version as our backbone. Unlike soft target [35] whose dimension is equal to the number of categories, the dimension of feature maps is related to the size of inputs and networks architecture. Sometimes number can be millions. Simply mimicking the whole feature maps is difficult for student network to converge. Faster R-CNN [38] and R-FCN [37] are region-based detectors and both of them use RoI-Pooling operation. So the region of interest plays more important role than other regions. We use mimic learning between the region of interest on student's and teacher's feature maps. The whole loss function of mimic learning is described as follows.

$$L = L_{cls}^{r} + L_{reg}^{r} + L_{cls}^{d} + L_{reg}^{d} + \lambda L_{m} \tag{4}$$

$$L_{m} = \frac{1}{2N} \sum_{i} \left\| f_{t}^{i} - r\left(f_{s}^{i}\right) \right\|_{2}^{2} \tag{5}$$

where L_{cls}^{r}, L_{reg}^{r} are the loss function of region proposal networks [15] while L_{cls}^{d}, L_{reg}^{d} are the function of R-FCN or Faster R-CNN detectors. We define L_m as the mimic-loss and λ is the loss weight. N is the number of region proposals. f_t^i and f_s^i represent the ith region proposal on teacher and student network's feature maps. Function r transfers the feature map from student network to the same size of teacher network. The mimic learning is on the last year of feature extractor networks.

Though RoI mimic learning reduces the dimension of feature maps and helps student network convergence, very tiny network is sensitive to mimic loss weight λ. If λ is small, it will weaken the effectiveness of mimic learning. In the contrast, large λ will also bring bad results. Due to the poor learning capacity of very tiny network, large λ will cause it focus on the learning of teacher network's feature map at the begining of training. In this way, it will ignore other loss. We name this phenomenon as 'gradient focus' and we set λ as 0.1, 1 and 10 for experiments.

3.3 Quantization Mimic

The pipeline of our algorithm is as follows: First we train a full-precision teacher network. Then we use function Q to compress full-precision teacher network to a quantized network. To get high performance compressed model, we finetune on full-precision network. Finally, we utilize quantized teacher network to teach student network using mimic loss as supervision. And during training, we both quantize the feature map of teacher and student network. Figure 3 illustrates our method.
Because of quantization operation, the mimic loss L_m is redefined as:

$$L_{m} = \frac{1}{2N} \sum_{i} \left\| Q\left(f_{t}^{i}\right) - Q\left(r\left(f_{s}^{i}\right)\right) \right\|_{2}^{2} \tag{6}$$

where quantization function Q is defined in Eq. 1

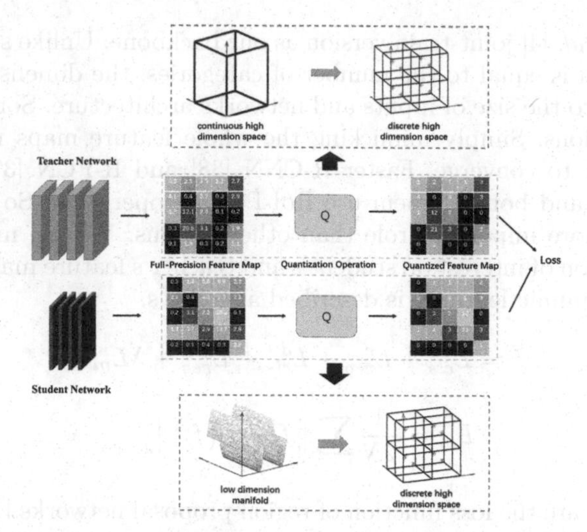

Fig. 3. The effect of quantizatuon operation. We use quantized teacher network to guide quantized student network. The quantization on teacher network can discretize its feature maps and convert a continous high dimension space to a discrete high dimension space. And for student network, quantization helps low dimension manifold to match a discrete high dimension feature map. In this way, mimic learning becomes easier.

3.4 Analysis

We will show that the quantization of both teacher and student networks will facilitate feature maps matching between student and teacher networks and help student network learn better. Figure 3 shows the effect of quantization operation. We assume that f_t^n is the feature map of full-precision teacher network with the input I_n. The width, height and channel numbers of f_t^n are W_t^n, H_t^n and C_t^n.We squeeze f_t^n as a column vector y_n whose dimension is $W_t^n H_t^n C_t^n$. The target of mimic learning is to get approximate solution of the following equation:

$$Y = w_s I \tag{7}$$

$$Y = [y_1, y_2, ..., y_n] \tag{8}$$

$$I = [I_1, I_2, ..., I_n] \tag{9}$$

where w_s is the weights of student network. However, due to the high dimensionality of y_n and large image numbers, the rank of Y can be very high. On the other hand, very tiny networks have few parameters and the rank of w_s is low. Therefore, it is difficult for very tiny student networks to mimic high dimension feature maps directly. The target of Quantization Mimic is changed as:

$$Q(Y) = Q(w_s I) \tag{10}$$

where Q is quantization function. The quantization operation on the output of teacher network discretizes its feature maps. Furthermore, because of the range

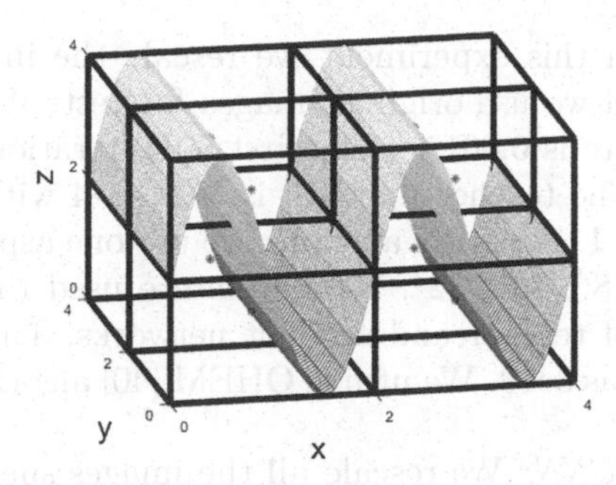

Fig. 4. A manifold in 3-dimension space. The manifold intersect all 8 cubes. The point '*' represent the center of cube, which is the vector after quantization operation.

of element in feature maps is bounded, the value of every entry in matrix $Q(Y)$ is discrete and finite. For example, if the range of element in f_t^n is $[0, 40]$ and the stride of uniform quantization is 8, the possible value of entry in $Q(Y)$ is from $\{0, 8, 16, 24, 32, 40\}$. In this way, we convert continuous high dimension space to discrete high dimension space.

The quantization on student networks makes it easier to match the $Q(f_t^n)$. Every axis of target space for student network can be separated by entries in code dictionary. And the whole space is separated by several high dimension cubes.

For simplicity, we assume the dimension of target space ϕ is 3, *i.e.* , the dimension of y_n is 3. The code dictionary is selected as $\{1, 3\}$. Because of quantization operation, this 3-dimension space is separated by 8 cubes (See Fig. 4). If a vector v is in cube c , after quantization operation, it will be the center of cube c. For example, $v = [1.2, 2.2, 1.8]^{\mathrm{T}}$, $Q(v) = [1, 3, 1]^{\mathrm{T}}$, and $[1, 3, 1]^{\mathrm{T}}$ is the center of a cube.

We suppose that feature maps of student network consist a low dimension manifold. The goal of mimic learning is to use this manifold to fit all 8 cube centers, *i.e.* , we want these 8 centers on the manifold. However, after introducing quantization on student network, if the manifold intersect a cube, the manifold can achieve the center of this cube. Thus, instead of matching all centers, we only need the manifold to intersect 8 cubes, which weaken matching conditions. And in this way, there are more suitable manifolds , which promotes feature maps matching between two networks. Experiments in Sect. 4.1 shows that our approach is still effective in high dimension case. Figure 4 illustrates a manifold in 3-dimension space which intersect all cubes.

3.5 Implementation Details

We train networks with Caffe [39] using C++ on 8 Nvidia GPU Titan X Pascal. We use stochastic gradient descent (SGD) algorithm. The weight decay is 0.0005 and momentum is 0.9. We set uniform quantization stride as 1 for all experiments.

VGG with R-FCN: In this experiment we rescale the images such that their shorter side is 600 and we use original images for test. We use gray images as input. The learning rate is 0.001 for the first 50K iterations and 0.0001 for the next 30K iterations. The teacher network is VGG-1-4 with R-FCN and we set mimic loss weight λ as 1. For RPN anchors, we use one aspect ratio and 4 scales with box areas of 4^2, 8^2, 16^2, 32^2. 2000 RoIs are used to sample the features on the feature maps of teacher and student networks. The ROI output size of R-FCN detector is set as 3×3. We utilize OHEM [40] algorithm to help training.

Resnet with Faster R-CNN: We rescale all the images such that shorter side is 600 for both training and test. We totally train 40K iterations. The learning rate is 0.001 for the first 30K iterations and 0.001 for the last 10k iterations. We set λ as 0.1, 1 and 10 for Resnet experiment respectively. And for RPN anchors, we use 2 aspect ratios (2:1, 3:1) and 3 scales with box areas of 4^2, 8^2 and 16^2. 128 RoIs are used to sample the features on the feature maps of teacher and student networks. The ROI output size of Faster R-CNN detector is set as 7×7.

4 Experiments

To prove the generalization ability of our method, we evaluate our approach for different frameworks on different datasets. In detail, we use VGG with R-FCN and Resnet with Faster R-CNN as our backbones. Results are reported on WIDER FACE [41] and Pascal VOC [42].

4.1 Experiments on WIDER FACE Dataset

WIDER FACE dataset [41] contains about 32K images with 394K annotated faces. The size of faces in WIDER FACE dataset vary a lot. The validation and Test set are divided into *easy* , *medium* and *hard* subsets. We find that VGG and VGG-1-4 have similar performance on WIDER FACE dataset (See Table 3) and we use VGG-1-4 with R-FCN detector as our teacher network (large model). To show the superiority of our algorithm, VGG-1-32 with R-FCN detector is selected as the student network (small model). Table 1 illustrate the speed and size of our very tiny model student network compared with large models. It has extremely small size and fast speed.

Main Results. We implement our algorithm on VGG-1-32 with R-FCN detector. We compare our method with Li *et al.* [4], He *et al.* [3] and group convolution based accelerating method including using Depthwise Convolution and Group Convolution. The results are shown in Table 2 (we set input as 1000×600 and compute the complexity). For fair comparison, we use the same implementation details for all experiments. We involve Depthwise Convolution and Group Convolution into VGG-1-32 structures, guaranteeing the similar complexity with the original network. For example, we extend the channel numbers of every convolution layers c to $\lceil\sqrt{3}c\rceil$ and we set group number as 3. We also compare with

Table 1. The comparision between VGG, VGG-1-4, VGG-1-32 with R-FCN detector on speed and size. The size is calculated theoretically. VGG-1-32 with R-FCN has tiny size and amazing speed, which can be applied on embedded devices. Tested on Titan X GPU with a single image of which the longer side is resized to 1024.

Method	Speed	Size
VGG with R-FCN	103.6 ms	79.8M
VGG-1-4 with R-FCN	30.2 ms	5.04 M
VGG-1-32 with R-FCN	**9.6 ms**	**0.13 2M**

Table 2. Comparison with other methods. The results show that our method outperforms others (higher is better). Group convolution based approach(Depthwise Convolution and Group Convolution) don't work well on the very tiny model. Quantization Mimic also outperforms than Li *et al.*, who only uses mimic learning.

Solution	Complexity (MFLOPS)	Easy	Medium	Hard
Scratch	227	71.3	55.4	23.8
Depthwise Convolution	232	69.1	51.1	21.6
Group Convolution(group 2)	286	67.8	51.9	22.4
Group Convolution(group 3)	273	65.8	50.8	22.1
He *et al.* [3]	227	68.0	50.7	22.1
Molchanov *et al.* [30]	227	73.2	58.2	25.2
Li *et al.* [4](only mimic)	227	71.9	58.2	25.6
Quantization Mimic	227	**73.9**	**62.1**	**27.6**

pruning methods [3,30]. The pruning ratio is set as 8, which means the model we get after pruning has the same size with VGG-1-32. The results demonstrate that our algorithm outperforms other methods. We find that group convolution based methods are not suitable for very tiny networks. This is mainly because very tiny networks usually have small channel numbers and using group convolutions will block the information flow. Compared with pruning methods [3,30], Quantization Mimic also works better. We argue that pruning methods can get good results on large models (*e.g.* , VGG and Resnet). However, none of these works try to prune a network to $\frac{1}{16}$ times. Compared with mimic method [4], Quantization Mimic outperforms it by 2.0 points, 3.9 points and 1.9 points on *easy*, *medium* and *hard* subsets. We find that quantized teacher network has better performance than full-precision teacher network. Ablation experiments are conducted to diagnose how Quantization Mimic brings improvement.

Table 3 further shows the effectiveness of our approach. We can see that our method can increase AP of very tiny models by 2.6 points, 6.7 points and 3.7 points on *easy*, *medium* and *hard* subsets respectively. Results on *medium* and *hard* subsets, the small model can even achieve comparable results with large model.

Table 3. The comparision between VGG and VGG-1-4 on the WIDER FACE dataset. We suggest that VGG has abundant structures and it has similar performance with VGG-1-4. And we choose VGG-1-4 as teacher model.

Model	Solution	Easy	Medium	Hard
VGG	Full-precision	83.9	61.0	26.8
VGG-1-4	Full-precision	82.4	62.5	26.3
	Quantized	83.7	65.0	27.4
VGG-1-32	Scratch	71.3	55.4	23.8
	Quantization mimic	73.9	62.1	27.6

Ablation Study on Quantization Operation. To verify the effectiveness of quantization operation, we do several experiments. As demonstrated in Table 4, the performance of teacher network directly impact the performance of student network. Also, the quantization operation help mimic learning and improves the performance of student network. For the same quantized teacher network, doing quantization operation on the student network increase AP by 0.9 point, 2.8 points and 2.0 points on three subsets.

Table 4. Quantization *vs.* Nonquantization: The ablation study shows that the performance of student network depends on the performance of teacher network. The results also suggest that quantization method do help mimic learning.

Teacher quantization?	Student quantization?	Easy	Medium	Hard
		71.9	58.2	25.6
✓		73.0	59.3	25.6
✓	✓	**73.9**	**62.1**	**27.6**

We notice that quantization operation has regularization effect on network. To exclude that it is the regularization that bring improvement of performance, we also do experiments with and without quantization on student network. In Table 5, we find that only doing quantization has no influence on the performance, *i.e.* , the improvement comes from Quantization Mimic.

Table 5. The influence of quantization only on small networks. The results suggest quantization only does not bring improvement.

Model	Quantization?	Easy	Medium	Hard
VGG-1-32	✓	71.9	55.2	23.7
		71.3	55.4	23.8

To further show that quantization operation can help student networks learn better, we illustrate the matching ratio of each RoI. In Sect. 3.4 we show that quantization operation promotes feature map matching between two networks. And in Sect. 3.2, we introduce that our mimic learning is based on RoIs. Thus, we consider the matching ratio of each RoI, *i.e.* , the percantage of elements in a RoI whose distance between two feature maps smaller than a threshold. We define the distance between ith entries of two feature maps as $|f_t^i - f_s^i|$, where f_t^i and f_s^i are the ith element of teacher and student feature maps. If this distance is smaller than a threshold (we set 0.3 in this paper), then these two entries match. We evaluate on the validation set of WIDER FACE. We compare the results between full-precision and quantized network. The horizontal axis represents bin of matching ratio, i.e. the percentage of matched entries in a RoI. Figure 5 demonstrates the results. The result shows that quantization operation can increase matching ratio of RoIs and promote feature maps matching process. Thus, quantization operation can help mimic learning.

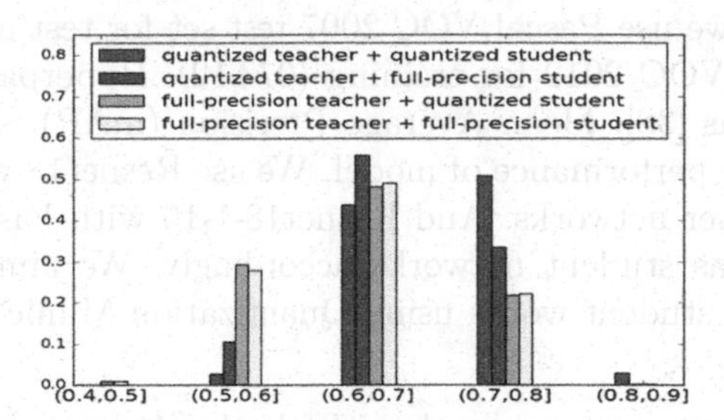

Fig. 5. Histogram of matching ratio. The plot suggests that using quantiation operation both on teacher and student networks can help student network's feature maps to better match teacher network's. The horizontal axis represents bin of matching ratio, *i.e.* the percentage of matched entries in a RoI. The vertical axis represents the frequency of RoIs within this bin.

Ablation Study on Quantization Method. Different quantization method will bring different effects. The quantization methods we use in our work is uniform quantization. Another popular quantization method is power of 2 quantization, constraining the output to be either zero or power of 2. Table 6 illustrates the comparison of uniform quantization and power of 2 quantization. Teacher networks using different quantization methods have similar performance. However, the student network using uniform quantization is much better than using power of 2 quantization. We think this is probably because that our mimic learning is based on RoIs and strong responses in these areas are more important. So we should describe large number more accurately. And for power of 2 quantization method, it describes small numbers (*e.g.* the number less than 1) accurately but roughly for large numbers. Thus, uniform quantization method is more reasonable and can bring better results.

Table 6. Uniform Quantization *vs.* Power of 2 Quantization: Using uniform quantization as quantization method can get better result than using power of 2 quantization.

Model	Quantization method	Easy	Medium	Hard
VGG-1-4 (teacher)	Power of 2	83.9	64.8	27.8
	Uniform(stride:1)	83.7	65.0	27.4
VGG-1-32 (student)	Power of 2	73.0	59.5	26.6
	Uniform(stride:1)	73.9	62.1	27.6

4.2 Experiments on Pascal VOC Dataset

We also carry out experiments on more complicated common object detection task. In this section we implement our approach on Resnet18 with Faster R-CNN detector for Pascal VOC object detection benchmark [42]. The experiments show that Quantization Mimic can extend to more complicated tasks.

Following [38], we use Pascal VOC 2007 test set for test and trainval images in VOC 2007 and VOC 2012 for training (07+12). Hyperparameters in Faster R-CNN are same as [38]. Mean Average Precision (mAP) is used as the criterion to evaluate the performance of model. We use Resnet18 with Faster R-CNN framework as teacher networks. And Resnet18-1-16 with Faster R-CNN framework are selected as student networks accordingly. We aim at improving the performance of the student works using Quantization Mimic method.

Main Results. First we compare the model using Quantization Mimic method with the model trained from scratch . Because of the poor learning ability of very tiny models, it is difficult to train them on complicated task, such as classification on Imagenet [43] and common object detections on Pascal VOC. Our method can improve a large margin of performance for very tiny networks on common object detections. Table 7 illustrates the results. We suggest that our method increase mAP 6.5 points for Resnet18-1-16 with Faster R-CNN framework. Relatively, we improve the performance for 16.0%. The experiments also show that Quantization Mimic is easy to implement and can be extended to different frameworks.

We also do experiments compared with other accelerating and compressing methods. Same as the experiments on WIDER FACE dataset, we compare our method with Li *et al.* [4], who only use mimic learning. In Table 8, our method outperforms than Li *et al.* [4]. Our results are 2.4 points higher than our backbone, Li *et al.* [4] on Resnet-1-16, which is a large margin.

Ablation Study on Mimic Loss Weight. We propose that very tiny networks can be sensitive to loss weight in multi-loss task. We do this experiment on Resnet18-1-16 to find a suitable mimic loss weight. In Table 9, we can see that the result of $\lambda = 1$ is much better than the result of $\lambda = 0.1$ and $\lambda = 10$. We suggest that if mimic loss is too small (*e.g.* $\lambda = 0.1$) , the effectiveness of

Table 7. The comparision between Resnet18-1-16 with Faster R-CNN detector finetuned on Imagenet dataset and using Quantization Mimic method. Our method can also bring huge improvement for very tiny networks on complicated common object tasks.

Model	Solution	mAP
Resnet18	Full-precision	72.9
	Quantized	73.3
Resnet18-1-16	Scratch	40.5
	Quantization Mimic	47.0

Table 8. Comparison with backbone on Resnet18-1-16 with Faster R-CNN framework. Our method outperforms our backbone Li *et al.* [4] methods for Resnet18 (higher is better).

Model	Solution	mAP
Resnet-1-16	Li *et al.* [4](only mimic)	44.6
	Quantization mimic	**47.0**

mimic learning will decline. However, if we set mimic loss weight too large (*e.g.* $\lambda = 10$), the very tiny network will mainly focus the gradient produced by mimic loss and ignore other gradients. And we call this phenomenon as 'gradient focus' phenomenon.

Table 9. Mimic Loss Weight λ: The results show that very tiny networks are sensitive to the mimic loss weight. Either too large or too small loss weight will decrease the effectiveness of mimic learning.

Model	Mimic loss weight	mAP
Resnet18-1-16	10	44.1
	1	**47.0**
	0.1	43.0

5 Conclusion

In this paper, we propose Quantization Mimic to improve the performance of very tiny CNNs. We show quantization operation on both teacher and student networks can promote feature map matching. It becomes easier for the student network to learn after quantization operation. The experiments on WIDER FACE and Pascal VOC dataset demonstrate that quantization mimic outperforms state-of-the-art methods. We hope our approach can facilitate future research on training very tiny CNNs for cutting-edge applications.

References

1. Courbariaux, M., Hubara, I., Soudry, D., El-Yaniv, R., Bengio, Y.: Binarized neural networks: training deep neural networks with weights and activations constrained to +1 or −1 (2016). arXiv preprint arXiv:1602.02830
2. Howard, A.G., et al.: Mobilenets: efficient convolutional neural networks for mobile vision applications (2017). arXiv preprint arXiv:1704.04861
3. He, Y., Zhang, X., Sun, J.: Channel pruning for accelerating very deep neural networks. In: Proceedings of the IEEE International Conference on Computer Vision (ICCV) (2017)
4. Li, Q., Jin, S., Yan, J.: Mimicking very efficient network for object detection. In: Proceedings of the IEEE Conference on Computer Vision and Pattern Recognition (CVPR) (2017)
5. Zeng, X.: Crafting GBD-Net for object detection. IEEE Trans. Pattern Anal. Mach. Intell. **40**, 2109–2123 (2017)
6. Liu, Y., Li, H., Yan, J., Wei, F., Wang, X., Tang, X.: Recurrent scale approximation for object detection in CNN. In: Proceedings of the IEEE International Conference on Computer Vision (ICCV) (2017)
7. Yan, J., Yu, Y., Zhu, X., Lei, Z., Li, S.Z.: Object detection by labeling superpixels. In: Proceedings of the IEEE Conference on Computer Vision and Pattern Recognition (CVPR) (2015)
8. Yan, J., Lei, Z., Wen, L., Li, S.Z.: The fastest deformable part model for object detection. In: Proceedings of the IEEE Conference on Computer Vision and Pattern Recognition (CVPR) (2014)
9. Ouyang, W., et al.: DeepID-Net: deformable deep convolutional neural networks for object detection. In: Proceedings of the IEEE Conference on Computer Vision and Pattern Recognition (CVPR) (2015)
10. Ouyang, W., Wang, K., Zhu, X., Wang, X.: Chained cascade network for object detection. In: Proceedings of the IEEE International Conference on Computer Vision (ICCV) (2017)
11. Wang, X., Han, T.X., Yan, S.: An HOG-LBP human detector with partial occlusion handling. In: Proceedings of the IEEE International Conference on Computer Vision (ICCV) (2009)
12. Lowe, D.G.: Distinctive image features from scale-invariant keypoints. Int. J. Comput. Vis. **60**(2), 91–110 (2004)
13. Girshick, R., Donahue, J., Darrell, T., Malik, J.: Rich feature hierarchies for accurate object detection and semantic segmentation. In: Proceedings of the IEEE Conference on Computer Vision and Pattern Recognition (CVPR) (2014)
14. He, K., Zhang, X., Ren, S., Sun, J.: Spatial pyramid pooling in deep convolutional networks for visual recognition. In: Fleet, D., Pajdla, T., Schiele, B., Tuytelaars, T. (eds.) ECCV 2014. LNCS, vol. 8691, pp. 346–361. Springer, Cham (2014). https://doi.org/10.1007/978-3-319-10578-9_23
15. Girshick, R.: Fast R-CNN. In: Proceedings of the IEEE International Conference on Computer Vision (ICCV)(2015)
16. Redmon, J., Divvala, S., Girshick, R., Farhadi, A.: You only look once: unified, real-time object detection. In: Proceedings of the IEEE Conference on Computer Vision and Pattern Recognition (CVPR) (2016)
17. Liu, W., et al.: SSD: single shot multibox detector. In: Leibe, B., Matas, J., Sebe, N., Welling, M. (eds.) ECCV 2016. LNCS, vol. 9905, pp. 21–37. Springer, Cham (2016). https://doi.org/10.1007/978-3-319-46448-0_2

18. Chollet, F.: Xception: deep learning with depthwise separable convolutions. In: Proceedings of the IEEE Conference on Computer Vision and Pattern Recognition (CVPR) (2017)
19. Zhang, T., Qi, G.J., Xiao, B., Wang, J.: Interleaved group convolutions for deep neural networks. In: Proceedings of the IEEE International Conference on Computer Vision (ICCV) (2017)
20. Zhang, X., Zhou, X., Lin, M., Sun, J.: ShuffleNet: An extremely efficient convolutional neural network for mobile devices (2017). arXiv preprint arXiv:1707.01083
21. Rastegari, M., Ordonez, V., Redmon, J., Farhadi, A.: XNOR-Net: ImageNet classification using binary convolutional neural networks. In: Leibe, B., Matas, J., Sebe, N., Welling, M. (eds.) ECCV 2016. LNCS, vol. 9908, pp. 525–542. Springer, Cham (2016). https://doi.org/10.1007/978-3-319-46493-0_32
22. Zhou, S., Wu, Y., Ni, Z., Zhou, X., Wen, H., Zou, Y.: DoReFa-net: Training low bitwidth convolutional neural networks with low bitwidth gradients. In: Proceedings of the IEEE Conference on Computer Vision and Pattern Recognition (CVPR) (2016)
23. Courbariaux, M., Bengio, Y., David, J.P.: BinaryConnect: training deep neural networks with binary weights during propagations. In: Advances in Neural Information Processing Systems (NIPS) (2015)
24. Juefei-Xu, F., Boddeti, V.N., Savvides, M.: Local binary convolutional neural networks. In: Proceedings of the IEEE Conference on Computer Vision and Pattern Recognition (CVPR) (2017)
25. Zhou, A., Yao, A., Guo, Y., Xu, L., Chen, Y.: Incremental network quantization: towards lossless CNNs with low-precision weights. In: International Conference of Learning Representation (ICLR) (2017)
26. Alvarez, J.M., Salzmann, M.: Learning the number of neurons in deep networks. In: Advances in Neural Information Processing Systems (NIPS) (2016)
27. Wen, W., Wu, C., Wang, Y., Chen, Y., Li, H.: Learning structured sparsity in deep neural networks. In: Advances in Neural Information Processing Systems (NIPS) (2016)
28. Anwar, S., Sung, W.: Compact deep convolutional neural networks with coarse pruning (2016). arXiv preprint arXiv:1610.09639
29. Li, H., Kadav, A., Durdanovic, I., Samet, H., Graf, H.P.: Pruning filters for efficient convnets. In: International Conference of Learning Representation (ICLR) (2017)
30. Molchanov, P., Tyree, S., Karras, T., Aila, T., Kautz, J.: Pruning convolutional neural networks for resource efficient inference. In: International Conference of Learning Representation (ICLR) (2017)
31. Guo, Y., Yao, A., Chen, Y.: Dynamic network surgery for efficient DNNs. In: Advances In Neural Information Processing Systems (NIPS) (2016)
32. Han, S., et al.: EIE: efficient inference engine on compressed deep neural network. In: Proceedings of the 43rd International Symposium on Computer Architecture (ISCA) (2016)
33. Han, S., Pool, J., Tran, J., Dally, W.: Learning both weights and connections for efficient neural network. In: Advances in Neural Information Processing Systems (NIPS) (2015)
34. Yang, T.J., Chen, Y.H., Sze, V.: Designing energy-efficient convolutional neural networks using energy-aware pruning. In: Proceedings of the IEEE Conference on Computer Vision and Pattern Recognition (CVPR) (2017)
35. Hinton, G., Vinyals, O., Dean, J.: Distilling the knowledge in a neural network (2015). arXiv preprint arXiv:1503.02531

36. Romero, A., Ballas, N., Kahou, S.E., Chassang, A., Gatta, C., Bengio, Y.: FitNets: hints for thin deep nets. In: International Conference of Learning Representation (ICLR) (2015)
37. Dai, J., Li, Y., He, K., Sun, J.: R-FCN: Object detection via region-based fully convolutional networks. In: Advances In Neural Information Processing Systems (NIPS) (2016)
38. Ren, S., He, K., Girshick, R., Sun, J.: Faster R-CNN: towards real-time object detection with region proposal networks. In: Advances in Neural Information Processing Systems (NIPS) (2015)
39. Jia, Y., et al. : Convolutional architecture for fast feature embedding. In: Proceedings of the 22nd ACM International Conference on Multimedia (ACMMM) (2014)
40. Shrivastava, A., Gupta, A., Girshick, R.: Training region-based object detectors with online hard example mining. In: Proceedings of the IEEE Conference on Computer Vision and Pattern Recognition (CVPR) (2016)
41. Yang, S., Luo, P., Loy, C.C., Tang, X.: Wider face: a face detection benchmark. In: Proceedings of the IEEE Conference on Computer Vision and Pattern Recognition (CVPR) (2016)
42. Everingham, M., Van Gool, L., Williams, C.K., Winn, J., Zisserman, A.: The Pascal visual object classes (VOC) challenge. Int. J. Comput. Vis. **88**(2), 303–338 (2010)
43. Deng, J., Dong, W., Socher, R., Li, L.J., Li, K., Fei-Fei, L.: ImageNet: a large-scale hierarchical image database. In: Proceedings of the IEEE Conference on Computer Vision and Pattern Recognition (CVPR) (2009)

Learning to Solve Nonlinear Least Squares for Monocular Stereo

Ronald Clark(✉), Michael Bloesch, Jan Czarnowski, Stefan Leutenegger, and Andrew J. Davison

Dyson Robotics Lab, Imperial College London, London SW7 2AZ, UK
{ronald.clark,michael.bloesch,jan.czarnowski,s.leutenegger, a.davison}@imperial.ac.uk
https://www.imperial.ac.uk/dyson-robotics-lab/projects/

Abstract. Sum-of-squares objective functions are very popular in computer vision algorithms. However, these objective functions are not always easy to optimize. The underlying assumptions made by solvers are often not satisfied and many problems are inherently ill-posed. In this paper, we propose a neural nonlinear least squares optimization algorithm which learns to effectively optimize these cost functions even in the presence of adversities. Unlike traditional approaches, the proposed solver requires no hand-crafted regularizers or priors as these are implicitly learned from the data. We apply our method to the problem of motion stereo ie. jointly estimating the motion and scene geometry from pairs of images of a monocular sequence. We show that our learned optimizer is able to efficiently and effectively solve this challenging optimization problem.

Keywords: Optimization · SLAM · Least squares · Gauss-Newton Levenberg-Marquadt

1 Introduction

Most algorithms in computer vision use some form of optimization to obtain a solution that best satisfies some objective function for the problem at hand. The optimization method itself can be seen as simply an intelligent means of searching the solution space for the answer, possibly exploiting the specific structure of the objective function to guide the search.

One particularly interesting form of objective function is one that is composed of a sum of many squared residual terms.

$$E = \frac{1}{2} \sum_j r_j^2(\mathbf{x}) \tag{1}$$

where r_j is the j-th residual term and E is the optimization objective.

In most cases the residual terms are a nonlinear function of the optimization variables and problems with this type of objective function are called nonlinear

V. Ferrari et al. (Eds.): ECCV 2018, LNCS 11212, pp. 291–306, 2018.
https://doi.org/10.1007/978-3-030-01237-3_18

least square (NLLS) problems (NLSPs). NLSPs can be efficiently solved using second-order methods [12].

However, the success in finding a good solution also depends on the characteristics of the problem itself. The set of residual functions can be likened to a system of equations with their solution at zero, $r_j(\mathbf{x}) = 0$. If the number of variables in this system is larger than the number of equations then the system is under determined, if they are equal then it is well-determined and if there are more equations than variables then it is overdetermined. Well-posed problems need to satisfy three conditions: (1) a solution must exist (2) there must be a unique solution and (3) the solution must be continuous as a function of its parameters [19].

Undetermined problems are ill-posed as they have infinitely many solutions and therefore no unique solution exists. To cope with this, traditional optimizers use hand-crafted regularizers and priors to make the ill-posed problem well-posed.

In this paper we aim to utilize strong and well-developed ideas from traditional nonlinear least squares solvers and integrate these with the promising new learning-based approaches. In doing so, we seek to capitalize on the ability of neural network-based methods to learn robust data-driven priors, and a traditional optimization-based approach to obtain refined solutions of high-precision. In particular, we propose to learn how to compute the update based on the current residual and Jacobian (and some extra parameters) to make the NLLS optimization algorithm more efficient and more robust to high noise.

We apply our optimizer to the problem of estimating the pose and depths of pairs of frames from a monocular image sequence known as monocular stereo as illustrated in Fig. 1.

To summarise, the contributions of our paper are the following:

1. We propose an end-to-end trainable optimization method that builds upon the powerful approximate Hessian-based optimization approaches to NLLS problems.
2. The implicit learning of priors and regularizers for least squares problems directly from data.
3. The first approach to use a learned optimizer for efficiently minimizing photometric residuals for monocular stereo reconstruction.

Compared to existing learning-based approaches, our method is designed to produce predictions that are accurate and photometrically consistent.

The rest of the paper is structured as follows. First we outline related work on dense reconstruction using traditional and learning-based approaches. We then visit some preliminaries such as the structure of traditional Gauss-Newton optimizers for nonlinear least square problems. We then introduce our proposed system and finally carry out an evaluation of our method in terms of structure and motion accuracy on a number of sequences from publicly available datasets.

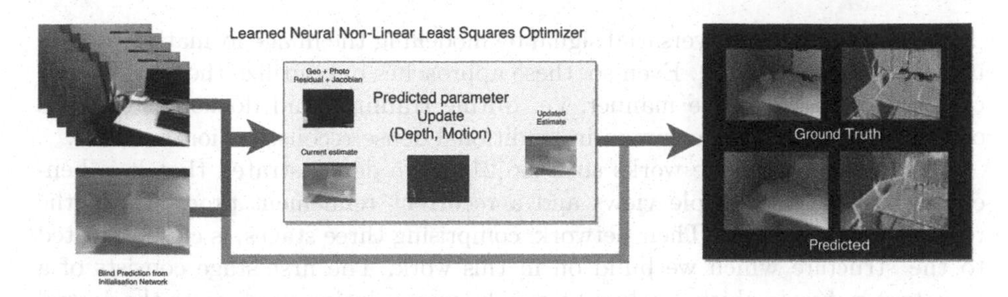

Fig. 1. Overview of our system for jointly optimizing a nonlinear least squares objective

2 Related Work

Optimization for SLAM. In visual SLAM we are faced with the problem of estimating both the geometry of the scene and the motion of the camera. This is most often formulated as an optimization over the pixel depths and transformation parameters between pairs of frames. The cost function comprises some form of reprojection error which may be formulated either in terms of geometric or photometric residuals. Geometric residuals require the correspondence of points to be known and thus are only feasible for sparse reconstructions. Photometric residuals are formulated in terms of intensity differences and can be computed across the entire image. However, this photometric optimization is difficult as the photometric residuals have high noise levels and various strategies have been proposed to cope with this. In DTAM [15], for example, this is accomplished by formulating a cost volume and integrating the residuals from multiple frames before performing the optimization. Even then, the residuals need to be combined with a TV-L1 regularization term to ensure noise does not dominate the reconstruction. Other approaches, such as LSD-SLAM [9], operate only on high-gradient pixels where the signal-to-noise ratio of the photometric residual is high. Even so, none of these systems are able to estimate the geometry and motion in a single joint optimization. Rather, they resort to an approach which swithches between independently optimizing the motion parameters and then the depths in an alternating fashion. CodeSLAM [2] overcomes this problem by using an autoencoder to compress the scene geometry into a small optimizable code, allowing for the joint optimization of both the geometry and motion.

Learning for Monocular Stereo. There has been much interest recently in using end-to-end learning to estimate the motion of a camera [5,6,22] and reconstruct scenes from monocular images [8]. Most of these [8,23] are based on feed-forward inference networks. The training signal for these networks can be obtained in many ways. The first approaches were based on a fully-supervised learning signal where labelled depth and pose information were used. Subsequent works have shown that the networks can be learned in a self-supervised manner using a learning signal derived, for example, from photometric error of pixel-wise reprojection [23], from the consistency of rays projected into a common volume

[20] or even using an adversarial signal by modelling the image formation process in a GAN framework [4]. Even so, these approaches only utilize the photometric consistency in an offline manner, i.e. during training, and do not attempt to optimize it online as is common in traditional dense reconstruction methods.

To this extent, some works such as [21], have demonstrated that it is beneficial to include multiple views and a recurrent refinement procedure in the reconstruction process. Their network, comprising three stages, is closely related to the structure which we build on in this work. The first stage consists of a *bootstrap network* which produces a rough low-resolution prediction; the second stage consists of an *iterative network* which iteratively refines the bootstrap prediction; and finally a *refinement network* which computes a refined and upscaled depth map.

In this paper, we adopt the same structure but formalize the iterative network as an optimization designed to enforce multiview photometric consistency where the bootstrap network acts as an initialization of the optimization and the refinement acts as an upscaling. In essence, our reconstruction is based on an optimization procedure that is itself optimized using data. This is commonly referred to in the machine-learning literature as a *meta-learned optimizer.*

Meta-learning and Learning to Optimize. A popular and very promising avenue of research which has been receiving increasing attention is that of meta-learned optimizers. Such approaches have shown great utility in performing few-shot learning without overfitting [17], for optimizing GANS which are traditionally very difficult to train [14], for optimizing general black box functions [3] and even for solving difficult combinatorial problems [7]. Perhaps the most important advantage is to learn data-driven regularization as demonstrated in [16] where the authors use a partially learned optimization approach for solving ill-posed inverse problems. In [13], the authors train through a multi-step inverse compositional Lukas Kanade algorithm for aligning 2D images. In our method, we utilize a learned multi-step optimization model by using a recurrent network to compute the update steps for the optimization variables. While most approaches that attempt to learn optimization updates, such as [3], have only used knowledge about the objective and first-order gradient information, we exploit the least-square structure of our problem and forward the full Jacobian matrix to provide the network with richer information. Our approach is – to the best of our knowledge – the first to use second-order approximations of the objective to learn optimization updates.

3 Preliminaries

3.1 Nonlinear Least Squares Solvers

Many optimization problems have an objective that takes the form of a sum of squared residual terms, $E = \frac{1}{2}\sum_j r_j^2(\mathbf{x})$ where r_j is the j-th residual term and E is the optimization objective. As such, much research has been devoted to finding efficient solvers for problems of this form. Two of the most successful and widely used approaches are the Gauss-Newton (GN) and Levenberg-Marquadt (LM) methods. Both of these are second-order, iterative optimization methods. However, instead of computing the true Hessian, they exploit the least-squares structure of the objective to compute an approximate Hessian that is used in the updates. Given an initial estimate of the variables, $\mathbf{x}_0$, these approaches compute updates to the optimization variable in the attempt to find a better solution, $\mathbf{x}_i$, at each step i. The incremental update, $\Delta\mathbf{x}_i$ is computed by solving a linear least squares problem which is formed by linearising the residual at the current estimate $\mathbf{r}(\mathbf{x}_i + \Delta\mathbf{x}_i) \approx \mathbf{r}_i + \mathbf{J}_i\Delta\mathbf{x}_i$ [12], with the abbreviations:

$$\mathbf{r}_i = \mathbf{r}(\mathbf{x}_i), \quad \mathbf{J}_i = \left.\frac{d\mathbf{r}}{d\mathbf{x}}\right|_{\mathbf{x}=\mathbf{x}_i}. \tag{2}$$

Using the linearized residual, the optimal update can be found as the solution to the quadratic problem [12]

$$\Delta\mathbf{x}_i = \arg\min_{\Delta\mathbf{x}_i} \frac{1}{2}||\mathbf{r}_i + \mathbf{J}_i\Delta\mathbf{x}_i||^2. \tag{3}$$

The well known Normal equations to this can be computed analytically by differentiating the problem and equating to zero. The update step used in GN is then given by solving:

$$\mathbf{J}_i^T\mathbf{J}_i\Delta\mathbf{x}_i = -\mathbf{J}_i^T\mathbf{r}_i \tag{4}$$

By comparing this to Newton's method which requires the computation of the true Hessian $\mathbf{H}(\mathbf{x}_i)$ for finding updates [10], we see that the GN method effectively approximates $\mathbf{H}(\mathbf{x}_i)$ using $\mathbf{J}_i^T\mathbf{J}_i$, which is usually more efficient to compute. LM extends GN by adding a damping factor λ to the update $\Delta\mathbf{x}_i = -(\mathbf{J}_i^T\mathbf{J}_i + \lambda\,\mathrm{diag}(\mathbf{J}_i^T\mathbf{J}_i))^{-1}\mathbf{J}_i^T\mathbf{r}_i$ to better condition the updates and make the optimization more robust [10].

In our proposed approach, we build on the GN method by not restricting the updates to be a static function of $\mathbf{J}_i$. Compared to LM which adaptively sets a single parameter, λ, we compute the entire update step by using a neural network which has as its input the full Jacobian $\mathbf{J}_i$. The details of this are described in Sect. 4.2.

3.2 Warping and Photometric Cost Function

The warping function we use for the least squares cost function is similar to the loss used in the unsupervised training in [23]. The warping is based on a spatial transformer which first transforms the coordinates of points in the target view to points in the source view and then samples the source view. The 4×4 transformation matrix, $\hat{T}_{t\rightarrow s}$ is obtained by applying an exponential map to the output of the network, i.e. $\hat{T}_{t\rightarrow s} = \exp(\mathbf{p}^{\times})$ where $\mathbf{p}$ (bold face) is the relative pose represented as a six-vector and p_s (non-bold face) is the pixel location in the source image and p_t (non-bold face) is a pixel location in the target image (consistent with the notation in the paper)

$$p_s \sim K\hat{T}_{t\rightarrow s}\hat{D}_t(p_t)K^{-1}p_t \tag{5}$$

Using these warped coordinates, a synthesized image $\hat{I}_s(p)$ is obtained through bilinear sampling of the the source view at the locations p_s computed in Eq. 5. The least squares loss function from which we derive $\mathbf{J}$ is then,

$$L = \sum_p ||I_t(p) - \hat{I}_s(p)||_2, \tag{6}$$

where I_t and I_s are the source and target intensity images and the residual corresponding to each pixel is $\mathbf{r}_p = I_t(p) - \hat{I}_s(p)$. The elements of the Jcaobian of the warping function, $\mathbf{J}$, can be easily computed using autodiff (in Tensorflow simply `tf.gradients(res[i],x))` for each residual. However, to speed up our implementation we analytically compute the elements of the Jacobian in our computation graph.

4 Model

The model is built around the optimization of the photometric consistency of the depth and motion predictions for a short sequence of input images. Each sequence of images has a single "target" keyframe (which we choose as the first frame) for which we optimize the depth values. In all cases, we operate on inverse depths, $z = \frac{1}{d}$ for better handling of large depths values. Our model additionally seeks to optimize for the relative transformations between each source frame s in the sequence and the target keyframe t, $\mathbf{p}_{t \to s}$. The full model consists of three stages. All iterative optimization procedures require an initial starting point and thus the initialization stage serves the purpose of predicting a good initial estimate. The optimization stage consists of a learned optimizer which benefits from explicitly computed residuals and Jacobians. To make the optimization computationally tractable, the optimization network operates on a down-sampled version of the input and exploits the sparsity of the problem. The final stage of the network upsamples the prediction to the original resolution. The networks (including those of the optimizer) are trained using a supervised loss. We now describe each of the three network components in detail.

Algorithm 1. Neuro-Adaptive Nonlinear Least Squares

Require: Residual function $\mathbf{r}(\mathbf{x})$, image sequence $\mathbf{I}_1, \mathbf{I}_2, \ldots$
  $\mathbf{x}_0 \leftarrow f_{\theta_0}(\mathbf{I}_1, \mathbf{I}_2, \ldots)$
  for $i = 0, 1, \ldots N-1$ **do**
    $\Delta\mathbf{x}_i, \mathbf{h}_{i+1} \leftarrow f_\theta(\Phi(\mathbf{J}_i, \mathbf{r}_i), \mathbf{h}_i)$
    if $||\Delta\mathbf{x}_i|| < \epsilon$ **then**
      return $\mathbf{x}_i$
    end if
    $\mathbf{x}_{i+1} \leftarrow \mathbf{x}_i + \Delta\mathbf{x}_i$
  end for

4.1 Initialization Network

The purpose of the initialization network is to predict a suitable starting point for the optimization stage. We provide the initialization network with both RGB images and thereby allow it to leverage stereopsis. The architecture of this stage is a simple convolutional network. For this stage we use 3 convolutions with stride 2, one convolution with stride 1 and one upsamplings + convolutional layers. This results in the output of the network being downscaled by a factor of 4 for feeding into the optimization stage. The network also produces an initial pose using a fully connected layer branched from the central layers of the network. Thus the output of the initialization stage consists of an initial depth image and pose.

4.2 Neuro-Adaptive Nonlinear Least Squares

The learnt optimization procedure is outlined in Algorithm 1. The optimization network attempts to optimize the photometric objective $E(\mathbf{x})$ where $\mathbf{x} = (\mathbf{z}, \mathbf{p})$ are the optimization variables (inverse depths $\mathbf{z}$ and pose $\mathbf{p}$). The objective $E(\mathbf{x})$ is a nonlinear least squares expression defined in terms of the photometric residual vector $\mathbf{r}(\mathbf{x})$

$$E(\mathbf{x}) = \frac{1}{2}||\mathbf{r}(\mathbf{x})||^2. \tag{7}$$

The updates of the parameters to be optimized, $\mathbf{x}$, follow a standard iterative optimization scheme, i.e.

$$\mathbf{x}_{i+1} = \mathbf{x}_i + \Delta\mathbf{x}_i. \tag{8}$$

In our case, the updates $\Delta\mathbf{x}_i$ are predicted using a Long Short Term Memory Recurrent Neural Network (LSTM-RNN) [11]. In order to compute the Jacobian we use automatic differentiation available in the Tensorflow library [1]. Using the automatic differentiation operation, we add operations to the Tensorflow computation graph [1] which compute the Jacobian of our residual vector with respect to the dense depth and motion. As the structure of the Jacobian often exhibits problem specific properties, we apply a transformation to the Jacobian, $\Phi(\mathbf{J}_i, \mathbf{r}_i)$ before feeding this Jacobian into our network. The operation Φ may involve element-wise matrix operations such as gather or other operations which simplify the Jacobian input. The operations we use for the problems addressed in this paper are detailed in Sect. 4.3.

To allow for the computation of parameter updates which are not restricted to those derived from the approximate Hessian, we turn to the powerful function approximation ability of the LSTM-RNN [11] to learn the final parameter update operation from data. As the number of coordinates are likely to be very large for most optimization problems, [3] propose to use one LSTM-RNN for each coordinate. For our problem, we have Jacobians with high spatial correlations and thus we replace the coordinate-wise LSTM with a convolutional LSTM. The per-iteration updates, $\Delta\mathbf{x}_i$ are predicted by a network which in this case is an LSTM-RNN,

$$\begin{bmatrix} \Delta x_i \\ h_{i+1} \end{bmatrix} = \mathrm{LSTM}_{cell}\left(\Phi(\mathbf{J}_i, \mathbf{r}_i), h_i, \mathbf{x}_i; \theta\right), \tag{9}$$

where θ are the parameters of the networks and LSTM_{cell} is a standard LSTM cell update function with hidden layer h_i.

4.3 The Jacobian Input Structure

Each type of least squares cost function gives rise to a special Jacobian structure. The input function, $\Phi(\mathbf{J}, \mathbf{r})$, to our network serves two purposes; one functional and the other structural. Firstly, Φ serves to compute the *approximate Hessian* as is done with the classical Gauss-Newton optimization method:

$$\Phi(\mathbf{J}, \mathbf{r}) = [\mathbf{J}^{\mathbf{T}}\mathbf{J}, \mathbf{r}]. \tag{10}$$

The structure of $\Phi(\mathbf{J}, \mathbf{r})$ is shown in Fig. 2. We note that we choose not to compute the full $(\mathbf{J}^T\mathbf{J})^{-1}\mathbf{J}$ as this adds additional computational complexity to the operation which is repeated many times during training. We also compress the sparse $\mathbf{J}^T\mathbf{J}$ into a compact form as illustrated in Fig. 2. The output of this restructuring yields the same image shape as the image. The compressed structure allows efficient processing of the matrix.

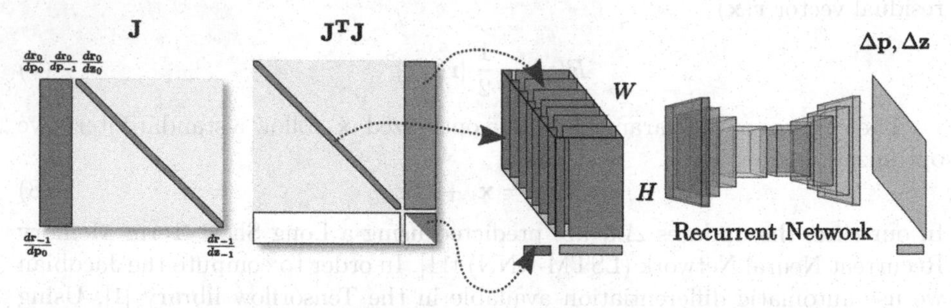

Fig. 2. The block-sparsity structure of $\mathbf{J}$ and $\mathbf{J}^T\mathbf{J}$ for the depth and egomotion estimation problem.

4.4 Upscaling Network

As the optimization network operates on low-resolution predictions, an upscaling network is used to produce outputs of the desired size. The upscaling network consists of a series of bilinear upsampling layers concatenated with convolutions and acts as a super-resolution network. The input to the upscaling network consists of the low-resolution depth prediction and the RGB image.

5 Loss Function

In this section we describe the loss function which we use to train the network weights of all three stages of our model.

The current state-of-the-art depth and motion prediction networks still rely on labelled images to provide a strong learning signal. We include a loss term based on labelled ground truth inverse depth images $\tilde{\mathbf{z}}$,

$$L_{depth}(\mathbf{x}) = \frac{1}{wh} \|\mathbf{z} - \tilde{\mathbf{z}}\|_1 \tag{11}$$

with image width w and height h, and where $\mathbf{z}$ is the predicted inverse depth image.

We also use a loss term based on the relative pose between the source (s) and target (t) frame, $\tilde{\mathbf{p}} = (\tilde{\mathbf{t}}_{t\to s}, \tilde{\boldsymbol{\alpha}}_{t\to s})$ with translation $\tilde{\mathbf{t}}_{t\to s}$ and rotation vector $\tilde{\boldsymbol{\alpha}}_{t\to s}$ from ground-truth data,

$$L_{pose}(\mathbf{x}) = \sum_s \|\boldsymbol{\alpha}_{t\to s} - \tilde{\boldsymbol{\alpha}}_{t\to s}\|_1 + \|\mathbf{t}_{t\to s} - \tilde{\mathbf{t}}_{t\to s}\|_1 \tag{12}$$

Note that this loss function need not be a sum of squares and can be computed using any other form using eg. L1 etc. The final loss function consists of a weighted combination of the individual loss terms:

$$L_{tot}(\theta) = \sum_i w_{pose} L_{pose}(\mathbf{x}_i(\theta)) + w_{depth} L_{depth}(\mathbf{x}_i(\theta)). \tag{13}$$

Note that our objective here includes the ground-truth inverse depth which we do not have access to when computing the residuals $\mathbf{r}$ (and then the Jacobian $\mathbf{J}$) in the recurrent optimization network in Sect. 4.2.

The optimization network is never directly privy to the ground truth depth and poses, it only benefits from these by what is learned in the network parameters during training. In this manner, we have a system which is trained offline to best minimize our objective online. During the offline training phase, our system learns robust priors for the optimization by using the large amounts of labelled data. During the online phase our system optimizes for photometric consistency only but is able to utilize the knowledge it has learned during the offline training to better condition the optimization process.

6 Training

During the training, we unroll our iterative optimization network for a set number of steps and backpropogate the loss through the network weights, θ. In order to find the parameters of the optimizer network, the meta-loss, $L_{tot}(\theta)$, is minimized using the ADAM optimizer where the total meta-loss is computed as the loss summed over the N iterations of the learned optimization (see Eq. 13). For each step i in the optimization process we update the state $\mathbf{x}_i$ of the optimization network according to Eq. 8.

As our loss depends on variables which are updated recurrently over a number of timesteps, we use backpropogation through time to train the network. Backpropogation through time unrolls each step and updates the parameters by computing the gradients through the unrolled network. In our experiments we unroll our optimization for 15 steps.

We find that training the whole network at once is difficult and thus train the initialization network first before adding the optimization stage.

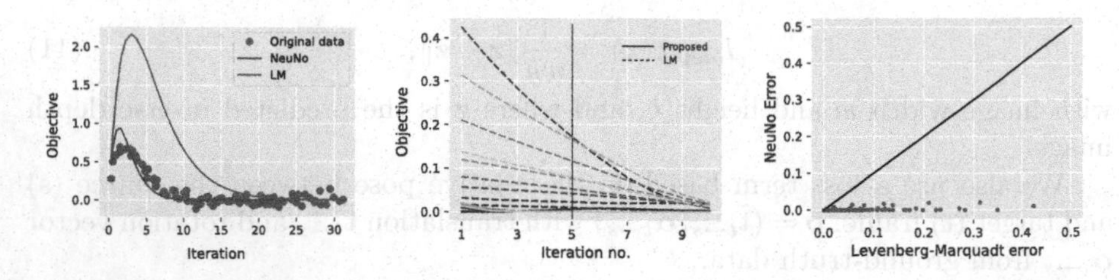

Fig. 3. Comparison between our method and standard least squares for fitting parametric functions to noisy data with a least-squares objective. In (a) the fitted functions limited to 5 iterations is shown, in (b) the error as a function of iteration no. is shown for 10 test functions and in (c) the LM error is plotted against the error of the proposed method for all iterations.

7 Evaluation

In this section we evaluate the proposed method on both synthetic and real datasets. We aim to determine the efficiency of our approach i.e. how quickly it converges to an optimum and how it compares to a network which does not explicitly incorporate the problem structure in its iterations.

7.1 Synthetic Data Experiments

In this section we evaluate the performance of our proposed method on a number of least squares curve fitting problems. We experiment on curves parameterized by two variables, $\mathbf{x} = (a, b)$. We chose a set of four functions to use for our experiment as follows

$$y = x\exp(at) + x\exp(bt) + \epsilon, \tag{14}$$

$$y = \sin(at + b) + \epsilon, \tag{15}$$

$$y = \text{sinc}(at + b) + \epsilon, \tag{16}$$

$$y = \mathcal{N}(t|\mu = a, \sigma = b) \text{ (fitting a Gaussian)} \tag{17}$$

For these experiments we generate the data by randomly sampling one of four parametric functions (Eqs. 14, 15, 16 and 17) as well as the two parameters a and b. For the training data we add noise $\epsilon \sim \mathcal{N}(0, 0.1)$ to the true function values. In Fig. 3 we show the results on a test set of sampled functions. Figure 3(a) shows the fitted function after 5 iterations (of a total of 15 iterations) for our method and standard LM. The learned approach clearly outperforms LM in terms of speed of convergence. In Fig. 3(b) we see the learned errors vs LM for all steps in the optimization, where again, the learned method clearly outperforms LM.

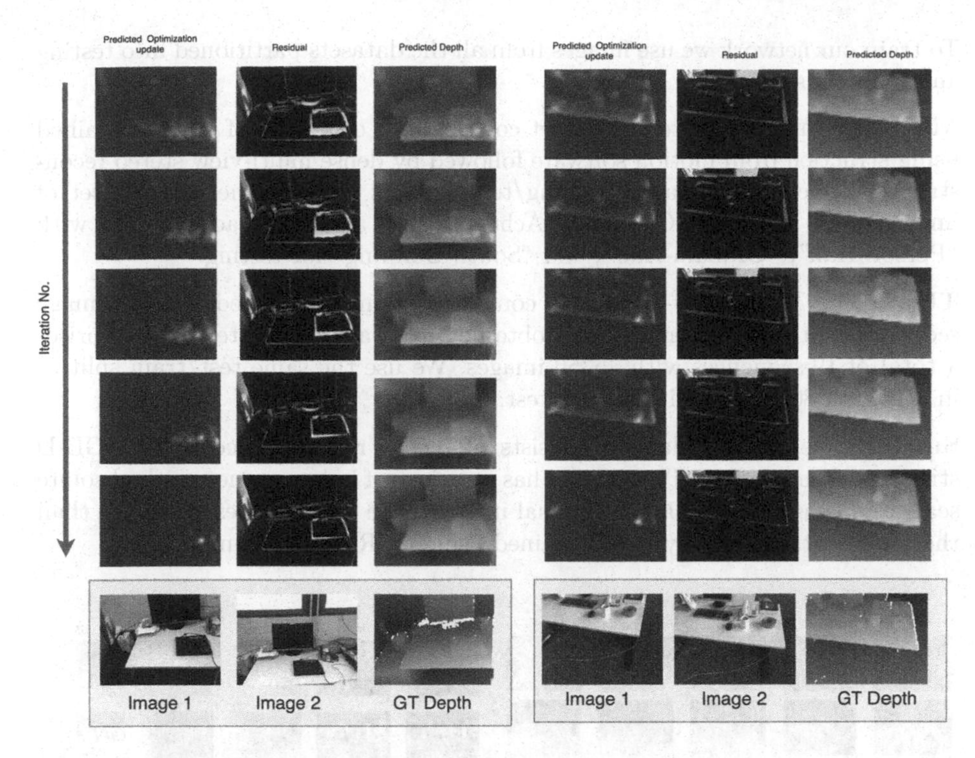

Fig. 4. Qualitative results on two challenging indoor scenes using only two frames. The figure shows the last 5 iterations of 15 of the optimization network. Even with this wide baseline, and only two frames, our method is able to optimize the photometric error reliably.

7.2 Real-World Test: Depth and Pose Estimation

In this section we test the ability of our proposed method on estimating the depth and egomotion of a moving camera. To provide a fair evaluation of the proposed approach, we use the same evaluation procedure as in [21] and report the same baselines, where oracle uses MVS with known poses, *SIFT* uses sparse-feature for correspondences, *FF* uses optical flow, *Matlab* uses the KLT tracker in Matlab as the basis of a bundle-adjusted reconstruction.

7.3 Metrics

We evaluate the performance of our approach on the depth as well as the motion prediction performance. For depth prediction we use the absolute, scale-invariant and relative performance metrics.

7.4 Datasets

The datasets which we use to evaluate the network consist of both indoor and outdoor scenes. For all the datasets, the camera undergoes free 6-DoF motion.

To train our network we use images from all the datasets partitioned into testing and training sets.

MVS. The multiview stereo dataset consists of a collection of scenes obtained using struction from motion software followed by dense multi-view stereo reconstruction. We use the same training/test split as in [21]. The training set of images used included "Citywall", "Achteckturm" and "Breisach" scenes with "Person-Hall", "Graham-Hall", and "South-Building" for testing.

TUM. The TUM RGB-D dataset consists of Kinect-captured RGB-D image sequences with ground truth poses obtained from a Vicon system. It comprises a total of 19 sequences with 45356 images. We use the same test/train split as in [21] with 80 held-out images for test.

Sun3D. The SUN3D dataset consists of scenes reconstructed using RGB-D structure-from-motion. The dataset has a variety of indoor scenes, with absolute scale and consists of 10,000 individual images. The poses are less accurate than the TUM dataset as they were obtained using an RGB-D reconstruction.

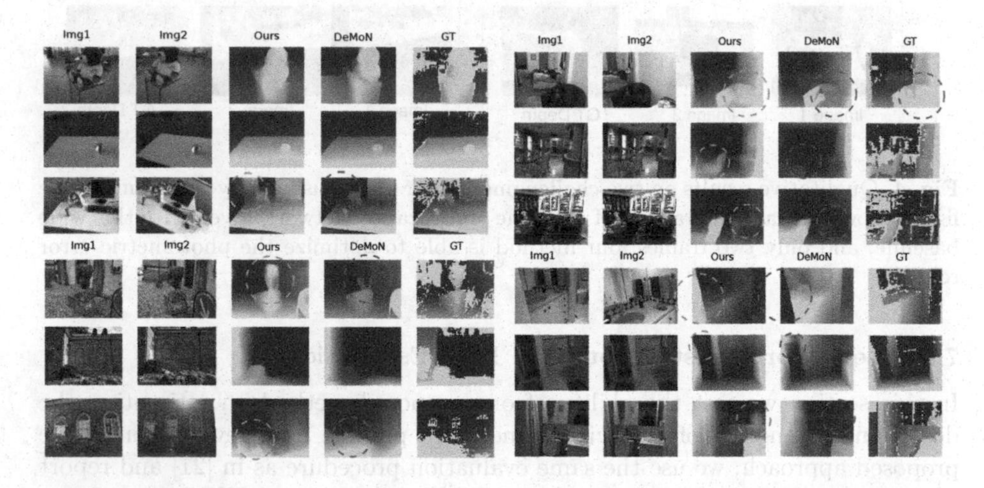

Fig. 5. Qualitative results on the NYU dataset. Compared to DeMoN our network has fewer "hallucinations" of structures which do not exist in the scene.

A qualitative evaluation of our method compared to standard multiview stereo and DeMoN [21] is shown in Fig. 5. Our method produces depth maps with sharper structures compared to DeMoN, even with a lower output resolution. Compared to COLMAP [18] our reconstruction is more dense and does not include as many outlier pixels. Numerical results on the testing data-sets are shown in Table 1. As is evident from the Table, our learned optimization approach outperforms most of the traditional baseline approaches, and performs better or on par with DeMoN on most cases. This may be due to our architectural choice as we do not include any alternating flow and depth predictions.

Table 1. Quantitative results on the evaluation datasets. Green highlights the best performing method for a particular task.

		Depth			Motion	
	Method	L1-inv	sc-inv	L1-rel	Rotation	Translation
MVS	MVS	0.019	0.197	0.105	0	0
	SIFT	0.056	0.309	0.361	21.180	60.516
	FF	0.055	0.308	0.322	4.834	17.252
	Matlab	-	-	-	10.843	32.736
	DeMoN	0.047	0.202	0.305	5.156	14.447
	Proposed	0.051	0.221	0.311	4.653	11.221
Scenes11	Oracle	0.023	0.618	0.349	0	0
	SIFT	0.051	0.900	1.027	6.179	56.650
	FF	0.038	0.793	0.776	1.309	19.425
	Matlab	-	-	-	0.917	14.639
	DeMoN	0.019	0.315	0.248	0.809	8.918
	Proposed	0.010	0.410	0.210	0.910	8.21
RGB-D	Oracle	0.026	0.398	0.336	0	0
	SIFT	0.050	0.577	0.703	12.010	56.021
	FF	0.045	0.548	0.613	4.709	46.058
	Matlab	-	-	-	12.831	49.612
	DeMoN	0.028	0.130	0.212	2.641	20.585
	Proposed	0.019	0.09	0.301	1.01	22.1
Sun3D	oracle	0.020	0.241	0.220	0	0
	SIFT	0.029	0.290	0.286	7.702	41.825
	FF	0.029	0.284	0.297	3.681	33.301
	Matlab	-	-	-	5.920	32.298
	DeMoN	0.019	0.114	0.172	1.801	18.811
	Proposed	0.015	0.189	0.650	1.521	14.347

8 Discussion

Table 2. Summary of the performance of our Neuro-Adaptive optimisation compared to standard LM. Table indicates the best performing method for criteria.

	Problem Size		
	Small	Medium	Large
Accuracy	Ours	Ours	Ours
Memory	Tie	Ours	Ours
Speed	Tie	Ours	Ours

In the context of optimisation, our network-based updates accomplish something which a classical optimisation approach cannot in that it is able to reliably optimise a large under-determined system with implicitly learned priors. For a large under-determined problem like in the depth and motion case, standard Levenberg-Marquadt (LM) fails to improve the objective and the required sparse matrix inversion for a $J^T J$ with $\approx 91K$ non-zero elements (128×96 size image) takes 532 ms, compared to our network forward pass which takes 25 ms. For small, overdetermined problems LM does work and for this reason, in Sect. 7.1, we have compared our approach to LM on a small curve fitting problem and found that our approach significantly outperforms it in terms of accuracy and convergence rate. For the small problem, the matrix inversion in the standard approach (LM) is very quick but we are also able to use a smaller network so our time per-iteration is tie with LM. This is summarised in Table 2.

8.1 Ablation Study

We conduct an experiment to verify the efficacy of the learned optimization procedure. The first part of our ablation study considers the effect of increasing the number of optimization iterations. These results are shown in Table 3 and a qualitative overview of the operation of our network is shown in Fig. 4 which visualizes the learned optimization process. The second part of our ablation study evaluates the efficacy of the learned optimizer compared to DeMoN's iterative network. This is show in Fig. 6.

8.2 Number of Parameters and Inference Speed

An advantage of our approach is its parameter efficiency. Compared to DeMoN, our model has significantly fewer parameters. The DeMoN network contains 45,753,883 wheres ours has only 11,438,470 – making it over 3× more parameter efficient. Ours also has an advantage in terms of inference speed, as although

Table 3. Results of the ablation study to evaluate the performance of the optimization iterations.

	Method	Depth			Motion	
		L1-inv	sc-inv	L1-rel	Rotation	Translation
RGB-D	Initialization	0.260	0.360	0.315	2.290	27.40
	Opt (5 steps)	0.220	0.15	0.308	2.11	25.63
	Opt (10 steps)	0.21	0.12	0.310	1.23	24.91
	Opt (15 steps)	0.019	0.09	0.301	1.01	22.14

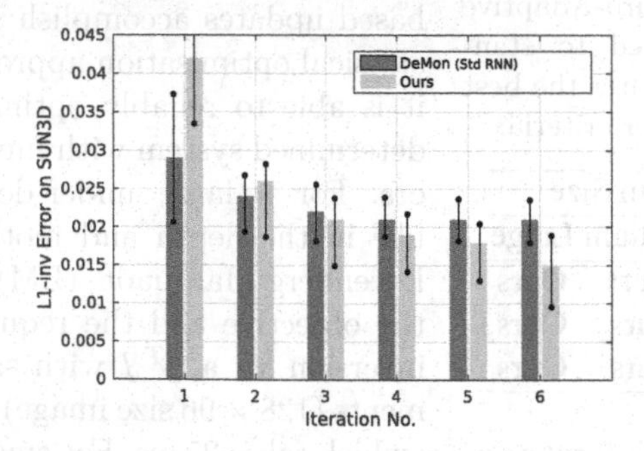

Fig. 6. Comparison between our learned optimizer and the (larger) RNN refinement network from DeMon.

we have to compute the large Jacobian, it still runs around 1.5× faster during inference compared to DeMoN.

9 Conclusion

In this paper we have presented an approach for robustly solving nonlinear least squares optimization problems by integrating deep neural models with traditional knowledge of the optimization structure. Our method is based on a novel neuro-adaptive nonlinear least squares optimizer which is trained to robustly optimize the residuals. Although it is generally applicable to any least squares problem, we have demonstrated the proposed method on the real-world problem of computing depth and egomotion for frames of a monocular video sequence. Our method can cope with images captured from a wide baseline. In future work we plan to investigate means of increasing the number of residuals that are optimized and thereby achieve an even more detailed prediction. We also plan to further study the interplay between the recurrent neural network and optimization structure and want to investigate the use of predicted confidence estimates in the learned optimization.

References

1. Abadi, M., et al.: Tensorflow: large-scale machine learning on heterogeneous distributed systems. arXiv preprint arXiv:1603.04467 (2016)
2. Bloesch, M., Czarnowski, J., Clark, R., Leutenegger, S., Davison, A.J.: CodeSLAM—learning a compact, optimisable representation for dense visual SLAM. In: Proceedings of the IEEE Conference on Computer Vision and Pattern Recognition (CVPR) (2018)
3. Chen, Y., et al.: Learning to learn without gradient descent by gradient descent. In: Proceedings of the 34th International Conference on Machine Learning, vol. 70, pp. 748–756. PMLR, 06–11 August 2017
4. Choy, C.B., Xu, D., Gwak, J.Y., Chen, K., Savarese, S.: 3D-R2N2: a unified approach for single and multi-view 3D object reconstruction. In: Leibe, B., Matas, J., Sebe, N., Welling, M. (eds.) ECCV 2016. LNCS, vol. 9912, pp. 628–644. Springer, Cham (2016). https://doi.org/10.1007/978-3-319-46484-8_38
5. Clark, R., Wang, S., Wen, H., Markham, A., Trigoni, N.: VidLoc: a deep spatio-temporal model for 6-DoF video-clip relocalization. In: Proceedings of the IEEE Conference on Computer Vision and Pattern Recognition (CVPR) (2017)
6. Clark, R., Wang, S., Wen, H., Markham, A., Trigoni, N.: VINet: visual-inertial odometry as a sequence-to-sequence learning problem. In: Proceedings of the National Conference on Artificial Intelligence (AAAI) (2017)
7. Dai, H., Khalil, E.B., Zhang, Y., Dilkina, B., Song, L.: Learning combinatorial optimization algorithms over graphs. arXiv preprint arXiv:1704.01665 (2017)
8. Eigen, D., Fergus, R.: Predicting depth, surface normals and semantic labels with a common multi-scale convolutional architecture. In: Proceedings of the International Conference on Computer Vision (ICCV) (2015)

9. Engel, J., Schöps, T., Cremers, D.: LSD-SLAM: large-scale direct monocular SLAM. In: Fleet, D., Pajdla, T., Schiele, B., Tuytelaars, T. (eds.) ECCV 2014. LNCS, vol. 8690, pp. 834–849. Springer, Cham (2014). https://doi.org/10.1007/978-3-319-10605-2_54
10. Fletcher, R.: Practical Methods of Optimization. Wiley, Chichester (2013)
11. Hochreiter, S., Younger, A.S., Conwell, P.R.: Learning to learn using gradient descent. In: Dorffner, G., Bischof, H., Hornik, K. (eds.) ICANN 2001. LNCS, vol. 2130, pp. 87–94. Springer, Heidelberg (2001). https://doi.org/10.1007/3-540-44668-0_13
12. Kelley, C.T.: Iterative Methods for Optimization, vol. 18. SIAM, Philadelphia (1999)
13. Lin, C.H., Lucey, S.: Inverse compositional spatial transformer networks. arXiv preprint arXiv:1612.03897 (2016)
14. Metz, L., Poole, B., Pfau, D., Sohl-Dickstein, J.: Unrolled generative adversarial networks. arXiv preprint arXiv:1611.02163 (2016)
15. Newcombe, R.A., et al.: KinectFusion: real-time dense surface mapping and tracking. In: Proceedings of the International Symposium on Mixed and Augmented Reality (ISMAR) (2011)
16. Öktem, O., Adler, J.: Solving ill-posed inverse problems using iterative deep neural networks. Inverse Prob. **33**(12), 124007 (2017)
17. Ravi, S., Larochelle, H.: Optimization as a model for few-shot learning. In: International Conference on Learning Representations (ICLR) (2016)
18. Schönberger, J.L., Zheng, E., Frahm, J.-M., Pollefeys, M.: Pixelwise view selection for unstructured multi-view stereo. In: Leibe, B., Matas, J., Sebe, N., Welling, M. (eds.) ECCV 2016. LNCS, vol. 9907, pp. 501–518. Springer, Cham (2016). https://doi.org/10.1007/978-3-319-46487-9_31
19. Tikhonov, A., Arsenin, V.: Solutions of Ill-Posed Problems. Winston, Washington (1977)
20. Tulsiani, S., Zhou, T., Efros, A.A., Malik, J.: Multi-view supervision for single-view reconstruction via differentiable ray consistency. In: Proceedings of the IEEE Conference on Computer Vision and Pattern Recognition (CVPR) (2017)
21. Ummenhofer, B., et al.: DeMoN: depth and motion network for learning monocular stereo. In: Proceedings of the IEEE Conference on Computer Vision and Pattern Recognition (CVPR)
22. Wang, S., Clark, R., Wen, H., Trigoni, N.: DeepVO: towards end to end visual odometry with deep recurrent convolutional neural networks. In: Proceedings of the IEEE International Conference on Robotics and Automation (ICRA) (2017)
23. Zhou, T., Brown, M., Snavely, N., Lowe, D.G.: Unsupervised learning of depth and ego-motion from video. In: Proceedings of the IEEE Conference on Computer Vision and Pattern Recognition (CVPR) (2017)

Extreme Network Compression via Filter Group Approximation

Bo Peng(✉), Wenming Tan, Zheyang Li, Shun Zhang, Di Xie, and Shiliang Pu

Hikvision Research Institute, Hangzhou, China
{pengbo7,tanwenming,lizheyang,zhangshun7,xiedi,pushiliang}@hikvision.com

Abstract. In this paper we propose a novel decomposition method based on filter group approximation, which can significantly reduce the redundancy of deep convolutional neural networks (CNNs) while maintaining the majority of feature representation. Unlike other low-rank decomposition algorithms which operate on spatial or channel dimension of filters, our proposed method mainly focuses on exploiting the filter group structure for each layer. For several commonly used CNN models, including VGG and ResNet, our method can reduce over 80% floating-point operations (FLOPs) with less accuracy drop than state-of-the-art methods on various image classification datasets. Besides, experiments demonstrate that our method is conducive to alleviating degeneracy of the compressed network, which hurts the convergence and performance of the network.

Keywords: Convolutional neural networks · Network compression
Low-rank decomposition · Filter group convolution
Image classification

1 Introduction

In recent years, CNNs have achieved great success on several computer vision tasks, such as image classification [19], object detection [27], instance segmentation [25] and many others. However, deep neural networks with high performance also suffer from a huge amount of computation cost, restricting applications of these networks on the resource-constrained devices. One of the classic networks, VGG16 [30] with 130 million parameters needs more than 30 billion FLOPs to classify a single 224×224 image. The heavy computation and memory cost can hardly be afforded by most of embedding-systems on real-time tasks. To address this problem, lots of studies have been proposed during last few years, including network compressing and accelerating [4,5,21,41], or directly designing more efficient architectures [10,14,37,40].

Low-rank decomposition is a common method to compress network by matrix or tensor factorization. A series of works [4,16,38,41] have achieved great progress on increasing efficiency of networks by representing the original weights

V. Ferrari et al. (Eds.): ECCV 2018, LNCS 11212, pp. 307–323, 2018.
https://doi.org/10.1007/978-3-030-01237-3_19

as a form of low-rank. However, these methods couldn't reach an extreme compression ratio with good performance since they may suffer from degeneration problem [26,29], which is harmful for the convergence and performance of the network. Filter group convolution [19] is another way to compact the network while keeping independencies among filters, which can alleviate the limitation of degeneration. In this work, we will show a novel method, which decompose a regular convolution to filter group structure [14] (Fig. 1), while achieve good performance and large compression ratio at the same time.

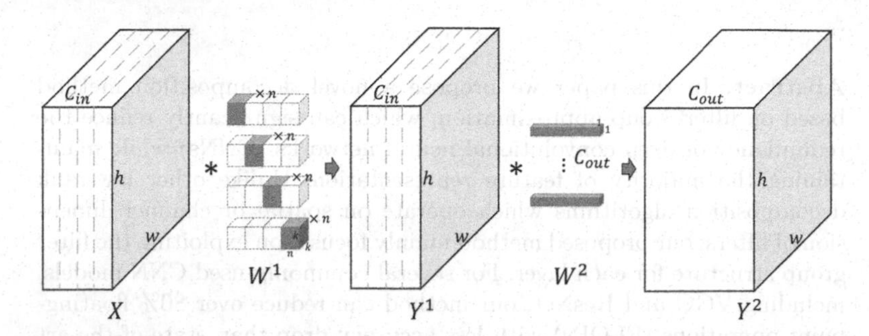

Fig. 1. The filter group structure is a linear combination of W^1 and W^2. X is the input feature with C_{in} channels and $h \times w$ spatial size. W^1 is a filter group convolutional layer with each filter size of $n \times k \times k$, W^2 is a 1×1 convolutional layer. Y^1 and Y^2 are outputs of W^1 and W^2 respectively

The concept of filter group convolution was first used in AlexNet [19] due to the shortage of GPU's memory. Surprisingly, independent filter groups in CNN learned a separation of responsibility, and the performance was close to that of corresponding network without filter groups, which means this lighter architecture has an equal ability of feature representation. After this work, filter group and depthwise convolution were widely used in designing efficient architectures [2,10,14,28,37,40] and achieved state-of-the-art performance among lightweight models. However, all of those well-designed architectures need to be trained from scratch with respect to specific tasks. Huang *et al.* [12] introduced CondenseNet, which learns filter group convolutions automatically during the training process, while several complicated stages with up to 300 epochs' training are needed to reach both sparsity and regularity of filters.

In this paper, we will show an efficient way to decompose the regular convolutional layer into the form of filter group structure which is a linear combination of filter group convolution and point-wise convolution (Fig. 1). Taking advantage of filter group convolution, computational complexity of the original network can be extremely compressed while preserve the diversity of feature representation, which leads to faster convergence and less accuracy drop. Besides, our method can be efficiently applied on most of regular pre-trained models without any additional training skill.

The contributions of this paper are summarized as follows:

- A filter group approximation method is proposed to decompose a regular convolutional layer into a filter group structure with tiny accuracy loss while mostly preserve feature representation diversity.
- Experiments and discussions provide new inspiration and promising research directions based on degeneracy problem in network compression.

2 Related Work

First of all, we briefly discuss related works including network pruning, low-rank decomposition and efficient architecture designing.

Network Pruning: Network pruning is an efficient method to reduce the redundancy in the deep neural network [31]. A straight forward way of pruning is to evaluate the importance of weights (*e.g.* the magnitude of weights [6,21], sparsity of activation [11], Taylor expansion [24], *etc.*), thus the less important weights could be pruned with less effect on performance. Yu *et al.* [39] proposed a Neuron Importance Score Propagation algorithm to propagate the importance scores to every weight. He *et al.* [9] utilized a Lasso regression based channel selection and least square reconstruction to compress the network. Besides, there are several training-based studies in which the structure of filters are forced to sparse during training [22,35]. Recently, Huang *et al.* [12] proposed an elaborate scheme to prune neuron connection with both sparsity and regularity during training process.

Low-Rank Decomposition: Instead of removing neurons of network, a series of works have been proposed to represent the original layer with low-rank approximation. Previous works [4,20] applied matrix or tensor factorization algorithms (*e.g.* SVD, CP-decomposition) on the weights of each layer to reduce computational complexity. Jaderberg *et al.* [16] proposed a joint reconstruction method to decompose $k \times k$ filter into a combination of $k \times 1$ and $1 \times k$ filters. These methods only gain limited compressions on shallow networks. Zhang *et al.* [41] improved the low-rank approximation of deeper networks on large dataset using a nonlinear asymmetric reconstruction method. Similarly, Masana *et al.* [23] proposed a domain adaptive low-rank decomposition method, which took the activations' statistics of the new domain into account. Alvarez *et al.* [1] regularized parameter matrix to low-rank during training, such that it could be decomposed easily in the post-processing stage.

Efficient Architecture Designing: The needs of applying CNNs on resource-constrained devices also encouraged the studies of efficient architecture designing. 'Residual' block in ResNet [7,8], 'Inception' block in GoogLeNet [32–34] and 'fire module' in SqueezeNet [13] achieved impressive performance with less complexity on spatial extents. AlexNet [19] utilized filter group convolution to solve the constraints of computational resources. ResNeXt [37] replaced the regular 3×3 convolutional layers in residual blocks of ResNet with group convolutional layers to achieve better results. Depthwise separable convolution proposed in Xception [2] promoted the performance of low-cost CNNs on embedded devices.

Benefiting from depthwise separable convolution, MobileNet v1 [10], v2 [28] and ShuffleNet [40] achieved state-of-the-art performance on several tasks with significantly reduced computational requirements.

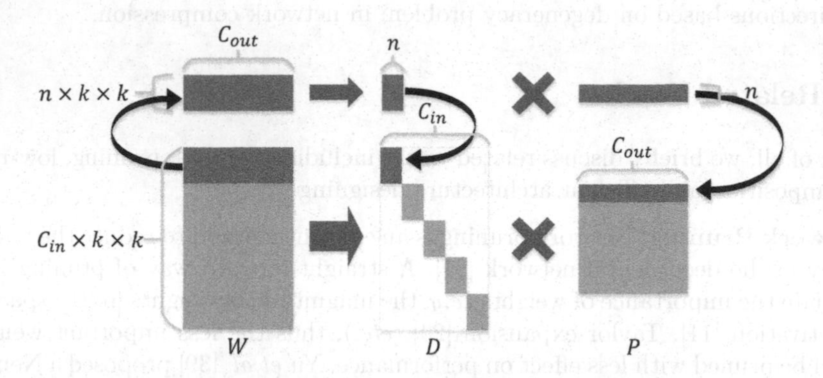

Fig. 2. Illustration of the decomposition. The original layer with weight matrix W is decomposed into two layer with weight matrices D and P respectively

3 Approaches

In this section we introduce a novel filter group approximation method to decompose a regular convolutional layer into the form of filter group structure. Furthermore, we discuss the degeneracy problem of the compressed network.

3.1 Filter Group Approximation of Weights

Weights of convolutional layer can be considered as tensor $W \in \mathbb{R}^{C_{in} \times k \times k \times C_{out}}$, where C_{out} and C_{in} are the number of output channels and input channels respectively, and k is the spatial size of filters. The response $Y \in \mathbb{R}^{N \times C_{out}}$ is computed by applying W on $X \in \mathbb{R}^{N \times C_{in} \times k \times k}$ which is sampled from $k \times k$ sliding window of the layer inputs. Thus the convolutional operation can be formulated as:

$$Y = X \times W. \tag{1}$$

The bias term is omitted for simplicity. X and W can be seen as matrices with shape N-by-$(C_{in}k^2)$ and $(C_{in}k^2)$-by-C_{out} respectively. The computational complexity of Eq. 1 is $O(C_{in}k^2C_{out})$.

Each row of matrix W is only multiplied with the corresponding column of matrix X. Let's consider each sub-matrix with $n \times k \times k$ rows of W and $n \times k \times k$ columns of X (n is divisible by C_{in}), which are denoted as W_i and X_i ($i = 1, 2, \ldots, C_{in}/n$) respectively. Equation 1 can be equally described as:

$$Y = \left[X_1\ X_2\ ...\ X_{C_{in}/n}\right] \begin{bmatrix} W_1 \\ W_2 \\ ... \\ W_{C_{in}/n} \end{bmatrix}. \tag{2}$$

Each sub-matrix W_i with rank d_i can be decomposed into two matrices D_i and P_i using SVD. Considering the redundancy of parameter in a layer, W_i can be approximated by $\widetilde{W_i} = D_{i,n} \times P_{i,n}^T$ with rank $n \leq d_i$. $D_{i,n}$ and $P_{i,n}$ are the first n columns of D_i and P_i related to the largest n singular values. By arranging $D_{i,n}$ and $P_{i,n}$ from each sub-matrices of W into two matrices denoted as D and P respectively, we can get an approximation of matrix W which is $W \approx D \times P$ (Fig. 2). The original layer with weights W can be replaced by two layers with weights D and P respectively. Thus the original response can be approximated by Y^* with:

$$Y \approx Y^* = X \times D \times P. \tag{3}$$

Table 1. Settings of n for each stage in whole network compression on ResNet34. '*Ours-Res34/A*', '*Ours-Res34/B*', '*Ours-Res34/C*' and '*Ours-Res34/D*' denote four compression networks using our method. '-' means no compression in this stage

Layer name	Output size	ResNet34	Ours-Res34/A	Ours-Res34/B	Ours-Res34/C	Ours-Res34/D
conv1	112×112	-				
conv2_x	56×56	-	$n = 8$	$n = 4$	$n = 1$	$n = 1$
conv3_x	28×28	-	$n = 32$	$n = 16$	$n = 4$	$n = 1$
conv4_x	14×14	-	$n = 128$	$n = 64$	$n = 16$	$n = 1$
conv5_x	7×7	-	-	$n = 256$	$n = 64$	$n = 1$
fc	1×1	-				
FLOPs		7.32×10^9	3.98×10^9	2.58×10^9	1.44×10^9	1.11×10^9

The matrix D is a block diagonal matrix as illustrated in Fig. 2, which can be implemented using a group convolutional layer with C_{in} filters of spatial size $k \times k$, and each filter convolve with n input channels sequentially. P is a 1×1 convolutional layer to create a linear combination of the output of D. So the computational complexity of Eq. 3 is $O(C_{in}k^2n + C_{in}C_{out})$. Compare with Eq. 1, the complexity reduces to $(n/C_{out} + 1/k^2)$. It shrinks to about $1/k^2$ of the original one in the case of $n = 1$, which is known as depthwise convolution.

3.2 Reconstruction and Fine-Tuning for the Compressed Network

Since our approximation is based on sub-matrices of W, the accumulative error and magnitude difference among approximated sub-matrices will damage the overall performance. Hence we further minimize the reconstruction error by:

$$A = arg \min_{A^*} \parallel Y - Y^* \times A^* \parallel_2^2, \tag{4}$$

where Y indicates the response of the original network, and Y^* is the response after approximation. Equation 4 is a typical linear regression problem without any constrains which can be solved by the least-square optimization. Matrix A can be implemented as a 1×1 convolutional layer, which can be merged into P in practice, thus there is no additional layer.

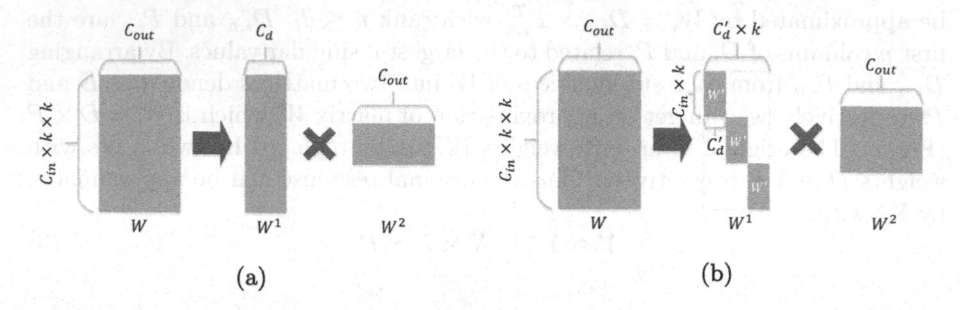

Fig. 3. Two low-rank decomposition strategies. (a) The SVD based method. The first C_d singular vectors are reserved in SVD. (b) The reconstruction method using $k \times 1$ and $1 \times k$ convolution. The block diagonal weight matrix W^1 is constructed using k replicas of W', which is weight matrix of the $k \times 1$ convolution. W^2 is weight matrix of the $1 \times k$ convolution

After reconstruction for each layer, the compressed network can maintain good performance even without fine-tuning. In our experiments, few epochs' fine-tuning (usually less than 20 epochs) with a very small learning rate is enough to achieve better accuracy.

3.3 Compression Degree for Each Layer

When compressing an entire network, a proper compression ratio need to be determined for each layer. One common strategy is removing the same proportion of parameters for each layer. However, it is not reasonable since different layers are not equally redundant. As mentioned by [9,41], deeper layers have less redundancy, which indicates less compression with increasing depth in whole network compression.

In our method, the compression ratio is controlled by n (see Sect. 3.1). For a whole network compression, we set larger n for deeper layers. Convolutional layers of the whole network can be separated into several stages according to the spatial size of corresponding output feature. Taking the experience of [14] for reference, we set the same n for those layers in the same stage, and the ratio of two values of n between adjacent stages is $1:4$ (shallow one *vs* deep one). Table 1 shows settings of n for each stage of ResNet34 in whole network compression, and '*Ours-Res34/D*' is a 'depthwise' compressed case in which n for all stages is 1. We will further discuss different degrees of compression with network depth in our experiment.

3.4 Consideration About the Degeneracy Problem

As mentioned in [29], the Jacobian of weights indicates the correlation between inputs and outputs, and degeneracy of Jacobian leads to poor backpropagation of gradients which impacts the convergence and performance of the network. Jacobian can be computed as: $J = \partial Y / \partial X$, where X and Y are inputs and outputs respectively. For linear case of two layers with weights W^1 and W^2, the Jacobian $J = W^1 \times W^2$.

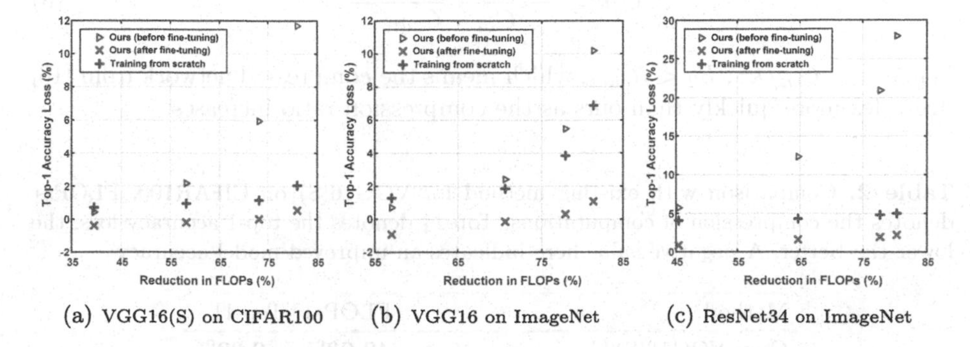

(a) VGG16(S) on CIFAR100 (b) VGG16 on ImageNet (c) ResNet34 on ImageNet

Fig. 4. Comparison with training from scratch. The green '▷' denotes the top-1 accuracy loss of compressed network without fine-tuning; the red '×' denotes the top-1 accuracy loss after fine-tuning; the blue '+' denotes the top-1 accuracy loss of training from scratch. A negative value of y-axis indicates an improved model accuracy (Color figure online)

Low-rank decomposition method achieves compression by representing the original layer with a linear combination of several layers on a low-rank subspace. Figure 3 illustrates two common low-rank decomposition strategies that decompose the weight matrix W into two matrices W^1 and W^2. C_{in} and C_{out} are numbers of input and output channels respectively, k is the spatial size of filters. Let's consider the case that $C_{in} \leq C_{out} < C_{in}k^2$ ($k > 1$), which is common in regular convolutional layers of classic networks like VGG [30], ResNet [7].

Figure 3(a) shows an instance of SVD based method [23,41]. The first C_d singular vectors are reserved in SVD. Thus the rank of Jacobian is $R_1 = C_d$,[1] and the computational complexity of the low-rank representation is $O(C_{in}k^2C_d + C_dC_{out})$. While in our method (Fig. 2), the rank R_{ours} can reach to C_{in} no matter how much the model is compressed, and the computational complexity is $O(C_{in}k^2n + C_{in}C_{out})$. Under the same compression ratio, we can get:

$$C_d = \frac{C_{in}k^2n + C_{in}C_{out}}{C_{in}k^2 + C_{out}}. \tag{5}$$

[1] We suppose that weight matrices after decomposition are full-rank which always holds in practice.

Since $n < C_{in}$, $R_1 < R_{ours}$. Equation 6 shows that, the more the model is compressed, the less C_d is, making the Jacobian more degenerate.

Jaderberg *et al.* [16] proposed a joint reconstruction method to represent a $k \times k$ filter with two $k \times 1$ and $1 \times k$ filters, which is equivalent to the representation of Fig. 3(b). W' is the weight matrix of the $k \times 1$ convolutional layer with C_d' output channels. The rank of Jacobian is $R_2 = \min(C_d' k, C_{out})$, and the computational complexity is $O(C_{in}C_d'k + C_d'kC_{out})$. Similarly, under the same compression ratio,

$$C_d' k = \frac{C_{in}k^2 n + C_{in}C_{out}}{C_{in} + C_{out}}. \tag{6}$$

When $n < C_{in}/k^2$, $R_2 < R_{ours}$, which means the compressed network from [16] degrades more quickly than ours as the compression ratio increases.

Table 2. Comparison with existing method for VGG16(S) on CIFAR100. FLOPs↓ denotes the compression of computations; Top-1↓ denotes the top-1 accuracy loss, the lower the better. A negative value here indicates an improved model accuracy

Method	FLOPs↓	Top-1↓
Ours-VGG16(S)/A	**40.03%**	**−0.39%**
Asym. [41] (*Fine-tuned, our impl.*)	39.77%	0.28%
Liu *et al.* [22]	37.00%	−0.22%
Ours-VGG16(S)/B	**73.40%**	**0.02%**
Asym. (*Fine-tuned, our impl.*)	73.21%	1.03%
Liu *et al.*	67.30%	2.34%
Ours-VGG16(S)/C	**84.82%**	**0.57%**
Asym. (*Fine-tuned, our impl.*)	84.69%	2.94%
Liu *et al.*	83.00%	3.85%
Ours-VGG16(S)/D	**88.58%**	**1.93%**
Asym. (*Fine-tuned, our impl.*)	87.33%	4.47%
Liu *et al.*[a]	–	–

[a] Liu *et al.* has not provided result with compression ratio about 88%.

4 Experiments

In this section, a set of experiments are performed on standard datasets with commonly used CNN networks to evaluate our method. Our implementations are based on Caffe [17].

Table 3. Comparison with existing method for VGG16 and ResNet34 on ImageNet. FLOPs↓ denotes the compression of computations; Top-1↓ and Top-5↓ denote the top-1 and top-5 accuracy losses, the lower the better

Network	Method	FLOPs↓	Top-1↓	Top-5↓
VGG16	Ours-VGG16/A	**56.99%**	**−0.82%**	**−0.94%**
	Asym. (*Fine-tuned, our impl.*)	56.17%	−0.18%	−0.27%
	He *et al.* [9]	≈ 50%	–	0.0%
	Ours-VGG16/B	**77.86%**	0.28%	0.07%
	Asym. (*Fine-tuned, our impl.*)	77.60%	1.81%	0.73%
	Asym. (3D) [41]	≈ 75%	–	0.3%
	He *et al.*	≈ 75%	–	1.0%
	He *et al.* (3C) [9]	≈ 75%	–	**0.0%**
	Jaderberg *et al.* [16] ([41]*'s impl.*)	≈ 75%	–	9.7%
	Ours-VGG16/C	**81.35%**	**1.06%**	**0.27%**
	Asym. (*Fine-tuned, our impl.*)	81.18%	4.53%	2.45%
	Asym. (3D)	≈ 80%	–	1.0%
	He *et al.*	≈ 80%	–	1.7%
	He *et al.* (3C)	≈ 80%	–	0.3%
	Kim *et al.* [18]	79.72%	–	0.5%
	Ours-VGG16/D	**85.80%**	**3.49%**	**2.03%**
	Asym. (*Fine-tuned, our impl.*)	83.91%	6.96%	5.14%
	Asym. (3D) (*Fine-tuned, our impl.*)	84.44%	4.51%	2.89%
	He *et al.* (3C)	85.55%	4.38%	2.96%
ResNet34	Ours-Res34/A	**45.63%**	**0.35%**	**0.04%**
	Li *et al.* [21]	24.20%	1.06%	–
	NISP-34-B [39]	43.76%	0.92%	–
	Asym. (*Fine-tuned, our impl.*)	44.60%	0.97%	0.21%
	Ours-Res34/B	**64.75%**	**1.02%**	**0.30%**
	Li *et al.* (*Fine-tuned, our impl.*)	63.98%	4.35%	2.29%
	Asym. (*Fine-tuned, our impl.*)	64.12%	2.91%	1.41%
	Ours-Res34/C	**80.33%**	**1.70%**	**0.44%**
	Li *et al.* (*Fine-tuned, our impl.*)	79.67%	8.23%	4.96%
	Asym. (*Fine-tuned, our impl.*)	79.95%	6.77%	4.10%
	Asym. (3D) (*Fine-tuned, our impl.*)	80.08%	3.79%	1.85%
	Ours-Res34/D	84.84%	**3.03%**	**1.22%**
	Li *et al.* (*Fine-tuned, our impl.*)	**84.99%**	13.27%	8.84%
	Asym. (*Fine-tuned, our impl.*)	84.79%	12.30%	8.27%
	Asym. (3D) (*Fine-tuned, our impl.*)	84.04%	5.35%	2.78%

Table 4. Comparison of actual running time (ms) per image (224×224).

Network	Methods	FLOPs↓	Top-5↓	GPU	CPU	TX1
VGG16	Baseline	-	-	2.91	2078	122.36
	Ours	**85.80%**	**2.03%**	2.17	**628**	**40.92**
	Asym.(3D)	84.44%	2.89%	1.78	778	97.36
	He *et al.*(3C)	85.55%	2.96%	1.65	741	94.27
ResNet34	Baseline	-	-	0.75	442	20.5
	Ours	**84.84%**	**1.22%**	**0.62**	**116**	**9.54**
	Asym.(3D)	84.04%	2.78%	0.67	128	18.33

4.1 Datasets and Experimental Setting

Focusing on the reduction of FLOPs and accuracy drops, we compare our method with training from scratch and several state-of-the-art methods on CIFAR100 and ImageNet-2012 datasets [3] for image classification task.

CIFAR100 dataset contains 50,000 training samples and 10,000 test samples with resolution 32×32 from 100 categories. We use a standard data augmentation scheme [7] including shifting and horizontal flipping in training. A variation of the original VGG16 from [22] (called VGG16(S) in our experiments) with top-1 accuracy 73.26% is used to evaluate the compression on CIFAR100 dataset.

ImageNet dataset consists of 1.2 million training samples and 50.000 validation samples from 1000 categories. We resize the input samples with short-side 256 and then adopt 224 × 224 crop (random crop in training and center crop in testing). Random horizontal flipping is also used in training. We evaluate single-view validation accuracy. On ImageNet dataset, we adopt the compression on VGG16 [30] and ResNet34 [7].

4.2 Comparison with Training-from-Scratch and Existing Methods

Comparison with Training-from-Scratch. Several compression ratios are adopted in our experiments to evaluate the performance. For the fine-tuning processes of the compressed networks, we use an initial learning rate of 1e–4, and divide it by 10 when training losses are stable. 5 $\sim$ 20 epochs are enough for fine-tuning to achieve convergence. For comparison, we directly train models with the same architecture as our compressed networks from scratch for more than 100 epochs, with the same initialization and learning strategies as proposed by the original works [7,30].

Comparison results are shown in Fig. 4. With 57% reduction of FLOPs for VGG16, the compressed network without fine-tuning only has a tiny accuracy loss on ImageNet, and it's comparable to the performance of the scratch counterpart. With a few epochs' fine-tuning, the compressed networks outperform training from scratch by a large margin. In some cases, our method even achieves higher accuracy than the original network.

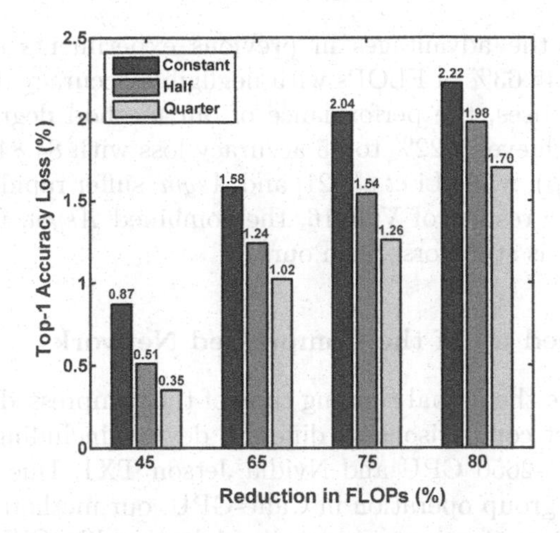

Fig. 5. Comparison results of three compression degrees with network depth for compression of ResNet34 on ImageNet

Comparison with Existing Methods. Next, we compare our method with several state-of-the-art methods under the same compression ratios. To be noted, results demonstrated in our experiments are all fine-tuned.

As shown in Table 2, for VGG16(S) on CIFAR100, 4 compressed architectures (*'Ours-VGG16(S)/A,B,C,D'*) are created by using different n as mentioned in Sect. 3.3. *'Ours-VGG16(S)/A'* increases top-1 accuracy by 0.39% with 40% FLOPs reduction, which is slightly better than the other two methods. Under larger compression ratios, our method outperforms the other two methods with much lower accuracy loss. With 88.58% reduction of FLOPs (8.5× speed-up), the increased error rate of *'Ours-VGG16(S)/D'* is 1.93% while *Asym.*'s is 4.47% under a similar compression ratio.

Networks trained on Imagenet with complex features are less redundant, which make compressing such networks much more challenging. The results of VGG16, ResNet34 and ResNet50 on ImageNet are shown in Table 3.

For VGG16, we adopt architectures *'Ours-VGG16/A,B,C,D'* with respect to 4 compression ratios. With 56.99% reduction of FLOPs, the top-5 accuracy of *'Ours-VGG16/A'* is 0.94% higher than the original network. When we speed the network up to 7×, *'Ours-VGG16/D'* can still achieve result of 2.03% top-5 accuracy drop, while for *Asym.* [41], it is much larger (5.14% drop on top-5 accuracy). *Asym.* (3D) and He *et al.* (3C) [9] improve their accuracy under the same compression ratios by combining with spatial decomposition [16]. However, the compressed architectures from combined methods are much inefficient on most of real-time devices since the original convolutional layer is decomposed into three layers with spatial filter size 3×1, 1×3 and 1×1. Besides, the combination can be also applied on our method. We will conduct the exploration in our future work.

For ResNet34, the advantages in previous experiments still hold. *'Ours-Res34/A'* reduces 45.63% of FLOPs with negligible accuracy drop. As the compression ratio increases, the performance of our method degrades very slowly. *'Ours-Res34/D'* achieves 1.22% top-5 accuracy loss with 84.84% FLOPs reduction (6.6× speed-up), while Li *et al.* [21] and *Asym.* suffer rapidly increased error rate. Similar to the results of VGG16, the combined *Asym.* (3D) outperforms *Asym.* a lot, but it is still worse than ours.

4.3 Actual Speed up of the Compressed Network

We further evaluate the actual running time of the compressed network. Table 4 illustrates time cost comparisons on different devices including Nvidia TITAN-XP GPU, Xeon E5-2650 CPU and Nvidia Jetson TX1. Due to the inefficient implementation of group operation in Caffe-GPU, our method shows large time cost. However, in most of resource-constrained devices, like CPU and TX1, bandwidth becomes the main bottleneck. In such case, our method achieves much significant actual speed up as shown in Table 4.

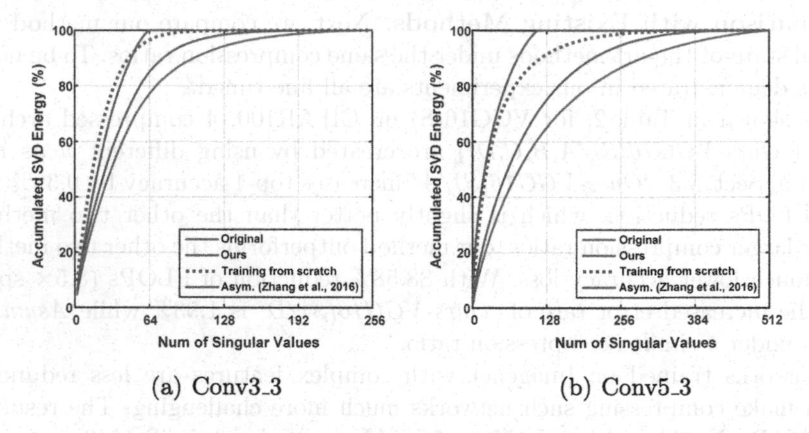

Fig. 6. SVD accumulative energy curves of Conv3_3 and Conv5_3 in VGG16 and its compressed networks. The red solid line denotes the original network; the green solid line denotes the compressed given by our method; the green dot line denotes training from scratch with the same architecture as our compressed model (Color figure online)

4.4 Compression Degree with Network Depth

As mentioned in Sect. 3.3, the ratio of n between adjacent stages is 1 : 4 (hereinafter called *'Quarter'*) in our experiments. In this part, we consider another two degrees of compression. The first one is *'Constant'*, which means the n for all stages maintain the same. The second one is *'Half'*, which means the ratio of n between adjacent stages is 1 : 2. We evaluate these three kinds of strategies on compression of ResNet34. Figure 5 illustrates the results. Compressed networks with *'Quarter'* degree give the best performance, which is consistent with [14]. These results also indicate that there should be less compression with increasing depth.

4.5 Degeneracy of the Extremely Compressed Network

Fine-tuning is a necessary process to recover the performance of a compressed network. However fine-tuning after low-rank decomposition may suffer from the instability problem [20]. In our experiments for VGG16 on ImageNet, the training of compressed models from *Asym.* shows gradient explosion problems, which was also mentioned in [41]. Besides, the performance degraded quickly when the compression ratio was getting larger. This phenomenon is caused by the degeneracy of the compressed network [26,29,36].

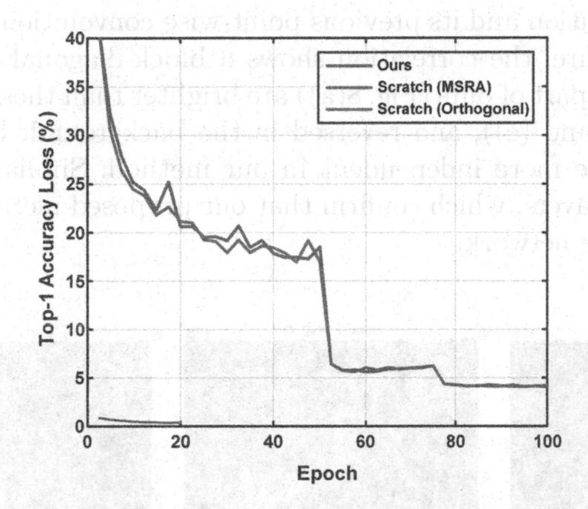

Fig. 7. Learning curves of compressed networks with initializations of ours, 'MSRA' and 'Orthogonal'

As we analyzed in Sect. 3.4, we calculate the singular values of Jacobian to analysis the degeneracy problem. Figure 6 illustrates SVD accumulative curves of two layers from the original VGG16 and compressed networks (5× speed-up) from *Asym.*, our method and training from scratch with the same architecture as our compressed model. The curves of the original network (denotes as red solid lines) are the most flat, indicate the least degenerate. Ours (green solid) are the second, training from scratch (green dotted) and *Asym.* (blue solid) are worse than ours. The rest layers hold similar phenomena. Thus it can be concluded that, our proposed method can alleviate the degeneracy problem efficiently, while *Asym.* is much affected due to more elimination of singular value. The result also proves that training from scratch can not provide enough dynamic to conquer the problem of degeneracy [36].

The problems of training instability are lightened in ResNet due to the existence of Batch Normalization [15] and short-cut connection [26]. However the performance of *Asym.* on ResNet still degraded quickly as the compression ratio increased. The degeneracy of network is still an open problem. We believe that it should be taken into account when studying network compression.

4.6 A Better Initialization of the Network

The comparison between training from scratch and our approximation method indicates that our compressed models provided a better initialization. For a further verification, we also evaluate the orthogonal initialization which could alleviate degeneracy in linear neural networks [29]. We compare models trained with the architecture of *'Ours-Res34/A'*. Figure 7 illustrates the learning curves. Our compressed network achieves much lower accuracy loss.

To give a better understanding, we conduct the inter-layer filter correlation analyses [14]. Figure 8 shows the correlation between the output feature maps of filter group convolution and its previous point-wise convolution. Enforced by the filter group structure, the correlation shows a block-diagonal matrix. Pixels in the block-diagonal part of ours (Fig. 8(a)) are brighter than those of training from scratch (Fig. 8(b) and (c)), and reversed in the background. It means features between groups are more independent in our method. Similar phenomena are observed in other layers, which confirm that our proposed method gives a better initialization of the network.

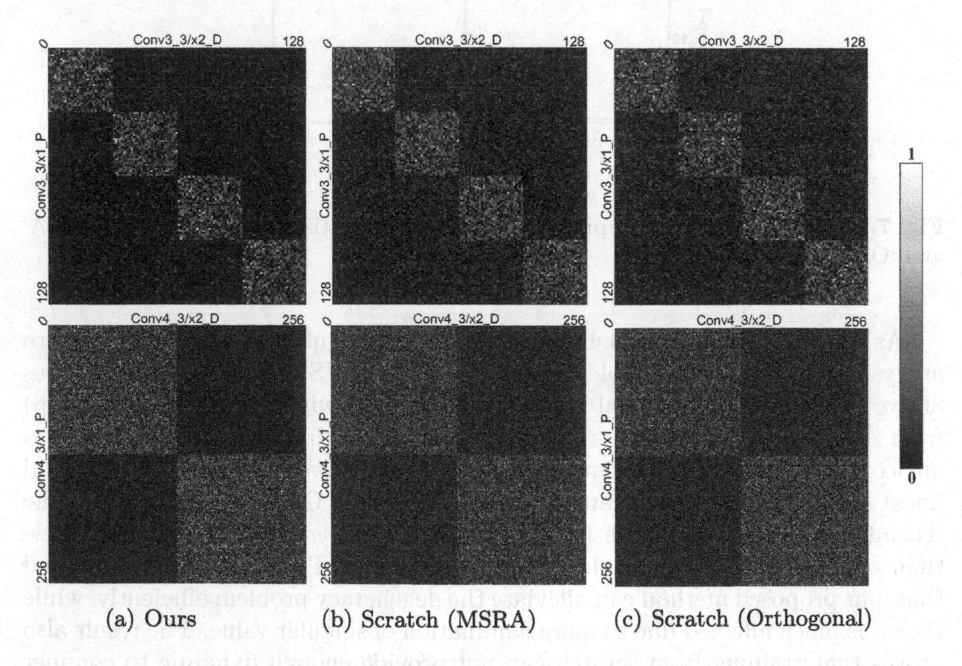

Fig. 8. Inter-layer filter correlation using initializations of ours, 'MSRA' and 'Orthogonal'. Brighter pixel indicates higher correlation

5 Conclusion

In this paper, we proposed a filter group approximation method to compress networks efficiently. Instead of compressing the spatial size of filters or the number of output channels in each layer, our method is aimed at exploiting a filter group structure of each layer. The experimental results demonstrated that our proposed method can achieve extreme compression ratio with tiny loss in accuracy. More importantly, our method can efficiently alleviate the degeneracy of the compressed networks. In the future, we will focus on solving the degeneracy problem on network compression.

References

1. Alvarez, J.M., Salzmann, M.: Compression-aware training of deep networks. In: Advances in Neural Information Processing Systems (2017)
2. Chollet, F.: Xception: deep learning with depthwise separable convolutions. In: IEEE Conference on Computer Vision and Pattern Recognition (2017)
3. Deng, J., et al.: Imagenet: a large-scale hierarchical image database. In: IEEE Conference on Computer Vision and Pattern Recognition (2009)
4. Denton, E., Zaremba, W., Bruna, J., Lecun, Y., Fergus, R.: Exploiting linear structure within convolutional networks for efficient evaluation. In: Advances in Neural Information Processing Systems (2014)
5. Han, S., Mao, H., Dally, W.J.: Deep compression: Compressing deep neural networks with pruning, trained quantization and huffman coding. In: International Conference on Learning Representations (2016)
6. Han, S., Pool, J., Tran, J., Dally, W.: Learning both weights and connections for efficient neural network. In: Advances in Neural Information Processing Systems (2015)
7. He, K., Zhang, X., Ren, S., Sun, J.: Deep residual learning for image recognition. In: IEEE Conference on Computer Vision and Pattern Recognition (2016)
8. He, K., Zhang, X., Ren, S., Sun, J.: Identity mappings in deep residual networks. In: Leibe, B., Matas, J., Sebe, N., Welling, M. (eds.) ECCV 2016. LNCS, vol. 9908, pp. 630–645. Springer, Cham (2016). https://doi.org/10.1007/978-3-319-46493-0_38
9. He, Y., Zhang, X., Sun, J.: Channel pruning for accelerating very deep neural networks. In: IEEE International Conference on Computer Vision (2017)
10. Howard, A.G., et al.: Mobilenets: efficient convolutional neural networks for mobile vision applications. arXiv:1704.04861 (2017)
11. Hu, H., Peng, R., Tai, Y.W., Tang, C.K.: Network trimming: a data-driven neuron pruning approach towards efficient deep architectures. arXiv:1607.03250 (2016)
12. Huang, G., Liu, S., Laurens, V.D.M., Weinberger, K.Q.: Condensenet: an efficient densenet using learned group convolutions. arXiv:1711.09224 (2017)
13. Iandola, F.N., Han, S., Moskewicz, M.W., Ashraf, K., Dally, W.J., Keutzer, K.: Squeezenet: alexnet-level accuracy with 50x fewer parameters and ¡0.5 mb model size. arXiv:1602.07360 (2016)
14. Ioannou, Y., Robertson, D., Cipolla, R., Criminisi, A.: Deep roots: Improving cnn efficiency with hierarchical filter groups. In: IEEE Conference on Computer Vision and Pattern Recognition (2017)

15. Ioffe, S., Szegedy, C.: Batch normalization: accelerating deep network training by reducing internal covariate shift. In: International Conference on International Conference on Machine Learning (2015)
16. Jaderberg, M., Vedaldi, A., Zisserman, A.: Speeding up convolutional neural networks with low rank expansions. In: British Machine Vision Conference (2014)
17. Jia, Y., Shelhamer, E., Donahue, J., Karayev, S., Long, J.: Caffe: convolutional architecture for fast feature embedding. In ACM International Conference on Multimedia, MM14 (2014)
18. Kim, Y.D., Park, E., Yoo, S., Choi, T., Yang, L., Shin, D.: Compression of deep convolutional neural networks for fast and low power mobile applications. In: International Conference on Learning Representations (2016)
19. Krizhevsky, A., Sutskever, I., Hinton, G.E.: Imagenet classification with deep convolutional neural networks. In: Advances in Neural Information Processing Systems (2012)
20. Lebedev, V., Ganin, Y., Rakhuba, M., Oseledets, I., Lempitsky, V.: Speeding-up convolutional neural networks using fine-tuned cp-decomposition. In: International Conference on Learning Representations (2015)
21. Li, H., Kadav, A., Durdanovic, I., Samet, H., Graf, H.P.: Pruning filters for efficient convnets. In: International Conference on Learning Representations (2017)
22. Liu, Z., Li, J., Shen, Z., Huang, G., Yan, S., Zhang, C.: Learning efficient convolutional networks through network slimming. In: IEEE International Conference on Computer Vision (2017)
23. Masana, M., Joost, V.D.W., Herranz, L.: Domain-adaptive deep network compression. In: IEEE International Conference on Computer Vision (2017)
24. Molchanov, P., Tyree, S., Karras, T., Aila, T., Kautz, J.: Pruning convolutional neural networks for resource efficient inference. In: International Conference on Learning Representations (2017)
25. Noh, H., Hong, S., Han, B.: Learning deconvolution network for semantic segmentation. In: IEEE International Conference on Computer Vision (2016)
26. Orhan, A.E., Pitkow, X.: Skip connections eliminate singularities. In: International Conference on Learning Representations (2018)
27. Ren, S., He, K., Girshick, R., Sun, J.: Faster R-CNN: towards real-time object detection with region proposal networks. IEEE Trans. Pattern Anal. Mach. Intell. **39**(6), 1137–1149 (2017)
28. Sandler, M., Howard, A., Zhu, M., Zhmoginov, A., Chen, L.C.: Inverted residuals and linear bottlenecks: Mobile networks for classification, detection and segmentation. arXiv:1801.04381 (2018)
29. Saxe, A.M., Mcclelland, J.L., Ganguli, S.: Exact solutions to the nonlinear dynamics of learning in deep linear neural networks. In: International Conference on Learning Representations (2013)
30. Simonyan, K., Zisserman, A.: Very deep convolutional networks for large-scale image recognition. In: International Conference on Learning Representations (2015)
31. Srinivas, S., Babu, R.V.: Data-free parameter pruning for deep neural networks. In: British Machine Vision Conference (2015)
32. Szegedy, C., Ioffe, S., Vanhoucke, V., Alemi, A.: Inception-v4, inception-resnet and the impact of residual connections on learning. In: AAAI Conference on Artificial Intelligence (2017)
33. Szegedy, C., et al.: Going deeper with convolutions. In: IEEE Conference on Computer Vision and Pattern Recognition (2015)

34. Szegedy, C., Vanhoucke, V., Ioffe, S., Shlens, J., Wojna, Z.: Rethinking the inception architecture for computer vision. In: IEEE Conference on Computer Vision and Pattern Recognition (2016)
35. Wen, W., Wu, C., Wang, Y., Chen, Y., Li, H.: Learning structured sparsity in deep neural networks. In: Advances in Neural Information Processing Systems (2016)
36. Xie, D., Xiong, J., Pu, S.: All you need is beyond a good init: Exploring better solution for training extremely deep convolutional neural networks with orthonormality and modulation. In: IEEE Conference on Computer Vision and Pattern Recognition (2017)
37. Xie, S., Girshick, R., Dollar, P., Tu, Z., He, K.: Aggregated residual transformations for deep neural networks. In: IEEE Conference on Computer Vision and Pattern Recognition (2017)
38. Xue, J., Li, J., Gong, Y.: Restructuring of deep neural network acoustic models with singular value decomposition. In: Conference of the International Speech Communication Association (2013)
39. Yu, R., et al.: Nisp: Pruning networks using neuron importance score propagation. arXiv:1711.05908 (2017)
40. Zhang, X., Zhou, X., Lin, M., Sun, J.: Shufflenet: An extremely efficient convolutional neural network for mobile devices. arXiv:1707.01083 (2017)
41. Zhang, X., Zou, J., He, K., Sun, J.: Accelerating very deep convolutional networks for classification and detection. IEEE Trans. Pattern Anal. Mach. Intell. **38**(10), 1943–1955 (2016)

ArticulatedFusion: Real-Time Reconstruction of Motion, Geometry and Segmentation Using a Single Depth Camera

Chao Li, Zheheng Zhao, and Xiaohu Guo(✉)

Department of Computer Science, The University of Texas at Dallas, Richardson, USA
{Chao.Li2,Zheheng.Zhao,xguo}@utdallas.edu

Abstract. This paper proposes a real-time dynamic scene reconstruction method capable of reproducing the motion, geometry, and segmentation simultaneously given live depth stream from a single RGB-D camera. Our approach fuses geometry frame by frame and uses a segmentation-enhanced node graph structure to drive the deformation of geometry in registration step. A two-level node motion optimization is proposed. The optimization space of node motions and the range of physically-plausible deformations are largely reduced by taking advantage of the articulated motion prior, which is solved by an efficient node graph segmentation method. Compared to previous fusion-based dynamic scene reconstruction methods, our experiments show robust and improved reconstruction results for tangential and occluded motions.

Keywords: Fusion · Articulated · Motion · Segmentation

1 Introduction

Dynamic scene reconstruction is a very important topic for digital world building. It includes capturing and reproducing geometry, appearance, motion, and skeleton, which enables more realistic rendering for VR/AR scenarios like Holoportation [5]. An example is that the reconstructed geometry can be directly used for a virtual scene, and the articulated motion can be retargeted to new models to generate new animations, making scene production more efficient.

Although many efforts have been devoted to this research field, the problem remains challenging due to extraordinarily large solution space but real-time rendering requirements for VR/AR applications. Recently, volumetric depth fusion

Electronic supplementary material The online version of this chapter (https://doi.org/10.1007/978-3-030-01237-3_20) contains supplementary material, which is available to authorized users.

V. Ferrari et al. (Eds.): ECCV 2018, LNCS 11212, pp. 324–340, 2018.
https://doi.org/10.1007/978-3-030-01237-3_20

methods for dynamic scene reconstruction, such as DynamicFusion [17], VolumeDeform [10], Fusion4D [5] and albedo based fusion [8] open a new gate for people in this field. This type of method enables quality improvements over temporal reconstruction models in terms of both accuracy and completeness of the surface geometry. Among all these works, fusion methods by a single depth camera [10,17] are more promising for popularization, because of their low cost and easy setup. However, this group of methods still faces some challenging issues, like high occlusion from the single view, limited computational resource to achieve real-time performance, and no geometry/skeleton prior knowledge, and thus are restricted to limited motions. DoubleFusion [30] can reconstruct both the inner body and outer surface for faster motions by adding body template as prior knowledge. Later, KillingFusion [21] and SobolevFusion [22] is proposed to reconstruct dynamic scenes with topology changes and fast inter-frame motions.

DynamicFusion is the pioneering work acheiving template-less non-rigid reconstruction in real time from single depth camera. However, its robustness can be significantly improved by utilizing skeleton prior, as been shown in work of BodyFusion [29]. In this paper, we propose to add articulated motion prior into the depth fusion system. Our method contributes to this field by pushing the limitation from skeleton-prior-based methods to skeleton-less ones. The motions of many objects in our world including human motion follows articulated structures. Thus, articulated motions can be represented by skeleton/cluster-based motion and can be extracted from non-rigid motion as a prior. Our self-adaption segmentation inherits the rigid feature of traditional skeleton structure while does not require any pre-defined skeleton. The segmentation constrains all nodes labeled to the same segment having transformation as close as possible and can reduce the solution space of the optimization problem. Therefore, the self-adapted segmentation can result in better reconstruction results.

Our method iteratively optimizes the motion field of a node graph and its segmentation, which helps each other to get a better reconstruction performance. Integrating the articulated motion prior into the reconstruction framework assists in the non-rigid surface registration and geometry fusion, while surface registration results improve the quality of segmentation and its reconstructed motion. Although the advantages of such unification is obvious, in practice, designing a real-time algorithm to take advantage of both merits of these two aspects is still an unstudied problem, especially on how to segment a node graph based on its motion trajectory in real-time. We have carefully designed our ArticulatedFusion system, to achieve simultaneous reconstruction of motion, geometry, and segmentation in real-time, given a single depth video input. The contributions in this paper are as follows:

1. We present ArticulatedFusion, a system that involves registration, segmentation, and fusion, and enables real-time reconstruction of motion, geometry, and segmentation for dynamic scenes of human and non-human subjects.
2. A two-level registration method which can narrow down the optimization solution space, and result in better reconstructed motions in many challenging cases, with the help of node graph segmentation.

3. A novel real-time segmentation method to solve the clustering of a set of deformed nodes based on their motion trajectories by merging and swapping operations.

2 Related Work

The most popular dynamic 3D scene reconstruction method is to use a predefined model or skeleton as prior knowledge. Most of these methods focus on the reconstruction of human body parts such as face [3,14], hands [24,25], and body [20,27]. Other techniques are proposed to reconstruct general objects by using a pre-scanned geometry [13,32] as a template instead of predefined models.

To further eliminate the dependency on geometry priors, some template-less methods were proposed to utilize more advanced structure to merge and store geometry information across the motion sequence. Wand et al. [28] proposed an algorithm to align and merge pairs of adjacent frames in a hierarchical fashion to gradually build the template shape. Recently, fine 3D models have been reconstructed without any shape priors by gradually fusing multi-frame depth images from a single view depth camera [5,10,17,18]. Innmann et al. [10] proposed to add SIFT features to the ICP registration framework, thereby improving the accuracy of motion reconstruction.

Our method is partly inspired by Pekelny and Gotsman's method [19], However their method requires the user to manually segment a range scan in advance, whereas we automatically solve for the segmentation in real-time. Chang and Zwicker's method [4] is also lack of real data of human motions and takes much time to reconstruct for each frame. Tzionas and Gall's recent work [26] introduces an algorithm to build rigged models of articulated objects from depth data of a single camera. But it requires to pre-scan the target object as the geometry prior knowledge.

Guo et al. [6] proposes an L_0 regularizer to constrain local non-rigid deformation only on joints of articulated motion, which reduces the solution space and yields a physically plausible and robust deformation. However, our method is designed to achieve real-time performance while their method requires around 60s for the L_0 optimization of each frame [7]. Ours directly solves the segmentation of human body in the proposed energy function while theirs implicitly involves the articulated motion property in an L_0 regularizer. Their method also needs a pre-scaned shape as a template. Yu et al.'s method [29] is the one most related to our work, but it requires the skeleton information of the first frame as initialization while our method does not need any prior information. Our method can estimate the segmentation of dynamic scene during the reconstruction process. Therefore, it also works for non-human objects where a predefined skeleton is not available, as illustrated in Figs. 6 and 8. There is also a rich body of work proposed on articulated decomposition of animated mesh sequences [11,12]. Both of these methods can only work on animated sequences with fixed mesh connectivity, and cannot meet our real-time reconstruction requirement.

3 Overview

Figure 1 illustrates the pipeline of processing one frame given the geometry, motion and segmentation reconstructed from earlier frames. [8,10,17], our system runs in a frame-by-frame manner. Two main data structures are used in our system. The geometry is represented in a volume with the Truncated Signed Distance Function (TSDF), while the segmentation and motions are defined in an embedded graph of controlling nodes similar to DynamicFusion [17].

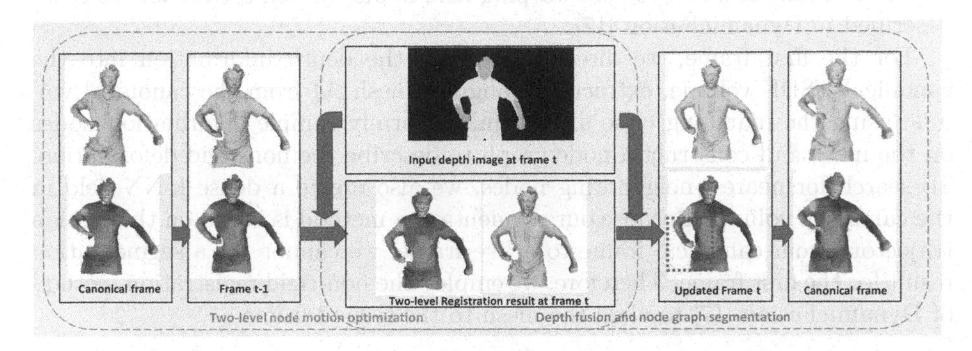

Fig. 1. Overview of our pipeline. The orange box represents our two-level node motion optimization, and the blue box represents fusion of depth and node graph segmentation. (Color figure online)

The first frame is selected as the *canonical frame*. The first step of our system is *two-level node motion optimization* (Sect. 4.2). In this step, motions of controlling nodes from the canonical frame to the current frame are estimated. This is achieved by first warping a mesh using reconstructed motion and segmentation from earlier frames, and followed by solving a two-level optimization problem to fit this mesh with the current depth image. The mesh is extracted from the TSDF volume by marching cube algorithm [15]. The first level of our node motion optimization is run on each segmented cluster, thus can reduce the solution space and make optimization converging faster. The second level of optimization is run on each individual node, so it can keep track of the high-frequency details of the target object. The depth is fused into the TSDF volume to obtain a new integrated geometry (Sect. 4.3). The final step is *node graph segmentation*, in which nodes are segmented by our novel clustering method to minimize the error between the articulated cluster deformation of nodes and their non-rigid deformation (Sect. 4.4). This segmentation makes the node motion estimation of next frame to perform better than employing non-rigid estimation only.

4 Method

4.1 Preliminaries and Initialization

Only a single depth camera is used to capture the depth information in our system. The input to our pipeline is a depth image sequence $\{\mathcal{D}^t\}$. The output of our pipeline includes a fused geometry $\mathcal{V}$ of the target object, the embedded graph segmentation $\mathcal{C}$, and the two-level warping field $\{\mathcal{W}^t\}$, where $\mathcal{W}^t$ represents the non-rigid node motion from the canonical frame to each live frame t. The TSDF volume and level-two warping field in our system is the same as those described in DynamicFusion [17].

For the first frame, we directly integrate the depth information into the canonical TSDF volume, extract a triangular mesh $\mathcal{M}$ from the canonical volume using the marching cube algorithm, uniformly sample deformation nodes on the mesh and construct a node graph to describe the non-rigid deformation. To search for nearest-neighboring nodes, we also create a dense k-NN field in the canonical volume. Because our segmentation method is based on the motion trajectory from canonical frame to a live frame, we cannot get a segmentation result for the first frame. Therefore, we employ the non-rigid registration method of DynamicFusion [17] to align the mesh to the second frame.

4.2 Registration

As mentioned above, the first step of our system is to fit the canonical mesh $\mathcal{M}$ to the depth image $\mathcal{D}^t$ of live frame t. We have the current mesh $\mathcal{M}$ (obtained by fusing the depth from earlier frames), the segmentation $\mathcal{C}$, and the motion field $\mathcal{W}^{t-1}$. Using the newly captured depth in frame t, the algorithm presented in this section estimates $\mathcal{W}^t$ to fit $\mathcal{M}$ with $\mathcal{D}^t$. For this purpose, we propose a two-level optimization framework based on Linear Blend Skinning (LBS) model and node graph motion representation. The optimization is solved by minimizing the following energy function first in LBS model and then in node graph model:

$$E_{total}(\mathcal{W}^t) = \omega_f E_{fit} + \omega_r E_{reg}, \tag{1}$$

where E_{fit} is the data term to minimize the fitting error between deformed vertex and its corresponding point on depth image, and E_{reg} regularizes the motion to be locally as rigid as possible. ω_f and ω_r are controlling weights to balance the influence of two energy terms. In all of our experiments, we set $\omega_f = 1.0$ and $\omega_r = 10.0$.

Before solving the energy function, we build the two-level deformation model based on the node graph and its segmentation by defining the following skinning weight for each vertex $\mathbf{v}_i$ on mesh $\mathcal{M}$:

$$\mathbf{w}_i^{(l)} = \begin{cases} \frac{1}{\Lambda}\sum_{j=1}^{k} \lambda_{i,j}\mathbf{g}_j & l = 1, \\ \frac{1}{\Lambda}\sum_{j=1}^{k} \lambda_{i,j}\mathbf{h}_j & l = 2, \end{cases} \tag{2}$$

where l denotes the level, and $\lambda_{i,j}$ is the weight describing the influence of the j-th node $\mathbf{x}_j$ on vertex $\mathbf{v}_i$ and is defined as $\lambda_{i,j} = exp\left(-\|\mathbf{v}_i - \mathbf{x}_j\|_2^2/\left(2\sigma_j\right)^2\right)$.

Λ is a normalization coefficient, the summation of all spatial weights $\lambda_{i,j}$ for the same i. Here, σ_j is the given influence radius of controlling node $\mathbf{x}_j$. When level $l = 1$, $\mathbf{g}_j = (g_{j,1}, g_{j,2}, ..., g_{j,m})$ is the binding of controlling node $\mathbf{x}_j$ to m clusters. Because each node only belongs to one cluster, only one element of $\mathbf{g}_j$ is 1 and all other elements are 0. $\mathbf{w}_i^{(1)} = \left(w_{i,1}^{(1)}, w_{i,2}^{(1)}, ..., w_{i,m}^{(1)}\right)$ includes the skinning weights of vertex $\mathbf{v}_i$ w.r.t. m clusters. When level $l = 2$, $\mathbf{h}_j = (h_{j,1}, h_{j,2}, ..., h_{j,k})$ is the binding of $\mathbf{v}_i$'s neighboring node $\mathbf{x}_j$ to itself. Thus only $h_{j,j}$ is 1 and all other elements are 0. $\mathbf{w}_i^{(2)} = \left(w_{i,1}^{(2)}, w_{i,2}^{(2)}, ..., w_{i,k}^{(2)}\right)$ includes the skinning weight of vertex $\mathbf{v}_i$ w.r.t. its k-NN controlling nodes.
The fitting term E_{fit} represents the point-to-plane energy, as follows:

$$E_{fit}(\mathcal{W}^t) = \sum_i \left(\mathbf{n}_{\mathbf{u}_i^t}^\top \left(\hat{\mathbf{v}}_i - \mathbf{u}_i^t\right)\right)^2, \tag{3}$$

where $\hat{\mathbf{v}}_i$ is the transformed vertex defined by the formula:

$$\hat{\mathbf{v}}_i = \sum_j w_{i,j}^{(l)} (\mathbf{R}_j^t \mathbf{v}_i + \mathbf{t}_j^t). \tag{4}$$

Here $\mathbf{v}_i$ is a vertex on $\mathcal{M}$, and $\{\mathbf{R}_j^t, \mathbf{t}_j^t\}$ are the unknown rotation and translation of either the j-th cluster (level $l = 1$) or the j-th node (level $l = 2$), which will be solved during the optimization process. $\mathbf{u}_i^t$ is the corresponding 3D point on depth frame D^t for $\mathbf{v}_i$, and $\mathbf{n}_{\mathbf{u}_i^t}$ represents its normal. To obtain the pair of such correspondences, we render the deformed mesh $\mathcal{M}$ with the current warping field to exclude occluded vertices and project visible vertices onto the screen space of D^t. Then we look up the corresponding pixel with the same coordinates. For vertices lying on the silhouette of projected 2D image, we employ Tagliasacchi et al.'s method [24] – using 2D Distance Transform (DT) to locate the corresponding pixel and back-projecting it to 3D camera space. This correspondence search mechanism can guarantee better convergence when meeting large deformations in the direction perpendicular to the screen space (tangential motions) between two adjacent frames. Figure 2 shows a comparison of results with and without distance transform correspondences. Figure 2(a) are point clouds from two adjacent frames. The subfigure on the right illustrates the computed distance transform based on depth image contour. Figure 2(b) represents the tracking reconstruction result without using distance transform correspondences for silhouette points while Fig. 2(c) represents the result with distance transform correspondences search which is converged better than the one in Fig. 2(b).
The regularity term E_{reg} is an as-rigid-as-possible constraint:

$$E_{reg}(\mathcal{W}^t) = \sum_{j_1} \sum_{j_2 \in \mathcal{N}(j_1)} \alpha^{(l)}(\mathbf{g}_{j_1}, \mathbf{g}_{j_2}) \cdot \|\mathbf{R}_{j_1}^t \mathbf{x}_{j_2} + \mathbf{t}_{j_1}^t - \mathbf{R}_{j_2}^t \mathbf{x}_{j_2} - \mathbf{t}_{j_2}^t\|^2, \tag{5}$$

where $\mathcal{N}(j_1)$ denotes the set of neighboring nodes of the j_1-th node. $\alpha^{(l)}(\mathbf{g}_{j_1}, \mathbf{g}_{j_2})$ is a clustering-awareness weight. In level $l = 1$, $\alpha^{(1)}(\mathbf{g}_{j_1}, \mathbf{g}_{j_2}) = 1$ when the j_1-th node and the j_2-th node belong to the same cluster, and $\alpha^{(1)}(\mathbf{g}_{j_1}, \mathbf{g}_{j_2}) = 0$

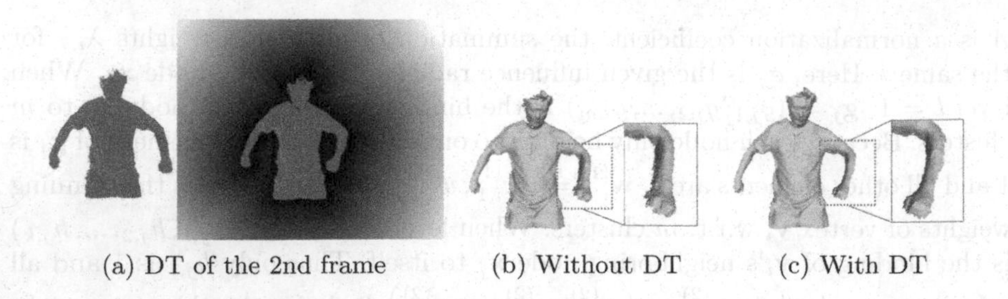

(a) DT of the 2nd frame (b) Without DT (c) With DT

Fig. 2. Tracking results comparison from one frame to its next frame without and with Distance Transform (DT) correspondences.

otherwise. In level $l = 2$, $\alpha^{(2)}(\mathbf{g}_{j_1}, \mathbf{g}_{j_2})$ is always equal to 1. This regularization term is important to ensure that all vertices will move with the visible regions as rigidly as possible if some object regions are occluded due to our single-camera capture environment.

The minimization of Eq. (1) is a nonlinear problem. In level $l = 1$, we solve the transformations of each cluster, while in level $l = 2$, we solve the transformations of each node. Both levels are solved through Gauss-Newton iterations. In each iteration, the problem is linearized around the transformations from the previous iteration: $\mathbf{J}^\top \mathbf{J}\hat{\mathbf{x}} = \mathbf{J}^\top \mathbf{f}$, where $\mathbf{J}$ is the Jacobian of function $\mathbf{f}(\hat{x})$ from the energy decomposition: $E_{total}(\hat{x}) = \mathbf{f}(\hat{x})^\top \mathbf{f}(\hat{x})$. Then, a linear system is solved to obtain the updated transformations of $\hat{\mathbf{x}}$ for the current iteration with the twist representation [16] to represent the 6D motion parameters of each cluster or node. In order to meet the real-time requirement, we use the same method as in Fusion4D [5]: $\mathbf{J}^\top \mathbf{J}$ and $\mathbf{J}^\top \mathbf{f}$ is constructed on GPU, and then Preconditioned Conjugate Gradient (PCG) method is employed to solve the transformations.

4.3 Depth Fusion

After solving for the deformation of each node, we integrate the depth information into the TSDF volume of canonical frame and uniformly sample the newly added surface to update the nodes [17]. However, this integration method may result in issues due to voxel collision: if several voxels are warped to the same position in the live frame, then the TSDF of all these voxels will be updated. To resolve this ambiguity, we modify the method presented in Fusion4D [5] to a stricter strategy. If two or more voxels in the canonical frame are warped to the same position, we reject their TSDF integration. This method avoids the generation of erroneous surfaces due to voxel collisions.

4.4 Segmentation

The optimal articulated clustering of node graph $\mathcal{C} = \{C_n\}$ can be solved based on the motion trajectory from the canonical frame to live frame t. We assume that each cluster is associated with a rigid transformation $\{\mathbf{R}_n^t, \mathbf{t}_n^t\}$. The following energy function measures the error between rigidly transformed node positions to their non-rigidly warped positions in live frame t:

$$E_{seg} = \sum_{n=1}^{m} \sum_{\mathbf{x} \in C_n} \|\mathbf{R}_n^t \mathbf{x} + \mathbf{t}_n^t - \mathbf{y}^t\|^2, \tag{6}$$

where t is the index of the live frame, n is the index of clusters, m is the total number of clusters, $\mathbf{x}$ is position of a node in the canonical frame and $\mathbf{y}^t$ is its corresponding node position after being warped into frame t. $\mathbf{x}$ and $\mathbf{y}^t$ have one-to-one correspondence because $\mathbf{y}^t$ are all deformed from the canonical frame.

The minimization of Eq. (6) implicitly includes the information of the motion trajectory – nodes with similar motions will be merged into the same cluster. By using our following method, the unknown clustering $\{C_n\}$ and per-cluster transformation $\{\mathbf{R}_n^t, \mathbf{t}_n^t\}$ can be solved simultaneously and efficiently. Although they are correlated, we find that $\{\mathbf{R}_n^t, \mathbf{t}_n^t\}$ has a closed-form solution for fixed clustering in Eq. (6) [9,23]. In this paper, we employ the merging and swapping idea as proposed by Cai et al. [1,2] to solve for $\{C_n\}$ and $\{\mathbf{R}_n^t, \mathbf{t}_n^t\}$ simultaneously.

Now we formulate the optimal clustering by minimizing the energy of Eq. (6) while keeping their rigid transformation $\{\mathbf{R}_n^t, \mathbf{t}_n^t\}$ fixed:

$$\{C_n\}_{n=1}^m = \min_{C_n} \sum_{n=1}^{m} \sum_{\mathbf{x} \in C_n} \|\mathbf{R}_n^t \mathbf{x} + \mathbf{t}_n^t - \mathbf{y}^t\|^2. \tag{7}$$

For each cluster C_n, we define its centroid in the canonical frame as $\mathbf{c}_n$:

$$\mathbf{c}_n = \frac{\sum_{\mathbf{x} \in C_n} \mathbf{x}}{\sum_{\mathbf{x} \in C_n} 1}, \tag{8}$$

and so is its corresponding vertex centroid $\mathbf{c}_n^t$ in live frame t. Then Eq. (7) can be rewritten by applying the closed-form solution of $\{\mathbf{R}_n^t, \mathbf{t}_n^t\}$:

$$\{C_n\}_{n=1}^m = \min_{C_n} \sum_{n=1}^{m} E^*(C_n), \tag{9}$$

where:

$$E^*(C_n) = \sum_{\mathbf{x} \in C_n} [(\mathbf{x} - \mathbf{c}_n)^\top (\mathbf{x} - \mathbf{c}_n) + (\mathbf{y}^t - \mathbf{c}_n^t)^\top (\mathbf{y}^t - \mathbf{c}_n^t)] - 2\sum_{q=1}^{3} \sigma_{nq}^t, \tag{10}$$

and σ_{nq}^t is the singular value of cross covariance matrix $\mathbf{A}^t(C_n)$:

$$\mathbf{A}^t(C_n) = \sum_{\mathbf{x} \in C_n} (\mathbf{x} - \mathbf{c}_n)(\mathbf{y}^t - \mathbf{c}_n^t)^\top. \tag{11}$$

Equation (9) can be solved in two stages: initial clustering by merging operations, and clustering optimization by swapping operations.

Initial Clustering by Merging Operations: Inspired by the surface simplification idea of Cai et al. [2], we define merging operations to partition the nodes of the canonical frame into m clusters as initialization. It will result in a good initial clustering for the next stage of swapping-based optimization.

In the first step of the merging operation, each node is treated as an individual cluster, which forms potential merging pairs with its neighboring clusters. When a pair of clusters is merged to a new cluster, a merge cost is calculated and associated with this merge operation. For a merging operation $(C_i, C_j) \rightarrow C_k$, the merging cost is defined as: $E^*(C_k) - E^*(C_i) - E^*(C_j)$. Figure 3 shows the concept of such an operation.

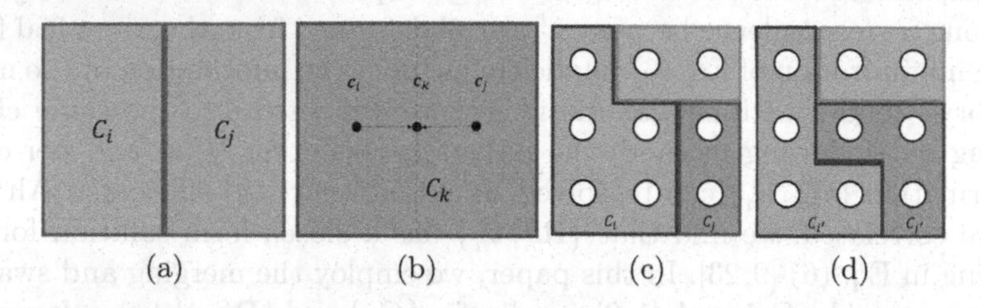

Fig. 3. Merging and swapping operation for a pair of clusters. C_i and C_j is merged to C_k. (a) Before merging. (b)After merging, the centroid of new cluster $\mathbf{c}_k$ is different from both $\mathbf{c}_i$ and $\mathbf{c}_j$. (c) The center node $\mathbf{x}_l$ is swapped from C_i to C_j. Clustering before swapping: region *Blue* is C_i, and region *Green* is C_j. *Circle* represents nodes in clusters. (d) Clustering after swapping: region *Blue* is $C_{i'}$, and region *Green* is $C_{j'}$. After the swapping operation, the belonging of node $\mathbf{x}_l$ is changed from $C_{i'}$ to $C_{j'}$. (Color figure online)

A heap is maintained to store all possible merging operations in the current clustering, paired with the corresponding costs as the key value. Next, the least-cost merging is performed. Each time after the least-cost pair is selected from the heap, only a local update is needed to maintain the validity of the merging heap: the remaining pairs of the two merged clusters in the heap are deleted, and the potential merging between the new cluster and its direct neighbors are inserted. This step is iteratively performed until the number of clusters reaches m. As shown in Supplementary Material, the merging cost can be computed with $O(1)$ complexity, which is independent of the number of nodes in each cluster.

Clustering Optimization by Swapping Operations: Only greedily merging the least-cost pair of clusters as initialization cannot guarantee the optimal solution for Eq. (9). The second stage of swapping operations can continue to optimize it based on the above initialization. In the greedy merging process, each time a pair of clusters is merged, nodes from both clusters are bound to reside in the same new cluster. Those nodes cannot freely decide where to go, so a swapping operation is necessary to relax the binding between nodes and clusters from the above initialization.

The swapping operation is defined as swapping a boundary node from its belonged cluster C_i to swapping-available clusters. A boundary node $\mathbf{x}_l$ is the node which resides in C_i and has at least a neighboring node $\mathbf{x}_j \in \mathcal{N}(\mathbf{x}_l)$ that does not belong to C_i. We denote the set of clusters that $\mathcal{N}(\mathbf{x}_l)$ reside in as swapping-available clusters $NC_{\mathbf{x}_l}$. Whether swapping $\mathbf{x}_l$ from C_i to $C_j \in NC_{\mathbf{x}_l}$ is determined by the sign of energy change after the swapping operation. We call this energy change as swapping cost.

If the swapping cost is less than 0, it means this swapping can decrease the energy of our objective function Eq. (6). Otherwise, the current clustering is best suitable for the tested node, and there is no further operation needed. If there is more than one cluster in $NC_{\mathbf{x}_l}$ that can optimize the clustering, we select the one that leads to the largest decrease of energy. To be more precise, as shown in the Supplementary Material, the swapping cost can be efficiently computed with $O(1)$ complexity, which is independent of the number of nodes in each cluster. Figure 3(c) and (d) illustrates a typical swapping operation by swapping the center node $\mathbf{x}_l$ from C_i to C_j which results in new clusters $C_{i'}$ and $C_{j'}$.

In order to achieve real-time reconstruction, we need to accelerate the segmentation step. We only employ the merging operation after registering the mesh of canonical frame with the second frame. For the segmentation step of later frames, we initialize the clustering with the previous result and then perform swapping based on such initialization. For newly added nodes after depth fusion, their cluster belongings are determined by their closest existing neighbor nodes. Because of such initialization, the maintenance of heap structure is no longer needed. We can use GPU to compute the cross covariance matrix $\mathbf{A}^t(C_n)$ and the energy $E^*(C_n)$ in parallel according to Eqs. (10) and (11).

Fig. 4. Segmentation improves the reconstruction result for fast inter-frame motion in direction parallel to the screen. In each group from left to right: input depth image, the reconstructed result of our method, and the result of DynamicFusion with only DT.

Figure 4 shows a comparison example between our method and DynamicFusion with DT in the registration step. Although both cases employ the DT-based correspondences computing, the reconstruction result of our method is much better because the introduction of segmentation.

The number of clusters can be given as a constant, or can be estimated dynamically by adding an energy threshold in the merging step. When the increased energy after one merging operation is bigger than the threshold, the merging step stops. This mechanism can automatically determine the number of clusters. Considering real-time performance, we can break any cluster with error higher than a given threshold into two new clusters and adjust the boundaries of new clusters in the swapping step. Cluster breaking can be achieved by merging all original nodes into two new clusters. Because only a small number of nodes in that cluster needs to be re-merged, the real-time performance can still hold. Due to the space limit of the paper, details about dynamic clustering such as how the number of clusters influences the results, and the comparison of reconstruction results can be found in our Supplementary Material.

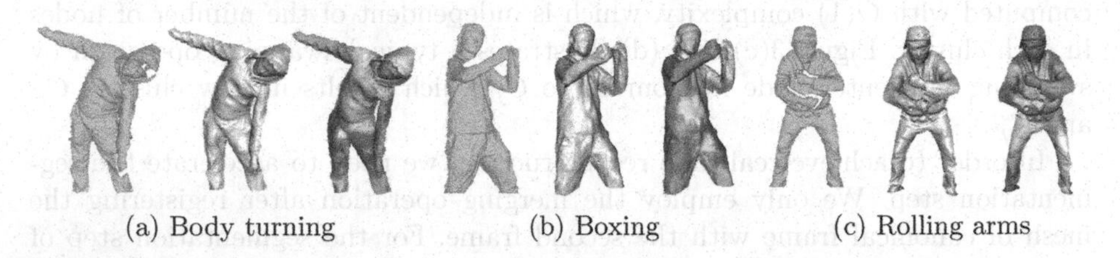

(a) Body turning (b) Boxing (c) Rolling arms

Fig. 5. Selected human motion reconstruction results by our system. From left to right for each motion: input depth, reconstructed geometry, segmentation.

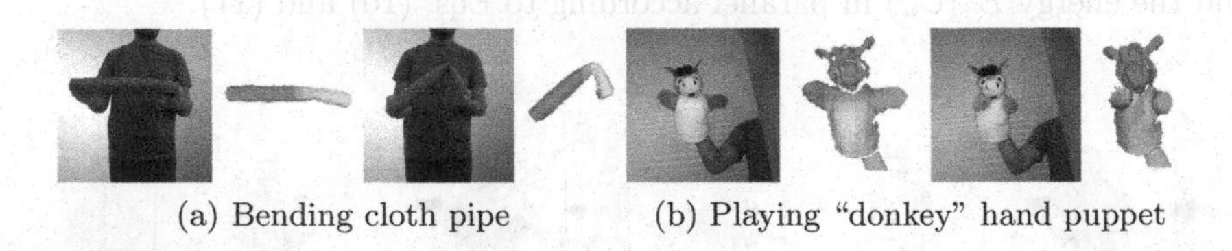

(a) Bending cloth pipe (b) Playing "donkey" hand puppet

Fig. 6. Selected non-human reconstruction results by our system. (a) shows our reconstructed results of bending a cloth pipe at the 1/4 location; (b) shows our results of playing a "donkey" hand puppet.

5 Results

In this section, we describe the performance of our system and details of its implementation, followed by qualitatively comparisons with state-of-the-art methods and evaluations. We captured more than 10 sequences with persons performing natural body motions like "Boxing", "Dancing", "Body turning", "Rolling arms", and "Crossing arms", etc. We have also experimented our algorithm on an existing dataset for articulated model reconstruction [26].

Figure 5 shows some of our reconstruction results for motions "Body turning", "Boxing", and "Rolling arms". Our ArticulatedFusion system enables simultaneous geometry, motion, and segmentation reconstruction. As shown in

Fig. 5(c), the human body is segmented by deformation clustering so hands, arms and head are segmented out because of their articulated motion property.

Figure 6 shows that our system can also reconstruct geometry, motion, and segmentation for non-human motion sequences without any prior skeleton information or template. It automatically learns the segmentation from control nodes clustering. As shown in the 2nd and 4th columns of Fig. 6(a) and (b), faithful segmentation can be automatically generated during the reconstruction process with motions and fine geometry.

5.1 Performance

Our system is fully implemented on a single NVIDIA GeForce GTX 1080 graphics processing unit using both the OpenGL API and the NVIDIA CUDA API. The pipeline runs at 34–40 ms per frame on average. The time breaking of main steps is as follows (Table 1): the preprocessing of the depth information (including bilateral filtering and calculation of the depth normals) requires 1 ms; the rendering of the results requires 1 ms. For two-level node motion optimization, we run 5 and 2 iterations respectively. In each iteration, to solve the linear equation, we run 10 iterations of PCG. The voxel resolution is 5 mm. For each vertex, 8 nearest nodes is used as its control node. The number of segments ranges from 6 to 40. In all examples, we capture the depth stream using a Kinect v2 with 512×424 depth image resolution.

Table 1. Average computation time per frame for several motions (ms). Column "Init" is the time to initialize and update node graph. Column "DT" is the time to calculate distance transform. Columns "Level 1" and "Level 2" represent the time to solve level-1 and level-2 registration. Column "TSDF" represents the time to perform TSDF integration. Column "Seg" is the time of segmetation.

	# of Segs	# of Nodes	Init (ms)	DT (ms)	Level 1 (ms)	Level 2 (ms)	TSDF (ms)	Seg (ms)	Total (ms)
Boxing	20	1442	2.7	4.9	8.3	13.9	4.7	2.5	37.0
Rolling arms	20	1914	3.4	4.6	8.5	15.0	4.9	2.7	39.1
Crossing arms	12	1130	2.5	4.6	7.1	13.4	5.1	1.9	34.6
Dancing	30	1569	3.0	4.7	9.0	14.4	5.2	3.0	39.3
Body turning	20	2002	3.5	4.7	8.6	14.5	4.8	2.8	38.9

5.2 Comparisons and Evaluations

We compare our ArticulatedFusion with two state-of-the-art methods DynamicFusion [17] and VolumeDeform [10]. Figure 7 shows visual comparisons on motion "Dancing". We can see both DynamicFusion and VolumeDeform fail in the left

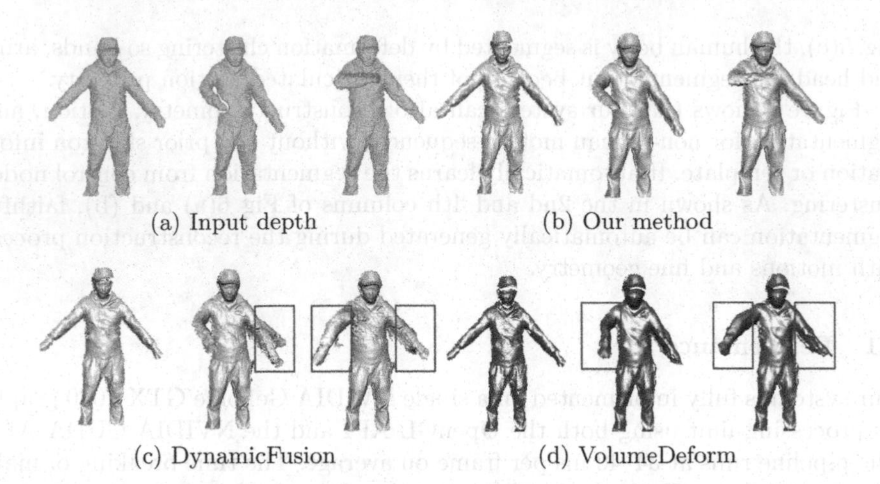

Fig. 7. Visual comparisons of the results between: (b) our method, (c) DynamicFusion [17], and (d) VolumeDeform [10], with input depth images shown in (a).

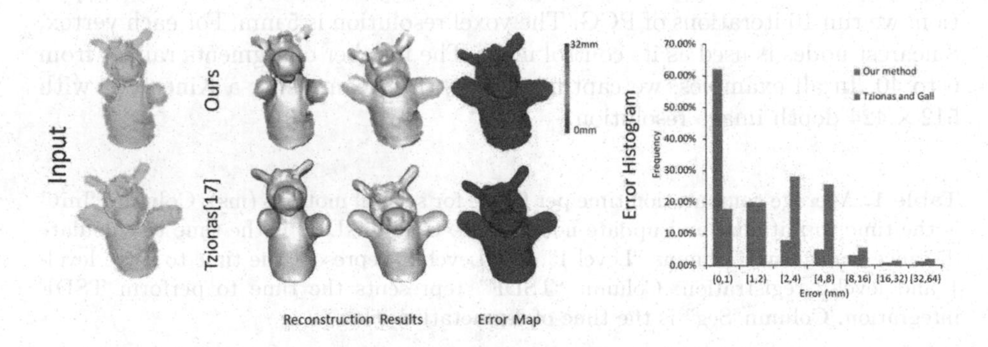

Fig. 8. Non-human object reconstruction comparison on "donkey" hand puppet.

and right arms region. Our method generates more faithful results for motions in tangential direction or motions having large occlusions.

To further quantitatively evaluate our reconstructed segmentation and motion, we compare our results with the other state-of-the-art methods by using the Vicon-captured groundtruth data from BodyFusion [29]. In Fig. 9, it is noted that our reconstruction error is comparative to BodyFusion (slightly higher though), but our method is more general and can be applied to dynamic scenes where Kinect-based skeleton is not available, such as non-human-body motions (Figs. 6, 8 and 10(b)) and human-body motions without initial skeleton information (Fig. 10(a)). In Fig. 10(a), the skeleton of the person on the back cannot be provided by Kinect because of high occlusion in the body. It is noted that the highlighted head and leg part is well reconstructed with the help of our segmentation, while they are not correctly tracked by DynamicFusion.

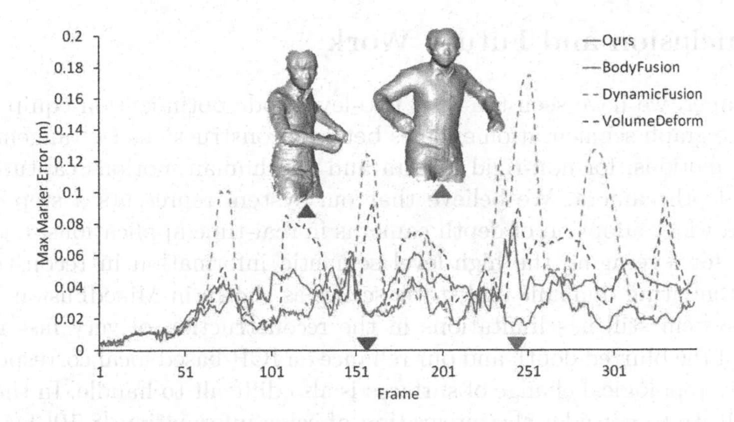

Fig. 9. Quantitative comparison: max marker errors of our method, BodyFusion, DynamicFusion and VolumeDeform for a motion sequence.

We compare our method with two other reconstruction methods that can reconstruct non-human objects. Figure 8 shows a detailed comparison of the near-articulated example "donkey" hand puppet with the template-based reconstruction result in Tzionas and Gall's work [26]. The first column of Fig. 8 shows two input depth images. From both the error map and the error histogram, we can find our method has better error distribution than theirs. In order to have a fair comparison in error histogram, we only count visible vertices in both cases. Because of the introduction of segmentaion in the registration step, our method is more robust for fast motion. Figure 10(b) shows another example of non-human object reconstruction. In VolumeDeform [10], their reconstruction fails when skipping 4 or more frames before next frame. But our method can still get a good result, while every petal of the sunflower is clustered as one segment.

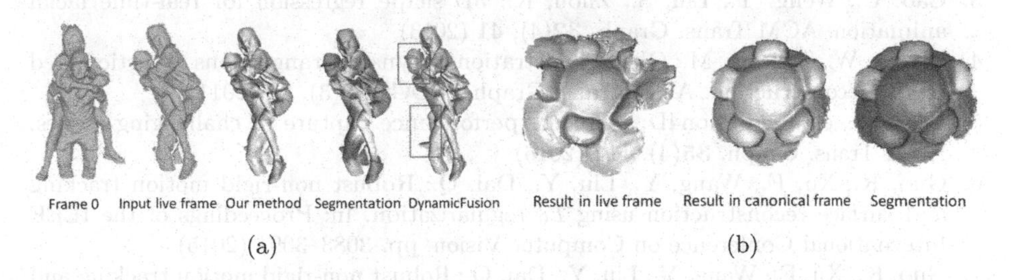

Fig. 10. (a) Reconstruction result comparison of our method and DynamicFusion [17]. (b) Reconstruction result of the failure case in VolumeDeform [10] (shown in their Fig. 9) for 5x speed input (skipping 5 frames).

6 Conclusion and Future Work

In this paper, we have seen that our two-level node optimization equipped efficient node graph segmentation enables better reconstructions for tangential and occluded motions, for non-rigid human and non-human motions captured with a single depth camera. We believe that our system represents a step forward towards a wider adoption of depth cameras in real-time applications, and opens the door for leveraging the high-level semantic information in reconstruction, e.g. differentiating dynamic and static scenes as shown in MixedFusion [31].

Our system still has limitations in the reconstruction of very fast motions because of the blurred depth and our reliance on ICP-based local correspondence matching. Topological change of surfaces is also difficult to handle. In the future we would like to consider the integration of color information [8,10] for further improvement on the motion optimization, and extracting a consistent tree-based skeleton structure from our segmentation.

Acknowledgement. We would like to thank the reviewers for their valuable comments. We are grateful to Matthias Innmann for the help on comparison results of VolumeDeform, Tao Yu for providing their Vicon-based ground-truth marker data in BodyFusion, and Dimitrios Tzionas for providing their data. This work was partially supported by National Science Foundation under grant number IIS-1149737. Chao would like to thank the support provided by Hua Guo during the preparation for this paper.

References

1. Cai, Y., Guo, X.: Anisotropic superpixel generation based on Mahalanobis distance. Comput. Graph. Forum **35**(7), 199–207 (2016)
2. Cai, Y., Guo, X., Liu, Y., Wang, W., Mao, W., Zhong, Z.: Surface approximation via asymptotic optimal geometric partition. IEEE Trans. Vis. Comput. Graph. **23**(12), 2613–2626 (2017)
3. Cao, C., Weng, Y., Lin, S., Zhou, K.: 3D shape regression for real-time facial animation. ACM Trans. Graph. **32**(4), 41 (2013)
4. Chang, W., Zwicker, M.: Global registration of dynamic range scans for articulated model reconstruction. ACM Trans. Graph. (TOG) **30**(3), 26 (2011)
5. Dou, M., et al.: Fusion4D: real-time performance capture of challenging scenes. ACM Trans. Graph. **35**(4), 114 (2016)
6. Guo, K., Xu, F., Wang, Y., Liu, Y., Dai, Q.: Robust non-rigid motion tracking and surface reconstruction using L_0 regularization. In: Proceedings of the IEEE International Conference on Computer Vision, pp. 3083–3091 (2015)
7. Guo, K., Xu, F., Wang, Y., Liu, Y., Dai, Q.: Robust non-rigid motion tracking and surface reconstruction using L_0 regularization. IEEE Trans. Vis. Comput. Graph. (2017)
8. Guo, K., Xu, F., Yu, T., Liu, X., Dai, Q., Liu, Y.: Real-time geometry, albedo, and motion reconstruction using a single RGB-D camera. ACM Trans. Graph. **36**(3), 32 (2017)
9. Horn, B.K.P.: Closed-form solution of absolute orientation using unit quaternions. J. Opt. Soc. Am. A **4**(4), 629–642 (1987)

10. Innmann, M., Zollhöfer, M., Nießner, M., Theobalt, C., Stamminger, M.: VolumeDeform: real-time volumetric non-rigid reconstruction. In: Leibe, B., Matas, J., Sebe, N., Welling, M. (eds.) ECCV 2016. LNCS, vol. 9912, pp. 362–379. Springer, Cham (2016). https://doi.org/10.1007/978-3-319-46484-8_22
11. James, D.L., Twigg, C.D.: Skinning mesh animations. ACM Trans. Graph. **24**(3), 399–407 (2005)
12. Le, B.H., Deng, Z.: Smooth skinning decomposition with rigid bones. ACM Trans. Graph. **31**(6), 199 (2012)
13. Li, H., Adams, B., Guibas, L.J., Pauly, M.: Robust single-view geometry and motion reconstruction. ACM Trans. Graph. (TOG) **28**(5), 175 (2009)
14. Li, H., Yu, J., Ye, Y., Bregler, C.: Realtime facial animation with on-the-fly correctives. ACM Trans. Graph. **32**(4), 42-1 (2013)
15. Lorensen, W.E., Cline, H.E.: Marching cubes: a high resolution 3D surface construction algorithm. In: ACM siggraph computer graphics, vol. 21, pp. 163–169. ACM (1987)
16. Murray, R.M., Li, Z., Sastry, S.S.: A Mathematical Introduction to Robotic Manipulation. CRC Press, Boca Raton (1994)
17. Newcombe, R.A., Fox, D., Seitz, S.M.: DynamicFusion: reconstruction and tracking of non-rigid scenes in real-time. In: IEEE Conference on Computer Vision and Pattern Recognition, pp. 343–352 (2015)
18. Newcombe, R.A., et al.: KinectFusion: real-time dense surface mapping and tracking. In: 10th IEEE international symposium on Mixed and Augmented Reality, pp. 127–136 (2011)
19. Pekelny, Y., Gotsman, C.: Articulated object reconstruction and markerless motion capture from depth video. Comput. Graph. Forum **27**(2), 399–408 (2008)
20. Pons-Moll, G., Baak, A., Helten, T., Müller, M., Seidel, H.P., Rosenhahn, B.: Multisensor-fusion for 3D full-body human motion capture. In: IEEE Conference on Computer Vision and Pattern Recognition, pp. 663–670 (2010)
21. Slavcheva, M., Baust, M., Cremers, D., Ilic, S.: KillingFusion: non-rigid 3D reconstruction without correspondences. In: IEEE Conference on Computer Vision and Pattern Recognition (CVPR) (2017)
22. Slavcheva, M., Baust, M., Ilic, S.: SobolevFusion: 3D reconstruction of scenes undergoing free non-rigid motion. In: IEEE/CVF Conference on Computer Vision and Pattern Recognition (CVPR) (2018)
23. Sorkine, O.: Least-squares rigid motion using SVD. Technical notes (2017)
24. Tagliasacchi, A., Schröder, M., Tkach, A., Bouaziz, S., Botsch, M., Pauly, M.: Robust articulated-ICP for real-time hand tracking. Comput. Graph. Forum **34**(5), 101–114 (2015)
25. Tkach, A., Pauly, M., Tagliasacchi, A.: Sphere-meshes for real-time hand modeling and tracking. ACM Trans. Graph. **35**(6), 222 (2016)
26. Tzionas, D., Gall, J.: Reconstructing articulated rigged models from RGB-D videos. In: Hua, G., Jégou, H. (eds.) ECCV 2016. LNCS, vol. 9915, pp. 620–633. Springer, Cham (2016). https://doi.org/10.1007/978-3-319-49409-8_53. http://files.is.tue.mpg.de/dtzionas/Skeleton-Reconstruction
27. Vlasic, D., Baran, I., Matusik, W., Popović, J.: Articulated mesh animation from multi-view silhouettes. ACM Trans. Graph. **27**(3), 97 (2008)
28. Wand, M., et al.: Efficient reconstruction of nonrigid shape and motion from real-time 3D scanner data. ACM Trans. Graph. **28**(2), 15 (2009)
29. Yu, T., et al.: Bodyfusion: real-time capture of human motion and surface geometry using a single depth camera. In: The IEEE International Conference on Computer Vision (ICCV). IEEE, October 2017

30. Yu, T., et al.: Doublefusion: real-time capture of human performances with inner body shapes from a single depth sensor. In: The IEEE International Conference on Computer Vision and Pattern Recognition(CVPR). IEEE, June 2018
31. Zhang, H., Xu, F.: MixedFusion: real-time reconstruction of an indoor scene with dynamic objects. IEEE Trans. Vis. Comput. Graph. (2017)
32. Zollhöfer, M., et al.: Real-time non-rigid reconstruction using an RGB-D camera. ACM Trans. Graph. **33**(4), 156 (2014)

MRF Optimization with Separable Convex Prior on Partially Ordered Labels

Csaba Domokos[1,2(✉)], Frank R. Schmidt[1,2], and Daniel Cremers[1]

[1] Technical University of Munich, Garching bei München, Germany
cremers@tum.de

[2] Bosch Center for Artificial Intelligence, Renningen, Germany
{csaba.domokos,frank.r.schmidt}@de.bosch.com

Abstract. Solving a multi-labeling problem with a convex penalty can be achieved in polynomial time if the label set is totally ordered. In this paper we propose a generalization to partially ordered sets. To this end, we assume that the label set is the Cartesian product of totally ordered sets and the convex prior is separable. For this setting we introduce a general combinatorial optimization framework that provides an approximate solution. More specifically, we first construct a graph whose minimal cut provides a lower bound to our energy. The result of this relaxation is then used to get a feasible solution via classical move-making cuts. To speed up the optimization, we propose an efficient coarse-to-fine approach over the label space. We demonstrate the proposed framework through extensive experiments for optical flow estimation.

Keywords: Multi-labeling problem · Poset · Sub-modular relaxation

1 Introduction

Many computer vision problems like stereo matching [1–3], semantic image segmentation [4] or optical flow estimation [5,6] can be formulated as a *multi-labeling problem*. For a set of variables $\mathcal{V}$ and a finite label set $\mathcal{L}$, a mapping $f\colon \mathcal{V} \to \mathcal{L}$ is called a *multi-labeling*. The multi-labeling problem aims to find a multi-labeling f that minimizes an energy $E(f)$. In general, this problem is known to be NP-hard, moreover, there is no algorithm that can approximate this general energy minimization with an approximation ratio better than some exponential function in the input size [7]. Nevertheless, by making some assumptions the multi-labeling problem becomes tractable [8–10].

C. Domokos—This work was done while the author was an Alexander von Humboldt Fellow at the Technical University of Munich.

Electronic supplementary material The online version of this chapter (https://doi.org/10.1007/978-3-030-01237-3_21) contains supplementary material, which is available to authorized users.

V. Ferrari et al. (Eds.): ECCV 2018, LNCS 11212, pp. 341–356, 2018.
https://doi.org/10.1007/978-3-030-01237-3_21

In this paper we address the problem of solving a multi-labeling problem. In order to find an optimal multi-labeling $f\colon \mathcal{V} \to \mathcal{L}$ we want to minimize an energy of the form

$$E(f) = \sum_{i \in \mathcal{V}} E_i(f_i) + \sum_{(i,j) \in \mathcal{E}} E_{ij}(f_i, f_j), \tag{1}$$

where $\mathcal{E} \subset \mathcal{V} \times \mathcal{V}$ denotes the pairwise dependencies of different variables. The energies $E_i\colon \mathcal{L} \to \mathbb{R}$ and $E_{ij}\colon \mathcal{L} \times \mathcal{L} \to \mathbb{R}_0^+$ describe the data fidelity terms and pairwise smoothness terms, respectively. While the data term E_i for all $i \in \mathcal{V}$ can be chosen arbitrarily, the smoothness terms E_{ij} are of the following form

$$E_{ij}(f_i, f_j) = w_{ij} \cdot d(f_i, f_j) \quad \text{for all } (i,j) \in \mathcal{E}. \tag{2}$$

The energy (1) corresponds to a Markov random field (MRF) formulation [8] over an undirected graph $\mathcal{G} = (\mathcal{V}, \mathcal{E})$, where $P(f) \sim \exp(-E(f))$. Here, $w_{ij} \geq 0$ depends on the input data and $d\colon \mathcal{L} \times \mathcal{L} \to \mathbb{R}_0^+$ is a *metric* on $\mathcal{L}$. Under these mild restrictions, it is known that (1) can be minimized globally in polynomial time if $|\mathcal{L}| = 2$ [11] or if $\mathcal{L}$ is the totally ordered set $\{1, \ldots, \ell\}$ and there is an even, convex function $g\colon \mathbb{R} \to \mathbb{R}_0^+$ such that $d(f_i, f_j) = g(f_i - f_j)$ [8].

In this paper we focus on a more general setting of partially ordered label sets $\mathcal{L}$. In particular, we assume that $\mathcal{L} = \mathcal{L}_1 \times \ldots \times \mathcal{L}_k$ can be written as the Cartesian product of k different totally ordered label sets. In addition, we assume that the function d that penalizes different labels for interacting pixels (*i.e.*for all $(i,j) \in \mathcal{E}$) has the form $d(f_i, f_j) = g(f_i - f_j)$, where g is an even, separable convex function, *i.e.*a sum of regularizers for each dimension of the label space.

The rest of this paper is organized as follows. We give a short overview of the related work in Sect. 1.1. In Sect. 2 we introduce the theoretical background of partially ordered sets, a.k.a. posets. The two main contributions of the paper can be summarized as follows:

- We propose a combinatorial optimization framework, which can be applied for minimizing energies defined on poset labelings. Namely, we show a general graph construction (see Sect. 2.2), whose minimal cut provides a lower bound to our energy. This relaxation is exploited to get a feasible solution by making use of classical move-making cuts [1]. The proposed graph construction can handle arbitrary data costs and separable convex smoothness costs.
- We also propose an efficient coarse-to-fine strategy in the label space (see Sect. 3), which effectively reduces the possible search space and results in a considerable speed-up of the algorithm.

As an illustration of the proposed optimization scheme we consider the problem of optical flow estimation. Comprehensive experiments in Sect. 4 show that the proposed method provides competitive results with other combinatorial optimization algorithms at reduced complexity. Section 5 concludes the paper.

1.1 Related Work

Partially ordered label sets are very common in several computer vision applications like optical flow estimation, image registration, stereo exposure fusion, *etc.*, where the label set $\mathcal{L}$ is the Cartesian product of totally ordered sets.

Schekhovtsov *et al.* [12] proposed an MRF model for image registration, where the deformation is described by a coupled field of discrete x- and y-displacements of pixels. The model consists of two layers of variables. The inter-layer interaction is used to encode the data term, and the intra-layer interactions encode pairwise (smoothness) constraints for neighboring pixels. This model leads to a simpler relaxation to which the sequential tree-reweighted message passing (TRW-S) algorithm [2] is applied. Chen and Koltun [6] addressed the problem of optical flow estimation, where the classical Horn-Schunck objective [13] is minimized over a regular grid by making use of the TRW-S algorithm [2]. Another discrete optimization approach was presented in [5] for optical flow estimation. The authors formulated the problem as a discrete inference and applied a block coordinate descent method, which iteratively optimizes all image rows and columns via dynamic programming.

Kohli *et al.* [14] considered the problem of optimizing multi-label pairwise MRFs. The multi-label MRF model is first converted into an equivalent binary MRF and then it is relaxed, which can be efficiently solved using a maximum flow algorithm [11]. The solution provides a partially optimal labeling of the binary variables, which is transferred to the multi-label problem. A detailed review for minimizing functions with both sub-modular[1] and non-submodular terms can be found in [15], referred to as the QPBO method (quadratic pseudo-Boolean optimization). The output of QPBO, however, is a *partial labeling*, which means there is a special label that is interpreted as "unknown".

Goldstein *et al.* [16] presented a general variational functional lifting technique for minimizing vector-valued problems. This technique allows to find global minimizers for optical flow. The authors consider total-variation as regularizer. In contrast to our approach, L_2^2 penalty cannot be considered in [16]. A continuous convex relaxation for multi-label problems was proposed in [17] for the case when the label space is a continuous product space and the regularizer is separable. Through the relaxed problem, various problems like optic flow, stereo matching and segmentation can be solved within provable bounds of the global optimum. This approach allows a very general class of continuous regularizers on multi-dimensional label spaces. The regularizers can be arbitrarily mixed, in the sense that each dimension of the label space can have its own type of regularity. We note that, in contrast to continuous relaxations, we focus on combinatorial optimization approaches in this paper.

[1] A set function $f : 2^{\mathcal{V}} \to \mathbb{R}$ is called sub-modular, if for any pair of subsets $A, B \subset \mathcal{V}$, $f(A) + f(B) \geq f(A \cup B) + f(A \cap B)$ is satisfied.

2 Energy Minimization on Posets

In the following, we address the problem of minimizing (1) if $\mathcal{L}$ is a partially ordered set (or poset). In Sect. 2.1 we provide a short introduction to posets [18] and explain their difficulties in an energy minimization framework. In Sect. 2.2 we show how to design a sub-modular energy that is a relaxed version of (1). In particular, we will show in Sect. 2.3 how to efficiently minimize this lifted energy by finding a minimal cut in a graph and how to employ a heuristic projection scheme in order to find a feasible solution of the original energy.

2.1 Posets, Lower Level Sets and Lower Ideals

A partially ordered set is a set $\mathcal{L}$ together with a relation that stores for any pair of elements $\alpha, \beta \in \mathcal{L}$ whether the statement $\alpha \leq \beta$ is true or not.

Definition 1 (Poset). *Given a set $\mathcal{L}$ and a relation $\leq$ on $\mathcal{L}$. We call $(\mathcal{L}, \leq)$ a* partially ordered set *or* poset *if the following conditions are satisfied for all $\alpha, \beta, \gamma \in \mathcal{L}$*

$$\alpha \leq \alpha \qquad \textit{(Reflexivity)}$$
$$\alpha \leq \beta,\ \beta \leq \alpha \Rightarrow \alpha = \beta \qquad \textit{(Antisymmetry)}$$
$$\alpha \leq \beta,\ \beta \leq \gamma \Rightarrow \alpha \leq \gamma \qquad \textit{(Transitivity)}$$

$(\mathcal{L}, \leq)$ is called a totally ordered set *if, for any pair $\alpha, \beta \in \mathcal{L}$ the statement $\alpha \leq \beta$ or $\beta \leq \alpha$ is true.*

The main difference between posets and totally ordered sets is that there may be two different elements $\alpha, \beta \in \mathcal{L}$ in a poset for which we cannot decide whether one element is larger than the other. From now on we use the notation $\alpha < \beta$ iff $\alpha \leq \beta$ and $\alpha \neq \beta$ holds. The easiest way to create a poset is to take the Cartesian product of two or more totally ordered sets.

Lemma 1 (Cartesian Product). *Let $(\mathcal{L}_1, \leq_1)$ and $(\mathcal{L}_2, \leq_2)$ be two totally ordered sets. The Cartesian product $\mathcal{L} := \mathcal{L}_1 \times \mathcal{L}_2$ becomes a poset $(\mathcal{L}, \leq)$ via*

$$(\alpha_1, \alpha_2) \leq (\beta_1, \beta_2) :\Leftrightarrow (\alpha_1 \leq_1 \beta_1) \wedge (\alpha_2 \leq_2 \beta_2).$$

Proof. Follows directly from the definition of posets.

A common way to visualize the internal structure of a poset is to consider its *Hasse diagram.*

Definition 2. (Hasse Diagram). *Let $(\mathcal{L}, \leq)$ be a finite poset. Then, the* Hasse diagram *of $\mathcal{L}$ is a directed graph $\mathcal{H} = (\mathcal{L}, \mathcal{E}_\mathcal{L})$ with the vertex set $\mathcal{L}$ and the edge set*

$$\mathcal{E}_\mathcal{L} := \{(\beta, \alpha) \in \mathcal{L} \times \mathcal{L} \mid \alpha < \beta,\ \forall \gamma \in \mathcal{L}\colon \neg(\alpha < \gamma < \beta)\}.$$

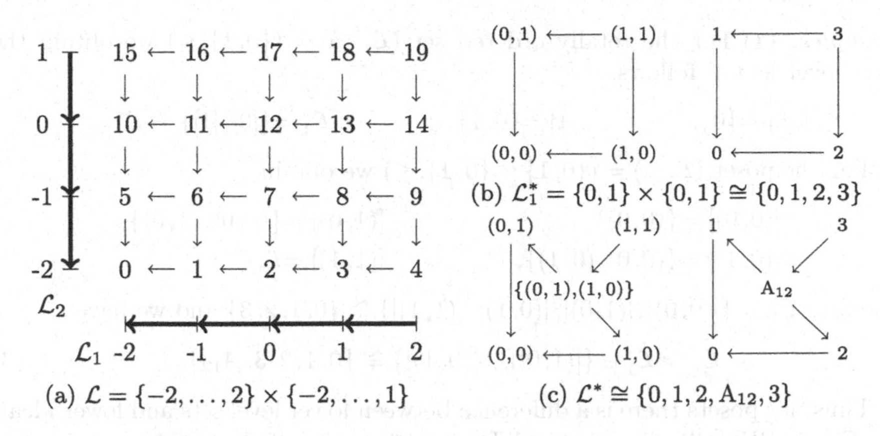

Fig. 1. Hasse diagrams. (a) Hasse diagram for the poset $\mathcal{L} = \mathcal{L}_1 \times \mathcal{L}_2$, where $\mathcal{L}_1 = \{-2, \ldots, 2\}$ and $\mathcal{L}_2 = \{-2, \ldots, 1\}$ are totally ordered sets. The Hasse diagrams of $\mathcal{L}_1$ and $\mathcal{L}_2$ are chains. (b) Two isomorphic Hasse diagrams for $\mathcal{L} = \{0,1\} \times \{0,1\} \cong \mathcal{L}_1^*$. (c) Two isomorphic Hasse diagrams for $\mathcal{L}^* = \mathcal{L}_1^* \cup \{[(1,0)] \cup [(0,1)]\} \cong \{0,1,2,3,\mathrm{A}_{12}\}$

For the totally ordered set $\mathcal{L} = \{1, \ldots, \ell\}$, the Hasse diagram has exactly $\ell - 1$ edges. These edges are of the form $(\alpha + 1, \alpha)$. Thus, the Hasse diagram of a totally ordered set is always a chain. If $\mathcal{L}$ is a poset on the other hand, the Hasse diagram becomes a DAG (directed acyclic graph) (see Fig. 1).

Of particular interest for the next section is the set of lower ideals.

Definition 3. *For each* $\alpha \in \mathcal{L}$, *we refer to the set*

$$[\alpha] := \{\beta \in \mathcal{L} \mid \beta \leq \alpha\}$$

as its lower level set. *Further, we call a subset* $I \subset \mathcal{L}$ *a* lower ideal *if the following holds*

$$\alpha \in I \Rightarrow [\alpha] \subset I.$$

We denote the set of all lower ideals as $\mathcal{L}^* \subset 2^{\mathcal{L}}$ *and the set of all lower level sets as* $\mathcal{L}_1^* \subset \mathcal{L}^*$.

In fact, every element of $\mathcal{L}^*$ can be represented as the union of elements included in $\mathcal{L}_1^*$. In other words, a lower ideal $L \in \mathcal{L}^*$ is a set that accumulates lower level sets, that is

$$L = \bigcup_{\alpha \in L} [\alpha].$$

Note that, by construction, both $\mathcal{L}$ and $\mathcal{L}_1^*$ have the same cardinality. Nevertheless, $\mathcal{L}^*$ can be larger than $\mathcal{L}_1^*$. We also remark that the elements of $\mathcal{L}_1^*$ are subsets of $\mathcal{L}$.

It is worth noting that for totally ordered sets, we always have $\mathcal{L}^* = \mathcal{L}_1^*$, which has the same cardinality as $\mathcal{L}$. Thus, the difference between lower ideals and lower level sets is only observable for posets.

Examples. (1) For the totally ordered set $(\mathcal{L}, \leq) = (\{0,1\}, \leq)$ we obtain the lower level sets as follows:

$$[0] = \{0\}, \qquad [1] = \{0,1\}, \qquad \mathcal{L}_1^* = \{[0],[1]\} = \mathcal{L}^*.$$

(2) For the poset $(\mathcal{L}, \leq) = (\{0,1\} \times \{0,1\}, \leq)$ we obtain

$$[(0,0)] = \{(0,0)\}, \qquad [(1,0)] = \{(0,0),(1,0)\},$$
$$[(0,1)] = \{(0,0),(0,1)\}, \qquad [(1,1)] = \mathcal{L},$$

therefore $\mathcal{L}_1^* = \{[(0,0)],[(1,0)],[(0,1)],[(1,1)]\} \cong \{0,1,2,3\}$ and we have

$$\mathcal{L}^* = \mathcal{L}_1^* \cup \{[(1,0)] \cup [(0,1)]\} \cong \{0,1,2,3,A_{12}\}. \tag{3}$$

Thus, for posets there is a difference between lower level sets and lower ideals (see Fig. 1). We will refer to this difference

$$\mathcal{L}^{\mathrm{A}} := \mathcal{L}^* - \mathcal{L}_1^* \subset 2^{\mathcal{L}} \tag{4}$$

as the *augmented label set*, or equivalently $\mathcal{L}^* = \mathcal{L}_1^* \cup \mathcal{L}^{\mathrm{A}}$. Please note that the cardinality of $\mathcal{L}^{\mathrm{A}}$ may grow exponentially with respect to $|\mathcal{L}|$. In Sect. 2.2 we will see how these augmented labels appear if we lift our energy (1). In fact, the augmented labels result in an infeasible solution. To obtain a feasible solution without augmented labels, we propose a heuristic projection scheme.

2.2 Energy Lifting

From now on we assume a poset $(\mathcal{L}, \leq) = (\mathcal{L}, \subset)$, where $\mathcal{L} = \mathcal{L}_1 \times \ldots \times \mathcal{L}_k$ is the Cartesian product of k totally ordered sets and $\mathcal{H} = (\mathcal{L}, \mathcal{E}_{\mathcal{L}})$ its Hasse diagram. Let E be of the form (1). Furthermore, we assume that the smoothness term E_{ij} is of the form (2) and that $d(f_i, f_j) = g(f_i - f_j)$ can be represented via an even, separable convex function g. We want to construct a graph $\mathcal{G}$ such that each labeling $f \colon \mathcal{V} \to \mathcal{L}$ corresponds to an s-t cut of $\mathcal{G}$ with $E(f)$ as its cut value [11].

Totally Ordered Label Set. In the simple case $k = 1$, thus $\mathcal{L} = \mathcal{L}_1$ is a totally ordered set and we can follow the construction of Ishikawa [8] to design a graph with the desired properties. The used vertices consist of a *source* s, a *sink* t and the *internal nodes* $\mathcal{V} \times \mathcal{L}$. The edges can be divided into three different classes.

The *constraint edges* between (i,ℓ) and $(i,\ell-1)$ of infinite capacities guarantee that in an optimal cut the binary labeling of the set $\{i\} \times \mathcal{L}$ has the form $(1,\ldots,1,0,\ldots,0)$, where 1 indicates that a vertex is connected with the source.

The *data edges* can be designed as terminal links between s, respectively t, and (i,ℓ). This formulation is due to [19] and differs from the original formulation of [8]. The *smoothness edges* of capacity $w_{ij} \cdot c_\delta$ between vertices $(i,\ell+\delta)$ and (j,ℓ) for all $(i,j) \in \mathcal{E}$ model the convex function g. This is done by using the non-negative values

$$c_0 = g_1 - g_0 \qquad \text{and} \qquad c_\delta = g_{\delta+1} - 2g_\delta + g_{\delta-1} \quad (\forall \delta > 0).$$

For more details we refer to [8].

Partially Ordered Label Set. For the general case $k > 1$ we want to design a different graph with the desired properties. Like before, the used vertices are the source s, the sink t and the internal vertices $\mathcal{V} \times \mathcal{L}$. Also, we introduce *constraint edges*, *data edges* and *smoothness edges*. While these edges will be different from Ishikawa's construction [8], they serve nonetheless the same purpose.

The *constraint edges* should also connect a label ℓ with its immediate predecessor ℓ'. Due to the partial ordering, ℓ' is not unique. Thus, we use the Hasse diagram $\mathcal{H} = (\mathcal{L}, \mathcal{E}_{\mathcal{L}})$ of $\mathcal{L}$ and introduce an edge of infinite capacity between (i, ℓ) and (i, ℓ') for each $(\ell, \ell') \in \mathcal{E}_{\mathcal{L}}$. As a consequence, we obtain a labeling $\hat{f} \colon \mathcal{V} \to \mathcal{L}^*$ instead of $f \colon \mathcal{V} \to \mathcal{L}$. Note that the set $\mathcal{L}^*$ of lower ideals contains the lower level sets $\mathcal{L}_1^*$ and the augmented labels $\mathcal{L}^A$. Since there is a one-to-one relationship between $\mathcal{L}_1^*$ and $\mathcal{L}$, *i.e.*they are isomorph[2], we can understand $\hat{f}$ as a *relaxation* of f and we will denote $\hat{f}$ as $\hat{f} \colon \mathcal{V} \to (\mathcal{L} \cup \mathcal{L}^A)$.

The *data edges* should reflect the data terms $E_i(f_i)$. Since a label $f_i \in \mathcal{L}$ is now represented by the lower level set $[f_i] \in \mathcal{L}_1^*$, we have to associate a unary data cost of $D_{i,\ell}$ with the vertex (i, ℓ) such that the following holds

$$\sum_{\ell \in [f_i]} D_{i,\ell} = E_i(f_i) \qquad \forall i \in \mathcal{V}, f_i \in \mathcal{L}. \tag{5}$$

Since the Hasse diagram is a DAG, the matrix of this system of linear equations is (after permutation) in upper triangular form. Therefore, the Problem (5) can be readily solved by successive substitution. If the resulting $D_{i,\ell}$ is positive, it results in an edge of capacity $D_{i,\ell}$ from (i, ℓ) to the sink t. Otherwise, it results in an edge of capacity $-D_{i,\ell}$ from the source s to (i, ℓ) [9].

The *smoothness edges* should reflect the pairwise smoothness terms, that is, $E_{ij}(f_i, f_j) = w_{ij} \cdot g(f_i - f_j)$. Here, the special structure of our posets comes into play. $\mathcal{L} = \mathcal{L}_1 \times \ldots \times \mathcal{L}_k$ results in k-dimensional labels, therefore, we write $f_i = (f_{i,1}, \ldots, f_{i,k})$ and $f_j = (f_{j,1}, \ldots, f_{j,k})$. Since we assume that g is an even, separable convex function, we have k even, convex functions g_κ for $\kappa = 1, \ldots, k$ such that

$$d(f_i, f_j) = \sum_{\kappa=1}^{k} g_\kappa(f_{i,\kappa} - f_{j,\kappa}). \tag{6}$$

Since a label $f_i \in \mathcal{L}$ is now represented by its lower level set $[f_i]$, this lower level set also contains

$$(0_1, \ldots, 0_{\kappa-1}, f_{i,\kappa}, 0_{\kappa+1}, \ldots, 0_k), \tag{7}$$

where $0_{\kappa'}$ denotes the minimal element of the totally ordered set $\mathcal{L}_{\kappa'}$. Therefore, it is enough to encode g_κ on

$$\hat{\mathcal{L}}_\kappa := \{0_1\} \times \ldots \times \{0_{\kappa-1}\} \times \mathcal{L}_\kappa \times \{0_{\kappa+1}\} \times \ldots \times \{0_k\}.$$

Note that $\hat{\mathcal{L}}_\kappa$ is a totally ordered set and we can therefore replicate Ishikawa's idea for all $\kappa = 1, \ldots, k$ in order to design the smoothness edges. Note that this is possible since g is separable convex. For more details we refer to Fig. 2.

[2] Two posets are said to be isomorph, when their Hasse diagrams as graphs are isomorph to each other.

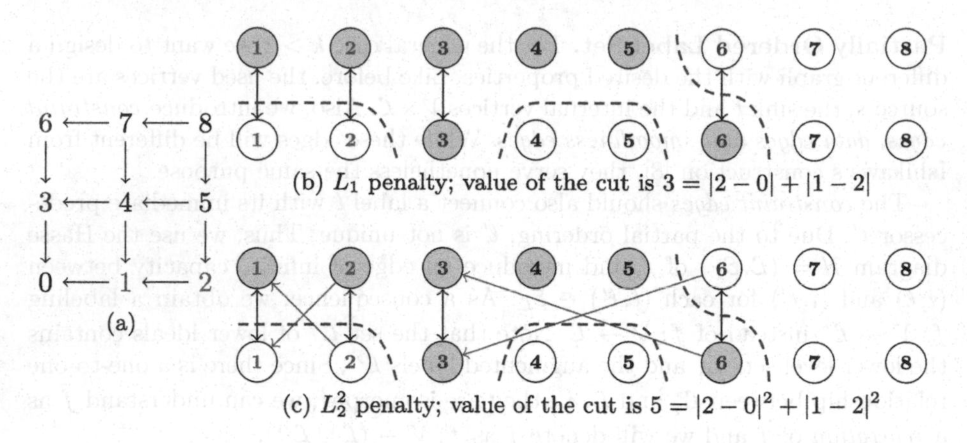

Fig. 2. Graph construction for smoothness terms. (a) Hasse diagram of the poset $\mathcal{L} = \{0,1,2\} \times \{0,1,2\}$. (b), (c) Graph construction for L_1 and L_2^2 penalties, resp., where the gray and white nodes connected to the source and sink (corresponding to 1 and 0), resp. This example shows the case that $f_i = (2,1) \in \mathcal{L}$, $f_j = (0,2) \in \mathcal{L}$. The cut is shown by the blue dashed lines. Note that only 1-0 edges should be cut (Color figure online)

Overall, we have proved the following theorem.

Theorem 1. *Let $\mathcal{L}$ be a poset that can be represented as the Cartesian product of k totally ordered sets $\mathcal{L}_\kappa$, $\kappa = 1,\dots,k$. Further consider the multi-labeling problem of minimizing the energy (1) for $f\colon \mathcal{V} \to \mathcal{L}$*

$$E(f) = \sum_{i\in\mathcal{V}} E_i(f_i) + \sum_{(i,j)\in\mathcal{E}} E_{i,j}(f_i, f_j),$$

where the smoothness term is given as

$$E_{ij}(f_i, f_j) = w_{ij} \cdot d(f_i, f_j) = w_{ij} \sum_{\kappa=1}^{k} g_\kappa(f_{i,\kappa} - f_{j,\kappa}) \qquad w_{ij} \geq 0$$

for even, convex functions g_κ for all $\kappa = 1,\dots,k$. Then we can define a lifted, sub-modular, graph-representable functional $D\colon \left[\mathcal{V} \to (\mathcal{L} \cup \mathcal{L}^A)\right] \to \mathbb{R}$ such that

$$D(f) = E(f) \qquad \text{if } f\colon \mathcal{V} \to \mathcal{L}. \tag{8}$$

So far, we found an optimal labeling $f\colon \mathcal{V} \to (\mathcal{L} \cup \mathcal{L}^A)$. If this labeling is in fact a labeling $f\colon \mathcal{V} \to \mathcal{L}$ that excludes augmented labels, we globally solved the original multi-labeling problem. This can happen if the considered data terms are very pronounced. Nonetheless, we should assume that in practice augmented labels will occur. While $D(f) = E(f)$ is satisfied for the lower level sets, we like to emphasize that our energy (1) is in general not sub-modular[3].

[3] The proof is contained in the supplementary material.

We consider an energy with sub-modular pairwise terms, however, the arbitrary unary terms make the energy non-submodular. The proposed relaxation is graph-representable, thus it is sub-modular[4]. Thus, we can compute the global optimum of the relaxed energy at the cost of having augmented labels. In the next section we provide a heuristics in order to remove these augmented labels.

2.3 Resolving Augmented Labels

Assume that $\mathcal{L}^A \ni f_i = \bigcup_{\mu=1}^m [\alpha_\mu]$. One way of resolving the ambiguity would be to apply move-making methods like $\alpha-\beta$ swaps [1] over the labels $[\alpha_1], \ldots, [\alpha_m]$. Nonetheless, we like to point to a different heuristic that takes the structure of the poset better into account. The idea is to also consider those labels that can be constructed by the join operation $\vee$

$$\alpha \vee \beta = \min\{\gamma \mid \alpha \leq \gamma \text{ and } \beta \leq \gamma\}.$$

Let us consider, for example, the label space $\mathcal{L} = \{0,1\} \times \{0,1\}$ and let $f_i = [(1,0)] \cup [(0,1)]$. In this case we consider all $\alpha - \beta$ swaps with respect to $\{(1,0),(0,1),(1,1)\}$. The rationale is that the energy with respect to f_i accumulated the data terms of $[(1,0)]$ and $[(0,1)]$. Since the energy with respect to $[(1,1)]$ also accumulates these data terms (and the data term of $(1,1)$), it makes sense to broaden the label space for the move-making methods.

Discussion. In many applications the label set is defined as a *lattice*[5], (*i.e.*regular grid). Topkis [18] presented a theory of sub-modular energy minimization on a lattice. Although our label set also forms a lattice, our energy (1) is not sub-modular. In [20] a general hierarchical model is introduced, where the label space forms an arbitrary tree specifying a partial ordering over the labels. The authors proposed effective multi-labeling moves, called Path-Moves [20]. The Path-Moves algorithm can be seen as a combination of well-known α-expansion [1] and Ishikawa's construction [8]. Nonetheless, the label set that we consider in this paper is a lattice, rather than a tree, therefore Path-Moves algorithm cannot be directly applied.

3 Coarse-to-fine Strategy

In practice, the minimization of the lifted energy (8) becomes quickly intractable as the number of labels grows. Therefore, it is beneficial to have the number of possible labels as small as possible. In addition, we deal with the relaxation to our original energy. There is no guarantee that we obtain a feasible solution. Accordingly, for some pixels we may obtain augmented labels (*i.e.*combination

[4] Graph-representability implies sub-modularity [9].

[5] If two elements α and β of a poset have a least upper bound (greatest lower bound), denoted by $\alpha \vee \beta$ $(\alpha \wedge \beta)$, it is their *join* (*meet*). A poset that contains the join and the meet for each pair of its element is a *lattice* [18].

of labels), that we need to resolve so as to get a feasible solution. Note that the number of the augmented labels grows exponentially by increasing the size of the label sets, which makes the augmented label removal very challenging. To overcome these issues, we consider the following *coarse-to-fine* approach.

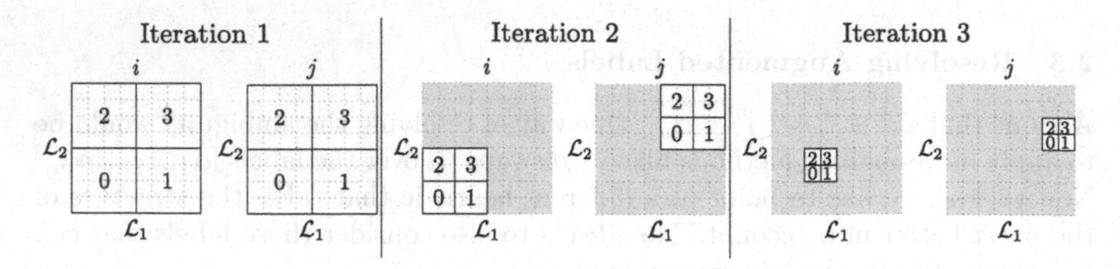

Fig. 3. Illustration of the proposed coarse-to-fine strategy over the label space $\mathcal{L} = \{0, \ldots, 7\} \times \{0, \ldots, 7\}$, where $m = n = 2$. In each iteration the search space for each pixel is partitioned into $mn = 4$ equal regions, indexed by, resp., 0, 1, 2 and 3, and the optimal region is sought. Only this optimal region of the labels space will be considered in the next iteration. The rest of the labels, shown in red, will be ignored

To simplify the notation we assume that $k = 2$ and $\mathcal{L} = \mathcal{L}_1 \times \mathcal{L}_2$. In the first iteration we consider only $m \times n$ labels for each pixel, where m and n are divisors of the size of $\mathcal{L}_1$ and $\mathcal{L}_2$, respectively. Each of the coarse labels correspond to a region of labels. After a decision on the coarsest level, the next iteration only considers the region, that has been selected in the previous iteration. This common approach is illustrated in Fig. 3. After some iterations either $\mathcal{L}_1$ or $\mathcal{L}_2$ cannot be divided anymore. This means that the remaining part of the optimization boils down the minimization over a totally ordered set, which can be globally solved via Ishikawa's construction [8].

For the data term on the coarse level we apply *min pooling* over the labels belonging to the same region. Thus, we have a strong guidance for the optimization at the current level. For the smoothness terms we are using the distance between the centers of the selected patches.

It is important to note that, in contrast to the previous works [21], we apply a coarse-to-fine approach in the label space instead of the image domain. Moreover, the goal of our method is to compute labelings that provide useful results in practice, even if not all labels can be chosen optimally. Like α-expansion, our method tries to find a local optimum as quickly as possible. For that reason we can only provide a weak-persistency guarantee, namely that the global optimum is found if no augmented label is inferred.

4 Numerical Experiments

In this section we discuss the implementation details of the proposed minimization scheme and illustrate it through optical flow estimation.

4.1 Implementation Details

We ran our experiments on a machine with Intel Xeon E5-2697 CPU@2.3GHz under Linux in `Matlab` with `C/C++ mex` extensions. For the maximum flow calculation and for move-making algorithms (*i.e.* $\alpha - \beta$ swap and α-expansion) we used the publicly available GCO library [1,9,11]. In order to have a fair comparison with other methods we used `float` representation of the energy terms. Our implementation is publicly available at https://github.com/csaba-domokos/MRFOptimizationOnPosets.

Minimization. In order to minimize our relaxed energy, we applied the BK algorithm [11]. During the flow graph construction, for each pixel an augmenting path is sought through the data edges and the constraint edges corresponding to the given pixel. This pre-processing has linear time complexity and ends up a better runtime of the BK algorithm, since the BK algorithm has the worst case complexity $\mathcal{O}(|\mathcal{E}|\,|\mathcal{V}|^2\,C)$, where C is the value of the minimum cut in the flow graph [11].

Augmented labels. In order to resolve augmented labels, *i.e.*unfeasible solutions, we applied the heuristics that we explored in Sect. 2.3. That is, we considered a 2×2 label space in each iteration of the proposed coarse-to-fine approach. Therefore we only have one augmented label, *i.e.*$\alpha = [(0,1)] \cup [(1,0)]$, and we select a feasible label among the labels $\{(0,1),(1,0),(1,1)\}$ via standard $\alpha - \beta$ swap moves [1]. More precisely, the augmented labels are replaced with a feasible label corresponding to the lowest data cost for the given pixel. Afterwards the $\alpha - \beta$ swap algorithm [1] is run over all three label pairs. The $\alpha - \beta$ swap algorithm requires the pairwise terms to be semi-metric, which is satisfied in our case, since we assume even functions in our energy.

4.2 Optical Flow Estimation

To substantiate the quality of our optimization we focus on the optical flow application. Assuming an input image pair I_1 and I_2, the classical optical flow estimation aims to find the displacement between pixels in I_1 and corresponding pixels in I_2 [13]. In a discrete setting one can consider totally ordered (finite) label sets $\mathcal{L}_1$ and $\mathcal{L}_2$ to model the horizontal and vertical displacements. The labels for each pixel is taken from the poset $\mathcal{L}_1 \times \mathcal{L}_2$. The goal is to find an optimal labeling $f\colon \mathcal{V} \to \mathcal{L}_1 \times \mathcal{L}_2$ such that $I_1(p_i) = I_2(p_i + f_i)$.

Recently, Chen and Koltun [6] have proposed an efficient solution for optical flow estimation. Here, we defined our energy, adopted from [6], as

$$E(f) = \sum_{i \in \mathcal{V}} E_i(f_i) + \lambda \sum_{(i,j) \in \mathcal{E}} w_{ij} |f_i - f_j|, \tag{9}$$

where $\lambda = 0.021$ and w_{ij} represents the contrast-sensitive weighting factors. The data cost has the form of $E_i(f_i) = 1 - \max(0, \mathrm{NCC}(i, f_i))$, where $\mathrm{NCC}(i, f_i)$ is the

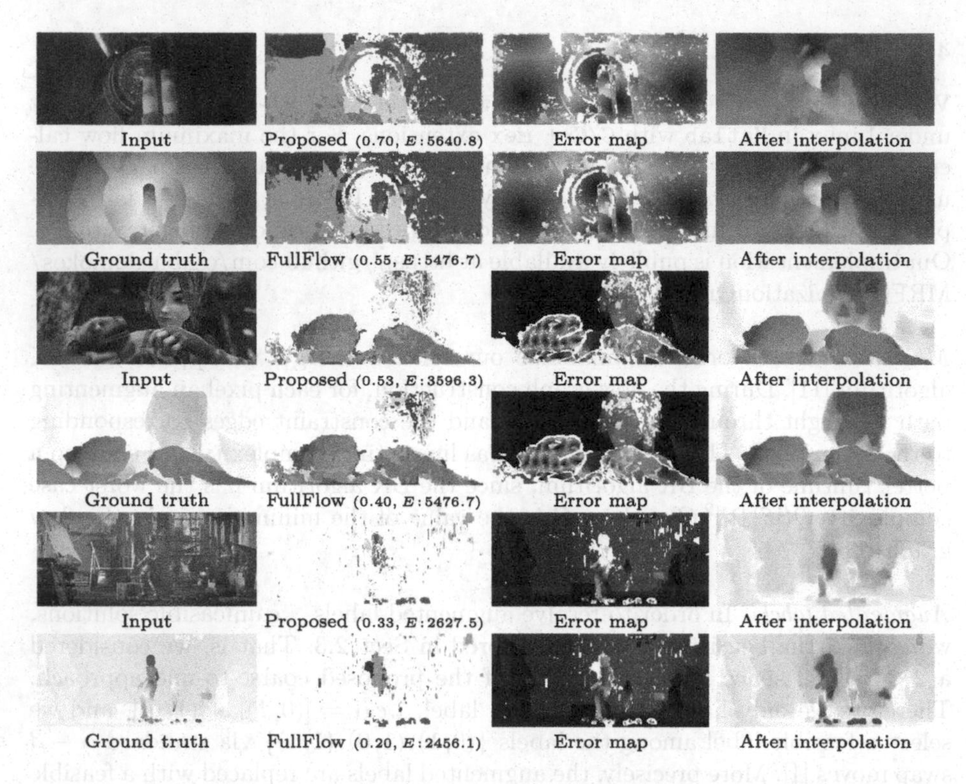

Fig. 4. Qualitative results on the Sintel dataset [22]. The input images along with the ground truth are in the first column. The results obtained by our method and the FullFlow [6] method, resp., are shown in the second column. The average endpoint errors and the energy values E are in parenthesis. The corresponding error maps are in the third column. The results in the last column are obtained after EpicFlow [23] interpolation

normalized cross-correlation between the patches of size 3×3 centered at pixels i and $i + f_i$, respectively. In order to prevent the penalty of negatively correlated patches, negative values are clamped to zero. The pairwise smoothness terms are defined as the *contrast-sensitive Potts model* [24], that is, the edge based weighting factors w_{ij} are calculated as

$$w_{ij} = \exp\left(-\frac{\|I_1(i) - I_2(j)\|_2^2}{2\sigma^2}\right), \qquad \text{where } \sigma = \frac{1}{\sqrt{6}}.$$

Post-processing. In several methods, the estimated optical flow is interpolated further to obtain sub-pixel accuracy [6,25]. Recently, it has been a common technique to apply EpicFlow interpolation [23] as post-processing. EpicFlow requires point matches as an input and the final result is achieved through variational optimization. We adopted the interpolation from the paper [6]. Accordingly, we also used EpicFlow interpolation [23] (see Fig. 4).

4.3 Evaluation

For evaluation we used the MPI Sintel dataset [22], which is a naturalistic optical flow dataset derived from a 3D animated film Sintel. Each image has a resolution of 438×1024 pixels. The data set includes a variety of challenging features like long sequences, large motions, specular reflections, motion blur, defocus blur and atmospheric effects. We ran our experiments on the *training* set with the *final* sequences, including motion blur. By following the settings in [6], we first rescaled the input images by a factor of 1/3. We considered sequences, having 50 images, with various maximum displacements of 10, 22, 46 and 94, which correspond to the label set of size 8×8, 16×16, 32×32 and 64×64, respectively, after rescaling. As evaluation measure the *average endpoint error* was used. Some qualitative results can be seen in Fig. 4.

Comparison. Our experiments were targeted at providing a comprehensive comparison to state of the art combinatorial optimization approaches. As a baseline we ran alternating optimization, initialized from the zero flow, where the global optimization method [8] was used for each direction. We considered classical move-making algorithms, that is, $\alpha - \beta$ swap and α-expansion [1]. In case of the TRW-S method, we used the implementation of the FullFlow method [6]. In contrast to [6], we ran the code on a single CPU core in order to have a fair runtime comparison. Only three iterations of the TRW-S method were computed. For the sake of completeness, we also ran the method of Shekhovtsov *et al.* [12]. We used the authors implementation with similar settings as in the case of other methods. We remark that the implementation of [12] applies the TRW-S method as inference, however, the considered energy is not the same as the energy (9), therefore, this comparison is not completely fair.

The quantitative results are shown in Table 1. We can observe that the classical move-making algorithms become quickly prohibitive as the size of the label

Table 1. Quantitative comparison to other combinatorial optimization approaches on the Sintel dataset [22]. EPE and rt., resp., stand for the mean value of the average endpoint error and the runtime (sec.). All experiments were ran on a single CPU core

		Baseline		$\alpha - \beta$ swap		α-expansion		FullFlow [6]		Proposed		[12]
Sequence	$\lvert\mathcal{L}\rvert$	EPE	rt.	EPE	rt.	EPE	rt.	EPE	rt.	EPE	rt.	EPE
sleeping_1	8×8	1.12	2.23	0.56	3.06	0.55	3.16	**0.52**	0.86	0.60	**0.35**	1.77
sleeping_2	8×8	0.71	1.50	0.53	2.82	0.53	2.52	**0.47**	0.86	0.53	**0.24**	1.46
shaman_3	16×16	1.10	6.44	0.76	27.48	0.73	14.19	**0.62**	2.74	0.85	**0.44**	1.45
alley_1	32×32	1.45	20.79	0.85	377.34	0.77	61.85	**0.58**	10.93	0.92	**0.56**	1.44
alley_2	32×32	3.69	29.45	1.24	445.39	1.16	74.93	**0.74**	11.23	1.32	**0.70**	3.48
bandage_2	32×32	0.93	19.44	0.54	314.45	0.53	59.49	**0.40**	10.94	0.57	**0.45**	0.93
shaman_2	32×32	1.29	16.03	0.65	377.79	0.58	67.21	**0.36**	10.97	0.95	**0.62**	0.92
ambush_7	64×64	1.97	57.80	1.58	9278.76	1.36	286.73	**0.65**	47.33	1.40	**0.89**	3.30
market_2	64×64	1.67	79.07	1.02	5851.91	1.19	306.62	**0.58**	47.96	1.61	**0.84**	1.27

set grows. Our proposed method provides comparable accuracy to those methods. The FullFlow method always provided the least average endpoint error, but its runtime grows linearly with respect to $|\mathcal{L}|$. Our method provided moderately worse results comparing to the FullFlow method, however, the runtime of our method increases very slowly and always stayed below a second. The method [12] provided larger errors than the other methods.

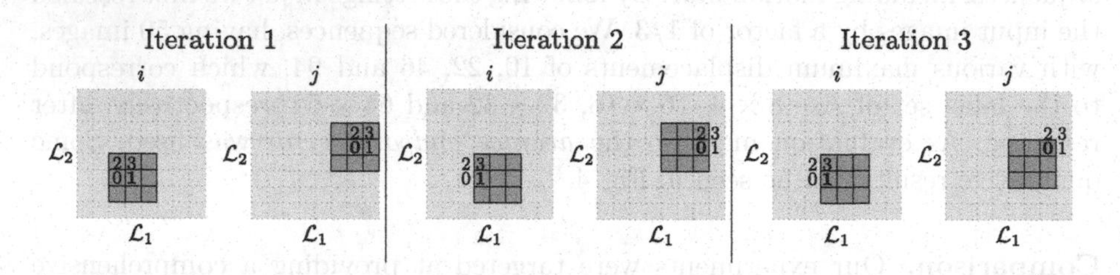

Fig. 5. Illustration of three iterations of label refinement. At the given level of the coarse-to-fine approach, we have the (coarse) labels $f_i = 1$ and $f_j = 0$, and consider their 3×3 neighborhoods in the (coarse) label space $\{0, \ldots, 7\} \times \{0, \ldots, 7\}$, shown by green, for refinement. In the next iteration the 3×3 neighborhood of the refined label is considered

Label Refinement. One can observe from Table 1 that the error obtained by our method grows with the size of the label set. In fact, there is an inherent limitation of our coarse-to-fine strategy. When it makes a decision for a pixel at a current level, then only the corresponding region of labels will be taken into an account in the later iterations. Although, the min-pooling operation provides a strong guidance, the labeling at the current level is not necessarily optimal. To overcome this limitation, we investigated a label refinement technique.

In each iteration, we get a feasible solution, which is then refined by applying local move-making cuts. More precisely, for the current labeling we consider only the labels at the given level of the coarse-to-fine approach, and explore 3×3 neighborhoods in the label space (see Fig. 5). The classical $\alpha - \beta$ swap algorithm is used over the 3×3 regions in order to refine the current labeling. We reconsider the resulting labels again and use the same process until no more improvement is possible. As the $\alpha - \beta$ swap always decreases the energy, convergence is guaranteed. We observed slightly improvement of the results, however, at the price of higher runtime (see the supplementary material).

5 Conclusions

In this work we have presented a new approach to compute a (locally) optimal labeling for a specific class of partially ordered label sets. We assume that the label set $\mathcal{L}$ can be represented as the Cartesian product of k different totally ordered label sets $\mathcal{L}_\kappa$. Under the assumption that the convex prior on $\mathcal{L}$ is separable with respect to the k totally ordered label sets, we were able to design a graph-representable sub-modular energy. While this energy leads to a relaxed solution, we could show that the relaxation helps us to guide local move-making methods. In combination with variational post-processing, we were able to provide optical flow results that are comparable with state-of-the-art methods, based on combinatorial approaches, at reduced time complexity.

Acknowledgment. This work was partially supported by the Alexander von Humboldt Foundation.

References

1. Boykov, Y., Veksler, O., Zabih, R.: Fast approximate energy minimization via graph cuts. IEEE Trans. Pattern Anal. Mach. Intell. **23**(11), 1222–1239 (2001)
2. Kolmogorov, V.: Convergent tree-reweighted message passing for energy minimization. IEEE Trans. Pattern Anal. Mach. Intell. **28**(10), 1568–1583 (2006)
3. Komodakis, N., Tziritas, G.: Approximate labeling via graph cuts based on linear programming. IEEE Trans. Pattern Anal. Mach. Intell. **28**(8), 1436–1453 (2007)
4. Ladický, L., Russell, C., Kohli, P., Torr, P.H.S.: Associative hierarchical random fields. IEEE Trans. Pattern Anal. Mach. Intell. **36**(6), 1056–1077 (2013)
5. Menze, M., Heipke, C., Geiger, A.: Discrete optimization for optical flow. In: Gall, J., Gehler, P., Leibe, B. (eds.) GCPR 2015. LNCS, vol. 9358, pp. 16–28. Springer, Cham (2015). https://doi.org/10.1007/978-3-319-24947-6_2
6. Chen, Q., Koltun, V.: Full flow: optical flow estimation by global optimization over regular grids. In: Proceedings of IEEE Conference on Computer Vision and Pattern Recognition, Las Vegas, NV, USA. IEEE (2015)
7. Li, M., Shekhovtsov, A., Huber, D.: Complexity of discrete energy minimization problems. In: Leibe, B., Matas, J., Sebe, N., Welling, M. (eds.) ECCV 2016. LNCS, vol. 9906, pp. 834–852. Springer, Cham (2016). https://doi.org/10.1007/978-3-319-46475-6_51
8. Ishikawa, H.: Exact optimization for Markov random fields with convex priors. IEEE Trans. Pattern Anal. Mach. Intell. **25**(10), 1333–1336 (2003)
9. Kolmogorov, V., Zabin, R.: What energy functions can be minimized via graph cuts? IEEE Trans. Pattern Anal. Mach. Intell. **26**(2), 147–159 (2004)
10. Ramalingam, S., Kohli, P., Alahari, K., Torr, P.H.S.: Exact inference in multi-label CRFs with higher order cliques. In: Proceedings of IEEE Conference on Computer Vision and Pattern Recognition, Anchorage, AK, USA. IEEE (2008)
11. Boykov, Y., Kolmogorov, V.: An experimental comparison of min-cut/max- flow algorithms for energy minimization in vision. IEEE Trans. Pattern Anal. Mach. Intell. **26**(9), 1124–1137 (2004)
12. Shekhovtsov, A., Kovtun, I., Hlaváč, V.: Efficient MRF deformation model for non-rigid image matching. Comput. Vis. Image Underst. **112**(1), 91–99 (2008)
13. Horn, B.K., Schunck, B.G.: Determining optical flow. Artif. Intell. **17**(1–3), 185–203 (1981)
14. Kohli, P., Shekhovtsov, A., Rother, C., Kolmogorov, V., Torr, P.H.S.: On partial optimality in multi-label MRFs. In: Proceedings of International Conference on Machine Learning, Helsinki, Finland, pp. 480–487. ACM (2008)

15. Kolmogorov, V., Rother, C.: Minimizing nonsubmodular functions with graph cuts-a review. IEEE Trans. Pattern Anal. Mach. Intell. **29**(7), 1274–1279 (2007)
16. Goldstein, T., Bresson, X., Osher, S.: Global minimization of Markov random fields with applications to optical flow. Inverse Prob. Imaging **6**(4), 623–644 (2012)
17. Goldluecke, B., Strekalovskiy, E., Cremers, D.: Tight convex relaxations for vector-valued labeling. SIAM J. Imaging Sci. **6**(3), 1626–1664 (2013)
18. Topkis, D.M.: Minimizing a submodular function on a lattice. Oper. Res. **26**(2), 305–321 (1978)
19. Li, K., Wu, X., Chen, D., Sonka, M.: Optimal surface segmentation in volumetric images - a graph-theoretic approach. IEEE Trans. Pattern Anal. Mach. Intell. **28**(1), 119–134 (2006)
20. Isack, H., Veksler, O., Oguz, I., Sonka, M., Boykov, Y.: Efficient optimization for hierarchically-structured interacting segments (HINTS). In: Proceedings of IEEE Conference on Computer Vision and Pattern Recognition, Honolulu, HI, USA. IEEE (2017)
21. Carr, P., Hartley, R.: Solving multilabel graph cut problems with multilabel swap. In: Proceedings of International Conference on Digital Image Computing, Melbourne, Australia. IEEE (2009)
22. Butler, D.J., Wulff, J., Stanley, G.B., Black, M.J.: A naturalistic open source movie for optical flow evaluation. In: Fitzgibbon, A., Lazebnik, S., Perona, P., Sato, Y., Schmid, C. (eds.) ECCV 2012. LNCS, vol. 7577, pp. 611–625. Springer, Heidelberg (2012). https://doi.org/10.1007/978-3-642-33783-3_44
23. Revaud, J., Weinzaepfel, P., Harchaoui, Z., Schmid, C.: EpicFlow: edge-preserving interpolation of correspondences for optical flow. In: Proceedings of IEEE Conference on Computer Vision and Pattern Recognition, Boston, MA, USA. IEEE (2015)
24. Kohli, P., Ladický, L., Torr, P.H.S.: Robust higher order potentials for enforcing label consistency. In: Proceedings of IEEE Conference on Computer Vision and Pattern Recognition, Anchorage, AK, USA. IEEE (2008)
25. Bailer, C., Taetz, B., Stricker, D.: Flow fields: dense correspondence fields for highly accurate large displacement optical flow estimation. In: Proceedings of IEEE International Conference on Computer Vision, Santiago, Chile, pp. 4015–4023. IEEE (2015)

Attend and Rectify: A Gated Attention Mechanism for Fine-Grained Recovery

Pau Rodríguez[1](✉), Josep M. Gonfaus[2], Guillem Cucurull[1], F. Xavier Roca[1], and Jordi Gonzàlez[1]

[1] Computer Vision Center and Universitat Autònoma de Barcelona (UAB), Campus UAB, 08193 Bellaterra, Catalonia, Spain
pau.rodriguez@cvc.uab.cat

[2] Visual Tagging Services, Parc de Recerca, Campus UAB, Bellaterra, Spain

Abstract. We propose a novel attention mechanism to enhance Convolutional Neural Networks for fine-grained recognition. It learns to attend to lower-level feature activations without requiring part annotations and uses these activations to update and rectify the output likelihood distribution. In contrast to other approaches, the proposed mechanism is modular, architecture-independent and efficient both in terms of parameters and computation required. Experiments show that networks augmented with our approach systematically improve their classification accuracy and become more robust to clutter. As a result, Wide Residual Networks augmented with our proposal surpasses the state of the art classification accuracies in CIFAR-10, the Adience gender recognition task, Stanford dogs, and UEC Food-100.

Keywords: Deep learning · Convolutional Neural Networks
Attention

1 Introduction

Humans and animals process vasts amounts of information with limited computational resources thanks to attention mechanisms which allow them to focus resources on the most informative chunks of information [1,3,29]

This work is inspired by the advantages of visual and biological attention mechanisms, for tackling fine-grained visual recognition with Convolutional Neural Networks (CNN) [17]. This is a particularly difficult task since it involves looking for details in large amounts of data (images) while remaining robust to deformation and clutter. In this sense, different attention mechanisms for fine-grained recognition exist in the literature: (i) iterative methods that process images using "glimpses" with recurrent neural networks (RNN) or long short-term memory (LSTM) [26,38], (ii) feed-forward attention mechanisms that augment vanilla CNNs, such as the Spatial Transformer Networks (STN) [11], or top-down feed-forward attention mechanisms (FAM) [23]. Although it is not applied to fine-grained recognition, the Residual Attention introduced by [32]

V. Ferrari et al. (Eds.): ECCV 2018, LNCS 11212, pp. 357–372, 2018.
https://doi.org/10.1007/978-3-030-01237-3_22

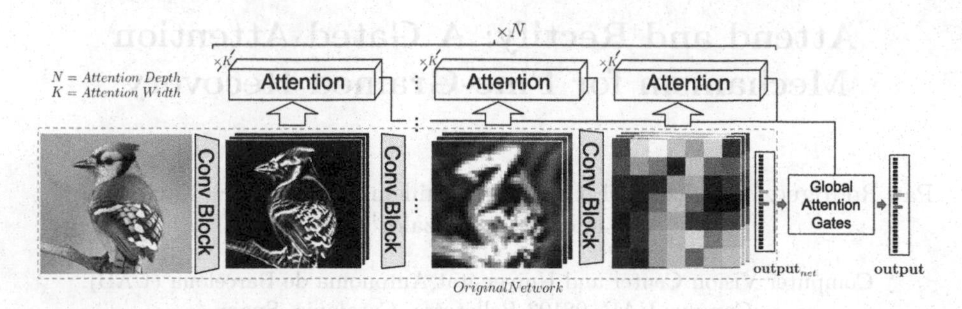

Fig. 1. The proposed mechanism. The original CNN is augmented with N attention modules at N different depths. Each attention module applies K attention heads to the network feature maps to make a class prediction based on local information. The original network $\mathbf{output}_{net}$ is then corrected based on the local features by means of the global attention gates, resulting in the final **output**.

is another example of feed-forward attention mechanism that takes advantage of residual connections [8] to enhance or dampen certain regions of the feature maps in an incremental manner.

Thus, most of the existing attention mechanisms are either limited by having to perform multiple passes through the data [26], by carefully designed architectures that should be trained from scratch [11], or by considerably increasing the needed amount of memory and computation, thus introducing computational bottlenecks [12]. Hence, there is still the need of models with the following learning properties: (i) Detect and process in detail the most informative parts of an image for learning models more robust to deformation and clutter [21]; (ii) feed-forward trainable with SGD for achieving faster inference than iterative models [26,38], together with faster convergence rate than Reinforcement Learning-based (RL) methods [19,26]; (iii) preserve low-level detail for a direct access to local low-level features before they are modified by residual identity mappings. This is important for fine-grained recognition, where low-level patterns such as textures can help to distinguish two similar classes. This is not fulfilled by Residual Attention, where low-level features are subject to noise after traversing multiple residual connections [32].

In addition, desirable properties for attention mechanisms applied to CNNs would be: (i) **Modular and incremental**, since the same structure can be applied at each layer on any convolutional architecture, and it is easy to adapt to the task at hand; (ii) **Architecture independent**, that is, being able to adapt any pre-trained architecture such as VGG [27] or ResNet [8]; (iii) **Low computational impact** implying that it does not result in a significant increase in memory and computation; and (iv) **Simple** in the sense that it can be implemented in few lines of code, making it appealing to be used in future work.

Based on all these properties, we propose a novel attention mechanism that learns to attend low-level features from a standard CNN architecture through a set of replicable Attention Modules and gating mechanisms (see Sect. 3). Concretely, as it can be seen in Fig. 1, any existing architecture can be augmented by applying the proposed model at different depths, and replacing the original loss by the proposed one. It is remarkable that the modules are independent of the original path of the network, so in practice, it can be computed in parallel to the rest of the network. The proposed attention mechanism has been included in a strong baseline like Wide Residual Networks (WRN) [35], and applied on CIFAR-10, CIFAR-100 [15], and five challenging fine-grained recognition datasets. The resulting network, called Wide Attentional Residual Network (WARN) systematically enhances the performance of WRNs and surpasses the state of the art in various classification benchmarks.

2 Related Work

There are different approaches to fine-grained recognition [37]: (i) vanilla deep CNNs, (ii) CNNs as feature extractors for localizing parts and do alignment, (iii) ensembles, (iv) attention mechanisms. In this work, we focus on (iv), the attention mechanisms, which aim to discover the most discriminative parts of an image to be processed in greater detail, thus ignoring clutter and focusing on the most distinctive traits. These parts are central for fine-grained recognition, where the inter-class variance is small and the intra-class variance is high.

Different fine-grained attention mechanisms can be found in the literature. [33] proposed a *two-level attention* mechanism for fine-grained classification on different subsets of the ILSVRC [25] dataset, and the CUB200_2011. In this model, images are first processed by a bottom-up object proposal network based on R-CNN [36] and selective search [28]. Then, the softmax scores of another ILSVRC2012 pre-trained CNN, which they call *FilterNet*, are thresholded to prune the patches with the lowest parent class score. These patches are then classified to fine-grained categories with a *DomainNet*. Spectral clustering is also used on the *DomainNet* filters in order to extract parts (head, neck, body, etc.), which are classified with an SVM. Finally, the part- and object-based classifier scores are merged to get the final prediction. The *two-level attention* obtained state of the art results on CUB200-2011 with only class-level supervision. However, the pipeline must be carefully fine-tuned since many stages are involved with many hyper-parameters.

Differently from *two-level attention*, which consists of independent processing and it is not end-to-end, Sermanet *et al.* proposed to use a deep CNN and a Recurrent Neural Network (RNN) to accumulate high multi-resolution "glimpses" of an image to make a final prediction [26]. However, reinforcement learning slows down convergence and the RNN adds extra computation steps and parameters.

A more efficient approach was presented by Liu *et al.* [19], where a fully-convolutional network is trained with reinforcement learning to generate confidence maps on the image and use them to extract the parts for the final classifiers whose scores are averaged. Compared to previous approaches, in the work done by [19], multiple image regions are proposed in a single timestep thus, speeding up the computation. A greedy reward strategy is also proposed in order to increase the training speed. The recent approach presented by [5] uses a classification network and a recurrent attention proposal network that iteratively refines the center and scale of the input (RA-CNN). A ranking loss is used to enforce incremental performance at each iteration.

Zhao *et al.* proposed to enforce multiple non-overlapped attention regions [38]. The overall architecture consists of an attention canvas generator, which extracts patches of different regions and scales from the original image; a VGG-16 [27] CNN is then used to extract features from the patches, which are aggregated with a long short-term memory [9] that attends to non-overlapping regions of the patches. Classification is performed with the average prediction in each region. Similarly, in [39], they proposed the Multi-Attention CNN (MA-CNN) to learn to localize informative patches from the output of a VGG-19 and use them to train an ensemble of part classifiers.

In [12], they propose to extract global features from the last layers of a CNN, just before the classifier and use them to attend relevant regions in lower level feature activations. The attended activations from each level are then spatially averaged, channel-wise concatenated, and fed to the final classifier. The main differences with [12] are: (i) attention maps are computed in parallel to the base model, while the model in [12] requires output features for computing attention maps; (ii) WARN uses fewer parameters, so dropout is not needed to obtain competitive performance (these two factors clearly reflect in gain of speed); and (iii) gates allow our model to ignore/attend different information to improve the performance of the original model, while in [12] the full output function is replaced. As a result, WARN obtains 3.44% error on CIFAR10, outperforming [12] while being 7 times faster w/o parallelization.

All the previously described methods involve multi-stage pipelines and most of them are trained using reinforcement learning (which requires sampling and makes them slow to train). In contrast, STNs, FAM, the model in [12], and our approach jointly propose the attention regions and classify them in a single pass. Moreover, different from STNs and FAM our approach only uses one CNN stream, it can be used on pre-trained models, and it is far more computationally efficient than STNs, FAM, and [12] as described next.

3 Our Approach

Our approach consists of a universal attention module that can be added after each convolutional layer without altering pre-defined information pathways of any architecture (see Fig. 1). This is helpful since it seamlessly augments any architecture such as VGG and ResNet with no extra supervision, *i.e.* no part labels are necessary. Furthermore, it also allows being plugged into any existing trained network to quickly perform transfer learning approaches.

The attention module consists of three main submodules depicted in Fig. 2(a): (i) the attention heads $\mathcal{H}$, which define the most relevant regions of a feature map, (ii) the output heads $\mathcal{O}$, generate an hypothesis given the attended

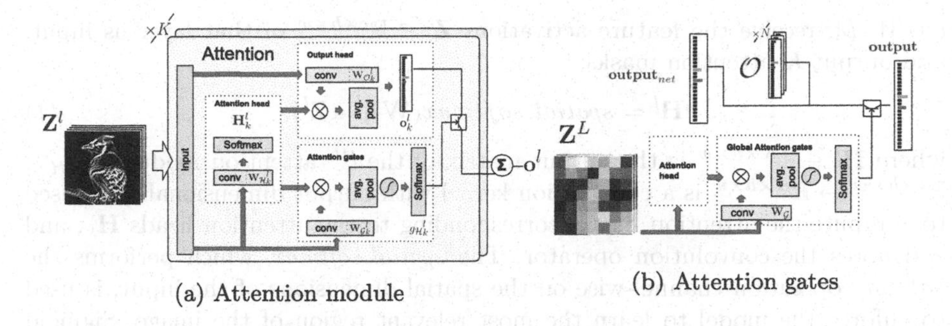

Fig. 2. (a) Attention Module: K attention heads $\mathbf{H}_k^l$ are applied to a feature map $\mathbf{Z}^l$, and information is aggregated with the layer attention gates. (b) Global attention: global information from the last feature map $\mathbf{Z}^L$ is used to compute the gating scores that produce the final **output** as the weighted average of the outputs of the attention modules and the original network $\mathbf{output}_{net}$

information, and (iii) the confidence gates $\mathcal{G}$, which output a confidence score for each attention head. Each of these modules is described in detail in the following subsections.

3.1 Overview

As it can be seen in Fig. 1, a convolution layer is applied to the output of the augmented layer, producing K attentional heatmaps. These attentional maps are then used to spatially average the local class probability scores for each of the feature maps, and produce the final class probability vector. This process is applied to an arbitrary number N of layers, producing N class probability vectors. Then, the model learns to correct the initial prediction by attending the lower-level class predictions. This is the final combined prediction of the network. In terms of probability, the network corrects the initial likelihood by updating the prior with local information.

3.2 Attention Head

Inspired by [38] and the *transformer* architecture presented by [30], and following the notation established by [35], we have identified two main dimensions to define attentional mechanisms: (i) the number of layers using the attention mechanism, which we call *attention depth* (AD), and (ii) the number of attention heads in each attention module, which we call *attention width* (AW). Thus, a desirable property for any universal attention mechanism is to be able to be deployed at any arbitrary *depth* and *width*.

This property is fulfilled by including K attention heads $\mathcal{H}_k$ (width), depicted in Fig. 1, into each attention module (depth)[1]. Then, the attention heads at layer

[1] Notation: $\mathcal{H}, \mathcal{O}, \mathcal{G}$ are the set of attention heads, output heads, and attention gates respectively. Uppercase letters refer to functions or constants, and lowercase ones to indices. Bold uppercase letters represent matrices and bold lowercase ones vectors.

$l \in [1..L]$, receive the feature activations $\mathbf{Z}^l \in \mathbb{R}^{c \times h \times w}$ of that layer as input, and output K attention masks:

$$\mathbf{H}^l = spatial\_softmax(\mathbf{W_{\mathcal{H}}}^l * \mathbf{Z}^l), \tag{1}$$

where $\mathbf{H}^l \in \mathbb{R}^{K \times h \times w}$ is the output matrix of the lth attention module, $\mathbf{W_{\mathcal{H}}}^l : \mathbb{R}^{c \times h \times w} \rightarrow \mathbb{R}^{K \times h \times w}$ is a convolution kernel with output dimensionality K used to compute the attention masks corresponding to the attention heads $\mathbf{H}_k$, and $*$ denotes the convolution operator. The *spatial_softmax*, which performs the *softmax* operation channel-wise on the spatial dimensions of the input, is used to enforce the model to learn the most relevant region of the image. Sigmoid units could also be used at the risk of degeneration to all-zeros or all-ones. To prevent the attention heads at the same depth to collapse into the same region, we apply the regularizer proposed in [38].

3.3 Output Head

To obtain the class probability scores, the input feature map $\mathbf{Z}^l_k$ is convolved with a kernel:

$$\mathbf{W_{\mathcal{O}}}^l_k \in \mathbb{R}^{channels \times h \times w} \rightarrow \mathbb{R}^{\#labels \times h \times w},$$

h, w represent the spatial dimensions, and *channels* is the number of input channels to the module. This results on a spatial map of class probability scores:

$$\mathbf{O}^l_k = \mathbf{W_{\mathcal{O}}}^l_k * \mathbf{Z}^l. \tag{2}$$

Note that this operation can be done in a single pass for all the K heads by setting the number of output channels to $\#labels \cdot K$. Then, class probability vectors $\mathbf{O}^l_k$ are weighted by the spatial attention scores and spatially averaged:

$$\mathbf{o}^l_k = \sum_{x,y} \mathbf{H}^l_k \odot \mathbf{O}^l_k, \tag{3}$$

where $\odot$ is the element-wise product, and $x \in \{1..width\}, y \in \{1..height\}$. The attention scores $\mathbf{H}^l_k$ are a 2d flat mask and the product with each of the input channels of $\mathbf{Z^l}$ is done by broadcasting, *i.e.* repeating $\mathbf{H}^l_k$ for each of the channels of $\mathbf{Z^l}$.

3.4 Layered Attention Gates

The final output $\mathbf{o}^l$ of an attention module is obtained by a weighted average of the K output probability vectors, through the use of head attention gates $\mathbf{g_{\mathcal{H}}}^l \in \mathbb{R}^{|\mathcal{H}|}$, $\sum_k g_{\mathcal{H}}{}^l_k = 1$.

$$\mathbf{o}^l = \sum_k g_{\mathcal{H}}{}^l_k o^l_k. \tag{4}$$

where $g_{\mathcal{H}}$ is obtained by first convolving $\mathbf{Z}^l$ with

$$\mathbf{W_g}^l \in \mathbb{R}^{channels \times h \times w} \rightarrow \mathbb{R}^{|\mathcal{H}| \times h \times w},$$

and then performing a spatial weighted average:

$$\mathbf{g}_{\mathcal{H}}{}^{l} = softmax(tanh(\sum_{x,y}(\mathbf{W_g}{}^{l} * \mathbf{Z}^{l}) \odot \mathbf{H}_{l})). \tag{5}$$

This way, the model learns to choose the attention head that provides the most meaningful output for a given attention module.

3.5 Global Attention Gates

In order to let the model learn to choose the most discriminative features at each depth to disambiguate the output prediction, a set of relevance scores $\mathbf{c}$ are predicted at the model output, one for each attention module, and one for the final prediction. This way, through a series of gates, the model can learn to query information from each level of the network conditioned to the global context. Note that, unlike in [12], the final predictions do not act as a bottleneck to compute the output of the attention modules.

The relevance scores are obtained with an inner product between the last feature activation of the network $\mathbf{Z}^L$ and the gate weight matrix $\mathbf{W}_{\mathcal{G}}$:

$$\mathbf{c} = tanh(\mathbf{W}_{\mathcal{G}}\mathbf{Z}^{L}). \tag{6}$$

The gate values $\mathbf{g}_{\mathcal{O}}$ are then obtained by normalizing the set of scores by means of a $softmax$ function:

$$g_{\mathcal{O}}{}_k^l = \frac{e^{c_k^l}}{\sum_{i=1}^{|\mathcal{G}|} e^{c_i}}, \tag{7}$$

where $|\mathcal{G}|$ is the total number of gates, and c_i is the ith confidence score from the set of all confidence scores. The final output of the network is the weighted sum of the attention modules:

$$\mathbf{output} = g_{net} \cdot \mathbf{output}_{net} + \sum_{l \in \{1..|\mathcal{O}|\}} g_{\mathcal{O}}^{l} \cdot \mathbf{o}^{l}, \tag{8}$$

where g_{net} is the gate value for the original network output ($\mathbf{output_{net}}$), and **output** is the final output taking the attentional predictions $\mathbf{o}^l$ into consideration. Note that setting the output of $\mathcal{G}$ to $\frac{1}{|\mathcal{O}|}$, corresponds to averaging all the outputs. Likewise, setting $\{\mathcal{G} \setminus G_{output}\} = 0, G_{output} = 1$, *i.e.* the set of attention gates is set to zero and the output gate to one, corresponds to the original pre-trained model without attention.

It is worth noting that all the operations that use $\mathbf{Z}^l$ can be aggregated into a single convolution operation. Likewise, the fact that the attention mask is generated by just one convolution operation, and that most masking operations are directly performed in the label space, or can be projected into a smaller dimensionality space, makes the implementation highly efficient. Additionally, the direct access to the output gradients makes the module fast to learn, thus being able to generate foreground masks from the beginning of the training and refining them during the following epochs.

Fig. 3. Samples from the five fine-grained datasets. (a) Adience, (b) CUB200 Birds, (c) Stanford Cars, (d) Stanford Dogs, (e) UEC-Food100

4 Experiments

We empirically demonstrate the impact on the accuracy and robustness of the different modules in our model on Cluttered Translated MNIST and then compare it with state-of-the-art models such as DenseNets and ResNeXt. Finally, we demonstrate the universality of our method for fine-grained recognition through a set of experiments on five fine-grained recognition datasets, as detailed next.

4.1 Datasets

Cluttered Translated MNIST[2]. Consists of 40×40 images containing a randomly placed MNIST [16] digit and a set of D randomly placed distractors, see Fig. 5b. The distractors are random 8×8 patches from other MNIST digits.

CIFAR[3]. The CIFAR dataset consists of 60K 32×32 images in 10 classes for CIFAR-10, and 100 for CIFAR-100. There are 50K training and 10K test images.

Stanford Dogs [13]. The Stanford Dogs dataset consists of 20.5K images of 120 breeds of dogs, see Fig. 3d. The dataset splits are fixed and they consist of 12k training images and 8.5K validation images.

UEC Food 100 [20]. A Japanese food dataset with 14K images of 100 different dishes, see Fig. 3e. In order to follow the standard procedure (*e.g.* [2,6]), bounding boxes are used to crop the images before training.

Adience dataset [4]. The adience dataset consists of 26.5K images distributed in eight age categories (02, 46, 813, 1520, 2532, 3843, 4853, 60+), and gender labels. A sample is shown in Fig. 3a. The performance on this dataset is measured using 5-fold cross-validation.

Stanford Cars [14]. The Cars dataset contains 16K images of 196 classes of cars, see Fig. 3c. The data is split into 8K training and 8K testing images.

Caltech-UCSD Birds 200 [31]. The CUB200-2011 birds dataset (see Fig. 3b) consists of 6K train and 5.8K test bird images distributed in 200 categories. Although bounding box, segmentation, and attributes are provided, we perform raw classification as done by [11].

[2] https://github.com/deepmind/mnist-cluttered.
[3] https://www.cs.toronto.edu/~kriz/cifar.html.

4.2 Ablation Study

We evaluate the submodules of our method on the Cluttered Translated MNIST following the same procedure as in [21]. The proposed attention mechanism is used to augment a CNN with five 3×3 convolutional layers and two fully-connected layers in the end. The three first convolution layers are followed by Batch-normalization and a spatial pooling. Attention modules are placed starting from the fifth convolution (or pooling instead) backward until AD is reached. Training is performed with SGD for 200 epochs, and a learning rate of 0.1, which is divided by 10 after epoch 60. Models are trained on a $200k$ images train set, validated on a $100k$ images validation set, and tested on $100k$ test images. Weights are initialized using He *et al.* [7]. Figure 4 shows the effects of the different hyperparameters of the proposed model. The performance without attention is labeled as `baseline`. Attention models are trained with softmax attention gates and regularized with [38], unless explicitly specified.

First, we test the importance of AD for our model by increasingly adding attention layers with $AW = 1$ after each pooling layer. As it can be seen in Fig. 4b, greater AD results in better accuracy, reaching saturation at $AD = 4$, note that for this value the receptive field of the attention module is 5×5 px, and thus the performance improvement from such small regions is limited. Figure 4c shows training curves for different values of AW, and $AD = 4$. As it can be seen, small performance increments are obtained by increasing the number of attention heads even with a single object present in the image.

Then, we use the best AD and AW, *i.e.* $AD, AW = 4$, to verify the importance of using softmax on the attention masks instead of sigmoid (1), the effect of using gates (Eq. 7), and the benefits of regularization [38]. Figure 4d confirms that ordered by importance: gates, softmax, and regularization result in accuracy improvement, reaching 97.8%. In particular, gates play an important role in discarding the distractors, especially for high AW and high AD

Finally, in order to verify that attention masks are not overfitting on the data, and thus generalize to any amount of clutter, we run our best model so far (Fig. 4d) on the test set with an increasing number of distractors (from 4 to 64). For the comparison, we included the baseline model before applying our approach and the same baseline augmented with an STN [11] that reached comparable performance as our best model in the validation set. All three models were trained with the same dataset with eight distractors. Remarkably, as it can be seen in Fig. 4e, the attention augmented model demonstrates better generalization than the baseline and the STN.

4.3 Training from Scratch

We benchmark the proposed attention mechanism on CIFAR-10 and CIFAR-100, and compare it with the state of the art. As a base model, we choose Wide Residual Networks, a strong baseline with a large number of parameters so that the additional parameters introduced by our model (WARN) could be considered negligible. The same WRN baseline is used to train an `att2` model

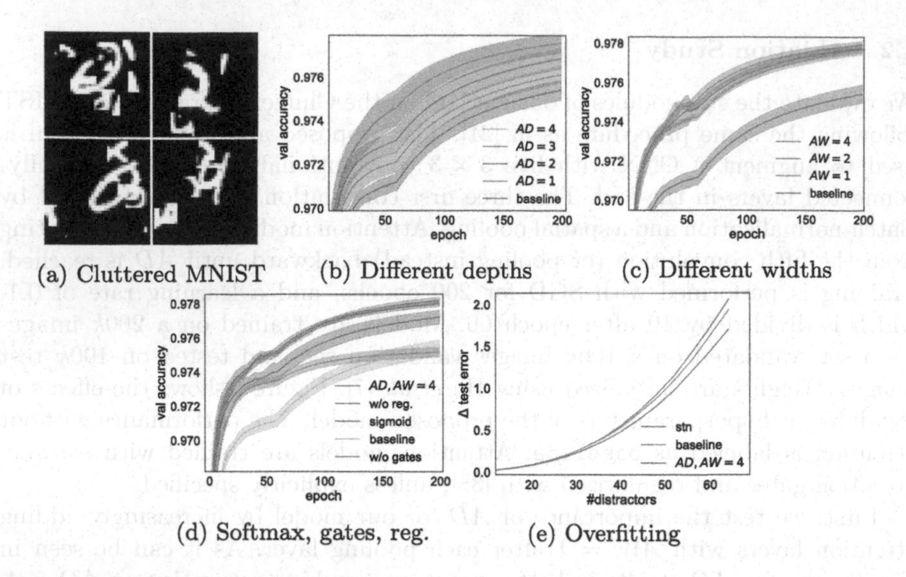

(a) Cluttered MNIST (b) Different depths (c) Different widths

(d) Softmax, gates, reg. (e) Overfitting

Fig. 4. Ablation experiments on Cluttered Translated MNIST. `baseline` indicates the original model before being augmented with attention. (a) shows a sample of the cluttered MNIST dataset. (b) the effect of increasing the attention depth (AD), for attention width $AW = 1$. (c) effect of increasing AW, for AD=4. (d) best performing model ($AD, AW = 4$, softmax attention gates, and regularization [38]) vs unregularized, sigmoid attention, and without gates. (e) test error of the baseline, attention ($AD, AW = 4$), and spatial transformer networks (stn), when trained with different amounts of distractors.

[12], we refer to this model as WRN-att2. Models are initialized and optimized following the same procedure as in [35]. Attention Modules are systematically placed after each of the three convolutional groups starting by the last one until the attention depth has been reached in order to capture information at different levels of abstraction and fine-grained resolution, this same procedure is followed in [12]. The model is implemented with pytorch [22] and run on a single workstation with two NVIDIA 1080Ti.[4]

First, the same ablation study performed in Sect. 4.2 is repeated on CIFAR100. We consistently reached the same conclusions as in Cluttered-MNIST: accuracy improves 1.5% by increasing attention depth from 1 to #residual_blocks, and width from 1 to 4. Gating performs 4% better than a simpler linear projection, and 3% with respect to simply averaging the output vectors. A 0.6% improvement is also observed when regularization is activated. Interestingly, we found sigmoid attention to perform similarly to softmax. With this setting, WARN reaches 17.82% error on CIFAR100. In addition, we perform an experiment blocking the gradients from the proposed attention modules to the original network to analyze whether the observed improvement is due to the attention mechanism or an optimization effect due to introducing shortcut paths to the loss function [18]. Interestingly, we

[4] https://github.com/prlz77/attend-and-rectify.

Table 1. Error rate on CIFAR-10 and CIFAR-100 (%). Results that surpass all other methods are in blue, results that surpass the baseline are in black bold font. Total network depth, attention depth, attention width, the usage of dropout, and the amount of floating point operations (Flop) are provided in columns 1–5 for fair comparison

	Net Depth	AD	AW	Dropout	GFlop	CIFAR-10	CIFAR-100
Resnext [34]	29	-	-		10.7	3.58	17.31
Densenet [10]	250	-	-		5.4	3.62	17.60
	190	-	-		9.3	3.46	17.18
WRN [35]	28	-	-		5.2	4	19.25
	28	-	-	✓	5.2	3.89	18.85
	40	-	-	✓	8.1	3.8	18.3
WRN-att2 [12]	28	2	-		5.7	4.10	21.20
	28	2	-	✓	5.7	**3.60**	20.00
	40	2	-	✓	8.6	3.90	19.20
WARN	28	2	4		5.2	**3.60**	18.72
	28	3	4		5.3	3.45	18.61
	28	3	4	✓	5.3	3.44	18.26
	40	3	4	✓	8.2	**3.46**	**17.82**

observed a 0.2% drop on CIFAR10, and 0.4% on CIFAR100, which are still better than the baseline. Note that a performance drop should be expected, even without taking optimization into account, since backpropagation makes intermediate layers learn to gather more discriminative features for the attention layers. It is also worth noting that fine-grained accuracy improves even when fine-tuning (gradients are multiplied by 0.1 in the base model), see Sect. 4.4. In contrast, the approach in [12] does not converge when gradients are not sent to the base model since classification is directly performed on intermediate feature maps (which continuously shift during training).

As seen in Table 1, the proposed Wide Attentional Residual Network (WARN) improves the baseline model for CIFAR-10 and CIFAR-100 even without the use of Dropout and outperforms the rest of the state of the art in CIFAR-10 while being remarkably faster, as it can be seen in Table 2. Remarkably, the performance on CIFAR-100 makes WARN competitive when compared with Densenet and Resnext, while being up to 36 times faster. We hypothesize that the increase in accuracy of the augmented model is limited by the base network and even better results could be obtained when applied on the best performing baseline. Interestingly, WARN shows superior performance even without the use of dropout; this was not possible with [12], which requires dropout to achieve competitive performances, since they introduce more parameters to the augmented network. The computing efficiency of the top performing models is shown in Fig. 5. WARN provides the highest accuracy per GFlop on CIFAR-10, and is more competitive than WRN, and WRN-att2 on CIFAR-100.

Table 2. Number of parameters, floating point operations (Flop), time (s) per validation epoch, and error rates (%) on CIFAR-10 and CIFAR-100. The "Time" column shows the amount of seconds to forward the validation dataset with batch size 256 on a single GPU

	Depth	Params	GFlop	Time	CIFAR-10	CIFAR-100
ResNext	29	68M	10.7	5.02 s	3.58	17.31
Densenet	190	**26M**	9.3	6.41 s	3.46	**17.18**
WRN	40	56M	8.1	0.18 s	3.80	18.30
WRN-att2	40	64M	8.6	0.24 s	3.90	19.20
WARN	28	37M	**5.3**	**0.17 s**	**3.44**	18.26
WARN	40	56M	8.2	0.18 s	3.46	17.82

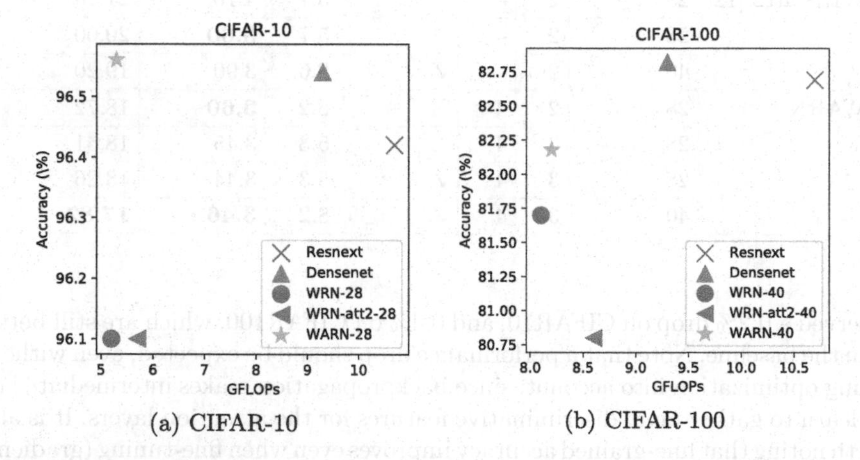

(a) CIFAR-10 (b) CIFAR-100

Fig. 5. Comparison of the best performing Resnext, Densenet, WRN, WRN-att2, and WARN on the CIFAR-10 and CIFAR-100. Validation accuracy is reported as a function of the number of GFLOPs.

4.4 Transfer Learning

We fine-tune an augmented WRN-50-4 pre-trained on Imagenet [25] and report higher accuracy on five different fine-grained datasets: Stanford Dogs, UEC Food-100, Adience, Stanford Cars, CUB200-2001 compared to the WRN baseline. All the experiments are trained for 100 epochs, with a batch size of 64. The learning rate is first set to 10^{-3} to all layers except the attention modules and the classifier, for which it ten times higher. The learning rate is reduced by a factor of 0.1 every 30 iterations and the experiment is automatically stopped if a plateau is reached. The network is trained with standard data augmentation, *i.e.* random 224 × 224 patches are extracted from 256 × 256 images with random horizontal flips. Since the aim of this work is to demonstrate that the proposed mechanism universally improves the baseline CNNs for fine-grained recognition, we follow the same training procedure in all datasets. Thus, we do

Table 3. Results on six fine-grained recognition tasks. *DSP* means that the cited model uses Domain Specific Pre-training. *HR* means the cited model uses high-resolution images. Accuracies that improve the baseline model are in black bold font, and highest accuracies are in blue

	Dogs	Food	Cars	Gender	Age	Birds
SotA	RA-CNN [5]	Inception [6]	MA-CNN [39]	FAM [23]	DEX [24]	MA-CNN [39]
DSP				✓	✓	
HR	✓		✓			✓
Accuracy	87.3	81.5	92.8	93.0	64.0	86.5
WRN	89.6	84.3	88.5	93.9	57.4	84.3
WARN	92.9	85.5	**90.0**	94.6	**59.7**	**85.6**

not use 512 × 512 images, which are central for state-of-the-art methods such as RA-CNNs, MA-CNNs, or color jitter [6] for food recognition. The proposed method is able to obtain state of the art results in Adience Gender, Stanford dogs and UEC Food-100 even when trained with lower resolution.

As seen in Table 3, WRN substantially increase their accuracy on all benchmarks by just fine-tuning them with the proposed attention mechanism. Moreover, we report the highest accuracy scores on Stanford Dogs, UEC Food, and Gender recognition, and obtain competitive scores when compared with models that use high resolution images, or domain-specific pre-training. For instance, in [24] a domain-specific model pre-trained on millions of faces is used for age recognition, while our baseline is a general-purpose WRN pre-trained on the Imagenet. It is also worth noting that the performance increase on CUB200-2011 (+1.3%) is higher than the one obtained in STNs with 224 × 224 images (+0.8%) even though we are augmenting a stronger baseline. This points out that the proposed mechanism might be extracting complementary information that is not extracted by the main convolutional stream. As seen in Table 4, WARN not only increases the absolute accuracy, but it provides a high efficiency per introduced parameter.

A sample of the attention masks for each dataset is shown on Fig. 6. As it can be seen, the attention heads learn to ignore the background and to attend the most discriminative parts of the objects. This matches the conclusions of Sect. 4.2.

Table 4. Increment of accuracy (%) per Million of parameters

	Dogs	Food	Cars	Gender	Age	Birds	Average
WRN	1.3	1.2	1.3	1.4	0.8	1.2	1.2
WARN	**6.9**	**2.5**	**3.1**	**1.5**	**4.0**	**2.5**	**3.4**

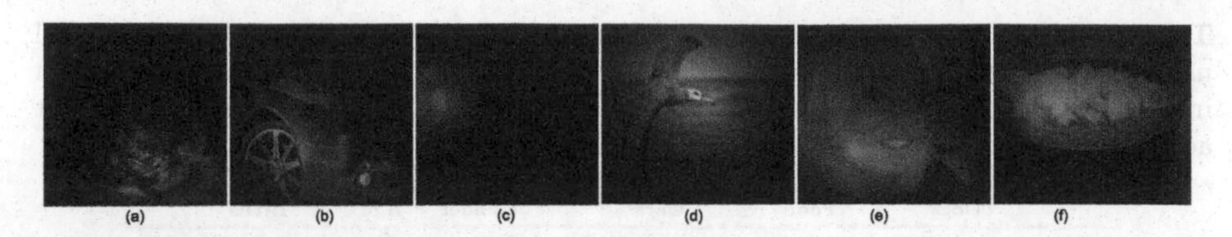

Fig. 6. Attention masks for each dataset: (a) Stanford dogs, (b) Stanford cars, (c) Adience gender, (d) CUB birds, (e) Adience age, (f) UEC food. As it can be seen, the masks help to focus on the foreground object. In (c), the attention mask focuses on ears for gender recognition, possibly looking for earrings

5 Conclusion

We have presented a novel attention mechanism to improve CNNs. The proposed model learns to attend the most informative parts of the CNN feature maps at different depth levels and combines them with a gating function to update the output distribution.

We suggest that attention helps to discard noisy uninformative regions, avoiding the network to memorize them. Unlike previous work, the proposed mechanism is modular, architecture independent, fast, simple, and yet WRN augmented with it obtain state-of-the-art results on highly competitive datasets while being 37 times faster than DenseNet, 30 times faster than ResNeXt, and making the augmented model more parameter-efficient. When fine-tuning on a transfer learning task, the attention augmented model showed superior performance in each recognition dataset. Moreover, state of the art performance is obtained on dogs, gender, and food. Results indicate that the model learns to extract local discriminative information that is otherwise lost when traversing the layers of the baseline architecture.

Acknowledgments. Authors acknowledge the support of the Spanish project TIN2015-65464-R (MINECO/FEDER), the 2016FI B 01163 grant of Generalitat de Catalunya, and the COST Action IC1307 iV&L Net. We also gratefully acknowledge the support of NVIDIA Corporation with the donation of a Tesla K40 GPU and a GTX TITAN GPU, used for this research.

References

1. Anderson, J.R.: Cognitive Psychology and Its Implications. WH Freeman/Times Books/Henry Holt and Co, New York (1985)
2. Chen, J., Ngo, C.W.: Deep-based ingredient recognition for cooking recipe retrieval. In: ACM MM, pp. 32–41. ACM (2016)
3. Desimone, R., Duncan, J.: Neural mechanisms of selective visual attention. Ann. Rev. Neurosci. **18**(1), 193–222 (1995)
4. Eidinger, E., Enbar, R., Hassner, T.: Age and gender estimation of unfiltered faces. TIFS **9**(12), 2170–2179 (2014)

5. Fu, J., Zheng, H., Mei, T.: Look closer to see better: recurrent attention convolutional neural network for fine-grained image recognition. In: CVPR (2017)
6. Hassannejad, H., Matrella, G., Ciampolini, P., De Munari, I., Mordonini, M., Cagnoni, S.: Food image recognition using very deep convolutional networks. In: MADIMA Workshop, pp. 41–49. ACM (2016)
7. He, K., Zhang, X., Ren, S., Sun, J.: Delving deep into rectifiers: surpassing human-level performance on imagenet classification. In: CVPR, pp. 1026–1034 (2015)
8. He, K., Zhang, X., Ren, S., Sun, J.: Deep residual learning for image recognition. In: CVPR, pp. 770–778 (2016)
9. Hochreiter, S., Schmidhuber, J.: Long short-term memory. Neural Comput. **9**(8), 1735–1780 (1997)
10. Huang, G., Liu, Z., Weinberger, K.Q., van der Maaten, L.: Densely connected convolutional networks. In: CVPR, vol. 1, p. 3 (2017)
11. Jaderberg, M., Simonyan, K., Zisserman, A., et al.: Spatial transformer networks. In: NIPS, pp. 2017–2025 (2015)
12. Jetley, S., Lord, N.A., Lee, N., Torr, P.: Learn to pay attention. In: ICLR (2018)
13. Khosla, A., Jayadevaprakash, N., Yao, B., Li, F.F.: Novel dataset for fine-grained image categorization: stanford dogs. In: FGVC, vol. 2, p. 1 (2011)
14. Krause, J., Stark, M., Deng, J., Fei-Fei, L.: 3D object representations for fine-grained categorization. In: CVPR, pp. 554–561 (2013)
15. Krizhevsky, A., Hinton, G.: Learning multiple layers of features from tiny images (2009)
16. LeCun, Y.: The MNIST database of handwritten digits (1998). http://yann.lecun.com/exdb/mnist/
17. LeCun, Y., Bottou, L., Bengio, Y., Haffner, P.: Gradient-based learning applied to document recognition. Proc. IEEE **86**(11), 2278–2324 (1998)
18. Lee, C.Y., Xie, S., Gallagher, P., Zhang, Z., Tu, Z.: Deeply-supervised nets. In: AISTATS, pp. 562–570 (2015)
19. Liu, X., Xia, T., Wang, J., Lin, Y.: Fully convolutional attention localization networks: efficient attention localization for fine-grained recognition. arXiv preprint arXiv:1603.06765 (2016)
20. Matsuda, Y., Hoashi, H., Yanai, K.: Recognition of multiple-food images by detecting candidate regions. In: ICME (2012)
21. Mnih, V., Heess, N., Graves, A., et al.: Recurrent models of visual attention. In: NIPS, pp. 2204–2212 (2014)
22. Paszke, A., Gross, S., Chintala, S., Chanan, G.: Pytorch (2017)
23. Rodriguez, P., Cucurull, G., Gonfaus, J.M., Roca, F.X., Gonzalez, J.: Age and gender recognition in the wild with deep attention. PR **72**, 563–571 (2017)
24. Rothe, R., Timofte, R., Gool, L.V.: Deep expectation of real and apparent age from a single image without facial landmarks. IJCV **126**, 144–157 (2016)
25. Russakovsky, O., Deng, J., Krause, J., Berg, A., Fei-Fei, L.: The ImageNet large scale visual recognition challenge 2012 (ILSVRC2012) (2012)
26. Sermanet, P., Frome, A., Real, E.: Attention for fine-grained categorization. In: ICLR (2015)
27. Simonyan, K., Zisserman, A.: Very deep convolutional networks for large-scale image recognition. arXiv preprint arXiv:1409.1556 (2014)
28. Uijlings, R., van de Sande, A., Gevers, T., Smeulders, M., et al.: Selective search for object recognition. IJCV **104**(2), 154–171 (2013)
29. Ungerleider, S.K.: Mechanisms of visual attention in the human cortex. Annu. Rev. Neurosci. **23**(1), 315–341 (2000)

30. Vaswani, A., et al.: Attention is all you need. In: NIPS, pp. 5998–6008 (2017)
31. Wah, C., Branson, S., Welinder, P., Perona, P., Belongie, S.: The Caltech-UCSD Birds-200-2011 Dataset. Technical report (2011)
32. Wang, F., et al.: Residual attention network for image classification. In: CVPR (2017)
33. Xiao, T., Xu, Y., Yang, K., Zhang, J., Peng, Y., Zhang, Z.: The application of two-level attention models in deep convolutional neural network for fine-grained image classification. In: CVPR, pp. 842–850 (2015)
34. Xie, S., Girshick, R., Dollár, P., Tu, Z., He, K.: Aggregated residual transformations for deep neural networks. In: CVPR, pp. 5987–5995. IEEE (2017)
35. Zagoruyko, S., Komodakis, N.: Wide residual networks. In: BMVC (2016)
36. Zhang, N., Donahue, J., Girshick, R., Darrell, T.: Part-based R-CNNs for fine-grained category detection. In: Fleet, D., Pajdla, T., Schiele, B., Tuytelaars, T. (eds.) ECCV 2014. LNCS, vol. 8689, pp. 834–849. Springer, Cham (2014). https://doi.org/10.1007/978-3-319-10590-1_54
37. Zhao, B., Feng, J., Wu, X., Yan, S.: A survey on deep learning-based fine-grained object classification and semantic segmentation. IJAC **14**, 1–17 (2017)
38. Zhao, B., Wu, X., Feng, J., Peng, Q., Yan, S.: Diversified visual attention networks for fine-grained object classification. IEEE Trans. Multimedia **19**(6), 1245–1256 (2017)
39. Zheng, H., Fu, J., Mei, T., Luo, J.: Learning multi-attention convolutional neural network for fine-grained image recognition. In: ICCV (2017)

LQ-Nets: Learned Quantization for Highly Accurate and Compact Deep Neural Networks

Dongqing Zhang[1], Jiaolong Yang[1](✉), Dongqiangzi Ye[1], and Gang Hua[2]

[1] Microsoft Research, Beijing, China
zdqzeros@gmail.com, eowinye@gmail.com, jiaoyan@microsoft.com
[2] Microsoft Cloud and AI, Redmond, USA
ganghua@microsoft.com

Abstract. Although weight and activation quantization is an effective approach for Deep Neural Network (DNN) compression and has a lot of potentials to increase inference speed leveraging bit-operations, there is still a noticeable gap in terms of prediction accuracy between the quantized model and the full-precision model. To address this gap, we propose to jointly train a quantized, bit-operation-compatible DNN and its associated quantizers, as opposed to using fixed, handcrafted quantization schemes such as uniform or logarithmic quantization. Our method for learning the quantizers applies to both network weights and activations with arbitrary-bit precision, and our quantizers are easy to train. The comprehensive experiments on CIFAR-10 and ImageNet datasets show that our method works consistently well for various network structures such as AlexNet, VGG-Net, GoogLeNet, ResNet, and DenseNet, surpassing previous quantization methods in terms of accuracy by an appreciable margin. Code available at https://github.com/Microsoft/LQ-Nets.

Keywords: Deep neural networks · Quantization · Compression

1 Introduction

Deep neural networks, especially the deep convolutional neural networks, have achieved tremendous success in computer vision and the broader artificial intelligence field. However, the large model size and high computation cost remain great hurdles for many applications, especially on some constrained devices with limited memory and computational resources.

To address this issue, there has been a surge of interests recently in reducing the model complexity of DNNs. Representative techniques include quantization [3,6,9,18,21,22,29,34,39,52–55], pruning [12,13,17,36], low-rank decomposition [7,8,24,27,38,49,51], hashing [4], and deliberate architecture

D. Zhang, J. Yang and D. Ye—Contributed equally. This work was done when DY was an intern at MSR.

V. Ferrari et al. (Eds.): ECCV 2018, LNCS 11212, pp. 373–390, 2018.
https://doi.org/10.1007/978-3-030-01237-3_23

design [19,23,50]. Among these approaches, quantization based methods represent the network weights with very low precision, thus yielding highly compact DNN models compared to their floating-point counterparts. Moreover, it has been shown that if both the network weights and activations are properly quantized, the convolution operations can be efficiently computed via bitwise operations [21,39], enabling fast inference without GPU.

Notwithstanding the promising results achieved by the existing quantization-based methods [3,6,9,18,21,22,29,34,39,52–55], there is still a sizeable accuracy gap between the quantized DNNs and their full-precision counterparts, especially when quantized with extremely low bit-widths such as 1 bit or 2 bits. For example, using the state-of-the-art method of [3], a 50-layer ResNet model [15] with 1-bit weights and 2-bit activations can achieve 64.6% top-1 image classification accuracy on ImageNet validation set [40]. However, the full-precision reference is 75.3% [15], i.e., the absolute accuracy drop induced by quantization is as large as 10.7%.

This work is devoted to pushing the limit of network quantization algorithms to achieve better accuracy with low precision weights and activations. We found that existing methods often use simple, hand-crafted quantizers (e.g., uniform or logarithmic quantization) [11,22,31,37,52,53] or otherwise pre-computed quantizers fixed during network training [3]. However, one can never be sure that the simple quantizers are the best choices for network quantization. Moreover, the distributions of weights and activations in different networks and even different network layers may differ a lot. We believe a better quantizer should be made adaptive to the weights and activations to gain more flexibility.

To this end, we propose to jointly train a quantized DNN and its associated quantizers. The proposed method not only makes the quantizers learnable, but also renders them compatible with bitwise operations so as to keep the fast inference merit of properly-quantized neural networks. Our quantizer can be optimized via backpropagation in a standard network training pipeline, and we further propose an algorithm based on quantization error minimization which yields better performance. The proposed quantization can be applied to both network weights and activations, and arbitrary bit-width can be achieved. Moreover, layer-wise quantizers with unshared parameters can be applied to gain further flexibility. We call the networks quantized by our method the "LQ-Nets".

We evaluate our LQ-Nets with image classification tasks on the CIFAR-10 [25] and ImageNet [40] datasets. The experimental results show that they perform remarkably well across various network structures such as AlexNet [26], VGG-Net [41], GoogLeNet [42], ResNet [15] and DenseNet [20], surpassing previous quantization methods by a wide margin.

2 Related Work

A large number of works have been devoted to reducing DNN model size and improving inference efficiency for practical applications. We briefly review the existing approaches as follows.

Compact Network Design: To achieve fast inference, one strategy is to carefully design a compact network architecture [19,23,32,42,50]. For example, Network in Network [32] enhanced the local modeling via the micro networks and replaced the costly fully-connected layer by global average pooling. GoogLeNet [42] and SqueezeNet [23] utilized 1×1 convolution layers to compute reductions before the expensive 3×3 or 5×5 convolutions. Similarly, ResNet [15] applied "bottleneck" structures with 1×1 convolutions when training deeper nets with enormous parameters. The recently proposed computation-efficient network structures MobileNet [19] and ShuffleNet [50] employed depth-wise convolution or group convolution advocated in [5,48] to reduce the computation cost.

Network Parameter Reduction: Considerable efforts have been devoted to reducing the number of parameters in an existing network [4,7,8,10,12,13,17,24, 27,28,35,36,38,45,46,49,51]. For example, by exploiting the redundancy of the filters weights, some methods substitute the pre-trained weights using their low-rank approximations [7,8,24,27,38,49,51]. Connection pruning was investigated in [12,13] to reduce the parameters of AlexNet and VGG-Net, where significant reduction was achieved on fully-connected layers. Promising results on modern network architectures such as ResNet were achieved recently by [17,36]. Another similar technique is to regularize the network by structured sparsity to obtain a hardware-friendly DNN model [28,35,45]. Some other approaches such as hashing and vector quantization [44] have also been explored to reduce DNN model complexity [4,10,46].

Network Quantization: Another category of existing methods, which our method also belongs to, train low-precision DNNs via quantization. These methods can be further divided into two subcategories: those performing quantization on *weights only* versus *both weights and activations.*

For weight-only quantization methods, Courbariaux et al. [6] constrained the weights to only two possible values of −1 and 1 (i.e., binarization or one-bit quantization). They obtained promising results on small datasets using stochastic binarization. Rastegari et al. [39] later demonstrated that deterministic binarization with optimized scale factors to approximate the full-precision weights work better on deeper network structures and larger datasets. To obtain better accuracy, ternary and other multi-bit quantization schemes were explored in [9,18,29,34,52,54]. It was shown in [52] that quantizing a network with five bits can achieve similar accuracy to its 32-bit floating-point counterpart by incremental group-wise quantization and re-training.

In the latter regard, Hubara et al. [21] and Rastegari et al. [39] proposed to binarize both weights and activations to −1 and +1. This way, the convolution operations can be implemented by efficient bit-wise operations for substantial speed-up. To address the significant accuracy drop, multi-bit quantization was further studied in [22,30,33,37,43,53]. A popular choice of the quantization function is the uniform quantization [22,53]. Miyashita et al. [37] used logarithmic quantization and improve the inference efficiency via the bitshift operation. Cai et al. [3] proposed to binarize the network weights while quantize the activations using multiple bits. A single activation quantizer computed by fitting the probability density function of a half-wave Gaussian distribution is applied to all network layers and fixed during training. In the multi-bit quantization methods of Tang et al. [43] and Li et al. [30], each bit is used to binarize the residue approximation error from previous bits.

Our proposed method can quantize both the weights and the activations with arbitrary bit-widths. Different from most of the previous methods, our quantizer is adaptively learned during network training.

3 LQ-Nets: Networks with Learned Quantization

In this section, we first briefly introduce the goal of neural network quantization. Then we present the details of our quantization method and how to train a quantized DNN model with it in a standard network training pipeline.

3.1 Preliminaries: Network Quantization

The main operations in deep neural networks are interleaved linear and non-linear transformations, expressed as

$$z = \sigma(\mathbf{w}^{\mathrm{T}}\mathbf{a}), \tag{1}$$

where $\mathbf{w} \in \mathbb{R}^N$ is the weight vector, $\mathbf{a} \in \mathbb{R}^N$ is the input activation vector computed by the previous network layer, $\sigma(\cdot)$ is a non-linear function, and z is the output activation.[1] The convolutional layers are composed by multiple convolution filters $\mathbf{w}_i \in \mathbb{R}^{C \cdot H \cdot W}$, where C, H and W are the number of convolution filter channels, kernel height, and kernel width, respectively. Fully-connected layers can be viewed as a special type of convolutional layer. Modern deep neural networks often have millions of weight parameters, which incur large memory footprints. Meanwhile, the large numbers of inner product operations between the weights and feature vectors lead to high computation cost. The memory and computation costs are great hurdles for many applications on resource-constrained devices such as mobile phones.

The goal of network quantization is to represent the floating-point weights $\mathbf{w}$ and/or activations $\mathbf{a}$ with few bits. In general, a quantization function is a piecewise-constant function which can be written as

$$Q(x) = q_l, \text{ if } x \in (t_l, t_{l+1}], \tag{2}$$

where q_l, $l = 1, ..., L$ are the quantization levels and $(t_l, t_{l+1}]$ are quantization intervals. The quantization function maps all the input values within a quantization interval to the corresponding quantization level, and a quantized value can be encoded by only $\log_2 L$ bits. Perhaps the simplest quantizer is the sign function used for binary quantization [21,39]: $Q(x) = +1$ if $x \geq 0$ or -1 otherwise. For quantization with 2 or more bits, the most commonly used quantizer

[1] For brevity, we omit the bias term in Eq. (1).

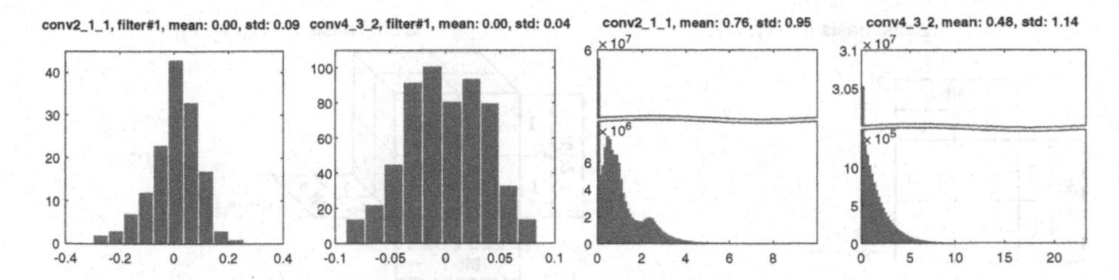

Fig. 1. Distributions of weights (left two columns) and activations (right two columns) at different layers of the ResNet-20 network trained on CIFAR-10. All the test-set images are used to get the activation statistics.

is the uniform quantization function where all the quantization steps $q_{l+1} - q_l$ are equal [22, 53]. Some methods use logarithmic quantization which uniformly quantizes the data in the *log*-domain [37].

Quantizing the network weights can generate highly compact and memory-efficient DNN models: using n-bit encoding, the compression rate is $\frac{32}{n}$ or $\frac{64}{n}$ compared to the 32-bit or 64-bit floating point representation. Moreover, if both weights and activations are quantized properly, the inner product in Eq. (1) can be computed by bitwise operations such as *xnor* and *popcnt*, where *xnor* is the exclusive-not-or logical operation and *popcnt* counts the number of 1's in a bit string. Both the two operations can process at least 64 bits in one or few clock cycle on most general computing platforms such as CPU and GPU, which potentially leads to 64× speedup.[2]

3.2 Learnable Quantizers

An optimal quantizer should yield minimal quantization error for the input data distribution:

$$Q^*(x) = \arg\min_{Q} \int p(x)(Q(x) - x)^2 dx, \tag{3}$$

where $p(x)$ is the probability density function of x. We can never be sure if the popular quantizers such as a uniform quantizer are the optimal selections for the network weights and activations. In Fig. 1 we present the statistical distributions of the weights and activations (after batch normalization (BN) and Rectified Linear Unit (ReLU) layers) in a trained floating-point network. It can be seen that the distributions can be complex and differ across layers, and a uniform quantizer is not optimal for them. Of course, if we train a quantized network the weight and activation distributions may change. But again we can never be sure if any pre-defined quantizer is optimal for our task, and an improper quantizer can easily jeopardize the final accuracy.

To get better network quantizers and improve the accuracy of a quantized network, we propose to jointly train the network and its quantizers. The insight

[2] We refer the readers to [21, 39] for more details regarding the bitwise operations and speed-up analysis on different hardware platforms.

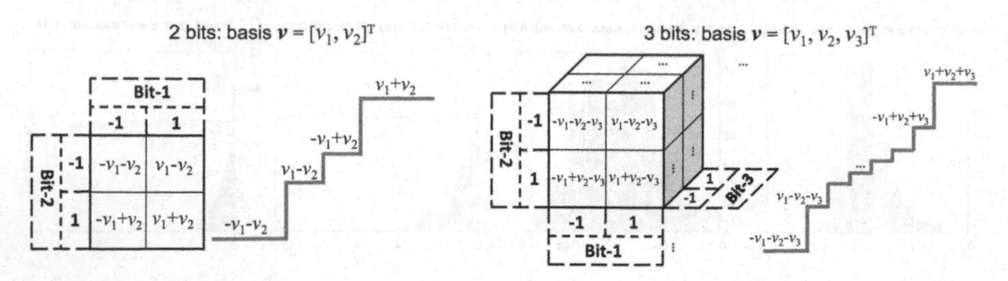

Fig. 2. Illustration of our learnable quantizer on the 2-bit (left) and 3-bit (right) cases. For each case, the left figure shows how quantization levels are generated by the basis vector, and the right figure illustrates the corresponding quantization function.

behind is that if the optimizers are learnable and optimized through network training, they can not only minimize the quantization error, but also adapt to the training goal thus improving the final accuracy. A naive way to train the quantizers would be directly optimizing the quantization levels $\{q_l\}$ in network training. However, such a naive strategy would render the quantization functions not compatible with bitwise operations, which is undesired as we want to keep the fast inference merit of quantized neural networks.

To resolve this issue, we need to confine our quantization functions into a *subspace* which is compatible with bitwise operations. But how to confine the quantizers into such a space during training? Our solution is inspired by the uniform quantization which is bit-op compatible (see [53]). The uniform quantization essentially maps floating-point numbers to their nearest fixed-point integers with a normalization factor, and the key property for it to be bit-op-compatible is that the quantized values can be decomposed by a linear combination of the bits. Specifically, an integer q represented by a K-bit binary encoding is actually the inner product between a basis vector and the binary coding vector $\mathbf{b} = [b_1, b_2, ..., b_K]^T$ where $b_i \in \{0, 1\}$, i.e.,

$$q = \left\langle \begin{bmatrix} 1 \\ 2 \\ ... \\ 2^{K-1} \end{bmatrix}, \begin{bmatrix} b_1 \\ b_2 \\ ... \\ b_K \end{bmatrix} \right\rangle. \tag{4}$$

In order to learn the quantizers while keeping them compatible with bitwise operations, we can simply learn the basis vector which consists of K scalars.

Concretely, our learnable quantization function is simply in the form of

$$Q_{\text{ours}}(x, \mathbf{v}) = \mathbf{v}^T \mathbf{e}_l, \qquad \text{if } x \in (t_l, t_{l+1}], \tag{5}$$

where $\mathbf{v} \in \mathbb{R}^K$ is the learnable floating-point basis and $\mathbf{e}_l \in \{-1, 1\}^K$ for $l = 1, \ldots, 2^K$ enumerates all the K-bit binary encodings from $[-1, \ldots, -1]$ to $[1, \ldots, 1]$.[3] For a K-bit quantization, the 2^K quantization levels are generated by

[3] Note that $\mathbf{e}_i$ can be either $\{0, 1\}$ encodings or $\{-1, 1\}$ encodings, both of which can yield quantizers compatible with bitwise operations. In our implementation, we adopt the $\{-1, 1\}$ encoding for weights and $\{0, 1\}$ encoding for activations. For convenience we will use the $\{-1, 1\}$ encoding in the remaining text as the example.

$q_l = \mathbf{v}^{\mathrm{T}}\mathbf{e}_l$ for $l = 1, \ldots, 2^K$. Given $\{q_l\}$ and assuming $q_1 < q_2 < \ldots < q_{2^K}$, it can be easily derived that for any x, the optimal $\{t_l\}$ minimizing the error in Eq. (3) are simply $t_l = (q_{l-1} + q_l)/2$ for $l = 2, \ldots, 2^K$ (note $t_1 = -\infty$ and $t_{2^K+1} = +\infty$). Figure 2 illustrates our quantizer with the 2-bit and 3-bit cases.

We now show how the inner products between our quantized weights and activations can be computed by bitwise operations. Let a weight vector $\mathbf{w} \in \mathbb{R}^N$ be encoded by the vectors $\mathbf{b}_i^w \in \{-1, 1\}^N$, $i = 1, \ldots, K_w$ where K_w is the bit-width for weights and $\mathbf{b}_i^w$ consists of the encoding of the i-th bit for all the values in $\mathbf{w}$. Similarly, for activation vector $\mathbf{a} \in \mathbb{R}^N$ we have $\mathbf{b}_j^a \in \{-1, 1\}^N$, $j = 1, \ldots, K_a$. It can be readily derived that

$$Q_{\mathrm{ours}}(\mathbf{w}, \mathbf{v}^w)^{\mathrm{T}} Q_{\mathrm{ours}}(\mathbf{a}, \mathbf{v}^a) = \sum_{i=1}^{K_w} \sum_{j=1}^{K_a} v_i^w v_j^a (\mathbf{b}_i^w \odot \mathbf{b}_j^a) \tag{6}$$

where $\mathbf{v}^w \in \mathbb{R}^{K_w}$ and $\mathbf{v}^a \in \mathbb{R}^{K_a}$ are the learned basis vectors for the weight and activation quantizers respectively, and $\odot$ denotes the inner product with bitwise operations *xnor* and *popcnt*.

In practice, we apply layer-wise quantizers for activations (i.e., one quantizer per layer) and channel-wise quantizers for weights (one quantizer for each conv filter). The number of extra parameters introduced by the quantizers is negligible compared to the large volume of network weights.

3.3 Training Algorithm

To train the LQ-Nets, we use floating-point network weights which are quantized before convolution and optimized with error back-propagation (BP) and gradient descent. After training, they can be discarded and their binary codes and quantizer bases are kept. We now present how we optimize the quantizers.

Quantizer Optimization: A simple and straightforward way to optimize our quantizers is through BP similar to weight optimization. Here we present an algorithm based on quantization error minimization which optimizes our quantizers in the forward passes during training. This algorithm leads to much better performance as we will show later in the experiments.

Let $\mathbf{x} = [x_1, \ldots, x_N]^{\mathrm{T}} \in \mathbb{R}^N$ be the full-precision data (weights or activations) and K be the specified bit number for quantization. Our goal is to find an optimal quantizer basis $\mathbf{v} \in \mathbb{R}^K$ as well as an encoding $B = [\mathbf{b}_1, \ldots, \mathbf{b}_N] \in \{-1, 1\}^{K \times N}$ that minimize the quantization error:

$$\mathbf{v}^*, B^* = \arg\min_{\mathbf{v}, B} \left\| B^{\mathrm{T}}\mathbf{v} - \mathbf{x} \right\|_2^2, \quad s.t.\ B \in \{-1, 1\}^{K \times N}. \tag{7}$$

Equation (7) is complex and to provably solve for the optimal solution via brute-force search is exponential in the size of B. For efficiency purposes, we alternately solve for $\mathbf{v}$ and B in a block coordinate descent fashion:

Algorithm 1. Training and testing the quantizers in LQ-Nets

1: **Parameters:** $\mathbf{v}$ - the current basis vector of the quantizer
2: **Input:** $\mathbf{x} = [x_1, x_2, ..., x_N]$ - the full-precision data (weights or activations)
3: **Output:** $B = [\mathbf{b}_1, ..., \mathbf{b}_N]$ - the binary encodings for the input data
4: **Procedure:**
5: **if** in the training stage **then** {//quantizer optimization with QEM in forward pass}
6: Set $\mathbf{v}^{(0)} = \mathbf{v}$
7: **for** $t = 1 \rightarrow T$ **do**
8: Compute $B^{(t)}$ with $\mathbf{v}^{(t-1)}$ per Eq. (5)
9: Compute $\mathbf{v}^{(t)}$ with $B^{(t)}$ per (8)
10: **end for**
11: Output $B = B^{(T)}$; Update current $\mathbf{v}$ with $\mathbf{v}^{(T)}$ via moving average
12: **else** {//simple quantization operation in the test stage}
13: Compute B with $\mathbf{v}$ per Eq. (5)
14: **end if**

- *Fix* $\mathbf{v}$ *and update* B. Given $\mathbf{v}$, the optimal encoding B^* can be simply found by looking up the quantization intervals $t_1, ..., t_{2^K+1}$.
- *Fix* B *and update* $\mathbf{v}$. Given B, Eq. (7) reduces to a linear regression problem with a closed form solution as

$$\mathbf{v}^* = (BB^{\mathrm{T}})^{-1}B\mathbf{x}. \tag{8}$$

We iterate the alternation T times. For brevity, we will refer to the above procedure as the QEM (Quantization Error Minimization) algorithm.

Network Training: We use the standard mini-batch based approach to train the LQ-Nets, and our quantizer learning is conducted in the forward passes with the QEM algorithm. Since, for activation quantization, only part of the input data is visible in one iteration due to mini-batch sampling, we apply moving average for the optimized quantizer parameters (i.e., basis vectors). We also apply the moving average strategy for the weight quantizers to gain more stability. The operations in our quantizers are summarized in Algorithm 1.

In a backward pass, direct error back-propagation would be problematic as the gradient of the quantization function is 0 at almost everywhere. To tackle this issue, we use the Straight-Through Estimator (STE) proposed in [2] to compute the gradients. Specifically, for activations we set the gradient of the quantization function to 1 for values between q_1 and q_{2^K} defined in Eq. (5) and 0 elsewhere; for weights, the gradient is set to 1 everywhere [3]. The QEM algorithm is unrelated to the backward pass so the quantizers will remain unchanged (unless BP is used to train them instead).

4 Experiments

In this section, we evaluate the proposed method on two image classification datasets: CIFAR-10 [25] and ImageNet (ILSVRC12) [40]. The CIFAR-10 dataset consists of 60,000 color images of size 32 × 32 belonging to 10 classes (6,000 images per class). There are 50,000 training and 10,000 test images. ImageNet ILSVRC12 contains about 1.2 million training and 50K validation images of 1,000 object categories.

Although our method is designed to quantize both weights and activations to facilitate fast inference through bitwise operations, we also conduct experiments of weight-only quantization and compare with the prior art.

4.1 Implementation Details

Our LQ-Nets are implemented with TensorFlow [1] and trained with the aid of the Tensorpack library [47].[4] We present our implementation details as follows.
Quantizer Implementation: We apply layer re-ordering to the networks similar to [3,39]: the typical Conv→BN→ReLU operations is re-organized as BN→ ReLU (→Quant.)→Conv. Following previous methods [3,21,39,53,54], we quantize all the convolution and fully-connected layers but the first and last layers, for which the speedup benefited by bitwise operations is low due to their small channel number or filter size [30,39].

Network Structures: We conduct experiments on AlexNet [26], ResNet [15], DenseNet [20], two variants of the VGG-Net [41] "VGG-Small"and"VGG-Variant" from [3], and a variant of GoogLeNet [42] also from [3]. VGG-Small is a simplified VGG-Net similar to that of [21,39] but with only one fully-connected layer. VGG-Variant is a smaller version of the model-A in [14]. The GoogLeNet structure in [3] contains some modifications of the original GoogLeNet (e.g., more filters in some 1 × 1 conv layers) and we denote it as "GoogleNet-Variant" in this paper. Detailed structures of these network variants can be found in [3]'s publicly-available implementation.[5] For ResNet-50, the parameter-free type-A shortcut [15] is adopted in this paper.

Initialization: In all the experiments, our LQ-Nets are trained from scratch (random initialization) without leveraging any pre-trained model. Our quantizers are initialized with uniform quantization (we also tried random initialization and initializing them via pre-computing the quantization levels using [3], however no noticeable difference on the results was observed).

Hyper-parameters and Other Setup: To train on various network architectures, we mostly follow the hyper-parameter settings (learning rate, batch size, training epoch, weight decay, etc.) of their original papers [15,16,20]. For fair comparisons with the method of [3], we use the hyper-parameters described in [3] to train all the networks with 1-bit weights and 2-bit activations. The iteration number T in our QEM algorithm is fixed as 1 (no significant benefit was observed with larger values; see Sect. 4.2). The moving average factor for quantizer learning is fixed as 0.9. Details of all our hyper-parameter settings can be found in the *supplementary material* as well as our released source code.

[4] Our source code is available at https://github.com/Microsoft/LQ-Nets/.
[5] https://github.com/zhaoweicai/hwgq (accessed July 10, 2018).

Table 1. Optimization method comparison on the ResNet-20 model.

Bit-width (W/A)	Optim. method	Accuracy (%)
2/32	BP	90.0
2/32	QEM	**91.8**
2/2	BP	88.2
2/2	QEM	**90.2**

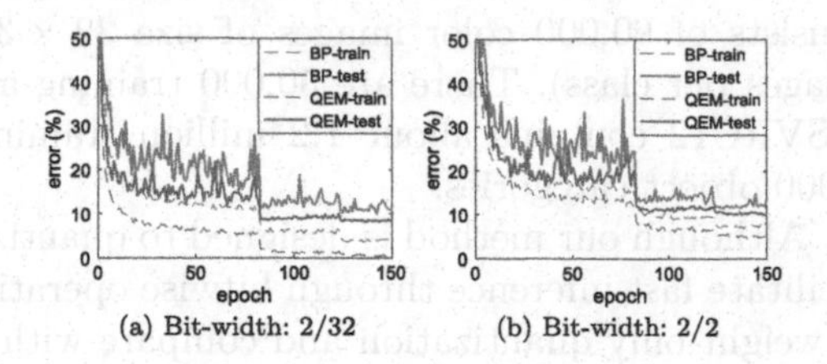

(a) Bit-width: 2/32 (b) Bit-width: 2/2

Fig. 3. Error curves with the two optimization methods

In the remaining text, we used "W/A" to denote the number of bits used for weights/activations. A bit-width of 32 indicates using 32-bit floating-point values without quantization (thus "w/32" with $w < 32$ indicates weight-only quantization and "32/32" are"full-precision" (FP) models). For the experiments on CIFAR-10, we run our method 5 times and report the mean accuracy.

4.2 Performance Analysis

Effectiveness of the QEM Algorithm: Our quantizer can be trained by either the proposed QEM algorithm or a naive BP procedure. In this experiment, we evaluate the effectiveness of the QEM algorithm and compare it against BP. Table 1 shows the performance of the quantized ResNet-20 models on CIFAR-10 test set, and Fig. 3 presents the corresponding training and testing curves. The quantized network trained using QEM is clearly better than BP for weight-only quantization as well as weight-and-activation quantization. In all the following experiments, we use the QEM algorithm to optimize our quantizers.

Table 2 shows the accuracy of quantized ResNet-20 models with different QEM solver iteration T. As can be seen, using $T = 2, 3$ or 4 did not show significant benefit compared to $T = 1$. Note that each time the solver starts from the result of the last training iteration (see Line 6 in Algorithm 1) which is a good starting point especially when the gradients become small after a few epochs. The good performance with $T = 1$ suggests that the iterations of the alternately-directional optimization can be effectively substituted by the training iterations. In this paper, we use $T = 1$ in all the experiments.

Table 2. Accuracy w.r.t. QEM iteration number T

Bit-width (W/A)	Accuracy (%; "mean ± std" of 5 runs) $T = 1$	$T = 2$	$T = 3$	$T = 4$
1/2	88.37 ± 0.26	88.38 ± 0.11	88.45 ± 0.12	88.51 ± 0.20
2/2	90.16 ± 0.08	9035 ± 0.12	90.33 ± 0.20	90.25 ± 0.14
3/3	91.58 ± 0.16	91.55 ± 0.16	91.62 ± 0.15	91.44 ± 0.14

Effectiveness of the Learnable Quantizers: The key idea of our method is to apply flexible quantizers and optimize them jointly with the network. Table 3 compares the results of our method and two previous methods: DoReFa-Net [53] and HWGQ [3], the former of which is based on fixed uniform quantizers and latter pre-computes the quantizer by fitting a half-wave Gaussian distribution. It

Table 3. Comparison of different quantization methods (ResNet-18 on ImageNet

Method	Bit-width (W/A)	Accuracy (%)	
		Top-1	Top-5
Uniform–DoReFa-Net [53]	1/4	59.2	-
Half-wave Gaussian–HWGQ [3]	1/2	59.6	82.2
Ours	1/2	**62.6**	**84.3**

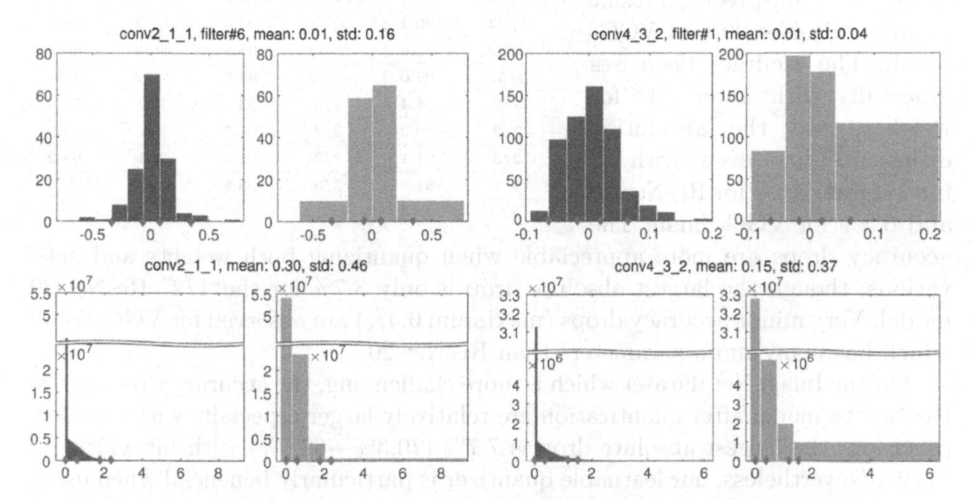

Fig. 4. Statistics of the weights (top row) and activations (bottom row) before (i.e., the floating-point values) and after quantization. A ResNet-20 model trained on CIFAR-10 with "2/2" quantization is used. The orange diamonds indicate the four quantization levels of our learned quantizers. Note that in the left figures for the floating-point values, the histogram bins are of equal step size, whereas in the right figures each of the four bins contains all the values quantized to its corresponding quantization levels.

can be seen that using 1-bit weights and 2-bit activations, the ResNet-18 model with our learnable quantizers outperformed HWGQ under the same setting and also outperformed DoReFa-Net with 4-bit activations on ImageNet. More result comparisons on various network structures can be found in Sect. 4.3.

Figure 4 presents the weight and activation statistics in two layers of a trained ResNet-20 model before (i.e., the floating-point values) and after quantization using our method. The network is quantized with "2/2" bits and the floating-point weights are obtained from the last iteration of training (these values can be discarded after training and only quantized values are used in the inference time). The floating-point activations are obtained using all the test images of CIFAR-10. It can be seen that our learned quantizers are not uniform ones and they differ at different layers. Statistical results with more bits can be found in the *supplementary material*.

Performance w.r.t. Bit-width: We now study the impact of bit-width on the performance of our LQ-Nets. Table 4 shows the results of three network structures: ResNet-20, VGG-Small and ResNet-18.

On the CIFAR-10 dataset, high accuracy can be achieved by our low-precision networks. The accuracy from "3/32" quantization has roughly reached our full-precision result for both ResNet-20 and VGG-Small. The accuracy decreases gracefully with lower bits for weights, and the absolution drops are low even with 1-bit weights: 2.0% for ResNet-20 and 0.3% for VGG-Small. The accuracy drops are more appreciable when quantizing both weights and activations, though the largest absolute drop is only 3.7% for the"1/2" ResNet-20 model. Very minor accuracy drops (maximum 0.4%) are observed for VGG-Small which has many more parameters than ResNet-20.

Table 4. Impact of bit-width on our LQ-Nets

ResNet-20 (CIFAR-10)		VGG-Small (CIFAR-10)		ResNet-18 (ImageNet)	
Bit-width (W/A)	Acc. (%)	Bit-width (W/A)	Acc. (%)	Bit-width (W/A)	Acc. (%)
32/32	92.1	32/32	93.8	32/32	70.3
1/32	90.1	1/32	93.5	2/32	68.0
2/32	91.8	2/32	93.8	3/32	69.3
3/32	92.0	3/32	93.8	4/32	70.0
1/2	88.4	1/2	93.4	1/2	62.6
2/2	90.2	2/2	93.5	2/2	64.9
2/3	91.1	2/3	93.8	3/3	68.2
3/3	91.6	3/3	93.8	4/4	69.3

On the ImageNet dataset which is more challenging, the accuracy drops of the ResNet-18 model after quantization are relatively larger especially with very low precision: the largest absolute drop is 7.7% (70.3%→62.6%) with bit-widths of "1/2". Nevertheless, our learnable quantizer is particularly beneficial when using 2 or more bits due to its high flexibility. The accuracy of the quantized ResNet-18 quickly increases with 2 or more bits as shown in Table 4. The accuracy gap is almost closed with"4/32" bits (0.3% absolute difference only), and the accuracy drop with the "4/4" case is as low as 1%.

4.3 Comparison with Previous Methods

In this section, we compare the performance of our quantization method with existing methods including TWN [29], TTQ [54], BNN [21], BWN [39], XNOR-Net [39], DoReFa-Net [53], HWQG [3] and ABC-Net [33], with various network architectures tested on CIFAR-10 and ImageNet classification tasks.

Comparison on CIFAR-10: Table 5 presents the results of the VGG-Small model quantized using different methods. All these methods quantize (or binarize) both weights and activations to achieve extremely low precision. With 1-bit weights and 2-bit activations, the accuracy using our method is significantly better than the state-of-the-art method HWGQ (93.4% vs. 92.5%).

Table 5. Comparison of quantized VGG-Small networks on CIFAR-10

Model	Methods	Bit-width (W/A)	Acc. (%) (%)
VGG-Small	FP-HWGQ[3]	32/32	93.2
	FP-ours	32/32	93.8
	BNN[21]	1/1	89.9
	XNOR-Net[39]	1/1	89.8
	HWGQ[3]	1/2	92.5
	Ours	1/2	**93.4**

Table 6. Comparison with state-of-the-art quantization methods on ImageNet. "FP" denotes "Full Precision"; the "W/A" values are the bit-widths of weights/activations.

Methods	Bit-width (W/A)	Accuracy(%) Top-1	Top-5
ResNet-18			
FP* [15]	32/32	69.6	89.2
FP-ours	32/32	70.3	89.5
BWN [39]	1/32	60.8	83.0
TWN [29]	2/32	61.8	84.2
TWN† [29]	2/32	65.3	86.2
TTQ† [54]	2/32	66.6	87.2
Ours	2/32	**68.0**	**88.0**
Ours	3/32	**69.3**	**88.8**
Ours	4/32	**70.0**	**89.1**
XNOR-Net [39]	1/1	51.2	73.2
DoReFa-Net‡ [53]	1/2	53.4	-
DoReFa-Net‡ [53]	1/4	59.2	-
HWGQ [3]	1/2	59.6	82.2
ABC-Net [33]	3/3	61.0	83.2
ABC-Net [33]	5/5	65.0	85.9
Ours	1/2	**62.6**	**84.3**
Ours	2/2	**64.9**	**85.9**
Ours	3/3	**68.2**	**87.9**
Ours	4/4	**69.3**	**88.8**
ResNet-34			
FP* [15]	32/32	73.3	91.3
FP-ours	32/32	73.8	91.4
HWGQ [3]	1/2	64.3	85.7
ABC-Net [33]	3/3	66.7	87.4
ABC-Net [33]	5/5	68.4	88.2
Ours	1/2	**66.6**	**86.9**
Ours	2/2	**69.8**	**89.1**
Ours	3/3	**71.9**	**90.2**
ResNet-50			
FP* [15]	32/32	76.0	93.0
FP-ours	32/32	76.4	93.2
Ours	2/32	**75.1**	**92.3**
Ours	4/32	**76.4**	**93.1**
HWGQ [3]	1/2	64.6	85.9
ABC-Net [33]	5/5	70.1	89.7
Ours	1/2	**68.7**	**88.4**
Ours	2/2	**71.5**	**90.3**
Ours	3/3	**74.2**	**91.6**
Ours	4/4	**75.1**	**92.4**

Methods	Bit-width (W/A)	Accuracy(%) Top-1	Top-5
AlexNet			
FP [26]	32/32	57.1	80.2
FP-ours	32/32	61.8	83.5
BWN [39]	1/32	56.8	79.4
DoReFa-Net§ [53]	1/32	53.9	76.3
TWN§ [29]	2/32	54.5	76.8
TTQ [54]	2/32	57.5	79.7
Ours	2/32	**60.5**	**82.7**
BNN§ [21]	1/1	41.8	67.1
XNOR-Net [39]	1/1	44.2	69.2
DoReFa-Net [53]	1/1	43.6	-
DoReFa-Net [53]	1/2	49.8	-
DoReFa-Net [53]	1/4	53.0	-
HWGQ [3]	1/2	52.7	76.3
Ours	1/2	**55.7**	**78.8**
Ours	2/2	**57.4**	**80.1**
DenseNet-121			
FP [20]	32/32	75.0	92.3
FP-ours	32/32	75.3	92.5
DoReFa-Net* [53]	2/2	67.7	88.4
Ours	2/2	**69.6**	**89.1**
VGG-Variant			
FP-HWGQ [3]	32/32	69.8	89.3
FP-ours	32/32	72.0	90.5
HWGQ [3]	1/2	64.1	85.6
Ours	1/2	**67.1**	**87.6**
Ours	2/2	**68.8**	**88.6**
GoogLeNet-Variant			
FP-HWGQ [3]	32/32	71.4	90.5
FP-ours	32/32	72.9	91.3
HWGQ [3]	1/2	63.0	84.9
Ours	1/2	**65.6**	**86.4**
Ours	2/2	**68.2**	**88.1**

*Results of the ResNet models trained in Torch: https://github.com/facebook/fb.resnet.torch (accessed July 10, 2018)
†Results of ResNet-18B [29] where the filter number in each block is 1.5× of ResNet-18
‡ Results quoted from the method's official webpage https://github.com/tensorpack/tensorpack/tree/master/examples/DoReFa-Net (accessed July 10, 2018)
*Results trained by us with the authors' code (same URL as above)
§Results quoted from [54] for TWN and DoReFa-Net, and [22] for BNN.

Comparison on ImageNet: The results on ImageNet validation set are presented in Table 6. For weight-only quantization, our LQ-Nets outperformed BWN, TWN, TTQ and DoReFa-Net by large margins.

As for quantizing both weights and activations, our results are significantly better than DoReFa-Net and HWGQ when using very low bit-widths (1 bit for weights and few for activations). Our method is even more advantageous when using larger bit-widths. Table 6 shows that with more bits (2, 3, or 4), the accuracy can be dramatically improved by our method. For example, with "4/4" bits, the top-1 accuracy of ResNet-50 is boosted from 68.7% (with "1/2" bits) to 75.1%. The absolute accuracy increase is as high as 6.4%, and the gap to its FP counterpart is reduced to 1.3%. According to Table 6, the accuracy of our LQ-Nets comprehensively surpassed the other competing methods under the same bit-width settings.

4.4 Training Time

Compared to training floating-point networks, our extra cost lies in quantizer optimization. In the QEM algorithm, the cost of solving B is negligible. For N input scalars, the time complexity of solving $\mathbf{v}$ of length K is $O(K^2N)$, which is a relatively small compared to the conv operations in theory.[6] Table 7 shows the total training time comparison based on our current unoptimized implementation. The network is ResNet-18 and no bitwise operation is used in all cases. Our training time increases gracefully with larger bit-widths.

Table 7. Training time

Bit-width (W/A)	Training time
32/32	1.0×
2/32	1.4×
3/32	1.7×
1/2	2.1×
2/2	2.3×
3/3	3.7×

5 Conclusions

We have presented a novel DNN quantization method that led to state-of-the-art accuracy for various network structures. The key idea is to apply learnable quantizers which can be jointly trained with the network parameters to gain more flexibility. Our quantizers can be applied to both weights and activations, and they are made compatible with bitwise operations facilitating fast inference. In future, we plan to deploy our LQ-Nets on some resource-constrained devices such as mobile phones and test their performance.

Acknowledgment. This work is partially supported by the National Natural Science Foundation of China under Grant 61629301.

[6] To solve for $\mathbf{v}$ in Eq. (8), we need $O(K^2N)$ for matrix multiplication BB^{T}, $O(K^3)$ for matrix inverse, and $O(KN)$ for matrix-vector multiplications. Note $K \ll N$. Let the input and output activation map sizes be (H, W, C_{in}) and (H, W, C_{out}). The input activation number is $N_a = C_{in}HW$. The time complexity of an $S \times S$ conv operation with stride 1 is $O(S^2C_{out}C_{in}HW) = O(S^2C_{out}N_a)$, whereas that of the quantizer optimization is $O(K_a^2N_a)$ for activations and $O(K_w^2N_w)$ for weights.

References

1. Abadi, M., et al.: TensorFlow: large-scale machine learning on heterogeneous systems (2015). https://www.tensorflow.org/
2. Bengio, Y., Léonard, N., Courville, A.: Estimating or propagating gradients through stochastic neurons for conditional computation. arXiv:1308.3432 (2013)
3. Cai, Z., He, X., Sun, J., Vasconcelos, N.: Deep learning with low precision by half-wave Gaussian quantization. In: IEEE Conference on Computer Vision and Pattern Recognition (CVPR), pp. 5918–5926 (2017)
4. Chen, W., Wilson, J.T., Tyree, S., Weinberger, K.Q., Chen, Y.: Compressing neural networks with the hashing trick. In: International Conference on Machine Learning (ICML), pp. 2285–2294 (2015)
5. Chollet, F.: Xception: Deep learning with depthwise separable convolutions. In: IEEE Conference on Computer Vision and Pattern Recognition (CVPR), pp. 1251–1258 (2017)
6. Courbariaux, M., Bengio, Y., David, J.P.: BinaryConnect: training deep neural networks with binary weights during propagations. In: Advances in Neural Information Processing Systems (NIPS), pp. 3123–3131 (2015)
7. Denil, M., Shakibi, B., Dinh, L., Ranzato, M., de Freitas, N.: Predicting parameters in deep learning. In: Advances in Neural Information Processing Systems (NIPS), pp. 2148–2156 (2013)
8. Denton, E., Zaremba, W., Bruna, J., LeCun, Y., Fergus, R.: Exploiting linear structure within convolutional networks for efficient evaluation. In: Advances in Neural Information Processing Systems (NIPS), pp. 1269–1277 (2014)
9. Dong, Y., Ni, R., Li, J., Chen, Y., Zhu, J., Su, H.: Learning accurate low-bit deep neural networks with stochastic quantization. In: British Machine Vision Conference (BMVC) (2017)
10. Gong, Y., Liu, L., Yang, M., Bourdev, L.: Compressing deep convolutional networks using vector quantization. arXiv:1412.6115 (2014)
11. Gupta, S., Agrawal, A., Gopalakrishnan, K., Narayanan, P.: Deep learning with limited numerical precision. In: International Conference on Machine Learning (ICML), pp. 1737–1746 (2015)
12. Han, S., Mao, H., Dally, W.J.: Deep compression: compressing deep neural networks with pruning, trained quantization and Huffman coding. In: International Conference on Learning Representations (ICLR) (2016)
13. Han, S., Pool, J., Tran, J., Dally, W.J.: Learning both weights and connections for efficient neural networks. In: Advances in Neural Information Processing Systems (NIPS), pp. 1135–1143 (2015)
14. He, K., Zhang, X., Ren, S., Sun, J.: Delving deep into rectifiers: surpassing human-level performance on ImageNet classification. In: International Conference on Computer Vision (ICCV), pp. 1026–1034 (2015)
15. He, K., Zhang, X., Ren, S., Sun, J.: Deep residual learning for image recognition. In: IEEE Conference on Computer Vision and Pattern Recognition (CVPR), pp. 770–778 (2016)

16. He, K., Zhang, X., Ren, S., Sun, J.: Identity mappings in deep residual networks. In: Leibe, B., Matas, J., Sebe, N., Welling, M. (eds.) ECCV 2016. LNCS, vol. 9908, pp. 630–645. Springer, Cham (2016). https://doi.org/10.1007/978-3-319-46493-0_38
17. He, Y., Zhang, X., Sun, J.: Channel pruning for accelerating very deep neural networks. In: International Conference on Computer Vision (ICCV), pp. 1389–1397 (2017)
18. Hou, L., Kwok, J.T.: Loss-aware weight quantization of deep networks. In: International Conference on Learning Representations (ICLR) (2018)
19. Howard, A.G., et al.: Mobilenets: efficient convolutional neural networks for mobile vision applications. arXiv:1704.04861 (2017)
20. Huang, G., Liu, Z., van der Maaten, L.: Densely connected convolutional networks. In: IEEE Conference on Computer Vision and Pattern Recognition (CVPR), pp. 2261–2269 (2017)
21. Hubara, I., Courbariaux, M., Soudry, D., El-Yaniv, R., Bengio, Y.: Binarized neural networks. In: Advances in Neural Information Processing Systems (NIPS), pp. 4107–4115 (2016)
22. Hubara, I., Courbariaux, M., Soudry, D., El-Yaniv, R., Bengio, Y.: Quantized neural networks: training neural networks with low precision weights and activations. arXiv:1609.07061 (2016)
23. Iandola, F.N., Han, S., Moskewicz, M.W., Ashraf, K., Dally, W.J., Keutzer, K.: SqueezeNet: AlexNet-level accuracy with 50x fewer parameters and ¡0.5MB model size. arXiv:1602.07360 (2016)
24. Jaderberg, M., Vedaldi, A., Zisserman, A.: Speeding up convolutional neural networks with low rank expansions. In: British Machine Vision Conference (BMVC) (2014)
25. Krizhevsky, A.: Learning multiple layers of features from tiny images. Technical report (2009)
26. Krizhevsky, A., Sutskever, I., Hinton, G.E.: ImageNet classification with deep convolutional neural networks. In: Advances in Neural Information Processing Systems (NIPS), pp. 1097–1105 (2012)
27. Lebedev, V., Ganin, Y., Rakhuba, M., Oseledets, I., Lempitsky, V.: Speeding-up convolutional neural networks using fine-tuned CP-decomposition. In: International Conference on Learning Representations (ICLR) (2015)
28. Lebedev, V., Lempitsky, V.: Fast convnets using group-wise brain damage. In: IEEE Conference on Computer Vision and Pattern Recognition (CVPR), pp. 2554–2564 (2016)
29. Li, F., Zhang, B., Liu, B.: Ternary weight networks. In: NIPS Workshop on Efficient Methods for Deep Neural Networks (2016)
30. Li, Z., Ni, B., Zhang, W., Yang, X., Gao, W.: Performance guaranteed network acceleration via high-order residual quantization. In: International Conference on Computer Vision (ICCV), pp. 2584–2592 (2017)
31. Lin, D., Talathi, S., Annapureddy, S.: Fixed point quantization of deep convolutional networks. In: International Conference on Machine Learning (ICML), pp. 2849–2858 (2016)
32. Lin, M., Chen, Q., Yan, S.: Network in network. In: International Conference on Learning Representations (ICLR) (2014)
33. Lin, X., Zhao, C., Pan, W.: Towards accurate binary convolutional neural network. In: Advances in Neural Information Processing Systems (NIPS), pp. 345–353 (2017)

34. Lin, Z., Courbariaux, M., Memisevic, R., Bengio, Y.: Neural networks with few multiplications. In: International Conference on Learning Representations (ICLR) (2016)
35. Liu, B., Wang, M., Foroosh, H., Tappen, M., Penksy, M.: Sparse convolutional neural networks. In: IEEE Conference on Computer Vision and Pattern Recognition (CVPR), pp. 806–814 (2015)
36. Luo, J.H., Wu, J., Lin, W.: Thinet: A filter level pruning method for deep neural network compression. In: International Conference on Computer Vision (ICCV), pp. 5058–5066 (2017)
37. Miyashita, D., Lee, E.H., Murmann, B.: Convolutional neural networks using logarithmic data representation. arXiv:1603.01025 (2016)
38. Novikov, A., Podoprikhin, D., Osokin, A., Vetrov, D.: Tensorizing neural networks. In: Advances in Neural Information Processing Systems (NIPS), pp. 442–450 (2015)
39. Rastegari, M., Ordonez, V., Redmon, J., Farhadi, A.: XNOR-Net: ImageNet classification using binary convolutional neural networks. In: Leibe, B., Matas, J., Sebe, N., Welling, M. (eds.) ECCV 2016. LNCS, vol. 9908, pp. 525–542. Springer, Cham (2016). https://doi.org/10.1007/978-3-319-46493-0_32
40. Russakovsky, O., et al.: ImageNet large scale visual recognition challenge. Int. J. Comput. Vis. (IJCV) **115**(3), 211–252 (2015)
41. Simonyan, K., Zisserman, A.: Very deep convolutional networks for large-scale image recognition. In: International Conference on Learning Representations (ICLR) (2015)
42. Szegedy, C., et al.: Going deeper with convolutions. In: IEEE Conference on Computer Vision and Pattern Recognition (CVPR), pp. 1–9 (2015)
43. Tang, W., Hua, G., Wang, L.: How to train a compact binary neural network with high accuracy? In: AAAI Conference on Artificial Intelligence (AAAI), pp. 2625–2631 (2017)
44. Wang, J., Zhang, T., Sebe, N., Shen, H.T., et al.: A survey on learning to hash. IEEE Trans. Pattern Anal. Mach. Intell. (TPAMI) **40**(4), 769–790 (2018)
45. Wen, W., Wu, C., Wang, Y., Chen, Y., Li, H.: Learning structured sparsity in deep neural networks. In: Advances in Neural Information Processing Systems (NIPS), pp. 2074–2082 (2016)
46. Wu, J., Leng, C., Wang, Y., Hu, Q., Cheng, J.: Quantized convolutional neural networks for mobile devices. In: IEEE Conference on Computer Vision and Pattern Recognition (CVPR), pp. 4820–4828 (2016)
47. Wu, Y., et al.: Tensorpack (2016). https://github.com/tensorpack/
48. Xie, S., Girshick, R., Dollár, P., Tu, Z., He, K.: Aggregated residual transformations for deep neural networks. In: IEEE Conference on Computer Vision and Pattern Recognition (CVPR), pp. 1492–1500 (2017)
49. Yu, X., Liu, T., Wang, X., Tao, D.: On compressing deep models by low rank and sparse decomposition. In: IEEE Conference on Computer Vision and Pattern Recognition (CVPR), pp. 7370–7379 (2017)
50. Zhang, X., Zhou, X., Lin, M., Sun, J.: ShuffleNet: an extremely efficient convolutional neural network for mobile devices. In: IEEE Conference on Computer Vision and Pattern Recognition (CVPR), pp. 6848–6856 (2017)
51. Zhang, X., Zou, J., He, K., Sun, J.: Accelerating very deep convolutional networks for classification and detection. IEEE Trans. Pattern Anal. Mach. Intell. (TPAMI) **38**(10), 1943–1955 (2016)
52. Zhou, A., Yao, A., Guo, Y., Xu, L., Chen, Y.: Incremental network quantization: towards lossless CNNs with low-precision weights. In: International Conference on Learning Representations (ICLR) (2017)

53. Zhou, S., Wu, Y., Ni, Z., Zhou, X., Wen, H., Zou, Y.: DoReFa-Net: Training low bitwidth convolutional neural networks with low bitwidth gradients. arXiv:1606.06160 (2016)
54. Zhu, C., Han, S., Mao, H., Dally, W.J.: Trained ternary quantization. In: International Conference on Learning Representations (ICLR) (2017)
55. Zhuang, B., Shen, C., Tan, M., Liu, L., Reid, I.: Towards effective low-bitwidth convolutional neural networks. In: IEEE Conference on Computer Vision and Pattern Recognition (CVPR), pp. 7920–7928 (2018)

Retrospective Encoders for Video Summarization

Ke Zhang[1], Kristen Grauman[2], and Fei Sha[3(✉)]

[1] Department of Computer Science, University of Southern California, Los Angeles, CA 90089, USA
zhang.ke@usc.edu

[2] Facebook AI Research, 300 W. Sixth St., Austin, TX 78701, USA
grauman@fb.com

[3] Netflix, 5808 Sunset Blvd, Los Angeles, CA 90028, USA
fsha@netflix.com

Abstract. Supervised learning techniques have shown substantial progress on video summarization. State-of-the-art approaches mostly regard the predicted summary and the human summary as two sequences (sets), and minimize discriminative losses that measure element-wise discrepancy. Such training objectives do not explicitly model how well the predicted summary preserves semantic information in the video. Moreover, those methods often demand a large amount of human generated summaries. In this paper, we propose a novel sequence-to-sequence learning model to address these deficiencies. The key idea is to complement the discriminative losses with another loss which measures if the predicted summary preserves the same information as in the original video. To this end, we propose to augment standard sequence learning models with an additional "retrospective encoder" that embeds the predicted summary into an abstract semantic space. The embedding is then compared to the embedding of the original video in the same space. The intuition is that both embeddings ought to be close to each other for a video and its corresponding summary. Thus our approach adds to the discriminative loss a metric learning loss that minimizes the distance between such pairs while maximizing the distances between unmatched ones. One important advantage is that the metric learning loss readily allows learning from videos without human generated summaries. Extensive experimental results show that our model outperforms existing ones by a large margin in both supervised and semi-supervised settings.

Keywords: Video summarization · Sequence-to-sequence learning

---

K. Grauman—On leave from University of Texas at Austin (grauman@cs.utexas.edu)
F. Sha—On leave from University of Southern California (feisha@usc.edu).

Electronic supplementary material The online version of this chapter (https://doi.org/10.1007/978-3-030-01237-3_24) contains supplementary material, which is available to authorized users.

V. Ferrari et al. (Eds.): ECCV 2018, LNCS 11212, pp. 391–408, 2018.
https://doi.org/10.1007/978-3-030-01237-3_24

1 Introduction

The amount of online video data is staggering: hundreds of hours of videos are uploaded to YouTube every minute [2], video posts on Facebook have been increasing by more than 90% annually, and by Cisco's estimate, traffic from online videos will constitute over 80% of all consumer Internet traffic by 2020.

As such, there has been a growing interest in automatic video summarization. The main objective is to shorten a video while still preserving the important and relevant information it contains. A shortened video is more convenient and efficient for both interactive use (such as exploratory browsing), fast indexing and matching (such as responding to search queries). To this end, a common type of summary is composed of a selected set of frames (*i.e.* keyframes) [15,19,30,32, 40,40,50,63], segments, or subshots (*i.e.* keyshots) [29,34,41,43]. Other formats are possible [12,14,25,46,51], though they are not the focus of this work.

Many methods for summarization have been proposed and studied. Among them, supervised learning based techniques have recently gained significant attention [6,15,18,19,49,54,64–66]. As opposed to unsupervised ones [21,25,26, 30,33,34,36,38,43,63], supervised techniques explicitly maximize the correspondence between the automatically generated summary and the human created one. As such, those techniques often achieve higher performance metrics.

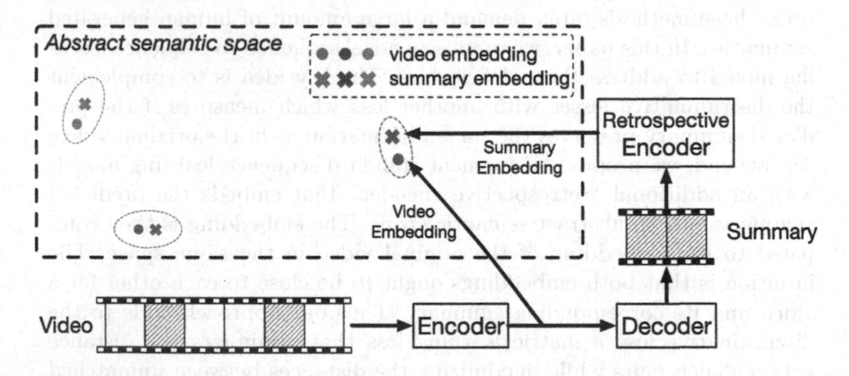

Fig. 1. Conceptual diagram of our approach. Our model consists of two components. First, we use SEQ2SEQ models to generate summaries. Secondly, we introduce an retrospective encoder that maps the generated summaries to an abstract semantic space so that we can measure how well the summaries preserve the information in the original videos, *i.e.* the summary (×) should be close to its original video (•) while distant from other videos ({•, •}) and summaries ({×, ×}). In this semantic space, we derive metric learning based loss functions and combine them with the discriminative loss by matching human generated summaries and predicted ones. See text for details. (Color figure online)

In particular, recent work on applying sequence-to-sequence learning techniques to video summarization has introduced several promising models [24, 38,64–66]. Viewing summarization as a structured prediction problem, those techniques model the long-range dependency in video using the popular long short-term memory units (LSTM) and its variants [7,17,20]. The key idea is to maximize the accuracy of which frames or subshots are selected in the summary. Figure 2 shows the basic concepts behind these modeling techniques to which we collectively refer as SEQ2SEQ.

The conventional overlap accuracy is a useful surrogate for measuring how good the generated summaries are. However, it suffers from several flaws. First, it emphasizes equally the local correspondence between human and machine summaries on all frames or subshots. For instance, for a video of a soccer game, while arguably the moment around a goal-shot is likely in every human annotator's summary, whether or not other less critical events (before or after the shot) are included could be quite varying – for example, subshots showing running across different sections of the play-field are equally good (or bad). Thus modeling those subshots in the summary is not always useful and necessary. Instead, we ought to assess whether the summary "holistically" preserves the *most important and relevant* information in the original video.

The second difficulty of employing overlap accuracy (and thus to a large degree, supervised learning techniques) is the demand of time-consuming and labor-intensive annotation procedures, which has been a limiting factor of existing datasets, cf. [65]. Thus supervised techniques have limited applicability when the annotated data is scarce.

To address these flaws, we propose a new sequence learning model—retrospective sequence-to-sequence learning (*re*-SEQ2SEQ). The key idea behind *re*-SEQ2SEQ is to measure how well the machine-generated summary is similar to **the original video** in an abstract semantic space.

Specifically, as the original video is processed by the encoder component of a SEQ2SEQ model, the encoder outputs a vector embedding which represents **the semantic meaning of the original video**. We then pass the outputs of the decoder, which should yield the desired summary, to a *retrospective* encoder to infer a vector embedding to represent **the semantic meaning of the summary**. If the summary preserves the important and relevant information in the original video, then we should expect that the two embeddings are similar (e.g. in Euclidean distance). Figure 1 schematically illustrates the idea. Besides learning to "pull" the summary close to the original video, our model also "pushes far away" the embeddings that do not form corresponding pairs.

The measure of similarity (or distance) is combined with the standard loss function (in SEQ2SEQ models) that measures how well the summary aligns locally on the frame/shot-level with what is provided by human annotators. However, the proposed learning of similarity in the abstract semantic space provides additional benefits. Since it does not use any human annotations, our measure can be computed on videos without any "ground-truth" summaries. This provides a natural basis for semi-supervised learning where we can leverage the large amount of unlabeled videos to augment training.

To summarize, our contributions are: (i) a novel sequence learning model for video summarization, which combines the benefits of discriminative learning by aligning human annotation with the model's output and semi-supervised/unsupervised learning which ensure the model's output is in accordance with the original video by embedding both in close proximity; (ii) an extensive empirical study demonstrating the effectiveness of the proposed approach on several benchmark datasets, and highlighting the advantages of using unlabeled data to improve summarization performance.

2 Related Work

Unsupervised video summarization methods mostly rely on manually designed criteria [8,11,21,25,27,30,31,33,34,36,43,45,50,63,67], e.g. importance, representativeness, and diversity. In addition, auxiliary cues such as web images [21, 26,27,50] or video categories [44,45] are also exploited in the unsupervised (weakly-supervised) summarization process.

Supervised learning for video summarization has made significant progress [6, 15,18,19,64]. Framing the task as a special case of structured prediction, Zhang *et al.* [65] proposed to use sequence learning methods, and in particular, sequence-to-sequence models [7,10,52] that have been very successful in other structured prediction problems such as machine translation [22,23,35,47,58], image or video caption generation [55,57,59], parsing [56], and speech recognition [4].

Several extensions of sequence learning models have since been studied [24,38,66,68]. Yang *et al.* [60] and Mahasseni *et al.* [38] bear a somewhat similar modeling intuition as our approach. In their works, the model is designed such that the video highlight/summary (as a sequence) can generate another (video) sequence similar to the original video. However, this desideratum is very challenging to achieve. In particular, the mapping from video to summary is lossy, making the reverse mapping almost unattainable: for instance, the objects that are in the discarded frames but missing from the summarization frames cannot be reliably recovered from the summary alone. In contrast, our model has a simpler architecture, and contains fewer LSTMs units (thus fewer parameters); our approach only desires that the *embeddings* of human created and predicted summaries be close. It attains better results than those reported in [38].

Zhou *et al.* [68] propose to use reinforcement learning to model the sequential decision-making process of selecting frames as a summary. While interesting, the design of reward functions with heuristic criteria can be as challenging as using unsupervised methods for summarization. It shows minor gains over the less competitive model in the fully supervised learning model of [65]. Both Zhao *et al.* [66] and Ji *et al.* [24] introduce hierarchical LSTMs and attention mechanisms for modeling videos. They focus on maximizing the alignment between the generated summaries and the human annotators'. Our approach also uses hierarchical LSTMs but further incorporates objectives to match the generated summaries and the original videos, *i.e.* aiming to preserve important information in the original videos. The experimental study demonstrates the advantages.

3 Approach

We start by stating the setting for the video summarization task, introducing the notations and (briefly) the background on sequence learning with LSTMs [20,39,52,61]. We then describe the proposed *retrospective encoder sequence-to-sequence (re-*SEQ2SEQ*)* approach in detail. The model extends the standard encoder-decoder LSTM by applying an additional encoder on the outputs of the decoder and introducing new loss functions.

3.1 Setting, Notations, and Sequence Learning Models

We represent a video as a sequence $\boldsymbol{X} = \{\boldsymbol{x}_1, \boldsymbol{x}_2, \cdots, \boldsymbol{x}_\mathsf{T}\}$ where $\boldsymbol{x}_t, t \in 1, \cdots, T$, is the feature vector characterizing the t-th frame in the video. We denote (sub)shots in the video by $\boldsymbol{B} = \{\boldsymbol{b}_1, \boldsymbol{b}_2, \cdots, \boldsymbol{b}_\mathsf{B}\}$. Each of the B shots refers to a consecutive subset of $\boldsymbol{X}$, and doesn't overlap with others.

Video Summarization Task. The task is to select a subset of shots as the summary, denoted as $\boldsymbol{Y} = \{\boldsymbol{y}_1, \boldsymbol{y}_2, \cdots, \boldsymbol{y}_\mathsf{L}\}$ where $\boldsymbol{y}_l$ indicates the feature vector for the l-th shot in the summary. Obviously we desire $\mathsf{L} < \mathsf{B} < \mathsf{T}$. The ground-truth keyshots are denoted as $\boldsymbol{Z} = \{\boldsymbol{z}_1, \boldsymbol{z}_2, \cdots, \boldsymbol{z}_\mathsf{L}\}$.

When $\boldsymbol{B}$ is not given (which is common in most datasets for the task), we use a shot-boundary detection model to infer the boundaries of the shots. This leads to misaligned shot boundaries between what is given in the ground-truth keyshots and what is inferred. We discuss how we handle this in the experimental details and in the Suppl. For clarity, we assume $\boldsymbol{B}$ is known and given throughout this section.

Sequence Learning. Long short-term memory (LSTMs) are a special kind of recurrent neural networks that are adept at modeling long-range dependencies. They have been used to model temporal (and sequential) data very successfully [13,20,61]. An LSTM has time-varying memory state variables $\boldsymbol{c}_t$ and an output variable $\boldsymbol{h}_t$. The values of those variables depend on the current input, past outputs, and memory states. The details of the basic LSTM cells that we use in this paper are documented in the Suppl. and [16,65].

SEQ2SEQ typically consists of a pair of LSTMs—the encoder and the decoder—which are combined to perform sequence transduction [3,55]. Specifically, the encoder reads the input sequence $\{\boldsymbol{x}_1, \boldsymbol{x}_2, \cdots, \boldsymbol{x}_\mathsf{T}\}$ sequentially (or in any predefined order), and calculates a sequence of hidden states $\boldsymbol{H} = \{\boldsymbol{h}_1, \boldsymbol{h}_2, \cdots, \boldsymbol{h}_\mathsf{T}\}$. Each hidden state $\boldsymbol{h}_t$ at step t feeds into the next step at $(t+1)$. The last hidden state $\boldsymbol{h}_\mathsf{T}$ feeds into the decoder. The decoder is similar to the encoder except for two changes: (1) the decoder has its own hidden state sequence $\boldsymbol{V} = \{\boldsymbol{v}_1, \boldsymbol{v}_2, \cdots, \boldsymbol{v}_\mathsf{L}\}$; (2) the decoder does not have external input. Instead, its input (*i.e.* its version of $\boldsymbol{x}_t$) at step $(l+1)$ is now its own output at step l, given by $\boldsymbol{y}_l = g(\boldsymbol{y}_{l-1}, \boldsymbol{v}_l)$. Note that the function $g(\cdot)$ as well as other parameters in the encoder/decoder are learnt from data. Figure 2 illustrates these steps, though in the context of hierarchical LSTMs.

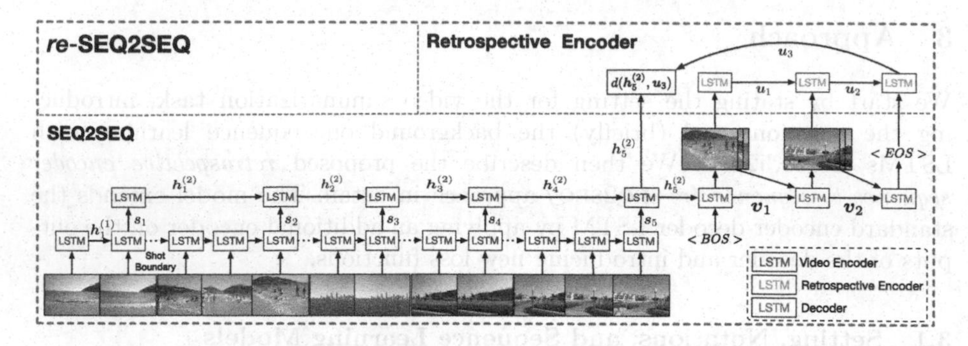

Fig. 2. Our proposed approach for video summarization. The model has several distinctive features. First, it uses hierarchical LSTMs: a bottom layer of LSTMs models shots composed of frames and an upper-layer LSTM models the video composed of shots. Secondly, the model has a *retrospective encoder* (green) that computes the embeddings of the outputs of the decoder (red). The training objective for the retrospective encoder is to ensure the embedding of the summary outputs matches the embedding computed from the original inputs, cf. Eq. (5). (Color figure online)

3.2 Retrospective-Encoder Sequence-to-sequence (*re*-seq2seq)

We propose several important extensions to the original SEQ2SEQ model: hierarchical modeling of frames and shots, and new loss functions for training.

Hierarchical Modeling. As shown in [42,55,66], the ideal length of video for LSTM modeling is less than 100 frames despite LSTMs' ability to model long-range dependencies. Thus, it is challenging to model long videos. To this end, we leverage the hierarchical structures in a video [66] to capture dependencies across longer time spans.

As shown in Fig. 2, there are two encoder layers made of LSTM units for modeling frames and shots, respectively. The first layer is responsible for modeling at the frame level and yielding a representation for all the frames in the current shot. This representation is then fed as input to the second LSTM layer. The final output of the second layer is then treated as the embedding for the whole video as it combines all the information from all the shots.

Concretely, for the first layer LSTMs, the input is $\boldsymbol{x}_t$, the feature vector for the tth frame. Assuming t is within a shot $\boldsymbol{b}_b$, the hidden state of this layer's LSTM unit is $\boldsymbol{h}_t^{(1)}$, encoding all frames from the beginning of the shot boundary by computing over the current feature $\boldsymbol{x}_t$ and the previous hidden state $\boldsymbol{h}_{t-1}^{(1)}$.

When t passes the shot's ending boundary, we denote the final hidden state of the LSTM unit as $\boldsymbol{s}_b$, the encoding vector for the current shot $\boldsymbol{b}_b$. The LSTM unit's memory $\boldsymbol{c}_t^{(1)}$ and the initial hidden state $\boldsymbol{h}_t^{(1)}$ are then reset to $\boldsymbol{c}_0^{(1)}$ and $\boldsymbol{h}_0^{(1)}$ which are both zero vectors in our model (one can also learn them).

After all the frames are processed, we have a sequence of encodings $\boldsymbol{S} = \{\boldsymbol{s}_b\}$ for $b = 1, 2, \cdots, \mathsf{B}$. We construct another LSTM layer over $\boldsymbol{S}$. The hidden states of this layer are denoted by $\boldsymbol{h}_b^{(2)}$. Of particular importance is $\boldsymbol{h}_{\mathsf{B}}^{(2)}$ which is regarded as the encoding vector for the whole video. (One can also introduce more layers for finer-grained modeling [9], and we leave that for future work.)

The decoder layer is similar to the one in a standard non-hierarchical LSTM (cf. Fig. 2). It does not have any input (except $\boldsymbol{h}_{\mathsf{B}}^{(2)}$ initializes the first LSTM unit in the layer), and its output is denoted by $\boldsymbol{y}_l$ for $l = 1, 2, \cdots, \mathsf{L}$. Its hidden states are denoted by $\boldsymbol{v}_l$, which is a function of the previous hidden state $\boldsymbol{v}_{l-1}$ and output $\boldsymbol{y}_{l-1}$. The output $\boldsymbol{y}_l$ is parameterized as a function of $\boldsymbol{v}_l$.

Regression Loss Function for Matching Summaries. In supervised learning for video summarization, we maximize the accuracy of whether a particular frame/subshot is selected. To this end, one would set the output of the decoder as a binary variable and use a cross-entropy loss function, cf. [65] for details.

In our model, however, we intend to treat the outputs as a shortened video sequence and regard $\boldsymbol{y}_l$ as visual feature vectors (of shots). Thus, the cross-entropy loss function is not applicable. Instead, we propose the following *regression loss*

$$\ell_{\text{SUMMARY}} = \sum_{i}^{\mathsf{L}} \|\boldsymbol{y}_l - \boldsymbol{g}_l\|_2^2, \tag{1}$$

where $\boldsymbol{g}_l$ is a target vector corresponding to the l-th shot in the ground-truth summary $\boldsymbol{Z}$. Suppose this shot corresponds to the b_l-th shot in the sequence of shots $\boldsymbol{B}$, where b_l is between 1 and B. We then compose $\boldsymbol{g}_l$ as the concatenation of two vectors: (1) the encoding $\boldsymbol{s}_{b_l}$ of the b_l-th shot as computed by the first LSTM layer, and (2) the average of frame-level vectors $\boldsymbol{x}_t$ within the b_l-th shot. We use $\bar{\boldsymbol{x}}_{b_l}$ to denote this average. $\boldsymbol{g}_l$ is thus given by

$$\boldsymbol{g}_l = [\boldsymbol{s}_{b_l}, \bar{\boldsymbol{x}}_{b_l}]. \tag{2}$$

This form of $\boldsymbol{g}_l$ is important. While the goal is to generate outputs $\boldsymbol{y}_l$ closely matching the encodings of shots, we could obtain trivial solutions where the LSTMs learn to encode shots as a constant vector and to output a constant vector as the summary. The inclusion of the video's raw feature vectors in the learning effectively eliminates trivial solutions.

Embedding Matching for the Summary and the Original. The intuition behind our modeling is that the outputs should convey the same amount of information as the inputs. For summarization, this is precisely the goal: a good summary should be such that after viewing the summary, users would get about the same amount of information as if they had viewed the original video.

How to measure and characterize the amount of information conveyed in the original sequence and the summary? Recall that the basic assumption about the encoder LSTMs is that they compress semantic information of their inputs into a semantic embedding, namely $\boldsymbol{h}_{\mathsf{B}}^{(2)}$, the final hidden state[1]. Likewise, if we add another encoder to the decoder output $\boldsymbol{Y}$, then this new encoder should also be

[1] Otherwise, we would not have expected $\boldsymbol{h}_{\mathsf{B}}^{(2)}$ to be able to generate the summary to begin with.

able to compress it into a semantic embedding with its final hidden state $\boldsymbol{u}_{\mathsf{L}}$. Figure 2 illustrates the new *re*-SEQ2SEQ model structure.

To learn this "retrospective" encoder, we use the following loss

$$\ell_{\text{MATCH}} = \|\boldsymbol{h}_{\mathsf{B}}^{(2)} - \boldsymbol{u}_{\mathsf{L}}\|_2^2. \tag{3}$$

Contrastive Embedding for Mismatched Summary and Original. We can further model the alignment between the summary and the original by adding penalty terms that penalize mismatched pairs:

$$\begin{aligned} \ell_{\text{MISMATCH}} = & \sum_{\boldsymbol{h}'} [m + \|\boldsymbol{h}_{\mathsf{B}}^{(2)} - \boldsymbol{u}_{\mathsf{L}}\|_2^2 - \|\boldsymbol{h}' - \boldsymbol{u}_{\mathsf{L}}\|_2^2]_+ \\ & + \sum_{\boldsymbol{u}'} [m + \|\boldsymbol{h}_{\mathsf{B}}^{(2)} - \boldsymbol{u}_{\mathsf{L}}\|_2^2 - \|\boldsymbol{h}_{\mathsf{B}}^{(2)} - \boldsymbol{u}'\|_2^2]_+, \end{aligned} \tag{4}$$

where $\boldsymbol{h}'$ (or $\boldsymbol{u}'$) is the hidden state in the shot-level LSTM layer (or the re-encoder LSTM layer) from a video other than $\boldsymbol{h}_{\mathsf{B}}^{(2)}$ (or a summary other than $\boldsymbol{u}_{\mathsf{L}}$). $m > 0$ is a margin parameter and $[\cdot]_+ = \max(0, \cdot)$ is the standard hinge loss function. In essence this loss function aims to push apart mismatched summaries and videos.

Final Training Objective. We train the models by balancing the different types of loss functions

$$\ell = \ell_{\text{SUMMARY}} + \lambda \ell_{\text{MATCH}} + \eta \ell_{\text{MISMATCH}}, \tag{5}$$

where the λ and η are tradeoff parameters.

Note that neither ℓ_{MATCH} nor ℓ_{MISMATCH} requires human annotated summaries. Thus they can also be used to incorporate unannotated video data which are disjoint from the annotated data from which ℓ_{SUMMARY} is computed. Our empirical results will show that learning with these two loss terms noticeably improves learning with only the discriminative loss.

The specific forms of ℓ_{MATCH} and ℓ_{MISMATCH} are also reminiscent of metric learning (for multi-way classification) [5]. In particular, we transform both the summary and the video into vectors (through a series of encoder/decoder LSTMs) and perform metric learning in that abstract semantic space. However, different from traditional metric learning methods, we also need to learn to infer the desired representations of the structured objects (*i.e.* sequences of frames).

Implementation Details. Throughout our empirical studies, we use standard LSTM units. The dimensions of the hidden units for all LSTM units are 256. All LSTM parameters are randomly initialized with a uniform distribution in $[-0.05, 0.05]$. The models are trained to converge with Adam [28] with an initial learning rate $4e-4$, and mini-batch size of 10. All experiments are on a single GPU. Please refer to the Suppl. for more details.

4 Experiments

We first introduce the experimental setting (datasets, features, metrics) in Sect. 4.1. We then present the main quantitative results in the supervised learning setting to demonstrate the advantages of the proposed approach over existing methods in Sect. 4.2. We further validate the proposed approach in the semi-supervised setting in Sect. 4.3. We perform ablation studies and analyze strengths and weaknesses of our approach in Sects. 4.4 and 4.5.

4.1 Setup

Datasets. We evaluate on 3 datasets. The first two have been widely used to benchmark summarization tasks [24,38,65,68]: **SumMe** [19] and **TVSum** [50]. **SumMe** consists of 25 user videos of a variety of events such as holidays and sports. **TVSum** contains 50 videos downloaded from YouTube in 10 categories. Both datasets provide multiple user-annotated summaries per video.

Following [65], we also use **Youtube** [11] and **Open Video Project (OVP)** [1,11] as auxiliary datasets to augment the training data. We use the same set of features, *i.e.* each frame $\boldsymbol{x}_i$ is represented by the output of the penultimate layer (pool 5) of GoogLeNet [53] (1024 dimensions). As pointed out in [65], the limited amount of annotated data limits the applicability of supervised learning techniques. Thus, we focus on the **augmented setting** (if not specified otherwise) as in that work and other follow-up ones[2]. In this setting, 20% of the dataset is used for evaluation, 20% is used for validation (in our experiments) and the other 60% is combined with auxiliary datasets for training. We tune hyperparameters, e.g. λ and η, w.r.t. the performance on the validation set.

We also demonstrate our model on a third dataset **VTW** [62] which is large-scale and originally proposed for video highlight detection. In [66], it is re-targeted for video summarization by converting the highlights into keyshots. VTW collects user-generated videos which are mostly shorter than ones in SumMe and TVSum. The dataset is split into 1500 videos for training and 500 videos for testing as in [66]. We have not been able to confirm the split details so our results in this paper are not directly comparable to their reported ones.

Shot Boundary Generation. As mentioned in Sect. 3, shot boundaries for each video are required for both training and testing. However, none of the datasets used in the experiments are annotated with ground-truth shot boundaries: VTW is annotated only for keyshots, SumMe is annotated by multiple users for keyshots, and TVSum is annotated by fix-length intervals (2 s). To this end, we train a single-layer LSTM for shot-boundary detection with another *disjoint* dataset, CoSum [8]. CoSum has 51 videos with human annotated shot-boundaries. The LSTM has 256−dim hidden units and is trained for 150 epochs

[2] Zhao *et al.* [66] use a larger dataset MED [45] to augment the training, which results in a larger number of videos (235), as opposed to 154 video in [24,38,65,68]. Since their code is unavailable, we have re-implemented their method to the best of our knowledge from their paper and experimented in the same setting as ours and others.

with learning rate $4e-4$. We then threshold the predictions on any new videos to detect the boundaries. The best thresholds are determined by the summarization performance on the validation set. Please refer to details on shot boundary detection in the Suppl.

Evaluation. Given the heterogeneous video types and summary formats in these datasets, we follow the procedures outlined in [65,66] to prepare training, validation, and evaluation data. In particular, we set the threshold of the total duration of keyshots as 15% of the original video length (for all datasets), following the protocols in [19,50,66]. Then we compare the generated summary A to the user summary B for evaluation, by computing the precision (P) and recall (R), according to the *temporal overlap* between the two, as well as their harmonic mean F-score [18,19,38,50,65,66]. Higher scores are better. Please refer to the Suppl. for details on the performance and evaluation with user summaries.

Table 1. Performance (F-score) of various supervised video summarization methods on three datasets. Published results are denoted in *italic*; our implementations are in normal font. Nonzero values of λ and η represent contributions from relevant terms in our models.

	SumMe	TVSum	VTW
dppLSTM [65]	*42.9*	*59.6*	44.3
SUM-GAN [38]	*43.6*	*61.2*	-
DR-DSN [68]	*43.9*	*59.8*	-
H-RNN [66]	43.6	61.5	46.9
SEQ2SEQ (frame only)	40.8	56.3	-
re-SEQ2SEQ ($\lambda = 0, \eta = 0$)	43.2	61.9	45.1
re-SEQ2SEQ ($\lambda = \lambda^*, \eta = \eta^*$)	**44.9**	**63.9**	**48.0**

4.2 Supervised Learning Results

In Table 1, we compare our approach to several state-of-the-art supervised methods for video summarization. We report published results in the table as well as results from our implementation of [66]. Only the best variants of all methods are quoted and presented. We have implemented a strong baseline *re*-SEQ2SEQ ($\lambda = 0, \eta = 0$), trained with the objective function Eq. (5) described in Sect. 3. This baseline is different from the LSTM-based SEQ2SEQ models in [65] where the model is frame-based, to which we refer as SEQ2SEQ (frame only). *re*-SEQ2SEQ ($\lambda = 0, \eta = 0$) has the advantage of hierarchical modeling. Optimal λ^* and η^* are tuned over the validation set and $\lambda^* = 0.1, 0.1, 0.2$ and $\eta^* = 0.15, 0.1, 0.2$ for SumMe, TVSum, and VTW, respectively. The cells with red-colored numbers indicate the best performing methods in each column.

Main Results. Our approach *re*-SEQ2SEQ ($\lambda = \lambda^*, \eta = \eta^*$) performs the best on all 3 datasets. Hierarchical modeling is clearly advantageous, evidenced by the performance of all our model variations and [66]. Our model *re*-SEQ2SEQ ($\lambda = 0, \eta = 0$) is slightly worse than [66], most likely due to the fact we use regression as summary loss while they use cross-entropy. Note that regression loss is needed in order to incorporate matching and mismatching losses in our model, cf. Eq. (5). The advantage of incorporating the retrospective encoder loss is clearly evidenced.

Table 2. F-scores on the TVSum dataset in the semi-supervised learning setting. n indicates the number of unannotated videos used for training.

	$n = 0$	$n = 150$	$n = 500$	$n = 1000$	$n = 1500$	$n = 1800$
pre-training	63.9	64.1	64.4	64.5	64.7	64.9
joint-training		64.1	64.7	64.9	65.1	**65.2**

Table 3. Performance of our model with different types of shot boundaries.

	SumMe	TVSum
re-SEQ2SEQ ($\lambda = \lambda^*, \eta = 0$) w/KTS	44.5	62.8
re-SEQ2SEQ ($\lambda = \lambda^*, \eta = 0$) w/LSTM	44.6	63.0
re-SEQ2SEQ ($\lambda = \lambda^*, \eta = \eta^*$) w/KTS	44.8	63.6
re-SEQ2SEQ ($\lambda = \lambda^*, \eta = \eta^*$) w/LSTM	**44.9**	**63.9**

4.3 Semi-Supervised Learning Results

Next we carry out experiments to show that the proposed approach can benefit from both unlabeled and labeled video data. For labeled data, we use the same train and test set as in the augmented setting, *i.e.* OVP + Youtube + SumMe + 80% TVSum, and 20% TVSum, respectively. For unlabeled data, we randomly sample n videos from the VTW dataset and ignore their annotations. We investigate two possible means of semi-supervised training:

(1) *pre-training*: the unlabeled data are used to pre-train *re*-SEQ2SEQ to minimize ℓ_{MATCH} and ℓ_{MISMATCH} only. The pre-trained model is further fine-tuned with labeled training data to minimize Eq. (5).
(2) *joint-training*: We jointly train the model with labeled training data and unlabeled data: we minimize Eq. (5) for labeled data, and minimize ℓ_{MATCH} and ℓ_{MISMATCH} for unlabeled data.

Note that the test set is only for testing and not used as either labeled or unlabeled data during training, which is different from the transductive setting [38]. Results are shown in Table 2. In general, both *pre-training* and *joint-training* show improvements over supervised learning, and joint-training seems slightly better with more unlabeled data. Results are also encouraging in showing that more unlabeled data can help improve more.

Table 4. Performances of transductive setting on SumMe and TVSum.

	SumMe	TVSum
SUM-GAN [38]	*43.6*	*61.2*
re-SEQ2SEQ ($\lambda = \lambda^*, \eta = \eta^*$)	**45.5**	**65.4**

Table 5. Performance of the proposed approach with different choices of λ and η

	SumMe	TVSum	VTW
re-SEQ2SEQ ($\lambda = 0, \eta = 0$)	43.2	61.9	45.1
re-SEQ2SEQ ($\lambda = \lambda^*, \eta = 0$)	44.6	63.0	47.7
re-SEQ2SEQ ($\lambda = 0, \eta = \eta^*$)	44.6	63.2	47.8
re-SEQ2SEQ ($\lambda = \lambda^*, \eta = \eta^*$)	**44.9**	**63.9**	**48.0**

4.4 Ablation Study

Shot-Boundaries. Shot boundaries play an important role in keyshot-based summarization methods. In this paper we learn an LSTM to infer the shot boundaries, while in [65] an unsupervised shot boundary detection method, KTS [45], is applied. Table 3 reports the performances of our model with shot boundaries generated by KTS and the learned LSTM, respectively. The main observation is better shot boundary detection in general improves summarization.

Transductive Setting. To make a fair comparison to [38], we next perform our model in the transductive setting, where the testing data are included in computing the two new loss terms ℓ_{MATCH} and ℓ_{MISMATCH}. The results are shown in Table 4 and they are clearly stronger than those in the supervised setting (Table 1). One possible interpretation for this case is that our model maps the video and its summary in close proximity while the reconstruction from a summary to the original video in [38] may be lossy or even unattainable.

Contributions of Each Loss Term. Table 5 reports experiments of the proposed approach with different combinations of ℓ_{MATCH} and ℓ_{MISMATCH} through their balancing parameters, *i.e.* λ and η. To summarize, jointly minimizing both loss terms brings the state-of-the-art performance on all datasets. Furthermore, the performances of different combinations of loss terms are consistent across the 3 datasets: using ℓ_{MISMATCH} alone gets the same or slightly better performances compared to using ℓ_{MATCH} alone, while combining both of them always obtains the best performance. Please refer to the Suppl. for model details.

Other Detailed Analysis in Suppl. We summarize additional discussions as follows. We show that summaries by our approach obtain comparable diversity to ones by dppLSTM [65]. We also show that our approach outperforms the autoencoder-based method [60]. We further analyze the correlation between our approach and recent works [48,49] on the query-focused summarization.

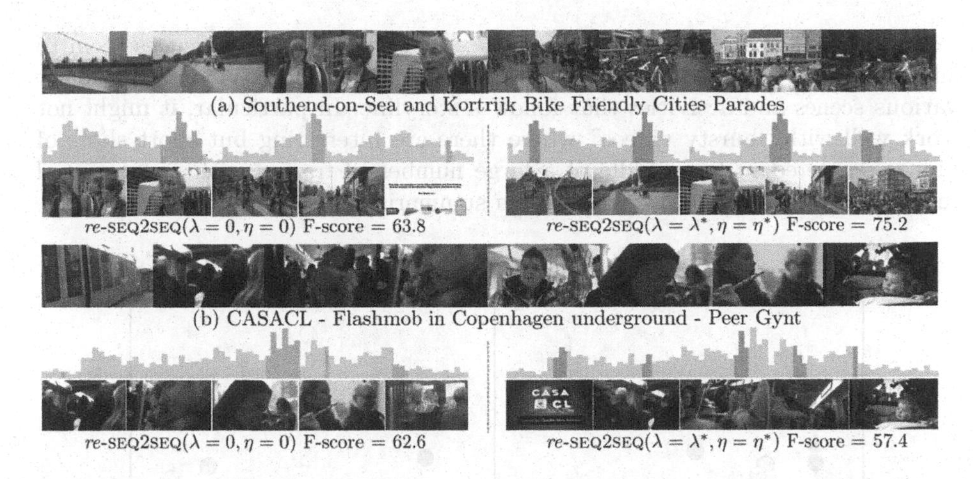

Fig. 3. Exemplar videos and predicted summaries by *re*-SEQ2SEQ ($\lambda = \lambda^*, \eta = \eta^*$) (blue) and *re*-SEQ2SEQ ($\lambda = 0, \eta = 0$) (red). Pictures on the top are sampled from the video and ones in the bottom are sampled from the corresponding summary. The ground-truth importance scores are shown as gray background. See text for details. (Color figure online)

4.5 Qualitative Results and Analysis

How Does *re*-seq2seq Summarize Differently than Regular seq2seq? We examine a few exemplar video summarization results in Fig. 3 to shed light on how the learning objective of *re*-SEQ2SEQ affects summarization results. Our approach aims to reduce the difference in semantic embeddings for both input videos and output summaries, cf. Eq. (5). Balancing the need to match between the outputs and human summaries, it would be sensible for our approach to summarize broadly. This will result in comprehensive coverage of visual features, and thus increase the chance of more similar embeddings. The opposite strategy of selecting from a concentrated area is unlikely to yield high similarity as the selected frames are unlikely to provide a sufficient coverage of the original.

Figure 3 precisely highlights the strategy adopted by our approach. The video of Fig. 3(a) is about bike parades. *re*-SEQ2SEQ ($\lambda = 0, \eta = 0$) summarizes the mid-section of the video, but completely misses the important part in the beginning, which tells us the parades actually start from suburb via a bridge to downtown. In contrast, *re*-SEQ2SEQ ($\lambda = \lambda^*, \eta = \eta^*$) selects broadly from video shots, which show much better consensus with the video. In Fig. 3(b), however, *re*-SEQ2SEQ ($\lambda = \lambda^*, \eta = \eta^*$) underperforms (slightly) *re*-SEQ2SEQ ($\lambda = 0, \eta = 0$). The video depicts a flash mob in Copenhagen. *re*-SEQ2SEQ ($\lambda = 0, \eta = 0$) gets a better F-score by focusing on the mid-section of the video where there are a lot of human activities and is able to correctly get the major events in that region. *re*-SEQ2SEQ ($\lambda = \lambda^*, \eta = \eta^*$), on the other hand, spreads out its selection and takes only a small part of the major event compared to *re*-SEQ2SEQ ($\lambda = 0, \eta = 0$).

While more error analysis is desirable, these preliminary evidences seem to suggest that *re*-SEQ2SEQ ($\lambda = \lambda^*, \eta = \eta^*$) would work well for videos that depict various scenes and activities that follow a storyline. In particular, it might not work well with "bursty videos" where there are interesting but short shots of videos scattered in the middle of a large number of frames with non-essential information likely to be discarded when summarized.

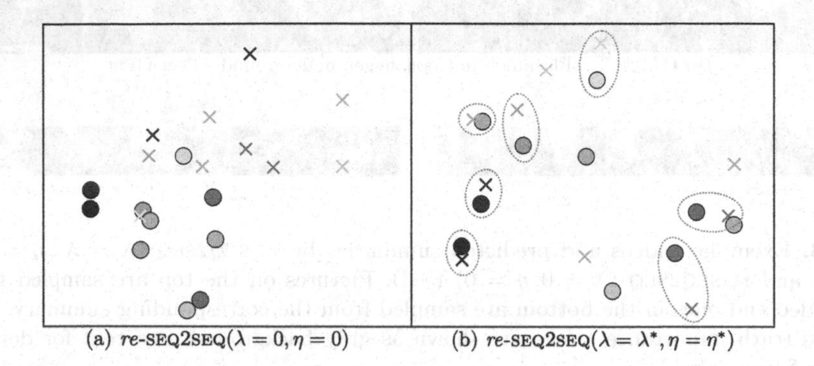

Fig. 4. t-SNE visualization of semantic encodings of videos (denoted as •) and their summaries (denoted as $\times$). Corresponding pairs are in the same color. The closer they are the better. Each dashed ellipsoid indicates that a video is the nearest neighbor to its summary after embedding. See text for details.

Can *re*-seq2seq Lead to Semantically Similar Embeddings Between the Video and Summary? Here we evaluate how well the video and summary can be embedded in close proximity. Videos used here are sampled from the TVSum dataset. For *re*-SEQ2SEQ ($\lambda = 0, \eta = 0$), we input the summary to the same encoder as for videos and obtain the outputs of the encoder as the embedding, and in *re*-SEQ2SEQ ($\lambda = \lambda^*, \eta = \eta^*$), we collect the embedding for the summary from the retrospective LSTM encoder. We then use t-SNE [37] to visualize the embeddings in $2d$ space as shown in Fig. 4. We use circles to denote video embeddings, and crosses for summary embeddings. Each video-summary pair is marked by the same color.

We can clearly observe that the video and its summary are mostly embedded much closer by *re*-SEQ2SEQ ($\lambda = \lambda^*, \eta = \eta^*$) (Fig. 4(b)) than ones by *re*-SEQ2SEQ ($\lambda = 0, \eta = 0$) (Fig. 4(a)). In particular the video embedded by *re*-SEQ2SEQ ($\lambda = \lambda^*, \eta = \eta^*$) mostly has its corresponding summary as the nearest neighbor, while this is usually not the case in ones by *re*-SEQ2SEQ ($\lambda = 0, \eta = 0$). Moreover, embeddings of videos and summaries in Fig. 4(a) are 'clustered' together compared to ones in Fig. 4(b), where different pairs of video and summary are relatively far away from each other. This shows the proposed approach embeds a summary and its original video into similar locations, while pushing apart mismatched summaries and original videos.

5 Conclusion

We propose a novel sequence-to-sequence learning model for video summarization that not only minimizes the discriminative loss for matching the generated and target summaries, but also embeds corresponding video and summary pairs in close proximity in an abstract semantic space. The proposed approach exploits both labeled and unlabeled videos to derive semantic embeddings. Extensive experimental results on multiple datasets show the advantage of our approach over existing methods in both supervised and semi-supervised settings. In the future, we plan to explore more delicate strategies to combine unlabeled data during training to improve summarization performance.

Acknowledgments. We appreciate the feedback from the reviewers. KG is partially supported by NSF IIS-1514118 and an AWS Machine Learning Research Award. Others are partially supported by USC Graduate Fellowships, NSF IIS-1065243, 1451412, 1513966/1632803/1833137, 1208500, CCF-1139148, a Google Research Award, an Alfred P. Sloan Research Fellowship, gifts from Facebook and Netflix, and ARO# W911NF-12-1-0241 and W911NF-15-1-0484.

References

1. Open video project. http://www.open-video.org/
2. Youtube statistics. https://www.youtube.com/yt/press/statistics.html
3. Bahdanau, D., Cho, K., Bengio, Y.: Neural machine translation by jointly learning to align and translate. In: ICLR (2015)
4. Bahdanau, D., Chorowski, J., Serdyuk, D., Brakel, P., Bengio, Y.: End-to-end attention-based large vocabulary speech recognition. In: ICASSP (2016)
5. Bellet, A., Habrard, A., Sebban, M.: Metric learning. Synth. Lect. Artif. Intell. Mach. Learn. **9**(1), 1–151 (2015)
6. Chao, W.L., Gong, B., Grauman, K., Sha, F.: Large-margin determinantal point processes. In: UAI (2015)
7. Cho, K., et al.: Learning phrase representations using RNN encoder-decoder for statistical machine translation. arXiv preprint (2014)
8. Chu, W.S., Song, Y., Jaimes, A.: Video co-summarization: video summarization by visual co-occurrence. In: CVPR (2015)
9. Chung, J., Ahn, S., Bengio, Y.: Hierarchical multiscale recurrent neural networks. arXiv preprint (2016)
10. Dai, A.M., Le, Q.V.: Semi-supervised sequence learning. In: NIPS (2015)
11. De Avila, S.E.F., Lopes, A.P.B., da Luz, A., de Albuquerque Araújo, A.: VSUMM: a mechanism designed to produce static video summaries and a novel evaluation method. Pattern Recognit. Lett. **32**(1), 56–68 (2011)
12. Furini, M., Geraci, F., Montangero, M., Pellegrini, M.: STIMO: still and moving video storyboard for the web scenario. Multimed. Tools Appl. **46**(1), 47–69 (2010)
13. Gers, F.A., Schmidhuber, J., Cummins, F.: Learning to forget: continual prediction with LSTM. Neural Comput. **12**(10), 2451–2471 (2000)
14. Goldman, D.B., Curless, B., Salesin, D., Seitz, S.M.: Schematic storyboarding for video visualization and editing. ACM Trans. Graph. **25**(3), 862–871 (2006)

15. Gong, B., Chao, W.L., Grauman, K., Sha, F.: Diverse sequential subset selection for supervised video summarization. In: NIPS (2014)
16. Graves, A., Jaitly, N.: Towards end-to-end speech recognition with recurrent neural networks. In: ICML (2014)
17. Graves, A., Schmidhuber, J.: Framewise phoneme classification with bidirectional LSTM and other neural network architectures. Neural Netw. **18**(5), 602–610 (2005)
18. Gygli, M., Grabner, H., Van Gool, L.: Video summarization by learning submodular mixtures of objectives. In: CVPR (2015)
19. Gygli, M., Grabner, H., Riemenschneider, H., Van Gool, L.: Creating summaries from user videos. In: Fleet, D., Pajdla, T., Schiele, B., Tuytelaars, T. (eds.) ECCV 2014. LNCS, vol. 8695, pp. 505–520. Springer, Cham (2014). https://doi.org/10.1007/978-3-319-10584-0_33
20. Hochreiter, S., Schmidhuber, J.: Long short-term memory. Neural Comput. **9**(8), 1735–1780 (1997)
21. Hong, R., Tang, J., Tan, H.K., Yan, S., Ngo, C., Chua, T.S.: Event driven summarization for web videos. In: SIGMM Workshop (2009)
22. Jean, S., Cho, K., Memisevic, R., Bengio, Y.: On using very large target vocabulary for neural machine translation. In: ACL (2015)
23. Jean, S., Firat, O., Cho, K., Memisevic, R., Bengio, Y.: Montreal neural machine translation systems for WMT'15. In: WMT (2015)
24. Ji, Z., Xiong, K., Pang, Y., Li, X.: Video summarization with attention-based encoder-decoder networks. arXiv preprint (2017)
25. Kang, H.W., Matsushita, Y., Tang, X., Chen, X.Q.: Space-time video montage. In: CVPR (2006)
26. Khosla, A., Hamid, R., Lin, C.J., Sundaresan, N.: Large-scale video summarization using web-image priors. In: CVPR (2013)
27. Kim, G., Xing, E.P.: Reconstructing storyline graphs for image recommendation from web community photos. In: CVPR (2014)
28. Kingma, D., Ba, J.: Adam: a method for stochastic optimization. arXiv preprint (2014)
29. Laganière, R., Bacco, R., Hocevar, A., Lambert, P., Païs, G., Ionescu, B.E.: Video summarization from spatio-temporal features. In: ACM TRECVid Video Summarization Workshop (2008)
30. Lee, Y.J., Ghosh, J., Grauman, K.: Discovering important people and objects for egocentric video summarization. In: CVPR (2012)
31. Li, Y., Merialdo, B.: Multi-video summarization based on video-MMR. In: WIAMIS Workshop (2010)
32. Liu, D., Hua, G., Chen, T.: A hierarchical visual model for video object summarization. IEEE Trans. Pattern Anal. Mach. Intell. **32**(12), 2178–2190 (2010)
33. Liu, T., Kender, J.R.: Optimization algorithms for the selection of key frame sequences of variable length. In: Heyden, A., Sparr, G., Nielsen, M., Johansen, P. (eds.) ECCV 2002. LNCS, vol. 2353, pp. 403–417. Springer, Heidelberg (2002). https://doi.org/10.1007/3-540-47979-1_27
34. Lu, Z., Grauman, K.: Story-driven summarization for egocentric video. In: CVPR (2013)
35. Luong, M.T., Pham, H., Manning, C.D.: Effective approaches to attention-based neural machine translation. arXiv preprint (2015)
36. Ma, Y.F., Lu, L., Zhang, H.J., Li, M.: A user attention model for video summarization. In: ACM MM (2002)
37. van der Maaten, L., Hinton, G.: Visualizing data using t-SNE. J. Mach. Learn. Res. **9**, 2579–2605 (2008)

38. Mahasseni, B., Lam, M., Todorovic, S.: Unsupervised video summarization with adversarial LSTM networks. In: CVPR (2017)
39. Mueller, J., Gifford, D., Jaakkola, T.: Sequence to better sequence: continuous revision of combinatorial structures. In: ICML, pp. 2536–2544 (2017)
40. Mundur, P., Rao, Y., Yesha, Y.: Keyframe-based video summarization using delaunay clustering. Int. J. Digit. Libr. **6**(2), 219–232 (2006)
41. Nam, J., Tewfik, A.H.: Event-driven video abstraction and visualization. Multimed. Tools Appl. **16**(1–2), 55–77 (2002)
42. Ng, J.Y.H., Hausknecht, M., Vijayanarasimhan, S., Vinyals, O., Monga, R., Toderici, G.: Beyond short snippets: deep networks for video classification. In: CVPR (2015)
43. Ngo, C.W., Ma, Y.F., Zhang, H.: Automatic video summarization by graph modeling. In: ICCV (2003)
44. Panda, R., Das, A., Wu, Z., Ernst, J., Roy-Chowdhury, A.K.: Weakly supervised summarization of web videos. In: ICCV (2017)
45. Potapov, D., Douze, M., Harchaoui, Z., Schmid, C.: Category-specific video summarization. In: Fleet, D., Pajdla, T., Schiele, B., Tuytelaars, T. (eds.) ECCV 2014. LNCS, vol. 8694, pp. 540–555. Springer, Cham (2014). https://doi.org/10.1007/978-3-319-10599-4_35
46. Pritch, Y., Rav-Acha, A., Gutman, A., Peleg, S.: Webcam synopsis: peeking around the world. In: ICCV (2007)
47. Ramachandran, P., Liu, P.J., Le, Q.V.: Unsupervised pretraining for sequence to sequence learning. arXiv preprint (2016)
48. Sharghi, A., Gong, B., Shah, M.: Query-focused extractive video summarization. In: Leibe, B., Matas, J., Sebe, N., Welling, M. (eds.) ECCV 2016. LNCS, vol. 9912, pp. 3–19. Springer, Cham (2016). https://doi.org/10.1007/978-3-319-46484-8_1
49. Sharghi, A., Laurel, J.S., Gong, B.: Query-focused video summarization: dataset, evaluation, and a memory network based approach. In: CVPR (2017)
50. Song, Y., Vallmitjana, J., Stent, A., Jaimes, A.: TVSum: summarizing web videos using titles. In: CVPR (2015)
51. Sun, M., Farhadi, A., Taskar, B., Seitz, S.: Salient montages from unconstrained videos. In: Fleet, D., Pajdla, T., Schiele, B., Tuytelaars, T. (eds.) ECCV 2014. LNCS, vol. 8695, pp. 472–488. Springer, Cham (2014). https://doi.org/10.1007/978-3-319-10584-0_31
52. Sutskever, I., Vinyals, O., Le, Q.V.: Sequence to sequence learning with neural networks. In: NIPS (2014)
53. Szegedy, C., et al.: Going deeper with convolutions. In: CVPR (2015)
54. Vasudevan, A.B., Gygli, M., Volokitin, A., Van Gool, L.: Query-adaptive video summarization via quality-aware relevance estimation. In: ACM MM (2017)
55. Venugopalan, S., Rohrbach, M., Donahue, J., Mooney, R., Darrell, T., Saenko, K.: Sequence to sequence-video to text. In: ICCV (2015)
56. Vinyals, O., Kaiser, Ł., Koo, T., Petrov, S., Sutskever, I., Hinton, G.: Grammar as a foreign language. In: NIPS (2015)
57. Vinyals, O., Toshev, A., Bengio, S., Erhan, D.: Show and tell: a neural image caption generator. In: CVPR (2015)
58. Wu, Y., et al.: Google's neural machine translation system: bridging the gap between human and machine translation. arXiv preprint (2016)
59. Xu, K., et al.: Show, attend and tell: neural image caption generation with visual attention. In: ICML (2015)
60. Yang, H., Wang, B., Lin, S., Wipf, D., Guo, M., Guo, B.: Unsupervised extraction of video highlights via robust recurrent auto-encoders. In: ICCV (2015)

61. Zaremba, W., Sutskever, I.: Learning to execute. arXiv preprint (2014)
62. Zeng, K.-H., Chen, T.-H., Niebles, J.C., Sun, M.: Title generation for user generated videos. In: Leibe, B., Matas, J., Sebe, N., Welling, M. (eds.) ECCV 2016. LNCS, vol. 9906, pp. 609–625. Springer, Cham (2016). https://doi.org/10.1007/978-3-319-46475-6_38
63. Zhang, H.J., Wu, J., Zhong, D., Smoliar, S.W.: An integrated system for content-based video retrieval and browsing. Pattern Recognit. **30**(4), 643–658 (1997)
64. Zhang, K., Chao, W.L., Sha, F., Grauman, K.: Summary transfer: exemplar-based subset selection for video summarization. In: CVPR (2016)
65. Zhang, K., Chao, W.-L., Sha, F., Grauman, K.: Video summarization with long short-term memory. In: Leibe, B., Matas, J., Sebe, N., Welling, M. (eds.) ECCV 2016. LNCS, vol. 9911, pp. 766–782. Springer, Cham (2016). https://doi.org/10.1007/978-3-319-46478-7_47
66. Zhao, B., Li, X., Lu, X.: Hierarchical recurrent neural network for video summarization. In: ACM MM (2017)
67. Zhao, B., Xing, E.P.: Quasi real-time summarization for consumer videos. In: CVPR (2014)
68. Zhou, K., Qiao, Y.: Deep reinforcement learning for unsupervised video summarization with diversity-representativeness reward. arXiv preprint (2017)

Constraint-Aware Deep Neural Network Compression

Changan Chen, Frederick Tung[(✉)], Naveen Vedula, and Greg Mori

School of Computing Science, Simon Fraser University, Burnaby, Canada
{cca278,ftung,nvedula}@sfu.ca, mori@cs.sfu.ca

Abstract. Deep neural network compression has the potential to bring modern resource-hungry deep networks to resource-limited devices. However, in many of the most compelling deployment scenarios of compressed deep networks, the operational constraints matter: for example, a pedestrian detection network on a self-driving car may have to satisfy a latency constraint for safe operation. We propose the first principled treatment of deep network compression under operational constraints. We formulate the compression learning problem from the perspective of constrained Bayesian optimization, and introduce a cooling (annealing) strategy to guide the network compression towards the target constraints. Experiments on ImageNet demonstrate the value of modelling constraints directly in network compression.

1 Introduction

Modern deep neural networks contain millions of parameters over dozens or even hundreds of layers [1,2]. Standard benchmarks such as ImageNet [3] have incentivized the design of increasingly expensive networks, as the additional expressiveness seems necessary to correctly handle the remaining hard test samples [4]. However, the deployment of deep networks in real-world systems requires consideration of the computation cost. The issue of computation cost has led to a natural surge in interest in deep network compression [5–22].

Constraints matter in many of the most compelling deployment scenarios for compressed deep neural networks. For example, deep neural network compression enables us to deploy powerful networks in systems such as self-driving vehicles with real-time operation requirements. A self-driving vehicle may have latency constraints for executing a scene segmentation routine: if the network cannot return predictions within 50 ms on average, for instance, the safe operation of the vehicle may be compromised. As another example, deep network compression enables us to deploy compact networks on embedded platforms with limited

Electronic supplementary material The online version of this chapter (https://doi.org/10.1007/978-3-030-01237-3_25) contains supplementary material, which is available to authorized users.

V. Ferrari et al. (Eds.): ECCV 2018, LNCS 11212, pp. 409–424, 2018.
https://doi.org/10.1007/978-3-030-01237-3_25

computing power. A drone may have fixed memory constraints and only be able to run a 12 MB network on-board.

Previous work on deep network compression has focused on achieving the highest compression rate while maintaining an acceptable level of accuracy (e.g. within 1–2% of the uncompressed network's accuracy). We refer to this general approach to network compression as *unconstrained* network compression because operational constraints are not considered in the training of the compressed network. In this paper, we propose *constraint-aware* network compression, in which we incorporate operational constraints directly in the compression process. This framework allows us to ensure that the compressed network satisfies the operational constraints of the system on which the network will be deployed. Figure 1 shows an overview of our approach.

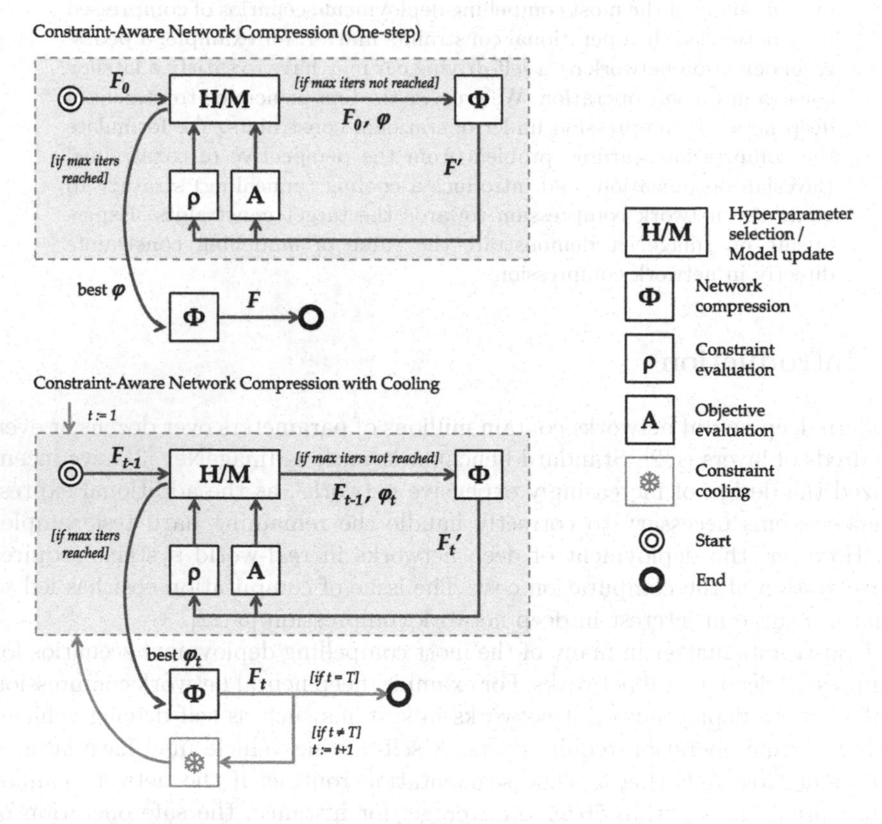

Fig. 1. We propose a framework for deep network compression under operational constraints (e.g. latency). The one-step model takes an uncompressed network F_0 and employs constrained Bayesian optimization to explore the space of compression hyperparameters ϕ such that the task objective (e.g. classification accuracy) is maximized and all constraints are satisfied. F' denotes a "proposed" compressed network. The cooling model guides network compression gradually towards the constraints via a sequence of easier intermediate targets.

For some types of operational constraints, such as latency, ensuring that a system always meets *hard* constraints requires verification on domain specific hardware. A wide range of systems design issues often need to be addressed to guarantee correct performance. For example, WCET (worst case execution times) analysis on multi-core processors is notoriously difficult and remains an open research challenge [23–25]. Verification on domain specific hardware is beyond the scope of this paper. Instead, we focus on ensuring that all constraints are satisfied *in expectation.* In computer vision, this regime is similar to that of budgeted batch classification, in which a fixed time budget is available to classify a set of images and the model is trained to ensure that the time budget is satisfied in expectation [4].

To the best of our knowledge, this paper presents the first principled framework for deep network compression under operational constraints. Experiments on Describable Textures [26] and ImageNet [3] demonstrate the value of modelling constraints directly in network compression.

2 Constraint-Aware Network Compression

The problem of deep network compression with constraints can be expressed as follows. Given a pre-trained deep neural network, we would like to obtain a compressed network that satisfies a fixed set of constraints $\mathcal{C}$, while preserving the original task performance of the network as closely as possible.

Suppose we have a network compression algorithm $\Phi(F, \phi)$ that takes as input a deep network F and a set of tunable compression-related hyperparameters ϕ, and outputs a compressed network. For example, ϕ might be a vector specifying magnitude thresholds for pruning each layer in the network [8].

In an unconstrained compression setting, it is difficult to compress the network using Φ while ensuring that the operational constraints $\mathcal{C}$ are satisfied. A straightforward approach would be to repeatedly try different compression configurations until a compressed network is found that satisfies $\mathcal{C}$; however, the configuration space might be very large and each compression attempt may be computationally expensive. Even if the repeated trials are feasible, the final compressed network may not provide satisfactory performance because its training does not directly take $\mathcal{C}$ into account during optimization.

We propose a principled framework for deep network compression under operational constraints. Let $A : F \rightarrow \mathbb{R}$ map a network F to a performance metric specific to the network's task; for example, if F is a network for image classification, then A could be the top-1 classification accuracy. Let $\rho_i : F \rightarrow \mathbb{R}$ map a network to a measurement of the ith constraint condition, such as latency, energy consumption, or memory, $i = \{1, ..., |\mathcal{C}|\}$. Let $\mathbf{c} \in \mathbb{R}^{|\mathcal{C}|}$ be a vector of constraint values. We define the constraint-aware network compression problem as

$$
\begin{aligned}
F = & \arg\max_{F} A(F) \qquad (1) \\
\text{subject to} \quad & \forall i \; \rho_i(F) \leq \mathbf{c}_i \\
& F = \Phi(F_0, \phi)
\end{aligned}
$$

where F_0 is the original network to compress. For example, suppose we wish to compress a semantic segmentation network and ensure that the compressed network satisfies a maximum latency constraint of 100 ms at inference time. A would be a semantic segmentation performance metric such as per-pixel accuracy, $|\mathcal{C}| = 1$, ρ_1 measures the latency of the network at inference time, and $\mathrm{c}_1 = 100$ ms.

To approach this difficult non-convex optimization problem, we employ constrained Bayesian optimization [27–29]. Bayesian optimization provides a general framework for optimizing black-box objective functions that are typically expensive to evaluate, non-convex, may not be expressible in closed form, and may not be easily differentiable [30]. Bayesian optimization iteratively constructs a probabilistic model of the objective function based on the outcomes of evaluating the function at various points in the input parameter space. In each iteration, the candidate point to evaluate next is determined by an acquisition function that trades off exploration (preferring regions of the input space with high model uncertainty) and exploitation (preferring regions of the input space that the model predicts will result in a high objective value). Constrained Bayesian optimization additionally models feasibility with respect to constraints.

In problem (1), we employ constrained Bayesian optimization to obtain compression hyperparameters ϕ that produce a compressed network F satisfying the constraints. We model the objective function as a Gaussian process [31]. A Gaussian process is an uncountable set of random variables, any finite subset of which is jointly Gaussian. Gaussian processes are commonly used in Bayesian optimization as they enable efficient computation of the posterior. For a more comprehensive treatment of Gaussian processes and Bayesian optimization, we refer the interested reader to [27,29,31]. In each iteration of our optimization, the next input ϕ is chosen using an expected improvement based acquisition function, the input network F_0 (or F_{t-1} if using a cooling schedule, discussed later) is compressed using Φ with hyperparameters ϕ, and the model is updated with the objective value and whether the constraints are satisfied. Figure 1 (top) illustrates the basic compression process.

Running the compression algorithm Φ to completion over a large number of Bayesian optimization iterations may be prohibitively expensive. In practice, we substitute Φ with a fast approximation of Φ that skips fine-tuning the network after compression. We also estimate the objective value using a small subset of images. After Bayesian optimization determines the most promising hyperparameters ϕ, we run the full compression algorithm Φ using ϕ to produce the compressed network F.

As described so far, the Bayesian optimization attempts to find a compression configuration that immediately satisfies the operational constraints; we will refer to this strategy as *one-step* constraint-aware compression. However, we find that pursuing a gradual trajectory towards the constraints leads to better performance, especially when the constraints are aggressive. This gradual trajectory provides a sequence of easier targets that approach the constraints, and

Algorithm 1. Constraint-aware network compression with cooling

Input: Network compression algorithm Φ, constraints $\mathcal{C}$ (implemented as measurement functions ρ_i and values $\mathbf{c}_i$ for $i = 1, 2, ..., |\mathcal{C}|$), uncompressed network F_0, number of cooling steps T, cooling function g

Output: Compressed network F

1: F[0] = F_0
2: **for** t = 1 to T **do**
3: Update cooled constraint values $g_i(t)$
4: **repeat**
5: Determine most promising compression hyperparameters ϕ to evaluate next based on expected improvement
6: Compress F[t-1] with Φ using hyperparameters ϕ
7: Update Gaussian process model based on objective and constraints evaluation
8: **until** maximum iterations of constrained Bayesian optimization reached
9: Compress F[t-1] with best hyperparameters ϕ discovered to obtain F[t]
10: Fine-tune F[t]
11: **end for**
12: F := F[T]

is governed by a cooling schedule. We write the constraint-aware network compression problem with cooling as a sequence of problems indexed by cooling step $t = 1, 2, ..., T$:

$$\begin{aligned} F_t = & \arg\max_{F_t} A(F_t) \\ \text{subject to} \quad & \forall i \; \rho_i(F_t) \leq g_i(t) \\ & F_t = \Phi(F_{t-1}, \phi_t) \end{aligned} \tag{2}$$

where T is the total number of cooling steps, and g_i is a cooling function that depends on T, the ith target constraint value $\mathbf{c}_i$, and $\rho_i(F_0)$, the initial value of the ith constraint variable (for the original uncompressed network). We require $g_i(T) = \mathbf{c}_i$ and return F_T as the final compressed network. Figure 1 (bottom) illustrates constraint-aware network compression with cooling. In each cooling step $t = 1, 2, ..., T$, constrained Bayesian optimization is used to compress the network while ensuring that the target constraints are satisfied. At the end of a cooling iteration, we have a compressed network that satisfies the target constraints, and the target constraints are updated according to the cooling function. In the final cooling iteration T, the target constraints are equal to the operational constraints $\mathbf{c}_i$. We consider two cooling functions in this paper. For linear cooling, we define

$$g_{i,\text{linear}}(t) = \rho_i(F_0) + t/T \cdot (\mathbf{c}_i - \rho_i(F_0)) \tag{3}$$

This cooling schedule sets the intermediate targets by linearly interpolating from the value of the uncompressed network $\rho_i(F_0)$ to the constraint $\mathbf{c}_i$. For exponential cooling, we define

$$g_{i,\exp}(t) = \mathbf{c}_i + (\rho_i(F_0) - \mathbf{c}_i) \cdot e^{-\alpha t} + (\mathbf{c}_i - \rho_i(F_0)) \cdot e^{-\alpha T} \tag{4}$$

The exponential cooling schedule sets more aggressive intermediate targets at first and cools more slowly when approaching the final constraint $\mathbf{c}_i$. The intuition is that the network may be initially easy to compress, but after several iterations of constrained compression it may become more difficult to make further progress. For exponential cooling, there is one parameter α, which controls the degree of cooling in each iteration. The process for constraint-aware network compression with cooling is summarized in Algorithm 1.

3 Experiments

We performed an initial set of experiments on the Describable Textures Dataset (DTD) [26] to explore a range of alternatives for performing network compression under operational constraints; we then performed final experiments on ImageNet (ILSVRC-2012) [3] to show the generalization of our technique to large-scale data. For concreteness, we used inference latency as a typical operational constraint in real-world systems. The performance of the classification networks is measured by top-1 accuracy.

3.1 Implementation Details

We used magnitude-based pruning [6,8,15,17] followed by fine-tuning as our compression strategy Φ. Magnitude-based pruning removes the weights in each layer with the lowest absolute value, with the intuition that these will have the least impact on the computation result. The compression hyperparameters ϕ are the pruning percentages for each layer. We used an ImageNet-pretrained CaffeNet (a variation of AlexNet [32]) as the original network. During constrained Bayesian optimization, the accuracy of a compressed network was measured on a subset of the training set. Fine-tuning was performed on the whole training set.

We implemented our networks in the open source library SkimCaffe [15], which can speed up sparse deep neural networks via direct convolution operation and sparse matrix multiplication on CPU. For constrained Bayesian optimization, we used the official Matlab implementation.

Latency is measured as stabilized (after model is loaded into memory) average forwarding time of one batch in SkimCaffe over 100 timing trials. As discussed in the introduction, we focus on satisfying the latency constraint in expectation, i.e. we assume an NHRT (Non Hard Real-Time) system [23,24] for testing. Since conv1 is memory bandwidth dominant, pruning this layer gives low speedup but makes it harder to preserve the accuracy [15]; by default, we do not prune conv1 in the latency experiments.

3.2 Methods Evaluated

We considered four approaches: an unconstrained baseline and three constraint-aware alternatives:

1. Unconstrained compression. This baseline repeatedly tries different compression configurations and returns the best compressed network found that satisfies the operational constraints. Starting from a compression rate of 50%, we discard half the weights in each layer, until the operational constraints are satisfied; we then iteratively increase and decrease the compression rate by binary search to satisfy the constraints as closely as possible, until the binary search interval is smaller than 0.001. We then prune the model using the found compression rate and fine-tune the whole model.
2. Constraint-aware compression with one step. This constraint-aware variation is illustrated in Fig. 1 (top), in which we do not use a cooling schedule and attempt to meet the operational constraint directly in a single step ($T = 1$).
3. Constraint-aware compression with linear cooling. This method is Fig. 1 (bottom) with a linear cooling schedule to gradually and uniformly approach the operational constraint.
4. Constraint-aware compression with exponential cooling. This method is Fig. 1 (bottom) with an exponential cooling schedule to gradually approach the operational constraint with more aggressive targets at the beginning.

3.3 Exploratory Experiments (DTD)

Our initial experiments for exploring alternatives were performed on the first train-validation-test split of the Describable Textures Dataset [26]. We performed multiple trials on a single split instead of single trials on multiple splits so that any variation in outcomes would be due to the stochastic elements of the algorithm instead of differences in the data split. The hardware platform for latency measurement was Intel(R) Core(TM) i7-7700 CPU @ 3.60 GHz. At a batch size of 32 and 4 threads, the inference latency of the original uncompressed network was 207 ms. We set the learning rate to 0.001, the number of constrained Bayesian optimization iterations to 100, the number of fine-tuning iterations in each cooling step to 1500, the number of cooling steps T to 5, and the exponential coefficient for exponential cooling to 0.5. The unconstrained and one-step baselines were fine-tuned to 3000 iterations, which was enough for convergence.

Table 1. Compression results for AlexNet on DTD with a latency constraint of 60 ms. Accuracy is top-1 classification accuracy. Results are averaged over five trials.

	Latency	Accuracy
Original network	207.3 ± 8.1 ms	60.7%
Unconstrained compression	59.7 ± 0.2 ms	56.3 ± 0.0%
Constraint-aware compression, one-step	57.1 ± 1.6 ms	53.9 ± 6.0%
Constraint-aware compression, linear cooling	58.4 ± 0.6 ms	57.8 ± 1.0%
Constraint-aware compression, exponential cooling	58.2 ± 0.5 ms	59.0 ± 0.4%

Method Comparisons. Table 1 shows the final latency and top-1 accuracy results under a latency constraint of 60 ms for all methods. Means and standard deviations were computed over five independent runs to account for stochastic elements of the algorithm. For a given run, the latency of the compressed network was obtained via 100 timing measurements to account for variance from the CPU environment; the standard deviation of the timing measurements was 0.3 ms on average. Compared to the unconstrained compression baseline, constraint-aware compression with cooling obtained 2.7% higher accuracy. The exponential cooling schedule led to a higher final accuracy than the linear cooling schedule, suggesting that rapid initial cooling followed by a more conservative final approach was an effective strategy in this case.

Why Does Cooling Provide Better Performance? One might ask whether a better hyperparameter sweep would suffice for the unconstrained or one-step baselines to match the performance of linear or exponential cooling. Why is cooling valuable? The cooling schedule induces a series of easier compression problems and allows the compression to adapt to the network structure as it changes over time [16]. Since the network is fine-tuned at the end of each cooling step, each round of Bayesian optimization starts from an initial network F_{t-1} with structure that is closer to the final compressed network. A one-step or unconstrained approach does not benefit from these intermediate network structures. We performed an additional experiment in which we ran the one-step baseline using the compression hyperparameters found in the final cooling step of exponential cooling. This resulted in an accuracy of $52.6 \pm 2.4\%$, which is worse than the result of the normal exponential cooling method, with compression performed over multiple steps. Interestingly, if instead of transferring only the compression hyperparameters from exponential cooling to the one-step baseline, we also transferred the network *structure* (i.e. the sparsity structure), then the accuracy improved to $58.3 \pm 1.2\%$. This suggests that the exponential cooling approach does not perform better simply because of a better hyperparameter search, but that the setting of progressive targets and the intermediate fine-tuning are helpful in evolving the network to the highest performing compressed structure.

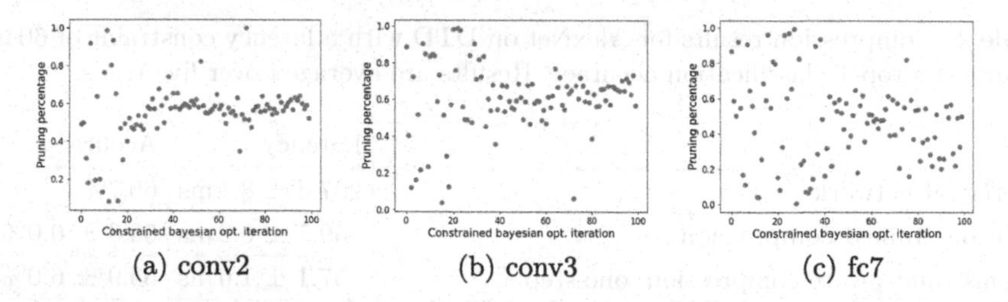

(a) conv2 (b) conv3 (c) fc7

Fig. 2. Visualization of the pruning rates proposed by constrained Bayesian optimization for the first cooling step of a single trial in Table 2.

Table 2. Layer-wise compression results for the constraint-aware compression with exponential cooling method in Table 1.

	Pruning rate	Latency before	Latency after
conv2	95.06 ± 1.85 %	52.9 ± 2.7 ms	7.8 ± 1.8 ms
conv3	92.19 ± 4.25 %	30.2 ± 1.6 ms	4.9 ± 2.3 ms
conv4	85.29 ± 4.26 %	25.6 ± 1.4 ms	6.5 ± 1.7 ms
conv5	77.61 ± 4.02 %	19.1 ± 1.2 ms	8.3 ± 1.0 ms
fc6	96.03 ± 2.33 %	15.6 ± 0.3 ms	2.4 ± 0.7 ms
fc7	90.05 ± 6.42 %	6.3 ± 0.2 ms	1.8 ± 0.8 ms
fc8	82.07 ± 8.35 %	0.1 ± 0.01 ms	0.07 ± 0.02 ms

Layer-Wise Results. Table 2 shows the average latency and pruning rate for each layer obtained by the constraint-aware compression with exponential cooling method in Table 1. Figure 2 shows the evolution of the individual pruning rates proposed by Bayesian optimization for the conv2, conv3, and fc7 layers, for the first cooling step of a single trial with exponential cooling. Bayesian optimization quickly clusters around an effective pruning rate range for conv2 and conv3, while the rates proposed for fc7 are more scattered, even at the maximum number of iterations. This suggests that the quality of the compressed solutions is more dependent on how conv2 and conv3 are pruned than on how fc7 is pruned, which is expected since convolution layers contribute more to the overall latency than fully connected layers. Likewise, we can observe from Table 2 that the variance in pruning rate is higher for fc7 and fc8 than for the convolution layers.

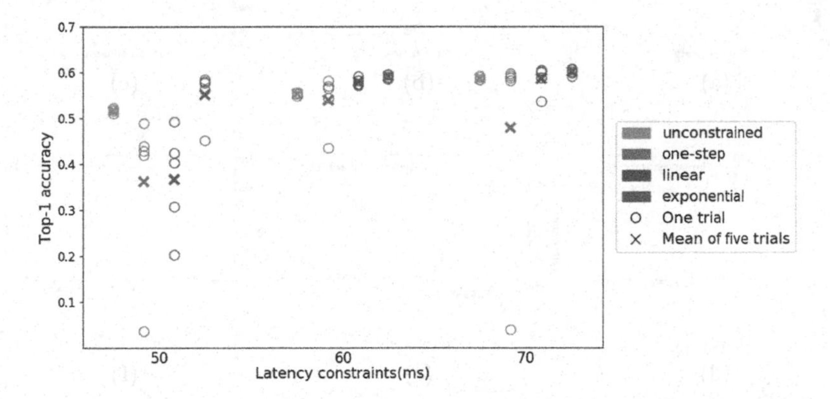

Fig. 3. Compression results for AlexNet on DTD for latency constraints of 50 ms, 60 ms, and 70 ms. Constraint-aware compression with exponential cooling provides the best overall performance for all three tested constraint values.

Generalization to Different Constraint Values. Figure 3 shows compression performance over a range of latency constraint values. Our observations about the importance of cooling generalize to other latency targets. The large variance in the one-step baseline in both the 50 ms and 70 ms experiments is due to failures in a single trial in the respective experiments. To explain these failures, Fig. 4(a) visualizes the compressed networks proposed by constrained Bayesian optimization for the 70 ms trial in which the single-step baseline failed. The saturation of the data points indicates the Bayesian optimization iteration in which that compressed network was proposed; deeper saturation corresponds to a later iteration. We can see that the feasible solutions proposed by Bayesian optimization (data points under the dotted line) are almost equally poor in terms of accuracy. In this case, the model is unable to distinguish between compressed networks that can be improved with sufficient fine-tuning and networks that cannot be improved with any amount of fine-tuning. Figure 4(b–f) visualize the compressed networks proposed by constrained Bayesian optimization for a trial of the exponential cooling method. In the case of exponential cooling, since compression is performed gradually with intermediate targets over several iterations, constrained Bayesian optimization is able to consistently converge to high-accuracy solutions that respect the operational constraint.

One way to mitigate this failure mode for the one-step baseline is to perform a look ahead step during constrained Bayesian optimization: for every compressed network proposed by Bayesian optimization, we partially fine-tune the proposed

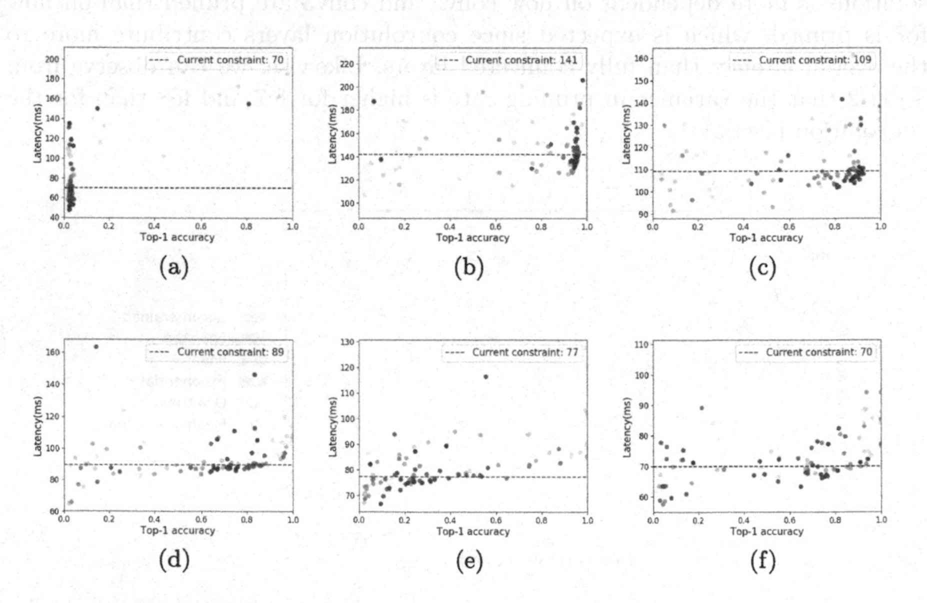

Fig. 4. A visualization of the compression solutions proposed by constrained Bayesian optimization for the 70 ms experiment in Fig. 3. Deeper saturation corresponds to a later iteration in the Bayesian optimization. (a) Single-step compression failure case. (b–f) Compression with exponential cooling. See text for discussion.

network (e.g. we look ahead one epoch) to obtain a better estimate of the final accuracy. We implemented this variation and found that looking ahead improves the average accuracy from 53.9% to 55.9% and reduces the standard deviation from 6.0% to 1.1%. However, fine-tuning each proposed network increases the computation overhead of Bayesian optimization and may not be suitable for large-scale datasets such as ImageNet.

Limitations. In our experiments, we have assumed that the operational constraint value is feasible given the selected network F and compression method Φ. If the constraint cannot be satisfied even if the network is maximally compressed using Φ (e.g. in our case, if the layers are pruned to the extent of leaving a single non-zero weight in each layer), then our framework cannot propose a feasible solution. The lower bound on the operational constraint depends on Φ: for instance, in knowledge distillation [9,14] the architecture of the compressed (student) network is typically different from that of the original (teacher) network, so it may be able to achieve more extreme latency targets than a method that keeps the original network architecture.

3.4 Large-Scale Experiments (ImageNet)

To demonstrate that our framework generalizes to large-scale data, we performed experiments on ImageNet (ILSVRC-2012). We performed three independent trials on the standard training and validation split. The hardware platform for latency measurement was Intel(R) Core(TM) i7-4790 CPU @ 3.60 GHz. We set the learning rate to 0.001, the number of constrained Bayesian optimization iterations to 200, the number of fine-tuning iterations in each cooling step to 10K, the number of cooling steps T to 10, and the exponential coefficient for exponential cooling to 0.5. We matched the total number of fine-tuning iterations to be 150K for all baselines.

Method Comparisons. Table 3 shows the averaged results for unconstrained compression, constraint-aware compression in one-step, and constraint-aware compression with exponential cooling, under an operational constraint of 70 ms latency. Compared to unconstrained compression, constraint-aware compression with exponential cooling obtains 3.1% higher top-1 accuracy while satisfying the operational constraint.

Table 3. Compression results for AlexNet on ImageNet with a latency constraint of 70 ms. Accuracy is top-1 classification accuracy. Results are averaged over three trials.

	Latency	Accuracy
Original network	237.0 ± 2.9 ms	57.41%
Unconstrained compression	69.2 ± 1.3 ms	50.62 ± 0.50%
Constraint-aware compression, one-step	62.2 ± 4.3 ms	47.27 ± 3.31%
Constraint-aware compression, exponential cooling	69.7 ± 0.7 ms	53.70 ± 0.15%

Layer-Wise Results. Detailed layer-wise results can be found in the supplementary material. Similar to the DTD experiments, Bayesian optimization quickly clusters around an effective pruning rate range for conv2 and conv3, while the rates proposed for fc7 are more scattered, even at the maximum number of iterations. The highest variances in pruning rate are for fc7 and fc8. Similar to DTD, the quality of the compressed solutions depends more on how the convolution layers are pruned than on how the fc7 and fc8 layers are pruned, which is expected given the constraint on inference latency.

Time Requirements. In one step of the cooling schedule, constrained Bayesian optimization is first used to search for the hyperparameters and then fine-tuning is performed. The constrained Bayesian optimization takes 1.5 h for 200 iterations. One iteration is roughly 30 s, and consists of 17 s of accuracy measurement, 10 s of latency test, and 3 s of Bayesian optimization calculation. We perform 150K fine-tuning iterations, which requires 30 h on a 1080Ti.

Generalization to Other Constraint Types. To demonstrate that our framework generalizes to different types of operational constraints, we performed a preliminary experiment on ImageNet with a constraint on the storage requirements of the network. We set the maximum storage cost to be 5% of the original cost and ran a single trial of constraint-aware compression with exponential cooling. We set the learning rate to 0.001, the number of constrained Bayesian optimization iterations to 200, the number of fine-tuning iterations in each cooling step to 10K, the number of cooling steps T to 10, and the exponential coefficient to 0.4. After the final cooling step, we fine-tuned for an additional 350K iterations in which we started with a learning rate of 0.001 and reduced the learning rate by a factor of 10 after every 150K iterations.

The storage cost of the original network is 232.56 MB. Constraint-aware compression with exponential cooling produces a compressed network with storage cost 11.33 MB (5% of the original cost) and top-1 accuracy of 54.84%. Table 4 shows the storage cost and pruning rate for each layer, and Fig. 5 visualizes the individual pruning rates proposed by Bayesian optimization for the conv2, fc6, and fc7 layers. In contrast to the previous experiments with latency constraints, given a storage constraint, our framework learns a policy that prioritizes the

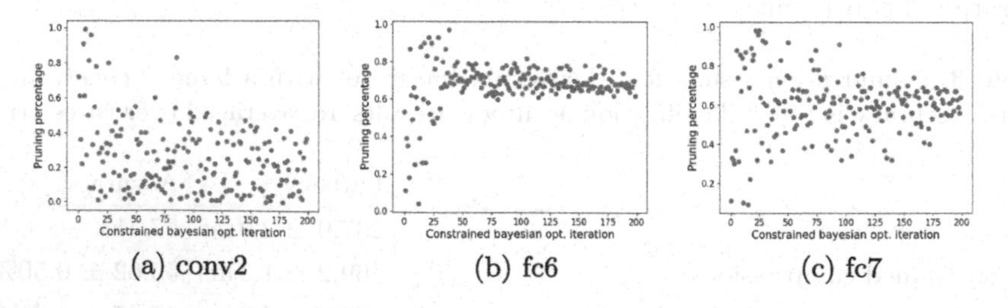

(a) conv2 (b) fc6 (c) fc7

Fig. 5. Visualization of the pruning rates proposed by constrained Bayesian optimization for the first cooling step of the storage-constraint experiment in Table 4.

Table 4. Layer-wise compression results for constraint-aware compression with a storage constraint of 5% of the original storage costs, AlexNet on ImageNet.

	Pruning rate	Storage before	Storage after
conv1	27.37 %	0.13 MB	0.10 MB
conv2	35.39 %	1.17 MB	0.76 MB
conv3	50.12 %	3.38 MB	1.68 MB
conv4	55.85 %	2.53 MB	1.12 MB
conv5	55.41 %	1.69 MB	0.75 MB
fc6	98.29 %	144.02 MB	2.46 MB
fc7	96.79 %	64.02 MB	2.05 MB
fc8	84.61 %	15.63 MB	2.41 MB
overall	95.13 %	232.56 MB	11.33 MB

fully connected layers: Bayesian optimization quickly converges for fc6 and fc7, while the proposed pruning rates for conv2 are more scattered, even at the maximum number of iterations; in Table 4, the fully connected layers are pruned more aggressively than the convolution layers. This contrasting behavior is expected because fully connected layers contribute more to the storage costs (they have more weights to store) than convolution layers. We can see that the compression behavior of constraint-aware compression automatically adapts to the type of operational constraint that the system is required to satisfy.

3.5 Comparison to Guided Sparsity Learning

The timing performance of compression algorithms is dependent on the hardware platform and software libraries used to implement key network operations such as convolution. We draw a comparison with Guided Sparsity Learning (GSL) [12] in SkimCaffe as our implementation is in SkimCaffe. GSL is specifically optimized for inference speed: compression is guided by a performance model that predicts the speedup potential of each layer, tuned to hardware characteristics (e.g. compute capability in FLOP/s, memory bandwidth). On DTD, GSL achieves a latency of 74.2 ms with a top-1 accuracy of 60.9%. This result motivated us to set successively harder latency targets of 70 ms, 60 ms, and 50 ms in our DTD experiments. Despite being hardware agnostic, and not specifically optimized for speed, our method obtains competitive performance at these aggressive targets: 60.1% at 70 ms and 59.0% at 60 ms. We also performed an additional comparison on ImageNet. On ImageNet, GSL achieves a latency of 78.2 ms with a top-1 accuracy of 57.5%. For a direct comparison, we set a latency target of 78.2 ms for constraint-aware compression. At 78.2 ms, constraint-aware compression achieves a top-1 accuracy of 57.4%. The results show that, in a fair comparison with the same hardware and software platforms, our method obtains comparable latency performance to optimized GSL, while requiring no hardware-specific tuning and providing generality to other constraint types besides latency.

4 Related Work

Network pruning methods sparsify the connections in a pre-trained network and then fine-tune the sparsified network to restore accuracy. The earliest pruning methods removed connections based on the second-order derivatives of the network loss [33,34]. A recent common pruning strategy removes the connections with the lowest magnitude weights, with the intuition that low-magnitude weights are likely to have less impact on the computation result if set to zero [6,8,15,17]. Structured pruning methods remove entire filters instead of individual connections [11,19,35]; this produces a speed-up in deep learning frameworks that implement convolutions as large matrix multiplications, at the possible cost of lower compression rates [15].

Weight quantization methods represent connections using a small set of permitted weight values, reducing the number of bits required to store each connection [12,18]. For example, if 64 unique values are permitted, then each connection can be represented using 6 bits. At the extreme, weights can be quantized to a single bit [7,13,20]. Weight quantization and pruning are complementary and can be combined sequentially or jointly [8,17].

Knowledge distillation uses a more expensive teacher network to guide the training of a smaller student network [9,14]. Low-rank approximation methods exploit the redundancy in filters and feature maps [5,10].

Any of these methods can in principle be plugged into our constraint-aware compression framework as the module Φ (see Fig. 1), provided that it exposes a set of tunable compression hyperparameters, accepts an uncompressed or partially compressed deep network as input, and outputs a compressed deep network. To the best of our knowledge, our study is the first principled treatment of deep network compression under operational constraints.

5 Conclusion

Advances in deep neural network compression have the potential to bring powerful networks to limited-compute platforms such as drones, mobile robots, and self-driving vehicles. We argue that our network compression algorithms should be constraint-aware, because in the real world, computation is not free and the operational constraints matter. In this paper, we have presented a general framework for training compressed networks that satisfy operational constraints in expectation. Our framework is complementary to specific compression techniques (e.g. distillation, pruning, quantization) and can accommodate any of these as its compression module Φ. In future, we plan to study whether the constraint cooling schedule can be learned, for example by using reinforcement learning.

Acknowledgements. This work was supported by the Natural Sciences and Engineering Research Council of Canada.

References

1. He, K., Zhang, X., Ren, S., Sun, J.: Deep residual learning for image recognition. In: IEEE Conference on Computer Vision and Pattern Recognition (2016)
2. Huang, G., Liu, Z., van der Maaten, L., Weinberger, K.Q.: Densely connected convolutional networks. In: IEEE Conference on Computer Vision and Pattern Recognition (2017)
3. Russakovsky, O., et al.: ImageNet Large Scale Visual Recognition Challenge. arXiv:1409.0575 (2014)
4. Huang, G., Chen, D., Li, T., Wu, F., van der Maaten, L., Weinberger, K.: Multi-scale dense networks for resource efficient image classification. In: International Conference on Learning Representations (2018)
5. Denton, E., Zaremba, W., Bruna, J., LeCun, Y., Fergus, R.: Exploiting linear structure within convolutional networks for efficient evaluation. In: Advances in Neural Information Processing Systems (2014)
6. Guo, Y., Yao, A., Chen, Y.: Dynamic network surgery for efficient DNNs. In: Advances in Neural Information Processing Systems (2016)
7. Guo, Y., Yao, A., Zhao, H., Chen, Y.: Network sketching: exploiting binary structure in deep CNNs. In: IEEE Conference on Computer Vision and Pattern Recognition (2017)
8. Han, S., Mao, H., Dally, W.J.: Deep compression: compressing deep neural networks with pruning, trained quantization and Huffman coding. In: International Conference on Learning Representations (2016)
9. Hinton, G., Vinyals, O., Dean, J.: Distilling the knowledge in a neural network. arXiv:1503.02531 (2015)
10. Jaderberg, M., Vedaldi, A., Zisserman, A.: Speeding up convolutional neural networks with low rank expansions. In: British Machine Vision Conference (2014)
11. Lebedev, V., Lempitsky, V.: Fast ConvNets using group-wise brain damage. In: IEEE Conference on Computer Vision and Pattern Recognition (2016)
12. Park, E., Ahn, J., Yoo, S.: Weighted-entropy-based quantization for deep neural networks. In: IEEE Conference on Computer Vision and Pattern Recognition (2017)
13. Rastegari, M., Ordonez, V., Redmon, J., Farhadi, A.: XNOR-Net: ImageNet classification using binary convolutional neural networks. In: Leibe, B., Matas, J., Sebe, N., Welling, M. (eds.) ECCV 2016. LNCS, vol. 9908, pp. 525–542. Springer, Cham (2016). https://doi.org/10.1007/978-3-319-46493-0_32
14. Romero, A., Ballas, N., Kahou, S.E., Chassang, A., Gatta, C., Bengio, Y.: FitNets: hints for thin deep nets. In: International Conference on Learning Representations (2015)
15. Park, J., et al.: Faster CNNs with direct sparse convolutions and guided pruning. In: International Conference on Learning Representations (2017)
16. Tung, F., Muralidharan, S., Mori, G.: Fine-pruning: joint fine-tuning and compression of a convolutional network with Bayesian optimization. In: British Machine Vision Conference (2017)
17. Tung, F., Mori, G.: CLIP-Q: deep network compression learning by in-parallel pruning-quantization. In: IEEE Conference on Computer Vision and Pattern Recognition (2018)
18. Ullrich, K., Meeds, E., Welling, M.: Soft weight-sharing for neural network compression. In: International Conference on Learning Representations (2017)

19. Wen, W., Wu, C., Wang, Y., Chen, Y., Li, H.: Learning structured sparsity in deep neural networks. In: Advances in Neural Information Processing Systems (2016)
20. Xu, F., Boddeti, V.N., Savvides, M.: Local binary convolutional neural networks. In: IEEE Conference on Computer Vision and Pattern Recognition (2017)
21. Yang, T.J., Chen, Y.H., Sze, V.: Designing energy-efficient convolutional neural networks using energy-aware pruning. In: IEEE Conference on Computer Vision and Pattern Recognition (2017)
22. Zhou, H., Alvarez, J.M., Porikli, F.: Less is more: towards compact CNNs. In: Leibe, B., Matas, J., Sebe, N., Welling, M. (eds.) ECCV 2016. LNCS, vol. 9908, pp. 662–677. Springer, Cham (2016). https://doi.org/10.1007/978-3-319-46493-0_40
23. Paolieri, M., Quiñones, E., Cazorla, F.J., Bernat, G., Valero, M.: Hardware support for WCET analysis of hard real-time multicore systems. In: International Symposium on Computer Architecture (2009)
24. Ungerer, T., et al.: Merasa: multicore execution of hard real-time applications supporting analyzability. IEEE Micro **30**(5), 66–75 (2010)
25. Abella, J., et al.: WCET analysis methods: pitfalls and challenges on their trustworthiness. In: IEEE International Symposium on Industrial Embedded Systems (2015)
26. Cimpoi, M., Maji, S., Kokkinos, I., Mohamed, S., Vedaldi, A.: Describing textures in the wild. In: IEEE Conference on Computer Vision and Pattern Recognition (2014)
27. Snoek, J., Larochelle, H., Adams, R.P.: Practical Bayesian optimization of machine learning algorithms. In: Advances in Neural Information Processing Systems (2012)
28. Gelbart, M.A., Snoek, J., Adams, R.P.: Bayesian optimization with unknown constraints. In: Conference on Uncertainty in Artificial Intelligence (2014)
29. Gardner, J.R., Kusner, M.J., Xu, Z., Weinberger, K.Q., Cunningham, J.P.: Bayesian optimization with inequality constraints. In: International Conference on Machine Learning (2014)
30. Wang, Z., Zoghi, M., Hutter, F., Matheson, D., de Freitas, N.: Bayesian optimization in high dimensions via random embeddings. In: International Joint Conference on Artificial Intelligence (2013)
31. Rasmussen, C.E., Williams, C.K.I.: Gaussian Processes for Machine Learning. MIT Press, Cambridge (2006)
32. Krizhevsky, A., Sutskever, I., Hinton, G.E.: ImageNet classification with deep convolutional neural networks. In: Advances in Neural Information Processing Systems (2012)
33. Hassibi, B., Stork, D.G.: Second order derivatives for network pruning: optimal brain surgeon. In: Advances in Neural Information Processing Systems (1992)
34. LeCun, Y., Denker, J.S., Solla, S.A.: Optimal brain damage. In: Advances in Neural Information Processing Systems (1990)
35. Luo, J.H., Wu, J., Lin, W.: ThiNet: a filter level pruning method for deep neural network compression. In: IEEE International Conference on Computer Vision (2017)

Video Compression Through Image Interpolation

Chao-Yuan Wu[✉], Nayan Singhal, and Philipp Krähenbühl

The University of Texas at Austin, Austin, USA
{cywu,nayans,philkr}@cs.utexas.edu

Abstract. An ever increasing amount of our digital communication, media consumption, and content creation revolves around videos. We share, watch, and archive many aspects of our lives through them, all of which are powered by strong video compression. Traditional video compression is laboriously hand designed and hand optimized. This paper presents an alternative in an end-to-end deep learning codec. Our codec builds on one simple idea: Video compression is repeated image interpolation. It thus benefits from recent advances in deep image interpolation and generation. Our deep video codec outperforms today's prevailing codecs, such as H.261, MPEG-4 Part 2, and performs on par with H.264.

1 Introduction

Video commands the lion's share of internet data, and today makes up three-fourths of all internet traffic [17]. We capture moments, share memories, and entertain one another through moving pictures, all of which are powered by ever powerful digital camera and video compression. Strong compression significantly reduces internet traffic, saves storage space, and increases throughput. It drives applications like cloud gaming, real-time high-quality video streaming [20], or 3D and 360-videos. Video compression even helps better understand and parse videos using deep neural networks [31]. Despite these obvious benefits, video compression algorithms are still largely hand designed. The most competitive video codecs today rely on a sophisticated interplay between block motion estimation, residual color patterns, and their encoding using discrete cosine transform and entropy coding [23]. While each part is carefully designed to compress the video as much as possible, the overall system is not jointly optimized, and has largely been untouched by end-to-end deep learning.

This paper presents, to the best of our knowledge, the first end-to-end trained deep video codec. The main insight of our codec is a different view on video compression: We frame video compression as repeated image interpolation, and draw on recent advances in deep image generation and interpolation. We first encode

Electronic supplementary material The online version of this chapter (https://doi.org/10.1007/978-3-030-01237-3_26) contains supplementary material, which is available to authorized users.

V. Ferrari et al. (Eds.): ECCV 2018, LNCS 11212, pp. 425–440, 2018.
https://doi.org/10.1007/978-3-030-01237-3_26

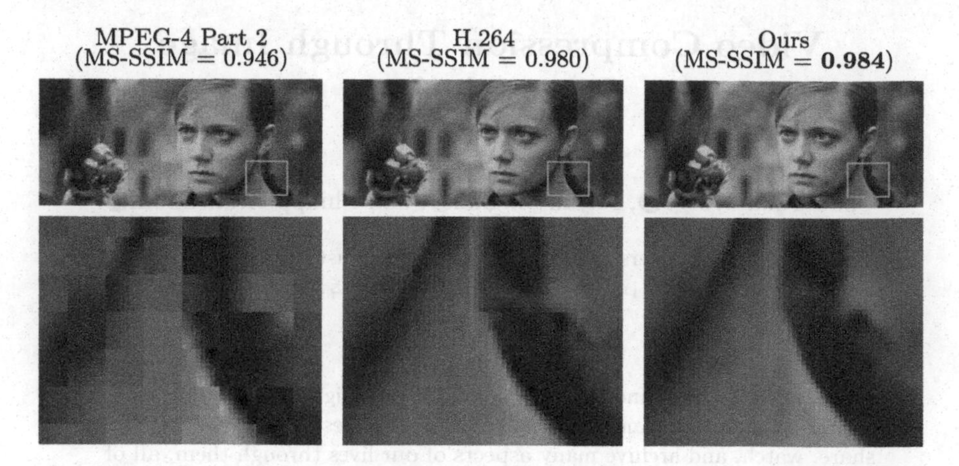

Fig. 1. Comparison of our end-to-end deep video compression algorithm to MPEG-4 Part 2 and H.264 on the Blender *Tears of Steel* movie. All methods use 0.080 BPP. Our model offers a visual quality better than MPEG-4 Part 2 and comparable to H.264. Unlike traditional methods, our method is free of block artifacts. The MS-SSIM [28] measures the image quality of the video clip compared to the raw uncompressed ground truth. (Best viewed on screen.)

a series of anchor frames (key frames), using standard deep image compression. Our codec then reconstructs all remaining frames by interpolating between neighboring anchor frames. However, this image interpolation is not unique. We additionally provide a small and compressible code to the interpolation network to disambiguate different interpolations, and encode the original video frame as faithfully as possible. The main technical challenge is the design of a compressible image interpolation network.

We present a series of increasingly powerful and compressible encoder-decoder architectures for image interpolation. We start by using a vanilla U-net interpolation architecture [22] for reconstructing frames other than the key frames. This architecture makes good use of repeating static patterns through time, but it struggles to properly disambiguate the trajectories for moving patterns. We then directly incorporate an offline motion estimate from either block-motion estimation or optical flow into the network. The new architecture interpolates spatial U-net features using the pre-computed motion estimate, and improves compression rates by an order of magnitude over deep image compression. This model captures most, but not all of the information we need to reconstruct a frame. We additionally train an encoder that extracts the content not present in either of the source images, and represents it compactly. Finally, we reduce any remaining spatial redundancy, and compress them using a 3D PixelCNN [19] with adaptive arithmetic coding [30].

To further reduce bitrate, our video codec applies image interpolation in a hierarchical manner. Each consecutive level in the hierarchy interpolates between ever closer reference frames, and is hence more compressible. Each level in the hierarchy uses all previously decompressed images.

We compare our video compression algorithm to state-of-the-art video compression (HEVC, H.264, MPEG-4 Part 2, H.261), and various image interpolation baselines. We evaluate all algorithms on two standard datasets of uncompressed video: Video Trace Library (VTL) [2] and Ultra Video Group (UVG) [1]. We additionally collect a subset of the Kinetics dataset [7] for both training and testing. The Kinetics subset contains high resolution videos, which we downsample to remove compression artifacts introduced by prior codecs on YouTube. The final dataset contains 2.8M frames. Our deep video codec outperforms all deep learning baselines, MPEG-4 Part 2, and H.261 in both compression rate and visual quality measured by MS-SSIM [28] and PSNR. We are on par with the state-of-the-art H.264 codec. Figure 1 shows a visual comparison. All the data is publicly available, and we will publish our code upon acceptance.

2 Related Work

Video compression algorithms must specify an encoder for compressing the video, and a decoder for reconstructing the original video. The encoder and the decoder together constitute a codec. A codec has one primary goal: Encode a series of images in the fewest number of bits possible. Most compression algorithms find a delicate trade-off between compression rate and reconstruction error. The simplest codecs, such as motion JPEG or GIF, encode each frame independently, and heavily rely on image compression.

Image Compression. For images, deep networks yield state-of-the-art compression ratios with impressive reconstruction quality [6,11,21,24,25]. Most of them train an autoencoder with a small binary bottleneck layer to directly minimize distortion [11,21,25]. A popular variant progressively encodes the image using a recurrent neural network [5,11,25]. This allows for variable compression rates with a single model. We extend this idea to variable rate video compression.

Deep image compression algorithms use fully convolutional networks to handle arbitrary image sizes. However, the bottleneck in fully convolutional networks still contains spatially redundant activations. Entropy coding further compresses this redundant information [6,16,21,24,25]. We follow Mentzer *et al.* [16] and use adaptive arithmetic coding on probability estimates of a Pixel-CNN [19].

Learning the binary representation is inherently non-differentiable, which complicates gradient based learning. Toderici *et al.* [25] use stochastic binarization and backpropagate the derivative of the expectation. Agustsson *et al.* [4] use soft assignment to approximate quantization. Balle *et al.* [6] replace the quantization by adding uniform noise. All of these methods work similarly and allow for gradients to flow through the discretization. In this paper, we use stochastic binarization [25].

Combining this bag of techniques, deep image compression algorithms offer a better compression rate than hand-designed algorithms, such as JPEG or

WebP [3], at the same level of image quality [21]. Deep image compression algorithms heavily exploit the spatial structure of an image. However, they miss out on a crucial signal in videos: time. Videos are temporally highly redundant. No deep image compression can compete with state-of-the-art (shallow) video compression, which exploits this redundancy.

Video Compression. Hand-designed video compression algorithms, such as H.263, H.264 or HEVC (H.265) [13] build on two simple ideas: They decompose each frame into blocks of pixels, known as macroblocks, and they divide frames into image (I) frames and referencing (P or B) frames. I-frames directly compress video frames using image compression. Most of the savings in video codecs come from referencing frames. P-frames borrow color values from preceding frames. They store a motion estimate and a highly compressible difference image for each macroblock. B-frames additionally allow bidirectional referencing, as long as there are no circular references. Both H.264 and HEVC encode a video in a hierarchical way. I-frames form the top of the hierarchy. In each consecutive level, P- or B-frames reference decoded frames at higher levels. The main disadvantages of traditional video compression is the intensive engineering efforts required and the difficulties in joint optimization. In this work, we build a hierarchical video codec using deep neural networks. We train it end-to-end without any hand-engineered heuristics or filters. Our key insight is that referencing (P or B) frames are a special case of image interpolation.

Learning-based video compression is largely unexplored, in part due to difficulties in modeling temporal redundancy. Tsai *et al.* propose a deep post-processing filter encoding errors of H.264 in domain specific videos [26]. However, it is unclear if and how the filter generalizes in an open domain. To the best of our knowledge, this paper proposes the first general deep network for video compression.

Image Interpolation and Extrapolation. Image interpolation seeks to hallucinate an unseen frame between two reference frames. Most image interpolation networks build on an encoder-decoder network architecture to move pixels through time [9,10,14,18]. Jia *et al.* [9] and Niklaus *et al.* [18] estimate a spatially-varying convolution kernel. Liu *et al.* [14] produce a flow field. All three methods then combine two predictions, forward and backward in time, to form the final output.

Image extrapolation is more ambitious and predicts a future video from a few frames [15], or a still image [27,32]. Both image interpolation and extrapolation works well for small timesteps, e.g. for creating slow-motion video [10] or predicting a fraction of a second into the future. However, current methods struggle for larger timesteps, where the interpolation or extrapolation is no longer unique, and additional side information is required. In this work, we extend image interpolation and incorporate few compressible bits of side information to reconstruct the original video.

3 Preliminary

Let $I^{(t)} \in \mathbb{R}^{W \times H \times 3}$ denote a series of frames for $t \in \{0, 1, \ldots\}$. Our goal is to compress each frame $I^{(t)}$ into a binary code $b^{(t)} \in \{0, 1\}^{N_t}$. An encoder $E : \{I^{(0)}, I^{(1)}, \ldots\} \rightarrow \{b^{(0)}, b^{(1)}, \ldots\}$ and decoder $D : \{b^{(0)}, b^{(1)}, \ldots\} \rightarrow \{\hat{I}^{(0)}, \hat{I}^{(1)}, \ldots\}$ compress and decompress the video respectively. E and D have two competing aims: Minimize the total bitrate $\sum_t N_t$, and reconstruct the original video as faithfully as possible, measured by $\ell(\hat{I}, I) = \|\hat{I} - I\|_1$.

Image Compression. The simplest encoders and decoders process each image independently: $E_I : I^{(t)} \rightarrow b^{(t)}$, $D_I : b^{(t)} \rightarrow \hat{I}^{(t)}$. Here, we build on the model of Toderici *et al.* [25], which encodes and reconstructs an image progressively over K iterations. At each iteration, the model encodes a residual r_k between the previously coded image and the original frame:

$$r_0 := I$$
$$b_k := E_I\left(r_{k-1}, g_{k-1}\right), \qquad r_k := r_{k-1} - D_I\left(b_k, h_{k-1}\right), \qquad \text{for } k = 1, 2, \ldots$$

where g_k and h_k are latent Conv-LSTM states that are updated at each iteration. All iterations share the same network architecture and parameters forming a recurrent structure. The training objective minimizes the distortion at all the steps $\sum_{k=1}^{K} \|r_k\|_1$. The reconstruction $\hat{I}_K = \sum_{k=1}^{K} D_I(b_k)$ allows for a variable bitrate encoding depending on the choice of K.

Both the encoder and the decoder consist of 4 Conv-LSTMs with stride 2. The bottleneck consists of a binary feature map with L channels and 16 times smaller spatial resolution in both width and height. Toderici *et al.* use a stochastic binarization to allow a gradient signal through the bottleneck. Mathematically, this reduces to *REINFORCE* [29] on sigmoidal activations. At inference time, the most likely state is selected.

This architecture yields state-of-the-art image compression performance. However, it fails to exploit any temporal redundancy.

Video Compression. Modern video codecs process I-frames using an image encoder E_I and decoder D_I. P-frames store a block motion estimate $\mathcal{T} \in \mathbb{R}^{W \times H \times 2}$, similar to an optical flow field, and a residual image $\mathcal{R}$, capturing the appearance changes not explained by motion. Both motion estimate and residual are jointly compressed using entropy coding. The original color frame is then recovered by

$$I_i^{(t)} = I_{i-\mathcal{T}_i^{(t)}}^{(t-1)} + \mathcal{R}_i^{(t)}, \tag{1}$$

for every pixel i in the image. The compression is uniquely defined by a block structure and motion estimate $\mathcal{T}$. The residual is simply the difference between the motion interpolated image and the original.

In this paper, we propose a more general view on video compression through image interpolation. We augment image interpolation network with motion information and add a compressible bottleneck layer.

4 Video Compression Through Interpolation

Our codec first encodes I-frames using the compression algorithm of Toderici *et al.*, see Fig. 2a. We chose every n-th frame as an I-frame. The remaining $n-1$ frames are interpolated. We call those frames R-frames, as they reference other frames. We choose $n = 12$ in practice, but also experimented with larger groups of pictures. We will first discuss our basic interpolation network, and then show a hierarchical interpolation setup, that further reduces the bitrate.

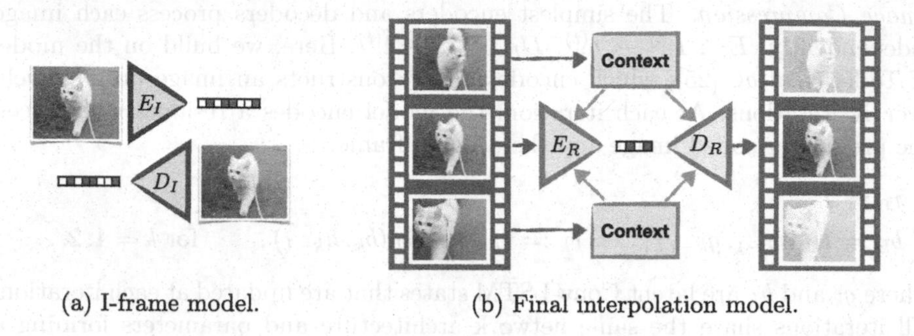

(a) I-frame model. (b) Final interpolation model.

Fig. 2. Our model is composed of an image compression model that compresses the key frames, and a conditional interpolation model that interpolates the remaining frames. Blue arrows represent motion compensated context features. Gray arrows represent input and output of the network.

4.1 Interpolation Network

In the simplest version of our codec, all R-frames use a blind interpolation network to interpolate between two key-frames I_1 and I_2. Specifically, we train a context network $C : I \rightarrow \{f^{(1)}, f^{(2)}, \ldots\}$ to extract a series of feature maps $f^{(l)}$ of various spatial resolutions. For notational simplicity let $f := \{f^{(1)}, f^{(2)}, \ldots\}$ be the collection of all context features. In our implementation, we use the upconvolutional feature maps of a U-net architecture with increasing spatial resolution $\frac{W}{8} \times \frac{H}{8}$, $\frac{W}{4} \times \frac{H}{4}$, $\frac{W}{2} \times \frac{H}{2}$, $W \times H$, in addition to the original image.

We extract context features f_1 and f_2 for key-frames I_1 and I_2 respectively, and train a network D to interpolate the frame $\hat{I} := D(f_1, f_2)$. C and D are trained jointly. This simple model favors a high compression rate over image quality, as none of the R-frames capture any information not present in the I-frames. Without further information, it is impossible to faithfully reconstruct a frame. What can we provide to the network to make interpolation easier?

Motion Compensated Interpolation. A great candidate is ground truth motion. It defines where pixels move through time and greatly disambiguates interpolation. We tried both optical flow [8] and block motion estimation [20]. Block motion estimates are easier to compress, but optical flow retains finer details.

We use the motion information to warp each context feature map

$$\tilde{f}_i^{(l)} = f_{i-\mathcal{T}_i}^{(l)}, \tag{2}$$

at every spatial location i. We scale the motion estimation with the resolution of the feature map, and use bilinear interpolation for fractional locations. The decoder now uses the warped context features $\tilde{f}$ instead, which allows it to focus solely on image creation, and ignore motion estimation.

Motion compensation greatly improves the interpolation network, as we will show in Sect. 5. However, it still only produces content seen in either reference image. Variations beyond motion, such as change in lighting, deformation, occlusion, etc. are not captured by this model.

Our goal is to encode the remaining information in a highly compact from.

Residual Motion Compensated Interpolation. Our final interpolation model combines motion compensated interpolation with a compressed residual information, capturing both the motion and appearance difference in the interpolated frames. Figure 2b show an overview of the model.

We jointly train an encoder E_R, context model C and interpolation network D_R. The encoder sees the same information as the interpolation network, which allows it to compress just the missing information, and avoid a redundant encoding. Formally, we follow the progressive compression framework of Toderici *et al.* [25], and train a variable bitrate encoder and decoder conditioned on the warped context $\tilde{f}$:

$$r_0 := I$$

$$b_k := E_R(r_{k-1}, \tilde{f}_1, \tilde{f}_2, g_{k-1}), \quad r_k := r_{k-1} - D_R(b_k, \tilde{f}_1, \tilde{f}_2, h_{k-1}), \quad \text{for } k = 1, 2, \ldots$$

This framework allows for learning a variable rate compression at high reconstruction quality. The interpolation network generally requires fewer bits to encode temporally close images and more bits for images that are farther apart. In one extreme, when key frames do not provide any meaningful signal to the interpolated frame, our algorithm reduces to image compression. In the other extreme, when the image content does not change, our method reduces to a vanilla interpolation, and requires close to zero bits.

In the next section, we use this to our advantage, and design a hierarchical interpolation scheme, maximizing the number of temporally close interpolations.

4.2 Hierarchical Interpolation

The basic idea of hierarchical interpolation is simple: We interpolate some frames first, and use them as key-frames for the next level of interpolations. See Fig. 3 for example. Each interpolation model $\mathcal{M}_{a,b}$ references a frames into the past and b frames into the future. There are a few things we need to trade off. First, every level in our hierarchical interpolation compounds error. The shallower the hierarchy, the fewer errors compound. In practice, the error propagation for more than three levels in the hierarchy significantly reduces the performance of our codec. Second, we need to train a different interpolation network $\mathcal{M}_{a,b}$ for each temporal offset (a, b), as different interpolations behave differently. To maximally use each trained model, we repeat the same temporal offsets as often as possible. Third, we need to minimize the sum of temporal offsets used in interpolation. The compression rate directly relates to the temporal offset, hence minimizing the temporal offset reduces the bitrate.

Considering just the bitrate and the number of interpolation networks, the optimal hierarchy is a binary tree cutting the interpolation range in two at each level. However, this cannot interpolate more than $n = 2^3 = 8$ consecutive frames, without significant error propagation. We extend this binary structure to $n = 12$ frames, by interpolating at a spacing of three frames in the last level of the hierarchy. For a sequence of four frames $I_1, \ldots, I_4$, we train an interpolation model $\mathcal{M}_{1,2}$ that predicts frame I_2, given I_1 and I_4. We use the exact same model $\mathcal{M}_{1,2}$ to predict I_3, but flip the conditioned images I_4 and I_1. This yields an equivalent model $\mathcal{M}_{2,1}$ predicting the third instead of the second image in the series. Combining this with an interpolation model $\mathcal{M}_{3,3}$ and $\mathcal{M}_{6,6}$ in a hierarchy, we extend the interpolation range from $n = 8$ frames to $n = 12$ frames while keeping the same number of models and levels. We tried applying the same trick to all levels in the hierarchy, extending the interpolation to $n = 27$ frames, but performance dropped, as we had more distant interpolations.

To apply this to a full video of N frames, we divide them into $\lceil N/n \rceil$ groups of pictures (GOPs). Two consecutive groups share the same boundary I-frame. We apply our hierarchical interpolation to each group independently.

Bitrate Optimization. Each interpolation model at a level l of the hierarchy, can choose to spend K_l bits to encode an image. Our goal is to minimize the overall bitrate, while maintaining a low distortion for all encoded frames. The challenge here is that each selection of K_l affects all lower levels, as errors propagate. Selecting a globally optimal set of $\{K_l\}$ thus requires iterating through all possible combinations, which is infeasible in practice.

We instead propose a heuristic bitrate selection based on beam search. For each level we chose from m different bitrates. We start by enumerating all m possibilities for the I-frame model. Next, we expand the first interpolation model with all m possible bitrates, leading to m^2 combinations. Out of these

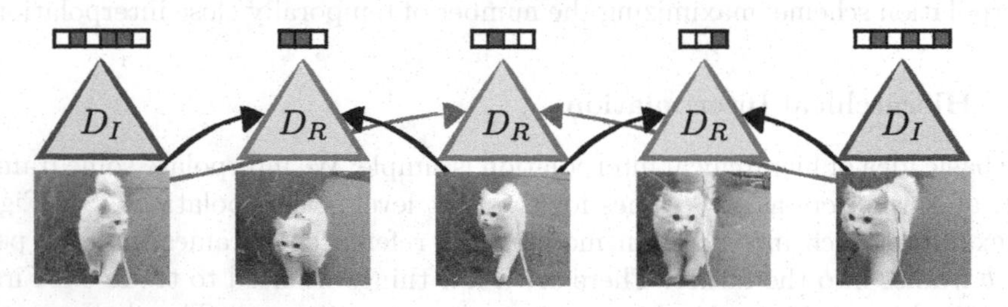

Fig. 3. We apply interpolation hierarchically. Each level in hierarchy uses previously decompressed images. Arrows represent motion compensated interpolation.

combinations, not all lead to a good MS-SSIM per bitrate, and we discard combinations not on the envelope of the MS-SSIM vs bitrate curve. In practice, only $O(m)$ combinations remain. We repeat this procedure for all levels of the hierarchy. This reduces the search space from m^L to $O(Lm^2)$ for an L-level hierarchy. In practice, this yields sufficiently good bitrates.

4.3 Implementation

Architecture. Our encoder and decoder (interpolation network) architecture follows the image compression model in Toderici *et al.* [25]. While Toderici *et al.* use $L = 32$ latent bits to compress an image, we found that for interpolation, $L = 8$ bits suffice for distance 3 and $L = 16$ for distance 6 and 12. This yields a bitrate of 0.0625 bits per pixel (BPP) and 0.03125 BPP for each iteration respectively.

We use the original U-net [22] as the context model. To speed-up training and save memory, we reduce the number of channels of all filters by half. We did not observe any significant performance degradation.

To make it compatible with our architecture, we remove the final output layer and takes the feature maps at the resolutions that are $2\times$, $4\times$, $8\times$ smaller than the original input image.

Conditional Encoder and Decoder. To add the information of the context frames into the encoder and decoder, we fuse the U-net features with the individual Conv-LSTM layers. Specifically, we perform the fusion before each Conv-LSTM layer by concatenating the corresponding U-net features of the same spatial resolution. To increase the computational efficiency, we selectively turn some of the conditioning off in both encoder and decoder. This was tuned for each interpolation network; see supplementary material for details.

To help the model compare context frames and the target frame side-by-side, we additionally stack the two context frames with target frame, resulting in a 9-channel image, and use that instead as the encoder input.

Entropy Coding. Since the model is fully-convolutional, it uses the same number of bits for all locations of an image. This disregards the fact that information is not distributed uniformly in an image. Following Mentzer *et al.* [16], we train a 3D Pixel-CNN on the $\{0,1\}^{W/16 \times H/16 \times L}$ binary codes to obtain the probability of each bit sequentially. We then use this probability with adaptive arithmetic coding to encode the feature map. See supplementary material for more details.

Motion Compression. We store forward and backward block motion estimates as a lossless 4-channel WebP [3] image. For optical flow we train a separate lossy deep compression model, as lossless WebP was unable to compress the flow field.

5 Experiments

In this section, we perform a detailed analysis on the series of interpolation models (Sect. 5.1), and present both quantitative and qualitative (Sect. 5.2) evaluation of our approach.

Datasets and Protocol. We train our models using videos from the Kinetics dataset [7]. We only use videos with a width and height greater than 720 px. To remove artifacts induced by previous compression, we downsample those high resolution videos to 352×288 px. We allow the aspect ratio to change. The resulting dataset contains 37K videos. We train on 27K, use 5K for validation, and 5K for testing. For training, we sample 100 frames per video. For faster testing on Kinetics, we only use a single group of $n = 12$ pictures per video.

We additionally test our method on two raw video datasets, Video Trace Library (VTL) [2] and Ultra Video Group (UVG) [1]. The VTL dataset contains ~40K frames of resolution 352×288 in 20 videos. The UVG dataset contains 3,900 frames of resolution 1920×1080 in 7 videos.

We evaluate our method based on the compression rate in bits per pixel (BPP), and the reconstruction quality in multi-scale structural similarity (MS-SSIM) [28] and peak signal-to-noise ratio (PSNR). We report the average performance of all videos, as opposed to the average of all frames, as our final performance. We use a GOP size of $n = 12$ frames, for all algorithms unless otherwise stated.

Training Details. All of our models are trained from scratch for 200K iterations using ADAM [12], with gradient norms clipped at 0.5. We use a batch size of 32 and a learning rate of 0.0005, which is divided by 2 when the validation MS-SSIM plateaus. We augment the data through horizontal flipping. For image models we train on 96×96 random crops, and for the interpolation models we train on 64×64 random crops. We train all models with 10 reconstruction iterations.

5.1 Ablation Study

We first evaluate the series of image interpolation models in Sect. 4 on the VTL dataset. Figure 4a shows the results.

We can see that image compression model requires by far the highest BPP to achieve high visual quality and performs poorly in the low bitrate region. This is not surprising as it does not exploit any temporal redundancy and needs to encode everything from scratch. Vanilla interpolation does not work much better. We present results for interpolation from 1 to 4 frames, using the best image compression model. While it exploits the temporal redundancy, it fails to accurately reconstruct the image.

Motion-compensated interpolation works significantly better. The additional motion information disambiguates the interpolation, improving the accuracy. The presented BPP includes the size of motion vectors.

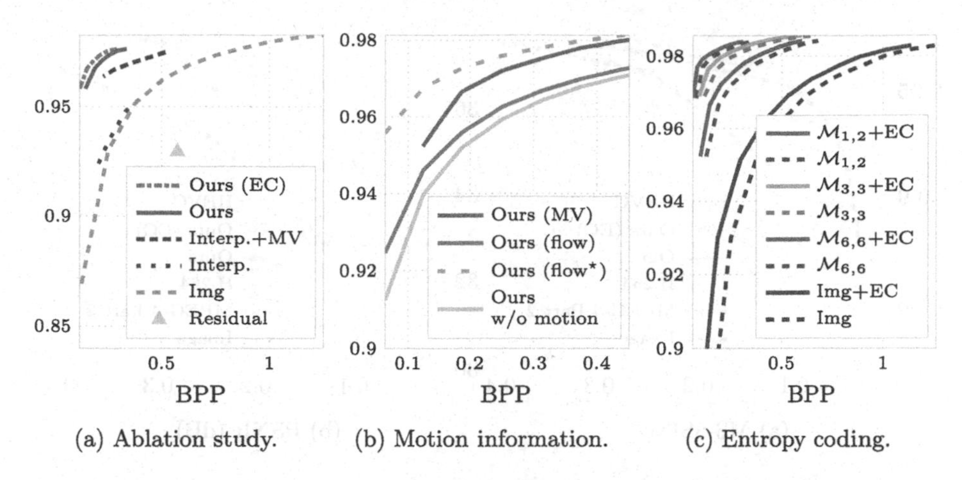

(a) Ablation study. (b) Motion information. (c) Entropy coding.

Fig. 4. MS-SSIM of different models evaluated on the VTL dataset.

Our final model efficiently encodes residual information and makes good use of hierarchical referencing. It achieves the best performance when combined with entropy coding. Note the large performance gap between our method and the image compression model in the low bitrate regime – our model effectively exploits context and achieves a good performance with very few bits per pixel.

As a sanity check, we further implemented a simple deep codec that uses image compression to encode the residual $\mathcal{R}$ in traditional codecs. This simple baseline stores the video as the encoded residuals, compressed motion vectors, in addition to key frames compressed by a separate deep image compression model. The residual model struggles to learn patterns from noisy residual images, and works worse than an image-only compression model. This suggests that trivially extending deep image compression to videos is not sufficient. Our end-to-end interpolation network performs considerably better.

Motion. Next, we analyze different motion estimation models, and compare optical flow to block motion vectors. For optical flow, we use the OpenCV implementation of the Farnebäck's algorithm [8]. For motion compensation, we use the same algorithm as H.264.

Figure 4b shows the results of the $\mathcal{M}_{6,6}$ model with both motion sources. Using motion information clearly helps improve the performance of the model, despite the overhead of motion compression. Block motion estimation (MV) works significantly better than the optical flow based model (flow). Almost all of this performance gain comes from better compressible motion information. The block motion estimates are smaller, easier to compress, and fit in a lossless compression scheme.

To understand whether the worse performance of optical flow is due to the errors in flow compression or the property of the flow itself, we further measure the *hypothetical* performance upper bound of an optical flow based model *assuming* a lossless flow compression at no additional cost (flow*). As shown

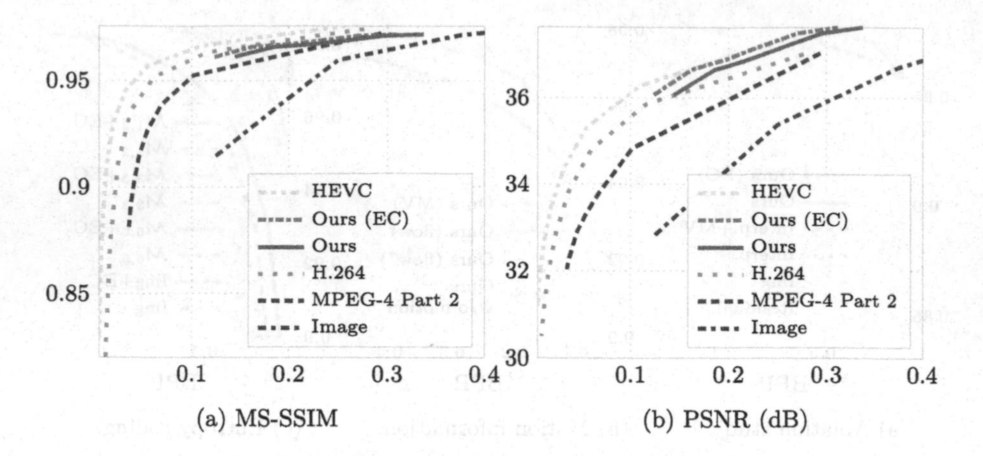

Fig. 5. Performance on the UVG dataset.

in Fig. 4b, this upper bound performs better than motion vectors, leaving room for improvement through compressible optical flow estimation. However, finding such a compressible flow estimate is beyond the scope of this paper. In the rest of this section, we use block motion estimates in all our experiments.

Individual Interpolation Models and Entropy Coding. Figure 4c shows the performance of different interpolation models with and without entropy coding. For all models, entropy coding saves up to 52% BPP, at a low bitrate, and at least 10%, at a high bitrate. More interestingly, the short time-frame interpolation is almost free, achieving the same visual quality as an image-based model at one or two orders of magnitude lower BPP. This shows that most of our bitrate saving comes from the interpolation models at lower levels in the hierarchy.

5.2 Comparison to Prior Work

We now quantitatively evaluate our method on all three datasets and compare our method with today's prevailing codecs, HEVC (H.265), H.264, MPEG-4 Part 2, and H.261. For consistent comparison, we use the same GOP size, 12, for H.264 and HEVC. We test H.261 on only VTL and Kinetics-5K, since it does not support high-resolution (1920 × 1080) videos of the UVG dataset.

Figures 5, 6 and 7 present the results. Despite its simplicity, our model greatly outperforms MPEG-4 Part 2 and H.261, performs on par with H.264, and close to state-of-the-art HEVC. In particular, on the high-resolution UVG dataset, it outperforms H.264 by a good margin and matches HEVC in terms of PSNR.

Our testing datasets are not just large in scale (>100K frames of >5K videos), they also consist of videos in a wide range of sizes (from 352 × 288 to 1920 × 1080), time (from 1990s for most VTL videos to 2018 for Kinetics), quality (from professional UVG to user uploaded Kinetics), and contents (from scenes,

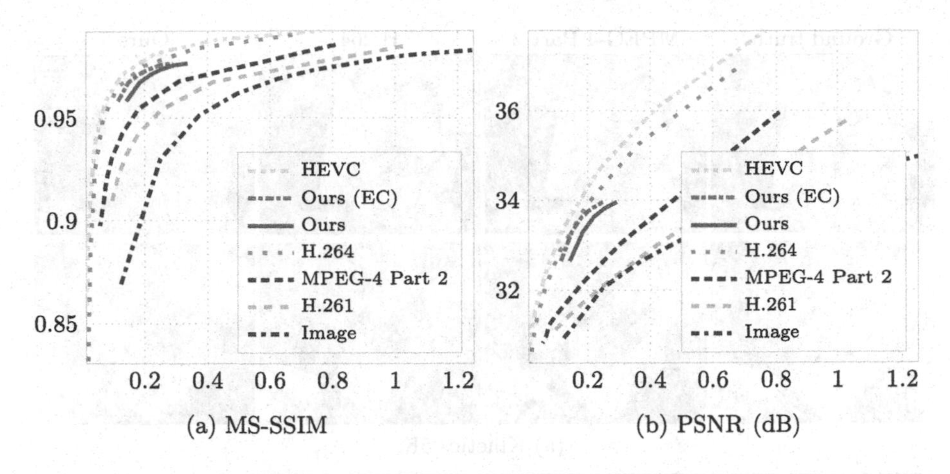

(a) MS-SSIM (b) PSNR (dB)

Fig. 6. Performance on the VTL dataset.

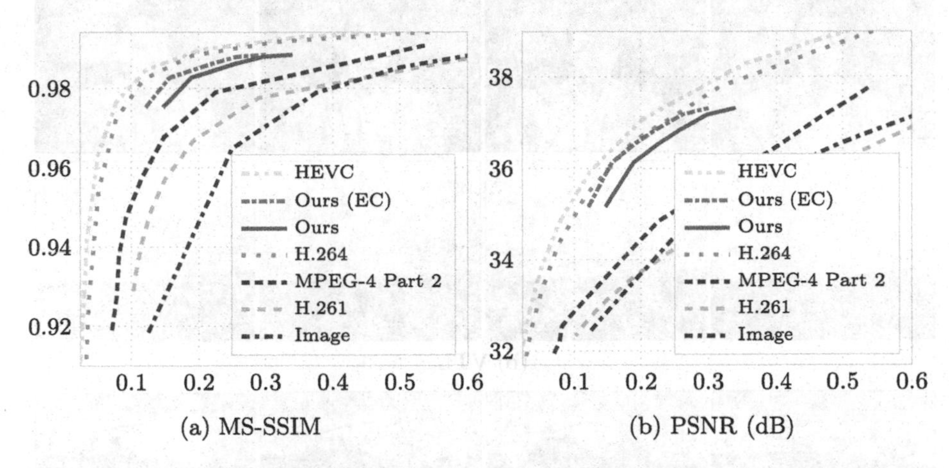

(a) MS-SSIM (b) PSNR (dB)

Fig. 7. Performance on the Kinetics-5K dataset.

animals, to the 400 human activities in Kinetics). Our model, trained on only one dataset, works well on all of them.

Finally, we present qualitative results of three of the best performing models, MPEG-4 Part 2, H.264 and ours in Fig. 8. All models here use 0.12 ± 0.01 BPP. We can see that in all datasets, our method shows faithful images without any blocky artifacts. It greatly outperforms MPEG-4 Part 2 without bells and whistles, and matches state-of-the-art H.264.

(a) Kinetics-5K

(b) VTL

(c) UVG

Fig. 8. Comparison of compression results at 0.12 ± 0.01 BPP. Our method shows faithful images without any blocky artifacts. (Best viewed on screen.) More examples and demo videos showing temporal coherence are available at https://chaoyuaw.github.io/vcii/.

6 Conclusion

This paper presents, to the best of our knowledge, the first end-to-end trained deep video codec. It relies on repeated deep image interpolation. To disambiguate the interpolation, we encode a few compressible bits of information representing information not inferred from the neighboring key frames. This yields a faithful reconstruction instead of pure hallucination. The network is directly trained to optimize reconstruction, without prior engineering knowledge.

Our deep codec is simple, and outperforms the prevailing codecs such as MPEG-4 Part 2 or H.261, matching state-of-the-art H.264. We have not considered the engineering aspects such as runtime or real-time compression. We think they are important directions for future research.

In short, video compression powered by deep image interpolation achieves state-of-the-art performance without sophisticated heuristics or excessive engineering.

Acknowledgment. We would like to thank Manzil Zaheer, Angela Lin, Ashish Bora, and Thomas Crosley for their valuable comments and feedback on this paper. This work was supported in part by Berkeley DeepDrive and an equipment grant from Nvidia.

References

1. Ultra video group test sequences. http://ultravideo.cs.tut.fi. Accessed 11 Mar 2018
2. Video trace library. http://trace.eas.asu.edu/index.html. Accessed 11 Mar 2018
3. WebP. https://developers.google.com/speed/webp/. Accessed 11 Mar 2018
4. Agustsson, E., et al.: Soft-to-hard vector quantization for end-to-end learning compressible representations. In: NIPS (2017)
5. Baig, M.H., Koltun, V., Torresani, L.: Learning to inpaint for image compression. In: NIPS (2017)
6. Ballé, J., Laparra, V., Simoncelli, E.P.: End-to-end optimized image compression. In: ICLR (2017)
7. Carreira, J., Zisserman, A.: Quo vadis, action recognition? A new model and the kinetics dataset. In: CVPR (2017)
8. Farnebäck, G.: Two-frame motion estimation based on polynomial expansion. In: Bigun, J., Gustavsson, T. (eds.) SCIA 2003. LNCS, vol. 2749, pp. 363–370. Springer, Heidelberg (2003). https://doi.org/10.1007/3-540-45103-X_50
9. Jia, X., De Brabandere, B., Tuytelaars, T., Gool, L.V.: Dynamic filter networks. In: NIPS (2016)
10. Jiang, H., Sun, D., Jampani, V., Yang, M.H., Learned-Miller, E., Kautz, J.: Super slomo: high quality estimation of multiple intermediate frames for video interpolation. In: CVPR (2018)
11. Johnston, N., et al.: Improved lossy image compression with priming and spatially adaptive bit rates for recurrent networks (2017). arXiv preprint: arXiv:1703.10114
12. Kingma, D.P., Ba, J.: Adam: a method for stochastic optimization (2014). arXiv preprint: arXiv:1412.6980
13. Le Gall, D.: MPEG: a video compression standard for multimedia applications. Commun. ACM **34**, 46–58 (1991)

14. Liu, Z., Yeh, R., Tang, X., Liu, Y., Agarwala, A.: Video frame synthesis using deep voxel flow. In: ICCV (2017)
15. Mathieu, M., Couprie, C., LeCun, Y.: Deep multi-scale video prediction beyond mean square error. In: ICLR (2016)
16. Mentzer, F., Agustsson, E., Tschannen, M., Timofte, R., Van Gool, L.: Conditional probability models for deep image compression. In: CVPR (2018)
17. Cisco Visual Networking Index: Forecast and methodology, 2016-2021. CISCO White paper (2016)
18. Niklaus, S., Mai, L., Liu, F.: Video frame interpolation via adaptive separable convolution. In: ICCV (2017)
19. van den Oord, A., Kalchbrenner, N., Kavukcuoglu, K.: Pixel recurrent neural networks. In: ICML (2016)
20. Richardson, I.E.: Video Codec Design: Developing Image and Video Compression Systems. John Wiley & Sons, Chichester (2002)
21. Rippel, O., Bourdev, L.: Real-time adaptive image compression. In: ICML (2017)
22. Ronneberger, O., Fischer, P., Brox, T.: U-Net: convolutional networks for biomedical image segmentation. In: Navab, N., Hornegger, J., Wells, W.M., Frangi, A.F. (eds.) MICCAI 2015, Part III. LNCS, vol. 9351, pp. 234–241. Springer, Cham (2015). https://doi.org/10.1007/978-3-319-24574-4_28
23. Schwarz, H., Marpe, D., Wiegand, T.: Overview of the scalable video coding extension of the H.264/AVC standard. TCSVT **17**(9), 1103–1120 (2007)
24. Theis, L., Shi, W., Cunningham, A., Huszár, F.: Lossy image compression with compressive autoencoders. In: ICLR (2017)
25. Toderici, G., et al.: Full resolution image compression with recurrent neural networks. In: CVPR (2017)
26. Tsai, Y.H., Liu, M.Y., Sun, D., Yang, M.H., Kautz, J.: Learning binary residual representations for domain-specific video streaming. In: AAAI (2018)
27. Vondrick, C., Pirsiavash, H., Torralba, A.: Generating videos with scene dynamics. In: NIPS (2016)
28. Wang, Z., Simoncelli, E.P., Bovik, A.C.: Multiscale structural similarity for image quality assessment. In: ACSSC (2003)
29. Williams, R.J.: Simple statistical gradient-following algorithms for connectionist reinforcement learning. In: Sutton, R.S. (ed.) Reinforcement Learning. The Springer International Series in Engineering and Computer Science (Knowledge Representation, Learning and Expert Systems), vol. 173, pp. 5–23. Springer, Boston (1992). https://doi.org/10.1007/978-1-4615-3618-5_2
30. Witten, I.H., Neal, R.M., Cleary, J.G.: Arithmetic coding for data compression. Commun. ACM **30**, 520–540 (1987)
31. Wu, C.Y., Zaheer, M., Hu, H., Manmatha, R., Smola, A.J., Krähenbühl, P.: Compressed video action recognition. In: CVPR (2018)
32. Xue, T., Wu, J., Bouman, K., Freeman, B.: Visual dynamics: Probabilistic future frame synthesis via cross convolutional networks. In: NIPS (2016)

Few-Shot Human Motion Prediction via Meta-learning

Liang-Yan Gui[(✉)], Yu-Xiong Wang, Deva Ramanan, and José M. F. Moura

Carnegie Mellon University, Pittsburgh, USA
{lgui,yuxiongw,deva,moura}@andrew.cmu.edu

Abstract. Human motion prediction, forecasting human motion in a few milliseconds conditioning on a historical 3D skeleton sequence, is a long-standing problem in computer vision and robotic vision. Existing forecasting algorithms rely on extensive annotated motion capture data and are brittle to novel actions. This paper addresses the problem of *few-shot* human motion prediction, in the spirit of the recent progress on few-shot learning and meta-learning. More precisely, our approach is based on the insight that having a good generalization from few examples relies on both a generic initial model and an effective strategy for adapting this model to novel tasks. To accomplish this, we propose *proactive and adaptive meta-learning (PAML)* that introduces a novel combination of model-agnostic meta-learning and model regression networks and unifies them into an *integrated, end-to-end* framework. By doing so, our meta-learner produces a generic initial model through aggregating contextual information from a variety of prediction tasks, while effectively adapting this model for use as a task-specific one by leveraging *learning-to-learn* knowledge about how to transform few-shot model parameters to many-shot model parameters. The resulting PAML predictor model significantly improves the prediction performance on the heavily benchmarked H3.6M dataset in the small-sample size regime.

Keywords: Human motion prediction · Few-shot learning
Meta-learning

1 Introduction

One of the hallmarks of human intelligence is the ability to predict the future based on past observations. Through perceiving and forecasting how the environment evolves and how a fellow human acts, a human learns to interact with the world [60]. Remarkably, humans acquire such a prediction ability from just a few experiences, which is yet generalizable across different scenarios [50]. Similarly, to allow natural and effective interaction with humans, artificial agents (*e.g.*, robots) should be able to do the same, *i.e.*, forecasting how a human moves or acts in the near future conditioning on a series of historical movements [29]. As a more concrete example illustrated in Fig. 1, when deployed in natural environments, robots are supposed to predict unfamiliar actions after seeing only a

V. Ferrari et al. (Eds.): ECCV 2018, LNCS 11212, pp. 441–459, 2018.
https://doi.org/10.1007/978-3-030-01237-3_27

Fig. 1. Illustration of the importance of few-shot human motion prediction as a first step towards seamless human-robot interaction and collaboration. In real-world scenarios, the prediction typically happens *in an on-line, streaming manner* with limited training data. Specifically, a robot has acquired a general-purpose prediction ability, *e.g.*, through learning on several known action classes using our meta-learning approach. The robot is then deployed in a natural environment. Now a person performs certain *never-before-seen* action, *e.g.*, greeting, while the robot is watching (a). The person then stops, and the robot has no sensory inputs, which is illustrated by blinding its eyes with a sheet of paper (b). The robot adapts the generic initial model for use as a task-specific predictor model, predicts the future motion of the person, and performs or demonstrates it in a human-like, realistic way (c) and (d).

few examples [20,27]. While human motion prediction has attracted increasing attention [9,16,19,26,32], the existing approaches rely on extensive annotated motion capture (mocap) data and are brittle to novel actions.

We believe that the significant gap between human and machine prediction arises from two issues. First, motion dynamics are difficult to model because they entangle physical constraints with goal-directed behaviors [32]. Beyond some action classes (*e.g.*, walking) [8,22], it is challenging to generate sophisticated physical models for general types of motion [42]. Second, there exists a lack of large-scale, annotated motion data. Current mocap datasets are constructed with dedicated sensored environments and so are *not scalable*. This motivates the exploration of motion models learned from limited training data. Unfortunately, a substantial amount of annotated data is required for the state-of-the-art deep recurrent encoder-decoder network based models [4,16,18,19,26,32] to learn the desired motion dynamics. One stark evidence of this is that a constant pose predictor [32], as a naïve approach that does not produce interesting motion, sometimes achieves the best performance. An attractive solution is learning a "basis" of underlying knowledge that is shared across a wide variety of action classes, including never-before-seen actions. This can be in principle achieved by transfer learning [3,38,44,68] in a way that fine-tunes a pre-trained network from another task which has more labeled data; nevertheless, the benefit of pre-training decreases as the source task diverges from the target task [70].

Here we make the first attempt towards *few-shot human motion prediction*. Inspired by the recent progress on few-shot learning and meta-learning [14,47,58, 61,66], we propose a general meta-learning framework—*proactive and adaptive meta-learning (PAML)*, which can be applied to human motion prediction. *Our key insight* is that having a good generalization from few examples relies on both a generic initial model and an effective strategy for adapting this model to novel tasks. We then introduce a novel combination of the state-of-the-art model-agnostic meta-learning (MAML) [14] and model regression networks (MRN) [66, 69], and unify them into an *integrated, end-to-end* framework. MAML enables the meta-learner to aggregate contextual information from various prediction tasks and thus produces a generic model initialization, while MRN allows the meta-learner to adapt a few-shot model and thus improves its generalization.

More concretely, a beneficial common initialization would serve as a good point to start training for a novel action being considered. This can be accomplished by explicitly learning the initial parameters of a predictor model in a way that the model has maximal performance on a new task after the parameters have been updated with a few training examples from that new task. Hence, we make use of MAML [14], which initializes the weights of a network such that standard stochastic gradient descent (SGD) can make rapid progress on a new task. We learn this initialization through a meta-learning procedure that learns from a large set of motion prediction tasks with small amounts of data. After obtaining the pre-trained model, MAML uses one or few SGD updates to adapt it to a novel task. Although the initial model is somewhat generic, plain SGD updates can only slightly modify its parameters [68] especially in the small-sample size regime; otherwise, it would lead to severe over-fitting to the new data [23]. This is still far from satisfactory, because the obtained task-specific model is different from the one that would be learned from a large set of samples.

To address this limitation, we consider meta-learning approaches that learn an update function or learning rule. Specifically, we leverage MRN [66, 69] as the adaptation strategy, which describes a method for learning from small datasets through estimating a generic model transformation. That is, MRN learns a meta-level network that operates on the space of model parameters, which is trained to regress many-shot model parameters (trained on large datasets) from few-shot model parameters (trained on small datasets). While MRN was developed in the context of convolutional neural networks, we extend it to recurrent neural networks. By unifying MAML with MRN, our resulting PAML model is not only directly initialized to produce the desired parameters that are useful for later adaptation, but it can also be effectively adapted to novel actions through exploiting the structure of model parameters shared across action classes.

Our contributions are three-fold. (1) To the best of our knowledge, this is the first time the few-shot learning problem for human motion prediction has been explored. We show how meta-learning can be operationalized for such a task. (2) We present a novel meta-learning approach, combining MAML with MRN, that jointly learns a generic model initialization and an effective model adaptation strategy. Our approach is general and can be applied to different tasks. (3) We show how our approach significantly facilitates the prediction of novel actions from few examples on the challenging mocap H3.6M dataset [25].

2 Related Work

Human motion prediction has great application potential in computer vision and robotic vision, including human-robot interaction and collaboration [29], motion generation for computer graphics [30], action anticipation [24,28], and proactive decision-making in autonomous driving systems [37]. It is typically addressed by state-space equations and latent-variable models. Traditional approaches focus on hidden Markov models [7], linear dynamic models [41], Gaussian process latent variable models [59,62], bilinear spatio-temporal basis models [1], and restricted Boltzmann machines [52–55]. In the deep learning era, recurrent neural networks (RNNs) based approaches have attracted more attention and significantly pushed the state of the art [16,18,19,26,32].

Flagship techniques include LSTM-3LR and ERD [16], SRNNs [26], and residual sup. [32]. LSTM-3LR (3-layer long short-term memory network) learns pose representation and temporal dynamics simultaneously via curriculum learning [16]. In additional to the concatenated LSTM units as in LSTM-3LR, ERD (encoder-recurrent-decoder) further introduces non-linear space encoders for data preprocessing [16]. SRNNs (structural RNNs) model human activity with a hand-designed spatio-temporal graph and introduce the encoded semantic knowledge into recurrent networks [26]. These approaches fail to consider the shared knowledge across action classes and they thus learn action-specific models and restrict the training process on the corresponding subsets of the mocap dataset. Residual sup. is a simple sequence-to-sequence architecture with a residual connection, which incorporates the action class information via one-hot vectors [32]. Despite their promise, these existing methods directly learn on the target task with large amounts of training data and cannot generalize well from a few examples or to novel action classes. There has been little work on few-shot motion prediction as ours, which is crucial for robot learning in practice. Our task is also significantly different from few-shot imitation learning: while this line of work aims to learn and mimic human motion from demonstration [11,15,39,71], our goal is to *predict unseen future* motion based on historical observations.

Few-shot or low-shot learning has long stood as one of the unsolved fundamental problems and been addressed from different perspectives [13,14,17,21,45, 56,61,63–67]. Our approach falls more into a classic yet recently renovated class of approaches, termed as meta-learning that frames few-shot learning itself as a "*learning-to-learn*" problem [47,57,58]. The idea is to use the common knowledge captured among a set of few-shot learning tasks during meta-training for a novel few-shot learning problem, in a way that (1) accumulates statistics over the training set using RNNs [61], memory-augmented networks [45], or multilayer perceptrons [12], (2) produces a generic network initialization [14,36,65], (3) embeds examples into a universal feature space [51], (4) estimates the model parameters that would be learned from a large dataset using a few novel class examples [6] or from a small dataset model [66,69], (5) modifies the weights of one network using another [46,48,49], and (6) learns to optimize through a learned update rule instead of hand-designed SGD [2,31,43].

Often, these prior approaches are developed with image classification in mind, and cannot be easily re-purposed to handle different model architectures or readily applicable to other domains such as human motion prediction. Moreover, they aim to either obtain a better model initialization [14,36,65] or learn an update function or learning rule [2,5,43,48,66], *but not both.* By contrast, we present a unified view by taking these two aspects into consideration and show how they complement each other in an end-to-end meta-learning framework. Our approach is also general and can be applied to other tasks as well.

3 Proactive and Adaptive Meta-learning

We now present our meta-learning framework for few-shot human motion prediction. The predictor (*i.e.*, learner) is a recurrent encoder-decoder network, which frames motion prediction as a sequence-to-sequence problem. To enable the predictor to rapidly produce satisfactory prediction from just a few training sequences for a novel task (*i.e.*, action class), we introduce proactive and adaptive meta-learning (PAML). Through meta-learning from a large collection of few-shot prediction tasks on known action classes, PAML jointly learns a generic model initialization and an effective model adaptation strategy.

3.1 Meta-learning Setup for Human Motion Prediction

Human motion is typically represented as sequential data. Given a historical motion sequence, we predict possible motion in the short-term or long-term future. In *few-shot motion prediction*, we aim to train a predictor model that can quickly adapt to a new task using only a few training sequences. To achieve this, we introduce a *meta-learning mechanism* that treats entire prediction tasks as training examples. During meta-learning, the predictor is trained on a set of prediction tasks guided by a *high-level meta-learner*, such that the trained predictor can accomplish the desired few-shot adaptation ability.

The predictor (*i.e.*, learner), represented by a parametrized function $\mathcal{P}_\theta$ with parameters θ, maps an input historical sequence $\mathbf{X}$ to an output future sequence $\widehat{\mathbf{Y}}$. We denote the input motion sequence of length n as $\mathbf{X} = \{\mathbf{x}^1, \mathbf{x}^2, \ldots, \mathbf{x}^n\}$, where $\mathbf{x}^i \in \mathbb{R}^d, i = 1, \ldots, n$ is a mocap vector consisting of a set of 3D body joint angles [35], and d is the number of joint angles. The learner predicts the future sequence $\widehat{\mathbf{Y}} = \{\widehat{\mathbf{x}}^{n+1}, \widehat{\mathbf{x}}^{n+2}, \ldots, \widehat{\mathbf{x}}^{n+m}\}$ in the next m timesteps, where $\widehat{\mathbf{x}}^j \in \mathbb{R}^d, j = n+1, \ldots, n+m$ is the predicted mocap vector at the j-th timestep. The groundtruth of the future sequence is denoted as $\mathbf{Y}^{gt} = \{\mathbf{x}^{n+1}, \mathbf{x}^{n+2}, \ldots, \mathbf{x}^{n+m}\}$.

During meta-learning, we are interested in training a *learning procedure* (*i.e.*, the meta-learner) that enables the predictor model to adapt to a large number of prediction tasks. For the k-shot prediction task, each task $\mathcal{T} = \{\mathcal{L}, \mathcal{D}_{\text{train}}, \mathcal{D}_{\text{test}}\}$ aims to predict a certain action from a few (k) examples. It consists of a loss function $\mathcal{L}$, a small training set $\mathcal{D}_{\text{train}} = \{(\mathbf{X}_u, \mathbf{Y}_u^{gt})\}, u = 1, \ldots, k$ with k action-specific past and future sequence pairs, and a test set $\mathcal{D}_{\text{test}}$ that has a set number of past and future sequence pairs for evaluation. A frame-wise Euclidean distance is commonly used as the loss function $\mathcal{L}$ for motion prediction. For each task, the meta-learner takes $\mathcal{D}_{\text{train}}$ as input and produces a predictor (*i.e.*, learner) that achieves high average prediction performance on its corresponding $\mathcal{D}_{\text{test}}$.

More precisely, we consider a distribution $p(\mathcal{T})$ over prediction tasks that we want our predictor to be able to adapt to. Meta-learning algorithms have two phases: meta-training and meta-test. During meta-training, a prediction task $\mathcal{T}_i$ is sampled from $p(\mathcal{T})$, and the predictor $\mathcal{P}$ is trained on its corresponding small training set $\mathcal{D}_{\text{train}}$ with the loss $\mathcal{L}_{\mathcal{T}_i}$ from $\mathcal{T}_i$. The predictor is then improved by considering how the test error on the corresponding test set $\mathcal{D}_{\text{test}}$ changes with respect to the parameters. This test error serves as the *training error* of the meta-learning process. During meta-test, a held-out set of prediction tasks drawn from $p(\mathcal{T})$ (*i.e.*, novel action classes), each with its own small training set $\mathcal{D}_{\text{train}}$ and test set $\mathcal{D}_{\text{test}}$, is used to evaluate the performance of the predictor.

3.2 Learner: Encoder-Decoder Architecture

We use the state-of-the-art recurrent encoder-decoder network based motion predictor in [32] as our learner $\mathcal{P}$. The encoder and decoder consist of GRU (gated recurrent unit) [10] cells as building blocks. The input sequence is passed through the encoder to infer a latent representation. This latent representation and a seed motion frame are then fed into the decoder to output the first timestep prediction. The decoder takes its own output as the next timestep input and generates further prediction sequentially. Different from [32], to deal with novel action classes, we do not use one-hot vectors to indicate the action class.

3.3 Proactive Meta-learner: Generic Model Initialization

Intuitively, if we have a *universal predictor* that is broadly applicable to a variety of tasks in $p(\mathcal{T})$ instead of a specific task, it would serve as a good point to start training for a novel target task. We explicitly learn such a general-purpose initial model by using model-agnostic meta-learning (MAML) [14]. MAML is developed for gradient-based learning rules (*e.g.*, SGD) and aims to learn a model in a way that a few SGD updates can make rapid progress on a new task.

Concretely, when adapting to a new task $\mathcal{T}_i$, the initial parameters θ of the predictor become θ'_i. In MAML, this is computed using one or more SGD updates on $\mathcal{D}_{\text{train}}$ of task $\mathcal{T}_i$. For the sake of simplicity and without loss of generality, we consider one SGD update:

$$\theta'_i = \theta - \alpha \nabla_\theta \mathcal{L}_{\mathcal{T}_i}\left(\mathcal{P}_\theta\right), \tag{1}$$

where α is the learning rate hyper-parameter. We optimize θ such that the updated θ'_i will produce maximal performance on $\mathcal{D}_{\text{test}}$ of task $\mathcal{T}_i$. When averaged across the tasks sampled from $p(\mathcal{T})$, we have the meta-objective function:

$$\min_\theta \sum_{\mathcal{T}_i \sim p(\mathcal{T})} \mathcal{L}_{\mathcal{T}_i}\left(\mathcal{P}_{\theta'_i}\right) = \min_\theta \sum_{\mathcal{T}_i \sim p(\mathcal{T})} \mathcal{L}_{\mathcal{T}_i}\left(\mathcal{P}_{\theta - \alpha \nabla_\theta \mathcal{L}_{\mathcal{T}_i}(\mathcal{P}_\theta)}\right). \tag{2}$$

Note that the meta-optimization is performed over the predictor parameters θ, whereas the objective is computed using the updated parameters θ'. This meta-optimization across tasks is performed via SGD in the form of

$$\theta \leftarrow \theta - \beta \nabla_\theta \sum_{\mathcal{T}_i \sim p(\mathcal{T})} \mathcal{L}_{\mathcal{T}_i}\left(\mathcal{P}_{\theta_i'}\right), \tag{3}$$

where β is the meta-learning rate hyper-parameter. During each iteration, we sample task mini-batch from $p(\mathcal{T})$ and perform the corresponding learner update in Eq. (1) and meta-learner update in Eq. (3).

3.4 Adaptive Meta-learner: Model Adaptation Strategy

In MAML, the model parameters θ_i' of a new task $\mathcal{T}_i$ are obtained by performing a few plain SGD updates on top of the initial θ using its small training set $\mathcal{D}_{\text{train}}$. After meta-training, θ tend to be generic. However, with limited training data from $\mathcal{D}_{\text{train}}$, SGD updates can only modify θ slightly, which is still far from the desired θ_i^* that would be learned from a large set of target samples. Higher-level knowledge is thus necessary to guide the model adaptation to novel tasks.

In fact, during meta-training, for each of the *known action classes*, we have a large training set of annotated sequences, and we sample from this original large set to generate few-shot training sequences. Note that for the novel classes during meta-test, there are no large annotated training sets. Such a setup—meta-learners are trained by sampling small training sets from a large universe of annotated examples—is common in few-shot image classification through meta-learning [14,21,61,66]. While the previous approaches (*e.g.*, MAML) only use this original large set for sampling few-shot training sets, we *explicitly* leverage it and learn the corresponding many-shot model θ_i^* for $\mathcal{T}_i$. During sampling, if some tasks are sampled from the same action class, while they have their own few-shot training sequences, these tasks correspond to the same θ_i^* of that action class. We then use model regression networks (MRN) [66,69] as the adaptation strategy. MRN is developed in image classification scenarios and obtains learning-to-learn knowledge about a generic transformation from few-shot to many-shot models.

Let θ_i^0 denote the model parameters learned from $\mathcal{D}_{\text{train}}$ by using SGD (*i.e.*, θ_i' in Eq. (1)). Let θ_i^* denote the *underlying* model parameters learned from a large set of annotated samples. We aim to make the updated θ_i' as close as to the desired θ_i^*. MRN assumes that there exists a generic non-linear transformation, represented by a regression function $\mathcal{H}_\phi$ parameterized by ϕ in the model parameter space, such that $\theta_i^* \approx \mathcal{H}_\phi\left(\theta_i^0\right)$ for a broad range of tasks $\mathcal{T}_i$. The square of the Euclidean distance is used as the regression loss. We then estimate $\mathcal{H}_\phi$ based on a large set of known tasks $\mathcal{T}_i$ drawn from $p(\mathcal{T})$ during meta-training:

$$\min_\phi \sum_{\mathcal{T}_i \sim p(\mathcal{T})} \left\|\mathcal{H}_\phi\left(\theta_i^0\right) - \theta_i^*\right\|_2^2. \tag{4}$$

Consistent with [66], we use multilayer feed-forward networks as $\mathcal{H}$.

Algorithm 1: PAML Meta-Training for k-Shot Human Motion Prediction

Require: Learner: motion predictor model $\mathcal{P}_\theta$ with parameters θ;
MRN adaptation meta-network: $\mathcal{H}_\phi$ with parameters ϕ
Require: $p(\mathcal{T})$: distribution over prediction tasks
Require: α, β, γ: learning or meta-learning rate hyper-parameters;
λ: trade-off hyper-parameter

1 Randomly initialize θ and ϕ
2 **while** *not done* **do**
3 Sample batch of tasks $\mathcal{T}_i \sim p(\mathcal{T})$
4 **for** *all* $\mathcal{T}_i$ **do**
5 Learn (or retrieve) θ_i^* from the original large set of annotated past and future sequence pairs of the corresponding action class
6 Sample k action-specific past and future sequence pairs $\mathcal{D}_{\text{train}} = \left\{\left(\mathbf{X}_u, \mathbf{Y}_u^{gt}\right)\right\}, u = 1, \dots, k$ from $\mathcal{T}_i$
7 Evaluate $\mathcal{L}_{\mathcal{T}_i}(\mathcal{P}_\theta)$ on $\mathcal{D}_{\text{train}}$
8 Compute adapted parameters using Eq. (5), *i.e.*, performing SGD updates then applying adaptation $\mathcal{H}$: $\theta_i' = \mathcal{H}_\phi\left(\theta - \alpha \nabla_\theta \mathcal{L}_{\mathcal{T}_i}(\mathcal{P}_\theta)\right)$
9 Sample $\mathcal{D}_{\text{test}} = \left\{\left(\mathbf{X}_v, \mathbf{Y}_v^{gt}\right)\right\}$ from $\mathcal{T}_i$ for the meta-update
10 Evaluate $\widetilde{\mathcal{L}}_{\mathcal{T}_i}\left(\mathcal{P}_{\theta_i'}\right) = \mathcal{L}_{\mathcal{T}_i}\left(\mathcal{P}_{\theta_i'}\right) + \frac{1}{2}\lambda \|\theta_i' - \theta_i^*\|_2^2$ on $\mathcal{D}_{\text{test}}$ using Eq. (6)
11 **end for**
12 Update θ and ϕ by performing SGD:
13 $\theta \leftarrow \theta - \beta \nabla_\theta \sum_{\mathcal{T}_i \sim p(\mathcal{T})} \widetilde{\mathcal{L}}_{\mathcal{T}_i}\left(\mathcal{P}_{\theta_i'}\right)$, $\phi \leftarrow \phi - \gamma \nabla_\phi \sum_{\mathcal{T}_i \sim p(\mathcal{T})} \widetilde{\mathcal{L}}_{\mathcal{T}_i}\left(\mathcal{P}_{\theta_i'}\right)$
14 **end while**

3.5 An Integrated Framework

We introduce the adaptation strategy in both the meta-training and meta-test phases. For task $\mathcal{T}_i$, after performing a few SGD updates on small training set $\mathcal{D}_{\text{train}}$, we then apply the transformation $\mathcal{H}$ to obtain θ_i'. Equation (1) is modified as

$$\theta_i' = \mathcal{H}_\phi\left(\theta - \alpha \nabla_\theta \mathcal{L}_{\mathcal{T}_i}(\mathcal{P}_\theta)\right). \tag{5}$$

During *meta-training*, for task $\mathcal{T}_i$, we also have the underlying parameters θ_i^*, which are obtained by performing SGD updates on the corresponding large sample set. Now, the meta-objective in Eq. (2) becomes

$$\min_{\theta,\phi} \sum_{\mathcal{T}_i \sim p(\mathcal{T})} \widetilde{\mathcal{L}}_{\mathcal{T}_i}\left(\mathcal{P}_{\theta_i'}\right) = \min_{\theta,\phi} \sum_{\mathcal{T}_i \sim p(\mathcal{T})} \mathcal{L}_{\mathcal{T}_i}\left(\mathcal{P}_{\theta_i'}\right) + \frac{1}{2}\lambda \|\theta_i' - \theta_i^*\|_2^2, \tag{6}$$

where λ is the trade-off hyper-parameter. This is a *joint optimization* with respect to both θ and ϕ, and we perform the meta-optimization across tasks using SGD, as shown in Algorithm 1. Hence, we integrate both model initialization and adaptation into an end-to-end meta-learning framework. The model is initialized to produce the parameters that are optimal for its adaptation; meanwhile, the model is adapted by leveraging "learning-to-learn" knowledge about

Table 1. Performance sanity check of our approach by comparing with some state-of-the-art meta-learning approaches to few-shot image classification on the widely used mini-ImageNet dataset. Our PAML outperforms these baselines, showing its general effectiveness for few-shot learning

Method	5-way accuracy	
	1-shot	5-shot
Matching networks [61]	$43.56\% \pm 0.84\%$	$55.31\% \pm 0.73\%$
MAML [14]	$48.70\% \pm 1.84\%$	$63.11\% \pm 0.92\%$
Meta-learner LSTM [43]	$43.44\% \pm 0.77\%$	$60.60\% \pm 0.71\%$
Prototypical networks [51]	$46.61\% \pm 0.78\%$	$65.77\% \pm 0.70\%$
Meta networks [34]	$49.21\% \pm 0.96\%$	– –
PAML (Ours)	$\mathbf{53.26\% \pm 0.52\%}$	$\mathbf{68.19\% \pm 0.61\%}$

the relationship between few-shot and many-shot models. During *meta-test*, for a novel prediction task, with the learned generic model initialization θ and model adaptation $\mathcal{H}_\phi$, we use Eq. (5) to obtain the task-specific predictor model.

4 Experimental Evaluation

In this section, we explore the use of our proactive and adaptive meta-learning (PAML). PAML is general and can be in principle applied to a broad range of few-shot learning tasks. For performance calibration, we begin with a sanity check of our approach on a standard few-shot image classification task and compare with existing meta-learning approaches. We then focus on our main task of human motion prediction. Through comparing with the state-of-the-art motion prediction approaches, we show that PAML significantly improves the prediction performance in the small-sample size regime.

4.1 Sanity Check on Few-Shot Image Classification

The majority of the existing few-shot learning and meta-learning approaches are developed in the scenario of classification tasks. As a sanity check, the first question is how our meta-learning approach compares with these prior techniques. For a fair comparison, we evaluate on the standard few-shot image classification task. The most common setup is an N-way, k-shot classification that aims to classify data into N classes when we only have a small number (k) of labeled instances per class for training. The loss function is the cross-entropy error between the predicted and true labels. Following [14, 33, 34, 43, 51, 61], we evaluate on the most widely used mini-ImageNet benchmark. It consists of 64 meta-training and 24 meta-test classes, with 600 images of size 84×84 per class.

During meta-training, each task is sampled as an N-way, k-shot classification problem: we first randomly sample N classes from the meta-training classes; for each class, we randomly sample k and 1 examples to form the training and test set, respectively. During meta-test, we report performance on the unseen classes from the meta-test classes. We use the convolutional network in [14] as the classifier (*i.e.*, learner). Our model adaptation meta-network is a 2-layer fully-connected network with Leaky ReLU nonlinearity.

Table 1 summarizes the performance comparisons in the standard 5-way, 1-/5-shot setting. Our PAML consistently outperforms all the baselines. In particular, there is a notable 5% performance improvement compared with MAML, showing the complementary benefits of our model adaptation strategy. This sanity check verifies the effectiveness of our meta-learning framework. Moreover, some of these existing methods, such as matching networks [61] and prototypical networks [51], are designed with few-shot classification in mind, and are not readily applicable to other domains such as human motion prediction.

4.2 Few-Shot Human Motion Prediction

We now focus on using our meta-learning approach for human motion prediction. To the best of our knowledge, we are the first ones that explore the few-shot learning problem for human motion prediction. Due to the lack of published protocols, we propose our evaluation protocol for this task.

Dataset. We evaluate on Human 3.6M (H3.6M) [25], a heavily benchmarked, large-scale mocap dataset that has been widely used in human motion analysis. H3.6M contains seven actors performing 15 varied actions. Following the standard experimental setup in [16,26,32], we down-sample the dataset by two, train on six subjects, and test on subject five. Each action contains hours of video from these actors performing such activity. Sequence clips are randomly taken from the training and test videos to construct the corresponding training and test sequences [26]. Given the past 50 mocap frames (2 s in total), we forecast the future 10 frames (400 ms in total) in short-term prediction and the future 25 frames (1 s in total) in long-term prediction.

Few-Shot Learning Task and Meta-learning Setup. We use 11 action classes for meta-training: directions, greeting, phoning, posing, purchases, sitting, sitting down, taking photo, waiting, walking dog, and walking together. And we use the remaining 4 action classes for meta-test: walking, eating, smoking, and discussion. These four actions are commonly used to evaluate motion prediction algorithms [16,26,32]. The *k-shot motion prediction task* which we address is: for a certain action, given a small collection of k *action-specific* past and future sequence pairs, we aim to learn a predictor model so that it is able to predict the possible future motion for a new past sequence from that action. Accordingly, the setup of k-shot prediction tasks in meta-learning is as follows. During meta-training, for each task, we randomly select one action out of 11, and we sample k action-specific sequence pairs as $\mathcal{D}_{\text{train}}$. During meta-test, for each of the 4 novel actions, we sample k sequence pairs from its training set to produce the small set $\mathcal{D}_{\text{train}}$. We then adapt our meta-learned predictor for use as the target action-specific predictor. We evaluate it on the corresponding test set. We run five trials for each action and report the average performance.

Table 2. Mean angle error comparisons between our PAML and variants of the state-of-the-art residual sup. [32] on the 4 novel actions of H3.6M for $k = 5$-shot human motion prediction. Our PAML consistently and significantly outperforms all the baselines. In particular, it is superior to the multi-task learning and transfer learning baselines on all the actions across different time horizons

milliseconds		Walking						Eating					
		80	160	320	400	560	1000	80	160	320	400	560	1000
residual sup. [32] w/ (Baselines)	$\text{Scratch}_{\text{spec}}$	1.90	1.95	2.16	2.18	1.99	2.00	2.33	2.31	2.30	2.30	2.31	2.34
	$\text{Scratch}_{\text{agn}}$	1.78	1.89	2.20	2.23	2.02	2.05	2.27	2.16	2.18	2.27	2.25	2.31
	$\text{Transfer}_{\text{ots}}$	0.60	0.75	0.88	0.93	1.03	1.26	0.57	0.70	0.91	1.04	1.19	1.58
	Multi-task	0.57	0.71	0.79	0.85	0.96	1.12	0.59	0.68	0.83	0.93	1.12	1.33
	$\text{Transfer}_{\text{ft}}$	0.44	0.55	0.85	0.95	0.74	1.03	0.61	0.65	0.74	0.78	0.86	1.19
Meta-learning (Ours)	PAML	**0.35**	**0.47**	**0.70**	**0.82**	**0.80**	**0.83**	**0.36**	**0.52**	**0.65**	**0.70**	**0.71**	**0.79**
milliseconds		Smoking						Discussion					
		80	160	320	400	560	1000	80	160	320	400	560	1000
residual sup. [32] w/ (Baselines)	$\text{Scratch}_{\text{spec}}$	2.88	2.86	2.85	2.83	2.80	2.99	3.01	3.13	3.12	2.95	2.62	2.99
	$\text{Scratch}_{\text{agn}}$	2.53	2.61	2.67	2.65	2.71	2.73	2.77	2.79	2.82	2.73	2.82	2.76
	$\text{Transfer}_{\text{ots}}$	0.70	0.84	1.18	1.23	1.38	2.02	0.58	0.86	1.12	1.18	1.54	2.02
	Multi-task	0.71	0.79	1.09	1.20	1.25	1.23	0.53	0.82	1.02	1.17	1.33	1.97
	$\text{Transfer}_{\text{ft}}$	0.87	1.02	1.25	1.30	1.45	2.06	0.57	0.82	1.11	1.11	1.37	2.08
Meta-learning (Ours)	PAML	**0.39**	**0.66**	**0.81**	**1.01**	**1.03**	**1.01**	**0.41**	**0.71**	**1.01**	**1.02**	**1.09**	**1.12**

Implementation Details. In our experiments, the predictor is residual sup., the state-of-the-art encoder-decoder network for motion prediction [32]. For the encoder and decoder, we use a single GRU cell [10] with hidden size 1,024, respectively. Following [32], we use tied weights between the encoder and decoder. We use fully-connected networks with Leaky ReLU nonlinearity as our model adaptation meta-networks. In most cases, k is set as 5 and we also evaluate how performance changes when k varies. By cross-validation, the trade-off hyper-parameter λ is set as 0.1, the learning rate α is set as 0.05, and the meta-learning rates β and γ are set as 0.0005. For the predictor, we clip the gradient to a maximum ℓ_2-norm of 5. We run 10,000 iterations during meta-training. We use PyTorch [40] to train our model.

Baselines. For a fair comparison, we compare with residual sup. [32], which is the same predictor as ours *but is not meta-learned.* In particular, we evaluate its variants in the small-sample size regime and consider learning both action-specific and action-agnostic models in the following scenarios.

- **Action-specific training from scratch:** for each of the 4 target actions, we learn an action-specific predictor from its k training sequences pairs.
- **Action-agnostic training from scratch:** we learn a single predictor for the 4 target actions from all their training sequence pairs.
- **Off-the-shelf transfer:** we learn a single predictor for the 11 meta-training actions from their large amounts of training sequence pairs, and directly use this predictor for the 4 target actions without modification.
- **Multi-task learning:** we learn a single predictor for all the 15 actions from large amounts of training sequence pairs of the 11 meta-training actions and k sequence pairs per action of the 4 target actions.

– **Fine-tuning transfer:** after learning a single predictor for the 11 meta-training actions from their large amounts of training sequence pairs, we fine-tune it to be an action-specific predictor for each of the 4 target actions, respectively, using its k training sequence pairs.

Evaluation Metrics. We evaluate our approach both quantitatively and qualitatively. For the quantitative evaluation, we use the standard metric—mean error between the predicted motion and the groundtruth motion in the angle space [16,26,32]. Following the preprocessing in [32,54], we exclude the translation and rotation of the whole body. We also qualitatively visualize the prediction frame by frame.

Comparison with the State-of-the-Art Approaches. Table 2 shows the quantitative comparisons between our PAML and a variety of variants of residual sup. While residual sup. has achieved impressive performance with a large amount of annotated mocap sequences [32], its prediction significantly degrades in the small-sample size regime. As expected, directly training the predictor from a few examples leads to poor performance (*i.e.*, with the angle error in range 2–3), due to severe over-fitting. In such scenarios of training from scratch, learning an action-agnostic model is slightly better than learning an action-specific one (*e.g.*, decreasing the angle error by 0.1 at 80 ms for walking), since the former allows the predictor to exploit some common motion regularities from multiple actions. By transferring knowledge from relevant actions with large sets of samples in a more principled manner, the prediction performance is slightly improved. This is achieved by multi-task learning, *e.g.*, training an action-agnostic predictor using both the 11 source and 4 target actions, or transfer learning, *e.g.*, first training an action-agnostic predictor using the source actions, and then using it either in an off-the-shelf manner or through fine-tuning.

However, modeling multiple actions is more challenging than modeling each action separately, due to the significant diversity of different actions. The performance improvement of these multi-task learning and transfer learning baselines is limited and their performance is also comparably low. This thus demonstrates the general difficulty of our few-shot motion prediction task. By contrast, our PAML *consistently and significantly* outperforms the baselines on almost all the actions across different time horizons, showing the effectiveness of our meta-learning mechanism. There is even a noticeable performance boost for the complicated motion (*e.g.*, decreasing the angle error by 0.3 at 80 ms for smoking). By explicitly learning from a large number of few-shot prediction tasks during meta-training, PAML is able to extract and leverage knowledge shared *both across different actions and across multiple few-shot prediction tasks*, thus improving the prediction of novel actions from a few examples by a large margin.

Moreover, as mentioned before, most of the current meta-learning approaches, such as matching networks [61] and prototypical networks [51], are developed for the simple tasks like image classification with task-specific model architectures (*e.g.*, learning an embedding space that is useful for nearest neighbor or prototype classifiers), which are not readily applicable to our problem. Unlike them, our approach is general and can be effectively used across a broad range of tasks, as shown in Tables 1 and 2. Figure 2 further visualizes our prediction and compares with one of the top performing baselines. From Fig. 2, we can see that our PAML generates lower-error, smoother, and more realistic prediction.

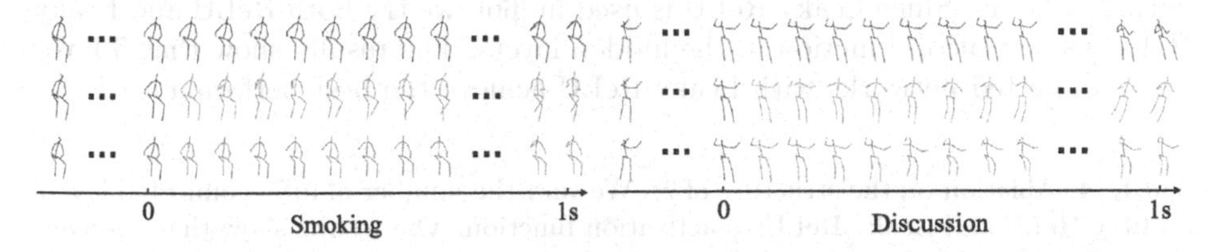

Fig. 2. Visualizations for $k = 5$-shot motion prediction on smoking and discussion. Top: the input sequence and the groundtruth of the prediction sequence. Middle: multi-task learning of residual sup. [32], one of the top performing baselines. Bottom: our prediction results. The groundtruth and the input sequences are shown in black, and the predictions are shown in color. Our PAML produces smoother and more human-like prediction. **Best viewed in color with zoom.** (Color figure online)

Table 3. Ablation on model initialization vs. adaptation. Each component by itself outperforms the fine-tuning baseline. Our full model achieves the best performance

milliseconds		Walking						Eating					
		80	160	320	400	560	1000	80	160	320	400	560	1000
Top baseline	Transfer_{ft}	0.44	0.55	0.85	0.95	0.74	1.03	0.61	0.65	0.74	0.78	0.86	1.19
Meta-learning (Ours)	PAML w/ init	0.40	0.51	0.76	0.86	0.89	0.92	0.49	0.55	0.68	0.74	0.77	0.94
	PAML w/ adapt	0.39	0.52	0.73	0.86	0.90	0.93	0.50	0.59	0.73	0.76	0.81	0.92
	full PAML	**0.35**	**0.47**	**0.70**	**0.82**	**0.80**	**0.83**	**0.36**	**0.52**	**0.65**	**0.70**	**0.71**	**0.79**
milliseconds		Smoking						Discussion					
		80	160	320	400	560	1000	80	160	320	400	560	1000
Top baseline	Transfer_{ft}	0.87	1.02	1.25	1.30	1.45	2.06	0.57	0.82	1.11	1.11	1.37	2.08
Meta-learning (Ours)	PAML w/ init	0.53	0.72	0.95	1.07	1.11	1.18	0.54	0.77	1.02	1.07	1.36	1.55
	PAML w/ adapt	0.58	0.79	0.86	1.03	1.09	1.12	0.47	0.79	1.12	1.15	1.16	1.26
	full PAML	**0.39**	**0.66**	**0.81**	**1.01**	**1.03**	**1.01**	**0.41**	**0.71**	**1.01**	**1.02**	**1.09**	**1.12**

Ablation Studies. In Tables 3 and 4 we evaluate the contributions of different factors in our approach to the results.

Model Initialization vs. Model Adaptation. Our meta-learning approach consists of two components: a generic model initialization and an effective model adaptation meta-network. In Table 3, we can see that each component by itself is superior to the baselines reported in Table 2 in almost all the scenarios. This shows that meta-learning, in general, by leveraging shared knowledge across relevant tasks, enables us to deal with a novel task in a sample-efficient way. Moreover, our full PAML model consistently outperforms its variants, showing the complementarity of each component. This verifies the importance of simultaneously learning a generic initial model and an effective adaptation strategy.

Structure of $\mathcal{H}$. In Table 4 we compare different implementations of the model adaptation meta-network $\mathcal{H}$: as a simple affine transformation, or as networks with 2–4 layers. Since Leaky ReLU is used in [66], we try both ReLU and Leaky ReLU as activation function in the hidden layers. The results show that 3-layer fully-connected networks with Leaky ReLU achieve the best performance.

Table 4. Ablation on the structure of $\mathcal{H}$. We vary the number of fully-connected layers and try ReLU and Leaky ReLU as activation function. The results show that "3-layer, Leaky ReLU" works best, but in general $\mathcal{H}$ is robust to specific implementation choices

milliseconds	Walking					
	80	160	320	400	560	1000
PAML w/ 1-layer, None	0.39	0.54	0.73	0.86	0.85	0.91
PAML w/ 2-layer, ReLU	0.39	0.51	0.75	0.85	0.86	0.92
PAML w/ 2-layer, Leaky ReLU	0.38	0.48	0.74	0.83	0.88	0.91
PAML w/ 3-layer, ReLU	0.37	0.50	0.71	**0.82**	0.83	0.88
PAML w/ 3-layer, Leaky ReLU	**0.35**	**0.47**	**0.70**	**0.82**	**0.80**	**0.83**
PAML w/ 4-layer, ReLU	0.37	0.51	0.72	0.86	0.83	0.90
PAML w/ 4-layer, Leaky ReLU	0.36	0.49	0.73	0.83	0.83	0.89

Impact of Training Sample Sizes. In the previous experiments, we focused on a fixed $k = 5$-shot motion prediction task. To test how our meta-learning approach benefits from more training sequences, we evaluate the performance change with respect to the sample size k. Figure 3 summarizes the comparisons with fine-tuning transfer, one of the top performing baselines reported in Table 2, when k varies from 1 to 100 at 80 ms. As a reference, we also include the *oracle* performance, which is the residual sup. baseline trained on the entire training set of the target action (*i.e.*, with thousands of annotated sequence pairs). Figure 3

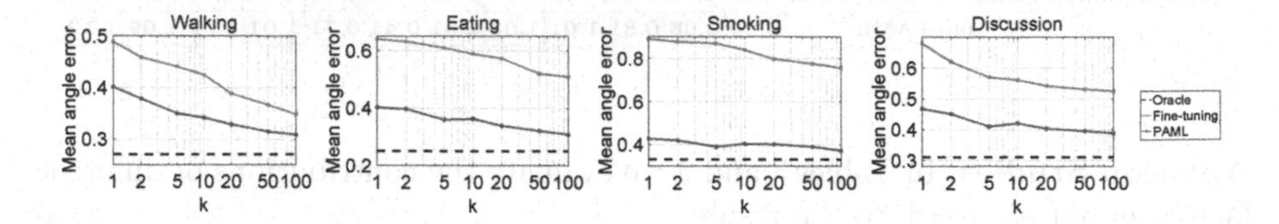

Fig. 3. Impact of the training sample size k for k-shot motion prediction. We compare our PAML with fine-tuning transfer of residual sup. [32], one of the top performing baselines. As a reference, we also include the oracle performance, which is residual sup. trained *from thousands of annotated sequence pairs*. X-axis: number of training sequence pairs k per task. Y-axis: mean angle error. Ours consistently outperforms fine-tuning and *with only* 100 *sequence pairs*, it achieves the performance close to the oracle.

shows that our approach consistently outperforms fine-tuning and improves its performance with more and more training sequences. Interestingly, through our meta-learning mechanism, *with only* 100 *sequence pairs*, we achieve the performance that is close to the oracle trained from thousands of sequence pairs.

5 Conclusions

In this work we have formulated a novel problem of few-shot human motion prediction and proposed a conceptually simple but powerful approach to address this problem. Our key insight is to jointly learn a generic model initialization and an effective model adaptation strategy through meta-learning. To do so, we utilize a novel combination of model-agnostic meta-learning and model regression networks, two meta-learning approaches that have complementary strengths, and unify them into an integrated, end-to-end framework. As a sanity check, we demonstrate that our approach significantly outperforms existing techniques on the most widely benchmarked few-shot image classification task. We then present the state-of-the-art results on few-shot human motion prediction.

Acknowledgments. The motivating example with a Pepper robot in the introduction section was done in the Laboratory of Professor Manuela Veloso at CMU. We thank Professor Veloso and Mr. Kevin Zhang for all their help.

References

1. Akhter, I., Simon, T., Khan, S., Matthews, I., Sheikh, Y.: Bilinear spatiotemporal basis models. ACM Trans. Graph. (TOG) **31**(2), 17:1–17:12 (2012)
2. Andrychowicz, M., et al.: Learning to learn by gradient descent by gradient descent. In: Advances in Neural Information Processing Systems (NIPS), Barcelona, Spain, pp. 3981–3989, December 2016
3. Azizpour, H., Sharif Razavian, A., Sullivan, J., Maki, A., Carlsson, S.: From generic to specific deep representations for visual recognition. In: IEEE Conference on Computer Vision and Pattern Recognition (CVPR) Workshops, Boston, MA, USA, pp. 36–45, June 2015
4. Barsoum, E., Kender, J., Liu, Z.: HP-GAN: Probabilistic 3D human motion prediction via GAN, November 2017. arXiv preprint: arXiv:1711.09561
5. Bengio, S., Bengio, Y., Cloutier, J., Gecsei, J.: On the optimization of a synaptic learning rule. In: Conference on Optimality in Biological and Artificial Networks. Dallas, TX, USA, February 1992
6. Bertinetto, L., Henriques, J.F., Valmadre, J., Torr, P., Vedaldi, A.: Learning feed-forward one-shot learners. In: Advances in Neural Information Processing Systems (NIPS), Barcelona, Spain, pp. 523–531, December 2016
7. Brand, M., Hertzmann, A.: Style machines. In: ACM International Conference on Computer Graphics and Interactive Techniques (SIGGRAPH), New Orleans, LA, USA, pp. 183–192, July 2000
8. Brubaker, M.A., Fleet, D.J., Hertzmann, A.: Physics-based person tracking using the anthropomorphic walker. Int. J. Comput. Vis. (IJCV) **87**(1–2), 140 (2010)

9. Bütepage, J., Black, M.J., Kragic, D., Kjellström, H.: Deep representation learning for human motion prediction and classification. In: IEEE Conference on Computer Vision and Pattern Recognition (CVPR), Honolulu, HI, USA, pp. 1591–1599, July 2017
10. Cho, K., Van Merriënboer, B., Bahdanau, D., Bengio, Y.: On the properties of neural machine translation: Encoder-decoder approaches. In: Syntax, Semantics and Structure in Statistical Translation (SSST), Doha, Qatar, pp. 103–111, October 2014
11. Duan, Y., et al.: One-shot imitation learning. In: Advances in Neural Information Processing Systems (NIPS), Long Beach, CA, USA, pp. 1087–1098, December 2017
12. Edwards, H., Storkey, A.: Towards a neural statistician. In: International Conference on Learning Representations (ICLR), Toulon, France, April 2017
13. Fei-Fei, L., Fergus, R., Perona, P.: One-shot learning of object categories. IEEE Trans. Pattern Anal. Mach. Intell. (TPAMI) **28**(4), 594–611 (2006)
14. Finn, C., Abbeel, P., Levine, S.: Model-agnostic meta-learning for fast adaptation of deep networks. In: International Conference on Machine Learning (ICML), Sydney, Australia, pp. 1126–1135, August 2017
15. Finn, C., Yu, T., Zhang, T., Abbeel, P., Levine, S.: One-shot visual imitation learning via meta-learning. In: Conference on Robot Learning (CoRL), Mountain View, CA, USA, November 2017
16. Fragkiadaki, K., Levine, S., Felsen, P., Malik, J.: Recurrent network models for human dynamics. In: IEEE International Conference on Computer Vision (ICCV), Las Condes, Chile, pp. 4346–4354, December 2015
17. Fu, Y., Xiang, T., Jiang, Y.G., Xue, X., Sigal, L., Gong, S.: Recent advances in zero-shot recognition: toward data-efficient understanding of visual content. IEEE Signal Process. Mag. (SPM) **35**(1), 112–125 (2018)
18. Ghosh, P., Song, J., Aksan, E., Hilliges, O.: Learning human motion models for long-term predictions. In: International Conference on 3D Vision (3DV), Qingdao, China, pp. 458–466, October 2017
19. Gui, L.Y., Wang, Y.X., Liang, X., Moura, J.M.F.: Adversarial geometry-aware human motion prediction. In: Ferrari, V., et al. (eds.) ECCV 2018, Part IV. LNCS, vol. 11208, pp. 823–842. Springer, Cham (2018)
20. Gui, L.Y., Zhang, K., Wang, Y.X., Liang, X., Moura, J.M.F., Veloso, M.M.: Teaching robots to predict human motion. In: IEEE/RSJ International Conference on Intelligent Robots (IROS), Madrid, Spain, October 2018
21. Hariharan, B., Girshick, R.: Low-shot visual recognition by shrinking and hallucinating features. In: IEEE International Conference on Computer Vision (ICCV), Venice, Italy, pp. 3037–3046, October 2017
22. Hauberg, S., Sommer, S., Pedersen, K.S.: Gaussian-like spatial priors for articulated tracking. In: Daniilidis, K., Maragos, P., Paragios, N. (eds.) ECCV 2010, Part I. LNCS, vol. 6311, pp. 425–437. Springer, Heidelberg (2010). https://doi.org/10.1007/978-3-642-15549-9_31
23. Held, D., Thrun, S., Savarese, S.: Robust single-view instance recognition. In: IEEE International Conference on Robotics and Automation (ICRA), Stockholm, Sweden, pp. 2152–2159, May 2016
24. Huang, D.-A., Kitani, K.M.: Action-reaction: Forecasting the dynamics of human interaction. In: Fleet, D., Pajdla, T., Schiele, B., Tuytelaars, T. (eds.) ECCV 2014, Part VII. LNCS, vol. 8695, pp. 489–504. Springer, Cham (2014). https://doi.org/10.1007/978-3-319-10584-0_32

25. Ionescu, C., Papava, D., Olaru, V., Sminchisescu, C.: Human3.6M: Large scale datasets and predictive methods for 3D human sensing in natural environments. IEEE Trans. Pattern Anal. Mach. Intell. (TPAMI) **36**(7), 1325–1339 (2014)
26. Jain, A., Zamir, A.R., Savarese, S., Saxena, A.: Structural-RNN: Deep learning on spatio-temporal graphs. In: IEEE Conference on Computer Vision and Pattern Recognition (CVPR), Las Vegas, NV, USA, pp. 5308–5317, June–July 2016
27. Jong, M.D., et al.: Towards a robust interactive and learning social robot. In: International Conference on Autonomous Agents and Multiagent Systems (AAMAS), Stockholm, Sweden, July 2018
28. Koppula, H., Saxena, A.: Learning spatio-temporal structure from RGB-D videos for human activity detection and anticipation. In: International Conference on Machine Learning (ICML), Atlanta, GA, USA, pp. 792–800, June 2013
29. Koppula, H.S., Saxena, A.: Anticipating human activities using object affordances for reactive robotic response. IEEE Trans. Pattern Anal. Mach. Intell. (TPAMI) **38**(1), 14–29 (2016)
30. Kovar, L., Gleicher, M., Pighin, F.: Motion graphs. In: ACM International Conference on Computer Graphics and Interactive Techniques (SIGGRAPH), San Antonio, TX, USA, pp. 473–482, July 2002
31. Li, K., Malik, J.: Learning to optimize. In: International Conference on Learning Representations (ICLR), Toulon, France, April 2017
32. Martinez, J., Black, M.J., Romero, J.: On human motion prediction using recurrent neural networks. In: IEEE Conference on Computer Vision and Pattern Recognition (CVPR), Honolulu, HI, USA, pp. 4674–4683, July 2017
33. Mishra, N., Rohaninejad, M., Chen, X., Abbeel, P.: A simple neural attentive meta-learner. In: International Conference on Learning Representations (ICLR), Vancouver, Canada, April–May 2018
34. Munkhdalai, T., Yu, H.: Meta networks. In: International Conference on Machine Learning (ICML), Sydney, Australia, pp. 2554–2563, August 2017
35. Murray, R.M., Li, Z., Sastry, S.S., Sastry, S.S.: A Mathematical Introduction to Robotic Manipulation, 1st edn. CRC Press, Boca Raton (1994)
36. Nichol, A., Schulman, J.: Reptile: A scalable metalearning algorithm, March 2018. arXiv preprint: arXiv:1803.02999
37. Paden, B., Čáp, M., Yong, S.Z., Yershov, D., Frazzoli, E.: A survey of motion planning and control techniques for self-driving urban vehicles. IEEE Trans. Intell. Veh. (T-IV) **1**(1), 33–55 (2016)
38. Pan, S.J., Yang, Q.: A survey on transfer learning. IEEE Trans. Knowl. Data Eng. (TKDE) **22**(10), 1345–1359 (2010)
39. Pastor, P., Hoffmann, H., Asfour, T., Schaal, S.: Learning and generalization of motor skills by learning from demonstration. In: IEEE International Conference on Robotics and Automation (ICRA), Kobe, Japan, pp. 763–768, May 2009
40. Paszke, A., et al.: Automatic differentiation in PyTorch. In: Advances in Neural Information Processing Systems (NIPS) Autodiff Workshop, Long Beach, CA, USA, December 2017
41. Pavlovic, V., Rehg, J.M., MacCormick, J.: Learning switching linear models of human motion. In: Advances in Neural Information Processing Systems (NIPS), Vancouver, Canada, pp. 981–987, December 2001
42. Poppe, R.: Vision-based human motion analysis: An overview. Comput. Vis. Image Underst. (CVIU) **108**(1–2), 4–18 (2007)
43. Ravi, S., Larochelle, H.: Optimization as a model for few-shot learning. In: International Conference on Learning Representations (ICLR), Toulon, France, April 2017

44. Razavian, A.S., Azizpour, H., Sullivan, J., Carlsson, S.: CNN features off-the-shelf: An astounding baseline for recognition. In: IEEE Conference on Computer Vision and Pattern Recognition (CVPR) Workshops, Columbus, OH, USA, pp. 806–813, June 2014
45. Santoro, A., Bartunov, S., Botvinick, M., Wierstra, D., Lillicrap, T.: Meta-learning with memory-augmented neural networks. In: International Conference on Machine Learning (ICML), New York City, NY, USA, pp. 1842–1850, June 2016
46. Schmidhuber, J.: Learning to control fast-weight memories: An alternative to dynamic recurrent networks. Neural Comput. **4**(1), 131–139 (1992)
47. Schmidhuber, J., Zhao, J., Wiering, M.: Shifting inductive bias with success-story algorithm, adaptive Levin search, and incremental self-improvement. Mach. Learn. **28**(1), 105–130 (1997)
48. Schmidhuber, J.: Evolutionary principles in self-referential learning. (On learning now to Learn: The Meta-Meta-Meta...-Hook). Diploma thesis, Technische Universitat Munchen, Munich, Germany, May 1987
49. Schmidhuber, J.: A neural network that embeds its own meta-levels. In: IEEE International Conference on Neural Networks (ICNN), San Francisco, CA, USA, pp. 407–412, March–April 1993
50. Schmidt, L.A.: Meaning and compositionality as statistical induction of categories and constraints. Ph.D. thesis, Massachusetts Institute of Technology, Boston, MA, USA, September 2009
51. Snell, J., Swersky, K., Zemel, R.S.: Prototypical networks for few-shot learning. In: Advances in Neural Information Processing Systems (NIPS), Long Beach, CA, USA, pp. 4077–4087, December 2017
52. Sutskever, I., Hinton, G.E., Taylor, G.W.: The recurrent temporal restricted Boltzmann machine. In: Advances in Neural Information Processing Systems (NIPS), Whistler, Canada, pp. 1601–1608, December 2009
53. Taylor, G.W., Hinton, G.E.: Factored conditional restricted Boltzmann machines for modeling motion style. In: International Conference on Machine Learning (ICML), Montreal, Canada, pp. 1025–1032, June 2009
54. Taylor, G.W., Hinton, G.E., Roweis, S.T.: Modeling human motion using binary latent variables. In: Advances in Neural Information Processing Systems (NIPS), Vancouver, Canada, pp. 1345–1352, December 2007
55. Taylor, G.W., Sigal, L., Fleet, D.J., Hinton, G.E.: Dynamical binary latent variable models for 3D human pose tracking. In: IEEE Conference on Computer Vision and Pattern Recognition (CVPR), San Francisco, CA, USA, pp. 631–638, June 2010
56. Thrun, S.: Is learning the n-th thing any easier than learning the first? In: Advances in Neural Information Processing Systems (NIPS), Denver, CO, USA, pp. 640–646, December 1996
57. Thrun, S.: Lifelong learning algorithms. In: Thrun S., Pratt L. (eds.) Learning to learn, pp. 181–209. Springer, Boston (1998). https://doi.org/10.1007/978-1-4615-5529-2_8
58. Thrun, S., Pratt, L.: Learning to learn: Introduction and overview. In: Thrun S., Pratt L. (eds.) Learning To Learn, pp. 3–17. Springer, Boston (1998). https://doi.org/10.1007/978-1-4615-5529-2_1
59. Urtasun, R., Fleet, D.J., Geiger, A., Popović, J., Darrell, T.J., Lawrence, N.D.: Topologically-constrained latent variable models. In: International Conference on Machine Learning (ICML), Helsinki, Finland, pp. 1080–1087, July 2008
60. Vernon, D., Von Hofsten, C., Fadiga, L.: A Roadmap for Cognitive Development in Humanoid Robots, vol. 11. Springer, Heidelberg (2011)

61. Vinyals, O., Blundell, C., Lillicrap, T., Kavukcuoglu, K., Wierstra, D.: Matching networks for one shot learning. In: Advances in Neural Information Processing Systems (NIPS), Barcelona, Spain, pp. 3630–3638, December 2016
62. Wang, J.M., Fleet, D.J., Hertzmann, A.: Gaussian process dynamical models for human motion. IEEE Trans. Pattern Anal. Mach. Intell. (TPAMI) **30**(2), 283–298 (2008)
63. Wang, Y.X., Hebert, M.: Model recommendation: Generating object detectors from few samples. In: IEEE Conference on Computer Vision and Pattern Recognition (CVPR), Boston, MA, USA, pp. 1619–1628, June 2015
64. Wang, Y.X., Hebert, M.: Learning by transferring from unsupervised universal sources. In: AAAI Conference on Artificial Intelligence (AAAI), Phoenix, AZ, USA, pp. 2187–2193, February 2016
65. Wang, Y.X., Hebert, M.: Learning from small sample sets by combining unsupervised meta-training with CNNs. In: Advances in Neural Information Processing Systems (NIPS), Barcelona, Spain, pp. 244–252, December 2016
66. Wang, Y.X., Hebert, M.: Learning to learn: Model regression networks for easy small sample learning. In: Leibe, B., Matas, J., Sebe, N., Welling, M. (eds.) ECCV 2016, Part VI. LNCS, vol. 9910, pp. 616–634. Springer, Cham (2016). https://doi.org/10.1007/978-3-319-46466-4_37
67. Wang, Y.X., Girshick, R., Hebert, M., Hariharan, B.: Low-shot learning from imaginary data. In: IEEE Conference on Computer Vision and Pattern Recognition (CVPR), Salt Lake City, UT, USA, pp. 7278–7286, June 2018
68. Wang, Y.X., Ramanan, D., Hebert, M.: Growing a brain: Fine-tuning by increasing model capacity. In: IEEE Conference on Computer Vision and Pattern Recognition (CVPR), Honolulu, HI, USA, pp. 3029–3038 (2017)
69. Wang, Y.X., Ramanan, D., Hebert, M.: Learning to model the tail. In: Advances in Neural Information Processing Systems (NIPS), Long Beach, CA, USA, pp. 7029–7039, December 2017
70. Yosinski, J., Clune, J., Bengio, Y., Lipson, H.: How transferable are features in deep neural networks? In: Advances in Neural Information Processing Systems (NIPS), Montréal, Canada, pp. 3320–3328, December 2014
71. Zhu, Y., et al.: Reinforcement and imitation learning for diverse visuomotor skills, February 2018. arXiv preprint: arXiv:1802.09564

Straight to the Facts: Learning Knowledge Base Retrieval for Factual Visual Question Answering

Medhini Narasimhan(✉) and Alexander G. Schwing

University of Illinois Urbana-Champaign, Champaign, USA
{medhini2,aschwing}@illinois.edu

Abstract. Question answering is an important task for autonomous agents and virtual assistants alike and was shown to support the disabled in efficiently navigating an overwhelming environment. Many existing methods focus on observation-based questions, ignoring our ability to seamlessly combine observed content with general knowledge. To understand interactions with a knowledge base, a dataset has been introduced recently and keyword matching techniques were shown to yield compelling results despite being vulnerable to misconceptions due to synonyms and homographs. To address this issue, we develop a learning-based approach which goes straight to the facts via a learned embedding space. We demonstrate state-of-the-art results on the challenging recently introduced fact-based visual question answering dataset, outperforming competing methods by more than 5%.

Keywords: Fact based visual question answering · Knowledge bases

1 Introduction

When answering questions given a context, such as an image, we seamlessly combine the observed content with general knowledge. For autonomous agents and virtual assistants which naturally participate in our day to day endeavors, where answering of questions based on context and general knowledge is most natural, algorithms which leverage both observed content and general knowledge are extremely useful.

To address this challenge, in recent years, a significant amount of research has been devoted to question answering in general and Visual Question Answering (VQA) in particular. Specifically, the classical VQA tasks require an algorithm to answer a given question based on the additionally provided context, given in the form of an image. For instance, significant progress in VQA was

---

Electronic supplementary material The online version of this chapter (https://doi.org/10.1007/978-3-030-01237-3_28) contains supplementary material, which is available to authorized users.

V. Ferrari et al. (Eds.): ECCV 2018, LNCS 11212, pp. 460–477, 2018.
https://doi.org/10.1007/978-3-030-01237-3_28

Question: Which object in the image can be used to eat with?
Relation: UsedFor
Associated Fact: (Fork, UsedFor, Eat)
Answer Source: Image
Answer: Fork

Question: What do the animals in the image eat?
Relation: RelatedTo
Associated Fact: (Sheep, RelatedTo, Grass Eater)
Answer Source: Knowledge Base
Answer: Grass

Question: Which equipment in this image is used to hit baseball?
Relation: CapableOf
Associated Fact: (Baseball bat, CapableOf, Hit a baseball)
Answer Source: Image
Answer: Baseball bat

Fig. 1. The FVQA dataset expects methods to answer questions about images utilizing information from the image, as well as fact-based knowledge bases. Our method makes use of the image, and question text features, as well as high-level visual concepts extracted from the image in combination with a learned fact-ranking neural network. Our method is able to answer both visually grounded as well as fact based questions.

achieved by introducing a variety of VQA datasets with strong baselines [1–8]. The images in these datasets cover a broad range of categories and the questions are designed to test perceptual abilities such as counting, inferring spatial relationships, and identifying visual cues. Some challenging questions require logical reasoning and memorization capabilities. However, the majority of the questions can be answered by solely examining the visual content of the image. Hence, numerous approaches to solve these problems [7–13] focus on extracting visual cues using deep networks.

We note that many of the aforementioned methods focus on the visual aspect of the question answering task, *i.e.*, the answer is predicted by combining representations of the question and the image. This clearly contrasts the described human-like approach, which combines observations with general knowledge. To address this discrepancy, in very recent meticulous work, Wang *et al.* [14] introduced a 'fact-based' VQA task (FVQA), an accompanying dataset, and a knowledge base of facts extracted from three different sources, namely WebChild [15], DBPedia [16], and ConceptNet [17]. Different from the classical VQA datasets, Wang *et al.* [14] argued that such a dataset can be used to develop algorithms which answer more complex questions that require a combination of observation and general knowledge. In addition to the dataset, Wang *et al.* [14] also developed a model which leverages the information present in the supporting facts to answer questions about an image.

To this end, Wang *et al.* [14] design an approach which extracts keywords from the question and retrieves facts that contain those keywords from the knowledge base. Clearly, synonyms and homographs pose challenges which are hard to recover from.

To address this issue, we develop a learning based retrieval method. More specifically, our approach learns a parametric mapping of facts and question-image pairs to an embedding space. To answer a question, we use the fact that is most aligned with the provided question-image pair. As illustrated in Fig. 1, our approach is able to accurately answer both more visual questions as well as more fact based questions. For instance, given the image illustrated on the left hand side along with the question, "Which object in the image can be used to eat with?", we are able to predict the correct answer, "fork." Similarly, the proposed approach is able to predict the correct answer for the other two examples. Quantitatively we demonstrate the efficacy of the proposed approach on the recently introduced FVQA dataset, outperforming state-of-the-art by more than 5% on the top-1 accuracy metric.

2 Related Work

We develop a framework for visual question answering that benefits from a rich knowledge base. In the following, we first review classical visual question answering tasks before discussing visual question answering methods that take advantage of knowledge bases.

Visual Question Answering. In recent years, a significant amount of research has been devoted to developing techniques which can answer a question about a provided context such as an image. Of late, visual question answering has also been used to assess reasoning capabilities of state-of-the-art predictors. Using a variety of datasets [2,3,5,8,10,11], models based on multi-modal representation and attention [18–25], deep network architectures [12,26–28], and dynamic memory nets [29] have been developed. Despite these efforts, assessing the reasoning capabilities of present day deep network-based approaches and differentiating them from mere memorization of training set statistics remains a hard task. Most of the methods developed for visual question answering [2,6–8,10,12,18–24,27,29–34] focus exclusively on answering questions related to observed content. To this end, these methods use image features extracted from networks such as the VGG-16 [35] trained on large image datasets such as ImageNet [36]. However, it is unlikely that all the information which is required to answer a question is encoded in the features extracted from the image, or even the image itself. For example, consider an image containing a dog, and a question about this image, such as *"Is the animal in the image capable of jumping in the air?"*. In such a case, we would want our method to combine common sense and general knowledge about the world, such as the ability of a healthy dog to jump, along with features and observations from the image, such as the presence of the dog. This motivates us to develop methods that can use knowledge bases encoding general knowledge.

Knowledge-Based Visual Question Answering. There has been interest in the natural language processing community in answering questions based on knowledge bases (KBs) using either semantic parsing [37–47] or information retrieval [48–54] methods. However, knowledge based visual question answering is still relatively unexplored, even though this is appealing from a practical standpoint as this decouples the reasoning by the neural network from the storage of knowledge in the KB. Notable examples in this direction are work by Zhu *et al.* [55], Wu *et al.* [56], Wang *et al.* [57], Krishnamurthy and Kollar [58], and Narasimhan *et al.* [59].

The works most related to our approach include *Ask Me Anything* (AMA) by Wu *et al.* [60], Ahab by Wang *et al.* [61], and FVQA by Wang *et al.* [14]. AMA describes the content of an image in terms of a set of attributes predicted about the image, and multiple captions generated about the image. The predicted attributes are used to query an external knowledge base, DBpedia [16], and the retrieved paragraphs are summarized to form a knowledge vector. The predicted attribute vector, the captions, and the database-based knowledge vector are passed as inputs to an LSTM that learns to predict the answer to the input question as a sequence of words. A drawback of this work is that it does not perform any explicit reasoning and ignores the possible structure in the KB. Ahab and FVQA, on the other hand, attempt to perform explicit reasoning. Ahab converts an input question into a database query, and processes the returned knowledge to form the final answer. Similarly, FVQA learns a mapping from questions to database queries through classifying questions into categories and extracting parts from the question deemed to be important. While both of these methods rely on fixed query templates, this very structure offers some insight into what information the method deems necessary to answer a question about a given image. Both these methods use databases with a particular structure: those that contain facts about visual concepts represented as tuples, for example, (*Cat*, *CapableOf*, *Climbing*), and (*Dog*, *IsA*, *Pet*). We develop our method on the dataset released as part of the FVQA work, referred to as the FVQA dataset [14], which is a subset of three structured databases – DBpedia [16], ConceptNet [17], and WebChild [15]. The method presented in FVQA [14] produces a query as an output of an LSTM which is fed the question as an input. Facts in the knowledge base are filtered on the basis of visual concepts such as objects, scenes, and actions extracted from the input image. The predicted query is then applied on the filtered database, resulting in a set of retrieved facts. A matching score is then computed between the retrieved facts and the question to determine the most relevant fact. The most correct fact forms the basis of the answer for the question.

In contrast to Ahab and FVQA, we propose to directly learn an embedding of facts and question-image pairs into a space that permits to assess their compatibility. This has two important advantages over prior work: (1) by avoiding the generation of an explicit query, we eliminate errors due to synonyms, homographs, and incorrect prediction of visual concept type and answer type; and (2) our technique is easy to extend to any knowledge base, even one with a different structure or size. We also do not require any ad-hoc filtering of knowledge, and can instead learn to transform extracted visual concepts into a vector close to a relevant fact in the learned embedding space. Our method also naturally produces a ranking of facts deemed to be useful for the given question and image.

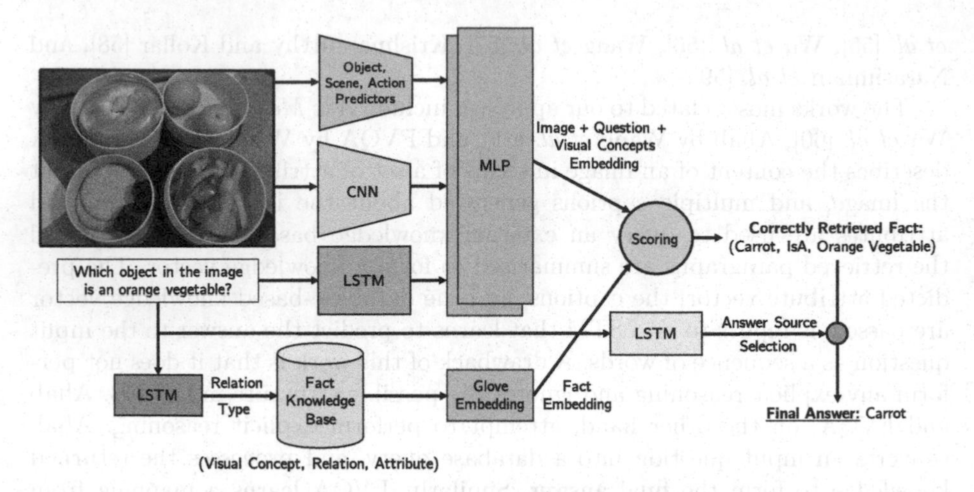

Fig. 2. Overview of the proposed approach. Given an image and a question about the image, we obtain an Image + Question Embedding through the use of a CNN on the image, an LSTM on the question, and a Multi Layer Perceptron (MLP) for combining the two modalities. In order to filter relevant facts from the Knowledge Base (KB), we use another LSTM to predict the fact relation type from the question. The retrieved structured facts are encoded using GloVe embeddings. The retrieved facts are ranked through a dot product between the embedding vectors and the top-ranked fact is returned to answer the question.

3 Learning Knowledge Base Retrieval

In the following, we first provide an overview of the proposed approach for knowledge based visual question answering before discussing our embedding space and learning formulation.

Overview. Our developed approach is outlined in Fig. 2. The task at hand is to predict an answer y for a question Q given an image x by using an external knowledge base KB, which consists of a set of facts f_i, *i.e.*, $\text{KB} = \{f_1, \ldots, f_{|\text{KB}|}\}$. Each fact f_i in the knowledge base is represented as a Resource Description Framework (RDF) triplet of the form $f_i = (a_i, r_i, b_i)$, where a_i is a visual concept in the image, b_i is an attribute or phrase associated with the visual entity a_i, and $r_i \in \mathcal{R}$ is a relation between the two entities. The dataset contains $|\mathcal{R}| = 13$ relations $r \in \mathcal{R} = \{$*Category*, *Comparative*, *HasA*, *IsA*, *HasProperty*, *CapableOf*, *Desires*, *RelatedTo*, *AtLocation*, *PartOf*, *ReceivesAction*, *UsedFor*, *CreatedBy*$\}$. Example triples of the knowledge base in our dataset are (*Umbrella*, *UsedFor*, *Shade*), (*Beach*, *HasProperty*, *Sandy*), (*Elephant*, *Comparative-LargerThan*, *Ant*).

To answer a question Q correctly given an image x, we need to retrieve the right supporting fact and choose the correct entity, *i.e.*, either a or b. Importantly, entity a is always derived from the image and entity b is derived from the fact base. Consequently we refer to this choice as the answer source $s \in \{\text{Image}, \text{KnowledgeBase}\}$. Using this formulation, we can extract the answer

y from a predicted fact $\hat{f} = (\hat{a}, \hat{r}, \hat{b})$ and a predicted answer source $\hat{s}$ using

$$y = \begin{cases} \hat{a}, & \text{from } \hat{f} \text{ if } \hat{s} = \text{Image} \\ \hat{b}, & \text{from } \hat{f} \text{ if } \hat{s} = \text{KnowledgeBase} \end{cases}. \tag{1}$$

It remains to answer, how to predict a fact $\hat{f}$ and how to infer the answer source $\hat{s}$. The latter is a binary prediction task and we describe our approach below. For the former, we note that the knowledge base contains a large number of facts. We therefore consider it infeasible to search through all the facts f_i $\forall i \in \{1, \ldots, |\text{KB}|\}$ using an expensive evaluation based on a deep net. We therefore split this task into two parts: (1) Given a question, we train a network to predict the relation $\hat{r}$, that the question focuses on. (2) Using the predicted relation, $\hat{r}$, we reduce the fact space to those containing only the predicted relation.

Subsequently, to answer the question Q given image x, we only assess the suitability of the facts which contain the predicted relation $\hat{r}$. To assess the suitability, we design a score function $S(g^{\text{F}}(f_i), g^{\text{NN}}(x, Q))$ which measures the compatibility of a fact representation $g^{\text{F}}(f_i)$ and an image-question representation $g^{\text{NN}}(x, Q)$. Intuitively, the higher the score, the more suitable the fact f_i for answering question Q given image x.
Formally, we hence obtain the predicted fact $\hat{f}$ via

$$\hat{f} = \arg \max_{i \in \{j : \text{rel}(f_j) = \hat{r}\}} S(g^{\text{F}}(f_i), g^{\text{NN}}(x, Q)), \tag{2}$$

where we search for the fact $\hat{f}$ maximizing the score S among all facts f_i which contain relation $\hat{r}$, *i.e.*, among all f_i with $i \in \{j : \text{rel}(f_j) = \hat{r}\}$. Hereby we use the operator $\text{rel}(f_i)$ to indicate the relation of the fact triplet f_i. Given the predicted fact using Eq. (2) we obtain the answer y from Eq. (1) after predicting the answer source $\hat{s}$.

This approach is outlined in Fig. 2. Pictorially, we illustrate the construction of an image-question embedding $g^{\text{NN}}(x, Q)$, via LSTM and CNN net representations that are combined via an MLP. We also illustrate the fact embedding $g^{\text{F}}(f_i)$. Both of them are combined using the score function $S(\cdot, \cdot)$, to predict a fact $\hat{f}$ from which we extract the answer as described in Eq. (1).

In the following, we first provide details about the score function S, before discussing prediction of the relation $\hat{r}$ and prediction of the answer source $\hat{s}$.

Scoring the Facts. Figure 2 illustrates our approach to score the facts in the knowledge base, *i.e.*, to compute $S(g^{\text{F}}(f_i), g^{\text{NN}}(x, Q))$. We obtain the score in three steps: (1) computing of a fact representation $g^{\text{F}}(f_i)$; (2) computing of an image-question representation $g^{\text{NN}}(x, Q)$; (3) combination of the fact and image-question representation to obtain the final score S. We discuss each of those steps in the following.

(1) Computing a Fact Representation. To obtain the fact representation $g^{\text{F}}(f_i)$, we concatenate two vectors, the averaged GloVe-100 [62] representation of the words of entity a_i and the averaged GloVe-100 representation of the words of

entity b_i. Note that this fact representation is non-parametric, *i.e.*, there are no trainable parameters.

(2) Computing an Image-Question Representation. We compute the image-question representation $g^{\text{NN}}(x, Q)$, by combining a visual representation $g_w^V(x)$, obtained from a standard deep net, *e.g.*, ResNet or VGG, with a visual concept representation $g_w^C(x)$, and a sentence representation $g_w^Q(Q)$, of the question Q, obtained using a trainable recurrent net. For notational convenience we concatenate all trainable parameters into one vector w. Making the dependence on the parameters explicit, we obtain the image-question representation via $g_w^{\text{NN}}(x, Q) = g_w^{\text{NN}}(g_w^V(x), g_w^Q(Q), g_w^C(x))$.

More specifically, for the question embedding $g_w^Q(Q)$, we use an LSTM model [63]. For the image embedding $g_w^V(x)$, we extract image features using ResNet-152 [64] pre-trained on the ImageNet dataset [65]. In addition, we also extract a visual concept representation $g_w^C(x)$, which is a multi-hot vector of size 1176 indicating the visual concepts which are grounded in the image. The visual concepts detected in the images are objects, scenes, and actions. For *objects*, we use the detections from two Faster-RCNN [66] models that are trained on the Microsoft COCO 80-object [67] and the ImageNet 200-object [36] datasets. In total, there are 234 distinct object classes, from which we use that subset of labels that coincides with the FVQA dataset. The *scene* information (such as pasture, beach, bedroom) is extracted by the VGG-16 model [35] trained on the MIT Places 365-class dataset [68]. Again, we use a subset of Places to construct the 1176-dimensional multi-hot vector $g_w^C(x)$. For detecting *actions*, we use the CNN model proposed in [69] which is trained on the HICO [70] and MPII [71] datasets. The HICO dataset contains labels for 600 human-object interaction activities while the MPII dataset contains labels for 393 actions. We use a subset of actions, namely those which coincide with the ones in the FVQA dataset.

All the three vectors $g_w^V(x), g_w^Q(Q), g_w^C(x)$ are concatenated and passed to the multi-layer perceptron $g_w^{\text{NN}}(\cdot, \cdot, \cdot)$.

(3) Combination of Fact and Image-Question Representation. For each fact representation $g^{\text{F}}(f_i)$, we compute a score

$$S_w(g^{\text{F}}(f_i), g_w^{\text{NN}}(x, Q)) = \cos(g^{\text{F}}(f_i), g_w^{\text{NN}}(x, Q)) = \frac{g^{\text{F}}(f_i) \cdot g_w^{\text{NN}}(x, Q)}{||g^{\text{F}}(f_i)|| \cdot ||g_w^{\text{NN}}(x, Q)||},$$

where $g_w^{\text{NN}}(x, Q)$ is the image question representation. Hence, the score S is the cosine similarity between the two normalized representations and represents the fit of fact f_i to the image-question pair (x, Q).

Predicting the Relation. To predict the relation $\hat{r} \in \mathcal{R} = h_{w_1}^r(Q)$, from the obtained question Q, we use an LSTM net. More specifically, we first embed and then encode the words of the question Q, one at a time, and linearly transform the final hidden representation of the LSTM to predict $\hat{r}$, from $|\mathcal{R}|$ possibilities using a standard multinomial classification. For the results presented in this work, we trained the relation prediction parameters w_1 independently of the score function. We leave a joint formulation to future work.

Algorithm 1. Training with hard negative mining

Input: (x, Q, f^*), KB
Output: parameters w
1: **for** $t = 0, \ldots, T$ **do**
2: Create dataset $\mathcal{D}^{(t)}$ by sampling negative facts randomly (if $t = 0$) or by retrieving facts predicted wrongly with $w^{(t-1)}$ (if $t > 0$)
3: Use $\mathcal{D}^{(t)}$ to obtain $w^{(t)}$ by optimizing the program given in Eq. (7)
4: **end for**
5: **return** $w^{(T)}$

Predicting the Answer Source. Prediction of the answer source $\hat{s} = h^s_{w_2}(Q)$ from a given question Q is similar to relation prediction. Again, we use an LSTM net to embed and encode the words of the question Q before linearly transforming the final hidden representation to predict $\hat{s} \in \{\text{Image}, \text{KnowledgeBase}\}$. Analogous to relation prediction, we train this LSTM net's parameters w_2 separately and leave a joint formulation to future work.

Learning. As mentioned before, we train the parameters w (score function), w_1 (relation prediction), and w_2 (answer source prediction) separately. To train w_1, we use a dataset $\mathcal{D}_1 = \{(Q, r)\}$ containing pairs of question and the corresponding relation which was used to obtain the answer. To learn w_2, we use a dataset $\mathcal{D}_2 = \{(Q, s)\}$, containing pairs of question and the corresponding answer source. For both classifiers we use stochastic gradient descent on the classical cross-entropy and binary cross-entropy loss respectively. Note that both the datasets are readily available from [14].

To train the parameters of the score function we adopt a successive approach operating in time steps $t = \{1, \ldots, T\}$. In each time step, we gradually increase the difficulty of the dataset $\mathcal{D}^{(t)}$ by mining hard negatives. More specifically, for every question Q, and image x, $\mathcal{D}^{(0)}$ contains the 'groundtruth' fact f^* as well as 99 randomly sampled 'non-groundtruth' facts. After having trained the score function on this dataset we use it to predict facts for image-question pairs and create a new dataset $\mathcal{D}^{(1)}$ which now contains, along with the groundtruth fact, another 99 non-groundtruth facts that the score function assigned a high score to.

Given a dataset $\mathcal{D}^{(t)}$, we train the parameters w of the representations involved in the score function $S_w(g^{\mathrm{F}}(f_i), g^{\mathrm{NN}}_w(x, Q))$, and its image, question, and concept embeddings by encouraging that the score of the groundtruth fact f^* is larger than the score of any other fact. More formally, we aim for parameters w which ensure the classical margin, *i.e.*, an SVM-like loss for deep nets:

$$S_w(f^*, x, Q) \geq L(f^*, f) + S_w(f, x, Q) \qquad \forall (f, x, Q) \in \mathcal{D}^{(t)}, \tag{3}$$

where $L(f^*, f)$ is the task loss (aka margin) comparing the groundtruth fact f^* to other facts f. In our case $L \equiv 1$. Since we may not find parameters w which ensure feasibility $\forall (f, x, Q) \in \mathcal{D}^{(t)}$, we introduce slack variables $\xi_{(f,x,Q)} \geq 0$ to obtain after reformulation:

$$\xi_{(f,x,Q)} \geq L(f^*, f) + S_w(f, x, Q) - S_w(f^*, x, Q) \qquad \forall (f, x, Q) \in \mathcal{D}^{(t)}. \tag{4}$$

Table 1. Accuracy of predicting relations given the question.

Method	Accuracy	
	@1	@3
FVQA [14]	64.94	82.42
Ours	**75.4**	**91.97**

Table 2. Accuracy of predicting answer source from a given question.

Method	Accuracy	
	@1	@3
Ours	97.3	100.00

Instead of enforcing the constraint $\forall(f, x, Q)$ in the dataset $\mathcal{D}^{(t)}$, it is equivalent to require [72]

$$\xi_{(x,Q)} \geq \max_f \{L(f^*, f) + S_w(f, x, Q)\} - S_w(f^*, x, Q) \quad \forall(x, Q) \in \mathcal{D}^{(t)}. \quad (5)$$

Using this constraint, we find the parameters w by solving

$$\min_{w, \xi_{(x,Q)} \geq 0} \frac{C}{2}\|w\|_2^2 + \sum_{(x,Q) \in \mathcal{D}^{(t)}} \xi_{(x,Q)} \quad \text{s.t. Constraints in Eq. (5).} \quad (6)$$

For applicability of the standard sub-gradient descent techniques, we reformulate the program given in Eq. (6) to read as

$$\min_w \frac{C}{2}\|w\|_2^2 + \sum_{(x,Q) \in \mathcal{D}^{(t)}} \left(\max_f \{L(f^*, f) + S_w(f, x, Q)\} - S_w(f^*, x, Q) \right), \quad (7)$$

which can be optimized using standard deep net packages. The proposed approach for learning the parameters w is summarized in Algorithm 1. In the following we now assess the suitability of the proposed approach.

4 Evaluation

In the following, we assess the proposed approach. We first provide details about the proposed dataset before presenting quantitative results for prediction of relations from questions, prediction of answer-source from questions, and prediction of the answer and the supporting fact. We also discuss mining of hard negatives. Finally, we show qualitative results.

Dataset and Knowledge Base. We use the publicly available FVQA dataset [14] and its knowledge base to evaluate our model. This dataset consists of 2,190 images, 5,286 questions, and 4,126 unique facts corresponding to the questions. The knowledge base, consisting of 193,449 facts, were constructed by extracting the top visual concepts for all the images in the dataset and querying for those concepts in the three knowledge bases, WebChild [15], ConceptNet [17], and DBPedia [16]. The dataset consists of 5 train-test folds, and all the scores we report are averaged across all splits.

Predicting Relations from Questions. We use an LSTM architecture as discussed in Sect. 3 to predict the relation $r \in \mathcal{R}$ given a question Q. The standard train-test split of the FVQA dataset is used to evaluate our model. Batch gradient descent with Adam optimizer was used on batches of size 100 and the model was trained over 50 epochs. LSTM embedding and word embeddings are of size 128 each. The learning rate is set to 1e−3 and a dropout of 0.7 is applied after the word embeddings as well as the LSTM embedding. Table 1 provides a comparison of our model to the FVQA baseline [14] using top-1 and top-3 prediction accuracy. We observe our results to improve the baseline by more than 10% on top-1 accuracy and by more than 9% when using the top-3 accuracy metric.

Predicting Answer Source from Questions. We assess the accuracy of predicting the answer source s given a question Q. To predict the source of the answer, we use an LSTM architecture as discussed in detail in Sect. 3. Note that for predicting the answer source, the size of the LSTM embedding and word embeddings was set to 64 each. Table 2 summarizes the accuracy of the prediction results of our model. We observe the prediction accuracy of the proposed approach to be close to perfect.

Predicting the Correct Answer. Our score function based model to retrieve the supporting fact is described in detail in Sect. 3. For the image embedding, we pass the 2048 dimensional feature vector returned by ResNet through a fully-connected layer and reduce it to a 64 dimensional vector. For the question embedding, we use an LSTM with a hidden layer of size 128. The two are then concatenated into a vector of size 192 and passed through a two layer perceptron with 256 and 128 nodes respectively. Note that the baseline doesn't use image features apart from the detected visual concepts.

The multi-hot visual concept embedding is passed through a fully-connected layer to form a 128 dimensional vector. This is then concatenated with the output of the perceptron and passed through another layer with 200 output nodes. We found a late fusion of the visual concepts to results in a better model as the facts explicitly contain these terms.

Fact embeddings are constructed using GloVe-100 vectors each, for entities a and b. If a or b contain multiple words, an average of all the embeddings is computed. We use cosine distance between the MLP and the fact embeddings to score the facts. The highest scoring fact is chosen as the answer. Ties are broken randomly.

Based on the answer source prediction which is computed using the aforementioned LSTM model, we choose either entity a or b of the fact to be the answer. See Eq. (1) for the formal description. Accuracy is computed based on exact match between the chosen entity and the groundtruth answer.

To assess the importance of particular features we investigate 5 variants of our model with varying features: two oracle approaches '*gt* Question + Image + Visual Concepts' and '*gt* Question + Visual Concepts' which make use of groundtruth relation type and answer type data. More specifically, '*gt* Question + Image + Visual Concepts' and '*gt* Question + Visual Concepts' use the groundtruth relations and answer sources respectively. We have three approaches

Table 3. Answer accuracy over the FVQA dataset.

Method	Accuracy	
	@1	@3
LSTM-Question+Image+Pre-VQA [14]	24.98	40.40
Hie-Question+Image+Pre-VQA [14]	43.14	59.44
FVQA [14]	56.91	64.65
Ensemble [14]	58.76	-
Ours - Question + Image	26.68	30.27
Ours - Question + Image + Visual Concepts	60.30	73.10
Ours - Question + Visual Concepts	**62.20**	**75.60**
Ours - *gt* Question + Image + Visual Concepts	69.12	80.25
Ours - *gt* Question + Visual Concepts	70.34	82.12

using a variety of features as follows: 'Question + Image + Visual Concepts,' 'Question + Visual Concepts,' and 'Question + Image.' We drop either the Image embeddings from ResNet or the Visual Concept embeddings to obtain two other models, 'Question + Visual Concepts' and 'Question + Image.'

Table 3 shows the accuracy of our model in predicting an answer and compares our results to other FVQA baselines. We observe the proposed approach to outperform the state-of-the-art ensemble technique by more than 3% and the strongest baseline without ensemble by over 5% on the top-1 accuracy metric. Moreover we note the importance of visual concepts to accurately predict the answer. By including groundtruth information we assess the maximally possible top-1 and top-3 accuracy. We observe the difference to be around 8%, suggesting that there is some room for improvement.

Question to Supporting Fact. To provide a complete assessment of the proposed approach we illustrate in Table 4 the top-1 and top-3 accuracy scores in retrieving the supporting facts of our model compared to other FVQA baselines. We observe the proposed approach to improve significantly both the top-1 and top-3 accuracy by more than 20%. We think this is a significant improvement towards efficiently including knowledge bases into visual question answering.

Mining Hard Negatives. We trained our model over three iterations of hard negative mining, *i.e.*, $T = 2$. In iteration 1 ($t = 0$), all the 193,449 facts were used to sample the 99 negative facts during train. At every 10th epoch of training, negative facts which received high scores were saved. In the next iteration, the trained model along with the negative facts is loaded and we ensure that the 99 negative facts are now sampled from the hard negatives. Table 5 shows the Top-1 and Top-3 accuracy for predicting the supporting facts over each of the three iterations. We observe significant improvements due to the proposed hard negative mining strategy. While naïve training of the proposed approach yields only 20.17% top-1 accuracy, two iterations improve the performance to 64.5%.

Table 4. Correct fact prediction precision over the FVQA dataset.

Method	Accuracy	
	@1	@3
FVQA-top-1 [14]	38.76	42.96
FVQA-top-3 [14]	41.12	45.49
Ours - Question + Image	28.98	32.34
Ours - Question + Image + Visual Concepts	62.30	74.90
Ours - Question + Visual Concepts	**64.50**	**76.20**

Table 5. Correct fact prediction precision with hard negative mining.

Iteration	# Hard negatives	Precision	
		@1	@3
1	0	20.17	23.46
2	84,563	38.65	45.49
3	6,889	64.5	76.2

Synonyms and Homographs. Here we show the improvements of our model compared to the baseline with respect to synonyms and homographs. To this end, we run additional tests using Wordnet to determine the number of question-fact pairs which contain synonyms. The test data contains 1105 such pairs out of which our model predicts 91.6% (1012) correctly, whereas the FVQA model predicts 78.0% (862) correctly. In addition, we manually generated 100 synonymous questions by replacing words in the questions with synonyms (*e.g.*, "What in the bowl can you eat?" is rephrased to "What in the bowl is edible?"). Tests on these 100 new samples find that our model predicts 89 of these correctly, whereas the key-word matching FVQA technique [14] gets 61 of these right. With regards to homographs, the test set has 998 questions which contain words that have multiple meanings across facts. Our model predicts correct answers for 79.4% (792), whereas the FVQA model gets 66.3% (662) correct.

Qualitative Results. Figure 3 shows the Visual Concepts (VCs) detected for a few samples along with the top 3 facts retrieved by our model. Providing these predicted VCs as input to our fact-scoring MLP helps improve supporting fact retrieval as well as answer accuracy by a large margin of over 30% as seen in Tables 3 and 4. As can be seen in Fig. 3, there is a close alignment between relevant facts and predicted VCs, as VCs provide a high-level overview of the salient content in the images.

In Fig. 4, we show success and failure cases of our method. There are 3 steps to producing the correct answer using our method: (1) correctly predicting the relation, (2) retrieving supporting facts containing the predicted relation, and relevant to the image, and (3) choosing the answer from the predicted answer

Question: Which object in this image is considered to be a shelter?
Scenes Detected:
Alley, Residential Neighborhood, Street, House, Motel
Predicted Relation: IsA
Top-3 Retrieved Facts:
(House, IsA, Shelter)
(Car, IsA, Heavier Than Horse)
(Car, IsA, Motorvehicle)
Predicted Answer: House

Fig. 3. Examples of Visual Concepts (VCs) detected by our framework. Here, we show examples of detected objects, scenes, and actions predicted by the various networks used in our pipeline. There is a clear alignment between useful facts, and the predicted VCs. As a result, including VCs in our scoring method helps improve performance.

source (Image/Knowledge Base). The top two rows of images show cases where all the 3 steps were correctly executed by our proposed method. Note that our method works for a variety of relations, objects, answer sources, and varying difficulty. It is correctly able to identify the object of interest, even when it is not the most prominent object in the image. For example, in the middle image of the first row, the frisbee is smaller than the dog in the image. However, we were correctly able to retrieve the supporting fact about the frisbee using information from the question, such as '*capable of*' and '*flying.*'

A mistake in any of the 3 steps can cause our method to produce an incorrect answer. The bottom row of images in Fig. 4 displays prototypical failure modes. In the leftmost image, we miss cues from the question such as '*round,*' and instead retrieve a fact about the person. In the middle image, our method makes a mistake at the final step and uses information from the wrong answer source. This is a very rare source of errors overall, as we are over 97% accurate in predicting the answer source, as shown in Table 2. In the rightmost image, our method makes a mistake at the first step of predicting the relation, making the remaining steps incorrect. Our relation prediction is around 75%, and 92% accurate by the top-1 and top-3 metrics, as shown in Table 1, and has some scope for improvement. For qualitative results regarding synonyms and homographs we refer the interested reader to the supplementary material.

Question: What is a bookshelf used for?

Predicted Relation: UsedFor
Predicted Supporting Fact:
(Bookshelf, UsedFor, Carrying Books)
Predicted Answer Source: KB

Predicted Answer: Carrying books
GT Answer: Carrying books

Question: What object in this image is capable of flying?

Predicted Relation: CapableOf
Predicted Supporting Fact:
(Frisbee, CapableOf, Flying)
Predicted Answer Source: Image

Predicted Answer: Frisbee
GT Answer: Frisbee

Question: Which property does the place in the image have?

Predicted Relation: HasProperty
Predicted Supporting Fact:
(Beach, HasProperty, Sandy)
Predicted Answer Source: KB

Predicted Answer: Sandy
GT Answer: Sandy

Question: What object in this image is cheaper than a taxi?

Predicted Relation: Comparative
Predicted Supporting Fact:
(Bus, Comparative-cheaper, Taxi)
Predicted Answer Source: Image

Predicted Answer: Bus
GT Answer: Bus

Question: Which kind of food is sweet in this image?

Predicted Relation: HasProperty
Predicted Supporting Fact:
(Cake, HasProperty, Sweet)
Predicted Answer Source: Image

Predicted Answer: Cake
GT Answer: Cake

Question: What is an item of office equipment in this image?

Predicted Relation: Category
Predicted Supporting Fact:
(Monitor, Category, Office Equipment)
Predicted Answer Source: Image

Predicted Answer: Monitor
GT Answer: Monitor

Question: What object in this image is round?
Predicted Relation: HasProperty
Predicted Supporting Fact:
(Person, HasProperty, Alive)
GT Supporting Fact:
(TennisBall, HasProperty, Round)

Predicted Answer Source: Image
GT Answer Source: Image

Predicted Answer: Person
GT Answer: TennisBall

Question: Which action is less strenuous than the action in the image?
Predicted Relation: Comparative
Predicted Supporting Fact:
(Jumping, Comparative-more strenuous, Dressage)

Predicted Answer Source: Image
GT Answer Source: KB

Predicted Answer: Jumping
GT Answer: Dressage

Question: What sort of food can you see in the image?
Predicted Relation: IsA
GT Relation: Category

Predicted Supporting Fact: (Lemon, isA, Fruit)
GT Supporting Fact: (Fruits, Category, Food)

Predicted Answer Source: Image

Predicted Answer: Lemon
GT Answer: Fruits

Fig. 4. Success and failure cases of our method. In the top two rows, our method correctly predicts the relation, the supporting fact, and the answer source to produce the correct answer for the given question. The bottom row of examples shows the failure modes of our method.

5 Conclusion

In this work, we addressed knowledge-based visual question answering and developed a method that learns to embed facts as well as question-image pairs into a space that admits efficient search for answers to a given question. In contrast to existing retrieval based techniques, our approach learns to embed questions and facts for retrieval. We have demonstrated the efficacy of the proposed method on the recently introduced and challenging FVQA dataset, producing state-of-the-art results. In the future, we hope to address extensions of our work to larger structured knowledge bases, as well as unstructured knowledge sources, such as online text corpora.

Acknowledgments. This material is based upon work supported in part by the National Science Foundation under Grant No. 1718221, Samsung, and 3M. We thank NVIDIA for providing the GPUs used for this research. We also thank Arun Mallya and Aditya Deshpande for their help.

References

1. Krishna, R., et al.: Visual genome: connecting language and vision using crowdsourced dense image annotations. IJCV **123**, 32–73 (2017)
2. Ren, M., Kiros, R., Zemel, R.: Exploring models and data for image question answering. In: NIPS (2015)
3. Zhu, Y., Groth, O., Bernstein, M., Fei-Fei, L.: Visual7W: grounded question answering in images. In: CVPR (2016)
4. Malinowski, M., Fritz, M.: Towards a visual turing challenge. In: NIPS (2014)
5. Johnson, J., Hariharan, B., van der Maaten, L., Fei-Fei, L., Zitnick, C.L., Girshick, R.: CLEVR: a diagnostic dataset for compositional language and elementary visual reasoning. In: CVPR (2017)
6. Jabri, A., Joulin, A., van der Maaten, L.: Revisiting visual question answering baselines. In: Leibe, B., Matas, J., Sebe, N., Welling, M. (eds.) ECCV 2016, Part VIII. LNCS, vol. 9912, pp. 727–739. Springer, Cham (2016). https://doi.org/10.1007/978-3-319-46484-8_44
7. Yu, L., Park, E., Berg, A., Berg, T.: Visual Madlibs: fill in the blank image generation and question answering. In: ICCV (2015)
8. Antol, S., et al.: VQA: visual question answering. In: ICCV (2015)
9. Goyal, Y., Khot, T., Summers-Stay, D., Batra, D., Parikh, D.: Making the V in VQA matter: elevating the role of image understanding in visual question answering. In: CVPR (2017)
10. Gao, H., Mao, J., Zhou, J., Huang, Z., Wang, L., Xu, W.: Are you talking to a machine? Dataset and methods for multilingual image question answering. In: NIPS (2015)
11. Malinowski, M., Fritz, M.: A multi-world approach to question answering about real-world scenes based on uncertain input. In: NIPS (2014)
12. Malinowski, M., Rohrbach, M., Fritz, M.: Ask your neurons: a neural-based approach to answering questions about images. In: ICCV (2015)
13. Hu, R., Andreas, J., Rohrbach, M., Darrell, T., Saenko, K.: Learning to reason: end-to-end module networks for visual question answering. CoRR, abs/1704.05526 3 (2017)

14. Wang, P., Wu, Q., Shen, C., Dick, A., van den Hengel, A.: FVQA: fact-based visual question answering. TPAMI (2018)
15. Tandon, N., de Melo, G., Suchanek, F., Weikum, G.: Webchild: harvesting and organizing commonsense knowledge from the web. In: WSDM (2014)
16. Auer, S., Bizer, C., Kobilarov, G., Lehmann, J., Cyganiak, R., Ives, Z.: DBpedia: a nucleus for a web of open data. In: Aberer, K. (ed.) ASWC/ISWC 2007. LNCS, vol. 4825, pp. 722–735. Springer, Heidelberg (2007). https://doi.org/10.1007/978-3-540-76298-0_52
17. Speer, R., Chin, J., Havasi, C.: ConceptNet 5.5: an open multilingual graph of general knowledge. In: AAAI (2017)
18. Lu, J., Yang, J., Batra, D., Parikh, D.: Hierarchical question-image co-attention for visual question answering. In: NIPS (2016)
19. Yang, Z., He, X., Gao, J., Deng, L., Smola, A.: Stacked attention networks for image question answering. In: CVPR (2016)
20. Andreas, J., Rohrbach, M., Darrell, T., Klein, D.: Deep compositional question answering with neural module networks. In: CVPR (2016)
21. Das, A., Agrawal, H., Zitnick, C.L., Parikh, D., Batra, D.: Human attention in visual question answering: do humans and deep networks look at the same regions? In: EMNLP (2016)
22. Fukui, A., Park, D.H., Yang, D., Rohrbach, A., Darrell, T., Rohrbach, M.: Multimodal compact bilinear pooling for visual question answering and visual grounding. In: EMNLP (2016)
23. Shih, K.J., Singh, S., Hoiem, D.: Where to look: focus regions for visual question answering. In: CVPR (2016)
24. Xu, H., Saenko, K.: Ask, attend and answer: exploring question-guided spatial attention for visual question answering. In: Leibe, B., Matas, J., Sebe, N., Welling, M. (eds.) ECCV 2016, Part VII. LNCS, vol. 9911, pp. 451–466. Springer, Cham (2016). https://doi.org/10.1007/978-3-319-46478-7_28
25. Schwartz, I., Schwing, A.G., Hazan, T.: High-order attention models for visual question answering. In: NIPS (2017)
26. Ben-younes, H., Cadene, R., Cord, M., Thome, N.: MUTAN: multimodal tucker fusion for visual question answering. In: ICCV (2017)
27. Ma, L., Lu, Z., Li, H.: Learning to answer questions from image using convolutional neural network. In: AAAI (2016)
28. Jain, U., Zhang, Z., Schwing, A.G.: Creativity: generating diverse questions using variational autoencoders. In: CVPR (2017)
29. Xiong, C., Merity, S., Socher, R.: Dynamic memory networks for visual and textual question answering. In: ICML (2016)
30. Kim, J.H., et al.: Multimodal residual learning for visual QA. In: NIPS (2016)
31. Zitnick, C.L., Agrawal, A., Antol, S., Mitchell, M., Batra, D., Parikh, D.: Measuring machine intelligence through visual question answering. AI Mag. **37**, 63–72 (2016)
32. Zhou, B., Tian, Y., Sukhbataar, S., Szlam, A., Fergus, R.: Simple baseline for visual question answering (2015). arXiv preprint: arXiv:1512.02167
33. Wu, Q., Shen, C., van den Hengel, A., Wang, P., Dick, A.: Image captioning and visual question answering based on attributes and their related external knowledge (2016). arXiv:1603.02814
34. Jain, U., Lazebnik, S., Schwing, A.G.: Two can play this game: visual dialog with discriminative question generation and answering. In: CVPR (2018)
35. Simonyan, K., Zisserman, A.: Very deep convolutional networks for large-scale image recognition (2014). arXiv preprint: arXiv:1409.1556

36. Russakovsky, O., et al.: ImageNet large scale visual recognition challenge. IJCV **115**, 211–252 (2015)
37. Zettlemoyer, L.S., Collins, M.: Learning to map sentences to logical form: structured classification with probabilistic categorial grammars. In: UAI (2005)
38. Zettlemoyer, L.S., Collins, M.: Learning context-dependent mappings from sentences to logical form. In: ACL (2005)
39. Berant, J., Chou, A., Frostig, R., Liang, P.: Semantic parsing on freebase from question-answer pairs. In: EMNLP (2013)
40. Cai, Q., Yates, A.: Large-scale semantic parsing via schema matching and lexicon extension. In: ACL (2013)
41. Liang, P., Jordan, M.I., Klein, D.: Learning dependency-based compositional semantics. Comput. Linguist. **39**, 389–446 (2013)
42. Kwiatkowski, T., Choi, E., Artzi, Y., Zettlemoyer, L.: Scaling semantic parsers with on-the-fly ontology matching. In: EMNLP (2013)
43. Berant, J., Liang, P.: Semantic parsing via paraphrasing. In: ACL (2014)
44. Fader, A., Zettlemoyer, L., Etzioni, O.: Open question answering over curated and extracted knowledge bases. In: KDD (2014)
45. Yih, W., Chang, M.W., He, X., Gao, J.: Semantic parsing via staged query graph generation: question answering with knowledge base. In: ACL-IJCNLP (2015)
46. Reddy, S., et al.: Transforming dependency structures to logical forms for semantic parsing. In: ACL (2016)
47. Xiao, C., Dymetman, M., Gardent, C.: Sequence-based structured prediction for semantic parsing. In: ACL (2016)
48. Unger, C., Bühmann, L., Lehmann, J., Ngomo, A.C.N., Gerber, D., Cimiano, P.: Template-based question answering over RDF data. In: WWW (2012)
49. Kolomiyets, O., Moens, M.F.: A survey on question answering technology from an information retrieval perspective. Inf. Sci. **181**, 5412–5434 (2011)
50. Yao, X., Durme, B.V.: Information extraction over structured data: question answering with freebase. In: ACL (2014)
51. Bordes, A., Chopra, S., Weston, J.: Question answering with sub-graph embeddings. In: EMNLP (2014)
52. Bordes, A., Weston, J., Usunier, N.: Open question answering with weakly supervised embedding models. In: Calders, T., Esposito, F., Hüllermeier, E., Meo, R. (eds.) ECML PKDD 2014, Part I. LNCS (LNAI), vol. 8724, pp. 165–180. Springer, Heidelberg (2014). https://doi.org/10.1007/978-3-662-44848-9_11
53. Dong, L., Wei, F., Zhou, M., Xu, K.: Question answering over freebase with multi-column convolutional neural networks. In: ACL (2015)
54. Bordes, A., Usunier, N., Chopra, S., Weston, J.: Large-scale simple question answering with memory networks. In: ICLR (2015)
55. Zhu, Y., Zhang, C., Ré, C., Fei-Fei, L.: Building a large-scale multimodal knowledge base for visual question answering. CoRR (2015)
56. Wu, Q., Wang, P., Shen, C., van den Hengel, A., Dick, A.: Ask me anything: free-form visual question answering based on knowledge from external sources. In: CVPR (2016)
57. Wang, P., Wu, Q., Shen, C., van den Hengel, A., Dick, A.: Explicit knowledge-based reasoning for visual question answering. In: IJCAI (2017)
58. Krishnamurthy, J., Kollar, T.: Jointly learning to parse and perceive: connecting natural language to the physical world. In: ACL (2013)
59. Narasimhan, K., Yala, A., Barzilay, R.: Improving information extraction by acquiring external evidence with reinforcement learning. In: EMNLP (2016)

60. Wu, Q., Wang, P., Shen, C., Dick, A., van den Hengel, A.: Ask me anything: free-form visual question answering based on knowledge from external sources. In: CVPR (2016)
61. Wang, P., Wu, Q., Shen, C., Dick, A., Van Den Henge, A.: Explicit knowledge-based reasoning for visual question answering. In: IJCAI (2017)
62. Pennington, J., Socher, R., Manning, C.D.: Glove: global vectors for word representation. In: EMNLP (2014)
63. Hochreiter, S., Schmidhuber, J.: Long short-term memory. Neural Comput. **9**, 1735–1780 (1997)
64. He, K., Zhang, X., Ren, S., Sun, J.: Deep residual learning for image recognition. In: CVPR (2016)
65. Deng, J., Dong, W., Socher, R., Li, L.J., Li, K., Fei-Fei, L.: Imagenet: a large-scale hierarchical image database. In: CVPR (2009)
66. Ren, S., He, K., Girshick, R., Sun, J.: Faster R-CNN: towards real-time object detection with region proposal networks. In: NIPS (2015)
67. Lin, T.-Y., et al.: Microsoft COCO: common objects in context. In: Fleet, D., Pajdla, T., Schiele, B., Tuytelaars, T. (eds.) ECCV 2014, Part V. LNCS, vol. 8693, pp. 740–755. Springer, Cham (2014). https://doi.org/10.1007/978-3-319-10602-1_48
68. Zhou, B., Lapedriza, A., Khosla, A., Oliva, A., Torralba, A.: Places: a 10 million image database for scene recognition. TPAMI **40**, 1452–1464 (2017)
69. Mallya, A., Lazebnik, S.: Learning models for actions and person-object interactions with transfer to question answering. In: Leibe, B., Matas, J., Sebe, N., Welling, M. (eds.) ECCV 2016, Part I. LNCS, vol. 9905, pp. 414–428. Springer, Cham (2016). https://doi.org/10.1007/978-3-319-46448-0_25
70. Chao, Y.W., Wang, Z., He, Y., Wang, J., Deng, J.: HICO: a benchmark for recognizing human-object interactions in images. In: ICCV (2015)
71. Andriluka, M., Pishchulin, L., Gehler, P., Schiele, B.: 2D human pose estimation: new benchmark and state of the art analysis. In: CVPR (2014)
72. Tsochantaridis, I., Joachims, T., Hofmann, T., Altun, Y.: Large margin methods for structured and interdependent output variables. JMLR **6**, 1453–1484 (2005)

Joint and Progressive Learning from High-Dimensional Data for Multi-label Classification

Danfeng Hong[1,2(✉)], Naoto Yokoya[3], Jian Xu[1], and Xiaoxiang Zhu[1,2]

[1] Remote Sensing Technology Institute (IMF), German Aerospace Center (DLR), Wessling, Germany
{danfeng.hong,jian.xu,xiao.zhu}@dlr.de
[2] Signal Processing in Earth Observation (SiPEO), Technical University of Munich, Munich, Germany
[3] RIKEN Center for Advanced Intelligence Project, Tokyo, Japan
naoto.yokoya@riken.jp

Abstract. Despite the fact that nonlinear subspace learning techniques (e.g. manifold learning) have successfully applied to data representation, there is still room for improvement in explainability (explicit mapping), generalization (out-of-samples), and cost-effectiveness (linearization). To this end, a novel linearized subspace learning technique is developed in a joint and progressive way, called joint and progressive learning strategy (J-Play), with its application to multi-label classification. The J-Play learns high-level and semantically meaningful feature representation from high-dimensional data by (1) jointly performing multiple subspace learning and classification to find a latent subspace where samples are expected to be better classified; (2) progressively learning multi-coupled projections to linearly approach the optimal mapping bridging the original space with the most discriminative subspace; (3) locally embedding manifold structure in each learnable latent subspace. Extensive experiments are performed to demonstrate the superiority and effectiveness of the proposed method in comparison with previous state-of-the-art methods.

Keywords: Alternating direction method of multipliers
High-dimensional data · Manifold regularization
Multi-label classification · Joint learning · Progressive learning

1 Introduction

High-dimensional data are often characterized by very rich and diverse information, which enables us to classify or recognize the targets more effectively and analyze data attributes more easily, but inevitably introduces some drawbacks (e.g. information redundancy, complex noise effects, high storage-consuming, etc.) due to *the curve of dimensionality*. A general way to address this problem

V. Ferrari et al. (Eds.): ECCV 2018, LNCS 11212, pp. 478–493, 2018.
https://doi.org/10.1007/978-3-030-01237-3_29

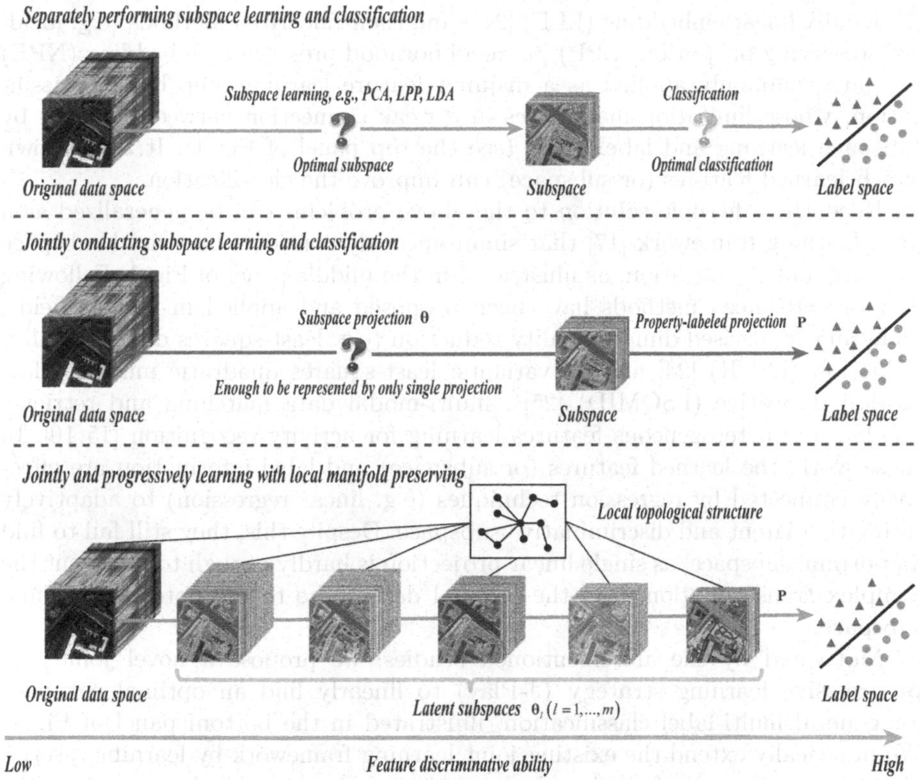

Fig. 1. The motivation interpolation from separately performing subspace learning and classification to joint learning to joint & progressive learning again. The subspaces learned from our model indicates the higher feature discriminative ability as explained by the green bottom line. (Color figure online)

is to learn a low-dimensional and high-discriminative feature representation. In general, it is also called as dimensionality reduction or subspace learning. In the past decades, a large number of subspace learning techniques have been developed in the machine learning community, with successful applications to biometrics [5,9,10,20], image/video analysis [26], visualization [22], hyperspectral data analysis (e.g., dimensionality reduction and unmixing) [12–14]. These subspace learning techniques are generally categorized into linear or nonlinear methods. Theoretically, nonlinear approaches are capable of curving the data structure in a more effective way. There is, however, no explicit mapping function (poor explainability), and meanwhile it is relatively hard to embed the out-of-samples into the learned subspace (weak generalization) as well as high computational cost (lack of cost-effectiveness). Additionally, for a task of multi-label classification, these classic subspace learning techniques, such as principal component analysis (PCA) [29], local discriminant analysis (LDA) [20], local fisher discriminant analysis (LFDA) [23], manifold learning (e.g. Laplacian eigenmaps (LE)

[1], locally linear embedding (LLE) [21]) and their linearized methods (e.g. locality preserving projection (LPP) [6], neighborhood preserving embedding (NPE) [4]), are commonly applied as a disjunct feature learning step before classification, whose limitation mainly lies in a weak connection between features by subspace learning and label space (see the top panel of Fig. 1). It is unknown which learned features (or subspace) can improve the classification.

Recently, a feasible solution to the above problems can be generalized as a joint learning framework [17] that simultaneously considers linearized subspace learning and classification, as illustrated in the middle panel of Fig. 1. Following it, more advanced methods have been proposed and applied in various fields, including supervised dimensionality reduction (e.g. least-squares dimensionality reduction (LSDR) [24] and its variants: least-squares quadratic mutual information derivative (LSQMID) [25]), multi-modal data matching and retrieval [27,28], and heterogeneous features learning for activity recognition [15,16]. In these work, the learned features (or subspace) and label information are effectively connected by regression techniques (e.g. linear regression) to adaptively estimate a latent and discriminative subspace. Despite this, they still fail to find an optimal subspace, as single linear projection is hardly enough to represent the complex transformation from the original data space to the potential optimal subspace.

Motivated by the aforementioned studies, we propose a novel **j**oint and **p**rogre-ssive **l**e**a**rning strateg**y** (J-Play) to linearly find an optimal subspace for general multi-label classification, illustrated in the bottom panel of Fig. 1. We practically extend the existing joint learning framework by learning a series of subspaces instead of single subspace, aiming at progressively converting the original data space to a potentially optimal subspace through multi-coupled intermediate transformations [18]. Theoretically, by increasing the number of subspaces, coupled subspace variations are gradually narrowed down to a very small range that can be represented effectively via a *linear transformation*. This renders us to find a good solution easier, especially when the model is complex and non-convex. We also contribute to structure learning in each latent subspace by locally embedding manifold structure.

The main highlights of our work can be summarized as follows:

- A linearized progressive learning strategy is proposed to describe the variations from the original data space to potentially optimal subspace, tending to find a better solution. A joint learning framework that simultaneously estimates subspace projections (connect the original space and the latent subspaces) and a property-labeled projection (connect the learned latent subspaces and label space) is considered to find a discriminative subspace where samples are expected to be better classified.
- Structure learning with local manifold regularization is performed in each latent subspace.
- Based on the above techniques, a novel joint and progressive learning strategy (J-Play) is developed for multi-label classification.

- An iterative optimization algorithm based on the alternating direction method of multipliers (ADMM) is designed to solve the proposed model.

2 Joint and Progressive Learning Strategy (J-Play)

2.1 Notations

Let $\mathbf{X} = [\mathbf{x}_1, ..., \mathbf{x}_k, ..., \mathbf{x}_N] \in \mathbb{R}^{d_0 \times N}$ be a data matrix with d_0 dimensions and N samples, and the matrix of corresponding class labels be $\mathbf{Y} \in \{0,1\}^{L \times N}$. The kth column of $\mathbf{Y}$ is $\mathbf{y}_k = [\mathbf{y}_{k1}, ..., \mathbf{y}_{kt}, ..., \mathbf{y}_{kL}]^T \in \mathbb{R}^{L \times 1}$ whose each element can be defined as follows:

$$\mathbf{y}_{kt} = \begin{cases} 1, & \text{if } \mathbf{y}_k \text{ belongs to the } t\text{-th class;} \\ 0, & \text{otherwise.} \end{cases} \tag{1}$$

In our task, we aim to learn a set of coupled projections $\{\mathbf{\Theta}_l\}_{l=1}^{m} \in \mathbb{R}^{d_l \times d_{l-1}}$ and a property-labeled projection $\mathbf{P} \in \mathbb{R}^{L \times d_m}$, where m stands for the number of subspace projections and $\{d_l\}_{l=1}^{m}$ are defined as the dimensions of those latent subspaces respectively, while d_0 is specified as the dimension of $\mathbf{X}$.

2.2 Basic Framework of J-Play from the View of Subspace Learning

Subspace learning is to find a low-dimensional space where we expect to maximize certain properties of the original data, e.g. variance (PCA), discriminative ability (LDA), and graph structure (manifold learning). Yan et al. [30] summarized these subspace learning methods in a general graph embedding framework.

Given an undirected similarity graph $G = \{\mathbf{X}, \mathbf{W}\}$ with the vertices $\mathbf{X} \in \{\mathbf{x}_1, ..., \mathbf{x}_N\}$ and the adjacency matrix $\mathbf{W} \in \mathbb{R}^{N \times N}$, we can intuitively measure the similarities among the data. By preserving the similarities relationship, the high-dimensional data can be well embedded into the low-dimensional space, which can be formulated by denoting the low-dimensional data representation as $\mathbf{Z} \in \mathbb{R}^{d \times N}$ ($d \ll d_0$) in the following

$$\min_{\mathbf{Z}} \operatorname{tr}(\mathbf{Z}\mathbf{L}\mathbf{Z}^{\mathrm{T}}), \quad \text{s.t.} \quad \mathbf{Z}\mathbf{D}\mathbf{Z}^{\mathrm{T}} = \mathbf{I}, \tag{2}$$

where $\mathbf{D}_{ii} = \sum_j \mathbf{W}_{ij}$ is a diagonal matrix, $\mathbf{L}$ is a Laplacian matrix defined by $\mathbf{L} = \mathbf{D} - \mathbf{W}$ [3], and $\mathbf{I}$ is the identity matrix. In our case, we aim at learning multi-coupled linear projections to find optimal mapping, therefore a linearized subspace learning problem can be reformulated on the basis of Eq. (2) by substituting $\mathbf{\Theta}\mathbf{X}$ for $\mathbf{Z}$

$$\min_{\mathbf{\Theta}} \operatorname{tr}(\mathbf{\Theta}\mathbf{X}\mathbf{L}\mathbf{X}^{\mathrm{T}}\mathbf{\Theta}^{\mathrm{T}}), \quad \text{s.t.} \quad \mathbf{\Theta}\mathbf{X}\mathbf{D}\mathbf{X}^{\mathrm{T}}\mathbf{\Theta}^{\mathrm{T}} = \mathbf{I}, \tag{3}$$

which can be solved by generalized eigenvalue decomposition.

Different from the previously mentioned subspace learning methods, a regression-based joint learning model [17] can explicitly bridge the learned latent subspace and labels, which can be formulated in a general form:

$$\min_{\mathbf{P},\mathbf{\Theta}} \frac{1}{2}\mathbf{E}(\mathbf{P},\mathbf{\Theta}) + \frac{\beta}{2}\mathbf{\Phi}(\mathbf{\Theta}) + \frac{\gamma}{2}\mathbf{\Psi}(\mathbf{P}), \tag{4}$$

where $\mathbf{E}(\mathbf{P},\mathbf{\Theta})$ is the error term defined as $\|\mathbf{Y} - \mathbf{P}\mathbf{\Theta}\mathbf{X}\|_{\mathrm{F}}^2$, $\|\bullet\|_{\mathrm{F}}$ represents a Frobenius norm, β and γ are the corresponding penalty parameters. $\mathbf{\Phi}$ and $\mathbf{\Psi}$ denote regularization functions, which might be l_1 norm, l_2 norm, $l_{2,1}$ norm or manifold regularization. Herein, the variable $\mathbf{\Theta}$ is called intermediate transformation and the corresponding subspace generated by $\mathbf{\Theta}$ is called latent subspace where the feature can be further structurally learned and represented in a more suitable way [16].

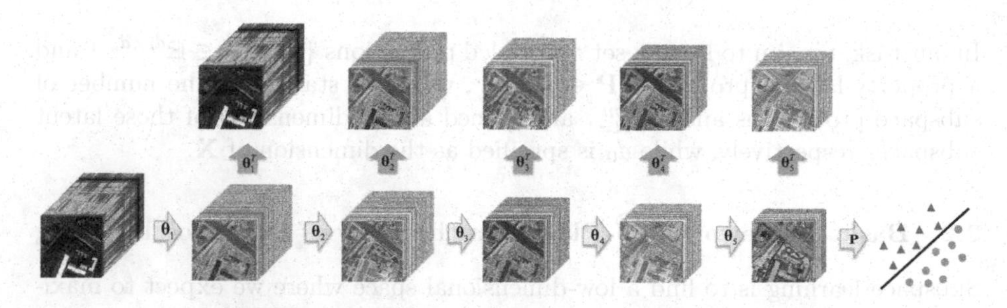

Fig. 2. The illustration of the proposed J-Play framework.

On the basis of Eq. (5), we further extend the framework by following a progressive learning strategy:

$$\min_{\mathbf{P},\{\mathbf{\Theta}_l\}_{l=1}^m} \frac{1}{2}\mathbf{E}(\mathbf{P},\{\mathbf{\Theta}_l\}_{l=1}^m) + \frac{\beta}{2}\mathbf{\Phi}(\{\mathbf{\Theta}_l\}_{l=1}^m) + \frac{\gamma}{2}\mathbf{\Psi}(\mathbf{P}), \tag{5}$$

where $\mathbf{E}(\mathbf{P},\{\mathbf{\Theta}_l\}_{l=1}^m)$ is specified as $\|\mathbf{Y} - \mathbf{P}\mathbf{\Theta}_m...\mathbf{\Theta}_l...\mathbf{\Theta}_1\mathbf{X}\|_{\mathrm{F}}^2$ and $\{\mathbf{\Theta}_l\}_{l=1}^m$ represent a set of intermediate transformations.

2.3 Problem Formulation

Following the general framework given in Eq. (6), the proposed J-Play can be formulated as the following constrained optimization problem:

$$\begin{aligned} \min_{\mathbf{P},\{\mathbf{\Theta}_l\}_{l=1}^m} & \frac{1}{2}\mathbf{\Upsilon}(\{\mathbf{\Theta}_l\}_{l=1}^m) + \frac{\alpha}{2}\mathbf{E}(\mathbf{P},\{\mathbf{\Theta}_l\}_{l=1}^m) + \frac{\beta}{2}\mathbf{\Phi}(\{\mathbf{\Theta}_l\}_{l=1}^m) + \frac{\gamma}{2}\mathbf{\Psi}(\mathbf{P}) \\ \text{s.t.} \quad & \mathbf{X}_l = \mathbf{\Theta}_l\mathbf{X}_{l-1}, \quad \mathbf{X}_l \succeq 0, \quad \|\mathbf{x}_{lk}\|_2 \preceq 1, \quad \forall l = 1,2,...,m, \end{aligned} \tag{6}$$

where $\mathbf{X}$ is assigned to $\mathbf{X}_0$, while α, β, and γ are three penalty parameters corresponding to the different terms, which aim at balancing the importance between the terms. Figure 2 illustrates the J-Play framework. Since Eq. (7) is a typically ill-posed problem, reasonable assumptions or priors need to be introduced to search a solution in a narrowed range effectively. More specifically, we cast Eq. (7) as a least-square regression problem with reconstruction loss term ($\mathbf{\Upsilon}(\bullet)$), prediction loss term ($\mathbf{E}(\bullet)$) and two regularization terms ($\mathbf{\Phi}(\bullet)$ and $\mathbf{\Psi}(\bullet)$). We detail these terms one by one as follows.

(1) Reconstruction Loss Term $\mathbf{\Upsilon}(\{\mathbf{\Theta}_l\}_{l=1}^m)$: Without any constraints or prior, directly estimating multi-coupled projections in J-Play is hardly performed with the increase of the number of estimated projections. This can be reasonably explained by gradient missing between the two neighboring variables estimated in the process of optimization. That is, the variations between these neighboring projections are made to be tiny and even zero. In particular, when the number of projections increases to a certain extent, most of learned projections tend to be zero and become meaningless. To this end, we adopt a kind of autoencoder-like scheme to make the learned subspace projected back to the original space as much as possible. The benefits of the scheme are, on one hand, to prevent the data over-fitting to some extent, especially avoiding overmuch noises from being considered; on the other hand, to establish an effective link between the original space and the subspace, making the learned subspace more meaningful. Therefore, the resulting expression is

$$\mathbf{\Upsilon}(\{\mathbf{\Theta}_l\}_{l=1}^m) = \sum\nolimits_{l=1}^{m} \|\mathbf{X}_{l-1} - \mathbf{\Theta}_l^T \mathbf{\Theta}_l \mathbf{X}_{l-1}\|_{\mathrm{F}}^2. \tag{7}$$

In our case, to fully utilize the advantages of this term, we consider it in each latent subspace as shown in Eq. (8).

(2) Predication Loss Term $\mathbf{E}(\mathbf{P}, \{\mathbf{\Theta}_l\}_{l=1}^m)$: This term is to minimize the empirical risk between the original data and the corresponding labels through multi-coupled projections in a progressive way, which can be formulated as

$$\mathbf{E}(\mathbf{P}, \{\mathbf{\Theta}_l\}_{l=1}^m) = \|\mathbf{Y} - \mathbf{P}\mathbf{\Theta}_m ... \mathbf{\Theta}_l ... \mathbf{\Theta}_1 \mathbf{X}\|_{\mathrm{F}}^2. \tag{8}$$

(3) Local Manifold Regularization $\mathbf{\Phi}(\{\mathbf{\Theta}_l\}_{l=1}^m)$: As introduced in [27], a manifold structure is an important prior for subspace learning. Superior to vector-based feature learning, such as artificial neural network (ANN), a manifold structure can effectively capture the intrinsic structure between samples. To facilitate structure learning in J-Play, we perform the local manifold regularization to each latent subspace. Specifically, this term can be expressed by

$$\mathbf{\Phi}(\{\mathbf{\Theta}_l\}_{l=1}^m) = \sum\nolimits_{l=1}^{m} \mathrm{tr}(\mathbf{\Theta}_l \mathbf{X}_{l-1} \mathbf{L} \mathbf{X}_{l-1}^{\mathrm{T}} \mathbf{\Theta}_l^{\mathrm{T}}). \tag{9}$$

(4) Regression Coefficient Regularization $\mathbf{\Psi}(\mathbf{P})$: The regularization term can promote us to derive a more reasonable solution with a reliable generalization to our model, which can be written as

$$\mathbf{\Psi}(\mathbf{P}) = \|\mathbf{P}\|_{\mathrm{F}}^2. \tag{10}$$

Algorithm 1. Joint & Progressive Learning Strategy (J-Play)

Input: $\mathbf{Y}, \mathbf{X}, \mathbf{L}$, and parameters α, β, γ and $maxIter$.
Output: $\{\boldsymbol{\Theta}_l\}_{l=1}^m$.
1 **Initialization Step:**
2 Greedily initialize $\boldsymbol{\Theta}_l$ corresponding to each latent subspace:
3 **for** $l = 1 : m$ **do**
4 $\quad \boldsymbol{\Theta}_l^0 \leftarrow LPP(\mathbf{X}_{l-1})$
5 $\quad \boldsymbol{\Theta}_l \leftarrow AutoRULe(\mathbf{X}_{l-1}, \boldsymbol{\Theta}_l^0, \mathbf{L})$
6 $\quad \mathbf{X}_l \leftarrow \boldsymbol{\Theta}_l \mathbf{X}_{l-1}$
7 **end**
8 **Fine-tuning Step:**
9 $t = 0, \zeta = 1e-4;$
10 **while** *not converged* or $t > maxIter$ **do**
11 $\quad$ Fix other variables to update $\mathbf{P}$ by solving a subproblem of $\mathbf{P}$;
12 $\quad$ **for** $i = 1 : m$ **do**
13 $\quad\quad$ Fix other variables to update $\boldsymbol{\Theta}_l^{t+1}$ by solving a subproblem of $\boldsymbol{\Theta}_l$;
14 $\quad$ **end**
15 $\quad$ Compute the objective function value Obj^{t+1} and check the convergence condition: **if** $|\frac{Obj^{t+1} - Obj^t}{Obj^t}| < \zeta$ **then**
16 $\quad\quad$ Stop iteration;
17 $\quad$ **else**
18 $\quad\quad$ $t \leftarrow t + 1;$
19 $\quad$ **end**
20 **end**

Moreover, the non-negativity constraint with respect to each learned dimension-reduced feature (e.g. $\{\mathbf{X}_l\}_{l=1}^m \succeq 0$) is considered since we aim to obtain a meaningful low-dimensional feature representation similar to original image data acquired in a non-negative unit. In addition to the non-negativity constraint, we also impose a norm constraint[1] for sample-based of each subspace: $\|\mathbf{x}_{lk}\|_2 \preceq 1, \forall k = 1, ..., N$ and $l = 1, ..., m$.

2.4 Model Optimization

Considering the complexity and the non-convexity of our model, we pretrain our model to have an initial approximation of subspace projections $\{\boldsymbol{\Theta}_l\}_{l=1}^m$ as this can greatly reduce the model's training time and also help finding an optimal solution easier. This is a common tactic that has been successfully employed in deep autoencoders [8]. Inspired by this trick, we propose a pre-training model with respect to $\boldsymbol{\Theta}_l, \forall l = 1, ..., m$ by simplifying Eq. (7) as

$$\min_{\boldsymbol{\Theta}_l} \frac{1}{2}\boldsymbol{\Upsilon}(\boldsymbol{\Theta}_l) + \frac{\eta}{2}\boldsymbol{\Phi}(\boldsymbol{\Theta}_l) \quad \text{s.t.} \quad \mathbf{X}_l \succeq 0, \quad \|\mathbf{x}_{lk}\|_2 \preceq 1, \tag{11}$$

which is named as **auto**-reconstructing **u**nsupervised **le**arning (AutoRULe). Given the outputs of AutoRULe, the problem of Eq. (7) can be more effectively solved by an alternatively minimizing strategy that separately solves two subproblems with respect to $\{\boldsymbol{\Theta}_l\}_{l=1}^m$ and $\mathbf{P}$. Therefore, the global algorithm of J-Play can be summarized in Algorithm 1, where AutoRULe is initialized by LPP.

[1] Regarding this constraint,please refer to [19] for more details.

The pre-training method (AutoRULe) can be effectively solved via the ADMM-based framework. Following this, we consider an equivalent form of Eq. (12) by introducing multiple auxiliary variables $\mathbf{H}$, $\mathbf{G}$, $\mathbf{Q}$ and $\mathbf{S}$ to replace $\mathbf{X}_l$, $\boldsymbol{\Theta}_l$, $\mathbf{X}_l^+$ and $\mathbf{X}_l^{\sim}$, respectively, where $()^+$ denotes an operator that converts each component of the matrix to its absolute value and $()^{\sim}$ is a proximal operator for solving the constraint of $\|\mathbf{x}_{lk}\|_2 \preceq 1$ [7], written as follows

$$\begin{aligned} \min_{\boldsymbol{\Theta}_l,\mathbf{H},\mathbf{G},\mathbf{Q},\mathbf{S}} \frac{1}{2}\boldsymbol{\Upsilon}(\mathbf{G},\mathbf{H}) + \frac{\eta}{2}\boldsymbol{\Phi}(\boldsymbol{\Theta}_l) = \frac{1}{2}\|\mathbf{X}_{l-1} - \mathbf{G}^{\mathrm{T}}\mathbf{H}\|_{\mathrm{F}}^2 + \frac{\eta}{2}\,\mathrm{tr}(\mathbf{X}_l\mathbf{L}\mathbf{X}_l^{\mathrm{T}}) \\ \text{s.t.} \quad \mathbf{Q} \succeq 0, \quad \|\mathbf{s}_k\|_2 \preceq 1, \quad \mathbf{X}_l = \boldsymbol{\Theta}_l\mathbf{X}_{l-1}, \\ \mathbf{X}_l = \mathbf{H}, \quad \boldsymbol{\Theta}_l = \mathbf{G}, \quad \mathbf{X}_l = \mathbf{Q}, \quad \mathbf{X}_l = \mathbf{S}. \end{aligned} \tag{12}$$

The augmented Lagrangian version of Eq. (13) is

$$\begin{aligned} &\mathscr{L}_\mu\left(\boldsymbol{\Theta}_l, \mathbf{H}, \mathbf{G}, \mathbf{Q}, \mathbf{S}, \{\boldsymbol{\Lambda}_n\}_{n=1}^4\right) \\ &= \frac{1}{2}\|\mathbf{X}_{l-1} - \mathbf{G}^{\mathrm{T}}\mathbf{H}\|_{\mathrm{F}}^2 + \frac{\eta}{2}\,\mathrm{tr}(\boldsymbol{\Theta}_l\mathbf{X}_{l-1}\mathbf{L}\mathbf{X}_{l-1}^{\mathrm{T}}\boldsymbol{\Theta}_l^{\mathrm{T}}) + \boldsymbol{\Lambda}_1^{\mathrm{T}}(\mathbf{H} - \boldsymbol{\Theta}_l\mathbf{X}_{l-1}) \\ &+ \boldsymbol{\Lambda}_2^{\mathrm{T}}(\mathbf{G} - \boldsymbol{\Theta}_l) + \boldsymbol{\Lambda}_3^{\mathrm{T}}(\mathbf{Q} - \boldsymbol{\Theta}_l\mathbf{X}_{l-1}) + \boldsymbol{\Lambda}_4^{\mathrm{T}}(\mathbf{S} - \boldsymbol{\Theta}_l\mathbf{X}_{l-1}) + \frac{\mu}{2}\|\mathbf{H} - \boldsymbol{\Theta}_l\mathbf{X}_{l-1}\|_{\mathrm{F}}^2 \\ &+ \frac{\mu}{2}\|\mathbf{G} - \boldsymbol{\Theta}_l\|_{\mathrm{F}}^2 + \frac{\mu}{2}\|\mathbf{Q} - \boldsymbol{\Theta}_l\mathbf{X}_{l-1}\|_{\mathrm{F}}^2 + \frac{\mu}{2}\|\mathbf{S} - \boldsymbol{\Theta}_l\mathbf{X}_{l-1}\|_{\mathrm{F}}^2 + l_R^+(\mathbf{Q}) + l_R^{\sim}(\mathbf{S}), \end{aligned} \tag{13}$$

where $\{\boldsymbol{\Lambda}_n\}_{n=1}^4$ are Lagrange multipliers and μ is the penalty parameter. The two terms $l_R^+(\bullet)$ and $l_R^{\sim}(\bullet)$ represent two kinds of projection operators, respectively. That is, $l_R^+(\bullet)$ is defined as

$$max(\bullet) = \begin{cases} \bullet, & \bullet \succ 0 \\ 0, & \bullet \preceq 0, \end{cases} \tag{14}$$

while $l_R^{\sim}(\bullet_k)$ is a vector-based operator defined by

$$prox_f(\bullet_k) = \begin{cases} \frac{\bullet_k}{\|\bullet_k\|_2}, & \|\bullet_k\|_2 \succ 1 \\ \bullet_k, & \|\bullet_k\|_2 \preceq 1, \end{cases} \tag{15}$$

where $\bullet_k$ is the kth column of matrix $\bullet$. Algorithm 2 details the procedures of AutoRULe.

The two subproblems in Algorithm 1 can be optimized alternatively as follows:

Optimization with respect to $\mathbf{P}$: This is a typical least square regression problem, which can be written as

$$\min_{\mathbf{P}} \frac{\alpha}{2}\mathbf{E}(\mathbf{P}) + \frac{\gamma}{2}\boldsymbol{\Psi}(\mathbf{P}) = \frac{\alpha}{2}\|\mathbf{Y} - \mathbf{P}\boldsymbol{\Theta}_m...\boldsymbol{\Theta}_l...\boldsymbol{\Theta}_1\mathbf{X}\|_{\mathrm{F}}^2 + \frac{\gamma}{2}\|\mathbf{P}\|_{\mathrm{F}}^2, \tag{16}$$

which has a closed-form solution

$$\mathbf{P} \leftarrow (\alpha\mathbf{Y}\mathbf{V}^{\mathrm{T}})(\alpha\mathbf{V}\mathbf{V}^{\mathrm{T}} + \gamma\mathbf{I})^{-1}, \tag{17}$$

where $\mathbf{V} = \boldsymbol{\Theta}_m...\boldsymbol{\Theta}_l...\boldsymbol{\Theta}_1, \forall l = 1, ..., m$.

Algorithm 2. Auto-reconstructing unsupervised learning (AutoRULe)

Input: $\mathbf{X}_{l-1}, \mathbf{\Theta}_l^0, \mathbf{L}$, and parameters η and *maxIter*.
Output: $\mathbf{\Theta}_l$.
1 **Initialization:** $\mathbf{H}^0 = \mathbf{\Theta}_l^0\mathbf{X}_{l-1}, \mathbf{G}^0 = \mathbf{0}, \mathbf{Q}^0 = \mathbf{P}^0 = \mathbf{0}, \mathbf{\Lambda}_2^0 = \mathbf{0}, \mathbf{\Lambda}_1^0 = \mathbf{\Lambda}_3^0 = \mathbf{\Lambda}_4^0 = \mathbf{0}, \mu^0 = 1e-3, \mu_{max} = 1e6, \rho = 2, \varepsilon = 1e-6, t = 0$.
2 **while** *not converged* or $t > maxIter$ **do**
3 Fix $\mathbf{H}^t, \mathbf{G}^t, \mathbf{Q}^t, \mathbf{P}^t$ to update $\mathbf{\Theta}_l^{t+1}$ by
$$\mathbf{\Theta}_l = (\mu\mathbf{H}\mathbf{X}_{l-1}^T + \mathbf{\Lambda}_1\mathbf{X}_{l-1}^T + \mu\mathbf{G} + \mathbf{\Lambda}_2 + \mu\mathbf{Q}\mathbf{X}_{l-1}^T + \mathbf{\Lambda}_3\mathbf{X}_{l-1}^T + \mu\mathbf{P}\mathbf{X}_{l-1}^T + \mathbf{\Lambda}_4\mathbf{X}_{l-1}^T)(\eta(\mathbf{X}_{l-1}\mathbf{L}\mathbf{X}_{l-1}^T) + 3\mu(\mathbf{X}_{l-1}\mathbf{X}_{l-1}^T) + \mu\mathbf{I})^{-1}.$$
4 Fix $\mathbf{\Theta}_l^{t+1}, \mathbf{G}^t, \mathbf{Q}^t, \mathbf{P}^t$ to update $\mathbf{H}^{t+1}$ by
$$\mathbf{H} = (\mathbf{G}\mathbf{G}^T + \mu\mathbf{I})^{-1}(\mathbf{G}\mathbf{X}_{l-1} + \mu\mathbf{\Theta}_l\mathbf{X}_{l-1} - \mathbf{\Lambda}_1).$$
5 Fix $\mathbf{H}^{t+1}, \mathbf{\Theta}_l^{t+1}, \mathbf{Q}^t, \mathbf{P}^t$ to update $\mathbf{G}^{t+1}$ by
$$\mathbf{G} = (\mathbf{H}\mathbf{H}^T + \mu\mathbf{I})^{-1}(\mathbf{H}\mathbf{X}_i + \mu\mathbf{\Theta}_l - \mathbf{\Lambda}_2).$$
6 Fix $\mathbf{H}^{t+1}, \mathbf{G}^{t+1}, \mathbf{\Theta}_l^{t+1}, \mathbf{P}^t$ to update $\mathbf{Q}^{t+1}$ by
$$\mathbf{Q} = max(\mathbf{\Theta}_l\mathbf{X}_{l-1} - \mathbf{\Lambda}_3/\mu, 0).$$
7 Fix $\mathbf{H}^{t+1}, \mathbf{G}^{t+1}, \mathbf{\Theta}_l^{t+1}, \mathbf{Q}^{t+1}$ to update $\mathbf{P}^{t+1}$ by
$$\mathbf{P} = prox_f(\mathbf{\Theta}_l\mathbf{X}_{l-1} - \mathbf{\Lambda}_4/\mu).$$
8 Update Lagrange multipliers by
$$\mathbf{\Lambda}_1^{t+1} = \mathbf{\Lambda}_1^t + \mu^t(\mathbf{H}^{t+1} - \mathbf{\Theta}_i^{t+1}\mathbf{X}_{l-1}), \mathbf{\Lambda}_2^{t+1} = \mathbf{\Lambda}_2^t + \mu^t(\mathbf{G}^{t+1} - \mathbf{\Theta}_i^{t+1}),$$
$$\mathbf{\Lambda}_3^{t+1} = \mathbf{\Lambda}_3^t + \mu^t(\mathbf{Q}^{t+1} - \mathbf{\Theta}_i^{t+1}\mathbf{X}_{l-1}), \mathbf{\Lambda}_4^{t+1} = \mathbf{\Lambda}_4^t + \mu^t(\mathbf{P}^{t+1} - \mathbf{\Theta}_i^{t+1}\mathbf{X}_{l-1}).$$
9 Update penalty parameter by
$$\mu^{t+1} = min(\rho\mu^t, \mu_{max}).$$
10 Check the convergence conditions: **if** $\|\mathbf{H}^{t+1} - \mathbf{\Theta}_l^{t+1}\mathbf{X}_{l-1}\|_F < \varepsilon$ *and* $\|\mathbf{G}^{t+1} - \mathbf{\Theta}_l^{t+1}\|_F < \varepsilon$ *and* $\|\mathbf{Q}^{t+1} - \mathbf{\Theta}_l^{t+1}\mathbf{X}_{l-1}\|_F < \varepsilon$ *and* $\|\mathbf{P}^{t+1} - \mathbf{\Theta}_l^{t+1}\mathbf{X}_{l-1}\|_F < \varepsilon$ **then**
11 Stop iteration;
12 **else**
13 $t \leftarrow t + 1$;
14 **end**
15 **end**

Optimization with respect to $\{\mathbf{\Theta}_l\}_{l=1}^m$: The variables $\{\mathbf{\Theta}_l\}_{l=1}^m$ can be individually optimized, and hence the optimization problem of each $\mathbf{\Theta}_l$ can be generally formulated by

$$\begin{aligned}\min_{\mathbf{\Theta}_l}\frac{1}{2}\mathbf{\Upsilon}(\mathbf{\Theta}_l) + \frac{\alpha}{2}\mathbf{E}(\mathbf{\Theta}_l) + \frac{\beta}{2}\mathbf{\Phi}(\mathbf{\Theta}_l) &= \frac{1}{2}\|\mathbf{X}_{l-1} - \mathbf{\Theta}_l^{\mathrm{T}}\mathbf{\Theta}_l\mathbf{X}_{l-1}\|_{\mathrm{F}}^2 \\ &+ \frac{\alpha}{2}\|\mathbf{Y} - \mathbf{P}\mathbf{\Theta}_m...\mathbf{\Theta}_l...\mathbf{\Theta}_1\mathbf{X}\|_{\mathrm{F}}^2 + \frac{\beta}{2}\mathrm{tr}(\mathbf{\Theta}_l\mathbf{X}_{l-1}\mathbf{L}\mathbf{X}_{l-1}^{\mathrm{T}}\mathbf{\Theta}_l^{\mathrm{T}}) \\ \text{s.t.}\quad \mathbf{X}_l = \mathbf{\Theta}_l\mathbf{X}_{l-1}, \quad \mathbf{X}_l \succeq 0, &\quad \|\mathbf{x}_{lk}\|_2 \preceq 1,\end{aligned} \tag{18}$$

which can be basically deduced by following the framework of Algorithm 2. The only difference lies in the optimization subproblem with respect to $\mathbf{H}$ whose solution can be collected by solving the following problem:

$$\begin{aligned}\min_{\mathbf{H}}\frac{1}{2}\|\mathbf{X}_{l-1} - \mathbf{G}^{\mathrm{T}}\mathbf{H}\|_{\mathrm{F}}^2 + \frac{\alpha}{2}\|\mathbf{Y} - \mathbf{P}_l\mathbf{H}\|_{\mathrm{F}}^2 + \mathbf{\Lambda}_1^{\mathrm{T}}(\mathbf{H} - \mathbf{\Theta}_l\mathbf{X}_{l-1}) \\ + \frac{\mu}{2}\|\mathbf{H} - \mathbf{\Theta}_l\mathbf{X}_{l-1}\|_{\mathrm{F}}^2 \quad \text{s.t.}\quad \mathbf{P}_l = \mathbf{P}_{l-1}\mathbf{\Theta}_{l+1}, \quad \mathbf{P}_0 = \mathbf{P}.\end{aligned} \tag{19}$$

The analytical solution of Eq. (20) is given by

$$\mathbf{H} \leftarrow (\alpha \mathbf{P}_l^{\mathrm{T}} \mathbf{P}_l + \mathbf{G}\mathbf{G}^{\mathrm{T}} + \mu \mathbf{I})^{-1} (\alpha \mathbf{P}_l^{\mathrm{T}} \mathbf{Y} + \mathbf{G}\mathbf{X}_{l-1} + \mu \mathbf{\Theta}_l \mathbf{X}_{l-1} - \mathbf{\Lambda}_1). \tag{20}$$

Finally, we repeat these optimization procedures until a stopping criterion is satisfied. Please refer to Algorithms 1 and 2 for more explicit steps.

3 Experiments

In this section, we conduct the classification to quantitatively evaluate the performance of the proposed method (J-Play) using three popular and advanced classifiers, namely the nearest neighbor (NN) based on the Euclidean distance, kernel support vector machines (KSVM) and canonical correlation forest (CCF), in comparison with previous state-of-the-art methods. Overall accuracy (OA) is given to quantify the classification performance.

3.1 Data Description

The experiments are performed on two different types of datasets: hyperspectral datasets and face datasets, as both of them easily suffer from the information redundancy and need to improve the representative ability of features. We have used the following two hyperspectral datasets and two face datasets:

(1) *Indian Pines AVIRIS Image:* The first hyperspectral cube was acquired by the AVIRIS sensor with the size of $145 \times 145 \times 220$, which consists of 16 class of vegetation. More specific classes and the arrangement of training and test samples can be found in [11]. The first image of Fig. 3 shows a false color image of Indian Pines data.

(2) *University of Houston Image:* The second hyperspectral cube was provided for the 2013 IEEE GRSS data fusion contest acquired by ITRES-CASI sensor with size of $349 \times 1905 \times 144$. The information regarding classes and corresponding train and test samples can be found in [13]. A false color image of the study scene is shown in the first image of Fig. 4.

(3) *Extended Yale-B Dataset:* We only choose a subset of the mentioned dataset with the frontal pose and the different illuminations of 38 subjects (2414 images in total), which can widely used in evaluating the performance of subspace learning [2,32]. These images were aligned and cropped to the size of 32×32, that is, 1024-dimensional vector-based representation. Each individual has 64 near frontal images under different illuminations.

(4) *AR Dataset:* Similar to [31], we choose a subset of AR under the conditions of illumination and expressions, which comprises of 100 subjects. Each person has 14 images with seven ones from Session 1 as training set and others from Session 2 as testing samples. The images are resized to 60×43.

3.2 Experimental Steup

As the fixed training and testing samples are given for the hyperspectral datasets, subspace learning techniques can directly be performed on training set to learn an optimal subspace where the testing set can be simply classified by NN, KSVM, and CCF. For the face datasets, since there is no standard training and testing sets, ten replications are performed for randomly selecting training and testing samples. A random subset with 10 facial images per individual is chosen with labels as the training set and the rest of it is considered to be the testing set. Furthermore, we compare the performance of the proposed method (J-Play) with the baseline (original features without dimensionality reduction) and six popular and advanced methods (PCA, LPP, LDA, LFDA, LSDR, and LSQMID). With learning the different number of coupled projections, the proposed method can be successively specified as J-Play$_1$,...,J-Play$_l$,...,J-Play$_m$, $\forall l = 1, ..., m$. To investigate the trend of OAs, m are uniformly set up to 7 on the four datasets.

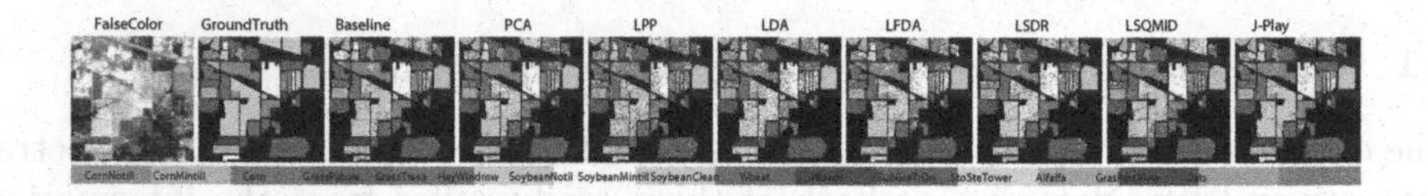

Fig. 3. A false color image, ground truth and classification maps of the different algorithms obtained using CCF on the Indian Pines dataset.

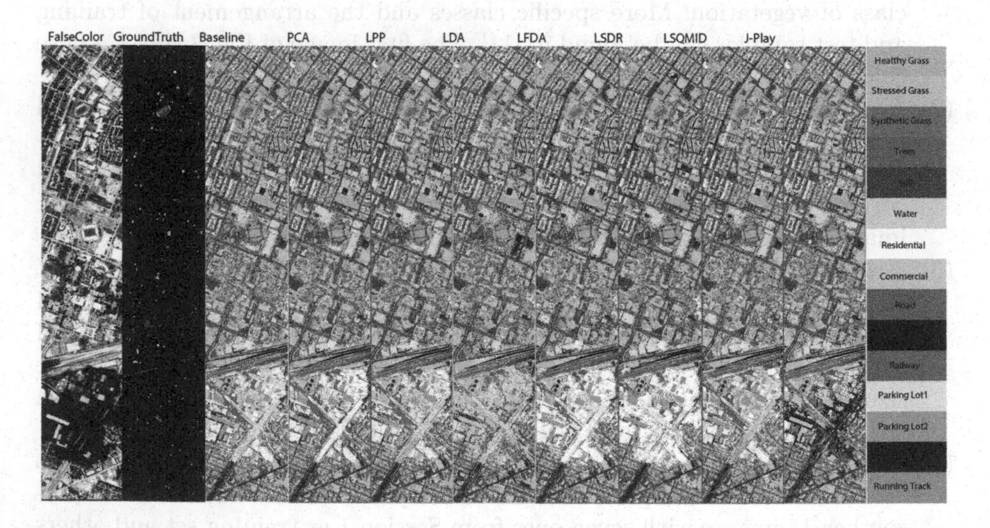

Fig. 4. A false color image, ground truth and classification maps of the different algorithms obtained using CCF on the Houston dataset. (Color figure online)

Table 1. Quantitative performance comparisons on two hyperspectral datasets. The best results for the different classifiers are shown in red.

Methods	Indian Pines dataset			Houston dataset		
	NN	KSVM	CCF	NN	KSVM	CCF
Baseline (220/144)	65.89%	66.56%	81.71%	72.83%	80.19%	82.60%
PCA (20/20)	65.40%	75.25%	79.26%	72.75%	79.54%	83.90%
LPP (20/30)	64.86%	63.02%	68.48%	75.31%	78.43%	81.77%
LDA (15/14)	64.14%	63.88%	65.61%	75.81%	76.66%	79.62%
LFDA (15/14)	73.86%	74.25%	75.17%	75.52%	80.46%	82.27%
LSDR (50/40)	73.67%	76.84%	77.38%	76.80%	80.39%	81.64%
LSQMID (60/80)	66.94%	78.90%	79.32%	76.31%	80.23%	81.69%
J-Play$_1$ (20/30)	78.81%	82.04%	82.24%	78.22%	83.32%	85.09%
J-Play$_2$ (20/30)	80.87%	83.75%	83.23%	79.16%	84.41%	85.15%
J-Play$_3$ (20/30)	83.59%	85.08%	84.44%	80.13%	83.68%	88.19%
J-Play$_4$ (20/30)	83.92%	85.21%	84.57%	79.64%	83.25%	85.63%
J-Play$_5$ (20/30)	83.76%	85.30%	84.41%	80.00%	82.21%	85.81%
J-Play$_6$ (20/30)	83.56%	84.79%	83.82%	79.69%	82.45%	84.82%
J-Play$_7$ (20/30)	82.70%	83.82%	83.04%	77.81%	81.03%	83.23%

3.3 Results of Hyperspectral Data

Initially, we conduct a 10-fold cross-validation for the different algorithms on the training set in order to estimate the optimal parameters which can be selected from $\{10^{-2}, 10^{-1}, 10^{0}, 10^{1}, 10^{2}\}$. Table 1 lists classification performances of the different methods with the optimal subspace dimensions obtained by cross-validation using three different classifiers. Correspondingly, the classification maps are given in Figs. 3 and 4 to intuitively highlight the difference.

Overall, PCA performs basically similar performance with the baseline using the three different classifiers on the two datasets. For LPP, due to its sensitivity to noise, it yields a poor performance on the first dataset, while on the relatively high-quality second dataset, LPP steadily outperforms the baseline and PCA. In the supervised algorithms, owing to the limitation of training samples and discriminative power, the classification accuracies of classic LDA is holistically lower than those previously mentioned. With a more powerful discriminative criterion, LFDA obtains more competitive results by locally focusing on discriminative information, which are generally better than those of the baseline, PCA, LPP, and LDA. However, the features learned by LFDA is sensitive to noise and the number of neighbors, resulting in the unstable performance particularly for the different classifiers. For LSDR and LSQMID, they aim to find a linear projection by maximizing the mutual information between input and output from the view of statistics. With fully considering the mutual information, they achieve the good performance on the two given hyperspectral datasets.

Remarkably, the performance of the proposed method (J-Play) is superior to the other methods on the two hyperspectral datasets. This indicates that J-Play is prone to learn a better feature representation and robust against noise. On the other hand, with the increase of m, the performance of J-Play steadily increases to the best with around 4 or 5 layers for the first dataset and 2 or 3 layers for the second one, and then gradually decreases with a slight perturbation since our model is only trained on the training set.

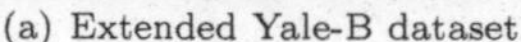

(a) Extended Yale-B dataset

(b) AR dataset

Fig. 5. Visualization of partial facial features learned by the proposed J-Play on two face datasets.

3.4 Results of Face Images

As J-Play is proposed as a general subspace learning framework for multi-label classiciation, we additionally used two popular face datasets to further assess its generalization capability. Similarly, cross-validation on training set is conducted for estimating the optimal parameter combination on the extended Yale-B and AR datasets. Considering the high-dimensional vector-based face images, we first perform the PCA for face images in order to roughly reduce the feature redundancy, whose results are further explored to the dimensionality reduction methods by following the previous work on face recognition (e.g. LDA (Fisherfaces) [20] and LPP (Laplacianfaces) [5]). Table 2 gives the corresponding OAs using the different methods on the two face datasets respectively.

By comparison, the performance of PCA and LPP is steadily superior to that of baseline, while PCA is even better than LPP. For supervised approaches, LDA performs better than baseline, PCA, LPP and even LFDA, showing an impressive result. Due to the less number of training samples from face datasets, LSDR and LSQMID are limited to effectively estimate the mutual information

Table 2. Quantitative performance comparisons on two face datasets. The best results for the different classifiers are shown in red.

Methods	Extended Yale-B dataset			AR dataset		
	NN	KSVM	CCF	NN	KSVM	CCF
Baseline (1024/2580)	45.77%	45.87%	76.99%	71.71%	72.29%	80.29%
PCA (120/80)	41.05%	81.47%	83.53%	68.43%	80.29%	81.43%
LPP (170/70)	70.75%	76.55%	77.48%	70.86%	74.00%	79.86%
LDA (37/99)	80.88%	78.37%	83.68%	81.43%	82.29%	85.38%
LFDA (37/99)	81.02%	80.88%	83.58%	71.29%	75.71%	80.38%
LSDR (60/80)	71.29%	76.40%	78.66%	75.14%	79.00%	80.14%
LSQMID (60/80)	71.48%	77.09%	78.37%	73.29%	74.29%	79.29%
J-Play$_1$ (170/210)	73.01%	79.30%	80.29%	73.57%	79.86%	77.86%
J-Play$_2$ (170/210)	81.17%	84.27%	85.22%	82.29%	86.00%	84.57%
J-Play$_3$ (170/210)	83.43%	85.50%	85.76%	85.43%	88.71%	87.43%
J-Play$_4$ (170/210)	84.07%	86.09%	86.55%	85.29%	87.71%	87.71%
J-Play$_5$ (170/210)	84.56%	86.14%	86.20%	85.71%	87.29%	88.86%
J-Play$_6$ (170/210)	85.35%	85.64%	86.53%	85.14%	87.29%	88.29%
J-Play$_7$ (170/210)	85.74%	85.45%	86.20%	86.57%	86.86%	88.71%

between the training samples and labels, resulting in the performance degradation compared to the hyperspectral data. The proposed method outperforms other algorithms, which indicates that this method can effectively learn an optimal mapping from original space to label space, further improving the classification accuracy. Likewise, there is a similar trend for the proposed method with the increase of m that J-Play can basically obtain the optimal OAs with around 4 or 5 layers and more layers would lead to the performance degradation. We also characterize and visualize each column of the learned projection, as shown in Fig. 5 where those high-level or semantically meaningful features, i.e. face features under the different pose and illumination, can be learned well, making the faces identified easier.

4 Conclusions

To effectively find an optimal subspace where the samples can be semantically represented and thereby be better classified or recognized, we proposed a novel linearized subspace learning framework (J-Play) which aims at learning the feature representation from the high-dimensional data in a joint and progressive way. Extensive experiments of multi-label classification are conducted on two types of datasets: hyperspectral images and face images, in comparison with some previously proposed state-of-the-art methods. The promising results using J-Play demonstrate its superiority and effectiveness. In the future, we will further build an unified framework based on J-Play by extending it to semi-supervised learning, transfer learning, or multi-task learning.

References

1. Belkin, M., Niyogi, P.: Laplacian eigenmaps for dimensionality reduction and data representation. Neural Comput. **15**(6), 1373–1396 (2003)
2. Cai, D., He, X., Han, J.: Spectral regression: a unified approach for sparse subspace learning. In: International Conference on Data Mining (ICDM), pp. 73–82 (2007)
3. Chung, F.R.K.: Spectral Graph Theory. American Mathematical Society, Providence (1997)
4. He, X., Cai, D., Yan, S., Zhang, H.J.: Neighborhood preserving embedding. In: International Conference on Computer Vision (ICCV), vol. 2, pp. 1208–1213 (2005)
5. He, X., Hu, S., Niyogi, P., Zhang, H.J.: Face recognition using laplacianfaces. IEEE Trans. Pattern Anal. Mach. Intell. (TPAMI) **27**(3), 328–340 (2005)
6. He, X., Niyogi, P.: Locality preserving projections. In: Advances in Neural Information Processing Systems (NIPS), pp. 153–160 (2004)
7. Heide, F., Heidrich, W., Wetzstein, G.: Fast and flexible convolutional sparse coding. In: IEEE Conference on Computer Vision and Pattern Recognition (CVPR), pp. 5135–5143 (2015)
8. Hinton, G.E., Salakhutdinov, R.R.: Reducing the dimensionality of data with neural networks. Science **313**(5786), 504–507 (2006)
9. Hong, D., Liu, W., Su, J., Pan, Z., Wang, G.: A novel hierarchical approach formultispectral palmprint recognition. Neurocomputing **151**, 511–521 (2015)
10. Hong, D., Liu, W., Wu, X., Pan, Z., Su, J.: Robust palmprint recognition based on the fast variation Vese-Osher model. Neurocomputing **174**, 999–1012 (2016)
11. Hong, D., Yokoya, N., Zhu, X.: The K-LLE algorithm for nonlinear dimensionality ruduction of large-scale hyperspectral data. In: IEEE Workshop on Hyperspectral Image and Signal Processing: Evolution in Remote Sensing (WHISPERS), pp. 1–5. IEEE (2016)
12. Hong, D., Yokoya, N., Zhu, X.: Local manifold learning with robust neighbors selection for hyperspectral dimensionality reduction. In: IEEE International Conference on Geoscience and Remote Sensing Symposium (IGARSS), pp. 40–43. IEEE (2016)
13. Hong, D., Yokoya, N., Zhu, X.: Learning a robust local manifold representation for hyperspectral dimensionality reduction. IEEE J. Sel. Top. Appl. Earth Obs. Remote Sens. (JSTARS) **10**(6), 2960–2975 (2017)
14. Hong, D., Yokoya, N., Chanussot, J., Zhu, X.X.: Learning a low-coherence dictionary to address spectral variability for hyperspectral unmixing. In: 2017 IEEE International Conference on Image Processing (ICIP), pp. 235–239. IEEE (2017)
15. Hu, J., Zheng, W., Lai, J., Zhang, J.: Jointly learning heterogeneous features for RGB-D activity recognition. In: IEEE Conference on Computer Vision and Pattern Recognition (CVPR), pp. 5344–5352 (2015)
16. Hu, J., Zheng, W., Lai, J., Zhang, J.: Jointly learning heterogeneous features for RGB-D activity recognition (2016)
17. Ji, S., Ye, J.: Linear dimensionality reduction for multi-label classification. In: International Joint Conference on Artifical Intelligence (IJCAI), vol. 9, pp. 1077–1082 (2009)
18. Kan, M., Shan, S., Chang, H., Chen, X.: Stacked progressive auto-encoders (SPAE) for face recognition across poses. In: IEEE Conference on Computer Vision and Pattern Recognition (CVPR), pp. 1883–1890 (2014)

19. Lee, H., Battle, A., Raina, R., Ng, A.Y.: Efficient sparse coding algorithms. In: Advances in Neural Information Processing Systems (NIPS), pp. 801–808 (2007)
20. Martínez, A.M., Avinash, C.K.: PCA versus LDA. IEEE Trans. Pattern Anal. Mach. Intell. (TPAMI) **23**(2), 228–233 (2001)
21. Roweis, S.T., Lawrence, K.S.: Nonlinear dimensionality reduction by locally linear embedding. Science **290**(5500), 2323–2326 (2000)
22. Saul, S.L., Roweis, S.T.: Think globally, fit locally: unsupervised learning of low dimensional manifolds. J. Mach. Learn. Res. (JMLR) **4**, 119–155 (2003)
23. Sugiyama, M.: Dimensionality reduction of multimodal labeled data by local fisher discriminant analysis. J. Mach. Learn. Res. (JMLR) **8**, 1027–1061 (2007)
24. Suzuki, T., Sugiyama, M.: Sufficient dimension reduction via squared-loss mutual information estimation. Neural Comput. **25**(3), 725–758 (2013)
25. Tangkaratt, V., Sasaki, H., Sugiyama, M.: Direct estimation of the derivative of quadratic mutual information with application in supervised dimension reduction. Neural Comput. **29**(8), 2076–2122 (2017)
26. Tosato, D., Farenzena, M., Spera, M., Murino, V., Cristani, M.: Multi-class classification on riemannian manifolds for video surveillance. In: Daniilidis, K., Maragos, P., Paragios, N. (eds.) ECCV 2010. LNCS, vol. 6312, pp. 378–391. Springer, Heidelberg (2010). https://doi.org/10.1007/978-3-642-15552-9_28
27. Wang, K., He, R., Wang, L., Wang, W., Tan, T.: Joint feature selection and subspace learning for cross-modal retrieval. IEEE Trans. Pattern Anal. Mach. Intell. (TPAMI) **38**(10), 2010–2023 (2016)
28. Wang, K., He, R., Wang, W., Wang, L., Tan, T.: Learning coupled feature spaces for cross-modal matching. In: International Conference on Computer Vision (ICCV), pp. 2088–2095 (2013)
29. Wold, S., Esbensen, K., Geladi, P.: Principal component analysis. Chemometr. Intell. Lab. Syst. **2**(1), 37–52 (1987)
30. Yan, S., Xu, D., Zhang, B., Zhang, H.J., Yang, Q., Lin, S.: Graph embedding and extensions: a general framework for dimensionality reduction. IEEE Trans. Pattern Anal. Mach. Intell. (TPAMI) **29**(1), 40–51 (2007)
31. Yang, M., Zhang, L., Yang, J., Zhang, D.: Robust sparse coding for face recognition. In: IEEE Conference on Computer Vision and Pattern Recognition (CVPR), pp. 625–632 (2011)
32. Zhang, L., Yang, M., Feng, X.: Sparse representation or collaborative representation: which helps face recognition?. In: International Conference on Computer Vision (ICCV), pp. 471–478 (2011)

Video Object Detection with an Aligned Spatial-Temporal Memory

Fanyi Xiao(✉) and Yong Jae Lee(✉)

University of California, Davis, USA
{fyxiao,yongjaelee}@ucdavis.edu

Abstract. We introduce Spatial-Temporal Memory Networks for video object detection. At its core, a novel Spatial-Temporal Memory module (STMM) serves as the recurrent computation unit to model long-term temporal appearance and motion dynamics. The STMM's design enables full integration of pretrained backbone CNN weights, which we find to be critical for accurate detection. Furthermore, in order to tackle object motion in videos, we propose a novel MatchTrans module to align the spatial-temporal memory from frame to frame. Our method produces state-of-the-art results on the benchmark ImageNet VID dataset, and our ablative studies clearly demonstrate the contribution of our different design choices. We release our code and models at http://fanyix.cs.ucdavis.edu/project/stmn/project.html.

Keywords: Aligned spatial-temporal memory · Video object detection

1 Introduction

Object detection is a fundamental problem in computer vision. While there has been a long history of detecting objects in *static images*, there has been much less research in detecting objects in *videos*. However, cameras on robots, surveillance systems, vehicles, wearable devices, etc., receive videos instead of static images. Thus, for these systems to recognize the key objects and their interactions, it is critical that they be equipped with accurate *video* object detectors.

The simplest way to detect objects in video is to run a static image-based detector independently on each frame. However, due to the different biases and challenges of video (e.g., motion blur, low-resolution, compression artifacts), an image detector usually does not generalize well. More importantly, videos provide *rich temporal and motion information* that should be utilized by the detector during both training and testing. For example, in Fig. 1, since the hamster's profile view (frames 1–2) is much easier to detect than the challenging viewpoint/pose in later frames, the image detector only succeeds in detecting the leading frame of the sequence. On the other hand, by learning to aggregate useful information over time, a video object detector can robustly detect the object under extreme viewpoint/pose.

V. Ferrari et al. (Eds.): ECCV 2018, LNCS 11212, pp. 494–510, 2018.
https://doi.org/10.1007/978-3-030-01237-3_30

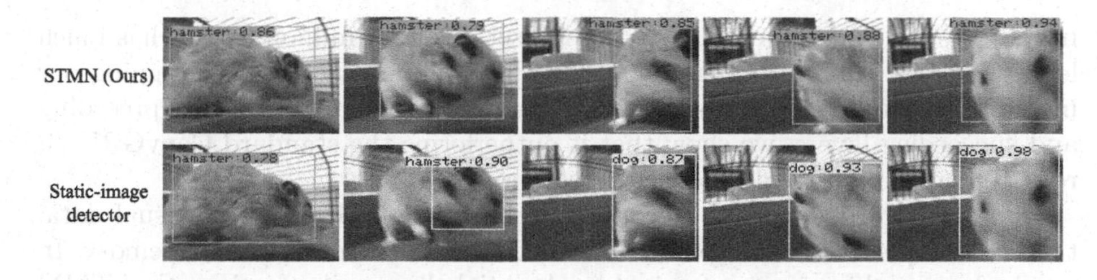

Fig. 1. Static image detectors (such as Fast-RCNN [17] or R-FCN [9]), tend to fail under occlusion or extreme pose (false detections shown in yellow). By learning to aggregate information across time, our STMN video object detector can produce correct detections in frames with challenging pose/viewpoints. In this example, it aggregates information from the easier profile views of the hamster (first two frames) to aid detection in occluded or extreme views of the hamster (third-fifth frames). (Color figure online)

Therefore, in recent years, there has been a growing interest in the community on designing video object detectors [14,18,19,25,29,50,51]. However, many existing methods exploit temporal information in an ad-hoc, post-processing manner – static object detections returned by an image detector like R-FCN [9] or Faster R-CNN [38] are linked across frames [19,25,29], or video segmentation is performed to refine the detection results [18]. Although these methods show improvement over a static image detector, exploiting temporal information as post-processing is sub-optimal since temporal and motion information are ignored during detector training. As such, they have difficulty overcoming consecutive failures of the static detector e.g., when the object-of-interest has large occlusion or unusual appearance for a long time.

More recent works [14,50,51] learn to exploit temporal information *during training* by either learning to combine features across neighboring frames or by predicting the displacement of detection boxes across frames. However, these methods operate on fixed-length temporal windows and thus have difficulty modeling *variable and long-term* temporal information. While the Tubelet Proposal Network [24] does model long-term dependencies, it uses *vectors* to represent the memory of the recurrent unit, and hence loses spatial information. To compensate, it computes the memory vectors at the region-level for each tube (sequence of proposals), but this can be very slow and depends strongly on having accurate initial tubes.

To address these limitations, we introduce the *Spatial-Temporal Memory Network* (STMN), which jointly learns to model and align an object's long-term appearance and motion dynamics in an end-to-end fashion for video object detection. At its core is the Spatial-Temporal Memory Module (STMM), which is a convolutional recurrent computation unit that fully integrates pre-trained weights learned from static images (e.g., ImageNet [11]). This design choice is critical in addressing the practical challenge of learning from contemporary video datasets, which largely lack intra-category object diversity; i.e., since video frames are highly redundant, a video dataset of e.g., 1 million frames has much lower diversity than an image dataset with 1 million images. By designing our memory unit to be compatible with pre-trained weights from both its preceding and succeeding layers, we show that it outperforms the standard ConvGRU [4] recurrent module for video object detection.

Furthermore, in order to account for the 2D spatial nature of visual data, the STMM preserves the spatial information of each frame in its memory. In particular, to achieve accurate pixel-level spatial alignment over time, the STMM uses a novel MatchTrans module to explicitly model the displacement introduced by motion across frames. Since the convolutional features for each frame are aligned and aggregated in the spatial memory, the feature for any particular object region is well-localized and contains information across multiple frames. Furthermore, each region feature can be extracted trivially via ROI pooling from the memory.

In summary, our main contribution is a novel spatial-temporal memory network for video object detection. Our ablative studies show the benefits provided by the STMM and MatchTrans modules – integrating pre-trained static image weights and providing spatial alignment across time. These design choices lead to state-of-the-art results on the ImageNet video object detection dataset (VID) [1] across different base detectors and backbone networks.

2 Related Work

Static image object detection. Recent work that adopt deep neural networks have significantly advanced the state-of-the-art in static image object detection [7,9, 16,17,31,37–40]. Our work also builds on the success of deep networks to learn the features, classifier, and bounding box localizer in an end-to-end framework. However, in contrast to most existing work that focus on detecting objects in static images, this paper aims to detect objects in *videos*.

Video object detection. Compared to static image-based object detection, there has been less research in detecting objects in videos. Early work processed videos captured from a static camera or made strong assumptions about the type of scene (e.g., highway traffic camera for detecting cars or an indoor room for detecting persons) [8,46]. Later work used hand-designed features by aggregating simple motion cues (based on optical flow, temporal differences, or tracking), and focused mostly on pedestrian detection [10,23,35,45].

With the introduction of ImageNet VID [1] in 2015, researchers have focused on more generic categories and realistic videos. However, many existing approaches combine per-frame detections from a static image detector via tracking in a two-stage pipeline [19,25,43]. Since the motion and temporal cues are used as a post-processing step only during testing, many heuristic choices are required, which can lead to sub-optimal results. In contrast, our approach directly *learns* to integrate the motion and temporal dependencies during training. Our end-to-end architecture also leads to a clean and fast runtime.

Sharing our goal of leveraging temporal information *during training*, the recent works of Zhu et al. [50,51] learn to combine features of different frames with a feed-forward network for improved detection accuracy. Our method differs in that it produces a *spatial-temporal memory* that can carry on information across long and variable number of frames, whereas the methods in [50,51] can only aggregate information over a small and fixed number of frames. In Sect. 4.3, we demonstrate the benefits gained from this flexibility. Although the approach of Kang et al. [24] uses memory to aggregate temporal information, it uses a vector representation. Since spatial information is lost, it computes a separate memory vector for each region tube (sequence of proposals) which can make the approach very slow. In contrast, our approach only needs to compute a single *frame-level* spatial memory, whose computation is independent of the number of proposals.

Finally, Detect and Track [14] aims to unify detection and tracking, where the correlation between consecutive *two* frames are used to predict the movement of the detection boxes. Unlike [14], our spatial-temporal memory aggregates information across $t > 2$ frames. Furthermore, while our approach also computes the correlation between neighboring frames with the proposed MatchTrans module, we use it to warp the entire feature map for alignment (i.e., at the coarse pixel-level), rather than use it to predict the displacement of the boxes. Overall, these choices lead to state-of-the-art detection accuracy on ImageNet VID.

Learning with videos. Apart from video object detection, other recent work use convolutional and/or recurrent networks for video classification [4,26,42]. These methods tend to model entire video frames instead of pixels, which means the fine-grained details required for localizing objects are often lost. Object tracking (e.g., [30,33]), which requires accurate localization, is also closely-related. The key difference is that in tracking, the bounding box of the first frame is given and the tracker does not necessarily need to know the semantic category of the object being tracked.

Modeling sequence data with RNNs. In computer vision, RNNs have been used for image captioning [12,27,44], visual attention [2,32,47], action/object recognition [4,12], human pose estimation [6,15], and semantic segmentation [49]. Recently, Tripathi et al. [43] adopted RNNs for video object detection. However, in their pipeline, the CNN-based detector is first trained, then an RNN is trained to refine the detection outputs of the CNN.

Despite the wide adoption of RNNs in various vision tasks, most approaches work with vector-form memory units (as in standard LSTM/GRU). To take spatial locality into account, Ballas et al. [4] proposed convolutional gated recurrent units (ConvGRU) and applied it to the task of action recognition. Built upon [4], Tokmakov et al. [41] used ConvGRUs for the task of video object segmentation. Our work differs in three ways: (1) we classify bounding boxes rather than frames or pixels; (2) we propose a new recurrent computation unit called STMM that makes better use of static image detector weights pre-trained on a large-scale image dataset like ImageNet; and (3) our spatial-temporal memory is aligned

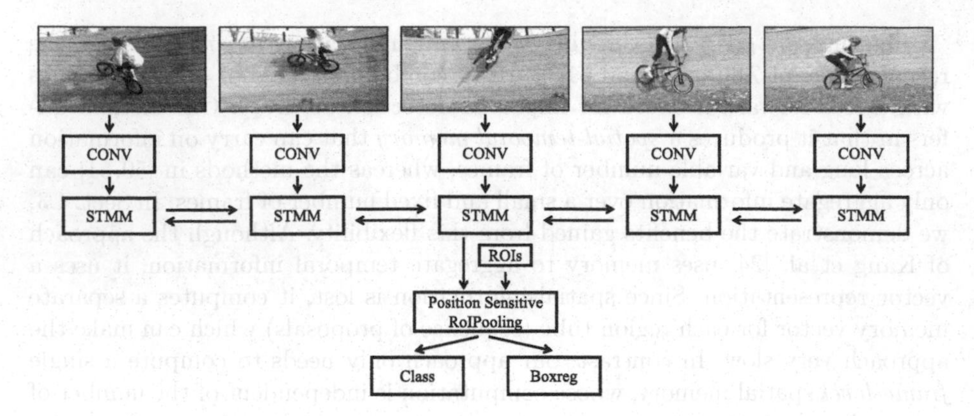

Fig. 2. Our STMN architecture. Consecutive frames are forwarded through the convolutional stacks to obtain spatial-preserving convolutional feature maps, which are then fed into the spatial-temporal memory module (STMM). In this example, in order to detect an object on the center frame, information flows into the center STMM from all five frames. The STMM output from the center frame is then fed into a classification and box regression sub-network.

frame-to-frame through our MatchTrans module. We show that these properties lead to better results than ConvGRU for video object detection.

3 Approach

We propose a novel RNN architecture called the Spatial-Temporal Memory Network (STMN) to model an object's changing appearance and motion over time for video object detection.

3.1 Overview

The overall architecture is shown in Fig. 2. Assuming a video sequence of length T, each frame is first forwarded through a convnet to obtain convolutional feature maps $F_1, F_2, ..., F_T$ as appearance features. To aggregate information along the temporal axis, the appearance feature of each frame is fed into the Spatial-Temporal Memory Module (STMM). The STMM at time step t receives the appearance feature for the current frame F_t, as well as a spatial-temporal memory $M_{t-1}^{\rightarrow}$, which carries the information of all previous frames up through timestep $t-1$. The STMM then updates the spatial-temporal memory for the current time step $M_t^{\rightarrow}$ conditioned on both F_t and $M_{t-1}^{\rightarrow}$. In order to capture information from both previous and later frames, we use two STMMs, one for each direction, to obtain both $M^{\rightarrow}$ and $M^{\leftarrow}$. These are then concatenated to produce the temporally modulated memory M for each frame.

The concatenated memory M, which also preserves spatial information, is then fed into subsequent convolution/fully-connected layers for both category classification and bounding box regression. This way, our approach combines information from both the current frame as well as temporally-neighboring frames when making its detections. This helps, for instance, in the case of detecting a frontal-view bicycle in the center frame of Fig. 2 (which is hard), if we have seen its side-view (which is easier) from nearby frames. In contrast, a static image detector would only see the frontal-view bicycle when making its detection.

Finally, to train the detector, we use the same loss function used in R-FCN [9]. Specifically, for each frame in a training sequence, we enforce a cross-entropy loss between the predicted class label and the ground-truth label, and enforce a smooth $L1$ loss on the predicted bounding box regression coefficients. During testing, we slide the testing window and detect on all frames within each sliding window, to be consistent with our training procedure.

3.2 Spatial-Temporal Memory Module

We next explain how the STMM models the temporal correlation of an object across frames. At each time step, the STMM takes as input F_t and M_{t-1} and computes the following:

$$z_t = \texttt{BN}^*(\texttt{ReLU}(W_z * F_t + U_z * M_{t-1})), \tag{1}$$
$$r_t = \texttt{BN}^*(\texttt{ReLU}(W_r * F_t + U_r * M_{t-1})), \tag{2}$$
$$\tilde{M}_t = \texttt{ReLU}(W * F_t + U * (M_{t-1} \odot r_t)), \tag{3}$$
$$M_t = (1 - z_t) \odot M_{t-1} + z_t \odot \tilde{M}_t, \tag{4}$$

where $\odot$ is element-wise multiplication, $*$ is convolution, and U, W, U_r, W_r, U_z, W_z are the 2D convolutional kernels, whose parameters are optimized end-to-end. Gate r_t masks elements of M_{t-1} (i.e., it allows the previous state to be forgotten) to generate candidate memory $\tilde{M}_t$. And gate z_t determines how to weight and combine the memory from the previous step M_{t-1} with the candidate memory $\tilde{M}_t$, to generate the new memory M_t.

To generate r_t and z_t, the STMM first computes an affine transformation of M_{t-1} and F_t, and then ReLU [28] is applied to the outputs. Since r_t and z_t are gates, their values need to be in the range of [0, 1]. Therefore, we make two changes to the standard BatchNorm [22] (and denote it as BN*) such that it normalizes its input to [0, 1], instead of zero mean and unit standard deviation.

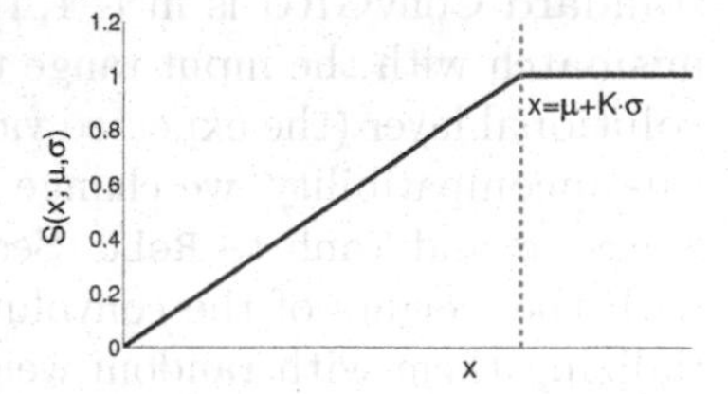

Fig. 3. $S(x; \mu, \sigma)$ squashes any value in $[0, +\inf)$ into range $[0, 1]$, with a linear scaling function thresholded at $\mu + K \cdot \sigma$. We set $K = 3$.

First, our variant of BatchNorm computes the mean $\mu(X)$ and standard deviation $\sigma(X)$ for an input batch X, and then normalizes values in X with the linear squashing function $S(X; \mu, \sigma)$ shown in Fig. 3. Second, we compute the mean and standard deviation for each batch independently instead of keeping running averages across training batches.

In this way, we do not need to store different statistics for different time-steps, which allows us to generate test results for sequence lengths not seen during training (e.g., we can compute detections on longer sequences than those seen during training as demonstrated in Sect. 4.3). Note that a key difference between `BN*` and instance/layer normalization [3,21] is that `BN*` guarantees that *each and every* value in its output is normalized within [0, 1] (which is necessary for gating variables), whereas neither instance nor layer normalization ensures this property. Although simple, we find `BN*` works well for our purpose.

Differences with ConvGRU [4]. A key practical challenge of learning video object detectors is the lack of intra-category object diversity in contemporary video datasets; i.e., since video frames are highly redundant, a video dataset of e.g., 1 million frames has much lower diversity than an image dataset with 1 million images. The cost of annotation is much higher in video, which makes it difficult to have the same level of diversity as an image dataset. Therefore, transferring useful information from large-scale *image* datasets like ImageNet [11]—into the memory processing unit itself—would benefit our video object detector by providing additional diversity.

Specifically, we would like to initialize our STMN detector with the weights of the state-of-the-art static image-based RFCN detector [9] which has been pretrained on ImageNet DET images, and continue to fine-tune it on ImageNet VID videos. In practice, this would entail converting the last convolution layer before the Position-Sensitive ROI pooling in RFCN into our STMM memory unit (see Fig. 2). However, this conversion is non-trivial with standard recurrent units like LSTM/GRU that employ `Sigmoid/Tanh` nonlinearities, since they are different from the `ReLU` nonlinearity employed in the R-FCN convolutional layers.

Thus, to transfer the weights of the pre-trained RFCN static image detector into our STMN video object detector, we make two changes to the ConvGRU [4]. First, in order to make full use of the pre-trained weights, we need to make sure the output of the recurrent computation unit is compatible with the pre-trained weights before and after it. As an illustrative example, since the output of the standard ConvGRU is in $[-1, 1]$ (due to `Tanh` non-linearity), there would be a mismatch with the input range that is expected by the ensuing pre-trained convolutional layer (the expected values should all be positive due to `ReLU`). To solve this incompatibility, we change the non-linearities in standard ConvGRU from `Sigmoid` and `Tanh` to `ReLU`. Second, we initialize W_z, W_r and W in Eqs. 1–3 with the weights of the convolution layer that is swapped out, rather than initializing them with random weights. Conceptually, this can be thought of as a way to initialize the memory with the pre-trained static convolutional feature maps. In Sect. 4.3, we show that these modifications allow us to make better use of pre-trained weights and achieve better detection performance.

3.3 Spatial-Temporal Memory Alignment

Next, we explain how to align the memory across frames. Since objects *move* in videos, their spatial features can be mis-aligned across frames. For example, the position of a bicycle in frame $t-1$ might not be aligned to the position of the bicycle in frame t (as in Fig. 2). In our case, this means that the spatial-temporal memory M_{t-1} may not be spatially aligned to the feature map for current frame F_t. This can be problematic, for example in the case of Fig. 4; without proper alignment, the spatial-temporal memory can have a hard time forgetting an object after it has moved to a different spatial position. This is manifested by a trail of saliency, in the fourth row of Fig. 4, due to the effect of overlaying multiple unaligned feature maps. Such hallucinated features can lead to false positive detections and inaccurate localizations, as shown in the third row of Fig. 4.

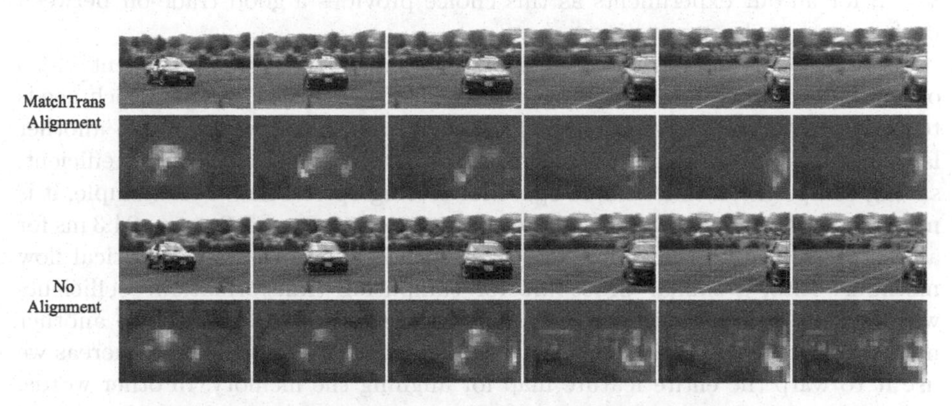

Fig. 4. Effect of alignment on spatial-temporal memory. In the first and second rows, we show the detection and the visualization of the spatial-temporal memory (by computing the $L2$ norm across feature channels at each spatial location to get a saliency map), respectively, with MatchTrans alignment. The detection and memory without alignment are shown in rows 3 and 4, respectively. Without proper alignment, the memory has a hard time forgetting an object after it has moved to a different spatial position (third row), which is manifested by a trail of saliency on the memory map due to overlaying multiple unaligned maps (fourth row). Alignment with MatchTrans helps generate a much cleaner memory (second row), which also results in better detections (first row). Best viewed in pdf. (Color figure online)

To alleviate this problem, we propose the MatchTrans module to align the spatial-temporal memory across frames. For a feature cell $F_t(x, y) \in 1 \times 1 \times D$ at location (x, y) in F_t, MatchTrans computes the affinity between $F_t(x, y)$ and feature cells in a small vicinity around location (x, y) in F_{t-1}, in order to transform the spatial-temporal memory M_{t-1} to align with frame t. More formally, the transformation coefficients Γ are computed as:

$$\Gamma_{x,y}(i, j) = \frac{F_t(x, y) \cdot F_{t-1}(x+i, y+j)}{\sum_{i,j \in \{-k,\dots,k\}} F_t(x, y) \cdot F_{t-1}(x+i, y+j)},$$

where both i and j are in the range of $[-k, k]$, which controls the size of the matching vicinity. With Γ, we transform the unaligned memory M_{t-1} to the aligned M'_{t-1} as follows:

$$M'_{t-1}(x,y) = \sum_{i,j \in \{-k,\ldots,k\}} \Gamma_{x,y}(i,j) \cdot M_{t-1}(x+i, y+j).$$

The intuition here is that given transformation Γ, we reconstruct the spatial memory $M'_{t-1}(x,y)$ as a weighted average of the spatial memory cells that are within the $(2k+1) \times (2k+1)$ vicinity around (x,y) on M_{t-1}; see Fig. 5. At this point, we can thus simply replace all occurrences of M_{t-1} with the spatially aligned memory M'_{t-1} in Eqs. 1–4. With proper alignment, our generated memory is much cleaner (second row of Fig. 4) and leads to more accurate detections (first row of Fig. 4). Since the computational cost is quadratic in k, we set $k = 2$ for all our experiments as this choice provides a good trade-off between performance and computation.

Our MatchTrans is related to the alignment module used in recent video object detection work by [50,51]. However, [50,51] use optical flow, which needs to be computed either externally e.g., using [5], or in-network through another large CNN e.g., FlowNet [13]. In contrast, our MatchTrans is much more efficient, saving computation time and/or space for storing optical flow. For example, it is nearly an order of magnitude faster to compute (on average, 2.9 ms vs. 24.3 ms for an 337×600 frame) than FlowNet [13], which is one of the fastest optical flow methods. Also, a similar procedure for computing transformation coefficients was used in [14]. However, in [14], the coefficients are fed as input to another network to regress the displacement of bounding boxes for tracking, whereas we use it to warp the entire feature map for aligning the memory. In other words, rather than use the transformation coefficients to track and connect detections, we instead use them to align the memory over time to produce better features for each candidate object region. We show in Sect. 4.1 that this leads to better performance on ImageNet VID.

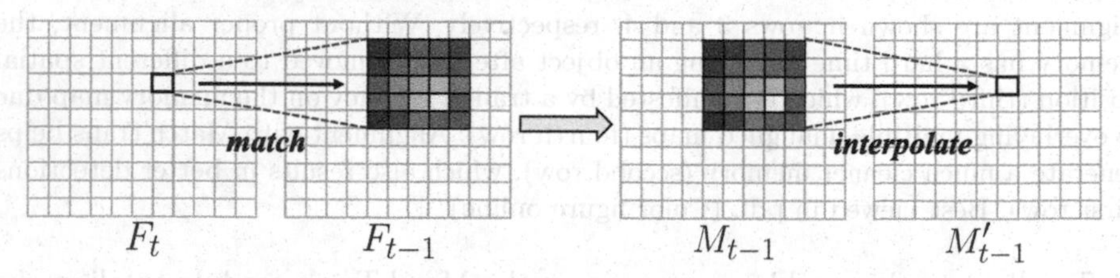

Fig. 5. The transformation coefficients Γ for position (x,y) are computed by matching $F_t(x,y)$ to $F_{t-1}(i,j)$, where i,j indexes a spatial neighborhood surrounding (x,y). The transformation coefficients are then used to synthesize $M'_{t-1}(x,y)$ by interpolating the corresponding $M_{t-1}(i,j)$ feature vectors.

3.4 Temporal Linkage During Testing

Finally, even though we enforce temporal smoothness in our spatial-temporal memory (i.e., at the feature level), we do not have an explicit smoothness constraint in the output space to ensure that detections in adjacent frames are spatially smooth. We therefore apply standard Seq-NMS [19] over our per-frame detections, following [14,51].

3.5 Approach Summary

Through the specially designed Spatial-Temporal Memory and MatchTrans modules, our STMN detector aggregates and aligns useful information from temporally nearby frames for video object detection.

4 Results

We show quantitative and qualitative results of our STMN video object detector, and compare to both state-of-the-art static image and video detectors. We also conduct ablation studies to analyze the different components of our model.

Dataset. We use ImageNet VID [1], which has 3862/555/937 videos for training/validation/testing for 30 categories. Bounding box annotation is provided for all frames. We choose ImageNet VID for its relatively large size as well as for ease of comparison to existing state-of-the-art methods [1,9,14,24,25,50,51].

Implementation details. For object proposals, we use DeepMask [36] for our method and our own baselines. We use the R-FCN detector [9] with ResNet-101 [20] as the backbone network. Following [14], we first train R-FCN on ImageNet DET, and then transfer its weights (using the method described in Sect. 3.2) to initialize our STMN detector and continue fine-tuning it on ImageNet VID. We set sequence length $T = 7$ during training. For testing, we observe better performance when using a longer sequence length; specifically, $T = 11$ frames provides a good balance between performance and GPU memory/computation (we later show the relationship between performance and test sequence length). We set the number of channels of the spatial memory to 512. To reduce redundancy within sequences, we form a sequence by sampling 1 in every 10 video frames with uniform stride. For training, we start with a learning rate of 1e-3 with SGD and lower it to 1e-4 when training loss plateaus. During testing we ensemble the detection results of the STMN detector with the initial R-FCN detector from which it started since it comes for free as a byproduct of the training procedure. We employ standard left-right flipping augmentation.

4.1 Comparison to State-of-the-Art

Table 1 shows the comparison to existing state-of-the-art image and video detectors. First, our STMN detector outperforms the static-image based R-FCN detector with a large margin (+7.1%). This demonstrates the effectiveness of our proposed spatial-temporal memory. Our STMN detector also achieves the best performance compared to all existing video object detection methods with ResNet-101 as the base network. Furthermore, in order to enable a fairer comparison to older methods that use Fast/Faster-RCNN + VGG-16 as the base detector and backbone network, we also train an STMN model with the Fast-RCNN as the base detector and VGG-16 as the backbone feature network. Specifically,

Table 1. mAP comparison to the state-of-the-art on ImageNet VID. For both the "R-FCN+ResNet-101" and the "Fast-RCNN+VGG-16" settings, our STMN detector outperforms all existing methods with the same base detector and backbone network. Furthermore, in both cases, our STMN outperforms the corresponding static-image detector by a large margin.

	Base network	Base detector	Test	Val
STMN (Ours)	ResNet-101	R-FCN	-	**80.5**
D&T [14]	ResNet-101	R-FCN	-	79.8
Zhu et al. [50]	ResNet-101+DCN	R-FCN	-	78.6
FGFA [51]	ResNet-101	R-FCN	-	78.4
T-CNN [25]	DeepID+Craft [34,48]	RCNN	67.8	73.8
R-FCN [9]	ResNet-101	R-FCN	-	73.4
TPN [24]	GoogLeNet	TPN	-	68.4
STMN (Ours)	VGG-16	Fast-RCNN	**56.5**	**61.7**
Faster-RCNN [1,19]	VGG-16	Faster-RCNN	48.2	52.2
ITLab VID - Inha [1]	VGG-16	Fast-RCNN	51.5	-

we first train a static-image Fast-RCNN detector and initialize the weights of STMN using a similar procedure as described in Sect. 3.2.[1] With this setting, our STMN achieves 61.7% val mAP, which is much higher than its static-image based counterpart (52.2%). This result shows that our method can be generalized across different base detectors and backbone networks.

When examining per-category results, our method shows the largest improvement on categories like "sheep", "rabbit", and "domestic cat" compared to methods like [14]. In these cases, we see a clear advantage of aggregating information across multiple frames (vs. 2 frames as in [14]), as there can be consecutive "hard" frames spanning multiple (>2) frames (e.g., a cat turning away from the camera for several frames). On the other hand, we find that the three categories on which we perform the worst are "monkey", "snake", and "squirrel". These are categories with large deformation and strong motion blur. When the per-frame appearance features fail to accurately model these objects due to such challenges, aggregating those features over time with our STMM does not help. Still, overall, we find that our model produces robust detection results across a wide range of challenges as demonstrated next in the qualitative results.

4.2 Qualitative Results

Figure 6 shows qualitative comparisons between our STMN detections and the static image R-FCN detections. Our STMN detections are more robust to motion blur; e.g., in the last frame of the "hamster" sequence, R-FCN gets confused

[1] Specifically, we convert the `conv5` layer in VGG-16 to an STMM module by initializing W_z, W_r and W in Eqs. 1–3 with the weights of `conv5`.

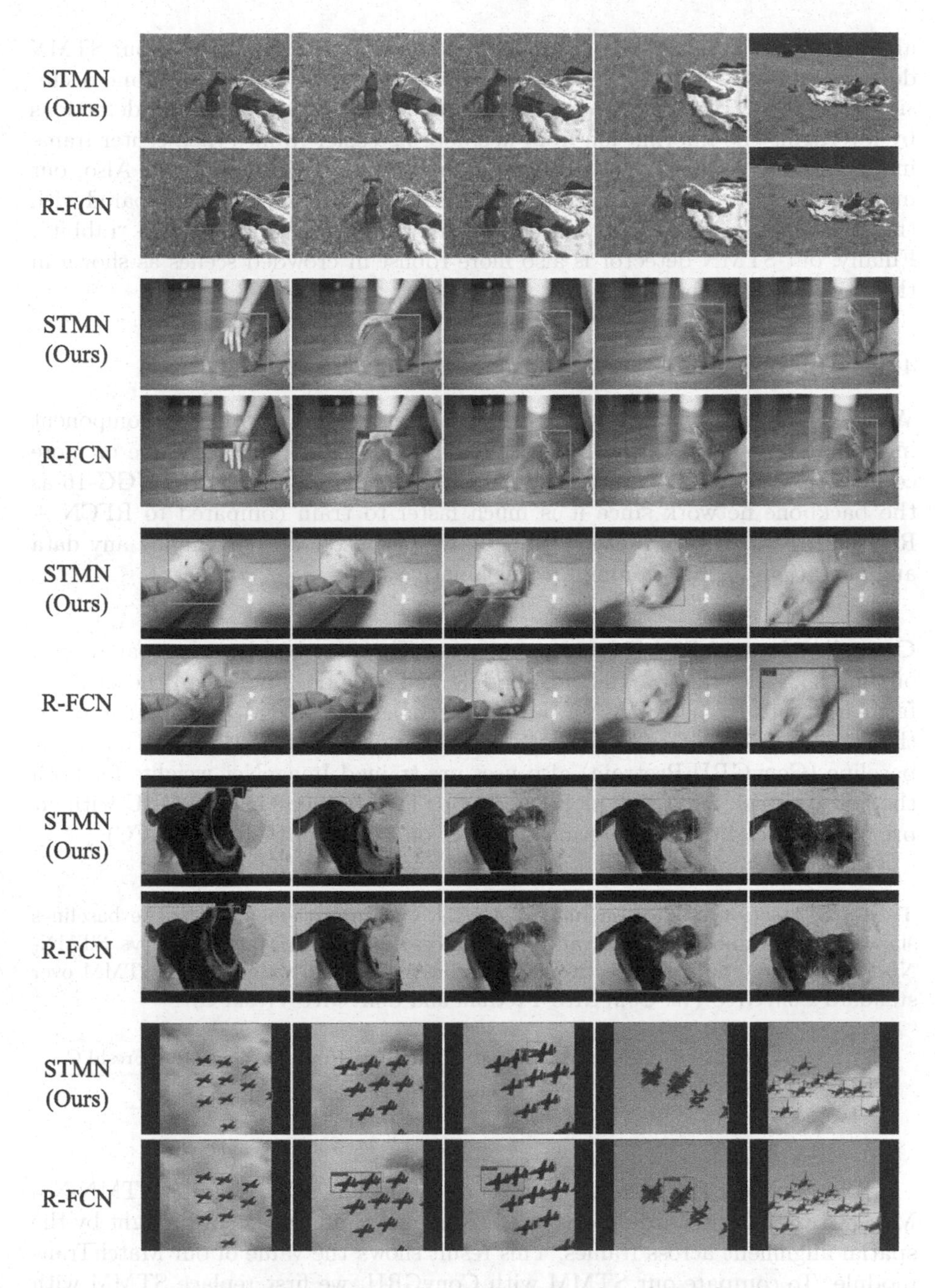

Fig. 6. Example detections produced by our STMN video object detector vs. R-FCN image detector. Green and red boxes indicate correct and incorrect detections, respectively. For any false positive detection due to misclassification or mislocalization, the predicted category label is shown at the top-left corner of the box. The ground-truth object in each sequence is: "squirrel","rabbit", "hamster","dog," and "airplane". Best viewed in pdf, zoomed-in. (Color figure online)

about the class label of the object due to large motion blur, whereas our STMN detector correctly detects the object. In the case of difficult viewpoint and occlusion ("dog" and "rabbit", respectively), our STMN produces robust detections by leveraging the information from neighboring easier frames (i.e., center frame in the"rabbit" sequence and the first frame in the "dog" sequence). Also, our model outputs detections that are more consistent across frames, compared with the static image detector, as can be seen in the case of "squirrel" and "rabbit". Finally, our STMN detector is also more robust in crowded scenes as shown in the "airplane" sequence.

4.3 Ablation Studies

We next conduct ablation studies to analyze the impact of each component in our model by comparing it to a number of baselines that lack one or more components. For this, we use Fast-RCNN as the base detector and VGG-16 as the backbone network since it is much faster to train compared to RFCN + ResNet-101. To ensure a clean analysis, we purposely do not employ any data augmentation during training for this ablative study.

Contribution of STMN Components. The first baseline, compared with our model, lacks the MatchTrans module and thus does not align the memory from frame to frame (STMN-No-MatchTrans). The second baseline computes the memory using ConvGRU [4], instead of our proposed STMM. Like ours, this baseline (ConvGRU-Pretrain) also uses pre-trained ImageNet weights for both the feature stack and prediction layers. Our final baseline is ConvGRU without pre-trained weights for the ensuing prediction FCs (ConvGRU-FreshFC).

Table 2. Ablation studies on ImageNet VID. Our improvements over the baselines show the importance of memory alignment across frames with MatchTrans (vs. STMN-No-MatchTrans), and the effectiveness of using pre-trained weights with STMM over standard ConvGRU (vs. ConvGRU-Pretrain and ConvGRU-FreshFC).

	STMN	STMN No-MatchTrans	ConvGRU Pretrain	ConvGRU FreshFC
Test mAP	50.7	49.0	48.0	44.8

Table 2 shows the results. First, comparing our STMN to the STMN-No-MatchTrans baseline, we observe a 1.7% test mAP improvement brought by the spatial alignment across frames. This result shows the value of our MatchTrans module. To compare our STMM with ConvGRU, we first replace STMM with ConvGRU and as with standard practice, randomly initialize the weights for the FC layers after the ConvGRU. With this setting (ConvGRU-FreshFC), we obtain a relatively low test mAP of 44.8%, due to the lack of data to train the large amount of weights in the FCs. This result shows that initializing the memory by only partially transferring the pre-trained ImageNet weights is sub-optimal. If we instead initialize the weights of the FCs after the ConvGRU with pre-trained weights (ConvGRU-Pretrain), we improve the test mAP from 44.8% to 48.0%. Finally, by replacing `Sigmoid` and `Tanh` with `ReLU`, which is our full model (STMN), we boost the performance even further to 50.7%. This shows the importance of utilizing pre-trained weights in both the feature stacks and prediction head, and the necessity of an appropriate form of recurrent computation that best matches its output to the input expected by the pre-trained weights.

Length of Test Window Size. We next analyze the relationship between detection performance and length of test window size. Specifically, we test our model's performance with test window size 3, 7, 11, and 15, on ImageNet VID validation set (the training window size is always 7). The corresponding mAP differences, with respect to that of window size 7, are −1.9%, 0.0%, +0.7%, +1.0%, respectively; as we increase the window size, the performance tends to keep increasing. This suggests the effectiveness of our memory: the longer the sequence, the more longer-range useful information is stored in the memory, which leads to better detection performance. However, increasing the test window size also increases computation cost and GPU memory consumption. Therefore, we find that setting the test window size to 11 provides a good balance.

4.4 Computational Overhead of STMN

Finally, we sketch the computational overhead of our memory module. To forward a batch of 11 frames of size 337×600, it takes 0.52 and 0.83 s for R-FCN and STMN respectively, on a Titan X GPU. The added 0.028 (=0.31/11) secs/frame is spent on STMM computation including MatchTrans alignment.

5 Conclusion

We proposed a novel spatial-temporal memory network (STMN) for video object detection. Our main contributions are a carefully-designed recurrent computation unit that integrates pre-trained image classification weights into the memory and an in-network alignment module that spatially-aligns the memory across time. Together, these lead to state-of-the-art results on ImageNet VID. Finally, we believe that our STMN could also be useful for other video understanding tasks that require accurate spatial information like action detection and keypoint detection.

Acknowledgments. This work was supported in part by the ARO YIP W911NF17-1-0410, NSF CAREER IIS-1751206, AWS Cloud Credits for Research Program, and GPUs donated by NVIDIA. The views and conclusions contained in this document are those of the authors and should not be interpreted as representing the official policies, either expressed or implied, of ARO or the U.S. Government. The U.S. Government is authorized to reproduce and distribute reprints for Government purposes notwithstanding any copyright notation herein.

References

1. http://image-net.org/challenges/LSVRC/2015/results#vid
2. Ba, J., Mnih, V., Kavukcuoglu, K.: Multiple object recognition with visual attention. arXiv preprint arXiv:1412.7755 (2014)
3. Ba, J.L., Kiros, J.R., Hinton, G.E.: Layer normalization. arXiv preprint arXiv:1607.06450 (2016)
4. Ballas, N., Yao, L., Pal, C., Courville, A.: Delving deeper into convolutional networks for learning video representations. In: ICLR (2016)
5. Brox, T., Malik, J.: Large displacement optical flow: descriptor matching in variational motion estimation. PAMI **33**(3), 500–513 (2011)
6. Carreira, J., Agrawal, P., Fragkiadaki, K., Malik, J.: Human pose estimation with iterative error feedback. In: CVPR (2016)
7. Chen, X., Gupta, A.: Spatial memory for context reasoning in object detection. In: ICCV (2017)
8. Coifman, B., Beymer, D., Mclauchlan, P., Malik, J.: A realtime computer vision system for vehicle tracking and traffic surveillance. Transp. Res. C **6C**(4), 271–288 (1998)
9. Dai, J., Li, Y., He, K., Sun, J.: R-FCN: object detection via region-based fully convolutional networks. In: NIPS (2016)
10. Dalal, N., Triggs, B., Schmid, C.: Human detection using oriented histograms of flow and appearance. In: Leonardis, A., Bischof, H., Pinz, A. (eds.) ECCV 2006. LNCS, vol. 3952, pp. 428–441. Springer, Heidelberg (2006). https://doi.org/10.1007/11744047_33
11. Deng, J., Dong, W., Socher, R., Li, L.J., Li, K., Fei-Fei, L.: ImageNet: a large-scale hierarchical image database. In: CVPR (2009)
12. Donahue, J., et al.: Long-term recurrent convolutional networks for visual recognition and description. In: CVPR (2015)
13. Dosovitskiy, A., et al.: FlowNet: learning optical flow with convolutional networks. In: ICCV (2015)
14. Feichtenhofer, C., Pinz, A., Zisserman, A.: Detect to track and track to detect. In: ICCV (2017)
15. Fragkiadaki, K., Levine, S., Felsen, P., Malik, J.: Recurrent network models for human dynamics. In: ICCV (2015)
16. Girshick, R., Donahue, J., Darrell, T., Malik, J.: Rich feature hierarchies for accurate object detection and semantic segmentation. In: CVPR (2014)
17. Girshick, R.: Fast R-CNN. In: ICCV (2015)
18. Han, P., Yuan, W., Lu, Z., Wen, J.R.: Video detection by learning with deep representation and spatio-temporal context (2015)
19. Han, W., et al.: Seq-NMS for video object detection. arXiv preprint arXiv:1602.08465 (2016)
20. He, K., Zhang, X., Ren, S., Sun, J.: Deep residual learning for image recognition. In: CVPR (2016)
21. Huang, X., Belongie, S.J.: Arbitrary style transfer in real-time with adaptive instance normalization. In: ICCV (2017)
22. Ioffe, S., Szegedy, C.: Batch normalization: Accelerating deep network training by reducing internal covariate shift. arXiv preprint arXiv:1502.03167 (2015)
23. Jones, M., Snow, D.: Pedestrian detection using boosted features over many frames. In: ICPR (2008)

24. Kang, K., et al.: Object detection in videos with tubelet proposal networks. In: CVPR (2017)
25. Kang, K., et al.: T-CNN: tubelets with convolutional neural networks for object detection from videos. TCSVT (2017)
26. Karpathy, A., Toderici, G., Shetty, S., Leung, T., Sukthankar, R., Fei-Fei, L.: Large-scale video classification with convolutional neural networks. In: CVPR (2014)
27. Kiros, R., Salakhutdinov, R., Zemel, R.S.: Unifying visual-semantic embeddings with multimodal neural language models. arXiv preprint arXiv:1411.2539 (2014)
28. Krizhevsky, A., Sutskever, I., Hinton, G.: ImageNet classification with deep convolutional neural networks. In: NIPS (2012)
29. Lee, B., Erdenee, E., Jin, S., Nam, M.Y., Jung, Y.G., Rhee, P.K.: Multi-class multi-object tracking using changing point detection. In: Hua, G., Jégou, H. (eds.) ECCV 2016. LNCS, vol. 9914, pp. 68–83. Springer, Cham (2016). https://doi.org/10.1007/978-3-319-48881-3_6
30. Li, Y., Zhu, J., Hoi, S.C.: Reliable patch trackers: robust visual tracking by exploiting reliable patches. In: CVPR (2015)
31. Liu, W., et al.: SSD: single shot multibox detector. In: Leibe, B., Matas, J., Sebe, N., Welling, M. (eds.) ECCV 2016. LNCS, vol. 9905, pp. 21–37. Springer, Cham (2016). https://doi.org/10.1007/978-3-319-46448-0_2
32. Mnih, V., Heess, N., Graves, A., et al.: Recurrent models of visual attention. In: NIPS (2014)
33. Nam, H., Han, B.: Learning multi-domain convolutional neural networks for visual tracking. In: CVPR (2016)
34. Ouyang, W., et al.: DeepID-Net: multi-stage and deformable deep convolutional neural networks for object detection. arXiv preprint arXiv:1409.3505 (2014)
35. Park, D., Zitnick, C.L., Ramanan, D., Dollar, P.: Exploring weak stabilization for motion feature extraction. In: CVPR (2013)
36. Pinheiro, P.O., Collobert, R., Dollar, P.: Learning to segment object candidates. In: NIPS (2015)
37. Redmon, J., Divvala, S., Girshick, R., Farhadi, A.: You only look once: unified, real-time object detection. In: CVPR (2016)
38. Ren, S., He, K., Girshick, R., Sun, J.: Faster R-CNN: towards real-time object detection with region proposal networks. In: NIPS (2015)
39. Sermanet, P., Eigen, D., Zhang, X., Mathieu, M., Fergus, R., LeCun, Y.: OverFeat: integrated recognition, localization and detection using convolutional networks. In: ICLR (2014)
40. Shrivastava, A., Gupta, A.: Contextual priming and feedback for faster R-CNN. In: Leibe, B., Matas, J., Sebe, N., Welling, M. (eds.) ECCV 2016. LNCS, vol. 9905, pp. 330–348. Springer, Cham (2016). https://doi.org/10.1007/978-3-319-46448-0_20
41. Tokmakov, P., Alahari, K., Schmid, C.: Learning video object segmentation with visual memory. In: ICCV (2017)
42. Tran, D., Bourdev, L., Fergus, R., Torresani, L., Paluri, M.: Learning spatiotemporal features with 3D convolutional networks. In: ICCV (2015)
43. Tripathi, S., Lipton, Z.C., Belongie, S., Nguyen, T.: Context matters: Refining object detection in video with recurrent neural networks. arXiv preprint arXiv:1607.04648 (2016)
44. Vinyals, O., Toshev, A., Bengio, S., Erhan, D.: Show and tell: a neural image caption generator. In: CVPR (2015)
45. Viola, P., Jones, M., Snow, D.: Detecting pedestrians using patterns of motion and appearance. IJCV **63**(2), 153–161 (2005)

46. Wren, C., Azarbayejani, A., Darrell, T., Pentland, A.: Pfinder: real-time tracking of the human body. PAMI **19**, 780–785 (1997)
47. Xu, K., et al.: Show, attend and tell: Neural image caption generation with visual attention. arXiv preprint arXiv:1502.03044 (2015)
48. Yang, B., Yan, J., Lei, Z., Li, S.Z.: Craft objects from images. In: CVPR (2016)
49. Zheng, S., et al.: Conditional random fields as recurrent neural networks. In: CVPR (2015)
50. Zhu, X., Dai, J., Yuan, L., Wei, Y.: Towards high performance video object detection. In: CVPR (2018)
51. Zhu, X., Wang, Y., Dai, J., Yuan, L., Wei, Y.: Flow-guided feature aggregation for video object detection. In: ICCV (2017)

Coded Illumination and Imaging for Fluorescence Based Classification

Yuta Asano[1], Misaki Meguro[1], Chao Wang[2], Antony Lam[3(✉)], Yinqiang Zheng[4], Takahiro Okabe[2], and Imari Sato[1,4]

[1] Tokyo Institute of Technology, Tokyo, Japan
{asano.y.ac,meguro.m.ab}@m.titech.ac.jp
[2] Kyushu Institute of Technology, Kitakyushu, Japan
c_wang@pluto.ai.kyutech.ac.jp, okabe@ai.kyutech.ac.jp
[3] Saitama University, Saitama, Japan
antonylam@cv.ics.saitama-u.ac.jp
[4] National Institute of Informatics, Tokyo, Japan
{yqzheng,imarik}@nii.ac.jp

Abstract. The quick detection of specific substances in objects such as produce items via non-destructive visual cues is vital to ensuring the quality and safety of consumer products. At the same time, it is well-known that the fluorescence excitation-emission characteristics of many organic objects can serve as a kind of "fingerprint" for detecting the presence of specific substances in classification tasks such as determining if something is safe to consume. However, conventional capture of the fluorescence excitation-emission matrix can take on the order of minutes and can only be done for point measurements. In this paper, we propose a coded illumination approach whereby light spectra are learned such that key visual fluorescent features can be easily seen for material classification. We show that under a single coded illuminant, we can capture one RGB image and perform pixel-level classifications of materials at high accuracy. This is demonstrated through effective classification of different types of honey and alcohol using real images.

Keywords: Fluorescence · Coded illumination · Classification

1 Introduction

The detection of specific substances in objects such as produce items via non-destructive visual cues is vital to applications for ensuring the quality and safety of consumer products. For example, in a factory setting, we may need to evaluate the quality of food products and whether they have been contaminated with harmful bacteria and substances. A promising approach is to use coded illumination, in which controlled, active lighting makes the distinctive features of different materials visually apparent. In fact, a number of coded illumination approaches for material classification have been proposed [1–4].

V. Ferrari et al. (Eds.): ECCV 2018, LNCS 11212, pp. 511–526, 2018.
https://doi.org/10.1007/978-3-030-01237-3_31

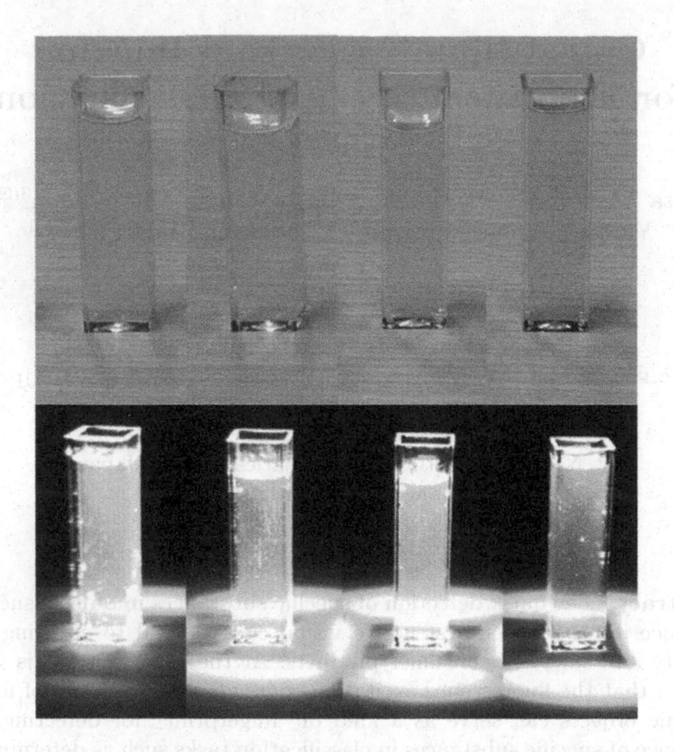

Fig. 1. In many cases, visually distinguishing something like different types of honey is difficult. In the top portion of the image, the left-most two vials contain honey made from acacia flowers. The right-most two vials contain Canadian clover honey. On the bottom, we have illuminated the samples with learned illuminants that make the fluorescent emissions of the substances in the honey show visually distinct appearances.

These aforementioned approaches are all promising but they do not consider fluorescent effects, which have been shown to be especially effective in the analysis of organic substances. In short, fluorescence is a process by which an incident wavelength of light excites a substance and causes it to emit light of typically longer wavelengths. Thus for a given substance, if we were to excite it with the right kind of incident light, we would clearly see its distinctive features (Fig. 1). Indeed, the distinctive excitation and emission characteristics from the fluorescent component of various materials have been used for effective detection of substances and classification tasks. For example, Sugiyama et al. [5] showed that the fluorescence excitation-emission matrix can be used as a kind of "fluorescence fingerprint" for detecting the presence of Mycotoxin in wheat (known to cause vomiting, diarrhea, and headaches) and aerobic bacteria on beef. Fluorescence has also been used to identify cheeses [6] and wines [7], differentiate between fresh or aged fish [8], determine the botanical origin of different types of honey [9], and more.

However, conventional fluorescence-based analysis setups can only make point measurements of the target object and are often slow. For example, [5] indicates that capture of the excitation-emission matrix for a single point takes on the order of minutes. On the other hand, a number of techniques for capturing the reflective and fluorescent spectral components of entire scenes have been proposed [10–13] but these either require multiple images or at least one hyperspectral image, which limits their applicability in machine vision applications.

In this paper, we propose directly learning optimal coded illuminants and weightings of the RGB channels in a camera to make fluorescent features for classification visually apparent in images. We explicitly model reflective and fluorescent effects and cast our formulation into an SVM framework [14] to jointly learn the illuminants and RGB channel weights in an alternating optimization scheme. We show that our final system is able to perform single-shot, pixel-level classification of organic materials, so our system is suited to fast quality control applications in settings such as factories. We demonstrate real sample applications in the classification of different types of honey and alcohol. To our knowledge, ours is the first approach for coded illumination-based classification using fluorescence.

2 Related Work

2.1 Material Classification Using Coded Illumination

The use of coded illumination to highlight discriminative features of material surfaces has shown great promise for machine vision classification applications. In their early work, Gu and Liu [1] proposed a per-pixel material classification approach using spectral bidirectional reflectance distribution functions (BRDFs). In their setup, they used formulations such as SVM or Fisher LDA to optimize the intensities of multispectral and multidirectional light sources for binary classification. They showed effective classification but their setup required capturing two grayscale images because they needed to simulate negative intensities via image subtraction. They also showed multiclass classification was possible by solving a set of one-versus-one classification problems but this required $K(K-1)/2+1$ grayscale images for K classes. Later, Liu and Gu [2] extended their work to use RGB images. Using the same lighting setup but with a three-channel camera, they then used the binary or multiclass Fisher LDA formulations to find the 3-D feature space that maximizes the ratio of the between-class to within-class scattering. However, they still needed to capture two RGB images to simulate negative intensities via image subtraction.

In Wang and Okabe [3], they proposed a coded illumination approach that would only require a single image for per-pixel material classification. This provided a great advantage because single-shot systems are well suited to situations where the objects are in motion. In a factory setting, one may expect objects to be moving along quickly on a conveyer belt. The single-shot capability of their system was made possible by enforcing non-negative constraints on the learned coded illuminants so that a second image for simulating negative intensities would not be needed. They also showed that it was possible to capture a scene using one fixed set of coded illuminants and an RGB camera but in postprocessing, achieve multiclass classification. This was made possible by jointly learning a single set of non-negative coded illuminants with multiple postprocessing grayscale conversions of the RGB image. The multiple grayscale images generated from a single captured RGB image would then highlight features effective for multiple binary classification decisions.

In Blasinski et al. [4], they also proposed a non-negative coded illumination approach to material classification. Specifically, they learned multiple illuminant spectra based on an SVM formulation or non-negative PCA. They then captured scenes using RGB camera spectral responses under the illuminants and show effective per-pixel classification in test scenes with different fruits. In general, they reported that about 3–4 illuminants gave good performance with only modest gains if more coded illuminants were added. Their paper differs from the previously mentioned papers in that they do not use multidirectional light but rather vary the illuminants primarily in the spectral domain.

2.2 Fluorescence for Classification and Detection of Substances

The previously mentioned coded illumination approaches showed promising results. However, they all assumed scenes to be purely reflective and did not consider fluorescent effects. We now briefly describe the difference between reflectance and fluorescence. In summary, reflectance is when both the incident and reflected light from the material are of the same wavelength. On the other hand, fluorescence is when light of a typically shorter wavelength "excites" a substance and then typically longer wavelengths of light are "emitted".

It is well-known that fluorescence can reveal a lot about the state of objects. In particular, organic objects exhibit distinctive fluorescent characteristics based on what kinds of substances and/or bacteria are present. For example, Sugiyama et al. [5] used a fluorescence spectrometer to make point measurements to determine the spectral excitation-emission matrix of different organic objects. They showed that the excitation-emission matrix could be treated as a kind of "fluorescence fingerprint" to identify the presence of Mycotoxin in wheat (known to cause vomiting, diarrhea, and headaches). They were also able to detect aerobic bacteria on beef. As mentioned earlier, fluorescence has also been used for varied tasks such as identifying different types of cheeses, wines, honey [6,7,9] and even to tell the difference between fresh and aged fish [8]. It is well-known that observing fluorescence is an effective means of analyzing various materials but conventional measurements such as that of [5] do not capture the entire scene and take on the order of minutes to capture the entire excitation-emission matrix. This precludes applications to settings such as quality control in a factory where numerous products could be moving quickly along a conveyer belt.

2.3 Fluorescence Imaging and Classification

In recent years, there have been a number of proposed techniques for capturing fluorescence spectral components for entire scenes. Lam and Sato [10] proposed using a sparse set of narrowband illuminants and images combined with basis vectors to estimate the fluorescence spectral components. Fu et al. [11] proposed capturing hyperspectral images under two high frequency light spectra to estimate the fluorescence spectral components. Later, Fu et al. [12] estimated the components using an RGB camera and multiple active illuminants. Zheng et al. [13] devised a means to estimate all the fluorescence spectral components using only a single hyperspectral image. All the aforementioned approaches require either multiple images or at least one hyperspectral image, which limits applications to static scenes.

In this paper, we propose directly learning coded illuminants for material classification tasks. We explicitly model fluorescence and derive a formulation that can be cast into an SVM learning framework. In doing so, we create illuminants that excite the fluorescent components of specific substances such that their distinctive features are easily seen under an RGB camera. Furthermore, our proposed system only requires a single image and so is applicable to scenes with moving objects (such as in a factory with conveyer belts). We demonstrate our system with real applications in classifying different types of honey and alcohol. In summary, our contributions are as follows:

1. We explicitly model the images of reflective-fluorescent materials under an RGB camera and show that this formulation can be cast into an SVM learning framework for optimizing coded illuminants.
2. We demonstrate that the resultant coded illuminants can make it so that visual features from the fluorescent components of substances are easily seen.
3. We provide a comparison between coded illuminants and standard illuminants in classification tasks to demonstrate the benefits of our proposed approach.
4. To our knowledge, we are the first to propose coded illuminants that leverage fluorescence for classification tasks–despite the well-known observation that fluorescence provides highly distinctive cues for detecting the presence of substances.

3 Coded Spectral Response and Illumination for Fluorescence-Based Classification

3.1 Imaging Model

Most fluorescent materials actually have a combination of reflectance and fluorescence. So we start with presenting a model for how reflective-fluorescent materials are observed under a given illumination spectrum for a single channel camera. It is well-known that the image of any given reflective-fluorescent material is a linear combination of the reflected incident light and the emitted light from the fluorescent component. This emitted light is typically shifted to longer wavelengths than the incident light. Thus for a given camera, the outgoing wavelength λ_o for a reflective-fluorescent material illuminated by incident light at wavelength λ_i can be modeled as

$$P(\lambda_o, \lambda_i) = R(\lambda_o)L(\lambda_i)\delta(\lambda_o - \lambda_i)C(\lambda_o) + E_m(\lambda_o)C(\lambda_o)E_x(\lambda_i)L(\lambda_i) \tag{1}$$

where $R(\lambda_o)$ is the reflectance at wavelength λ_o, $L(\lambda_i)$ is the illuminant at wavelength λ_i, and $C(\lambda_o)$ is the camera spectral response at wavelength λ_o. $E_m(\lambda_o)$ and $E_x(\lambda_i)$ are the emission and excitation of the fluorescent component at their respective wavelengths. The excitation term $E_x(\lambda_i)$ determines how much the energy from incident light at wavelength λ_i is able to excite the fluorescent component. On the other hand, the emission term $E_m(\lambda_o)$ determines how much light at wavelength λ_o, the fluorescent component is able to emit relative to the amount of energy from the excitation. $\delta(\lambda_o - \lambda_i)$ is the unit impulse function where $\delta(0) = 1$ and $\delta(x) = 0$ for $x \neq 0$. The unit impulse function ensures only the incident wavelength is reflected for the reflective component.

Then to determine the image of the material under wideband light for a wideband camera, we can simply sum over all the possible combinations of wavelengths λ_o and λ_i:

$$I = \iint P(\lambda_o, \lambda_i) d\lambda_o d\lambda_i \approx \sum_{m=1}^{M} \sum_{x=1}^{X} P(\lambda_o^{(m)}, \lambda_i^{(x)}) \Delta\lambda_o \Delta\lambda_i. \tag{2}$$

The right hand side of Eq. 2 is the discrete approximation that is used in practice. In our setup, we calculate the P term at intervals of 10 nm for both wavelength parameters.

4 Learning the Coded Illumination

We now describe how the imaging model in Eq. 2 can be used to formulate a framework for learning an illuminant spectrum and weighting for the RGB channels so that distinctive fluorescent features for classification are easily seen. We could then perform pixel-wise classification of the types of materials present with just a single image.

For convenience, let $T(\lambda_o, \lambda_i) = R(\lambda_o)L(\lambda_i)\delta(\lambda_o - \lambda_i) + E_m(\lambda_o)E_x(\lambda_i)$. Then Eq. 2 can be written in matrix form as

$$\begin{aligned} I &= \begin{pmatrix} C(\lambda_o^{(1)}) \ldots C(\lambda_o^{(M)}) \end{pmatrix} \begin{pmatrix} T(\lambda_o^{(1)}, \lambda_i^{(1)}) & \ldots & T(\lambda_o^{(1)}, \lambda_i^{(X)}) \\ \vdots & \vdots & \vdots \\ T(\lambda_o^{(M)}, \lambda_i^{(1)}) & \ldots & T(\lambda_o^{(M)}, \lambda_i^{(X)}) \end{pmatrix} \begin{pmatrix} L(\lambda_i^{(1)}) \\ \vdots \\ L(\lambda_i^{(X)}) \end{pmatrix} \\ &= \boldsymbol{c}^T \mathrm{T} \boldsymbol{l} = \boldsymbol{f}^T \boldsymbol{l}. \end{aligned} \tag{3}$$

Note that T is basically the fluorescence excitation-emission matrix of the material (but with reflectance terms added in), $\boldsymbol{c}$ is the vector representing the camera spectral response, and $\boldsymbol{l}$ is the vector representing the illuminant spectrum. We define vector $\boldsymbol{f}$ as the reflective-fluorescent feature of the given material under camera spectral response $\boldsymbol{c}$. Thus for a given camera spectral response and material's T matrix, the image of the material under illuminant $\boldsymbol{l}$ is the inner-product between reflective-fluorescent feature $\boldsymbol{f}$ and illuminant $\boldsymbol{l}$.

In the case of an RGB camera, we have three channels. So for a single illuminant, the reflective-fluorescent material's image would consist of three values computed as

$$\begin{pmatrix} I_r \\ I_g \\ I_b \end{pmatrix} = \begin{pmatrix} \boldsymbol{f}_r^T \\ \boldsymbol{f}_g^T \\ \boldsymbol{f}_b^T \end{pmatrix} \boldsymbol{l}. \tag{4}$$

For discussion purposes, we also define the weighting of the RGB values:

$$I = (w_r \; w_g \; w_b) \begin{pmatrix} I_r \\ I_g \\ I_b \end{pmatrix} = w_r \boldsymbol{l}^T \boldsymbol{f}_r + w_g \boldsymbol{l}^T \boldsymbol{f}_g + w_b \boldsymbol{l}^T \boldsymbol{f}_b \tag{5}$$

where w_r, w_g, and w_b are weights in the summation of the image of the materials under each RGB channel.

From Eq. 5, we can see that for an RGB camera, the combination of illuminant spectrum $\boldsymbol{l}$ and RGB weighting values w_r, w_g, and w_b constitute a linear discriminant hyperplane of the form

$$I + b = w_r \boldsymbol{l}^T \boldsymbol{f}_r + w_g \boldsymbol{l}^T \boldsymbol{f}_g + w_b \boldsymbol{l}^T \boldsymbol{f}_b + b = 0 \tag{6}$$

where b is a bias term. Then given a set of features $\boldsymbol{f}_r, \boldsymbol{f}_g, \boldsymbol{f}_b$, and class labels $y \in \{1, -1\}$, we might try to learn an appropriate hyperplane using a soft-margin SVM [14]. This is similar to previous work that used soft-margin SVM optimization inspired approaches to learn coded illuminants [1–4]. However, past approaches have only considered the reflectance of incident light but not fluorescence excitation-emissions as we do here. Going back to our discussion, Eq. 6 shows that we have unknown illuminant spectrum $\boldsymbol{l}$ and unknown RGB weighting values w_r, w_g, and w_b. In addition, the first three terms in the summation are all dependent on illuminant spectrum $\boldsymbol{l}$. Thus the standard SVM soft-margin optimization procedure cannot be used. Fortunately, we have found that although Wang and Okabe [3] worked in the domain of reflectance BRDFs and did not optimize light spectra, their reformulated SVM soft-margin optimization can be used in the spectral domain for learning our proposed fluorescence-based coded illuminants. For clarity, we present the optimization formulation with our fluorescence terms integrated here:

$$\begin{aligned} &\min_{\boldsymbol{l}, w_r, w_g, w_b, b, \xi_n} \frac{1}{2} |\boldsymbol{l}|^2 (w_r^2 + w_g^2 + w_b^2) + \beta \sum_{n=1}^{N} \xi_n \\ s.t. \;\; & y_n[\boldsymbol{l}^T (w_r \boldsymbol{f}_{nr} + w_g \boldsymbol{f}_{ng} + w_b \boldsymbol{f}_{nb}) + b] \geq 1 - \xi_n \quad (n = 1, 2, ..., N), \\ & \xi_n \geq 0 \quad (n = 1, 2, ..., N), \\ & l_k \geq 0 \quad (k = 1, 2, ..., K). \end{aligned} \tag{7}$$

N is the number of training samples, $\boldsymbol{f}_{nm}$ denotes the nth reflective-fluorescent training sample for camera color channel m. ξ_n is the slack variable and β is the weight penalty term. In our setup, we use coded illuminants ranging from 350 nm–640 nm in increments of 10 nm so $K = 30$.

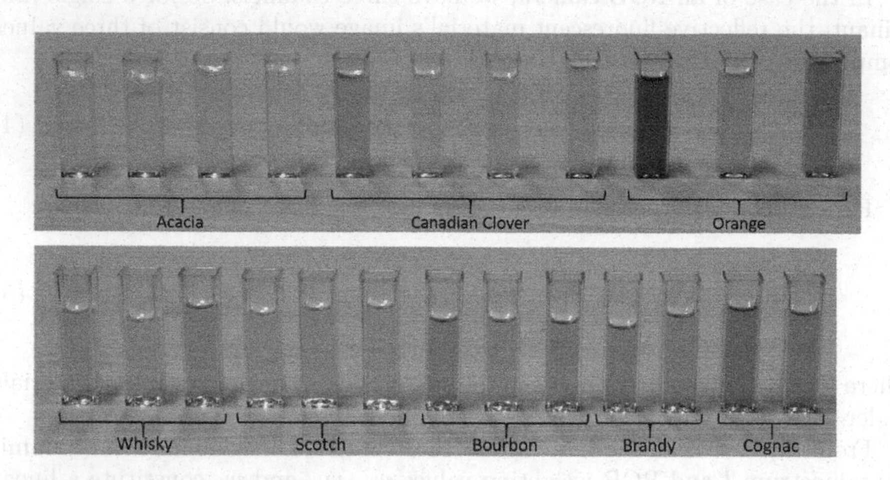

Fig. 2. Consumer products collected for our dataset. Various types of honey (top) and alcohol (bottom) spanning different brands are shown.

The above formulation has an unknown illuminant spectrum $\boldsymbol{l}$ and unknown set of RGB weighting values w_r, w_g, w_b. In our setup, we solve for the RGB weights and then the illuminant spectrum and bias using alternating iterations of quadratic programming. Specifically, we initialize the illuminant spectrum $\boldsymbol{l} = (11\ldots1)^T$ and bias $b = 1$ and solve for the RGB weighting values. Then the RGB weights are fixed and we solve for the illuminant spectrum and bias. The iterations are repeated until convergence or a preset maximum number of iterations is reached.

5 Experiments

5.1 Data Collection

We built a dataset consisting of various types of honey and alcohol (Fig. 2). Specifically, we obtained acacia honey (4 brands), Canadian clover honey (4 brands), orange honey (3 brands), whisky (3 brands), scotch (3 brands), bourbon (3 brands), brandy (2 brands), and cognac (2 brands). For each product, we used a fluorescence spectrometer to capture 20×20 hyperspectral images of the given sample at multiple narrowbands ranging from 350 nm–640 nm in increments of 10 nm. The narrowband lights were all normalized in postprocessing so that they would have equal intensity.

5.2 Experiment Setup and Classification Tasks

System Setup: Our proposed system consists of an RGB camera and coded illuminant spectrum as the light source. We use a PointGrey GS3-U3-23S6 camera with color filters as our RGB camera. Note that this camera has a linear response function with manual settings for gamma correction and white balance. Thus our setup assumes a linear response function. However, we can still use an sRGB camera with a non-linear response function by first obtaining its response function in advance and then converting it to give a linear response image. For the first part of our classification experiments, we take the 20×20 hyperspectral images from our dataset and simulate the image of each sample under our RGB camera's known set of RGB spectral response functions and coded illuminants (ranging from 350 nm–640 nm in increments of 10 nm). In the next phase of our tests, we demonstrate an implementation of our system using our PointGrey GS3-U3-23S6 RGB camera and a Nikon ELS programmable light source for generating coded illuminant spectra. For a given coded illuminant we can then capture an RGB image and classify each pixel using the discriminant hyperplane defined in Eq. 6.

Classification Tasks: For the classification tasks, our aim is to differentiate between different types of honey and alcohol in a one-versus-one manner. As an example, consider the problem of classifying acacia honey versus Canadian clover honey. In this case, we use two samples (one sample from each type of honey) and learn a coded illuminant spectrum to separate them. (Each sample is an image that consists of 20×20 pixels so this means we have 400 datapoints per sample to learn the coded illuminant.) The coded illuminant spectrum is then used as the light source for the 2D RGB images of all instances of acacia honey and Canadian clover honey in our dataset that were not used in the training data. We note that all these different instances of honey come from different brands.

Training-Testing Splits: In our example on acacia versus Canadian clover honey, we described a single training-testing split in our classification tests. To thoroughly test the classification of acacia honey versus Canadian clover honey, we exhaustively try all combinations of training-testing splits of the data in which the training set always consists of one sample of each type of honey. We then determine the average accuracy of all the pixel-level classifications on the test set (containing exclusively different brands from the training set) and report them. We also repeat the same test procedure for various combinations of one-versus-one classification problems for different types of honey as well as different types of alcohol.

Comparisons to Non-coded Illuminants: We also repeat our experiments with three conventional illuminants (Fig. 3). We conduct these tests by using the same formulation as Eq. 7 to learn a discriminant hyperplane but the illuminant spectrum is kept fixed. In other words, only the bias term and RGB weighting values are learned for the classification task. Then for testing, the fixed standard

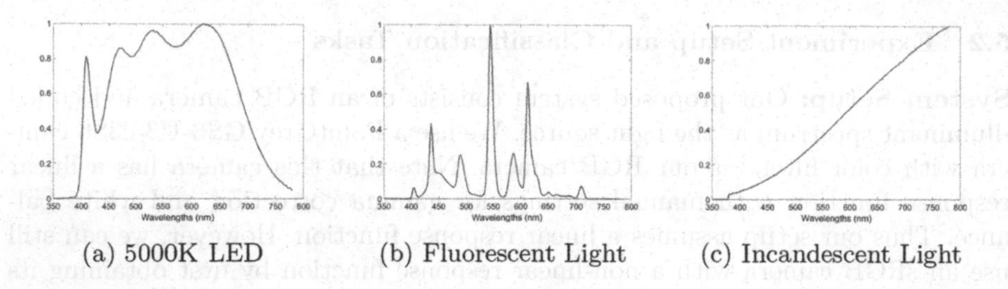

(a) 5000K LED (b) Fluorescent Light (c) Incandescent Light

Fig. 3. Conventional (non-coded) illuminants used for comparisons to coded illuminants for classification tasks.

illuminant, learned bias term, and learned RGB weights are used for pixel-level classification as is done in the coded illumination tests.

6 Results

We report the average accuracies on classifying different types of honey based on botanical origin (which kinds of flowers they were made from) in Table 1. We see that the proposed coded illuminants can be used for effective classification. In Fig. 4, we show examples of the excitation-emission matrices of different instances of honey and their categories. We also include examples of learned coded illuminants for separating classes based on these excitation-emission characteristics. We can see that the coded illuminants will emphasize the range of wavelengths where the material exhibits high excitation and emission. As mentioned earlier, for tests with conventional illuminants, we used Eq. 7 to learn weights for the RGB channels and the bias term but kept the illuminant fixed. We found that the resultant classifiers using conventional illuminants would output the same class label for input test data in almost all the cases. Thus many of the average accuracies in Table 1 appear to be the same (e.g. 40% appears because the number of instances in the testing set consisted of 60% of one class versus 40% of the other class). On the other hand, using our proposed coded illuminant approach, we achieved effective classification of different types of honey despite only training on two samples of particular brands of honey and then testing on multiple brands. We note though, that in the case of Canadian clover honey versus orange honey, our accuracy was lower. However, our proposed approach still allowed for effective discrimination of other types of honey whereas conventional non-coded lighting could not classify any honey in most of the cases.

In Table 2, we can see classification results on various types of whisky versus brandy. Since whisky is distilled beer and brandy is distilled wine, we would expect various categories of whisky to be separable from brandy. Indeed, we can see in Table 2, that the classification accuracies using our coded illumination approach indicate we can differentiate between different types of whisky and brandy. In Table 3, we show results from tests on various types of whisky versus various types of whisky. Since they are more similar to each other than in the

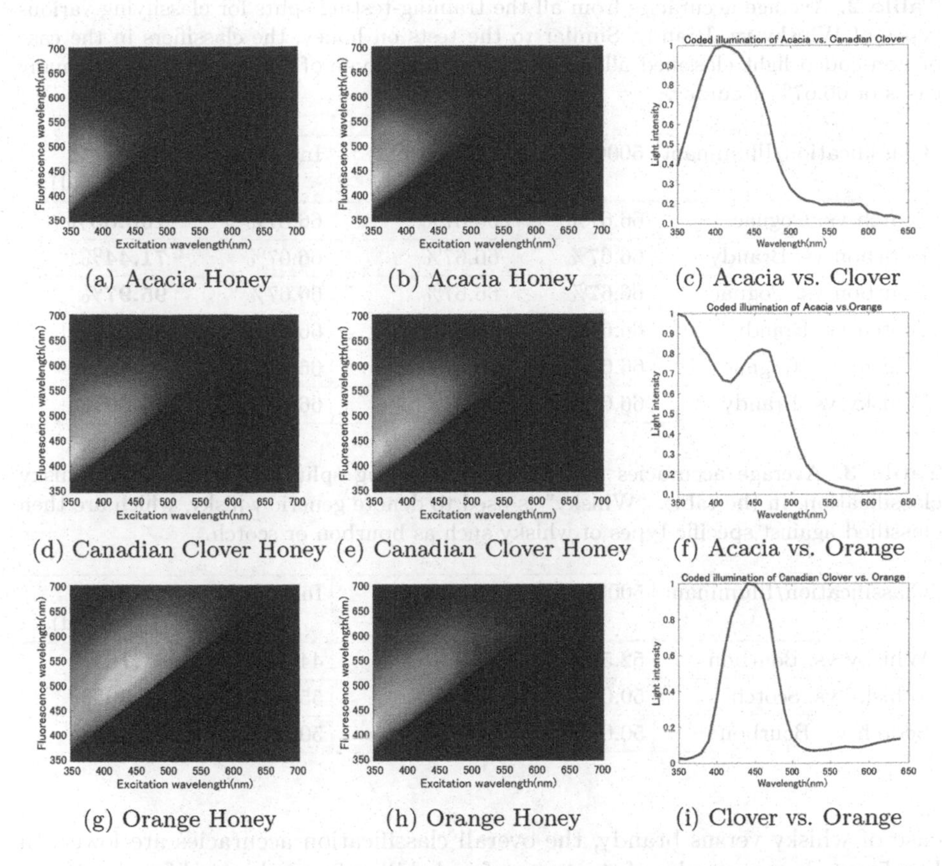

(a) Acacia Honey (b) Acacia Honey (c) Acacia vs. Clover

(d) Canadian Clover Honey (e) Canadian Clover Honey (f) Acacia vs. Orange

(g) Orange Honey (h) Orange Honey (i) Clover vs. Orange

Fig. 4. Examples of Excitation-Emission Matrices and Coded Illuminants for Differentiating Between Types of Honey

Table 1. Average accuracies from all the training-testing splits for classifying different types of honey. For the non-coded illuminants, many of the classifications gave the same output label regardless of the test input. Thus there are many cases with 40% accuracy because the test sets in those cases had 60% of one class versus 40% of the other class.

Classification/Illuminant	5000K LED	Fluorescent Light	Incandescent	Coded (Proposed)
Acacia vs. Canadian Clover	50.00%	50.67%	50.67%	**91.17%**
Acacia vs. Orange	40.00%	40.00%	40.00%	**78.26%**
Canadian Clover vs. Orange	41.67%	40.00%	45.00%	**52.03%**

Table 2. Average accuracies from all the training-testing splits for classifying various types of Whisky vs. Brandy. Similar to the tests on honey, the classifiers in the case of non-coded light classified all input data as some type of whisky so there are many cases of 66.67% accuracy.

Classification/Illuminant	5000K LED	Fluorescent Light	Incandescent	Coded (Proposed)
Scotch vs. Cognac	66.67%	66.67%	66.67%	**100.00%**
Bourbon vs. Brandy	66.67%	66.67%	66.67%	**71.44%**
Bourbon vs. Cognac	66.67%	66.67%	66.67%	**95.97%**
Scotch vs. Brandy	66.67%	66.67%	66.67%	**99.43%**
Whisky vs. Cognac	66.67%	66.67%	66.67%	**99.50%**
Whisky vs. Brandy	66.67%	66.67%	66.67%	**93.00%**

Table 3. Average accuracies on the training-testing splits for Whisky vs. Whisky classification. In the table, "Whisky" is used to denote generic whisky, which are then classified against specific types of whisky such as bourbon or scotch.

Classification/Illuminant	5000K LED	Fluorescent Light	Incandescent	Coded (Proposed)
Whisky vs. Bourbon	52.58%	50.00%	44.27%	**61.10%**
Whisky vs. Scotch	50.00%	50.00%	55.00%	**77.30%**
Scotch vs. Bourbon	50.00%	50.00%	50.00%	**58.16%**

case of whisky versus brandy, the overall classification accuracies are lower. In Fig. 5, we show examples of the types of coded illuminants learned for classifying alcohol. There is a good amount of variety in their characteristics.

Up to this point, we have presented binary classification results but our formulation also allows for multiclass classification. Typically, multiclass classification is performed by using multiple binary classifiers to decide on class membership. Our formulation actually allows for obtaining V linear discriminant hyperplanes with only a single image. This is because it is possible to take a single image under only *one coded illuminant* and then learn a set of RGB weights w_{vr}, w_{vg}, w_{vb}, and biases b_v for each linear discriminant hyperplane v. Thus using basically the same optimization formulation as binary classification, we start with a single fixed illuminant spectrum and biases b_v. We then iteratively update each set of RGB weights for each binary classification problem. Then the multiple sets of RGB weights are all fixed and we update the single illuminant spectrum and biases b_v. This alternating process is repeated until convergence or a preset number of iterations is reached. For final classification, these multiple hyperplanes can then be used to vote for the class labels of test cases. In Table 4, we can see results on four-class classification of alcohol. Multiple training-testing splits were chosen in each case such that the test sets would have four test cases, one from each class. We can see that the mul-

Table 4. Average accuracies from all the training-testing splits for classifying four-class types of alcohol.

Classification/Illuminant	Coded (Proposed)
Whisky vs. Scotch vs. Bourbon vs. Brandy	**55.10%**
Whisky vs. Scotch vs. Bourbon vs. Cognac	**51.04%**
Whisky vs. Scotch vs. Brandy vs. Cognac	**62.65%**
Whisky vs. Bourbon vs. Brandy vs. Cognac	**68.93%**
Scotch vs. Bourbon vs. Brandy vs. Cognac	**64.84%**

ticlass classification accuracies using our coded illumination approach indicate we can differentiate between four different types of alcohol. For the non-coded illuminants, many of the classifications gave the same output label regardless of the test input. We found that many cases using the non-coded illuminants resulted in 25% accuracy, which is the same as random guessing.

Overall, our proposed coded illumination fluorescence-based classification approach showed significant improvement over using conventional light sources. As expected, when intraclass variation is high for both the classes in question, the accuracies are lower. Likewise, separation of different categories of items with very similar characteristics was, as expected, difficult. However, in all our tests, we only used one sample per class and tested on more instances than training data. Thus the overall good classification performance despite the difficult tests shows the effectiveness of our approach.

The experiments presented so far made use of real images but they were narrowband images that were used to simulate an RGB camera using a given set of spectral response functions. This allowed us to perform a large number of extensive tests. We now demonstrate a single-shot setup using a PointGrey GS3-U3-23S6 RGB camera and Nikon ELS programmable light source to generate coded illuminants (Fig. 6). We chose to compare the results from our programmable light source setup to two training-testing splits from our previous tests. The results are presented in Table 5. In the table, we can see the two training-testing splits and the average pixel classification accuracies. The column denoted "ideal" shows results from our tests using the real captured narrowband images that are then used to simulate RGB images using spectral response functions. In this case, the tests show what accuracies ideally generated illuminants could yield. Not surprisingly the coded illuminant generated by the Nikon ELS results in a lower accuracy for the honey classification test. It is interesting that in some cases, such as in the bourbon versus scotch test, the results were similar between the programmable light source and ideal setups. Future work will investigate the differences between the programmable light source setup and ideal light setup.

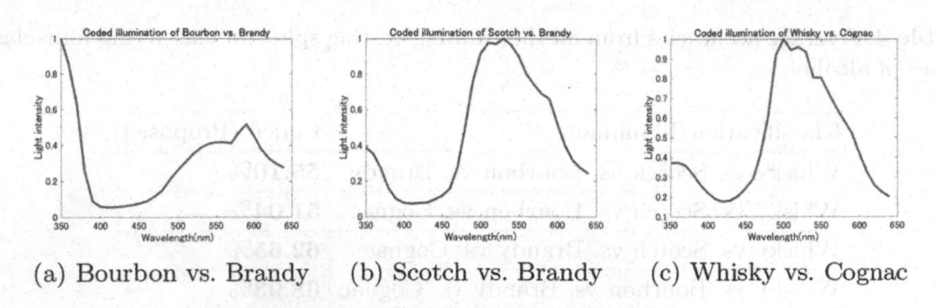

(a) Bourbon vs. Brandy (b) Scotch vs. Brandy (c) Whisky vs. Cognac

Fig. 5. Coded illumination for alcohol classification

Fig. 6. Setup with programmable light source

Table 5. Comparison of ideal setup vs. programmable light source for two specific training-testing splits. "Ideal" denotes the results from our narrowband images that were used to simulate RGB images under coded illuminants.

	Ideal	Programmable Light Source
Acacia vs. Canadian Clover	92.69%	85.96%
Bourbon vs. Scotch	85.06%	85.75%

7 Conclusion

We have demonstrated the effectiveness of learning coded illumination to leverage the particular excitation-emission characteristics of substances in materials for classification purposes. In addition, our system only requires a single image under one illuminant and thus is applicable for use in such settings as factory quality and safety control. We also demonstrated the use of a programmable light source to show that coded illuminants can be generated in reality. There are some cases where our system could not classify well. These are likely due to a combination of high intraclass variability and low interclass difference (e.g. differentiating different kinds of whisky). In the future, we will investigate ways to capture unique excitation-emission characteristics with more detail. One possible approach is to learn coded camera spectral responses instead of just weighting the RGB channels. Building a larger dataset to obtain more training data may also allow us to build stronger classifiers.

Acknowledgements. This work was supported in part by JSPS KAKENHI Grant Numbers JP15H05918, JP16H01676, and JP17H01766.

References

1. Gu, J., Liu, C.: Discriminative illumination: per-pixel classification of raw materials based on optimal projections of spectral BRDF. In: IEEE Conference on Computer Vision and Pattern Recognition (CVPR), pp. 797–804, June 2012
2. Liu, C., Gu, J.: Discriminative illumination: per-pixel classification of raw materials based on optimal projections of spectral BRDF. IEEE Trans. Pattern Anal. Mach. Intell. (PAMI) **36**(1), 86–98 (2014)
3. Wang, C., Okabe, T.: Joint optimization of coded illumination and grayscale conversion for one-shot raw material classification. In: British Machine Vision Conference (BMVC) (2017)
4. Blasinski, H., Farrell, J., Wandell, B.: Designing illuminant spectral power distributions for surface classification. In: IEEE Conference on Computer Vision and Pattern Recognition (CVPR), July 2017
5. Sugiyama, J., Fujita, K., Yoshimura, M., Tsuta, M., Shibata, M., Kokawa, M.: Detection of food hazards using fluorescence fingerprint. IFAC Proc. Vol. **46**(18), 70–74 (2013). 4th IFAC Conference on Modelling and Control in Agriculture, Horticulture and Post Harvest Industry
6. Karoui, R., Dufour, E., Schoonheydt, R., Baerdemaeker, J.D.: Characterisation of soft cheese by front face fluorescence spectroscopy coupled with chemometric tools: effect of the manufacturing process and sampling zone. Food Chem. **100**(2), 632–642 (2007)
7. Chabreyrie, D., Chauvet, S., Guyon, F.: Salagoty M.H., Antinelli, J.F., Medina, B.: Characterization and quantification of grape variety by means of shikimic acid concentration and protein fingerprint in still white wines. J. Agric. Food Chem. **56**(16), 6785–6790 (2008). PMID: 18624410
8. Dufour, E., Frencia, J.P., Kane, E.: Development of a rapid method based on front-face fluorescence spectroscopy for the monitoring of fish freshness. Food Res. Int. **36**(5), 415–423 (2003)
9. Lenhardt, L., Zekovic, I., Dramicanin, T., Dramicanin, M.D., Bro, R.: Determination of the botanical origin of honey by front-face synchronous fluorescence spectroscopy. Appl. Spectrosc. **68**(5), 557–563 (2014)
10. Lam, A., Sato, I.: Spectral modeling and relighting of reflective-fluorescent scenes. In: IEEE Conference on Computer Vision and Pattern Recognition (CVPR), pp. 1452–1459, June 2013
11. Fu, Y., Lam, A., Sato, I., Okabe, T., Sato, Y.: Separating reflective and fluorescent components using high frequency illumination in the spectral domain. IEEE Trans. Pattern Anal. Mach. Intell. (PAMI) **38**(5), 965–978 (2016)

12. Fu, Y., Lam, A., Sato, I., Okabe, T., Sato, Y.: Reflectance and fluorescence spectral recovery via actively lit RGB images. IEEE Trans. Pattern Anal. Mach. Intell. (PAMI) **38**(7), 1313–1326 (2016)
13. Zheng, Y., Fu, Y., Lam, A., Sato, I., Sato, Y.: Separating fluorescent and reflective components by using a single hyperspectral image. In: IEEE International Conference on Computer Vision (ICCV), pp. 3523–3531, December 2015
14. Cortes, C., Vapnik, V.: Support-vector networks. Mach. Learn. **20**(3), 273–297 (1995)

Multi-scale Residual Network for Image Super-Resolution

Juncheng Li[1], Faming Fang[1(✉)], Kangfu Mei[2], and Guixu Zhang[1]

[1] Shanghai Key Laboratory of Multidimensional Information Processing, and Department of Computer Science and Technology, East China Normal University, Shanghai, China
cvjunchengli@gmail.com, {fmfang,gxzhang}@cs.ecnu.edu.cn

[2] School of Computer Science and Information Engineering, Jiangxi Normal University, Nanchang, China
meikangfu@jxnu.edu.cn

Abstract. Recent studies have shown that deep neural networks can significantly improve the quality of single-image super-resolution. Current researches tend to use deeper convolutional neural networks to enhance performance. However, blindly increasing the depth of the network cannot ameliorate the network effectively. Worse still, with the depth of the network increases, more problems occurred in the training process and more training tricks are needed. In this paper, we propose a novel multi-scale residual network (MSRN) to fully exploit the image features, which outperform most of the state-of-the-art methods. Based on the residual block, we introduce convolution kernels of different sizes to adaptively detect the image features in different scales. Meanwhile, we let these features interact with each other to get the most efficacious image information, we call this structure Multi-scale Residual Block (MSRB). Furthermore, the outputs of each MSRB are used as the hierarchical features for global feature fusion. Finally, all these features are sent to the reconstruction module for recovering the high-quality image.

Keywords: Super-resolution · Convolutional neural network
Multi-scale residual network

1 Introduction

Image super-resolution (SR), particularly single-image super-resolution (SISR), has attracted more and more attention in academia and industry. SISR aims to reconstruct a high-resolution (HR) image from a low-resolution (LR) image which is an ill-posed problem since the mapping between LR and HR has multiple solutions. Thence, learning methods are widely used to learn a mapping from LR to HR images via applying large image datasets.

Currently, convolutional neural networks (CNNs) have indicated that they can provide remarkable performance in the SISR problem. In 2014, Dong et al.

V. Ferrari et al. (Eds.): ECCV 2018, LNCS 11212, pp. 527–542, 2018.
https://doi.org/10.1007/978-3-030-01237-3_32

proposed a model for SISR problem termed SRCNN [1], which was the first successful model adopting CNNs to SR problem. SRCNN was an efficient network that could learn a kind of end-to-end mapping between the LR and HR images without requiring any engineered features and reached the most satisfactory performance at that time. Since then, many studies focused on building a more efficient network to learn the mapping between LR and HR images so that a series of CNNs-based SISR models [2–9] were proposed. EDSR [9] was the champion of the NTIRE2017 SR Challenge. It based on SRResNet [8] while enhanced the network by removing the normalization layers as well as using deeper and wider network structures. These models received excellent performance in terms of peak signal-to-noise ratio (PSNR) and structural similarity index (SSIM [10]) in the SISR problem. Nevertheless, all of these models tend to construct deeper and more complex network structures, which means training these models consumes more resources, time, and tricks. In this work, we have reconstructed some classic SR models, such as SRCNN [1], EDSR [9] and SRResNet [8]. During the reconstruction experiments, we find most existing SR models have the following problems:

(a) Hard to Reproduce: The experimental results manifest that most SR models are sensitive to the subtle network architectural changes and some of them are difficult to reach the level of the original paper due to the lack of the network configuration. Also, the same model achieves different performance by using different training tricks, such as weight initialization, gradient truncation, data normalization and so on. This means that the improvement of the performance may not be owing to the change of the model architecture, but the use of some unknown training tricks.

(b) Inadequate of Features Utilization: Most methods blindly increase the depth of the network in order to enhance the performance of the network but ignore taking full use of the LR image features. As the depth of the network increases, the features gradually disappear in the process of transmission. How to make full use of these features is crucial for the network to reconstruct high-quality images.

(c) Poor Scalability: Using the preprocessed LR image as input will add computational complexity and produce visible artifacts. Therefore, recent approaches pay more attention to amplifying LR images directly. As a result, it is difficult to find a simple SR model that can accommodate to any upscaling factors, or can migrate to any upscaling factors with only minor adjustments to the network architecture.

In order to solve the mentioned problems, we propose a novel multi-scale residual network (MSRN) for SISR. In addition, a multi-scale residual block (MSRB) is put forward as the building module for MSRN. Firstly, we use the MSRB to acquire the image features on different scales, which is considered as local multi-scale features. Secondly, the outputs of each MSRB are combined for global feature fusion. Finally, the combination of local multi-scale features and global features can maximize the use of the LR image features and completely solve the problem that features disappear in the transmission process. Besides, we introduce a convolution layer with 1×1 kernel as a bottleneck layer to obtain global feature fusion. Furthermore, we utilize a well-designed reconstruction structure that is simple but efficient, and can easily migrate to any upscaling factors.

We train our models on the DIV2K [11] dataset without special weight initialization method or other training tricks. Our base-model shows superior performance over most state-of-the-art methods on benchmark test-datasets. Besides, the model can achieve more competitive results by increasing the number of MSRB or the size of training images. It is more exciting that our MSRB module can be migrate to other restoration models for feature extraction. Contributions of this paper are as follows:

- Different from previous works, we propose a novel multi-scale residual block (MSRB), which can not only adaptively detect the image features, but also achieve feature fusion at different scales. This is the first multi-scale module based on the residual structure. What's more, it is easy to train and outperform the existing modules.
- We extend our work to computer vision tasks and the results exceed those of the state-of-the-art methods in SISR without deep network structure. Besides, MSRB can be used for feature extraction in other restoration tasks which show promising results.
- We propose a simple architecture for hierarchical features fusion (HFFS) and image reconstruction. It can be easily extended to any upscaling factors.

2 Related Works

2.1 Single-Image Super-Resolution

The SISR problem can be divided into three major stages roughly. Early approaches use interpolation techniques based on sampling theory like linear or bicubic. Those methods run fast, but can not rebuild the detailed, realistic textures. Improved works aim to establish complex mapping functions between LR and HR images. Those methods rely on techniques ranging from neighbor embedding to sparse coding.

Recent works tend to build an end-to-end CNNs model to learn mapping functions from LR to HR images by using large training datasets. Since Dong et al. proposed the SRCNN [1] model, various CNNs architectures have been used on SISR problem. Previous work often used pre-processed LR image as input, which was upscaled to HR space via an upsampling operator as bicubic. However, this method has been proved [2] that it will add computational complexity and produce visible artifacts. To avoid this, new methods are proposed, such as Fast Super-Resolution Convolutional Neural Networks (FSRCNN [3]) and Efficient Sub-pixel Convolutional Networks (ESPCN [2]). All of the models mentioned above are shallow networks (less than 5 layers). Kim et al. [12] first introduced the residual architecture for training much deeper network (20 layers) and achieved

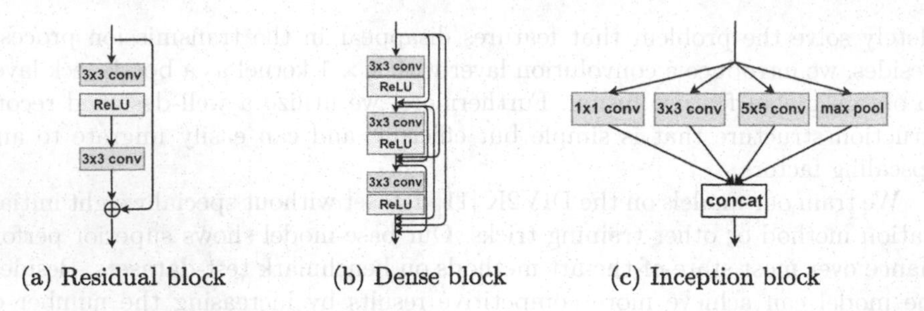

Fig. 1. The structure of feature extraction blocks: (a) residual block, (b) dense block, and (c) inception block.

great performance. After that, many SR models have been proposed, including DRCN [5], DRNN [7], LapSRN [6], SRResNet [8], and EDSR [9]. Unfortunately, these models become more and more deeper and extremely difficult to train.

2.2 Feature Extraction Block

Nowadays, many feature extraction blocks have been proposed. The main idea of the inception block [13] (Fig. 1(c)) is to find out how an optimal local sparse structure works in a convolutional network. However, these different scale features simply concatenate together, which leads to the underutilization of local features. In 2016, Kim et al. [12] proposed a residual learning framework (Fig. 1(a)) to ease the training of networks so that they could achieve more competitive results. After that, Huang et al. introduced the dense block (Fig. 1(b)). Residual block and dense block use a single size of convolutional kernel and the computational complexity of dense blocks increases at a higher growth rate. In order to solve these drawbacks, we propose a multi-scale residual block.

Based on the residual structure, we introduce convolution kernels of different sizes, which designed for adaptively detecting the features of images at different scales. Meanwhile, a skip connection is applied between different scale features so that the features information can be shared and reused with each other. This helps to fully exploit the local features of the image. In addition, a 1×1 convolution layer at the end of the block can be used as a bottleneck layer, which contributes to feature fusion and reduces computation complexity. We will give a more detailed description in Sect. 3.1.

3 Proposed Method

In this work, our intent is to reconstruct a super-resolution image I^{SR} from a low-resolution image I^{LR}. The I^{LR} is the low-resolution version of I^{HR}, which is obtained by the bicubic operation. We convert the image to the YCbCr color space and train only on the Y channel. For an image with C color channels, we describe the I^{LR} with a tensor of size $W \times H \times C$ and denote the I^{HR}, I^{SR}

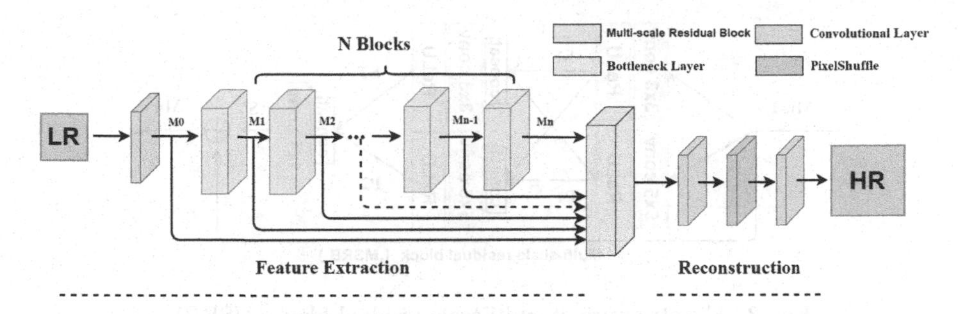

Fig. 2. The complete architecture of our proposed model. The network is divided into feature extraction and reconstruction, different color squares represent different operations, the top-right of the picture gives a specific description.

with $rW \times rH \times C$, where $C = 1$, represents the Y channel and r represents the upscaling factor.

Our ultimate goal is to learn an end-to-end mapping function F between the I^{LR} and the I^{HR}. Given a training dataset $\{I_i^{LR}, I_i^{HR}\}_{i=1}^{N}$, we solve the following problem:

$$\hat{\theta} = arg \min_{\theta} \frac{1}{N} \sum_{i=1}^{N} \mathcal{L}^{SR}(F_\theta(I_i^{LR}), I_i^{HR}), \tag{1}$$

where $\theta = \{W_1, W_2, W_3...W_m, b_1, b_2, b_3...b_m\}$, denotes the weights and bias of our m-layer neural network. $\mathcal{L}^{SR}$ is the loss function used to minimize the difference between I_i^{SR} and I_i^{HR}. Recently, researchers also focus on finding a superior loss function to improve the network performance. The most widely-used image objective optimization functions are the MSE function and L2 function. Although these methods can obtain high PSNR/SSIM, solutions for MSE optimization and L2 optimization problems often produce excessively smooth textures. Now, a variety of loss functions have been proposed such as VGG [4] function and Charbonnier Penalty function [6]. On the contrary, we find that their performance improvement is marginal. In order to avoid introducing unnecessary training tricks and reduce computations, we finally choose the L1 function. Thus, the loss function $\mathcal{L}^{SR}$ can be defined as:

$$\mathcal{L}^{SR}(F_\theta(I_i^{LR}), I_i^{HR}) = \left\| F_\theta(I_i^{LR}) - I_i^{HR} \right\|_1. \tag{2}$$

As shown in Fig. 2, it is the complete architecture of our proposed model. Our model takes the unprocessed LR images as input, which are directly upsampled to high-resolution space via the network. Our model can be divided into two parts: the feature extraction module and the image reconstruction module. The feature extraction module is composed of two structures: multi-scale residual block (MSRB) and hierarchical feature fusion structure (HFFS).

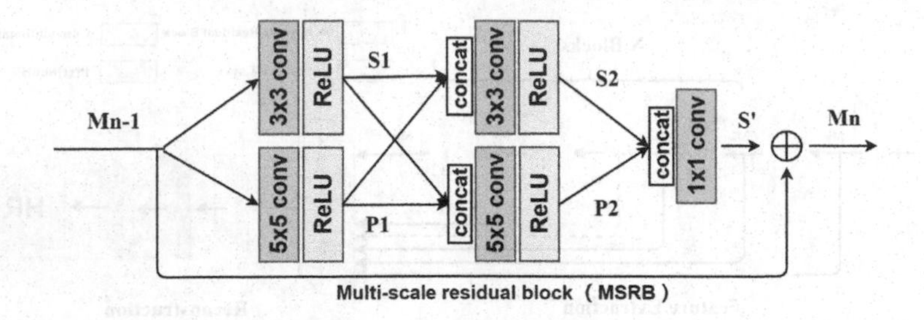

Fig. 3. The structure of multi-scale residual block (MSRB).

3.1 Multi-scale Residual Block (MSRB)

In order to detect the image features at different scales, we propose multi-scale residual block (MSRB). Here we will provide a detailed description of this structure. As shown in Fig. 3, our MSRB contains two parts: multi-scale features fusion and local residual learning.

Multi-scale Features Fusion: Different from previous works, we construct a two-bypass network and different bypass use different convolutional kernel. In this way, the information between those bypass can be shared with each other so that able to detect the image features at different scales. The operation can be defined as:

$$S_1 = \sigma(w^1_{3\times3} * M_{n-1} + b^1), \tag{3}$$

$$P_1 = \sigma(w^1_{5\times5} * M_{n-1} + b^1), \tag{4}$$

$$S_2 = \sigma(w^2_{3\times3} * [S_1, P_1] + b^2), \tag{5}$$

$$P_2 = \sigma(w^2_{5\times5} * [P_1, S_1] + b^2), \tag{6}$$

$$S^{'} = w^3_{1\times1} * [S_2, P_2] + b^3, \tag{7}$$

where w and b represent the weights and bias respectively, and the superscripts represent the number of layers at which they are located, while the subscripts represent the size of the convolutional kernel used in the layer. $\sigma(x) = max(0, x)$ stands for the ReLU function, and $[S_1, p_1]$, $[P_1, S_1]$, $[S_2, P_2]$ denote the concatenation operation.

Let M denote the number of feature maps sent to the MSRB. So the input and output of the first convolutional layer have M feature maps. And the second convolutional layer has 2M feature maps, either input or output. All of these feature maps are concatenated and sent to a 1×1 convolutional layer. This layer reduces the number of these feature maps to M, thus the input and output of our MSRB have the same number of feature maps. The distinctive architecture allows multiple MSRBs to be used together.

Local Residual Learning: In order to make the network more efficient, we adopt residual learning to each MSRB. Formally, we describe a multi-scale residual block (MSRB) as:

$$M_n = S^{'} + M_{n-1}, \tag{8}$$

where M_n and M_{n-1} represent the input and output of the MSRB, respectively. The operation $S^{'} + M_{n-1}$ is performed by a shortcut connection and element-wise addition. It is worth mentioning that the use of local residual learning makes the computational complexity greatly reduced. Simultaneously, the performance of the network is improved.

3.2 Hierarchical Feature Fusion Structure (HFFS)

For SISR problem, input and output images are highly correlated. It is crucial to fully exploit the features of the input image and transfer them to the end of the network for reconstruction. However, as the depth of the network increases these features gradually disappear during transmission. Driven by this problem, various methods have been proposed, among which the skip connection is the most simple and efficient method. All of these methods try to create different connections between different layers. Unfortunately, these methods can't fully utilize the features of the input image, and generate too much redundant information for aimlessness.

In the experiment, we notice that with the growth of depth, the spatial expression ability of the network gradually decreases while the semantic expression ability gradually increases. Additionally, the output of each MSRB contains distinct features. Therefore, how to make full use of these hierarchical features will directly affect the quality of reconstructed images. In this work, a simple hierarchical feature fusion structure is utilized. We send all the output of the MSRB to the end of the network for reconstruction. On the one hand, these feature maps contain a large amount of redundant information. On the other hand, using them directly for reconstruction will greatly increase the computational complexity. In order to adaptively extract useful information from these hierarchical features, we introduce a bottleneck layer which is essential for a convolutional layer with 1×1 kernel. The output of hierarchical feature fusion structure (HFFS) can be formulated as:

$$F_{LR} = w * [M_0, M_1, M_2, ..., M_N] + b, \tag{9}$$

where M_0 is the output of the first convolutional layer, $M_i (i \neq 0)$ represents the output of the ith MSRB, and $[M_0, M_1, M_2, ..., M_N]$ denotes the concatenation operation.

3.3 Image Reconstruction

The previous work paid close attention to learn a mapping function between LR and HR images, where the LR image was upsampled to the same dimensions as HR by bicubic. Yet, this approach introduced redundant information and increased the computational complexity. Inspired by it, recent work tends to use the un-amplified LR as the input image to train a network that can be directly upsampled to HR dimensions. Instead, it is difficult to find an SR model which is able to migrate to any upscaling factors with only minor adjustments

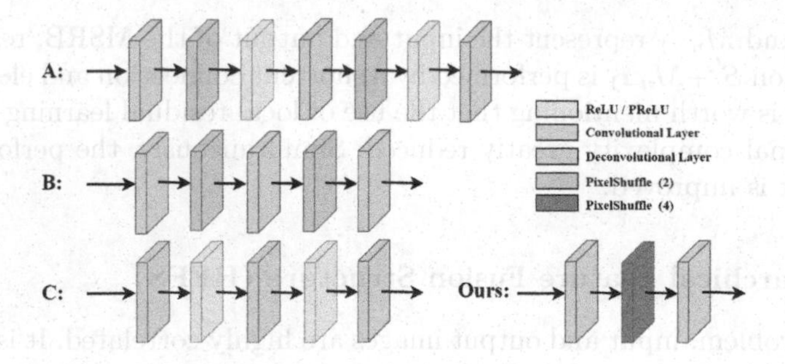

Fig. 4. Comparison of some common image reconstruction structure (×4).

to the network architecture. Moreover, most of these networks tend to be a fixed upscaling factor (x4), with no specific instructions given to migrate to other upscaling factors.

PixelShuffle [2] and deconvolutional layer are widely used in SISR tasks. As shown in Fig. 4, there are several common reconstruction modules. Taking the upscaling factor of ×4 as an example, all of these modules use pixelShuffle or deconvolution operation and the SR image is reconstructed gradually with upscaling factor 2 as the base. However, as the upscaling factor increases (e.g. ×8), the network becomes deeper accompanied with more uncertain training problems. Moreover, these methods does not work on odd upscaling factors, while one might expect a tardy growth in upscaling factor (e.g. ×2, ×3, ×4, ×5) rather than exponential increase.

For this purpose, we put forward a new reconstruction module (Fig. 4(ours)), which is a simple, efficient, and flexible structure. Thanks to pixelshuffle [2], our modules can be migrated to any upscaling factor with minor adjustments. In Table 1. We provide thorough configuration information about the reconstruction structure. In our network, for different upscaling factors, we only need to change the value of M whose change is negligible. Experiments indicate that this structure performs well on different upscaling factors.

4 Experiments

In this section, we evaluate the performance of our model on several benchmark test-datasets. We first introduce the dataset used for training and testing, then we give implementation details. Next, we compare our model with several state-of-the-art methods. Finally, we give a series of qualitative analysis experiments results. In addition, we show some of the results on other low-level computer vision tasks with our MSRB.

4.1 Datasets

The most widely used training dataset in previous studies includes 291 images, of which 91 images are from [14] and the other 200 images are from [15]. And

Table 1. Detailed configuration information about the reconstruction structure. For different upscaling factors, we only need to change the value of M.

Laye_name	Input_channel	Output_channel	Kernel_size
conv_input	64	64 × 2 × 2	3 × 3
PixelShuffle(×2)	64 × 2 × 2	64	/
conv_output	64	1	3 × 3
conv_input	64	64 × 3 × 3	3 × 3
PixelShuffle(×3)	64 × 3 × 3	64	/
conv_output	64	1	3 × 3
conv_input	64	64 × 4 × 4	3 × 3
PixelShuffle(×4)	64 × 4 × 4	64	/
conv_output	64	1	3 × 3
conv_input	64	64 × 8 × 8	3 × 3
PixelShuffle(×8)	64 × 8 × 8	64	/
conv_output	64	1	3 × 3
conv_input	64	64 × M × M	3 × 3
PixelShuffle(×M)	64 × M × M	64	/
conv_output	64	1	3 × 3

some methods take ImageNet [16] as training dataset, since it contains richer samples. In our work, we choose DIV2K [11] as our training dataset, a new high-quality image dataset for image restoration challenge. During testing, we choose five widely used benchmark datasets: Set5 [17], Set14 [18], BSDS100 [19], Urban100 [20] and Manga109 [21]. These datasets contain a wide variety of images that can fully verify our model. Following previous works, all our training and testing are based on luminance channel in YCbCr colour space, and upscaling factors: ×2, ×3, ×4, ×8 are used for training and testing.

4.2 Implementation Details

Following [6], we augment the training data in three ways: (1) scaling (2) rotation (3) flipping. In each training batch, we randomly extract 16 LR patches with the size of 64×64 and an epoch having 1000 iterations of back-propagation. We train our model with ADAM optimizer [22] by setting the learning rate $lr = 0.0001$. In our final model, we use 8 multi-scale residual blocks (MSRB, $N = 8$) and the output of each MSRB has 64 feature maps. Simultaneously, the output of each bottleneck layer (1 × 1 convolutional layer) has 64 feature maps. We implement MSRN with the Pytorch framework and train them using NVIDIA Titan Xp GPU. We do not use a special weight initialization method or other training tricks, and code is available at https://github.com/MIVRC/MSRN-PyTorch.

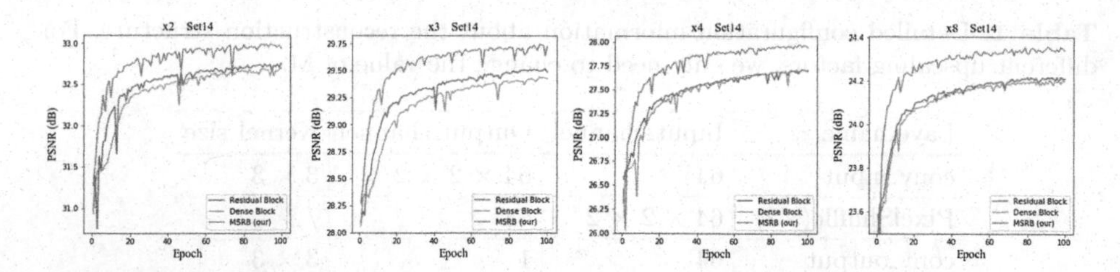

Fig. 5. Quantitative comparison of three different feature extraction blocks (residual block [12], dense block [24], and MSRB(our)) on SISR. The green line represents our model and it achieves the best results under different upscaling factors.

4.3 Comparisons with State-of-the-art Methods

We compare our model with 10 state-of-the-art SR methods, including Bicubic, A+ [23], SelfExSR [20], SRCNN [1], ESPCN [2], FSRCNN [3], VDSR [4], DRCN [5], LapSRN [6] and EDSR [9]. For fair, we retrain most of these models (except for EDSR [9], the results of EDSR provided by their original papers). Taking the equality of comparison into account, we evaluate the SR images with two commonly-used image quality metrics: PSNR and SSIM. Moreover, all the reported PSNR/SSIM measures are calculated on the luminance channel and remove M-pixel from each border (M stands for the upscaling factor).

The evaluation results of the SR method including our model and 10 state-of-art methods are demonstrated in Table 2. Our model outperforms by a large margin on different upscaling factors and test-datasets. It can be seen that our results are slightly lower than EDSR [9]. But it is worth noting that EDSR [9] use RGB channels for training, meanwhile, the data augment methods are different. To better illustrate the difference with EDSR [9], we show a comparison of model specifications in Table 3. EDSR [9] is an outstanding model gained amazing results. However, it is a deep and wide network which contains large quantities of convolutional layers and parameters. In other words, training this model will cost more memory, space and datasets. In contrast, the specifications of our model is much smaller than EDSR [9], which makes it easier to reproduce and promote.

In Figs. 6 and 7 we present visual performance on different datasets with different upscaling factors. Our model can reconstruct sharp and natural images, as well as outperforms other state-of-the-art methods. This is probably owing to the MSRB module can detect the image features at different scales and use them for reconstruction. For better illustration, more SR images reconstructed by our model can be found at https://goo.gl/bGnZ8D.

4.4 Qualitative Analysis

Benefit of MSRB: In this work, we propose an efficient feature extraction structure: multi-scale residual block. This module can adaptively detect image features at different scales and fully exploit the potential features of the image.

Table 2. Quantitative comparisons of state-of-the-art methods. Red text indicates the best performancen and blue text indicate the second best performance. Notice that the EDSR results were not retrained by us, but were provided by their original paper.

Algorithm	Scale	Set5 PSNR/SSIM	Set14 PSNR/SSIM	BSDS100 PSNR/SSIM	Urban100 PSNR/SSIM	Manga109 PSNR/SSIM
Bicubic	x2	33.69/0.9284	30.34/0.8675	29.57/0.8434	26.88/0.8438	30.82/0.9332
A+ [23]	x2	36.60/0.9542	32.42/0.9059	31.24/0.8870	29.25/0.8955	35.37/0.9663
SelfExSR [20]	x2	36.60/0.9537	32.46/0.9051	31.20/0.8863	29.55/0.8983	35.82/0.9671
SRCNN [1]	x2	36.71/0.9536	32.32/0.9052	31.36/0.8880	29.54/0.8962	35.74/0.9661
ESPCN [2]	x2	37.00/0.9559	32.75/0.9098	31.51/0.8939	29.87/0.9065	36.21/0.9694
FSRCNN [3]	x2	37.06/0.9554	32.76/0.9078	31.53/0.8912	29.88/0.9024	36.67/0.9694
VDSR [4]	x2	37.53/0.9583	33.05/0.9107	31.92/0.8965	30.79/0.9157	37.22/0.9729
DRCN [5]	x2	37.63/0.9584	33.06/0.9108	31.85/0.8947	30.76/0.9147	37.63/0.9723
LapSRN [6]	x2	37.52/0.9581	33.08/0.9109	31.80/0.8949	30.41/0.9112	37.27/0.9855
EDSR [9]	x2	38.11/0.9601	33.92/0.9195	32.32/0.9013	-/-	-/-
MSRN(our)	x2	38.08/0.9605	33.74/0.9170	32.23/0.9013	32.22/0.9326	38.82/0.9868
Bicubic	x3	30.41/0.8655	27.64/0.7722	27.21/0.7344	24.46/0.7411	26.96/0.8555
A+ [23]	x3	32.63/0.9085	29.25/0.8194	28.31/0.7828	26.05/0.8019	29.93/0.9089
SelfExSR [20]	x3	32.66/0.9089	29.34/0.8222	28.30/0.7839	26.45/0.8124	27.57/0.7997
SRCNN [1]	x3	32.47/0.9067	29.23/0.8201	28.31/0.7832	26.25/0.8028	30.59/0.9107
ESPCN [2]	x3	33.02/0.9135	29.49/0.8271	28.50/0.7937	26.41/0.8161	30.79/0.9181
FSRCNN [3]	x3	33.20/0.9149	29.54/0.8277	28.55/0.7945	26.48/0.8175	30.98/0.9212
VDSR [4]	x3	33.68/0.9201	29.86/0.8312	28.83/0.7966	27.15/0.8315	32.01/0.9310
DRCN [5]	x3	33.85/0.9215	29.89/0.8317	28.81/0.7954	27.16/0.8311	32.31/0.9328
LapSRN [6]	x3	33.82/0.9207	29.89/0.8304	28.82/0.7950	27.07/0.8298	32.21/0.9318
EDSR [9]	x3	34.65/0.9282	30.52/0.8462	29.25/0.8093	-/-	-/-
MSRN(our)	x3	34.38/0.9262	30.34/0.8395	29.08/0.8041	28.08/0.8554	33.44/0.9427
Bicubic	x4	28.43/0.8022	26.10/0.6936	25.97/0.6517	23.14/0.6599	24.91/0.7826
A+ [23]	x4	30.33/0.8565	27.44/0.7450	26.83/0.6999	24.34/0.7211	27.03/0.8439
SelfExSR [20]	x4	30.34/0.8593	27.55/0.7511	26.84/0.7032	24.83/0.7403	27.83/0.8598
SRCNN [1]	x4	30.50/0.8573	27.62/0.7453	26.91/0.6994	24.53/0.7236	27.66/0.8505
ESPCN [2]	x4	30.66/0.8646	27.71/0.7562	26.98/0.7124	24.60/0.7360	27.70/0.8560
FSRCNN [3]	x4	30.73/0.8601	27.71/0.7488	26.98/0.7029	24.62/0.7272	27.90/0.8517
VDSR [4]	x4	31.36/0.8796	28.11/0.7624	27.29/0.7167	25.18/0.7543	28.83/0.8809
DRCN [5]	x4	31.56/0.8810	28.15/0.7627	27.24/0.7150	25.15/0.7530	28.98/0.8816
LapSRN [6]	x4	31.54/0.8811	28.19/0.7635	27.32/0.7162	25.21/0.7564	29.09/0.8845
EDSR [9]	x4	32.46/0.8968	28.80/0.7876	27.71/0.7420	-/-	-/-
MSRN(our)	x4	32.07/0.8903	28.60/0.7751	27.52/0.7273	26.04/0.7896	30.17/0.9034
Bicubic	x8	24.40/0.6045	23.19/0.5110	23.67/0.4808	20.74/0.4841	21.46/0.6138
A+ [23]	x8	25.53/0.6548	23.99/0.5535	24.21/0.5156	21.37/0.5193	22.39/0.6454
SelfExSR [20]	x8	25.49/0.6733	24.02/0.5650	24.19/0.5146	21.81/0.5536	22.99/0.6907
SRCNN [1]	x8	25.34/0.6471	23.86/0.5443	24.14/0.5043	21.29/0.5133	22.46/0.6606
ESPCN [2]	x8	25.75/0.6738	24.21/0.5109	24.37/0.5277	21.59/0.5420	22.83/0.6715
FSRCNN [3]	x8	25.42/0.6440	23.94/0.5482	24.21/0.5112	21.32/0.5090	22.39/0.6357
VDSR [4]	x8	25.73/0.6743	23.20/0.5110	24.34/0.5169	21.48/0.5289	22.73/0.6688
DRCN [5]	x8	25.93/0.6743	24.25/0.5510	24.49/0.5168	21.71/0.5289	23.20/0.6686
LapSRN [6]	x8	26.15/0.7028	24.45/0.5792	24.54/0.5293	21.81/0.5555	23.39/0.7068
MSRN(our)	x8	26.59/0.7254	24.88/0.5961	24.70/0.5410	22.37/0.5977	24.28/0.7517

Table 3. Specifications comparison (x4). 'RGB' means the model is trained on RGB channels, 'Y' means the model is trained on luminance channel in YCbCr colour space, and 'M' means million.

Algorithm	Feature extraction	Filters	Layers	Depth	Parameters	Updates	Channel
EDSR [9]	32 blocks	256	69	69	43M	1×10^6	RGB
MSRN (our)	8 blocks	64	44	28	6.3M	4×10^5	Y

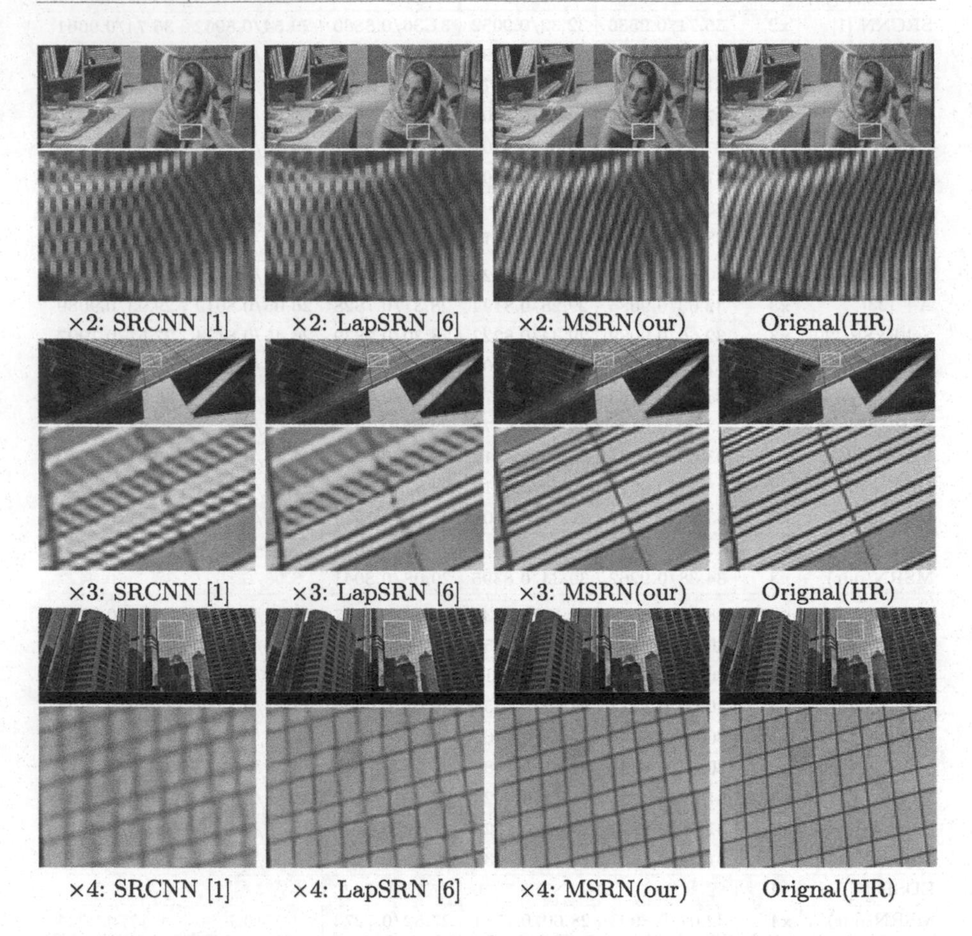

Fig. 6. Visual comparison for ×2, ×3, ×4 SR images. Our MSRN can reconstruct realistic images with sharp edges.

To validate the effectiveness of our module, we design a set of comparative experiments to compare the performance with residual block [12], dense block [24] and MSRB in SISR tasks. Based on the MSRN architecture, we replace the feature extraction block in the network. The three networks contain different feature extraction block, and each network contains only one feature extraction block.

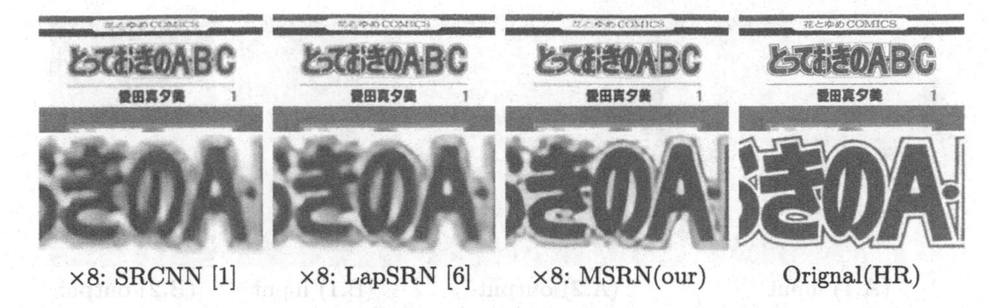

Fig. 7. Visual comparison of MSRN with other SR methods on large-scale (×8) SR task. Obviously, MSRN can reconstruct realistic images with sharp edges.

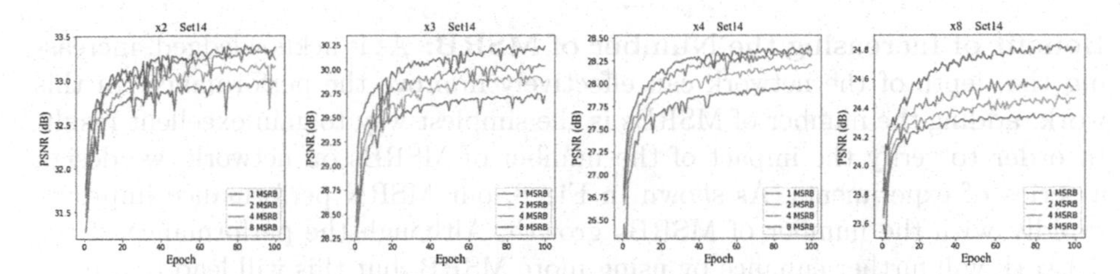

Fig. 8. Performance comparison of MSRN with different number of MSRBs.

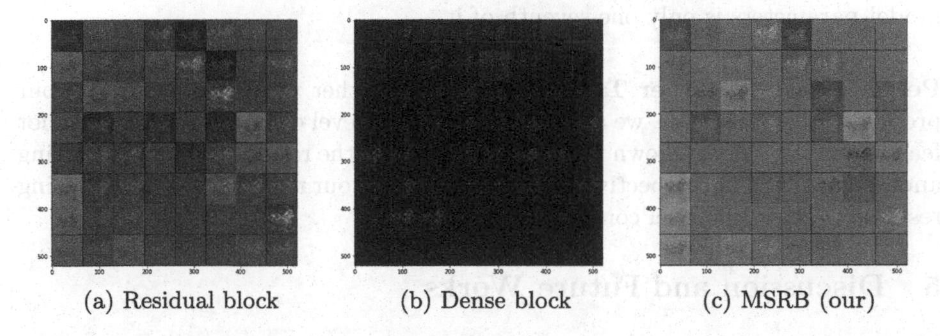

Fig. 9. Feature maps visualization. Represent the output of the residual block [12], the dense block [24], and our MSRB, respectively.

For quick verification, we use a small training dataset in this part, and all these models are trained in the same environment by 10^5 iterations. The results (Fig. 5) show that our MSRB module is superior to other modules at all upsampling factors. As shown in Fig. 9, we visualize the output of these feature extraction blocks. It deserves to notice that the activations are sparse (most values are zero, as the visualization shown in black) and some activation maps may be all zero which indicates dead filters. It is obvious that the output of the MSRB contains more valid activation maps, which further proves the effectiveness of the structure.

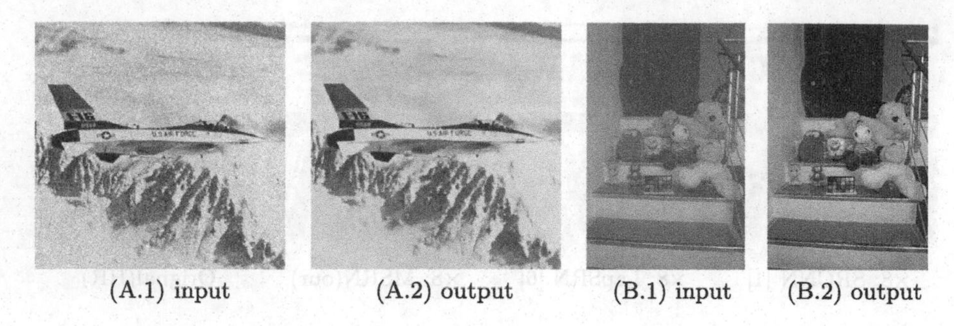

(A.1) input (A.2) output (B.1) input (B.2) output

Fig. 10. Application examples for image denoising and image dehazing, respectively.

Benefit of Increasing the Number of MSRB: As is acknowledged, increasing the depth of the network can effectively improve the performance. In this work, adding the number of MSRBs is the simplest way to gain excellent result. In order to verify the impact of the number of MSRBs on network, we design a series of experiments. As shown in Fig. 8, our MSRN performance improves rapidly with the number of MSRBs growth. Although the performance of the network will further enhance by using more MSRB, but this will lead to a more complex network. While weighing the network performance and network complexity, we finally use 8 MSRBs, the result is close to EDSR, but the number of model parameters is only one-seventh of it.

Performance on Other Tasks: In order to further verify the validity of our proposed MSRB module, we apply it to other low-level computer vision tasks for feature extraction. As shown in Fig. 10, we provide the results of image-denoising and image-dehazing, respectively. It is obvious that our model achieves promising results on other low-level computer vision tasks.

5 Discussion and Future Works

Many training tricks have been proposed to make the reconstructed image more realistic in SISR. For example, multi-scale (the scale here represents the upscaling factor) mixed training method is used in [4,9], and geometric selfensemble method is proposed in [9]. We believe that these training tricks can also improve our model performance. However, we are more inclined to explore an efficient model rather than use training tricks. Although our model has shown superior performance, the reconstructed image is still not clear enough under large upscaling factors. In the future work, we will pay more attention to large-scale downsampling image reconstruction.

6 Conclusions

In this paper, we proposed an efficient multi-scale residual block (MSRB), which is used to adaptively detect the image features at different scales. Based on

MSRB, we put forward multi-scale residual network (MSRN). It is a simple and efficient SR model so that we can fully utilize the local multi-scale features and the hierarchical features to obtain accurate SR image. Additionally, we achieved promising results by applying the MSRB module to other computer vision tasks such as image-denoising and image-dehazing.

Acknowledgments. This work are sponsored by the key project of the National Natural Science Foundation of China (No. 61731009), the National Science Foundation of China (No. 61501188), the "Chenguang Program" supported by Shanghai Education Development Foundation and Shanghai Municipal Education Commission (No. 17CG25) and East China Normal University.

References

1. Dong, C., Loy, C.C., He, K., Tang, X.: Learning a deep convolutional network for image super-resolution. In: Fleet, D., Pajdla, T., Schiele, B., Tuytelaars, T. (eds.) ECCV 2014. LNCS, vol. 8692, pp. 184–199. Springer, Cham (2014). https://doi.org/10.1007/978-3-319-10593-2_13
2. Shi, W. et al.: Real-time single image and video super-resolution using an efficient sub-pixel convolutional neural network. In: Proceedings of the IEEE Conference on Computer Vision and Pattern Recognition, pp. 1874–1883 (2016)
3. Dong, C., Loy, C.C., Tang, X.: Accelerating the super-resolution convolutional neural network. In: Leibe, B., Matas, J., Sebe, N., Welling, M. (eds.) ECCV 2016. LNCS, vol. 9906, pp. 391–407. Springer, Cham (2016). https://doi.org/10.1007/978-3-319-46475-6_25
4. Kim, J., Kwon Lee, J., Mu Lee, K.: Accurate image super-resolution using very deep convolutional networks. In: Proceedings of the IEEE Conference on Computer Vision and Pattern Recognition, pp. 1646–1654 (2016)
5. Kim, J., Kwon Lee, J., Mu Lee, K.: Deeply-recursive convolutional network for image super-resolution. In: Proceedings of the IEEE Conference on Computer Vision and Pattern Recognition, pp. 1637–1645 (2016)
6. Lai, W.S., Huang, J.B., Ahuja, N., Yang, M.H.: Deep laplacian pyramid networks for fast and accurate superresolution. In: IEEE Conference on Computer Vision and Pattern Recognition, vol. 2, p. 5 (2017)
7. Tai, Y., Yang, J., Liu, X.: Image super-resolution via deep recursive residual network. In: Proceedings of the IEEE Conference on Computer Vision and Pattern Recognition, vol. 1, p. 5 (2017)
8. Ledig, C., et al.: Photo-realistic single image superresolution using a generative adversarial network. In: The IEEE Conference on Computer Vision and Pattern Recognition, vol. 2, p. 4 (2017)
9. Lim, B., Son, S., Kim, H., Nah, S., Lee, K.M.: Enhanced deep residual networks for single image super-resolution. In: The IEEE Conference on Computer Vision and Pattern Recognition Workshops. vol. 1, p. 4 (2017)
10. Wang, Z., Bovik, A.C., Sheikh, H.R., Simoncelli, E.P.: Image quality assessment: from error visibility to structural similarity. IEEE Trans. Image Process. **13**(4), 600–612 (2004)
11. Agustsson, E., Timofte, R.: Ntire 2017 challenge on single image super-resolution: dataset and study. In: The IEEE Conference on Computer Vision and Pattern Recognition Workshops, vol. 3, p. 2 (2017)

12. He, K., Zhang, X., Ren, S., Sun, J.: Deep residual learning for image recognition. In: Proceedings of the IEEE Conference on Computer Vision and Pattern Recognition, pp. 770–778 (2016)
13. Szegedy, C., et al.: Going deeper with convolutions. In: Proceedings of the IEEE Conference on Computer Vision and Pattern Recognition, pp. 1–9 (2015)
14. Yang, J., Wright, J., Huang, T.S., Ma, Y.: Image super-resolution via sparse representation. IEEE Trans. Image Process. **19**(11), 2861–2873 (2010)
15. Martin, D., Fowlkes, C., Tal, D., Malik, J.: A database of human segmented natural images and its application to evaluating segmentation algorithms and measuring ecological statistics. In: Proceedings Eighth IEEE International Conference on Computer Vision, pp. 416–423 (2001)
16. Russakovsky, O., Deng, J., Su, H., Krause, J., Satheesh, S., Ma, S., Huang, Z., Karpathy, A., Khosla, A., Bernstein, M.: Imagenet large scale visual recognition challenge. Int. J. Comput. Vis. **115**(3), 211–252 (2015)
17. Bevilacqua, M., Roumy, A., Guillemot, C., Alberi-Morel, M.L.: Low-complexity single-image super-resolution based on nonnegative neighbor embedding. In: Proceedings of the 23rd British Machine Vision Conference. (2012)
18. Zeyde, R., Elad, M., Protter, M.: On single image scale-up using sparse-representations. In: Boissonnat, J.-D., Chenin, P., Cohen, A., Gout, C., Lyche, T., Mazure, M.-L., Schumaker, L. (eds.) Curves and Surfaces 2010. LNCS, vol. 6920, pp. 711–730. Springer, Heidelberg (2012). https://doi.org/10.1007/978-3-642-27413-8_47
19. Arbelaez, P., Maire, M., Fowlkes, C., Malik, J.: Contour detection and hierarchical image segmentation. IEEE Trans. Pattern Anal. Mach. Intell. **33**(5), 898–916 (2011)
20. Huang, J.B., Singh, A., Ahuja, N.: Single image super-resolution from transformed self-exemplars. In: Proceedings of the IEEE Conference on Computer Vision and Pattern Recognition, pp. 5197–5206 (2015)
21. Matsui, Y., Ito, K., Aramaki, Y., Fujimoto, A., Ogawa, T., Yamasaki, T., Aizawa, K.: Sketch-based manga retrieval using manga109 dataset. Multimed. Tools Appl. **76**(20), 21811–21838 (2017)
22. Kingma, D.P., Ba, J.L.: Adam: a method for stochastic optimization. In: Proceedings of the 3rd International Conference on Learning Representations (2014)
23. Timofte, R., De Smet, V., Van Gool, L.: A+: adjusted anchored neighborhood regression for fast super-resolution. In: Cremers, D., Reid, I., Saito, H., Yang, M.-H. (eds.) ACCV 2014. LNCS, vol. 9006, pp. 111–126. Springer, Cham (2015). https://doi.org/10.1007/978-3-319-16817-3_8
24. Huang, G., Liu, Z., Weinberger, K.Q., van der Maaten, L.: Densely connected convolutional networks. In: Proceedings of the IEEE Conference on Computer Vision and Pattern Recognition, vol. 1, p. 3 (2017)

A Dataset for Lane Instance Segmentation in Urban Environments

Brook Roberts, Sebastian Kaltwang(✉), Sina Samangooei, Mark Pender-Bare, Konstantinos Tertikas, and John Redford

FiveAI Ltd., Cambridge CB2 1NS, UK
{brook,sebastian,sina,mark.pender-bare,konstantinos,john}@five.ai

Abstract. Autonomous vehicles require knowledge of the surrounding road layout, which can be predicted by state-of-the-art CNNs. This work addresses the current lack of data for determining lane instances, which are needed for various driving manoeuvres. The main issue is the time-consuming manual labelling process, typically applied per image. We notice that driving the car is itself a form of annotation. Therefore, we propose a semi-automated method that allows for efficient labelling of image sequences by utilising an estimated road plane in 3D based on where the car has driven and projecting labels from this plane into all images of the sequence. The average labelling time per image is reduced to 5 s and only an inexpensive dash-cam is required for data capture. We are releasing a dataset of 24,000 images and additionally show experimental semantic segmentation and instance segmentation results.

Keywords: Dataset · Urban driving · Road · Lane
Instance segmentation · Semi-automated annotation · Partial labels

1 Introduction

Autonomous vehicles have the potential to revolutionise urban transport. Mobility will be safer, always available, more reliable and provided at a lower cost. Yet we are still at the beginning of implementing fully autonomous systems, with many unsolved challenges remaining [1]. One important problem is giving the autonomous system knowledge about surrounding space: a self-driving car needs to know the road layout around it in order to make informed driving decisions. In this work, we address the problem of detecting driving lane instances from a camera mounted on a vehicle. Separate, space-confined lane instance regions are needed to perform various challenging driving manoeuvres, including lane changing, overtaking and junction crossing.

Electronic supplementary material The online version of this chapter (https://doi.org/10.1007/978-3-030-01237-3_33) contains supplementary material, which is available to authorized users.

V. Ferrari et al. (Eds.): ECCV 2018, LNCS 11212, pp. 543–559, 2018.
https://doi.org/10.1007/978-3-030-01237-3_33

Typical state-of-the-art CNN models need large amounts of labelled data to detect lane instances reliably (e.g. [2–4]). However, few labelled datasets are publicly available, mainly due to the time consuming annotation process; it takes from several minutes up to more than one hour per image [5–7] to annotate images completely for semantic segmentation tasks. In this work, we introduce a new video dataset for road segmentation, ego lane segmentation and lane instance segmentation in urban environments. We propose a semi-automated annotation process, that reduces the average time per image to the order of seconds. This speed-up is achieved by (1) noticing that driving the car is itself a form of annotation and that cars mostly travel along lanes, (2) propagating manual label adjustments from a single view to all images of the sequence and (3) accepting non-labelled parts in ambiguous situations.

Previous lane detection work has focused on detecting the components of lane boundaries, and then applying clustering to identify the boundary as a whole [2,8–10]. More recent methods use CNN based segmentation [2,4], and RNNs [11] for detecting lane boundaries. However, visible lane boundaries can be interrupted by occlusion or worn markings, and by themselves are not associated with a specific lane instance. Hence, we target lane instance labels in our dataset, which provide a consistent definition of the lane surface (from which lane boundaries can be derived). Some work focuses on the road markings [12], which are usually present at the border of lanes. However, additional steps are needed to determine the area per lane. Much of the work has only been evaluated on proprietary datasets and only few public datasets are available [13]. Various datasets include road area as a detection task, in addition to many other semantic segmentation classes [5–7,14–17]. Some datasets also includes the

Fig. 1. Example image from our dataset (top left), including annotations for road (top right), ego-lane (bottom left) and lane instance (bottom right). Road and lanes below vehicles are annotated despite being occluded. Non-coloured parts have not been annotated, i.e. the class is not known.

Table 1. Comparison of the available datasets. Label time per image is only shown if provided by the authors. Many datasets are not only targeting the road layout, and thus the labelling includes more classes.

Name	Year	#labeled frames	#videos	img. seq.	road area	ego lane	lane instances	label time per img.
Caltech Lanes [19]	2008	1,224	4	✓	✓ [b]	-	✓	-
CamVid [5,14]	2008	701	4	✓	✓	-	-	20 min
Yotta [15]	2012	86	1	✓	✓	-	-	-
Daimler USD [16]	2013	500	-	-	✓ [c]	-	-	-
KITTI-Road [18]	2013	600	-	-	✓	✓	-	-
NYC3DCars [17]	2013	1,287	-	-	✓	-	-	-
Cityscapes [6] (fine)	2016	5,000	-	✓ [a]	✓	-	-	90 min
Cityscapes [6] (coarse)	2016	20,000	-	✓ [a]	✓	-	-	7 min
Mapillary Vistas [7]	2017	20,000	-	-	✓	-	-	94 min
TuSimple [20]	2017	3,626	3,626	✓ [a]	✓ [b]	✓	✓ [d]	-
Our Lanes	2018	23,980	402	✓	✓	✓	✓	5 sec

[a] Only single images are annotated, but additional (non-annotated) image sequences are provided.
[b] Road area is implicitly annotated by the given lanes.
[c] Annotated ground instead of road, i.e. it includes non-drivable area.
[d] Limited to three instances: ego-lane and left/right of ego-lane.

ego-lane [18], which is useful for lane following tasks. Few datasets provide lane instances [19,20], which are needed for more sophisticated driving manoeuvres. Aly et. al. [19] provide a relatively limited annotation of 4 single coordinates per lane border. TuSimple [20] offer a large number of sequences, but for highway driving only. Table 1 provides an overview of the publicly available datasets. Our average annotation time per image is much lower. However, our provided classes are different, since we focus on lane instances (and thus ignore other semantic segmentation classes like vehicle, building, person, etc.). Furthermore, our data provides road surface annotations in dense traffic scenarios despite occlusions, i.e. we provide the road label below the vehicles (see Fig. 1). This is different from typical semantic segmentation labels, which provide a label for the occluding object instead [5–7,14–16]. Another approach to efficiently obtain labels is to create a virtual world where everything is known a-priori [21–23]. However, current methods do not reach the fidelity of real images.

Some previous work has aimed at creating semi-automated object detections in autonomous driving scenarios. [17,24] use structure-from-motion (SFM) to estimate the scene geometry and dynamic objects. [25] proposes to annotate lanes in the birds-eye view and then back-project and interpolate the lane boundaries into the sequence of original camera images. [26] uses alignment with OpenStreetMap to generate ground-truth for the road. [27] allows for bounding box annotations of Lidar point-clouds in 3D for road and other static scene components. These annotations are then back-projected to each camera image as semantic labels and they report a similar annotation speed-up as ours: 13.5 sec per image. [28] propose to detect and project the future driven path in images, without the focus of lane annotations. This means the path is not adapted to lane widths and crosses over lanes and junctions. Both [27,28] require an expensive sensor suite, which includes calibrated cameras and Lidar. In contrast, our method is applicable to data from a GPS enabled dash-cam. The overall contributions of this work include: (1) The release of a new dataset for lane instance and road segmentation, (2) A semi-automated annotation method for lane instances in 3D, requiring only inexpensive dash-cam equipment, (3) Road surface annotations in dense traffic scenarios despite occlusion, and (4) Experimental results for road, ego-lane and lane instance segmentation using a CNN.

2 Video Collection

Videos and associated GPS data were captured with a standard Nextbase 402G dashcam recording at a resolution of 1920×1080 at 30 fps and compressed with the H.264 standard. The camera was mounted on the inside of the car windscreen, roughly along the centre line of the vehicle and approximately aligned with the axis of motion. Figure 1 (top left) shows an example image from our collected data. In order to remove parts where the car moves very slowly or stands still (which is common in urban environments), we only include frames that are at least 1 m apart according to the GPS. Finally, we split the recorded data into sequences of 200 m in length, since smaller sequences are easier to handle (e.g. no need for key-frame bundle adjustment, and faster loading times).

3 Video Annotation

The initial annotation step is automated and provides an estimate of the road surface in 3D space, along with an estimate for the ego-lane (see Sect. 3.1). Then the estimates are corrected manually and further annotations are added in the road surface space. The labels are then projected into the 2D camera views, allowing the annotation of all images in the sequence at once (see Sect. 3.2).

3.1 Automated Ego-Lane Estimation in 3D

Given a dash-cam video sequence of N frames from a camera with unknown intrinsic and extrinsic parameters, the goal is to determine the road surface in 3D and project an estimate of the ego-lane onto this surface. To this end, we first apply OpenSfM [29], a structure from motion algorithm, to obtain the 3D camera locations $\mathbf{c}_i$ and poses $\mathbf{R}_i$ for each frame $i \in \{1, ..., N\}$ in a global coordinate system, as well as the camera projective transform $P(\cdot)$, which includes the estimated focal length and distortion parameters ($\mathbf{R}_i \in \mathbb{R}^{3\times3}$ are 3D rotation matrices). OpenSfM reconstructions are not perfect, and failure cases are filtered during the manual annotation process.

We assume that the road is a 2D manifold embedded in the 3D world. The local curvature of the road is low, and thus the orientation of the vehicle wheels

Fig. 2. Estimation of the lane border points $\mathbf{b}_i^{left}, \mathbf{b}_i^{right}$ at frame i. $\mathbf{c}_i$ is the camera position at frame i (obtained via SfM), $\mathbf{g}_i$ is point on the road below the camera, h is the height of the camera above the road, $\mathbf{f}$ is the forward direction, $\mathbf{n}$ is the normal vector of the road plane, $\mathbf{r}$ is the horizontal vector across the lane ($\mathbf{f}$, $\mathbf{n}$ and $\mathbf{r}$ are relative to the camera orientation) and w_i^{left}, w_i^{right} are the distances to the left and right ego-lane borders.

provide a good estimate of the local surface gradient. The camera is fixed within the vehicle with a static translation and rotation from the current road plane (i.e. we assume the vehicle body follows the road plane and neglect suspension movement). Thus the ground point $\mathbf{g}_i$ on the road below the camera at frame i is calculated as $\mathbf{g}_i = \mathbf{c}_i + h\mathbf{R}_i\mathbf{n}$, where h is the height of the camera above the road and $\mathbf{n}$ is the surface normal of the road relative to the camera (see Fig. 2, left). The left and right ego-lane borders $\mathbf{b}_i^{left}, \mathbf{b}_i^{right}$ can then be derived as

$$\begin{aligned} \mathbf{b}_i^{left} &= \mathbf{g}_i + w_i^{left}\mathbf{R}_i\mathbf{r} \\ \mathbf{b}_i^{right} &= \mathbf{g}_i + w_i^{right}\mathbf{R}_i\mathbf{r} \end{aligned} \tag{1}$$

where $\mathbf{r}$ is the vector within the road plane, that is perpendicular to the driving direction and w_i^{left}, w_i^{right} are the offsets to the left and right ego-lane borders. See Fig. 2 (right) for an illustration. We make the simplifying assumption that the road surface is flat perpendicular to the direction of the car motion (but we don't assume that the road is flat generally - if our ego path travels over hills, this is captured in our ego path).

Given a frame i, we can project all future lane borders $\mathbf{b}_j$ ($\mathbf{b}_j \in \{\mathbf{b}_j^{left}, \mathbf{b}_j^{right}\}$ and $j > i$) into the local pixel coordinate system via

$$\hat{\mathbf{b}_j} = P\left(\mathbf{R}_i^{-1}(\mathbf{b}_j - \mathbf{c}_i)\right) \tag{2}$$

where $P()$ is the camera perspective transform obtained via OpenSfM [29], that projects a 3D point in camera coordinates to a 2D pixel location in the image. Then the lane annotations can be drawn as polygons of neighbouring future frames, i.e. with the corner points $\hat{\mathbf{b}}_j^{left}, \hat{\mathbf{b}}_j^{right}, \hat{\mathbf{b}}_{j+1}^{right}, \hat{\mathbf{b}}_{j+1}^{left}$. This makes implicitly the assumption that the lane is piece-wise straight and flat between captured images. In the following part, we describe how to get the quantities h, $\mathbf{n}$, $\mathbf{r}$, w_i^{left} and w_i^{right}. Note that h, $\mathbf{n}$ and $\mathbf{r}$ only need to be estimated once for all sequences with the same camera position.

The camera height above the road h is easy to measure manually. However, in case this cannot be done (e.g. for dash-cam videos downloaded from the web) it is also possible to obtain the height of the camera using the estimated mesh of the road surface obtained from OpenSfM. A rough estimate for h is sufficient, since it is corrected via manual annotation, see the following section.

In order to estimate the road normal $\mathbf{n}$, we use the fact that when the car moves around a turn, the vectors representing it's motion $\mathbf{m}$ will all lie in the road plane, and thus taking the cross product of them will result in the road normal, see Fig. 3. Let $\mathbf{m}_{i,j}$ be the normalised motion vector between frames i and j, i.e. $\mathbf{m}_{i,j} = \frac{\mathbf{c}_j - \mathbf{c}_i}{\|\mathbf{c}_j - \mathbf{c}_i\|}$. The estimated road normal at frame i (in camera coordinates) is $\mathbf{n}_i = \mathbf{R}_i^{-1}(\mathbf{m}_{i-1,i} \otimes \mathbf{m}_{i,i+1})$, where $\otimes$ denotes the cross-product (see Fig. 3). The quality of this estimate depends highly on the degree of our previous assumptions being correct. To get a more reliable estimate, we average all $\mathbf{n}_i$ across the journey, and weight them implicitly by the magnitude of the cross product:

$$\mathbf{n} = \frac{1}{\sum_{i=2}^{N-2} \|\mathbf{n}_i\|} \sum_{i=2}^{N-2} \mathbf{n}_i \tag{3}$$

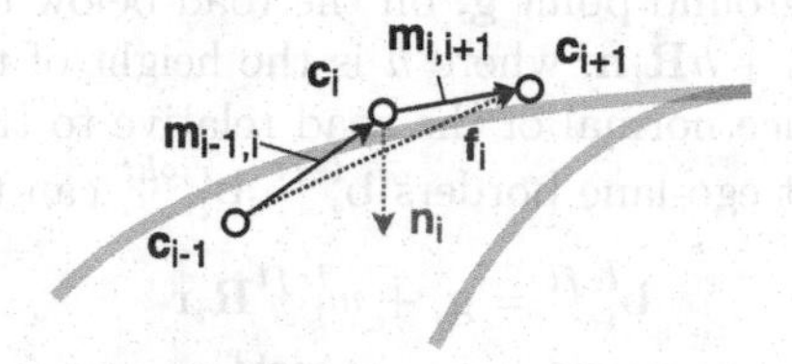

Fig. 3. Estimation of the road normal $\mathbf{n}_i$ and forward direction $\mathbf{f}_i$ at a single frame i. The final estimate is an aggregate over all frames.

We can only estimate the normal during turns, and thus this weighting scheme emphasises tight turns and ignores straight parts of the journey. $\mathbf{r}$ is perpendicular to the forward direction $\mathbf{f}$ and within the road plane, thus

$$\mathbf{r} = \mathbf{f} \otimes \mathbf{n} \tag{4}$$

The only quantity left is $\mathbf{f}$, which can be derived by using the fact that $\mathbf{m}_{i-1,i+1}$ is approximately parallel to the tangent at $\mathbf{c}_i$, if the rate of turn is low. Thus we can estimate the forward point at frame i via $\mathbf{f}_i = \mathbf{R}_i^{-1}\mathbf{m}_{i-1,i+1}$, see Fig. 3. As for the normal, we average all $\mathbf{f}_i$ over the journey to get a more reliable estimate:

$$\mathbf{f} = \frac{1}{\sum_i a_i} \sum_{i=2}^{N-2} a_i \mathbf{f}_i \tag{5}$$

$$a_i = \max(\mathbf{m}_{i-1,i}^\top \mathbf{m}_{i,i+1}, 0) \tag{6}$$

In this case, we weight the movements according the inner product a_i in order to up-weight parts with a low rate of turn, while the max assures forward movement.

w_i^{left} and w_i^{right} are crucial quantities to get the correct alignment of the annotated lane borders with the visible boundary, however automatic detection is non-trivial. Therefore we assume initially that the ego-lane has a fixed width w and the car has travelled exactly in the centre, i.e. $w_i^{left} = \frac{1}{2}w$ and $w_i^{right} = -\frac{1}{2}w$ are both constant for all frames. Later (see the following section), we relax this assumption and get an improved estimate through manual annotation.

In practice, we select a sequence with a lot of turns within the road plane to estimate $\mathbf{n}$ and a straight sequence to estimate $\mathbf{f}$. Then the same values are re-used for all sequences with the same static camera position. We only annotate the first part of the sequence, up until 100 m from the end. We do this to avoid partial annotations on the final frames of a sequence which result from too few lane border points remaining ahead of a given frame. A summary of the automated ego-lane annotation procedure is provided in Algorithm 1 and a visualisation of the automated border point estimation is shown in Fig. 4 (in blue).

Algorithm 1. Automated ego-lane estimation

1: Measure height of the camera above road h
2: Apply OpenSFM to get $\mathbf{c}_i, \mathbf{R}_i$
3: Estimate road normal $\mathbf{n}$ according Eq. (3)
4: Estimate forward direction $\mathbf{f}$ according Eq. (5)
5: Derive vector across road $\mathbf{r}$ according Eq. (4)
6: Set $w_i^{left} = \frac{1}{2}w$ and $w_i^{right} = -\frac{1}{2}w$, where w is the default lane width
7: Derive border points $\mathbf{b}_i^{left}, \mathbf{b}_i^{right}$ according Eq. (1)
8: **for** each frame i **do**
9: Get all future border points $\hat{\mathbf{b}}_j^{left}, \hat{\mathbf{b}}_j^{right}$, $j > i$ according Eq. (2)
10: Draw polygons with edges $\hat{\mathbf{b}}_j^{left}, \hat{\mathbf{b}}_j^{right}, \hat{\mathbf{b}}_{j+1}^{right}, \hat{\mathbf{b}}_{j+1}^{left}$

3.2 Manual Corrections and Additional Annotations

Manual annotations serve three goals: (1) exclude erroneous OpenSfM reconstructions (2) to improve the automated estimate for the ego-lane, (3) annotate additional lanes left and right of the ego-lane and (4) annotate non-road areas.

OpenSfM failures happened a few times, but they are easy to spot by the annotator and subsequently excluded from the dataset. In order to improve the ego-lane positions, the annotators are provided with a convenient interface to edit h, w_i^{left} and w_i^{right}. Note that these quantities are only scalars (in contrast to 3D points), and are thus easily adjusted via keyboard input. We provide a live rendered view at a particular frame (see Fig. 5, left), and immediate feedback is provided after changes. Also, it is easy to move forward or backward in the sequence. For improving the ego-lane, the annotators have the options to:

1. Adjust h (applies to the whole sequence)
2. Adjust all w_i^{left} or all w_i^{right} (applies to the whole sequence)

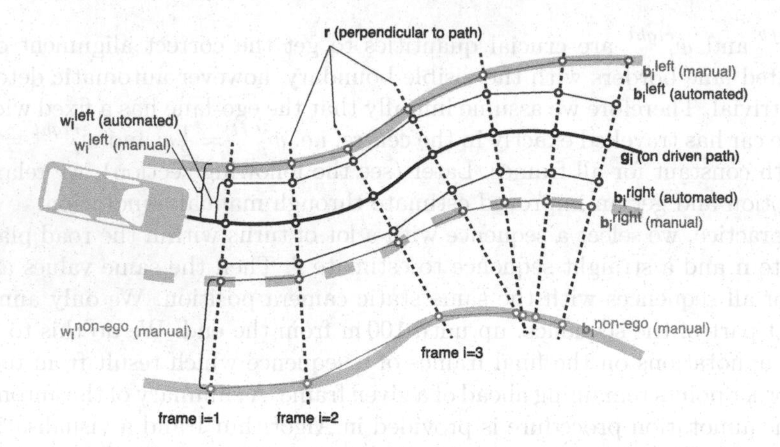

Fig. 4. Visualisation of the lane estimates, seen from above. The automated estimate is shown in blue, while the manual correction is shown in red. A manually annotated additional lane is shown in green. Initially, all w_i^{left} and w_i^{right} are set to a constant value, and thus the estimate is parallel the driven path, which only approximately follows the true lane borders (in blue). Then the annotators can correct w_i^{left} and w_i^{right} for each frame, which moves the border points along **r** (shown as dotted black line) until they align with the true border (shown in red). Furthermore, annotators can add additional (non-ego) lanes and adjust their width $w_i^{non-ego}$. (Color figure online)

3. Adjust all w_j^{left} or all w_j^{right} from the current frame i on, $j > i$ (applies to all future frames, relative to the current view)

In order to keep the interface complexity low, only one scalar is edited at a time. We observed that during a typical drive, the car is moving parallel to the ego-lane *most of the time*. Also, lanes have a constant width *most of the time*. If both holds, then it is sufficient to use (2) to edit the lane borders for the whole sequence. Only in the case that the car deviates from the parallel path, or the lane width changes, the annotator needs option (3).

New lanes can be placed adjacent to current ones by a simple button click. This generates a new sequence of $\mathbf{b}_i^{non-ego}$, either on the left or right of the current lanes (see Fig. 4). As for the ego-lane, the annotator can adjust the corresponding $w_i^{non-ego}$. Equivalently, a non-road surface can be added next to current lanes, in the same way as if it were a lane, i.e. by getting its own set of $\mathbf{b}_i^{non-ego}$ and $w_i^{non-ego}$. In addition to that, a fixed part on top of the image can be annotated with non-road, as the road is usually found in the lower part of the image (except for very hilly regions or extreme camera angles).

Figure 5 (left) shows the interface used by the annotators. In the centre of the image, the ego-path can be seen projected into this frame. In the bottom-left, the annotator is provided with controls to manipulate rendered lanes (narrow, widen, move to the left or right, move the boundaries of the lane etc.) and add new lanes. In the top right of the screen (not visible), the annotator is provided with the means to adjust the camera height, to match the reconstruction to

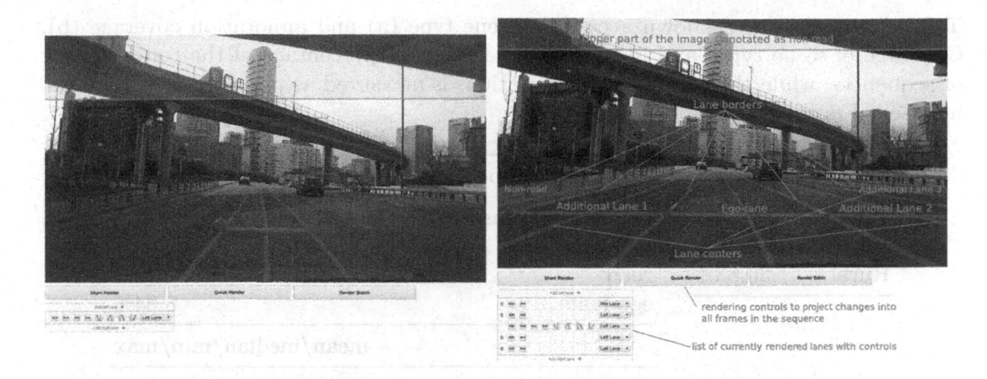

Fig. 5. Annotator interface with the automated initial ego-lane estimate, given by the future driven path (left) and after manual corrections and additional lane annotations (right). The red text and lines are overlaid descriptions, all other colours are part of the interface. (Color figure online)

the road surface, and the crop height, to exclude the vehicle's dash or bonnet. All annotations are performed in the estimated 3D road plane, but immediate feedback is provided via projection in the 2D camera view. The annotator can easily skip forward and backward in the sequence to determine if the labels align with the image, and correct them if needed. An example of a corrected sequence is shown in Fig. 4 (in red). Figure 1 shows an example of the rendered annotations and the supplementary material contains an example video.

4 Dataset Statistics and Split

The full annotated set includes 402 sequences, 23,979 images in total, and thus on average 60 images per sequence. Table 2b shows a breakdown of the included annotation types. In total, there were 47,497 lane instances annotated, i.e. 118.2 per sequence. Instance IDs are consistent across a sequence, i.e. consecutive frames will use the same instance ID for the same lane. Furthermore, the annotators have been instructed to categorise each sequence according the scene type: urban, highway or rural. The breakdown of the sequences is shown in Table 2a. We plan to update the dataset with new sequences, once they become available.

We split the data into two sets, for training and testing. The train set comprises 360 sequences and a total of 21,355 frames, while the test set includes 42 sequences and 2,624 frames. The test set was selected to include the same urban/motorway/rural distribution as the train set. The frames of the training set are made available[1] with both images and annotations while only the images are provided for the testing set.

Furthermore, we have measured the average annotation time per scene type, and find that there is a large variation, with an urban scene taking roughly 3

[1] online at https://five.ai/datasets.

Table 2. Dataset breakdown according scene type (a) and annotation coverage (b). Coverage of scene types and instances is measured as percentage of the total number of sequences, while the coverage of annotations is measured as percentage of the total number of pixels.

Scene type	
Urban	58.61%
Highway	10.56%
Rural	30.83%

(a)

Annotation type	
annotation density	77.53%
non-road	62.13%
road	15.40%
ego-lane	8.84%
	mean/median/min/max
#instances (per sequence)	2.2/2/1/6

(b)

Table 3. Average annotation time in seconds.

Scene type	Urban	Highway	Rural
Per sequence	361	100	140
Per image	5	2	2

Table 4. Agreement of the annotators

Task	IoU	std
Road vs non-road	97.2	± 1.5
Ego vs road vs non-road	94.3	± 3.4
	AP@50	AP
Lane instance segmentation	99.0	84.4

times longer than a highway or countryside scene of similar length (see Table 3). This is due to the varying complexity in terms of the road layout, which is caused by various factors: the frequency of junctions and side roads, overall complexity of lane structure and additional features such as traffic islands and cycle lanes that are typically not found outside of an urban setting (Table 2).

The annotation quality is measured through agreement between the two annotators on 12 randomly selected sequences. 84.3% of the pixels have been given a label by at least 1 annotator, with 67.3% of these being given an annotation by both annotators; i.e. 56.8% of all pixels were given an annotation by both annotators. We measure the agreement on these overlapping labels via Intersection-over-Union (IoU) and agreement of instances using Average Precision (AP) and AP@50 (average precision with instance IoU greater than 50%). The results are shown in Table 4. The standard deviation is calculated over the 12 sequences.

5 Experiments

To demonstrate the results achievable using our annotations we present evaluation procedures, models and results for two example tasks: semantic segmentation of the road and ego-lane, as well as lane instance segmentation.

5.1 Road and Ego-Lane Segmentation

The labels and data described in Sect. 4 directly allow for two segmentation tasks: Road/Non-Road detection (ROAD) and Ego/Non-Ego/Non-Road lane detection (EGO). For our baseline we used the well studied SegNet [30] architecture, trained independently for both the EGO and ROAD experiments. In addition to an evaluation on our data, we provide ROAD and EGO cross-database results for CityScapes (fine), Mapillary and KITTI Lanes. We have selected a simple baseline model and thus the overall results are lower than those reported for models tailored to the respective datasets, as can be seen in the leaderboards of CityScapes, Mapillary and KITTI. Thus our results should not be seen as an upper performance limit. Nevertheless, we deem them a good indicator on how models generalise across datasets.

For each dataset, we use 10% of training sequences for validation. During training, we pre-process each input image by resizing it to have a height of 330 px and extracting a random crop of 320×320 px. We use the ADAM optimiser [31] with a learning rate of 0.001 which we decay to 0.0005 after 25,000 steps and then to 0.0001 after 50,000 steps. We trained for 100,000 training steps, and select the model with the best validation loss. Our mini batch size was 2 and the optimisation was performed on a per pixel cross entropy loss.

We train one separate model per dataset and per task. This leads to 4 models for ROAD, trained on our data, CityScapes (fine), Mapillary and KITTI Lanes. EGO labels are only available for the UM portion of KITTI Lanes and our data, hence we train 2 models for EGO.

For each model we report the IoU, and additionally the F1 score as it is the default for KITTI. We measure each model on held out data from every dataset. For CityScapes and Mapillary the held out sets are their respective predefined validation sets, for our dataset the held out set is our test set (as defined in Sect. 4). The exception to this scheme is KITTI Lanes which is very small and has no available annotated held out set. Therefore we use the entire set for training the KITTI model, and the same set for the evaluation of other models. We report the average IoU and F1 across classes for each task. Note that we cropped the car hood and ornament from the CityScapes data, since it is not present in other datasets (otherwise the results drop significantly). It should also be noted that the results are not directly comparable to the intended evaluation of CityScapes, Mapillary or KITTI Lanes due to the different treatment of the road occluded by vehicles.

The ROAD results are shown in Table 5 and the EGO results in Table 6. First, we note that IoU and F1 follow the same trend, while F1 is a bit larger in absolute values. We see a clear trend between the datasets. Firstly, the highest IoUs are achieved when training and testing subsets are from the same data. This points to an overall generalisation issue; no dataset (including our own) achieves the same performance on other data. The model trained on KITTI shows the worst cross-dataset average. This is not surprising, since it is also the smallest set (it contains only 289 images for the ROAD task and 95 images for the EGO task). Cityscapes does better, but there is still a bigger gap to ours

Table 5. Results for the ROAD task, measured by IoU and F1 score. Off-diagonal results are from cross-dataset experiments. The column determines which set the model was trained on, and the row determines the source of the evaluation set. The reported column average includes only cross-dataset experiments.

IoU		Trained On			
		Ours	Mapillary	CityScapes	KITTI
Tested On	Our Test Set	95.0	85.4	73.2	71.0
	Mapillary Val	82.9	90.0	79.6	69.6
	CityScapes Val	85.2	85.2	90.0	60.4
	KITTI Train	83.8	72.6	74.6	-
	Cross-dataset Average	84.0	81.1	75.8	67.0
F1		**Trained On**			
		Ours	Mapillary	CityScapes	KITTI
Tested On	Our Test Set	97.4	91.9	83.7	81.6
	Mapillary Val	90.4	94.7	88.3	81.0
	CityScapes Val	91.9	91.9	94.7	74.0
	KITTI Train	90.9	83.5	84.8	
	Cross-dataset Average	91.1	89.1	85.6	75.8

Table 6. Results for the EGO task, measured by IoU and F1 score.

Train	Test	IoU	F1
Ours	Ours	88.5	93.7
Ours	KITTI	61.2	72.6
KITTI	Ours	39.2	48.3

Table 7. Results for lane instance segmentation

Metric	Score
AP	0.250
AP@50	0.507

and Mapillary, probably due to lower diversity. Mapillary is similar to ours in size and achieves almost the same performance. The slightly lower results could be due to its different viewpoints, since it contains images taken from non-road perspectives, e.g. side-walks.

5.2 Lane Instance Segmentation

The annotation of multiple distinct lanes per image, the number of which is variable across images and potentially sequences, naturally suggests an instance segmentation task for our dataset. Though it has been postulated that "Stuff" is uncountable and therefore doesn't have instances [32,33], we present this lane instance segmentation task as a counter example. Indeed it would seem many stuff-like classes (parking spaces, lanes in a swimming pool, fields in satellite imagery) can have meaningful delineations and therefore instances applied.

Providing a useful baseline for this lane instance segmentation task presents its own challenges. The current state of the art for instance segmentation on Cityscapes is MaskRCNN [34]. This approach is based on the RCNN object detector and is therefore optimised for the detection of compact objects which fit inside broadly non overlapping bounding boxes, traditionally called "Things". In the case of lanes detected in the perspective view, a bounding box for any given lane greatly overlaps neighbouring lanes, making the task potentially challenging for standard bounding boxes. This becomes more apparent when the road undergoes even a slight curve in which case the bounding boxes are almost on top of one another even though the instance pixels are quite disjoint. Recently, a few works have explored an alternative approach to RCNN based algorithms which use pixel embeddings to perform instance segmentation [35–38]; we provide a baseline for our dataset using pixel embeddings.

Specifically we train a model based on [35]. We follow their approach of learning per pixel embeddings whose value is optimised such that pixels within the same training instance are given similar embeddings, while the mean embedding of separate instances are simultaneously pushed apart. A cost function which learns such pixel embeddings can be written down exactly and is presented in Eqs. 1, 2, 3 and 4 of [35], we use the same hyper parameters reported in that work, and thus use an 8-dimensional embedding space. We impose this loss as an extra output of a ROAD SegNet model trained along side the segmentation task from scratch.

At run time we follow a variant of the approach proposed by [35], predicting an embedding per pixel. We use our prediction of road to filter away pixels which are not likely to be lanes. We then uniformly sample pixels in the road area and cluster their embeddings using the Mean Shift [39] algorithm, identifying the centres of our detected lane instances. Finally, all pixels in the road area are assigned to their closest lane instance embedding using the euclidean distance to the pixel's own embedding; pixels assigned to the same centroid are in the same instance.

For evaluation, we use the Average Precision (AP) measures calculated as described for the MS-COCO [40] instance segmentation task. Specifically: we calculate the AP across images and across IoU thresholds of detected lanes (pixels assigned to embedding cluster centroids) and ground truth lanes. True and false positives are counted in the following way: (1) A detection is a **true positive** when it overlaps a ground truth instance with an IoU above some threshold and (2) a detection is a **false positive** when it does not sufficiently overlap any ground truth instance. Using these definitions we report average precision at 50% IoU and an average AP across multiple thresholds from 50% to 95% in increments of 5%. Table 7 shows the instance segmentation baseline results. Qualitatively, the lane instances are well separated, as can be seen in Fig. 6.

Fig. 6. An example image from our test set (top left) including predictions for the ROAD (top right), EGO (bottom left) and instance (bottom right) tasks. The colours of the ROAD and EGO models match those in Fig. 1. The predicted instances are represented by red, green and blue. (Color figure online)

6 Conclusions

We have created a dataset for road detection and lane instance segmentation in urban environments, using only un-calibrated low-cost equipment. Moreover, we have done this using an efficient annotation procedure that minimises manual work. The initial experiments presented show promising generalisation results across datasets. Despite this step towards autonomous driving systems, our data has various limitations: (1) Annotations of many other object classes of the static road layout are not included, like buildings, traffic signs and traffic lights. (2) All annotated lanes are parallel to the future driven path, thus currently lane splits and perpendicular lanes (e.g. at junctions) have been excluded. (3) Positions of dynamic objects, like vehicles, pedestrians and cyclists, are not included. In future work, those limitations could be addressed by adding further annotations of different objects in 3D, inspired by [27]. Non-parallel lanes could be handled by extending our annotator tool to allow for variable angles for the lanes in the road plane. Also, a pre-trained segmentation model could be used to better initialise the annotations. Furthermore, the position of dynamic objects could be estimated by including additional sensor modalities, like stereo vision or LIDAR.

Acknowledgements. We would like to thank our colleagues Tom Westmacott, Joel Jakubovic and Robert Chandler, who have contributed to the implementation of the annotation software.

References

1. Janai, J., Güney, F., Behl, A., Geiger, A.: Computer Vision for Autonomous Vehicles: Problems, Datasets and State-of-the-Art (2017)
2. Huval, B., et al.: An empirical evaluation of deep learning on highway driving (2015). arXiv preprint arXiv:1504.01716
3. Oliveira, G.L., Burgard, W., Brox, T.: Efficient deep methods for monocular road segmentation. In: IEEE/RSJ International Conference on Intelligent Robots and Systems (IROS 2016), pp. 4885–4891 (2016)
4. Neven, D., De Brabandere, B., Georgoulis, S., Proesmans, M., Van Gool, L.: Towards End-to-End Lane Detection: an Instance Segmentation Approach (2018). arXiv preprint arXiv:1802.05591
5. Brostow, G.J., Fauqueur, J., Cipolla, R.: Semantic object classes in video: a high-definition ground truth database. Pattern Recognit. Lett. **30**(2), 88–97 (2009)
6. Cordts, M., et al.: The cityscapes dataset for semantic urban scene understanding. In: CVPR (2016)
7. Neuhold, G., Ollmann, T., Bulò, S.R., Kontschieder, P.: The mapillary vistas dataset for semantic understanding of street scenes. In: Proceedings of the International Conference on Computer Vision (ICCV), Venice, pp. 22–29 (2017)
8. McCall, J.C., Trivedi, M.M.: Video-based lane estimation and tracking for driver assistance: survey, system, and evaluation. IEEE Trans. Intell. Transp. Syst. **7**(1), 20–37 (2006)
9. Kim, Z.: Robust lane detection and tracking in challenging scenarios. IEEE Trans. Intell. Transp. Syst. **9**(1), 16–26 (2008)
10. Gopalan, R., Hong, T., Shneier, M., Chellappa, R.: A learning approach towards detection and tracking of lane markings. IEEE Trans. Intell. Transp. Syst. **13**(3), 1088–1098 (2012)
11. Li, J., Mei, X., Prokhorov, D., Tao, D.: Deep neural network for structural prediction and lane detection in traffic scene. IEEE Trans. Neural Netw. Learn. Syst. **28**(3), 690–703 (2017)
12. Mathibela, B., Newman, P., Posner, I.: Reading the road: road marking classification and interpretation. IEEE Trans. Intell. Transp. Syst. **16**(4), 2072–2081 (2015)
13. Hillel, A.B., Lerner, R., Levi, D., Raz, G.: Recent progress in road and lane detection: a survey. Mach. Vis. Appl. **25**(3), 727–745 (2014)
14. Brostow, G.J., Shotton, J., Fauqueur, J., Cipolla, R.: Segmentation and recognition using structure from motion point clouds. In: Forsyth, D., Torr, P., Zisserman, A. (eds.) ECCV 2008. LNCS, vol. 5302, pp. 44–57. Springer, Heidelberg (2008). https://doi.org/10.1007/978-3-540-88682-2_5
15. Sengupta, S., Sturgess, P., Torr, P.H.S., et al.: Automatic dense visual semantic mapping from street-level imagery. In: IEEE/RSJ International Conference on Intelligent Robots and Systems (IROS), pp. 857–862. IEEE (2012)
16. Scharwächter, T., Enzweiler, M., Franke, U., Roth, S.: Efficient multi-cue scene segmentation. In: Weickert, J., Hein, M., Schiele, B. (eds.) GCPR 2013. LNCS, vol. 8142, pp. 435–445. Springer, Heidelberg (2013). https://doi.org/10.1007/978-3-642-40602-7_46
17. Matzen, K., Snavely, N.: NYC3DCars: a dataset of 3D vehicles in geographic context. In: ICCV, pp. 761–768. IEEE (2013)

18. Fritsch, J., Kuehnl, T., Geiger, A.: A new performance measure and evaluation benchmark for road detection algorithms. In: 16th International IEEE Conference on Intelligent Transportation Systems (ITSC 2013), pp. 1693–1700. IEEE (2013)
19. Aly, M.: Real time detection of lane markers in urban streets. In: IEEE Intelligent Vehicles Symposium, Proceedings, pp. 7–12. IEEE (2008)
20. TuSimple: Lane Detection Challenge (Dataset) (2017). http://benchmark.tusimple.ai
21. Richter, S.R., Vineet, V., Roth, S., Koltun, V.: Playing for data: ground truth from computer games. In: Leibe, B., Matas, J., Sebe, N., Welling, M. (eds.) ECCV 2016. LNCS, vol. 9906, pp. 102–118. Springer, Cham (2016). https://doi.org/10.1007/978-3-319-46475-6_7
22. Ros, G., Sellart, L., Materzynska, J., Vazquez, D., Lopez, A.M.: The synthia dataset: a large collection of synthetic images for semantic segmentation of urban scenes. In: Proceedings of the IEEE Conference on Computer Vision and Pattern Recognition, pp. 3234–3243 (2016)
23. Gaidon, A., Wang, Q., Cabon, Y., Vig, E.: Virtual Worlds as Proxy for Multi-Object Tracking Analysis. In: CVPR (2016)
24. Leibe, B., Cornelis, N., Cornelis, K., Van Gool, L.: Dynamic 3D scene analysis from a moving vehicle. In: CVPR, pp. 1–8. IEEE (2007)
25. Borkar, A., Hayes, M., Smith, M.T.: A novel lane detection system with efficient ground truth generation. IEEE Trans. Intell. Transp. Syst. **13**(1), 365–374 (2012)
26. Laddha, A., Kocamaz, M.K., Navarro-Serment, L.E., Hebert, M.: Map-supervised road detection. In: IEEE Intelligent Vehicles Symposium (IV), pp. 118–123. IEEE (2016)
27. Xie, J., Kiefel, M., Sun, M.T., Geiger, A.: Semantic instance annotation of street scenes by 3D to 2D label transfer. In: Proceedings of the IEEE Conference on Computer Vision and Pattern Recognition, pp. 3688–3697 (2016)
28. Barnes, D., Maddern, W., Posner, I.: Find your own way: weakly-supervised segmentation of path proposals for urban autonomy. In: ICRA (2017)
29. Mapillary: OpenSfM (Software) (2014). https://github.com/mapillary/OpenSfM
30. Badrinarayanan, V., Kendall, A., Cipolla, R.: Segnet: A deep convolutional encoder-decoder architecture for image segmentation (2015). arXiv preprint arXiv:1511.00561
31. Kingma, D.P., Ba, J.: Adam: A method for stochastic optimization. CoRR (2014)
32. Caesar, H., Uijlings, J., Ferrari, V.: Coco-stuff: Thing and Stuff Classes in Context (2017). arXiv preprint. arXiv:1612.03716
33. Adelson, E.H.: On seeing stuff: the perception of materials by humans and machines. In: Rogowitz, B.E., Pappas, T.N. (Eds.): Society of Photo-Optical Instrumentation Engineers (SPIE) Conference Series, vol. 4299, pp. 1–12, June 2001
34. He, K., Gkioxari, G., Dollár, P., Girshick, R.B.: Mask R-CNN. CoRR (2017)
35. Brabandere, B.D., Neven, D., Gool, L.V.: Semantic instance segmentation with a discriminative loss function. CoRR (2017)
36. Li, S., Seybold, B., Vorobyov, A., Fathi, A., Huang, Q., Kuo, C.C.J.: Instance embedding transfer to unsupervised video object segmentation. In: Proceedings of the IEEE Conference on Computer Vision and Pattern Recognition, pp. 6526–6535 (2018)
37. Fathi, A., Wojna, Z., Rathod, V., Wang, P., Song, H.O., Guadarrama, S., Murphy, K.P.: Semantic instance segmentation via deep metric learning. CoRR (2017)
38. Kong, S., Fowlkes, C.: Recurrent pixel embedding for instance grouping (2017)

39. Comaniciu, D., Meer, P.: Mean shift: a robust approach toward feature space analysis. IEEE Trans. Pattern Anal. Mach. Intell. **24**(5), 603–619 (2002)
40. Lin, T.-Y., Maire, M., Belongie, S., Hays, J., Perona, P., Ramanan, D., Dollár, P., Zitnick, C.L.: Microsoft COCO: common objects in context. In: Fleet, D., Pajdla, T., Schiele, B., Tuytelaars, T. (eds.) ECCV 2014. LNCS, vol. 8693, pp. 740–755. Springer, Cham (2014). https://doi.org/10.1007/978-3-319-10602-1_48

Out-of-Distribution Detection Using an Ensemble of Self Supervised Leave-Out Classifiers

Apoorv Vyas[1,3], Nataraj Jammalamadaka[1(✉)], Xia Zhu[2], Dipankar Das[1], Bharat Kaul[1], and Theodore L. Willke[2]

[1] Intel Labs, Bangalore, India
natraj.j@gmail.com, {dipankar.das,bharat.kaul}@intel.com
[2] Intel Labs, Hillsboro, OR 97124, USA
{xia.zhu,ted.willke}@intel.com
[3] Idiap Research Institute, Martigny, Switzerland
apoorv.vyas@idiap.ch

Abstract. As deep learning methods form a critical part in commercially important applications such as autonomous driving and medical diagnostics, it is important to reliably detect out-of-distribution (OOD) inputs while employing these algorithms. In this work, we propose an OOD detection algorithm which comprises of an ensemble of classifiers. We train each classifier in a self-supervised manner by leaving out a random subset of training data as OOD data and the rest as in-distribution (ID) data. We propose a novel margin-based loss over the softmax output which seeks to maintain at least a margin m between the average entropy of the OOD and in-distribution samples. In conjunction with the standard cross-entropy loss, we minimize the novel loss to train an ensemble of classifiers. We also propose a novel method to combine the outputs of the ensemble of classifiers to obtain OOD detection score and class prediction. Overall, our method convincingly outperforms Hendrycks *et al.* [7] and the current state-of-the-art ODIN [13] on several OOD detection benchmarks.

Keywords: Anomaly detection · Out-of-distribution

1 Introduction

Deep learning has significantly improved the performance of machine learning systems in fields such as computer vision, natural language processing, and

A. Vyas, N. Jammalamadaka and X. Zhu—Equal contribution. Work done when the authors were working at Intel labs.

Electronic supplementary material The online version of this chapter (https://doi.org/10.1007/978-3-030-01237-3_34) contains supplementary material, which is available to authorized users.

V. Ferrari et al. (Eds.): ECCV 2018, LNCS 11212, pp. 560–574, 2018.
https://doi.org/10.1007/978-3-030-01237-3_34

speech. In turn, these algorithms are integral in commercial applications such as autonomous driving, medical diagnosis, and web search. In these applications, it is critical to detect sensor failures, unusual environments, novel biological phenomena, and cyber attacks. To accomplish this, systems must be capable of detecting when inputs are anomalous or out-of-distribution (OOD). In this work, we propose an out-of-distribution detection method for deep neural networks and demonstrate its performance across several out-of-distribution classification tasks on the state-of-the-art deep neural networks such as DenseNet [8] and Wide ResNet(WRN) [22].

We propose a novel margin-based loss term, added to cross-entropy loss over in-distribution samples, which maintains a margin of at least m between the average entropy of OOD and ID samples respectively. We propose an ensemble of K leave-out classifiers for OOD detection. The training dataset with N classes is partitioned into K subsets such that the classes of each partition are mutually exclusive with respect to each other. Each classifier samples one of the K subsets without replacement as *out-of-distribution training data* and the rest of the $K-1$ subsets as *in-distribution training data*. We also propose a new OOD detection score which combines both softmax prediction score and entropy with temperature scaling [13]. We demonstrate the efficacy of our method on standard benchmarks proposed in ODIN [13] and *outperform them*. Our contributions are (i) proposing a novel loss for OOD detection, (ii) demonstrating a self-supervised OOD detection method, and (iii) moving the state-of-the-art by outperforming the current best methods.

The rest of the paper is organized as follows. Section 2 describes the previous work on the OOD detection. Section 3 describes our method in detail. Section 4 describes various evaluation metrics to measure the performance of OOD detection algorithms. The ablation results of various design choices and hyper-parameters are also presented. We then compare our method against the recently proposed ODIN algorithm [13] and demonstrate that it outperforms it on various OOD detection benchmarks. Finally, Sect. 5 discusses observations about our method, future directions and conclusions.

2 Related Work

Traditionally, based on the availability of the data labels, OOD detection methods can be categorized into supervised [16], semi-supervised [4] and unsupervised methods [3,15]. All these classes of methods have access to the OOD data while training but differ in access to labels. It is assumed that the classifier has labels for normal as well as OOD classes during training for supervised OOD detection, while labels for only the normal classes are available in case of semi-supervised methods, and no labels are provided for unsupervised OOD detection methods which typically rely on the fact that anomalies occur in much less frequency than normal data. Our method is able to detect anomalies in test OOD datasets the very first time it encounters them during testing. We use one OOD dataset as validation set to search for hyper-parameters.

Notable OOD detection algorithms which work in the same setting as ours are isolation forests [14], Hendrycks and Gimpel [7], ODIN [13] and Lee *et al.* [12]. The work reported in isolation forests [14] exploits the fact that anomalies are scarce and different and while constructing the isolation tree, it is observed that the anomalous samples appear close to the root of the tree. These anomalies are then identified by measuring the length of the path from the root to a terminating node; the closer a node is to the root, the higher is its chance of representing an OOD. Hendrycks and Gimpel [7] is based on the observation that prediction probability of incorrect and out-of-distribution samples tends to be lower than the prediction probability of correct samples. Lee *et al.* modify the formulation of generative adversarial networks [6] to generate OOD samples for the given in-distribution. They achieve this by simultaneously training GAN [6] and standard supervised neural network. The joint loss consists of individual losses and an additional connecting term which reduces the KL divergence between the generated sample's softmax distribution and the uniform distribution.

Another set of related works are open set classification methods [1,2,17–19]. Scheirer *et al.* [19] introduces and formalizes "open space risk" which intuitively is the risk associated with labeling those areas in the output feature space as positive where there is no density support from the training data. Thus the approximation to the ideal risk is defined as a linear combination of "open space risk" and the standard "empirical risk". Bendale and Boult [1] extend the definition of "open set risk" to open world recognition where the unknown samples are not static set. The open world recognition defines a *multi-class open set recognition function*, a *labeling process* and an *incremental learning function*. The *multi-class open set recognition function* detects novel classes which are labeled using the *labeling process* and finally are fed to *incremental learning function* which updates the model. The OSDN [2] work proposes openMax function which extends the softmax function by adding an additional unknown class to the classification layer. The value for unknown class is computed by taking the weighted average of all other classes. The weights are obtained from Weibull distribution learnt over the pairwise distances between penultimate activation vectors (AV) of the top farthest correctly classified samples. For an OOD test sample these weights will be high while for an in-distribution sample these scores will be low. The final activation vector is re-normalized using softmax function.

The current state-of-the-art is ODIN [13] which proposes to increase the difference between the maximum softmax scores of in-distribution and OOD samples by (i) calibrating the softmax scores by scaling the logits that feed into softmax by a large constant (referred to as temperature) and (ii) pre-processing the input by perturbing it with the loss gradient. ODIN [13] demonstrated that at high temperature values, the softmax score for the predicted class is proportional to the relative difference between largest unnormalized output (logit) and the remaining outputs (logits). Moreover, they empirically showed that the difference between the largest logit and the remaining logits is higher for the in-distribution images than for the out-of-distribution images. Thus temperature scaling pushes the softmax scores of in- and out-of-distribution images further apart when compared to plain softmax. Perturbing the input image through gradient ascent w.r.t to the score of predicted label was demonstrated [13] to have stronger effect on the in-distribution images than that on out-of-distribution images, thereby, further pushing apart the softmax scores of in- and out-of-distribution images. We leverage the effectiveness of both these methods. The proposed method outperforms all the above methods by considerable margins.

3 Out-of-Distribution (OOD) Classifier

In this section, we introduce three important components of our method: entropy based margin-loss function Sect. 3.1, training ensemble of leave-out classifiers Sect. 3.2, and OOD detection scores Sect. 3.3.

Algorithm 1. Algorithm to train K Leave Out Classifiers

Input : Training Data X, Number of classes N, K Partitions, δ accuracy bound, Validation OOD Data X_{valOOD}
Output: K Leave Out Classifiers

```
1  for i ← 1 to K do
2      X_ood ← X_i, X_in ← X − X_i;
3      while Not Converged do
4          ood_batch ← Sample OOD minibatch;
5          in_batch ← Sample in-distribution minibatch;
6          update the classifier F_i by minimizing loss (Equation 1) using SGD;
7          save model with least OOD error on X_valOOD within δ accuracy of
            current best accuracy.;
8      end
9  end
10 return {F_i};
```

3.1 Entropy Based Margin-Loss

Given a labeled set $(x_i \in X_{in}, y_i \in Y_{in})$ of in-distribution (ID) samples and $(x_o \in X_{ood})$ of out-of-distribution (OOD) samples, we propose a novel loss term in addition to the standard cross-entropy loss on ID samples. This loss term seeks to maintain a margin of at least m between the average entropy of OOD and ID samples. Formally, a multi-layer neural network $F : x \rightarrow p$ which maps an input x to probability over classes and parametrized by W is learned by minimizing the margin-loss over the difference of average entropies over OOD samples and ID samples, and cross entropy loss on ID samples. The loss function is given by Eq. 1,

$$\mathcal{L} = -\frac{1}{|X_{in}|} \sum_{x_i \in X_{in}} \log(F_{y_i}(x_i)) + \beta * \max\left(m + \frac{\sum_{x_i \in X_{in}} H(F(x_i))}{|X_{in}|} - \frac{\sum_{x_o \in X_{ood}} H(F(x_o))}{|X_{ood}|}, 0\right) \quad (1)$$

where $F_{y_i}(x_i)$ is the predicted probability of sample x_i whose ground truth class y_i, $H(\cdot)$ is the entropy over the softmax distribution, m is the margin and β is the weight on margin entropy loss.

The new loss term evaluates to its minimum value *zero* when the difference between the average entropy of OOD and ID samples is greater than the margin m. For ID samples, the entropy loss encourages the softmax probabilities of non ground-truth classes to decrease and the cross-entropy loss encourages the softmax probability of ground-truth class to increase. For OOD samples, the entropy loss encourages the probabilities of all the classes to be equal. When the OOD entropy is higher than ID entropy by a margin m, the new loss term evaluates to *zero*. Our experiments suggest that maximizing OOD entropy leads to overfitting. Bounding the difference of average entropies of ID samples and OOD samples entropies with margin has helped in preventing overfitting, and thus is better for model generalization [11].

Algorithm 2. Algorithm for OOD Detection using K Leave Out Classifiers

Input : Test Image x_t, K leave-out Classifiers $F_i, i \in 1, ..., K$ and their temperature scaled versions $F_i(x_t; T)$, perturbation factor ϵ, number of classes N

Output: Class prediction C_t, OOD score O_t

1 $S_t \leftarrow \{0\}^N$, $O_t \leftarrow 0$;
2 **for** $i \leftarrow 1$ ***to*** K **do**
3 $\quad S_t \leftarrow S_t + F_i(x_t)$;
4 $\quad \hat{x}_t \leftarrow x_t - \epsilon * \text{sign}(\frac{\partial H(F_i(\hat{x}_t; T))}{\partial x_t})$;
5 $\quad O_t \leftarrow O_t + \max_N(F_i(\hat{x}_t; T)) - H(F_i(\hat{x}_t; T))$;
6 **end**
7 $C_t \leftarrow \text{argmax}(S_t)$;
8 **return** C_t, O_t;

3.2 Training Ensemble of Leave-Out Classifiers

Given an in-distribution training data X which consists of N classes, the data is divided into K partitions $X_i, i \in \{1, ..., K\}$ such that the classes of each partition are mutually exclusive to all other partitions. A set of K classifiers are learned where classifier $F_i, i \in \{1, ..., K\}$ uses the partition X_i as OOD data X_{ood} and rest of the data $X - X_i$ as in-distribution data X_{in}. A particularly simple way of partitioning the classes is to divide them into partitions with equal number of classes. For example, dividing a dataset of $N = 100$ classes into $K = 5$ random and equal partitions gives us a partition with size of 20 classes. Each of the K classifiers would then use 20 classes for OOD and 80 classes as ID. Each classifier F_i is learned by minimizing the proposed margin entropy loss (Eq. 1) using the assigned OOD and ID data. During the training, we also assume a small number of out-of-distribution images to be available as a validation dataset. At every epoch, we save the model with best OOD detection rate on this small OOD validation data and within a δ accuracy bound of the current best accuracy. The complete algorithm for training the leave-out classifiers in presented in Algorithm 1.

3.3 OOD Detection Score for Test Image

At the time of testing, an input image is forward propagated through all the K leave-out classifiers and the softmax vectors of all the networks are remapped to their original class indices. For the left-out classes, a score of zero is assigned. For classification of an input sample, first the softmax vectors of all the classifiers are averaged and the class with the highest averaged softmax score is considered as the prediction. For the OOD detection score, for each of the K classifiers, we first compute both the maximum value and negative entropy of the softmax vectors with temperature scaling. We then compute the average of all these values to obtain the OOD detection score.

An in-distribution sample with class labels y_i acts as an OOD for exactly one of the K classifiers. This is because the classes are divided into K mutually exclusive partitions and class y_i can be part of only one of these partitions. When an in-distribution sample (x_i, y_i) is forward propagated through these K classifiers, we would expect the negative entropy and maximum softmax score to be high for $K - 1$ classifiers where it was sampled as in-distribution dataset. However, for an OOD sample x_o we expect the negative entropy and maximum softmax score to be relatively low for all the K classifiers. We thus expect a higher OOD detection score for ID samples than the OOD samples thus differentiating them.

Following the work of ODIN [13], we use both temperature scaling and input preprocessing while testing. In temperature scaling, the logits feeding into softmax layer are scaled by a constant factor T. It has been established that temperature scaling can calibrate the classification score and in the context of OOD detection [13], it pushes the softmax scores of in- and out-of-distribution samples further apart when compared to plain softmax. We modify input preprocessing by perturbing over entropy loss instead of cross-entropy loss used by ODIN [13]. Perturbing using the entropy loss decreases the entropy of the ID samples much more than the OOD samples. For an input test image x_t, after it is forward propagated through the neural network F_i, the gradient of the entropy loss with respect to x_t is computed and the input is perturbed with Eq. 2. The OOD detection score is then calculated by the combination of maximum softmax value and entropy as described previously, both with temperature scaling.

$$\hat{x_t} = x_t - \epsilon * \text{sign}(\frac{\partial L(F_i(x_t;T))}{\partial x_t}) \tag{2}$$

The complete algorithm for OOD detection on a test image is presented in Algorithm 2.

4 Experimental Results

In this section, we describe our experimental results. The details such as in-distribution and OOD datasets, the neural network architectures and evaluation metrics are described in detail. The ablation studies on various hyper-parameters of the algorithms are described and conclusions are drawn. Finally, our method is compared against the current state-of-the-art ODIN [13] and is shown to significantly outperform it.

Table 1. Test error rates on CIFAR-10 and CIFAR-100

Architecture	CIFAR-10	CIFAR-100
DenseNet-BC	5.0	19.9
WRN-28-10	5.0	20.4

4.1 Experimental Setup

We use CIFAR-10 (contains 10 classes) and CIFAR-100 (contains 100 classes) [10] datasets as in-distribution datasets to train deep neural networks for image classification. They both consist of 50,000 images for training, and 10,000 images for testing. The dimensions of an image in both the datasets is 32×32. The classes of both CIFAR-10 and CIFAR-100 are randomly divided into five parts. As described in Sect. 3.2, each part is assigned as OOD to a unique network which is then trained. For each network, the other parts act as in-distribution samples.

Following the benchmarks given in [13], the following OOD datasets are used in our experiments. The datasets are described in ODIN [13] and provided as a part of their code release; here we are simply restating the description for comprehensiveness.

- **TinyImageNet** [9] **(TIN)** is a subset of ImageNet dataset [13]. Tiny ImageNet contains 200 classes which is drawn from original 1,000 classes of ImageNet. In total, there are 10,000 images in the Tiny ImageNet. By randomly cropping and downsampling each image to 32×32, two datasets *TinyImageNetcrop* (*TINc*) and *TinyImageNetresize* (*TINr*) are constructed.
- **LSUN** is the Large Scale UNderstanding dataset (LSUN) [21] created by Princeton, using deep learning classifiers with humans in the loop. It contains 10,000 images of 10 scene categories. By randomly cropping and downsampling each image to size 32×32, two datasets *LSUNc* and *LSUNr* are constructed.
- **iSUN** [20] is collected by gaze tracking from Amazon Mechanical Turk using a webcam. It contains 8925 scene images. Similar to the above dataset as other datasets, images are down-sampled to size 32×32.
- **Uniform Noise (UNFM)** is synthetic dataset consists of 10,000 noise images. The RGB value of each pixel in an image is drawn from uniform distribution in the range $[0, 1]$.

– **Gaussian Noise (GSSN)** is synthetic dataset consists of 10,000 noise images. The RGB value of each pixel is drawn from independent and identically distributed Gaussian with mean 0.5 and unit variance and each pixel value is clipped to the range $[0, 1]$.

Neural Network Architecture. Following ODIN [13], two state-of-the-art neural network architectures, *DenseNet* [8] and *Wide ResNet*(WRN) [22], are adopted to evaluate our method. For DenseNet, we use the DenseNet-BC setup as in [8], with depth $L = 100$, growth rate $k = 12$ and dropout rate 0. For Wide ResNet, we use WRN-28-10 setup, with depth 28, width 10 and dropout rate of 0.3. We train both DenseNet-BC and Wide ResNet on CIFAR-10 and CIFAR-100 for 100 epochs with batch size 100, momentum 0.9, weight decay 0.0005, and margin 0.4. The initial training rate is 0.1 and it is linearly dropped to 0.0001 over the whole training process. During training, we augment our training data with random flip and random cropping. We use the smallest OOD dataset, iSUN, as validation data for hyper-parameter search. We test the rest four out-of-distribution datasets except iSUN on our trained network. During testing, we use batch size 100. Similar to ODIN [13], input preprocessing with $\epsilon = 0.002$ is used.

Table 1 shows the test error rates when our method is trained and tested on CIFAR-10 and CIFAR-100 respectively using the Algorithms 1 and 2. For CIFAR-10, the vanilla DenseNet-BC [8] and the proposed method gives error rates of 4.51% and 5.0% respectively. For CIFAR-100, the error rates are 22.27% and 19.9% respectively. On both these datasets, the difference in error rates is marginal. For WRN [22] with depth 40, $k = 10$, the test error rate on CIFAR-10 for the vanilla network is 4.17% and for the proposed network is 5.0%. For CIFAR-100, the error rates are 20.5% and 20.4% for the vanilla network and the proposed network respectively. The small difference in the performance on CIFAR-10 can be explained by the fact that the our method did not use the ZCA whitening preprocessing while the vanilla network did.

4.2 Evaluation Metrics

To measure the effectiveness of our method to distinguish between in-distribution and out-of-distribution samples, we adopt five different metrics, same as what was used in ODIN [13] paper. We restate these metrics below for comprehensiveness. In the rest of manuscript, TP, TN, FP, FN are used to denote true positives, true negatives, false positives and false negatives respectively.

FPR at 95% TPR measures the probability that an out-of-distribution sample is misclassified as in-distribution when the true positive rate (TPR) is 95%. In this metric, TPR is computed by $TP/(TP+TN)$, and FPR is computed by $FP/(FP+TN)$.

Detection Error measures the minimum misclassification probability over all possible score thresholds, as defined in ODIN [13]. To have a fair comparison with ODIN, the same number of positive and negative samples are used during testing.

AUROC is the Area Under the Receiver Operating Characteristic curve. In a ROC curve, the TPR is plotted as a function of FPR for different threshold settings. AUROC equals to the probability that a classifier will rank a randomly chosen positive sample higher than a randomly chosen negative one. AUROC score of 100% means perfect separation between positive and negative samples.

AUPR-In measures the Area Under the Precision-Recall curve. In a PR curve, the $precision = TP/(TP + FP)$, is plotted as a function of $recall = TP/(TP + FN)$, for different threshold settings. Since precision is directly influenced by class imbalance (due to FP), PR curves can highlight performance differences that are lost in ROC curves for imbalanced datasets [5]. AUPR score of 100% means perfect distinguish between positive and negative samples. For AUPR-In metric, in-distribution images are specified as positive.

AUPR-Out is similar to the metric AUPR-In. The difference lies in that for AUPR-Out metric, out-of-distribution images are specified as positive.

CLS Acc is the classification accuracy for ID samples.

Table 2. Ablation studies on CIFAR-100 as in-distribution data and iSUN as out-of-distribution data on DenseNet-100 network. All values are percentages. ↑ indicates larger value is better, and ↓ indicates lower value is better.

Ablation Studies	Parameters	FPR at 95% TPR ↓	Detection Error ↓	AUROC ↑	AUPR In ↑	AUPR Out ↑	CLS Acc ↑
Number of Splits	3	32.37	13.94	93.50	94.39	92.22	76.41
	5	**22.95**	**10.79**	**95.69**	**96.55**	94.3	80.01
	10	28.71	12.53	94.48	95.37	93.26	81.94
	20	23.85	10.95	95.49	96.24	**94.36**	**82.33**
Type of splits	Random	**22.95**	**10.79**	**95.69**	**96.55**	**94.3**	**80.01**
	Manual	40.16	16.26	91.57	92.90	89.57	79.79
Epsilon	0.000000	53.51	16.37	90.75	93.16	86.71	**80.32**
	0.000313	41.62	14.37	92.8	94.52	90.16	80.22
	0.000625	34.64	12.83	94.09	95.4	92.19	80.17
	0.001250	25.74	11.19	95.38	96.31	94.04	80.08
	0.002000	**22.95**	**10.79**	**95.69**	**96.55**	**94.3**	80.01
	0.003000	29.07	11.79	94.73	95.9	92.43	79.97
Temp-rature	1	38.57	17.32	91.44	92.7	90.12	**80.01**
	10	27.84	11.93	94.86	95.81	93.39	**80.01**
	100	24.44	10.86	95.6	96.5	94.17	**80.01**
	1000	22.95	**10.79**	**95.69**	**96.55**	**94.3**	**80.01**
	5000	**22.7**	10.81	95.66	96.53	94.28	**80.01**
Loss Function	SFX	84.09	36.55	68.96	72.38	63.77	54.18
	SFX+MaxEntropyDiff	50.70	19.65	88.26	89.71	86.18	72.99
	SFX+MarginEntropy	**22.95**	**10.79**	**95.69**	**96.55**	**94.3**	**80.01**
OOD Detection Score	SFX	50.52	19.91	88.69	90.91	86.19	**80.01**
	Entropy	36.23	16.48	91.92	93.03	90.74	**80.01**
	SFX+Entropy	38.57	17.32	91.44	92.7	90.12	**80.01**
	SFX@Temp	**22.71**	10.83	95.65	96.52	94.26	**80.01**
	Entropy@Temp	37.0	14.05	93.33	94.76	91.04	**80.01**
	(SFX+Entropy)@Temp	22.95	**10.79**	**95.69**	**96.55**	**94.3**	**80.01**

4.3 Ablation Studies

In this section, we perform ablation studies to study the effects of various hyper parameters used in our model. We perform the ablation studies on DenseNet-BC [8] network with CIFAR-100 [10] as in-distribution while training and iSUN [20] as the OOD validation data while testing. By default, we use 5 random splits for CIFAR-100, $\epsilon = 0.002$, *SFX+MarginEntropy* loss to train network, accuracy bound $\delta = 2\%$ to save the models, and use *(Softmax + Entropy)@Temperature* with $T = 1000$ to detect out-of-distribution samples. Results are given in Table 2.

(1) **Number of splits:** This analysis characterizes the sensitivity of our algorithm to the number of splits of the training classes which is same as the number of classifiers in the ensemble. As the number of splits increase, the number of times a particular training class being in-distribution for the leave-out classifiers increases too. This enables the ensemble to discriminate an in-distribution sample from the OOD sample. But it also increases the computational cost. For CIFAR-100, we studied 3, 5, 10 and 20 splits. Our results show that while 5 splits gave the best result, 3 splits also provides a good trade-off between accuracy and computational cost. We choose the number of splits as 5 as default value.

(2) **Type of splits:** This study characterizes the way in which the classes are split into mutually exclusive sets. We experiment with splitting the classes manually using prior knowledge and splitting randomly. For the manual split, the class labels are first clustered into semantically consistent groups and classes from each group are then distributed across the splits. The results show that the OOD detection rates for random selections are better than the manual selection.This ensures that we can achieve good OOD detection rates even by random selection of classes when the number of classes is huge.

(3) **Different ϵ for input preprocessing:** For input preprocessing, we sweep over $\epsilon \in [0, 0.000313, 0.000625, 0.00125, 0.002, 0.003]$. Our results show that as ϵ increases from 0, the performance of out-of-distribution detector increases, and it reaches the best performance at 0.002. The further increase of ϵ does not help performance.

(4) **Different T for temperature scaling:** For temperature scaling, we sweep over $T \in [1, 10, 100, 1000, 5000]$. Our results show that for DenseNet-BC with CIFAR-100, as T increases from 1 to 1000, the performance of out-of-distribution detector increases. Beyond $T = 1000$, the performance does not change much.

(5) **Loss function variants:** We study the effects of training our method with different types of losses. The training regime follows the strategy given in Sect. 3.2, where the training data X is split into K partitions $X_i, i \in \{1, ..., K\}$. A total of K classifiers are trained where classifier F_i uses the partition X_i as OOD data and $X - X_i$ as in-distribution data.

- *SFX*: We assign an additional label to all the OOD samples and train classification network using the cross entropy loss.
- *SFX+MaxEntropyDiff*: Along with the cross entropy loss, we maximize the difference between the entropy of in- and out-of-distribution samples across all in-distribution classes.
- *SFX+MarginEntropy*: Along with the cross entropy, we maximize the difference between the entropy of in- and out-of-distribution samples across all in-distribution classes, but is bounded by a margin as given in Eq. 1.

Our results show that the proposed *SFX+MarginEntropy* loss works dramatically better than all other types of losses for detecting out-of-distribution samples as well as for accurate classification. The results demonstrate that the proposed novel loss function *SFX+MarginEntropy* (Eq. 1) is the major factor in significant improvements over the current state-of-the-art ODIN [13].

(6) **Out-of-distribution detector:** We study different OOD scoring methods to discriminate out-of-distribution samples from in-distribution samples.

- *Softmax score*: Given an input image, the score is given by the average of maximum softmax outputs over all the classifiers in the ensemble.
- *Entropy score*: Given an input image, the score is given by the average of entropy of softmax vector over all the classifiers in the ensemble.
- *Softmax + Entropy*: Given an input image, both the above scores are added.
- *Softmax@Temperature*: Given an input image, the above described *S*oftmax score is computed on temperature scaled ($T = 1000$) softmax vectors.
- *Entropy@Temperature*: Given an input image, the above described *E*ntropy score is computed on temperature scaled ($T = 1000$) softmax vectors.
- *(Softmax + Entropy)@Temperature*: Given an input image, the above described *E*ntropy@Temperature and *S*oftmax@Temperature are computed ($T = 1000$) on softmax vectors and then added.

Among the above OOD scoring methods, the *(Softmax + Entropy)@Temperature* ($T = 1000$) achieved the best performance. *Softmax@Temperature* ($T = 1000$) achieved the second best performance.

4.4 Results and Analysis

Table 3 shows the comparison between our results and ODIN [13] on various benchmarks. The results are reported on all neural network, in-dataset and OOD dataset combinations. Our hyperparameters are tuned using iSUN dataset. From the Table 3, it is very clear that our approach significantly outperforms ODIN [13] across all neural network architectures on almost all of the dataset pairs. The combination of novel loss function, OOD scoring method, and the ensemble of models has enabled our method to significantly improve the performance of OOD detection on more challenging datasets, such as LSUN (resized), iSUN and ImageNet(resized), where the images contain full objects as opposed to the cropped parts of objects. The proposed method is slightly worse on the uniform and some of Gaussian distribution results. Moreover, our method achieves significant gains on both CIFAR-10 and CIFAR-100 with the same number of splits which is 5, even though the number of classes have increased by a factor of ten from CIFAR-10 to CIFAR-100. Thus the number of splits need not be scaled linearly with the number of classes, making our method practical. We implicitly outperform Hendrycks and Gimpel [7] and Lee *et al.* [12] as ODIN outperforms both these works and our method outperform ODIN on all but two benchmarks.

All three components in our method, namely novel loss function, the ensemble of leave-out classifiers and improved OOD detection metric contributed to the improvement in performance over state-of-the-art ODIN (refer to Table 2). The contribution of these components can be seen in Table 2 in the rows marked as "Loss function", "Number of splits" and "OOD detection scores".

Our algorithm has stochasticity in the form of random splits of the classes. Given 100 classes in CIFAR-100, there are many ways to split 100 classes into 5 partitions. Table 4 gives the mean and standard deviation across five random

Table 3. Distinguishing in- and out-of-distribution test set data for the image classification. All values are percentages. ↑ indicates larger value is better, and ↓ indicates lower value is better. Each value cell is in "ODIN [13]/Our Method" format.

	OOD Dataset	**FPR at 95% TPR** ↓	**Detection Error** ↓	**AUROC** ↑	**AUPR In** ↑	**AUPR Out** ↑
		each cell in **ODIN[13]/Our Method** format				
DenseNet-BC CIFAR-10	TINc	4.30/**1.23**	4.70/**2.63**	99.10/**99.65**	99.10/**99.68**	99.10/**99.64**
	TINr	7.50/**2.93**	6.10/**3.84**	98.50/**99.34**	98.60/**99.37**	98.50/**99.32**
	LSUNc	8.70/**3.42**	6.00/**4.12**	98.20/**99.25**	98.50/**99.29**	97.80/**99.24**
	LSUNr	3.80/**0.77**	4.40/**2.1**	99.20/**99.75**	99.30/**99.77**	99.20/**99.73**
	UNFM	**0.00**/2.61	**0.20**/3.6	**100**/98.55	**100**/98.94	**100**/97.52
	GSSN	**0.00/0.00**	**0.50**/0.2	**99.90**/99.84	**100**/99.89	**99.90**/99.6
DenseNet-BC CIFAR-100	TINc	17.30/**8.29**	8.80/**6.27**	97.10/**98.43**	97.40/**98.58**	96.80/**98.3**
	TINr	44.30/**20.52**	17.50/**9.98**	90.70/**96.27**	91.40/**96.66**	90.10/**95.82**
	LSUNc	17.60/**14.69**	9.40/**8.46**	96.80/**97.37**	97.10/**97.62**	96.50/**97.18**
	LSUNr	44.00/**16.23**	16.80/**8.77**	91.50/**97.03**	92.40/**97.37**	90.60/**96.6**
	UNFM	**0.50**/79.73	**2.50**/9.46	**99.50**/92.0	**99.60**/94.77	**99.00**/83.81
	GSSN	**0.20**/38.52	**1.90**/8.21	**99.60**/94.89	**99.70**/96.36	**99.10**/90.01
WRN-28-10 CIFAR-10	TINc	23.40/**0.82**	11.60/**2.24**	94.20/**99.75**	92.80/**99.77**	94.70/**99.75**
	TINr	25.50/**2.94**	13.40/**3.83**	92.10/**99.36**	89.00/**99.4**	93.60/**99.36**
	LSUNc	21.80/**1.93**	9.80/**3.24**	95.90/**99.55**	95.80/**99.57**	95.50/**99.55**
	LSUNr	17.60/**0.88**	9.70/**2.52**	95.40/**99.7**	93.80/**99.72**	96.10/**99.68**
	UNFM	**0.00**/16.39	**0.20**/5.39	**100**/96.77	**100**/97.78	**100**/94.18
	GSSN	**0.00/0.00**	**0.10**/1.03	**100**/99.58	**100**/99.71	**100**/99.2
WRN-28-10 CIFAR-100	TINc	43.90/**9.17**	17.20/**6.67**	90.80/**98.22**	91.40/**98.39**	90.00/**98.07**
	TINr	55.90/**24.53**	23.30/**11.64**	84.00/**95.18**	82.80/**95.5**	84.40/**94.78**
	LSUNc	39.60/**14.22**	15.60/**8.2**	92.00/**97.38**	92.40/**97.62**	91.60/**97.16**
	LSUNr	56.50/**16.53**	21.70/**9.14**	86.00/**96.77**	86.20/**97.03**	84.90/**96.41**
	UNFM	**0.10**/99.9	**2.20**/14.86	**99.10**/83.44	**99.40**/89.43	**97.50**/71.2
	GSSN	**1.00**/98.26	**2.90**/16.88	**98.50**/93.04	**99.10**/88.64	**95.90**/71.62

Table 4. Mean and standard deviation of FPR at 95% TPR

OOD Dataset	DenseNet-BC CIFAR-10	DenseNet-BC CIFAR-100	WRN-28-10 CIFAR-10	WRN-28-10 CIFAR-100
TINc	1.49 ± 0.23	10.26 ± 1.33	1.3 ± 0.33	10.35 ± 2.21
TINr	3.95 ± 0.75	26.58 ± 4.16	4.56 ± 1.29	29.84 ± 5.12
LSUNc	4.54 ± 1.42	16.95 ± 1.27	3.81 ± 1.22	15.51 ± 1.4
LSUNr	1.3 ± 0.6	20.22 ± 2.79	1.53 ± 0.41	22.51 ± 6.08
UNFM	14.37 ± 31.84	38.79 ± 19.41	0.75 ± 1.24	47.67 ± 47.19
GSSN	27.09 ± 40.02	82.24 ± 12.81	31.47 ± 33.95	67.48 ± 44.33

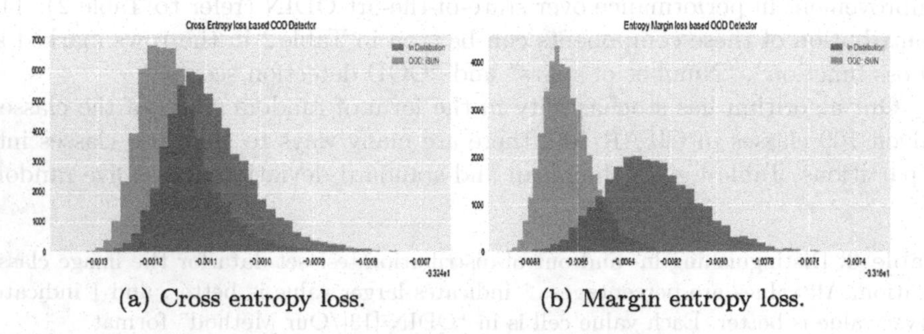

(a) Cross entropy loss. (b) Margin entropy loss.

Fig. 1. Histogram of ID and OOD detection scores of the proposed method and ODIN [13]

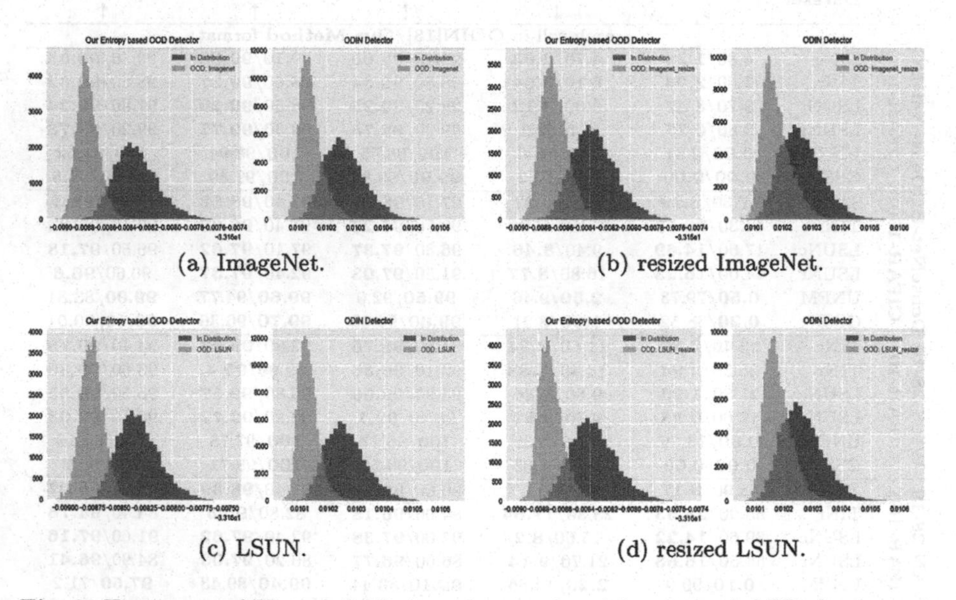

(a) ImageNet. (b) resized ImageNet.

(c) LSUN. (d) resized LSUN.

Fig. 2. Histogram of ID and OOD detection scores with proposed OOD detector vs. ODIN OOD detector

ways to partition data when we use 5 number of splits for training. We note that even our worst case results outperform ODIN [13] on more challenging datasets.

Figure 1 compares the histogram of OOD detection scores on ID and OOD samples when different loss functions are used for training. Figure 1(a) is trained with only cross entropy loss, while Fig. 1(b) is trained with proposed margin entropy loss and cross entropy, the proposed OOD detector is used in both bases. As shown in Fig. 1, the proposed margin entropy loss helps to better separate ID and OOD distributions than using cross entropy loss alone. Figure 2 presents the histogram plot of OOD detection scores on ID and OOD samples for both our method and ODIN [13]. As shown in Fig. 2, the proposed method has less overlap between OOD samples and ID samples compared to ODIN [13] and thus separates ID and OOD distributions better.

5 Conclusion and Future Work

As deep learning is widely adopted in many commercially important applications, it is very important that anomaly detection algorithms are developed for these algorithms. In this work, we have proposed an anomaly detection algorithm for deep neural networks which is an ensemble of leave-out-classifiers. These classifiers are learned by maximizing the margin-loss between the entropy of OOD samples and in-distribution samples. A random subset of training data serves as OOD data while the rest of the data serves as in-distribution. We show our algorithm significantly outperforms the current state-of-art methods [7,12,13] across almost all the benchmarks. Our method contains three important components, novel loss function, the ensemble of leave-out classifiers, and novel out-of-distribution detector. Each of this component improves OOD detection performance. Each of them can be applied independently on top of other methods.

We also note that this method opens up several directions of research to pursue. First, the proposed method of the ensemble of neural networks requires large memory and computational resources. This can potentially be alleviated by all the networks sharing most of the parameters and branch away individually. Also, the number of splits can be used to trade off between detection performance and computational overhead. Notice that based on ablation study (Table 2) and detailed 3 splits results in supplementary document, even 3 splits outperform ODIN [13]. For use cases where reducing computational time is critical, we recommend to use 3 splits. Please see supplementary material for detailed results on 3 splits. Our current work requires an OOD dataset for hyper-parameter search. This problem can potentially be solved by investigating other surrogate functions for entropy which are better behaved with the epochs.

References

1. Bendale, A., Boult, T.E.: Towards open world recognition. In: IEEE Conference on Computer Vision and Pattern Recognition (CVPR), pp. 1893–1902 (2015)
2. Bendale, A., Boult, T.E.: Towards open set deep networks. In: IEEE Conference on Computer Vision and Pattern Recognition (CVPR), pp. 1563–1572 (2016)
3. Chandola, V., Banerjee, A., Kumar, V.: Anomaly detection: a survey. ACM Comput. Surv. **41**(3), 15:1–15:58 (2009)
4. Fujimaki, R., Yairi, T., Machida, K.: An approach to spacecraft anomaly detection problem using kernel feature space. In: KDD, pp. 401–410 (2005)
5. Goadrich, M., Oliphant, L., Shavlik, J.: Creating ensembles of first-order clauses to improve recall-precision curves. Mach. Learn. **64**, 231–262 (2006)
6. Goodfellow, I., et al.: Generative adversarial nets. In: Ghahramani, Z., Welling, M., Cortes, C., Lawrence, N.D., Weinberger, K.Q. (eds.) Advances in Neural Information Processing Systems (NIPS) (2014)
7. Hendrycks, D., Gimpel, K.: A baseline for detecting misclassified and out-of-distribution examples in neural networks. In: International Conference on Learning Representations (ICLR) (2017)
8. Huang, G., Liu, Z., Weinberger, K.Q.: Densely connected convolutional networks (2016). arXiv preprint arXiv:1608.06993
9. https://tiny-imagenet.herokuapp.com
10. Krizhevsky, A., Hinton, G.: Learning multiple layers of features from tiny images
11. LeCun, Y., Chopra, S., Hadsell, R., Ranzato, M., Huang, F.: A tutorial on energy-based learning. In: Predicting structured data (2006)
12. Lee, K., Lee, H., Lee, K., Shin, J.: Training confidence-calibrated classifiers for detecting out-of-distribution samples. In: International Conference on Learning Representations (ICLR) (2018). https://openreview.net/forum?id=ryiAv2xAZ
13. Liang, S., Li, Y., Srikant, R.: Enhancing the reliability of out-of-distribution image detection in neural networks. In: International Conference on Learning Representations (ICLR) (2018)
14. Liu, F.T., Ting, K.M., Zhou, Z.: Isolation forest. In: ICDM, pp. 413–422 (2008)
15. Lu, W., Traoré, I.: Unsupervised anomaly detection using an evolutionary extension of k-means algorithm. IJICS **2**(2), 107–139 (2008)
16. Phua, C., Alahakoon, D., Lee, V.C.S.: Minority report in fraud detection: classification of skewed data. SIGKDD Explor. **6**(1), 50–59 (2004)
17. Rudd, E.M., Jain, L.P., Scheirer, W.J., Boult, T.E.: The extreme value machine. IEEE Trans. Pattern Anal. Mach. Intell. **40**(3), 762–768 (2018)
18. Scheirer, W.J., Jain, L.P., Boult, T.E.: Probability models for open set recognition. IEEE Trans. Pattern Anal. Mach. Intell. **36**(11), 2317–2324 (2014)
19. Scheirer, W.J., de Rezende Rocha, A., Sapkota, A., Boult, T.E.: Toward open set recognition. IEEE Trans. Pattern Anal. Mach. Intell. **35**(7), 1757–1772 (2013)
20. Xu, P., Ehinger, K.A., Zhang, Y., Finkelstein, A., Kulkarni, S.R., Xiao, J.: Turkergaze: crowdsourcing saliency with webcam based eye tracking. arXiv preprint arXiv:1504.06755 (2015)
21. Yu, F., Zhang, Y., Song, S., Seff, A., Xiao, J.: LSUN: construction of a large-scale image dataset using deep learning with humans in the loop. arXiv preprint arXiv:1506.03365 (2015)
22. Zagoruyko, S., Komodakis, N.: Wide residual networks. arXiv preprint arXiv:1605.07146 (2016)

Structure-from-Motion-Aware PatchMatch for Adaptive Optical Flow Estimation

Daniel Maurer[1(✉)], Nico Marniok[2], Bastian Goldluecke[2], and Andrés Bruhn[1]

[1] Institute for Visualization and Interactive Systems, University of Stuttgart, Stuttgart, Germany
{maurer,bruhn}@vis.uni-stuttgart.de

[2] Computer Vision and Image Analysis Group, University of Konstanz, Konstanz, Germany
{nico.marniok,bastian.goldluecke}@uni-konstanz.de

Abstract. Many recent energy-based methods for optical flow estimation rely on a good initialization that is typically provided by some kind of feature matching. So far, however, these initial matching approaches are rather general: They do not incorporate any additional information that could help to improve the accuracy or the robustness of the estimation. In particular, they do not exploit potential cues on the camera poses and the thereby induced rigid motion of the scene. In the present paper, we tackle this problem. To this end, we propose a novel structure-from-motion-aware PatchMatch approach that, in contrast to existing matching techniques, combines two hierarchical feature matching methods: a recent two-frame PatchMatch approach for optical flow estimation (general motion) and a specifically tailored three-frame PatchMatch approach for rigid scene reconstruction (SfM). While the motion PatchMatch serves as baseline with good accuracy, the SfM counterpart takes over at occlusions and other regions with insufficient information. Experiments with our novel SfM-aware PatchMatch approach demonstrate its usefulness. They not only show excellent results for all major benchmarks (KITTI 2012/2015, MPI Sintel), but also improvements up to 50% compared to a PatchMatch approach without structure information.

1 Introduction

Since almost four decades the estimation of optical flow from image sequences is one of the most challenging tasks in computer vision. Despite of the recent success of learning-based approaches [2,9,18,23,36], global energy-based methods are still among the most accurate techniques for solving this task [16,17,22,44]. Even if combined with partial learning [1,33,41,42] such methods offer the advantage

Electronic supplementary material The online version of this chapter (https://doi.org/10.1007/978-3-030-01237-3_35) contains supplementary material, which is available to authorized users.

V. Ferrari et al. (Eds.): ECCV 2018, LNCS 11212, pp. 575–592, 2018.
https://doi.org/10.1007/978-3-030-01237-3_35

that they allow for a transparent modeling, since assumptions are explicitly stated in the underlying energy functional. However, since the complexity of the models has significantly grown within the last few years – recent methods try to estimate segmentation [33,41,44], occlusions [17,44] or illumination changes [8] jointly with the optical flow – the minimization of the resulting non-convex energies has become an increasingly challenging problem.

In this context, many energy-based approaches [14,22,33,41] rely on a suitable initialization provided by other methods. Among the most popular approaches that are considered useful as initialization are EpicFlow [30], Coarse-to-fine PatchMatch [15] and DiscreteFlow [25] – approaches that rely on the interpolation or fusion of *feature matches*. This has two main reasons: On the one hand, feature matching approaches are known to provide good results in the context of large displacements. On the other hand, they are typically based on some kind of filtering or a-posteriori regularization which renders the initialization sufficiently smooth and outlier-free. As a consequence, the initial flow field offers already a reasonable quality and the energy minimization starts with a good solution and is hence less likely to end up in undesired local minima.

While recent methods promote the use of feature-based approaches for initialization, they also show that integrating *additional information* in the estimation can be highly beneficial w.r.t. both accuracy and robustness [1,16,17,33,41]. Apart from considering domain-dependent semantic information [1,5,16,33], it has proven useful to integrate structure constraints and symmetry cues. For instance, [41] proposed a method that jointly estimates the rigidity of each pixel together with its optical flow. Thereby structure constraints are imposed only on rigid parts of the scene. In contrast, [17] suggested an approach that exploits symmetry and consistency cues to jointly estimate forward and backward flows. This in turn, allows to infer occlusion information together with the optical flow.

Given the fact that the two aforementioned approaches as well as many other recent methods from the literature rely on a suitable initialization from feature-based methods, it is surprising that such information has *hardly entered* the initial feature matching step so far. While symmetry and consistency cues are at least considered in terms of simple forward-backward checks to detect occlusions and remove the corresponding outliers [9,15,30], structure constraints in terms of a rigid background motion have not found their way into feature matching approaches for computing the optical flow at all. Hence, it would be desirable to develop a feature-based method that allows to exploit structure information while still being able to estimate independently moving objects at the same time.

Contributions. In our paper, we develop such a hybrid method. In this context, our contributions are threefold. (i) First, we introduce a coarse-to-fine three-frame PatchMatch approach for estimating structure matches (SfM) that combines a depth-driven parametrization with different temporal selection strategies. While the parametrization robustifies the estimation by reducing the search space, the hierarchical optimization and the temporal selection improve the accuracy. (ii) Second, we propose a consistency-based selection scheme for combining matches from this structure-based PatchMatch approach and an unconstrained

PatchMatch approach. Thereby, the backward flow allows us to identify reliable structure matches, while a robust voting scheme decides on the remaining cases. (iii) Finally, we embed the resulting matches into a full estimation pipeline. Using recent approaches for interpolation and refinement, our method provides dense results with sub-pixel accuracy. Experiments on all major benchmarks demonstrate the benefits of our novel SfM-aware PatchMatch approach.

1.1 Related Work

As mentioned, integrating additional information can render the estimation of the optical flow significantly more accurate and robust. We first comment on related work regarding the integration of such information, while afterwards we focus on related PatchMatch approaches for optical flow and scene structure.

Rigid Motion. In order to improve accuracy and robustness in case of a rigid background, one may enforce geometric assumptions such as the epipolar constraint [29,38,43,44]. However, if this assumption is forced to hold for the entire scene, as proposed by Oisel *et al.* [29] and Yamaguchi *et al.* [43,44], the approach is only applicable to fully rigid scenes, e.g. to those of the KITTI 2012 benchmark [11]. Although this problem can be slightly alleviated by soft constraints as proposed by Valgaerts *et al.* [37,38], results for non-rigid scenes are typically not good. Hence, Wedel *et al.* [40] suggested to turn off the epipolar constraint for sequences with independent object motion. This, however, does not allow to exploit rigid body priors at all in the standard optical flow setting. Consequently, Gerlich and Eriksson [12] presented a more advanced approach that segments the scene into different regions with independent rigid body motions. While this strategy allows to handle automotive scenes with other rigdly moving objects quite well, e.g. sequences similar to the KITTI 2015 benchmark [24], it cannot model any type of non-rigid motion, e.g. as required for the different characters in the MPI Sintel benchmark [7]. In contrast, our SfM-aware PatchMatch approach combines information from general and SfM-based motion estimation. Hence, it is not restricted to fully rigid or object-wise rigid scenes.

Mostly Rigid Motion. Compared to [12], Wulff *et al.* [41] went a step further. Instead of requiring the scene to be object-wise rigid they assume the scene to be only mostly rigid. To this end, they suggested a complex iterative model that jointly segments the scene into foreground and background using semantic information as well as motion and structure cues while estimating the background motion with a dedicated epipolar stereo algorithm. In contrast to this approach, that uses the general optical flow method [25] as initialization and adaptively integrates strong rigidity priors later on in the estimation, our SfM-aware PatchMatch approach aims at integrating such priors already in the estimation of feature matches at the *very beginning* of the estimation – and this without the use of semantic information. Hence, our results are relevant for all methods relying on a suitable initialization – including the work of Wulff *et al.* [41] and other recent methods such as [17] or [33].

Parametrized Models. An alternative strategy that recently became very popular is to refrain from using global or object-wise rigidity priors and to model motions that are pixel- or piecewise rigid. Typically this is done by means of a suitable flow (over-)parametrization; see e.g. [13,16,24,28,39,45]. For instance, Hornaček *et al.* [13] proposed a 9 DoF flow parametrization that models a locally rigid motion of planes. Similar, Yang *et al.* [45] and Hur and Roth [16,17] suggested approaches that use a spatially coherent 8 DoF homography based on superpixels. In contrast to those methods, our SfM-aware PatchMatch approach does not explicitly rely on an over-parametrization. Vice versa, it gains robustness by restricting the search space to 1D when calculating the SfM matches. Moreover, it estimates the flow pixel-wise instead of segment-wise. Hence, it is more suitable for general scenes with non-rigid motion and fine motion details.

Semantic Information. Another way to improve the accuracy and the robustness of the estimation is to consider semantic. For instance, Bai *et al.* [1] proposed to use instance-level segmentation to identify independently moving traffic participants before computing separate rigid motions for both the background and the participants. Similarly, Hur and Roth [16] make use of a CNN to integrate semantic information into a joint approach for estimating the flow and a temporally consistent semantic segmentation. Furthermore, Sevilla-Lara *et al.* [33] suggested a layered approach that relies on semantic information when switching between different motion models. Finally, there is also the method of Wulff *et al.* [41] (see mostly rigid motion). While semantic information often improves the results, it has to be particularly adapted to the given domain. As a consequence, the corresponding approaches do typically not generalize well across different applications or benchmarks. Hence, we do not rely on such information.

PatchMatch. In the context of unconstrained matching (optical flow), PatchMatch has been originally proposed by Barnes *et al.* [4]. Recent developments include the work of Bao *et al.* [3] that introduces an edge-preserving weighting scheme as well as the approach of Hu *et al.* [15] that improves accuracy and speed with a hierarchical matching strategy. Moreover, Gadot and Wolf [9] and Bailer *et al.* [2], have recently shown that feature learning can be beneficial. Despite of all the progress, however, none of the aforementioned optical flow methods includes structure information. In contrast, our SfM-aware approach exploits such information by explicitly using feature matches from a specifically tailored three-view stereo/SfM PatchMatch method. Also in the stereo/SfM context, there exists a vast literature on PatchMatch algorithms. There, PatchMatch has been first introduced by Bleyer et al. [6] who proposed a plane-fitting variant for the rectified case. Recent developments include the approaches of Shen [34] and Galliani *et al.* [10] who extended PatchMatch to the non-rectified two-view and multi-view case, respectively; see also [32,46]. In contrast to all those methods, our SfM-aware PatchMatch approach not only extracts pure stereo information. Instead, it combines information from optical flow and stereo and is hence also applicable to non-rigid scenes with independent object motion. Moreover, it relies on a hierarchical optimization [15] which has not been used in the context of

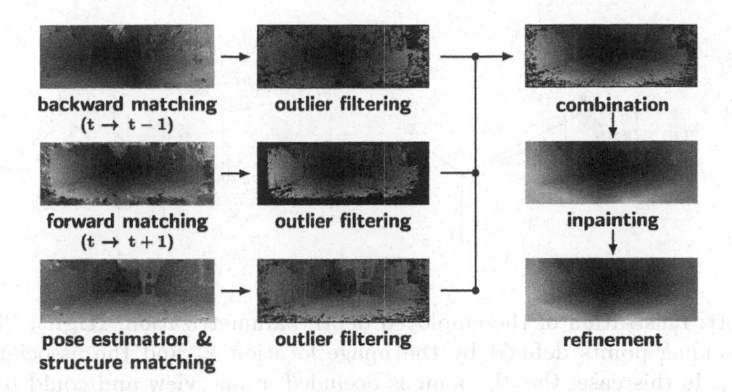

Fig. 1. Schematic overview over our SfM-aware PatchMatch approach.

PatchMatch stereo so far. Finally, the SfM part of our algorithm uses a direct depth-parametrization. This, in turn, makes both the estimation very robust.

2 Method Overview

Let us start by giving a brief overview over the proposed method. As many recent optical flow techniques it relies on a multi-stage approach which includes steps for computing and refining an initial flow field; see e.g. [14,17,22,33,41]. However, in contrast to most of these approaches that typically aim at improving an already given flow field, our method focuses on the generation of an accurate and robust initial flow field itself. To achieve this goal, our method integrates structure information into the feature matching process, which plays an essential role for the initialization [15,25,30]. This integration is motivated by the observation that many sequences contain a significant amount of rigid motion induced by the ego-motion of the camera [41]. Since this motion is constrained by the underlying stereo geometry, structure information can significantly improve the estimation.

In our multi-stage method, we realize this integration by combining two hierarchical feature matching approaches that complement each other: On the one hand, we use a recent two-frame PatchMatch approach for optical flow estimation [15]. This allows our method to estimate the unconstrained motion in the scene (forward and backward matches). On the other hand, we rely on a specifically tailored three-frame stereo/SfM PatchMatch approach (see Sect. 3) with preceding pose estimation [26]. This in turn, allows us our method to compute the rigid motion of the scene induced by the moving camera (structure matches). In order to discard outliers and combine the remaining matches, we perform a filtering approach for all matches followed by a consistency-based selection (see Sect. 4). Finally, we inpaint and refine the combined matches using recent methods from the literature [14,22]. An overview of the entire approach is given in Fig. 1.

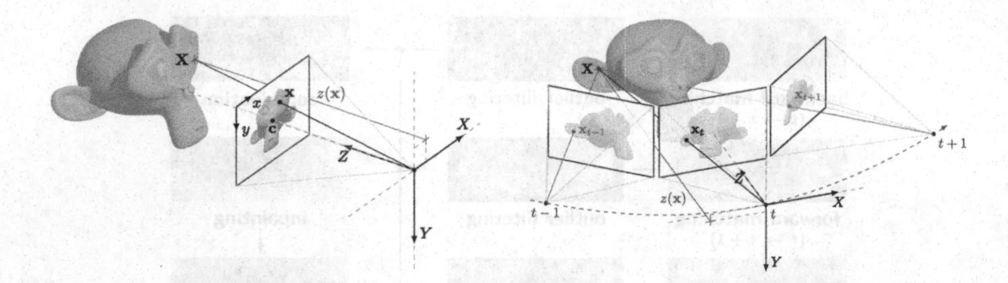

Fig. 2. Left: Illustration of the employed depth parametrization. **Right:** Illustration of corresponding points defined by the image location $\mathbf{x}_t$ and the associated depth value $z(\mathbf{x}_t)$. In this case, the 3D point is occluded in one view and could be handled with the idea of temporal selection. i.e. by the view from the other time step.

3 Structure Matching

In this section, we present our structure matching framework which builds upon the PatchMatch algorithm [4] – a randomized, iterative algorithm for approximate patch matching. In this context, we adopt ideas of the recently proposed Coarse-to-fine PatchMatch (CPM) for optical flow [15] and apply them in the context stereo/SfM estimation that relies on a depth-based parametrization [10,31]. This not only enables the straightforward integration of multiple frames, but also allows to consider the concepts of temporal averaging and temporal selection [19], the latter one being a strategy for implicit occlusion handling.

3.1 Depth-Based Parametrization

Let us start by deriving the employed depth-based parametrization. To this end, we assume that all images are captured by a calibrated perspective camera that possibly moves in space, i.e. the corresponding projection matrices $P_t = K\,[R_t|\mathbf{t}_t]$ are known. Here R_t is a 3×3 rotation matrix and $\mathbf{t}_t$ a translation 3-vector that together describe the pose of the camera at a certain time step t. In addition, the 3×3 matrix K denotes the intrinsic camera calibration matrix given by

$$K = \begin{pmatrix} s_x & 0 & c_x \\ 0 & s_y & c_y \\ 0 & 0 & 1 \end{pmatrix}, \tag{1}$$

where (s_x, s_y) denotes the scaled focal length and $\mathbf{c} = (c_x, c_y)^\top$ denotes the principal point offset. Given the projection matrix P_t, a 3D point $\mathbf{X} \in \mathbb{R}^3$ is projected onto a 2D point $\mathbf{x} \in \mathbb{R}^2$ on the image plane by $\mathbf{x} = \pi(P_t\tilde{\mathbf{X}})$, where the tilde denotes homogeneous coordinates, such that

$$\tilde{\mathbf{X}} = \left(\mathbf{X}^\top, 1\right)^\top, \tag{2}$$

and π maps a homogeneous coordinate $\tilde{\mathbf{x}}$ to its Euclidean counterpart $\mathbf{x}$

$$\pi(\tilde{\mathbf{x}}) = \begin{pmatrix} \tilde{x}_1/\tilde{x}_3 \\ \tilde{x}_2/\tilde{x}_3 \end{pmatrix}, \quad \text{with} \quad \tilde{\mathbf{x}} = \left(\tilde{x}_1, \tilde{x}_2, \tilde{x}_3\right)^\top. \tag{3}$$

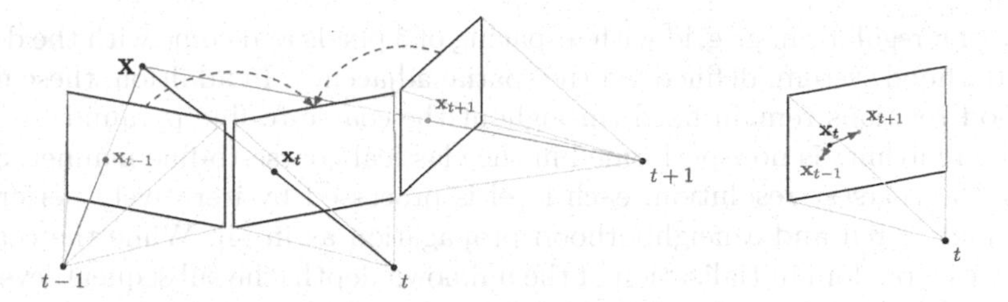

Fig. 3. Illustration showing the conversion procedure from a 3D point to the displacement vectors w.r.t. to the forward frame $t+1$ and backward frame $t-1$.

Now, to define our parametrization, we assume w.l.o.g. that the camera pose of the reference camera, i.e. the camera associated with the image taken at time t, is aligned with the world coordinate system and invert the previous described projection to specify a 3D point on the surface $\mathbf{s}$ by an image location $\mathbf{x}$ and the corresponding depth $z(\mathbf{x})$ along the optical axis; see Fig. 2. This leads to

$$\mathbf{X} = \mathbf{s}(\mathbf{x}, z(\mathbf{x})) = z(\mathbf{x})K^{-1}\tilde{\mathbf{x}}, \tag{4}$$

which allows us to describe correspondences throughout multiple images with a single unknown, the depth $z(\mathbf{x})$, by projecting onto the respective image planes using the corresponding projection matrices; see Fig. 2. Finally, given three frames as in our case, with projection matrices P_{t+1}, P_t, and P_{t-1}, one can directly convert the estimated depth values to the corresponding displacement vectors w.r.t. to the forward frame $t+1$ and the backward frame $t-1$ (Fig. 3):

$$\mathbf{u}_{\text{st,fw}}(\mathbf{x}, z(\mathbf{x})) = \pi(P_{t+1}\tilde{\mathbf{s}}(\mathbf{x}, z(\mathbf{x})) - \pi(P_t\tilde{\mathbf{s}}(\mathbf{x}, z(\mathbf{x})), \tag{5}$$

$$\mathbf{u}_{\text{st,bw}}(\mathbf{x}, z(\mathbf{x})) = \pi(P_{t-1}\tilde{\mathbf{s}}(\mathbf{x}, z(\mathbf{x})) - \pi(P_t\tilde{\mathbf{s}}(\mathbf{x}, z(\mathbf{x})). \tag{6}$$

3.2 Hierarchical Matching

With the depth parametrization at hand we now turn to the actual matching. While applying the classical PatchMatch approach [4] directly to the problem typically yields noisy results due to non-existent explicit regularization, we resort to the idea of integrating a hierarchical coarse-to-fine scheme, which has shown to be less prone to noise in the context of optical flow estimation [15].

As in [15] we do not estimate the unknowns for all pixel locations, but for multiple collections of seeds $\mathcal{S}^l = \{s_m^l\}$ that are defined on each resolution level $l \in \{0, 1, \ldots, k-1\}$ of the coarse-to-fine pyramid. While the number of seeds remains the same for each resolution level, their spatial locations are given by

$$\mathbf{x}(s_m^l) = \lfloor \eta \cdot \mathbf{x}(s_m^{l-1}) \rceil \quad \text{for} \quad l \geq 1, \tag{7}$$

where $\lfloor \cdot \rceil$ is a function that returns the nearest integer value and $\eta = 0.5$ is the employed downsampling factor between two consecutive pyramid levels. Furthermore, the locations for $l = 0$ (full image resolution) are located at the cross points of a regular image grid with a spacing of 3 pixels and come with the default neighborhood system, defined via the spatial adjacency. In addition, these neighborhood relations remain fixed throughout the coarse-to-fine pyramid.

The matching is now performed in the classical coarse-to-fine manner: Starting at the coarsest resolution, each level is processed by iteratively performing a random search and a neighborhood propagation as in [4]. While the coarsest level uses a random initialization of the unknown depth, the subsequent levels are initialized with the depth values of the corresponding seeds of the next coarser level. Furthermore, the search radius for the random sampling is reduced exponentially throughout the coarse-to-fine pyramid, such that the random search is restricted to values near the current best depth estimate.

3.3 Cost Computation and Temporal Averaging/Selection

Since we consider three images, there are several possibilities how to compute the matching cost between corresponding patches. One possible choice is to compute all pairwise similarity measures w.r.t. the reference patch and average the costs. While this renders the estimation more robust if the actual 3D point is visible in all views, it may lead to deteriorated results in case of occlusions. In order to deal with this, one can apply the idea of temporal selection [19] and compute all pairwise similarity measures w.r.t. the reference patch, but only consider the lowest pairwise cost as overall cost. Thereby it can be ensured that, as long as the reference patch can be found in at least one view and is occluded in the remaining ones, the correct correspondence retains a small cost. In our experiments we will use both approaches, temporal averaging and temporal selection.

Finally, we utilize SIFT descriptors [15,20,21] in order to compute the similarity between two corresponding locations. This also renders the matching more robust than operating directly on the intensity values. Regarding the cost function we follow [15] and apply a robust L^1-loss. The resulting forward and backward structure matching costs C_{t+1} and C_{t-1} are then given by

$$C_{t+1}(\mathbf{x}, z(\mathbf{x})) = ||\mathbf{f}_{\text{SIFT}}(\pi(P_{t+1}\tilde{\mathbf{s}}(\mathbf{x}, z(\mathbf{x}))) - \mathbf{f}_{\text{SIFT}}(\pi(P_t\tilde{\mathbf{s}}(\mathbf{x}, z(\mathbf{x}))||_1, \quad (8)$$

$$C_{t-1}(\mathbf{x}, z(\mathbf{x})) = ||\mathbf{f}_{\text{SIFT}}(\pi(P_{t-1}\tilde{\mathbf{s}}(\mathbf{x}, z(\mathbf{x}))) - \mathbf{f}_{\text{SIFT}}(\pi(P_t\tilde{\mathbf{s}}(\mathbf{x}, z(\mathbf{x}))||_1, \quad (9)$$

where $\mathbf{f}_{\text{SIFT}}$ denotes the SIFT-feature and $||\cdot||_1$ is the L^1-norm. The corresponding temporal averaging and temporal selection costs read

$$C_{\text{avg}}(\mathbf{x}, z(\mathbf{x})) = \tfrac{1}{2}(C_{t+1}(\mathbf{x}, z(\mathbf{x})) + C_{t-1}(\mathbf{x}, z(\mathbf{x}))), \quad (10)$$

$$C_{\text{ts}}(\mathbf{x}, z(\mathbf{x})) = \min(C_{t+1}(\mathbf{x}, z(\mathbf{x})), C_{t-1}(\mathbf{x}, z(\mathbf{x}))). \quad (11)$$

3.4 Outlier Handling

Finally, we extend the classical bi-directional consistency check to our three-view setting. Therefore, we not only estimate the depth values with frame t as reference view but also with the other two frames as reference. Then we take the estimated depth value $z_t(\mathbf{x})$ at frame t, project it into the frames $t+1$ and

$t-1$, take the estimated depth values $z_{t+1}(\mathbf{x})$ and $z_{t-1}(\mathbf{x})$ there, and project them back to frame t. Only if at least one of the two backprojections maps to the starting point $\mathbf{x}$, the depth value $z_t(\mathbf{x})$ is considered valid. In this case, the forward/backward structure matches can be computed from $z_t(\mathbf{x})$ via Eqs. (5) and (6).

4 Combining Matches

At this point, we have computed filtered forward and backward structure matches from frame t to frames $t+1$ and $t-1$. For the sake of clarity let us denote these matches by $\hat{\mathbf{u}}_{\mathrm{st,fw}}$ and $\hat{\mathbf{u}}_{\mathrm{st,bw}}$. Moreover, as indicated in Fig. 1. we have also computed the corresponding forward and backward optical flow matches between the same frames with a hierarchical PatchMatch approach for unconstrained motion [15]. Since these optical flow matches underwent a classical bi-directional consistency check to remove outliers (which requires to additionally compute matches from frames $t+1$ and $t-1$ to frame t), let us denote them by $\hat{\mathbf{u}}_{\mathrm{of,fw}}$ and $\hat{\mathbf{u}}_{\mathrm{of,bw}}$.

The goal of the combination step is now to fuse these four matches in such a way such that rigid parts of the scene can benefit from the structure matches. Thereby one has to keep in mind that optical flow matches may explain rigid motion, while structure matches are typically wrong in the context of independent object motion. To avoid using structural matches at inappropriate locations, we propose a conservative approach: We augment the optical flow matches with the matches obtained from the structure matching. This means that we always keep the match of the forward flow, if it has passed the outlier filtering. Otherwise, however, we consider to augment the final matches at this location by the match of the structure matching approach. In order to decide if such a structure match should really be considered, we propose three different approaches (see Fig. 4):

Permissive Approach. The first approach is the most permissive approach. It includes all structure matches $\hat{\mathbf{u}}_{\mathrm{st,fw}}$ that have passed the outlier filtering at locations where no forward optical flow match $\hat{\mathbf{u}}_{\mathrm{of,fw}}$ is available.

Restrictive Approach. The second approach is more restrictive. Instead of including all structure matches, we enforce an additional consistency check. This allows to reduce the probability of blindly including possibly false matches. For this consistency check we make use of the backward optical flow match $\hat{\mathbf{u}}_{\mathrm{of,bw}}$. We only consider the forward structure match $\hat{\mathbf{u}}_{\mathrm{st,fw}}$, if its backward variant $\hat{\mathbf{u}}_{\mathrm{st,bw}}$ is consistent with the backward optical flow match $\hat{\mathbf{u}}_{\mathrm{of,bw}}$. In case the additional consistency check cannot be performed, because the backward optical flow match did not pass the outlier filtering, we do not consider the structure match.

Voting Approach. Finally, we propose a voting approach that enforces the additional consistency check as in the restrictive approach but still allows to include structure matches in case the additional consistency check cannot be performed. The decision if such non-checkable structure matches should be included is conducted for each sequence separately. It is based on a voting scheme: All locations, that contain a valid match for the forward, backward and structure match are eligible to vote. If the structure match is consistent with both the forward and the backward match, we count this as a vote in favor of including non-checkable matches. If the votes surpass a certain threshold (80% in our experiments) all non-checkable structure matches are added. This can be seen as a detection scheme that allows to identify scenes with a large amount of ego-motion.

5 Evaluation

Evaluation Setup. In order to evaluate our new approach, we used the following components within our pipeline (cf. Fig. 1): The pose estimation uses the OpenMVG [27] implementation of the incremental SfM approach [26], the forward and backward matching employ the Coarse-to-fine PatchMatch (CPM) [15] approach, the structure matching and consistent combination are performed as described in Sects. 3 and 4, respectively, followed by a robust interpolation of the combined correspondences (RIC) using [14]. Finally, the inpainted matches are refined using the order-adaptive illumination-aware refinement method (OIR) [22]. Except for the refinement, where we optimized [35] the three weighting parameters per benchmark using the training data, we used the default parameters.

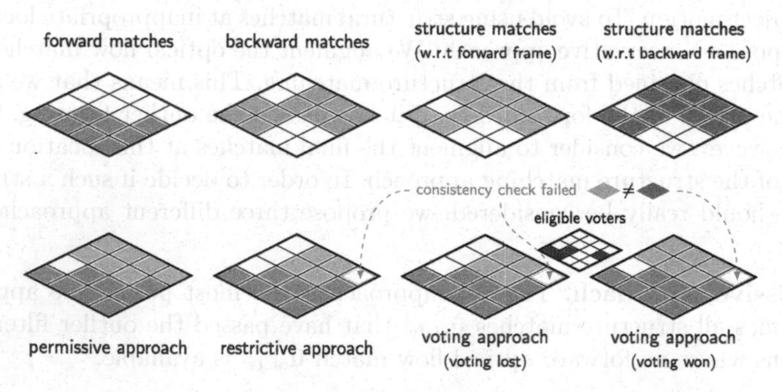

Fig. 4. Illustration showing the different strategies to combine the computed matches. **Top:** Color coded input matches. White denotes no match. **Bottom:** Fusion results. (Color figure online)

Benchmarks. To evaluate the performance of our approach, we consider three different benchmarks: the KITTI 2012 [11], the KITTI 2015 [24], and the MPI Sintel [7] benchmark. These benchmarks exhibit an increasing amount of ego-motion induced optical flow. While KITTI 2012 consists of pure ego-motion, KITTI 2015 additionally includes motion of other traffic participants. Finally, MPI Sintel also contains non-rigid motion from animated characters.

Baseline. To measure improvements, we establish a baseline that does not use structure information and only relies on forward optical flow matches (CPM).

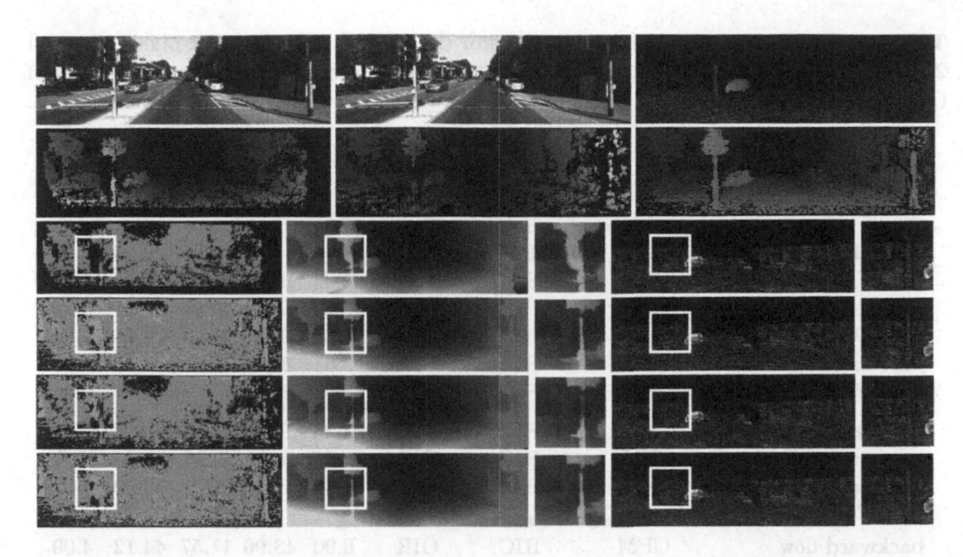

Fig. 5. Example for the KITTI 2015 benchmark [24] (#186). **First row:** Reference frame, subsequent frame, ground truth. **Second row:** Forward matches, structure matches (depth visualization). **Following rows. From left to right:** Used matches (color-coding see Fig. 4), final result, bad pixel visualization. **From top to bottom:** Baseline, permissive approach, restrictive approach, voting approach. (Color figure online)

As Table 1 shows, our baseline outperforms most of the related approaches. Only DF+OIR [22] performs slightly better, due to the advanced DF matches [25].

Structure Matching. Next, we investigate the performance of our novel structure matching approach on its own. Therefore, we replace the matching approach (CPM) in our baseline with three variants of our structure matching approach (CPMz): a two-frame variant, a three-frame variant with temporal averaging and a three-frame variant with temporal selection. As the results in Table 1 show, structure matching significantly outperforms the baseline in pure ego-motion scenes, while it naturally has problems in scenes with independent motion. Moreover, they show that the use of multiple frames pays off. However, while for the KITTI benchmarks the robustness of temporal averaging is more beneficial than the occlusion handling of temporal selection, the opposite holds for the MPI Sintel benchmark. This, in turn, might be attributed to the fact that MPI Sintel contains a larger amount of occlusions. Since both strategies have their advantages, we consider both variants for our further evaluation.

Unconstrained Matching. Apart from the baseline we also evaluated two additional variants solely based on unconstrained matching: a variant only using backward matches and a variant that augments the forward matches with backward matches. To this end, we assume a constant motion model, i.e. $\hat{\mathbf{u}}_{\text{of,fw}} = -\hat{\mathbf{u}}_{\text{of,bw}}$. The results for the backward flow in Table 1 show that such a

Table 1. Results for the training datasets of the KITTI 2012 [11] (all pixels), KITTI 2015 [24] (all pixels) and the MPI Sintel [7] benchmarks (clean render path) in terms of the average endpoint error (AEE) and the percentage of bad pixels (BP, 3px threshold).

method name	matching	inpainting	refinement	KITTI 2012 AEE	KITTI 2012 BP	KITTI 2015 AEE	KITTI 2015 BP	Sintel AEE
related approaches (+ baseline)								
CPM-Flow [15]	CPM	EPIC	EPIC	3.00	14.58	7.78	22.86	2.00
RIC-Flow [14]	CPM	RIC	OpenCV	2.94	10.94	7.24	21.46	2.16
CPM+OIR [22]	CPM	EPIC	OIR	2.78	9.68	7.36	19.21	1.99
DF+OIR [22]	DF	EPIC	OIR	**2.34**	9.29	**5.89**	**18.10**	**1.91**
baseline	CPM	RIC	OIR	2.61	**8.98**	6.82	18.70	1.95
only structure matching								
two-frame	CPMz	RIC	OIR	2.25	9.47	9.15	23.02	17.09
temporal averaging	CPMz	RIC	OIR	**1.25**	**6.51**	**7.85**	**19.11**	20.68
temporal selection	CPMz	RIC	OIR	1.43	6.69	8.06	19.52	**15.69**
only unconstrained matching								
backward flow	CPM	RIC	OIR	6.90	43.96	11.57	44.12	4.00
forward flow	CPM	RIC	OIR	**2.61**	**8.98**	**6.82**	**18.70**	**1.95**
combined fw&bw	CPM	RIC	OIR	4.53	18.93	9.54	27.42	2.05
combined (temporal selection)								
permissive approach	CPM/CPMz	RIC	OIR	**1.47**	5.91	4.95	14.12	2.53
restrictive approach	CPM/CPMz	RIC	OIR	1.60	6.22	5.20	15.10	**1.88**
voting approach	CPM/CPMz	RIC	OIR	1.48	**5.82**	**4.91**	**13.95**	1.90
combined (temporal averaging)								
permissive approach	CPM/CPMz	RIC	OIR	**1.30**	5.71	4.21	13.72	2.92
restrictive approach	CPM/CPMz	RIC	OIR	1.59	6.17	5.04	14.97	**1.90**
voting approach	CPM/CPMz	RIC	OIR	**1.30**	**5.67**	**4.16**	**13.61**	1.92
recent literature								
PWC-Net [36]	CVPR '18			4.14	–	10.35	33.67	2.55
FlowNet2 [18]	CVPR '18			4.09	–	10.06	30.37	2.02
UnFlow [23]	AAAI '18			**3.29**	–	**8.10**	23.27	
DCFlow [42]	CVPR '17			–	–	–	15.09	–
MR-Flow [41]	CVPR '17			–	–	–	14.09	**1.83**
Mirror Flow [17]	ICCV '17			–	–	–	**9.98**	–
learning approaches (fine tuned)								
PWC-Net-ft[36]	CVPR '18			(1.45)	–	(2.16)	(9.80)	(1.70)
FlowNet2-ft [18]	CVPR '17			(1.28)	–	(2.30)	(8.61)	(1.45)
UnFlow-ft [23]	AAAI '18			(1.14)	–	(1.86)	(7.40)	–

simple model does not allow to leverage useful information to predict the forward flow. Even the augmented variant does not improve compared to the baseline.

Combined Approach. Let us now turn towards the evaluation of our combined approach. In this context, we compare the impact of the different combination strategies. As one can see in Table 1, the permissive approach is not an option. While it works well for dominating ego-motion, it includes too many false structure matches in case of independent object motion. In contrast, the restric-

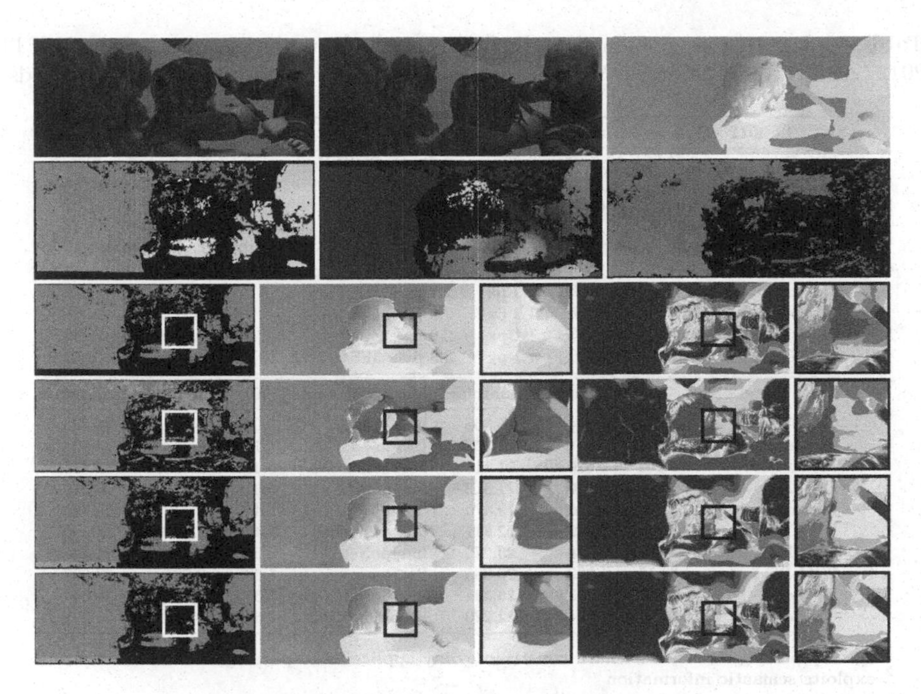

Fig. 6. Example for the MPI Sintel benchmark [7] (ambush5 #44). **First row:** Reference frame, subsequent frame, ground truth. **Second row:** Forward matches, structure matches (forward match visualization). **Following rows. From left to right:** Used matches (color-coding see Fig. 4), final result, bad pixel visualization. **From top to bottom:** Baseline, permissive approach, restrictive approach, voting approach. (Color figure online)

tive approach prevents the inclusion of false structure matches, but cannot make use of the full potential of such matches in scenes with dominating ego-motion. Nevertheless, it already outperforms the baseline significantly and gives the best results for MPI Sintel. Finally, the voting approach combines the advantages of both schemes. It yields the best results for KITTI 2012/2015 with improvements up to 50% compared to the baseline, while still offering an improvement w.r.t. MPI Sintel. This observation is also confirmed by the examples in Figs. 5 and 6. They show the usefulness of including structure matches in occluded areas and the importance of filtering false structure matches in general.

Comparison to the Literature. Finally, we compare our method to other approaches from the literature. To this end, we consider both the training and the test data sets; see Tables 1 and 2, respectively. Regarding the training data sets, our method generally yields better results than recent learning approaches without fine-tuning (PWC-Net [36], FlowNet2 [18], UnFlow [23]). Moreover, it also outperforms DCFlow [42] and MR-Flow [41] on the KITTI 2015 benchmark. Only MirrorFlow [17] (KITTI 2015) and MR-Flow (MPI Sintel) provide better results. This good performance holds for the test data sets as well, for which we

Table 2. Top 10 non-anonymous optical flow methods on the test data of the KITTI 2012/2015 [11,24] and of the MPI Sintel benchmark [7], excluding scene flow methods.

KITTI 2012	Out-Noc	Out-All	Avg-Noc	Avg-All	KITTI 2015	Fl-bg	Fl-fg	Fl-all
SPS-Fl[1]	3.38 %	10.06 %	0.9 px	2.9 px	PWC-Net	9.66 %	9.31 %	9.60 %
PCBP-Flow[1]	3.64 %	8.28 %	0.9 px	2.2 px	MirrorFlow	8.93 %	17.07 %	10.29 %
SDF[2]	3.80 %	7.69 %	1.0 px	2.3 px	SDF[2]	8.61 %	23.01 %	11.01 %
MotionSLIC[1]	3.91 %	10.56 %	0.9 px	2.7 px	UnFlow	10.15 %	15.93 %	11.11 %
our approach	**4.02 %**	**6.15 %**	**1.0 px**	**1.5 px**	CNNF+PMBP	10.08 %	18.56 %	11.49 %
PWC-Net	4.22 %	8.10 %	0.9 px	1.7 px	**our approach**	**9.66 %**	**22.73 %**	**11.83 %**
UnFlow	4.28 %	8.42 %	0.9 px	1.7 px	MR-Flow[2]	10.13 %	22.51 %	12.19 %
MirrorFlow	4.38 %	8.20 %	1.2 px	2.6 px	DCFlow	13.10 %	23.70 %	14.86 %
ImpPB+SPCI	4.65 %	13.47 %	1.1 px	2.9 px	SOF[2]	14.63 %	22.83 %	15.99 %
CNNF+PMBP	4.70 %	14.87 %	1.1 px	3.3 px	JFS[2]	15.90 %	19.31 %	16.47 %

MPI Sintel clean	all	matched	unmatched	MPI Sintel final	all	matched	unmatched
MR-Flow[2]	2.527	0.954	15.365	PWC-Net	5.042	2.445	26.221
our approach	**2.910**	**1.016**	**18.357**	DCFlow	5.119	2.283	28.228
FlowFields+	3.102	0.820	21.718	FlowFieldsCNN	5.363	2.303	30.313
CPM2	3.253	0.980	21.812	MR-Flow[2]	5.376	2.818	26.235
MirrorFlow	3.316	1.338	19.470	S2F-IF	5.417	2.549	28.795
DF+OIR	3.331	0.942	22.817	**our approach**	**5.466**	**2.683**	**28.147**
S2F-IF	3.500	0.988	23.986	InterpoNet_ff	5.535	2.372	31.296
SPM-BPv2	3.515	1.020	23.865	RicFlow	5.620	2.765	28.907
DCFlow	3.537	1.103	23.394	InterpoNet_cpm	5.627	2.594	30.344
RicFlow	3.550	1.264	22.220	ProbFlowFields	5.696	2.545	31.371

[1] uses epipolar geometry as a hard constraint, only applicable to pure ego-motion
[2] exploits semantic information

Table 3. Impact of refinement parameter optimization.

method name	parameters	KITTI 2012 AEE	KITTI 2012 BP	KITTI 2015 AEE	KITTI 2015 BP	Sintel AEE
voting approach	individually optimized	**1.30**	**5.67**	**4.16**	**13.61**	**1.92**
voting approach	single parameter set	1.31	5.70	**4.16**	13.70	1.93

evaluated the approaches that had performed best on the training data. Here, on KITTI 2012, our method performs favorably (all pixels) even compared to methods based on pure ego-motion and semantic information. Moreover, it also outperforms recent approaches with an explicit SfM background estimation (MR-Flow) on KITTI 2015. Finally, ranking second and sixth our method also yields an excellent performance on the clean and final set of MPI Sintel, respectively. This shows that our method not only works well in the context of pure ego-motion but can also handle a significant amount of independent object motion.

Fixed Parameter Set. Finally, we investigate how the results change when not optimizing the refinement parameters individually for each benchmark. To this end, we considered the voting approach with temporal averaging and conducted an experiment on the training data with *all parameters fixed.* As Table 3 shows the results hardly deteriorate when using a single parameter set for all benchmarks.

Runtime. The runtime of the pipeline excluding the pose estimation is 32s for one frame of size 1024 × 436 (MPI Sintel) using three cores on an Intel® Core^{TM} i7-7820X CPU @ 3.6 GHz, which splits into: 5.5s matching (incl. outlier filtering), <0.1s combination, 1.5s inpainting and 25s refinement. The pose estimation is run on the entire image sequence, which takes 83s for a sequence with 50 frames.

6 Conclusion

In this paper, we addressed the problem of integrating structure information into feature matching approaches for computing the optical flow. To this end, we developed a hierarchical depth-parametrized three-frame SfM/stereo PatchMatch approach with temporal selection and preceding pose estimation. By adaptively combining the resulting matches with those of a recent PatchMatch approach for general motion estimation, we obtained a novel SfM-aware method that benefits from a global rigidity prior, while still being able to estimate independently moving objects. Experiments not only showed excellent results on all major benchmarks (KITTI 2012/2015, MPI Sintel), they also demonstrated consistent improvements over a baseline without structure information. Since our approach is based on inpainting and refining advanced feature matches, it offers another advantage: Other optical flow methods can easily benefit from it by incorporating its matches or the resulting dense flow fields as initialisation.

Acknowledgments. We thank the German Research Foundation (DFG) for financial support within projects B04 and B05 of SFB/Transregio 161.

References

1. Bai, M., Luo, W., Kundu, K., Urtasun, R.: Exploiting semantic information and deep matching for optical flow. In: Leibe, B., Matas, J., Sebe, N., Welling, M. (eds.) ECCV 2016, Part VI. LNCS, vol. 9910, pp. 154–170. Springer, Cham (2016). https://doi.org/10.1007/978-3-319-46466-4_10
2. Bailer, C., Varanasi, K., Stricker, D.: CNN-based patch matching for optical flow with thresholded Hinge embedding loss. In: Proceedings of the IEEE Conference on Computer Vision and Pattern Recognition, pp. 2710–2719 (2017)
3. Bao, L., Yang, Q., Jin, H.: Fast edge-preserving PatchMatch for large displacement optical flow. In: Proceedings of the IEEE Conference on Computer Vision and Pattern Recognition, pp. 1510–1517 (2014)
4. Barnes, C., Shechtman, E., Finkelstein, A., Goldman, D.B.: PatchMatch: a randomized correspondence algorithm for structural image editing. ACM Trans. Graph. **28**(3), 24 (2009)
5. Behl, A., Jafari, O., Mustikovela, S., Alhaija, H., Rother, C., Geiger, A.: Bounding boxes, segmentations and object coordinates: how important is recognition for 3D scene flow estimation in autonomous driving scenarios? In: Proceedings of the IEEE International Conference on Computer Vision, pp. 2574–2583 (2017)
6. Bleyer, M., Rhemann, C., Rother, C.: PatchMatch stereo - stereo matching with slanted support windows. In: Proceedings of the British Machine Vision Conference, pp. 14:1–14:11 (2011)

7. Butler, D.J., Wulff, J., Stanley, G.B., Black, M.J.: A naturalistic open source movie for optical flow evaluation. In: Fitzgibbon, A., Lazebnik, S., Perona, P., Sato, Y., Schmid, C. (eds.) ECCV 2012, Part VI. LNCS, vol. 7577, pp. 611–625. Springer, Heidelberg (2012). https://doi.org/10.1007/978-3-642-33783-3_44
8. Demetz, O., Stoll, M., Volz, S., Weickert, J., Bruhn, A.: Learning brightness transfer functions for the joint recovery of illumination changes and optical flow. In: Fleet, D., Pajdla, T., Schiele, B., Tuytelaars, T. (eds.) ECCV 2014, Part I. LNCS, vol. 8689, pp. 455–471. Springer, Cham (2014). https://doi.org/10.1007/978-3-319-10590-1_30
9. Gadot, D., Wolf, L.: PatchBatch: a batch augmented loss for optical flow. In: Proceedings of the IEEE Conference on Computer Vision and Pattern Recognition, pp. 4236–4245 (2016)
10. Galliani, S., Lasinger, K., Schindler, K.: Massively parallel multiview stereopsis by surface normal diffusion. In: Proceedings of the IEEE International Conference on Computer Vision, pp. 873–881 (2015)
11. Geiger, A., Lenz, P., Urtasun, R.: Are we ready for autonomous driving? The KITTI vision benchmark suite. In: Proceedings of the IEEE Conference on Computer Vision and Pattern Recognition, pp. 3354–3361 (2012)
12. Gerlich, T., Eriksson, J.: Optical flow for rigid multi-motion scenes. In: Proceedings of the IEEE International Conference on 3D Vision, pp. 212–220 (2016)
13. Hornáček, M., Besse, F., Kautz, J., Fitzgibbon, A., Rother, C.: Highly overparameterized optical flow using PatchMatch belief propagation. In: Fleet, D., Pajdla, T., Schiele, B., Tuytelaars, T. (eds.) ECCV 2014, Part III. LNCS, vol. 8691, pp. 220–234. Springer, Cham (2014). https://doi.org/10.1007/978-3-319-10578-9_15
14. Hu, Y., Li, Y., Song, R.: Robust interpolation of correspondences for large displacement optical flow. In: Proceedings of the IEEE Conference on Computer Vision and Pattern Recognition, pp. 481–489 (2017)
15. Hu, Y., Song, R., Li, Y.: Efficient Coarse-to-fine PatchMatch for large displacement optical flow. In: Proceedings of the IEEE Conference on Computer Vision and Pattern Recognition, pp. 5704–5712 (2016)
16. Hur, J., Roth, S.: Joint optical flow and temporally consistent semantic segmentation. In: Hua, G., Jégou, H. (eds.) ECCV 2016, Part I. LNCS, vol. 9913, pp. 163–177. Springer, Cham (2016). https://doi.org/10.1007/978-3-319-46604-0_12
17. Hur, J., Roth, S.: MirrorFlow: exploiting symmetries in joint optical flow and occlusion estimation. In: Proceedings of the IEEE International Conference on Computer Vision, pp. 312–321 (2017)
18. Ilg, E., Mayer, N., Saikia, T., Keuper, M., Dosovitskiy, A., Brox, T.: FlowNet 2.0: evolution of optical flow estimation with deep networks. In: Proceedings of the IEEE Conference on Computer Vision and Pattern Recognition, pp. 1647–1655 (2017)
19. Kang, S.B., Szeliski, R., Chai, J.: Handling occlusions in dense multi-view stereo. In: Proceedings of the IEEE Conference on Computer Vision and Pattern Recognition, pp. 103–110 (2001)
20. Liu, C., Yuen, J., Torralba, A.: SIFT flow: dense correspondence across scenes and its applications. IEEE Trans. Pattern Anal. Mach. Intell. **33**(5), 978–994 (2011)
21. Lowe, D.G.: Distinctive image features from scale-invariant keypoints. Int. J. Comput. Vis. **60**(2), 91–110 (2004)

22. Maurer, D., Stoll, M., Bruhn, A.: Order-adaptive and illumination-aware variational optical flow refinement. In: Proceedings of the British Machine Vision Conference, pp. 662:1–662:13 (2017)
23. Meister, S., Hur, J., Roth, S.: UnFlow: unsupervised learning of optical flow with a bidirectional census loss. In: Proceedings of the AAAI Conference on Artificial Intelligence (2018)
24. Menze, M., Geiger, A.: Object scene flow for autonomous vehicles. In: Proceedings of the IEEE Conference on Computer Vision and Pattern Recognition, pp. 3061–3070 (2015)
25. Menze, M., Heipke, C., Geiger, A.: Discrete optimization for optical flow. In: Gall, J., Gehler, P., Leibe, B. (eds.) GCPR 2015. LNCS, vol. 9358, pp. 16–28. Springer, Cham (2015). https://doi.org/10.1007/978-3-319-24947-6_2
26. Moulon, P., Monasse, P., Marlet, R.: Adaptive structure from motion with *a Contrario* model estimation. In: Lee, K.M., Matsushita, Y., Rehg, J.M., Hu, Z. (eds.) ACCV 2012, Part IV. LNCS, vol. 7727, pp. 257–270. Springer, Heidelberg (2013). https://doi.org/10.1007/978-3-642-37447-0_20
27. Moulon, P., Monasse, P., Marlet, R., Others: OpenMVG. An Open Multiple View Geometry library. https://github.com/openMVG/openMVG
28. Nir, T., Bruckstein, A.M., Kimmel, R.: Over-parameterized variational optical flow. Int. J. Comput. Vis. **76**(2), 205–216 (2007)
29. Oisel, L., Memin, E., Morin, L., Labit, C.: Epipolar constrained motion estimation for reconstruction from video sequences. In: Proceedings of the SPIE, vol. 3309, pp. 460–468 (1998)
30. Revaud, J., Weinzaepfel, P., Harchaoui, Z., Schmid, C.: Epicflow: edge-preserving interpolation of correspondences for optical flow. In: Proceedings of the IEEE Conference on Computer Vision and Pattern Recognition, pp. 1164–1172 (2015)
31. Robert, L., Deriche, R.: Dense depth map reconstruction: a minimization and regularization approach which preserves discontinuities. In: Buxton, B., Cipolla, R. (eds.) ECCV 1996. LNCS, vol. 1064, pp. 439–451. Springer, Heidelberg (1996). https://doi.org/10.1007/BFb0015556
32. Schönberger, J.L., Zheng, E., Frahm, J.-M., Pollefeys, M.: Pixelwise view selection for unstructured multi-view stereo. In: Leibe, B., Matas, J., Sebe, N., Welling, M. (eds.) ECCV 2016, Part III. LNCS, vol. 9907, pp. 501–518. Springer, Cham (2016). https://doi.org/10.1007/978-3-319-46487-9_31
33. Sevilla-Lara, L., Sun, D., Jampani, V., Black, M.J.: Optical flow with semantic segmentation and localized layers. In: Proceedings of the IEEE Conference on Computer Vision and Pattern Recognition, pp. 3889–3898 (2016)
34. Shen, S.: Accurate multiple view 3D reconstruction using patch-based stereo for large-scale scenes. IEEE Trans. Image Process. **22**(5), 1901–1914 (2013)
35. Stoll, M., Volz, S., Maurer, D., Bruhn, A.: A time-efficient optimisation framework for parameters of optical flow methods. In: Sharma, P., Bianchi, F.M. (eds.) SCIA 2017, Part I. LNCS, vol. 10269, pp. 41–53. Springer, Cham (2017). https://doi.org/10.1007/978-3-319-59126-1_4
36. Sun, D., Yang, X., Liu, M.Y., Kautz, J.: PWC-Net: CNNs for optical flow using pyramid, warping, and cost volume. In: Proceedings of the IEEE Conference on Computer Vision and Pattern Recognition (2018)
37. Valgaerts, L., Bruhn, A., Mainberger, M., Weickert, J.: Dense versus sparse approaches for estimating the fundamental matrix. Int. J. Comput. Vis. **96**(2), 212–234 (2012)

38. Valgaerts, L., Bruhn, A., Weickert, J.: A variational model for the joint recovery of the fundamental matrix and the optical flow. In: Rigoll, G. (ed.) DAGM 2008. LNCS, vol. 5096, pp. 314–324. Springer, Heidelberg (2008). https://doi.org/10.1007/978-3-540-69321-5_32
39. Vogel, C., Schindler, K., Roth, S.: 3D scene flow estimation with a piecewise rigid scene model. Int. J. Comput. Vis. **115**(1), 1–28 (2015)
40. Wedel, A., Cremers, C., Pock, T., Bischof, H.: Structure-and motion-adaptive regularization for high accuracy optic flow. In: Proceedings of the IEEE International Conference on Computer Vision, pp. 1663–1668 (2009)
41. Wulff, J., Sevilla-Lara, L., Black, M.J.: Optical flow in mostly rigid scenes. In: Proceedings of the IEEE Conference on Computer Vision and Pattern Recognition, pp. 6911–6920 (2017)
42. Xu, J., Ranftl, R., Koltun, V.: Accurate optical flow via direct cost volume processing. In: Proceedings of the IEEE Conference on Computer Vision and Pattern Recognition, pp. 5807–5815 (2017)
43. Yamaguchi, K., McAllester, D., Urtasun, R.: Robust monocular epipolar flow estimation. In: Proceedings of the IEEE Conference on Computer Vision and Pattern Recognition, pp. 1862–1869 (2013)
44. Yamaguchi, K., McAllester, D., Urtasun, R.: Efficient joint segmentation, occlusion labeling, stereo and flow estimation. In: Fleet, D., Pajdla, T., Schiele, B., Tuytelaars, T. (eds.) ECCV 2014, Part V. LNCS, vol. 8693, pp. 756–771. Springer, Cham (2014). https://doi.org/10.1007/978-3-319-10602-1_49
45. Yang, J., Li, H.: Dense, accurate optical flow estimation with piecewise parametric model. In: Proceedings of the IEEE Conference on Computer Vision and Pattern Recognition, pp. 1019–1027 (2015)
46. Zheng, E., Dunn, E., Jojic, V., Frahm, J.M.: PatchMatch based joint view selection and depthmap estimation. In: Proceedings of the IEEE Conference on Computer Vision and Pattern Recognition, pp. 1510–1517 (2014)

Universal Sketch Perceptual Grouping

Ke Li[1,2](✉), Kaiyue Pang[2], Jifei Song[2], Yi-Zhe Song[2], Tao Xiang[2], Timothy M. Hospedales[3], and Honggang Zhang[1]

[1] Beijing University of Posts and Telecommunications, Beijing, China
{like1990,zhhg}@bupt.edu.cn
[2] SketchX, Queen Mary University of London, London, UK
{kaiyue.pang,j.song,yizhe.song,t.xiang}@qmul.ac.uk
[3] The University of Edinburgh, Edinburgh, UK
t.hospedales@ed.ac.uk

Abstract. In this work we aim to develop a universal sketch grouper. That is, a grouper that can be applied to sketches of any category in any domain to group constituent strokes/segments into semantically meaningful object parts. The first obstacle to this goal is the lack of large-scale datasets with grouping annotation. To overcome this, we contribute the largest sketch perceptual grouping (SPG) dataset to date, consisting of 20, 000 unique sketches evenly distributed over 25 object categories. Furthermore, we propose a novel deep universal perceptual grouping model. The model is learned with both generative and discriminative losses. The generative losses improve the generalisation ability of the model to unseen object categories and datasets. The discriminative losses include a local grouping loss and a novel global grouping loss to enforce global grouping consistency. We show that the proposed model significantly outperforms the state-of-the-art groupers. Further, we show that our grouper is useful for a number of sketch analysis tasks including sketch synthesis and fine-grained sketch-based image retrieval (FG-SBIR).

Keywords: Sketch perceptual grouping · Universal grouper
Deep grouping model · Dataset

1 Introduction

Humans effortlessly detect objects and object parts out of a cluttered background. The Gestalt school of psychologists [1,2] argued that this ability to perceptually group visual cues/patterns into objects is built upon a number of grouping principles, termed Gestalt laws of grouping. These include five categories, namely proximity, similarity, continuity, closure, and symmetry [3].

Computer vision research in grouping or segmentation has long exploited these perceptual grouping principles. For example, in image segmentation [4–7], pixel visual appearance similarity and local proximity are often used to group pixels into objects. These principles are exploited by the human visual system to

V. Ferrari et al. (Eds.): ECCV 2018, LNCS 11212, pp. 593–609, 2018.
https://doi.org/10.1007/978-3-030-01237-3_36

robustly perform perceptual grouping in diverse contexts and for diverse object categories. Exploiting them is important for a universal grouping algorithm.

We aim to develop such a universal grouper for human free-hand sketches which takes a sketch as input and groups the constituent strokes into semantic parts. Note that this is different from semantic segmentation for either photos [7] or sketches [8–10], where each segmented part is given a label, and the labels are often object category-dependent. Only the group relationship between strokes is predicted so that the grouper can *universally* be applied to any object category.

Fig. 1. Examples of the SPG dataset. Stroke groups are colour coded. (Color figure online)

Very few existing studies [11,12] investigate sketch perceptual grouping. These approaches compute hand-crafted features from each stroke and use the proximity and continuity principles to compute a stroke affinity matrix for subsequent clustering/grouping. They thus have a number of limitations: (i) Only two out of the five principles are exploited, while the unused ones such as closure are clearly useful in grouping human sketches which can be fragmented (see Fig. 1). (ii) How the principles are formulated is determined manually rather than learned from data. (iii) Fixed weightings of different principles are used which are either manually set [11] or learned [12]. However, for different sketches, different principles could be used by humans with different weightings. Therefore a more dynamic sketch-specific grouping strategy is preferable. Nevertheless, the existing sketch perceptual grouping datasets [8,12] are extremely small, containing 2,000 annotated sketches at most. This prevents more powerful and flexible deep neural network models from being developed.

The first contribution of this paper is to provide the first large-scale sketch perceptual grouping (SPG) dataset consisting of 20,000 sketches with ground truth grouping annotation, i.e., 10 times larger than the largest dataset to date [12]. The sketches are collected from 25 representative object categories with 800 sketches per category. Some examples of the sketches and their annotation can be seen in Fig. 1. A dataset of such size makes the development of a deep universal grouper possible.

Even with sufficient training samples, learning a deep universal sketch grouper is non-trivial. In particular, there are two challenges: how to make the deep grouper generalisable to unseen object categories and domains without any training data from them; and how to design training losses that enforce both local (stroke pairwise) grouping consistency and global (whole sketch level) grouping consistency given variable number of strokes per sketch. Most losses used by existing deep models are for supervised classification tasks; grouping is closer to clustering than classification so few options exist.

In this paper, we propose a novel deep sketch grouping model to overcome both challenges. Specifically, treating a sketch as a sequence of strokes/segments, our model is a sequence-to-sequence variational autoencoder (VAE). The reconstruction loss in this deep generative model forces the learned representation to preserve information richer than required for the discriminative grouping task alone. This has been proven to be useful for improving model generalisation ability [13], critical for making the grouper universal. As for the discriminative grouping learning objectives, we deploy two losses: a pairwise stroke grouping loss enforcing local grouping consistency and a global grouping loss to enforce global grouping consistency. This separation of the local and global grouping losses enables us to balance the two and makes our model more robust against annotation noise. Based on the proposed grouper we develop a simple sketch synthesis model by grouping and abstracting photo edge maps. The synthesised sketches can be used to learn a strong *unsupervised* fine-grained sketch-based image retrieval (FG-SBIR) model, i.e., using photos only.

Our contributions are as follows: (1) We contribute the largest sketch perceptual grouping dataset to date with extensive human annotation. To drive future research, we will make the dataset publicly available. (2) For the first time, a deep universal sketch grouper is developed based on a novel deep sequence-to-sequence VAE with both generative and discriminative losses. (3) Extensive experiments show the superiority of our grouper against existing ones, especially when evaluated on new categories or new domains. Its usefulness on a number of sketch analysis tasks including sketch synthesis and FG-SBIR is also demonstrated.

2 Related Work

Perceptual Grouping: Humans can easily extract salient visual structure from apparent noise. Gestalt psychologists referred to this phenomenon as perceptual organisation [1,2] and introduced the concept of perceptual grouping, which accounts for the observation that humans naturally group visual patterns into objects. A set of simple Gestalt principles were further developed, including proximity, similarity and continuity [3], with closure, connectedness and common fate introduced later, primarily for studying human vision systems [4,14].

Sketch Groupers: Very few studies exist on grouping sketch strokes into parts. The most related studies are [11,12]. They compute an affinity matrix between strokes using hand-crafted features based on proximity and continuity principles. The two principles are combined with fixed weights learned from human annotated stroke groups. In contrast, we assume that when humans draw sketches and annotate them into groups, all grouping principles could be used. Importantly, using which ones and by how much are dependent on the specific sketch instance. Our model is thus a deep neural network that takes the sketch as input and aims to model all principles implicitly via both generative and discriminative grouping losses. It thus has the potential to perform principle selection and weighting dynamically according to the sketch input. We also provide a much larger dataset compared to the one provided in [12]. We show that on both datasets, our model outperforms that in [12] by a big margin. Note that perceptual grouping has been modelled using a deep autoencoder in [15]. However, the objective is to group discrete graphical patterns which has richer visual cues that make them more akin to the problem of image segmentation, and thus easier than grouping line drawings in sketches.

Sketch Semantic Segmentation: A closely related problem to sketch grouping is sketch semantic segmentation [8–10][1]. The key difference is that a sketch grouper is universal in that it can be applied to any object category as it only predicts whether strokes belong to the same group rather than what group. In contrast, sketch segmentation models need to predict the label of each group. As a result, typically one model is needed for each object category. Note that although two different problems are tackled, our work can potentially benefit sketch semantic segmentation in two ways: (i) The grouping principles modelled implicitly in our grouping model could be used for semantic segmentation, e.g., by modifying/fine-tuning our model to a fully supervised one. (ii) The SPG dataset also contains group ID labels for each category so can be used for developing deep segmentation models, which has not been possible to date due to the small sizes of existing sketch segmentation datasets [8–10].

Sketch Stroke Analysis: Like our model, a number of recent sketch models are based on stroke modelling. [10] studied stroke semantic segmentation. A sequence-to-sequence variational autoencoder is used in [16] for a different purpose of conditional sketch synthesis. The work in [17] uses a sketch RNN for sketch abstraction problem by sequentially removing redundant strokes. A stroke-based model is naturally suited for perceptual grouping. Modelling Gestalt principles is harder if a sketch is treated as a 2D pixel array instead of strokes.

Fine-grained SBIR: FG-SBIR has been a recent focus in sketch analysis [18–23]. Training a FG-SBIR model typically requires expensive photo-sketch pair collection, which severely restricts its applicability to large number of object categories. In this work, we show that our universal grouper is general enough to be applied to edge maps computed from object photos. The edge maps can then be abstracted by removing the least important groups. The abstracted edge map can be used to substitute human sketches and form synthetic sketch-photo pairs for training a FG-SBIR model. We show that the performance of a model trained in this way approaches that of the same model trained with human labelled data, and is superior to the state-of-the-art unsupervised alternative [17].

[1] Their relationship is analogous to that between unsupervised image segmentation [5,6] and semantic segmentation [7].

3 Free-Hand Sketch Perceptual Grouping Dataset

We contribute the Sketch Perceptual Grouping dataset, the largest free-hand sketch perceptual grouping dataset to date. It contains 20,000 sketches distributed over 25 categories with each sketch manually annotated into parts.

Category Selection: The sketches come from the QuickDraw dataset [16], which is by far the largest sketch dataset. It contains 345 categories of everyday objects. Out of these, 25 are selected for SPG (see Table 1) based on following criteria: (i) Complexity: the category should contain at least three semantic parts, meaning categories such as cloud and moon are out. (ii) Variety: The selected categories need to be sufficiently different from each other to be appropriate for testing the grouper's generalisation ability to unseen classes. For example, only one of the four-legged animal classes is chosen.

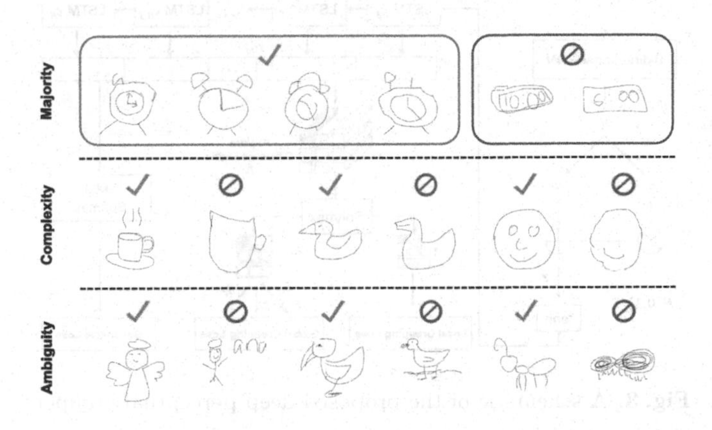

Fig. 2. Examples to illustrate our sketch selection process. See details in text.

Sketch Instance Selection: Each QuickDraw category contains at least 100,000 sketches. Annotating all of them is not feasible. So 800 sketches are chosen from each category. First, some quality screening is performed. Specifically, since all QuickDraw sketches were drawn within 20 seconds, there are a large number of badly drawn sketches that are unrecognisable by humans, making part grouping impossible. We thus first discard sketches which could not be recognised by an off-the-shelf sketch classifier [24]. The remaining sketches are then subject to the following instance selection criteria: (i) **Majority**: Sketches in each category can form subcategories which can be visually very different from each other. Only the sketches from the majority subcategory are selected. For example, the top row of Fig. 2 shows that most sketches from the alarm clock category belong to the "with hand" subcategory, whilst a small minority depicts digital clocks without hands. Only sketches from the former are selected. (ii) **Complexity:** Over-abstract sketches with less than three parts are removed.

(iii) **Ambiguity:** Finally, we eliminate sketches that contain both the target object and other objects/background to avoid ambiguity of the object category. Figure 2 shows examples of how these criteria are enforced during instance selection.

Annotation: Now given a sketch, each annotator is asked to group the strokes into groups. Each group has a semantic meaning and typically corresponds to an object part. So apart from the grouping label, the group ID is also annotated. Even though the group ID information is not used in our perceptual grouping model, it can be used when the task is sketch semantic segmentation. To obtain consistent grouping annotation, 25 annotators are recruited and each only annotates one category. Examples of the annotation can be seen in Fig. 1.

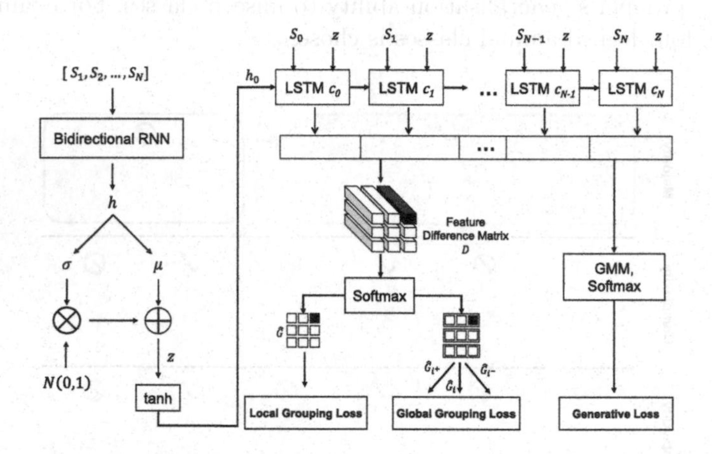

Fig. 3. A schematic of the proposed deep perceptual grouper.

4 Deep Universal Sketch Perceptual Grouper

4.1 Model Overview

Our deep sketch grouper is a variant of the sequence-to-sequence variational autoencoder (VAE) [25,26]. As shown in Fig. 3, it is essentially a deep encoder-decoder with both the encoder and decoder being RNNs for modelling a sketch as a set of strokes. The encoder produces a global representation of the sketch, which is used as a condition for a variational decoder that aims to reconstruct the input sketch. Such sketch synthesis is a side task here. Our main aim is for the decoder to produce a representation of each stroke useful for grouping them. Once learned, the decoder should implicitly model all the grouping principles used by the annotators in producing the grouping labels, so that the learned stroke representation can be used to compute a stroke affinity matrix indicating the correct stroke grouping. To this end, the decoder has two branches: a generative branch to reconstruct the input sketch; and a discriminative branch that produces the discriminative stroke feature/affinity matrix.

4.2 Encoder and Decoder Architecture

Traditional perceptual grouping methods treat sketches as images composed of static pixels, thus neglecting the dependency between different segments and strokes (each stroke consists of a variable number of line segments). In our dataset, all the sketches are captured in a vectorised format, making sequential modelling of sketches possible. More specifically, we first represent a sketch as a sequence of N stroke-segments $[S_1, S_2, ..., S_N]$. Each segment is a tuple $(\Delta x, \Delta y, p)$, where Δx and Δy denote the offsets along the horizontal and vertical directions respectively, while p represents the drawing state, following the same representation used for human handwriting [27].

With these stroke segments as inputs, both the encoder and decoder are RNNs. In particular, we adopt the same architecture as in sketch-rnn [16] for conditional sketch synthesis. That is, a bi-directional RNN [28] is used as the encoder to extract the global embedding of the input sketch. The final state output of the encoder is then projected to a mean and a variance vector, to define an IID Gaussian distribution. That distribution is then sampled to produce a random vector z as the representation of the input sketch. Thus z is not a deterministic output of the encoder given a sketch, but a random vector conditional on the input. The decoder is an LSTM model. Its initial state is conditional on z via a single fully connected (FC) layer. At each time step, it then predicts the offset for each stroke segment in order to reconstruct the input sketch. For further details on the encoder/decoder architecture, please refer to [16].

4.3 Formulation

The decoder splits into two branches after the LSTM hidden cell outputs: a generative branch to synthesise a sketch and a discriminative branch for grouping. Different learning objectives are used for the two branches: in the generative branch, two losses encourage the model to reconstruct the input sketch; in the discriminative branch, the sketch grouping annotation is used to train the decoder to produce an accurate stroke affinity matrix for grouping.

Group Affinity Matrix: The grouping annotation is represented as a sparse matrix denoting the group relationship between segments $\mathbf{G} \in \mathbb{R}^{N \times N}$. Denoting the ith sketch segment as $S_i, i \in [1, N]$, we have:

$$G_{i,j} = \begin{cases} 1, & if\ S_i, S_j\ are\ from\ the\ same\ group \\ 0, & otherwise \end{cases} \quad (1)$$

Where each element of the matrix indicates whether the ith and j^{th} segments belong to the same group or not. A straightforward design of the discriminative learning objective is to make the affinity matrix computed using the learned stroke feature $f_i = \phi(S_i)$ as similar as possible to $\mathbf{G}$, via an l_1 or l_2 loss. However, we found that in practice this works very poorly. This is because $\mathbf{G}$ conveys two types of grouping constraints: each element enforces a binary pairwise constraint for two segments, whilst the whole matrix also enforces global grouping constraint, e.g., if S_1 and S_2 are in the same group, and S_2 and S_5 are also in the same group, then global grouping consistency dictates that S_1 and S_5 must also belong to the same group. Balancing these two is critical because pairwise grouping predictions are typically noisy and can lead to global grouping inconsistency. However, using a single loss makes it impossible to achieve a balance. We thus propose to use two losses to implements the two constraints.

Local Grouping Loss: This loss requires that the pairwise relationship between two segments are kept when the pairwise affinity is measured using the learned stroke segment feature. The decoder LSTM learns a mapping function ϕ and map the ith stroke segment S_i to a 128D feature vector f_i. To measure the affinity of any two segments in the input sketch, the absolute element-wise feature difference is computed to obtain a symmetric absolute feature difference matrix, $\mathbf{D} \in \mathbb{R}^{N \times N \times 128}$ as:

$$\mathbf{D} = \{D_{i,j} \mid i, j \in [1, N]\} = \{|f_i - f_j| \mid i, j \in [1, N]\}. \tag{2}$$

Each vector $D_{i,j} \in \mathbb{R}^{128}$ is then subject to a binary classification loss (cross-entropy) to obtain the local affinity prediction $\hat{G}_{i,j}$, between the ith and j^{th} segments. The local grouping loss, $\mathcal{L}_A$, is thus computed as:

$$\mathcal{L}_A = \sum_{i=1}^{N} \sum_{j=1}^{N} \left[-G_{i,j} \log(\hat{G}_{i,j}) - (1 - G_{i,j}) \log(1 - \hat{G}_{i,j}) \right]. \tag{3}$$

Global Grouping Loss: Using only a local grouping loss may lead to global grouping inconsistency. However, formulating the global grouping consistency into a loss for a deep neural network is not straightforward. Our strategy is to first derive a global grouping representation for each segment using the local affinity prediction $\hat{G}_{i,j}$. We then use a triplet ranking loss to enforce that the segments belonging the same group have more similar grouping relationships to each other, than to a segment outside the group. Although the triplet ranking loss involves three segments only, since each segment is represented by its grouping relationship to all other segments, this loss is a global grouping loss. More concretely, we first construct the local affinity prediction matrix $\hat{\mathbf{G}}$ with $\hat{G}_{i,j}$ as elements. Each row vector of $\hat{\mathbf{G}}$, $\hat{G}_{i,:}$ is then used as a global grouping relationship vector to represent S_i. The final global grouping loss $\mathcal{L}_G$ is:

$$\mathcal{L}_G = \max(0, \Delta + d(\hat{G}_{i,:}, \hat{G}_{i^+,:}) - d(\hat{G}_{i,:}, \hat{G}_{i^-,:})), \tag{4}$$

where i represents an anchor segment, i^+ a positive segment in the same group and i^- a negative segment from a different group, Δ is a margin and $d(\cdot)$ denotes a distance function between two feature inputs. Here we take the squared Euclidean distance under the l_2 normalisation.

Generative Losses: For the generative branch, we use the same generative losses as in [16]. These include a reconstruction loss $\mathcal{L}_R$ and a KL loss $\mathcal{L}_{KL}$

measuring the difference between the latent random vector z and a IID Gaussian vector with zero-mean and unit variance.

Full Learning Objective: Our full loss $\mathcal{L}_F$ can be written as:

$$\mathcal{L}_F = \lambda_a \mathcal{L}_A + \lambda_g \mathcal{L}_G + \lambda_r (\mathcal{L}_R + \mathcal{L}_{KL}) \tag{5}$$

where the hyper-parameters λ_a, λ_g, and λ_r describe the relative importance of the different losses in the full training objective.

Model Testing: During testing stage, given a sketch, the trained model is used to compute an estimated segment affinity matrix, $\hat{G}$. This affinity matrix is then used to generate the final grouping. Since the number of groups varies for different sketches, the group number also needs to be estimated. To this end, we adopt a recent agglomerative clustering method [29] to obtain the final grouping. Note that the method does not introduce any additional free parameters.

4.4 Applications to Sketch Analysis

Sketch Synthesis from Edge Map: A simple sketch synthesis method can be developed based on the proposed universal grouper. The method is based on grouping edge maps extracted from photo images and removing the least important groups. Assume that the N segments of an edge map have been grouped in K groups, denoted as $P_k, k \in [1, K]$. An importance measure is defined as:

$$I(P_k) = I_L(P_k) \cdot I_N(P_k) + I_D(P_k) \tag{6}$$

where $I_L(P_k)$, $I_N(P_k)$ and $I_D(P_k)$ measure the importance from the perspectives of length, numbers and distribution of the segments in group P_k respectively. A less important group has smaller number of segments with shorter lengths but occupies a bigger region. We thus have:

$$I_L(P_k) = \frac{\sum_{i=1}^{N_{P_k}} L_{S_i}}{\sum_{i=1}^{N} L_{S_i}}, \; I_N(P_k) = \frac{N_{P_k}}{N}, \; I_D(P_k) = \frac{\max(w,h) N_{P_k}}{\sum_{i=1}^{N_{P_k}} d(M_{P_k}, M_{S_i})} \tag{7}$$

where N_{P_k} is the number of segments in P_k, L_{S_i} is the length of segment S_i, w and h are the width and height of the object, respectively, M_{P_k} denotes the average position of group P_k in the image plane, M_{S_i} represents the average position of segment S_i, and Euclidean distance $d(\cdot)$ is used. With the importance measure $I(P_k)$ computed for each group, we can then drop the least important groups defined as those with $I(P_k) < I_\delta$ where I_δ is a threshold.

Fine-Grained Sketch Based Image Retrieval: We further develop an unsupervised FG-SBIR method following [17]. Specifically, we apply our grouper to edge maps extracted from photos to synthesise human style sketches. Three threshold values of I_δ are used for each photo to accounts for the variable levels of abstraction among human sketchers. The photos and corresponding synthesised sketches are then used as data to train an off-the-shelf FG-SBIR model

[19]. During testing, the grouping and group removal processes are applied to the human sketches, again with three different thresholds. The matching scores using the three abstracted sketches plus the original query sketch are then fused to produce the final retrieval results. Note that for this unsupervised FG-SBIR model to work well, our grouper must be truly universal: it needs to work well on both human sketches which it was trained on, and photo edge maps.

5 Experiments

5.1 Datasets and Settings

Dataset Splits and Preprocessing: Among the 25 categories in the new SPG dataset, we randomly select 20 as **seen categories**, and use the remaining 5 categories as **unseen categories** to test the generalisation of our universal grouper. In each seen category, we select 650 sketches for training, 50 for validation, and 100 for testing. For the unseen categories, no data are used for training and we randomly select 100 sketches per category for testing to have the same per-category size as the seen categories. We normalise all the sketch strokes, and augment the sketch via stroke removal and distortion [24].

Implementation Details: Our deep grouper is implemented on Tensorflow on a single Titan X GPU. For model training, we set the importance weights λ_r, λ_a and λ_g for different losses (Eq. (4)) to 0.5, 0.6, and 1, respectively. The Adam optimiser [30] is applied with the parameters $\beta_1 = 0.5$, $\beta_2 = 0.9$, $\epsilon = 10^{-8}$. The initial learning rate is set to 0.0003 with exponential weight decay. The model is trained for 22,000 iterations with a batch size of 100.

Evaluation Metrics: Sketch perceptual grouping shares many common characteristics with the unsupervised image segmentation problem [5]. We thus adopt the same metrics including variation of information (VOI), probabilistic rand index (PRI), and segmentation covering (SC) as defined in [31]. More detailed definition of these metrics in the context of sketch grouping are: (i) **Variation of Information:** In this metric, the distance between two groups in terms of their average conditional entropy is calculated. (ii) **Probabilistic Rand Index:** Rand index compares the compatibility of assignments between pairs of stroke segments in each group. (iii) **Segmentation Covering:** the overlapping between the machine grouping and human grouping is measured. For SC and PRI, higher scores are better, while for VOI, a lower score indicates better results.

Competitors: Very few sketch perceptual grouping methods exist. The state-of-the-art model **Edge-PG** [12] uses two Gestalt principles, namely proximity (spatial closeness) and continuity (slope trend) to compute an affinity matrix and feeds the matrix to a graph cut algorithm to get the groups. The weightings of the two principles are learned from data using RankSVM. This method thus differs from ours in that hand-crafted features are used and only two principles are modelled. Beyond sketch grouping, many semantic image segmentation methods have been proposed lately based on fully convolutional networks (FCN).

We choose one of the state-of-the-art models, **DeepLab** [7] as a baseline. It is trained to take images as input and output the semantic grouping, i.e., each pixel is assigned a class label. A conditional random field (CRF) is integrated to the network to enforce the proximity and similarity principles. Note that: (1) DeepLab is a supervised semantic segmentation method. It thus needs not only grouping annotation as our model does, but also group ID annotation, which is not used by our model and Edge-PG. This gives it an unfair advantage. (2) It performs grouping at the pixel level whilst both our model and Edge-FG do it at the stroke/segment level.

5.2 Results on Perceptual Grouping

Results on Seen Categories: In this experiment, the model are trained on the seen category training set and tested on the seen category testing set. From Table 1, we can see that: (i) Our model achieves the best performance across all 25 categories on each metric, except the VOI metric on face where our model is slightly inferior to DeepLab. The improvement on VOI is particularly striking indicating that the groups discovered by our model in each sketch are distinctive to each other. In contrast, the two compared models tend to split a semantic part into multiple groups resulting similar groups (see Fig. 4). (ii) Edge-PG is much worse than our method because it is based on hand-crafted features for only two principles, while our model implicitly learns the features and combination strategy based on end-to-end learning from human group annotation. (iii) Although DeepLab also employs a deep neural network and uses additional annotations, its result is no better than Edge-PG. This suggests that for sketch perceptual grouping, it is important to treat sketches as a set of strokes rather than pixels, as strokes already grouping pixels. These constraints are ignored by the DeepLab types of models designed for photo image segmentation.

Some examples of the grouping results are shown in Fig. 4. As expected, ignoring the stroke level grouping constraint on pixels, each stroke is often split into multiple groups by DeepLab [7]. Edge-PG [12] does not suffer from that problem. However, it suffers from the limitations on modelling only two principles. For example, to group the clock contour (second column) into one group, the closure principle needs to be used. It is also unable to model even the two principles effectively due to the limited expressive power of hand-crafted features: in the airplane example (first column), the two wings should be grouped together using the continuity principle, but broken into two by Edge-PG. In contrast, our model produces more consistent groupings using multiple principles dynamically. For instance, both DeepLab and our model successfully deploy the similarity principle to group the two legs of both the alarm clock (second column) and duck (third column) together. But DeepLab does so by explicitly encoding the principle in its CRF layer, while our model does it implicitly. In the cactus example (last column), to produce the correct grouping of those spikes, both continuity, similarity and less prevalent principles such as common fate need to be combined. Only our model is able to do that because it has implicitly learned to model all the principles used by humans to annotate the groupings.

Table 1. Comparative grouping results on seen categories.

Category	Ours			Edege-PG [12]			DeepLab [7]		
	VOI ↓	PRI ↑	SC ↑	VOI ↓	PRI ↑	SC ↑	VOI ↓	PRI ↑	SC ↑
Airplane	**0.58**	**0.88**	**0.78**	0.72	0.80	0.71	1.09	0.72	0.65
Alarm clock	**0.46**	**0.93**	**0.83**	0.59	0.84	0.73	0.86	0.80	0.70
Ambulance	**0.67**	**0.86**	**0.77**	1.35	0.67	0.60	1.19	0.71	0.63
Ant	**0.86**	**0.83**	**0.69**	1.32	0.68	0.62	1.38	0.69	0.60
Apple	**0.25**	**0.92**	**0.91**	0.54	0.88	0.79	0.82	0.83	0.72
Backpack	**0.57**	**0.88**	**0.79**	1.29	0.70	0.61	1.59	0.67	0.59
Basket	**0.76**	**0.84**	**0.74**	1.27	0.71	0.59	1.37	0.69	0.61
Butterfly	**0.83**	**0.76**	**0.65**	1.30	0.69	0.58	1.58	0.66	0.58
Cactus	**0.51**	**0.90**	**0.83**	0.86	0.82	0.71	0.90	0.79	0.68
Calculator	**0.50**	**0.86**	**0.83**	0.98	0.77	0.68	1.17	0.72	0.64
Camp fire	**0.28**	**0.95**	**0.91**	1.05	0.71	0.65	0.77	0.85	0.74
Candle	**0.89**	**0.78**	**0.69**	1.47	0.65	0.57	1.54	0.67	0.60
Coffee cup	**0.38**	**0.91**	**0.86**	0.85	0.83	0.68	0.98	0.79	0.66
Crab	**0.69**	**0.81**	**0.74**	1.29	0.69	0.56	1.58	0.67	0.60
Duck	**0.86**	**0.83**	**0.69**	0.95	0.74	0.68	1.63	0.65	0.57
Face	0.81	**0.84**	**0.74**	1.24	0.69	0.61	**0.80**	0.82	0.73
Ice-cream	**0.41**	**0.94**	**0.85**	0.79	0.82	0.71	1.40	0.68	0.62
Pig	**0.63**	**0.84**	**0.78**	1.55	0.63	0.50	0.98	0.77	0.67
Pineapple	**0.50**	**0.93**	**0.82**	0.63	0.83	0.72	1.05	0.74	0.65
Suitcase	**0.54**	**0.89**	**0.83**	0.58	0.82	0.75	1.10	0.73	0.64
Average	**0.59**	**0.87**	**0.79**	1.03	0.75	0.65	1.20	0.73	0.65

Table 2. Perceptual grouping results on unseen categories.

Category	Ours			Edge-PG [12]		
	VOI ↓	PRI ↑	SC ↑	VOI ↓	PRI ↑	SC ↑
Angel	**0.70**	**0.87**	**0.73**	1.19	0.69	0.60
Bulldozer	**0.81**	**0.85**	**0.73**	1.37	0.65	0.58
Drill	**0.67**	**0.78**	**0.77**	1.45	0.61	0.53
Flower	**0.39**	**0.90**	**0.84**	0.79	0.75	0.64
House	**0.46**	**0.91**	**0.83**	0.85	0.77	0.69
Average	**0.64**	**0.86**	**0.77**	1.13	0.69	0.61

Results on Unseen Categories: In this experiment, models learned using seen categories are tested directly on unseen categories without any fine-tuning. This experiment is thus designed to evaluate whether the grouper is indeed universal,

Fig. 4. Qualitative grouping results on seen categories.

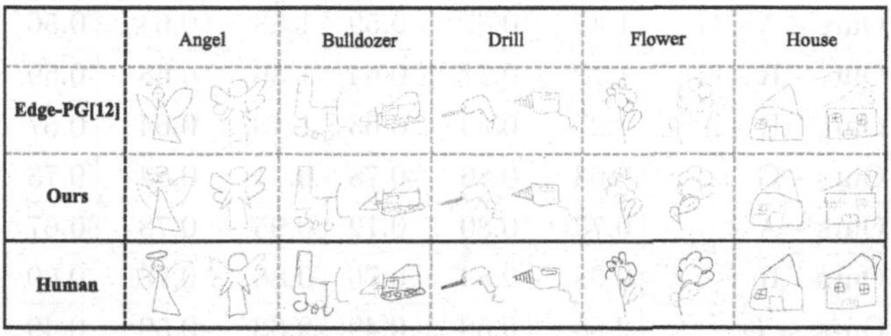

Fig. 5. Qualitative grouping results on unseen categories.

i.e., can be applied to any new object category. Note that as a supervised segmentation method, DeepLab cannot be applied here because each category has a unique set of group IDs. The results of our model and Edge-GP are shown in Table 2. It can been seen that our model outperforms Edge-GP by a big margin. Importantly, comparing Table 2 with Table 1, our model's performance on PRI and SC hardly changed. In contrast, the Edge-PG's performance on the unseen categories is clearly worse than that on the seen categories. This suggests that our grouper is more generalisable and universal. Some qualitative results are shown in Fig. 5. It again shows that the lack of powerful feature learning and limitation on only two principles contribute to the weaker results of Edge-GP.

Results on Unseen Dataset: To further demonstrate the generalisation ability of our universal grouper, we test the trained model on a different dataset. Specifically, we choose 10 categories from the dataset in [33] including 5 categories overlapping with our dataset and 5 new categories. Note that the sketches in this datasets are from the database proposed in [34], which are drawn without the 20 second constraint, thus exhibiting much more details with better quality in general. This dataset thus represents a different domain. Table 3 shows that our model again demonstrates better generalisation ability than Edge-PG.

Ablation Study: Our model is trained with a combination of generative and discriminative losses (Sect. 4.3). These include the local grouping loss $\mathcal{L}_A$, global grouping loss $\mathcal{L}_G$, reconstruction loss $\mathcal{L}_R$ and KL loss $\mathcal{L}_{KL}$. Among them, all but the KL loss can be removed, leading to six variants of our model, e.g., Ours - A - G is obtained by removing $\mathcal{L}_A$ and $\mathcal{L}_G$. In addition, we implement Ours +

Table 3. Compare Edge-PG [12] with ours on Edge-PG [12]'s datasets.

Method	VOI ↓	PRI ↑	SC ↑
Edge-PG [12]	1.69	0.62	0.53
Ours	**0.96**	**0.78**	**0.71**

Table 4. Performance of different variants of our model on seen and unseen categories.

Method	Seen categories			Unseen categories		
	VOI ↓	PRI ↑	SC ↑	VOI ↓	PRI ↑	**SC** ↑
Ours - A - G	1.45	0.65	0.59	1.53	0.64	0.56
Ours - R - G	1.12	0.71	0.64	1.36	0.68	0.59
Ours - R - A	1.27	0.69	0.63	1.48	0.64	0.57
Ours - G	0.63	0.86	0.78	0.71	0.84	0.73
Ours - A	0.75	0.80	0.72	0.95	0.78	0.67
Ours - R	0.68	0.83	0.76	0.86	0.78	0.69
Ours + l_2	2.68	0.58	0.49	2.63	0.59	0.49
Ours full model	**0.59**	**0.87**	**0.79**	**0.64**	**0.86**	**0.77**

l_2 which is having an l_2 loss on the predicted affinity matrix $\hat{G}$ w.r.t. the ground truth matrix G to examine the importance of having separate local and global grouping losses. The results are shown in Table 4. Clearly all three losses contribute to the performance of our model. The poorest result was obtained when an l_2 loss is added on the predicted affinity matrix, suggesting that balancing the local and global grouping losses is critical for learning a good grouper. We further show that the improvement of our full model over Ours - R on the unseen categories (0.64 vs 0.86) is bigger on the seen categories (0.59 vs. 0.68). This indicates that the generative loss helps the model generalise to unseen categories.

5.3 Applications on Sketch Synthesis and FG-SBIR

One application of our grouper is to use it as an abstraction model so that edge maps extracted from photos can be grouped and abstracted to synthesise human-like sketches. Figure 6 shows some examples of edge map grouping results and the synthesised sketches. It can be seen that our grouper is generalisable to photo edges and our abstraction method produces visually appealing sketches. The synthesised sketches are then used to train a state-of-the-art FG-SBIR model [19] without using any real human sketches. We use the largest FG-SBIR datasets QMUL Shoe-V2 and Chair-V2 [35]. We first compare with the same FG-SBIR model trained using synthesised sketches from the deep conditional GAN network in [32] (denoted as Scribbler). As can be seen in Table 5, our model performs much better. This suggests that our edge abstraction model, albeit simple, synthesises more realistic sketches from edge maps. We further compare with a recently proposed unsupervised FG-SBIR model LDSA [17] which is also based on abstracting photo edge maps to synthesise sketches. Table 5 shows that our model outperforms LDSA model by 5.71% and 3.63% on top 1 accuracy on Shoe-V2 and Chair-V2, respectively. The results are not far off the upper-bound which is obtained using the same FG-SBIR model trained with the real sketch-photo pairs in Shoe-V2 and Chair-V2. This shows that our method enables FG-SBIR to be used without the expensive collection of sketch-photo pairs.

Table 5. FG-SBIR performance on Shoe-V2 and Chair-V2 dataset

Method	Shoe-V2		Chair-V2	
	Top1	Top10	Top1	Top10
Scribbler [32]	8.86%	32.28%	31.27%	78.02%
LDSA [17]	21.17%	55.86%	41.80%	84.21%
Ours	**26.88%**	**61.86%**	**45.57%**	**88.61%**
Upper Bound	34.38%	79.43%	48.92%	90.71%

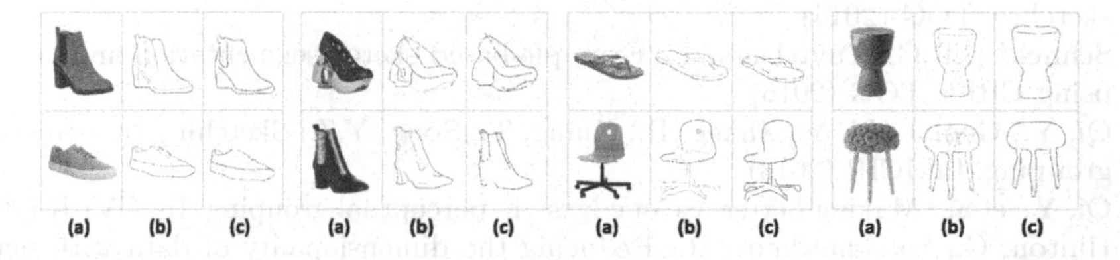

Fig. 6. Applying our grouper to synthesise abstract sketches from photo edge map. **(a)** columns show the photos; **(b)** columns give the edge maps extracted from the photos and the grouping results; **(c)** columns provide synthesised abstract sketches.

6 Conclusion

We have proposed an end-to-end sketch perceptual grouping model. This is made possible by collecting a new large-scale sketch grouping dataset SPG. Our grouper is trained with generative losses to make it generalisable to new object categories and datasets/domains. Two grouping losses were also formulated to balance the local and global grouping constraints. Extensive experiments showed that our model significantly outperforms existing groupers. We also demonstrated our grouper's application to sketch synthesis and FG-SBIR.

References

1. Wagemans, J., et al.: A century of gestalt psychology in visual perception: I. Perceptual grouping and figure-ground organization. Psychol. Bull. **138**(6), 1172–1217 (2012)
2. Wagemans, J.: A century of gestalt psychology in visual perception: II. Conceptual and theoretical foundations. Psychol. Bull. **138**(6), 1218–1252 (2012)
3. Wertheimer, M.: Laws of Organization in Perceptual Forms. Kegan Paul, Trench, Trubner & Company, London, England (1938)
4. Ren, X., Malik, J.: Learning a classification model for segmentation. In: ICCV (2003)
5. Xia, X., Kulis, B.: W-net: A deep model for fully unsupervised image segmentation. ArXiv e-prints (2017)
6. Wang, C., Yang, B., Liao, Y.: Unsupervised image segmentation using convolutional autoencoder with total variation regularization as preprocessing. In: ICASSP (2017)
7. Chen, L.C., Papandreou, G., Kokkinos, I., Murphy, K., Yuille, A.L.: Deeplab: Semantic image segmentation with deep convolutional nets, atrous convolution, and fully connected CRFs. arXiv:1606.00915 (2016)
8. Sun, Z., Wang, C., Zhang, L., Zhang, L.: Free hand-drawn sketch segmentation. In: Fitzgibbon, A., Lazebnik, S., Perona, P., Sato, Y., Schmid, C. (eds.) ECCV 2012. LNCS, vol. 7572, pp. 626–639. Springer, Heidelberg (2012). https://doi.org/10.1007/978-3-642-33718-5_45
9. Huang, Z., Fu, H., Lau, R.W.: Data-driven segmentation and labeling of freehand sketches. TOG (2014)
10. Schneider, R.G., Tuytelaars, T.: Example-based sketch segmentation and labeling using CRFs. TOG (2016)
11. Qi, Y., Guo, J., Li, Y., Zhang, H., Xiang, T., Song, Y.Z.: Sketching by perceptual grouping. In: ICIP (2013)
12. Qi, Y., et al.: Making better use of edges via perceptual grouping. In: CVPR (2015)
13. Hinton, G., Salakhutdinov, R.: Reducing the dimensionality of data with neural networks. Science **313**, 504–507 (2006)
14. Amir, A., Lindenbaum, M.: A generic grouping algorithm and its quantitative analysis. TPAMI **20**(2), 168–185 (1998)
15. Lun, Z., et al.: Learning to group discrete graphical patterns. TOG (2017)
16. Ha, D., Eck, D.: A neural representation of sketch drawings. arXiv preprint arXiv:1704.03477 (2017)
17. Muhammad, U.R., Song, Y.Z., Xiang, T., Hospedales, T.: Learning deep sketch abstraction. In: CVPR (2018)
18. Li, Y., Hospedales, T.M., Song, Y.Z., Gong, S.: Fine-grained sketch-based image retrieval by matching deformable part models. In: BMVC (2014)
19. Yu, Q., Liu, F., Song, Y.Z., Xiang, T., Hospedales, T.M., Loy, C.C.: Sketch me that shoe. In: CVPR (2016)
20. Song, J., Song, Y.Z., Xiang, T., Hospedales, T., Ruan, X.: Deep multi-task attribute-driven ranking for fine-grained sketch-based image retrieval. In: BMVC (2016)
21. Pang, K., Song, Y.Z., Xiang, T., Hospedales, T.M.: Cross-domain generative learning for fine-grained sketch-based image retrieval. In: BMVC (2017)
22. Hu, C., Li, D., Song, Y.Z., Xiang, T., Hospedales, T.: Sketch-a-classifier: Sketch-based photo classifier generation. In: CVPR (2018)

23. Song, J., Qian, Y., Song, Y.Z., Xiang, T., Hospedales, T.: Deep spatial-semantic attention for fine-grained sketch-based image retrieval. In: ICCV (2017)
24. Yu, Q., Yang, Y., Liu, F., Song, Y.Z., Xiang, T., Hospedales, T.M.: Sketch-a-net: A deep neural network that beats humans. IJCV (2017)
25. Bowman, S.R., Vilnis, L., Vinyals, O., Dai, A.M., Jozefowicz, R., Bengio, S.: Generating sentences from a continuous space. Computer Science (2015)
26. Kingma, D.P., Welling, M.: Auto-encoding variational bayes. ArXiv e-prints (2013)
27. Graves, A.: Generating sequences with recurrent neural networks. arXiv preprint arXiv:1308.0850 (2013)
28. Schuster, M., Paliwal, K.K.: Bidirectional recurrent neural networks. TSP **45**, 2673–2681 (1997)
29. Yang, J., Parikh, D., Batra, D.: Joint unsupervised learning of deep representations and image clusters. In: CVPR (2016)
30. Kingma, D., Ba, J.: Adam: A method for stochastic optimization. arXiv preprint arXiv:1412.6980 (2014)
31. Arbelez, P., Maire, M., Fowlkes, C., Malik, J.: Contour detection and hierarchical image segmentation. TPAMI **33**, 898–916 (2011)
32. Sangkloy, P., Lu, J., Fang, C., Yu, F., Hays, J.: Scribbler: Controlling deep image synthesis with sketch and color. In: CVPR (2017)
33. Qi, Y., Guo, J., Song, Y.Z., Xiang, T., Zhang, H., Tan, Z.H.: Im2sketch: Sketch generation by unconflicted perceptual grouping. Neurocomputing **165**, 338–349 (2015)
34. Eitz, M., Hays, J., Alexa, M.: How do humans sketch objects? TOG (2012)
35. Yu, Q., Song, Y.Z., Xiang, T., Hospedales, T.M.: SketchX - Shoe/Chair fine-grained SBIR dataset (2017). http://sketchx.eecs.qmul.ac.uk

Imagine This! Scripts to Compositions to Videos

Tanmay Gupta[1(✉)], Dustin Schwenk[2], Ali Farhadi[2,3], Derek Hoiem[1], and Aniruddha Kembhavi[2]

[1] University of Illinois Urbana-Champaign, Champaign, USA
tgupta6@illinois.edu
[2] Allen Institute for Artificial Intelligence (AI2), Seattle, USA
[3] University of Washington, Seattle, USA

Abstract. Imagining a scene described in natural language with realistic layout and appearance of entities is the ultimate test of spatial, visual, and semantic world knowledge. Towards this goal, we present the **C**omposition, **R**etrieval **a**nd **F**usion Ne**t**work (CRAFT), a model capable of learning this knowledge from video-caption data and applying it while generating videos from novel captions. CRAFT explicitly predicts a temporal-layout of mentioned entities (characters and objects), retrieves spatio-temporal entity segments from a video database and fuses them to generate scene videos. Our contributions include sequential training of components of CRAFT while *jointly* modeling layout and appearances, and losses that encourage learning compositional representations for retrieval. We evaluate CRAFT on *semantic fidelity* to caption, *composition consistency*, and *visual quality*. CRAFT outperforms direct pixel generation approaches and generalizes well to unseen captions and to unseen video databases with no text annotations. We demonstrate CRAFT on FLINTSTONES (FLINTSTONES is available at https://prior.allenai.org/projects/craft), a new richly annotated video-caption dataset with over 25000 videos. For a glimpse of videos generated by CRAFT, see https://youtu.be/688Vv86n0z8.

1 Introduction

Consider the scene description: *Fred is wearing a blue hat and talking to Wilma in the living room. Wilma then sits down on a couch.* Picturing the scene in our mind requires the knowledge of plausible locations, appearances, actions, and interactions of characters and objects being described, as well as an ability to understand and translate the natural language description into a plausible visual instantiation. In this work, we introduce Semantic Scene Generation (SSG), the task of generating complex scene videos from rich natural language descriptions which requires jointly modeling the layout and appearances of entities mentioned

T. Gupta—Majority of this work was done during an internship at AI2 and is partly supported by the Office of Naval Research grant ONR MURI N00014-16-1-2007.

V. Ferrari et al. (Eds.): ECCV 2018, LNCS 11212, pp. 610–626, 2018.
https://doi.org/10.1007/978-3-030-01237-3_37

in the description. SSG models are trained using a densely annotated video dataset with scene descriptions and entity bounding boxes. During inference, the models must generate videos for novel descriptions (unseen during training) (Fig. 1).

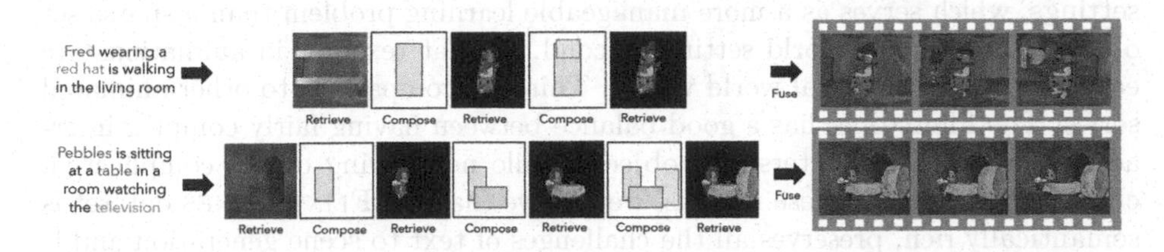

Fig. 1. Given a novel description, CRAFT sequentially composes a scene layout and retrieves entities from a video database to create complex scene videos.

Modelling the layout and appearances of entities for descriptions like the one above poses several challenges: (a) **Entity Recall** - the video must contain the relevant characters (Fred, Wilma), objects (blue hat, couch) and background (setting that resembles a living room); (b) **Layout Feasibility** - characters and objects must be placed at plausible locations and scales (Fred, Wilma and the couch should be placed on the ground plane, the hat must lie on top of Fred's head); (c) **Appearance Fidelity** - entity appearance, which may be affected by identity, pose, action, attributes and layout, should respect the scene description; (d) **Interaction Consistency** - appearance of characters and objects must be *consistent with each other* given the described, sometimes implicit, interaction (Fred and Wilma should face each other as do people when they talk to each other); (f) **Language Understanding** - the system must be able to understand and translate a natural language description into a plausible visual instantiation.

Currently, the dominant approaches to conditional generation of visual data from text rely on directly learning distributions in a *high dimensional pixel space*. While these approaches have shown impressive results for aligned images of objects (faces, birds, flowers, etc.), they are often inadequate for addressing the above challenges, due to the *combinatorial explosion* of the image space arising from multiple characters and objects with significant appearance variations arranged in a large number of possible layouts. In contrast, our proposed **C**omposition, **R**etrieval **a**nd **F**usion Network (CRAFT) explicitly models the spatio-temporal layout of characters and objects in the scene jointly with entity appearances. Unlike pixel generation approaches, our appearance model is based on text to entity segment retrieval from a video database. Spatio-temporal segments are extracted from the retrieved videos and fused together to generate the final video. The layout composition and entity retrieval work in a sequential manner which is determined by the language input. Factorization of our model into composition and retrieval stages alleviates the need to directly model pixel spaces, results in an architecture that exploits location and appearance contextual cues, and renders an interpretable output.

Towards the goal of SSG, we introduce FLINTSTONES, a densely annotated dataset based on *The Flintstones* animated series, consisting of over 25000 videos, each 75 frames long. FLINTSTONES has several advantages over using a random sample of internet videos. First, in a closed world setting such as a television series, the most frequent characters are present in a wide variety of settings, which serves as a more manageable learning problem than a sparse set obtained in an open world setting. Second, the flat textures in animations are easier to model than real world videos. Third, in comparison to other animated series, The Flintstones has a good balance between having fairly complex interactions between characters and objects while not having overly complicated, cluttered scenes. For these reasons, we believe that the FLINTSTONES dataset is semantically rich, preserves all the challenges of text to scene generation and is a good stepping stone towards real videos. FLINTSTONES consists of an 80-10-10 train-val-test split. The train and val sets are used for learning and model selection respectively. Test captions serve as novel descriptions to generate videos at test time. To quantitatively evaluate our model, we use two sets of metrics. The first measures *semantic fidelity* of the generated video to the desired description using entity noun, adjective, and verb recalls. The second measures *composition consistency*, *i.e.* the consistency of the appearances, poses and layouts of entities with respect to other entities in the video and the background.

We use FLINTSTONES to evaluate CRAFT and provide a detailed ablation analysis. CRAFT outperforms baselines that generate pixels directly from captions as well as a whole video retrieval approach (as opposed to modeling entities). It generalizes well to unseen captions as well as unseen videos in the target database. Our quantitative and qualitative results show that for simpler descriptions, CRAFT exploits location and appearance contextual cues and outputs videos that have consistent layouts and appearances of described entities. However, there is tremendous scope for improvement. CRAFT can fail catastrophically for complex descriptions (containing large number of entities, specially infrequent ones). The adjective and verb recalls are also fairly low. We believe SSG on FLINTSTONES presents a challenging problem for future research.

2 Related Work

Generative Models. Following pioneering work on Variational Autoencoders [15] and Generative Adversarial Networks [9], there has been tremendous interest in generative modelling of visual data in a high dimensional pixel space. Early approaches focused on unconditional generation [2,4,10,24], whereas recent works have explored models conditioned on simple textual inputs describing objects [20,26,27,33,34]. While the visual quality of images generated by these models has been steadily improving [14,22], success stories have been limited to generating images of aligned objects (e.g. faces, birds, flowers), often training one model per object class. In contrast, our work deals with generating complex scenes which requires modelling the layout and appearances of multiple entities in the scene.

Of particular relevance is the work by Hong *et al.* [12] who first generate a coarse semantic layout of bounding boxes, refine that to segmentation masks and then generate an image using an image-to-image translation model [6,13]. A limitation of this approach is that it assumes a fixed number of object classes (80 in their experiments) and struggles with the usual challenge of modeling high dimensional pixel spaces such as generating coherent entities. Formulating appearance generation in terms of entity retrieval from a database allows our model to scale to a large number of entity categories, guarantee intra-entity coherence and allows us to focus on the semantic aspects of scene generation and inter-entity consistency. The retrieval approach also lends itself to generating videos without significant modification. There have been attempts at extending GANs for unconditional [30,31] as well as text conditional [18,21] video generation, but quality of generated videos is usually worse than that of GAN generated images unless used in very restrictive settings. A relevant generative modelling approach is by Kwak *et al.* [17] who proposed a model in which parts of the image are generated sequentially and combined using alpha blending. However, this work does not condition on text and has not been demonstrated on complex scenes. Another relevant body of work is by Zitnick *et al.* [35–37] who compose static images from descriptions with clipart images using a Conditional Random Field formulation.

To control the structure of the output image, a growing body of literature conditions image generation on a wide variety of inputs ranging from keypoints [25] and sketches [19] to semantic segmentation maps [13]. In contrast to these approaches which condition on *provided* location, our model *generates* a plausible scene layout and then conditions entity retrieval on this layout.

Phrase Grounding and Caption-Image Retrieval. The entity retriever in CRAFT is related to caption based image retrieval models. The caption-image embedding space is typically learned by minimizing a ranking loss such as a triplet loss [7,8,8,16,32]. Phrase grounding [23] is another closely related task where the goal is to localize a region in an image described by a phrase.

One of our contributions is enriching the semantics of embeddings learned through triplet loss by simultaneously minimizing an auxiliary classification loss based on noun, adjective and verb words associated with an entity in the text description. This is similar in principle to [29] where auxiliary autoencoding losses were used in addition to a primary binary prediction loss to learn robust visual semantic embeddings. Learning shared representations across multiple related tasks is a key concept in multitask learning [5,11].

3 Model

Figure 2 presents an overview of **C**omposition, **R**etrieval **a**nd **F**usion Network which consists of three parts: *Layout Composer*, *Entity Retriever*, and *Background Retriever*. Each is a neural network that is trained independently using ground truth supervision. During inference, CRAFT begins with an empty video and adds entities in the scene sequentially based on the order of appearance in the description. At each step, the *Layout Composer* predicts a location and scale for an entity given the text and the video constructed so far. Then, conditioned on the predicted location, text, and the partially constructed video, the *Entity Retriever* produces a query embedding that is looked up against the embeddings of entities in the target video database. The entity is cropped from the retrieved video and placed at the predicted location and scale in the video being generated. Alternating between the *Layout Composer* and *Entity Retriever* allows the model to condition the layout of entities on the appearance and vice versa. Similar to *Entity Retriever*, the *Background Retriever* produces a query embedding for the desired scene from text and retrieves the closest background video from the target database. The retrieved spatio-temporal entity segments and background are fused to generate the final video. We now present the notation used in the rest of the paper, followed by architecture and training details for the three components.

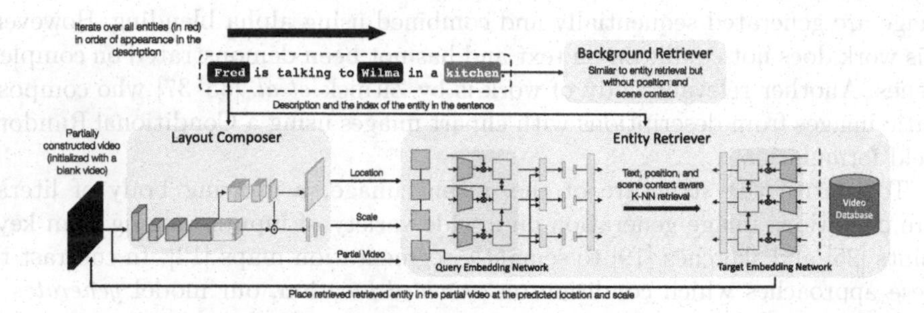

Fig. 2. Overview of **C**omposition, **R**etrieval **a**nd **F**usion Ne**t**work (CRAFT), consisting of three parts: *Layout Composer*, *Entity Retriever* and *Background Retriever*. CRAFT begins with an empty video and sequentially adds entities mentioned in the input description at locations and scales predicted by the Layout Composer.

Caption	
T	Caption with length $\|T\|$
$\{E_i\}_{i=1}^n$	n entities in T in order of appearance
$\{e_i\}_{i=1}^n$	entity noun positions in T
Video	
F	number of frames in a video
$\{(l_i, s_i)\}_{i=1}^n$	position of entities in the video
l_i	entity bounding box at each frame ($\{(x_{if}, y_{if}, w_{if}, h_{if})\}_{f=1}^F$)
s_i	entity pixel segmentation mask at each frame
V_{i-1}	partially constructed video with entities $\{E_j\}_{j=1}^{i-1}$
$V\ (= V_n)$	full video containing all entities
$\{(V^{[m]}, T^{[m]})\}_{m=1}^M$	training data points, where M = number of data points

3.1 Layout Composer

The layout composer is responsible for generating a plausible layout of the scene consisting of the locations and scales of each character and object mentioned in the scene description. Jointly modeling the locations of all entities in a scene presents fundamentally unique challenges for spatial knowledge representation beyond existing language-guided localization tasks. Predicting plausible locations and scales for objects not yet in an image requires a significant amount of *spatial knowledge* about people and objects, in contrast to text based object localization which relies heavily on appearance cues. This includes knowledge like – a hat goes on top of a person's head, a couch goes under the person sitting on it, a person being talked to faces the person speaking instead of facing away, tables are short and wide while standing people are tall and thin, etc.

Figure 3 presents a schematic for the layout composer. Given the varying number of entities across videos, the layout composer is setup to run in a sequential manner over the set of distinct entities mentioned in a given description. At each step, a text embedding of the desired entity along with a partially constructed video (consisting of entities fused into the video at previous steps) are input to the model which predicts distributions for the location and scale of the desired entity.

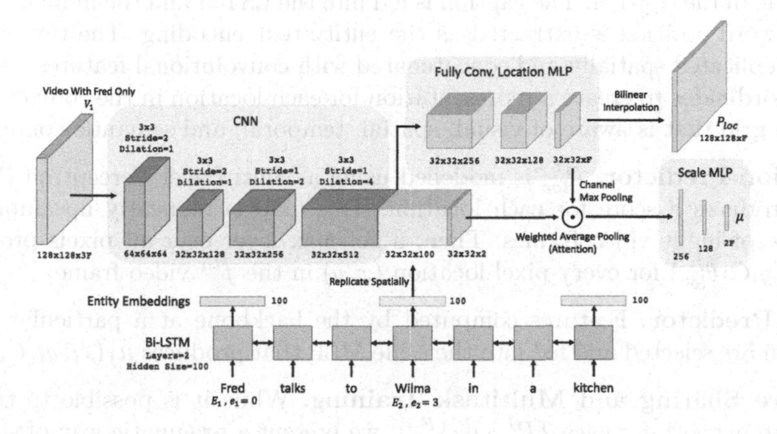

Fig. 3. Layout Composer is run sequentially through the set of entities in the description, predicting the distributions for the location and scale of the desired entity.

The layout composer models $P(l_i|V_{i-1}, T, e_i; \theta_{loc}, \theta_{sc})$, the conditional distribution of the location and scale (width and height normalized by image size) of the ith entity given the text, entity noun position in tokenized text, and the partial video with previous entities. Let C_i denote the conditioning information, (V_{i-1}, T, e_i). We factorize the position distribution into location and scale components as follows:

$$P(l_i|C_i; \theta_{loc}, \theta_{sc}) = \prod_{f=1}^{F} P^f_{loc}(x_{if}, y_{if}|C_i; \theta^f_{loc}) \cdot P^f_{sc}(w_{if}, h_{if}|x_{if}, y_{if}, C_i; \theta^f_{sc}) \quad (1)$$

$\theta_{loc} = \{\theta_{loc}^f\}_{f=1}^F$ and $\theta_{sc} = \{\theta_{sc}^f\}_{f=1}^F$ are learnable parameters. P_{loc}^f is modelled using a network that takes C_i as input and produces a distribution over all pixel locations for the fth image frame. We model P_{sc}^f using a Gaussian distribution whose mean μ_f and covariance Σ_f are predicted by a network given (x_i, y_i, C_i). Parameters θ_{loc} and θ_{sc} are learned from ground truth position annotations by minimizing the following maximum likelihood estimation loss:

$$\sum_{m=1}^{M}\sum_{i=1}^{n^{[m]}}\sum_{f=1}^{F}\Big[-\log(P_{loc}^f(x_{if}^{[m]}, y_{if}^{[m]}|C_i^{[m]};\theta_{loc}^f)) + 0.5\cdot\log(\det(\Sigma(x_{if}, y_{if}, C_i;\theta_{sc}^f)))+$$
$$0.5\cdot(z_{if}^{[m]} - \mu_f(D_i^{[m]};\theta_{sc}^f))^T\Sigma_f{}^{-1}(z_{if}^{[m]} - \mu_f(D_i^{[m]};\theta_{sc}^f)) + \log(2\pi)\Big] \quad (2)$$

where $z_{if} = [w_{if}; h_{if}]$ & $D_i^{[m]} = (x_i^{[m]}, y_i^{[m]}, C_i^{[m]})$. For simplicity, we manually set and freeze Σ to an isometric diagonal covariance matrix with variance of 0.005.

Feature Computation Backbone. The location and scale predictors have an identical feature computation backbone comprising of a CNN and a bidirectional LSTM. The CNN encodes V_{i-1} (8 sub-sampled frames concatenated along the channel dimension) as a set of convolutional feature maps which capture appearance and positions of previous entities in the scene. The LSTM is used to encode the entity E_i for which the prediction is to be made along with semantic context available in the caption. The caption is fed into the LSTM and the hidden output at e_i^{th} word position is extracted as the entity text encoding. The text encoding is replicated spatially and concatenated with convolutional features and 2-D grid coordinates to create a representation for each location in the convolutional feature grid that is aware of visual, spatial, temporal, and semantic context.

Location Predictor. P_{loc}^f is modelled using a Multi Layer Perceptron (MLP) that produces a score for each location. This map is bilinearly upsampled to the size of input video frames. Then, a softmax layer over all pixels produces $P_{loc}^f(x, y|C;\theta_{loc}^f)$ for every pixel location (x, y) in the fth video frame.

Scale Predictor. Features computed by the backbone at a particular (x, y) location are selected and fed into the scale MLP that produces $\mu_f(x_i, y_i, C_i;\theta_{sc}^f)$.

Feature Sharing and Multitask Training. While it is possible to train a separate network for each $\{P_{loc}^f, \mu_f\}_{f=1}^F$, we present a pragmatic way of sharing features and computation for different frames and also between the location and scale networks. To share features and computation across frames, the location network produces F probability maps in a single forward pass. This is equivalent to sharing all layers across all P_{loc}^f nets except for the last layer of the MLP that produces location scores. Similarly, all the μ_f nets are also combined into a single network. We refer to the combined networks by P_{loc} and μ.

In addition, we also share features across the location and scale networks. First, we share the feature computation backbone, the output from which is then passed into location and scale specific layers. Second, we use a soft-attention mechanism to select likely positions for feeding into the scale layers. This conditions the scale prediction on the plausible locations of the entity. We combine the

F spatial maps into a single attention map through max pooling. This attention map is used to perform weighted average pooling on backbone features and then fed into the scale MLP. Note that this is a differentiable greedy approximation to find the most likely location (by taking argmax of spatial probability maps) and scale (directly using output of μ, the mode for a gaussian distribution) in a single forward pass. To keep training consistent with inference, we use the soft-attention mechanism instead of feeding ground-truth locations into μ.

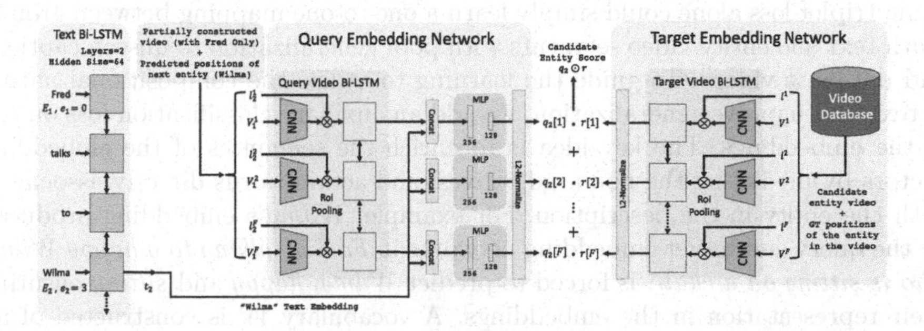

Fig. 4. Entity Retriever retrieves spatio-temporal patches from a target database that match entity description as encoded by the query embedding network.

3.2 Entity Retriever

The task of the entity retriever is to find a spatio-temporal patch within a target database that matches an entity in the description *and* is consistent with the video constructed thus far – the video with all previous entities retrieved and placed in the locations predicted by the layout network. We adopt an embedding based lookup approach for entity retrieval. This presents several challenges beyond traditional image retrieval tasks. Not only does the retrieved entity need to match the semantics of the description but it also needs to respect the implicit relational constraints or context imposed by the appearance and locations of other entities. E.g. for *Fred is talking to Wilma*, it is not sufficient to retrieve *a Wilma*, but one who is also facing in the right direction, i.e. towards *Fred*.

The Entity Retriever is shown in Fig. 4 and consists of two parts: (i) query embedding network Q, and (ii) target embedding network R. Q and R are learned using the query-target pairs $\langle(T^{[m]}, e_i^{[m]}, l_i^{[m]}, V_{i-1}^{[m]}), (V^{[m]}, l_i^{[m]}, s_i^{[m]})\rangle_{i,m}$ in the training data. For clarity, we abbreviate $Q(T^{[m]}, e_i^{[m]}, l_i^{[m]} V_{i-1}^{[m]})$ as $q_i^{[m]}$ and $R(V^{[m]}, l_i^{[m]}, s_i^{[m]})$ as $r_i^{[m]}$. At each training iteration, we sample a mini-batch of B pairs without replacement and compute embeddings $\{(q_{i_b}^{[m_b]}, r_{i_b}^{[m_b]})\}_{b=1}^{B}$ where q and r are each sequence of F embeddings corresponding to F video frames. The model is trained using a triplet loss computed on *all possible* triplets in the mini-batch. Let δ_b denote the set of all indices from 1 to B except b. The loss can then be defined as

$$\mathcal{L}_{triplet} = \frac{1}{B \cdot (B-1)} \sum_{b=1}^{B} \sum_{b^- \in \delta_b} \Big[\max(0, \gamma + q_{i_b}^{[m_b]} \odot r_{i_{b^-}}^{[m_{b^-}]} - q_{i_b}^{[m_b]} \odot r_{i_b}^{[m_b]}) + \max(0, \gamma + q_{i_{b^-}}^{[m_{b^-}]} \odot r_{i_b}^{[m_b]} - q_{i_b}^{[m_b]} \odot r_{i_b}^{[m_b]}) \Big] \quad (3)$$

where $q \odot r = \frac{1}{F} \sum_{f=1}^{F} q[f] \cdot r[f]$ is the average dot product between corresponding query and target frame embeddings. We use a margin of $\gamma = 0.1$.

Auxiliary Multi-label Classification Loss. We found that models trained using triplet loss alone could simply learn a one-to-one mapping between ground truth text and entity video segments with poor generalization to unseen captions and database videos. To guide the learning to utilize the compositional nature of text and improve generalization, we add an auxiliary classification loss on top of the embeddings. The key idea is to enrich the semantics of the embedding vectors by predicting the noun, adjectives, and action words directly associated with the entity in the description. For example, *Wilma*'s embedding produced by the query and target embedding networks in *Fred is talking to a happy Wilma who is sitting on a chair.* is forced to predict *Wilma*, *happy* and *sitting* ensuring their representation in the embeddings. A vocabulary $\mathcal{W}$ is constructed of all nouns, adjectives and verbs appearing in the training data. Then for each sample in the mini-batch, an MLP is used as a multi-label classifier to predict associated words from the query and target embeddings. Note that a single MLP is used to make these noun, adjective and verb predictions on *both* query and target embeddings.

Query Embedding Network (Q). Similar to the layout composer's feature computation backbone, Q consists of a CNN to independently encode every frame of V_{i-1} and an LSTM to encode (T, e_i) which are concatenated together along with a 2-D coordinate grid to get per-frame feature maps. However, unlike layout composer, the query embedding network also needs to be conditioned on the position l_i where entity E_i is to be inserted in V_{i-1}. To get location and scale specific query embeddings, we use a simplified RoIAlign (RoIPool with RoI quantization and bilinear interpolation) mechanism to crop out the per-frame feature maps using the corresponding bounding box l_i^f and scaling it to a 7×7 receptive field. The RoIAlign features are then averaged along the spatial dimensions to get the vector representations for each time step independently. An LSTM applied over the sequence of these embeddings is used to capture temporal context. The hidden output of the LSTM at each time step is normalized and used as the frame query embedding $q[f]$.

Target Embedding Network (R). Since during inference, R needs to embed entities in the target database which do not have text annotations, it does not use T as an input. Thus, R is similar to Q but without the LSTM to encode the text. In our experiments we found that using 2-D coordinate features in both query and target networks made the network susceptible to ignoring all other features since it provides an easy signal for matching ground truth query-target pairs during training. This in turn leads to poor generalization. Thus, R has no 2-D coordinate features.

3.3 Background Retriever

The task of the background retriever is to find a background scene that matches the setting described in the description. To construct a database of backgrounds without characters in them, we remove characters from videos (given bounding boxes) and perform hole filling using PatchMatch [3]. The background retriever model is similar to the entity retriever with two main differences. First, since the whole background scene is retrieved instead of entity segments, the conditioning on position is removed from both query and database embedding networks replacing RoI pooling with global average pooling. Second, while ideally we would like scene and entity retrieval to be conditioned on each other, for simplicity we leave this to future work and currently treat them independently. These modifications essentially reduce the query embedding network to a text Bi-LSTM whose output at the background word location in the description is used as the query embedding, and the target embedding network to a video Bi-LSTM without RoI pooling. The model is trained using just the triplet loss.

4 The Flintstones Dataset

Composition. The FLINTSTONES dataset is composed of 25184 densely annotated video clips derived from the animated sitcom *The Flintstones.* Clips are chosen to be 3 seconds (75 frames) long to capture relatively small action sequences, limit the number of sentences needed to describe them and avoid scene and shot changes. Clip annotations contain clip's characters, setting, and objects being interacted with marked in text as well as their bounding boxes in all frames. FLINTSTONES has a 80-10-10 train-val-test split[1].

Clip Annotation. Dense annotations are obtained in a multi-step process: identification and localization of characters in keyframes, identification of the scene setting, scene captioning, object annotation, and entity tracking to provide annotations for all frames. The dataset also contains segmentation masks for characters and objects. First, a rough segmentation mask is produced by using SLIC [1] followed by hierarchical merging. This mask is then used to initialize GrabCut [28], which further refines the segmentation. The dataset also contains a clean background for each clip. Foreground characters and objects are excised, and the resulting holes are filled using PatchMatch [3].

5 Experiments

5.1 Layout Composer Evaluation

Training. We use the Adam optimizer (learning rate = 0.001, decay factor = 0.5 per epoch, weight decay = 0.0001) and a batch size of 32.

[1] See https://prior.allenai.org/projects/craft for more details on dataset split, annotation visualization, and dataset statistics.

Metrics. We evaluate layout composer using 2 metrics: (a) negative log-likelihood (NLL) of ground truth (GT) entity positions under the predicted distribution, and (b) average normalized pixel distance (coordinates normalized by image height and width) of the ground truth from the most likely predicted entity location. While NLL captures both location and scale, pixel distance only measures location accuracy. We report metrics on unseen test descriptions using ground truth locations and appearances for previous entities in the partial video.

Table 1. Layout Composer Analysis. Evaluation of our model (last row) and ablations on test set. First row provides theoretically computed values assuming a uniform location distribution while making no assumptions about the scale distribution.

Text	Scene context	2D Coord. grid	Dil. conv	NLL	Pixel dist.
Uniform Distribution				>9.704	>0.382
✗	✓	✓	✓	9.845	0.180
✓	✗	✓	✓	8.167	0.185
✓	✓	✗	✓	8.250	0.287
✓	✓	✓	✗	7.780	0.156
✓	✓	✓	✓	**7.636**	**0.148**

Feature Ablation. The ablation study in Table 1 shows that the layout composer benefits from each of the 3 input features – text, scene context (partial video), and 2D coordinate grid. The significant drop in NLL without text features indicates the importance of entity identity, especially in predicting scale. The lack of spatial awareness in convolutional feature maps without the 2D coordinate grid causes pixel distance to approximately double. The performance drop on removing scene context is indicative of the relevance of knowing *what* entities are *where* in the scene in predicting the location of next entity. Finally, replacing vanilla convolutions by dilated convolutions increases the spatial receptive field without increasing the number of parameters improves performance, which corroborates the usefulness of scene context in layout prediction.

5.2 Entity Retriever Evaluation.

Training. We use the Adam optimizer (learning rate = 0.001, decay factor = 0.5 every 10 epochs) and a batch size of 30.

Metrics. To evaluate semantic fidelity of retrieved entities to the query caption, we measure noun, adjective, and verb recalls (@1 and @10) averaged across entities in the test set. The captions are automatically parsed to identify nouns, adjectives and verbs associated with each entity both in the query captions and target database (using GT database captions for evaluation only). Note that captions often contain limited adjective and verb information. For example, a *red hat* in the video may only be referred to as a *hat* in the caption, and *Fred standing and talking* may be described as *Fred is talking.* We also do not take synonyms (*talking-speaking*) and hypernyms (*person-woman*) into account. Thus the proposed metric underestimates performance of the entity retriever.

Feature Ablation. Table 2 shows that text and location features are critical to noun, adjective and verb recall[2]. Scene context only marginally affects noun recall but causes significant drop in adjective and verb recalls.

Table 2. Entity retriever feature ablation. Top-1 and top-10 recalls of our model (last row) and ablations while generating videos for unseen test captions.

QueryFeatures			Recall@1			Recall@10		
Text	Context	Location	Noun	Adj.	Verb	Noun	Adj.	Verb
✗	✓	✓	24.88	3.04	9.48	55.22	19.39	37.18
✓	✗	✓	60.54	9.5	11.2	**77.71**	39.92	43.58
✓	✓	✗	56.14	8.56	11.34	73.03	39.35	41.48
✓	✓	✓	**61.19**	**12.36**	**14.77**	75.98	**47.72**	**46.86**

Table 3. Entity retriever loss ablation. Top-1 and top-10 recalls of our model (last row) and ablations while generating videos for unseen test captions.

	Auxiliary Loss		Recall@1			Recall@10		
Triplet	Query	Target	Noun	Adj.	Verb	Noun	Adj.	Verb
✗	✓	✓	35.75	7.79	8.83	63.62	43.35	33.12
✓	✗	✓	51.68	3.8	8.66	67.86	25.28	39.46
✓	✓	✗	50.54	4.94	9.94	66.36	28.52	39.5
✓	✗	✗	48.59	3.04	9.34	65.64	20.15	37.95
✓	✓	✓	**61.19**	**12.36**	**14.77**	**75.98**	**47.72**	**46.86**

Table 4. Generalization to Unseen Database Videos. Retrieval results for CRAFT when queried against seen videos vs unseen videos.

Video Database	Recall@1			Recall@10		
	Noun	Adj.	Verb	Noun	Adj.	Verb
Seen (Train)	61.19	12.36	14.77	75.98	47.72	46.86
Unseen (Test)	50.52	11.98	10.4	69.1	41.25	42.57

[2] For context, most frequent entity prediction baselines are on our project page.

Effect of Auxiliary Loss. Table 3 shows that triplet loss alone does significantly worse than in combination with auxiliary classification loss. Adding the auxiliary classification loss on either query or target embeddings improves over triplet only but is worse than using all three. Interestingly, using both auxiliary losses outperforms triplet loss with a single auxiliary loss (and triplet only) on adjective and verb recall. This strongly suggests the benefits of multi-task training in entity retrieval.

Background Retriever. Similar to the entity recall evaluation, we computed a top-1 background recall of 57.5 for CRAFT.

Generalization to Unseen Videos. A key advantage of the embedding based text to entity video retrieval approach over text only methods is that the embedding approach can use any unseen video databases without any text annotations, potentially in entirely new domains (eg. learning from synthetic video caption datasets and applying the knowledge to generate real videos). However, this requires a model that generalizes well to unseen captions as well as unseen videos. In Table 4 we compare entity recall when using the train set (seen) videos as the target database vs using the test set (unseen) video as the target database.

OHEM vs All Mini-Batch Triplets. We experimented with online hard example mining (OHEM) where negative samples that most violate triplet constraints are used in the loss. All triplets achieved similar or higher top-1 noun, adjective and verb recall than OHEM when querying against seen videos (1.8, 75.3, 8.5% relative gain) and unseen videos (1.7, 42.8, −5.0% relative gain).

Modelling Whole Video vs Entities. A key motivation to composing a scene from entities is the combinatorial nature of complex scenes. To illustrate this point we compare CRAFT to a text-to-text based whole video retrieval baseline. For a given test caption, we return a video in the database whose caption has the highest BLEU-1 score. This approach performs much worse than our model except on verb recall (BLEU: 49.57, 5.18, 26.64; Ours: 62.3, 21.7, 16.0). This indicates that novel captions often do not find a match in the target database with all entities and their attributes present in the same video. However, it is more likely that each entity and attribute combination appears in some video in the database. Note that text-to-text matching also prevents extension to unseen video databases without text annotations.

5.3 Human Evaluation

Metrics. In addition to the automated recall metrics which capture semantic fidelity of the generated videos to the captions, we run a human evaluation study to estimate the *compositional consistency* of entities in the scene (given the description) and the overall *visual quality* (independent of the description). The consistency metric requires humans to rate each entity in the video on a 0-4 scale on three aspects: (a) *position* in the scene, (b) *size* relative to other entities or the background, and (c) appearance and consistency of described *interactions* with other entities in the scene. The visual quality metric measures the aesthetic and realism of the generated scenes on a 0-4 scale along three axes: (a) *foreground quality*, (b) *background quality*, and (c) *sharpness*. See supplementary material for the design of these experiments.

Table 5. Human evaluation to estimate consistency and quality of generated videos.

	Composition consistency			Visual quality		
	Position	Rel. Size	Interact.	FG	BG	Sharpness
Pixel Generation L1	0.69	0.65	0.55	0.96	1.44	1.07
Ours (GT Position)	1.69	1.69	1.34	1.49	1.65	**2.16**
Ours	**1.78**	**1.86**	**1.46**	**1.98**	**1.95**	1.82

Modelling Pixels vs Retrieval. We experimented extensively with text conditioned whole video generation using models with and without adversarial losses and obtained poor results. Since generative models tend to work better on images with single entities, we swapped out the target embedding network in the entity retriever by a generator. Given the query embedding at each of the F time steps, the generator produces an appearance image and a segmentation mask. The model is trained using an $L1$ loss between the masked appearance image and the masked ground truth image, and an $L1$ loss between the generated and ground truth masks. See supplementary material for more details. This baseline produced blurry results with recognizable colors and shapes for most common characters like *Fred, Wilma, Barney,* and *Betty* at best. We also tried GAN and VAE based approaches and got only slightly less blur. Table 5 shows that this model performs poorly on the Visual Quality metric compared to CRAFT. Moreover, since the visual quality of the generated previous entities affects the performance of the layout composer, this also translates into poor ratings on the composition consistency metric. Since the semantic fidelity metrics can not be computed for this pixel generation approach, we ran a human evaluation to compare this model to ours. Humans were asked to mark nouns, adjectives and verbs in the sentence missing in the generated video. CRAFT significantly outperformed the pixel generation approach on noun, adjective, and verb recall (CRAFT 61.0, 54.5, 67.8, L1: 37.8, 45.9, 48.1) (Fig. 5).

Joint vs Independent Modelling of Layout. We compare CRAFT to a model that uses the same entity retriever but with ground truth (GT) positions. Using GT positions performed worse than CRAFT (GT:62.2, 18.1, 12.4; Full:62.3, 21.7, 16.0 Recall@1). This is also reflected in the composition consistency metric (GT:1.69, 1.69, 1.34; Full:1.78, 1.89, 1.46). This emphasizes the need to model layout composition and entity retrieval jointly. When using GT layouts, the retrieval gets conditioned on the layout but not vice versa.

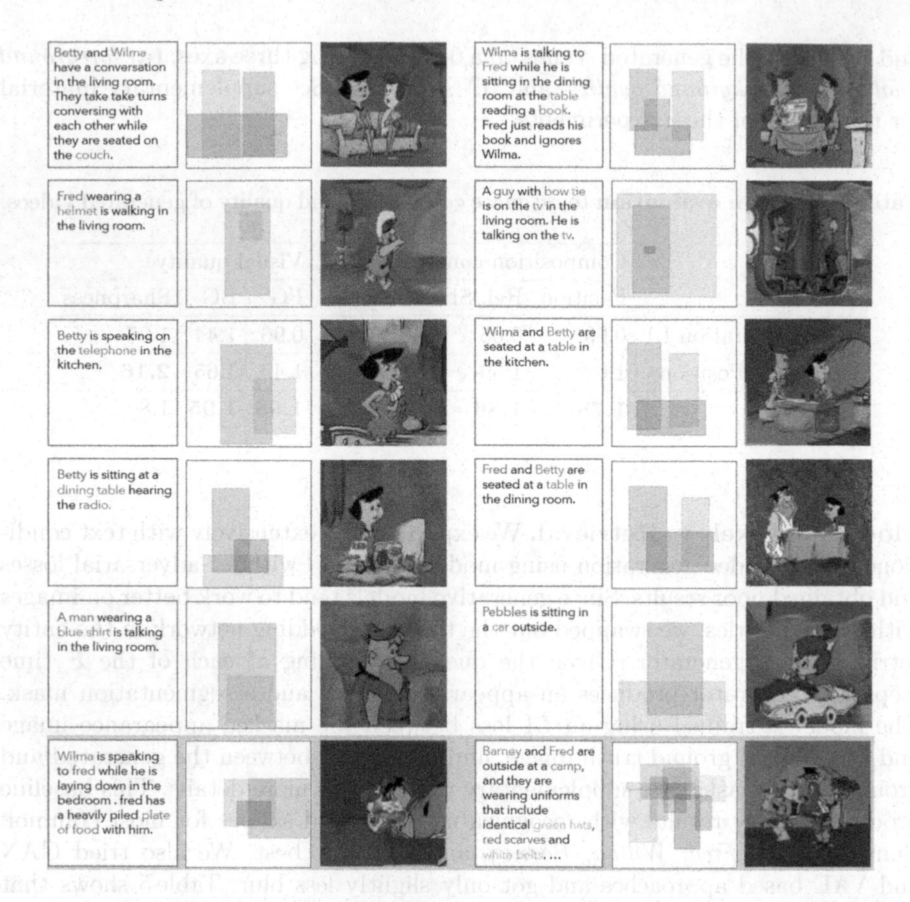

Fig. 5. Qualitative results for CRAFT. Last row shows failures of the layout composer (left) and the entire system (right). See https://youtu.be/688Vv86n0z8 for video examples, failure cases, and visualization of predicted location and scale distributions

References

1. Achanta, R., Shaji, A., Smith, K., Lucchi, A., Fua, P., Süsstrunk, S.: Slic superpixels compared to state-of-the-art superpixel methods. IEEE Trans. Pattern Anal. Mach. Intell. **34**(11), 2274–2282 (2012)
2. Arjovsky, M., Chintala, S., Bottou, L.: Wasserstein gan. CoRR abs/1701.07875 (2017)
3. Barnes, C., Shechtman, E., Finkelstein, A., Goldman, D.B.: Patchmatch: a randomized correspondence algorithm for structural image editing. ACM Trans. Graph.-TOG **28**(3), 24 (2009)
4. Bengio, Y., Mesnil, G., Dauphin, Y., Rifai, S.: Better mixing via deep representations. In: ICML (2013)
5. Caruana, R.: Multitask learning. In: Thrun, S., Pratt, L. (eds.) Learning to Learn, pp. 95–133. Springer, Boston (1998). https://doi.org/10.1007/978-1-4615-5529-2_5
6. Chen, Q., Koltun, V.: Photographic image synthesis with cascaded refinement networks. CoRR abs/1707.09405 (2017)

7. Faghri, F., Fleet, D.J., Kiros, J.R., Fidler, S.: Vse++: Improved visual-semantic embeddings. arXiv preprint arXiv:1707.05612 (2017)
8. Frome, A., Corrado, G.S., Shlens, J., Bengio, S., Dean, J., Mikolov, T., et al.: Devise: a deep visual-semantic embedding model. In: Advances in Neural Information Processing Systems, pp. 2121–2129 (2013)
9. Goodfellow, I.J., et al.: Generative adversarial nets. In: NIPS (2014)
10. Gregor, K., Danihelka, I., Graves, A., Rezende, D.J., Wierstra, D.: Draw: a recurrent neural network for image generation. In: ICML (2015)
11. Gupta, T., et al.: Aligned image-word representations improve inductive transfer across vision-language tasks. arXiv preprint arXiv:1704.00260 (2017)
12. Hong, S., Yang, D., Choi, J., Lee, H.: Inferring semantic layout for hierarchical text-to-image synthesis. CoRR abs/1801.05091 (2018)
13. Isola, P., Zhu, J.Y., Zhou, T., Efros, A.A.: Image-to-image translation with conditional adversarial networks. CoRR abs/1611.07004 (2016)
14. Karras, T., Aila, T., Laine, S., Lehtinen, J.: Progressive growing of gans for improved quality, stability, and variation. CoRR abs/1710.10196 (2017)
15. Kingma, D.P., Welling, M.: Auto-encoding variational bayes. CoRR abs/1312.6114 (2013)
16. Kiros, R., Salakhutdinov, R., Zemel, R.S.: Unifying visual-semantic embeddings with multimodal neural language models. arXiv preprint arXiv:1411.2539 (2014)
17. Kwak, H., Zhang, B.T.: Generating images part by part with composite generative adversarial networks. CoRR abs/1607.05387 (2016)
18. Li, Y., Min, M.R., Shen, D., Carlson, D., Carin, L.: Video generation from text. arXiv preprint arXiv:1710.00421 (2017)
19. Liu, Y., Qin, Z., Luo, Z., Wang, H.: Auto-painter: Cartoon image generation from sketch by using conditional generative adversarial networks. CoRR abs/1705.01908 (2017)
20. Mansimov, E., Parisotto, E., Ba, J., Salakhutdinov, R.: Generating images from captions with attention. In: ICLR (2016)
21. Marwah, T., Mittal, G., Balasubramanian, V.N.: Attentive semantic video generation using captions. CoRR abs/1708.05980 (2017)
22. Odena, A., Olah, C., Shlens, J.: Conditional image synthesis with auxiliary classifier gans. In: ICML (2017)
23. Plummer, B.A., Wang, L., Cervantes, C.M., Caicedo, J.C., Hockenmaier, J., Lazebnik, S.: Flickr30k entities: collecting region-to-phrase correspondences for richer image-to-sentence models. In: 2015 IEEE International Conference on Computer Vision (ICCV), pp. 2641–2649. IEEE (2015)
24. Radford, A., Metz, L., Chintala, S.: Unsupervised representation learning with deep convolutional generative adversarial networks. CoRR abs/1511.06434 (2015)
25. Reed, S., van den Oord, A., Kalchbrenner, N., Bapst, V., Botvinick, M., de Freitas, N.: Generating interpretable images with controllable structure. In: OpenReview.net (2017)
26. Reed, S.E., Akata, Z., Mohan, S., Tenka, S., Schiele, B., Lee, H.: Learning what and where to draw. In: NIPS (2016)
27. Reed, S.E., Akata, Z., Yan, X., Logeswaran, L., Schiele, B., Lee, H.: Generative adversarial text to image synthesis. In: ICML (2016)
28. Rother, C., Kolmogorov, V., Blake, A.: Grabcut: Interactive foreground extraction using iterated graph cuts. In: ACM Transactions on Graphics (TOG), vol. 23, pp. 309–314. ACM (2004)
29. Tsai, Y.H.H., Huang, L.K., Salakhutdinov, R.: Learning robust visual-semantic embeddings. arXiv preprint arXiv:1703.05908 (2017)

30. Villegas, R., Yang, J., Zou, Y., Sohn, S., Lin, X., Lee, H.: Learning to generate long-term future via hierarchical prediction. arXiv preprint arXiv:1704.05831 (2017)
31. Vondrick, C., Pirsiavash, H., Torralba, A.: Generating videos with scene dynamics. In: NIPS (2016)
32. Wang, L., Li, Y., Lazebnik, S.: Learning deep structure-preserving image-text embeddings. In: Proceedings of the IEEE Conference on Computer Vision and Pattern Recognition, pp. 5005–5013 (2016)
33. Yan, X., Yang, J., Sohn, K., Lee, H.: Attribute2Image: conditional image generation from visual attributes. In: Leibe, B., Matas, J., Sebe, N., Welling, M. (eds.) ECCV 2016. LNCS, vol. 9908, pp. 776–791. Springer, Cham (2016). https://doi.org/10.1007/978-3-319-46493-0_47
34. Zhang, H., et al.: Stackgan: Text to photo-realistic image synthesis with stacked generative adversarial networks. CoRR abs/1612.03242 (2016)
35. Zitnick, C.L., Parikh, D.: Bringing semantics into focus using visual abstraction. In: 2013 IEEE Conference on Computer Vision and Pattern Recognition, pp. 3009–3016 (2013)
36. Zitnick, C.L., Parikh, D., Vanderwende, L.: Learning the visual interpretation of sentences. In: 2013 IEEE International Conference on Computer Vision, pp. 1681–1688 (2013)
37. Zitnick, C.L., Vedantam, R., Parikh, D.: Adopting abstract images for semantic scene understanding. IEEE Trans. Pattern Anal. Mach. Intell. **38**, 627–638 (2016)

Urban Zoning Using Higher-Order Markov Random Fields on Multi-View Imagery Data

Tian Feng[1], Quang-Trung Truong[2], Duc Thanh Nguyen[3](✉), Jing Yu Koh[2], Lap-Fai Yu[4], Alexander Binder[2], and Sai-Kit Yeung[5]

[1] University of New South Wales, Kensington, Australia
[2] Singapore University of Technology and Design, Singapore, Singapore
[3] Deakin University, Geelong, Australia
duc.nguyen@deakin.edu.au
[4] University of Massachusetts Boston, Boston, USA
[5] Hong Kong University of Science and Technology, Clear Water Bay, Hong Kong

Abstract. Urban zoning enables various applications in land use analysis and urban planning. As cities evolve, it is important to constantly update the zoning maps of cities to reflect urban pattern changes. This paper proposes a method for automatic urban zoning using higher-order Markov random fields (HO-MRF) built on multi-view imagery data including street-view photos and top-view satellite images. In the proposed HO-MRF, top-view satellite data is segmented via a multi-scale deep convolutional neural network (MS-CNN) and used in lower-order potentials. Street-view data with geo-tagged information is augmented in higher-order potentials. Various feature types for classifying street-view images were also investigated in our work. We evaluated the proposed method on a number of famous metropolises and provided in-depth analysis on technical issues.

Keywords: Urban zoning · Street-view images · Satellite images Higher-order Markov random fields

1 Introduction

Urban zoning is a common practice adopted by many developed countries for urban planning [1]. The primary purpose of urban zoning is to segregate an urban area into distinct zones with regard to the use of spaces (e.g., residential, commercial, industrial), while specifying the height and bulk of structures, the lot dimensions, and open space requirements [2]. Urban planners, administrators, and policy makers rely on urban zoning maps to analyze, predict, and plan for urban development.

T. Feng and Q.-T. Truong—Co-first author

V. Ferrari et al. (Eds.): ECCV 2018, LNCS 11212, pp. 627–644, 2018.
https://doi.org/10.1007/978-3-030-01237-3_38

Conventional urban zoning approaches [2] require tremendous manual efforts; hence, they are time-consuming, prone to error, and non-scalable. Routine processes in updating a zoning map typically require several months of intensive labor work. Therefore, an automatic approach for urban zoning is highly favorable and deserves in-depth studies.

Existing efforts (e.g., [3–16]) have been classifying land use and land cover using remotely sensed data (i.e., satellite and aerial images). Several methods (e.g., [3, 9–11]) applied image segmentation techniques on aerial images. However, manually segmenting those images is laborious and challenging: human efforts are needed for visually interpreting every pixel from single or multiple band(s). Hence, automatic semantic segmentation techniques (e.g., [4–8, 14, 16]) have also been proposed.

Thanks to the rise of social networking services (e.g., Flickr, Facebook), an enormous amount of street-view photos with geo-tagged information are publicly shared. This sort of data carry detailed semantic information about different places and thus could help to interpret zoning information. In this paper, we explore the use of street-view photos and satellite images for automatic urban zoning. Specifically, we propose an urban zoning method using multi-source data including top-view satellite images and street-view photos. This multi-source data is fused into a higher order Markov random fields (HO-MRF) model. In the model, a multi-scale deep convolutional neural network (MS-CNN) is built to segment the top-view data and used in lower-order potentials while the street-view photos are classified and added in higher-order potentials. We conducted extensive experiments to investigate various aspects of our proposed solution. In particular, we investigated different features and classifiers that could be used for classifying street-view photos. We compared the use of multi-source vs single-source data. We also compared our proposed HO-MRF model with conventional MRF and our deep neural network with existing network architectures.

It is important to note that urban zoning conceptually differs from land cover or land use despite their correlation. Land cover refers to the observed physical cover on the earth surface. Land use refers to the activities people undertake on a certain type of land cover to change or maintain it, or to produce [17]. Urban zoning, on the other hand, refers to segregating an urban area into distinct zones by the use of buildings and spaces within a zone. It provides a convenient mean to visualize patterns of social and economic developments.

The remainder of the paper is organized as follows. Section 2 reviews the related work. Our proposed method is presented in Sect. 3. Datasets and experiments are described in Sect. 4. Section 5 concludes the paper and provides remarks.

2 Related Work

2.1 Land Use and Land Cover Classification

Early works (e.g., [18,19]) have successfully applied satellite sensor technology for monitoring agricultural land use, which motivate recent attempts on applying similar technologies for analyzing land use and land cover. Barnsley and Barr [20] proposed to extract land use information using land cover classification from multi-spectral images captured by a satellite sensor. However, the degree of sensitivity between land use patterns and the accuracy of initial land cover classification is yet to be determined.

Brown et al. [3] analyzed the relationship between land use and land cover from a spatial-temporal perspective using a Markov transition probability model. Porway et al. [12,13] proposed a hierarchical and contextual model for aerial image understanding. Lienou et al. [15] annotated satellite images using semantic concepts related to land use. The annotation task combined the classification of image patches and the integration of the spatial information between these patches. Rozenstein and Karnieli [4] introduced Geographical Information Systems (GIS) to facilitate land use classification based on hybrid supervised and unsupervised learning on remote sensing data. Hu and Wang [14] used a decision tree with remote-sensing data to classify urban land use classes. Banerjee et al. [7] applied cluster ensemble techniques to support self-training-based, unsupervised land cover classification on satellite images, to overcome the challenge of limited information in data distribution. Luus et al. [16] introduced multi-view deep learning to the field of land use classification.

There are also recent works on applying semantic segmentation techniques to land use and land cover classification. For example, Frohlich et al. [6] used iterative context forests to classify land cover from satellite images by considering contextual information. Volpi and Ferrari [9] segmented satellite images using conditional random fields. Albert et al. [11] proposed a method for the simultaneous classification of land cover and land use, taking the consideration of spatial context.

2.2 Urban Understanding from Street-View Photos

The abundance of street-view photos provides new opportunities for computer vision research on understanding urban areas. For example, previous works have demonstrated using such data for city identification [21,22], geo-informative social attributes prediction [23] and urban perception [24,25]. Recently, Dubey et al. quantified the perception of urban environment at the global scale by training a convolutional neural architecture on a new crowd-sourced dataset [26].

An early attempt was made by Leung and Newsam [27] on using street-view photos for classifying land use and land cover. To measure social development, they formulated the problem as supervised binary classification. Oba et al. [28] proposed text features in addition to visual features to improve land cover classification. Frey et al. [29] applied unsupervised learning to automatically characterize large geographical regions into location types.

2.3 Correlation Between Top-View and Street-View Imagery Data

Recently the correlation between top-view and street-view imagery data has been exploited for scene understanding. For example, Lin et al. [30] proposed to learn features using deep networks for cross-view image matching. In this work, the geo-location of a street-view query image on an aerial image is determined via feature matching. In [31], Máttyus et al. proposed an automatic road segmentation method for vehicles using both aerial and ground-view imagery data. Specifically, ground-view images of a road are captured using a stereo camera built in vehicles and paired with aerial imagery obtained from GPS to reasoning the road surface and perform road segmentation. In [32], functions of buildings were classified using both ground-level and overhead images. Convolutional neural networks (CNNs) were used to learn visual features at both ground and overhead levels. The ground-level feature map for an input overhead image was then constructed by applying kernel regression on the ground-level features extracted by the CNNs on ground-level images.

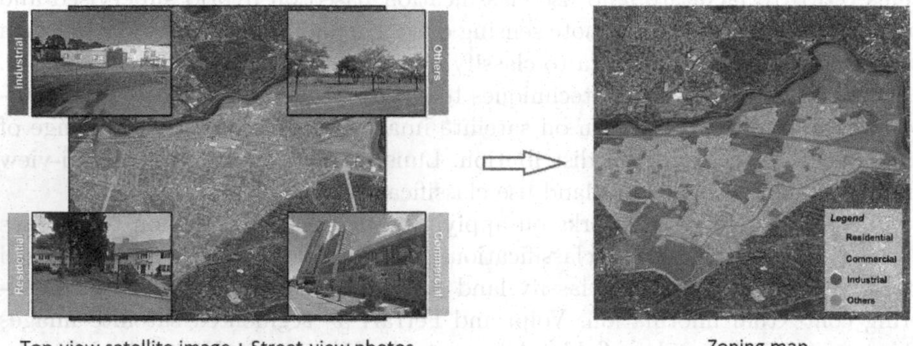

Fig. 1. Our approach infers a reliable urban zoning map from top-view satellite images and street-view photos.

3 Proposed Method

3.1 Higher-Order Markov Random Fields

The problem of urban zoning can be described as follows. Given a satellite image S covering an urban area U and a set of randomly downloaded street-view photos $G = \{g_i\}$ located within U and associated with geo-tagged information, the problem is to infer possible zoning maps of U at metropolis-level. Figure 1 illustrates the proposed urban zoning system.

We formulate the problem of urban zoning as segmenting the satellite image S into a number of regions, called *zones*, and identifying the zone types of the regions. The zone type of each region is determined by the visual information extracted from the pixels of that region and the associated street-view photos.

According to the definition of the uses of urban buildings and spaces [2], we categorize urban zones into 4 types: *Residential*, *Commercial*, *Industrial*, and *Others* in this paper. This categorization ensures the generality of the problem. Let Z be the set of zone types. $|Z| = 4$ in our case. Figure 2 shows some examples of street-view photos under different zone types.

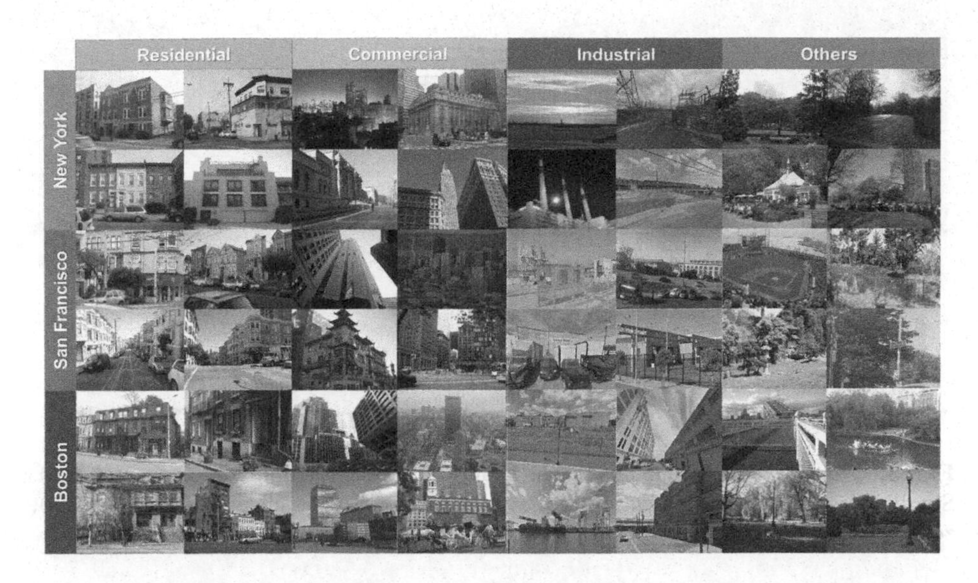

Fig. 2. Examples of street-view photos from New York, San Francisco, and Boston.

Technically, the problem stated above can be regarded as *semantic segmentation* of the satellite image S. Following this idea, we propose a higher-order Markov random fields (HO-MRF) model to solve the problem. In our HO-MRF model, unary terms are computed from visual features extracted on the satellite image S via a deep convolutional neural network. The relationships between the satellite image S and its associated street-view photos G are encoded in higher order potentials and augmented to the HO-MRF model. Figure 3 summarizes the workflow of this solution.

The HO-MRF model is constructed as follows. The input satellite image S is represented as a lattice of pixels. Each pixel $\mathbf{p}_i \in S$ is considered as a node and its label is denoted as l_i taking value in Z. Akin to fully connected MRFs [33], each pixel is connected to all other pixels.

The zoning problem is equivalent to finding the best configuration $\mathcal{L} = (l_1, l_2, ..., l_{|S|})$ for $|S|$ pixels of the satellite image S. In particular, we minimize the energy function,

$$\mathcal{L}^* = \arg\min_{\mathcal{L} \in \mathbf{L}^{|S|}} \left[\sum_{i \in S} \psi_i(l_i) + \sum_{(i,j), i<j} \psi_{i,j}(l_i, l_j) + \sum_{i \in S} \varphi(l_i, G) + \sum_{g \in G} \varphi(g) \right], \quad (1)$$

The unary potential $\psi_i(l_i)$ in (1) is defined as,

$$\psi_i(l_i = z) \propto -\log C(S, \mathbf{p}_i | l_i = z), \quad (2)$$

where C is the classification scores of assigning the zone type of pixel $\mathbf{p}_i$ (i.e., l_i) to z based on the input satellite image S. The computation of C will be presented in details in Sect. 3.2.

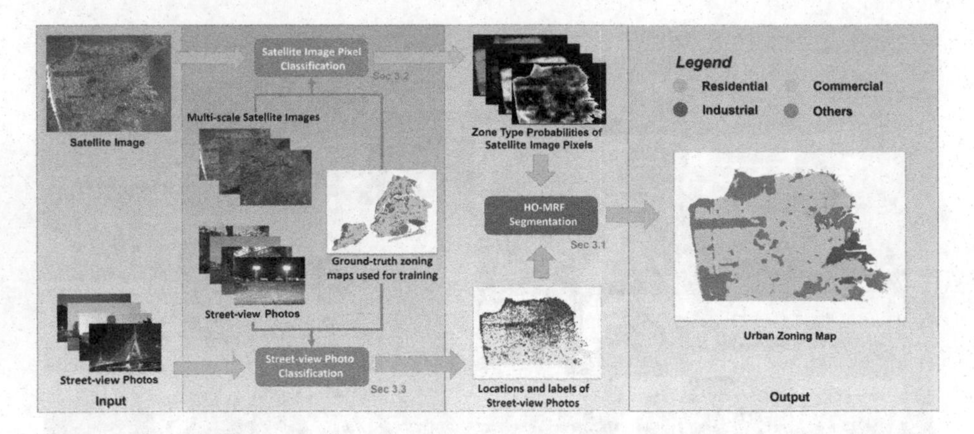

Fig. 3. The workflow of our approach. From left to right: Input data (1st column), Satellite image pixel classification and street-view photo classification (2nd column), zoning using HO-MRF (3rd column), output (4th column).

The pairwise potential $\psi_{ij}(l_i, l_j)$ is defined as a mixture of Gaussians of the location and color information of image pixels on S. In particular,

$$\psi_{ij}(l_i, l_j) = \mu_{ij} \left[\exp\left(- \frac{|\mathbf{p}_i - \mathbf{p}_j|^2}{2\alpha^2} - \frac{|\mathbf{c}_i - \mathbf{c}_j|^2}{2\beta^2} \right) + \exp\left(- \frac{|\mathbf{p}_i - \mathbf{p}_j|^2}{2\gamma^2} \right) \right] \quad (3)$$

where $\mathbf{c}_i/\mathbf{c}_j$ is the color vector at pixel $\mathbf{p}_i/\mathbf{p}_j$ and $\mathbf{p}_i$ is the location vector (i.e., x- and y-coordinate) of $\mathbf{p}_i$, μ_{ij} is the Pott label compatibility function [33], e.g.,

$$\mu_{ij} = \begin{cases} -1, & \text{if } l_i = l_j \\ 1, & \text{otherwise.} \end{cases} \quad (4)$$

In the HO-MRF model, we introduce higher-order potentials (e.g., $\varphi(g)$) capturing the relationships between S and G. The term $\varphi(l_i, G)$ encodes the zone consistency between a point $\mathbf{p}_i$ on S and its nearest street-view photo in G. Note that since every street-view photo is associated with a geo-location, the distance between a pixel $\mathbf{p}_i \in S$ to a street-view photo can be determined. In particular, we define,

$$\varphi(l_i, G) \propto \min_{g \in G, f(g) = l_i} \left\{ -\log \left[\frac{1}{d(\mathbf{p}_i, g)} \right] \right\}, \quad (5)$$

where $f(g)$ is a function returning the zone type of g and is described in Sect. 3.3; $d(\mathbf{p}_i, g)$ is the spatial distance between $\mathbf{p}_i$ and g. Intuitively, $\varphi(l_i, G)$ is inverse to the distance from $\mathbf{p}_i$ to its closest street-view photo whose zone type is l_i. In other words, the zone type of $\mathbf{p}_i$ would be more biased by its nearest street-view photo.

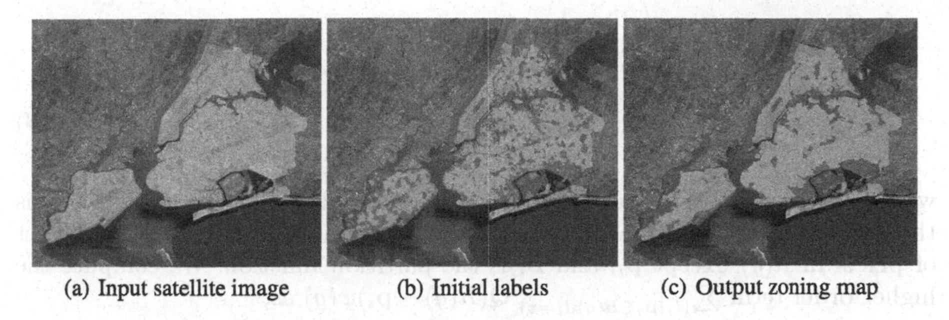

(a) Input satellite image
(b) Initial labels
(c) Output zoning map

Fig. 4. Zoning of New York City. Initial label of each pixel is determined by the zone type of its nearest street-view photo.

Note that $\varphi(l_i, G)$ needs to be computed for every $\mathbf{p}_i$. To save the computational cost, the Distance Transform proposed in [34] is applied on grids formed by the locations of street-view photos G. In particular, the zone type of each street-view photo is first obtained (see Sect. 3.3). For every zone type $z \in Z$, a Distance Transform D_z is applied on the street-view photos that have been classified as zone type z. The potential $\varphi(l_i, G)$ can then be rewritten as,

$$\varphi(l_i, G) \propto -\log \frac{1}{D_{l_i}(\mathbf{p}_i)}, \tag{6}$$

where $D_{l_i}(\mathbf{p}_i)$ is the value of the Distance Transform D_{l_i} at location $\mathbf{p}_i$.

The term $\varphi(g)$ represents the zone consistency of pixels in a local image region (on S), at which the street-view photo g could be captured. Specifically, given g, its geo-location on S can be obtained and, at this geo-location, a local image region $R(g)$ of size $W \times W$ is extracted. In our implementation, W is set to 46, which is also the size of image patches used in classifying pixels on the satellite image S (see Sect. 3.2). We then construct a probability distribution $P_g(l_k)$ over the labels $l_k \in \mathcal{L}$ conditioned on pixels k inside $R(g)$. The cost $\varphi(g)$ is then computed from the entropy of $P_g(l_k)$ as,

$$\varphi(g) \propto - \sum_{l_k \in \mathcal{L} | \mathbf{p}_k \in R(g)} P_g(l_k) \log P_g(l_k) \tag{7}$$

The optimization problem in (1) can be solved using the variational mean field method [35,36]. In particular, (1) is equivalent to finding a maximum of a posteriori (MAP) $p(L|S = \{\mathbf{p}_i\})$. In variational mean field, this can be approximated by a variational distribution Q which is fully factorized, i.e. $Q(L) = \prod_i Q_i(l_i)$. The solution of (1) is finally achieved by iteratively updating $Q_i(l_i)$ as follows,

$$Q_i(l_i = z) \leftarrow \frac{1}{Z_i} \exp \Bigg[- \psi_i(l_i = z) - \sum_{z' \in Z} \sum_{j \neq i} Q_j(l_j = z') \psi_{ij}(l_i, l_j) - \varphi(l_i = z, G) - \sum_{g \in G} \sum_{\{l_j | \mathbf{p}_j \in R(g), l_i = z\}} \mathbf{Q}(R(g) - \mathbf{p}_i) \varphi(g) \Bigg] \quad (8)$$

where $R(g)$ is an image patch on S that is centered at the location of g, $\mathbf{Q}$ is the variational distribution of the higher order terms [37], $R(g) - \mathbf{p}_i$ is the set of pixels in $R(g)$ except $\mathbf{p}_i$, and Z_i is the partition function. We compute the higher order term $\sum_{\{l_j | \mathbf{p}_j \in R(g), l_i = z\}} \mathbf{Q}(R(g) - \mathbf{p}_i) \varphi(g)$ as,

$$\sum_{\{l_j | \mathbf{p}_j \in R(g), l_i = z\}} \mathbf{Q}(R(g) - \mathbf{p}_i) \varphi(g) = - \sum_{l_k \in \mathcal{L} | \mathbf{p}_k \in R(g)} P_g(l_k) \log P_g(l_k) \Bigg[\prod_{\substack{\mathbf{p}_m \in R(g), \\ m \neq i}} Q_m(l_m = z) \Bigg] - \sum_{l_k \in \mathcal{L} | \mathbf{p}_k \in R(g)} P_g(l_k) \log P_g(l_k) \Bigg[1 - \prod_{\substack{\mathbf{p}_m \in R(g), \\ m \neq i}} Q_m(l_m = z) \Bigg] \quad (9)$$

In our implementation, the label of each pixel on the satellite image S was initialized by the label of its nearest street-view photo. Figure 4 shows an example of zone segmentation of New York city.

3.2 Classifying Satellite Image Pixels

This section describes the classification of the zone type of pixels $\mathbf{p}_i$ on the satellite image S, i.e., estimation of $C(S, \mathbf{p}_i | l_i)$ in (2). Like the work by Farabet et al. [38], our network receives input the YUV image of S. A pyramid including three scales ($S^0 = S$, $S^1 = \frac{1}{2} S$, $S^2 = \frac{1}{2} S^1$) is then created. For each pixel $\mathbf{p}_i$, three local image patches I_i^0, I_i^1, and I_i^2 of size 46 × 46-pixels centered at $\mathbf{p}_i$ on S^0, S^1, and S^2 are extracted.

A multi-scale convolutional neural network (MS-CNN) is then constructed to learn the appearance features and classify local image patches at various scales. Utilizing the multi-scale approach would enable learning scale-invariant features. In addition, multi-scale regions at a pixel would allow the incorporation of context information and thus could be useful for the classification. In the MS-CNN, for each scale, a 5-layer sub-CNN is formed with the interchange of convolutional and max-pooling layers. For example, the 1st and 3rd layers are obtained from the banks of 16 7 × 7 filters, of which 10 filters connect to the Y channel and the other 6 filters connect to the U and V channels. The 2nd and 4th are results of 16 and 64 2 × 2 max-pooling operations respectively. The 5th layer is formed by 256 7 × 7 filters. The outputs of all sub-CNNs are then concatenated to a layer fed to a 2 fully connected layer structure for classification. The first layer of this fully connected network includes 1024 nodes and the second layer contains 4 nodes corresponding to 4 different zone types. Figure 5 illustrates the

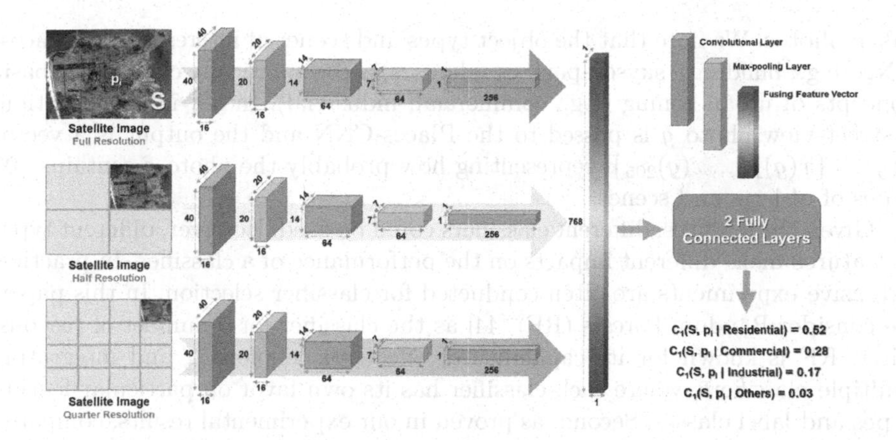

Fig. 5. MS-CNN for classifying satellite image pixels.

MS-CNN. In the network, *softmax* is used as the activation function for the last layer of the sub-CNNs and the last layer of the fully connected network, and *tanh* is used for all other layers.

The MS-CNN is trained via optimizing a cross-entropy loss and using stochastic gradient descent method. The batch size is set to 100 and the learning rate is set to 10^{-3}. We found that these settings achieved the best performance. Since the training data may be biased, the loss function is weighted relatively to the proportion of the class labels in the training dataset. In addition, all sub-CNNs share the same parameters including weight and bias. As indicated by Farabet et al. [38], imposing complete weight sharing across scales is a natural way of forcing the network to learn scale-invariant features, and at the same time, to reduce the chances of over-fitting. Given the MS-CNN, $C(S, \mathbf{p}_i | l_i = z)$ is computed as classification score of pixel $\mathbf{p}_i$ to the zone type z, i.e., the response of the MS-CNN at the zone type z.

3.3 Classifying Street-View Photos

Recall that in (5), the HO-MRF requires a function $f(g)$ that returns the zone type of a street-view photo g. Intuitively, if the geo-location of each photo could be paired with the corresponding zone type, we would have a reasonable zoning map. To recognize street-view photos, features need to be determined. Well-known features such as GIST [39], HOG [40], local binary patterns (LBP) [41] have been proposed in the literature. However, those features are handcrafted and thus require the specific knowledge in particular fields. Recently, deep neural networks have been used for automatically learning features and training classifiers [42].

Inspired by the relevance of the information conveyed by deep networks for scene recognition, we choose the *Places-CNN*, a CNN trained on Places Database [43]. Places-CNN is able to recognize 205 object types and scenes from daily taken photos. We note that the object types and scenes of interest in the Places-CNN (e.g., buildings, skyscrapers, warehouses) are semantically close to the basic concepts of urban zoning (e.g., commercial, industrial). In our implementation, a street-view photo g is passed to the Places-CNN and the output is a vector $\mathbf{x}(g) = \{x(g)_1, ..., x(g)_{205}\}$, representing how probably the photo g contains 205 types of objects and scenes.

Given the features, different classifiers could be used. However, different types of features make different impacts on the performance of a classifier. In practice, extensive experiments are often conducted for classifier selection. In this paper, we consider Random Forests (RF) [44] as the classifier for a number of reasons. First, RF is known for its capability of effectively exploiting and integrating multiple classifiers, where each classifier has its own favor on particular feature types and label classes. Second, as proven in our experimental results, compared with other classifiers, RF based on the features generated by the Places-CNN works well on our problem.

Our RF classifier f includes multiple weak classifiers [45]. The predicted label of f given an input photo g is a weighted majority vote of the predictions made by individual classifiers. Specifically, let $h_1, ..., h_M$ be M weak classifiers. The predicted label of a photo g is denoted as $f(g)$ and can be computed as,

$$f(g) = \arg\max_{z \in Z} \left(\sum_{k=1}^{M} w_k I(h_k(\mathbf{x}(g)) = z) \right), \tag{10}$$

where $\mathbf{x}(g)$ is the 205-dimensional feature vector extracted using the Places-CNN, $I(\cdot)$ is the indicator function, and w_k is the weight of the k-th weak classifier h_k.

4 Experiments

4.1 Dataset

Our experiments were conducted on the map data of three metropolises: **New York, San Francisco** and **Boston**.

Satellite Data. Satellite images are our top-view imagery data that could be obtained without expensive devices or professional expertise. We downloaded the satellite image tiles for each city by its corresponding geographical boundary from the National Map service operated by U.S. Geology Survey [46].

Table 1. Numbers of street-view photos.

	Residential	Commercial	Industrial	Others	Total
New York	59,906	77,193	25,109	56,570	218,778
San Francisco	49,543	46,454	11,553	41,140	148,690
Boston	32,412	37,588	10,179	42,682	122,861

Street-View Data. Popular social network services provide public access to many of their street-view photos and associated geo-tagged information. We collected 490, 329 photos of the three metropolises from Flickr and Panoramio. Specifically, we queried the URLs of outdoor photos by calling the APIs of Flickr and Panoramio within the geographical boundary (the minimum bounding box) of each city. Photos within each city were downloaded after their coordinates were verified by GIS. Table 1 summarizes the number of street-view photos used for each metropolis. Figure 6 shows the distribution of street-view photos in New York.

Table 2. Proportion of zones in ground-truth zoning maps.

	Residential	Commercial	Industrial	Others
New York	64.21%	4.90%	14.15%	16.74%
San Francisco	53.82%	8.88%	6.49%	30.81%
Boston	40.91%	12.07%	3.42%	43.60%

Urban Zoning Maps. We collected urban zoning maps from the websites of local governments, which were stored in the standard GIS format, SHAPEFILE [47]. The zone types include: *Residential*, *Commercial*, *Industrial* and *Others*. The mentioned maps served as the ground-truth for evaluations. Table 2 shows the percentage of each type of zones in the ground truth zoning maps.

4.2 Classifying Street-View Photos

We first evaluated street-view photo classification. In this experiment, we investigated different feature types and classifiers that are well-known for scene classification. Specifically, for features, we evaluated the GIST [39], HOG [40], and Places-CNN [43].

For classifiers, we compared RBF-kernel SVM, k-nearest neighbors, and RF. We found that RBF-kernel SVM significantly outperformed linear SVM. For the k-nearest neighbors, we set k to 10 which gave the best performance on this technique. To measure the similarity between samples, we used the Euclidean distance. For the RF, 15 trees were used. All the classifiers were evaluated using 3-fold cross validation.

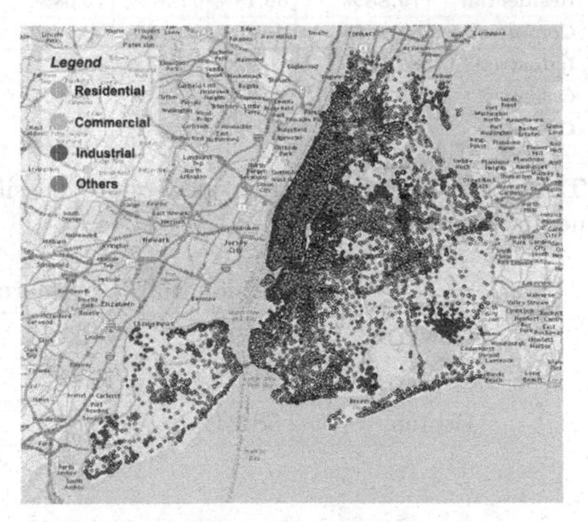

Fig. 6. The plot map of street-view photos in New York city. Each photo is marked with a color corresponding to its zone type.

Table 3 summarizes the results of this experiment. As shown, in most cases, the combination of Places-CNN with RF achieves the best performance. It is also worthwhile to notice that compared with handcrafted features, the features learned by the Places-CNN often gain higher classification accuracy and achieve the best overall performance irrespective of the classifiers.

We also evaluated the use of neural network for street-view photo classification. Specifically, we directly connected the outputs of Places-CNN to a fully connected neural network (with one hidden layer and 4 outputs corresponding to 4 zone types). The results of this experiment are reported in Table 4. As shown in both Tables 3 and 4, applying RF on-top of Places-CNN achieves the best overall performance.

Table 3. Accuracy of street-view photo classification.

	Random Forest			SVM with RBF kernel			k-Nearest Neighbors		
	Places-CNN	GIST	HOG	Places-CNN	GIST	HOG	Places-CNN	GIST	HOG
New York									
Residential	**79.04%**	70.56%	71.75%	71.32%	64.12%	65.33%	65.21%	60.59%	61.44%
Commercial	**81.65%**	65.19%	69.22%	73.74%	62.90%	64.78%	67.31%	57.57%	62.16%
Industrial	71.75%	66.21%	**72.80%**	68.46%	54.31%	62.10%	61.43%	57.53%	54.12%
Others	**81.26%**	67.78%	69.13%	72.97%	68.49%	66.31%	67.06%	61.53%	58.73%
Overall	**79.76%**	67.51%	70.35%	72.33%	62.32%	65.07%	66.05%	59.47%	60.20%
San Francisco									
Residential	**78.19%**	69.25%	70.67%	74.19%	67.39%	68.11%	73.33%	65.38%	67.14%
Commercial	**82.55%**	72.54%	72.34%	71.52%	68.10%	67.55%	65.71%	60.44%	59.76%
Industrial	70.88%	65.81%	**70.96%**	73.73%	63.54%	68.91%	64.32%	63.92%	65.88%
Others	**86.18%**	80.55%	83.48%	76.26%	74.62%	76.39%	69.09%	66.79%	68.42%
Overall	**81.19%**	73.13%	74.76%	73.89%	69.31%	70.29%	69.07%	64.11%	65.10%
Boston									
Residential	**79.88%**	69.18%	71.57%	75.08%	64.11%	70.02%	72.57%	66.53%	67.82%
Commercial	**82.25%**	71.20%	70.88%	70.26%	68.29%	69.23%	68.45%	65.78%	65.93%
Industrial	**86.45%**	70.09%	69.47%	74.31%	67.54%	65.33%	69.13%	66.91%	65.02%
Others	**82.39%**	72.34%	73.59%	77.29%	69.51%	74.87%	73.29%	67.52%	70.19%
Overall	**82.08%**	70.96%	71.77%	74.01%	67.58%	70.22%	71.21%	66.60%	67.67%

Table 4. Accuracy of street-view photo classification using Places-CNN and fully connected neural network.

	Residential	Commercial	Industrial	Others	Overall
New York	79.97%	44.22%	27.89%	66.11%	60.89%
San Francisco	74.01%	45.69%	24.84%	78.43%	68.13%
Boston	58.24%	25.82%	9.41%	80.95%	65.38%

4.3 Zoning

Since zoning is formulated as semantic segmentation of satellite images, its performance can be evaluated via the segmentation accuracy, i.e., the accuracy of classifying of satellite image pixels using the proposed MS-CNN. In our implementation, the MS-CNN was trained/tested in 3-fold cross fashion (i.e. two cities

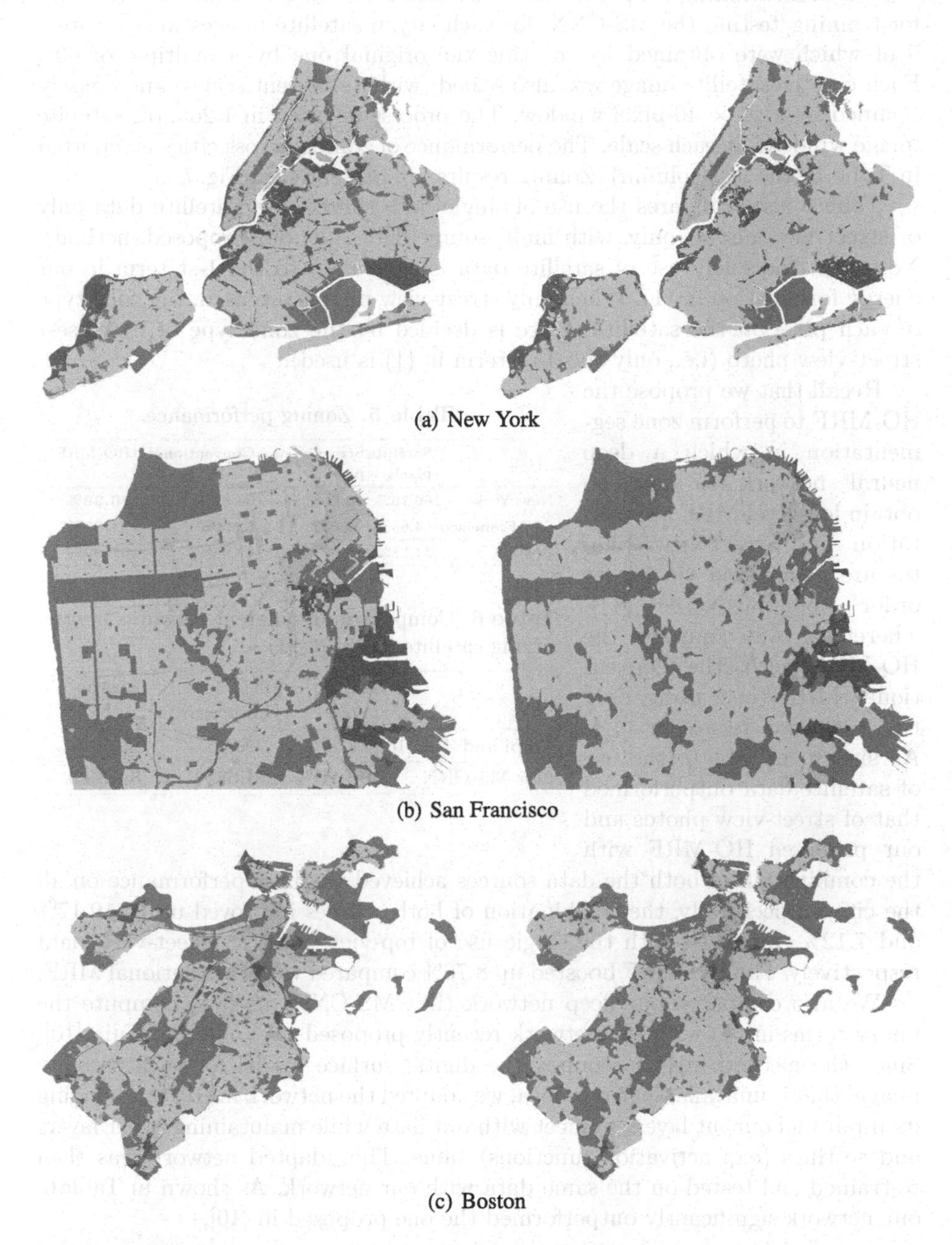

(a) New York

(b) San Francisco

(c) Boston

Fig. 7. Zoning results. For each city, the ground-truth is shown on the left and the zoning map result is shown on the right.

were used for training while the other was used for testing). To increase the data for training/testing the MS-CNN, for each city, 6 satellite images were created, 5 of which were obtained by rotating the original one by a multiple of 60°. Each created satellite image was also scaled (with 3 different scales) and densely scanned by a 46 × 46-pixel window. The process resulted in 1,265,572 satellite image windows at each scale. The performance of zoning across cities is reported in Table 5 (the last column). Zoning results are presented in Fig. 7.

Table 5 also compares the use of single data source, e.g. satellite data only or street-view photos only, with multi-source data (i.e., our proposed method). Note that the solely use of satellite data is equivalent to the 1-st term in our energy formulation in (1). When only street-view photos are used, the zone type of each pixel on the satellite image is decided by the zone type of its closest street-view photo (i.e., only the 3-rd term in (1) is used).

Recall that we propose the HO-MRF to perform zone segmentation in which a deep neural network is used to obtain low-level MRF segmentation and street-view photos are augmented via higher order potentials (see (1)). Therefore, we compare the HO-MRF with the conventional MRF (i.e., using only the first two terms in (1)). As shown in Table 5, the use of satellite data outperformed that of street-view photos and our proposed HO-MRF with the combination of both the data sources achieved the best performance on all the cities. Specifically, the combination of both sources improved up to 10.17% and 7.12% compared with the single use of top-view data or street-view data respectively. The HO-MRF boosted up 8.76% compared with conventional MRF.

Table 5. Zoning performance.

	Satellite pixels	Street-view photos	Conventional MRF	HO-MRF
New York	66.70%	60.50%	66.87%	**70.33%**
San Francisco	64.68%	61.63%	62.99%	**71.80%**
Boston	51.33%	48.08%	47.95%	**57.09%**

Table 6. Comparison of different networks in classifying satellite image pixels.

	New York	San Francisco	Boston
Volpi and Tuia[10]	20.50%	10.10%	22.50%
Our MS-CNN	**66.70%**	**64.68%**	**51.33%**

We also compared our deep network (i.e., MS-CNN) used to compute the unary terms in (1) with the network recently proposed by Volpi and Tuia [10]. Since the method in [10] requires the digital surface model for each satellite image, that is unavailable in our data, we adapted the network in [10] by changing its input and output layers to meet with our data while maintaining other layers and settings (e.g. activation functions) same. The adapted network was then re-trained and tested on the same data with our network. As shown in Table 6, our network significantly outperformed the one proposed in [10].

4.4 Discussion

We have found that larger improvement with the HO-MRF was obtained on Boston and San Francisco compared to only using satellite imagery as opposed to New York probably because New York contains more industrial regions (e.g., as shown in Table 2 industrial takes 14.15% in New York, compared with 6.49% and 3.42% in San Francisco and Boston). However, as shown in Table 3, industrial street-view photos are recognized with lower accuracy compared with other zone types.

Experimental results (e.g., Fig. 7) also show our method fails to segment tiny/thin regions. This is because those regions occupy small portions in local image windows and thus are biased by nearby larger regions. We have also found that the method may fail at regions with less street-view images captured. Note that street-view photos are captured sparsely and non-uniformly (see Fig. 6). We believe that, 3D data such as digital surface models, digital elevation models (if available or achievable approximately) would be useful to resolve these issues.

5 Conclusion

We proposed a higher-order Markov random fields model for urban zoning based on multi-view imagery data including top-view satellite and street-view images. We also developed a multi-scale deep convolutional neural network used for classifying satellite image pixels. By integrating different sources of imagery data, our approach can achieve urban zoning automatically, and hence overcome the scalability bottleneck faced by the conventional practice of creating zoning maps manually. We investigated various implementation strategies including feature types, classification models, deep architectures, and conducted extensive experiments and comparisons to verify our approach.

Acknowledgement. Quang-Trung Truong was supported by Singapore MOE Academic Research Fund MOE2016-T2-2-154. Tian Feng was supported by the UNSW Art & Design Faculty Research Grant PS49003. Lap-Fai Yu was supported in part by the National Science Foundation under award number 1565978. Alexander Binder was supported by the SUTD grant SRIS15105.

This research was partially funded by the Heritage Research Grant of the National Heritage Board, Singapore NRF under its IDM Futures Funding Initiative and Virtual Singapore Award No. NRF2015VSGAA3DCM001-014, and by an internal grant from HKUST (R9429).

References

1. Whitnall, G.: History of zoning. Ann. Am. Acad. Polit. Soc. Sci. **155**, 1–14 (1931)
2. GoLdberg, M., Horwood, P., Block, W.: Zoning: Its Costs and Relevance for the 1980s. Fraser Institute's housing and land economics series, Fraser Institute (1980)
3. Brown, D., Pijanowski, B., Duh, J.: Modeling the relationships between land use and land cover on private lands in the upper midwest, USA. J. Environ. Manag. **59**(4), 247–263 (2000)
4. Rozenstein, O., Karnieli, A.: Comparison of methods for land-use classification incorporating remote sensing and GIS inputs. Appl. Geogr. **31**(2), 533–544 (2011)

5. Tuia, D., Muñoz-Marí, J., Kanevski, M., Camps-Valls, G.: Structured output svm for remote sensing image classification. J. Signal Process. Syst. **65**(3), 301–310 (2011)
6. Frohlich, B., Bach, E., Walde, I., Hese, S., Schmullius, C., Denzler, J.: Land cover classification of satellite images using contextual information. Ann. Photogramm. Remote. Sens. Spat. Inf. Sci. **1**, 1–6 (2013)
7. Banerjee, B., Bovolo, F., Bhattacharya, A., Bruzzone, L., Chaudhuri, S., Mohan, B.: A new self-training-based unsupervised satellite image classification technique using cluster ensemble strategy. IEEE Geosci. Remote. Sens. Lett. **12**(4), 741–745 (2015)
8. Tokarczyk, P., Wegner, J., Walk, S., Schindler, K.: Features, color spaces, and boosting: new insights on semantic classification of remote sensing images. IEEE Trans. Geosci. Remote. Sens. **53**(1), 280–295 (2015)
9. Volpi, M., Ferrari, V.: Semantic segmentation of urban scenes by learning local class interactions. In: Proceedings of the IEEE Computer Vision and Pattern Recognition Workshops (2015)
10. Volpi, M., Tuia, D.: Dense semantic labeling of sub-decimeter resolution images with convolutional neural networks. IEEE Trans. Geosci. Remote. Sens. **55**(2), 881–893 (2017)
11. Albert, L., Rottensteiner, F., Heipke, C.: An Iterative Inference Procedure Applying Conditional Random Fields for Simultaneous Classification of Land Cover and Land Use. ISPRS Annals of Photogrammetry, Remote Sensing and Spatial Information Sciences, pp. 369–376, August 2015
12. Porway, J., Wang, K., Yao, B., Zhu, S.C.: A hierarchical and contextual model for aerial image understanding. In: Proceedings of the IEEE International Conference on Computer Vision and Pattern Recognition, pp. 1–8 (2008)
13. Porway, J., Wang, Q., Zhu, S.C.: A hierarchical and contextual model for aerial image parsing. Int. J. Comput. Vis. **88**(2), 254–283 (2010)
14. Hu, S., Wang, L.: Automated urban land-use classification with remote sensing. Int. J. Remote. Sens. **34**(3), 790–803 (2013)
15. Lienou, M., Maitre, H., Datcu, M.: Semantic annotation of satellite images using latent dirichlet allocation. IEEE Geosci. Remote. Sens. Lett. **7**, 28–32 (2010)
16. Luus, F.P.S., Salmon, B.P., van den Bergh, F., Maharaj, B.T.J.: Multiview deep learning for land-use classification. IEEE Geosci. Remote. Sens. Lett. **12**(12), 2448–2452 (2015)
17. Food and Agriculture Organization of the United Nations: Land Cover Classification System (LCCS): classification concepts and user manual (2000)
18. Forster, B.C.: An examination of some problems and solutions in monitoring urban areas from satellite platforms. Int. J. Remote. Sens. **6**(1), 139–151 (1985)
19. Gong, P., Howarth, P.J.: Land-use classification of spot hrv data using a cover-frequency method. Int. J. Remote. Sens. **13**(8), 1459–1471 (1991)
20. Barnsley, M.J., Barr, S.L.: Inferring urban land use from satellite sensor images using kernel-based spatial reclassification. Photogramm. Eng. Remote. Sens. **62**(8), 949–958 (1996)
21. Doersch, C., Singh, S., Gupta, A., Sivic, J., Efros, A.A.: What makes paris look like paris? ACM Trans. Graph. **31**(4), 101:1–101:9 (2012)
22. Zhou, B., Liu, L., Oliva, A., Torralba, A.: Recognizing city identity via attribute analysis of geo-tagged images. In: Fleet, D., Pajdla, T., Schiele, B., Tuytelaars, T. (eds.) ECCV 2014. LNCS, vol. 8691, pp. 519–534. Springer, Cham (2014). https://doi.org/10.1007/978-3-319-10578-9_34

23. Lee, S., Zhang, H., Crandall, D.J.: Predicting geo-informative attributes in large-scale image collections using convolutional neural networks. In: Proceedings of the IEEE International Winter Conference on Applications of Computer Vision, pp. 550–557 (2015)
24. Ordonez, V., Berg, T.L.: Learning high-level judgments of urban perception. In: Fleet, D., Pajdla, T., Schiele, B., Tuytelaars, T. (eds.) ECCV 2014. LNCS, vol. 8694, pp. 494–510. Springer, Cham (2014). https://doi.org/10.1007/978-3-319-10599-4_32
25. Quercia, D., O'Hare, N.K., Cramer, H.: Aesthetic capital: What makes London look beautiful, quiet, and happy? In: Proceedings of the 17th ACM Conference on Computer Supported Cooperative Work and Social Computing, pp. 945–955. ACM, New York (2014)
26. Dubey, A., Naik, N., Parikh, D., Raskar, R., Hidalgo, C.A.: Deep learning the city: quantifying urban perception at a global scale. In: Leibe, B., Matas, J., Sebe, N., Welling, M. (eds.) ECCV 2016. LNCS, vol. 9905, pp. 196–212. Springer, Cham (2016). https://doi.org/10.1007/978-3-319-46448-0_12
27. Leung, D., Newsam, S.: Proximate sensing: inferring what-is-where from georeferenced photo collections. In: Proceedings of the IEEE International Conference on Computer Vision and Pattern Recognition, pp. 2955–2962 (2010)
28. Oba, H., Hirota, M., Chbeir, R., Ishikawa, H., Yokoyama, S.: Towards better land cover classification using geo-tagged photographs. In: Proceedings of the IEEE International Symposium on Multimedia, pp. 320–327 (2014)
29. Frey, N., Torralba, A., Stauffer, C.: Unsupervised non-parametric geospatial modeling from ground imagery. In: Proceedings of the IEEE International Winter Conference on Applications of Computer Vision, pp. 698–705 (2014)
30. Lin, T.Y., Cui, Y., Belongie, S., Hays, J.: Learning deep representations for ground-to-aerial geolocalization. In: Proceedings of the IEEE International Conference on Computer Vision and Pattern Recognition, pp. 5007–5015 (2015)
31. Máttyus, G., Wang, S., Fidler, S., Urtasun, R.: Hd maps: Fine-grained road segmentation by parsing ground and aerial images. In: Proceedings of the IEEE International Conference on Computer Vision and Pattern Recognition, pp. 3611–3619 (2016)
32. Workman, S., Zhai, M., Crandall, D.J., Jacobs, N.: A unified model for near and remote sensing. In: Proceedings of the IEEE International Conference on Computer Vision, pp. 2688–2697 (2017)
33. Krähenbühl, P., Koltun, V.: Efficient inference in fully connected CRFs with gaussian edge potentials. In: Proceedings of the Conference on Neural Information Processing Systems, pp. 109–117 (2011)
34. Felzenszwalb, P.F., Huttenlocher, D.P.: Distance transforms of sampled functions. Technical report, Cornell Computing and Information Science (2004)
35. Jordan, M.I., Ghahramani, Z., Jaakkola, T.S., Saul, L.: An introduction to variational methods for graphical models. Mach. Learn. **37**, 183–233 (1999)
36. Wainwright, M.J., Jordan, M.I.: Graphical models, exponential families, and variational inference. Found. Trends Mach. Learn. **1**(1–2), 1–305 (2008)
37. Vineet, V., Warrell, J., Torr, P.H.S.: Filter-based mean-field inference for random fields with higher-order terms and product label-spaces. Int. J. Comput. Vis. **110**(3), 290–307 (2014)
38. Farabet, C., Couprie, C., Najman, L., LeCun, Y.: Learning hierarchical features for scene labeling. IEEE Trans. Pattern Anal. Mach. Intell. **35**(8), 1915–1929 (2013)
39. Oliva, A., Torralba, A.: Modeling the shape of the scene: a holistic representation of the spatial envelope. Int. J. Comput. Vis. **42**(3), 145–175 (2001)

40. Dalal, N., Triggs, B.: Histograms of oriented gradients for human detection. In: Proceedings of the IEEE International Conference on Computer Vision and Pattern Recognition, pp. 886–893 (2005)
41. Ojala, T., Pietikăinen, M., Harwood, D.: A comparative study of texture measures with classification based on featured distributions. Pattern Recognit. **29**(1), 51–59 (1996)
42. Krizhevsky, A., Sutskever, I., Hinton, G.E.: Imagenet classification with deep convolutional neural networks. In: Proceedings of the Conference on Neural Information Processing Systems, pp. 1106–1114 (2012)
43. Zhou, B., Lapedriza, À., Xiao, J., Torralba, A., Oliva, A.: Learning deep features for scene recognition using places database. In: Proceedings of the Conference on Neural Information Processing Systems, pp. 487–495 (2014)
44. Breiman, L.: Random forests. Mach. Learn. **45**(1), 5–32 (2001)
45. Kuncheva, L.I.: Combining Pattern Classifiers: Methods and Algorithms. Wiley-Interscience (2004)
46. USGS: The national map. https://viewer.nationalmap.gov/basic/
47. Esri Inc.: ESRI Shapefile Technical Description. Environmental Systems Research Institute, Inc., July 1998

Quaternion Convolutional Neural Networks

Xuanyu Zhu[1], Yi Xu[1(✉)], Hongteng Xu[2,3], and Changjian Chen[1]

[1] Shanghai Jiao Tong University, Shanghai, China
{others_sing,xuyi}@sjtu.edu.cn, ccj1988@gmail.com
[2] Infinia ML, Inc., Durham, USA
[3] Duke University, Durham, NC, USA
hongteng.xu@duke.edu

Abstract. Neural networks in the real domain have been studied for a long time and achieved promising results in many vision tasks for recent years. However, the extensions of the neural network models in other number fields and their potential applications are not fully-investigated yet. Focusing on color images, which can be naturally represented as quaternion matrices, we propose a quaternion convolutional neural network (QCNN) model to obtain more representative features. In particular, we re-design the basic modules like convolution layer and fully-connected layer in the quaternion domain, which can be used to establish fully-quaternion convolutional neural networks. Moreover, these modules are compatible with almost all deep learning techniques and can be plugged into traditional CNNs easily. We test our QCNN models in both color image classification and denoising tasks. Experimental results show that they outperform the real-valued CNNs with same structures.

Keywords: Quaternion convolutional neural network
Quaternion-based layers · Color image denoising
Color image classification

1 Introduction

As a powerful feature representation method, convolutional neural networks (CNNs) have been widely applied in the field of computer vision. Since the success of AlexNet [20], many novel CNNs have been proposed, *e.g.*, VGG [31], ResNet [13], and DenseNet [16], etc., which achieved state-of-the-art performance in almost all vision tasks [4,12,23]. One key module of CNN model is the convolution layer, which extracts features from high-dimensional structural

Electronic supplementary material The online version of this chapter (https://doi.org/10.1007/978-3-030-01237-3_39) contains supplementary material, which is available to authorized users.

V. Ferrari et al. (Eds.): ECCV 2018, LNCS 11212, pp. 645–661, 2018.
https://doi.org/10.1007/978-3-030-01237-3_39

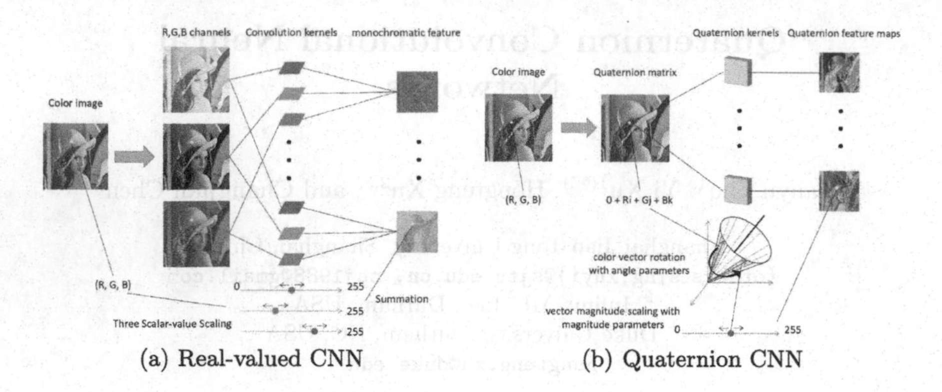

(a) Real-valued CNN (b) Quaternion CNN

Fig. 1. Illustration of the difference between CNN and QCNN on convolution layers. (Color figure online)

data efficiently by a set of convolution kernels. When dealing with multi-channel inputs (*e.g.*, color images), the convolution kernels merges these channels by summing up the convolution results and output one single channel per kernel accordingly, as Fig. 1(a) shows.

Although such a processing strategy performs well in many practical situations, it congenitally suffers from some drawbacks in color image processing tasks. Firstly, for each kernel it just sums up the outputs corresponding to different channels and ignores the complicated interrelationship between them. Accordingly, we may lose important structural information of color and obtain non-optimal representation of color image [36]. Secondly, simply summing up the outputs gives too many degrees of freedom to the learning of convolution kernels, and thus we may have a high risk of over-fitting even if imposing heavy regularization terms. How to overcome these two challenges is still not fully-investigated.

Focusing on the problems mentioned above, we propose a novel quaternion convolutional neural network (QCNN) model, which represents color image in the quaternion domain. Figure 1 illustrates the scheme of QCNN model. In particular, each color pixel in a color image (*i.e.*, the yellow dot in Fig. 1) is represented as a quaternion, and accordingly, the image is represented as a quaternion matrix rather than three independent real-valued matrices. Taking the quaternion matrix as the input of our network, we design a series of basic modules, *e.g.*, quaternion convolution layer, quaternion fully-connected layer. While the traditional real-valued convolution is only capable to enforce scaling transformation on the input, specifically, the quaternion convolution achieves the scaling and the rotation of input in the color space, which provides us with more structural representation of color information. Based on these modules, we can establish fully-quaternion CNNs to represent color images in a more effective way. Moreover, we study the relationship between our QCNN model and existing real-valued CNNs and find a compatible way to combine them together in a same algorithmic framework.

Essentially, our QCNN imposes an implicit regularizer on the architecture of network, which ensures that the representations of color image under the guidance of quaternion operations. Such a strategy considers more complicated relationships across different channels while suppress the degrees of freedom of model's parameters during training. As a result, using quaternion CNNs, we can achieve better learning results with fewer parameters compared with real-valued CNNs. Additionally, a color image is represented as a quaternion matrix in our QCNN, so that we can transform a color pixel throughout the color space using independent and physically-meaningful parameters (*i.e.*, the magnitude and the angle on the color cone shown in Fig. 1(b)), which enhances the interpretability of the model. As Fig. 1 shows, our QCNN preserves more color information than real-valued CNN, which is suitable for color image processing, especially for low-level color feature extraction. Experimental results show that our QCNN model provides benefits for both high-level vision task (*i.e.*, color image classification) and low-level vision task (*i.e.*, color image denoising), which outperforms its competitors.

2 Related Works

2.1 Quaternion-Based Color Image Processing

Quaternion is a kind of hyper complex numbers, which is first described by Hamilton in 1843 and interpreted as points in three-dimensional space. Mathematically, a quaternion $\hat{q}$ in the quaternion domain $\mathbb{H}$, *i.e.*, $q \in \mathbb{H}$, can be represented as $\hat{q} = q_0 + q_1 i + q_2 j + q_3 k$, where $q_l \in \mathbb{R}$ for $l = 0, 1, 2, 3$, and the imaginary units i, j, k obey the quaternion rules that $i^2 = j^2 = k^2 = ijk = -1$.

Accordingly, a N-dimensional quaternion vector can be denoted as $\hat{\boldsymbol{q}} = [\hat{q}_1, ..., \hat{q}_N]^\top \in \mathbb{H}^N$. Similar to real numbers, we can define a series of operations for quaternions:

- **Addition:** $\hat{p} + \hat{q} = (p_0 + q_0) + (p_1 + q_1)i + (p_2 + q_2)j + (p_3 + q_3)k$.
- **Scalar multiplication:** $\lambda\hat{q} = \lambda q_0 + \lambda q_1 i + \lambda q_2 j + \lambda q_3 k$.
- **Element multiplication:**

$$\begin{aligned}\hat{p}\hat{q} = &(p_0 q_0 - p_1 q_1 - p_2 q_2 - p_3 q_3) + (p_0 q_1 + p_1 q_0 + p_2 q_3 - p_3 q_2)i \\ &+ (p_0 q_2 - p_1 q_3 + p_2 q_0 + p_3 q_1)j + (p_0 q_3 + p_1 q_2 - p_2 q_1 + p_3 q_0)k.\end{aligned}$$

- **Conjugation:** $\hat{q}^* = q_0 - q_1 i - q_2 j - q_3 k$.

These quaternion operations can be used to represent rotations in a three-dimensional space. Suppose that we rotate a 3D vector $\boldsymbol{q} = [q_1\ q_2\ q_3]^\top$ to get a new vector $\boldsymbol{p} = [p_1\ p_2\ p_3]^\top$, with an angle θ and along a rotation axis $\boldsymbol{w} = [w_1\ w_2\ w_3]^\top$, $w_1^2 + w_2^2 + w_3^2 = 1$. Such a rotation is equivalent to the following quaternion operation:

$$\hat{p} = \hat{w}\hat{q}\hat{w}^*, \tag{1}$$

where $\hat{q} = 0 + q_1 i + q_2 j + q_3 k$ and $\hat{p} = 0 + p_1 i + p_2 j + p_3 k$ are pure quaternion representations of these two vectors, and

$$\hat{w} = \cos\frac{\theta}{2} + \sin\frac{\theta}{2}(w_1 i + w_2 j + w_3 k). \tag{2}$$

Since its convenience in representing rotations of 3-D vectors, quaternion is widely used in mechanics and physics [10]. In recent years, the theory of quaternion-based harmonic analysis has been well developed and many algorithms have been proposed, *e.g.*, quaternion Fourier transform (QFT) [29], quaternion wavelet transform (QWT) [1,35], and quaternion Kalman filter [2,39]. Most of these algorithms have been proven to work better for 3D objects than real-valued ones. In the field of computer vision and image processing, quaternion-based methods also show its potentials in many tasks. The advantages of quaternion wavelet transform [1,17], quaternion principal component analysis [40] and other quaternion color image processing techniques [37] have been proven to extract more representative features for color images and achieved encouraging results in high-level vision tasks like color image classification. In low-level vision tasks like image denoising and super-resolution, the quaternion-based methods [8,38] preserve more interrelationship information across different channels, and thus, can restore images with higher quality. Recently, a quaternion-based neural network is also put forward and used for classification tasks [3,27,30]. However, how to design a quaternion CNN is still an open problem.

2.2 Real-Valued CNNs and Their Extensions

Convolutional neural network is one of the most successful models in many vision tasks. Since the success of LeNet [21] in digit recognition, great progresses have been made. AlexNet [20] is the first deep CNN that greatly outperforms all past models in image classification task. Then, a number of models with deep and complicated structures are proposed, such as VGG [31] and ResNet [13], which achieve incredible success in ILSVRC [6]. Recently, the CNN models are also introduced for low-level vision tasks. For example, SRCNN [7] applies convolutional neural networks to image super-resolution and outperforms classical methods. For other tasks like denoising [24] and inpainting [34], CNNs also achieve encouraging results.

Some efforts have been made to extend real-valued neural networks to other number fields. Complex-valued neural networks have been built and proved to have advantage on generalization ability [15] and can be more easily optimized [26]. Audio signals can be naturally represented as complex numbers, so the complex CNNs are more suitable for such a kind of tasks than real-valued CNNs. It has been proven that deep complex networks can obtain competitive results with real-valued models on audio-related tasks [32]. In [9], a deep quaternion network is proposed. However, its convolution simply replaces the real multiplications with quaternion ones, and its quaternion kernel is not further parameterized. Our proposed quaternion convolution, however, is physically-meaningful for color image processing tasks.

3 Proposed Quaternion CNNs

3.1 Quaternion Convolution Layers

Focusing on color image representation, our quaternion CNN treats a color image as a 2D pure quaternion matrix, denoted as $\widehat{\boldsymbol{A}} = [\hat{a}_{nn'}] \in \mathbb{H}^{N\times N}$, where N represents the size of the image.[1] In particular, the quaternion matrix $\widehat{\boldsymbol{A}}$ is

$$\widehat{\boldsymbol{A}} = \boldsymbol{0} + \boldsymbol{R}i + \boldsymbol{G}j + \boldsymbol{B}k, \tag{3}$$

where $\boldsymbol{R}, \boldsymbol{G}, \boldsymbol{B} \in \mathbb{R}^{N\times N}$ represent red, green and blue channels, respectively.

Suppose that we have an $L \times L$ quaternion convolution kernel $\widehat{W} = [\hat{w}_{ll'}] \in \mathbb{H}^{L\times L}$. We aim to design an effective and physically-meaningful quaternion convolution operation, denoted as "$\circledast$", between the input $\widehat{\boldsymbol{A}}$ and the kernel $\widehat{W}$. Specifically, this operation should (i) apply rotations and scalings to color vectors in order to find the best representation in the whole color space; (ii) play the same role as real-valued convolution when processing grayscale images. To achieve this aim, we take advantage of the rotational nature of quaternion shown in (1, 2) and propose a quaternion convolution in a particular form. Specifically, we set the element of the quaternion convolution kernel as

$$\hat{w}_{ll'} = s_{ll'}(\cos\frac{\theta_{ll'}}{2} + \sin\frac{\theta_{ll'}}{2}\mu), \tag{4}$$

where $\theta_{ll'} \in [-\pi, \pi]$ and $s_{ll'} \in \mathbb{R}$. μ is the gray axis with unit length (*i.e.*, $\frac{\sqrt{3}}{3}(i+j+k)$). As shown in Eq. 2, we want a unit quaternion to perform rotation. Accordingly, the quaternion convolution is defined as

$$\widehat{\boldsymbol{A}} \circledast \widehat{W} = \widehat{\boldsymbol{F}} = [\hat{f}_{kk'}] \in \mathbb{H}^{(N-L+1)\times(N-L+1)}, \tag{5}$$

where

$$\hat{f}_{kk'} = \sum\nolimits_{l=1}^{L}\sum\nolimits_{l'=1}^{L}\frac{1}{s_{ll'}}\hat{w}_{ll'}\hat{a}_{(k+l)(k'+l')}\hat{w}_{ll'}^{*}. \tag{6}$$

The collection of all such convolution kernels formulates the proposed quaternion convolution layer.

Different from real-valued convolution operation, whose elementary operation is the multiplication between real numbers, the elementary operation of quaternion convolution in (6) actually applies a series of rotations and scalings to the quaternions $\hat{a}_{nn'}$'s in each patch. The rotation axis is set as $(\frac{\sqrt{3}}{3}, \frac{\sqrt{3}}{3}, \frac{\sqrt{3}}{3})$

[1] Without the loss of generality, we assume that both the width and the height of image are equal to N in the following content.

(*i.e.*, grayscale axis in color space) for all operations, while the rotation angle and the scaling factor are specified for each operation by $\theta_{ll'}$ and $s_{ll'}$, respectively.

The advantage of such a definition is interpretable. As shown in Fig. 1(a), the convolution in traditional CNNs operates triple scaling transforms to each pixel independently to walk through three color axes and it needs to find the best representation in the whole color space accordingly. For our QCNNs, one pixel is a quaternion or a 3D vector in color space, but the proposed convolution find its best representation in a small part of the color space because we restrict the convolution to apply only a rotate and a scaling transform. Such a convolution actually impose implicit regularizers on the model, such that we can suppress the risk of over-fitting brought by too many degrees of freedom to the learning of kernels. Additionally, in real-valued CNNs, the input layer transfers 3-channel images to single-channel feature maps, ignoring the interrelationship among channels, which causes information loss. Although the loss can be recovered with multiple different filters, the recovery requires redundant iterations, and there's no guarantee that the loss can be recovered perfectly. In QCNNs, the convolution causes no order reduction in the input layer, thus the information of interrelationship among channels can be fully conserved.

Although our convolution operation is designed for color image, it can be applied to grayscale image as well. For grayscale images, they can be seen as color images whose channels are the same. Because all the corresponding color vectors are parallel to the gray axis, the rotate transform equals to identical transformation, thus the quaternion convolution performs the same function as real-valued convolution. From this viewpoint, real-valued convolution is a special case of quaternion convolution for grayscale image.

According to the rule of quaternion computations, if we represent each $\hat{a}_{nn'}$ as a 3D vector $\boldsymbol{a}_{nn'} = [a_1\ a_2\ a_3]^\top$, then the operation in (6) can be represented by a set of matrix multiplications:

$$\boldsymbol{f}_{kk'} = \sum\nolimits_{l=1}^{L} \sum\nolimits_{l'=1}^{L} s_{ll'} \begin{pmatrix} f_1 & f_2 & f_3 \\ f_3 & f_1 & f_2 \\ f_2 & f_3 & f_1 \end{pmatrix} \boldsymbol{a}_{(k+l)(k'+l')}, \tag{7}$$

where $\boldsymbol{f}_{kk'}$ is a vectorized representation of quaternion $\hat{f}_{kk'}$, and

$$f_1 = \frac{1}{3} + \frac{2}{3}\cos\theta_{ll'},\ f_2 = \frac{1}{3} - \frac{2}{3}\cos(\theta_{ll'} - \frac{\pi}{3}),\ f_3 = \frac{1}{3} - \frac{2}{3}\cos(\theta_{ll'} + \frac{\pi}{3}). \tag{8}$$

The detailed derivation from (6) to (7) is given in the supplementary file. Additionally, because the inputs and outputs of quaternion convolutions are both pure quaternion matrices, quaternion convolution layers can be stacked like what we do in real-valued CNNs and most architectures of real-valued CNNs can also be used in QCNNs. In other words, the proposed quaternion convolution is compatible with traditional real-valued convolution.

According to (7), we can find that a quaternion convolution layer has twice as many parameters as the real-valued convolution layer with same structure and same number of filtering kernels since an arbitrary element of quaternion convolution kernel has two trainable parameters s and θ. Denote K as the number of kernels, L as kernel size and C as the number of input channels. A real-valued convolution layer with K $L \times L \times C$ kernels has KCL^2 parameters, and we require L^2N^2KC multiplications to process C $N \times N$ feature maps. A quaternion layer with K $L \times L \times C$ kernels has $2KCL^2$ parameters: each kernel has CL^2 angle parameters $[\theta_{ll'c}]$ and CL^2 scaling parameters $[s_{ll'c}]$. To process C $N \times N \times 3$ color feature maps, we need $9L^2N^2KC$ multiplications because each output quaternion $\boldsymbol{f}_{kk'}$ requires $9L^2$ multiplications, as shown in the (7). By reducing the number of the kernels and channels to $\frac{K}{\sqrt{2}}$ and $\frac{C}{\sqrt{2}}$, the number of the quaternion layer's parameters is halved and equal to that of real-valued layer. Since the number of channels C in one layer is equal to the number of kernels K in the previous layer, by reducing the number of the kernels in all layers with the ratio $\frac{1}{\sqrt{2}}$, we half the number of QCNN's parameters and half the number of operations to 4.5 times as that of the real-valued CNN. Note that the matrix multiplication in the (7) can be optimized and parallelized when implemented by Tensorflow. In our experiments, our QCNNs only takes about twice as much time as real-valued CNNs with same number of parameters. According to our following experiments, such a simplification will not do harm to our QCNN model — experimental results show that the QCNNs with comparable number of parameters to real-valued CNNs can still have superior performance.

3.2 Quaternion Fully-Connected Layers

The quaternion convolution layer mentioned above preserves more interrelationship information and extracting better features than real-valued one. However, if we had to connect it to a common fully-connected layer, that kind of information preserved would be lost. Therefore, here we design a quaternion fully-connected layer that performs same operation as quaternion convolution layer to keep the interrelationship information between channels. Specifically, similar to the real-valued CNNs, whose fully-connected layers can be seen as special cases of one-dimensional convolution layers with kernels having same shapes with inputs, our quaternion fully-connected layers follow the same rule. Suppose that the input is an N-dimensional quaternion vector $\hat{\boldsymbol{a}} = [\hat{a}_i] \in \mathbb{H}^N$, for $i = 1, 2, 3...N$. Applying M 1D quaternion filtering kernels, *i.e.*, $\hat{\boldsymbol{w}}^m = [\hat{w}_i^m] \in \mathbb{H}^M$ for $m = 1, .., M$, we obtain an output $\hat{\boldsymbol{b}} = [\hat{b}_m] \in \mathbb{H}^M$ with element

$$\hat{b}_m = \sum\nolimits_{i=1}^{N} \frac{1}{s_i} \hat{w}_i^m \hat{a}_i \hat{w}_i^{m*}, \tag{9}$$

where s_i is the magnitude of $\hat{w}_i^m$.

Similar to our quaternion convolution layer, the computation of the proposed quaternion fully-connected layer can also be reformulated as a set of matrix multiplications, and thus, it is also compatible with real-valued CNNs.

3.3 Typical Nonlinear Layers

Pooling and activation are import layers to achieve nonlinear operations. For our QCNN model, we extend those widely-used real-valued nonlinear layers to quaternion versions. For average-pooling, the average operation of quaternion is same as averaging the 3 imaginary parts respectively. For max-pooling, we can define various criterions such as magnitude or projection to gray axis to judge which element to choose.

In our experiments, we find that simply applying max-pooling to 3 imaginary parts respectively can provides us with good learning results. Similarly, we use same activation functions with real-valued CNNs for each channel respectively in QCNNs. For ReLU, if a vector of quaternion is rotated out of valid value range in color space, e.g. negative color value for RGB channels, we reset it to the nearest point in color space.

For softmax, we split the output of the quaternion layer in to real numbers and connect them to real-valued softmax layers and train classifiers accordingly.

3.4 Connecting with Real-Valued Networks

Using the modules mentioned above, we can establish arbitrary fully-quaternion CNNs easily. Moreover, because of the compatibility of these modules, we can also build hybrid convolutional neural networks using both quaternion-based layers and common real-valued layers. In particular,

- **Connect to real-valued convolution layer:** The feature map that a quaternion layer outputs can be split into 3 grayscale feature maps, each corresponding to one channel. Then, we can connect each of these three maps to real-valued convolution layers independently, or concatenate them together and connect with a single real-valued convolution layers.
- **Connect to real-valued fully-connected layer:** Similarly, we flatten the output of a quaternion layer and treat each quaternion element as 3 real numbers. Thus, we obtain a real-valued and vectorized output which can be connected to real-valued fully-connected layer easily.

4 Learning Quaternion CNNs

4.1 Weight Initialization

Proper weight initialization is essential for a network to be successfully trained. This principle is also applicable to our QCNN model. According to our analysis above, the scaling factor s corresponds to the parameters in real-valued CNNs, which controls the magnitude of transformed vector, while the rotation angle θ is an additional parameter, which only makes the transformed vector an rotation of input vector. Additionally, when transformed vectors are added together, though the magnitude is affected by θ, its projection to gray axis is still independent of θ. Therefore, we follow the suggestion proposed in [11] and perform normalized initialization in order to keep variance of the gradients same during training. Specifically, for each scaling factor and each rotation factor of the j-th layer, *i.e.*, s_j and θ, and we initialize them as two uniform random variables:

$$s_j \sim U\left[-\frac{\sqrt{6}}{\sqrt{n_j+n_{j+1}}}, \frac{\sqrt{6}}{\sqrt{n_j+n_{j+1}}}\right], \quad \theta \sim U\left[-\frac{\pi}{2}, \frac{\pi}{2}\right]. \tag{10}$$

where $U[\cdot]$ represents a uniform distribution, and n_j means the dimension of the j-th layer's input.

4.2 Backpropagation

Backpropagation is the key of training a network, which applies the chain rule to compute gradients of the parameters and updates them. Denote L as the real-valued loss function used to train our quaternion CNN model. $\hat{p} = p_1 i + p_2 j + p_3 k$ and $\hat{q} = q_1 i + q_2 j + q_3 k$ are two pure quaternion variables. For the operation we perform in the QCNN, *i.e.*, $\hat{p} = \frac{1}{s}\hat{w}\hat{q}\hat{w}^*$, it can be equivalently represented by a set of matrix multiplications. So is the corresponding quaternion gradient. Particularly, we have:

$$\frac{\partial L}{\partial \boldsymbol{q}} = \frac{\partial L}{\partial \boldsymbol{p}}\frac{\partial \boldsymbol{p}}{\partial \boldsymbol{q}}, \quad \frac{\partial L}{\partial \theta} = \frac{\partial L}{\partial \boldsymbol{p}}\frac{\partial \boldsymbol{p}}{\partial \theta}, \quad \frac{\partial L}{\partial s} = \frac{\partial L}{\partial \boldsymbol{p}}\frac{\partial \boldsymbol{p}}{\partial s}, \tag{11}$$

where $\boldsymbol{p} = [p_1, p_2, p_3]^\top$ and $\boldsymbol{q} = [q_1, q_2, q_3]^\top$ are vectors corresponding to $\hat{p}$ and $\hat{q}$. When $\boldsymbol{p}$ and $\boldsymbol{q}$ are arbitrary elements of feature maps and filtering kernels, corresponding to $\boldsymbol{a}_{nn'}$ and $\boldsymbol{w}_{ll'}$ in (7), we have

$$\frac{\partial \boldsymbol{p}}{\partial \boldsymbol{q}} = s\begin{pmatrix} f_1 & f_2 & f_3 \\ f_3 & f_1 & f_2 \\ f_2 & f_3 & f_1 \end{pmatrix}, \quad \frac{\partial \boldsymbol{p}}{\partial \theta} = s\begin{pmatrix} f_1' & f_2' & f_3' \\ f_3' & f_1' & f_2' \\ f_2' & f_3' & f_1' \end{pmatrix}\begin{pmatrix} q_1 \\ q_2 \\ q_3 \end{pmatrix}, \quad \frac{\partial \boldsymbol{p}}{\partial s} = \begin{pmatrix} f_1 & f_2 & f_3 \\ f_3 & f_1 & f_2 \\ f_2 & f_3 & f_1 \end{pmatrix}\begin{pmatrix} q_1 \\ q_2 \\ q_3 \end{pmatrix} \tag{12}$$

where f_i, $i = 1, 2, 3$, is defined as (8) does. The matrix of f_i's is exactly same as that in (7), but the operation switches from left multiplication to right multiplication. In other words, the backward process can be explained as a rotate transform with the same axis and a reverse angle.

4.3 Loss and Activation Functions

In neural networks, loss and activation functions must be differentiable for the gradient to generate and propagate. For fully-quaternion CNNs, any functions which are differentiable with respect to each part of the quaternion variables also make the quaternion chain rule hold, and thus, can be used as loss (and activation) functions. For hybrid CNNs, we select loss functions according to the category of tasks. In classification tasks, the top of the networks are real-valued fully-connected layers, before which the quaternion inputs are flattened as Sect. 3.4 suggested, and the loss function is cross entropy loss. In other tasks (*e.g.*, regression tasks) that the network outputs images, quaternion outputs of the top layer are regarded as the 3-channel images, and the loss function can be mean square error (MSE) or other similar functions.

5 Experiments

To demonstrate the superiority and the universality of our QCNN model, we test it on two typical vision tasks: color image classification and color image

Table 1. Experiment results in classification tasks

Model	Dataset	Test accuracy
Shallow real network	Cifar-10	0.7546
Shallow quaternion network	Cifar-10	**0.7778**
Real-valued VGG-S	102 flowers	0.7308
Quaternion VGG-S	102 flowers	**0.7695**
Quaternion VGG-S with fewer filters	102 flowers	**0.7603**

denoising. These two tasks represent typical high-level and low-level vision tasks. Compared with real-valued CNN models in these two tasks, our QCNN models show improvements on learning results consistently. **Some typical experimental results are shown and analyzed below, and more representative results and details are given in the supplementary file.**

5.1 Color Image Classification

We have tested two QCNN architectures in our research, a shallow network for cifar-10 [19], and a relatively deep one for 102 Oxford flowers [25]. For comparison, real-valued networks with same structure and comparable number of parameters are also trained in the same datasets. Both quaternion and real-valued networks use a real-valued fully-connected layer with softmax function, or a softmax layer to classify the input images. The real-valued networks use ReLU as activation functions, while the quaternion ones adapt ReLU for each imaginary part separately. All those networks are trained with cross entropy loss. Input data is augmented by shifting and flipping.

The proposed shallow network for cifar-10 contains 2 convolution blocks, each has 2 convolution layers and a max-pooling layer, and ends with 2 fully-connected layers. In the experiment, each layer of real-valued CNN and QCNN are of same number of filters, so actually QCNN has more parameters. Both models are optimized using RMSProp [14] with learning rate set at 0.0001, and learning rate decay set at 1e-6. The training ends at epoch 80.

The network for 102 Oxford flowers is VGG-S [5], which has 5 convolution layers, 3 pooling layers and 3 fully-connected layers. In this experiment, a QCNN with same number of filters as real-valued one and another one with fewer filters to keep the similar number of parameters are both tested. Models are optimized using Adam [18] with learning rate set at 0.0001. The training ends at epoch 50.

In Fig. 2, we can find that the performance of our QCNNs is consistently better than that of real-valued CNNs. For each data set, the loss function of our QCNN converges more quickly than that of real-valued CNNs in the training phase and reaches smaller loss finally. The classification accuracy on the testing set obtained by our QCNN is also better than that of real-valued CNN even in the very beginning of training phase. Moreover, even if we reduce the number of QCNN's parameters, the proposed QCNN model is still superior to

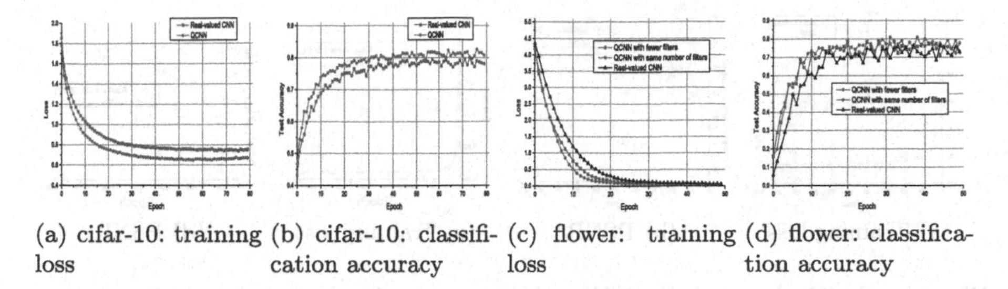

(a) cifar-10: training loss (b) cifar-10: classification accuracy (c) flower: training loss (d) flower: classification accuracy

Fig. 2. (a, b) The loss and the test accuracy of the shallow networks during training on cifar-10. (c, d) The loss and the test accuracy of the VGG-S networks during training on 102 Oxford flower data set (256 test images picked randomly from the test set for each epoch).

Table 2. Experiment results in denoising tasks

Model	Dataset	Test PSNR (dB)	Dataset	Test PSNR (dB)
Real-valued CNN	102 flowers	30.9792	Subset of COCO	30.4900
Quaternion CNN	102 flowers	**31.3176**	Subset of COCO	**30.7256**

the real-valued CNN with the same size. These phenomena verify our claims before. Firstly, although a QCNN can have more parameters than real-valued CNN, it can suffer less from the risk of over-fitting because of the implicit regularizers imposed by the computation of quaternions. Secondly, the quaternion convolution achieves both the scaling and the rotation of inputs in color space, which preserves more discriminative information for color images, and this information is beneficial for classifying color images, especially for classifying those images in which the objects have obvious color attributes (*i.e.*, the flowers in 102 Oxford flower data set). The quantitative experimental results are given in Table 1, which further demonstrates the superiority of our model.

5.2 Color Image Denoising

Besides the high-level vision tasks like image classification, the proposed QCNN can also obtain improvements in the low-level vision tasks. In fact, because our QCNN model can obtain more structural representation of color information, it is naturally suitable for extracting low-level features and replacing the bottom convolution layers of real-valued CNNs. To demonstrate our claim, we test our QCNN model in color image denoising task. Inspired from the encoder-decoder networks with symmetric skip connections for image restoration [24] and denoising autoencoders [33], a U-Net-like [28] encoder-decoder structure with skip connections is used for denoising in our research. The encoder contains two 2×2 average-pooling layers, each following after two 3×3 convolution layers, then two 3×3 convolution layers and a fully-connected layer. The decoder is symmetrical to the encoder, containing up-sampling and transposed convolution layers.

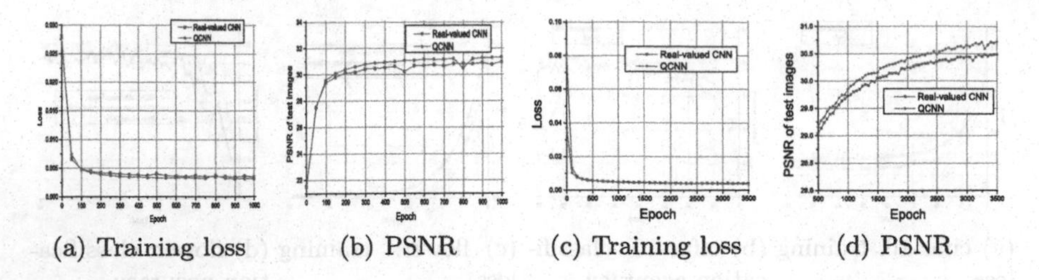

(a) Training loss (b) PSNR (c) Training loss (d) PSNR

Fig. 3. (a, b) The loss and the PSNR of test images using proposed denoising networks during training on 102 Oxford flower data set. (c, d) The loss and the PSNR of test images using proposed denoising networks during training on COCO subset.

The layers before pooling and that after up-sampling are connected by shortcuts. A QCNN and a real-valued CNN with this structure are both built, and the QCNN has fewer filters each layer to ensure a similar number of parameters to the real-valued CNN. Similar to networks for classification, both networks use ReLU as activation functions except the top layer, whose activation function is "tanh" function. Both networks are trained with MSE loss.

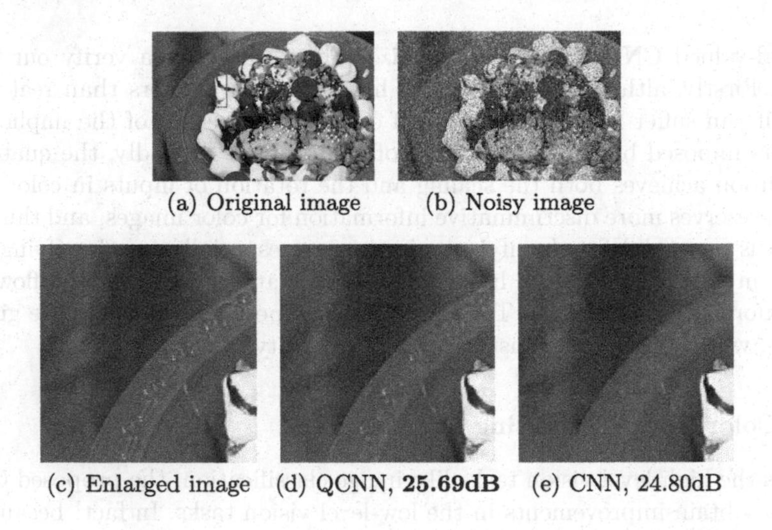

(a) Original image (b) Noisy image

(c) Enlarged image (d) QCNN, **25.69dB** (e) CNN, 24.80dB

Fig. 4. Denoising experiment on a image of snacks.

We trained and tested these two models on two data sets: the 102 Oxford flower data set and a subset of COCO data set [22]. These two data sets are representative for our research: the flower data set is a case having colorful images, which is used to prove the superiority of our QCNN model conceptually; while the COCO subset is a more general set of natural images, which have both colorful and colorless images and can be used to prove the performance of our model in practice.

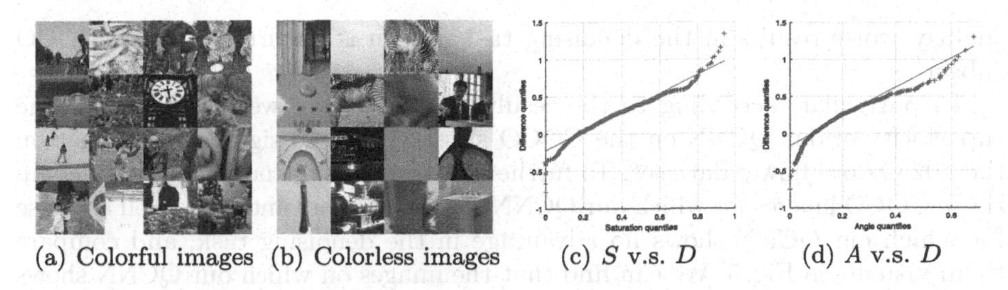

(a) Colorful images (b) Colorless images (c) S v.s. D (d) A v.s. D

Fig. 5. In the denoising task, QCNN shows at least 0.5dB higher PSNR than CNN for images in (a). For images in (b), CNN offers better result. (c) The quantile-quantile plot of saturation versus PSNR difference. (d) The quantile-quantile plot of average angle between color vectors and gray axis versus PSNR difference.

In our experiments, both the training and the testing images are cut and resized to 128×128 pixels with values normalized to $[0, 1]$. Then a salt and pepper noise which corrupts 30% of pixels and a Gaussian noise with zero mean and 0.01 variance are added. The inputs of networks are corrupted images, and target outputs are original images. For both real-valued CNN and our QCNN model, the optimizer is Adam with 0.001 learning rate, and the batch size is 64 for the 102 Oxford flower data set and 32 for the COCO subset, respectively.

Table 2 shows quantitative comparisons for the real-valued CNN model and the proposed QCNN model. We can find that our QCNN model obtains higher PSNR values consistently on both data sets. The change of loss function and that of PSNR on testing set are given in Fig. 3 for the two data sets. Similar to the experiments in color image classification task, the loss function of our QCNN converges more quickly to a smaller value and its PSNR on testing images becomes higher than that of the real-valued CNN after 100 epochs. Furthermore, we show a visual comparison for the denosing results of the real-valued CNN and our QCNN in Fig. 4. We can find that our QCNN preserves more detailed structures in the image (*e.g.*, the pattern on the plate) than the real-valued CNN does. Suffering from information loss during feature encoding, real-valued CNNs cannot perfectly preserve the details of color images, especially when the structure presents sharp color variations. Our QCNN, on the contrary, can avoid this information loss and learn more texture features even in bottom layers, so it outputs images of higher fidelity. High-resolution visual comparisons can be found in the supplementary file.

5.3 Discussion on Advantages and Limitations

As aforementioned, our QCNN is motivated for color image representation. When it comes to the images with little variety of colors, our QCNN degrades to a model similar to real-valued CNN,[2] and thus, obtains just comparable or

[2] As we mentioned in Sect. 3.1, for grayscale images, QCNNs perform exactly the same as real-valued CNNs with same number of filters.

slightly worse results in the denoising task, which is confirmed on the COCO subset.

In particular, according to the results shown above, we can find that the superiority of our QCNN on the COCO subset is not so significant as that on the 102 Oxford flower data set. To further analysis this phenomenon, we pick up those COCO images for which our QCNN shows great advantage as well as those for which our QCNN shows no advantage in the denoising task, and compare them visually in Fig. 5. We can find that the images on which our QCNN shows better performance are often colorful, while images where our QCNN is inferior to the real-valued CNN are close to grayscale images.

To further investigate QCNN's advantages, we use two metrics as quantitative descriptions of "colorful images". The first metric is the mean saturation of color image, denoted as S. For an image, a low S indicates that this image is similar to a grayscale image, while a high S value implies this image is with high color saturation (*i.e.* many colorful parts). The second metric is the averaged angle between the pixel (color vector) of color image and grayscale axis, denoted as A. For an image, the larger the averaged angle is, the colorful the image is. We show the quantile-quantile plots of these two metrics with respect to the difference between PSNR value of real-valued CNN and that of our QCNN (denoted as D) in Fig. 5(c) and (d), respectively. We can find that both S and A are correlated with D positively. It means that our QCNN can show its dominant advantages over real-valued CNNs when the target images are colorful. Otherwise, its performance is almost the same with that of real-valued CNNs.

6 Conclusions and Future Work

In this paper, we introduce QCNN, a quaternion-based neural network, which obtains better performance on both color image classification and color image denoising than traditional real-valued CNNs do. A novel quaternion convolution operation is defined to represent color information in a more structural way. A series of quaternion-based layers are designed with good compatibility to existing real-valued networks and reasonable computational complexity. In summary, the proposed model is a valuable extension of neural network model in other number fields. In the future, we plan to explore more efficient algorithms for the learning of QCNNs. For example, as we mentioned in Sect. 4.2, for QCNNs their backpropagation of gradients can be represented by reverse rotations of color vectors with respect to the forward propagation of inputs. Such a property provides us a chance to reduce the computation of the backpropagation given the intermediate information of forward propagation and accelerate the learning of QCNNs accordingly. Additionally, we will extend our QCNN model to large-scale data and more applications.

Acknowledgment. This work was supported in part by National Science Foundation of China (61671298, U1611461, 61502301, 61521062), STCSM (17511105400, 17511105402, 18DZ2270700), China's Thousand Youth Talents Plan, the 111 project

B07022, the MoE Key Lab of Artificial Intelligence, AI Institute of Shanghai Jiao Tong University, and the SJTU-UCLA Joint Center for Machine Perception and Inference. The corresponding author of this paper is Yi Xu (xuyi@sjtu.edu.cn).

References

1. Bayro-Corrochano, E.: The theory and use of the quaternion wavelet transform. J. Math. Imaging Vis. **24**(1), 19–35 (2006)
2. Bayro-Corrochano, E., Zhang, Y.: The motor extended Kalman filter: a geometric approach for rigid motion estimation. J. Math. Imaging Vis. **13**(3), 205–228 (2000)
3. Bayro-Corrochano, E.J.: Geometric neural computing. IEEE Trans. Neural Netw. **12**(5), 968–986 (2001)
4. Cao, Z., Simon, T., Wei, S.E., Sheikh, Y.: Realtime multi-person 2D pose estimation using part affinity fields. In: CVPR, vol. 1, p. 7 (2017)
5. Chatfield, K., Simonyan, K., Vedaldi, A., Zisserman, A.: Return of the devil in the details: Delving deep into convolutional nets. arXiv preprint arXiv:1405.3531 (2014)
6. Deng, J., Dong, W., Socher, R., Li, L.J., Li, K., Fei-Fei, L.: ImageNet: a large-scale hierarchical image database. In: IEEE Conference on Computer Vision and Pattern Recognition, CVPR 2009, pp. 248–255. IEEE (2009)
7. Dong, C., Loy, C.C., He, K., Tang, X.: Learning a deep convolutional network for image super-resolution. In: Fleet, D., Pajdla, T., Schiele, B., Tuytelaars, T. (eds.) ECCV 2014. LNCS, vol. 8692, pp. 184–199. Springer, Cham (2014). https://doi.org/10.1007/978-3-319-10593-2_13
8. Gai, S., Wang, L., Yang, G., Yang, P.: Sparse representation based on vector extension of reduced quaternion matrix for multiscale image denoising. IET Image Process. **10**(8), 598–607 (2016)
9. Gaudet, C., Maida, A.: Deep quaternion networks. arXiv preprint arXiv:1712.04604 (2017)
10. Girard, P.R.: The quaternion group and modern physics. Eur. J. Phys. **5**(1), 25 (1984)
11. Glorot, X., Bengio, Y.: Understanding the difficulty of training deep feedforward neural networks. J. Mach. Learn. Res. **9**, 249–256 (2010)
12. He, K., Gkioxari, G., Doll, P., Girshick, R.: Mask R-CNN (2017)
13. He, K., Zhang, X., Ren, S., Sun, J.: Deep residual learning for image recognition. In: Proceedings of the IEEE Conference on Computer Vision and Pattern Recognition, pp. 770–778 (2016)
14. Hinton, G., Srivastava, N., Swersky, K.: Neural networks for machine learning lecture 6a overview of mini-batch gradient descent (2012)
15. Hirose, A., Yoshida, S.: Generalization characteristics of complex-valued feedforward neural networks in relation to signal coherence. IEEE Trans. Neural Netw. Learn. Syst. **23**(4), 541–551 (2012)
16. Huang, G., Liu, Z., Weinberger, K.Q., van der Maaten, L.: Densely connected convolutional networks. In: Proceedings of the IEEE Conference on Computer Vision and Pattern Recognition, vol. 1, p. 3 (2017)
17. Jones, C.F., Abbott, A.L., Chair, R.W., Conners, R.W., Ehrich, I., Jacobs, S., Midkiff: Color face recognition using quaternionic gabor filters (2003)
18. Kingma, D.P., Ba, J.: Adam: A method for stochastic optimization. arXiv preprint arXiv:1412.6980 (2014)

19. Krizhevsky, A., Hinton, G.: Learning multiple layers of features from tiny images (2009)
20. Krizhevsky, A., Sutskever, I., Hinton, G.E.: ImageNet classification with deep convolutional neural networks. In: Advances in Neural Information Processing Systems, pp. 1097–1105 (2012)
21. LeCun, Y., et al.: Backpropagation applied to handwritten zip code recognition. Neural Comput. **1**(4), 541–551 (1989)
22. Lin, T.-Y., et al.: Microsoft COCO: common objects in context. In: Fleet, D., Pajdla, T., Schiele, B., Tuytelaars, T. (eds.) ECCV 2014. LNCS, vol. 8693, pp. 740–755. Springer, Cham (2014). https://doi.org/10.1007/978-3-319-10602-1_48
23. Long, J., Shelhamer, E., Darrell, T.: Fully convolutional networks for semantic segmentation. In: Proceedings of the IEEE Conference on Computer Vision and Pattern Recognition, pp. 3431–3440 (2015)
24. Mao, X., Shen, C., Yang, Y.B.: Image restoration using very deep convolutional encoder-decoder networks with symmetric skip connections. In: Advances in Neural Information Processing Systems, pp. 2802–2810 (2016)
25. Nilsback, M.E., Zisserman, A.: Automated flower classification over a large number of classes. In: Sixth Indian Conference on Computer Vision, Graphics & Image Processing, ICVGIP 2008, pp. 722–729. IEEE (2008)
26. Nitta, T.: On the critical points of the complex-valued neural network. In: International Conference on Neural Information Processing, pp. 1099–1103, vol. 3 (2002)
27. Nitta, T.: A quaternary version of the back-propagation algorithm. In: IEEE International Conference on Neural Networks, 1995 Proceedings, vol. 5, pp. 2753–2756. IEEE (1995)
28. Ronneberger, O., Fischer, P., Brox, T.: U-Net: convolutional networks for biomedical image segmentation. In: Navab, N., Hornegger, J., Wells, W.M., Frangi, A.F. (eds.) MICCAI 2015. LNCS, vol. 9351, pp. 234–241. Springer, Cham (2015). https://doi.org/10.1007/978-3-319-24574-4_28
29. Sangwine, S.J.: Fourier transforms of colour images using quaternion or hypercomplex, numbers. Electron. Lett. **32**(21), 1979–1980 (1996)
30. Shang, F., Hirose, A.: Quaternion neural-network-based polsar land classification in poincare-sphere-parameter space. IEEE Trans. Geosci. Remote Sens. **52**(9), 5693–5703 (2014)
31. Simonyan, K., Zisserman, A.: Very deep convolutional networks for large-scale image recognition. arXiv preprint arXiv:1409.1556 (2014)
32. Trabelsi, C., et al.: Deep complex networks. arXiv preprint arXiv:1705.09792 (2017)
33. Vincent, P., Larochelle, H., Bengio, Y., Manzagol, P.A.: Extracting and composing robust features with denoising autoencoders. In: Proceedings of the 25th International Conference on Machine Learning, pp. 1096–1103. ACM (2008)
34. Xie, J., Xu, L., Chen, E.: Image denoising and inpainting with deep neural networks. In: Advances in Neural Information Processing Systems, pp. 341–349 (2012)
35. Xu, Y., Yang, X., Song, L., Traversoni, L., Lu, W.: QWT retrospective and new applications. In: Bayro-Corrochano, E., Scheuermann, G. (eds.) Geometric Algebra Computing, pp. 249–273. Springer, London (2010). https://doi.org/10.1007/978-1-84996-108-0_13
36. Xu, Y., Yu, L., Xu, H., Zhang, H., Nguyen, T.: Vector sparse representation of color image using quaternion matrix analysis. IEEE Trans. Image Process. **24**(4), 1315–1329 (2015)

37. Yu, L., Xu, Y., Xu, H., Zhang, H.: Quaternion-based sparse representation of color image. In: 2013 IEEE International Conference on Multimedia and Expo (ICME), pp. 1–7. IEEE (2013)
38. Yu, M., Xu, Y., Sun, P.: Single color image super-resolution using quaternion-based sparse representation. In: 2014 IEEE International Conference on Acoustics, Speech and Signal Processing (ICASSP), pp. 5804–5808. IEEE (2014)
39. Yun, X., Bachmann, E.R.: Design, implementation, and experimental results of a quaternion-based Kalman filter for human body motion tracking. IEEE Trans. Robot. **22**(6), 1216–1227 (2006)
40. Zeng, R., et al.: Color image classification via quaternion principal component analysis network. Neurocomputing **216**, 416–428 (2016)

Stereo Relative Pose from Line and Point Feature Triplets

Alexander Vakhitov[1(✉)], Victor Lempitsky[1], and Yinqiang Zheng[2]

[1] Skoltech, Moscow Nobelya Ulitsa 3, 121207, Russia
{a.vakhitov,lempitsky}@skoltech.ru
[2] NII, 2-1-2 Hitotsubashi, Chiyoda-ku, Tokyo 101-8430, Japan
yqzheng@nii.ac.jp

Abstract. Stereo relative pose problem lies at the core of stereo visual odometry systems that are used in many applications. In this work we present two minimal solvers for the stereo relative pose. We specifically consider the case when a minimal set consists of three point or line features and each of them has three known projections on two stereo cameras. We validate the importance of this formulation for practical purposes in our experiments with motion estimation. We then present a complete classification of minimal cases with three point or line correspondences each having three projections, and present two new solvers that can handle all such cases. We demonstrate a considerable effect from the integration of the new solvers into a visual SLAM system.

Keywords: Minimal solver · Stereo visual odometry
Generalized camera · Relative pose · Line features

1 Introduction

Minimal solvers in computer vision are used to generate camera motion hypotheses from required minimal sets of feature correspondences, e.g. five feature point correspondences for single camera relative pose estimation [1]. Such solvers are mostly used as a source of motion hypotheses inside a RANSAC loop [2]. They are useful in providing initialization for the optimization procedures at the core of state-of-the-art SLAM systems [3]. For many pose estimation problems, such solvers have already been developed and are extensively used, e.g. to create large-scale structure from motion reconstructions involving thousands of images [4]. It

The work is funded by the Russian MES grant RFMEFI61516X0003; a part of this work was finished when Alexander Vakhitov was visiting the National Institute of Informatics (NII), Japan, funded by the NII MOU/Non-MOU International Exchange Program.

Electronic supplementary material The online version of this chapter (https://doi.org/10.1007/978-3-030-01237-3_40) contains supplementary material, which is available to authorized users.

V. Ferrari et al. (Eds.): ECCV 2018, LNCS 11212, pp. 662–677, 2018.
https://doi.org/10.1007/978-3-030-01237-3_40

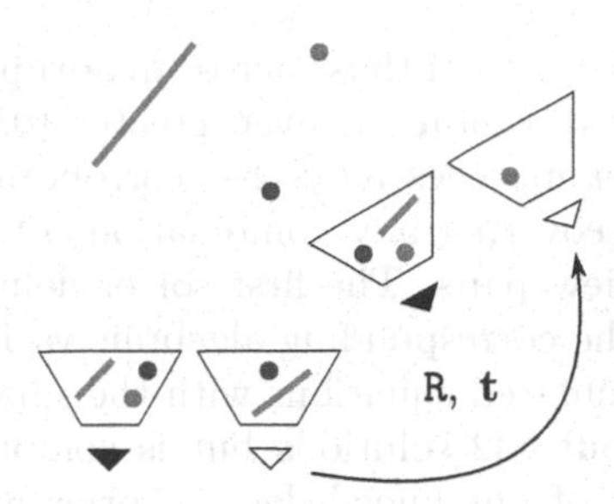

Fig. 1. Left:using three line or point features, each having exactly three projections, we seek to determine the relative pose of the two stereoviews. Right: the use of three-view matches (bottom) by the proposed solvers results in higher number of inliers compared to the use of four-view matches (top). We show the projections of the inlier correspondences on one of the images of KITTI sequence 0 chosen by the method Pradeep [8] using four-view matches (top) and by the proposed EpiSEgo solver using three-view matches (bottom).

is important to develop minimal solvers taking line segment correspondences as input in addition to points. As recent works demonstrated [5,6], the use of line segment features can considerably improve accuracy and robustness of visual SLAM and structure from motion systems.

To the best of our knowledge, there is no minimal solver for stereo camera relative pose estimation which is efficient enough for real-time use and does not rely on simplifying assumptions limiting its applicability. Thus, [7] is computationally heavy for real-time use, [8] is non-minimal and [9] employs an approximate rotation model that is valid only for small rotations. In this work, we describe two solvers that aim to close this gap, giving an efficient minimal solution to the stereo camera egomotion from three feature triplets. We assume that there are two stereo cameras with projection matrices $\mathtt{P}_{1,1} = [\mathbf{I},\ \mathbf{0}]$, $\mathtt{P}_{1,2} = [\mathbf{I},\ \mathbf{b}]$ for the first camera, $\mathtt{P}_{2,1} = [\mathbf{R},\ \mathbf{t}]$ and $\mathtt{P}_{2,2} = [\mathbf{R},\ \mathbf{b}+\mathbf{t}]$ for the second one, where the baseline $\mathbf{b}$ is known. The goal of the solvers is to find $\mathbf{R}$ and $\mathbf{t}$. In each case, we use three feature triplets, where each triplet is a set of three[1] projections of a 3D line or a 3D point computed using $\{\mathtt{P}_\alpha, \mathtt{P}_\beta, \mathtt{P}_\gamma\}$, $\alpha \neq \beta \neq \gamma$.

While the ability to use features with three rather than four known projections may seem unnecessary for a stereo system, we show that such ability actually provides considerable benefits. To illustrate this, we made a motivation experiment using the first sequence of the KITTI Odometry dataset [11]. We use ORB [12] and LBD [13] features and matched them between neighboring frames and across stereo-views. We then use the provided ground truth poses to estimate the ratio of inlier matches. We observe that for ORB matches the ratio

[1] In the presence of two-view correspondences only, the overlapped stereo can be regarded as a non-overlapped stereo, and some solutions have been proposed as in [7,9,10]. We exclude this case from consideration because the major focus of this work is on overlapped stereo systems.

of inlier matches across triplets of views is greater than those across quadruplets (0.121 vs 0.077). For LBD line matches, the advantage is even greater (0.019 vs 0.005). The advantage of relying on triplet matches is further corroborated in our experiments. We develop two solvers covering any combinations of the point/line correspondences among the two view pairs. The first solver delivers 16 solutions, which is equal to the degree of the corresponding algebraic variety. It is impossible to obtain a solver for the formulated equations with the smaller number of solutions. The second solver outputs 32 solutions but is computationally simpler. Both are novel: to the best of our knowledge, no prior work describes a solution to the stereo camera relative pose problem for any combination of line/point features with three projections or even only for the point features.

Experiments show that our solvers are numerically stable and computationally efficient. More interestingly, by using point and line features simultaneously, our solvers work reliably for real scenarios. The use of three-view correspondences allows increasing the inlier cardinality and ratio, which not only facilitates the RANSAC procedure, but also reduces the risk of drifting in the case of long trajectories.

To summarize, we make the following contributions. Firstly, we systematically explore the stereo ego-motion estimation problem in the case of a minimal set of three point and line features with three correspondences. Secondly, we develop new minimal solvers, which output a minimal number of solutions, and demonstrate the increase in accuracy and robustness of stereo egomotion estimation on simulated and real data.

In Sect. 2, we review the most closely related works on ego-motion estimation. In Sect. 3, we show the problem formulation and the complete categorization of the minimal point and line sets in any three views. We present the experiment results in Sect. 4.

2 Related Work

Non-overlapping fields of view: To increase the coverage of the field of view (FoV) and to decrease the costs as much as possible, it became popular in recent years to use multiple cameras without overlapped FoVs. The generalized relative pose method proposed in [7] can be applied to estimate the relative pose of such multicamera systems, however it returns up to 64 solutions and is too computationally expensive for real-time use. To solve the problem in real-time, authors introduce certain approximations, e.g. Kneip and Li [10] proposed to use non-minimal point sets and developed an approximated iterative optimization method, whose running speed is inappropriate for realtime applications. For acceleration, Ventura et al. [9] linearized the rotation between two consecutive time frames, so the solver does not apply in the general visual odometry setting.

Overlapping fields of view: Binocular stereo systems with partially overlapping FoVs are preferable in terms of system calibration and metric reconstruction. To estimate the ego-motion of an overlapping stereo rig, Nister et al. [14] proposed to use three points or two lines matched across all four views via triangulation. Chandraker et al. [15] showed that the triangulation of four-view correspondences for ego-motion estimation is unstable, especially when the baseline is small. They proposed instead to use three four-view line correspondences. Pradeep and Lim [8] used assorted point and line features and developed several minimal solvers for any point and line combinations, as long as these features are simultaneously visible in all four views. Clipp et al. [16] used point features in a mixed number of views, and Dunn et al. [17] used similar input data and accelerated the solving speed by using the constraints in proper ways. Discarding the correspondences without projections onto both views of one stereo camera, one can use generalized absolute pose solvers [18–23]. To summarize, no prior work addresses stereo relative pose problem for three features with three projections. Most of the studies consider the case of 4-view correspondences of only point features.

3 Stereo Egomotion Solvers

We address the problem of feature-based relative pose estimation for the binocular stereo camera, assuming that each line or point has exactly three projections. The minimal set in this case consists of three features. Trifocal tensors provide a way to formulate constraints for the line and point features arising from three perspective views. Using the translation and rotation parameterizations (1), (2)

Table 1. The table enumerates all possible cases (excluding symmetries) and points to the section that discusses each case. Latin letters are for points and Greek are for lines (the details of the notation are discussed in the beginning of Sect. 3.2).

Case	Sect.	Example			
		1st cam		2nd cam	
S3P	3.5	a, b, c	a, b, c	a	b, c
S2P1L	3.5	a, b, ξ	a, b, ξ	a, ξ	b
S1P2L	3.5	a, ξ, θ	a, ξ, θ	a	ξ, θ
S3L	3.4	ξ, θ, γ	ξ, θ, γ	ξ, θ	γ
S2L-1L	3.4	ξ, θ	ξ, θ, γ	ξ, θ, γ	γ
S2P-1L	3.3	a, b	a, b, ξ	a, ξ	b, ξ
S1P1L-1P	3.3	a, ξ	a, ξ, b	a, ξ, b	b
S1P-2L	3.3	a, ξ	a, θ	a, ξ, θ	ξ, θ
S1P1L-1L	3.3	a, ξ, θ	a, ξ	a, θ	ξ, θ
S2P-1P	3.3	a, b, c	a, b	a, c	b, c
S1P-1P1L	Reduces to S1P1L-1P				
S1P-2P	Reduces to S2P-1P				

which are explained below, these trifocal constraints become third-order equations. While for each line feature there are two such equations, for every point feature nine equations are obtained [24], of which only two are linearly independent. This effect complicates the solver construction.

At the same time, in our problem formulation, for each feature there always exists a stereo camera such that the feature is projected onto both of its views (the *main camera*). This simplifies the problem and allows to use projection constraints or two-view epipolar constraints between each view of the main camera and the view of the other camera. We use these approaches below and show that we can obtain 16 or 8 solutions using the proposed solvers, compared to 64 solutions using the solver [7] for the same problem.

3.1 Problem

We assume that there are two binocular rectified and calibrated stereo cameras with the same known baseline. We are given a set of triplet feature correspondences. Each correspondence is a triplet. For point feature, a triplet is $(\mathbf{x}_{i_1,\beta_1}, \mathbf{x}_{i_2,\beta_2}, \mathbf{x}_{i_3,\beta_3})$, where $\mathbf{x}_{i,\beta}$ denotes a homogeneous vector of point projection's coordinates onto a view β of a camera i. For a line feature, a triplet is $(\mathbf{l}_{i_1,\beta_1}, \mathbf{l}_{i_2,\beta_2}, \mathbf{l}_{i_3,\beta_3})$ where $\mathbf{l}_{i,\beta}$ denotes a vector of 2D line's coefficients of a 3D line's projection onto a view β of a camera i.

W.l.o.g., we assume that the baseline has unit length ($\mathbf{b} = [1.0.0]^T$) and the projection matrices $\mathtt{P}_{i,\beta}$ for a view β of a camera i are $\mathtt{P}_{1,1} = [\mathtt{I},\ \mathbf{0}]$, $\mathtt{P}_{1,2} = [\mathtt{I},\ \mathbf{b}]$, $\mathtt{P}_{2,1} = [\mathbf{R},\ \mathbf{t}]$ and $\mathtt{P}_{2,2} = [\mathbf{R},\ \mathbf{b} + \mathbf{t}]$. Our goal is to find $\mathbf{R}, \mathbf{t}$.

3.2 Analysis of Feature Combinations

As long as there are exactly three projections for each feature, we use the following definition.

Definition: *If a feature is projected onto both views of some stereo camera, this camera is called the* **main camera** *for this feature.*

We use the following notation for feature/correspondence combinations. We refer to problem as $S\alpha P\beta L - \gamma P\delta L$ when the first camera is the main for α points and β lines, while the second one is the main for γ points and δ lines. To simplify the analysis, for those combinations having points we assume that the first camera is the main for at least one point feature. Some combinations are reducible to other ones by swapping the first and second cameras.

The categorization of the possible feature combinations is summarized in Table 1. For a homogeneous minimal set, there are two possible feature divisions between the cameras: S2L-1L and S3L for lines, or S2P-1P and S3P for points. If we have two points and one line, we can get only S2P1L, S2P-1L, S1P1L-1P cases. For one point and two lines, there are S1P2L, S1P1L-1L and S2L-1P cases. No other feature/correspondence combinations are possible.

If all the features have the same main camera (i.e. S3L, S3P, S2P1L, S1L2P), they can be triangulated in the coordinate frame of this camera, and the problem reduces to generalized absolute pose [20] for lines and points known to have 8 possible solutions. If a minimal set consists only of lines (S3L and S2L-1L), it admits a particular straightforward scheme of solution ("easy" cases).

The other situations (S2P-1L, S1P1L-1P, S1P-2L, S1P1L-1L, S2P-1P) are the "hard" cases. They share two common properties: the features have different main cameras and there is at least one point in the feature set. Minimal solvers for them are the main contributions of the paper.

In the next section, we propose two polynomial solver-based approaches for the "hard" cases. After that, we show how the other cases can be reduced to finding the roots of a single eight-degree polynomial, and then a recently proposed method [23] can be used. For the degeneracy analysis, see Supp. Mat.

3.3 "Hard" Cases

In this section, we consider the situation when the features have different main cameras and there is at least one point in the minimal set. Without loss of generality, a camera is the first one if the first (and maybe the only) point feature is projected onto both views of this camera. We also assume that it is projected onto the first view of the second camera. We use the first point to express the translation $\mathbf{t}$ in terms of the point's depth and rotation matrix elements, as in [7]. In particular, from an equation describing the point's projection onto the first view of the second camera we get

$$\mathbf{t} = \alpha \mathbf{u} - \mathbf{R}\mathbf{S}, \tag{1}$$

where $\mathbf{S}$ is the point's position triangulated in its main camera's coordinates, $\mathbf{u}$ is the homogeneous vector of the point's projection, α is the depth constant. We will denote as $\mathbf{t}_\beta = \delta_{\beta,2}\mathbf{b}$ the translation of the view β w.r.t. the stereo camera coordinate system, where $\delta_{i,j} = 1$ iff $i = j$, else $\delta_{i,j} = 0$. We use the unit quaternion-based rotation parameterization:

$$\mathbf{R} = \begin{bmatrix} a^2 + b^2 - c^2 - d^2 & 2bc - 2ad & 2bd + 2ac \\ 2bc + 2ad & a^2 - b^2 + c^2 - d^2 & 2cd - 2ab \\ 2bd - 2ac & 2cd + 2ab & a^2 - b^2 - c^2 + d^2 \end{bmatrix}, \tag{2}$$

$$a^2 + b^2 + c^2 + d^2 = 1. \tag{3}$$

We have experimented with two ways of formulation of the polynomial equations for the stereo egomotion problem explained in the following paragraphs.

Solver Based on Epipolar/Pluecker Constraints. We describe next a solver for the 'hard' cases which uses generalized epipolar constraints as in [7]. If the feature is a point, we analyze the epipolar constraint arising from its projection onto the view β of the first camera and onto the view γ of the second camera. The epipolar line has the equation in homogeneous coordinates $\mathbf{E}_{1,\beta\to2,\gamma}\mathbf{x}_{1,\beta}$ using the essential matrix $\mathbf{E}_{1,\beta\to2,\gamma}(\alpha, \mathbf{R}) = [\mathbf{e}_{\beta,\gamma}]_\times \mathbf{R}$ where $\mathbf{e}_{\beta,\gamma} = \mathbf{t} + \mathbf{t}_\gamma \mathbf{b} + \mathbf{R}\mathbf{t}_\beta$,

$[\mathbf{a}]_\times$ is a matrix of a cross product with a vector $\mathbf{a}$. Then, the point's projection lies on the epipolar line, which translates to the following constraint:

$$\mathbf{x}_{2,\gamma}^T \mathbf{E}_{1,\beta\to 2,\gamma}(\alpha, \mathbf{R})\mathbf{x}_{1,\beta} = 0. \tag{4}$$

For the point feature, we will get two constraints of the form (4) with the unknowns $\mathbf{R}$ and α. Using 3D line's projections onto the views of its main camera j we compute a pair of 3D points lying on the line $\mathbf{X}_1, \mathbf{X}_2$. Assuming that $j = 1$, we get the following expression for the line through projections of the points $\mathbf{X}_1$ and $\mathbf{X}_2$:

$$\lambda \mathbf{l}_{i,\beta} = (\mathbf{R}\mathbf{X}_1 + \mathbf{t} + \mathbf{t}_\beta) \times (\mathbf{R}\mathbf{X}_2), \tag{5}$$

where λ is a scaling parameter. It leads to the following constraint:

$$[\mathbf{l}_{i,\beta}]_\times \mathbf{R}\big((\mathbf{X}_1 + \alpha\mathbf{u} + \mathbf{t}_\beta) \times \mathbf{X}_2 - \mathbf{X}_2 \times \mathbf{t}_\beta\big) = 0. \tag{6}$$

Likewise, we obtain the following constraint for $j = 2$:

$$[\mathbf{l}_{i,\beta}]_\times \mathbf{R}^T\big((\mathbf{X}_1 - \alpha\mathbf{u}) \times \mathbf{X}_2 - \mathbf{X}_2 \times \mathbf{t}_\beta\big). \tag{7}$$

A system of the constraints (4), (6) or (7) can be formulated as

$$\mathtt{A}\mathbf{r} + \alpha\mathtt{B}\mathbf{r} = \mathbf{0}, \tag{8}$$

where $\mathbf{r}$ is a vectorized matrix $\mathbf{R}$, and $\mathtt{A}$ and $\mathtt{B}$ are coefficient matrices.

Substituting the parameterization (2) into (8), we get four equations of degree three w.r.t. a, b, c, d, α and add to them the constraint (3). After formulating these equations over $\mathbb{Z}p$, we find using Maple [25] that the dimension of the quotient ring for the polynomial ideal is 32, see [26] for details. Each term in the Eq. (8) after substitution of (2) is of degree 2 w.r.t. a, b, c, d. We divide the equations by a^2, and denote $\tilde{b} = b/a$, $\tilde{c} = c/a$, $\tilde{d} = d/a$. We choose a as a divisor because it is close to one if the rotation is not big, which is the typical case for the SLAM systems. Finally, we get the constraints in the vector form:

$$\mathtt{C}(\tilde{b}, \tilde{c}, \tilde{d})[1,\ \alpha]^T = \mathbf{0}, \tag{9}$$

where $\mathtt{C}(\tilde{b}, \tilde{c}, \tilde{d})$ is a 4×2 matrix consisting of second-degree polynomials. All the 2×2 sub-matrices of $\mathtt{C}(\tilde{b}, \tilde{c}, \tilde{d})$ must have zero determinants. It gives six equations of degree four, which we multiply with all the monomials of $\tilde{b}, \tilde{c}, \tilde{d}$ of degree three and obtain 240 equations and then use them to construct an elimination template.

After the LU-decomposition of the template matrix, using the action monomial $\tilde{d}$ to construct an action matrix, we obtain the solutions by eigen-decomposition, find α from the null-space of $\mathtt{C}(\tilde{b}, \tilde{c}, \tilde{d})$, find a using the unit-norm constraint (3) and $\mathbf{t}$ using (1).

Solver Based on Point Projection Constraints. For the this solver, we apply the known preprocessing rotation $\tilde{\mathbf{R}}$ to the projections of all the features to the views of the second camera. $\tilde{\mathbf{R}}$ is chosen so that the first point's projection is in the image center: $\mathbf{u} = [0, 0, 1]^T$, see (1) for the definition of $\mathbf{u}$. The baseline vectors of the cameras become different, we denote them as $\mathbf{b}_j$, where $j = 1, 2$ is the stereo camera index, and get $\mathbf{b}_1 = \mathbf{b}$ and $\mathbf{b}_2 = \tilde{\mathbf{R}}\mathbf{b}$.

We define a function $\pi_{1,\beta}(\mathbf{R}, \alpha, \mathbf{X})$ describing the point projection process, which takes a 3D point $\mathbf{X}$ expressed in the first camera's coordinate frame and outputs the homogeneous point projection coordinates to view β of the second camera:

$$\pi_{1,\beta}(\mathbf{R}, \alpha, \mathbf{X}) = \mathbf{R}(\mathbf{X} - \mathbf{S}) + \alpha\mathbf{u} + \mathbf{t}_\beta, \tag{10}$$

which is a standard point projection equation after we substitute the translation according to (1). By noting that the rotation from the second to the first camera is $\mathbf{R}^T$ and the translation is $-\mathbf{R}^T\mathbf{t} = -\alpha\mathbf{R}^T\mathbf{u} + \mathbf{S}$, using (1), we formulate a similar function $\pi_{2,\beta}(\mathbf{R}, \alpha, \mathbf{X})$ returning a projection of a 3D point $\mathbf{X}$ expressed in the second camera's coordinate frame to a view β of a first camera:

$$\pi_{2,\beta}(\mathbf{R}, \alpha, \mathbf{X}) = \mathbf{R}^T(\mathbf{X} - \alpha\mathbf{u}) + \mathbf{S} + \mathbf{t}_\beta. \tag{11}$$

We assume that the camera j is the main one for the feature, and that the feature also has a projection onto a view β of a camera $i \neq j$. The constraint for the point feature is obtained from $\pi_{i,\beta}(\mathbf{R}, \alpha, \mathbf{X}) = \lambda_x\mathbf{x}_{i,\beta}$ by expressing and substituting the depth parameter λ_x:

$$\pi_{i,\beta}^{(k)}(\mathbf{R}, \alpha, \mathbf{X}_p) - \mathbf{x}_{i,\beta}^{(k)}\pi_{i,\beta}^{(3)}(\mathbf{R}, \alpha, \mathbf{X}_p) = 0, \quad k = 1, 2, \tag{12}$$

where k is the coordinate index of the feature projection, and $\mathbf{X}_p$ is found by triangulation using the point's projections onto the main camera views. The constraint for the line feature is:

$$\mathbf{l}_{i,\beta}^T\pi_{i,\beta}(\mathbf{R}, \alpha, \mathbf{X}_j) = 0, \quad j = 1, 2. \tag{13}$$

Using these constraints and substituting the parameterization (2), we get a system of four equations:

$$\mathtt{D}(a, b, c, d)[1, \ \alpha]^T = \mathbf{0}, \tag{14}$$

where $\mathtt{D}$ is a matrix of second-degree polynomials.

Generating in $\mathbb{Z}p$ the systems for all the possible feature combinations together with a constraint (3) and using Maple [25] we find that the quotient ring dimension and the number of solutions is 16.

From the system (14) by subtracting equations we obtain one or two (S2L-1P) linearly independent second-degree equations free of α. As before, by computing determinants we get fourth-degree equations. The final system consists of six fourth degree equations (or five for SP-2L, because one of the determinants is identically zero), one (or two, for SP-2L) α-free second-degree equations, and a quadratic constraint (3). This system also leads to 16 solutions.

The basis of the remainder quotient ring as a vector space is not the same for different feature combinations. In particular, for the S1P1L-1P and S1P1L-1L cases there is one particular basis, and another one for the combinations S2P-1L, S2P-1P, S2L-1P (see Supp. Mat.).

We solve the obtained system by constructing an elimination template. Denote the second degree equation obtained after subtraction as $f_1 = 0$, the unit norm constraint as $f_2 = 0$, the other equations as $g_i = 0$, $i = 1..6$. We form an equation set F from f_1 multiplied with a^2, f_2 multiplied with ab, ac, b^2, bc, c^2, and f_1, f_2, g_i for $i = 1..6$. We multiply every equation from F by a, b, c, d, then by a, b, c, then by a, b, then by a, and add all the equations obtained after every multiplication operation to a set G of cardinality 975. It allows us to express all the basis monomials times the action variable a. We use LU decomposition and get the action matrix of size 16×16. It is four times smaller than in the case of the Epipolar/Pluecker constraints, so the eigendecomposition can be performed faster, but template construction and LU decomposition will be slower.

3.4 Only Line Features

The previous analysis is missing two situations: when all the features are lines or when they all have the same main camera. Next, we describe how both situations lead to a second-degree polynomial system in three unknowns, and therefore can be addressed by an already developed method for this type of geometric computer vision problems.

The coefficients of the 3D line's projection coincide with the direction of the normal to the plane through the camera center and the 3D line. If we observe the line from three views, we know normals of three different planes containing the line: $\mathbf{n}_1, \mathbf{n}_2, \mathbf{n}_3$, and their triple product is equal to zero: $\mathbf{n}_1 \cdot (\mathbf{n}_2 \times \mathbf{n}_3) = 0$. We are going to use this fact to formulate the constraints as follows:

$$\mathbf{l}_{j,\gamma}^T \mathbf{R}^T (\mathbf{l}_{i,1} \times \mathbf{l}_{i,2}) = 0, \tag{15}$$

for $i = 1, j = 2$ or $i = 2, j = 1$ depending on whether the main camera for the feature is the first or the second one, $\gamma = 1, 2$ is the view number. Three such constraints formulated using (2) result in a second-degree system with 4 unknowns, the fourth equation being the unit norm constraint.

3.5 Single Main Camera

If all the features have the same main camera, their 3D coordinates w.r.t. this camera can be computed, and then the problem becomes a particular case of the generalized absolute pose problem (gP3P). In the case of three point features several methods are available in this case, e.g. [23]. To the best of our knowledge, there are no papers analyzing the generalized absolute pose problem for the mixed point/line minimal sets.

We propose to use the earlier introduced constraints (12, 13) here as well. Without loss of generality, we assume that the first camera is the main one for all the features, so we use the constraints with $\pi_{1,\beta}$ for $\beta = 1, 2$. The depth α enters the system linearly. It can be expressed as a linear combination of terms involving other unknowns. This way we obtain a system of three equations w.r.t the unknown rotation matrix parameters.

In both cases, we transform a system with four unknowns into a system of three quadrics in three unknowns $\tilde{b} = b/a, \tilde{c} = c/a, \tilde{d} = d/a$ by the use of the constraint (3) to remove the zero-order terms and division by a^2.

The recent work [23] provides a framework to which our problem fits well, proposing a way to reduce a problem of three quadrics intersection to root-finding of a single eighth-degree polynomial by using the hidden variable method to construct a single eight-order polynomial w.r.t. b, and we customize the method by adaptively choosing the variable to hide using the condition numbers (see Supp. Mat.).

To sum up, we have considered all possible feature and correspondence combinations up to symmetries. In the cases for three line features or when all features share the same main camera, the method [23] can be applied. The remaining cases are the most difficult and we have proposed two new polynomial solvers to cope with them. Next, we demonstrate the benefits of using the proposed solvers in synthetic experiments and on real data (Fig. 2).

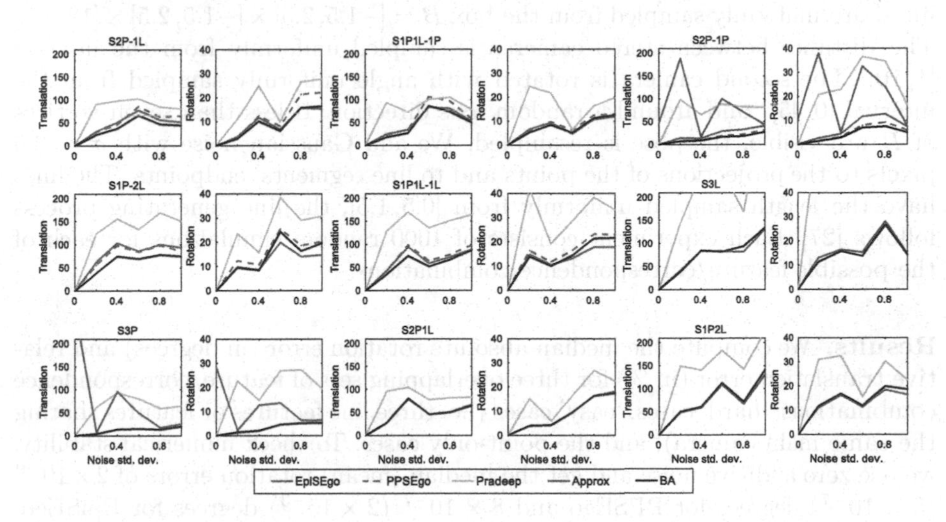

Fig. 2. The effect of additive noise variation on median relative translation and absolute rotation for each feature/correspondence combination. The accuracy of the methods degrades when noise is added. When fewer points are available, the translation error also grows. The new solvers PPSEgo and EpiSEgo are more accurate than the baselines and show almost the same accuracy as bundle adjustment (BA) started from the true solution and fitting to the noisy projections. The decrease in the error with growing noise happens simultaneously for BA and the proposed methods and can be explained by the non-linear nature of dependency between the projections and the SE3 transforms.

4 Experiments

4.1 Simulated Data

Setup: We perform a number of synthetic experiments to evaluate our method against the non-minimal assorted features solver [8] (*Pradeep*). For point-only configurations, we also compare to an approximate minimal solver for generalized relative pose from points for small rotation [9] (*Approx*). Finally, we evaluate bundle adjustment (*BA*) initialized with a true pose that uses the "gold standard" geometric feature reprojection error. We use BA with oracle initialization as a reference to demonstrate the best realistically achievable accuracy. While our methods and Approx use minimal feature sets, Pradeep needs four projections for every feature. We have re-implemented Pradeep and used the original code of Approx. We evaluate both of the proposed solvers, namely the epipolar constraint-based (EpiSEgo) solver and the point projection constraint-based solver (PPSEgo).

We assume that the stereo camera is rectified and the baseline is $\mathbf{b} = [1; 0; 0]^T$. We also consider square images with the side of 1000 pixels and the vertical and horizontal view angle of 90°. We fix the first stereo camera at the origin and randomly place the second camera. The points, as well as the 3D endpoints of the lines, are uniformly sampled from the box $B = [-1.5, 2.5] \times [-1.5, 2.5] \times [12, 16]$. The distance between stereo cameras is sampled uniformly from the interval $[1, 10]$. The second camera is rotated with angle uniformly sampled from the interval $[0, 45]°$ and around a random axis direction. If less than seven vertices of B are visible, the pose is resampled. We add Gaussian noise with $\sigma = 0.5$ pixels to the projections of the points and to line segments' endpoints. The lines have the length sampled uniformly from $[0.5, 1.5]$, the line generating process follows [27]. Each experiment consists of 1000 random simulations for each of the possible feature/correspondence combinations.

Results. We compute the median absolute rotation error (in degrees) and relative translation error (in %) for three overlapping sets of feature/correspondence combinations: 'hard' cases, 'easy' cases (i.e. three line features or features sharing the same main camera), and the point-only cases. To check numerical stability, we use zero additive noise and get the median (mean) rotation errors of 2×10^{-9} (5×10^{-7}) degrees for PPSEgo and 8×10^{-7} (2×10^{-3}) degrees for EpiSEgo, which is comparable to errors reported for similar solvers [7]. PPSEgo is thus more numerically stable.

The next experiment (Fig. 2) shows that the difference diminishes when the noise is present. Here we vary σ from 0.0 to 1.0. The errors for all methods increase with the noise level, and the accuracy of the proposed solvers is close to the reference one of the BA and better than the one of Pradeep and Approx. The translation errors tend to be higher if more line features are in the minimal set.

Next, we vary the rotation magnitude from 0 to 45° (Fig. 3-left). The rotation accuracy for the SEgo methods approaches BA accuracy, while translation errors are bigger. The accuracy of both rotation and translation of Approx drops rapidly due to the use of small angle rotation approximation. We then vary the translation magnitude from 1 to 33 (Fig. 3-right). Due to the choice of relative error to measure translation, we observe that translation accuracy increases, while the rotation errors grow and then stabilize. PPSEgo has slightly better translation and slightly worse rotation accuracy than EpiSEgo. Again, the accuracy of the new solvers approaches the reference (BA) and outperforms the baselines Pradeep and Approx.

4.2 Real Experiments

Matching Between Frames. We use the processed and rectified grayscale stereo sequences of the KITTI dataset as input [11]. Given four views, we detect and match lines and points using the EDLines + LBD [13,28] and ORB [12] algorithms implemented in OpenCV (Fig. 3).

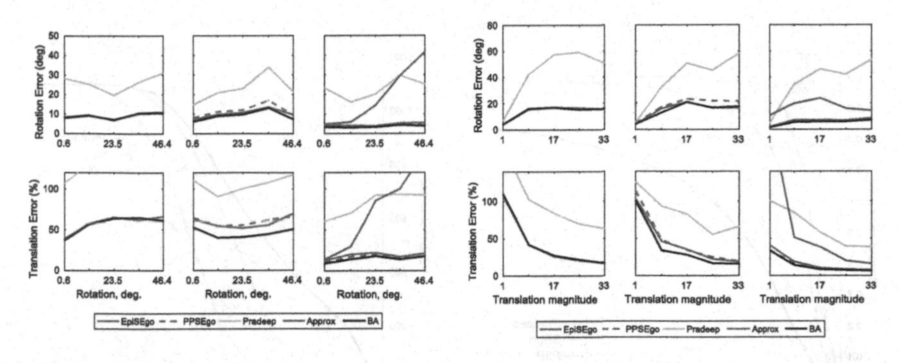

Fig. 3. The effects of rotation (left) and translation (right) magnitude variation on median relative translation and absolute rotation. The columns (left to right) correspond to: easy cases, hard cases, point-only combinations (S3P, S2P-1P). The new solvers PPSEgo and EpiSEgo have the lowest errors approaching the reference method (bundle adjustment with ground truth initialization). The new solvers PPSEgo and EpiSEgo are more accurate than the baselines (*Pradeep* and *Approx*, which is evaluated for point-only case).

We evaluate one of our solvers **EpiSEgo** against the baselines **Pradeep** [8], **Approx** [9] and **P3P** [29]. The Pradeep method takes as input four-view point and line correspondences. The P3P method emulates the classical approach of visual SLAM and takes the three-view correspondences constructed from both views of the first camera and the first view of the second camera. The Approx and our EpiSEgo methods work with three-view correspondences. While Approx uses only point features, our method employs both types of features.

To match point features between two images I_l and I_r, for each feature from I_l we find the closest one in I_r by the descriptor distance. We reject the match if its reprojection error after triangulation is less than $\tau = 5$ pixels. We match line segments in the same way, but without the reprojection validation. To find four-view correspondences, we match left and right images in both stereo pairs, and then match left images of the first and the second pairs. Denote the first stereo pair images as I_l, I_r, and the second stereo pair images as I_l', I_r'. We find three view correspondences for each possible triplet of four images.

Then we run the classical RANSAC loop [2] with the threshold of τ pixels, $p = 0.999$ and the initial outlier ratio of 0.5. For the three-view correspondences, we triangulate a feature using its main camera, project onto the remaining view and compare the reprojection error to τ. For the four-view correspondences, we choose one stereo pair, triangulate the feature using the projections onto its views, and then test the reprojection errors onto the views of the other stereo pair.

In Fig. 4 we show the results of the motion estimation experiment with the consecutive frame pairs of KITTI [30] sequence 6. The use of three-view correspondences and point and line features helps the EpiSEgo to achieve high inlier ratios and lower pose estimation errors compared to the baselines.

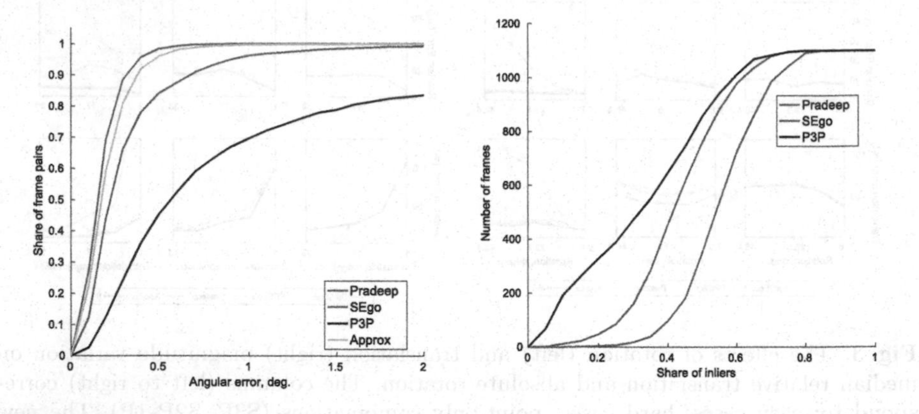

Fig. 4. Results of the experiment on a KITTI sequence 6. Left: cumulative distribution for the rotation error in degrees. Right: cumulative distribution for the ratio of inliers. The proposed EpiSEgo using line and point feature triplets has higher accuracy compared to the baselines. It has higher inlier ratio than P3P and Pradeep. The use of all possible types of feature triplets rather than quadruplets (Pradeep) is beneficial in motion estimation. We also see a benefit from new solvers compared to the classical approach (P3P). Approx is excluded from the inlier plot because it relies only on point feature triplets.

Integration into Visual SLAM Pipeline. While the previous experiment compares stereo egomotion methods at the task of relative pose estimation between stereo pairs, we also validate that such task can be used to improve modern stereo visual odometry pipelines. For this, we evaluate the system that integrates the proposed EpiSEgo solver into the ORB-SLAM2 [31] pipeline.

The ORB-SLAM2 pipeline uses the previous frame pose as an initial guess to estimate the next frame pose within bundle adjustment. We modify it to run

Table 2. The study of the robustness of the ORB-SLAM2 pipeline to the framerate decrease on the KITTI sequences 00-10. To make the task harder, we drop every second frame of each sequence. We compare the original and the modified pipeline that uses EpiSEgo solver for initialization in case of track loss. We report the percentage of runs where tracking was lost (F%), the relative pose estimation errors as proposed by the dataset authors [30]. After every second frame is dropped, there is the only sequence, which the original ORB-SLAM2 can track with probability more than 50%. At the same time, the modified version shows radical improvement, as it tracks ten out of eleven sequences with probability more than 50%.

Sequence	ORB-SLAM2			ORB-SLAM2+EpiSEgo		
	F%	t_{rel}	r_{rel}	F%	t_{rel}	r_{rel}
00	100%	-	-	0%	62%	$5 * 10^{-3}$
01	40%	3%	10^{-4}	40%	1.6%	10^{-4}
02	100%	-	-	0%	53%	$3.6 * 10^{-3}$
03	60%	0.8%	10^{-5}	0%	3%	10^{-4}
04	40%	0.8%	10^{-5}	0%	0.8%	10^{-5}
05	100%	-	-	0%	55%	$4.8 * 10^{-3}$
06	100%	-	-	0%	7%	10^{-4}
07	80%	1.3%	10^{-4}	0%	7%	10^{-4}
08	100%	-	-	0%	63%	$4.6 * 10^{-3}$
09	100%	-	-	80%	63%	$4.6 * 10^{-3}$
10	100%	-	-	0%	36%	$2.8 * 10^{-3}$

the EpiSEgo solver (point-only version) inside the RANSAC loop. The pose and the inliers estimated by RANSAC are used to initialize bundle adjustment. We run this algorithm each time the standard system loses the track. We do not include line features as they are absent in the original system.

While ORB-SLAM2 works well for the original sequences, it is important to study the robustness of the pipeline to the framerate decrease (which is equivalent to faster observer motion) which can happen in a real system. To do that, we drop *every second* frame of the sequence. Note that the uniform frame drop still enables the use of velocity-based pose prediction on which ORB-SLAM2 relies, provided the frames are separated by equal time periods. At the same time, it shows what can happen if motions become less predictable. Our experiments show that the ORB-SLAM2 often becomes unable to recover and loses the track, while the use of EpiSEgo solver can enable successful recovery from tracking losses. In Table 2, we show the results of 5 runs for the original and modified ORB-SLAM2 on 0–10 KITTI sequences. We report the percentage of failures as well as relative rotation and translation errors proposed by the dataset authors. The modified version does not lose track with probability more than 50% for all the sequences except the 9th, where a lack of tracked features in one moment is a possible problem. The original version is able to track with probability greater than 50% for only one sequence out of 11. The experiment shows that the integration of the stereo egomotion solver considerably increases the robustness of the system.

5 Summary

In this paper, we have proposed new minimal solvers that can handle the stereo relative pose problem for any combinations of point and line three-view correspondences. This case was not addressed in the previous literature. We demonstrate that the problem is practical and leads to improved performance of a well-known SLAM system.

References

1. Nister, D.: An efficient solution to the five-point relative pose problem. TPAMI **26**(6), 756–770 (2004)
2. Fischler, M.A., Bolles, R.C.: Random sample consensus: a paradigm for model fitting with applications to image analysis and automated cartography. In: Readings in Computer Vision, pp. 726–740. Elsevier (1987)
3. Cadena, C., et al.: Past, present, and future of simultaneous localization and mapping: toward the robust-perception age. IEEE Trans. Robot. **32**(6), 1309–1332 (2016)
4. Agarwal, S., et al.: building Rome in a day. Commun. ACM **54**(10), 105–112 (2011)
5. Micusik, B., Wildenauer, H.: Structure from motion with line segments under relaxed endpoint constraints. Int. J. Comput. Vis. **124**(1), 65–79 (2017)
6. Xu, C., Zhang, L., Cheng, L., Koch, R.: Pose estimation from line correspondences: a complete analysis and a series of solutions. IEEE Trans. Pattern Anal. Mach. Intell. **39**(6), 1209–1222 (2017)
7. Stewénius, H., Nistér, D., Oskarsson, M., Åström, K.: Solutions to minimal generalized relative pose problems. In: Workshop on Omnidirectional Vision, vol. 1, p. 3 (2005)
8. Pradeep, V., Lim, J.: Egomotion estimation using assorted features. Int. J. Comput. Vis. **98**(2), 202–216 (2012)
9. Ventura, J., Arth, C., Lepetit, V.: An efficient minimal solution for multi-camera motion. In: ICCV, pp. 747–755. IEEE (2015)
10. Kneip, L., Li, H.: Efcient computation of relative pose for multi-camera systems. In: CVPR, pp. 1–8. IEEE (2014)
11. Menze, M., Geiger, A.: Object scene flow for autonomous vehicles. In: Conference on Computer Vision and Pattern Recognition (CVPR) (2015)
12. Rublee, E., Rabaud, V., Konolige, K., Bradski, G.: ORB: An efficient alternative to sift or surf. In: International Conference on Computer Vision, pp. 2564–2571. IEEE (2011)
13. Zhang, L., Koch, R.: An efficient and robust line segment matching approach based on lbd descriptor and pairwise geometric consistency. J. Vis. Commun. Image Represent. **24**(7), 794–805 (2013)
14. Nister, D., Naroditsky, O., Bergen, J.: Visual odometry. In: CVPR, pp. 652–659. IEEE (2004)

15. Manmohan, C., Jongwoo, L., David, K.: Moving in stereo: efficient structure and motion using lines. In: International Conference on Computer Vision, pp. 1741–1748. IEEE (2009)
16. Brian, C., Christopher, Z., Jan-Michael, F., Marc, P.: A new minimal solution to the relative pose of a calibrated stereo camera with small field of view overlap. In: International Conference on Computer Vision, pp. 1725–1732. IEEE (2009)
17. Dunn, E., Clipp, B., Frahm, J.M.: A geometric solver for calibrated stereo egomotion. In: IEEE International Conference on Computer Vision (ICCV), pp. 1187–1194. IEEE (2011)
18. Nister, D.: A minimal solution to the generalised 3-point pose problem. In: IEEE Computer Society Conference on Computer Vision and Pattern Recognition (2004)
19. Ramalingam, S., Lodha, S.K., Sturm, P.: A generic structure-from-motion framework. Comput. Vis. Image Underst. **103**(3), 218–228 (2006)
20. Nistér, D., Stewénius, H.: A minimal solution to the generalised 3-point pose problem. J. Math. Imaging Vis. **27**(1), 67–79 (2007)
21. Merzban, M.H., Abdellatif, M., Abouelsoud, A.: A simple solution for the non perspective three point pose problem. In: International Conference on 3D Imaging (IC3D), pp. 1–6. IEEE (2014)
22. Miraldo, P., Araujo, H.: Direct solution to the minimal generalized pose. IEEE Trans. Cybern. **45**(3), 404–415 (2015)
23. Kukelova, Z., Heller, J., Fitzgibbon, A.: Efficient intersection of three quadrics and applications in computer vision. In: Proceedings of the IEEE Conference on Computer Vision and Pattern Recognition, pp. 1799–1808 (2016)
24. Hartley, R., Zisserman, A.: Multiple View Geometry in Computer Vision. Cambridge University Press, Cambridge (2003)
25. Char, B.W., Geddes, K.O., Gonnet, G.H., Leong, B.L., Monagan, M.B., Watt, S.: Maple V Library Reference Manual. Springer, New York (2013)
26. Cox, D.A., Little, J., O'shea, D.: Using algebraic geometry. Volume 185. Springer Science & Business Media (2006)
27. Vakhitov, A., Funke, J., Moreno-Noguer, F.: Accurate and linear time pose estimation from points and lines. In: Leibe, B., Matas, J., Sebe, N., Welling, M. (eds.) ECCV 2016. LNCS, vol. 9911, pp. 583–599. Springer, Cham (2016). https://doi.org/10.1007/978-3-319-46478-7_36
28. Akinlar, C., Topal, C.: Edlines: a real-time line segment detector with a false detection control. Pattern Recognit. Lett. **32**(13), 1633–1642 (2011)
29. Gao, X.S., Hou, X.R., Tang, J., Cheng, H.F.: Complete solution classification for the perspective-three-point problem. IEEE Trans. Pattern Anal. Mach. Intell. **25**(8), 930–943 (2003)
30. Geiger, A., Lenz, P., Urtasun, R.: Are we ready for autonomous driving? the KITTI vision benchmark suite. In: IEEE Conference on Computer Vision and Pattern Recognition (CVPR), pp. 3354–3361. IEEE (2012)
31. Mur-Artal, R., Tardós, J.D.: ORB-SLAM2: An open-source slam system for monocular, stereo, and RGB-D cameras. IEEE Trans. Robot. **33**(5), 1255–1262 (2017)

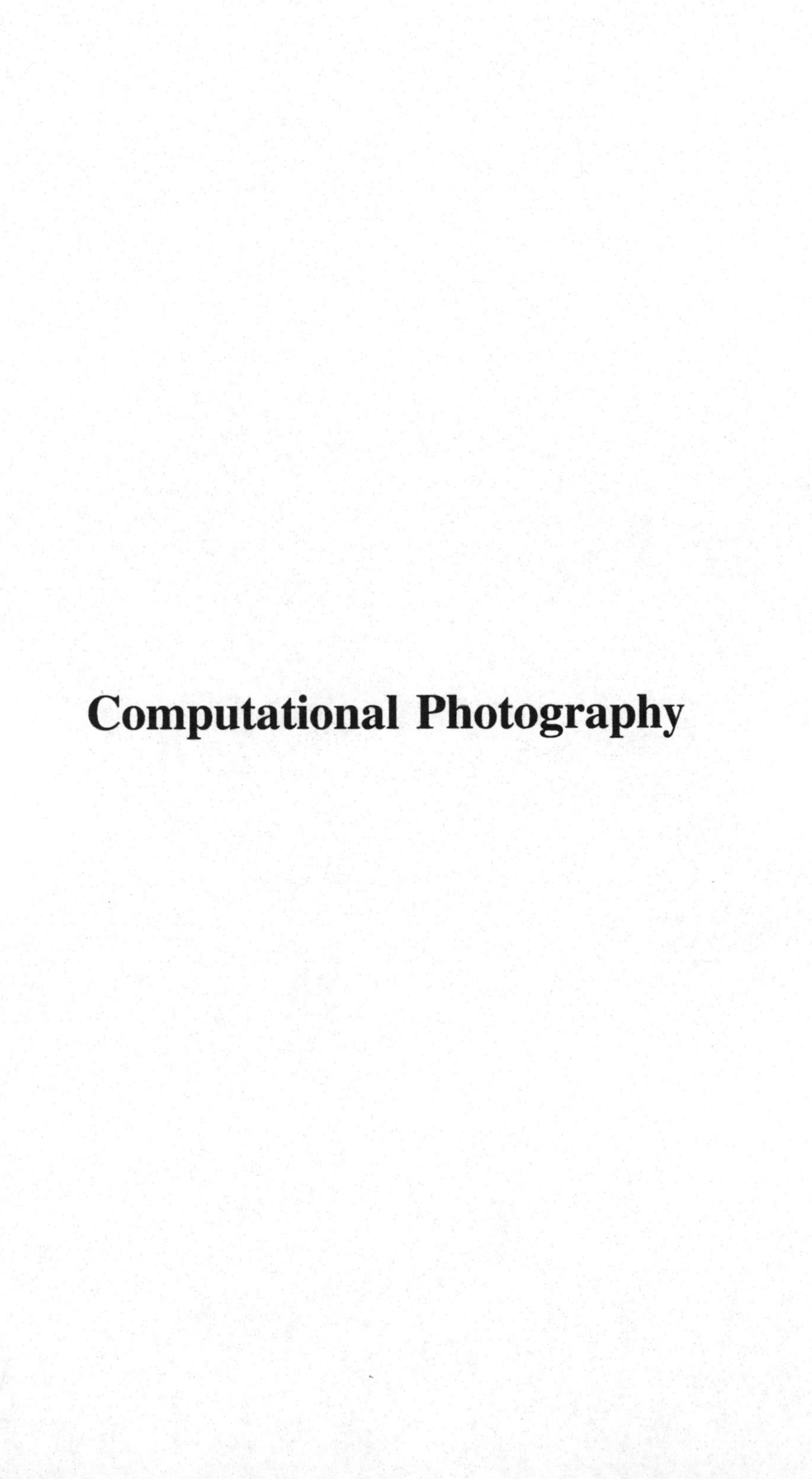

Computational Photography

3D Scene Flow from 4D Light Field Gradients

Sizhuo Ma, Brandon M. Smith, and Mohit Gupta(✉)

Department of Computer Sciences, University of Wisconsin-Madison, Madison, USA
{sizhuoma,bmsmith,mohitg}@cs.wisc.edu

Abstract. This paper presents novel techniques for recovering 3D dense scene flow, based on differential analysis of 4D light fields. The key enabling result is a per-ray linear equation, called the ray flow equation, that relates 3D scene flow to 4D light field gradients. The ray flow equation is invariant to 3D scene structure and applicable to a general class of scenes, but is underconstrained (3 unknowns per equation). Thus, additional constraints must be imposed to recover motion. We develop two families of scene flow algorithms by leveraging the structural similarity between ray flow and optical flow equations: local 'Lucas-Kanade' ray flow and global 'Horn-Schunck' ray flow, inspired by corresponding optical flow methods. We also develop a combined local-global method by utilizing the correspondence structure in the light fields. We demonstrate high precision 3D scene flow recovery for a wide range of scenarios, including rotation and non-rigid motion. We analyze the theoretical and practical performance limits of the proposed techniques via the light field structure tensor, a 3×3 matrix that encodes the local structure of light fields. We envision that the proposed analysis and algorithms will lead to design of future light-field cameras that are optimized for motion sensing, in addition to depth sensing.

1 Introduction

The ability to measure dense 3D scene motion has numerous applications, including robot navigation, human-computer interfaces and augmented reality. Imagine a head-mounted camera tracking the 3D motion of hands for manipulation of objects in a virtual environment, or a social robot trying to determine a person's level of engagement from subtle body movements. These applications require precise measurement of per-pixel 3D scene motion, also known as scene flow [31]. In this paper, we present a novel approach for measuring 3D scene flow with light field sensors [1,24]. This approach is based on the derivation of a new constraint,

Electronic supplementary material The online version of this chapter (https://doi.org/10.1007/978-3-030-01237-3_41) contains supplementary material, which is available to authorized users.

V. Ferrari et al. (Eds.): ECCV 2018, LNCS 11212, pp. 681–698, 2018.
https://doi.org/10.1007/978-3-030-01237-3_41

the *ray flow equation*, which relates dense 3D motion field of a scene to gradients of the measured light field, as follows:

$$\boxed{L_X V_X + L_Y V_Y + L_Z V_Z + L_t = 0},$$

where V_X, V_Y, V_Z are per-pixel 3D scene flow components, L_X, L_Y, L_Z are spatio-angular gradients of the 4D light field, and L_t is the temporal light field derivative. This simple, linear equation describes the *ray flow*, defined as local changes in the 4D light field, due to small, differential, 3D scene motion. The ray flow equation is independent of the scene depth, and is broadly applicable to a general class of scenes.

The ray flow equation is an under-constrained linear equation with three unknowns (V_X, V_Y, V_Z) per equation. Therefore, it is impossible to recover the full 3D scene flow without imposing further constraints. Our key observation is that, due to the structural similarity between ray flow and the classical optical flow equations [14], the regularization techniques developed over three decades of optical flow research can be easily adapted to constrain ray flow. The analogy between ray flow and optical flow provides a general recipe for designing ray flow based algorithms for recovering 3D dense scene flow directly from measured light field gradients.

We develop two basic families of scene flow recovery algorithms: local *Lucas-Kanade* methods, and global *Horn-Schunck* methods, based on local and global optical flow [14,20]. We also design a high-performance combined local-global method by utilizing the correspondence structure in the light fields. We adopt best practices and design choices from modern, state-of-the-art optical flow algorithms (*e.g.*, techniques for preserving motion discontinuities, recovering large motions). Using these techniques, we demonstrate 3D flow computation with *sub-millimeter* precision along all three axes, for a wide range of scenarios, including complex non-rigid motion.

Theoretical and Practical Performance Analysis: What is the space of motions that are recoverable by the proposed techniques? What factors influence their ability to recover 3D motion? To address these fundamental questions, we define the *light field structure tensor*, a 3×3 matrix that encodes local light field structure. We show that the space of recoverable motions is determined by the properties (rank and eigenvalues) of the light field structure tensor, which depends on the scene texture. We also analyze the performance dependence of ray flow techniques on the imaging parameters of the light field camera (*e.g.*, angular resolution, aperture size and field of view [11]). This analysis determines theoretical and practical performance limits of the proposed algorithms, and can also inform design of future light field cameras optimized for motion sensing.

Scope and Implications: The main goal of the paper is to establish theoretical foundations of 3D scene flow computation from light field gradients. In doing so, this paper takes the first steps towards positioning light field cameras as effective 3D motion sensors, in addition to their depth estimation capabilities. Although we have implemented several proof-of-concept ray flow methods, it is possible to leverage the vast body of optical flow research and design novel, practical ray flow algorithms in the future. These algorithms, along with novel light field camera designs optimized for motion sensing, can potentially provide high-precision 3D motion sensing capabilities in a wide range of applications, including robotic manipulation, user interfaces, and augmented reality.

2 Related Work

Light Field Scene Flow: State-of-the-art scene flow methods compute the 3D motion by combining optical flow and change of depths (*e.g.*, via stereo [15,34] or RGB-D cameras [12,29]). Scene flow methods for light fields cameras have also been proposed before [13,21,27], where light fields are used for recovering depths. Our goal is different: we use light fields for recovering 3D scene motion directly. Thus, the proposed approaches are not adversely affected by errors in measured depths, resulting in precise motion estimation, especially for subtle motions.

Light Field Odometry: Light fields have been used for recovering a camera's ego-motion [10,22], and to compute high-quality 3D scene reconstructions via structure-from-motion techniques [17,35]. These methods are based on a constraint relating camera motion and light fields. This constraint has the same structural form as the equation derived in this paper, although they are derived in different contexts (camera motion vs. non-rigid scene motion) with different assumptions. These works aim to recover 6-degrees-of-freedom (6DOF) camera motion, which is an over-constrained problem. Our focus is on recovering 3D non-rigid scene motion at every pixel, which is under-constrained due to considerably higher number of degrees of freedom.

Shape Recovery from Differential Motion: Chandraker *et al.* developed a comprehensive theory for recovering shape and reflectance from differential motion of the light source, object or camera [7–9,19,32]. While our approach is also based on a differential analysis of light fields, our goal is different – to recover scene motion itself.

3 The Ray Flow Equation

Consider a scene point P at 3D location $\mathbf{X} = (X, Y, Z)$. Let $L(\mathbf{X}, \theta, \phi)$ be the radiance of P along direction (θ, ϕ), where θ, ϕ are the polar angle and azimuth angle as defined in spherical coordinates. The function $L(\mathbf{X}, \theta, \phi)$ is called the *plenoptic function*: it defines the radiance at all positions, along all possible ray directions. Assuming the radiance does not change along a ray, the 5D function $L(\mathbf{X}, \theta, \phi)$ can be simplified to the 4D *light field* $L(x, y, u, v)$, with each ray parameterized by its intersections with two parallel planes $Z = 0$ and $Z = \Gamma$, where Γ is a fixed constant. This is shown in Fig. 1(a). Let the ray intersect the planes at points $(x, y, 0)$ and $(x + u, y + v, \Gamma)$, respectively. Then, the ray is represented by the coordinates (x, y, u, v). Note that (u, v) are *relative coordinates*; they represent the differences in the X and Y coordinates of the two intersection

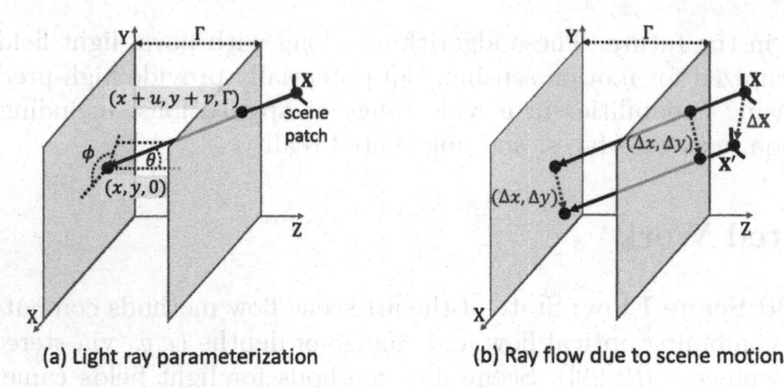

Fig. 1. (**a**) A light ray is parameterized by 4D coordinates (x, y, u, v), which are determined by the ray's intersection points $(x, y, 0)$ and $(x+u, y+v, \Gamma)$ with planes $Z=0$ and $Z=\Gamma$, where Γ is a fixed constant. (**b**) Motion (translation) of the scene point that emits or reflects the ray results in a change in the (x, y) coordinates of the ray, but the (u, v) coordinates remain constant.

points. This is called the *two-plane parameterization* of the light field [18,24], and is widely used to represent light fields captured by cameras.

By basic trigonometry, the relationship between the *scene-centric* coordinates (X, Y, Z, θ, ϕ) of a light ray, and its *camera-centric* coordinates (x, y, u, v) is given by:

$$x = X - Z\tan\theta\cos\phi, \qquad u = \Gamma\tan\theta\cos\phi,$$
$$y = Y - Z\tan\theta\sin\phi, \qquad v = \Gamma\tan\theta\sin\phi. \tag{1}$$

Effect of Scene Motion on Light Fields: Let the 3D locations of a scene point P at time t and $t+\Delta t$ be $\mathbf{X}$ and $\mathbf{X}' = \mathbf{X} + \Delta\mathbf{X}$, where $\Delta\mathbf{X} = (\Delta X, \Delta Y, \Delta Z)$ is the small (differential) 3D motion (shown in Fig. 1(b)). Consider a ray reflected (emitted) by P. We assume that the scene patch containing P only translates during motion[1], so that the ray only moves parallel to itself, *i.e.*, (u, v) coordinates of the ray remain constant. Let the coordinates of the ray before and after motion be (x, y, u, v) and $(x+\Delta x, y+\Delta y, u, v)$. Then, assuming that the ray brightness remains constant during motion[2]:

$$L(x, y, u, v, t) = L(x+\Delta x, y+\Delta y, u, v, t+\Delta t). \tag{2}$$

This *ray brightness constancy assumption* is similar to the *scene brightness constancy assumption* made in optical flow. First-order Taylor expansion of Eq. 2 gives:

$$\frac{\partial L}{\partial x}\Delta x + \frac{\partial L}{\partial y}\Delta y + \frac{\partial L}{\partial t}\Delta t = 0. \tag{3}$$

[1] For a rotating object, in general, the motion of small scene patches can be modeled as translation, albeit with a change in the surface normal. For small rotations (small changes in surface normal), the brightness of a patch can be assumed to be approximately constant [31].

[2] This is true under the assumption that the light sources are distant such that $\mathbf{N}\cdot\mathbf{L}$, the dot-product of surface normal and lighting direction, does not change [31].

We define *ray flow* as the change $(\Delta x, \Delta y)$ in a light ray's coordinates due to scene motion. Equation 3 relates ray flow and light field gradients $(\frac{\partial L}{\partial x}, \frac{\partial L}{\partial y}, \frac{\partial L}{\partial t})$. From Eq. 1, we can also find a relationship between ray flow and scene motion:

$$\begin{aligned} \Delta x &= \frac{\partial x}{\partial X}\Delta X + \frac{\partial x}{\partial Z}\Delta Z = \Delta X - \frac{u}{\Gamma}\Delta Z, \\ \Delta y &= \frac{\partial y}{\partial Y}\Delta Y + \frac{\partial y}{\partial Z}\Delta Z = \Delta Y - \frac{v}{\Gamma}\Delta Z. \end{aligned} \quad (4)$$

By substituting Eq. 4 in Eq. 3 and using symbols L_* for light field gradients, we get:

$$\boxed{L_X V_X + L_Y V_Y + L_Z V_Z + L_t = 0}, \quad (5)$$

where $L_X = \frac{\partial L}{\partial x}$, $L_Y = \frac{\partial L}{\partial y}$, $L_Z = -\frac{u}{\Gamma}\frac{\partial L}{\partial x} - \frac{v}{\Gamma}\frac{\partial L}{\partial y}$, $L_t = \frac{\partial L}{\partial t}$, $\mathbf{V} = (V_X, V_Y, V_Z) = (\frac{\Delta X}{\Delta t}, \frac{\Delta Y}{\Delta t}, \frac{\Delta Z}{\Delta t})$. We call this the *ray flow equation*; it relates the 3D scene motion and the measured light field gradients. This simple, yet powerful equation enables recovery of dense scene flow from measured light field gradients, as we describe in Sects. 4 to 6. In the rest of this section, we discuss salient properties of the ray flow equation in order to gain intuitions and insights into its implications.

3.1 Ray Flow Due to Different Scene Motions

Ray flows due to different scene motions have interesting qualitative differences. To visualize the difference, we represent a 4D light field sensor as a 2D array of pinhole cameras, each with a 2D image plane. In this representation (u, v) coordinates of the light field $L(x, y, u, v)$ denote the pixel indices within individual images (sub-aperture images). (x, y) coordinates denote the locations of the cameras, as shown in Fig. 2.

For X/Y scene motion, a light ray *shifts horizontally/vertically* across sub-aperture images. The amount of shift $(\Delta x, \Delta y)$ is *independent* of the ray's original coordinates, as evident from Eq. 4. For Z-motion, the ray *shifts radially* across sub-aperture images. The amount of shift *depends* on the ray's (u, v) coordinates (c.f. Eq. 4). For example, rays at the center of each sub-aperture image $(u = 0, v = 0)$ do not shift. In all cases, rays retain the *same pixel index* (u, v) after the motion, but in a *different sub-aperture image* (x, y), since scene motion results in rays translating parallel to themselves.

3.2 Invariance of Ray Flow to Scene Depth

An important observation is that the ray flow equation does not involve the depth or 3D position of the scene point. In conventional motion estimation techniques, depth and motion estimation are coupled together, and thus need to be performed simultaneously [2]. In contrast, the ray flow equation decouples depth and motion estimation. This has important practical implications: 3D scene motion can then be directly recovered from the light field gradients, without explicitly recovering scene depths, thereby avoiding the errors due to the intermediate depth estimation step.

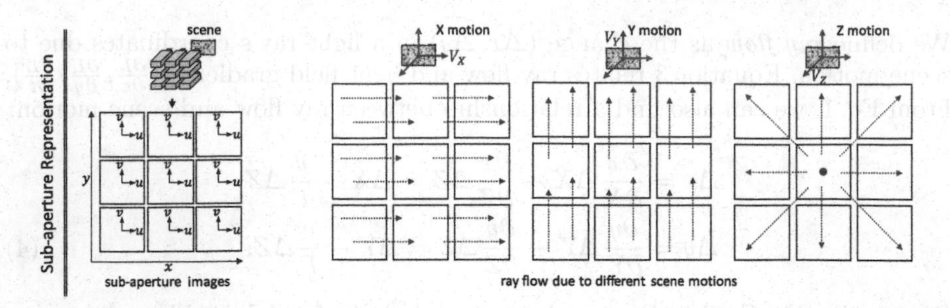

Fig. 2. Ray flow due to different scene motions. (**Left**) We represent a light field sensor as a 2D array of pinhole cameras, each of which captures a 2D image (sub-aperture images). (u, v) denotes the pixel indices within each sub-aperture image. (x, y) denotes the locations of the cameras. (**Right**) For X/Y scene motion, rays move horizontally/vertically, across sub-aperture images. The amount of change $(\Delta x, \Delta y)$ in the sub-aperture index is independent of the rays' coordinates. For Z-motion, rays shift radially across sub-aperture images. The shift depends on each ray's (u, v) coordinates. Rays at the center of each sub-aperture image $(u = 0, v = 0)$ do not shift. In all cases, rays retain the same pixel index (u, v), but move to a different sub-aperture image.

Notice that although motion estimation via ray flow does not need depth estimation, the accuracy of the estimated motion depends on scene depth. For distant scenes, the captured light field is convolved with a 4D low-pass point spread function, which makes gradient computation unreliable. As a result, scene motion cannot be estimated reliably.

3.3 Similarities Between Ray Flow and Optical Flow

For every ray in the captured light field, we have one ray flow equation with three unknowns to solve, which gives us an under-constrained system. Therefore additional assumptions need to be made to further constrain the problem. This is similar to the well-known *aperture problem* in 2D optical flow, where the optical flow equation $I_x u_x + I_y u_y + I_t = 0$ is also under-constrained (1 equation, 2 unknowns (u_x, u_y)). There are some interesting differences between ray flow and optical flow (see Table 1), but the key similarity is that both ray flow and optical flow are *under-constrained linear equations.*

Fortunately, optical flow is one of the most researched problems in computer vision. Broadly, there are two families of differential optical flow techniques, based on the additional constraints imposed for regularizing the problem. The first is local methods (*e.g.*, Lucas-Kanade [20]), which assume that the optical flow is constant within small image neighborhoods. Second is global methods (*e.g.*, Horn-Schunck [14]), which assume that the optical flow varies smoothly across the image. By exploiting the structural similarity between the optical flow and ray flow equations, we develop two families of ray flow techniques accordingly: local ray flow (Sect. 4) and global ray flow (Sect. 5).

Table 1. Comparisons between optical flow and ray flow.

Optical flow	Ray flow
Linear equation: $I_x u_x + I_y u_y + I_t = 0$	Linear equation: $L_X V_X + L_Y V_Y + L_Z V_Z + V_t = 0$
Coefficients: Image gradients (I_x, I_y, I_t)	Coefficients: Light field gradients (L_X, L_Y, L_Z, L_t)
2 unknowns per pixel: Pixel motion (u_x, u_y)	3 unknowns per pixel: Scene motion (V_X, V_Y, V_Z)
Motion (u_x, u_y) computed in 2D image space (pixels)	Motion (V_X, V_Y, V_Z) computed in 3D scene space
Gradients (I_x, I_y) defined on 2D image grid	Gradients (L_X, L_Y, L_Z) defined on 4D light-field grid
u_x and u_y flow computations are symmetric	X/Y and Z motion computations are asymmetric
Size of structure tensor: 2 × 2	Size of structure tensor: 3 × 3
Possible ranks of structure tensor: [0, 1, 2]	Possible ranks of structure tensor: [0, 2, 3]

4 Local 'Lucas-Kanade' Ray Flow

In this section, we develop the local ray flow based scene flow recovery methods, inspired by Lucas-Kanade optical flow [20]. This class of ray flow methods assume that the motion vector $\mathbf{V}$ is constant in local 4D light field windows. Consider a ray with coordinates $\mathbf{x}_c = (x, y, u, v)$. We stack all the equations of form Eq. 5 from rays in a local neighborhood of $\mathbf{x}_c$, $\mathbf{x}_i \in \mathcal{N}(\mathbf{x}_c)$ into a linear system $\mathbf{AV} = \mathbf{b}$, where:

$$\mathbf{A} = \begin{bmatrix} L_X(\mathbf{x}_1) & L_Y(\mathbf{x}_1) & L_Z(\mathbf{x}_1) \\ \vdots & \vdots & \vdots \\ L_X(\mathbf{x}_n) & L_Y(\mathbf{x}_n) & L_Z(\mathbf{x}_n) \end{bmatrix}, \mathbf{b} = \begin{bmatrix} -L_t(\mathbf{x}_1) \\ \vdots \\ -L_t(\mathbf{x}_n) \end{bmatrix}. \tag{6}$$

Then, the motion vector $\mathbf{V}$ can be estimated by the normal equation:

$$\mathbf{V} = (\mathbf{A}^T\mathbf{A})^{-1}\mathbf{A}^T\mathbf{b}. \tag{7}$$

4.1 What Is the Space of Recoverable Motions?

In the previous section, we discussed that it is impossible to recover the complete 3D motion vector from a single ray flow equation. A natural question to ask is: what is the space of recoverable motions with the additional local constancy constraint? Intuitively it depends on the local structure of the light field. For example, if the local window corresponds to a textureless scene, then no motion is recoverable. One way to address this question is by understanding the properties of the 3 × 3 symmetric matrix $\mathbf{S} = \mathbf{A}^T\mathbf{A}$.

$$\mathbf{S} = \begin{bmatrix} \sum_{i=1}^n L_{Xi}^2 & \sum_{i=1}^n L_{Xi}L_{Yi} & \sum_{i=1}^n L_{Xi}L_{Zi} \\ \sum_{i=1}^n L_{Yi}L_{Xi} & \sum_{i=1}^n L_{Yi}^2 & \sum_{i=1}^n L_{Yi}L_{Zi} \\ \sum_{i=1}^n L_{Zi}L_{Xi} & \sum_{i=1}^n L_{Zi}L_{Yi} & \sum_{i=1}^n L_{Zi}^2 \end{bmatrix}, \tag{8}$$

where L_{*i} is short for $L_*(\mathbf{x}_i)$. We define $\mathbf{S}$ as the *light field structure tensor*; it encodes the local structure of the light field.[3] To estimate motion using Eq. 7, $\mathbf{S}$

[3] Structure tensors have been researched and defined differently in the light field community (*e.g.*, [23]). Here it is defined by the gradients w.r.t. the 3D motion and is thus a 3 × 3 matrix.

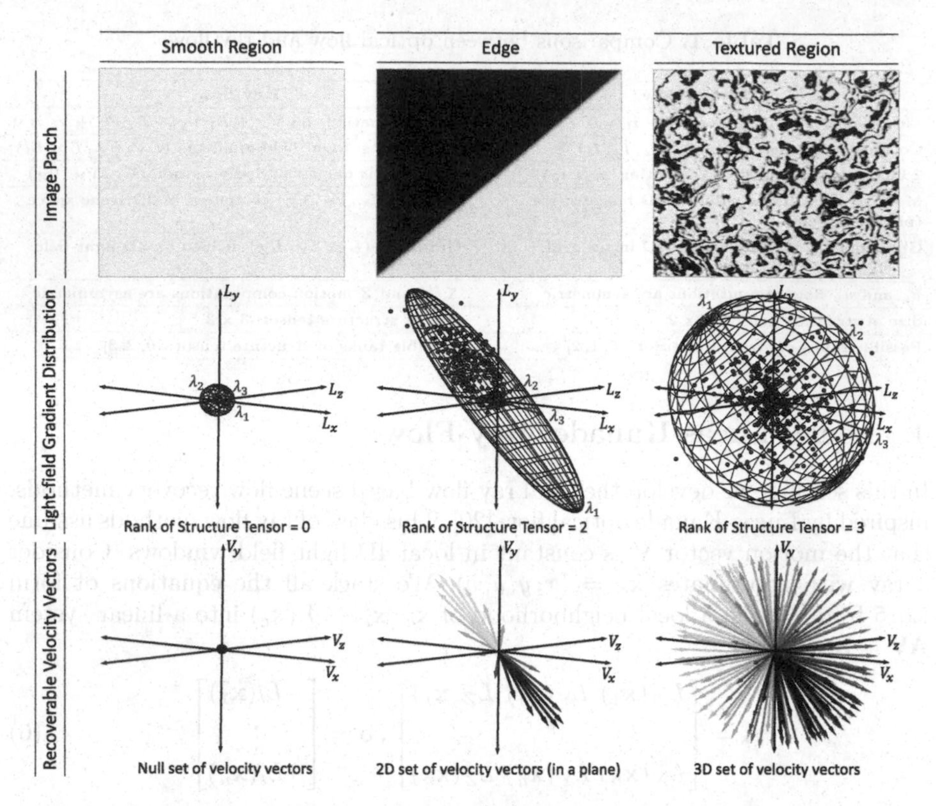

Fig. 3. Relationship between scene texture, rank of the light field structure tensor, and the space of recoverable motions. (**Top**) Scene patches. (**Middle**) Distribution of light field gradients; each dot represents the gradient (L_X, L_Y, L_Z) computed at one location in a light field window. The covariance of the gradients is represented by ellipsoids whose principal axes are proportional to the three eigenvalues $\lambda_1, \lambda_2, \lambda_3$ of the structure tensor. (**Bottom**) Set of recoverable motion vectors. **(Left)** For a light field window corresponding to a smooth patch, the gradients (L_X, L_Y, L_Z) are approximately zero, and concentrated around the origin in the gradient space. The rank of the structure tensor is 0, implying that no motion vector can be recovered reliably. **(Center)** For a patch with a single edge, non-zero gradients are distributed approximately along a plane in the gradient space, resulting in a rank 2 structure tensor (1-D null space). As a result, a 2D family of motions (orthogonal to the edge) can be recovered. (**Right**) For a patch with 2D texture, non-zero gradients are distributed nearly isotropically in the gradient space. Therefore, structure tensor has rank = 3. Thus, the entire space of 3D motions are recoverable.

must be invertible. Thus, the performance of the local method can be understood in terms of $rank(\mathbf{S})$.

Result (Rank of Structure Tensor). Structure tensor **S** has three possible ranks: 0, 2, and 3 for a local 4D light field window. These correspond to scene patches with no texture (smooth regions), an edge, and 2D texture, respectively.

Intuition: In the following, we provide an intuition for the above result by considering three cases. A detailed proof is given in the supplementary technical report.

Case 1: Smooth Region. In this case, $L_X = L_Y = L_Z = 0$ for all the locations in the light field window. Therefore, all the entries of the structure tensor (given in Eq. 8) are zero, resulting in it being a rank 0 matrix. All three eigenvalues $\lambda_1, \lambda_2, \lambda_3 = 0$, as shown in the left column of Fig. 3. As a result, it has a 3-D null space, and no motion vector can be recovered reliably for this window.

Case 2: Single Step Edge. Without loss of generality, suppose the light field window corresponds to a fronto-parallel scene patch with a vertical edge, *i.e.*, $L_Y = 0$. The middle row of the structure tensor is all zeros, resulting in a rank 2 matrix, with a 1-D null space (only one eigenvalue $\lambda_3 = 0$). As a result, a 2D family of motions (motion orthogonal to the edge) can be recovered, as illustrated in the second column of Fig. 3.

Case 3: 2D Texture. All three derivatives are non-zero and independent. The structure tensor is full rank (rank = 3) and the entire space of 3D motions are recoverable.

Comparisons with Structure Tensor for Optical Flow: The structure tensor for 2D optical flow is a 2×2 matrix and can have all possible ranks from 0 to 2 [26]. *For light fields, the structure tensor cannot have rank* 1. This is because even a 4D window with a single step edge results in a rank 2 structure tensor.[4] For more conceptual comparisons between optical flow and ray flow, please refer to Table 1.

Dependence on Camera Parameters. Besides scene texture and light field structure, the imaging parameters of the light field camera also influences the performance of ray flow methods. Using the ray flow equation requires computing angular light field gradients (L_X and L_Y), whose accuracy depends on the angular resolution of the light field camera. Most off-the-shelf light field cameras have a relatively low angular resolution (*e.g.*, 15×15 for Lytro Illum), resulting in aliasing [22]. To mitigate aliasing, we apply Gaussian pre-filtering before computing the gradients. Another important parameter is the aperture size, which limits the range of recoverable motion. This is because ray flow changes the (x, y) coordinates of the ray. When the motion is too large, most of the rays will escape the aperture and the motion cannot be recovered (see Fig. 2). See the supplementary report for a detailed discussion on the effects of various camera parameters.

[4] Although the structure tensor theoretically has rank 2, the ratio $\frac{\lambda_1}{\lambda_2}$ of the largest and second largest eigenvalues can be large. This is because the eigenvalue corresponding to Z motion depends on the range of (u, v) coordinates, which is limited by the size of the light field window. Therefore, a sufficiently large window size is required for motion recovery.

4.2 Enhanced Local Methods

Our analysis so far assumes small (differential) scene motion. If the inter-frame scene motion is large, then the simple linear ray flow equation is not valid. Another way to relate the scene motion and the resulting change in the captured light field is to define a warp function on the light field, which describes the change in coordinates $\mathbf{x} = (x, y, u, v)$ of a light ray due to scene motion $\mathbf{V}$ (Eq. 1):

$$\mathbf{w}(\mathbf{x},\mathbf{V}) = (x + V_X - \frac{u}{\Gamma}V_Z, y + V_Y - \frac{v}{\Gamma}V_Z, u, v). \tag{9}$$

Then, the local method can be formulated as a local light field registration problem:

$$\min_{\mathbf{V}} \sum_{\mathbf{x_i} \in \mathscr{N}(\mathbf{x_c})} (L_0(\mathbf{x_i}) - L_1(\mathbf{w}(\mathbf{x_i}, \mathbf{V})))^2. \tag{10}$$

The method described by Eq. 7 is *the same* as locally linearizing Eq. 10. Using this formulation, we develop an enhanced local method where the motion vector $\mathbf{V}$ is solved over a light field pyramid for dealing with large (non-differential) scene motions.

5 Global 'Horn-Schunck' Ray Flow

The local constancy assumption made by the local ray-flow methods is too restrictive when dealing with non-rigid motion. In this section, we propose a family of global ray flow methods that are inspired by global 'Horn-Schunck' optical flow [14]. The basic, less limiting assumption is that the 3D flow field varies smoothly over the scene. Therefore, we regularize the flow computation by introducing a smoothness term that penalizes large variations of $\mathbf{V}$ and minimize a global functional:

$$E(\mathbf{V}) = E_D(\mathbf{V}) + E_S(\mathbf{V}), \quad \text{where} \tag{11}$$

$$E_D(\mathbf{V}) = \int_\Omega (L_X V_X + L_Y V_Y + L_Z V_Z + L_t)^2 \, dx\, dy\, du\, dv,$$

$$E_S(\mathbf{V}) = \int_\Omega (\lambda|\nabla V_X|^2 + \lambda|\nabla V_Y|^2 + \lambda_Z|\nabla V_Z|^2) \, dx\, dy\, du\, dv.$$

Note that Ω is the 4D light field domain, and ∇p is the 4D gradient of a scalar field p: $\nabla p = (\frac{\partial p}{\partial x}, \frac{\partial p}{\partial y}, \frac{\partial p}{\partial u}, \frac{\partial p}{\partial v})$. Since the computation of X/Y flow and Z flow are asymmetric, we use different weights for the X/Y and Z smoothness terms. In practice we use $\lambda = 8$ and $\lambda_Z = 1$. $E(\mathbf{V})$ is a convex functional, and its minimum can be found by the Euler-Lagrange equations. See the supplementary technical report for details.

Enhanced Global Methods. The quadratic penalty functions used in the basic global ray flow method (Eq. 11) penalizes flow discontinuities, leading to over-smoothing around motion boundaries. In the optical flow community [3,5,25], it has been shown that robust penalty functions perform significantly better around motion discontinuities. Based on this, we developed an enhanced global method that uses the generalized Charbonnier function $\rho(x) = (x^2 + \epsilon^2)^a$ with $a = 0.45$ as suggested in [28].

6 Combined Local-Global Ray Flow

The ray flow methods considered so far treat the motion of each light ray separately. However, a light field camera captures multiple rays from the same scene point, all of which share the same motion. Can we exploit this constraint to further improve the performance of ray flow based motion recovery methods? Consider a ray with coordinates (x, y, u, v), coming from a scene point $S = (X, Y, Z)$. The coordinates of all the rays coming from S form a 2D plane $\mathscr{P}(u, v)$ [10,17,27] in the 4D light-field:

$$\mathscr{P}(u,v) = \{(x_i, y_i, u_i, v_i) \mid u_i = u - \alpha(x_i - x), v_i = v - \alpha(y_i - y)\}, \tag{12}$$

where the parameter $\alpha = \frac{\Gamma}{Z}$ is the disparity between sub-aperture images, and is a function of the depth Z of S. All these rays share the same flow vector $\mathbf{V} = (V_X, V_Y, V_Z)$. Therefore, we can estimate $\mathbf{V}$ by minimizing the following function:

$$\min_{\mathbf{V}} \sum_{\mathbf{x}_i \in \mathscr{P}(u,v)} (L_{Xi}V_X + L_{Yi}V_Y + L_{Zi}V_Z + L_{ti})^2. \tag{13}$$

Given the parameter α (which can be determined using light-field based depth estimation [33]), this function can be minimized similarly as the local method (Sect. 4), which assumes constancy of ray motion in a local 4D ray neighborhood $\mathscr{N}(u, v)$. While the local constancy assumption is only approximate, the constancy of motion over the 2D plane described in Eq. 12 is an *exact constraint*, resulting in better performance. Moreover, in order to further regularize the problem, we can leverage the global smoothness of motion assumption used in global methods in Sect. 5. Based on these observations, we propose a *combined local-global* (CLG) ray flow method [6], whose data term is given by minimizing the local term (Eq. 13) for each ray *in the central view* Ω_c:

$$E_D(\mathbf{V}) = \int_{\Omega_c} \sum_{\mathbf{x}_i \in \mathscr{P}(u,v)} (L_{Xi}V_X + L_{Yi}V_Y + L_{Zi}V_Z + L_{ti})^2 du\, dv. \tag{14}$$

This local data term is combined with a global smoothness term defined on Ω_c.

$$E_S(\mathbf{V}) = \int_{\Omega_c} (\lambda|\nabla V_X|^2 + \lambda|\nabla V_Y|^2 + \lambda_Z|\nabla V_Z|^2)\, du\, dv. \tag{15}$$

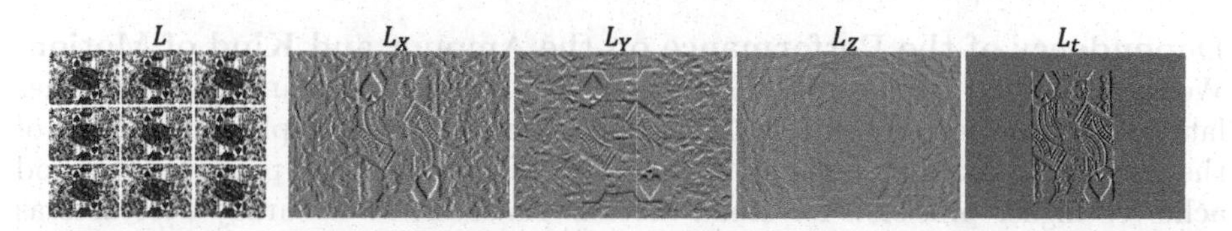

Fig. 4. Measured light field gradients. Light field for an example scene (a card moving in the X-Z plane in front of a static background) is shown as a 3 × 3 subset of sub-aperture images (left). Light field gradients are only shown for the central sub-aperture. **Zoom in for details.**

This formulation estimates motion only for the 2D central view Ω_c while utilizing the information from the whole light field, thereby simultaneously achieving computational efficiency and high accuracy. Furthermore, by adopting the enhancements of local and global methods, the CLG method outperforms individual local and global methods. Therefore, in the rest of the paper, we show results only for the CLG method. Also notice that the CLG ray flow method uses the estimated depths only *implicitly* as an additional constraint for regularization. Therefore, unlike previous methods [13,21,27], estimating depths accurately is not critical for recovering motion. Please see the supplementary technical report for implementation details of the CLG method, a comparison between the local, global and CLG methods and simulation results demonstrating the effect of depth accuracy on the CLG method.

7 Experimental Results

For our experiments, we use a Lytro Illum camera, calibrated using a geometric calibration toolbox [4]. We extract the central 9×9 subaperture images, each of which has a spatial resolution of 552×383. Figure 4 shows an example light field and the computed gradients. We compare our combined local-global method (CLG) with the RGB-D scene flow method (PD-Flow) of Jaimez *et al.* [16] and light field scene flow method (called OLFW in this paper) of Srinivasan *et al.* [27]. For a fair comparison, we use the same modality (light fields) for depth estimation in PD-Flow (depth estimated from light field is the depth channel input), using the same algorithm as in OLFW [30]. Please refer to the supplementary video for a better visualization of the scene motion.

Controlled Experiments on a Translation Stage. Figure 5 shows scene flow recovery results for a scene that is intentionally chosen to have simple geometry and sufficient texture to compare the baseline performance of the methods. The moving objects (playing cards) are mounted on controllable translation stages such that they can move in the X-Z plane with measured ground truth motion. Mean absolute error (MAE) for the three dimensions (ground truth Y-motion is zero) are computed and shown in the table. All three methods perform well for recovering the X-motion. However, PD-Flow and OLFW cannot recover the Z-motion reliably because errors in depth estimation are large compared to the millimeter-scale Z-motion. The proposed ray flow methods estimates the Z-motion directly, thereby achieving higher accuracy.

Dependency of the Performance on the Amount and Kind of Motion. We mount a textured plastic sheet on the translation stage and move it either laterally (X-motion) or axially (Z-motion). Figures 6(a), (b) plot the RMSE of the estimated motion, against the amount of motion. The proposed method achieves higher precision for small motion. However, its accuracy decreases as the amount of motion increases. This is because of the limit imposed by the aperture size, as discussed in Sect. 4.1. On the other hand, previous depth-based methods [27] can recover motion over a large range, albeit with lower precision. This complementary set of capabilities of our method and previous methods are

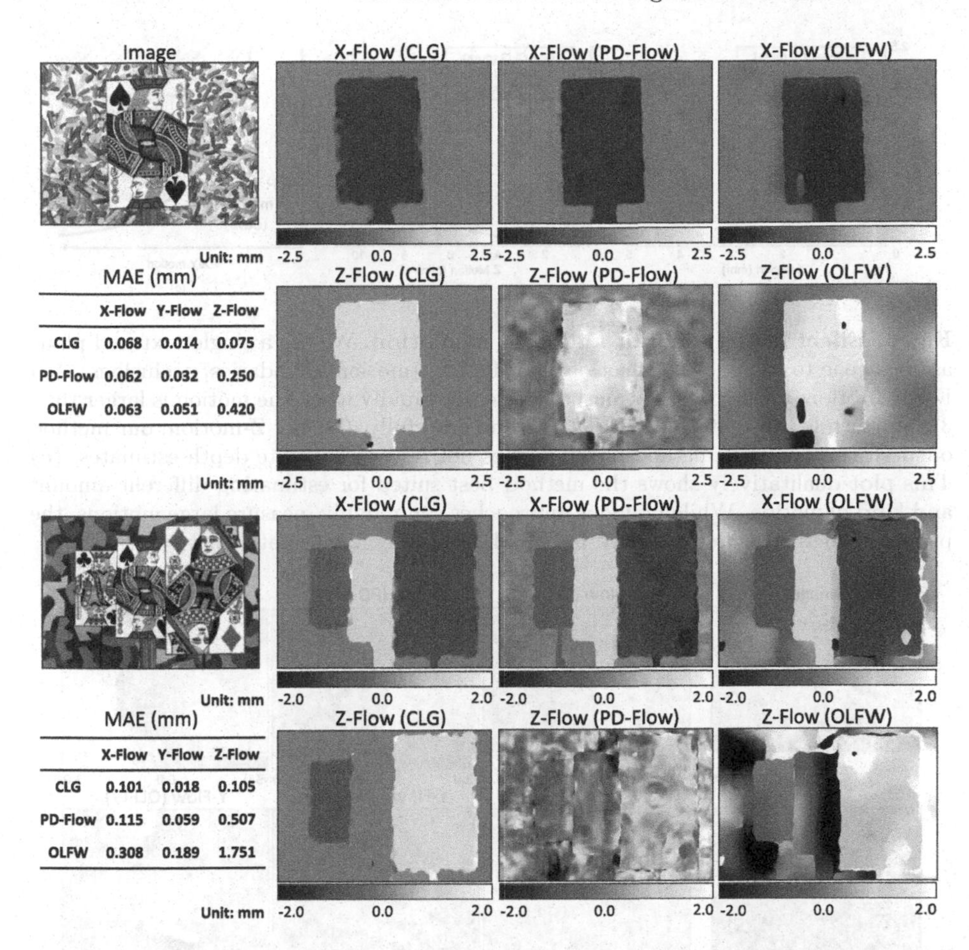

MAE (mm)

	X-Flow	Y-Flow	Z-Flow
CLG	0.068	0.014	0.075
PD-Flow	0.062	0.032	0.250
OLFW	0.063	0.051	0.420

MAE (mm)

	X-Flow	Y-Flow	Z-Flow
CLG	0.101	0.018	0.105
PD-Flow	0.115	0.059	0.507
OLFW	0.308	0.189	1.751

Fig. 5. Controlled experiments on a translation stage. (**Top**) A single card moving diagonally. (**Bottom**) Three cards moving diagonally forward, laterally, and diagonally backward, respectively. Mean absolute error (MAE) for the three motion components are shown in the tables. While all methods recover the lateral motion relatively accurately, the proposed CLG ray-flow approach estimates the Z-motion more accurately than previous approaches. This is because previous approaches rely on, and are thus prone to errors in, depth estimation. In contrast, our approach estimates the motion directly from light-field gradients, thereby achieving high accuracy.

shown qualitatively in Fig. 6(c). Although for the rest of the paper we focus on showing our methods' capability in recovering small motion (*e.g.*, for applications in finger gesture and facial expression recognition), previous approaches [27] may perform better for measuring large scale motion, such as gait recognition.

Qualitative Comparisons. Figures 7, 8, 9 and 10 shows qualitative comparisons of the three methods for complex, non-rigid motion and in challenging natural environments. For each experiment we only show one component of the recovered 3D flow. Please see the supplementary report for the full 3D flow

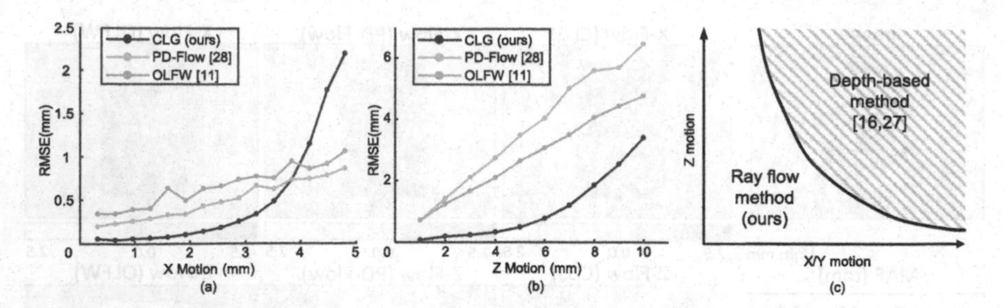

Fig. 6. Effect of the amount and kind of motion. We use a single textured plane as the scene to exclude the effect of other factors (motion boundaries, occlusions). **(a)** For X-motion, the error of our method increases rapidly when the motion is larger than 3.5 mm, while PD-Flow and OLFW degrade gracefully. **(b)** For Z-motion, our method outperforms previous methods since it does not rely on accurate depth estimates. **(c)** This plot qualitatively shows the method best suited for estimating different amount and kind of motion. While previous approaches can reliably measure large motions, the proposed method is better suited for small, especially axial, motions.

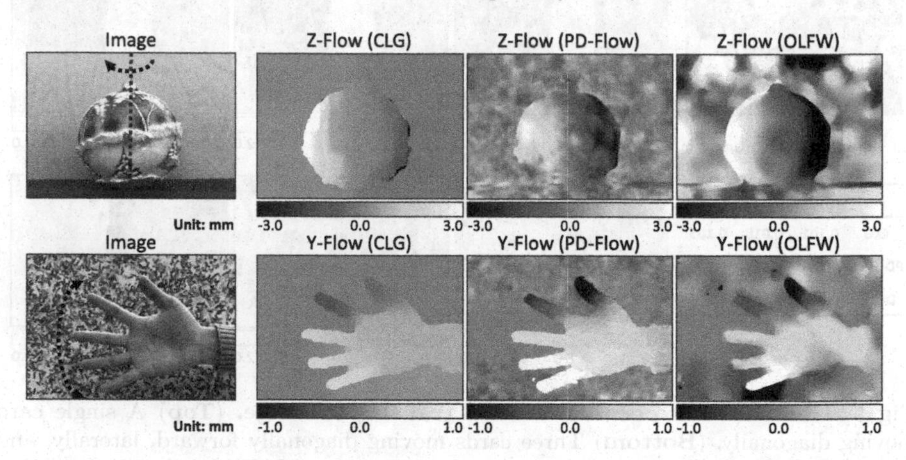

Fig. 7. Recovering non-planar and non-rigid motion. (Top) A rotating spherical ornament. All methods can estimate the gradually changing Z-motion, but only our method recovers the background correctly. **(Bottom)** An expanding hand. The expansion is demonstrated by the different Y-motion of the fingers.

visualization and more experiments. In all the examples, our method is able to estimate the complex, gradually changing motion fields and preserve the motion boundaries better than the other methods, especially for experiments involving small Z-motion, and where depth estimation is unreliable (*e.g.*, scenes with occlusions or reflections in the background). In Fig. 10 (bottom) all three methods have difficulty in preserving the object boundaries due to shadows, which is a inherent drawback of the brightness constancy assumption.

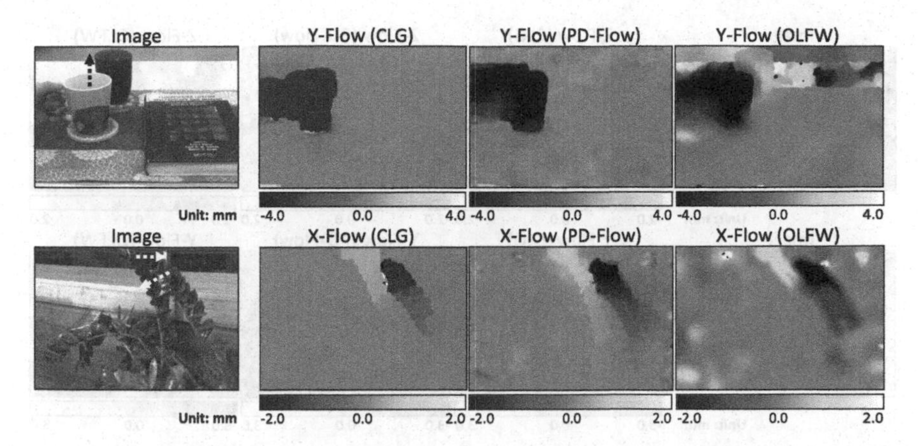

Fig. 8. Recovering motion in natural environments with occlusions. (Top) The mug on the left is picked up by a hand. Our method estimates the motion boundaries accurately. **(Bottom)** The top two vertical branches of the plant quiver in the wind. Our method can correctly compute the motion of the two complex-shaped branches.

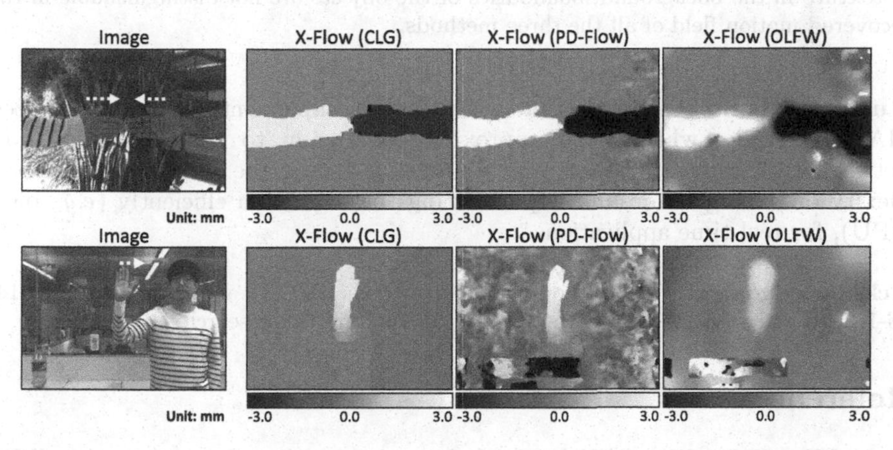

Fig. 9. Recovering human actions. (Top) Handshaking. All the three methods compute the joining movements of the hands correctly, while our method preserves the hand boundary best. **(Bottom)** Waving hand. Our method correctly estimates the motion in spite of the reflections and textureless regions in the background, which is challenging for depth estimation algorithms.

8 Limitations

Recoverable Range of Motion: As discussed in Sects. 4.1 and 7, the maximum recoverable amount of motion for ray flow methods is limited by the aperture size. A future research direction is to develop hybrid methods that combine the ray flow method and depth-based methods [16,27] according to the amount and nature of scene motion.

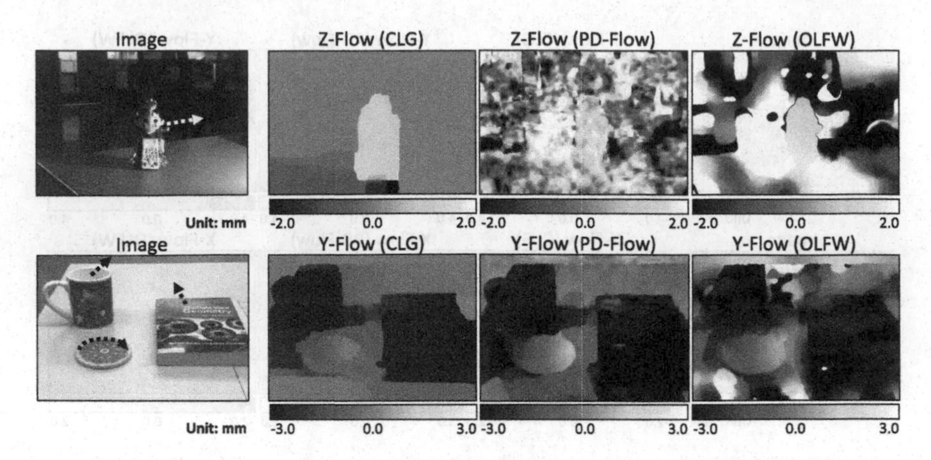

Fig. 10. Recovering motion under challenging lighting conditions. (**Top**) A figurine moves under weak, directional lighting. Our method still preserves the overall shape of the object, although its reflection on the table is also regarded as moving. (**Bottom**) **F**ailure case: a few objects move independently. Due to shadows and lack of texture in the background, boundaries of the objects are not distinguishable in the recovered motion field of all the three methods.

Running Time: Currently our methods are implemented via unoptimized MATLAB code, which takes approximately 10 min to compute scene flow between two frames. Further work includes reducing the computational complexity of the algorithm and implementing the algorithm efficiently (*e.g.*, on a GPU), for real-time applications.

Acknowledgement. The authors would like to thank ONR grant number N00014-16-1-2995 and DARPA REVEAL program for funding this research.

References

1. Adelson, E.H., Wang, J.Y.A.: Single lens stereo with a plenoptic camera. IEEE Trans. Pattern Anal. Mach. Intell. (TPAMI) **14**(2), 99–106 (1992)
2. Alexander, E., Guo, Q., Koppal, S., Gortler, S., Zickler, T.: Focal flow: measuring distance and velocity with defocus and differential motion. In: Leibe, B., Matas, J., Sebe, N., Welling, M. (eds.) ECCV 2016. LNCS, vol. 9907, pp. 667–682. Springer, Cham (2016). https://doi.org/10.1007/978-3-319-46487-9_41
3. Black, M.J., Anandan, P.: The robust estimation of multiple motions: parametric and piecewise-smooth flow fields. Comput. Vis. Image Underst. **63**(1), 75–104 (1996)
4. Bok, Y., Jeon, H.G., Kweon, I.S.: Geometric calibration of micro-lens-based light field cameras using line features. IEEE Trans. Pattern Anal. Mach. Intell. (TPAMI) **39**(2), 287–300 (2017)
5. Brox, T., Bruhn, A., Papenberg, N., Weickert, J.: High accuracy optical flow estimation based on a theory for warping. In: Pajdla, T., Matas, J. (eds.) ECCV 2004. LNCS, vol. 3024, pp. 25–36. Springer, Heidelberg (2004). https://doi.org/10.1007/978-3-540-24673-2_3

6. Bruhn, A., Weickert, J., Schnörr, C.: Lucas/Kanade meets Horn/Schunck: combining local and global optic flow methods. Int. J. Comput. Vis. (IJCV) **61**(3), 211–231 (2005)
7. Chandraker, M.: On shape and material recovery from motion. In: Fleet, D., Pajdla, T., Schiele, B., Tuytelaars, T. (eds.) ECCV 2014. LNCS, vol. 8695, pp. 202–217. Springer, Cham (2014). https://doi.org/10.1007/978-3-319-10584-0_14
8. Chandraker, M.: What camera motion reveals about shape with unknown BRDF. In: IEEE Conference on Computer Vision and Pattern Recognition (CVPR), pp. 2171–2178. IEEE, Washington (2014)
9. Chandraker, M.: The information available to a moving observer on shape with unknown, isotropic brdfs. IEEE Trans. Pattern Anal. Mach. Intell. (TPAMI) **38**(7), 1283–1297 (2016)
10. Dansereau, D.G., Mahon, I., Pizarro, O., Williams, S.B.: Plenoptic flow: closed-form visual odometry for light field cameras. In: IEEE/RSJ International Conference on Intelligent Robots and Systems (IROS), pp. 4455–4462. IEEE, Washington (2011)
11. Dansereau, D.G., Schuster, G., Ford, J., Wetzstein, G.: A wide-field-of-view monocentric light field camera. In: IEEE Conference on Computer Vision and Pattern Recognition (CVPR). IEEE, Washington (2017)
12. Gottfried, J.-M., Fehr, J., Garbe, C.S.: Computing range flow from multi-modal *Kinect* data. In: Bebis, G., et al. (eds.) ISVC 2011. LNCS, vol. 6938, pp. 758–767. Springer, Heidelberg (2011). https://doi.org/10.1007/978-3-642-24028-7_70
13. Heber, S., Pock, T.: Scene flow estimation from light fields via the preconditioned primal-dual algorithm. In: Jiang, X., Hornegger, J., Koch, R. (eds.) GCPR 2014. LNCS, vol. 8753, pp. 3–14. Springer, Cham (2014). https://doi.org/10.1007/978-3-319-11752-2_1
14. Horn, B.K., Schunck, B.G.: Determining optical flow. Artif. Intell. **17**(1–3), 185–203 (1981)
15. Hung, C.H., Xu, L., Jia, J.: Consistent binocular depth and scene flow with chained temporal profiles. Int. J. Comput. Vis. (IJCV) **102**(1–3), 271–292 (2013)
16. Jaimez, M., Souiai, M., Gonzalez-Jimenez, J., Cremers, D.: A primal-dual framework for real-time dense RGB-D scene flow. In: IEEE International Conference on Robotics and Automation (ICRA), pp. 98–104. IEEE, Washington (2015)
17. Johannsen, O., Sulc, A., Goldluecke, B.: On linear structure from motion for light field cameras. In: IEEE International Conference on Computer Vision (ICCV), pp. 720–728. IEEE, Washington (2015)
18. Levoy, M., Hanrahan, P.: Light field rendering. In: SIGGRAPH Conference on Computer Graphics and Interactive Techniques, pp. 31–42. ACM, New York (1996)
19. Li, Z., Xu, Z., Ramamoorthi, R., Chandraker, M.: Robust energy minimization for BRDF-invariant shape from light fields. In: IEEE Conference on Computer Vision and Pattern Recognition (CVPR), vol. 1. IEEE, Washington (2017)
20. Lucas, B.D., Kanade, T., et al.: An iterative image registration technique with an application to stereo vision. In: International Joint Conference on Artificial Intelligence, pp. 674–679. Morgan Kaufmann, San Francisco (1981)
21. Navarro, J., Garamendi, J.: Variational scene flow and occlusion detection from a light field sequence. In: International Conference on Systems. Signals and Image Processing (IWSSIP), pp. 1–4. IEEE, Washington (2016)
22. Neumann, J., Fermuller, C., Aloimonos, Y.: Polydioptric camera design and 3D motion estimation. In: IEEE Conference on Computer Vision and Pattern Recognition (CVPR), vol. 2, p. II-294. IEEE, Washington (2003)
23. Neumann, J., Fermüller, C., Aloimonos, Y.: A hierarchy of cameras for 3D photography. Comput. Vis. Image Underst. **96**(3), 274–293 (2004)

24. Ng, R., Levoy, M., Brédif, M., Duval, G., Horowitz, M., Hanrahan, P.: Light field photography with a hand-held plenoptic camera. Comput. Sci. Tech. Rep. CSTR **2**(11), 1–11 (2005)
25. Odobez, J.M., Bouthemy, P.: Robust multiresolution estimation of parametric motion models. J. Vis. Commun. Image Represent. **6**(4), 348–365 (1995)
26. Shi, J., Tomasi, C.: Good features to track. In: IEEE Conference on Computer Vision and Pattern Recognition (CVPR), pp. 593–600. IEEE, Washington (1994)
27. Srinivasan, P.P., Tao, M.W., Ng, R., Ramamoorthi, R.: Oriented light-field windows for scene flow. In: IEEE International Conference on Computer Vision (ICCV), pp. 3496–3504. IEEE, Washington (2015)
28. Sun, D., Roth, S., Black, M.J.: Secrets of optical flow estimation and their principles. In: IEEE Conference on Computer Vision and Pattern Recognition (CVPR), pp. 2432–2439. IEEE, Washington (2010)
29. Sun, D., Sudderth, E.B., Pfister, H.: Layered RGBD scene flow estimation. In: IEEE Conference on Computer Vision and Pattern Recognition (CVPR), pp. 548–556. IEEE, Washington (2015)
30. Tao, M.W., Hadap, S., Malik, J., Ramamoorthi, R.: Depth from combining defocus and correspondence using light-field cameras. In: IEEE International Conference on Computer Vision (ICCV), pp. 673–680. IEEE, Washington (2013)
31. Vedula, S., Baker, S., Rander, P., Collins, R., Kanade, T.: Three-dimensional scene flow. In: IEEE International Conference on Computer Vision (ICCV), vol. 2, pp. 722–729. IEEE, Washington (1999)
32. Wang, T.C., Chandraker, M., Efros, A.A., Ramamoorthi, R.: SVBRDF-invariant shape and reflectance estimation from light-field cameras. In: IEEE Conference on Computer Vision and Pattern Recognition (CVPR), pp. 5451–5459. IEEE, Washington (2016)
33. Wanner, S., Goldluecke, B.: Variational light field analysis for disparity estimation and super-resolution. IEEE Trans. Pattern Anal. Mach. Intell. (TPAMI) **36**(3), 606–619 (2014)
34. Wedel, A., Rabe, C., Vaudrey, T., Brox, T., Franke, U., Cremers, D.: Efficient dense scene flow from sparse or dense stereo data. In: Forsyth, D., Torr, P., Zisserman, A. (eds.) ECCV 2008. LNCS, vol. 5302, pp. 739–751. Springer, Heidelberg (2008). https://doi.org/10.1007/978-3-540-88682-2_56
35. Zhang, Y., Li, Z., Yang, W., Yu, P., Lin, H., Yu, J.: The light field 3D scanner. In: IEEE International Conference on Computational Photography (ICCP), pp. 1–9. IEEE, Washington (2017)

Direct Sparse Odometry with Rolling Shutter

David Schubert(✉), Nikolaus Demmel, Vladyslav Usenko, Jörg Stückler, and Daniel Cremers

Technical University of Munich, Garching b. München, Germany
{schubdav,demmeln,usenko,stueckle,cremers}@in.tum.de

Abstract. Neglecting the effects of rolling-shutter cameras for visual odometry (VO) severely degrades accuracy and robustness. In this paper, we propose a novel direct monocular VO method that incorporates a rolling-shutter model. Our approach extends direct sparse odometry which performs direct bundle adjustment of a set of recent keyframe poses and the depths of a sparse set of image points. We estimate the velocity at each keyframe and impose a constant-velocity prior for the optimization. In this way, we obtain a near real-time, accurate direct VO method. Our approach achieves improved results on challenging rolling-shutter sequences over state-of-the-art global-shutter VO.

Keywords: Direct monocular visual odometry · Rolling shutter

1 Introduction

Visual odometry for global-shutter cameras has been extensively studied in the last decades (e.g. [6,18]). Global-shutter cameras capture all pixels in the image within the same time of exposure. Most consumer grade devices such as smartphones or tablets, however, include rolling-shutter cameras which read out image rows sequentially and hence start to expose the rows at sequentially increasing capture times. This leads to image distortions when the camera is moving. Hence, it is necessary to consider the camera pose as a function of the capture time, i.e. row index. Simply neglecting this effect and assuming global shutter can lead to significant drift in the trajectory and 3D reconstruction estimate – see Fig. 1.

For visual odometry two major paradigms exist: direct methods (e.g. [6]) align image intensities based on the photoconsistency assumption, while indirect methods (e.g. [18]) align pixel coordinates of matched keypoints, i.e. they minimize keypoint reprojection error. Direct methods are particularly advantageous in weakly textured and repetitive regions. However, as demonstrated in [6], geometric noise as caused by neglecting rolling shutter significantly downgrades

Electronic supplementary material The online version of this chapter (https://doi.org/10.1007/978-3-030-01237-3_42) contains supplementary material, which is available to authorized users.

V. Ferrari et al. (Eds.): ECCV 2018, LNCS 11212, pp. 699–714, 2018.
https://doi.org/10.1007/978-3-030-01237-3_42

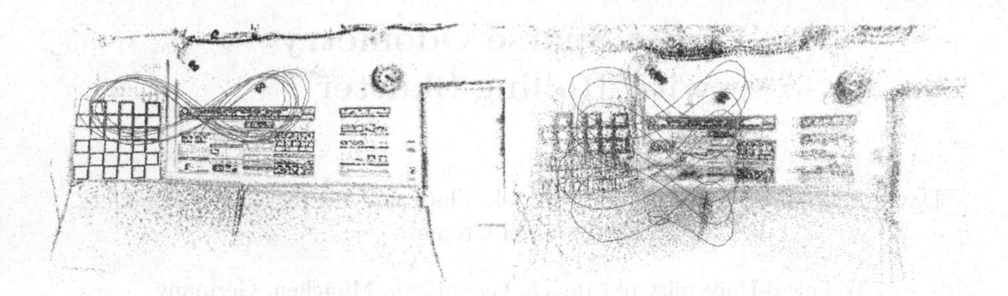

Fig. 1. Qualitative result of our method (DSORS, left) versus DSO (right) on the sequence *infinity-1*. The keyframe trajectory in red shows significant drift without a rolling shutter model. DSORS also produces much cleaner edges in the sparse 3D reconstruction than DSO.

the performance of direct methods. Thus, for direct methods, it is important to model rolling shutter.

While in indirect methods, the row and, hence, the capture time of corresponding keypoints can be assumed known through the extraction process, in direct methods, one has to impose the *rolling shutter constraint* [17] in order to retrieve the capture time. In this paper, we propose a novel direct visual odometry method for rolling-shutter cameras. Our approach performs direct bundle adjustment of a set of recent keyframe poses and the depths of a sparse set of image points. We extend direct sparse odometry (DSO, [6]) by estimating the velocity at each keyframe, imposing a constant-velocity prior for the optimization and incorporating rolling-shutter into the projection model.

We evaluate our method on challenging datasets recorded with rolling-shutter cameras and compare our method to a state-of-the-art approach for global shutter cameras, demonstrating the benefits of modeling rolling shutter adequately in our method.

2 Related Work

Indirect Methods: The vast set of literature on indirect methods for visual odometry and SLAM considers global-shutter cameras [18,19]. Some approaches investigate the proper treatment of rolling-shutter effects. Hedborg et al. [9] propose rolling shutter bundle adjustment which assumes constant-velocity motion between camera poses to determine the camera pose for the row of a keypoint through linear interpolation. Insights into degenerate cases of rolling-shutter bundle adjustment are given in [4]. Essentially, 3D reconstructions collapse to a plane when the camera frame directions are parallel in which the shutter is traversing. Ait-Aider et al. [1] recover 3D reconstruction and motion of a rigidly moving object using a snapshot of a rolling-shutter stereo camera. The method assumes linear motion and solves a non-linear system of equations resulting from the keypoint correspondences. They argue that the use of rolling-shutter cameras can be beneficial over global-shutter cameras for kinetics estimation of fast moving objects. Another line of work addresses the problem of recovering pose and motion in the case of known structure from a single rolling-shutter image [2,3,15,16]. Dai et al. [5] generalize epipolar geometry to the rolling-shutter case and propose linear and non-linear algorithms to solve for the rolling-shutter essential matrix that relates two rolling-shutter images by the relative pose and rotational and translational velocities of their cameras. Some approaches fuse vision with inertial measurements which allows for going beyond constant-velocity assumptions for inter-frame camera motion. Lovegrove et al. [14] approximate the continuous camera motion using B-splines. The approach of [13] considers rolling-shutter for extended Kalman filter based visual-inertial odometry. Saurer et al. [21] develop a pipeline for sparse-to-dense 3D reconstruction that incorporates GPS/INS readings in a rolling-shutter-aware bundle adjustment, prior to performing rolling-shutter stereo to create a dense reconstruction.

Direct Methods: Direct methods have been recently shown to achieve state of-the-art performance for visual odometry and SLAM with global-shutter cameras [6,7]. Since in direct methods, image correspondences are found through projective warping from one image to another, they are more susceptible to errors introduced by neglecting rolling-shutter effects than indirect methods. Estimating the time of projection in the other image requires the solution of the rolling-shutter constraint [17]. The constraint implicitly relates the reprojected image row of a pixel with its capture time, i.e. image row, in the other image. Meingast et al. [17] develop approximations to the constraint for several special cases of camera motion. Saurer et al. [20] present dense multi-view stereo reconstruction for rolling-shutter cameras including image distortion by wide-angle lenses, while they assume the camera motion known. Kerl et al. [11] use B-splines to represent the trajectory estimate continuously for visual odometry with rolling-shutter RGB-D. While we propose a direct method for monocular cameras, similar to our approach they also incorporate the rolling-shutter constraint as a hard constraint by solving for the observation time in the target frame. Most closely related to our method is the approach by Kim et al. [12]. It extends LSD-SLAM [7] to rolling-shutter cameras based on a spline trajectory representation. In contrast to our method they require depth initialization and do not incorporate lens distortion in their model. Their method explicitly incorporates residuals for the rolling-shutter constraint into the non-linear least squares problem by introducing variables for the capture time of each pixel while we directly solve for the capture time. Their implementation runs at approx. 120 s per frame, while our method is faster by orders of magnitude. While their approach separates tracking and mapping, we incorporate a rolling-shutter projection model into a windowed sparse direct bundle adjustment framework (DSO [6]), and represent trajectories using camera poses and velocities at the keyframes. This way, we achieve accurate but run-time efficient visual odometry for rolling-shutter cameras.

3 Direct Sparse Odometry with Rolling Shutter Cameras

We formulate visual odometry as direct bundle adjustment in a recent window of keyframes: we concurrently estimate the camera poses of the keyframes and reconstruct a sparse set of points from direct image alignment residuals (DSO [6]). The method comprises a visual odometry front-end and an optimization back-end. The front-end has been left unmodified compared to DSO. It provides initial parameters for the optimization back-end and is responsible for frame and point management. New frames are tracked with respect to the latest keyframe using direct image alignment assuming a constant camera pose across the image.

The need for a new keyframe is determined based on a heuristic that takes optical flow, camera translation and exposure changes into account. The front-end also decides for the marginalization of keyframes and points which drop out of the optimization window: Keyframes are dropped if they do not have at least 5% of their points visible in the latest keyframe. Also, if the number of keyframes exceeds a threshold ($N = 7$), a keyframe is selected for marginalization using a heuristic that keeps keyframes well-distributed in space, with more keyframes close to the latest one. When a keyframe is marginalized, first all points hosted in the keyframe are marginalized, then the keyframe variables are marginalized. Observations of other points visible in the marginalized keyframe are dropped to maintain the sparsity structure of the Hessian.

The point management aims at keeping a fixed number of active points in the optimization window. The method is sparse, i.e. it does not use all available information. Using more than 2000 image points hardly improves the tracking results of the global shutter method [6], and we also found for our method that the results do not justify the increase in runtime when using more points (see supplementary material). Candidate points are chosen in every new keyframe based on the image gradient, tracked in subsequent frames using epipolar line search and added to the set of active points for the bundle adjustment after old points are marginalized.

Our contribution lies in the optimization backend, where we introduce a model that explicitly accounts for rolling shutter. The energy contains residuals across the window of keyframes and is optimized with respect to all variables jointly using Gauss-Newton optimization.

3.1 Model

In the following, we detail our formulation of direct image alignment in the optimization backend of DSO for rolling shutter cameras. As the rows of an image are not taken at the same time, it is now necessary to find the camera pose as a function of time t. Camera poses $\mathbf{T}_i(t)$ are elements of the special Euclidean group SE(3). We choose a constant velocity model, such that the parametrization of the camera motion while frame i is being taken is given by

$$\mathbf{T}_i(t) = \exp(\hat{\mathbf{v}}_i t)\mathbf{T}_{0,i}, \tag{1}$$

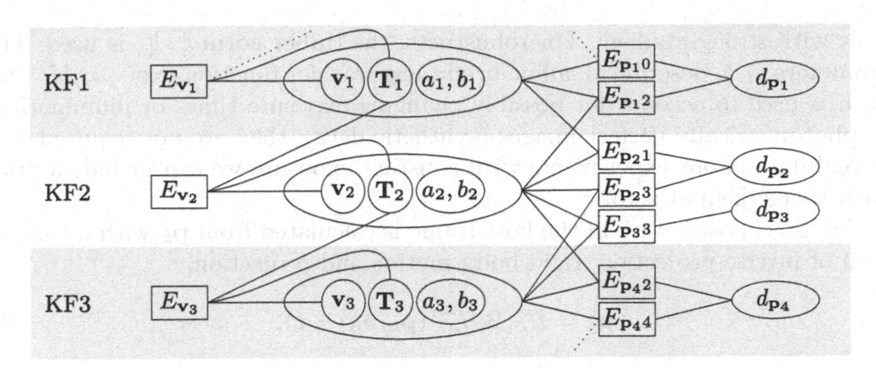

Fig. 2. Factor graph of the objective energy. The ith point observed in the jth keyframe contributes a photometric energy $E_{\mathbf{p}_i j}$, which depends on the variables of the host and the target keyframe plus the point's inverse depth in the host frame. In addition, energy terms $E_{\mathbf{v}_i}$ representing the velocity prior create correlations between velocities and poses. Not shown are the camera intrinsics, which influence every photometric residual.

where $\mathbf{v}_i \in \mathbb{R}^6$ is a velocity vector that includes both translational and rotational components and $\hat{\mathbf{v}}_i \in \mathfrak{se}(3) \subset \mathbb{R}^{4\times4}$ the corresponding Lie Algebra element. We assume that the time t when a pixel is read out is linearly related to the vertical y-coordinate of the pixel, i.e.

$$t(x, y) = y - y_0 \tag{2}$$

which usually is well satisfied for rolling shutter cameras (though technically the shutter might also be along the horizontal x-coordinate, in which case the image can simply be rotated). The optimization backend estimates the reference poses $\mathbf{T}_{0,i} \in \mathrm{SE}(3)$ of the keyframes and the velocities $\mathbf{v}_i \in \mathbb{R}^6$.

In our model, the row y_0 has been taken at the camera pose $\mathbf{T}_{0,i}$. We set y_0 in the middle of the vertical range of the image. Of course, y_0 can be chosen arbitrarily in the image and we could just choose $y_0 = 0$, but with our choice we assume that the optimal $\mathbf{T}_{0,i}$ is in best agreement with its initialization from tracking towards the last keyframe which assumes global shutter.

If a point $\mathbf{p}$ that is hosted in image I_i is observed in image I_j, it contributes to the energy as

$$E_{\mathbf{p}j} = \sum_{k \in \mathcal{N}_\mathbf{p}} w_{\mathbf{p}_k} \|r_k\|_\gamma, \tag{3}$$

with photometric residuals

$$r_k = (I_j[\mathbf{p}'_k] - b_j) - e^{a_j - a_i}(I_i[\mathbf{p}_k] - b_i). \tag{4}$$

The indices in $\mathcal{N}_\mathbf{p}$ denote pixels in the neighborhood of point $\mathbf{p}$. As in [6], we use an 8-pixel neighborhood and a gradient-based weighting $w_{\mathbf{p}_k}$ that down-weights pixels with strong gradient. For robustness, the Huber norm $\|\cdot\|_\gamma$ is used. The parameters a_i, b_i describe an affine brightness transfer function $\exp(-a_i)(I_i - b_i)$ which is used to account for possibly changing exposure times or illumination. For photometrically perfect images (synthetic data), they are not required. For the real data in our experiments with constant exposure we can include a prior which keeps them at zero.

The pixel position $\mathbf{p}'_k$ in the host frame is calculated from $\mathbf{p}_k$ with a composition of inverse projection, rigid body motion and projection,

$$\mathbf{p}'_k = \Pi_\mathbf{c}(\mathbf{R}\Pi_\mathbf{c}^{-1}(\mathbf{p}_k, d_\mathbf{p}) + \mathbf{t}), \tag{5}$$

where $d_\mathbf{p}$ is the depth of point $\mathbf{p}$ in its host frame and the projection $\Pi_\mathbf{c}$ depends on the four internal camera parameters f_x, f_y, c_x, c_y which are the components of the vector $\mathbf{c}$.

The rotation $\mathbf{R}$ and the translation $\mathbf{t}$ are calculated as

$$\begin{bmatrix}\mathbf{R} & \mathbf{t} \\ \mathbf{0} & 1\end{bmatrix} = \mathbf{T}_j(t^*)\mathbf{T}_i^{-1}(t(\mathbf{p})) \tag{6}$$

$$= \exp(\hat{\mathbf{v}}_j t^*)\mathbf{T}_{0,j}\mathbf{T}_{0,i}^{-1}\exp(-\hat{\mathbf{v}}_i t(\mathbf{p})) \tag{7}$$

Note that we know the time when the point has been observed in the host frame, as we know its pixel coordinates. It is not straightforward, however, to obtain the time t^* of observation in the target frame. It depends on the y-coordinate $\mathbf{p}'_y$ of the projected point (Eq. (2)), but the y-coordinate of the projected point also depends on time through the time-dependent pose $\mathbf{T}_j(t)$. This interdependency is formulated as the *rolling shutter constraint* [17], where we choose t^* such that it satisfies

$$t^* = t(\mathbf{p}'(t^*)). \tag{8}$$

In short: pose time equals row time. Here, t is the function defined in Eq. (2). Apart from some specific cases, there is no closed-form solution for t^* [17]. In practice, it turns out to be sufficient to iterate the update $t^* \leftarrow t(\mathbf{p}'(t^*))$ for a few times to obtain a solution.

We remove lens distortion from the images through undistortion in a preprocessing step. Consequently, the mapping between pixel coordinates and time in Eq. (2) changes: Instead of the row in the undistorted image, we need to consider the row of the corresponding point in the original distorted image,

$$t(x, y) = f_\mathrm{d}(x, y)_y - \tilde{y}_0. \tag{9}$$

A point in the undistorted image with coordinates x and y is mapped by the distortion function f_d into the original image, where the y-coordinate determines the time. The offset $\tilde{y}_0 = f_\mathrm{d}(x_0, y_0)_y$ is chosen to be the original y-coordinate of the midpoint (x_0, y_0) of the undistorted image. We calculate $f_\mathrm{d}(x, y)_y$ for all pixels as a preprocessing step and then interpolate. This is computationally less expensive than using the distortion function each time. Also, it facilitates the incorporation of new distortion models, as we later need the derivatives of the function.

The first component of the total energy is the summation over all photometric residuals,

$$E_{\text{ph}} = \sum_{i \in \mathcal{F}} \sum_{\mathbf{p} \in \mathcal{P}_i} \sum_{j \in \text{obs}(\mathbf{p})} E_{\mathbf{p}j}, \tag{10}$$

where $\mathcal{F}$ is the set of frames, $\mathcal{P}_i$ the set of points in frame i and $\text{obs}(\mathbf{p})$ the set of frames in which $\mathbf{p}$ is visible.

Optimizing E_{ph} alone, however, is not reliable. It has been shown that rolling shutter images are prone to ambiguities [4] and we also found out that softly constraining the velocities leads to a more stable system. Thus, we add an additional energy term E_{vel} to the total energy,

$$E = E_{\text{ph}} + \lambda E_{\text{vel}}. \tag{11}$$

The term

$$E_{\text{vel}} = \sum_{i \in \mathcal{F}} \|\mathbf{v}_i - \mathbf{v}_{i,\text{prior}}\|^2 \tag{12}$$

is a prior on the velocities, with

$$\mathbf{v}_{i,\text{prior}} = \log(\mathbf{T}_i^{-1}\mathbf{T}_{i-1})^{\vee} \frac{\Delta t_{\text{r}}}{t_i - t_{i-1}}, \tag{13}$$

where $\log(\cdot)^{\vee}$ is the composition of the matrix logarithm and the inverse hat transform which extracts twist coordinates from Lie algebra elements, so that $\mathbf{v}_{i,\text{prior}} \in \mathbb{R}^6$. Here, we need actual times: $t_i - t_{i-1}$ is the time difference between the capture of the ith and the $(i-1)$th keyframe and Δt_{r} is the time difference between two consecutive pixel rows due to the rolling shutter. The prior intuitively favors that the velocity between the latest existing keyframe and the new keyframe is similar to the velocity while taking the new keyframe. As initially many keyframes are taken, such a smoothness assumption is reasonable. The resulting constraints are visualized in Fig. 2, where a factor graph of the different energy terms is shown. After marginalizing a keyframe's variables, the prior still acts through the marginalization term.

3.2 Optimization

We minimize the cost in Eq. (11) using Gauss-Newton optimization. The linearized system is

$$\mathbf{H}\boldsymbol{\delta} = \mathbf{b}, \tag{14}$$

with

$$\mathbf{H} = \mathbf{J}^T\mathbf{W}\mathbf{J}, \tag{15}$$

$$\mathbf{b} = -\mathbf{J}^T\mathbf{W}\mathbf{r}. \tag{16}$$

The matrix $\mathbf{J}$ is the Jacobian of the residual vector $\mathbf{r}$ for the variables to optimize. The diagonal weight matrix $\mathbf{W}$ contains the weights of the residuals. The Hessian $\mathbf{H}$ has a large diagonal block of correlations between the depth variables, which makes efficient inversion using the Schur complement possible. Compared to [6], which has 8 variables per frame (6 for the camera pose plus 2 for the affine brightness transfer function), we now additionally have 6 velocity components, which gives 14 variables per frame. In addition, there are 4 internal camera parameters $\mathbf{c}$ shared among all keyframes. Each point adds one inverse depth variable.

One single row in the Jacobian, belonging to one single pixel $\mathbf{p}_k$ in the neighborhood of $\mathbf{p}$, is given by

$$\mathbf{J}_k = \frac{\partial r_k(\boldsymbol{\delta} \boxplus \boldsymbol{\zeta})}{\partial \boldsymbol{\delta}}. \tag{17}$$

The state vector $\boldsymbol{\zeta}$ contains all variables in the system, i.e. keyframe poses, velocities, affine brightness parameters, inverse depths and intrinsic camera parameters. The symbol $\boxplus$ denotes standard addition for all variables except for poses where it means $\boldsymbol{\delta}_\mathrm{p} \boxplus \mathbf{T} = \exp(\hat{\boldsymbol{\delta}}_\mathrm{p})\mathbf{T}$, with $\boldsymbol{\delta}_\mathrm{p} \in \mathbb{R}^6$ and $\mathbf{T} \in \mathrm{SE}(3)$.

The Jacobian can be decomposed as

$$\mathbf{J}_k = \left[\mathbf{J}_I \mathbf{J}_\mathrm{geo}, \mathbf{J}_\mathrm{photo}\right]. \tag{18}$$

The image gradient

$$\mathbf{J}_I = \frac{\partial I_j}{\partial \mathbf{p}'_k} \tag{19}$$

as well as the photometric Jacobian

$$\mathbf{J}_\mathrm{photo} = \frac{\partial r_k(\boldsymbol{\delta} \boxplus \boldsymbol{\zeta})}{\partial \boldsymbol{\delta}_\mathrm{photo}} \tag{20}$$

are evaluated at pixel $\mathbf{p}'_k$, where $\boldsymbol{\delta}_\mathrm{photo}$ corresponds to the photometric variables a_i, b_i, a_j, b_j. The geometric Jacobian $\mathbf{J}_\mathrm{geo}$ contains derivatives of the pixel location (not the intensity, as it is multiplied with $\mathbf{J}_I$) with respect to the geometric variables $\mathbf{T}_i, \mathbf{T}_j, \mathbf{v}_i, \mathbf{v}_j, d, \mathbf{c}$. It is approximated as the derivative of the central pixel $\mathbf{p}'$ for all pixels $\mathbf{p}'_k$ in the neighborhood. For $\mathbf{J}_\mathrm{geo}$, we also have to take into account that the observation time t^* depends on the geometric variables. Thus,

$$\mathbf{J}_\mathrm{geo} = \frac{\partial \mathbf{p}'}{\partial \delta_\mathrm{geo}} + \frac{\partial \mathbf{p}'}{\partial t^*} \frac{\mathrm{d}t^*}{\mathrm{d}\boldsymbol{\delta}_\mathrm{geo}}. \tag{21}$$

The derivative of a function $y(x)$ that is defined as the root of a function $R(x, y)$ is given as

$$\frac{\mathrm{d}y}{\mathrm{d}x} = -\frac{\partial R/\partial x}{\partial R/\partial y}. \tag{22}$$

As t^* is defined by Eq. (8), we can use this rule to calculate $\frac{\mathrm{d}t^*}{\mathrm{d}\delta_{\text{geo}}}$. In our case,

$$R(\boldsymbol{\zeta}, t^*) = t^* - t(\mathbf{p}'(\boldsymbol{\zeta}, t^*)) \tag{23}$$

$$= t^* - (f_{\mathrm{d}}(\mathbf{p}'(\boldsymbol{\zeta}, t^*))_y - \tilde{y}_0), \tag{24}$$

so that

$$\frac{\mathrm{d}t^*}{\mathrm{d}\boldsymbol{\delta}_{\text{geo}}} = \frac{\frac{\partial f_{\mathrm{d},y}}{\partial \mathbf{p}'} \frac{\partial \mathbf{p}'}{\partial \boldsymbol{\delta}_{\text{geo}}}}{1 - \frac{\partial f_{\mathrm{d},y}}{\partial \mathbf{p}'} \frac{\partial \mathbf{p}'}{\partial t^*}}. \tag{25}$$

The Jacobians $\mathbf{J}_{\text{geo}}$ and $\mathbf{J}_{\text{photo}}$ are approximated using first-estimates Jacobians [10]. This means that the evaluation point of these Jacobians does not change once a variable is part of the marginalization term, while the image gradient $\mathbf{J}_I$ and the residual r_k are always evaluated at the current state. The authors of [6] argue that $\mathbf{J}_{\text{geo}}$ and $\mathbf{J}_{\text{photo}}$ are smooth so that we can afford evaluating them at a slightly different location for the benefit of keeping a consistent system in the presence of non-linear null-spaces such as absolute pose and scale. As the translational component of the velocity is also affected by scale ambiguity, we decide to include velocities in the first-estimate Jacobian approximation.

When variables are marginalized, we follow the procedure of [6]: We start from a quadratic approximation of the energy that contains residuals which depend on variables to be marginalized. Variables are marginalized using the Schur complement, which results in an energy that only depends on variables which are still active in the optimization window. This energy acts like a prior and can be added to the energy of active residuals. We also include our velocity priors in the marginalization term if they depend on a variable that is marginalized, so that velocities of active keyframes are still constrained by marginalized keyframes which are temporally and spatially close. We refer the reader to [6] for further details on the marginalization process.

4 Experimental Evaluation on Real and Synthetic Data

4.1 Datasets

Along with the rolling shutter RGB-D SLAM method in [11], **synthetic sequences** were published. They are re-renderings of the ICL-NUIM dataset [8], containing 4 different trajectories in a living room, named *kt1*, *kt2*, *kt3*, and *kt4*. As the data is photometrically perfect, we do not estimate affine brightness parameters on these sequences.

We also show results for the sequence *freiburg1_desk*, an **office sequence** from the TUM RGB-D benchmark [22]. It has already been used by [12], but a quantitative comparison is not possible, as they only show a trajectory plot. The row time difference Δt_{r} is not available. We were successful with our first guess of $\Delta t_{\mathrm{r}} = 0.06\,\mathrm{ms}$, a value that leaves only a small time gap between the last row and the first row of the next image.

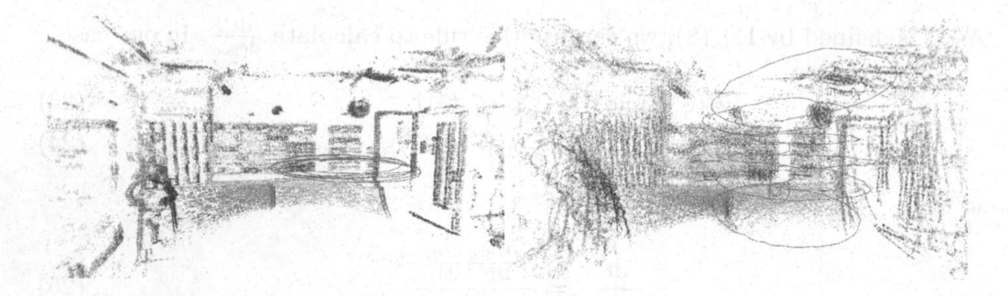

Fig. 3. Qualitative result of DSORS (left) versus DSO (right) on the sequence *alt-circle-1*. Even after many circles, the sparse 3D reconstruction of DSORS shows little drift, whereas DSO shows the same edges at clearly distinct locations.

Fig. 4. Our faster sequences show significant distortion and blur due to motion (from *alt-circle-2*).

Due to the lack of rolling shutter datasets for monocular visual odometry, we recorded six **own sequences** with ground truth. Sequences were captured at 1280×1024 resolution with a handheld uEye UI-3241LE-M-GL camera by IDS and a Lensagon BM4018S118 lens by Lensation. The camera was operated at 20 HZ and provides an approximate value of $\Delta t_\mathrm{r} = 0.033\,\mathrm{ms}$. Ground truth was recorded with a Flex 13 motion capture system by OptiTrack. It uses IR-reflective markers and 16 cameras distributed around the room. The ground truth poses are hand-eye and time shift calibrated, meaning that they provide poses of the camera frame to an external world system and timestamps of the ground truth poses are given in the same time system as timestamps for the camera frames. We fixed the exposure, which means our algorithm uses a prior that prefers small affine brightness parameters. We also use lens vignetting correction on our own sequences. The sequences can be divided into three categories:

- **infinity:** The camera motion repeatedly draws an infinity symbol in front of a wall.
- **circle:** The camera moves on a circle that lies in the horizontal plane while the camera is pointing outwards.
- **alt-circle:** Same as *circle*, but with alternating directions.

Each of the categories has been captured twice (e.g. *infinity-1* and *infinity-2*), with the second one always being faster than the first one, but none of them is really slow in order to have sufficient rolling shutter effect.

Our camera includes two identical cameras in a stereo setup. For comparison with methods processing global shutter images, we simultaneously recorded sequences using the second camera set to global shutter mode.

Our dataset contains significant blur and rolling-shutter distortion due to fast motion as can be seen in Fig. 4. Due to flickering of the illumination in our recording room, the rolling-shutter images contain alternating stripes of brighter and darker illumination which are also visible in Fig. 4. While this is not consistent with the illumination model in DSO and DSORS, none of the two has an obvious advantage. Note that the global shutter images do not exhibit this effect.

4.2 Evaluation Method

For each sequence, we compare the performance of DSORS versus DSO. DSO originally allows a maximum of 6 iterations for each Gauss-Newton optimization. We found slight improvements for our method if we increase them to 10. To make the comparison fair, we also allow a maximum of 10 iterations for DSO, though still both methods can break early when convergence is reached. The number of active points is set to 2000, and there are maximally 6 old plus one new keyframe in the optimization window, which are the standard settings for DSO. Compared to DSO, we only introduced one model parameter, the weight of the velocity prior λ. The same value is used for all sequences.

We use the *absolute trajectory error* (ATE) to evaluate our results quantitatively. Given ground truth keyframe positions $\hat{\mathbf{p}}_i \in \mathbb{R}^3$ and corresponding tracking results $\mathbf{p}_i \in \mathbb{R}^3$, it is defined as

$$e_{\text{ate}} = \min_{\mathbf{T} \in \text{Sim}(3)} \sqrt{\frac{1}{n} \sum_{i=1}^{n} \|\mathbf{T}(\mathbf{p}_i) - \hat{\mathbf{p}}_i\|^2}. \tag{26}$$

It is necessary to align with a 7D similarity transform[1] $\mathbf{T} \in \text{Sim}(3)$, since scale is not observable for monocular methods. We run the methods 20 times on each sequence. To randomize the results, different random number seeds are used for the point selection. We show two types of visualization for the quantitative results: the color plots show e_{ate} for each run and for each sequence individually. The cumulative error histograms contain all sequences of each dataset. Here, the function value at position e gives the number of sequences with $e_{\text{ate}} \leq e$.

4.3 Results

On the **synthetic sequences**, DSORS clearly outperforms DSO, as can be seen in Fig. 5. Not only is the overall performance in the cumulative error histogram visibly more accurate, but also on each sequence as can be seen in the color plot. Only on the sequence *kt0* it is not entirely stable, but here DSO also has outliers. The RGB-D method in [11] reports ATEs of (0.0186, 0.0054, 0.0079, 0.0210) (after SE(3) alignment) for the four trajectories, while our median ATEs over 20 runs are (0.0037, 0.0197, 0.0045, 0.0062) (after Sim(3) alignment).

For the **office sequence**, the difference between DSORS and DSO in the cumulative error histogram in Fig. 6 is even more obvious. The performance of DSORS is much more stable and accurate. On the right side of the figure, typical

[1] In Eq. (26) $\mathbf{T}$ is used as an operator on 3D points $\mathbf{T} : \mathbb{R}^3 \to \mathbb{R}^3, \mathbf{p} \mapsto \mathbf{T}(\mathbf{p})$.

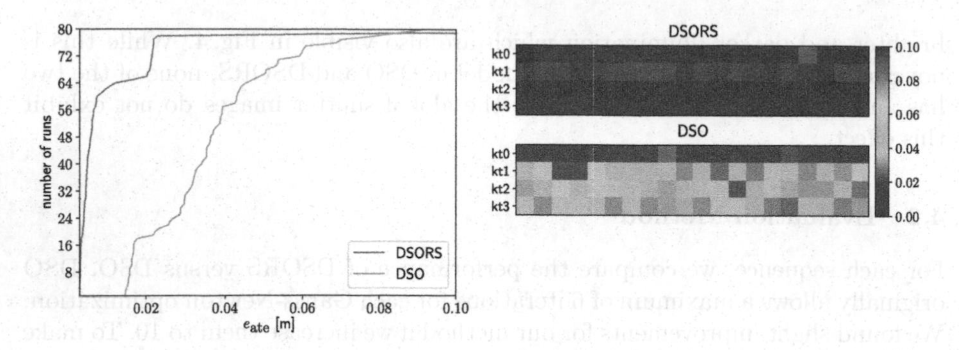

Fig. 5. On the left, the cumulative error histogram for 20 runs on each synthetic sequence clearly shows that DSORS produces more accurate results than DSO. The plot on the left indicates the error for each individual run and shows that DSORS is also superior on each sequence.

tracked trajectories are plotted with ground truth after Sim(3) alignment. The red lines between corresponding points make visible how large the error is for DSO, compared to much smaller errors for DSORS.

The results on our **own sequences** also demonstrate that DSORS is superior to DSO when dealing with rolling shutter data. Qualitatively, this is clearly visible in Figs. 1 and 3. The sparse 3D reconstructions look much cleaner for DSORS, while DSO produces inconsistent edges when revisiting a section of the room. Even more striking is the large systematic drift of the camera trajectories.

In Fig. 7, the quantitative difference also becomes apparent. DSORS outperforms DSO both in terms of accuracy and stability. Only the sequence *infinity-2*

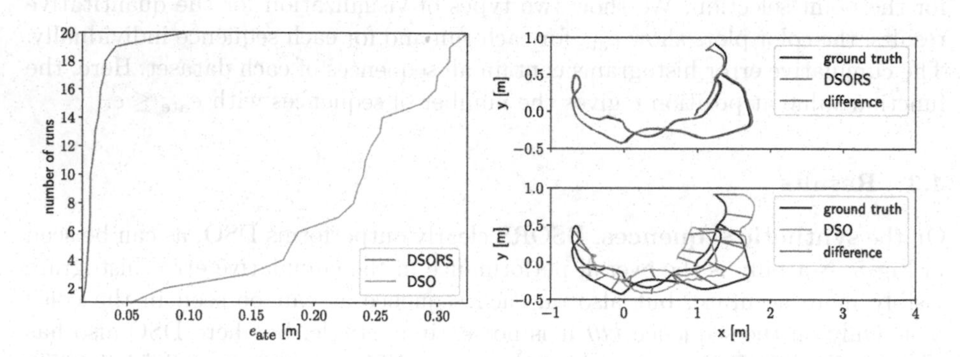

Fig. 6. On the left, the cumulative error histogram over 20 iterations on the *freiburg1_desk* sequence from the TUM-RGBD benchmark shows that DSORS can repeatably track the sequence accurately while DSO has large drift. On the right, the top down view shows the ground truth and estimated trajectories after Sim(3) alignment. For each method we select the iteration with median e_{ate} (DSORS: 0.022 m, DSO: 0.241 m). The red lines indicate corresponding points for every 10th keyframe. (Color figure online)

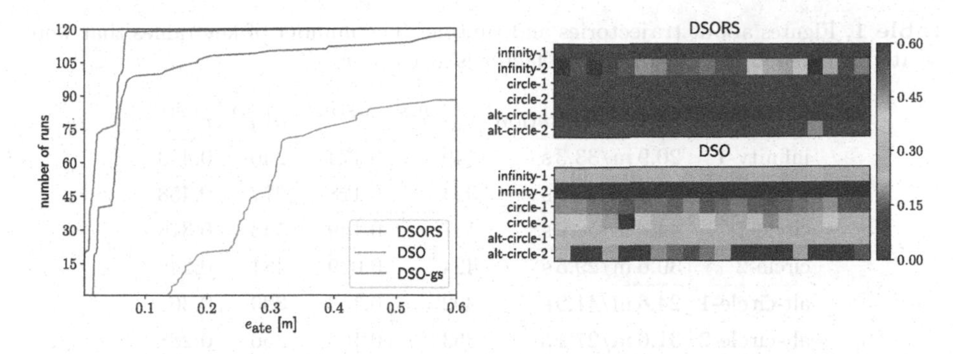

Fig. 7. Cumulative error histogram and color plot for the absolute trajectory error e_{ate} on our new sequences. In the cumulative histogram, the green line also gives a comparison to DSO running on global shutter data, which has been captured in parallel with a stereo setup. For trajectory plots as in Fig. 6, see supplementary material.

remains a challenge, but DSORS in approximately half of the cases produces reasonable results, whereas DSO always fails in our runs.

We also show results of DSO operating on global shutter data. The sequences are very comparable to the rolling shutter sequences, as they use the same hardware, and cameras are triggered at the same time in a stereo setup. Running DSO on global shutter images is still better than running DSORS on rolling shutter images. The difference in stability visible in the cumulative histogram mainly comes from the challenging sequence *infinity-2*. On the remaining sequences, the advantage of using global shutter images is not as dominant.

4.4 Runtime

The computationally most expensive part of our method is the creation of a new keyframe, i.e. calculating derivatives, accumulating the Hessian and solving the linear system. Our derivatives are more involved compared to DSO, and the number of variables is larger. As keyframes are not selected with equal time spacing, but based on motion, it is not possible to specify how many frames per second we can process in general. With a fast moving camera, more new keyframes are required per time, which affects the runtime. In Table 1, some figures about the trajectories and the performance of DSORS and DSO run on an Intel Core i5-2500 CPU are given. The realtime factor r is calculated as the real duration of the sequence divided by the processing time of the algorithm. By comparing each slower sequence (*...-1*) to its faster variant (*...-2*), one can confirm that the realtime factor depends on the speed of the camera motion. Only r^{DSO} for the sequence *infinity-2* is an exception, but this sequence is very unstable for DSO, thus many outlier points are dropped during the optimization, which speeds up the execution. Also, the number of keyframes is rather related to the total length of the trajectory than to the duration.

The results also prove that DSORS is slower than DSO, by a factor roughly around 2.5 (except for *infinity-2*). It might seem surprising that not even DSO

Table 1. Figures about trajectories and runtime. The number of keyframes that were created is denoted n_{KF}, the realtime factor is given by r.

Sequence	Length/Duration	$n_{\mathrm{KF}}^{\mathrm{DSORS}}$	r^{DSORS}	$n_{\mathrm{KF}}^{\mathrm{DSO}}$	r^{DSO}
infinity-1	20.9 m/33.3 s	249	0.174	240	0.433
infinity-2	36.3 m/29.9 s	324	0.128	277	0.458
circle-1	44.8 m/58.9 s	547	0.149	543	0.378
circle-2	30.6 m/29.5 s	424	0.099	431	0.248
alt-circle-1	24.6 m/41.9 s	392	0.153	399	0.362
alt-circle-2	31.6 m/27.1 s	353	0.109	356	0.288

is real-time here, but this is due to the fact that all results were created in a linearized mode, where the coarse tracking waits for the keyframe creation to finish. Given that DSO is generally a real-time capable method, further optimization of our method or using a faster processor might produce real-time results in the future. In fact, by reducing the number of active points to 800 and enforcing real-time execution (with the coarse tracking continuing while a new keyframe is created), it was possible to obtain results for the slower sequences that were close to our non-real-time results, but not yet for the faster sequences.

5 Conclusions

In this paper, we have integrated a rolling shutter model into direct sparse visual odometry. By extending keyframe poses with a velocity estimate and imposing a constant-velocity prior in the optimization, we obtain a near real-time but accurate direct visual odometry method.

Our experiments on sequences from rolling shutter cameras have demonstrated that the model is well-suited and can drastically improve accuracy and stability over methods that neglect rolling shutter. Our method makes accurate direct visual odometry available to rolling shutter cameras which are often present in consumer grade devices such as smartphones or tablets and in the automotive domain.

For direct rolling shutter approaches, real-time capability is a challenge. With our formulation, we are already much closer to real-time processing than the alternative approach in [12]. In future work, we will investigate further speedups of our implementation. The integration with inertial sensing could further increase the accuracy and stability of the visual odometry.

Acknowledgment. This work was partially supported through the grant "For3D" by the Bavarian Research Foundation and through the grant CR 250/9-2 "Mapping on Demand" by the German Research Foundation.

References

1. Ait-Aider, O., Berry, F.: Structure and kinematics triangulation with a rolling shutter stereo rig. In: IEEE International Conference on Computer Vision, pp. 1835–1840 (2009)
2. Ait-Aider, O., Andreff, N., Lavest, J.M., Martinet, P.: Simultaneous object pose and velocity computation using a single view from a rolling shutter camera. In: Leonardis, A., Bischof, H., Pinz, A. (eds.) ECCV 2006. LNCS, vol. 3952, pp. 56–68. Springer, Heidelberg (2006). https://doi.org/10.1007/11744047_5
3. Albl, C., Kukelova, Z., Pajdla, T.: R6P - rolling shutter absolute pose problem. In: IEEE Conference on Computer Vision and Pattern Recognition, pp. 2292–2300 (2015)
4. Albl, C., Sugimoto, A., Pajdla, T.: Degeneracies in rolling shutter SfM. In: Leibe, B., Matas, J., Sebe, N., Welling, M. (eds.) ECCV 2016. LNCS, vol. 9909, pp. 36–51. Springer, Cham (2016). https://doi.org/10.1007/978-3-319-46454-1_3
5. Dai, Y., Li, H., Kneip, L.: Rolling shutter camera relative pose: generalized epipolar geometry. In: IEEE Conference on Computer Vision and Pattern Recognition, pp. 4132–4140 (2016)
6. Engel, J., Koltun, V., Cremers, D.: Direct sparse odometry. IEEE Trans. Pattern Anal. Mach. Intell. **40**(3), 611–625 (2018)
7. Engel, J., Schöps, T., Cremers, D.: LSD-SLAM: large-scale direct monocular SLAM. In: Fleet, D., Pajdla, T., Schiele, B., Tuytelaars, T. (eds.) ECCV 2014. LNCS, vol. 8690, pp. 834–849. Springer, Cham (2014). https://doi.org/10.1007/978-3-319-10605-2_54
8. Handa, A., Whelan, T., McDonald, J., Davison, A.J.: A benchmark for RGB-D visual odometry, 3D reconstruction and SLAM. In: IEEE International Conference on Robotics and Automation, pp. 1524–1531 (2014)
9. Hedborg, J., Forssén, P.E., Felsberg, M., Ringaby, E.: Rolling shutter bundle adjustment. In: IEEE Conference on Computer Vision and Pattern Recognition, pp. 1434–1441 (2012)
10. Huang, G.P., Mourikis, A.I., Roumeliotis, S.I.: A first-estimates Jacobian EKF for improving SLAM consistency. In: Khatib, O., Kumar, V., Pappas, G.J., et al. (eds.) Experimental Robotics. Springer, Heidelberg (2009). https://doi.org/10.1007/978-3-642-00196-3_43
11. Kerl, C., Stückler, J., Cremers, D.: Dense continuous-time tracking and mapping with rolling shutter RGB-D cameras. In: IEEE International Conference on Computer Vision, pp. 2264–2272 (2015)
12. Kim, J.H., Cadena, C., Reid, I.: Direct semi-dense SLAM for rolling shutter cameras. In: IEEE International Conference on Robotics and Automation, pp. 1308–1315 (2016)
13. Li, M., Kim, B.H., Mourikis, A.I.: Real-time motion tracking on a cellphone using inertial sensing and a rolling-shutter camera. In: IEEE International Conference on Robotics and Automation, pp. 4712–4719 (2013)
14. Lovegrove, S., Patron-Perez, A., Sibley, G.: Spline fusion: a continuous-time representation for visual-inertial fusion with application to rolling shutter cameras. In: Burghardt, T., Damen, D., Mayol-Cuevas, W., Mirmehdi, M. (eds.) Proceedings of the British Machine Vision Conference. pp. 93.1–93.12. BMVA Press (2013)
15. Magerand, L., Bartoli, A.: A generic rolling shutter camera model and its application to dynamic pose estimation. In: International Symposium on 3D Data Processing, Visualization and Transmission (2010)

16. Magerand, L., Bartoli, A., Ait-Aider, O., Pizarro, D.: Global optimization of object pose and motion from a single rolling shutter image with automatic 2D-3D matching. In: Fitzgibbon, A., Lazebnik, S., Perona, P., Sato, Y., Schmid, C. (eds.) ECCV 2012. LNCS, vol. 7572, pp. 456–469. Springer, Heidelberg (2012). https://doi.org/10.1007/978-3-642-33718-5_33
17. Meingast, M., Geyer, C., Sastry, S.: Geometric models of rolling-shutter cameras. arXiv preprint arXiv:cs/0503076 (2005)
18. Mur-Artal, R., Tardós, J.D.: ORB-SLAM2: an open-source SLAM system for monocular, stereo, and RGB-D cameras. IEEE Trans. Robot. **33**(5), 1255–1262 (2017)
19. Nister, D., Naroditsky, O., Bergen, J.: Visual odometry. In: IEEE Conference on Computer Vision and Pattern Recognition, vol. 1, pp. I652–I659 (2004)
20. Saurer, O., Köser, K., Bouguet, J.Y., Pollefeys, M.: Rolling shutter stereo. In: IEEE International Conference on Computer Vision, pp. 465–472 (2013)
21. Saurer, O., Pollefeys, M., Lee, G.H.: Sparse to dense 3D reconstruction from rolling shutter images. In: IEEE Conference on Computer Vision and Pattern Recognition, pp. 3337–3345 (2016)
22. Sturm, J., Engelhard, N., Endres, F., Burgard, W., Cremers, D.: A benchmark for the evaluation of RGB-D SLAM systems. In: IEEE/RSJ International Conference on Intelligent Robots and Systems, pp. 573–580 (2012)

A Style-Aware Content Loss for Real-Time HD Style Transfer

Artsiom Sanakoyeu(✉), Dmytro Kotovenko, Sabine Lang, and Björn Ommer

Heidelberg Collaboratory for Image Processing, IWR, Heidelberg University, Heidelberg, Germany

{artsiom.sanakoyeu,dmytro.kotovenko, sabine.lang,bjorn.ommer}@iwr.uni-heidelberg.de

Abstract. Recently, style transfer has received a lot of attention. While much of this research has aimed at speeding up processing, the approaches are still lacking from a principled, art historical standpoint: a style is more than just a single image or an artist, but previous work is limited to only a single instance of a style or shows no benefit from more images. Moreover, previous work has relied on a direct comparison of art in the domain of RGB images or on CNNs pre-trained on ImageNet, which requires millions of labeled object bounding boxes and can introduce an extra bias, since it has been assembled without artistic consideration. To circumvent these issues, we propose a style-aware content loss, which is trained jointly with a deep encoder-decoder network for real-time, high-resolution stylization of images and videos. We propose a quantitative measure for evaluating the quality of a stylized image and also have art historians rank patches from our approach against those from previous work. These and our qualitative results ranging from small image patches to megapixel stylistic images and videos show that our approach better captures the subtle nature in which a style affects content.

Keywords: Style transfer · Generative network · Deep learning

1 Introduction

A picture may be worth a thousand words, but at least it contains a lot of very diverse information. This not only comprises *what* is portrayed, e.g., composition of a scene and individual objects, but also *how* it is depicted, referring to the artistic style of a painting or filters applied to a photo. Especially when considering artistic images, it becomes evident that not only content but also style is

A. Sanakoyeu and D. Kotovenko—Contributed equally to this work.

Electronic supplementary material The online version of this chapter (https://doi.org/10.1007/978-3-030-01237-3_43) contains supplementary material, which is available to authorized users.

V. Ferrari et al. (Eds.): ECCV 2018, LNCS 11212, pp. 715–731, 2018.
https://doi.org/10.1007/978-3-030-01237-3_43

a crucial part of the message an image communicates (just imagine van Gogh's Starry Night in the style of Pop Art). Here, we follow the common wording of our community and refer to 'content' as a synonym for 'subject matter' or 'sujet', preferably used in art history. A vision system then faces the challenge to decompose and separately represent the content and style of an image to enable a direct analysis based on each individually. The ultimate test for this ability is style transfer [12] – exchanging the style of an image while retaining its content (Fig. 1).

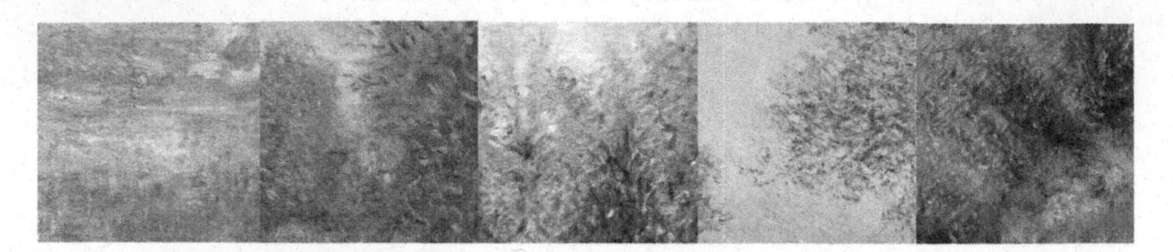

Fig. 1. Evaluating the fine details preserved by our approach. Can you guess which of the cut-outs are from Monet's artworks and which are generated? Solution is on p. xx.

In contrast to the seminal work of Gatys et al. [12], who have relied on powerful but slow iterative optimization, there has recently been a focus on feed-forward generator networks [6,20,22,27,40,41,44]. The crucial representation in all these approaches has been based on a VGG16 or VGG19 network [39], pre-trained on ImageNet [34]. However, a recent trend in deep learning has been to avoid supervised pre-training on a million images with tediously labeled object bounding boxes [43]. In the setting of style transfer this has the particular benefit of avoiding from the outset any bias introduced by ImageNet, which has been assembled without artistic consideration. Rather than utilizing a separate pre-trained VGG network to measure and optimize the quality of the stylistic output [6,12,22,27,40,41,44], we employ an encoder-decoder architecture with adversarial discriminator, Fig. 3, to stylize the input content image and also use the encoder to measure the reconstruction loss. In essence the stylized output image is again run through the encoder and compared with the encoded input content image. Thus, we learn a style-specific content loss from scratch, which adapts to the specific way in which a particular style retains content and is more adaptive than a comparison in the domain of RGB images [48].

Most importantly, however, previous work has only been based on a *single* style image. This stands in stark contrast to art history which understands "style as an expression of a collective spirit" resulting in a "distinctive manner which permits the grouping of works into related categories" [9]. As a result, art history developed a scheme, which allows to identify groups of artworks based on shared qualities. Artistic style consists of a diverse range of elements, such as form, color, brushstroke, or use of light. Therefore, it is insufficient to only use a single artwork, because it might not represent the full scope of an artistic style. Today, freely available art datasets such as Wikiart [23] easily contain more than 100K

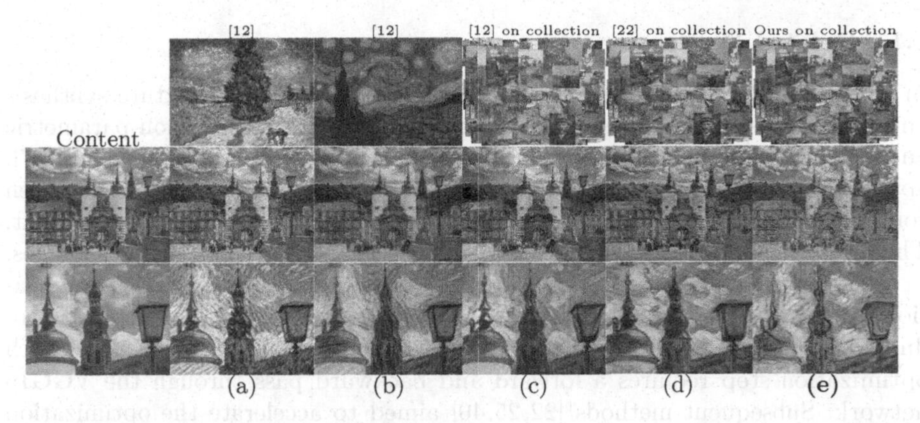

Fig. 2. Style transfer using different approaches on 1 and a collection of reference style images. (a) [12] using van Gogh's "Road with Cypress and Star" as reference style image; (b) [12] using van Gogh's "Starry night"; (c) [12] using the average Gram matrix computed across the collection of Vincent van Gogh's artworks; (d) [22] trained on the collection of van Gogh's artworks alternating target style images every SGD mini-batch; (e) our approach trained on the same collection of van Gogh's artworks. Stylizations *(a)* and *(b)* depend significantly on the particular style image, but using a collection of the style images *(c)*, *(d)* does not produce visually plausible results, due to oversmoothing over the numerous Gram matrices. In contrast, our approach *(e)* has learned how van Gogh is altering particular content in a specific manner (edges around objects also stylized, cf. bell tower)

images, thus providing numerous examples for various styles. Previous work [6,12,22,27,40,41,44] has represented style based on the Gram matrix, which captures highly image-specific style statistics, cf. Fig. 2. To combine several style images in [6,12,22,27,40,41,44] one needs to aggregate their Gram matrices. We have evaluated several aggregation strategies and averaging worked the best, Fig. 2(c). But, obviously, neither art history, nor statistics suggests aggregating Gram matrices. Additionally, we investigated alternating the target style images in every mini-batch while training [22], Fig. 2(d). However, all these methods cannot make proper use of several style images, because combining the Gram matrices of several images forfeits the details of style, cf. the analysis in Fig. 2. In contrast, our proposed approach allows to combine an arbitrary number of instances of a style during training.

We conduct extensive evaluations of the proposed style transfer approach; we quantitatively and qualitatively compare it against numerous baselines. Being able to generate high quality artistic works in high-resolution, our approach produces visually more detailed stylizations than the current state of the art style transfer approaches and yet shows real-time inference speed. The results are quantitatively validated by experts from art history and by adopting in this paper a *deception rate* metric based on a deep neural network for artist classification.

1.1 Related Work

In recent years, a lot of research efforts have been devoted to texture synthesis and style transfer problems. Earlier methods [17] are usually non-parametric and are build upon low-level image features. Inspired by Image Analogies [17], approaches [10,28,37,38] are based on finding dense correspondence between content and style image and often require image pairs to depict similar content. Therefore, these methods do not scale to the setting of arbitrary content images.

In contrast, Gatys et al. [11,12] proposed a more flexible iterative optimization approach based on a pre-trained VGG19 network [39]. This method produces high quality results and works on arbitrary inputs, but is costly, since each optimization step requires a forward and backward pass through the VGG19 network. Subsequent methods [22,25,40] aimed to accelerate the optimization procedure [12] by approximating it with feed-forward convolutional neural networks. This way, only one forward pass through the network is required to generate a stylized image. Beyond that, a number of methods have been proposed to address different aspects of style transfer, including quality [4,13,21,44,46], diversity [26,41], photorealism [30], combining several styles in a single model [3,6,42] and generalizing to previously unseen styles [14,20,27,36]. However, all these methods rely on the fixed style representation which is captured by the features of a VGG [39] network pre-trained on ImageNet. Therefore they require a supervised pre-training on millions of labeled object bounding boxes and have a bias introduced by ImageNet, because it has been assembled without artistic consideration. Moreover, the image quality achieved by the costly optimization in [12] still remains an upper bound for the performance of recent methods. Other works like [1,5,8,32,45] learn how to discriminate different techniques, styles and contents in the latent space. Zhu et al. [48] learn a bidirectional mapping between a domain of content images and paintings using generative adversarial networks. Employing cycle consistency loss, they directly measure the distance between a backprojection of the stylized output and the content image in the RGB pixel space. Measuring distances in the RGB image domain is not just generally prone to be coarse, but, especially for abstract styles, a pixel-wise comparison of backwards mapped stylized images is not suited. Then, either content is preserved and the stylized image is not sufficiently abstract,

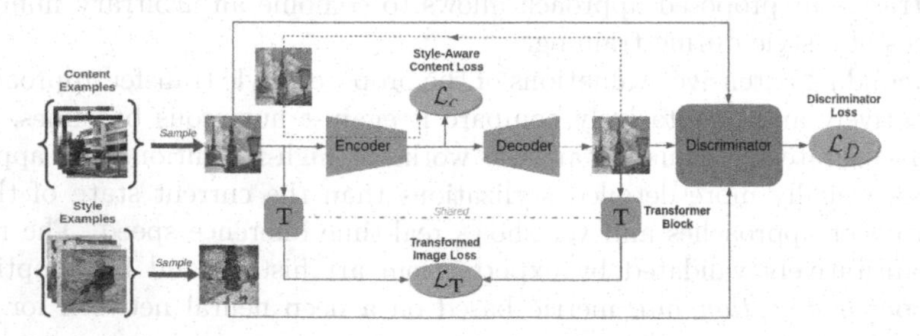

Fig. 3. Encoder-decoder network for style transfer based on style-aware content loss.

e.g., not altering object boundaries, or the stylized image has a suitable degree of abstractness and so a pixel-based comparison with the content image must fail. Moreover, the more abstract the style is, the more potential backprojections into the content domain exist, because this mapping is underdetermined (think of the many possible content images for a single cubistic painting). In contrast, we spare the ill-posed backward mapping of styles and compare stylized and content images in the latent space which is trained jointly with the style transfer network. Since both content and stylized images are run through our encoder, the latent space is trained to only pay attention to the commonalities, i.e., the content present in both. Another consequence of the cycle consistency loss is that it requires content and style images used for training to represent similar scenes [48], and thus training data preparation for [48] involves tedious manual filtering of samples, while our approach can be trained on arbitrary unpaired content and style images.

2 Approach

To enable a fast style transfer that instantly transfers a content image or even frames of a video according to a particular style, we need a feed-forward architecture [22] rather than the slow optimization-based approach of [12]. To this end, we adopt an encoder-decoder architecture that utilizes an encoder network E to map an input content image x onto a latent representation $z = E(x)$. A generative decoder G then plays the role of a painter and generates the stylized output image $y = G(z)$ from the sketchy content representation z. Stylization then only requires a single forward pass, thus working in real-time.

2.1 Training with a Style-Aware Content Loss

Previous approaches have been limited in that training worked only with a single style image [6,12,20,22,27,40,44] or that style images used for training had to be similar in content to the content images [48]. In contrast, given a single style image y_0 we include a set Y of related style images $y_j \in Y$, which are automatically selected (see Sect. 2.2) from a large art dataset (Wikiart). We do *not* require the y_j to depict similar content as the set X of arbitrary content images $x_i \in X$, which we simply take from Places365 [47]. Compared to [48], we thus can utilize standard datasets for content and style and need no tedious manual selection of the x_i and y_j as described in Sects. 5.1 and 7.1 of [48].

To train E and G we employ a standard adversarial discriminator D [15] to distinguish the stylized output $G(E(x_i))$ from real examples $y_j \in Y$,

$$\mathcal{L}_D(E,G,D) = \mathop{\mathbb{E}}_{y \sim p_Y(y)} [\log D(y)] + \mathop{\mathbb{E}}_{x \sim p_X(x)} [\log (1 - D(G(E(x))))] \quad (1)$$

However, the crucial challenge is to decide which details to retain from the content image, something which is not captured by Eq. 1. Contrary to previous work, we want to directly enforce E to strip the latent space of all image details

Fig. 4. 1st row - results of style transfer for different styles. 2nd row - sketchy content visualization reconstructed from the latent space $E(x)$ using method of [31]. (a) The encoder for Pollock does not preserve much content due to the abstract style; (b) only rough structure of the content is preserved (coarse patches) because of the distinct style of El Greco; (c) latent space highlights surfaces of the same color and that fine object details are ignored, since Gauguin was less interested in details, often painted plain surfaces and used vivid colors; (d) encodes the thick, wide brushstrokes Cézanne used, but preserves a larger palette of colors. (Color figure online)

that the target style disregards. Therefore, the details that need to be retained or ignored in z depend on the style. For instance, Cubism would disregard texture, whereas Pointillism would retain low-frequency textures. Therefore, a pre-trained network or fixed similarity measure [12] for measuring the similarity in content between x_i and y_i is violating the art historical premise that the manner, in which content is preserved, depends on the style. Similar issues arise when measuring the distance after projecting the stylized image $G(E(x_i))$ back into the domain X of original images with a second pair of encoder and decoder $G_2(E_2(G(E(x_i))))$. The resulting loss proposed in [48],

$$\mathcal{L}_{cycleGAN} = \mathop{\mathbb{E}}_{x \sim p_X(x)} \left[\|x - G_2(E_2(G(E(x))))\|_1 \right], \quad (2)$$

fails where styles become abstract, since the backward projection of abstract art to the original image is highly underdetermined.

Therefore, we propose a style-aware content loss that is being optimized, while the network learns to stylize images. Since encoder training is coupled with training of the decoder, which produces artistic images of the specific style, the latent vector z produced for the input image x can be viewed as its style-dependent sketchy content representation. This latent space representation is changing during training and hence *adapts* to the style. Thus, when measuring the similarity in content between input image x_i and the stylized image $y_i = G(E(x_i))$ in the latent space, we focus only on those details which are relevant for the style. Let the latent space have d dimensions, then we define a style-aware content loss as normalized squared Euclidean distance between $E(x_i)$ and $E(y_i)$:

$$\mathcal{L}_c(E, G) = \mathop{\mathbb{E}}_{x \sim p_X(x)} \left[\frac{1}{d} \|E(x) - E(G(E(x)))\|_2^2 \right] \quad (3)$$

To show the additional intuition behind the style-aware content loss we used the method [31] to reconstruct the content image from latent representations trained on different styles and illustrated it in Fig. 4. It can be seen that latent space encodes a sketchy, style-specific visual content, which is implicitly used by the loss function. For example, Pollock is famous for his abstract paintings, so reconstruction (a) shows that the latent space ignores most of the object structure; Gauguin was less interested in details, painted a lot of plain surfaces and used vivid colors which is reflected in the reconstruction (c), where latent space highlights surfaces of the same color and fine object details are ignored.

Since we train our model for altering the artistic style without supervision and from scratch, we now introduce extra signal to initialize training and boost the learning of the primary latent space. The simplest thing to do is to use an autoencoder loss which computes the difference between x_i and y_i in the RGB space. However, this loss would impose a high penalty for any changes in image structure between input x_i and output y_i, because it relies only on low-level pixel information. But we aim to learn image stylization and want the encoder to discard certain details in the content depending on style. Hence the autoencoder loss will contradict with the purpose of the style-aware loss, where the style determines which details to retain and which to disregard. Therefore, we propose to measure the difference after applying a weak image transformation on x_i and y_i, which is learned while learning E and G. We inject in our model a transformer block **T** which is essentially a one-layer fully convolutional neural network taking an image as input and producing a transformed image of the same size. We apply T to images x_i and $y_i = G(E(x_i))$ before measuring the difference. We refer to this as *transformed image loss* and define it as

$$\mathcal{L}_{\mathbf{T}}(E,G) = \mathop{\mathbb{E}}_{x \sim p_X(x)} \left[\frac{1}{CHW} ||\mathbf{T}(x) - \mathbf{T}(G(E(x))||_2^2 \right], \quad (4)$$

where $C \times H \times W$ is the size of image x and for training T is initialized with uniform weights.

Figure 3 illustrates the full pipeline of our approach. To summarize, the full objective of our model is:

$$\mathcal{L}(E,G,D) = \mathcal{L}_c(E,G) + \mathcal{L}_t(E,G) + \lambda \mathcal{L}_D(E,G,D), \quad (5)$$

where λ controls the relative importance of adversarial loss. We solve the following optimization problem:

$$E, G = \arg \min_{E,G} \max_{D} \mathcal{L}(E,G,D). \quad (6)$$

2.2 Style Image Grouping

In this section we explain an automatic approach for gathering a set of related style images. Given a single style image y_0 we strive to find a set Y of related style images $y_j \in Y$. Contrary to [48] we avoid tedious manual selection of style images and follow a fully automatic approach. To this end, we train a VGG16 [39] network C from scratch on the Wikiart [23] dataset to predict an artist given the artwork. The network is trained on the 624 largest (by number of works) artists from the Wikiart dataset. Note that our ultimate goal is stylization and numerous artists can share the same style, e.g., Impressionism, as well as a single artist can exhibit different styles, such as the different stylistic periods of Picasso. However, we do *not* use any *style* labels. Artist classification in this case is the surrogate task for learning meaningful features in the artworks' domain, which allows to retrieve similar artworks to image y_0.

Let $\phi(y)$ be the activations of the fc6 layer of the VGG16 network C for input image y. To get a set of related style images to y_0 from the Wikiart dataset $\mathcal{Y}$ we retrieve all nearest neighbors of y_0 based on the cosine distance δ of the activations $\phi(\cdot)$, i.e.

$$Y = \{y \mid y \in \mathcal{Y}, \delta(\phi(y), \phi(y_0)) < t\}, \tag{7}$$

where $\delta(a, b) = 1 + \frac{\phi(a)\phi(b)}{||a||_2||b||_2}$ and t is the 10% quantile of all pairwise distances in the dataset $\mathcal{Y}$.

3 Experiments

To compare our style transfer approach with the state-of-the-art, we first perform extensive qualitative analysis, then we provide quantitative results based on the *deception score* and evaluations of experts from art history. Afterwards in Sect. 3.3 we ablate single components of our model and show their importance.

Implementation Details: The basis for our style transfer model is an encoder-decoder architecture, cf. [22]. The encoder network contains 5 `conv` layers: 1×`conv-stride-1` and 4×`conv-stride-2`. The decoder network has 9 residual blocks [16], 4 upsampling blocks and 1×`conv-stride-1`. For upsampling blocks we used a sequence of nearest-neighbor upscaling and `conv-stride-1` instead of fractionally strided convolutions [29], which tend to produce heavier artifacts [33]. Discriminator is a fully convolutional network with 7×`conv-stride-2` layers. For a detailed network architecture description we refer to the supplementary material. We set $\lambda = 0.001$ in Eq. 5. During the training process we sample 768×768 content image patches from the training set of Places365 [47] and 768×768 style image patches from the Wikiart [23] dataset. We train for 300000 iterations with batch size 1, learning rate 0.0002 and Adam [24] optimizer. The learning rate is reduced by a factor of 10 after 200000 iterations.

Baselines: Since we aim to generate high-resolution stylizations, for comparison we run style transfer on our method and all baselines for input images of size 768×768, unless otherwise specified. We did not exceed this resolution when comparing, because some other methods were reaching the GPU memory limit. We optimize Gatys et al. [12] for 500 iterations using L-BFGS. For Johnson et al. [22] we used the implementation of [7] and trained a separate network for every reference style image on the same content images from Places365 [47] as our method. For Huang et al. [20], Chen et al. [4] and Li et al. [27] implementations and pre-trained models provided by the authors were used. Zhu et al. [48] was trained on exactly the same content and style images as our approach using the source code provided by the authors. Methods [4,12,20,22,27] utilized only one example per style, as they cannot benefit from more (cf. the analysis in Fig. 2).

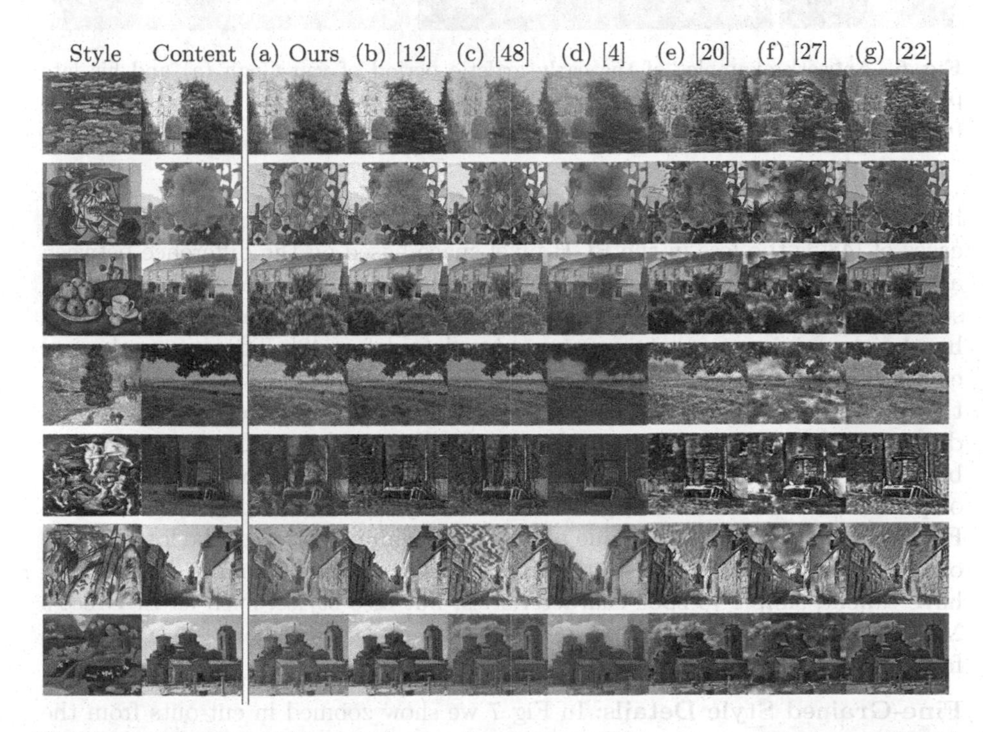

Fig. 5. Results from different style transfer methods. We compare methods on different styles and content images.

3.1 Qualitative Results

Full Image Stylization: In Fig. 5 we demonstrate the effectiveness of our approach for stylizing different contents with various styles. Chen et al. [4] work on the overlapping patches extracted from the content image, swapping the features of the original patch with the features of the most similar patch in the style image, and then averages the features in the overlapping regions, thus producing an over-smoothed image without fine details (Fig. 5(d)). [20] produces a lot of repetitive artifacts, especially visible on flat surfaces, cf. Fig. 5(e, rows 1, 4–6). Method [27] fails to understand the content of the image and applies different colors in the wrong locations (Fig. 5(f)). Methods [22,48] often fail to alter content image and their effect may be characterized as shifting the color

Fig. 6. Artwork examples of the early artistic period of van Gogh (a) and his late period (c). Style transfer of the content image (1st column) onto the early period is presented in (b) and the late period in (d).

histogram, e.g., Fig. 5(g, rows 3, 7; c, rows 1, 3–4). One reason for such failure cases of [48] is the loss in the RGB pixel space based on the difference between a backward mapping of the stylized output and the content image. Another reason for this is that we utilized the standard Places365 [47] dataset and did not hand-pick training content images, as is advised for [48]. Thus, artworks and content images used for training differed significantly in their content, which is the ultimate test for a stylization that truly alters the input and goes beyond a direct mapping between regions of content and style images. The optimization-based method [12] often works better than other baselines, but produces a lot of prominent artifacts, leading to details of stylizations looking unnatural, cf. Fig. 5(b, rows 4, 5, 6). This is due to an explicit minimization of the loss directly on the pixel level. In contrast to this, our model can not only handle styles, which have salient, simple to spot characteristics, but also styles, such as El Greco's Mannerism, with less graspable stylistic characteristics, where other methods fail (Fig. 5, b–g, 5th row).

Fine-Grained Style Details: In Fig. 7 we show zoomed in cut-outs from the stylized images. Interestingly, the stylizations of methods [4,12,19,20,27] do not change much across styles (compare Fig. 7(d, f–i, rows 1–3)). Zhu et al. [48] produce more diverse images for different styles, but obviously cannot alter the edges of the content (blades of grass are *clearly visible* on all the cutouts in Fig. 7(e)). Figure 7(c) shows the stylized cutouts of our approach, which exhibit significant changes from one style to another. Another interesting example is the style of Pollock, Fig. 7 (row 8), where the style-aware loss allows our model to properly alter content to the point of discarding it – as would be expected from a Pollock action painting. Our approach is able to generate high-resolution stylizations with a lot of style specific details and retains those content details which are necessary for the style.

Style Transfer for Different Periods of van Gogh: We now investigate our ability to properly model fine differences in style *despite* using a group of style images. Therefore, we take two reference images Fig. 6(a) and (c) from van Gogh's early and late period, respectively, and acquire related style images for both from Wikiart. It can be clearly seen that the stylizations produced for

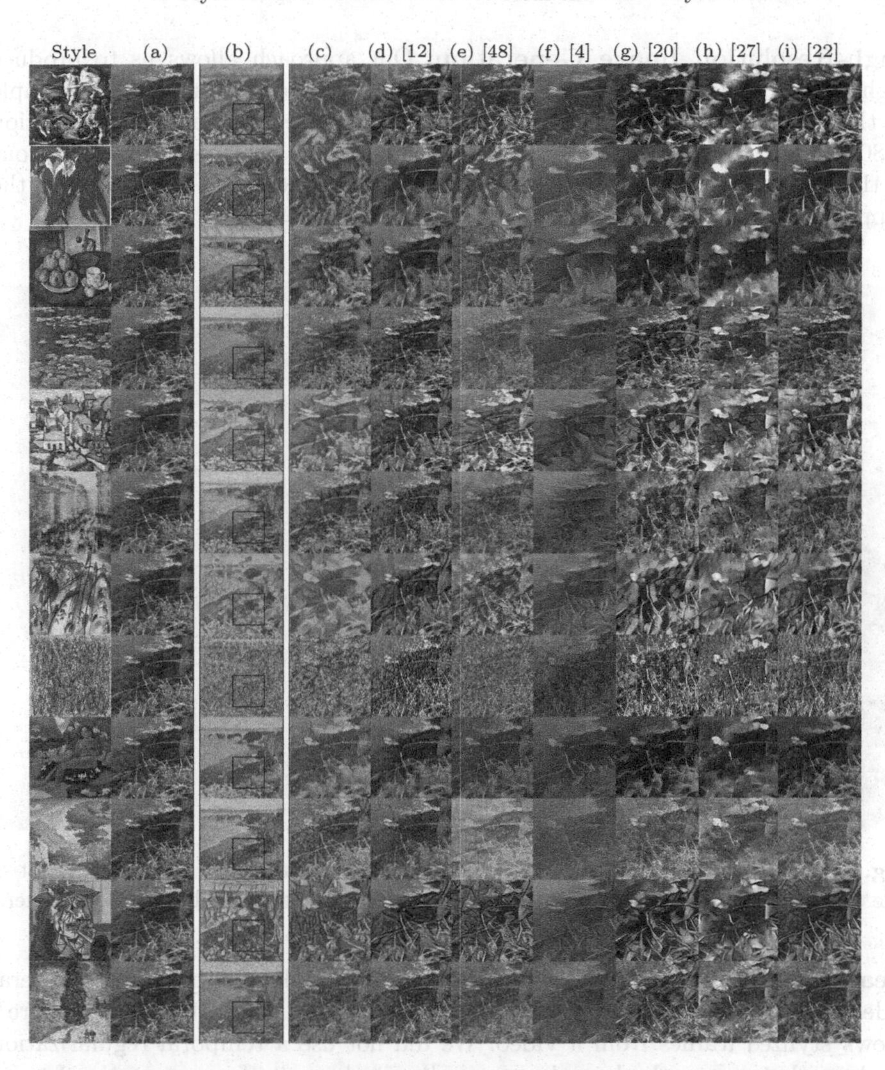

Fig. 7. Details from stylized images produced for different styles for a fixed content image (a). (b) is our entire stylized image, (c) the zoomed in cut-out and (d)–(i) the same region for competitors. Note the variation across different styles along the *column* for our method compared to other approaches. This highlights the ability to adapt content (not just colors or textures) where demanded by a style. Fine grained artistic details with sharp boundaries are produced, while altering the original content edges.

either period Fig. 6(b, d) are fairly different and indeed depict the content in correspondence with the style of early (b) and late (d) periods of van Gogh. This highlights that collections of style images are properly used and do not lead to an averaging effect.

High-Resolution Image Generation: Our approach allows us to produce high quality stylized images in high-resolution. Figure 8 illustrates an example of the generated piece of art in the style of Berthe Morisot with resolution 1280 × 1280. The result exhibits a lot of fine details such as color transitions of the oil paint and brushstrokes of different sizes. More HD images are in the supplementary.

Fig. 8. High-resolution image (1280 × 1280 pix) generated by our approach. A lot of fine details and brushstrokes are visible. A style example is in the bottom left corner.

Real-Time HD Video Stylization: We also apply our method to several videos. Our approach can stylize HD videos (1280 × 720) at 9 FPS. Figure 9 shows stylized frames from a video. We did not use a temporal regularization to show that our method produces equally good results for consecutive frames with varying appearance w/o extra constraints. Stylized videos are in the supplementary.

3.2 Quantitative Evaluation

Style Transfer Deception Rate: While several metrics [2,18,35] have been proposed to evaluate the quality of image generation, until now no evaluation metric has been proposed for an automatic evaluation of style transfer results. To measure the quality of the stylized images, we introduce the *style transfer deception rate.* We use a VGG16 network trained from scratch to classify 624 artists on Wikiart. Style transfer deception rate is calculated as the fraction of generated images which were classified by the network as the artworks of an artist for which the stylization was produced. For fair comparison with other approaches,

Fig. 9. Results of our approach applied to the HD video of Eadweard Muybridge "The horse in motion" (1878). Every frame was *independently* processed (no smoothing or post-processing) by our model in the style of Picasso. Video resolution 1920 × 1280 pix, here the original aspect ratio was changed to save space.

which used only one style image y_0 (hence only one artist), we restricted Y to only contain samples coming from the same artist as the query example y_0. We selected 18 different artists (i.e. styles). For every method we generated 5400 stylizations (18 styles, 300 per style). In Table 1 we report mean deception rate for 18 styles. Our method achieves 0.393 significantly outperforming the baselines. For comparison, mean accuracy of the network on hold-out real images of aforementioned 18 artists from Wikiart is 0.616.

Human Art History Experts Perceptual Studies: Three experts (with a PhD in art history with focus on modern and pre-modern paintings) have compared results of our method against recent work. Each expert was shown 1000 groups of images. Each group consists of stylizations which were generated by different methods based on the same content and style images. Experts were asked to choose one image which best and most realistically reflects the current style. The score is computed as the fraction of times a specific method was chosen as the best in the group. We calculate a mean expert score for each method using 18 different styles and report them in Table 1. Here, we see that the experts selected our method in around 50% of the cases.

Speed and Memory: Table 2 shows the time and memory required for stylization of a single image of size 768 × 768 px for different methods. One can see that our approach and that of [22,48] have comparable speed and only very modest demands on GPU memory, compared to modern graphics cards.

3.3 Ablation Studies

Effect of Different Losses: We study the effect of different components of our model in Fig. 10. Removing the style-aware content loss significantly degrades the results, (c). We observe that without the style-aware loss training becomes instable and often stalls. If we remove the transformed image loss, which we introduced for a proper initialization of our model that is trained from scratch, we notice mode collapse after 5000 iterations. Training directly with pixel-wise L2 distance causes a lot of artifacts (grey blobs and flaky structure), (d). Training only with a discriminator neither exhibits the variability in the painting nor in the content, (e). Therefore we conclude that both the style-aware content loss and the transformed image loss are critical for our approach.

Table 1. Mean deception rate and mean expert score for different methods. The higher the better.

Method	Deception rate	Expert score
Content images	0.002	–
AdaIn [20]	0.074	0.060
PatchBased [4]	0.040	0.132
Johnson et al. [22]	0.051	0.048
WCT [27]	0.035	0.044
CycleGan [48]	0.139	0.044
Gatys et al. [12]	0.147	0.178
Ours	**0.393**	**0.495**

Table 2. Average inference time and GPU memory consumption, measured on a Titan X Pascal, for different methods with batch size 1 and input image of 768 × 768 pix.

Method	Time	GPU memory
Gatys et al. [12]	200 s	3887 MiB
CycleGan [48]	0.07 s	1391 MiB
AdaIn [20]	0.16 s	8872 MiB
PatchBased [4]	8.70 s	4159 MiB
WCT [27]	5.22 s	10720 MiB
Johnson et al. [22]	**0.06 s**	**671 MiB**
Ours	0.07 s	1043 MiB

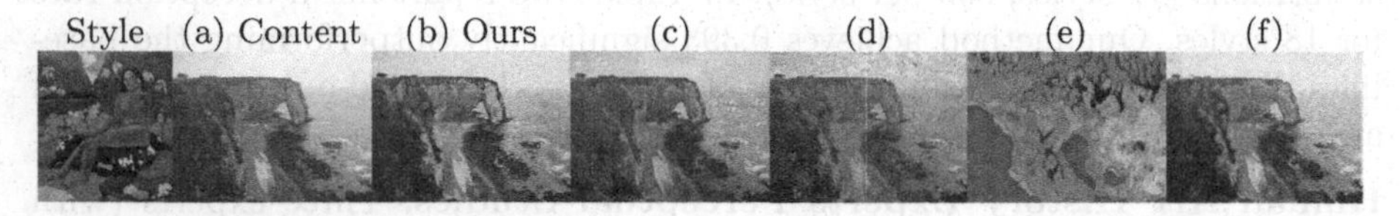

Fig. 10. Different variations of our method for Gauguin stylization. See Sect. 3.3 for details. (a) Content image; (b) full model ($\mathcal{L}_c$, $\mathcal{L}_{rgb}$ and $\mathcal{L}_D$); (c) $\mathcal{L}_{rgb}$ and $\mathcal{L}_D$; (d) without transformer block; (e) only $\mathcal{L}_D$; (f) trained with all of Gauguin's artworks as style images. Please zoom in to compare.

Single vs Collection of Style Images: Here, we investigate the importance of the style image grouping. First, we trained a model with only one style image of Gauguin, which led to mode collapse. Second, we trained with all of Gauguin's artworks as style images (without utilizing style grouping procedure). It produced unsatisfactory results, cf. Fig. 10(f), because style images comprised several distinct styles. Therefore we conclude that to learn a good style transfer model it is important to group style images according to their stylistic similarity.

Encoder Ablation: To investigate the effect of our encoder E, we substitute it with VGG16 [39] encoder (up to `conv5_3`) pre-trained on ImageNet. The VGG encoder retains features that separate object classes (since it was trained discriminatively), as opposed to our encoder which is trained to retain style-specific

Fig. 11. Encoder ablation studies: (a) stylization using our model; (b) stylization using pre-trained VGG16 encoder instead of E.

content details. Hence, our encoder is not biased towards class-discriminative features, but is style specific and trained from scratch. Figure 11(a, b) show that our approach produces better results than with pre-trained VGG16 encoder.

4 Conclusion

This paper has addressed major conceptual issues in state-of-the-art approaches for style transfer. We overcome the limitation of only a single style image or the need for style and content training images to show similar content. Moreover, we exceed a mere pixel-wise comparison of stylistic images or models that are pre-trained on millions of ImageNet bounding boxes. The proposed style-aware content loss enables a real-time, high-resolution encoder-decoder based stylization of images and videos and significantly improves stylization by capturing how style affects content.

Solution to Fig. 1*: patches* 3 *and* 5 *were generated by our approach, others by artists.*

Acknowledgement. This work has been supported in part by a DFG grant, the Heidelberg Academy of Science, and an Nvidia hardware donation.

References

1. Bautista, M.A., Sanakoyeu, A., Tikhoncheva, E., Ommer, B.: CliqueCNN: deep unsupervised exemplar learning. In: Advances in Neural Information Processing Systems, pp. 3846–3854 (2016)
2. Che, T., Li, Y., Jacob, A.P., Bengio, Y., Li, W.: Mode regularized generative adversarial networks. arXiv preprint arXiv:1612.02136 (2016)
3. Chen, D., Yuan, L., Liao, J., Yu, N., Hua, G.: Stylebank: an explicit representation for neural image style transfer. In: Proceedings of CVPR (2017)
4. Chen, T.Q., Schmidt, M.: Fast patch-based style transfer of arbitrary style. arXiv preprint arXiv:1612.04337 (2016)
5. Collomosse, J., Bui, T., Wilber, M.J., Fang, C., Jin, H.: Sketching with style: visual search with sketches and aesthetic context. In: The IEEE International Conference on Computer Vision (ICCV), October 2017
6. Dumoulin, V., Shlens, J., Kudlur, M.: A learned representation for artistic style. In: Proceedings of ICLR (2017)
7. Engstrom, L.: Fast style transfer (2016). https://github.com/lengstrom/fast-style-transfer/. Commit 55809f4e
8. Esser, P., Sutter, E., Ommer, B.: A variational U-Net for conditional appearance and shape generation. In: The IEEE Conference on Computer Vision and Pattern Recognition (CVPR), July 2018
9. Fernie, E.: Art History and Its Methods: A Critical Anthology, p. 361. Phaidon, London (1995)
10. Frigo, O., Sabater, N., Delon, J., Hellier, P.: Split and match: example-based adaptive patch sampling for unsupervised style transfer. In: Proceedings of the IEEE Conference on Computer Vision and Pattern Recognition, pp. 553–561 (2016)

11. Gatys, L.A., Ecker, A.S., Bethge, M.: Texture synthesis and the controlled generation of natural stimuli using convolutional neural networks. arXiv preprint arXiv:1505.07376 12 (2015)
12. Gatys, L.A., Ecker, A.S., Bethge, M.: Image style transfer using convolutional neural networks. In: IEEE Conference on Computer Vision and Pattern Recognition (CVPR), pp. 2414–2423. IEEE (2016)
13. Gatys, L.A., Ecker, A.S., Bethge, M., Hertzmann, A., Shechtman, E.: Controlling perceptual factors in neural style transfer. In: IEEE Conference on Computer Vision and Pattern Recognition (CVPR) (2017)
14. Ghiasi, G., Lee, H., Kudlur, M., Dumoulin, V., Shlens, J.: Exploring the structure of a real-time, arbitrary neural artistic stylization network. arXiv preprint arXiv:1705.06830 (2017)
15. Goodfellow, I., et al.: Generative adversarial nets. In: Advances in Neural Information Processing Systems, pp. 2672–2680 (2014)
16. He, K., Zhang, X., Ren, S., Sun, J.: Deep residual learning for image recognition. In: Proceedings of the IEEE Conference on Computer Vision and Pattern Recognition, pp. 770–778 (2016)
17. Hertzmann, A., Jacobs, C.E., Oliver, N., Curless, B., Salesin, D.H.: Image analogies. In: Proceedings of the 28th Annual Conference on Computer Graphics and Interactive Techniques, pp. 327–340. ACM (2001)
18. Heusel, M., Ramsauer, H., Unterthiner, T., Nessler, B., Hochreiter, S.: Gans trained by a two time-scale update rule converge to a local nash equilibrium. In: Advances in Neural Information Processing Systems, pp. 6629–6640 (2017)
19. Hinton, G.E., Salakhutdinov, R.R.: Reducing the dimensionality of data with neural networks. Science **313**(5786), 504–507 (2006). https://doi.org/10.1126/science.1127647
20. Huang, X., Belongie, S.: Arbitrary style transfer in real-time with adaptive instance normalization. In: ICCV (2017)
21. Jing, Y., Liu, Y., Yang, Y., Feng, Z., Yu, Y., Song, M.: Stroke controllable fast style transfer with adaptive receptive fields. arXiv preprint arXiv:1802.07101 (2018)
22. Johnson, J., Alahi, A., Fei-Fei, L.: Perceptual losses for real-time style transfer and super-resolution. In: Leibe, B., Matas, J., Sebe, N., Welling, M. (eds.) ECCV 2016. LNCS, vol. 9906, pp. 694–711. Springer, Cham (2016). https://doi.org/10.1007/978-3-319-46475-6_43
23. Karayev, S., et al.: Recognizing image style. arXiv preprint arXiv:1311.3715 (2013)
24. Kingma, D.P., Ba, J.: Adam: a method for stochastic optimization. arXiv preprint arXiv:1412.6980 (2014)
25. Li, C., Wand, M.: Precomputed real-time texture synthesis with markovian generative adversarial networks. In: Leibe, B., Matas, J., Sebe, N., Welling, M. (eds.) ECCV 2016. LNCS, vol. 9907, pp. 702–716. Springer, Cham (2016). https://doi.org/10.1007/978-3-319-46487-9_43
26. Li, Y., Fang, C., Yang, J., Wang, Z., Lu, X., Yang, M.H.: Diversified texture synthesis with feed-forward networks. In: IEEE Conference on Computer Vision and Pattern Recognition (2017)
27. Li, Y., Fang, C., Yang, J., Wang, Z., Lu, X., Yang, M.H.: Universal style transfer via feature transforms. In: Advances in Neural Information Processing Systems, pp. 385–395 (2017)
28. Liao, J., Yao, Y., Yuan, L., Hua, G., Kang, S.B.: Visual attribute transfer through deep image analogy. arXiv preprint arXiv:1705.01088 (2017)

29. Long, J., Shelhamer, E., Darrell, T.: Fully convolutional networks for semantic segmentation. In: Proceedings of the IEEE Conference on Computer Vision and Pattern Recognition, pp. 3431–3440 (2015)
30. Luan, F., Paris, S., Shechtman, E., Bala, K.: Deep photo style transfer. In: IEEE Conference on Computer Vision and Pattern Recognition (CVPR) (2017)
31. Mahendran, A., Vedaldi, A.: Understanding deep image representations by inverting them. In: Proceedings of the IEEE Conference on Computer Vision and Pattern Recognition (CVPR) (2015)
32. Mao, H., Cheung, M., She, J.: DeepArt: learning joint representations of visual arts. In: Proceedings of the 2017 ACM on Multimedia Conference, pp. 1183–1191. ACM (2017)
33. Odena, A., Dumoulin, V., Olah, C.: Deconvolution and checkerboard artifacts. Distill (2016). https://doi.org/10.23915/distill.00003
34. Russakovsky, O.: ImageNet large scale visual recognition challenge. Int. J. Comput. Vis. (IJCV) **115**(3), 211–252 (2015). https://doi.org/10.1007/s11263-015-0816-y
35. Salimans, T., Goodfellow, I., Zaremba, W., Cheung, V., Radford, A., Chen, X.: Improved techniques for training GANs. In: Advances in Neural Information Processing Systems, pp. 2234–2242 (2016)
36. Shen, F., Yan, S., Zeng, G.: Meta networks for neural style transfer. arXiv preprint arXiv:1709.04111 (2017)
37. Shih, Y., Paris, S., Barnes, C., Freeman, W.T., Durand, F.: Style transfer for headshot portraits. ACM Trans. Graph. (TOG) **33**(4), 148 (2014)
38. Shih, Y., Paris, S., Durand, F., Freeman, W.T.: Data-driven hallucination of different times of day from a single outdoor photo. ACM Trans. Graph. (TOG) **32**(6), 200 (2013)
39. Simonyan, K., Zisserman, A.: Very deep convolutional networks for large-scale image recognition. arXiv preprint arXiv:1409.1556 (2014)
40. Ulyanov, D., Lebedev, V., Vedaldi, A., Lempitsky, V.S.: Texture networks: feed-forward synthesis of textures and stylized images. In: ICML, pp. 1349–1357 (2016)
41. Ulyanov, D., Vedaldi, A., Lempitsky, V.: Improved texture networks: maximizing quality and diversity in feed-forward stylization and texture synthesis. In: Proceedings of CVPR (2017)
42. Wang, H., Liang, X., Zhang, H., Yeung, D.Y., Xing, E.P.: ZM-Net: real-time zero-shot image manipulation network. arXiv preprint arXiv:1703.07255 (2017)
43. Wang, X., Gupta, A.: Unsupervised learning of visual representations using videos. arXiv preprint arXiv:1505.00687 (2015)
44. Wang, X., Oxholm, G., Zhang, D., Wang, Y.F.: Multimodal transfer: a hierarchical deep convolutional neural network for fast artistic style transfer. In: The IEEE Conference on Computer Vision and Pattern Recognition (CVPR), July 2017
45. Wilber, M.J., Fang, C., Jin, H., Hertzmann, A., Collomosse, J., Belongie, S.: BAM! The behance artistic media dataset for recognition beyond photography. In: The IEEE International Conference on Computer Vision (ICCV), October 2017
46. Wilmot, P., Risser, E., Barnes, C.: Stable and controllable neural texture synthesis and style transfer using histogram losses. arXiv preprint arXiv:1701.08893 (2017)
47. Zhou, B., Lapedriza, A., Xiao, J., Torralba, A., Oliva, A.: Learning deep features for scene recognition using places database. In: Advances in Neural Information Processing Systems, pp. 487–495 (2014)
48. Zhu, J.Y., Park, T., Isola, P., Efros, A.A.: Unpaired image-to-image translation using cycle-consistent adversarial networks. In: IEEE International Conference on Computer Vision (2017)

Scale-Awareness of Light Field Camera Based Visual Odometry

Niclas Zeller[1,2,3(✉)], Franz Quint[2], and Uwe Stilla[1]

[1] Technische Universität München, Munich, Germany
{niclas.zeller,stilla}@tum.de
[2] Karlsruhe University of Applied Sciences, Karlsruhe, Germany
franz.quint@hs-karlsruhe.de
[3] Visteon, Karlsruhe, Germany

Abstract. We propose a novel direct visual odometry algorithm for micro-lens-array-based light field cameras. The algorithm calculates a detailed, semi-dense 3D point cloud of its environment. This is achieved by establishing probabilistic depth hypotheses based on stereo observations between the micro images of different recordings. Tracking is performed in a coarse-to-fine process, working directly on the recorded raw images. The tracking accounts for changing lighting conditions and utilizes a linear motion model to be more robust. A novel scale optimization framework is proposed. It estimates the scene scale, on the basis of keyframes, and optimizes the scale of the entire trajectory by filtering over multiple estimates. The method is tested based on a versatile dataset consisting of challenging indoor and outdoor sequences and is compared to state-of-the-art monocular and stereo approaches. The algorithm shows the ability to recover the absolute scale of the scene and significantly outperforms state-of-the-art monocular algorithms with respect to scale drifts.

Keywords: Light field · Plenoptic camera · SLAM · Visual odometry

1 Introduction

Over the last years, significant improvements in monocular visual odometry (VO) as well as simultaneous localization and mapping (SLAM) were achieved. Traditionally, the task of tracking a single camera was solved by indirect approaches [1]. These approaches extract a set of geometric interest points from the recorded images and estimate the underlying model parameters (3D point coordinates and camera orientation) based on these points. Recently, it was shown that so-called direct approaches, which work directly on pixel intensities, significantly outperform indirect methods [2]. These newest monocular VO and SLAM approaches succeed in versatile and challenging environments. However, a significant drawback remains for all monocular algorithms, by nature. This is that a pure monocular VO system will never be able to recover the scale of the scene.

V. Ferrari et al. (Eds.): ECCV 2018, LNCS 11212, pp. 732–747, 2018.
https://doi.org/10.1007/978-3-030-01237-3_44

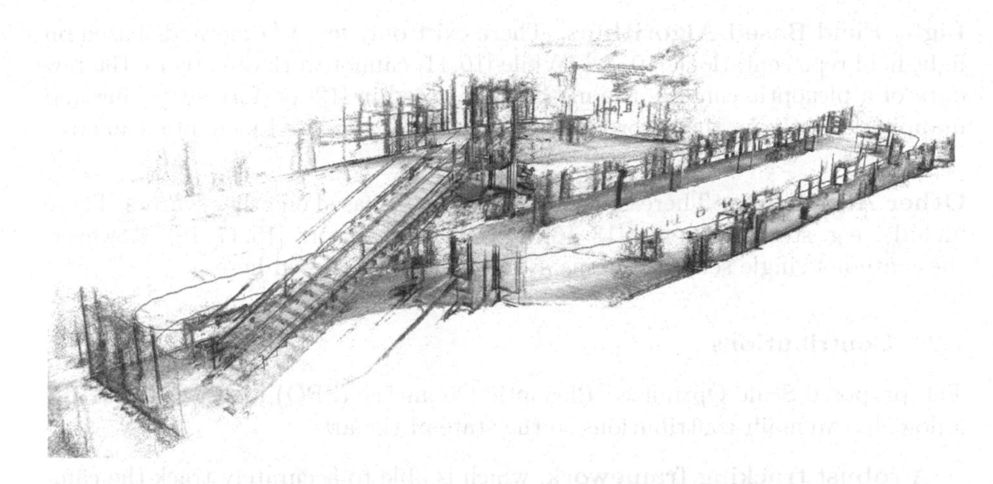

Fig. 1. Example of a point cloud calculated by the proposed Scale-Optimized Plenoptic Odometry (SPO) algorithm. Estimated camera trajectory is shown in green. (Color figure online)

In contrast, a light field camera (or plenoptic camera) is a single-sensor camera which is able to obtain depth from a single image and therefore, can also recover the scale of the scene – at least in theory. Although, the camera still has a size similar to that of a monocular camera.

In this paper, we present Scale-Optimized Plenoptic Odometry (SPO), a completely direct VO algorithm. The algorithm works directly on the raw images recorded by a focused plenoptic camera. It reliably tracks the camera motion and establishes a probabilistic semi-dense 3D point cloud of the environment. At the same time it obtains the absolute scale of the camera trajectory and thus, the scale of the 3D world. Figure 1 shows, by way of example, a 3D map calculated by the algorithm.

1.1 Related Work

Monocular Algorithms. During the last years several indirect (feature-based) and direct VO and SLAM algorithms were published. Indirect approaches split the overall task into two sequential steps. Geometric features are extracted from the images and afterwards the camera position and scene structure are estimated solely based on these features [1,3,4].

Direct approaches estimate the camera position and scene structure directly based on pixel intensities [2,5–8]. This way, all image information can be used for the estimation, instead of only those regions which conform to a certain feature descriptor. In [9] a direct tracking front-end in combination with a feature-based optimization back-end is proposed.

Light Field Based Algorithms. There exist only few VO methods based on light field representations [10–12]. While [10,11] cannot work directly on the raw data of a plenoptic camera, the method presented in [12] performs tracking and mapping directly on the recorded micro images of a focused plenoptic camera.

Other Algorithms. There exist various methods based on other sensors. These include, e.g. stereo cameras [13–16] and RGB-D sensors [15,17–19]. However, these are not single sensor systems as the method proposed here.

1.2 Contributions

The proposed Scale-Optimized Plenoptic Odometry (SPO) algorithm adds the following two main contributions to the state of the art:

- A **robust tracking framework**, which is able to accurately track the camera in versatile and challenging environments. Tracking is performed in a coarse-to-fine approach, directly on the recorded micro images. Robustness is achieved by compensating changes in the lighting conditions and performing a weighted Gauss-Newton optimization which is constrained by a linear motion prediction.
- A **scale optimization framework**, which continuously estimates the absolute scale of the scene based on keyframes. It is filtered over multiple estimates to obtain a globally optimized scale. The framework allows to recover the absolute scale and simultaneously scale drifts along the trajectory are significantly reduced.

Furthermore, we evaluated SPO based on a versatile and challenging dataset [20] and compare it to state-of-the-art monocular and stereo VO algorithms.

2 The Focused Plenoptic Camera

In contrast to a monocular camera, a focused plenoptic camera does not only capture a 2D image, but the entire light field of the scene as a 4D function. This is achieved by simply placing a micro lens array (MLA) in front of the image sensor, as it is visualized in Fig. 2(a). The MLA has the effect that multiple micro images are formed on the sensor. These micro images encode both spatial and angular information about the light rays emitted by the scene in front of the camera.

In this paper we will concentrate on so-called focused plenoptic cameras [21, 22]. For this type of camera, each micro image is a focused image which contains a small portion of the entire scene. Neighboring micro images show similar portions from slightly different perspectives (see Fig. 2(b)). Hence, the depth of a certain object point can be recovered from correspondences in the micro images [23]. Furthermore, using this depth, one is able to synthesize the intensities of the so-called virtual image (see Fig. 2(a)) which is created by the main lens [22]. This image is called totally focused (or total focus) image (Fig. 2(c)).

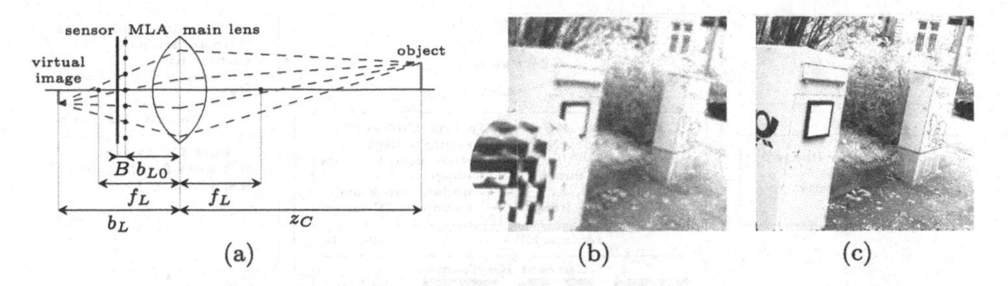

Fig. 2. Focused plenoptic camera. (a) Cross view: the MLA is placed in front of the sensor and creates multiple focused micro images of the same point of the virtual main lens image. (b) Raw image recorded by a focused plenoptic camera. (c) Totally focused image calculated from the raw image. This image is the virtual image.

3 SPO: Scale-Optimized Plenoptic Odometry

Section 3.1 introduces some notations, which will be used in this section. Furthermore, Sect. 3.2 gives an overview of the entire Scale-Optimized Plenoptic Odometry (SPO) algorithm. Afterwards, the main components of the algorithm are presented in detail.

3.1 Notations

In the following, we denote vectors by bold, lower-case letters $\boldsymbol{\xi}$ and matrices by bold, upper case letters $\boldsymbol{G}$. For vectors defining points we do not differentiate between homogeneous and non-homogeneous representations. However, this should be clear from the context. Frame poses are defined either in $\boldsymbol{G} \in \mathrm{SE}(3)$ (3D rigid body transformation) or in $\boldsymbol{S} \in \mathrm{Sim}(3)$ (3D similarity transformation):

$$\boldsymbol{G} := \begin{bmatrix} \boldsymbol{R}\,\boldsymbol{t} \\ \boldsymbol{0}\,1 \end{bmatrix} \quad \text{and} \quad \boldsymbol{S} := \begin{bmatrix} s\boldsymbol{R}\,\boldsymbol{t} \\ \boldsymbol{0}\quad 1 \end{bmatrix} \qquad \text{with } \boldsymbol{R} \in \mathrm{SO}(3), \boldsymbol{t} \in \mathbb{R}^3, s \in \mathbb{R}^+. \quad (1)$$

These transformations are represented by their corresponding tangent space vector of the respective Lie-Algebra. Here, the exponential map and its inverse are denoted as follows:

$$\boldsymbol{G} = \exp_{\mathfrak{se}(3)}(\boldsymbol{\xi}) \qquad \boldsymbol{\xi} = \log_{\mathrm{SE}(3)}(\boldsymbol{G}) \qquad \text{with } \boldsymbol{\xi} \in \mathbb{R}^6 \text{and } \boldsymbol{G} \in \mathrm{SE}(3), \quad (2)$$

$$\boldsymbol{S} = \exp_{\mathfrak{sim}(3)}(\boldsymbol{\xi}) \qquad \boldsymbol{\xi} = \log_{\mathrm{Sim}(3)}(\boldsymbol{S}) \qquad \text{with } \boldsymbol{\xi} \in \mathbb{R}^7 \text{and } \boldsymbol{S} \in \mathrm{Sim}(3). \quad (3)$$

3.2 Algorithm Overview

SPO is a direct VO algorithm which uses only the recordings of a focused plenoptic camera to estimate the camera motion and a semi-dense 3D map of the environment. The entire workflow of the algorithm is visualized in Fig. 3 and consists of the following main components:

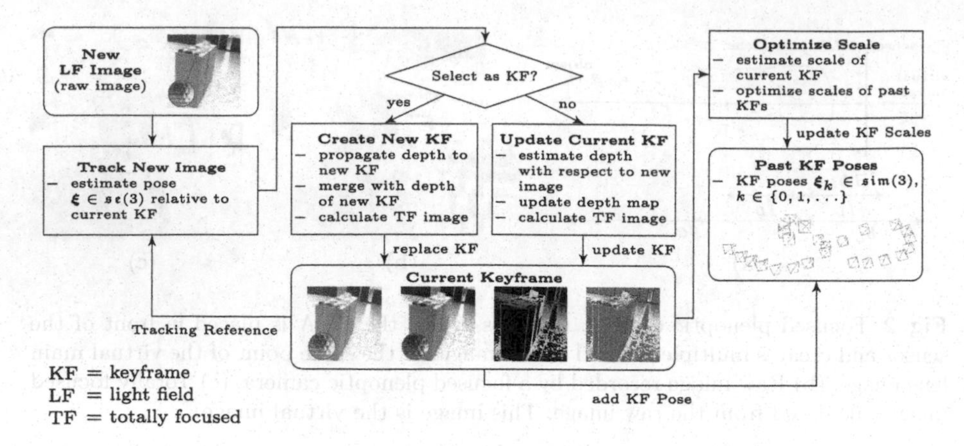

Fig. 3. Flowchart of the Scale-Optimized Plenoptic Odometry (SPO) algorithm.

– New recorded light field images are tracked continuously. Here, the pose $\boldsymbol{\xi} \in \mathfrak{se}(3)$ of the new image, relative to the current keyframe, is estimated. The tracking is constrained by a linear motion model and accounts for changing lighting conditions.
– In addition to its raw light field image, for each keyframe two depth maps (a micro image depth map (used for mapping) and a virtual image depth map (used for tracking)) as well as a totally focused intensity image are stored (see Fig. 5). While depth can be estimated from a single light field image already, the depth maps are gradually refined based on stereo observations, which are obtained with respect to the newly tracked images.
– A scale optimization framework estimates the absolute scale for every replaced keyframe. By filtering over multiple scale estimates a globally optimized scale is obtained. The poses of past keyframes are stored as 3D similarity transformations ($\boldsymbol{\xi}_k \in \mathfrak{sim}(3), k \in \{0, 1, \ldots\}$). This way, their scales can simply be updated.

Due to lacking depth information, the initialization is always an issue for monocular VO. This is not the case for SPO, as depth can be obtained for the first recorded image already.

3.3 Camera Model and Calibration

In [12], a new model for plenoptic cameras was proposed. This model is visualized in Fig. 4(a). Here, the plenoptic camera is represented as a virtual array of cameras with a very narrow field of view, at a distance z_{C0} to the main lens:

$$z_{C0} = \frac{f_L \cdot b_{L0}}{f_L - b_{L0}}. \tag{4}$$

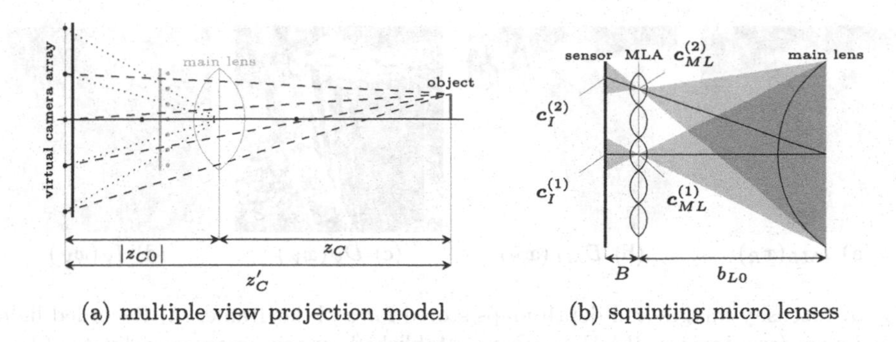

(a) multiple view projection model (b) squinting micro lenses

Fig. 4. Plenoptic camera model used in SPO. (a) The model of a focused plenoptic camera proposed in [12]. As shown in the figure, a plenoptic camera forms, in fact, the equivalent to a virtual array of cameras with a very narrow field of view. (b) Squinting micro lenses in a plenoptic camera. It is very often claimed that micro image centers $\boldsymbol{c}_I$ which can be estimated from a white image recorded by the plenoptic camera would be equivalent to the centers $\boldsymbol{c}_{ML}$ of the micro lenses in the MLA. This, in fact, is not the case as micro lenses distant from the optical axis squint, as it is shown in the figure.

In Eq. (4) f_L is the focal length of the main lens and b_{L0} the distance between main lens and real MLA. As this model forms the equivalent to a standard camera array, stereo correspondences between light field images from different perspectives can be found directly in the recorded micro images.

In this model, the relationship between regular 3D camera coordinates $\boldsymbol{x}_C = [x_C, y_C, z_C]^T$ of an object point and the homogeneous coordinates $\boldsymbol{x}_p = [x_p, y_p, 1]^T$ of the corresponding 2D point in the image of a virtual camera (or projected micro lens) is given as follows:

$$\boldsymbol{x}_C := z'_C \cdot \boldsymbol{x}_p + \boldsymbol{p}_{ML} = \boldsymbol{x}'_C + \boldsymbol{p}_{ML}. \tag{5}$$

In Eq. (5), $\boldsymbol{p}_{ML} = [p_{MLx}, p_{MLy}, -z_{C0}]^T$ is the optical center of a specific virtual camera. The vector $\boldsymbol{x}'_C = [x'_C, y'_C, z'_C]^T$ represents the so-called effective camera coordinates of the object point. Effective camera coordinates have their origin in the respective virtual camera center $\boldsymbol{p}_{ML}$. Below, we will rather use the definitions $\boldsymbol{c}_{ML}$ and $\boldsymbol{x}_R$ for the real micro lens centers and raw image coordinates, respectively, instead of their projected equivalents $\boldsymbol{p}_{ML}$ and $\boldsymbol{x}_p$. However, as the maps from one representation into the other are uniquely defined, we can simply switch between both representation. The definitions of these maps as well as further details about the model can be found in [12].

For SPO, this model is extended by some peculiarities of a real plenoptic camera. As the micro lenses in a real plenoptic camera squint (see Fig. 4(b)), this effect is considered in the camera model. Hence, the relationship between a micro image center $\boldsymbol{c}_I$, which can be detected from a recorded white image [24], and the corresponding micro lens center $\boldsymbol{c}_{ML}$ is defined as follows:

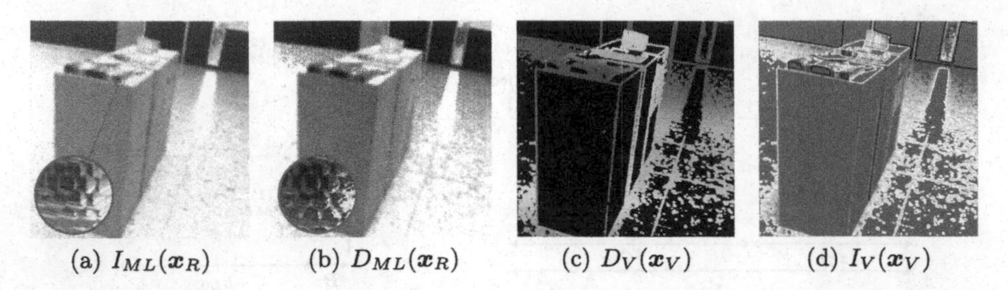

(a) $I_{ML}(\boldsymbol{x}_R)$ (b) $D_{ML}(\boldsymbol{x}_R)$ (c) $D_V(\boldsymbol{x}_V)$ (d) $I_V(\boldsymbol{x}_V)$

Fig. 5. Intensity images and depth maps stored for each keyframe. (a) Recorded light field image (raw image). (b) Depth map established on raw image coordinates (This depth map is refined in the mapping process). (c) Depth map on virtual image coordinates (This depth map can be calculated from (b) and is used for tracking). (d) Totally focused intensity image (represents intensities of the virtual image). In (d), for the red pixels (black pixels in (c)) no depth value, and therefore no intensity, was calculated.

$$\boldsymbol{c}_{ML} = \begin{bmatrix} c_{MLx} \\ c_{MLy} \\ b_{L0} \end{bmatrix} = \boldsymbol{c}_I \frac{b_{L0}}{b_{L0} + B} = \begin{bmatrix} c_{Ix} \\ c_{Iy} \\ b_{L0} + B \end{bmatrix} \frac{b_{L0}}{b_{L0} + B}. \tag{6}$$

Both, $\boldsymbol{c}_I$ and $\boldsymbol{c}_{ML}$ are defined as 3D coordinates with their origin in the optical center of the main lens. In addition, we define a standard lens distortion model [25], considering radial symmetric and tangential distortion, directly in the recorded raw image (on raw image coordinates $\boldsymbol{x}_R$).

While in this paper the plenoptic camera representation of [12] is used, a similar representation was described in [26].

3.4 Depth Map Representations in Keyframes

SPO establishes for each keyframe two separate representations: one on raw image coordinates $\boldsymbol{x}_R$ (raw image or micro image representation), and one on virtual image coordinates $\boldsymbol{x}_V$ (virtual image representation).

Raw Image Representation. The raw intensity image $I_{ML}(\boldsymbol{x}_R)$ (Fig. 5(a)) is the image which is recorded by the plenoptic camera and consists of thousands of micro images. For each pixel in the image which has a sufficiently high intensity gradient a depth estimate is established and gradually refined based on stereo observations between the keyframe and new tracked frames. This is done in a way similar to [12]. This raw image depth map $D_{ML}(\boldsymbol{x}_R)$ is shown in Fig. 5(b).

Virtual Image Representation. Between the object space and the raw image representation there exists a one-to-many mapping, as one object point is mapped to multiple micro images. From the raw image representation a virtual image representation, consisting of a depth map $D_V(\boldsymbol{x}_V)$ in virtual image coordinates (Fig. 5(c)) and the corresponding totally focused intensity image $I_V(\boldsymbol{x}_V)$

(Fig. 5(d)) can be calculated. Here, raw image points corresponding the same object point are combined and hence, a one-to-one mapping between object and image space is established. The virtual image representation is used to track new images, as will be described in Sect. 3.7.

Probabilistic Depth Model. Rather than representing depths as absolute values, they are represented as probabilistic hypotheses:

$$D(\boldsymbol{x}) := \mathcal{N}\left(d, \sigma_d^2\right), \tag{7}$$

where d defines the inverse effective depth $z_C'^{-1}$ of a point in either of the two representations. The depth hypotheses are established in a way similar to [12], where the variance σ_d^2 is calculated based on a disparity error model, which takes multiple error sources into account.

3.5 Final Map Representation

The final 3D map is a collection of virtual image representations as well as the respective keyframe poses combined to a global map. The keyframe poses are a concatenation of 3D similarity transformations $\boldsymbol{\xi}_k \in \mathfrak{sim}(3)$, where the respective scale is optimized by the scale optimization framework (Sect. 3.8).

3.6 Selecting Keyframes

When a tracked image is selected to become a new keyframe, depth estimation is performed in the new image. Afterwards, the raw image depth map of the current keyframe is propagated to the new one and the depth hypotheses are merged.

3.7 Tracking New Light Field Images

For a new recorded frame (index j), its pose $\boldsymbol{\xi}_{kj} \in \mathfrak{se}(3)$, relative to the current keyframe (index k), is estimated by direct image alignment. The problem is solved in a coarse-to-fine approach to increase the region of convergence.

We build pyramid levels of the new recorded raw image $I_{MLj}(\boldsymbol{x}_R)$ and of the virtual image representation $\{I_{Vk}(\boldsymbol{x}_V), D_{Vk}(\boldsymbol{x}_V)\}$ of the current keyframe, by simply binning pixels. As long as the size of a raw image pixel, on a certain pyramid level, is smaller than a micro image, the image of reduced resolution still is a valid light field image. At coarse levels, where the pixel size exceeds the size of a micro image, the raw image turns into a (slightly blurred) central perspective image.

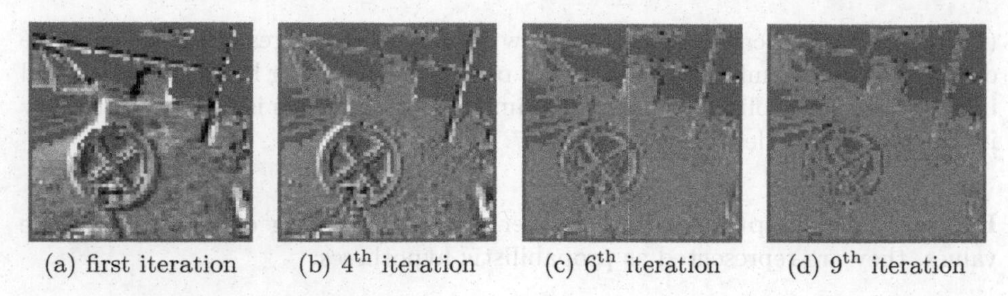

(a) first iteration (b) 4th iteration (c) 6th iteration (d) 9th iteration

Fig. 6. Tracking residual after various numbers of iterations. The figure shows residuals in virtual image coordinates of the tracking reference. The gray value represents the value of the tracking residual. Black signifies a negative residual with high absolute values and white signifies a positive residual with high absolute value. Red regions are invalid depth pixels and therefore have no residual.

At each of the pyramid levels, a energy function is defined, and optimized with respect to $\boldsymbol{\xi}_{kj} \in \mathfrak{se}(3)$:

$$E(\boldsymbol{\xi}_{kj}) = \sum_i \sum_l \left\| \left(\frac{r^{(i,l)}}{\sigma_r^{(i,l)}} \right)^2 \right\|_\delta + \tau \cdot E_{\text{motion}}(\boldsymbol{\xi}_{kj}), \tag{8}$$

$$r^{(i,l)} := I_{Vk}\left(\boldsymbol{x}_V^{(i)}\right) - I_{MLj}\left(\pi_{ML}\left(\boldsymbol{G}(\boldsymbol{\xi}_{kj})\pi_V^{-1}(\boldsymbol{x}_V^{(i)}), \boldsymbol{c}_{ML}^{(l)}\right)\right), \tag{9}$$

$$\left(\sigma_r^{(i,l)}\right)^2 := \sigma_n^2 \left(\frac{1}{N_k} + 1\right) + \left|\frac{\partial r(\boldsymbol{x}_V, \boldsymbol{\xi}_{kj})}{\partial d(\boldsymbol{x}_V)}\right|^2 \sigma_d^2(\boldsymbol{x}_V^{(i)}). \tag{10}$$

Here, $\pi_{ML}(\boldsymbol{x}_C, \boldsymbol{c}_{ML})$ defines the projection from camera coordinates $\boldsymbol{x}_C$ to raw image coordinates $\boldsymbol{x}_R$ through a certain micro lens $\boldsymbol{c}_{ML}$, and $\pi_V^{-1}(\boldsymbol{x}_V)$ the inverse projection from virtual image coordinates $\boldsymbol{x}_V$ to camera coordinates $\boldsymbol{x}_C$. To calculate $\boldsymbol{x}_C$ out of $\boldsymbol{x}_V$ one needed the corresponding depth value $D_V(\boldsymbol{x}_V)$. A detailed definition of this projection can be found in [27, Eqs. (3)–(6)]. The expression $\|\cdot\|_\delta$ is the robust Huber norm [28]. In Eq. (8), the second summand denotes a motion prior term, as it will be defined in Eq. (12). The parameter τ weights the motion prior with respect to the photometric error (first summand). In Eq. (10), the first summand defines the photometric noise on the residual, while the second summand is the geometric noise component, resulting from noise in the depth estimates.

An intensity value $I_{Vk}(\boldsymbol{x}_V)$ (Eq. (9)) in the virtual image of the keyframe is calculated as the average of multiple (N_k) micro image intensities. Considering the noise in the different micro images to be uncorrelated, the variance of the noise is N_k times smaller than for an intensity value $I_{MLj}(\boldsymbol{x}_R)$ in the new raw images. The variance of the sensor noise σ_n^2 is constant over the entire raw image.

Only for the final (finest) pyramid level, a single reference point $\boldsymbol{x}_V^{(i)}$ is projected to all micro images in the new frame which actually see this point. This is modeled by the sum over l in Eq. (8). This way we are able to implicitly incorporate the parallaxes in the micro images of the new light field image into the optimization. For all other levels the sum over l is omitted and $\boldsymbol{x}_V^{(i)}$ is projected only through the closest micro lens $\boldsymbol{c}_{ML}^{(0)}$. Figure 6 shows the tracking residual for different iterations in the optimization on a coarse pyramid level.

Motion Prior. A motion prior, based on a linear motion model, is used to constrain the optimization. This way, the region of convergence is shifted to an area where the optimal solution is more likely located.

A linear prediction $\widetilde{\boldsymbol{\xi}}_{kj} \in \mathfrak{se}(3)$ of $\boldsymbol{\xi}_{kj}$ is obtained from the pose $\boldsymbol{\xi}_{k(j-1)}$ of the previous image as follows:

$$\widetilde{\boldsymbol{\xi}}_{kj} = \log_{\mathrm{SE}(3)}\left(\exp_{\mathfrak{se}(3)}(\dot{\boldsymbol{\xi}}_{j-1}) \cdot \exp_{\mathfrak{se}(3)}(\boldsymbol{\xi}_{k(j-1)})\right). \tag{11}$$

In Eq. (11) $\dot{\boldsymbol{\xi}}_{j-1} \in \mathfrak{se}(3)$ is the motion vector at the previous image.

Using the pose prediction $\widetilde{\boldsymbol{\xi}}_{kj}$, we define the motion term $E_{\mathrm{motion}}(\boldsymbol{\xi}_{kj})$ to constrain the tracking:

$$E_{\mathrm{motion}}(\boldsymbol{\xi}_{kj}) = (\delta\boldsymbol{\xi})^T \delta\boldsymbol{\xi}, \quad \text{with}$$
$$\delta\boldsymbol{\xi} = \log_{\mathrm{SE}(3)}\left(\exp_{\mathfrak{se}(3)}(\boldsymbol{\xi}_{kj}) \cdot \exp_{\mathfrak{se}(3)}(\widetilde{\boldsymbol{\xi}}_{kj})^{-1}\right). \tag{12}$$

For coarse pyramid levels we are very uncertain about the correct frame pose and therefore a high weight τ is chosen in Eq. (8). This weight is decreased as the optimization moves down in the pyramid. On the final level, the weight is set to $\tau = 0$. This way, an error in the motion prediction does not influence the final estimate.

Lighting Compensation. To compensate for changing lighting conditions between the current keyframe and the new image, the residual term defined in Eq. (9) is extended by an affine transformation of the reference intensities $I_{Vk}(\boldsymbol{x}_V)$:

$$r^{(i,l)} := I_{Vk}\left(\boldsymbol{x}_V^{(i)}\right) \cdot a + b - I_{MLj}\left(\pi_{ML}\left(\boldsymbol{G}(\boldsymbol{\xi}_{kj})\pi_V^{-1}(\boldsymbol{x}_V^{(i)}), \boldsymbol{c}_{ML}^{(l)}\right)\right). \tag{13}$$

The parameters a and b must also be estimated in the optimization process. We initialize the parameters based on first- and second-order statistics calculated from the intensity images $I_{Vk}(\boldsymbol{x}_V)$ and $I_{MLj}(\boldsymbol{x}_R)$ as follows:

$$a_{\mathrm{init}} := \sigma_{I_{MLj}} / \sigma_{I_{Vk}} \quad \text{and} \quad b_{\mathrm{init}} := \overline{I}_{MLj} - \overline{I}_{Vk}. \tag{14}$$

In Eq. (14) $\overline{I}_{MLj}$ and $\overline{I}_{Vk}$ are the average intensity values over the entire images respectively, while $\sigma_{I_{MLj}}$ and $\sigma_{I_{Vk}}$ are the empirical standard deviations.

3.8 Optimizing the Global Scale

Scale Estimation in Finalized Keyframes. Scale estimation can be viewed as tracking a light field frame based on its own virtual image depth map $D_V(\boldsymbol{x}_V)$. However, instead of optimizing all pose parameters, a logarithmized scale (log-scale) parameter ρ is optimized. We work on the log-scale ρ to transform the scale $s = e^\rho$, which is applied on 3D camera coordinates $\boldsymbol{x}_C$, into a Euclidean space.

As for the tracking approach (Sect. 3.7), an energy function $E(\rho)$ is defined:

$$E(\rho) = \sum_i \sum_{l \neq 0} \left\| \left(\frac{r^{(i,l)}}{\sigma_r^{(i,l)}} \right)^2 \right\|_\delta, \tag{15}$$

$$r^{(i,l)} := I_{MLk}\left(\pi_{ML}\left(\pi_V^{-1}(\boldsymbol{x}_V^{(i)}) \cdot e^\rho, \boldsymbol{c}_{ML}^{(0)}\right)\right) - I_{MLk}\left(\pi_{ML}\left(\pi_V^{-1}(\boldsymbol{x}_V^{(i)}) \cdot e^\rho, \boldsymbol{c}_{ML}^{(l)}\right)\right), \tag{16}$$

$$\left(\sigma_r^{(i,l)}\right)^2 := 2\sigma_n^2 + \left| \frac{\partial r^{(i,l)}(\boldsymbol{x}_V^{(i)}, \rho)}{\partial \sigma_d(\boldsymbol{x}_V^{(i)})} \right|^2 \sigma_d^2(\boldsymbol{x}_V^{(i)}). \tag{17}$$

Instead of defining the photometric residual r with respect to the intensities of the totally focused image, the residuals are defined between the centered micro image and all surrounding micro images, which still see the virtual image point $\boldsymbol{x}_V^{(i)}$. This way, a wrong initial scale, which affects the intensities in the totally focused image, can not negatively affect the optimization.

In conjunction to the log-scale estimate ρ, its variance σ_ρ^2 is calculated:

$$\sigma_\rho^2 = \frac{N}{\sum_{i=0}^{N-1} \sigma_{\rho i}^{-2}} \quad \text{with} \quad \sigma_{\rho i}^2 = \left| \frac{\partial \rho}{\partial d(\boldsymbol{x}_V^{(i)})} \right|^2 \cdot \sigma_d(\boldsymbol{x}_V^{(i)})^2. \tag{18}$$

Far points do not contribute to a reliable scale estimate because for these points the ratio between the micro lens stereo baseline and the effective object distance $z'_C = d^{-1}$ becomes negligibly small. Hence, the N points used to define the scale variance are only the closest N points or, in other words, the points with the highest inverse effective depth d.

Scale Optimization. Since refined depth maps are propagated from keyframe to keyframe, the scales of subsequent keyframes are highly correlated and scale drifts between them are marginal. Hence, the estimated log-scale ρ can be filtered over multiple keyframes.

We formulate the following estimator which calculates the filtered log-scale value $\hat{\rho}^{(l)}$ for a certain keyframe with time index l based on a neighborhood of keyframes:

$$\hat{\rho}^{(l)} = \left(\sum_{m=-M}^{M} \rho^{(m+l)} \cdot \frac{c^{|m|}}{\left(\sigma_\rho^{(m+l)}\right)^2} \right) \cdot \left(\sum_{m=-M}^{M} \frac{c^{|m|}}{\left(\sigma_\rho^{(m+l)}\right)^2} \right)^{-1}. \tag{19}$$

In Eq. (19), the variable m is the discrete time index in keyframes. The parameter c ($0 \leq c \leq 1$) defines the correlation between subsequent keyframes. Since we consider a high correlation, c will be close to one. While each log-scale estimate $\rho^{(i)}$ ($i \in \{0, 1, \ldots, k\}$) is weighted by its inverse variance, estimates of keyframes which are farther from the keyframe of interest (index l) are down weighted by the respective power of c. The parameter M defines the influence length of the filter.

Due to the linearity of the filter, it can be solved recursively, in a way similar to a Kalman filter.

4 Results

Aside from the proposed SPO, there are no light field camera based VO algorithms available which succeed in challenging environments. Same holds true for datasets to evaluate such algorithms. Hence, we compare our method to state-of-the-art monocular and stereo VO approaches based on a new dataset [20].

The dataset presented in [20] contains various synchronized sequences recorded by a plenoptic camera and a stereo camera system, both mounted on a single hand-held platform. The dataset consists of 11 sequences, all recorded at a frame rate of 30 fps. Similar as for the dataset presented in [29], all sequences end in a very large loop, where start and end of the sequence capture the same scene (see Fig. 8). Hence, the accuracies of a VO algorithm can be measured by the accumulated drift over the entire sequence.

SPO is compared to the state-of-the-art in monocular and stereo VO, namely to DSO [2] and ORB-SLAM2 (monocular and stereo version of it) [1,15]. For ORB-SLAM2, we disabled relocalization and the detection of loop closures to be able to measure the accumulated drift of the algorithm. Figure 7 shows the results with respect to the dataset [20] as cumulative error plots. That is, the ordinate counts the number of sequences for which an algorithm performed better than a value x on the axis of abscissa. The figure shows the absolute scale error d'_s, the scale drift e'_s, and the alignment error e_{align}. All error metrics where calculates as defined in [20].

In comparison to SPO, the stereo algorithm has a much lower absolute scale error. However, the stereo system does also benefit from a much larger stereo baseline. Furthermore, the ground truth scale is obtained on the basis of the stereo data. Hence, the absolute scale error of the stereo system is rather reflecting the accuracy of the ground truth data. SPO is able to estimate the absolute scale with accuracy of 10%, and better, for most of the sequences. The algorithm performs significantly better with scale optimization than without. Regarding the scale drift over the entire sequence, SPO significantly outperforms existing monocular approaches. Regarding the alignment error SPO seems to perform equally well or only sightly worse than DSO [2]. However, the plenoptic images have a field of view which is much smaller than the one of the regular cameras (see [20]). Figure 8 shows, by way of example, two complete trajectories estimated by SPO. Here, the accumulated drift from start to end is clearly visible.

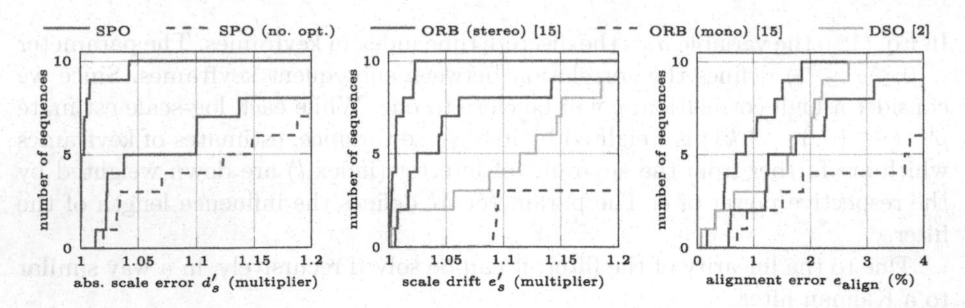

Fig. 7. Cumulative error plots obtained based on the synchronized stereo and plenoptic VO dataset [20]. d'_s and e'_s are multiplicative error, while e_{align} is given in percentages of the sequence length. By nature, no absolute scale error is obtained for the monocular approaches.

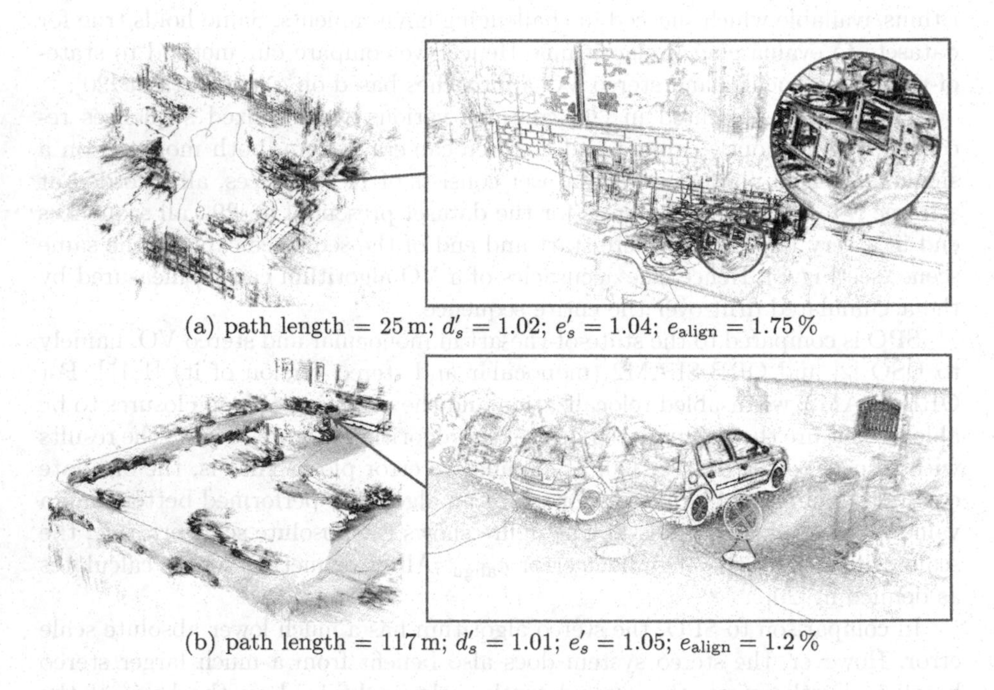

(a) path length = 25 m; $d'_s = 1.02$; $e'_s = 1.04$; $e_{\text{align}} = 1.75\,\%$

(b) path length = 117 m; $d'_s = 1.01$; $e'_s = 1.05$; $e_{\text{align}} = 1.2\,\%$

Fig. 8. Point clouds and trajectories calculated by SPO. Left: Entire point cloud and trajectory. Right: Subsection showing beginning and end of the trajectory. In the point clouds on the right the accumulated drift from beginning to end is clearly visible. The estimated camera trajectory is shown in green. (Color figure online)

A major drawback in comparison to monocular approaches is that the focal length of the plenoptic camera can not be chosen freely, but instead directly affects the depth range of the camera. Hence, the plenoptic camera will have a field of view which is always smaller than that of a monocular camera. While this makes tracking more challenging, on the other side it implicates a smaller

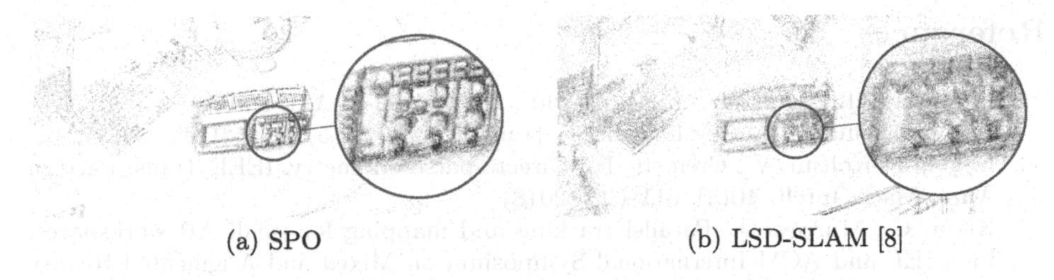

(a) SPO (b) LSD-SLAM [8]

Fig. 9. Point clouds of the same scene: (a) calculated by SPO and (b) calculated by LSD-SLAM. Because of its narrow field of view, the plenoptic camera has much smaller ground sampling distance, which, in turn, results in more detailed 3D map than for the monocular camera. However, as a result the reconstructed map is less complete.

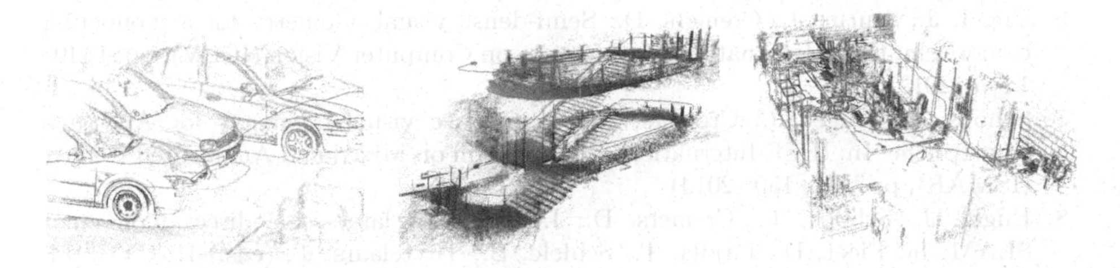

Fig. 10. Examples of point clouds calculated by SPO in various environments. Green line is the estimated camera trajectory. (Color figure online)

ground sampling distance for the plenoptic camera than for the monocular one. Therefore, SPO generally results in point clouds which are more detailed than their monocular (or stereo camera based) equivalent. This can be seen from Fig. 9. Figure 10 shows further results of SPO, demonstrating the quality and versatility of the algorithm.

5 Conclusions

In this paper we presented Scale-Optimized Plenoptic Odometry (SPO), which is a direct and semi-dense VO algorithms working on the recordings of a focused plenoptic camera. In contrast to previous algorithms based on plenoptic cameras and other light field representation [10–12], SPO is able to succeed in challenging real-life scenarios. It was shown that SPO is able to recover the absolute scale of a scene with an accuracy of 10% and better for most of the tested sequences. SPO significantly outperforms state-of-the-art monocular algorithms with respect to scale drifts, while showing similar overall tracking accuracies. In our opinion SPO represents a promising alternative to existing VO and SLAM systems.

Acknowledgment. This research is financed by the Baden-Württemberg Stiftung gGmbH and the Federal Ministry of Education and Research (Germany) in its program FHProfUnt.

References

1. Mur-Artal, R., Montiel, J.M.M., Tardós, J.D.: ORB-SLAM: a versatile and accurate monocular SLAM system. IEEE Trans. Robot. **31**(5), 1147–1163 (2015)
2. Engel, J., Koltun, V., Cremers, D.: Direct sparse odometry. IEEE Trans. Pattern Anal. Mach. Intell. **40**(3), 611–625 (2018)
3. Klein, G., Murray, D.: Parallel tracking and mapping for small AR workspaces. In: IEEE and ACM International Symposium on Mixed and Augmented Reality (ISMAR), vol. 6, pp. 225–234 (2007)
4. Eade, E., Drummond, T.: Edge landmarks in monocular SLAM. Image Vis. Comput. **27**(5), 588–596 (2009)
5. Newcombe, R.A., Lovegrove, S.J., Davison, A.J.: DTAM: dense tracking and mapping in real-time. In: IEEE International Conference on Computer Vision (ICCV) (2011)
6. Engel, J., Sturm, J., Cremers, D.: Semi-dense visual odometry for a monocular camera. In: IEEE International Conference on Computer Vision (ICCV), pp. 1449–1456 (2013)
7. Schöps, T., Engel, J., Cremers, D.: Semi-dense visual odometry for AR on a smartphone. In: IEEE International Symposium on Mixed and Augmented Reality (ISMAR), pp. 145–150 (2014)
8. Engel, J., Schöps, T., Cremers, D.: LSD-SLAM: large-scale direct monocular SLAM. In: Fleet, D., Pajdla, T., Schiele, B., Tuytelaars, T. (eds.) ECCV 2014. LNCS, vol. 8690, pp. 834–849. Springer, Cham (2014). https://doi.org/10.1007/978-3-319-10605-2_54
9. Forster, C., Pizzoli, M., Scaramuzza, D.: SVO: fast semi-direct monocular visual odometry. In: IEEE International Conference on Robotics and Automation (ICRA), pp. 15–22 (2014)
10. Dansereau, D., Mahon, I., Pizarro, O., Williams, S.: Plenoptic flow: closed-form visual odometry for light field cameras. In: IEEE/RSJ International Conference on Intelligent Robots and Systems (IROS), pp. 4455–4462 (2011)
11. Dong, F., Ieng, S.H., Savatier, X., Etienne-Cummings, R., Benosman, R.: Plenoptic cameras in real-time robotics. Int. J. Robot. Res. **32**(2), 206–217 (2013)
12. Zeller, N., Quint, F., Stilla, U.: From the calibration of a light-field camera to direct plenoptic odometry. IEEE J. Sel. Top. Signal Process. **11**(7), 1004–1019 (2017)
13. Engel, J., Stückler, J., Cremers, D.: Large-scale direct SLAM with stereo cameras. In: IEEE/RSJ International Conference on Intelligent Robots and Systems (IROS), pp. 1935–1942 (2015)
14. Usenko, V., Engel, J., Stückler, J., Cremers, D.: Direct visual-inertial odometry with stereo cameras. In: International Conference on Robotics and Automation (ICRA) (2016)
15. Mur-Artal, R., Tardós, J.D.: ORB-SLAM2: an open-source SLAM system for monocular, stereo, and RGB-D cameras. IEEE Trans. Robot. **33**(5), 1255–1262 (2017)
16. Wang, R., Schwörer, M., Cremers, D.: Stereo DSO: large-scale direct sparse visual odometry with stereo cameras. In: International Conference on Computer Vision (ICCV) (2017)
17. Izadi, S., et al.: KinectFusion: real-time 3D reconstruction and interaction using a moving depth camera. In: 24th Annual ACM Symposium on User Interface Software and Technology, pp. 559–568. ACM (2011)

18. Kerl, C., Sturm, J., Cremers, D.: Dense visual SLAM for RGB-D cameras. In: IEEE/RSJ International Conference on Intelligent Robots and Systems (IROS), pp. 2100–2106 (2013)
19. Kerl, C., Stückler, J., Cremers, D.: Dense continuous-time tracking and mapping with rolling shutter RGB-D cameras. In: IEEE International Conference on Computer Vision (ICCV), pp. 2264–2272 (2015)
20. Zeller, N., Quint, F., Stilla, U.: A synchronized stereo and plenoptic visual odometry dataset. arXiv:1807.09372 (2018)
21. Lumsdaine, A., Georgiev, T.: Full resolution lightfield rendering. Technical report, Adobe Systems, Inc. (2008)
22. Perwaß, C., Wietzke, L.: Single lens 3D-camera with extended depth-of-field. In: SPIE 8291, Human Vision and Electronic Imaging XVII (2012)
23. Zeller, N., Quint, F., Stilla, U.: Establishing a probabilistic depth map from focused plenoptic cameras. In: International Conference on 3D Vision (3DV), pp. 91–99 (2015)
24. Dansereau, D., Pizarro, O., Williams, S.: Decoding, calibration and rectification for lenselet-based plenoptic cameras. In: IEEE Conference on Computer Vision and Pattern Recognition (CVPR), pp. 1027–1034 (2013)
25. Brown, D.C.: Decentering distortion of lenses. Photogramm. Eng. **32**(3), 444–462 (1966)
26. Mignard-Debise, L., Restrepo, J., Ihrke, I.: A unifying first-order model for light-field cameras: the equivalent camera array. IEEE Trans. Comput. Imaging **3**(4), 798–810 (2017)
27. Zeller, N., Noury, C.A., Quint, F., Teulière, C., Stilla, U., Dhôme, M.: Metric calibration of a focused plenoptic camera based on a 3D calibration target. ISPRS Ann. Photogramm., Remote. Sens. Spat. Inf. Sci. **III-3**, 449–456 (2016). (Proceedings of ISPRS Congress 2016)
28. Huber, P.J.: Robust estimation of a location parameter. Ann. Math. Stat. **35**(1), 73–101 (1964)
29. Engel, J., Usenko, V., Cremers, D.: A photometrically calibrated benchmark for monocular visual odometry. arXiv:1607.02555 (2016)

Burst Image Deblurring Using Permutation Invariant Convolutional Neural Networks

Miika Aittala(✉) and Frédo Durand

Massachusetts Institute of Technology, Cambridge, MA 02139, USA
miika@csail.mit.edu, fredo@mit.edu

Abstract. We propose a neural approach for fusing an arbitrary-length burst of photographs suffering from severe camera shake and noise into a sharp and noise-free image. Our novel convolutional architecture has a simultaneous view of all frames in the burst, and by construction treats them in an order-independent manner. This enables it to effectively detect and leverage subtle cues scattered across different frames, while ensuring that each frame gets a full and equal consideration regardless of its position in the sequence. We train the network with richly varied synthetic data consisting of camera shake, realistic noise, and other common imaging defects. The method demonstrates consistent state of the art burst image restoration performance for highly degraded sequences of real-world images, and extracts accurate detail that is not discernible from any of the individual frames in isolation.

Keywords: Burst imaging · Image processing · Deblurring
Denoising · Convolutional neural networks

1 Introduction

Motion blur and noise remain a significant problem in photography despite advances in light efficiency of digital imaging devices. Mobile phone cameras are particularly suspect to handshake and noise due to the small optics and the typical unsupported free-hand shooting position. Shortcomings of optical systems can be in part ameliorated by computational procedures such as denoising and sharpening. One line of work that has recently had significant impact relies on *burst imaging*. A notable example is the imaging pipeline supplied in Android mobile phones: transparently to the user, the camera shoots a sequence of low-quality frames and fuses them computationally into a higher-quality photograph than could be achieved with a conventional exposure in same time [12].

We address the problem of *burst deblurring*, where one is presented with a set of images depicting the same target, each suffering from a different realization of

Electronic supplementary material The online version of this chapter (https://doi.org/10.1007/978-3-030-01237-3_45) contains supplementary material, which is available to authorized users.

V. Ferrari et al. (Eds.): ECCV 2018, LNCS 11212, pp. 748–764, 2018.
https://doi.org/10.1007/978-3-030-01237-3_45

camera shake. While each frame might be hopelessly blurred in isolation, they still retain pieces of partial information about the underlying sharp image. The aim is to recover it by fusing whatever information is available.

Convolutional neural networks (CNN's) have led to breakthroughs in a wide range of image processing tasks, and have also been applied to burst deblurring [33,34]. Observing that bursts can have arbitrarily varying lengths, the recent work of Wieschollek et al. [33] maintains an estimate of the sharp image, and updates it in a recurrent manner by feeding in the frames one at a time. While this is shown to produce good results, it is well known that recurrent architectures struggle with learning to fuse information they receive over a number of steps – even a task as simple as summing together a set of numbers can be difficult [36]. Indeed, our evaluation shows that the architecture of Wieschollek et al. [33] fails to e.g. fully use a lucky sharp image present in a burst (see Fig. 7). This suggests that it generally does not make full use of the information available.

The problem, we argue, is that a recurrent architecture puts the different frames into a highly asymmetric position. The first and the most recently seen frames can have a disproportionate influence on the solution, and complementary cues about individual image details are difficult to combine if they appear multiple frames apart.

We propose a fundamentally different architecture, which considers all of the frames simultaneously as an *unordered set* of arbitrary size. The key idea is to enforce *permutation invariance* by construction: when the ordering of the frames cannot affect the output, no frame is in a special position in relation to others, and consequently each one receives the same consideration. Any piece of useful information can directly influence the solution, and subtle cues scattered around in the burst can be combined effectively. The approach is similar in spirit to classical maximum likelihood or Bayesian inference, where contributions from each observation are symmetrically accumulated onto a likelihood function, from which the desired estimate is then derived.

We achieve this by extending recent ideas on permutation invariance in neural networks [24,36] to a convolutional image translation context. Our proposed network is a U-Net-inspired [25] CNN architecture that maps an unordered set of images into a single output image in a perfectly permutation-invariant manner, and facilitates repeated back-and-forth exchanges of feature information between the frames during the network evaluation. Besides deblurring, we believe that this general-purpose architecture has potential applications to a variety of problems involving loosely structured sets of image-valued observations.

We train our network with synthetically degraded bursts consisting of a range of severe image defects beyond just blur. The presence of noise changes the character of the deblurring problem, and in practice many deblurring algorithms struggle with the high noise levels in full-resolution low-light photographs, and images from low-end cameras. Of course, these are exactly the scenarios where deblurring would be most needed. Our training data simulates the noise characteristics of real-world cameras, and also considers some often overlooked details such as unknown gamma correction, and high dynamic range effects.

Figure 1 demonstrates the effectiveness of our approach compared to the state of the art recurrent architecture of Wieschollek et al. [33] on a challenging real-world burst involving significant image degradations: our method successfully recovers image content that appears to be all but lost in the individual frames of the burst, and markedly improves the overall image quality.

2 Related Work

2.1 Image Restoration

Deblurring. Restoring sharp images from blurred observations is a long-standing research topic. Wang and Tao [32] present a recent survey of approaches to this problem. Deconvolution algorithms seek to stably invert the linear convolution operation when the blur kernel is known. *Blind* deconvolution concerns the more challenging case when the kernel is unknown [2,10,20].

Various methods use neural networks to estimate blur kernels from images and apply classical non-blind deconvolution algorithms to perform the actual deblurring, either as a separate step or as an integrated part of the network [4,28,31,35]. Other approaches sidestep the classical deconvolution, and train a CNN to output a sharp image directly. Nah et al. [22] and Noroozi et al. [23] deblur single images using multi-scale end-to-end convolutional architectures.

Nah et al. [22] and Kupyn et al. [19] use a discriminator-based loss, which encourages the network to produce realistic-looking content in the deblurred image. The downside is that the network may in principle need to invent fictional detail in order to achieve an appearance of realism. We view this direction as largely orthogonal to ours, and focus on extracting the maximum amount of real information from the input burst.

Multi-frame Methods. A variety of deblurring methods consider combining information from multiple blurred frames [3,29,37–39]. Delbracio et al. [7] showed that for static scenes, the typical difficulties with multi-frame blind deconvolution can be sidestepped by combining the well-preserved parts of the power spectra of each frame in the Fourier domain. Wieschollek et al. [34] extend this by determining the deconvolution filters and the spectral averaging weights using a neural network. Recently Wieschollek et al. [33] proposed a neural method for directly predicting a sharp image from an arbitrary-length burst of blurred images, by using a recurrent neural architecture that updates the estimate when fed with new frames. Our method targets the same problem with a fundamentally different network architecture that instead considers all images simultaneously as a *set* of arbitrary size.

Some methods also aim to remove local blur caused by movement of individual objects in videos [5,15,30,33]. Our method focuses on blur caused by camera shake, where the correlations between frames are weak and the frame ordering carries a minor significance. We nonetheless demonstrate that in practice our approach is applicable to flow-aligned general motion data of Su et al. [30].

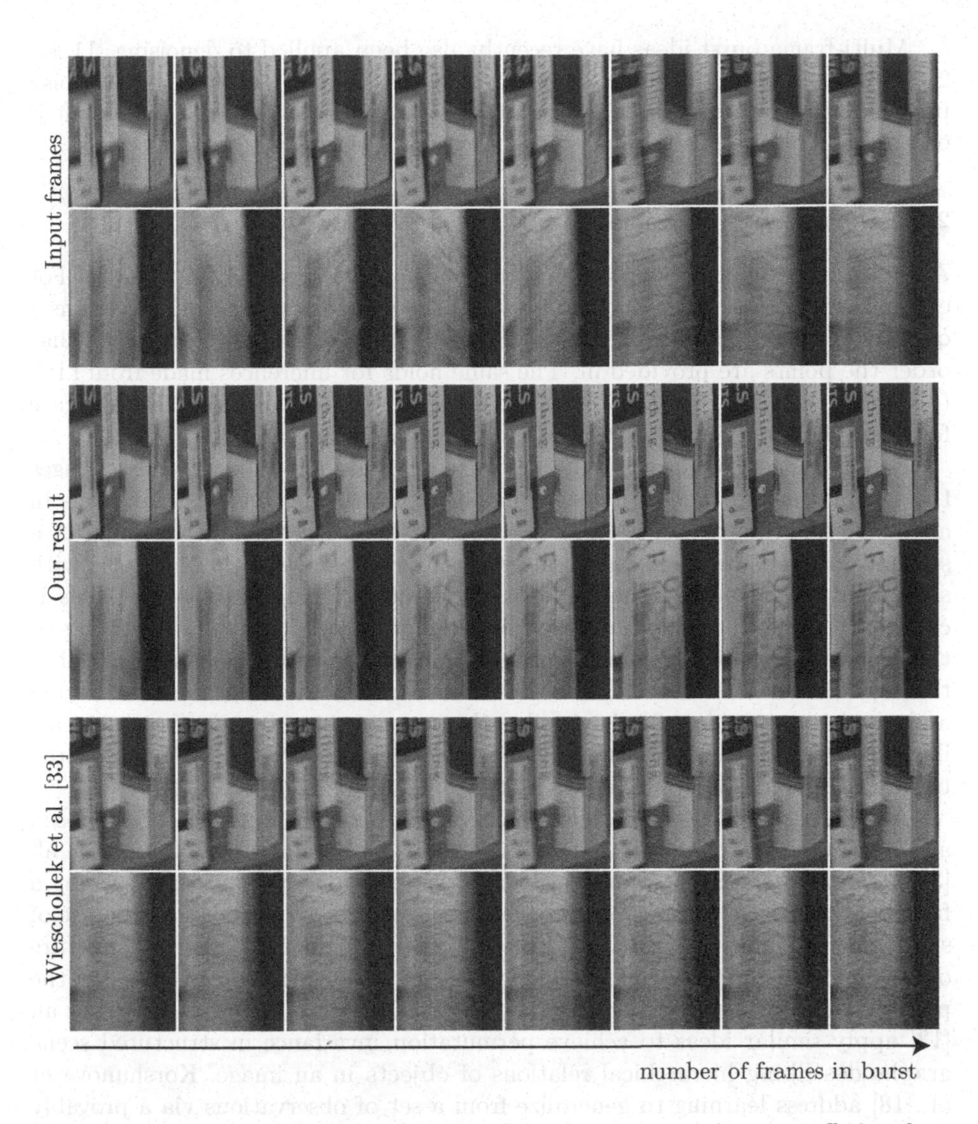

Fig. 1. Given a burst of full-resolution mobile phone camera images suffering from significant camera shake and noise (top rows), our method recovers a sharp estimate of the underlying image (middle rows). The horizontal sequence shows our solution for a growing number of input frames; the rightmost result uses all eight images. The bottom row shows the same progression for the state of the art neural burst deblurring method of Wieschollek et al. [33] (computed using their software implementation). Note how our method has resolved details that are difficult or impossible to reliably discern by eye in any of the inputs: for example the numbers 023-002 at the right edge (shown in blow-up) appear in the solution somewhere around the fourth frame, and become gradually sharper as images are added. These are the actual numbers on the subject (see the supplemental material for a verification photo). Note also the substantial reduction in noise. Images in this paper are best viewed digitally.

Multi-frame burst ideas have recently also been applied to denoising [11,12, 21]. While our main concern is deblurring, we train our model with heavily noisy images to promote robustness against real-world imaging defects. Consequently, our method also learns to denoise the bursts to a significant degree.

2.2 Permutation Invariance

A wide range of inference problems concern unordered sets of input data. For example, point clouds in Euclidian space have no natural ordering, and consequently any global properties we compute from them should not depend on what order the points are provided in. The same holds for inferences made from i.i.d. (or more generally, exchangeable) realizations of random variables, as is the case for example in maximum likelihood and Bayesian estimation.

For neural networks, switching the places of a pair of inputs generally changes the output, and for a good reason: the particular arrangement of the pixels in an image is strongly indicative of the subject depicted, and the meaning of a sentence depends on the order of the words. This is, however, problematic with set-valued data, because one cannot opt out of assigning an ordering. This is counterproductive, as the network will attempt to attribute some meaning to the order. A common argument is that in practice the network should learn that the input order is irrelevant, but this claim is both theoretically unsatisfying and empirically dubious. It is possible that permutation invariance is not easily learnable, and a significant amount of network capacity must be allocated towards achieving an approximation of it.

A variety of recent works have recognized this shortcoming and proposed architectures that handle unordered inputs in a principled way. Zaheer et al. [36] analyze the general characteristics of set-valued functions, and present a framework for constructing permutation invariant neural networks by the use of symmetric pooling layers. Qi et al. [24] propose a similar pooling architecture on point cloud data. Edwards and Storkey [8] use symmetric pooling for the purpose of learning to extract meaningful statistics out of datasets. Herzig et al. [13] apply similar ideas to achieve permutation invariance in structured scene graphs describing hierarchical relations of objects in an image. Korshunova et al. [18] address learning to generalize from a set of observations via a provably permutation invariant recurrent architecture. We discuss these ideas in detail in Sect. 3.1 and extend them to image translation CNN's.

3 Method

Our method consists of a convolutional neural network, which outputs a restored image when fed with a set of blurry and noisy images that have been approximately pre-aligned using homographies. We describe the network architecture in Sect. 3.1, and the synthetic data generation pipeline we use for training it in Sect. 3.2.

3.1 Network Architecture

Zaheer et al. [36] and Qi et al. [24] show that any function that maps an unordered set into a regular vector (or an image) can be approximated by a neural network as follows. The individual members of the set are first processed separately by *identical* neural networks with tied weights, yielding a vector (or an image) of features for each of them. The features are then *pooled* by a symmetric operation, by evaluating either the mean or maximum value of each feature across the members. That is, if the i'th output feature for the k'th member in the set is denoted as x_i^k, then a max-pooling operation returns the features $x_i^{\text{pooled}} = \max_k x_i^k$. The individual members are then forgotten, and the pooled features are processed by further neural network layers in the regular fashion. The key idea is that through end-to-end training, the per-member network will learn to output features for which the pooling is meaningful; intuitively, the pooling acts as a "vote" over the joint consensus on the global features. The remaining layers then extract the desired output from this consensus. Note that the symmetry of the pooling makes this scheme perfectly permutation invariant, and indifferent to the cardinality of the input set.

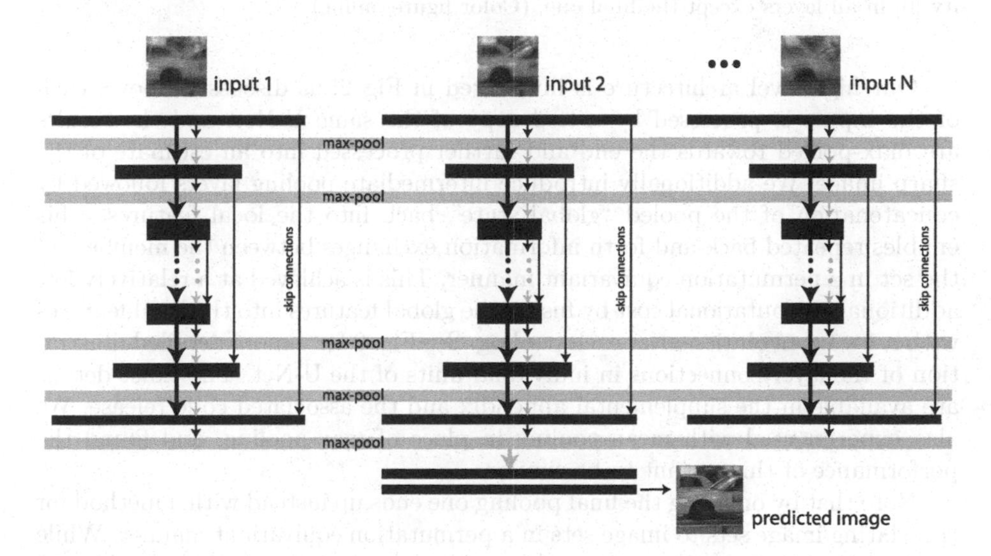

Fig. 2. Overview of our network architecture. Each input frame is processed by a copy of the same U-Net [25] with tied weights, but information is repeatedly exchanged between the copies. This is achieved by computing the maximum value of each activation between all the tracks, and concatenating these "global features" back into the per-frame local features. After the encoder-decoder cycle, the tracks are collapsed by a final max-pooling and processed into a joint estimate of the clean image. Observe that permuting the ordering of the inputs cannot change the output, and that their number can be arbitrary. See Fig. 3 for a detailed view of the layers.

In our context, this scheme gives the individual frames in the burst a principled mechanism for contributing their local findings about the likely content of the sharp image. We apply it on a U-Net-style architecture [25], which is a proven general-purpose model for transforming images [14]. The U-Net is a hourglass-shaped network consisting of an "encoder" that sequentially reduces the image to a low resolution, and a "decoder" that expands it back into a full image. Skip connections are used between correspondingly sized layers in the encoder and decoder to aid reconstruction of details at different scales.

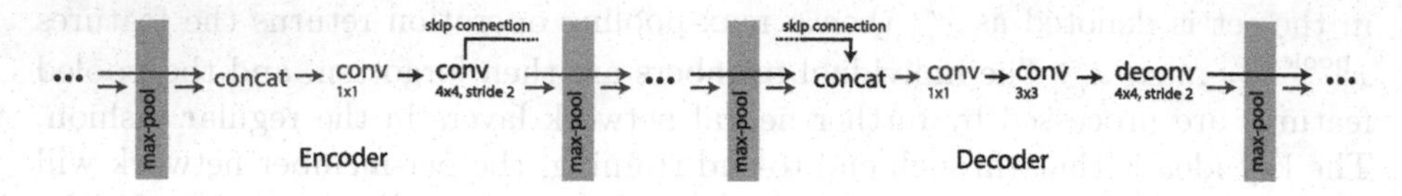

Fig. 3. A zoomed-in view of a single encoder downsampling unit (left) and a corresponding decoder upsampling unit (right) for a U-Net in Fig. 2, connected by a skip connection. The green-colored nodes indicate the layers we introduce. The max-pool layers transmit information to and from other tracks; notice that without them the architecture reduces to a regular U-Net. We use the exponential linear unit nonlinearity [6] in all layers except the final one. (Color figure online)

Our high-level architecture is illustrated in Fig. 2: as discussed above, each of the inputs is processed by a tied copy of the same U-Net, and the results are max-pooled towards the end and further processed into an estimate of the sharp image. We additionally introduce intermediate pooling layers followed by concatenation of the pooled "global state" back into the local features. This enables repeated back-and-forth information exchanges between the members of the set in a permutation equivariant manner. This is achieved at a relatively low additional computational cost by fusing the global features into the local features with a 1×1 convolution after each pooling. See Fig. 3 for a more detailed illustration of the layer connections in individual units of the U-Net. The exact details are available in the supplemental appendix and the associated code release. We also experimented with mean-pooling in place of max-pooling, and found the performance of this variant to be similar.

Note that by omitting the final pooling one ends up instead with a method for translating image sets to image sets in a permutation equivariant manner. While we don't make use of this variant, it may have applicability to other problems.

3.2 Training Data

We train our method with bursts of synthetically degraded crops of photographs from the Imagenet [26] dataset. The degradations are generated on the fly in TensorFlow [1]. Severity and intra-burst variation of the effects is randomized, so as to encourage the network to robustly take advantage of different cues. We also consider noise with inter-pixel correlations, unknown gamma correction, and streaks caused by blurring of overexposed image regions.

We generate training pairs of resolution 160×160, where the input is a degraded burst, and the target is a corresponding clean image. The length of the burst is randomized between 1 and 8 for each minibatch. Figure 4 shows examples of individual kernels and noises, as well as full degraded bursts from our pipeline. We give an overview of each component below.

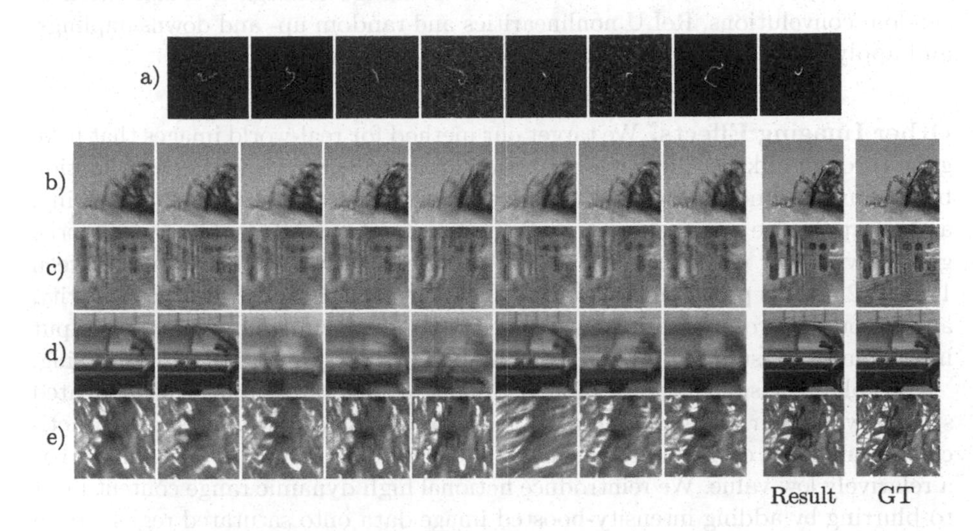

Fig. 4. (a): Blur kernels and noises generated by our synthetic training data generation pipeline. Notice that many of the kernels span several dozen pixels. (b)–(e): Synthetically degraded bursts from a held-out validation set, along with our network's prediction and the ground truth target. Notice the varying difficulty of the bursts, and the streaks from our dynamic range expansion scheme on the saturated skylight (e).

Kernel Generation. We simulate camera shake by convolving the clean photographs with random kernels. Each kernel is generated as a random walk of 128 steps by first drawing 2D acceleration vectors from unit normal distribution, and integrating them into velocities and positions by a pair of (damped) cumulative sums, taking care to choose the initial velocity from the stationary distribution.

We then center each kernel at the origin to avoid random misalignment between the frames and the training target, and standardize them to a unit variance. We apply a random scale to the entire burst's kernels, and then scale individual kernels in the burst randomly. The individual variations are randomized so that some bursts have uniformly sized kernels and others are mixtures of small and large ones. To encourage modest defocus deblurring, we perturb the points with small random offsets. Finally, the random walk positions are accumulated into bitmaps of size 51×51 by an additive scattering operation, yielding the desired convolution kernels.

Noise Generation. Various factors introduce pixel correlations in imaging noise and give it a characteristic "chunky" appearance: Bayer interpolation, camera software's internal denoising, smearing between pixels as they are aligned, compression, and so on. We simulate these effects with a heuristic noise-generation pipeline that mimics the visual appearance of typical camera noise. To this end, we feed an i.i.d. Gaussian noise image through a combination of random convolutions, ReLU nonlinearities and random up- and downsamplings, and apply it in random proportions additively and multiplicatively.

Other Imaging Effects. We target our method for real-world images that have gone through unknown gamma correction and color processing. Because motion blur occurs in linear space, we linearize the synthetic images prior to blurring, and re-apply the gamma correction afterwards. As we do not know the true gamma value for each Imagenet image, we simply pick a random value between 1.5 and 2.5. This procedure introduces the correct kind of post-blur nonlinearity, and encourages robustness against a variety of unknown nonlinearities the input image may have suffered. At test time, we perform no gamma-related processing.

Visible light sources and bright highlight regions often appear as elongated streaks when blurred (see e.g. Fig. 10c). This effect is not reproduced in synthetically blurred low dynamic range images, as their pixel intensities are saturated at a relatively low value. We reintroduce fictional high dynamic range content prior to blurring by adding intensity-boosted image data onto saturated regions from other images in the same minibatch. After blurring, we clip the image values again. The effect is often surprisingly convincing (see Fig. 4e).

3.3 Technical Details

We use the loss function $L(a, b) = \frac{1}{10}||a - b||_1 + ||\nabla a - \nabla b||_1$, where ∇ computes the (unnormalized) horizontal and vertical direction finite differences. This weighting assigns extra importance on reconstructing image edges.

We use weight normalization [27] and the associated data-dependent initialization scheme on all layers to stabilize the training.

The method is implemented in TensorFlow [1]. We train the model using the Adam [16] optimization algorithm with a learning rate of 0.003 and per-iteration decay of 0.999997. We train for 400 000 iterations with minibatch size of 8 split across two NVIDIA GTX 1080 Ti GPU's. This takes roughly 55 h.

For large images, we apply the network in overlapping sliding windows, with smooth blending across the overlap. The downscaling cycle of the U-Net gives the network a moderately wide receptive field. The method naturally handles inputs for which the kernel slowly varies across the image.

The runtime depends roughly linearly on both the number of input images as well as their pixel count. For a 12-megapixel 8-frame burst, the evaluation takes 1.5 m on a single GPU. The model has approximately 40M parameters.

The burst frames are pre-aligned with homographies using dense correspondences with the ECC algorithm [9]. This takes around 18 seconds per 12-megapixel frame. Pixel-perfect alignment does not appear to be critical; a small amount of parallax can be seen in many of our evaluation datasets.

4 Results

Figures 1 and 5 illustrate a selection of results from our method for a variety of challenging bursts shot under low light conditions with a shaky hand. The bursts were shot with the back camera of an iPhone SE. We use the raw format to bypass the (for us) counterproductive denoising of the camera software. We believe that this dataset is significantly more challenging than the existing ones in literature. The photographs are in their original resolution, which means that the shake kernels are relatively large and the noise has not been averaged down. We avoided including significantly lucky images, which might lead to overly optimistic results.

Overall, our method recovers significantly sharper images than any of those in the input burst. The results are largely free of high-frequency noise, and do not exhibit systematic artifacts besides blurriness in ambiguous regions for low frame counts. The method often extracts information that is collectively preserved by the full burst, but arguably not recoverable from any of the individual frames – see for example the text highlighted in Fig. 1, or try to count the number of cars on the sidewalk in Fig. 5 (top).

4.1 Comparisons and Experiments

Burst Deblurring. We compare our method to the state of the art neural burst deblurring method of Wieschollek et al. [33] in Figs. 1, 6 and 7. In Fig. 6 we use result images provided by the authors, and elsewhere we used their publicly available software implementation. Please refer to the supplemental material for further results on their and other methods [7,29,34,38].

Figure 6 shows comparison results on the dataset of Delbracio et al. [7], which contains various real-world bursts shot with different cameras (we also include their results). While all of the methods provide good results on this dataset, our method consistently reveals more detail, while producing fewer artifacts and exhibiting lower levels of noise. Many of these bursts contain lucky sharp frames and only modest blur and noise. In the more challenging dataset we captured, the method of Wieschollek et al. [33] does not reach a comparable quality, as shown in Fig. 1.

Figure 7 shows a result on the dataset of Köhler et al. [17], which contains a mixture of sharp and extremely blurry frames. Our method successfully picks up the lucky frame in the sequence, while the recurrent architecture of Wieschollek et al. [33] fails to properly integrate it into its running estimate. This behavior is confirmed by numerical comparisons to the ground thuth; see the supplemental appendix document for these results and further numerical experiments.

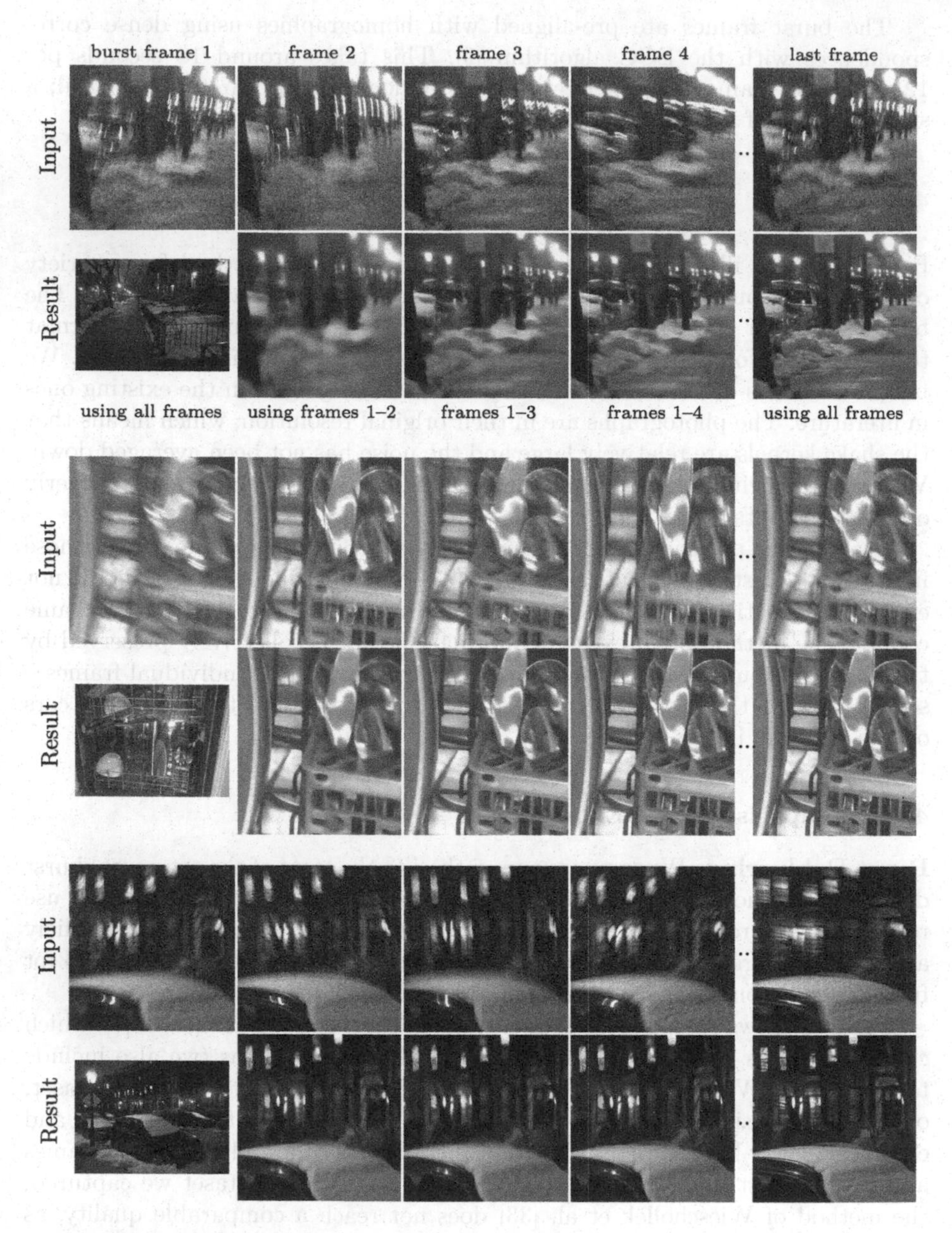

Fig. 5. A selection of results for challenging bursts from a mobile phone camera in full resolution. The full lengths of these bursts are 12, 5 and 10 frames, respectively. We show the first four and the last input, as well as the full-resolution output for the entire burst, and crops of intermediate and full burst outputs. Please refer to the supplemental material for full-size images, as well as results from recurrent neural model of Wieschollek et al. [33] on these images.

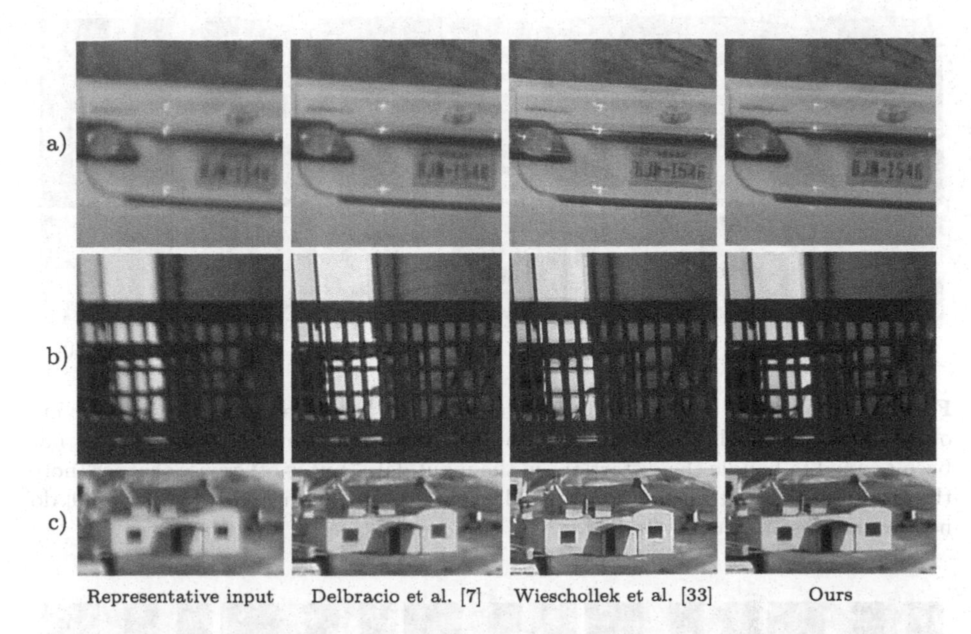

Fig. 6. Representative results on the dataset of Delbracio et al. [7], for methods of Delbracio et al. [7] (FBA), Wieschollek et al. [33] (RDN), and our method. Overall, our result is sharper and suffers from fewer artifacts such as oversharpening. Notice in particular the clean detail resolved in the license plate, the properly removed streaks in specular highlights on the car paint, and the artifact-free grid on the balcony railing. For (c), the ground truth is available: SSIM values achieved are 0.9456, 0.8764 and 0.9578 for FBA, RDN and our method, respectively.

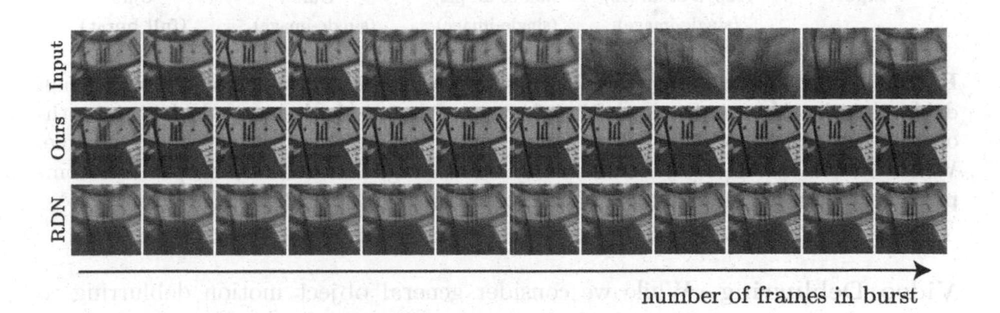

Fig. 7. When interpreted as a burst (and aligned by homographies), the standard deconvolution benchmark dataset of Köhler et al. [17] contains a "lucky" sharp frame in the third position. Our method successfully picks it up, and produces a consistently sharp estimate once it gets included in the burst. The poor-quality frames towards the end are also successfully ignored. In contrast, the RDN method of Wieschollek et al. [33] fails to take the lucky frame into account, and focuses on gradually improving the initial estimate. This suggests that a recurrent architecture struggles to give a uniform consideration to all frames it is presented with.

Fig. 8. Our method applied on flow-aligned five-frame video segments with moving objects from Su et al. [30]. Our result shows artifacts on the car hood, as it has not been trained to handle the distortions in the input data, but is otherwise sharper (note the tires and the text on the signs). Applied to our data from Fig. 1, Su et al. [30] do not reach the same quality (right).

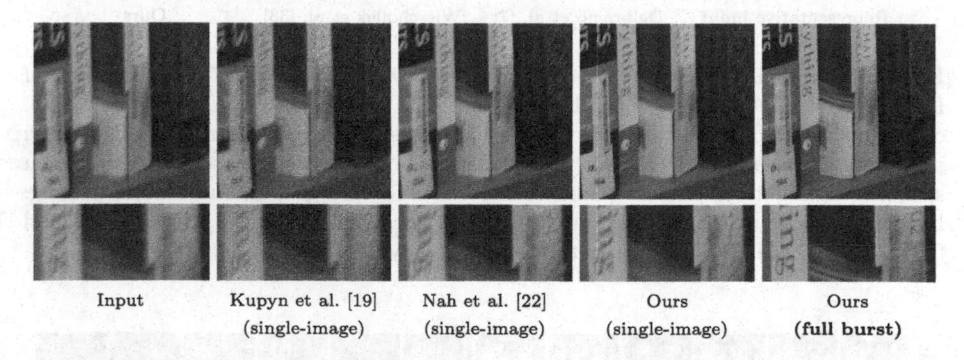

Fig. 9. Using our method on the full burst produces a significantly better result than deblurring the sharpest frame (left) with state of the art single-image deblurring methods [19,22]. This is to be expected, as the burst contains more information as a whole. When trained exclusively for single-image deblurring, our method also provides comparable or better single-image performance when the input suffers from heavy noise.

Video Deblurring. While we consider general object motion deblurring to be out of our scope, our method is in principle compatible with the flow-based frame registration scheme of Deep Video Deblurring method of Su et al. [30], as demonstrated in Fig. 8. The input is a sequence of five frames where moving objects have been deformed by optical flow to match the center frame (i.e. the third). Our network is not trained to handle the deformation artifacts, and fails to clean them up, but aside from this our result is sharper. Conversely, when applied to a five-frame sequence from Fig. 1 (centered around the sharpest frame), the result from Su et al. [30] is noisier and blurrier than ours.

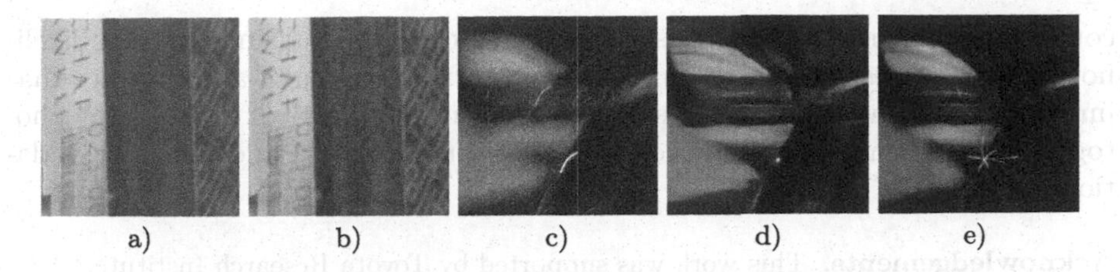

Fig. 10. Impact of noise and dynamic range expansion during training. (a) Our result for dataset of Fig. 1 when trained with our full noise model. (b) When trained with a simple non-correlated noise model, the method still exhibits state of the art burst deblurring performance, but leaves in more mid-frequency noise. (c) Representative frame from an extremely degraded burst. (d) Result from our full model. (e) Trained with a simple noise model and no dynamic range expansion, the method underestimates the intensity of noisy dark regions, and fails to concentrate the streaks into a point.

Single-Image Blind Deconvolution. To verify that considering the entire burst using our method provides a benefit over simply deblurring the sharpest individual frame, we tested state of the art blind single-image deconvolution methods [19,22] on our data. Figure 9 shows that considering the entire burst with our method results in a significantly better image. As a curiosity, we also tried training our method on solely single-image "bursts"; we reach a comparable or better performance than these dedicated single-image methods on our noisy data, but fall somewhat short in less noisy ones.

Significance of Noise and Dynamic Range in Training Data. While we have emphasized the importance of noise modeling, the main benefit of our method is still derived from the permutation invariant architecture. To test this, we trained our method with a naive noise model, simply adding independent normally distributed noise of standard deviation 0.02 on every training input. Figure 10 shows the result: while the output is much noisier, it is still state of the art in terms of detail resolved. Also shown is the effect of omitting the dynamic range expansion scheme.

5 Conclusions

We have presented a method for restoring sharp and noise-free images from bursts of photographs suffering from severe hand tremor and noise. The method reveals accurate image detail and produces pleasing image quality in challenging but realistic datasets that state of the art methods struggle with.

We attribute the success of our method largely to the network architecture that facilitates uniform order-independent handling of the input data, and hope that these ideas will find more widespread use with neural networks. A wide array of interesting problems have the character of fusing together evidence that is scattered in a loosely structured set of observations; one need only think of countless problems that are classically approached by stacking together likelihood terms corresponding to measurement data. Our results also indicate that image restoration methods targeting low-end imaging devices or low-light photography can benefit from considering more complex noise and image degradation models.

Acknowledgements. This work was supported by Toyota Research Institute.

References

1. Abadi, M., et al.: TensorFlow: large-scale machine learning on heterogeneous systems (2015). https://www.tensorflow.org/
2. Babacan, S.D., Molina, R., Do, M.N., Katsaggelos, A.K.: Bayesian Blind deconvolution with general sparse image priors. In: Fitzgibbon, A., Lazebnik, S., Perona, P., Sato, Y., Schmid, C. (eds.) ECCV 2012. LNCS, vol. 7577, pp. 341–355. Springer, Heidelberg (2012). https://doi.org/10.1007/978-3-642-33783-3_25
3. Cai, J.F., Ji, H., Liu, C., Shen, Z.: Blind motion deblurring using multiple images. J. Comput. Phys. **228**(14), 5057–5071 (2009)
4. Chakrabarti, A.: A neural approach to blind motion deblurring. In: Leibe, B., Matas, J., Sebe, N., Welling, M. (eds.) ECCV 2016. LNCS, vol. 9907, pp. 221–235. Springer, Cham (2016). https://doi.org/10.1007/978-3-319-46487-9_14
5. Chen, H., Gu, J., Gallo, O., Liu, M., Veeraraghavan, A., Kautz, J.: Reblur2deblur: deblurring videos via self-supervised learning. In: 2018 IEEE International Conference on Computational Photography, ICCP 2018, Pittsburgh, PA, USA, 4–6 May 2018, pp. 1–9. IEEE Computer Society (2018)
6. Clevert, D., Unterthiner, T., Hochreiter, S.: Fast and accurate deep network learning by exponential linear units (ELUs). In: ICLR (2016)
7. Delbracio, M., Sapiro, G.: Removing camera shake via weighted fourier burst accumulation. IEEE Trans. Image Process. **24**(11), 3293–3307 (2015)
8. Edwards, H., Storkey, A.J.: Towards a neural statistician. In: ICLR (2017)
9. Evangelidis, G.D., Psarakis, E.Z.: Parametric image alignment using enhanced correlation coefficient maximization. IEEE Trans. Pattern Anal. Mach. Intell. **30**(10), 1858–1865 (2008)
10. Fergus, R., Singh, B., Hertzmann, A., Roweis, S.T., Freeman, W.T.: Removing camera shake from a single photograph. ACM Trans. Graph. **25**(3), 787–794 (2006)
11. Godard, C., Matzen, K., Uyttendaele, M.: Deep burst denoising. CoRR abs/1712.05790 (2017)
12. Hasinoff, S.W., et al.: Burst photography for high dynamic range and low-light imaging on mobile cameras. ACM Trans. Graph. **35**(6), 192:1–192:12 (2016). (Proceedings of SIGGRAPH Asia)
13. Herzig, R., Raboh, M., Chechik, G., Berant, J., Globerson, A.: Mapping images to scene graphs with permutation-invariant structured prediction. CoRR abs/1802.05451 (2018)
14. Isola, P., Zhu, J.Y., Zhou, T., Efros, A.A.: Image-to-image translation with conditional adversarial networks. In: CVPR (2017)
15. Kim, T.H., Lee, K.M., Schölkopf, B., Hirsch, M.: Online video deblurring via dynamic temporal blending network. In: Proceedings IEEE International Conference on Computer Vision (ICCV), pp. 4038–4047. IEEE, Piscataway, October 2017
16. Kingma, D.P., Ba, J.: Adam: a method for stochastic optimization. In: ICLR (2015)

17. Köhler, R., Hirsch, M., Mohler, B., Schölkopf, B., Harmeling, S.: Recording and playback of camera shake: benchmarking blind deconvolution with a real-world database. In: Fitzgibbon, A., Lazebnik, S., Perona, P., Sato, Y., Schmid, C. (eds.) ECCV 2012. LNCS, vol. 7578, pp. 27–40. Springer, Heidelberg (2012). https://doi.org/10.1007/978-3-642-33786-4_3
18. Korshunova, I., Degrave, J., Huszár, F., Gal, Y., Gretton, A., Dambre, J.: A Generative Deep Recurrent Model for Exchangeable Data. ArXiv e-prints, February 2018
19. Kupyn, O., Budzan, V., Mykhailych, M., Mishkin, D., Matas, J.: DeblurGAN: blind motion deblurring using conditional adversarial networks. In: CVPR (2018)
20. Levin, A., Weiss, Y., Durand, F., Freeman, W.T.: Understanding blind deconvolution algorithms. IEEE Trans. Pattern Anal. Mach. Intell. **33**(12), 2354–2367 (2011)
21. Mildenhall, B., Barron, J.T., Chen, J., Sharlet, D., Ng, R., Carroll, R.: Burst denoising with kernel prediction networks. In: CVPR (2018)
22. Nah, S., Kim, T.H., Lee, K.M.: Deep multi-scale convolutional neural network for dynamic scene deblurring. In: The IEEE Conference on Computer Vision and Pattern Recognition (CVPR), July 2017
23. Noroozi, M., Chandramouli, P., Favaro, P.: Motion deblurring in the wild. In: Roth, V., Vetter, T. (eds.) GCPR 2017. LNCS, vol. 10496, pp. 65–77. Springer, Cham (2017). https://doi.org/10.1007/978-3-319-66709-6_6
24. Qi, C.R., Su, H., Mo, K., Guibas, L.J.: PointNet: deep learning on point sets for 3D classification and segmentation. In: 2017 IEEE Conference on Computer Vision and Pattern Recognition, CVPR 2017, Honolulu, HI, USA, 21–26 July 2017, pp. 77–85. IEEE Computer Society (2017)
25. Ronneberger, O., Fischer, P., Brox, T.: U-Net: convolutional networks for biomedical image segmentation. In: Navab, N., Hornegger, J., Wells, W.M., Frangi, A.F. (eds.) MICCAI 2015. LNCS, vol. 9351, pp. 234–241. Springer, Cham (2015). https://doi.org/10.1007/978-3-319-24574-4_28
26. Russakovsky, O., et al.: ImageNet large scale visual recognition challenge. Int. J. Comput. Vis. (IJCV) **115**(3), 211–252 (2015)
27. Salimans, T., Kingma, D.P.: Weight normalization: a simple reparameterization to accelerate training of deep neural networks. In: NIPS (2016)
28. Schuler, C.J., Hirsch, M., Harmeling, S., Schölkopf, B.: Learning to deblur. IEEE Trans. Pattern Anal. Mach. Intell. **38**(7), 1439–1451 (2016)
29. Sroubek, F., Milanfar, P.: Robust multichannel blind deconvolution via fast alternating minimization. IEEE Trans. Image Process. **21**(4), 1687–1700 (2012)
30. Su, S., Delbracio, M., Wang, J., Sapiro, G., Heidrich, W., Wang, O.: Deep video deblurring for hand-held cameras. In: Proceedings of the IEEE Conference on Computer Vision and Pattern Recognition, pp. 1279–1288 (2017)
31. Sun, J., Cao, W., Xu, Z., Ponce, J.: Learning a convolutional neural network for non-uniform motion blur removal. In: 2015 IEEE Conference on Computer Vision and Pattern Recognition (CVPR), pp. 769–777 (2015)
32. Wang, R., Tao, D.: Recent progress in image deblurring. CoRR abs/1409.6838 (2014)
33. Wieschollek, P., Hirsch, M., Schölkopf, B., Lensch, H.: Learning blind motion deblurring. In: IEEE International Conference on Computer Vision (ICCV 2017), pp. 231–240 (2017)

34. Wieschollek, P., Schölkopf, B., Lensch, H.P.A., Hirsch, M.: End-to-end learning for image burst deblurring. In: Lai, S.-H., Lepetit, V., Nishino, K., Sato, Y. (eds.) ACCV 2016. LNCS, vol. 10114, pp. 35–51. Springer, Cham (2017). https://doi.org/10.1007/978-3-319-54190-7_3
35. Xu, X., Pan, J., Zhang, Y.J., Wu, Y.: Motion blur kernel estimation via deep learning. IEEE Trans. Image Process. **27**, 194–205 (2017)
36. Zaheer, M., Kottur, S., Ravanbakhsh, S., Póczos, B., Salakhutdinov, R.R., Smola, A.J.: Deep sets. In: Guyon, I., von Luxburg, U., Bengio, S., Wallach, H.M., Fergus, R., Vishwanathan, S.V.N., Garnett, R. (eds.) Advances in Neural Information Processing Systems 30: Annual Conference on Neural Information Processing Systems 2017, pp. 3394–3404 (2017)
37. Zhang, H., Carin, L.: Multi-shot imaging: joint alignment, deblurring, and resolution-enhancement. In: 2014 IEEE Conference on Computer Vision and Pattern Recognition, pp. 2925–2932, June 2014
38. Zhang, H., Wipf, D., Zhang, Y.: Multi-observation blind deconvolution with an adaptive sparse prior. IEEE Trans. Pattern Anal. Mach. Intell. **36**(8), 1628–1643 (2014)
39. Zhang, H., Yang, J.: Intra-frame deblurring by leveraging inter-frame camera motion. In: 2015 IEEE Conference on Computer Vision and Pattern Recognition (CVPR), pp. 4036–4044, June 2015

Stereo and Reconstruction

PlaneMatch: Patch Coplanarity Prediction for Robust RGB-D Reconstruction

Yifei Shi[1,2], Kai Xu[1,2(✉)], Matthias Nießner[3], Szymon Rusinkiewicz[1], and Thomas Funkhouser[1,4]

[1] Princeton University, Princeton, USA
kevin.kai.xu@gmail.com
[2] National University of Defense Technology, Changsha, China
[3] Technical University of Munich, Munich, Germany
[4] Google, Mountain View, USA

Abstract. We introduce a novel RGB-D patch descriptor designed for detecting coplanar surfaces in SLAM reconstruction. The core of our method is a deep convolutional neural network that takes in RGB, depth, and normal information of a planar patch in an image and outputs a descriptor that can be used to find coplanar patches from other images. We train the network on 10 million triplets of coplanar and non-coplanar patches, and evaluate on a new coplanarity benchmark created from commodity RGB-D scans. Experiments show that our learned descriptor outperforms alternatives extended for this new task by a significant margin. In addition, we demonstrate the benefits of coplanarity matching in a robust RGBD reconstruction formulation. We find that coplanarity constraints detected with our method are sufficient to get reconstruction results comparable to state-of-the-art frameworks on most scenes, but outperform other methods on established benchmarks when combined with traditional keypoint matching.

Keywords: RGB-D registration · Co-planarity · Loop closure

1 Introduction

With the recent proliferation of inexpensive RGB-D sensors, it is now becoming practical for people to scan 3D models of large indoor environments with hand-held cameras, enabling applications in cultural heritage, real estate, virtual reality, and many other fields. Most state-of-the-art RGB-D reconstruction algorithms either perform frame-to-model alignment [1] or match keypoints for global pose estimation [2]. Despite the recent progress in these algorithms, registration

Electronic supplementary material The online version of this chapter (https://doi.org/10.1007/978-3-030-01237-3_46) contains supplementary material, which is available to authorized users.

V. Ferrari et al. (Eds.): ECCV 2018, LNCS 11212, pp. 767–784, 2018.
https://doi.org/10.1007/978-3-030-01237-3_46

of hand-held RGB-D scans remains challenging when local surface features are not discriminating and/or when scanning loops have little or no overlaps.

An alternative is to detect planar features and associate them across frames with coplanarity, parallelism, and perpendicularity constraints [3–9]. Recent work has shown compelling evidence that planar patches can be detected and tracked robustly, especially in indoor environments where flat surfaces are ubiquitous. In cases where traditional features such as keypoints are missing (e.g., wall), there seems tremendous potential to support existing 3D reconstruction pipelines.

Even though coplanarity matching is a promising direction, current approaches lack strong per-plane feature descriptors for establishing putative matches between disparate observations. As a consequence, coplanarity priors have only been used in the context of frame-to-frame tracking [3] or in post-process steps for refining a global optimization [4]. We see this as analogous to the relationship between ICP and keypoint matching: just as ICP only converges with a good initial guess for pose, current methods for exploiting coplanarity are unable to initialize a reconstruction process from scratch due to the lack of discriminative coplanarity features.

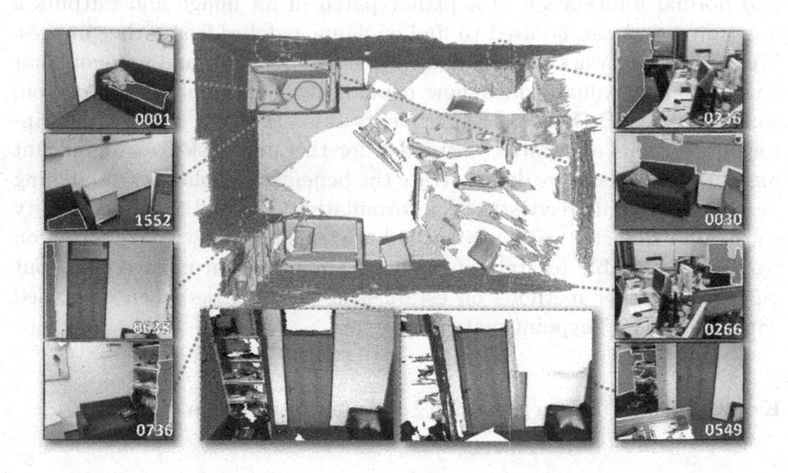

Fig. 1. Scene reconstruction based on coplanarity matching of patches across different views (numbers indicate frame ID) for both overlapping (left two pairs) and non-overlapping (right two pairs) patch pairs. The two pairs to the right are long-range, without overlapping. The bottom shows a zoomed-in comparison between our method (left) and key-point matching based method [2] (right).

This paper aims to enable global, *ab initio* coplanarity matching by introducing a discriminative feature descriptor for planar patches of RGB-D images. Our descriptor is learned from data to produce features whose L2 difference is predictive of *whether or not two RGB-D patches from different frames are coplanar.*

It can be used to detect pairs of coplanar patches in RGB-D scans *without an initial alignment*, which can be used to find loop closures or to provide coplanarity constraints for global alignment (see Fig. 1).

A key novel aspect of this approach is that it focuses on detection of coplanarity rather than overlap. As a result, our plane patch features can be used to discover long-range alignment constraints (like "loop closures") between distant, non-overlapping parts of the same large surface (e.g., by recognizing carpets on floors, tiles on ceilings, paneling on walls, etc.). In Fig. 1, the two patch pairs shown to the right helped produce a reconstruction with globally flat walls.

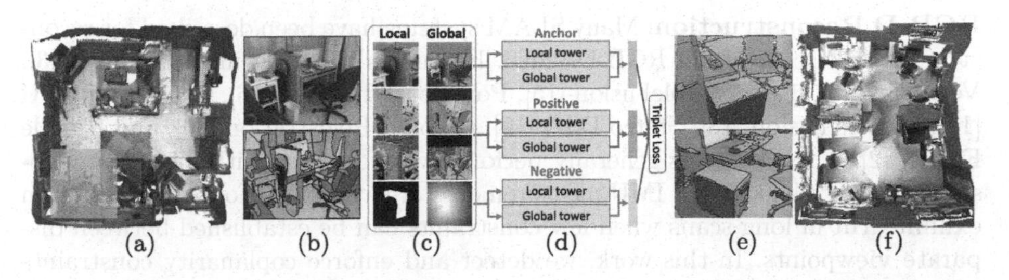

Fig. 2. An overview of our method. We train an embedding network (c–d) to predict coplanarity for a pair of planar patches across different views, based on the co-planar patches (b) sampled from training sequences with ground-truth camera poses (a). Given a test sequence, our robust optimization performs reconstruction (f) based on predicted co-planar patches (e).

To learn our planar patch descriptor, we design a deep network that takes in color, depth, normals, and multi-scale context for pairs of planar patches extracted from RGB-D images, and predicts whether they are coplanar or not. The network is trained in a self-supervised fashion where training examples are automatically extracted from coplanar and noncoplanar patches from ScanNet [10].

In order to evaluate our descriptor, we introduce a new coplanarity matching datasets, where we can see in series of thorough experiments that our new descriptor outperforms existing baseline alternatives by significant margins. Furthermore, we demonstrate that by using our new descriptor, we are able to compute strong coplanarity constraints that improve the performance of current global RGB-D registration algorithms. In particular, we show that by combining coplanarity and point-based correspondences reconstruction algorithms are able to handle difficult cases, such as scenes with a low number of features or limited loop closures. We outperform other state-of-the-art algorithms on the standard TUM RGB-D reconstruction benchmark [11]. Overall, the research contributions of this paper are:

– A new task: predicting coplanarity of image patches for the purpose of RGB-D image registration.

- A self-supervised process for training a deep network to produce features for predicting whether two image patches are coplanar or not.
- An extension of the robust optimization algorithm [12] to solve camera poses with coplanarity constraints.
- A new training and test benchmark for coplanarity prediction.
- Reconstruction results demonstrating that coplanarity can be used to align scans where keypoint-based methods fail to find loop closures.

2 Related Work

RGB-D Reconstruction: Many SLAM systems have been described for reconstructing 3D scenes from RGB-D video. Examples include KinectFusion [1,13], VoxelHashing [14], ScalableFusion [15], Point-based Fusion [16], Octrees on CPU [17], Elastic Fusion [18], Stereo DSO [19], Colored Registration [20], and Bundle Fusion [2]. These systems generally perform well for scans with many loop closures and/or when robust IMU measurements are available. However, they often exhibit drift in long scans when few constraints can be established between disparate viewpoints. In this work, we detect and enforce coplanarity constraints between planar patches to address this issue as an alternative feature channel for global matching.

Feature Descriptors: Traditionally, SLAM systems have utlized *keypoint* detectors and descriptors to establish correspondence constraints for camera pose estimation. Example keypoint descriptors include SIFT [21], SURF [22], ORB [23], etc. More recently, researchers have learned keypoint descriptors from data – e.g., MatchNet [24], Lift [25], SE3-Nets [26], 3DMatch [27], Schmidt et al. [28]. These methods rely upon repeatable extraction of keypoint positions, which is difficult for widely disparate views. In contrast, we explore the more robust method of extracting planar patches without concern for precisely positioning the patch center.

Planar Features: Many previous papers have leveraged planar surfaces for RGB-D reconstruction. The most common approach is to detect planes in RGB-D scans, establish correspondences between matching features, and solve for the camera poses that align the corresponding features [29–36]. More recent approaches build models comprising planar patches, possibly with geometric constraints [4,37], and match planar features found in scans to planar patches in the models [4–8]. The search for correspondences is often aided by hand-tuned descriptors designed to detect overlapping surface regions. In contrast, our approach finds correspondences between *coplanar patches* (that may not be overlapping); we learn descriptors for this task with a deep network.

Global Optimization: For large-scale surface reconstruction, it is common to use off-line or asynchronously executed global registration procedures. A common formulation is to compute a pose graph with edges representing pairwise transformations between frames and then optimize an objective function penalizing deviations from these pairwise alignments [38–40]. Recent methods [12,41] use indicator variables to identify loop closures or matching points during global optimization using a least-squares formulation. We extend this formulation by setting indicator variables for individual coplanarity constraints.

3 Method

Our method consists of two components: (1) a deep neural network trained to generate a descriptor that can be used to discover coplanar pairs of RGB-D patches without an initial registration, and (2) a global SLAM reconstruction algorithm that takes special advantage of detected pairs of coplanar patches.

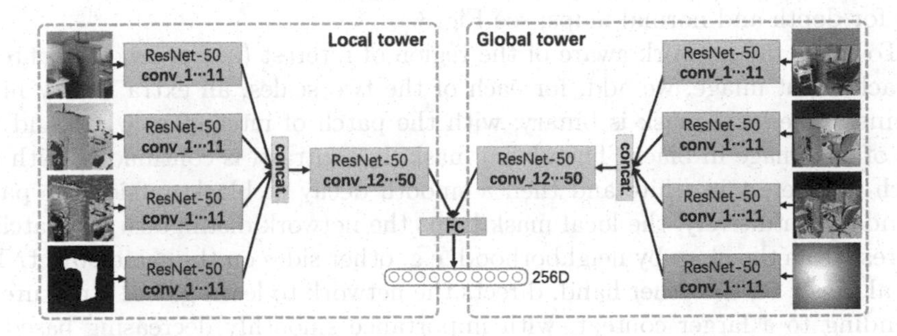

Fig. 3. Network architecture of the local and global towers. Layers shaded in the same color share weights. (Color figure online)

3.1 Coplanarity Network

Coplanarity of two planar patches is by definition geometrically measurable. However, for two patches that are observed from different, yet unknown views, whether they are coplanar is not determinable based on geometry alone. Furthermore, it is not clear that coplanarity can be deduced solely from the local appearance of the imaged objects. We argue that the prediction of coplanarity across different views is a structural, or even semantic, visual reasoning task, for which neither geometry nor local appearance alone is reliable.

Humans infer coplanarity by perceiving and understanding the structure and semantics of objects and scenes, and contextual information plays a critical role in this reasoning task. For example, humans are able to differentiate different facets of an object, from virtually *any* view, by reasoning about the structure of the facets and/or by relating them to surrounding objects. Both involve inference with a context around the patches being considered, possibly at multiple scales. This motivates us to learn to predict cross-view coplanarity from appearance and geometry, using *multi-scale contextual information*. We approach this task by learning an embedding network that maps coplanar patches from different views nearby in feature space.

Network Design: Our coplanarity network (Figs. 2 and 3) is trained with triplets of planar patches, each involving an anchor, a coplanar patch (positive) and a noncoplanar patch (negative), similar to [42]. Each patch of a triplet is fed into a convolutional network based on ResNet-50 [43] for feature extraction, and a triplet loss is estimated based on the relative proximities of the three features. To learn coplanarity from both appearance and geometry, our network takes multiple channels as input: an RGB image, depth image, and normal map.

We encode the contextual information of a patch at two scales, local and global. This is achieved by cropping the input images (in all channels) to rectangles of 1.5 and 5 times the size of the patch's bounding box, respectively. All cropped images are clamped at image boundaries, padded to a square, and then resized to 224×224. The padding uses 50% gray for RGB images and a value of 0 for depth and normal maps; see Fig. 3.

To make the network aware of the region of interest (as opposed to context) in each input image, we add, for each of the two scales, an extra binary mask channel. The local mask is binary, with the patch of interest in white and the rest of the image in black. The global mask, in contrast, is continuous, with the patch of interest in white and then a smooth decay to black outside the patch boundary. Intuitively, the local mask helps the network distinguish the patch of interest from the close-by neighborhood, e.g. other sides on the same object. The global mask, on the other hand, directs the network to learn global structure by attending to a larger context, with importance smoothly decreasing based on distance to the patch region. Meanwhile, it also weakens the effect of specific patch shape, which is unimportant when considering global structure.

In summary, each scale consists of RGB, depth, normal, and mask channels. These inputs are first encoded independently. Their feature maps are concatenated after the 11-th convolutional layer, and then pass through the remaining 39 layers. The local and global scales share weights for the corresponding channels, and their outputs are finally combined with a fully connected layer (Fig. 3).

Network Training: The training data for our network are generated from datasets of RGB-D scans of 3D indoor scenes, with high-quality camera poses provided with the datasets. For each RGB-D frame, we segment it into planar patches using agglomerative clustering on the depth channel. For each planar patch, we also estimate its normal based on the depth information. The extracted patches are projected to image space to generate all the necessary channels of input to our network. Very small patches, whose local mask image contains less than 300 pixels with valid depths, are discarded.

Triplet Focal Loss: When preparing triplets to train our network, we encounter the well-known problem of a severely imbalanced number of negative and positive patch pairs. Given a training sequence, there are many more negative pairs, and most of them are too trivial to help the network learn efficiently. Using randomly sampled triplets would overwhelm the training loss by the easy negatives.

We opt to resolve the imbalance issue by dynamically and discriminatively scaling the losses for hard and easy triplets, inspired by the recent work of focal loss for object detection [44]. Specifically, we propose the *triplet focal loss*:

$$L_{\text{focal}}(x_a, x_p, x_n) = \max\left(0, \frac{\alpha - \Delta d_{\text{f}}}{\alpha}\right)^{\lambda}, \tag{1}$$

where x_a, x_p and x_n are the feature maps extracted for anchor, positive, and negative patches, respectively; $\Delta d_{\text{f}} = d_{\text{f}}(x_n, x_a) - d_{\text{f}}(x_p, x_a)$, with d_{f} being the L2 distance between two patch features. Minimizing this loss encourages the anchor to be closer to the positive patch than to the negative in descriptor space, but with less weight for larger distances.

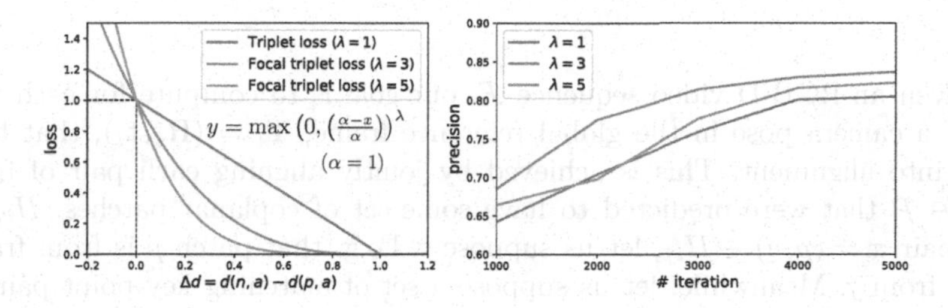

Fig. 4. Visualization and comparison (prediction accuracy over #iter.) of different triplet loss functions.

See Fig. 4, left, for a visualization of the loss function with $\alpha = 1$. When $\lambda = 1$, this loss becomes the usual margined loss, which gives non-negligible loss to easy examples near the margin α. When $\lambda > 1$, however, we obtain a focal loss that down-weights easy-to-learn triplets while keeping high loss for hard ones. Moreover, it smoothly adjusts the rate at which easy triplets are down-weighted. We found $\lambda = 3$ to achieve the best training efficiency (Fig. 4, right). Figure 5 shows a t-SNE visualization of coplanarity-based patch features.

3.2 Coplanarity-Based Robust Registration

To investigate the utility of this planar patch descriptor and coplanarity detection approach for 3D reconstruction, we have developed a global registration algorithm that estimates camera poses for an RGB-D video using pairwise constraints derived from coplanar patch matches in addition to keypoint matches.

Our formulation is inspired by the work of Choi et al. [12], where the key feature is the robust penalty term used for automatically selecting the correct matches from a large pool of hypotheses, thus avoiding iterative rematching as in ICP. Note that this formulation does not require an initial alignment of camera poses, which would be required for other SLAM systems that leverage coplanarity constraints.

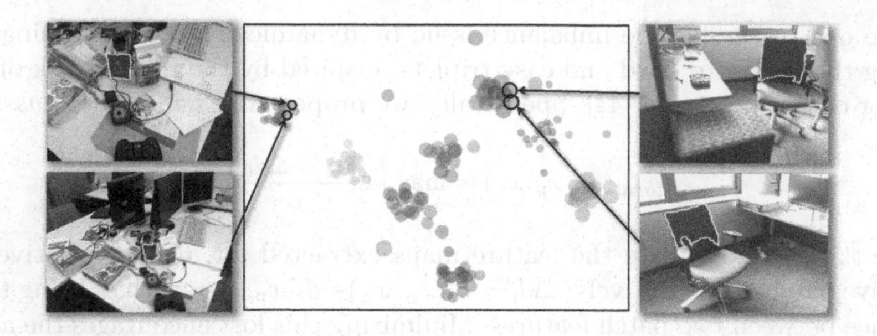

Fig. 5. t-SNE visualization of coplanarity-based features of planar patches from different views. Ground-truth coplanarity (measured by mutual RMS point-to-plane distance) is encoded by color and physical size of patches by dot size. (Color figure online)

Given an RGB-D video sequence $\mathcal{F}$, our goal is to compute for each frame $i \in \mathcal{F}$ a camera pose in the global reference frame, $\mathbf{T}_i = (\mathbf{R}_i, \mathbf{t}_i)$, that brings them into alignment. This is achieved by jointly aligning each pair of frames $(i, j) \in \mathcal{P}$ that were predicted to have some set of coplanar patches, Π_{ij}. For each pair $\pi = (p, q) \in \Pi_{ij}$, let us suppose w.l.o.g. that patch p is from frame i and q from j. Meanwhile, let us suppose a set of matching key-point pairs Θ_{ij} is detected and matched between frame i and j. Similarly, we assume for each point pair $\theta = (\mathbf{u}, \mathbf{v}) \in \Theta_{ij}$ that key-point $\mathbf{u}$ is from frame i and $\mathbf{v}$ from j.

Objective Function: The objective of our coplanarity-based registration contains four terms, responsible for coplanar alignment, coplanar patch pair selection, key-point alignment, and key-point pair selection:

$$E(T, s) = E_{\text{data-cop}}(T, s) + E_{\text{reg-cop}}(s) + E_{\text{data-kp}}(T, s) + E_{\text{reg-kp}}(s). \quad (2)$$

Given a pair of coplanar patches predicted by the network, the *coplanarity data term* enforces the coplanarity, via minimizing the point-to-plane distance from sample points on one patch to the plane defined by the other patch:

$$E_{\text{data-cop}}(T, s) = \sum_{(i,j)\in\mathcal{P}} \sum_{\pi\in\Pi_{ij}} w_\pi \, s_\pi \, \delta^2(\mathbf{T}_i, \mathbf{T}_j, \pi), \quad (3)$$

where δ is the *coplanarity distance* of a patch pair $\pi = (p, q)$. It is computed as the root-mean-square point-to-plane distance over both sets of sample points:

$$\delta^2 = \frac{1}{|\mathcal{V}_p|} \sum_{\mathbf{v}_p\in\mathcal{V}_p} d^2(\mathbf{T}_i\mathbf{v}_p, \phi_q^G) + \frac{1}{|\mathcal{V}_q|} \sum_{\mathbf{v}_q\in\mathcal{V}_q} d^2(\mathbf{T}_j\mathbf{v}_q, \phi_p^G),$$

where $\mathcal{V}_p$ is the set of sample points on patch p and d is point-to-plane distance:

$$d(\mathbf{T}_i\mathbf{v}_p, \phi_q^G) = (\mathbf{R}_i\mathbf{v}_p + \mathbf{t}_i - \mathbf{p}_q) \cdot \mathbf{n}_q.$$

$\phi_q^G = (\mathbf{p}_q, \mathbf{n}_q)$ is the plane defined by patch q, which is estimated in the *global* reference frame using the corresponding transformation $\mathbf{T}_j$, and is updated in every iteration. s_π is a control variable (in $[0, 1]$) for the selection of patch pair π, with 1 standing for selected and 0 for discarded. w_π is a weight that measures the confidence of pair π's being coplanar. This weight is another connection between the optimization and the network, besides the predicted patch pairs themselves. It is computed based on the feature distance of two patches, denoted by $d_{\text{f}}(p, q)$, extracted by the network: $w_{(p,q)} = e^{-d_{\text{f}}^2(p,q)/(\sigma^2 d_{\text{fm}}^2)}$, where d_{fm} is the maximum feature distance and $\sigma = 0.6$.

The *coplanarity regularization term* is defined as:

$$E_{\text{reg-cop}}(s) = \sum_{(i,j)\in\mathcal{P}} \sum_{\pi\in\Pi_{ij}} \mu\, w_\pi\, \Psi(s_\pi), \tag{4}$$

where the penalty function is defined as $\Psi(s) = (\sqrt{s} - 1)^2$. Intuitively, minimizing this term together with the data term encourages the selection of pairs incurring a small value for the data term, while immediately pruning those pairs whose data term value is too large and deemed to be hard to minimize. w_π is defined the same as before, and μ is a weighting variable that controls the emphasis on pair selection.

The *key-point data term* is defined as:

$$E_{\text{data-kp}}(T, s) = \sum_{(i,j)\in\mathcal{P}} \sum_{\theta\in\Theta_{ij}} s_\theta \left\|\mathbf{T}_i\mathbf{u} - \mathbf{T}_j\mathbf{v}\right\|, \tag{5}$$

Similar to coplanarity, a control variable s_θ is used to determine the selection of point pair θ, subjecting to the *key-point regularization term*:

$$E_{\text{reg-kp}}(s) = \sum_{(i,j)\in\mathcal{P}} \sum_{\theta\in\Theta_{ij}} \mu\, \Psi(s_\theta), \tag{6}$$

where μ shares the same weighting variable with Eq. (4).

Optimization: The optimization of Eq. (2) is conducted iteratively, where each iteration interleaves the optimization of transformations T and selection variables s. Ideally, the optimization could take every pair of frames in a sequence as an input for global optimization. However, this is prohibitively expensive since for each frame pair the system scales with the number of patch pairs and key-point pairs. To alleviate this problem, we split the sequence into a list of overlapping fragments, optimize frame poses within each fragment, and then perform a final global registration of the fragments, as in [12].

For each fragment, the optimization takes all frame pairs within that fragment and registers them into a rigid point cloud. After that, we take the matching pairs that have been selected by the intra-fragment optimization, and solve the inter-fragment registration based on those pairs. Inter-fragment registration benefits more from long-range coplanarity predictions.

The putative matches found in this manner are then pruned further with a rapid and approximate RANSAC algorithm applied for each pair of fragments. Given a pair of fragments, we randomly select a set of three matching feature pairs, which could be either planar-patch or key-point pairs. We compute the transformation aligning the selected triplet, and then estimate the "support" for the transformation by counting the number of putative match pairs that are aligned by the transformation. For patch pairs, alignment error is measures by the root-mean-square closest distance between sample points on the two patches. For key-point pairs, we simply use the Euclidean distance. Both use the same threshold of 1cm. If a transformation is found to be sufficiently supported by the matching pairs (more than 25% consensus), we include all the supporting pairs into the global optimization. Otherwise, we simply discard all putative matches.

Once a set of pairwise constraints have been established in this manner, the frame transformations and pair selection variables are alternately optimized with an iterative process using Ceres [45] for the minimization of the objective function at each iteration. The iterative optimization converges when the relative value change of each unknown is less than 1×10^{-6}. At a convergence, the weighting variable μ, which was initialized to 1m in the beginning, is decreased by half and the above iterative optimization continues. The whole process is repeated until μ is lower than 0.01 m, which usually takes less than 50 iterations. The supplementary material provides a study of the optimization behavior, including convergence and robustness to incorrect pairs.

4 Results and Evaluations

4.1 Training Set, Parameters, and Timings

Our training data is generated from the ScanNet [10] dataset, which contains 1513 scanned sequences of indoor scenes, reconstructed by BundleFusion [2]. We adopt the training/testing split provided with ScanNet and the training set (1045 scenes) are used to generate our training triplets. Each training scene contributes $10K$ triplets. About $10M$ triplets in total are generated from all training scenes. For evaluating our network, we build a *coplanarity benchmark* using 100 scenes from the testing set. For hierarchical optimization, the fragment size is 21, with a 5-frame overlap between adjacent fragments. The network training takes about 20 h to converge. For a sequence of $1K$ frames with 62 fragments and 30 patches per frame, the running time is 10 min for coplanarity prediction (0.1 s per patch pair) and 20 min for optimization (5 min for intra-fragment and 15 min for inter-fragment).

4.2 Coplanarity Benchmark

We create a benchmark **COP** for evaluating RGB-D-based coplanarity matching of planar patches. The benchmark dataset contains $12K$ patch pairs with ground-truth coplanarity, which are organized according to the physical size/area of patches (COP-S) and the centroid distance between pairs of patches (COP-D). COP-S contains $6K$ patch pairs which are split uniformly into three subsets with *decreasing* average patch size, where the patch pairs are sampled at random distances. COP-D comprises three subsets (each containing $2K$ pairs) with *increasing* average pair distance but uniformly distributed patch size. For all subsets, the numbers of positive and negative pairs are equal. Details of the benchmark are provided in the supplementary material.

4.3 Network Evaluation

Our network is the first, to our knowledge, that is trained for coplanarity prediction. Therefore, we perform comparison against baselines and ablation studies. See visual results of coplanarity matching in the supplementary material.

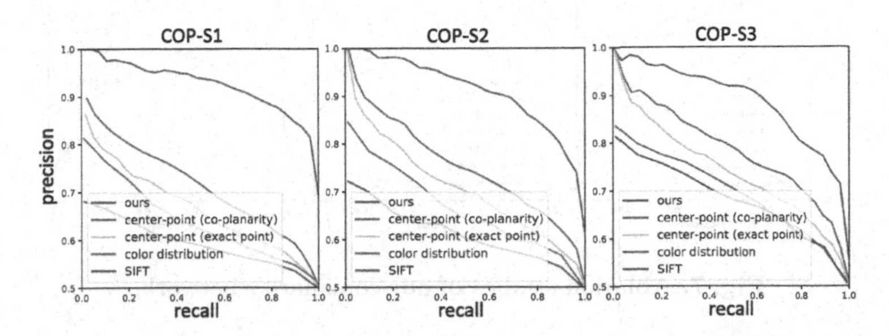

Fig. 6. Comparing to baselines including center-point matching networks trained with coplanarity and exact point matching, respectively, SIFT-based point matching and color distribution based patch matching.

Comparing to Baseline Methods: We first compare to two hand-crafted descriptors, namely the color histogram within the patch region and the SIFT feature at the patch centroid. For the task of key-point matching, a commonly practiced method (e.g., in [46]) is to train a neural network that takes image patches centered around the key-points as input. We extend this network to the task of coplanarity prediction, as a non-trivial baseline. For a fair comparison, we train a triplet network with ResNet-50 with only one tower per patch taking three channels (RGB, depth, and normal) as input. For each channel, the image is cropped around the patch centroid, with the same padding and resizing scheme as before. Thus, no mask is needed since the target is always at the image center. We train two networks with different triplets for the task of (1) exact center point matching and (2) coplanarity patch matching, respectively.

The comparison is conducted over COP-S and the results of precision-recall are plotted in Fig. 6. The hand-crafted descriptors fail on all tests, which shows the difficulty of our benchmark datasets. Compared to the two alternative center-point-based networks (point matching and coplanarity matching), our method performs significantly better, especially on larger patches.

Ablation Studies: To investigate the need for the various input channels, we compare our full method against that with the RGB, depth, normal, or mask input disabled, over the COP benchmark. To evaluate the effect of multi-scale context, our method is also compared to that without local or global channels. The PR plots in Fig. 7 show that our full method works the best for all tests.

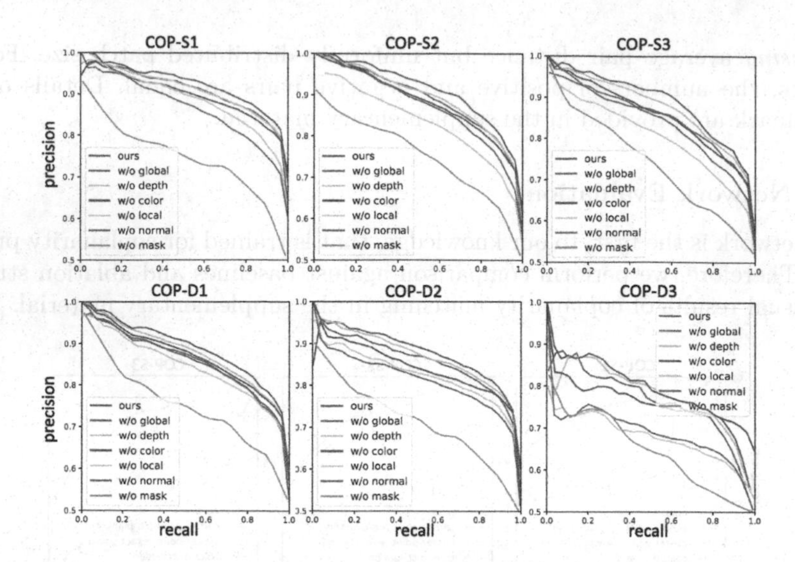

Fig. 7. Ablation studies of our coplanarity network.

From the experiments, several interesting phenomena can be observed. First, the order of overall importance of the different channels is: mask > normal > RGB > depth. This clearly shows that coplanarity prediction across different views can neither rely on appearance or geometry alone. The important role of masking in concentrating the network's attention is quite evident. We provide a further comparison to justify our specific masking scheme in the supplementary material. Second, the global scale is more effective for bigger patches and more distant pairs, for which the larger scale is required to encode more context. The opposite goes for the local scale due the higher resolution of its input channels. This verifies the complementary effect of the local and global channels in capturing contextual information at different scales.

4.4 Reconstruction Evaluation

Quantitative Results: We perform a quantitative evaluation of reconstruction using the TUM RGB-D dataset by [11], for which ground-truth camera trajectories are available. Reconstruction error is measured by the absolute trajectory error (ATE), i.e., the root-mean-square error (RMSE) of camera positions along a trajectory. We compare our method with six state-of-the-art reconstruction methods, including RGB-D SLAM [47], VoxelHashing [14], ElasticFusion [18], Redwood [12], BundleFusion [2], and Fine-to-Coarse [4]. Note that unlike the other methods, Redwood does not use color information. Fine-to-Coarse is the most closely related to our method, since it uses planar surfaces for structurally-constrained registration. This method, however, relies on a good initialization of camera trajectory to bootstrap, while our method does not. Our method uses SIFT features for key-point detection and matching. We also implement an enhanced version of our method where the key-point matchings are pre-filtered by BundleFusion (named 'BundleFusion+Ours').

As an ablation study, we implement five baseline variants of our method. (1) 'Coplanarity' is our optimization with only coplanarity constraints. Without key-point matching constraint, our optimization can sometimes be under-determined and needs reformulation to achieve robust registration when not all degrees of freedom (DoFs) can be fixed by coplanarity. The details on the formulation can be found in the supplementary material. (2) 'Keypoint' is our optimization with only SIFT key-point matching constraints. (3) 'No D. in RANSAC' stands for our method where we did not use our learned patch descriptor during the voting in frame-to-frame RANSAC. In this case, any two patch pairs could cast a vote if they are geometrically aligned by the candidate transformation. (4) 'No D. in Opt' means that the optimization objective for coplanarity is not weighted by the matching confidence predicted by our network (w_π in Eqs. (3) and (4)). (5) 'No D. in Both' is a combination of (3) and (4).

Table 1. Comparison of ATE RMSE (in cm) with alternative and baseline methods on TUM sequences [11]. Colors indicate the best and second best results.

Method	fr1/desk	fr2/xyz	fr3/office	fr3/nst
RGB-D SLAM	2.3	0.8	3.2	1.7
VoxelHashing	2.3	2.2	2.3	8.7
Elastic Fusion	2.0	1.1	1.7	1.6
Redwood	2.7	9.1	3.0	192.9
Fine-to-Coarse	5.0	3.0	3.9	3.0
BundleFusion	1.6	1.1	2.2	1.2
Ours	1.4	1.1	1.6	1.5
BundleFuison+Ours	1.3	0.8	1.5	0.9

(a) Comparison to alternatives.

Method	fr1/desk	fr2/xyz	fr3/office	fr3/nst
No D. in RANSAC	9.6	4.8	12.6	2.3
No D. in Opt.	4.8	2.7	2.5	1.9
No D. in Both	18.9	8.3	16.4	2.4
Key-point Only	5.6	4.4	5.2	2.6
Coplanarity Only	2.5	2.1	3.7	–
Ours	1.4	1.1	1.7	1.5

(b) Comparison to baselines.

Table 1 reports the ATE RMSE comparison. Our method achieves state-of-the-art results for the first three TUM sequences (the fourth is a flat wall). This is achieved by exploiting our long-range coplanarity matching for robust large-scale loop closure, while utilizing key-point based matching to pin down the possible free DoFs which are not determinable by coplanarity. When being combined with BundleFusion key-points, our method achieves the best results over all sequences. Therefore, our method complements the current state-of-the-art methods by providing a means to handle limited frame-to-frame overlap.

The ablation study demonstrates the importance of our learned patch descriptor in our optimization – i.e., our method performs better than all variants that do not include it. It also shows that coplanarity constraints alone are superior to keypoints only for all sequences except the flat wall (fr3/nst). Using coplanar and keypoint matches together provides the best method overall.

Qualitative Results: Figure 8 shows visual comparisons of reconstruction on sequences from ScanNet [10] and new ones scanned by ourselves. We compare reconstruction results of our method with a state-of-the-art key-point based method (BundleFusion) and a planar-structure-based method (Fine-to-Coarse). The low frame overlap makes the key-point based loop-closure detection fail in BundleFusion. Lost tracking of successive frames provides a poor initial alignment for Fine-to-Coarse, causing it to fail. In contrast, our method can successfully detect non-overlapping loop closures through coplanar patch pairs and achieve good quality reconstructions for these examples without an initial registration. More visual results are shown in the supplementary material.

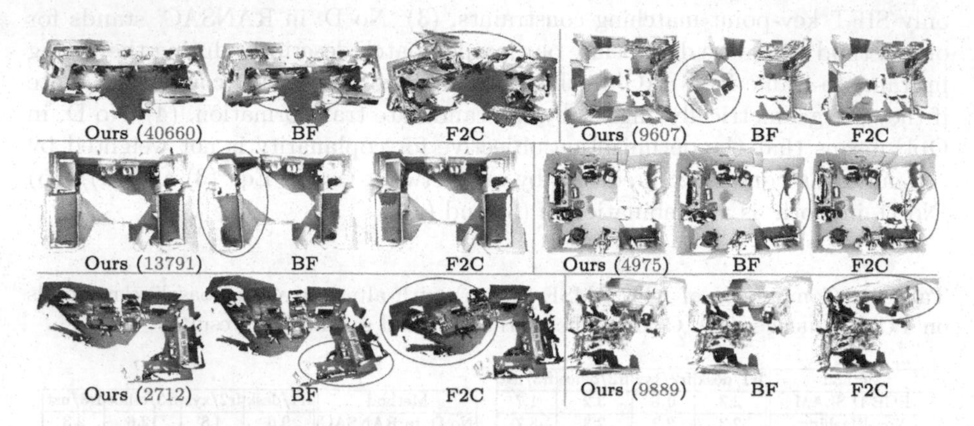

Fig. 8. Visual comparison of reconstructions by our method, BundleFusion (BF) [2], and Fine-to-Coarse (F2C) [4], on six sequences. Red ellipses indicate parts with misalignment. For our results, we give the number of long-range coplanar pairs selected by the optimization. (Color figure online)

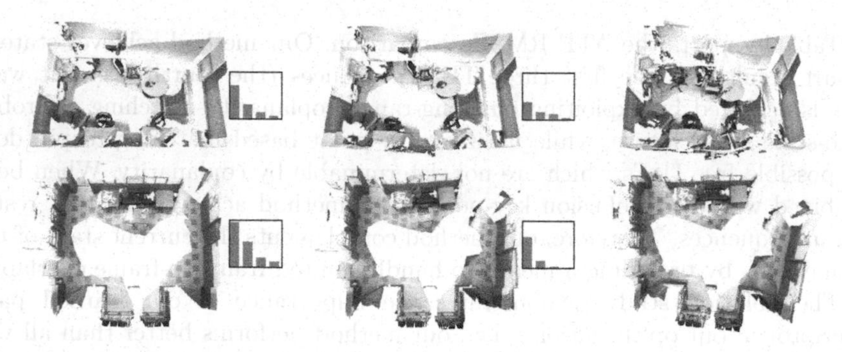

Fig. 9. Reconstruction results with 100% (left column), 50% (middle) and 0% (right) of long-range coplanar pairs detected, respectively. The histograms of long-range coplanar patch pairs (count over patch distance (1–5 m)) are given.

Effect of Long-Range Coplanarity. To evaluate the effect of long-range coplanarity matching on reconstruction quality, we show in Fig. 9 the reconstruction results computed with all, half, and none of the long-range coplanar pairs predicted by our network. We also show a histogram of coplanar pairs survived the optimization. From the visual reconstruction results, the benefit of long-range coplanar pairs is apparent. In particular, the larger scene (bottom) benefits more from long-range coplanarity than the smaller one (top). In Fig. 8, we also give the number of non-overlapping coplanar pairs after optimization, showing that long-range coplanarity did help in all examples.

5 Conclusion

We have proposed a new planar patch descriptor designed for finding coplanar patches without a priori global alignment. At its heart, the method uses a deep network to map planar patch inputs with RGB, depth, and normals to a descriptor space where proximity can be used to predict coplanarity. We expect that deep patch coplanarity prediction provides a useful complement to existing features for SLAM applications, especially in scans with large planar surfaces and little inter-frame overlap.

Acknowledgement. We are grateful to Min Liu, Zhan Shi, Lintao Zheng, and Maciej Halber for their help on data preprocessing. We also thank Yizhong Zhang for the early discussions. This work was supported in part by the NSF (VEC 1539014/ 1539099, IIS 1421435, CHS 1617236), NSFC (61532003, 61572507, 61622212), Google, Intel, Pixar, Amazon, and Facebook. Yifei Shi was supported by the China Scholarship Council.

References

1. Izadi, S., et al.: KinectFusion: real-time 3D reconstruction and interaction using a moving depth camera. In: Proceedings of UIST, pp. 559–568 (2011)
2. Dai, A., Nießner, M., Zollhöfer, M., Izadi, S., Theobalt, C.: BundleFusion: real-time globally consistent 3D reconstruction using on-the-fly surface reintegration. ACM Trans. on Graph. **36**(3), 24 (2017)
3. Zhang, Y., Xu, W., Tong, Y., Zhou, K.: Online structure analysis for real-time indoor scene reconstruction. ACM Trans. Graph. (TOG) **34**(5), 159 (2015)
4. Halber, M., Funkhouser, T.: Fine-to-coarse global registration of RGB-D scans. arXiv preprint arXiv:1607.08539 (2016)
5. Lee, J.K., Yea, J.W., Park, M.G., Yoon, K.J.: Joint layout estimation and global multi-view registration for indoor reconstruction. arXiv preprint arXiv:1704.07632 (2017)
6. Ma, L., Kerl, C., Stückler, J., Cremers, D.: CPA-SLAM: Consistent plane-model alignment for direct RGB-D SLAM. In: 2016 IEEE International Conference on Robotics and Automation (ICRA), pp. 1285–1291. IEEE (2016)
7. Trevor, A.J., Rogers, J.G., Christensen, H.I.: Planar surface slam with 3D and 2D sensors. In: 2012 IEEE International Conference on Robotics and Automation (ICRA), pp. 3041–3048. IEEE (2012)

8. Zhang, E., Cohen, M.F., Curless, B.: Emptying, refurnishing, and relighting indoor spaces. ACM Trans. Graph. (TOG) **35**(6), 174 (2016)
9. Huang, J., Dai, A., Guibas, L., Nießner, M.: 3Dlite: towards commodity 3D scanning for content creation. ACM Trans. Graph. (TOG) (2017)
10. Dai, A., Chang, A.X., Savva, M., Halber, M., Funkhouser, T., Nießner, M.: ScanNet: richly-annotated 3D reconstructions of indoor scenes. In: CVPR (2017)
11. Sturm, J., Engelhard, N., Endres, F., Burgard, W., Cremers, D.: A benchmark for the evaluation of RGB-D SLAM systems. In: Proceedings of IROS, October 2012
12. Choi, S., Zhou, Q.Y., Koltun, V.: Robust reconstruction of indoor scenes. In: Proceedings of the IEEE Conference on Computer Vision and Pattern Recognition, pp. 5556–5565 (2015)
13. Newcombe, R.A., et al.: KinectFusion: real-time dense surface mapping and tracking. In: Proceedings of ISMAR, pp. 127–136 (2011)
14. Nießner, M., Zollhöfer, M., Izadi, S., Stamminger, M.: Real-time 3D reconstruction at scale using voxel hashing. ACM TOG (2013)
15. Chen, J., Bautembach, D., Izadi, S.: Scalable real-time volumetric surface reconstruction. ACM TOG **32**(4), 113 (2013)
16. Keller, M., Lefloch, D., Lambers, M., Izadi, S., Weyrich, T., Kolb, A.: Real-time 3D reconstruction in dynamic scenes using point-based fusion. In: Proceedings of 3DV, pp. 1–8. IEEE (2013)
17. Steinbruecker, F., Sturm, J., Cremers, D.: Volumetric 3D mapping in real-time on a CPU. In: 2014 IEEE International Conference on Robotics and Automation (ICRA), Hongkong, China (2014)
18. Whelan, T., Leutenegger, S., Salas-Moreno, R.F., Glocker, B., Davison, A.J.: ElasticFusion: dense SLAM without a pose graph. In: Proceedings of RSS, Rome, Italy, July 2015
19. Wang, R., Schwörer, M., Cremers, D.: Stereo DSO: large-scale direct sparse visual odometry with stereo cameras. arXiv preprint arXiv:1708.07878 (2017)
20. Park, J., Zhou, Q.Y., Koltun, V.: Colored point cloud registration revisited. In: Proceedings of the IEEE Conference on Computer Vision and Pattern Recognition, pp. 143–152 (2017)
21. Lowe, D.G.: Object recognition from local scale-invariant features. In: The Proceedings of the Seventh IEEE International Conference on Computer Vision, vol. 2, pp. 1150–1157. IEEE (1999)
22. Bay, H., Tuytelaars, T., Van Gool, L.: SURF: speeded up robust features. In: Leonardis, A., Bischof, H., Pinz, A. (eds.) ECCV 2006. LNCS, vol. 3951, pp. 404–417. Springer, Heidelberg (2006). https://doi.org/10.1007/11744023_32
23. Rublee, E., Rabaud, V., Konolige, K., Bradski, G.: ORB: an efficient alternative to SIFT or SURF. In: 2011 IEEE International Conference on Computer Vision (ICCV), pp. 2564–2571. IEEE (2011)
24. Han, X., Leung, T., Jia, Y., Sukthankar, R., Berg, A.C.: MatchNet: unifying feature and metric learning for patch-based matching. In: Proceedings of the IEEE Conference on Computer Vision and Pattern Recognition, pp. 3279–3286 (2015)
25. Yi, K.M., Trulls, E., Lepetit, V., Fua, P.: LIFT: learned invariant feature transform. In: Leibe, B., Matas, J., Sebe, N., Welling, M. (eds.) ECCV 2016. LNCS, vol. 9910, pp. 467–483. Springer, Cham (2016). https://doi.org/10.1007/978-3-319-46466-4_28
26. Byravan, A., Fox, D.: SE3-Nets: learning rigid body motion using deep neural networks. In: 2017 IEEE International Conference on Robotics and Automation (ICRA), pp. 173–180. IEEE (2017)

27. Zeng, A., Song, S., Niessner, M., Fisher, M., Xiao, J., Funkhouser, T.: 3DMatch: learning local geometric descriptors from RGB-D reconstructions. In: Proceedings of the IEEE Conference on Computer Vision and Pattern Recognition, pp. 1802–1811 (2017)
28. Schmidt, T., Newcombe, R., Fox, D.: Self-supervised visual descriptor learning for dense correspondence. IEEE Robot. Autom. Lett. **2**(2), 420–427 (2017)
29. Concha, A., Civera, J.: DPPTAM: dense piecewise planar tracking and mapping from a monocular sequence. In: 2015 IEEE/RSJ International Conference on Intelligent Robots and Systems (IROS), pp. 5686–5693. IEEE (2015)
30. Dou, M., Guan, L., Frahm, J.-M., Fuchs, H.: Exploring high-level plane primitives for indoor 3D reconstruction with a hand-held RGB-D camera. In: Park, J.-I., Kim, J. (eds.) ACCV 2012. LNCS, vol. 7729, pp. 94–108. Springer, Heidelberg (2013). https://doi.org/10.1007/978-3-642-37484-5_9
31. Hsiao, M., Westman, E., Zhang, G., Kaess, M.: Keyframe-based dense planar slam. In: Proceedings of International Conference on Robotics and Automation (ICRA). IEEE (2017)
32. Pietzsch, T.: Planar features for visual SLAM. In: Dengel, A.R., Berns, K., Breuel, T.M., Bomarius, F., Roth-Berghofer, T.R. (eds.) KI 2008. LNCS (LNAI), vol. 5243, pp. 119–126. Springer, Heidelberg (2008). https://doi.org/10.1007/978-3-540-85845-4_15
33. Proença, P.F., Gao, Y.: Probabilistic combination of noisy points and planes for RGB-D odometry. arXiv preprint arXiv:1705.06516 (2017)
34. Salas-Moreno, R.F., Glocken, B., Kelly, P.H., Davison, A.J.: Dense planar SLAM. In: 2014 IEEE International Symposium on Mixed and Augmented Reality (ISMAR), pp. 157–164. IEEE (2014)
35. Taguchi, Y., Jian, Y.D., Ramalingam, S., Feng, C.: Point-plane slam for hand-held 3D sensors. In: 2013 IEEE International Conference on Robotics and Automation (ICRA), pp. 5182–5189. IEEE (2013)
36. Weingarten, J., Siegwart, R.: 3D SLAM using planar segments. In: 2006 IEEE/RSJ International Conference on Intelligent Robots and Systems, pp. 3062–3067. IEEE (2006)
37. Stuckler, J., Behnke, S.: Orthogonal wall correction for visual motion estimation. In: IEEE International Conference on Robotics and Automation, ICRA 2008, pp. 1–6. IEEE (2008)
38. Grisetti, G., Kummerle, R., Stachniss, C., Burgard, W.: A tutorial on graph-based SLAM. IEEE Intell. Transp. Syst. Mag. **2**(4), 31–43 (2010)
39. Henry, P., Krainin, M., Herbst, E., Ren, X., Fox, D.: RGB-D mapping: using depth cameras for dense 3D modeling of indoor environments. In: The 12th International Symposium on Experimental Robotics ISER. Citeseer (2010)
40. Zhou, Q.Y., Koltun, V.: Dense scene reconstruction with points of interest. ACM Trans. Graph. (TOG) **32**(4), 112 (2013)
41. Zhou, Q.-Y., Park, J., Koltun, V.: Fast global registration. In: Leibe, B., Matas, J., Sebe, N., Welling, M. (eds.) ECCV 2016. LNCS, vol. 9906, pp. 766–782. Springer, Cham (2016). https://doi.org/10.1007/978-3-319-46475-6_47
42. Schroff, F., Kalenichenko, D., Philbin, J.: FaceNet: a unified embedding for face recognition and clustering. In: Proceedings of the IEEE Conference on Computer Vision and Pattern Recognition, pp. 815–823 (2015)
43. He, K., Zhang, X., Ren, S., Sun, J.: Deep residual learning for image recognition. In: Proceedings of the IEEE Conference on Computer Vision and Pattern Recognition, pp. 770–778 (2016)

44. Lin, T.Y., Goyal, P., Girshick, R., He, K., Dollár, P.: Focal loss for dense object detection. arXiv preprint arXiv:1708.02002 (2017)
45. Agarwal, S., Mierle, K.: Ceres solver: Tutorial & reference, vol. 2, p. 72. Google Inc., Mountain View (2012)
46. Chang, A., et al.: Matterport3D: learning from RGB-D data in indoor environments. In: Proceedings of the International Conference on 3D Vision (3DV) (2017)
47. Endres, F., Hess, J., Engelhard, N., Sturm, J., Cremers, D., Burgard, W.: An evaluation of the RGB-D SLAM system. In: 2012 IEEE International Conference on Robotics and Automation (ICRA), pp. 1691–1696. IEEE (2012)

MVSNet: Depth Inference for Unstructured Multi-view Stereo

Yao Yao[1(✉)], Zixin Luo[1], Shiwei Li[1], Tian Fang[2], and Long Quan[1]

[1] The Hong Kong University of Science and Technology, Hong Kong, China
{yyaoag,zluoag,slibc,quan}@cse.ust.hk
[2] Shenzhen Zhuke Innovation Technology (Altizure), Shenzhen, China
fangtian@altizure.com

Abstract. We present an end-to-end deep learning architecture for depth map inference from multi-view images. In the network, we first extract deep visual image features, and then build the 3D cost volume upon the reference camera frustum via the differentiable homography warping. Next, we apply 3D convolutions to regularize and regress the initial depth map, which is then refined with the reference image to generate the final output. Our framework flexibly adapts arbitrary N-view inputs using a variance-based cost metric that maps multiple features into one cost feature. The proposed MVSNet is demonstrated on the large-scale indoor *DTU* dataset. With simple post-processing, our method not only significantly outperforms previous state-of-the-arts, but also is several times faster in runtime. We also evaluate MVSNet on the complex outdoor *Tanks and Temples* dataset, where our method ranks first before April 18, 2018 without any fine-tuning, showing the strong generalization ability of MVSNet.

Keywords: Multi-view stereo · Depth map · Deep learning

1 Introduction

Multi-view stereo (MVS) estimates the dense representation from overlapping images, which is a core problem of computer vision extensively studied for decades. Traditional methods use hand-crafted similarity metrics and engineered regularizations (e.g., normalized cross correlation and semi-global matching [12]) to compute dense correspondences and recover 3D points. While these methods have shown great results under ideal Lambertian scenarios, they suffer from some common limitations. For example, low-textured, specular and reflective regions

---

Yao Yao and Zixin Luo were summer interns, and Shiwei Li was an intern at Everest Innovation Technology (Altizure).

Electronic supplementary material The online version of this chapter (https://doi.org/10.1007/978-3-030-01237-3_47) contains supplementary material, which is available to authorized users.

V. Ferrari et al. (Eds.): ECCV 2018, LNCS 11212, pp. 785–801, 2018.
https://doi.org/10.1007/978-3-030-01237-3_47

of the scene make dense matching intractable and thus lead to incomplete reconstructions. It is reported in recent MVS benchmarks [1,18] that, although current state-of-the-art algorithms [7,8,32,36] perform very well on the *accuracy*, the reconstruction *completeness* still has large room for improvement.

Recent success on convolutional neural networks (CNNs) research has also triggered the interest to improve the stereo reconstruction. Conceptually, the learning-based method can introduce global semantic information such as specular and reflective priors for more robust matching. There are some attempts on the two-view stereo matching, by replacing either hand-crafted similarity metrics [10,11,23,39] or engineered regularizations [17,19,34] with the learned ones. They have shown promising results and gradually surpassed traditional methods in stereo benchmarks [9,25]. In fact, the stereo matching task is perfectly suitable for applying CNN-based methods, as image pairs are rectified in advance and thus the problem becomes the horizontal pixel-wise disparity estimation without bothering with camera parameters.

However, directly extending the learned two-view stereo to multi-view scenarios is non-trivial. Although one can simply pre-rectify all selected image pairs for stereo matching, and then merge all pairwise reconstructions to a global point cloud, this approach fails to fully utilize the multi-view information and leads to less accurate result. Unlike stereo matching, input images to MVS could be of arbitrary camera geometries, which poses a tricky issue to the usage of learning methods. Only few works acknowledge this problem and try to apply CNN to the MVS reconstruction: SurfaceNet [14] constructs the Colored Voxel Cubes (CVC) in advance, which combines all image pixel color and camera information to a single volume as the input of the network. In contrast, the Learned Stereo Machine (LSM) [15] directly leverages the differentiable projection/unprojection to enable the end-to-end training/inference. However, both the two methods exploit the volumetric representation of regular grids. As restricted by the huge memory consumption of 3D volumes, their networks can hardly be scaled up: LSM only handles synthetic objects in low volume resolution, and SurfaceNet applies a heuristic divide-and-conquer strategy and takes a long time for large-scale reconstructions. For the moment, the leading boards of modern MVS benchmarks are still occupied by traditional methods [7,8,32].

To this end, we propose an end-to-end deep learning architecture for depth map inference, which computes one depth map at each time, rather than the whole 3D scene at once. Similar to other depth map based MVS methods [3,8,32,35], the proposed network, MVSNet, takes one reference image and several source images as input, and infers the depth map for the reference image. The key insight here is the differentiable homography warping operation, which implicitly encodes camera geometries in the network to build the 3D cost volumes from 2D image features and enables the end-to-end training. To adapt arbitrary number of source images in the input, we propose a variance-based metric that maps multiple features into one cost feature in the volume. This cost volume then undergoes multi-scale 3D convolutions and regress an initial depth map.

Finally, the depth map is refined with the reference image to improve the accuracy of boundary areas. There are two major differences between our method and previous learned approaches [14,15]. First, for the purpose of depth map inference, our 3D cost volume is built upon the camera frustum instead of the regular Euclidean space. Second, our method decouples the MVS reconstruction to smaller problems of per-view depth map estimation, which makes large-scale reconstruction possible.

We train and evaluate the proposed MVSNet on the large-scale *DTU* dataset [1]. Extensive experiments show that with simple post-processing, MVSNet outperforms all competing methods in terms of completeness and overall quality. Besides, we demonstrate the generalization power of the network on the outdoor *Tanks and Temples* benchmark [18], where MVSNet ranks first (before April. 18, 2018) over all submissions including the open-source MVS methods (e.g., COLMAP [32] and OpenMVS [29]) and commercial software (Pix4D [30]) without any fine-tuning. It is also noteworthy that the runtime of MVSNet is several times or even several orders of magnitude faster than previous state-of-the-arts.

2 Related Work

MVS Reconstruction. According to output representations, MVS methods can be categorized into (1) direct point cloud reconstructions [7,22], (2) volumetric reconstructions [14,15,20,33] and (3) depth map reconstructions [3,8,32,35,38]. Point cloud based methods operate directly on 3D points, usually relying on the propagation strategy to gradually densify the reconstruction [7,22]. As the propagation of point clouds is proceeded sequentially, these methods are difficult to be fully parallelized and usually take a long time in processing. Volumetric based methods divide the 3D space into regular grids and then estimate if each voxel is adhere to the surface. The downsides for this representation are the space discretization error and the high memory consumption. In contrast, depth map is the most flexible representation among all. It decouples the complex MVS problem into relatively small problems of per-view depth map estimation, which focuses on only one reference and a few source images at a time. Also, depth maps can be easily fused to the point cloud [26] or the volumetric reconstructions [28]. According to the recent MVS benchmarks [1,18], current best MVS algorithms [8,32] are both depth map based approaches.

Learned Stereo. Rather than using traditional handcrafted image features and matching metrics [13], recent studies on stereo apply the deep learning technique for better pair-wise patch matching. Han *et al.* [10] first propose a deep network to match two image patches. Zbontar *et al.* [39] and Luo *et al.* [23] use the learned features for stereo matching and semi-global matching (SGM) [12] for post-processing. Beyond the pair-wise matching cost, the learning technique is also applied in cost regularization. SGMNet [34] learns to adjust the parameters used in SGM, while CNN-CRF [19] integrates the conditional random field optimization in the network for the end-to-end stereo learning. The recent state-of-the-art method is GCNet [17], which applies 3D CNN to regularize the cost volume and regress the disparity by the soft argmin operation.

It has been reported in KITTI banchmark [25] that, learning-based stereos, especially those end-to-end learning algorithms [17,19,24], significantly outperform the traditional stereo approaches.

Learned MVS. There are fewer attempts on learned MVS approaches. Hartmann *et al.* propose the learned multi-patch similarity [11] to replace the traditional cost metric for MVS reconstruction. The first learning based pipeline for MVS problem is SurfaceNet [14], which pre-computes the cost volume with sophisticated voxel-wise view selection, and uses 3D CNN to regularize and infer the surface voxels. The most related approach to ours is the LSM [15], where camera parameters are encoded in the network as the projection operation to form the cost volume, and 3D CNN is used to classify if a voxel belongs to the surface. However, due to the common drawback of the volumetric representation, networks of SurfaceNet and LSM are restricted to only small-scale reconstructions. They either apply the divide-and-conquer strategy [14] or is only applicable to synthetic data with low resolution inputs [15]. In contrast, our network focus on producing the depth map for one reference image at each time, which allows us to adaptively reconstruct a large scene directly.

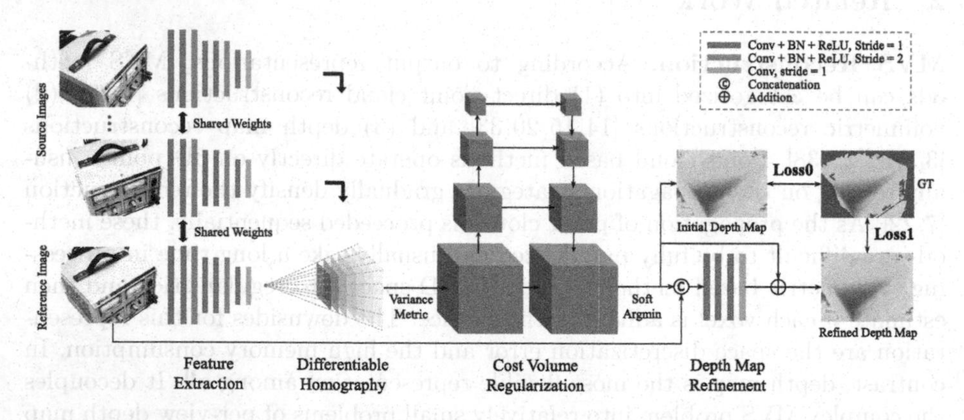

Fig. 1. The network design of MVSNet. Input images will go through the 2D feature extraction network and the differentiable homograph warping to generate the cost volume. The final depth map output is regressed from the regularized probability volume and refined with the reference image

3 MVSNet

This section describes the detailed architecture of the proposed network. The design of MVSNet strongly follows the rules of camera geometry and borrows the insights from previous MVS approaches. In following sections, we will compare each step of our network to the traditional MVS methods, and demonstrate the advantages of our learning-based MVS system. The full architecture of MVSNet is visualized in Fig. 1.

3.1 Image Features

The first step of MVSNet is to extract the deep features $\{\mathbf{F}_i\}_{i=1}^N$ of the N input images $\{\mathbf{I}_i\}_{i=1}^N$ for dense matching. An eight-layer 2D CNN is applied, where the strides of layer 3 and 6 are set to two to divide the feature towers into three scales. Within each scale, two convolutional layers are applied to extract the higher-level image representation. Each convolutional layer is followed by a batch-normalization (BN) layer and a rectified linear unit (ReLU) except for the last layer. Also, similar to common matching tasks, parameters are shared among all feature towers for efficient learning.

The outputs of the 2D network are N 32-channel feature maps downsized by four in each dimension compared with input images. It is noteworthy that though the image frame is downsized after feature extraction, the original neighboring information of each remaining pixel has already been encoded into the 32-channel pixel descriptor, which prevents dense matching from losing useful context information. Compared with simply performing dense matching on original images, the extracted feature maps significantly boost the reconstruction quality (see Sect. 5.3).

3.2 Cost Volume

The next step is to build a 3D cost volume from the extracted feature maps and input cameras. While previous works [14,15] divide the space using regular grids, for our task of depth map inference, we construct the cost volume upon the reference camera frustum. For simplicity, in the following we denote $\mathbf{I}_1$ as the reference image, $\{\mathbf{I}_i\}_{i=2}^N$ the source images, and $\{\mathbf{K}_i, \mathbf{R}_i, \mathbf{t}_i\}_{i=1}^N$ the camera intrinsics, rotations and translations that correspond to the feature maps.

Differentiable Homography. All feature maps are warped into different fronto-parallel planes of the reference camera to form N feature volumes $\{\mathbf{V}_i\}_{i=1}^N$. The coordinate mapping from the warped feature map $\mathbf{V}_i(d)$ to $\mathbf{F}_i$ at depth d is determined by the planar transformation $\mathbf{x}' \sim \mathbf{H}_i(d) \cdot \mathbf{x}$, where '$\sim$' denotes the projective equality and $\mathbf{H}_i(d)$ the homography between the ith feature map and the reference feature map at depth d. Let $\mathbf{n}_1$ be the principle axis of the reference camera, the homography is expressed by a 3×3 matrix:

$$\mathbf{H}_i(d) = \mathbf{K}_i \cdot \mathbf{R}_i \cdot \left(\mathbf{I} - \frac{(\mathbf{t}_1 - \mathbf{t}_i) \cdot \mathbf{n}_1^T}{d}\right) \cdot \mathbf{R}_1^T \cdot \mathbf{K}_1^T. \tag{1}$$

Without loss of generality, the homography for reference feature map $\mathbf{F}_1$ itself is an 3×3 identity matrix. The warping process is similar to that of the classical plane sweeping stereo [5], except that the differentiable bilinear interpolation is used to sample pixels from feature maps $\{\mathbf{F}_i\}_{i=1}^N$ rather than images $\{\mathbf{I}_i\}_{i=1}^N$. As the core step to bridge the 2D feature extraction and the 3D regularization networks, the warping operation is implemented in differentiable manner, which enables end-to-end training of depth map inference.

Cost Metric. Next, we aggregate multiple feature volumes $\{\mathbf{V}_i\}_{i=1}^N$ to one cost volume $\mathbf{C}$. To adapt arbitrary number of input views, we propose a variance-based cost metric $\mathcal{M}$ for N-view similarity measurement. Let W, H, D, F be the input image width, height, depth sample number and the channel number of the feature map, and $V = \frac{W}{4} \cdot \frac{H}{4} \cdot D \cdot F$ the feature volume size, our cost metric defines the mapping $\mathcal{M} : \underbrace{\mathbb{R}^V \times \cdots \times \mathbb{R}^V}_{N} \rightarrow \mathbb{R}^V$ that:

$$\mathbf{C} = \mathcal{M}(\mathbf{V}_1, \cdots, \mathbf{V}_N) = \frac{\sum\limits_{i=1}^{N} (\mathbf{V}_i - \overline{\mathbf{V}_i})^2}{N} \tag{2}$$

where $\overline{\mathbf{V}_i}$ is the average volume among all feature volumes, and all operations above are element-wise.

Most traditional MVS methods aggregate pairwise costs between the reference image and all source images in a heuristic way. Instead, our metric design follows the philosophy that all views should contribute equally to the matching cost and gives no preference to the reference image [11]. We notice that recent work [11] applies the mean operation with multiple CNN layers to infer the multi-patch similarity. Here we choose the 'variance' operation instead because the 'mean' operation itself provides no information about the feature differences, and their network requires pre- and post- CNN layers to help infer the similarity. In contrast, our variance-based cost metric explicitly measures the multi-view feature difference. In later experiments, we will show that such explicit difference measurement improves the validation accuracy.

Cost Volume Regularization. The raw cost volume computed from image features could be noise-contaminated (e.g., due to the existence of non-Lambertian surfaces or object occlusions) and should be incorporated with smoothness constraints to infer the depth map. Our regularization step is designed for refining the above cost volume $\mathbf{C}$ to generate a probability volume $\mathbf{P}$ for depth inference. Inspired by recent learning-based stereo [17] and MVS [14,15] methods, we apply the multi-scale 3D CNN for cost volume regularization. The four-scale network here is similar to a 3D version UNet [31], which uses the encoder-decoder structure to aggregate neighboring information from a large receptive field with relatively low memory and computation cost. To further lessen the computational requirement, we reduce the 32-channel cost volume to 8-channel after the first 3D convolutional layer, and change the convolutions within each scale from 3 layers to 2 layers. The last convolutional layer outputs a 1-channel volume. We finally apply the *softmax* operation along the depth direction for probability normalization.

The resulting probability volume is highly desirable in depth map inference that it can not only be used for per-pixel depth estimation, but also for measuring the estimation confidence. We will show in Sect. 3.3 that one can easily determine the depth reconstruction quality by analyzing its probability distribution, which leads to a very concise yet effective outlier filtering strategy in Sect. 4.2.

3.3 Depth Map

Initial Estimation. The simplest way to retrieve depth map $\mathbf{D}$ from the probability volume $\mathbf{P}$ is the pixel-wise winner-take-all [5] (i.e., *argmax*). However, the *argmax* operation is unable to produce sub-pixel estimation, and cannot be trained with back-propagation due to its indifferentiability. Instead, we compute the *expectation* value along the depth direction, i.e., the probability weighted sum over all hypotheses:

$$\mathbf{D} = \sum_{d=d_{min}}^{d_{max}} d \times \mathbf{P}(d) \tag{3}$$

where $\mathbf{P}(d)$ is the probability estimation for all pixels at depth d. Note that this operation is also referred to as the *soft argmin* operation in [17]. It is fully differentiable and able to approximate the argmax result. While the depth hypotheses are uniformly sampled within range $[d_{min}, d_{max}]$ during cost volume construction, the expectation value here is able to produce a continuous depth estimation. The output depth map (Fig. 2(b)) is of the same size to 2D image feature maps, which is downsized by four in each dimension compared to input images.

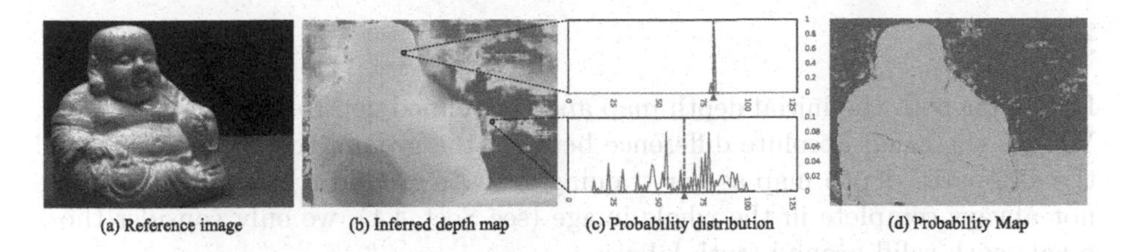

Fig. 2. Illustrations on inferred depth map, probability distributions and probability map. (a) One reference image of *scan* 114, *DTU* dataset [1]; (b) the inferred depth map; (c) the probability distributions of an inlier pixel (top) and an outlier pixel (bottom), where the x-axis is the index of depth hypothesis, y-axis the probability and red lines the soft argmin results; (d) the probability map. As shown in (c), the outlier's distribution is scattered and results in a low probability estimation in (d)

Probability Map. The probability distribution along the depth direction also reflects the depth estimation quality. Although the multi-scale 3D CNN has very strong ability to regularize the probability to the single modal distribution, we notice that for those falsely matched pixels, their probability distributions are scattered and cannot be concentrated to one peak (see Fig. 2(c)). Based on this observation, we define the quality of a depth estimation $\hat{d}$ as the probability that the ground truth depth is within a small range near the estimation. As depth hypotheses are discretely sampled along the camera frustum, we simply take the probability sum over the four nearest depth hypotheses to measure the estimation quality. Notice that other statistical measurements, such as standard deviation or entropy can also be used here, but in our experiments we observe no significant improvement from these measurements for depth map filtering. Moreover, our probability sum formulation leads to a better control of thresholding parameter for outliers filtering.

Depth Map Refinement. While the depth map retrieved from the probability volume is a qualified output, the reconstruction boundaries may suffer from oversmoothing due to the large receptive field involved in the regularization, which is similar to the problems in semantic segmentation [4] and image matting [37]. Notice that the reference image in natural contains boundary information, we thus use the reference image as a guidance to refine the depth map. Inspired by the recent image matting algorithm [37], we apply a depth residual learning network at the end of MVSNet. The initial depth map and the resized reference image are concatenated as a 4-channel input, which is then passed through three 32-channel 2D convolutional layers followed by one 1-channel convolutional layer to learn the depth residual. The initial depth map is then added back to generate the refined depth map. The last layer does not contain the BN layer and the ReLU unit as to learn the negative residual. Also, to prevent being biased at a certain depth scale, we pre-scale the initial depth magnitude to range [0, 1], and convert it back after the refinement.

3.4 Loss

Losses for both the initial depth map and the refined depth map are considered. We use the mean absolute difference between the ground truth depth map and the estimated depth map as our training loss. As ground truth depth maps are not always complete in the whole image (see Sect. 4.1), we only consider those pixels with valid ground truth labels:

$$Loss = \sum_{p \in \mathbf{p}_{valid}} \underbrace{\|d(p) - \hat{d}_i(p)\|_1}_{Loss0} + \lambda \cdot \underbrace{\|d(p) - \hat{d}_r(p)\|_1}_{Loss1} \tag{4}$$

where $\mathbf{p}_{valid}$ denotes the set of valid ground truth pixels, $d(p)$ the ground truth depth value of pixel p, $\hat{d}_i(p)$ the initial depth estimation and $\hat{d}_r(p)$ the refined depth estimation. The parameter λ is set to 1.0 in experiments.

4 Implementations

4.1 Training

Data Preparation. Current MVS datasets provide ground truth data in either point cloud or mesh formats, so we need to generate the ground truth depth maps ourselves. The *DTU* dataset [1] is a large-scale MVS dataset containing more than 100 scenes with different lighting conditions. As it provides the ground truth point cloud with normal information, we use the screened Poisson surface reconstruction (SPSR) [16] to generate the mesh surface, and then render the mesh to each viewpoint to generate the depth maps for our training. The parameter, *depth-of-tree* is set to 11 in SPSR to acquire the high quality mesh result. Also, we set the mesh *trimming-factor* to 9.5 to alleviate mesh artifacts in surface edge areas. To fairly compare MVSNet with other learning based methods, we choose the same training, validation and evaluation sets as in SurfaceNet [14][1]. Considering each scan contains 49 images with 7 different lighting conditions, by setting each image as the reference, *DTU* dataset provides 27097 training samples in total.

View Selection. A reference image and two source images ($N = 3$) are used in our training. We calculate a score $s(i, j) = \sum_{\mathbf{p}} \mathcal{G}(\theta_{ij}(\mathbf{p}))$ for each image pair according to the sparse points, where $\mathbf{p}$ is a common track in both view i and j, $\theta_{ij}(\mathbf{p}) = (180/\pi)\arccos((\mathbf{c}_i - \mathbf{p}) \cdot (\mathbf{c}_j - \mathbf{p}))$ is $\mathbf{p}$'s baseline angle and $\mathbf{c}$ is the camera center. $\mathcal{G}$ is a piecewise Gaussian function [40] that favors a certain baseline angle θ_0:

$$\mathcal{G}(\theta) = \begin{cases} \exp(-\frac{(\theta-\theta_0)^2}{2\sigma_1^2}), \theta \leq \theta_0 \\ \exp(-\frac{(\theta-\theta_0)^2}{2\sigma_2^2}), \theta > \theta_0 \end{cases}$$

In the experiments, θ_0, σ_1 and σ_2 are set to 5, 1 and 10 respectively.

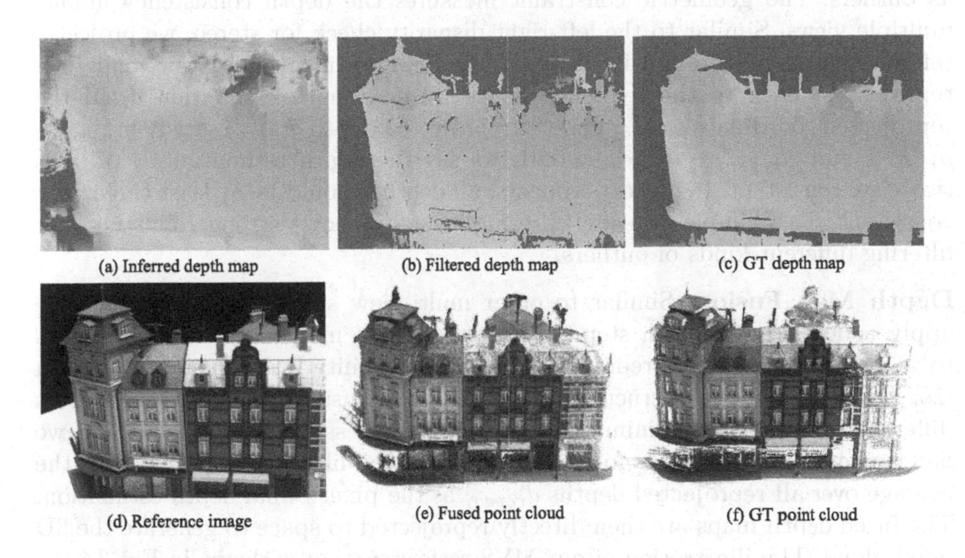

Fig. 3. Reconstructions of *scan* 9, *DTU* dataset [1]. From top left to bottom right: (a) the inferred depth map from MVSNet; (b) the filtered depth map after photometric and geometric filtering; (c) the depth map rendered from the ground truth mesh; (d) the reference image; (e) the final fused point cloud; (f) the ground truth point cloud

[1] Validation set: scans {3, 5, 17, 21, 28, 35, 37, 38, 40, 43, 56, 59, 66, 67, 82, 86, 106, 117}. Evaluation set: scans {1, 4, 9, 10, 11, 12, 13, 15, 23, 24, 29, 32, 33, 34, 48, 49, 62, 75, 77, 110, 114, 118}. Training set: the other 79 scans.

Notice that images will be downsized in feature extraction, plus the four-scale encoder-decoder structure in 3D regularization part, the input image size must be divisible by a factor of 32. Considering this requirement also the limited GPU memories, we downsize the image resolution from 1600×1200 to 800×600, and then crop the image patch with $W = 640$ and $H = 512$ from the center as the training input. The input camera parameters are changed accordingly. The depth hypotheses are uniformly sampled from 425 mm to 935 mm with a 2 mm resolution ($D = 256$). We use TensorFlow [2] to implement MVSNet, and the network is trained on one Tesla P100 graphics card for around 100,000 iterations.

4.2 Post-processing

Depth Map Filter. The above network estimates a depth value for every pixel. Before converting the result to dense point clouds, it is necessary to filter out outliers at those background and occluded areas. We propose two criteria, namely *photometric* and *geometric* consistencies for the robust depth map filtering.

The photometric consistency measures the matching quality. As discussed in Sect. 3.3, we compute the probability map to measure the depth estimation quality. In our experiments, we regard pixels with probability lower than 0.8 as outliers. The geometric constraint measures the depth consistency among multiple views. Similar to the left-right disparity check for stereo, we project a reference pixel p_1 through its depth d_1 to pixel p_i in another view, and then reproject p_i back to the reference image by p_i's depth estimation d_i. If the reprojected coordinate p_{reproj} and the reprojected depth d_{reproj} satisfy $|p_{reproj} - p_1| < 1$ and $|d_{reproj} - d_1|/d_1 < 0.01$, we say the depth estimation d_1 of p_1 is two-view consistent. In our experiments, all depths should be at least three view consistent. This simple two-step filtering strategy shows strong robustness for filtering different kinds of outliers.

Depth Map Fusion. Similar to other multi-view stereo methods [8,32], we apply a depth map fusion step to integrate depth maps from different views to a unified point cloud representation. The visibility-based fusion algorithm [26] is used in our reconstruction, where depth occlusions and violations across different viewpoints are minimized. To further suppress reconstruction noises, we determine the visible views for each pixel as in the filtering step, and take the average over all reprojected depths $\overline{d_{reproj}}$ as the pixel's final depth estimation. The fused depth maps are then directly reprojected to space to generate the 3D point cloud. The illustration of our MVS reconstruction is shown in Fig. 3.

5 Experiments

5.1 Benchmarking on *DTU* dataset

We first evaluate our method on the 22 evaluation scans of the *DTU* dataset [1]. The input view number, image width, height and depth sample number are set to $N = 5$, $W = 1600$, $H = 1184$ and $D = 256$ respectively. For quantitative evaluation, we calculate the *accuracy* and the *completeness* of both the distance metric [1] and the percentage metric [18]. While the matlab code for the distance metric is given by *DTU* dataset, we implement the percentage evaluation ourselves. Notice that the percentage metric also measures the overall performance of accuracy and completeness as the *f-score*. To give a similar measurement for the distance metric, we define the *overall score*, and take the average of mean accuracy and mean completeness as the reconstruction quality.

Quantitative results are shown in Table 1. While Gipuma [35] performs best in the accuracy, our MVSNet outperforms all methods in both the completeness and the overall quality **with a significant margin**. As shown in Fig. 4, MVSNet produces the most complete point clouds especially in those textureless and reflected areas, which are commonly considered as the most difficult parts to recover in MVS reconstruction.

Table 1. Quantitative results on the *DTU*'s evaluation set [1]. We evaluate all methods using both the distance metric [1] (lower is better), and the percentage metric [18] (higher is better) with respectively 1 *mm* and 2 *mm* thresholds

	Mean Distance (mm)			Percentage (<1 mm)			Percentage (<2 mm)		
	Acc.	Comp.	*overall*	Acc.	Comp.	*f-score*	Acc.	Comp.	*f-score*
Camp [3]	0.835	0.554	0.695	71.75	64.94	66.31	84.83	67.82	73.02
Furu [7]	0.613	0.941	0.777	69.55	61.52	63.26	78.99	67.88	70.93
Tola [35]	0.342	1.190	0.766	90.49	57.83	68.07	93.94	63.88	73.61
Gipuma [8]	**0.283**	0.873	0.578	**94.65**	59.93	70.64	**96.42**	63.81	74.16
SurfaceNet[14]	0.450	1.04	0.745	83.8	63.38	69.95	87.15	67.99	74.4
MVSNet (Ours)	0.396	**0.527**	**0.462**	86.46	**71.13**	**75.69**	91.06	**75.31**	**80.25**

5.2 Generalization on *Tanks and Temples* dataset

The *DTU* scans are taken under well-controlled indoor environment with fixed camera trajectory. To further demonstrate the generalization ability of MVSNet, we test the proposed method on the more complex outdoor *Tanks and Temples* dataset [18], using the model trained on *DTU* **without any fine-tuning**. While we choose $N = 5$, $W = 1920$, $H = 1056$ and $D = 256$ for all reconstructions, the depth range and the source image set for the reference image are determined according to sparse point cloud and camera positions, which are recovered by the open source SfM software OpenMVG [27].

Our method ranks first before April 18, 2018 among all submissions of the *intermediate set* [18] according to the online benchmark (Table 2). Although the model is trained on the very different *DTU* indoor dataset, MVSNet is still able to produce the best reconstructions on these outdoor scenes, demonstrating the strong generalization ability of the proposed network. The qualitative point cloud results of the *intermediate set* are visualized in Fig. 5.

5.3 Ablations

This section analyzes several components in MVSNet. For all following studies, we use the validation loss to measure the reconstruction quality. The 18 validation scans (see Sect. 4.1) are pre-processed as the training set that we set $N = 3$, $W = 640$, $H = 512$ and $D = 256$ for the validation loss computation.

View Number. We first study the influence of the input view number N and demonstrate that our model can be applied to arbitrary views of input. While the model in Sect. 4.1 is trained using $N = 3$ views, we test the model using $N = 2, 3, 5$ respectively. As expected, it is shown in Fig. 6(a) that adding input views can lower the validation loss, which is consistent with our knowledge about MVS reconstructions. It is noteworthy that testing with $N = 5$ performs better than with $N = 3$, even though the model is trained with the 3 views setting. This highly desirable property makes MVSNet flexible enough to be applied the different input settings.

Image Features. We demonstrate in this study that the learning based image feature could significantly boost the MVS reconstruction quality. To model the traditional patch-based image feature in MVSNet, we replace the original 2D feature extraction network with a single 32-channel convolutional layer. The filter kernel is set to a large number of 7×7 and the stride is set to 4. As shown in Fig. 6(b), network with the 2D feature extraction significantly outperforms the single layer one on validation loss.

Cost Metric. We also compare our variance operation based cost metric with the mean operation based metric [11]. The element-wise variance operation in

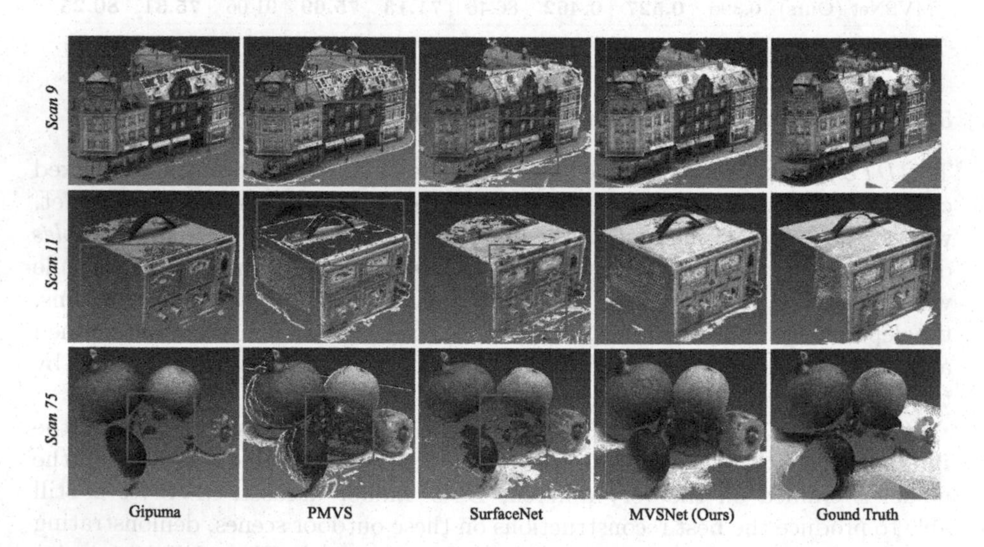

Fig. 4. Qualitative results of *scans* 9, 11 and 75 of *DTU* dataset [1]. Our MVSNet generates the most complete point clouds especially in those textureless and reflective areas. **Best viewed on screen**

Table 2. Quantitative results on *Tanks and Temples* benchmark [18]. MVSNet achieves best *f-score* result among all submissions without any fine-tuning

Method	Rank	Mean	Family	Francis	Horse	Lighthouse	M60	Panther	Playground	Train
MVSNet (Ours)	**3.00**	**43.48**	55.99	28.55	25.07	50.79	**53.96**	**50.86**	47.90	34.69
Pix4D [30]	3.12	43.24	**64.45**	31.91	**26.43**	54.41	50.58	35.37	47.78	34.96
COLMAP [32]	3.50	42.14	50.41	22.25	25.63	**56.43**	44.83	46.97	**48.53**	**42.04**
OpenMVG [27] + OpenMVS [29]	3.62	41.71	58.86	**32.59**	26.25	43.12	44.73	46.85	45.97	35.27
OpenMVG [27] + MVE [6]	6.00	38.00	49.91	28.19	20.75	43.35	44.51	44.76	36.58	35.95
OpenMVG [27] + SMVS [21]	10.38	30.67	31.93	19.92	15.02	39.38	36.51	41.61	35.89	25.12
OpenMVG-G [27] + OpenMVS [29]	10.88	22.86	56.50	29.63	21.69	6.55	39.54	28.48	0.00	0.53
MVE [6]	11.25	25.37	48.59	23.84	12.70	5.07	39.62	38.16	5.81	29.19
OpenMVG [27] + PMVS [7]	11.88	29.66	41.03	17.70	12.83	36.68	35.93	33.20	31.78	28.10

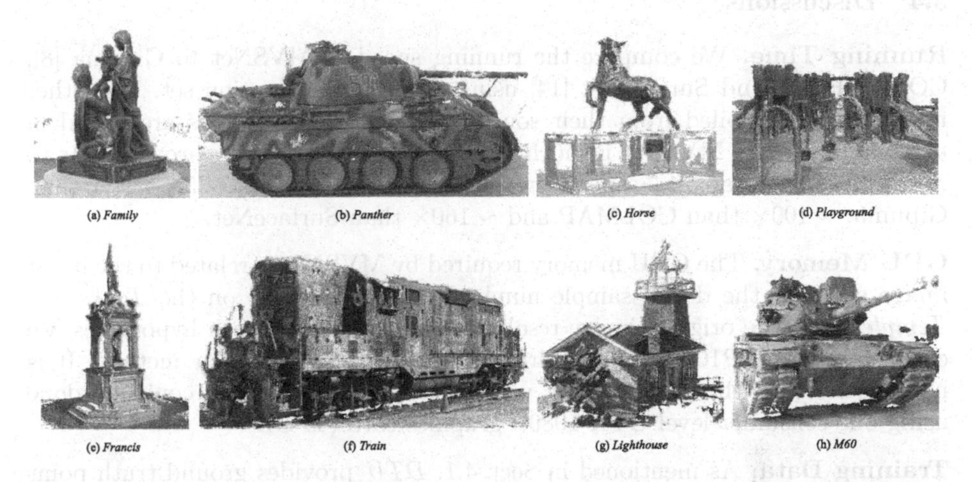

(a) *Family* (b) *Panther* (c) *Horse* (d) *Playground* (e) *Francis* (f) *Train* (g) *Lighthouse* (h) *M60*

Fig. 5. Point cloud results of the *intermediate set* of *Tanks and Temples* [18] dataset, which demonstrates the generalization power of MVSNet on complex outdoor scenes

Eq. 2 is replaced with the mean operation to train the new model. It can be found in Fig. 6(b) that our cost metric results in a faster convergence with lower validation loss, which demonstrates that it is more reasonable to use the explicit difference measurement to compute the multi-view feature similarity.

Depth Refinement. Lastly, we train MVSNet with and without the depth map refinement network. The models are also tested on *DTU* evaluation set as in Sect. 5.1, and we use the percentage metric [18] to quantitatively compare the two models. While Fig. 6(b) shows that the refinement does not affect the validation loss too much, the refinement network improves the evaluation results from 75.58 to 75.69 (<1 mm *f-score*) and from 79.98 to 80.25 (<2 mm *f-score*).

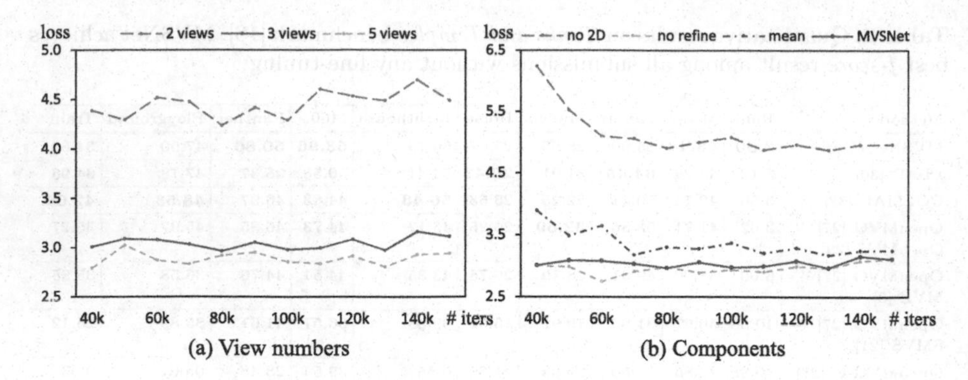

Fig. 6. Ablation studies. (a) Validation losses of different input view numbers. (b) Ablations on 2D image feature, cost metric and depth map refinement

5.4 Discussions

Running Time. We compare the running speed of MVSNet to Gipuma [8], COLMAP [32] and SurfaceNet [14] using the *DTU* evaluation set. The other methods are compiled from their source codes and all methods are tested in the same machine. MVSNet is much more efficient that it takes around 230 s to reconstruct one scan (**4.7 s** per view). The running speed is $\sim 5\times$ faster than Gipuma, $\sim 100\times$ than COLMAP and $\sim 160\times$ than SurfaceNet.

GPU Memory. The GPU memory required by MVSNet is related to the input image size and the depth sample number. In order to test on the *Tanks and Temples* with the original image resolution and sufficient depth hypotheses, we choose the Tesla P100 graphics card (16 GB) to implement our method. It is noteworthy that the training and validation on *DTU* dataset could be done using one consumer level GTX 1080ti graphics card (11 GB).

Training Data. As mentioned in Sect. 4.1, *DTU* provides ground truth point clouds with normal information so that we can convert them into mesh surfaces for depth maps rendering. However, currently *Tanks and Temples* dataset does not provide the normal information or mesh surfaces, so we are unable to fine-tune MVSNet on *Tanks and Temples* for better performance.

Although using such rendered depth maps have already achieved satisfactory results, some limitations still exist: (1) the provided ground truth meshes are not 100% complete, so some triangles behind the foreground will be falsely rendered to the depth map as the valid pixels, which may deteriorate the training process. (2) If a pixel is occluded in all other views, it should not be used for training. However, without the complete mesh surfaces we cannot correctly identify the occluded pixels. We hope future MVS datasets could provide ground truth depth maps with complete occlusion and background information.

6 Conclusion

We have presented a deep learning architecture for MVS reconstruction. The proposed MVSNet takes unstructured images as input, and infers the depth map for the reference image in an end-to-end fashion. The core contribution of MVSNet is to encode the camera parameters as the differentiable homography to build the cost volume upon the camera frustum, which bridges the 2D feature extraction and 3D cost regularization networks. It has been demonstrated on *DTU* dataset that MVSNet not only significantly outperforms previous methods, but also is more efficient in speed by several times. Also, MVSNet have produced the state-of-the-art results on *Tanks and Temples* dataset without any fine-tuning, which demonstrates its strong generalization ability.

Acknowledgement. This work is supported by T22-603/15N, Hong Kong ITC PSKL12EG02 and the Special Project of International Scientific and Technological Cooperation in Guangzhou Development District (No. 2017GH24).

References

1. Aanæs, H., Jensen, R.R., Vogiatzis, G., Tola, E., Dahl, A.B.: Large-scale data for multiple-view stereopsis. Int. J. Comput. Vis. (IJCV) **120**, 153–168 (2016)
2. Abadi, M., et al.: TensorFlow: Large-scale machine learning on heterogeneous systems (2015). https://www.tensorflow.org/
3. Campbell, N.D.F., Vogiatzis, G., Hernández, C., Cipolla, R.: Using multiple hypotheses to improve depth-maps for multi-view stereo. In: Forsyth, D., Torr, P., Zisserman, A. (eds.) ECCV 2008. LNCS, vol. 5302, pp. 766–779. Springer, Heidelberg (2008). https://doi.org/10.1007/978-3-540-88682-2_58
4. Chen, L.C., Papandreou, G., Kokkinos, I., Murphy, K., Yuille, A.L.: DeepLab: semantic image segmentation with deep convolutional nets, atrous convolution, and fully connected CRFs. IEEE Trans. Pattern Anal. Mach. Intell. (TPAMI) **40**, 834–848 (2017)
5. Collins, R.T.: A space-sweep approach to true multi-image matching. In: Computer Vision and Pattern Recognition (CVPR) (1996)
6. Fuhrmann, S., Langguth, F., Goesele, M.: MVE-a multi-view reconstruction environment. In: Eurographics Workshop on Graphics and Cultural Heritage (GCH) (2014)
7. Furukawa, Y., Ponce, J.: Accurate, dense, and robust multiview stereopsis. IEEE Trans. Pattern Anal. Mach. Intell. (TPAMI) **32**, 1362–1376 (2010)
8. Galliani, S., Lasinger, K., Schindler, K.: Massively parallel multiview stereopsis by surface normal diffusion. In: International Conference on Computer Vision (ICCV) (2015)
9. Geiger, A., Lenz, P., Urtasun, R.: Are we ready for autonomous driving? the KITTI vision benchmark suite. In: Computer Vision and Pattern Recognition (CVPR) (2012)
10. Han, X., Leung, T., Jia, Y., Sukthankar, R., Berg, A.C.: MatchNet: unifying feature and metric learning for patch-based matching. In: Computer Vision and Pattern Recognition (CVPR) (2015)

11. Hartmann, W., Galliani, S., Havlena, M., Van Gool, L., Schindler, K.: Learned multi-patch similarity. In: International Conference on Computer Vision (ICCV) (2017)
12. Hirschmuller, H.: Stereo processing by semiglobal matching and mutual information. IEEE Trans. Pattern Anal. Mach. Intell. (TPAMI) **30**, 328–341 (2008)
13. Hirschmuller, H., Scharstein, D.: Evaluation of cost functions for stereo matching. In: Computer Vision and Pattern Recognition (CVPR) (2007)
14. Ji, M., Gall, J., Zheng, H., Liu, Y., Fang, L.: SurfaceNet: an end-to-end 3D neural network for multiview stereopsis. In: International Conference on Computer Vision (ICCV) (2017)
15. Kar, A., Häne, C., Malik, J.: Learning a multi-view stereo machine. In: Advances in Neural Information Processing Systems (NIPS) (2017)
16. Kazhdan, M., Hoppe, H.: Screened poisson surface reconstruction. ACM Trans. Graph. (TOG) **32**, 29 (2013)
17. Kendall, A., Martirosyan, H., Dasgupta, S., Henry, P.: End-to-end learning of geometry and context for deep stereo regression. In: Computer Vision and Pattern Recognition (CVPR) (2017)
18. Knapitsch, A., Park, J., Zhou, Q.Y., Koltun, V.: Tanks and temples: benchmarking large-scale scene reconstruction. ACM Trans. Graph. (TOG) **36**, 78 (2017)
19. Knöbelreiter, P., Reinbacher, C., Shekhovtsov, A., Pock, T.: End-to-end training of hybrid CNN-CRF models for stereo. In: Computer Vision and Pattern Recognition (CVPR) (2017)
20. Kutulakos, K.N., Seitz, S.M.: A theory of shape by space carving. Int. J. Comput. Vis. (IJCV) **38**, 199–218 (2000)
21. Langguth, F., Sunkavalli, K., Hadap, S., Goesele, M.: Shading-aware multi-view stereo. In: Leibe, B., Matas, J., Sebe, N., Welling, M. (eds.) ECCV 2016. LNCS, vol. 9907, pp. 469–485. Springer, Cham (2016). https://doi.org/10.1007/978-3-319-46487-9_29
22. Lhuillier, M., Quan, L.: A quasi-dense approach to surface reconstruction from uncalibrated images. IEEE Trans. Pattern Anal. Mach. Intell. (TPAMI) **27**, 418–433 (2005)
23. Luo, W., Schwing, A.G., Urtasun, R.: Efficient deep learning for stereo matching. In: Computer Vision and Pattern Recognition (CVPR) (2016)
24. Mayer, N., et al.: A large dataset to train convolutional networks for disparity, optical flow, and scene flow estimation. In: Computer Vision and Pattern Recognition (CVPR) (2016)
25. Menze, M., Geiger, A.: Object scene flow for autonomous vehicles. In: Computer Vision and Pattern Recognition (CVPR) (2015)
26. Merrell, P., et al.: Real-time visibility-based fusion of depth maps. In: International Conference on Computer Vision (ICCV) (2007)
27. Moulon, P., Monasse, P., Marlet, R., et al.: OpenMVG: an open multiple view geometry library. https://github.com/openMVG/openMVG
28. Newcombe, R.A., et al.: KinectFusion: real-time dense surface mapping and tracking. In: IEEE International Symposium on Mixed and Augmented Reality (ISMAR) (2011)
29. OpenMVS: open multi-view stereo reconstruction library. https://github.com/cdcseacave/openMVS
30. Pix4D: https://pix4d.com/

31. Ronneberger, O., Fischer, P., Brox, T.: U-Net: convolutional networks for biomedical image segmentation. In: Navab, N., Hornegger, J., Wells, W.M., Frangi, A.F. (eds.) MICCAI 2015. LNCS, vol. 9351, pp. 234–241. Springer, Cham (2015). https://doi.org/10.1007/978-3-319-24574-4_28
32. Schönberger, J.L., Zheng, E., Frahm, J.-M., Pollefeys, M.: Pixelwise view selection for unstructured multi-view stereo. In: Leibe, B., Matas, J., Sebe, N., Welling, M. (eds.) ECCV 2016. LNCS, vol. 9907, pp. 501–518. Springer, Cham (2016). https://doi.org/10.1007/978-3-319-46487-9_31
33. Seitz, S.M., Dyer, C.R.: Photorealistic scene reconstruction by voxel coloring. Int. J. Comput. Vis. (IJCV) **35**, 151–173 (1999)
34. Seki, A., Pollefeys, M.: SGM-Nets: semi-global matching with neural networks. In: Computer Vision and Pattern Recognition Workshops (CVPRW) (2017)
35. Tola, E., Strecha, C., Fua, P.: Efficient large-scale multi-view stereo for ultra high-resolution image sets. In: Machine Vision and Applications (MVA) (2012)
36. Vu, H.H., Labatut, P., Pons, J.P., Keriven, R.: High accuracy and visibility-consistent dense multiview stereo. IEEE Trans. Pattern Anal. Mach. Intell. (TPAMI) **34**, 889–901 (2012)
37. Xu, N., Price, B., Cohen, S., Huang, T.: Deep image matting. In: Computer Vision and Pattern Recognition (CVPR) (2017)
38. Yao, Y., Li, S., Zhu, S., Deng, H., Fang, T., Quan, L.: Relative camera refinement for accurate dense reconstruction. In: 3D Vision (3DV) (2017)
39. Zbontar, J., LeCun, Y.: Stereo matching by training a convolutional neural network to compare image patches. J. Mach. Learn. Res. (JMLR) **17**, 2 (2016)
40. Zhang, R., Li, S., Fang, T., Zhu, S., Quan, L.: Joint camera clustering and surface segmentation for large-scale multi-view stereo. In: International Conference on Computer Vision (ICCV) (2015)

ActiveStereoNet: End-to-End Self-supervised Learning for Active Stereo Systems

Yinda Zhang[1,2](✉), Sameh Khamis[1], Christoph Rhemann[1], Julien Valentin[1], Adarsh Kowdle[1], Vladimir Tankovich[1], Michael Schoenberg[1], Shahram Izadi[1], Thomas Funkhouser[1,2], and Sean Fanello[1]

[1] Google Inc., Mountain View, USA
[2] Princeton University, Princeton, USA
yindaz@cs.princeton.edu

Abstract. In this paper we present ActiveStereoNet, the first deep learning solution for active stereo systems. Due to the lack of ground truth, our method is fully self-supervised, yet it produces precise depth with a subpixel precision of $1/30th$ of a pixel; it does not suffer from the common over-smoothing issues; it preserves the edges; and it explicitly handles occlusions. We introduce a novel reconstruction loss that is more robust to noise and texture-less patches, and is invariant to illumination changes. The proposed loss is optimized using a window-based cost aggregation with an adaptive support weight scheme. This cost aggregation is edge-preserving and smooths the loss function, which is key to allow the network to reach compelling results. Finally we show how the task of predicting invalid regions, such as occlusions, can be trained end-to-end without ground-truth. This component is crucial to reduce blur and particularly improves predictions along depth discontinuities. Extensive quantitatively and qualitatively evaluations on real and synthetic data demonstrate state of the art results in many challenging scenes.

Keywords: Active Stereo · Depth estimation
Self-supervised learning · Neural network · Occlusion handling
Deep learning

1 Introduction

Depth sensors are revolutionizing computer vision by providing additional 3D information for many hard problems, such as non-rigid reconstruction [8,9], action recognition [10,15] and parametric tracking [47,48]. Although there are many types of depth sensor technologies, they all have significant limitations.

Electronic supplementary material The online version of this chapter (https://doi.org/10.1007/978-3-030-01237-3_48) contains supplementary material, which is available to authorized users.

V. Ferrari et al. (Eds.): ECCV 2018, LNCS 11212, pp. 802–819, 2018.
https://doi.org/10.1007/978-3-030-01237-3_48

Time of flight systems suffer from motion artifacts and multi-path interference [4,5,39]. Structured light is vulnerable to ambient illumination and multi-device interference [12,14]. Passive stereo struggles in texture-less regions, where expensive global optimization techniques are required - especially in traditional non-learning based methods.

Active stereo offers a potential solution: an infrared stereo camera pair is used, with a pseudorandom pattern projectively texturing the scene via a patterned IR light source. (Fig. 1). With a proper selection of sensing wavelength, the camera pair captures a combination of active illumination and passive light, improving quality above that of structured light while providing a robust solution in both indoor and outdoor scenarios. Although this technology was introduced decades ago [41], it has only recently become available in commercial products (e.g., Intel R200 and D400 family [2]). As a result, there is relatively little prior work targeted specifically at inferring depths from active stereo images, and large scale training data with ground truth is not available yet.

Several challenges must be addressed in an active stereo system. Some are common to all stereo problems – for example, it must avoid matching occluded pixels, which causes oversmoothing, edge fattening, and/or flying pixels near contour edges. However, other problems are specific to active stereo – for example, it must process very high-resolution images to match the high-frequency patterns produced by the projector; it must avoid the many local minima arising from alternative alignments of these high frequency patterns; and it must compensate for luminance differences between projected patterns on nearby and distant surfaces. Additionally, of course, it cannot be trained with supervision from a large active stereo dataset with ground truth depths, since none is available.

This paper proposes the first end-to-end deep learning approach for active stereo that is trained fully self-supervised. It extends recent work on self-supervised passive stereo [58] to address problems encountered in active stereo. First, we propose a new reconstruction loss based on local contrast normalization (LCN) that removes low frequency components from passive IR and re-calibrates the strength of the active pattern locally to account for fading of active stereo patterns with distance. Second, we propose a window-based loss aggregation with adaptive weights for each pixel to increase its discriminability and reduce the effect of local minima in the stereo cost function. Finally, we detect occluded pixels in the images and omit them from loss computations. These new aspects of the algorithm provide significant benefits to the convergence during training and improve depth accuracy at test time. Extensive experiments demonstrate that our network trained with these insights outperforms previous work on active stereo and alternatives in ablation studies across a wide range of experiments.

2 Related Work

Depth sensing is a classic problem with a long history of prior work. Among the **active sensors**, Time of Flight (TOF), such as Kinect V2, emits a modulated light source and uses multiple observations of the same scene (usually 3–9) to

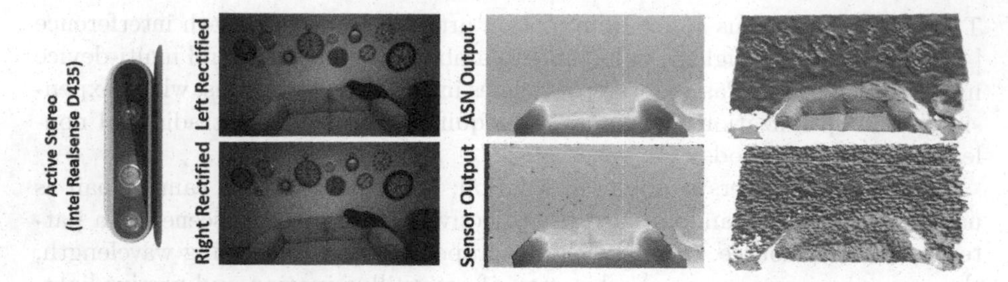

Fig. 1. ActiveStereoNet (ASN) produces smooth, detailed, quantization free results using a pair of rectified IR images acquired with an Intel Realsense D435 camera. In particular, notice how the jacket is almost indiscernible using the sensor output, and in contrast, how it is clearly observable in our results.

predict a single depth map. The main issues with this technology are artifacts due to motion and multipath interference [4,5,39]. Structure light (SL) is a viable alternative, but it requires a known projected pattern and is vulnerable to multi-device inference [12,14]. Neither approach is robust in outdoor conditions under strong illumination.

Passive stereo provides an alternative approach [21,43]. Traditional methods utilize hand-crafted schemes to find reliable local correspondences [6,7, 23,24,52] and global optimization algorithms to exploit context when matching [3,16,31,32]. Recent methods address these problems with deep learning. Siamese networks are trained to extract patch-wise features and/or predict matching costs [37,54–56]. More recently, end-to-end networks learn these steps jointly, yielding better results [19,25,28,36,38,42,44]. However all these deep learning methods rely on a strong supervised component. As a consequence, they outperform traditional handcrafted optimization schemes only when a lot of ground-truth depth data is available, which is not the case in active stereo settings.

Self-supervised passive stereo is a possible solution for absence of ground-truth training data. When multiple images of the same scene are available, the images can warp between cameras using the estimated/calibrated pose and the depth, and the loss between the reconstruction and the raw image can be used to train depth estimation systems without ground truth. Taking advantage of spatial and temporal coherence, depth estimation algorithms can be trained unsupervised using monocular images [18,20,35], video [51,59], and stereo [58]. However, their results are blurry and far from comparable with supervised methods due to the required strong regularization such as left-right check [20,58]. Also, they struggle in textureless and dark regions, as do all passive methods.

Active stereo is an extension of the traditional passive stereo approach in which a texture is projected into the scene with an IR projector and cameras are augmented to perceive IR as well as visible spectra [33]. Intel R200 was the first attempt of commercialize an active stereo sensor, however its accuracy is poor compared to (older) structured light sensors, such as Kinect V1 [12,14]. Very recently, Intel released the D400 family [1,2], which provides higher resolution,

1280×720, and therefore has the potential to deliver more accurate depth maps. The build-in stereo algorithm in these cameras uses a handcrafted binary descriptor (CENSUS) in combination with a semi-global matching scheme [29]. It offers reasonable performance in a variety of settings [46], but still suffers from common stereo matching issues addressed in this paper (edge fattening, quadratic error, occlusions, holes, etc.).

Learning-based solutions for active stereo are limited. Past work has employed shallow architectures to learn a feature space where the matching can be performed efficiently [13,14,50], trained a regressor to infer disparity [12], or learned a direct mapping from pixel intensity to depth [11]. These methods fail in general scenes [11], suffer from interference and per-camera calibration [12], and/or do not work well in texture-less areas due to their shallow descriptors and local optimization schemes [13,14]. Our paper is the first to investigate how to design an end-to-end deep network for active stereo.

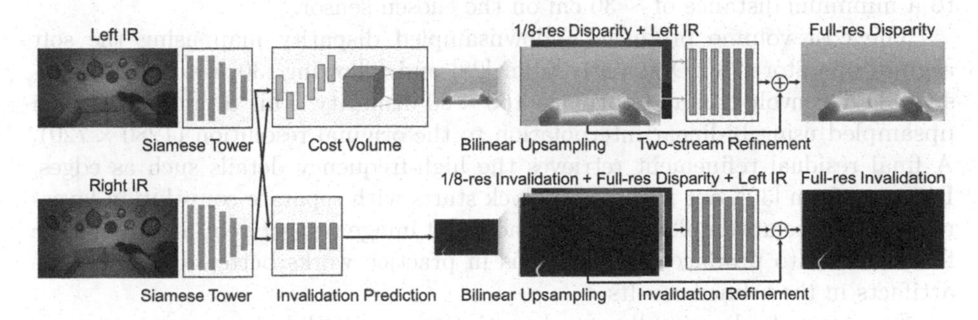

Fig. 2. ActiveStereoNet architecture. We use a two stage network where a low resolution cost volume is built and infers the first disparity estimate. A bilinear upsampling followed by a residual network predicts the final disparity map. An "Invalidation Network" (bottom) is also trained end-to-end to predict a confidence map.

3 Method

In this section, we introduce the network architecture and training procedure for ActiveStereoNet. The input to our algorithm is a rectified, synchronized pair of images with active illumination (see Fig. 1), and the output is a pair of disparity maps at the original resolution. For our experiments, we use the recently released Intel Realsense D435 that provides synchronized, rectified 1280×720 images at 30 fps. The focal length f and the baseline b between the two cameras are assumed to be known. Under this assumption, the depth estimation problem becomes a disparity search along the scan line. Given the output disparity d, the depth is obtained via $Z = \frac{bf}{d}$.

Since no ground-truth training data is available for this problem, our main challenge is to train an end-to-end network that is robust to occlusion and illumination effects without direct supervision. The following details our algorithm.

3.1 Network Architecture

Nowadays, in many vision problems, the choice of the architecture plays a crucial role, and most of the efforts are spent in designing the right network. In active stereo, instead, we found that the most challenging part is the training procedure for a given deep network. In particular, since our setting is unsupervised, designing the optimal loss function has the highest impact on the overall accuracy. For this reason, we extend the network architecture proposed in [30], which has shown superior performances in many passive stereo benchmarks. Moreover, the system is computationally efficient and allows us to run on full resolution at 60 Hz on a high-end GPU, which is desirable for real-time applications.

The overall pipeline is shown in Fig. 2. We start from the high-resolution images and use a siamese tower to produces feature map in 1/8 of the input resolution. We then build a low resolution cost volume of size $160 \times 90 \times 18$, allowing for a maximum disparity of 144 in the original image, which corresponds to a minimum distance of ~ 30 cm on the chosen sensor.

The cost volume produces a downsampled disparity map using the soft argmin operator [28]. Differently from [28] and following [30] we avoid expensive 3D deconvolution and output a 160×90 disparity. This estimation is then upsampled using bi-linear interpolation to the original resolution (1280×720). A final residual refinement retrieves the high-frequency details such as edges. Different from [30], our refinement block starts with separate convolution layers running on the upsampled disparity and input image respectively, and merge the feature later to produce residual. This in practice works better to remove dot artifacts in the refined results.

Our network also simultaneously estimates an invalidation mask to remove uncertain areas in the result, which will be introduced in Sect. 3.4.

3.2 Loss Function

The architecture described is composed of a low resolution disparity and a final refinement step to retrieve high-frequency details. A natural choice is to have a loss function for each of these two steps. Unlike [30], we are in an unsupervised setting due to the lack of ground truth data. A viable choice for the training loss L then is the photometric error between the original pixels on the left image I^l_{ij} and the reconstructed left image $\hat{I}^l_{ij}$, in particular $L = \sum_{ij} \|I^l_{ij} - \hat{I}^l_{ij}\|_1$. The reconstructed image $\hat{I}^l$ is obtained by sampling pixels from the right image I^r using the predicted disparity d, i.e. $\hat{I}^l_{ij} = I^r_{i,j-d}$. Our sampler uses the Spatial Transformer Network (STN) [26], which uses a bi-linear interpolation of 2 pixels on the same row and is fully differentiable.

However, as shown in previous work [57], the photometric loss is a poor choice for image reconstruction problems. This is even more dramatic when dealing with active setups. We recall that active sensors flood the scenes with texture and the intensity of the received signal follows the inverse square law $I \propto \frac{1}{Z^2}$, where Z is the distance from the camera. In practice this creates an explicit dependency between the intensity and the distance (i.e. brighter pixels

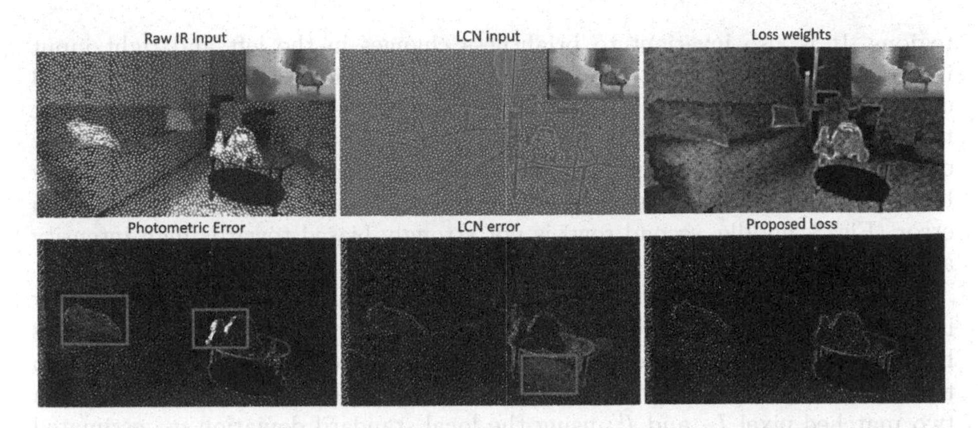

Fig. 3. Comparisons between photometric loss (left), LCN loss (middle), and the proposed weighted LCN loss (right). Our loss is more robust to occlusions, it does not depend on the brightness of the pixels and does not suffer in low texture regions.

are closer). A second issue, that is also present in RGB images, is that the difference between two bright pixels is likely to have a bigger residual when compared to the difference between two dark pixels. Indeed if we consider image I, to have noise proportional to intensity [17], the observed intensity for a given pixel can be written as: $I_{ij} = I^{\star}_{ij} + \mathcal{N}(0, \sigma_1 I^{\star}_{ij} + \sigma_2)$, where $I^{\star}_{ij}$ is the noise free signal and the standard deviations σ_1 and σ_2 depend on the sensor [17]. It is easy to show that the difference between two correctly matched pixels I and $\hat{I}$ has a residual: $\epsilon = \mathcal{N}(0, \sqrt{(\sigma_1 I^{\star}_{ij} + \sigma_2)^2 + (\sigma_3 \hat{I}^{\star}_{ij} + \sigma_4)^2})$, where its variance depends on the input intensities. This shows that for brighter pixels (i.e. close objects) the residual ϵ will be bigger compared to one of low reflectivity or farther objects.

In the case of passive stereo, this could be a negligible effect, since in RGB images there is no correlation between intensity and disparity, however in the active case the aforementioned problem will bias the network towards closeup scenes, which will have always a bigger residual. The architecture will learn mostly those easy areas and smooth out the rest. The darker pixels, mostly in distant, requiring higher matching precision for accurate depth, however, are overlooked. In Fig. 3 (left), we show the reconstruction error for a given disparity map using the photometric loss. Notice how bright pixels on the pillow exhibits high reconstruction error due to the input dependent nature of the noise.

An additional issue with this loss occurs in the occluded areas: indeed when the intensity difference between background and foreground is severe, this loss will have a strong contribution in the occluded regions, forcing the network to learn to fit those areas that, however, cannot really be explained in the data.

Weighted Local Contrast Normalization. We propose to use a Local Contrast Normalization (LCN) scheme, that not only removes the dependency between intensity and disparity, but also gives a better residual in occluded regions. It is also invariant to brightness changes in the left and right input image. In particular, for each pixel, we compute the local mean μ and standard deviation σ in a small 9×9 patch. These local statistics are used to normalize the current pixel intensity $I_{LCN} = \frac{I-\mu}{\sigma+\eta}$, where η is a small constant. The result of this normalization is shown in Fig. 3, middle. Notice how the dependency between disparity and brightness is now removed, moreover the reconstruction error (Fig. 3, middle, second row) is not strongly biased towards high intensity areas or occluded regions.

However, LCN suffers in low texture regions when the standard deviation σ is close to zero (see the bottom of the table in Fig. 3, middle). Indeed these areas have a small σ which will would amplify any residual together with noise between two matched pixels. To remove this effect, we re-weight the residual ϵ between two matched pixel I_{ij} and $\hat{I}^l_{ij}$ using the local standard deviation σ_{ij} estimated on the reference image in a 9×9 patch around the pixel (i, j). In particular our reconstruction loss becomes: $L = \sum_{ij} \|\sigma_{ij}(I^l_{LCNij} - \hat{I}^l_{LCNij})\|_1 = \sum_{ij} C_{ij}$. Example of weights computed on the reference image are shown in Fig. 3, top right and the final loss is shown on the bottom right. Notice how these residuals are not biased in bright areas or low textured regions.

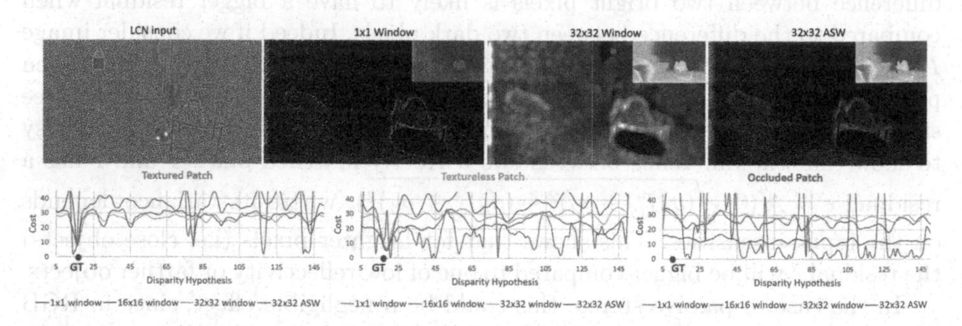

Fig. 4. Cost volume analysis for a textured region (green), textureless patch (orange) and occluded pixel (red). Notice how the window size helps to resolve ambiguous (textureless) areas in the image, whereas in occluded pixels the lowest cost will always lead to the wrong solution. However large windows oversmooth the cost function and they do not preserve edges, where as the proposed Adaptive Support Weight loss aggregates costs preserving edges. (Color figure online)

3.3 Window-Based Optimization

We now analyze in more details the behavior of the loss function for the whole search space. We consider a textured patch (green), a texture-less one (orange) and an occluded area (red) in an LCN image (see Fig. 4). We plot the loss function for every disparity candidate in the range of [5, 144]. For a single pixel cost (blue curve), notice how the function exhibits a highly non-convex behavior (w.r.t. the disparity) that makes extremely hard to retrieve the ground truth value (shown as purple dots). Indeed a single pixel cost has many local minima, that could lie far from the actual optimum. In traditional stereo matching pipelines, a cost aggregation robustifies the final estimate using evidence from neighboring pixels. If we consider a window around each pixel and sum all the costs, we can see that the loss becomes smoother for both textured and textureless patch and the optimum can be reached (see Fig. 4, bottom graphs). However as a drawback for large windows, small objects and details can be smooth out by the aggregation of multiple costs and cannot be recovered in the final disparity.

Traditional stereo matching pipelines aggregate the costs using an adaptive support (ASW) scheme [53], which is very effective, but also slow hence not practical for real-time systems where approximated solutions are required [34]. Here we propose to integrate the ASW scheme in the training procedure, therefore it does not affect the runtime cost. In particular, we consider a pixel (i, j) with intensity I_{ij} and instead of compute a per-pixel loss, we aggregate the costs C_{ij} around a $2k \times 2k$ window following: $\hat{C}_{ij} = \frac{\sum_{x=i-k}^{i+k-1} \sum_{y=j-k}^{j+k-1} w_{x,y} C_{ij}}{\sum_{x=i-k}^{i+k-1} \sum_{y=j-k}^{j+k-1} w_{x,y}}$, where $w_{xy} = \exp(-\frac{|I_{ij} - I_{xy}|}{\sigma_w})$, with $\sigma_w = 2$. As shown in Fig. 4 right, this aggregates the costs (i.e. it smooths the cost function), but it still preserves the edges. In our implementation we use a 32×32 during the whole training phase. We also tested a graduated optimization approach [22,40], where we first optimized our network using 64×64 window and then reduce it every 15000 iterations by a factor of 2, until we reach a single pixel loss. However this solution led to very similar results compared to a single pixel loss during the whole training.

3.4 Invalidation Network

So far the proposed loss does not deal with occluded regions and wrong matches (i.e. textureless areas). An occluded pixel does not have any useful information in the cost volume even when brute-force search is performed at different scales (see in Fig. 4, bottom right graph). To deal with occlusions, traditional stereo matching methods use a so called left-right consistency check, where a disparity is first computed from the left view point (d_l), then from the right camera (d_r) and invalidate those pixels with $|d_l - d_r| > \theta$. Related work use a left-right consistency in the loss minimization [20], however this leads to oversmooth edges which become flying pixels (outliers) in the pointcloud. Instead, we propose to use the left-check as a hard constraint by defining a mask for a pixel (i, j): $m_{ij} = |d_l - d_r| < \theta$, with $\theta = 1$ disparity. Those pixels with $m_{ij} = 0$ are ignored in the loss computation. To avoid a trivial solution (i.e. all the pixels are invalidated), similarly to [59], we enforce a regularization on the number of valid pixels by minimizing the cross-entropy loss with constant label 1 in each pixel location. We use this mask in both the low-resolution disparity as well as the final refined one.

At the same time, we train an invalidation network (fully convolutional), that takes as input the features computed from the Siamese tower and produces first a low resolution invalidation mask, which is then upsampled and refined with a similar architecture used for the disparity refinement. This allows, at runtime, to avoid predicting the disparity from both the left and the right viewpoint to perform the left-right consistency, making the inference significantly faster.

4 Experiments

We performed a series of experiments to evaluate ActiveStereoNet (ASN). In addition to analyzing the accuracy of depth predictions in comparison to previous work, we also provide results of ablation studies to investigate how each component of the proposed loss affects the results. In the supplementary material we also evaluate the applicability of our proposed self-supervised loss in passive (RGB) stereo, showing improved generalization capabilities and compelling results on many benchmarks.

4.1 Dataset and Training Schema

We train and evaluate our method on both real and synthetic data.

For the *real dataset*, we used an Intel Realsense D435 camera [2] to collect 10000 images for training in an office environment, plus 100 images in other *unseen* scenes for testing (depicting people, furnished rooms and objects).

For the *synthetic dataset*, we used Blender to render IR and depth images of indoor scenes such as living rooms, kitchens, and bedrooms, as in [14]. Specifically, we render synthetic stereo pairs with 9 cm baseline using projective textures to simulate projection of the Kinect V1 dot pattern onto the scene. We randomly move the camera in the rendered rooms and capture left IR image, right IR image as well as ground truth depth. Examples of the rendered scenes are showed in Fig. 8, left. The synthetic training data consists of 10000 images and the test set is composed of 1200 frames comprehending new scenes.

For both real and synthetic experiments, we trained the network using RMSprop [49]. We set the learning rate to 1e−4 and reduce it by half at $\frac{3}{5}$ iterations and to a quarter at $\frac{4}{5}$ iterations. We stop the training after 100000 iterations, that are usually enough to reach the convergence. Although our algorithm is self-supervised, we *did not* fine-tune the model on any of the test data since it reduces the generalization capability in real applications.

4.2 Stereo Matching Evaluation

In this section, we compare our method on real data with state of the art stereo algorithms qualitatively and quantitatively using traditional stereo matching metrics, such as jitter and bias.

Bias and Jitter. It is known that a stereo system with baseline b, focal length f, and a subpixel disparity precision of δ, has a depth error ϵ that increases quadratically with respect to the depth Z according to $\epsilon = \frac{\delta Z^2}{bf}$ [45]. Due to the variable impact of disparity error on the depth, naive evaluation metrics, like mean error of disparity, does not effectively reflect the quality of the estimated depth. In contrast, we first show error of depth estimation and calculate corresponding error in disparity.

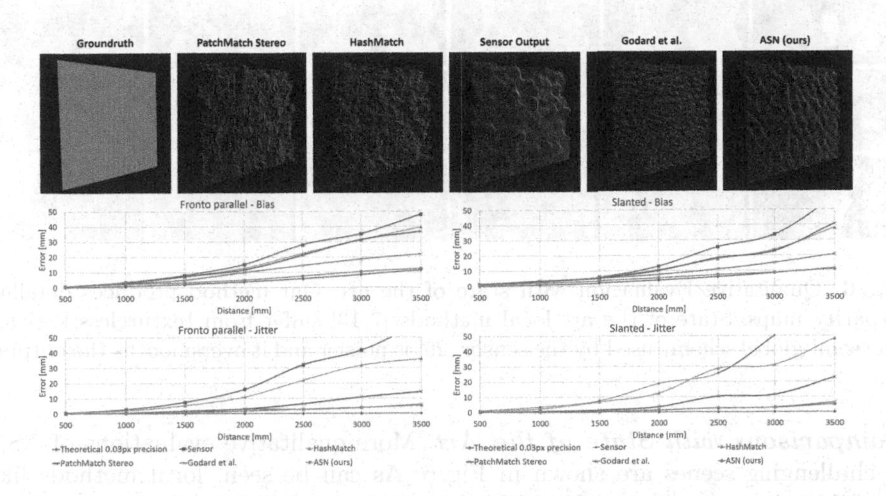

Fig. 5. Quantitative Evaluation with state of the art. We achieve one order of magnitude less bias with a subpixel precision of 0.03 pixels with a very low jitter (see text). We also show the predicted pointclouds for various methods of a wall at 3000 mm distance. Notice that despite the large distance (3m), our results is the less noisy compared to the considered approaches.

To assess the subpixel precision of ASN, we recorded 100 frames with the camera in front of a flat wall at distances ranging from 500 mm to 3500 mm, and also 100 frames with the camera facing the wall at an angle of 50° to assess the behavior on slanted surfaces. In this case, we evaluate by comparing to "ground truth" obtained with robust plane fitting.

To characterize the precision, we compute *bias* as the average ℓ_1 error between the predicted depth and the ground truth plane. Figure 5 shows the bias with regard to the depth for our method, sensor output [29], the state of the art local stereo methods (PatchMatch [7], HashMatch [13]), and our model trained using the state of the art unsupervised loss [20], together with visualizations of point clouds colored by surface normal. Our system performs significantly better than the other methods at all distances, and its error does not increase dramatically with depth. The corresponding subpixel disparity precision of our system is $1/30th$ of a pixel, which is obtained by fitting a curve using the above mentioned equation (also shown in Fig. 5). This is one order of magnitude lower than the other methods where the precision is not higher than 0.2 pixel.

To characterize the noise, we compute the *jitter* as the standard deviation of the depth error. Figure 5 shows that our method achieves the lowest jitter at almost every depth in comparison to other methods.

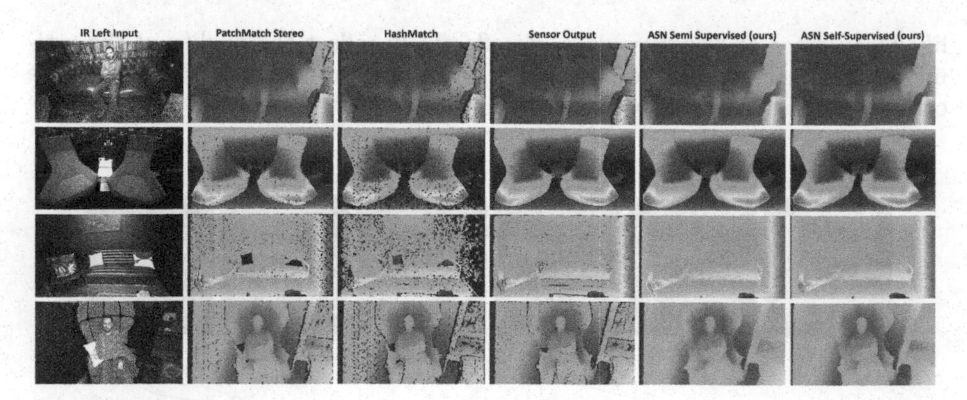

Fig. 6. Qualitative Evaluation with state of the art. Our method produces detailed disparity maps. State of the art local methods [7,13] suffer from textureless regions. The semi-global scheme used by the sensor [29] is noisier and it oversmooths the output.

Comparisons with State of the Art. More qualitative evaluations of ASN in challenging scenes are shown in Fig. 6. As can be seen, local methods like PatchMatch stereo [7] and HashMatch [13] do not handle mixed illumination with both active and passive light, and thus produce incomplete disparity images (missing pixels shown in black). The sensor output using a semi-global scheme is more suitable for this data [29], but it is still susceptible to image noise (note the noisy results in the fourth column). In contrast, our method produces complete disparity maps and preserves sharp boundaries.

More examples on real sequences are shown in Fig. 8 (right), where we show point clouds colored by surface normal. Our output preserves all the details and exhibits a low level of noise. In comparison, our network trained with the self-supervised method by Godard et al. [20] over-smooths the output, hallucinating geometry and flying pixels. Our results are also free from the texture copying problem, most likely because we use a cost volume to explicitly model the matching function rather than learn directly from pixel intensity. Even though the training data is mostly captured from office environment, we find ASN generalize well to various testing scenes, e.g. living room, play room, dinning room, and objects, e.g. person, sofas, plants, table, as shown in figures.

4.3 Ablation Study

In this section, we evaluate the importance of each component in the ASN system. Due to the lack of ground truth data, most of the results are qualitative – when looking at the disparity maps, please pay particular attention to noise, bias, edge fattening, flying pixels, resolution, holes, and generalization capabilities.

Self-supervised vs Supervised. Here we perform more evaluations of our self-supervised model on synthetic data when supervision is available as well as on real data using the depth from the sensor as supervision (together with the proposed loss). Quantitative evaluation on synthetic data (Fig. 8, left bottom), shows that the supervised model (blue) achieves a higher percentage of pixels with error less than 5 disparity, however for more strict requirements (error less than 2 pixels) our self-supervised loss (red) does a better job. This may indicate overfitting of the supervised model on the training set. This behavior is even more evident on real data: the model was able to fit the training set with high precision, however on test images it produces blur results compared to the self-supervised model (see Fig. 6, ASN Semi Supervised vs ASN Self-Supervised).

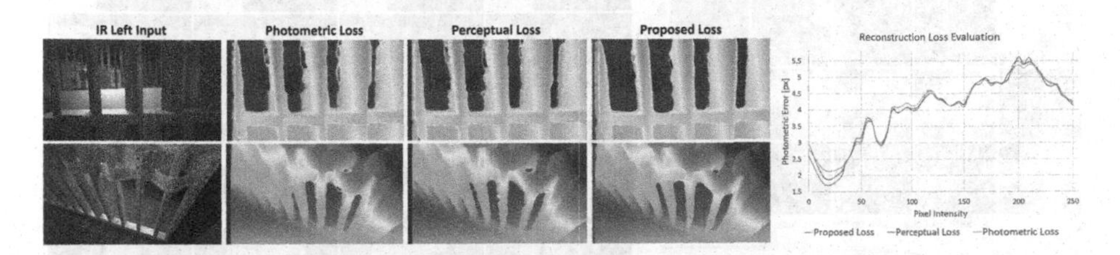

Fig. 7. Ablation study on reconstruction loss. Same networks, trained on 3 different reconstruction losses. Notice how the proposed WLCN loss infers disparities that better follow the edges in these challenging scenes. Photometric and Perceptual losses have also a higher level of noise. On the right, we show how our loss achieves the lowest reconstruction error for low intensity pixels thanks to the proposed WLCN.

Reconstruction Loss. We next investigate the impact of our proposed WLCN loss (as described in Sect. 3.2) in comparison to a standard photometric error (L1) and a perceptual loss [27] computed using feature maps from a pre-trained VGG network. In this experiment, we trained three networks with the same parameters, changing only the reconstruction loss: photometric on raw IR, VGG conv-1, and the proposed WLCN, and investigate their impacts on the results.

To compute accurate metrics, we labeled the occluded regions in a subset of our test case manually (see Fig. 9). For those pixels that were not occluded, we computed the photometric error of the raw IR images given the predicted disparity image. In total we evaluated over 10M pixels. In Fig. 7 (right), we show the photometric error of the raw IR images for the three losses with respect to the pixel intensities. The proposed WLCN achieves the lowest error for small intensities, showing that the loss is not biased towards bright areas. For the rest of the range the losses get similar numbers. Please notice that our loss achieves the lowest error even we did not explicitly train to minimize the photometric reconstruction. Although the numbers may seem similar, the effect on the final disparity map is actually very evident. We show some examples of predicted disparities for each of the three different losses in Fig. 7 (left). Notice how the proposed WLCN loss suffers from less noise, produces crisper edges, and has a lower percentage of outliers. In contrast, the perceptual loss highlights the high frequency texture in the disparity maps (i.e. dots), leading to noisy estimates. Since VGG conv-1 is pre-trained, we observed that the responses are high on bright dots, biasing the reconstruction error again towards close up scenes.

We also tried a variant of the perceptual loss by using the output from our Siamese tower as the perceptual feature, however the behavior was similar to the case of using the VGG features.

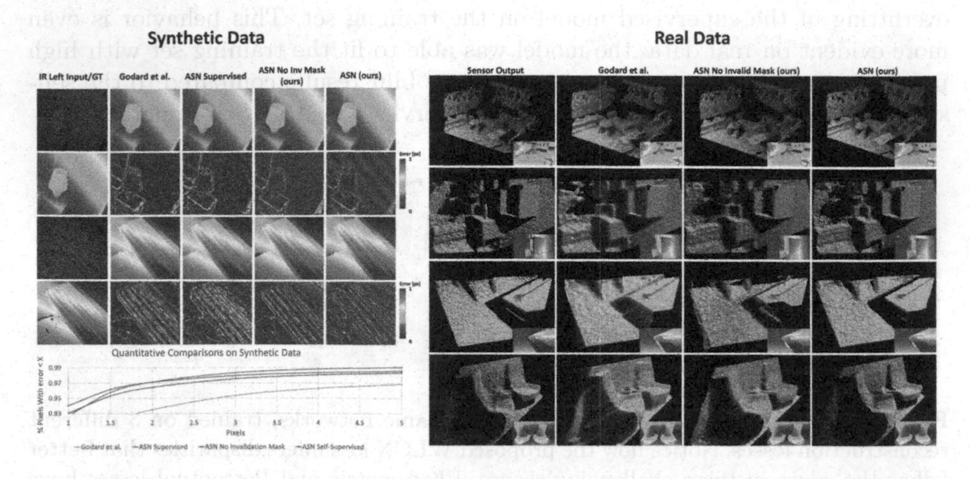

Fig. 8. Evaluation on Synthetic and Real Data. On synthetic data (left), notice how our method has the highest percentage of pixels with error smaller than 1 disparity. We also produce sharper edges and less noisy output compared to other baselines. The state of the art self-supervised method by Godard et al. [20] is very inaccurate near discontinuities. On the right, we show real sequences from an Intel RealSense D435 where the gap between [20] and our method is even more evident: notice flying pixels and oversmooth depthmaps produced by Godard et al. [20]. Our results has higher precision than the sensor output. (Color figure online)

Invalidation Network. We next investigate whether excluding occluded region from the reconstruction loss is important to train a network – i.e., to achieve crisper edges and less noisy disparity maps. We hypothesize that the architecture would try to overfit occluded regions without this feature (where there are no matches), leading to higher errors throughout the images. We test this quantitatively on synthetic images by computing the percentage of pixels with disparity error less than $x \in [1, 5]$. The results are reported in Fig. 8. With the invalidation mask employed, our model outperforms the case without for all the error threshold (Red v.s Purple curve, higher is better). We further analyze the produced disparity and depth maps on both synthetic and real data. On synthetic data, the model without invalidation mask shows gross error near the occlusion boundary (Fig. 8, left top). Same situation happens on real data (Fig. 8, right), where more flying pixels exhibiting when no invalidation mask is enabled.

As a byproduct of the invalidation network, we obtain a confidence map for the depth estimates. In Fig. 9 we show our predicted masks compared with the ones predicted with a left-right check and the photometric error. To assess the performances, we used again the images we manually labeled with occluded regions and computed the average precision (AP). Our invalidation network and left right check achieved the highest scores with an AP of 80.7% and 80.9% respectively, whereas the photometric error only reached 51.3%. We believe that these confidence maps could be useful for many higher-level applications.

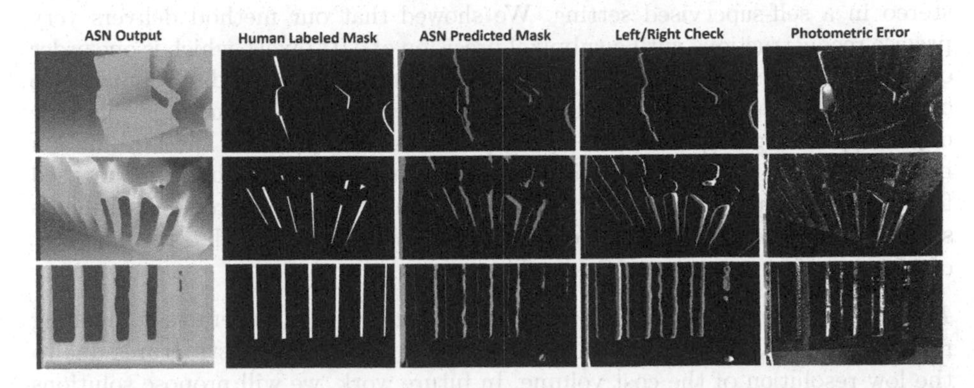

Fig. 9. Invalidation mask prediction. Our invalidation mask is able to detect occluded regions and it reaches an average precision of 80.7% (see text).

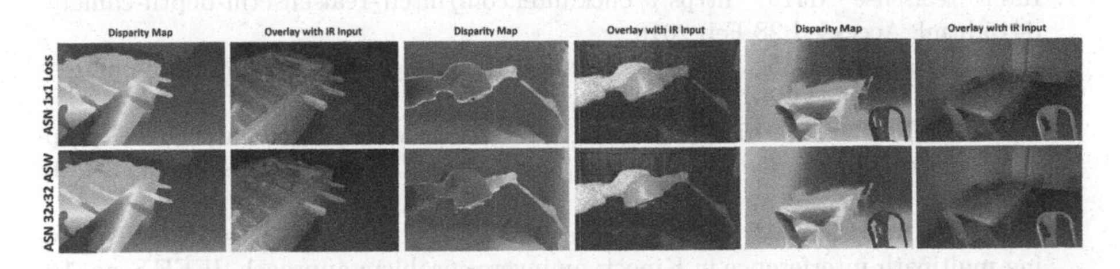

Fig. 10. Comparison between single pixel loss and the proposed window based optimization with adaptive support scheme. Notice how the ASW is able to recover more thin structures and produce less edge fattening.

Window Based Optimization. The proposed window based optimization with Adaptive Support Weights (ASW) is very important to get more support for thin structures that otherwise would get a lower contribution in the loss and treated as outliers. We show a comparison of this in Fig. 10. Notice how the loss with ASW is able to recover hard thin structures with higher precision. Moreover, our window based optimization also produces smoother results while preserving edges and details. Finally, despite we use a window-based loss, the proposed ASW strategy has a reduced amount of edge fattening.

5 Discussion

We presented ActiveStereoNet (ASN) the first deep learning method for active stereo systems. We designed a novel loss function to cope with high-frequency patterns, illumination effects, and occluded pixels to address issues of active stereo in a self-supervised setting. We showed that our method delivers very precise reconstructions with a subpixel precision of 0.03 pixels, which is one order of magnitude better than other active stereo matching methods. Compared to other approaches, ASN does not oversmooth details, and it generates complete depthmaps, crisp edges, and no flying pixels. As a byproduct, the invalidation network is able to infer a confidence map of the disparity that can be used for high level applications requiring occlusions handling. Numerous experiments show state of the art results on different challenging scenes with a runtime cost of 15ms per frame using an NVidia Titan X.

Limitations and Future Work. Although our method generates compelling results there are still issues with transparent objects and thin structures due to the low resolution of the cost volume. In future work, we will propose solutions to handle these cases with high level cues, such as semantic segmentation.

References

1. Intel realsense d415. https://click.intel.com/intelr-realsensetm-depth-camera-d415.html. Accessed 28 Feb 2018
2. Intel realsense d435. https://click.intel.com/intelr-realsensetm-depth-camera-d435.html. Accessed 28 Feb 2018
3. Besse, F., Rother, C., Fitzgibbon, A., Kautz, J.: PMBP: patchmatch belief propagation for correspondence field estimation. Int. J. Comput. Vis. **110**(1), 2–13 (2014)
4. Bhandari, A., Feigin, M., Izadi, S., Rhemann, C., Schmidt, M., Raskar, R.: Resolving multipath interference in Kinect: an inverse problem approach. IEEE Sens. **16**, 3419–3427 (2014)
5. Bhandari, A., et al.: Resolving multi-path interference in time-of-flight imaging via modulation frequency diversity and sparse regularization. CoRR (2014)
6. Bleyer, M., Gelautz, M.: Simple but effective tree structures for dynamic programming-based stereo matching. In: VISAPP, no. 2, pp. 415–422 (2008)
7. Bleyer, M., Rhemann, C., Rother, C.: Patchmatch stereo-stereo matching with slanted support windows. In: BMVC, vol. 11, pp. 1–11 (2011)
8. Dou, M., et al.: Motion2fusion: real-time volumetric performance capture. In: SIGGRAPH Asia (2017)
9. Dou, M., et al.: Fusion4D: real-time performance capture of challenging scenes. In: SIGGRAPH (2016)
10. Fanello, S.R., Gori, I., Metta, G., Odone, F.: Keep it simple and sparse: real-time action recognition. JMLR **14**, 2617–2640 (2013)
11. Fanello, S.R.: Learning to be a depth camera for close-range human capture and interaction. ACM SIGGRAPH Trans. Graph. **33**, 86 (2014)
12. Fanello, S.R., et al.: HyperDepth: learning depth from structured light without matching. In: CVPR (2016)

13. Fanello, S.R., et al.: Low compute and fully parallel computer vision with Hash-Match (2017)
14. Fanello, S.R., et al.: Ultrastereo: efficient learning-based matching for active stereo systems. In: 2017 IEEE Conference on Computer Vision and Pattern Recognition (CVPR), pp. 6535–6544. IEEE (2017)
15. Fanello, S.R., Gori, I., Metta, G., Odone, F.: One-shot learning for real-time action recognition. In: Sanches, J.M., Micó, L., Cardoso, J.S. (eds.) IbPRIA 2013. LNCS, vol. 7887, pp. 31–40. Springer, Heidelberg (2013). https://doi.org/10.1007/978-3-642-38628-2_4
16. Felzenszwalb, P.F., Huttenlocher, D.P.: Efficient belief propagation for early vision. Int. J. Comput. Vis. **70**(1), 41–54 (2006)
17. Foi, A., Trimeche, M., Katkovnik, V., Egiazarian, K.: Practical Poissonian-Gaussian noise modeling and fitting for single-image raw-data. IEEE Trans. Image Process. **17**, 1737–1754 (2008)
18. Garg, R., Vijay Kumar, B.G., Carneiro, G., Reid, I.: Unsupervised CNN for single view depth estimation: geometry to the rescue. In: Leibe, B., Matas, J., Sebe, N., Welling, M. (eds.) ECCV 2016. LNCS, vol. 9912, pp. 740–756. Springer, Cham (2016). https://doi.org/10.1007/978-3-319-46484-8_45
19. Gidaris, S., Komodakis, N.: Detect, replace, refine: deep structured prediction for pixel wise labeling. In: Proceedings of the IEEE Conference on Computer Vision and Pattern Recognition, pp. 5248–5257 (2017)
20. Godard, C., Mac Aodha, O., Brostow, G.J.: Unsupervised monocular depth estimation with left-right consistency. In: CVPR, vol. 2, p. 7 (2017)
21. Hamzah, R.A., Ibrahim, H.: Literature survey on stereo vision disparity map algorithms. J. Sens. **2016**, 23 (2016)
22. Hazan, E., Levy, K.Y., Shalev-Shwartz, S.: On graduated optimization for stochastic non-convex problems. In: ICML (2016)
23. Hirschmuller, H.: Stereo processing by semiglobal matching and mutual information. IEEE Trans. Pattern Anal. Mach. Intell. **30**(2), 328–341 (2008)
24. Hosni, A., Rhemann, C., Bleyer, M., Rother, C., Gelautz, M.: Fast cost-volume filtering for visual correspondence and beyond. IEEE Trans. Pattern Anal. Mach. Intell. **35**(2), 504–511 (2013)
25. Ilg, E., Mayer, N., Saikia, T., Keuper, M., Dosovitskiy, A., Brox, T.: FlowNet 2.0: evolution of optical flow estimation with deep networks. In: IEEE Conference on Computer Vision and Pattern Recognition (CVPR), vol. 2 (2017)
26. Jaderberg, M., Simonyan, K., Zisserman, A., Kavukcuoglu, K.: Spatial transformer networks. In: NIPS (2015)
27. Johnson, J., Alahi, A., Li, F.: Perceptual losses for real-time style transfer and super-resolution. CoRR (2016)
28. Kendall, A., et al.: End-to-end learning of geometry and context for deep stereo regression. CoRR, vol. abs/1703.04309 (2017)
29. Keselman, L., Iselin Woodfill, J., Grunnet-Jepsen, A., Bhowmik, A.: Intel realsense stereoscopic depth cameras. In: CVPR Workshops (2017)
30. Khamis, S., Fanello, S., Rhemann, C., Valentin, J., Kowdle, A., Izadi, S.: StereoNet: guided hierarchical refinement for edge-aware depth prediction. In: ECCV (2018)
31. Klaus, A., Sormann, M., Karner, K.: Segment-based stereo matching using belief propagation and a self-adapting dissimilarity measure. In: 18th International Conference on Pattern Recognition, ICPR 2006, vol. 3, pp. 15–18. IEEE (2006)
32. Kolmogorov, V., Zabih, R.: Computing visual correspondence with occlusions using graph cuts. In: Eighth IEEE International Conference on Computer Vision, ICCV 2001 Proceedings, vol. 2, pp. 508–515. IEEE (2001)

33. Konolige, K.: Projected texture stereo. In: ICRA (2010)
34. Kowalczuk, J., Psota, E.T., Perez, L.C.: Real-time stereo matching on CUDA using an iterative refinement method for adaptive support-weight correspondences. IEEE Trans. Circuits Syst. Video Technol. **23**, 94–104 (2013)
35. Kuznietsov, Y., Stückler, J., Leibe, B.: Semi-supervised deep learning for monocular depth map prediction. In: Proceedings of the IEEE Conference on Computer Vision and Pattern Recognition, pp. 6647–6655 (2017)
36. Liang, Z., et al.: Learning deep correspondence through prior and posterior feature constancy. arXiv preprint arXiv:1712.01039 (2017)
37. Luo, W., Schwing, A.G., Urtasun, R.: Efficient deep learning for stereo matching. In: Proceedings of the IEEE Conference on Computer Vision and Pattern Recognition, pp. 5695–5703 (2016)
38. Mayer, N., et al.: A large dataset to train convolutional networks for disparity, optical flow, and scene flow estimation. In: Proceedings of the IEEE Conference on Computer Vision and Pattern Recognition, pp. 4040–4048 (2016)
39. Naik, N., Kadambi, A., Rhemann, C., Izadi, S., Raskar, R., Kang, S.: A light transport model for mitigating multipath interference in TOF sensors. In: CVPR (2015)
40. Neil, T., Tim, C.: Multi-resolution methods and graduated non-convexity. In: Vision Through Optimization (1997)
41. Nishihara, H.K.: PRISM: a practical mealtime imaging stereo matcher. In: Intelligent Robots: 3rd International Conference on Robot Vision and Sensory Controls, vol. 449, pp. 134–143. International Society for Optics and Photonics (1984)
42. Pang, J., Sun, W., Ren, J., Yang, C., Yan, Q.: Cascade residual learning: a two-stage convolutional neural network for stereo matching. In: International Conference on Computer Vision-Workshop on Geometry Meets Deep Learning (ICCVW 2017), vol. 3 (2017)
43. Scharstein, D., Szeliski, R.: A taxonomy and evaluation of dense two-frame stereo correspondence algorithms. Int. J. Comput. Vis. **47**(1–3), 7–42 (2002)
44. Shaked, A., Wolf, L.: Improved stereo matching with constant highway networks and reflective confidence learning. CoRR, vol. abs/1701.00165 (2017)
45. Szeliski, R.: Computer Vision: Algorithms and Applications, 1st edn. Springer, London (2010). https://doi.org/10.1007/978-1-84882-935-0
46. Tankovich, V., et al.: Sos: Stereo matching in o(1) with slanted support windows. In: IROS (2018)
47. Taylor, J., et al.: Efficient and precise interactive hand tracking through joint, continuous optimization of pose and correspondences. In: SIGGRAPH (2016)
48. Taylor, J., et al.: Articulated distance fields for ultra-fast tracking of hands interacting. In: SIGGRAPH Asia (2017)
49. Tieleman, T., Hinton, G.: Lecture 6.5-RMSprop: divide the gradient by a running average of its recent magnitude. In: COURSERA: Neural Networks for Machine Learning (2012)
50. Wang, S., Fanello, S.R., Rhemann, C., Izadi, S., Kohli, P.: The global patch collider. In: CVPR (2016)
51. Xie, J., Girshick, R., Farhadi, A.: Deep3D: fully automatic 2D-to-3D video conversion with deep convolutional neural networks. In: Leibe, B., Matas, J., Sebe, N., Welling, M. (eds.) ECCV 2016. LNCS, vol. 9908, pp. 842–857. Springer, Cham (2016). https://doi.org/10.1007/978-3-319-46493-0_51
52. Yoon, K.J., Kweon, I.S.: Locally adaptive support-weight approach for visual correspondence search. In: IEEE Computer Society Conference on Computer Vision and Pattern Recognition, CVPR 2005, vol. 2, pp. 924–931. IEEE (2005)

53. Yoon, K.J., Kweon, I.S.: Adaptive support-weight approach for correspondence search. PAMI **28**, 650–656 (2006)
54. Zagoruyko, S., Komodakis, N.: Learning to compare image patches via convolutional neural networks. In: 2015 IEEE Conference on Computer Vision and Pattern Recognition (CVPR), pp. 4353–4361. IEEE (2015)
55. Zbontar, J., LeCun, Y.: Computing the stereo matching cost with a convolutional neural network. In: Proceedings of the IEEE Conference on Computer Vision and Pattern Recognition, pp. 1592–1599 (2015)
56. Zbontar, J., LeCun, Y.: Stereo matching by training a convolutional neural network to compare image patches. J. Mach. Learn. Res. **17**(1–32), 2 (2016)
57. Zhao, H., Gallo, O., Frosio, I., Kautz, J.: Loss functions for image restoration with neural networks. IEEE Trans. Comput. Imaging **3**, 47–57 (2017)
58. Zhong, Y., Dai, Y., Li, H.: Self-supervised learning for stereo matching with self-improving ability. arXiv preprint arXiv:1709.00930 (2017)
59. Zhou, T., Brown, M., Snavely, N., Lowe, D.G.: Unsupervised learning of depth and ego-motion from video. In: CVPR, vol. 2, p. 7 (2017)

GAL: Geometric Adversarial Loss for Single-View 3D-Object Reconstruction

Li Jiang[1](✉), Shaoshuai Shi[1], Xiaojuan Qi[1], and Jiaya Jia[1,2]

[1] The Chinese University of Hong Kong, Hong Kong, China
[2] Tencent YouTu Lab, Shenzhen, China
{lijiang,xjqi,leojia}@cse.cuhk.edu.hk, ssshi@ee.cuhk.edu.hk

Abstract. In this paper, we present a framework for reconstructing a point-based 3D model of an object from a single-view image. We found distance metrics, like Chamfer distance, were used in previous work to measure the difference of two point sets and serve as the loss function in point-based reconstruction. However, such point-point loss does not constrain the 3D model from a global perspective. We propose adding geometric adversarial loss (GAL). It is composed of two terms where the geometric loss ensures consistent shape of reconstructed 3D models close to ground-truth from different viewpoints, and the conditional adversarial loss generates a semantically-meaningful point cloud. GAL benefits predicting the obscured part of objects and maintaining geometric structure of the predicted 3D model. Both the qualitative results and quantitative analysis manifest the generality and suitability of our method.

Keywords: 3D Reconstruction · Adversarial loss
Geometric consistency · Point cloud · 3D Neural network

1 Introduction

Single-view 3D object reconstruction is a fundamental task in computer vision with various applications in robotics, CAD, virtual reality and augmented reality. Recently, data-driven 3D object reconstruction attracts much attention [3,4,7] with the availability of large-scale ShapeNet dataset [2] and advent of deep convolutional neural networks.

Previous approaches [3,4,7,21] adopted two types of representations for 3D objects. The first is voxel-based representation that requires the network to directly predict the occupancy of each voxel [3,7,21]. Albeit easy to integrate into deep neural networks, voxel-based representation suffers from efficiency and memory issues, especially in high-resolution prediction. To address these issues,

Electronic supplementary material The online version of this chapter (https://doi.org/10.1007/978-3-030-01237-3_49) contains supplementary material, which is available to authorized users.

V. Ferrari et al. (Eds.): ECCV 2018, LNCS 11212, pp. 820–834, 2018.
https://doi.org/10.1007/978-3-030-01237-3_49

Fan *et al.* [4] proposed point-based representation, in which the object is composed of discrete points. In this paper, we design our system based on point-based representation considering its scalability and flexibility.

Along the line of forming point-based representation, researchers focused on designing loss functions to measure the distance between prediction point set and ground-truth set. Chamfer distance and Earth Mover distance were used in [4] to train the model. These functions penalize prediction deviating from the ground-truth location. The limitation is that there is no guarantee that the predicted points follow the geometric shape of objects. It is possible that the result does not lie in the manifold of the real 3D objects.

We address this problem in this paper and propose a new complementary loss function – *geometric adversarial loss (GAL)*. It regularizes prediction globally by enforcing the prediction to be consistent with the ground-truth among different 2D views and following the 3D semantics of point cloud.

GAL is composed of two important components, namely, geometric loss and conditional adversarial loss. Geometric loss lets the prediction in different views consistent with the ground truth. Regarding conditional adversarial loss, the conditional discriminator network combines a 2D CNN, to extract image semantic features, with PointNet [16], which extracts global features of the predicted/ground-truth point cloud. Features from the 2D CNN serve as a condition to enforce predicted 3D point cloud with respect to the semantic class of the input. In this regard, GAL regularizes predictions in a global perspective and thus can work in complement with previous CD [4] loss for better object reconstruction from a single image.

Figure 1 preliminarily illustrates the reconstruction quality. When measured using chamfer distance, predictions by previous method [4] are similar to ours with just 0.5% difference. However, when viewed from different viewpoints, there come many noisy points as shown in Fig. 1(b) & (d) in the predicted point cloud produced by previous work. This is because the global 3D geometry is not respected, and only local point-to-point loss is adopted. With geometric adversarial loss (GAL) to regularize prediction globally, our method produces geometrically more reasonable results as shown in Fig. 1(c) & (e). Our main contribution is threefold.

- We propose a loss function, namely GAL, to geometrically regularize prediction from a global perspective.
- We extensively analyze contribution of different loss functions in generating 3D objects.
- Our method achieves better results both quantitatively and qualitatively in ShapeNet dataset.

2 Related Work

2.1 3D Reconstruction from Single Images

Traditional 3D reconstruction methods [1,5,8,10,11,13] require multiple view correspondence. Recently, data-driven 3D reconstruction from single images

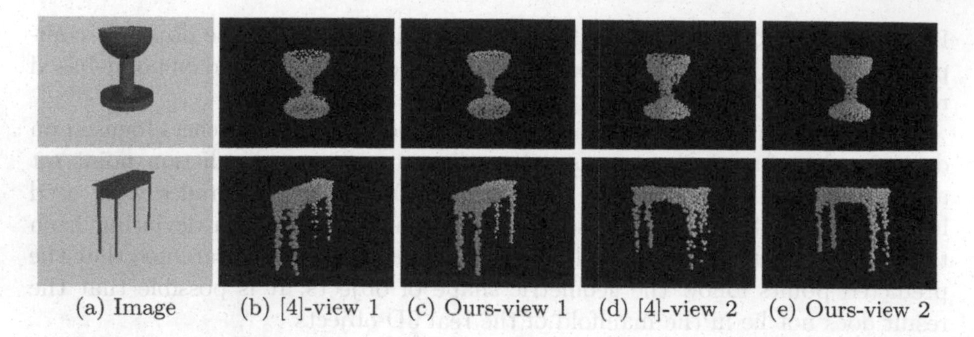

Fig. 1. Illustration of predictions. (a) Original image including the objects to be reconstructed. (b) & (d) Results of [4] when viewed in two different angles. (c) & (f) Our prediction results from corresponding views. Color represents the relative distance to the camera in (b)–(e).

[3,4,7,19,21] has gained more attention. Reconstructing 3D shapes from single images is ill-posed but desirable in real-world applications. Moreover, human actually have the ability to infer 3D shapes of objects given only a single view of it by using prior knowledge and visual experience of the 3D world. Previous work in this setting can be coarsely cast into two categories.

Voxel-based Reconstruction. One stream of research focuses on voxel-based representation [3,7,21]. Choy *et al.* [3] proposed applying 2D convolutional neural networks to encode prior knowledge about the shape into a vector representation and then 3D convolutional neural network was used to decode the latent representation into 3D object shapes. Follow-up work [7] proposed the adversarial constraint to regularize predictions in the real manifold with a large amount of unlabeled realistic 3D shapes. Tulsiani *et al.* [20] adopted an unsupervised solution for 3D object reconstruction by jointly learning a pose estimation network and 3D object voxel prediction network with the multi-view consistency constraint.

Point Cloud Reconstruction. Voxel-based representation may suffer from memory and computation issues when scaled to high resolutions. To address this issue, point cloud based representation for 3D reconstruction was introduced by Fan *et al.* [4]. Unordered point cloud is directly derived from a single image, which can encode more details of 3D shape. The end-to-end framework directly regresses point location. Chamfer distance is adopted to measure the difference between predicted point cloud and ground truth. We follow this line of research. Yet we make our contribution on a new differentiable multi-view geometric loss to measure results from different viewpoints, which is complementary to chamfer distance. We also use conditional adversarial loss as a manifold regularizer to make the predicted point cloud more reasonable and realistic.

2.2 Point Cloud Feature Extraction

Point cloud feature extraction is a challenging problem since points lie in a non-regular space and cannot be processed easily with common CNNs. Qi *et al.* [16] proposed PointNet to extract unordered point representation by using multilayer perceptron and global pooling. Transformer network is incorporated to learn robust transformation invariant features. PointNet is a simple and yet elegant framework to extract point features. As a follow-up work, PointNet++ was proposed in [17] to integrate global and local representations with much increased computation cost. In our work, we adopt pointNet as our feature extractor for predicted and ground truth point clouds.

2.3 Generative Adversarial Networks

There is a large body of work for generative adversarial networks [6,9,12,14,22] to create 2D images by regularizing prediction in the manifold of the target space. Generative adversarial networks were used in reconstructing 3D models from single-view images in [7,21]. Gwak *et al.* [7] better utilized unlabeled data for 3D voxel based reconstruction. Yang *et al.* [21] reconstructed 3D object voxels from single depth images. They show promising results in a simpler setting since one view of the 3D model is given with accurate 3D position. Different from these approaches, we design a conditional adversarial network for 3D point cloud based reconstruction to enforce prediction in the same semantic space under the condition of using single-view images.

3 Method Overview

Our approach produces 3D point cloud from a single-view image. The network architecture is shown in Fig. 2.

In the following, I_{in} denotes the input RGB image, and P_{gt} denotes the ground-truth point cloud. As illustrated in Fig. 2, the framework consists of two networks, i.e., generator network (G) and conditional discriminator network (D). G is the same as the one used in [4] composed of several encoder-decoder hourglass [15] modules and a fully connected branch to produce point locations. It is responsible for producing point locations that map input image I_{in} to its corresponding point cloud P_{pred}. Since it is not our major contribution, we refer readers to the supplementary material for more details.

The other component – conditional discriminator (D) (Fig. 2) – contains a PointNet [16] to extract features of the generated and ground-truth point clouds, and a CNN takes I_{in} as input to extract semantic features of the object. The extracted features are combined together as the final representation. The goal is to distinguish between the generated 3D prediction and the real 3D object.

Built upon the above network architecture, our loss function GAL regularizes the prediction globally to enforce it to follow the 3D geometry. GAL is composed of two components as shown in Fig. 2, i.e., multi-view geometric loss detailed

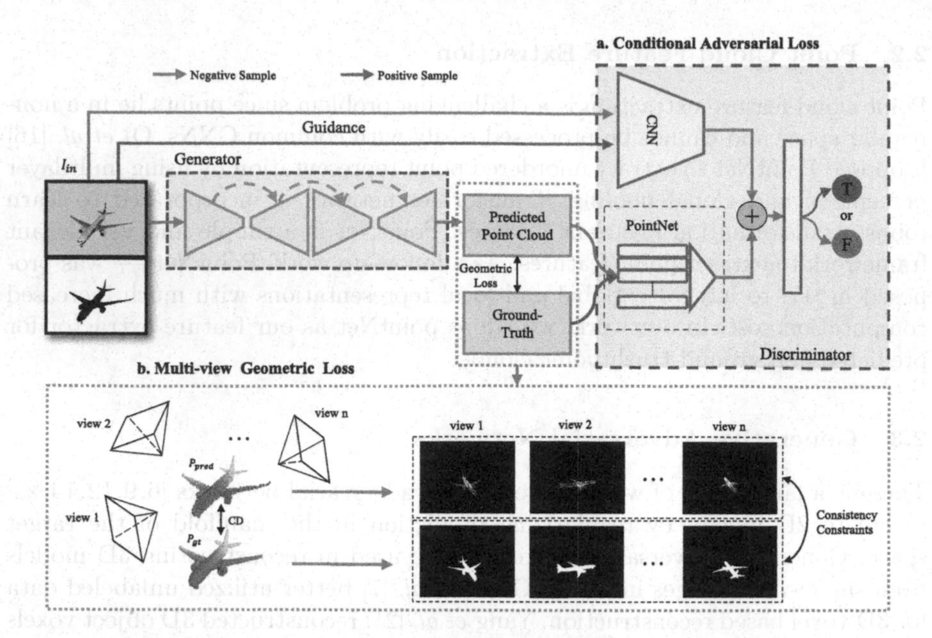

Fig. 2. Overview of our framework. The whole network consists of two parts: a generator network taking a single image as input and producing a point cloud modeling the 3D object, and a discriminator for judging the ground-truth and generated model conditioned on the input image. Our proposed geometric adversarial loss (GAL) is composed of conditional adversarial loss (a) and multi-view geometric loss (b).

in Sect. 4.1 and conditional adversarial loss detailed in Sect. 4.2. They work in synergy with the point-to-point chamfer-distance-based loss function [4] for both global and local regularization.

4 GAL: Geometric Adversarial Loss

4.1 Multi-view Geometric Loss

Human can naturally figure out the shape of an object even if only one view is available. It is because of prior knowledge and knowing the overall shape of the objects. In this section, we add multi-view geometric constraints to inject such prior in neural networks. Multi-view geometric loss shown in Fig. 2 measures the inconsistency of geometric shapes between the predicted points P_{pred} and ground-truth P_{gt} in different views.

We first normalize the point clouds to be centered at the origin of the world coordinate. The numbers of points in P_{gt} and P_{pred} are respectively denoted as n_{gt} and n_p. n_p is pre-assigned to 1024 following [4]. n_{gt} is generally much larger than n_p.

To measure multi-view geometric inconsistency between P_{gt} and P_{pred}, we synthesize an image for each view given the point set and view parameters, and

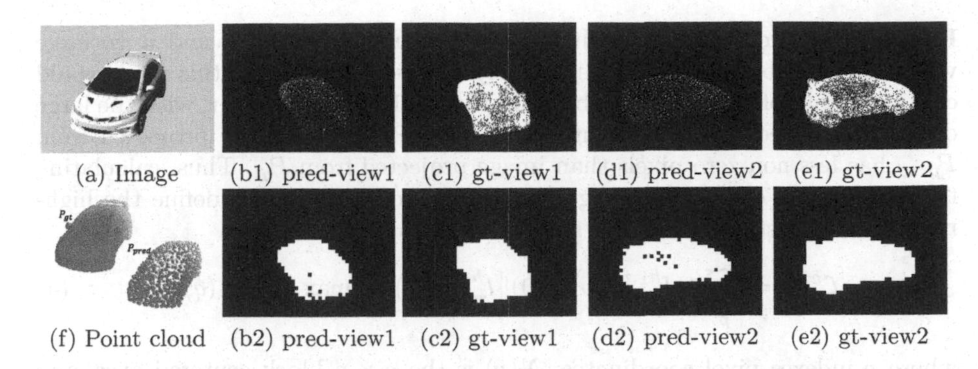

Fig. 3. (a) is the original image. (b1) & (d1) show the high resolution 2D projection of predicted point cloud in two different views. (c1) & (e1) show the high resolution 2D projection of the ground-truth point cloud. (b2)–(e2) show the corresponding low resolution results. (f) shows the ground-truth and predicted point cloud.

then compare each pair of images synthesized from P_{gt} and P_{pred}. Two examples are shown in Fig. 3(b1)–(e1).

To project the 3D point cloud to an image, we first transform point p_w with 3D world coordinate $p_w = (x_w, y_w, z_w)$ to camera coordinates $p_c = (x_c, y_c, z_c)$ as Eq. (1). R and d represent the rotation and translation parameters of the camera regarding the world coordinate. The rotation angles over $\{x, y, z\}$-axis are randomly sampled from $[0, 2\pi)$. Finally, point p_w is projected to the camera plane with function f as

$$p_c = Rp_w + d, \;\; f(p_w|K) = Kp_c, \tag{1}$$

where K is the camera intrinsic matrix.

We set the intrinsic parameters of our view camera as Eq. (2) to guarantee that the object is completely included in the image plane and the projected region occupies the image as much as possible.

$$u_0 = 0.5h, \;\; v_0 = 0.5w, \;\; f_u = f_v = \frac{0.5 \min(\{z_c\}) \min(h, w)}{\max(\{x_c\} \bigcup \{y_c\})} \tag{2}$$

where h and w are the height and width of the projected image.

Then, the projected images of ground-truth and predicted point cloud with size (h, w) could be respectively formulated as

$$I_{gt}^{h,w}(p) = \begin{cases} 1, & \text{if } p \in f(P_{gt}) \\ 0, & \text{otherwise} \end{cases}, \;\; I_{pred}^{h,w}(p) = \begin{cases} 1, & \text{if } p \in f(P_{pred}) \\ 0, & \text{otherwise} \end{cases} \tag{3}$$

where p indexes over all the pixels of the projected image.

The synthesized views (Fig. 3) are with different densities in high resolutions. The projection images from ground-truth shown in Fig. 3(c1) & (e1) is much denser than our corresponding prediction shown in Fig. 3(b1) & (d1). To resolve the above discrepancy, multi-view geometric consistency loss is added in multiple resolutions detailed in the following.

High Resolution Mode. In high resolution mode, we set h and w to large values denoted by h_1 and w_1 respectively. Images projected in this mode could contain details of the object as shown in Fig. 3(b1)–(e1). However, with the large difference between point amounts in P_{gt} and P_{pred}, the image projected from P_{pred} has less non-zero pixels than image projected from P_{gt}. Thus, calculating the L2 distance of the two images directly is not feasible. We define the high-resolution consistency loss for a single view v as

$$\mathcal{L}_v^{high} = \sum_p \mathbb{1}(I_{pred}^{h_1,w_1}(p) > 0) \| I_{pred}^{h_1,w_1}(p) - \max_{q \in N(p)} I_{gt}^{h_1,w_1}(q) \|_2^2, \quad (4)$$

where p indexes pixel coordinates, $N(p)$ is the $n \times n$ block centered at p, and $\mathbb{1}(.)$ is an indicator function set to 1 when the condition is satisfied. Since the predicted point cloud is sparser than the ground-truth, we only use the non-zero pixels in the predicted image to measure the inconsistency. For each non-zero pixel in I_{pred}, we find the corresponding position in I_{gt} and search its neighbors for non-zero pixels to reduce the influence of projection errors.

Low Resolution Mode. In the high-resolution mode, we only check whether the non-zero pixels in I_{pred} appear in I_{gt}. Note that the constraint needs to be bidirectional. We make I_{pred} the same density as I_{gt} by setting h and w to small values h_2 and w_2. Low-resolution projection images are shown in Fig. 3(b2)–(e2). Although details are lost in the low resolution, rough shape is still visible and can be used to check the consistency. Thus, we define the low-resolution consistency loss for a single view v as

$$\mathcal{L}_v^{low} = \sum_p \| I_{pred}^{h_2,w_2}(p) - I_{gt}^{h_2,w_2}(p) \|_2^2, \quad (5)$$

Where $I_{pred}^{h_2,w_2}$ and $I_{gt}^{h_2,w_2}$ represent the low resolution projection images and h_2 and w_2 are the corresponding height and width. The low-resolution loss constrains that the shapes of ground-truth and predicted objects are similar, while the high-resolution loss ensures the details.

Total Multi-view Geometric Loss. We denote v as the view index. The total multi-view geometric loss is defined as

$$\mathcal{L}_{mv} = \sum_v (\mathcal{L}_v^{high} + \mathcal{L}_v^{low}). \quad (6)$$

The objective regularizes the geometric shape of predicted point cloud from different viewpoints.

4.2 Point-Based Conditional Adversarial Loss

To generate a more plausible point cloud, we propose using a conditional adversarial loss to regularize the predicted 3D object points. The generated 3D model should be consistent with the semantic information provided by the image. We adopt PointNet [16] to extract the global feature of the predicted point cloud. Also, with the 2D semantic feature provided by the original image, the discriminator could better distinguish between the real 3D model and the generated fake one. Thus, the RGB image of the object is also fed into the discriminator. P_{pred} along with the corresponding I_{in} serve as a negative sample, while P_{gt} and I_{in} become positive when training the discriminator. During the course of training the generator, the conditional adversarial loss forces the generated point cloud to respect the semantics of the input image.

The CNN part of the discriminator is a pre-trained classification network to extract 2D semantic features, which are then concatenated with feature produced by PointNet [16] for identifying real and fake samples. We note that the point cloud from our prediction is sparser than ground-truth. Hence, we uniformly sample n_p points from ground-truth with a total of n_{gt} points.

Different from traditional GAN, which may be unstable and has low convergence rate, we apply LSGAN as our adversarial loss. LSGAN replaces logarithmic loss function with least-squared loss, which makes it easier for the generated data distribution to converge to the decision boundary. The conditional adversarial loss function is defined as

$$\begin{aligned}\mathcal{L}_{LSGAN}(D) &= \frac{1}{2}[\mathbb{E}_{P_{gt}\sim p(P_{gt})}(D(P_{gt}|I_{in})-1)^2 + \mathbb{E}_{I_{in}\sim p(I_{in})}(D(G(I_{in})|I_{in})-0)^2] \\ \mathcal{L}_{LSGAN}(G) &= \frac{1}{2}[\mathbb{E}_{I_{in}\sim p(I_{in})}(D(G(I_{in})|I_{in})-1)^2]\end{aligned} \tag{7}$$

During the training process, G and D are optimized alternately. G minimizes $\mathcal{L}_{LSGAN}(G)$, which aims to generate a point cloud similar to the real model, while D minimizes $\mathcal{L}_{LSGAN}(D)$ to discriminate between real and predicted point sets. In the testing process, only the well-trained generator needs to be used to reconstruct a point cloud model from a single-view image.

5 Total Objective

To better generate a 3D point cloud model from a single-view image, we combine the conditional adversarial loss and the geometric consistency loss as GAL for global regularization. We also follow the distance metric in [4] to use Chamfer distance to measure the point-to-point similarity of two point sets as a local constraint. Chamfer distance loss is defined as

$$\mathcal{L}_{cd}(I_{in}, P_{gt}|G) = \frac{1}{n_{gt}}\sum_{p\in P_{gt}}\min_{q\in G(I_{in})}\|p-q\|_2^2 + \frac{1}{n_p}\sum_{p\in G(I_{in})}\min_{q\in P_{gt}}\|p-q\|_2^2. \tag{8}$$

With global GAL and point-to-point distance constraint, the total objective becomes

$$\begin{aligned}G^* &= arg\min_G[\mathcal{L}_{LSGAN}(G) + \lambda_1\mathcal{L}_{mv} + \lambda_2\mathcal{L}_{cd}] \\ D^* &= arg\min_D\mathcal{L}_{LSGAN}(D)\end{aligned} \tag{9}$$

where λ_1 and λ_2 control the ratio of different losses.

The generator is responsible for fooling the discriminator, and reconstructing a 3D point set approximating the ground-truth. The adversarial part ensures the reconstructed 3D object to be reasonable with respect to the semantics of the original image. Multi-view geometric consistency loss makes the predicted point cloud a valid prediction when viewed in different directions.

6 Experiments

We perform our experiments on the ShapeNet dataset [2], which has a large collection of textured CAD models. Our detailed network architecture and implementation strategies are the following.

Generator Architecture. Our generator G is built upon the network structure in [4], which takes a 192×256 image as input and consists of a convolution branch producing 768 points and a fully connected branch producing 256 points, resulting in total 1024 points.

Discriminator Architecture. Our discriminator D contains a CNN part to extract semantic features from the input image and a PointNet part to extract features from point cloud as shown in Fig. 2. The backbone of the CNN part is VGG16 [18]. A fully connected layer is added after the $fc8$ layer to reduce the feature dimension to 40.

The major building block in PointNet is multi-layer perceptron (MLP) and global pooling as in [16]. The MLP utilized on points contains 5 hidden layers with layer sizes $(64, 64, 64, 128, 1024)$. The MLP after max pooling layer consists of 3 layers with sizes $(512, 256, 40)$. The features from CNN and PointNet are concatenated together for final discrimination.

Implementation Details. The whole network is trained in an end-to-end fashion using ADAM optimizer with batch size 32. The view number for multi-view geometric loss is set to 7, which is determined by experimenting with different view numbers and selecting the one that gives the best performance. h_1, w_1, h_2, and w_2 are set to 192, 256, 48, and 64 respectively. The block size for neighborhood searching in high resolution mode is set to 3×3.

6.1 Ablation Studies

Evaluation Metric. We evaluate the predicted point clouds of different methods using three metrics: point cloud based Chamfer Distance (CD), voxel based Intersection over Union (IoU) and 2D projection IoU. CD measures the distance between ground-truth point set and predicted one. The definition of CD is in Sect. 5. The lower CD value represents the better reconstructed results.

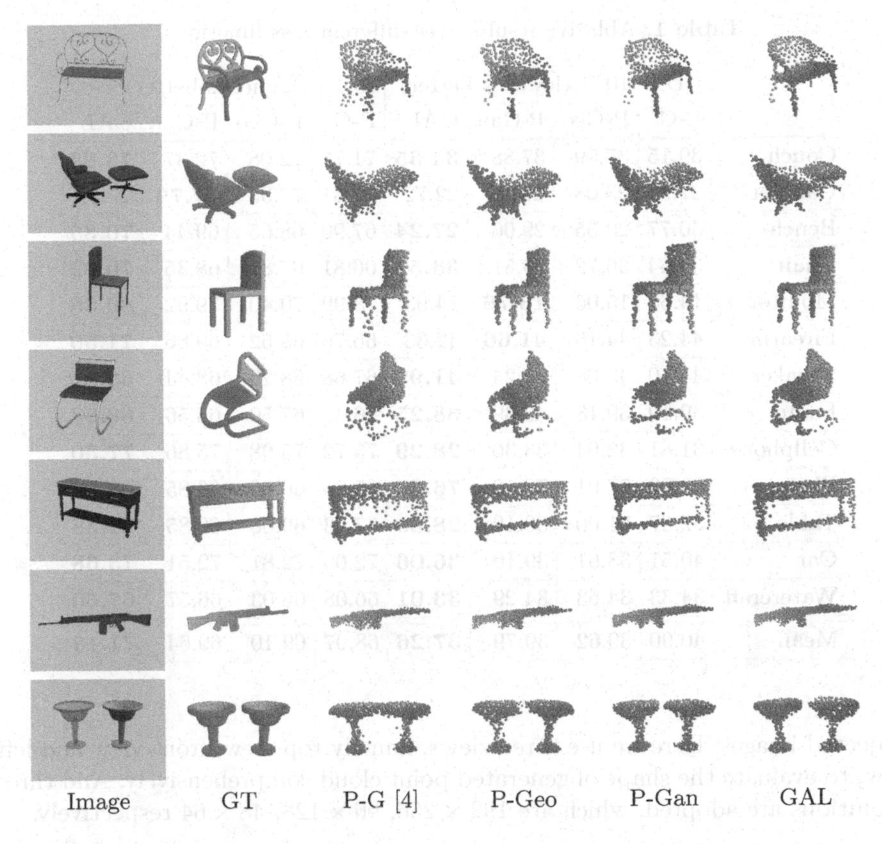

Fig. 4. Qualitative results of single image 3D reconstruction from different methods. For the same object, all the point clouds are visualized from the same viewpoint.

To compute IoU of two point sets, each point set will be voxelized by distributing points into $32 \times 32 \times 32$ grids. We treat each point as a $1 \times 1 \times 1$ grid centered at this point, namely point grid. For each voxel, we consider the maximum intersecting volume ratio of each point grid and this voxel as the occupancy probability. It is then translated into two-value form by a threshold t. The calculation formula of IoU is

$$IoU = \frac{\sum_i \mathbb{1}[V_{gt}(i)V_p(i) > 0]}{\sum_i \mathbb{1}[V_{gt}(i) + V_p(i) > 0]}, \tag{10}$$

where i indexes all voxels, $\mathbb{1}$ is an indicator function, V_{gt} and V_p are respectively the voxel-based ground-truth and voxel-based prediction. The higher IoU value indicates more precise point cloud prediction.

To better evaluate our generated point cloud, we propose a new projected view evaluation metric, i.e. 2D projection IoU, where we project the point clouds into images from different views, and then compute 2D intersection over union (IoU) between the ground-truth projected images and the reconstruction

Table 1. Ablative results over different loss functions.

	CD $\times$ 10^{-4} (lower is better)				IoU% (higher is better)			
	P-G	P-Geo	P-Gan	GAL	P-G	P-Geo	P-Gan	GAL
Couch	39.15	37.59	37.88	**34.35**	71.71	72.08	72.37	**73.87**
Cabinet	22.94	23.08	**22.27**	22.72	77.61	77.33	**77.79**	77.22
Bench	30.77	29.55	29.06	**27.24**	67.90	68.65	69.44	**70.85**
Chair	37.54	36.72	36.51	**33.59**	66.81	67.81	68.35	**70.02**
Monitor	14.65	15.06	**13.76**	14.93	78.99	79.40	79.92	**80.39**
Firearm	44.23	44.16	**41.66**	42.33	66.76	68.62	69.86	**71.50**
Speaker	44.10	43.08	47.24	**41.99**	67.68	68.20	68.44	**69.81**
Lamp	39.19	39.18	42.39	**38.25**	66.48	67.50	68.56	**69.98**
Cellphone	31.81	32.04	33.30	**28.29**	75.72	75.98	75.86	**77.30**
Plane	80.20	77.01	78.10	**76.34**	65.20	66.86	66.85	**68.53**
Table	32.67	31.00	30.10	**28.30**	67.93	69.08	69.85	**71.38**
Car	40.51	38.61	39.10	**36.06**	72.05	72.81	72.51	**73.68**
Watercraft	34.33	34.63	34.29	**33.01**	66.08	66.03	66.57	**67.50**
Mean	40.90	39.62	39.79	**37.26**	68.07	69.10	69.64	**71.16**

projected images. Here we use three views, namely top view, front view and left view, to evaluate the shape of generated point cloud comprehensively. And three resolutions are adopted, which are 192×256, 96×128, 48×64 respectively.

Comparison Among Different Methods. To thoroughly investigate our proposed GAL loss, we consider the following settings for ablation studies.

- *PointSetGeneration*(P-G) [4], which is a point-form single image 3D object reconstruction method. We directly use the model trained by the author-released code as our baseline.
- *PointGeo*(P-Geo), which combines the geometric loss proposed in Sect. 4.1 with our baseline to evaluate the effectiveness of geometric loss.
- *PointGan*(P-Gan), which combines the point-based conditional adversarial loss with our baseline to evaluate the effectiveness of adversarial loss.
- *PointGAL*(GAL), which is the complete framework as shown in Fig. 2 to evaluate the effectiveness of our proposed GAL loss.

Table 1 shows quantitative results regarding CD and IoU for 13 major categories following the setting of [4]. The statistics show that our PointGeo and PointGan models outperform the baseline method [4] in terms of both CD and IoU metrics. The final GAL model can further boost the performance and outperforms the baseline by a large margin. As shown in Table 2, GAL consistently improves 2D projection IoU in all viewpoints, which demonstrates the effectiveness of constraining geometric shape across different viewpoints.

Table 2. 2D projection IoU comparison. The images are projected with three resolutions for three different view points.

	Resolution 192 × 256				Resolution 96 × 128				Resolution 48 × 64			
	P-G	P-Geo	P-Gan	GAL	P-G	P-Geo	P-Gan	GAL	P-G	P-Geo	P-Gan	GAL
Front view	0.328	0.333	0.334	**0.340**	0.601	0.611	0.613	**0.622**	0.773	0.780	0.782	**0.792**
Left view	0.325	0.330	0.330	**0.337**	0.586	0.594	0.594	**0.606**	0.750	0.757	0.758	**0.770**
Top view	0.343	0.346	0.349	**0.355**	0.652	0.657	0.663	**0.673**	0.823	0.829	0.832	**0.839**
Mean-IoU	0.332	0.337	0.338	**0.344**	0.613	0.621	0.623	**0.634**	0.782	0.789	0.791	**0.801**

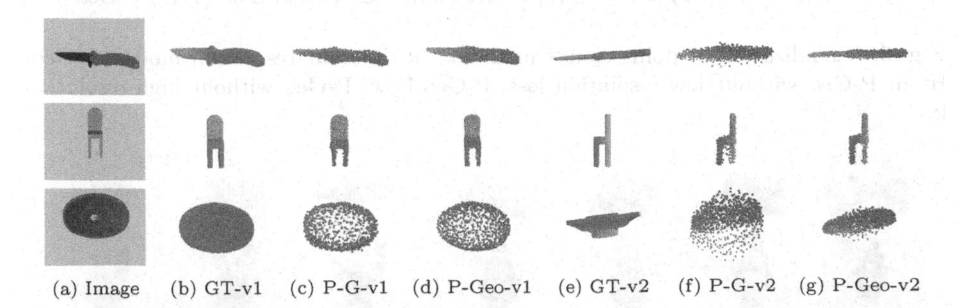

(a) Image (b) GT-v1 (c) P-G-v1 (d) P-Geo-v1 (e) GT-v2 (f) P-G-v2 (g) P-Geo-v2

Fig. 5. Visualization of point clouds predicted by the baseline model (P-G) and our network with geometric loss (P-Geo) from two representative viewpoints. (b)-(d) are visualized from the viewpoint of the input image (v1), while (e)-(g) are synthesized from another view (v2).

Qualitative comparison is shown in Fig. 4. P-G [4] predicts less accurate structure where shape distortion arises (see the leg of furnitures and the connection between two objects). On the contrary, our method can handle these challenges and produce better results, since GAL penalizes inaccurate points from different views and regularizes prediction with semantic information from 2D input images.

Analysis of Multi-view Geometric Loss. We analyze the importance of our multi-view geometric loss by checking the shape of the 3D models from different views. Figure 5 shows two different views of the 3D model produced by the baseline model (P-G) and the baseline model with multi-view consistency loss (P-Geo).

P-G result seems to be comparable (Fig. 5(c)) with ours shown in Fig. 5(d) when observed from the input image view angle. However, when the viewpoint changes, the generated 3D model of P-G (Fig. 5(f)) may not fit the geometry of the object. The predicted shape is much different from the real shape (Fig. 5(b)). In contrast, our reconstructed point cloud in Fig. 5(e) is still consistent with the ground-truth. When trained with multi-view geometric loss, the network penalizes incorrect geometric appearance from different views.

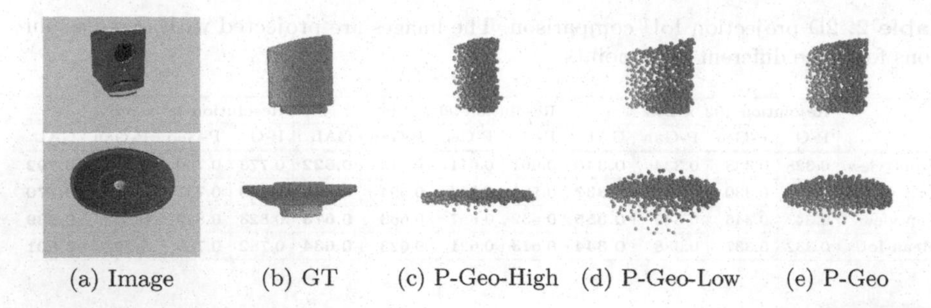

Fig. 6. Visualization of point clouds predicted in different resolution modes. P-Geo-High: P-Geo without low-resolution loss. P-Geo-Low: P-Geo without high-resolution loss.

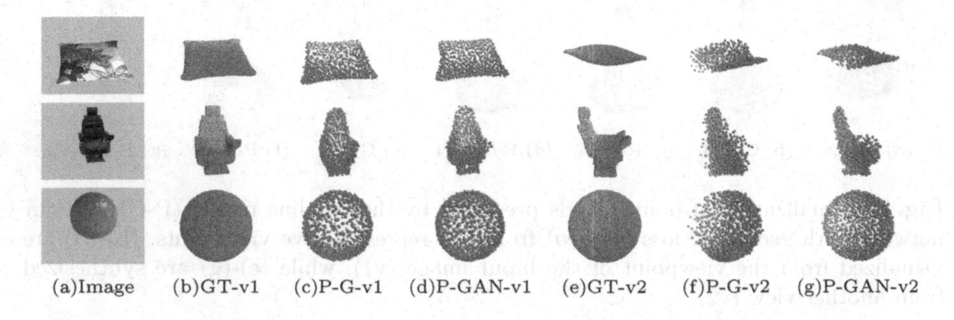

Fig. 7. P-G denotes our baseline model, P-GAN denotes the baseline model with conditional adversarial loss. Two different views are denoted by "v1" and"v2".

Analysis of Different Resolution Modes. We have conducted the ablation study to analyze the effectiveness of different resolution modes. With only the high-resolution geometric loss, the predicted points may lie inside the geometric shape of the object and do not cover the whole object as shown in Fig. 6(c). However, with only the low-resolution geometric loss, points may cover the whole object; but noisy points appear out of the shape as shown in Fig. 6(d). Combining the high and low-resolution loss, our trained model produces the best results as shown in Fig. 6(e).

Analysis of Point-Based Conditional Adversarial Loss. Our point-based conditional adversarial loss helps produce better semantically meaningful 3D object models.

Figure 7 shows the pairwise comparison between the baseline model (P-G) and baseline model with conditional adversarial loss (P-GAN) from two different views. Without exploring the semantic information, the generated point clouds from P-G (Fig. 7(c) & (f)) seem contrived, while our results (Fig. 7(d) & (g)) look more natural from different views. For example, the chair generated by P-G cannot be recognized as a chair when observing from the side view (Fig. 7(f)), while our results have much better appearance seen from different directions.

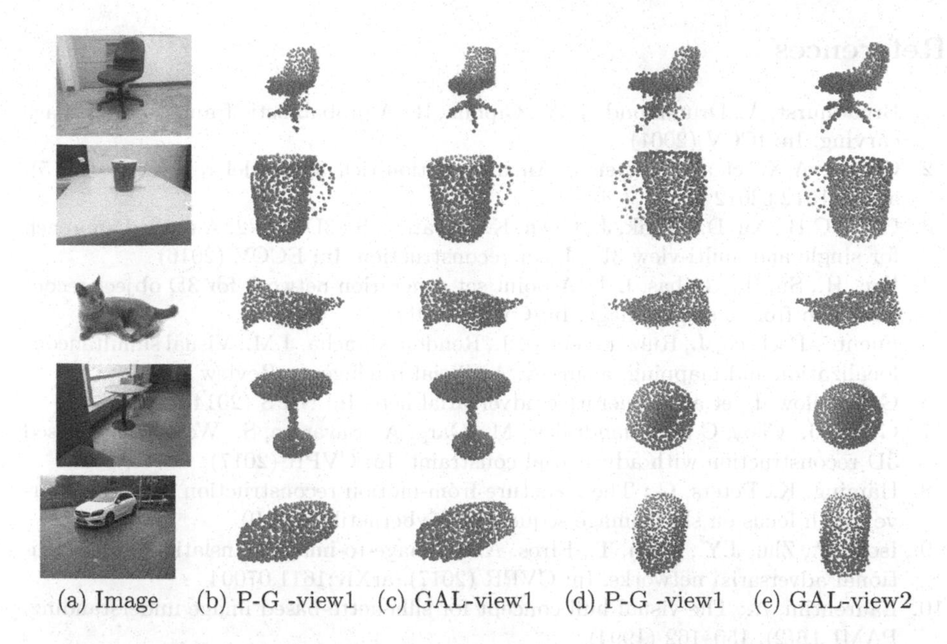

Fig. 8. Illustration of the real-world cases. (a) is the input image. (b) and (d) show results of P-G [4] from two different view angles. (c) and (f) show our prediction results from corresponding views.

6.2 Results on Real-World Objects

We also test the baseline and our GAL model on the real-world images. The images are manually annotated to get the mask of objects. The final results are shown in Fig. 8. Compared with the baseline method, the point clouds generated by our model capture more details. And in most cases, the geometric shape of our predicted point cloud seems to be more accurate in various views.

7 Conclusion

We have presented the geometric adversarial loss (GAL) to regularize single-view 3D object reconstruction from a global perspective. GAL includes two components, i.e. multi-view geometric loss and conditional adversarial loss. Multi-view geometric loss enforces the network to learn to reconstruct multiple-view valid 3D models. Conditional adversarial loss stimulates the system to reconstruct 3D object regarding semantic information in the original image. Results and analysis in the experiment section show that the model trained by our GAL achieves better performance on ShapeNet dataset than others. It can also generate precise point cloud from the real-world images. In the future, we plan to extend GAL to large-scale general reconstruction tasks.

References

1. Broadhurst, A., Drummond, T.W., Cipolla, R.: A probabilistic framework for space carving. In: ICCV (2001)
2. Chang, A.X., et al.: Shapenet: An information-rich 3d model repository (2015). arXiv:1512.03012
3. Choy, C.B., Xu, D., Gwak, J., Chen, K., Savarese, S.: 3D-R2N2: A unified approach for single and multi-view 3D object reconstruction. In: ECCV (2016)
4. Fan, H., Su, H., Guibas, L.J.: A point set generation network for 3D object reconstruction from a single image. In: CVPR (2017)
5. Fuentes-Pacheco, J., Ruiz-Ascencio, J., Rendón-Mancha, J.M.: Visual simultaneous localization and mapping: a survey. Artificial Intelligence Review (2015)
6. Goodfellow, I., et al.: Generative adversarial nets. In: NIPS (2014)
7. Gwak, J., Choy, C.B., Chandraker, M., Garg, A., Savarese, S.: Weakly supervised 3D reconstruction with adversarial constraint. In: CVPR (2017)
8. Häming, K., Peters, G.: The structure-from-motion reconstruction pipeline-a survey with focus on short image sequences. Kybernetika (2010)
9. Isola, P., Zhu, J.Y., Zhou, T., Efros, A.A.: Image-to-image translation with conditional adversarial networks. In: CVPR (2017). arXiv:1611.07004
10. Laurentini, A.: The visual hull concept for silhouette-based image understanding. PAMI **16**(2), 150–162 (1994)
11. Liu, S., Cooper, D.B.: Ray Markov random fields for image-based 3D modeling: model and efficient inference. In: CVPR (2010)
12. Lu, Y., Tai, Y.W., Tang, C.K.: Conditional cyclegan for attribute guided face image generation. In: CVPR (2017). arXiv:1705.09966
13. Matusik, W., Buehler, C., Raskar, R., Gortler, S.J., McMillan, L.: Image-based visual hulls. In: Proceedings of the 27th annual conference on Computer graphics and interactive techniques (2000)
14. Mirza, M., Osindero, S.: Conditional generative adversarial nets (2014). arXiv:1411.1784
15. Newell, A., Yang, K., Deng, J.: Stacked hourglass networks for human pose estimation. In: ECCV (2016) arXiv:1603.06937
16. Qi, C.R., Su, H., Mo, K., Guibas, L.J.: PointNet: Deep learning on point sets for 3D classification and segmentation (2017). arXiv:1612.00593
17. Qi, C.R., Yi, L., Su, H., Guibas, L.J.: PointNet++: Deep hierarchical feature learning on point sets in a metric space. In: NIPS (2017). arXiv:1706.02413
18. Simonyan, K., Zisserman, A.: Very deep convolutional networks for large-scale image recognition (2014). arXiv:1409.1556
19. Tatarchenko, M., Dosovitskiy, A., Brox, T.: Multi-view 3D models from single images with a convolutional network. In: ECCV (2016). arXiv:1511.06702
20. Tulsiani, S., Efros, A.A., Malik, J.: Multi-view consistency as supervisory signal for learning shape and pose prediction (2018). arXiv:1801.03910
21. Yang, B., Wen, H., Wang, S., Clark, R., Markham, A., Trigoni, N.: 3D object reconstruction from a single depth view with adversarial learning (2017). arXiv:1708.07969
22. Zhu, J.Y., Park, T., Isola, P., Efros, A.A.: Unpaired image-to-image translation using cycle-consistent adversarial networks (2017). arXiv:1703.10593

Deep Virtual Stereo Odometry: Leveraging Deep Depth Prediction for Monocular Direct Sparse Odometry

Nan Yang[1,2](✉), Rui Wang[1,2], Jörg Stückler[1], and Daniel Cremers[1,2]

[1] Technical University of Munich, Munich, Germany
{yangn,wangr,stueckle,cremers}@in.tum.de
[2] Artisense, Munich, Germany

Abstract. Monocular visual odometry approaches that purely rely on geometric cues are prone to scale drift and require sufficient motion parallax in successive frames for motion estimation and 3D reconstruction. In this paper, we propose to leverage deep monocular depth prediction to overcome limitations of geometry-based monocular visual odometry. To this end, we incorporate deep depth predictions into Direct Sparse Odometry (DSO) as direct virtual stereo measurements. For depth prediction, we design a novel deep network that refines predicted depth from a single image in a two-stage process. We train our network in a semi-supervised way on photoconsistency in stereo images and on consistency with accurate sparse depth reconstructions from Stereo DSO. Our deep predictions excel state-of-the-art approaches for monocular depth on the KITTI benchmark. Moreover, our Deep Virtual Stereo Odometry clearly exceeds previous monocular and deep-learning based methods in accuracy. It even achieves comparable performance to the state-of-the-art stereo methods, while only relying on a single camera.

Keywords: Monocular depth estimation
Monocular visual odometry · Semi-supervised learning

1 Introduction

Visual odometry (VO) is a highly active field of research in computer vision with a plethora of applications in domains such as autonomous driving, robotics, and augmented reality. VO with a single camera using traditional geometric approaches inherently suffers from the fact that camera trajectory and map can only be estimated up to an unknown scale which also leads to scale drift. Moreover, sufficient motion parallax is required to estimate motion and structure

---

Electronic supplementary material The online version of this chapter (https://doi.org/10.1007/978-3-030-01237-3_50) contains supplementary material, which is available to authorized users.

V. Ferrari et al. (Eds.): ECCV 2018, LNCS 11212, pp. 835–852, 2018.
https://doi.org/10.1007/978-3-030-01237-3_50

Fig. 1. DVSO achieves monocular visual odometry on KITTI on par with state-of-the-art stereo methods. It uses deep-learning based left-right disparity predictions (lower left) for initialization and virtual stereo constraints in an optimization-based direct visual odometry pipeline. This allows for recovering accurate metric estimates.

from successive frames. To avoid these issues, typically more complex sensors such as active depth cameras or stereo rigs are employed. However, these sensors require larger efforts in calibration and increase the costs of the vision system.

Metric depth can also be recovered from a single image if a-priori knowledge about the typical sizes or appearances of objects is used. Deep learning based approaches tackle this by training deep neural networks on large amounts of data. In this paper, we propose a novel approach to monocular visual odometry, Deep Virtual Stereo Odometry (DVSO), which incorporates deep depth predictions into a geometric monocular odometry pipeline. We use deep stereo disparity for virtual direct image alignment constraints within a framework for windowed direct bundle adjustment (e.g. Direct Sparse Odometry [8]). DVSO achieves comparable performance to the state-of-the-art stereo visual odometry systems on the KITTI odometry benchmark. It can even outperform the state-of-the-art geometric VO methods when tuning scale-dependent parameters such as the virtual stereo baseline.

As an additional contribution, we propose a novel stacked residual network architecture that refines disparity estimates in two stages and is trained in a semi-supervised way. In typical supervised learning approaches [6,24,25], depth ground truth needs to be acquired for training with active sensors like RGB-D cameras and 3D laser scanners which are costly to obtain. Requiring a large amount of such labeled data is an additional burden that limits generalization to new environments. Self-supervised [11,14] and unsupervised learning approaches [49], on the other hand, overcome this limitation and do not require additional active sensors. Commonly, they train the networks on photometric consistency, for example in stereo imagery [11,14], which reduces the effort for collecting training data. Still, the current self-supervised approaches are not as accurate as supervised methods [23]. We combine self-supervised and supervised training, but avoid the costly collection of LiDAR data in our approach. Instead, we make use of Stereo Direct Sparse Odometry (Stereo DSO [40]) to provide accurate sparse 3D reconstructions on the training set. Our deep depth prediction network outperforms the current state-of-the-art methods on KITTI.

A video demonstrating our methods as well as the results is available at https://youtu.be/sLZOeC9z_tw.

1.1 Related Work

Deep Learning for Monocular Depth Estimation. Deep learning based approaches have recently achieved great advances in monocular depth estimation. Employing deep neural network avoids the hand-crafted features used in previous methods [19,36]. Supervised deep learning [6,24,25] has recently shown great success for monocular depth estimation. Eigen et al. [5,6] propose a two scale CNN architecture which directly predicts the depth map from a single image. Laina et al. [24] propose a residual network [17] based fully convolutional encoder-decoder architecture [27] with a robust regression loss function. The aforementioned supervised learning approaches need large amounts of ground-truth depth data for training. Self-supervised approaches [11,14,44] overcome this limitation by exploiting photoconsistency and geometric constraints to define loss functions, for example, in a stereo camera setup. This way, only stereo images are needed for training which are typically easier to obtain than accurate depth measurements from active sensors such as 3D lasers or RGB-D cameras. Godard et al. [14] achieve the state-of-the-art depth estimation accuracy for a fully self-supervised approach. The semi-supervised scheme proposed by Kuznietsov et al. [23] combines the self-supervised loss with supervision with sparse LiDAR ground truth. They do not need multi-scale depth supervision or left-right consistency in their loss, and achieve better performance than the self-supervised approach in [14]. The limitation of this semi-supervised approach is the requirement for LiDAR data which are costly to collect. In our approach we use Stereo Direct Sparse Odometry to obtain sparse depth ground-truth for semi-supervised training. Since the extracted depth maps are even sparser than LiDAR data, we also employ multi-scale self-supervised training and left-right consistency as in Godard et al. [14]. Inspired by [20,34], we design a stacked network architecture leveraging the concept of residual learning [17].

Deep Learning for VO/SLAM. In recent years, large progress has been achieved in the development of monocular VO and SLAM methods [8,9,31,32]. Due to projective geometry, metric scale cannot be observed with a single camera [37] which introduces scale drift. A popular approach is hence to use stereo cameras for VO [8,10,31] which avoid scale ambiguity and leverage stereo matching with a fixed baseline for estimating 3D structure. While stereo VO delivers more reliable depth estimation, it requires self-calibration for long-term operation [4,46]. The integration of a second camera also introduces additional costs. Some recent monocular VO approaches have integrated monocular depth estimation [39,46] to recover the metric scale by scale-matching. CNN-SLAM [39] extends LSD-SLAM [9] by predicting depth with a CNN and refining the depth maps using Bayesian filtering [7,9]. Their method shows superior performance over monocular SLAM [9,30,35,45] on indoor datasets [15,38]. Yin et al. [46] propose to use convolutional neural fields and consecutive frames to improve the monocular depth estimation from a CNN. Camera motion is estimated using the refined depth. CodeSLAM [2] focuses on the challenge of dense 3D reconstruction. It jointly optimizes a learned compact representation of the dense

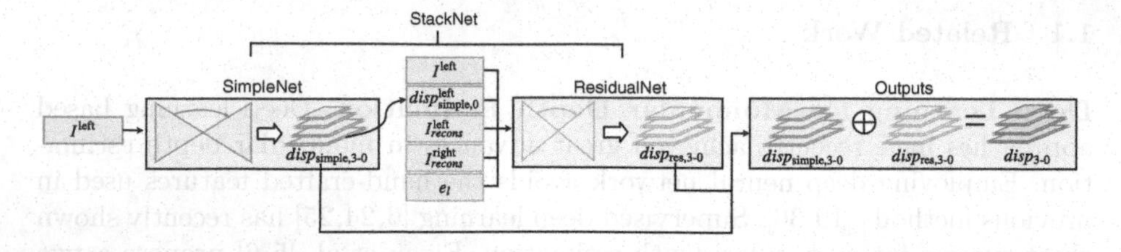

Fig. 2. Overview of StackNet architecture.

geometry with camera poses. Our work tackles the problem of odometry with monocular cameras and integrates deep depth prediction with multi-view stereo to improve camera pose estimation. Another line of research trains networks to directly predict the ego-motion end-to-end using supervised [41] or unsupervised learning [26,49]. However, the estimated ego-motion of these methods is still by far inferior to geometric visual odometry approaches. In our approach, we phrase visual odometry as a geometric optimization problem but incorporate photoconsistency constraints with state-of-the-art deep monocular depth predictions into the optimization. This way, we obtain a highly accurate monocular visual odometry that is not prone to scale drift and achieves comparable results to traditional stereo VO methods.

2 Semi-Supervised Deep Monocular Depth Estimation

In this section, we will introduce our semi-supervised approach to deep monocular depth estimation. It builds on three key ingredients: self-supervised learning from photoconsistency in a stereo setup similar to [14], supervised learning based on accurate sparse depth reconstruction by Stereo DSO, and two-stage refinement of the network predictions in a stacked encoder-decoder architecture.

2.1 Network Architecture

We coin our architecture StackNet since it stacks two sub-networks, SimpleNet and ResidualNet, as depicted in Fig. 2. Both sub-networks are fully convolutional deep neural network adopted from DispNet [28] with an encoder-decoder scheme. ResidualNet has fewer layers and takes the outputs of SimpleNet as inputs. Its purpose is to refine the disparity maps predicted by SimpleNet by learning an additive residual signal. Similar residual learning architectures have been successfully applied to related deep learning tasks [20,34]. The detailed network architecture is illustrated in the supplementary material.

SimpleNet. SimpleNet is an encoder-decoder architecture with a ResNet-50 based encoder and skip connections between corresponding encoder and decoder layers. The decoder upprojects the feature maps to the original resolution and generates 4 pairs of disparity maps $disp^{left}_{simple,s}$ and $disp^{right}_{simple,s}$ in different resolutions $s \in [0,3]$. The upprojection is implemented by resize-convolution [33], i.e. a nearest-neighbor upsampling layer by a factor of two followed by a convolutional layer. The usage of skip connections enables the decoder to recover high-resolution results with fine-grained details.

ResidualNet. The purpose of ResidualNet is to further refine the disparity maps predicted by SimpleNet. ResidualNet learns the residual signals $disp_{res,s}$ to the disparity maps $disp_{simple,s}$ (both left and right and for all resolutions). Inspired by FlowNet 2.0 [20], the inputs to ResidualNet contain various information on the prediction and the errors made by SimpleNet: we input I^{left}, $disp^{left}_{simple,0}$, I^{right}_{recons}, I^{left}_{recons} and e_l, where

- I^{right}_{recons} is the reconstructed right image by warping I^{left} using $disp^{right}_{simple,0}$.
- I^{left}_{recons} is the generated left image by back-warping I^{right}_{recons} using $disp^{left}_{simple,0}$.
- e_l is the $\ell 1$ reconstruction error between I^{left} and I^{left}_{recons}

For the warping, rectified stereo images are required while stereo camera intrinsics and extrinsics are not needed as our network directly outputs disparity.

The final refined outputs $disp_s$ are $disp_s = disp_{simple,s} \oplus disp_{res,s}$, $s \in [0,3]$, where $\oplus$ is element-wise summation. The encoder of ResidualNet contains 12 residual blocks in total and predicts 4 scales of residual disparity maps as SimpleNet. Adding more layers does not further improve performance in our experiments. Notably, only the left image is used as an input to either SimpleNet and ResidualNet, while the right image is not required. However, the network outputs a refined disparity map for the left and right stereo image. Both facts will be important for our monocular visual odometry approach.

2.2 Loss Function

We define a loss $\mathcal{L}_s$ at each output scale s, resulting in the total loss $\mathcal{L} = \sum_{s=0}^{3} \mathcal{L}_s$. The loss at each scale $\mathcal{L}_s$ is a linear combination of five terms which are symmetric in left and right images,

$$\begin{aligned}\mathcal{L}_s = {} & \alpha_U \left(\mathcal{L}_U^{left} + \mathcal{L}_U^{right}\right) + \alpha_S \left(\mathcal{L}_S^{left} + \mathcal{L}_S^{right}\right) + \alpha_{lr} \left(\mathcal{L}_{lr}^{left} + \mathcal{L}_{lr}^{right}\right) \\ & + \alpha_{smooth} \left(\mathcal{L}_{smooth}^{left} + \mathcal{L}_{smooth}^{right}\right) + \alpha_{occ} \left(\mathcal{L}_{occ}^{left} + \mathcal{L}_{occ}^{right}\right), \end{aligned} \quad (1)$$

where $\mathcal{L}_U$ is a self-supervised loss, $\mathcal{L}_S$ is a supervised loss, $\mathcal{L}_{lr}$ is a left-right consistency loss, $\mathcal{L}_{smooth}$ is a smoothness term encouraging the predicted disparities to be locally smooth and $\mathcal{L}_{occ}$ is an occlusion regularization term. In the following, we detail the left components $\mathcal{L}^{left}$ of the loss function at each scale. The right components $\mathcal{L}^{right}$ are defined symmetrically.

Self-supervised Loss. The self-supervised loss measures the quality of the reconstructed images. The reconstructed image is generated by warping the input image into the view of the other rectified stereo image. This procedure is fully (sub-)differentiable for bilinear sampling [21]. Inspired by [14,47], the quality of the reconstructed image is measured with the combination of the ℓ_1 loss and single scale structural similarity (SSIM) [42]:

$$\mathcal{L}_U^{left} = \frac{1}{N} \sum_{x,y} \alpha \frac{1 - \text{SSIM}\left(I^{left}(x,y), I_{recons}^{left}(x,y)\right)}{2} + (1-\alpha) \|I^{left}(x,y) - I_{recons}^{left}(x,y)\|_1, \tag{2}$$

with a 3×3 box filter for SSIM and α set to 0.84.

Supervised Loss. The supervised loss measures the deviation of the predicted disparity map from the disparities estimated by Stereo DSO at a sparse set of pixels:

$$\mathcal{L}_s^{left} = \frac{1}{N} \sum_{(x,y) \in \Omega_{DSO,left}} \beta_\epsilon \left(disp^{left}(x,y) - disp_{DSO}^{left}(x,y) \right) \tag{3}$$

where $\Omega_{DSO,left}$ is the set of pixels with disparities estimated by DSO and $\beta_\epsilon(x)$ is the reverse Huber (berHu) norm introduced in [24] which lets the training focus more on larger residuals. The threshold ϵ is adaptively set as a batch-dependent value $\epsilon = 0.2 \max_{(x,y) \in \Omega_{DSO,left}} \left| disp^{left}(x,y) - disp_{DSO}^{left}(x,y) \right|$.

Left-Right Disparity Consistency Loss. Given only the left image as input, the network predicts the disparity map of the left as well as the right image as in [14]. As proposed in [14,47], consistency between the left and right disparity image is improved by

$$\mathcal{L}_{lr}^{left} = \frac{1}{N} \sum_{x,y} \left| disp^{left}(x,y) - disp^{right}(x - disp^{left}(x,y), y) \right|. \tag{4}$$

Disparity Smoothness Regularization. Depth reconstruction based on stereo image matching is an ill-posed problem on its own: the depth of homogeneously textured areas and occluded areas cannot be determined. For these areas, we apply the regularization term

$$\mathcal{L}_{smooth}^{left} = \frac{1}{N} \sum_{x,y} \left| \nabla_x^2 disp^{left}(x,y) \right| e^{-\left\| \nabla_x^2 I^{left}(x,y) \right\|} + \left| \nabla_y^2 disp^{left}(x,y) \right| e^{-\left\| \nabla_y^2 I^{left}(x,y) \right\|} \tag{5}$$

that assumes that the predicted disparity map should be locally smooth. We use a second-order smoothness prior [43] and downweight it when the image gradient is high [18].

Occlusion Regularization. $\mathcal{L}_{smooth}^{left}$ itself tends to generate a shadow area where values gradually change from foreground to background due to stereo occlusion. To favor background depths and hard transitions at occlusions [48], we impose $\mathcal{L}_{occ}^{left}$ which penalizes the total sum of absolute disparities. The combination of smoothness- and occlusion regularizer prefers to directly take the (smaller) closeby background disparity which better corresponds to the assumption that the background part is uncovered

$$\mathcal{L}_{occ}^{left} = \frac{1}{N}\sum_{x,y}\left| disp^{left}(x,y)\right|. \tag{6}$$

3 Deep Virtual Stereo Odometry

Deep Virtual Stereo Odometry (DVSO) builds on the windowed sparse direct bundle adjustment formulation of monocular DSO. We use our disparity predictions for DSO in two key ways: Firstly, we initialize depth maps of new keyframes from the disparities. Beyond this rather straight-forward approach, we also incorporate virtual direct image alignment constraints into the windowed direct bundle adjustment of DSO. We obtain these constraints by warping images with the estimated depth by bundle adjustment and the predicted right disparities by our network assuming a virtual stereo setup. As shown in Fig. 3, DVSO integrates both the predicted left disparities and right disparities for the left image. The right image of the stereo setup is not used for our VO method at any stage, making it a monocular VO method.

In the following, we use D^L and D^R as shorthands to represent the predicted left ($disp_0^{left}$) and right disparity map ($disp_0^{right}$) at scale $s = 0$, respectively. When using purely geometric cues, scale drift is one of the main sources of error of monocular VO due to scale unobservability [37]. In DVSO we use the left disparity map D^L predicted by StackNet for initialization instead of randomly initializing the depth like in monocular DSO [8]. The disparity value of an image point with coordinate $\mathbf{p}$ is converted to the inverse depth $d_{\mathbf{p}}$ using the rectified camera intrinsics and stereo baseline of the training set of StackNet [16], $d_{\mathbf{p}} = \frac{D^L(\mathbf{p})}{f_x b}$. In this way, the initialization of DVSO becomes more stable than monocular DSO and the depths are initialized with a consistent metric scale.

The point selection strategy of DVSO is similar to monocular DSO [8], while we also introduce a left-right consistency check (similar to Equation (4)) to filter out the pixels which likely lie in the occluded area

$$e_{lr} = \left|D^L(\mathbf{p}) - D^R(\mathbf{p}')\right| \quad \text{with} \quad \mathbf{p}' = \mathbf{p} - \left[D^L(\mathbf{p})\ 0\right]^\top. \tag{7}$$

The pixels with $e_{lr} > 1$ are not selected.

Every new frame is firstly tracked with respect to the reference keyframe using direct image alignment in a coarse-to-fine manner [8]. Afterwards DVSO decides if a new keyframe has to be created for the new frame following the criteria proposed by [8]. When a new keyframe is created, the temporal multi-view energy function $E_{photo} := \sum_{i\in\mathcal{F}}\sum_{\mathbf{p}\in\mathcal{P}_i}\sum_{j\in\mathrm{obs}(\mathbf{p})} E_{ij}^{\mathbf{p}}$ needs to be optimized, where $\mathcal{F}$ is a fixed-sized window containing the active keyframes, $\mathcal{P}_i$ is the set of points selected from its host keyframe with index i and $j \in \mathrm{obs}(\mathbf{p})$ is the index of the keyframe which observes $\mathbf{p}$. $E_{ij}^{\mathbf{p}}$ is the photometric error of the point $\mathbf{p}$ when projected from the host keyframe I_i onto the other keyframe I_j:

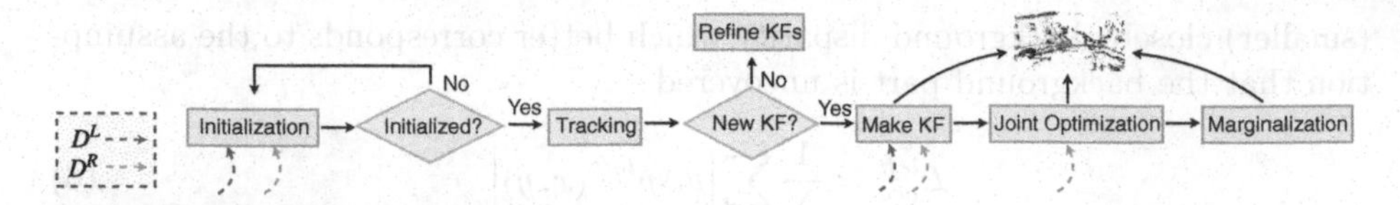

Fig. 3. System overview of DVSO. Every new frame is used for visual odometry and fed into the proposed StackNet to predict left and right disparity. The predicted left and right disparities are used for depth initialization, while the right disparity is used to form the virtual stereo term in direct sparse bundle adjustment.

$$E_{ij}^{\mathbf{p}} := \omega_{\mathbf{p}} \left\| (I_j[\tilde{\mathbf{p}}] - b_j) - \frac{e^{a_j}}{e^{a_i}} (I_i[\mathbf{p}] - b_i) \right\|_\gamma , \tag{8}$$

where $\tilde{\mathbf{p}}$ is the projected image coordinate using the relative rotation matrix $\mathbf{R} \in SO(3)$ and translation vector $\mathbf{t} \in \mathbb{R}^3$ [16], $\tilde{\mathbf{p}} = \Pi_c \left(\mathbf{R} \Pi_c^{-1} (\mathbf{p}, d_{\mathbf{p}}) + \mathbf{t} \right)$, where $\Pi_{\mathbf{c}}$ and $\Pi_{\mathbf{c}}^{-1}$ are the camera projection and back-projection functions. The parameters a_i, a_j, b_i and b_j are used for modeling the affine brightness transformation [8]. The weight $\omega_{\mathbf{p}}$ penalizes the points with high image gradient [8] with the intuition that the error originating from bilinear interpolation of the discrete image values is larger. $\|\cdot\|_\gamma$ is the Huber norm with the threshold γ. For the detailed explanation of the energy function, please refer to [8].

To further improve the accuracy of DVSO, inspired by Stereo DSO [40] which couples the static stereo term with the temporal multi-view energy function, we introduce a novel *virtual stereo* term $E^{\dagger\mathbf{p}}$ for each point $\mathbf{p}$

$$E_i^{\dagger\mathbf{p}} = \omega_{\mathbf{p}} \left\| I_i^{\dagger} \left[\mathbf{p}^{\dagger} \right] - I_i[\mathbf{p}] \right\|_\gamma \quad \text{with} \quad I_i^{\dagger} \left[\mathbf{p}^{\dagger} \right] = I_i \left[\mathbf{p}^{\dagger} - \left[D^R \left(\mathbf{p}^{\dagger} \right) 0 \right]^\top \right], \tag{9}$$

where $\mathbf{p}^{\dagger} = \Pi_{\mathbf{c}}(\Pi_{\mathbf{c}}^{-1}(\mathbf{p}, d_{\mathbf{p}}) + \mathbf{t}_b)$ is the virtual projected coordinate of $\mathbf{p}$ using the vector $\mathbf{t}_b$ denoting the virtual stereo baseline which is known during the training of StackNet. The intuition behind this term is to optimize the estimated depth of the visual odometry to become consistent with the disparity prediction of StackNet. Instead of imposing the consistency directly on the estimated and predicted disparities, we formulate the residuals in photoconsistency which better reflects the uncertainties of the prediction of StackNet and also keeps the unit of the residuals consistent with the temporal direct image alignment terms.

We then optimize the total energy

$$E_{photo} := \sum_{i \in \mathcal{F}} \sum_{\mathbf{p} \in \mathcal{P}_i} \left(\lambda E_i^{\dagger\mathbf{p}} + \sum_{j \in \mathrm{obs}(\mathbf{p})} E_{ij}^{\mathbf{p}} \right), \tag{10}$$

where the coupling factor λ balances the temporal and the virtual stereo term. All the parameters of the total energy are jointly optimized using the Gauss Newton method [8]. In order to keep a fixed size of the active window ($N = 7$ keyframes in our experiments), old keyframes are removed from the system by marginalization using the Schur complement [8]. Unlike sliding window bundle

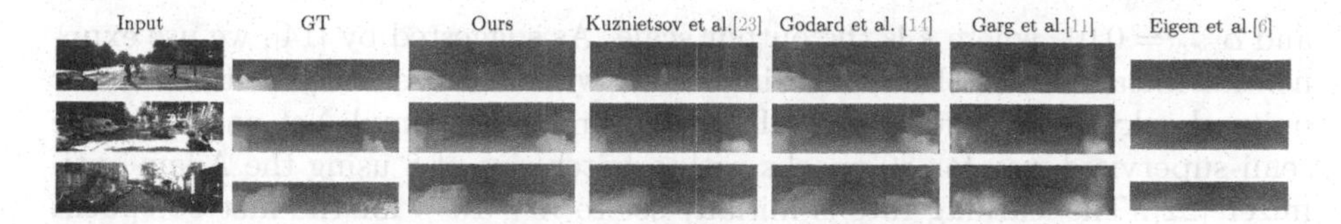

Fig. 4. Qualitative comparison with state-of-the-art methods. The ground truth is interpolated for better visualization. Our approach shows better prediction on thin structures than the self-supervised approach [14], and delivers more detailed disparity maps than the semi-supervised approach using LiDAR data [23].

adjustment, the parameter estimates outside the optimization window including camera poses and depths in a marginalization prior are also incorporated into the optimization. In contrast to the MSCKF [29], the depths of pixels are explicitly maintained in the state and optimized for. In our optimization framework we trade off predicted depth and triangulated depth using robust norms.

4 Experiments

We quantitatively evaluate our StackNet with other state-of-the-art monocular depth prediction methods on the publicly available KITTI dataset [12]. In the supplementary materials, we demonstrate results on the Cityscapes dataset [3] and the Make3D dataset [36] to show the generalization ability. For DVSO, we evaluate its tracking accuracy on the KITTI odometry benchmark with other state-of-the-art monocular as well as stereo visual odometry systems. In the supplementary material, we also demonstrate its results on the *Frankfurt* sequence of the Cityscapes dataset to show the generalization of DVSO.

4.1 Monocular Depth Estimation

Dataset. We train StackNet using the train/test split (**K**) of Eigen et al. [6]. The training set contains 23488 images from 28 scenes belonging to the categories "city", "residential" and "road". We used 22600 images of them for training and the remaining ones for validation. We further split **K** into 2 subsets $\mathbf{K}_o$ and $\mathbf{K}_r$. $\mathbf{K}_o$ contains the images of the sequences which appear in the training set (but not the test set) of the KITTI odometry benchmark on which we use Stereo DSO [40] to extract sparse ground-truth depth data. $\mathbf{K}_r$ contains the remaining images in **K**. Specifically, $\mathbf{K}_o$ contains the images of sequences 01, 02, 06, 08, 09 and 10 of the KITTI odometry benchmark.

Implementation Details. StackNet is implemented in TensorFlow [1] and trained from scratch on a single Titan X Pascal GPU. We resize the images to 512×256 for training and it takes less than 40 ms for inference including the I/O overhead. The weights are set to $\alpha_u = 1$, $\alpha_s = 10$, $\alpha_{lr} = 1$, $\alpha_{smooth} = 0.1/2^s$

and $\alpha_{occ} = 0.01$, where s is the output scale. As suggested by [14], we use exponential linear units (ELUs) for SimpleNet, while we use leaky rectified linear units (Leaky ReLUs) for ResidualNet. We first train SimpleNet on $\mathbf{K}_o$ in the semi-supervised way for 80 epochs with a batch size of 8 using the Adam optimizer [22]. The learning rate is initially set to $\lambda = 10^{-4}$ for the first 50 epochs and halved every 15 epochs afterwards until the end. Then we train SimpleNet with $\lambda = 5 \times 10^{-5}$ on $\mathbf{K}_r$ for 40 epochs in the self-supervised way without $\mathcal{L}_S$. In the end, we train again on $\mathbf{K}_o$ without $\mathcal{L}_U$ using $\lambda = 10^{-5}$ for 5 epochs. We explain the dataset schedule as well as the parameter tuning in detail in the supplementary material.

After training SimpleNet, we freeze its weights and train StackNet by cascading ResidualNet. StackNet is trained with $\lambda = 5 \times 10^{-5}$ in the same dataset schedules but with less epochs, i.e. 30, 15, 3 epochs, respectively. We apply random gamma, brightness and color augmentations [14]. We also employ the post-processing for left disparities proposed by Godard et al. [14] to reduce the effect of stereo disocclusions. In the supplementary material we also provide an ablation study on the various loss terms.

KITTI. Table 1 shows the evaluation results with the error metrics used in [6]. We crop the images as applied by Eigen et al. [6] to compare with [14], [23] within different depth ranges. The best performance of our network is achieved with the dataset schedule $\mathbf{K}_o \rightarrow \mathbf{K}_r \rightarrow \mathbf{K}_o$ as we described above. We outperform the state-of-the-art self-supervised approach proposed by Godard et al. [14] by a large margin. Our method also outperforms the state-of-the-art semi-supervised method using the LiDAR ground truth proposed by Kuznietsov et al. [23] on all the metrics except for the less restrictive $\delta < 1.25^2$ and $\delta < 1.25^3$.

Figure 4 shows a qualitative comparison with other state-of-the-art methods. Compared to the semi-supervised approach, our results contain more details and deliver comparable prediction on thin structures like the poles. Although the results of Godard et al. [14] appear more detailed on some parts, they are not actually accurate, which can be inferred by the quantitative evaluation. In general, the predictions of Godard et al. [14] on thin objects are not as accurate as our method. In the supplementary material, we show the error maps for the predicted depth maps. Figure 5 further show the advantages of our method compared to the state-of-the-art self-supervised and semi-supervised approaches. The results of Godard et al. [14] are predicted by the network trained with both the Cityscapes dataset and the KITTI dataset. On the wall of the far building in the left figure, our network can better predict consistent depth on the surface, while the prediction of the self-supervised network shows strong checkerboard artifact, which is apparently inaccurate. The semi-supervised approach also shows checkerboard artifact (but much slighter). The right side of the figure shows shadow artifacts for the approach of Godard et al. [14] around the boundaries of the traffic sign, while the result of Kuznietsov et al. [23] fails to predict the structure. Please refer to our supplementary material for further results. We also demonstrate how our trained depth prediction network generalizes to other datasets in the supplementary material.

Table 1. Evaluation results on the KITTI [13] Raw test split of Eigen et al. [6]. **CS** refers to the Cityscapes dataset [3]. Upper part: depth range 0-80 m, lower part: 1-50 m.All results are obtained using the crop from [6]. Our SimpleNet trained on $\mathbf{K}_o$ outperforms [14] (self-supervised) trained on **CS** and **K**. StackNet also outperforms semi-supervision with LiDAR [23] on most metrics.

Approach	Dataset	RMSE	RMSE (log)	ARD	SRD	$\delta < 1.25$	$\delta < 1.25^2$	$\delta < 1.25^3$
		Lower is better				Higher is better		
Godard et al. [14], ResNet	**CS**→**K**	4.935	0.206	0.114	0.898	0.861	0.949	0.976
Kuznietsov et al. [23]	**K**	*4.621*	*0.189*	0.113	*0.741*	0.862	**0.960**	**0.986**
Ours, SimpleNet	$\mathbf{K}_o$	4.886	0.209	0.112	0.888	0.862	0.950	0.976
Ours, SimpleNet	$\mathbf{K}_o \rightarrow \mathbf{K}_r$	4.817	0.202	0.108	0.862	*0.867*	0.950	0.977
Ours, SimpleNet	$\mathbf{K}_r \rightarrow \mathbf{K}_o$	4.890	0.208	0.115	0.870	0.863	0.950	0.977
Ours, SimpleNet	$\mathbf{K}_o \rightarrow \mathbf{K}_r \rightarrow \mathbf{K}_o$	4.785	0.199	*0.107*	0.852	0.866	0.950	0.978
Ours, StackNet	$\mathbf{K}_o \rightarrow \mathbf{K}_r \rightarrow \mathbf{K}_o$	**4.442**	**0.187**	**0.097**	**0.734**	**0.888**	*0.958*	*0.980*
Garg et al. [11] L12 Aug 8×	**K**	5.104	0.273	0.169	1.080	0.740	0.904	0.962
Godard et al. [14], ResNet	**CS**→**K**	3.729	0.194	0.108	0.657	0.873	0.954	0.979
Kuznietsov et al. [23]	**K**	*3.518*	*0.179*	*0.108*	*0.595*	*0.875*	**0.964**	**0.988**
Ours, StackNet	$\mathbf{K}_o \rightarrow \mathbf{K}_r \rightarrow \mathbf{K}_o$	**3.390**	**0.177**	**0.092**	**0.547**	**0.898**	*0.962*	*0.982*

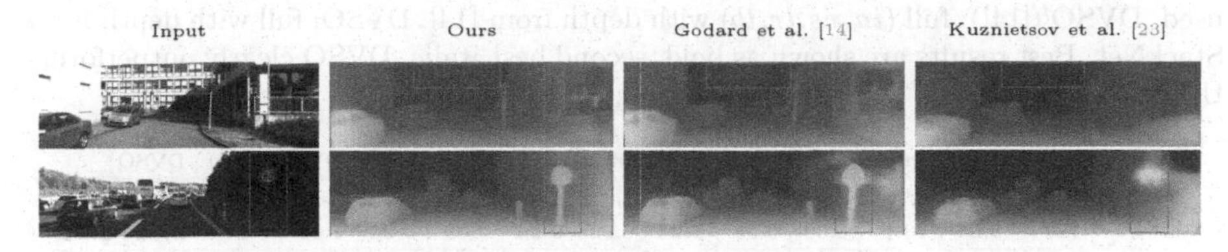

Fig. 5. Qualitative results on Eigen et al.'s KITTI Raw test split. The result of Godard et al. [14] shows a strong shadow effect around object contours, while our result does not. The result of Kuznietsov [23] shows failure on predicting the traffic sign. Both other methods [14,23] predict checkerboard artifacts on the far building, while our approach predicts such artifacts less.

4.2 Monocular Visual Odometry

KITTI Odometry Benchmark. The KITTI odometry benchmark contains 11 (0–10) training sequences and 11 (11–21) test sequences. Ground-truth 6D poses are provided for the training sequences, whereas for the test sequences evaluation results are obtained by submitting to the KITTI website. We use the error metrics proposed in [12].

We firstly provide an ablation study for DVSO to show the effectiveness of the design choices in our approach. In Table 2 we give results for DVSO in different variants with the following components: initializing the depth with the left disparity prediction (*in*), using the right disparity for the virtual stereo term in windowed bundle adjustment (*vs*), checking left-right disparity consistency for point selection (*lr*), and tuning the virtual stereo baseline *tb*. The intuition behind the virtual stereo baseline is that StackNet is trained over various camera parameters and hence provides a depth scale for an average baseline. For *tb*, we therefore tune the scale factors of different sequences with different cameras intrinsics, to better align the estimated scale with the ground truth. Baselines are tuned for each of the 3 different camera parameter sets in the training set individually using grid search on one training sequence. Specifically, we tuned the baselines on sequences 00, 03 and 05 which correspond to 3 different camera parameter sets. The test set contains the same camera parameter sets as the training set and we map the virtual baselines for *tb* correspondingly. Monocular DSO (after Sim(3) alignment) is also shown as the baseline. The results show that our full approach achieves the best average performance. Our StackNet also adds significantly to the performance of DVSO compared with using depth predictions from [14].

Table 2. Ablation study for DVSO. * and † indicate the sequences used and not used for training StackNet, respectively. t_{rel}(%) and r_{rel}(°) are translational- and rotational RMSE, respectively. Both t_{rel} and r_{rel} are averaged over 100 to 800 m intervals. *in*: D^L is used for depth initialization. *vs*: virtual stereo term is used with D^R. *lr*: left-right disparity consistency is checked using predictions. *tb*: tuned virtual baseline is used. DVSO'([14]): full (*in*, *vs*, *lr*, *tb*) with depth from [14]. DVSO: full with depth from StackNet. Best results are shown as bold, second best italic. DVSO clearly outperforms the other variants.

	Mono DSO		*in*		*in*, *vs*		*in*, *vs*, *lr*		*in*, *vs*, *tb*		DVSO'([14])		DVSO	
Seq.	t_{rel}	r_{rel}	t_{rel}	r_{rel}	t_{rel}	r_{rel}	t_{rel}	r_{rel}	t_{rel}	r_{rel}	t_{rel}	r_{rel}	t_{rel}	r_{rel}
00†	188	*0.25*	13.1	0.30	0.95	**0.24**	0.93	**0.24**	*0.73*	*0.25*	1.02	0.28	**0.71**	**0.24**
03†	17.7	**0.17**	9.10	0.29	2.56	0.19	2.56	*0.18*	**0.78**	0.19	4.78	0.18	*0.79*	*0.18*
04†	0.82	0.16	0.83	0.29	0.69	**0.06**	0.67	*0.07*	*0.36*	**0.06**	2.03	0.14	**0.35**	**0.06**
05†	72.6	*0.23*	12.7	*0.23*	0.67	*0.23*	0.64	*0.23*	*0.61*	0.23	2.11	**0.21**	**0.58**	0.22
07†	48.4	**0.32**	18.5	0.91	0.85	0.41	*0.80*	0.38	0.81	0.40	1.09	0.39	**0.73**	*0.35*
01*	9.17	*0.12*	4.30	0.41	1.50	**0.11**	1.52	*0.12*	**1.15**	**0.11**	1.23	**0.11**	*1.18*	**0.11**
02*	114	**0.22**	9.58	0.26	1.08	*0.23*	1.05	*0.23*	*0.86*	*0.23*	0.87	*0.23*	**0.84**	**0.22**
06*	42.2	**0.20**	11.2	0.30	0.84	*0.23*	0.80	0.24	*0.73*	*0.23*	0.87	0.24	**0.71**	**0.20**
08*	177	*0.26*	14.9	0.28	1.11	*0.26*	1.10	*0.26*	*1.05*	*0.26*	*1.05*	*0.26*	**1.03**	**0.25**
09*	28.1	**0.21**	14.2	*0.23*	1.03	**0.21**	0.95	**0.21**	0.88	**0.21**	*0.87*	**0.21**	**0.83**	**0.21**
10*	24.0	*0.22*	9.93	0.27	**0.58**	0.23	*0.59*	*0.22*	0.74	*0.22*	**0.68**	**0.21**	0.74	**0.21**
Mean†	65.50	0.23	10.85	0.40	1.14	0.23	1.12	*0.22*	*0.66*	0.23	2.21	0.24	**0.63**	**0.21**
Mean*	65.75	*0.21*	10.69	0.29	1.02	*0.21*	1.00	*0.21*	*0.90*	*0.21*	0.93	*0.21*	**0.89**	**0.20**
Overall mean	65.64	*0.21*	10.76	0.34	1.08	0.22	1.06	0.22	*0.79*	0.22	1.51	0.22	**0.77**	**0.20**

We also compare DVSO with other state-of-the-art *stereo* visual odometry systems on the sequences 00–10. The sequences with marker * are used for training StackNet and the sequences with marker † are not used for training the network. In Table 3 and the following tables, DVSO means our full approach with baseline tuning (*in*, *vs*, *lr*, *tb*). The average RMSE of DVSO without baseline

Table 3. Comparison with state-of-the-art stereo visual odometry. DVSO: our full approach (*in*, *vs*, *lr*, *tb*). Global optimization and loop-closure are turned off for stereo ORB-SLAM2 and Stereo LSD-SLAM. DVSO (monocular) achieves comparable performance to these stereo methods.

	St. LSD-VO [10]		ORB-SLAM2 [31]		St. DSO [40]		*in*, *vs*, *lr*		DVSO	
Seq.	t_{rel}	r_{rel}	t_{rel}	r_{rel}	t_{rel}	r_{rel}	t_{rel}	r_{rel}	t_{rel}	r_{rel}
00†	1.09	0.42	*0.83*	0.29	0.84	*0.26*	0.93	**0.24**	**0.71**	**0.24**
03†	1.16	0.32	**0.71**	*0.17*	0.92	**0.16**	2.56	0.18	*0.77*	0.18
04†	*0.42*	0.34	0.45	0.18	0.65	0.15	0.67	*0.07*	**0.35**	**0.06**
05†	0.90	0.34	*0.64*	0.26	0.68	**0.19**	*0.64*	0.23	**0.58**	*0.22*
07†	1.25	0.79	*0.78*	0.42	0.83	*0.36*	0.80	0.38	**0.73**	**0.35**
01*	2.13	0.37	**1.38**	0.20	1.43	**0.09**	1.52	0.12	**1.18**	*0.11*
02*	1.09	0.37	*0.81*	0.28	**0.78**	**0.21**	1.05	0.23	0.84	*0.22*
06*	1.28	0.43	0.82	0.25	**0.67**	**0.20**	0.80	*0.24*	*0.71*	**0.20**
08*	1.24	0.38	1.07	0.31	**0.98**	**0.25**	1.10	*0.26*	**1.03**	**0.25**
09*	1.22	0.28	**0.82**	0.25	0.98	**0.18**	0.95	*0.21*	*0.83*	*0.21*
10*	0.75	0.34	*0.58*	0.28	**0.49**	**0.18**	0.59	0.22	0.74	*0.21*
mean†	0.96	0.44	*0.68*	0.26	0.78	*0.22*	1.12	*0.22*	**0.63**	**0.21**
mean*	1.29	0.36	*0.91*	0.26	**0.89**	**0.19**	1.00	0.21	**0.89**	*0.20*
overall mean	1.14	0.40	**0.81**	0.26	0.84	**0.20**	1.06	*0.22*	**0.77**	**0.20**

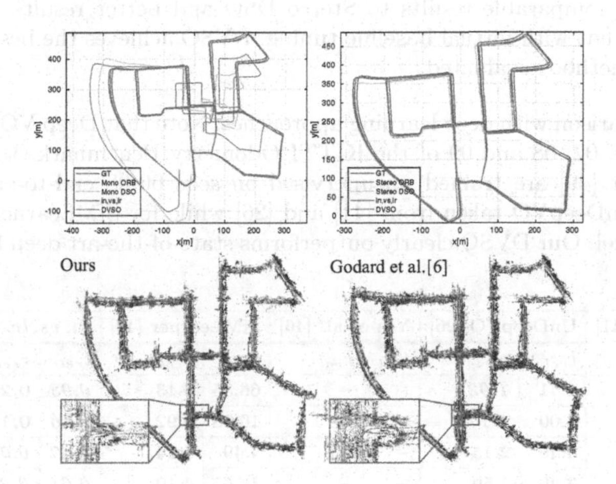

Fig. 6. Results on KITTI odometry seq. 00. Top: comparisons with monocular methods (Sim(3)-aligned) and stereo methods. DVSO provides significantly more consistent trajectories than other monocular methods and compares well to stereo approaches. Bottom: DVSO with StackNet produces more accurate trajectory and map than with [14].

tuning is better than Stereo LSD-VO, but not as good as Stereo DSO [40] or ORB-SLAM2 [31] (stereo, without global optimization and loop closure). Importantly, DVSO uses only monocular images. With the baseline tuning, DVSO achieves even better average performance than all other stereo systems on both rotational and translational errors. Figure 6 shows the estimated trajectory on sequence 00. Both monocular ORB-SLAM2 and DSO suffer from strong scale drift, while DVSO achieves superior performance on eliminating the scale drift. We also show the estimated trajectory on 00 by running DVSO using the depth map predicted by Godard et al. [14] with the model trained on the Cityscapes and the KITTI dataset. For the results in Fig. 6 our depth predictions are more

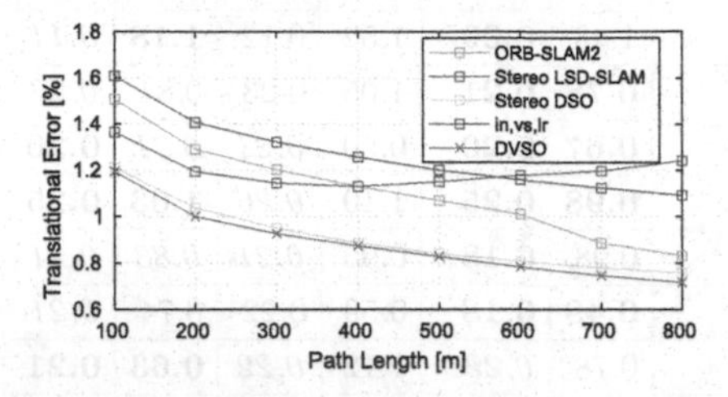

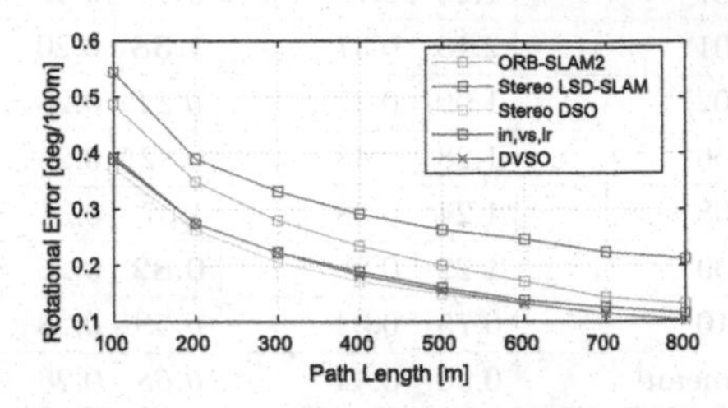

Fig. 7. Evaluation results on the KITTI odometry test set. We show translational and rotational errors with respect to path length intervals. For translational errors, DVSO achieves comparable performance to Stereo LSD-SLAM, while for rotational errors, DVSO achieves comparable results to Stereo DSO and better results than all other methods. Note that with virtual baseline tuning, DVSO achieves the best performance among all the methods evaluated.

Table 4. Comparison with deep learning approaches. Note that Deep VO [41] is trained on sequences 00, 02, 08 and 09 of the KITTI Odometry Benchmark. UnDeepVO [26] and SfMLearner [49] are trained unsupervised on seqs 00-08 end-to-end. Results of DeepVO and UnDeepVO taken from [41] and [26] while for SfMLearner we ran their pre-trained model. Our DVSO clearly outperforms state-of-the-art deep learning based VO methods.

	DeepVO [41]		UnDeepVO [26]		Yin et al. [46]		SfMLearner [49]		in, vs, lr		DVSO	
Seq.	t_{rel}	r_{rel}	t_{rel}	r_{rel}	t_{rel}	r_{rel}	t_{rel}	r_{rel}	t_{rel}	r_{rel}	t_{rel}	r_{rel}
00†	–	–	4.41	*1.92*	–	–	66.35	6.13	*0.93*	**0.24**	**0.71**	**0.24**
03†	8.49	6.89	5.00	*6.17*	–	–	10.78	3.92	*2.56*	**0.18**	**0.77**	**0.18**
04†	7.19	6.97	4.49	2.13	–	–	4.49	5.24	*0.67*	*0.07*	**0.35**	**0.06**
05†	2.62	3.61	3.40	1.50	–	–	18.67	4.10	*0.64*	*0.23*	**0.58**	**0.22**
07†	3.91	4.60	3.15	2.48	–	–	21.33	6.65	*0.80*	*0.38*	**0.73**	**0.35**
01*	–	–	69.07	1.60	–	–	35.17	2.74	*1.52*	*0.12*	**1.18**	**0.11**
02*	–	–	5.58	2.44	–	–	58.75	3.58	*1.05*	*0.23*	**0.84**	**0.22**
06*	5.42	5.82	6.20	1.98	–	–	25.88	4.80	*0.80*	*0.24*	**0.71**	**0.20**
08*	–	–	4.08	1.79	2.22	**0.10**	21.90	2.91	*1.10*	0.26	**1.03**	*0.25*
09*	–	–	7.01	3.61	4.14	**0.11**	18.77	3.21	0.95	*0.21*	**0.83**	*0.21*
10*	8.11	8.83	10.63	4.65	1.70	**0.17**	14.33	3.30	**0.59**	0.22	*0.74*	*0.21*

accurate. Figure 7 shows the evaluation result of the sequences 11–21 by submitting results of DVSO with and without baseline tuning to the KITTI odometry benchmark. Note that in Fig. 7, Stereo LSD-SLAM and ORB-SLAM2 are both full stereo SLAM approaches with global optimization and loop closure. For qualitative comparisons of further estimated trajectories, please refer to our supplementary material.

We also compare DVSO with DeepVO [41], UnDeepVO [26] and SfM-Learner [49] which are deep learning based visual odometry systems trained end-to-end on KITTI. As shown in Table 4, on all available sequences, DVSO achieves better performance than the other two end-to-end approaches. Table 4 also shows the comparison with the deep learning based scale recovery methods for monocular VO proposed by Yin et al. [46]. DVSO also outperforms their method. In the supplementary material, we also show the estimated trajectory on the Cityscapes *Frankfurt* sequence to demonstrate generalization capabilities.

5 Conclusion

We presented a novel monocular visual odometry system, DVSO, which recovers metric scale and reduces scale drift in geometric monocular VO. A deep learning approach predicts monocular depth maps for the input images which are used to initialize sparse depths in DSO to a consistent metric scale. Odometry is further improved by a novel virtual stereo term that couples estimated depth in windowed bundle adjustment with the monocular depth predictions. For monocular depth prediction we have presented a semi-supervised deep learning approach, which utilizes a self-supervised image reconstruction loss and sparse depth predictions from Stereo DSO as ground truth depths for supervision. A stacked network architecture predicts state-of-the-art refined disparity estimates.

Our evaluation conducted on the KITTI odometry benchmark demonstrates that DVSO outperforms the state-of-the-art monocular methods by a large margin and achieves comparable results to stereo VO methods. With virtual baseline tuning, DVSO can even outperform state-of-the-art stereo VO methods, i.e., Stereo LSD-VO, ORB-SLAM2 without global optimization and loop closure, and Stereo DSO, while using only monocular images.

The key practical benefit of the proposed method is that it allows us to recover accurate and scale-consistent odometry with only a single camera. Future work could comprise fine-tuning of the network inside the odometry pipeline end-to-end. This could enable the system to adapt online to new scenes and camera setups. Given that the deep net was trained on driving sequences, in future work we also plan to investigate how much the proposed approach can generalize to other camera trajectories and environments.

Acknowledgements. We would like to thank Clément Godard, Yevhen Kuznietsov, Ruihao Li and Tinghui Zhou for providing the data and code. We also would like to thank Martin Schwörer for the fruitful discussion.

References

1. Abadi, M., et al.: Tensorflow: a system for large-scale machine learning. OSDI **16**, 265–283 (2016)
2. Bloesch, M., Czarnowski, J., Clark, R., Leutenegger, S., Davison, A.J.: Codeslam-learning a compact, optimisable representation for dense visual slam. arXiv preprint arXiv:1804.00874 (2018)
3. Cordts, M., et al.: The cityscapes dataset for semantic urban scene understanding. In: Proceedings of the IEEE Conference on Computer Vision and Pattern Recognition (CVPR) (2016)
4. Dang, T., Hoffmann, C., Stiller, C.: Continuous stereo self-calibration by camera parameter tracking. IEEE Trans. Image Process. **18**(7), 1536–1550 (2009)
5. Eigen, D., Fergus, R.: Predicting depth, surface normals and semantic labels with a common multi-scale convolutional architecture. In: Proceedings of the IEEE International Conference on Computer Vision, pp. 2650–2658 (2015)
6. Eigen, D., Puhrsch, C., Fergus, R.: Depth map prediction from a single image using a multi-scale deep network. In: Advances in Neural Information Processing Systems, pp. 2366–2374 (2014)
7. Engel, J., Sturm, J., Cremers, D.: Semi-dense visual odometry for a monocular camera. In: IEEE International Conference on Computer Vision (ICCV) (2013)
8. Engel, J., Koltun, V., Cremers, D.: Direct sparse odometry. IEEE Trans. Pattern Anal. Mach. Intell. **40**(3), 611–625 (2017)
9. Engel, J., Schöps, T., Cremers, D.: LSD-SLAM: large-scale direct monocular SLAM. In: Fleet, D., Pajdla, T., Schiele, B., Tuytelaars, T. (eds.) ECCV 2014. LNCS, vol. 8690, pp. 834–849. Springer, Cham (2014). https://doi.org/10.1007/978-3-319-10605-2_54
10. Engel, J., Stückler, J., Cremers, D.: Large-scale direct slam with stereo cameras. In: IEEE/RSJ International Conference on Intelligent Robots and Systems (IROS), pp. 1935–1942. IEEE (2015)
11. Garg, R., B.G., V.K., Carneiro, G., Reid, I.: Unsupervised CNN for single view depth estimation: geometry to the rescue. In: Leibe, B., Matas, J., Sebe, N., Welling, M. (eds.) ECCV 2016. LNCS, vol. 9912, pp. 740–756. Springer, Cham (2016). https://doi.org/10.1007/978-3-319-46484-8_45
12. Geiger, A., Lenz, P., Stiller, C., Urtasun, R.: Vision meets robotics: The KITTI dataset. Int. J. Robot. Res. (IJRR) **32**(11), 1231–1237 (2013)
13. Geiger, A., Lenz, P., Urtasun, R.: Are we ready for autonomous driving? the KITTI vision benchmark suite. In: Conference on Computer Vision and Pattern Recognition (CVPR) (2012)
14. Godard, C., Mac Aodha, O., Brostow, G.J.: Unsupervised monocular depth estimation with left-right consistency. arXiv preprint arXiv:1609.03677 (2016)
15. Handa, A., Whelan, T., McDonald, J., Davison, A.J.: A benchmark for RGB-D visual odometry, 3D reconstruction and SLAM. In: IEEE international conference on Robotics and automation (ICRA), pp. 1524–1531. IEEE (2014)
16. Hartley, R., Zisserman, A.: Multiple View Geometry in Computer Vision. Cambridge University Press, Cambridge (2003)
17. He, K., Zhang, X., Ren, S., Sun, J.: Deep residual learning for image recognition. In: Proceedings of the IEEE Conference on Computer Vision and Pattern Recognition, pp. 770–778 (2016)
18. Heise, P., Klose, S., Jensen, B., Knoll, A.: Pm-huber: Patchmatch with huber regularization for stereo matching. In: IEEE International Conference on Computer Vision (ICCV), pp. 2360–2367. IEEE (2013)

19. Hoiem, D., Efros, A.A., Hebert, M.: Automatic photo pop-up. In: ACM Transactions on Graphics (TOG), vol. 24, pp. 577–584. ACM (2005)
20. Ilg, E., Mayer, N., Saikia, T., Keuper, M., Dosovitskiy, A., Brox, T.: Flownet 2.0: Evolution of optical flow estimation with deep networks. In: IEEE Conference on Computer Vision and Pattern Recognition (CVPR), vol. 2, p. 6 (2017)
21. Jaderberg, M., Simonyan, K., Zisserman, A., et al.: Spatial transformer networks. In: Advances in Neural Information Processing Systems, pp. 2017–2025 (2015)
22. Kingma, D.P., Ba, J.: Adam: A method for stochastic optimization. arXiv preprint arXiv:1412.6980 (2014)
23. Kuznietsov, Y., Stückler, J., Leibe, B.: Semi-supervised deep learning for monocular depth map prediction. arXiv preprint arXiv:1702.02706 (2017)
24. Laina, I., Rupprecht, C., Belagiannis, V., Tombari, F., Navab, N.: Deeper depth prediction with fully convolutional residual networks. In: Fourth International Conference on 3D Vision (3DV), pp. 239–248. IEEE (2016)
25. Li, B., Shen, C., Dai, Y., van den Hengel, A., He, M.: Depth and surface normal estimation from monocular images using regression on deep features and hierarchical CRFS. In: Proceedings of the IEEE Conference on Computer Vision and Pattern Recognition, pp. 1119–1127 (2015)
26. Li, R., Wang, S., Long, Z., Gu, D.: UnDeepVO: Monocular visual odometry through unsupervised deep learning. arXiv preprint arXiv:1709.06841 (2017)
27. Long, J., Shelhamer, E., Darrell, T.: Fully convolutional networks for semantic segmentation. In: Proceedings of the IEEE Conference on Computer Vision and Pattern Recognition, pp. 3431–3440 (2015)
28. Mayer, N., et al.: A large dataset to train convolutional networks for disparity, optical flow, and scene flow estimation. In: Proceedings of the IEEE Conference on Computer Vision and Pattern Recognition, pp. 4040–4048 (2016)
29. Mourikis, A.I., Roumeliotis, S.I.: A multi-state constraint kalman filter for vision-aided inertial navigation. In: IEEE International Conference on Robotics and Automation, pp. 3565–3572. IEEE (2007)
30. Mur-Artal, R., Montiel, J.M.M., Tardos, J.D.: Orb-slam: a versatile and accurate monocular slam system. IEEE Trans. Robot. **31**(5), 1147–1163 (2015)
31. Mur-Artal, R., Tardós, J.D.: Orb-slam2: An open-source slam system for monocular, stereo, and rgb-d cameras. IEEE Trans. Robot. **33**(5), 1255–1262 (2017)
32. Newcombe, R.A., Lovegrove, S.J., Davison, A.J.: Dtam: Dense tracking and mapping in real-time. In: IEEE International Conference on Computer Vision (ICCV), pp. 2320–2327. IEEE (2011)
33. Odena, A., Dumoulin, V., Olah, C.: Deconvolution and checkerboard artifacts. Distill (2016). https://doi.org/10.23915/distill.00003, http://distill.pub/2016/deconv-checkerboard
34. Pang, J., Sun, W., Ren, J., Yang, C., Yan, Q.: Cascade residual learning: A two-stage convolutional neural network for stereo matching. In: International Conference on Computer Vision-Workshop on Geometry Meets Deep Learning (ICCVW 2017), vol. 3 (2017)
35. Pizzoli, M., Forster, C., Scaramuzza, D.: Remode: Probabilistic, monocular dense reconstruction in real time. In: IEEE International Conference on Robotics and Automation (ICRA), pp. 2609–2616. IEEE (2014)
36. Saxena, A., Chung, S.H., Ng, A.Y.: Learning depth from single monocular images. In: Advances in Neural Information Processing Systems, pp. 1161–1168 (2006)
37. Strasdat, H., Montiel, J., Davison, A.J.: Scale drift-aware large scale monocular SLAM. Robotics: Science and Systems VI 2 (2010)

38. Sturm, J., Engelhard, N., Endres, F., Burgard, W., Cremers, D.: A benchmark for the evaluation of RGB-D slam systems. In: IEEE/RSJ International Conference on Intelligent Robots and Systems (IROS), pp. 573–580. IEEE (2012)
39. Tateno, K., Tombari, F., Laina, I., Navab, N.: Cnn-slam: Real-time dense monocular slam with learned depth prediction. arXiv preprint arXiv:1704.03489 (2017)
40. Wang, R., Schwörer, M., Cremers, D.: Stereo dso: Large-scale direct sparse visual odometry with stereo cameras. In: International Conference on Computer Vision (ICCV). Venice, Italy, October 2017
41. Wang, S., Clark, R., Wen, H., Trigoni, N.: Deepvo: Towards end-to-end visual odometry with deep recurrent convolutional neural networks. In: IEEE International Conference on Robotics and Automation (ICRA), pp. 2043–2050. IEEE (2017)
42. Wang, Z., Bovik, A.C., Sheikh, H.R., Simoncelli, E.P.: Image quality assessment: from error visibility to structural similarity. IEEE Trans. Image Process. **13**(4), 600–612 (2004)
43. Woodford, O., Torr, P., Reid, I., Fitzgibbon, A.: Global stereo reconstruction under second-order smoothness priors. IEEE Trans. Pattern Anal. Mach. Intell. **31**(12), 2115–2128 (2009)
44. Xie, J., Girshick, R., Farhadi, A.: Deep3D: Fully automatic 2D-to-3D video conversion with deep convolutional neural networks. In: Leibe, B., Matas, J., Sebe, N., Welling, M. (eds.) ECCV 2016. LNCS, vol. 9908, pp. 842–857. Springer, Cham (2016). https://doi.org/10.1007/978-3-319-46493-0_51
45. Yang, N., Wang, R., Gao, X., Cremers, D.: Challenges in monocular visual odometry: photometric calibration, motion bias and rolling shutter effect. IEEE Robot. Autom. Lett. (RA-L) **3**, 2878–2885 (2018). https://doi.org/10.1109/LRA.2018.2846813
46. Yin, X., Wang, X., Du, X., Chen, Q.: Scale recovery for monocular visual odometry using depth estimated with deep convolutional neural fields. In: Proceedings of the IEEE Conference on Computer Vision and Pattern Recognition, pp. 5870–5878 (2017)
47. Zhao, H., Gallo, O., Frosio, I., Kautz, J.: Is l2 a good loss function for neural networks for image processing?. ArXiv e-prints 1511 (2015)
48. Zhong, Y., Dai, Y., Li, H.: Self-supervised learning for stereo matching with self-improving ability. arXiv preprint arXiv:1709.00930 (2017)
49. Zhou, T., Brown, M., Snavely, N., Lowe, D.G.: Unsupervised learning of depth and ego-motion from video. In: CVPR, vol. 2, p. 7 (2017)

Author Index

Printed in the United States
By Bookmasters

Printed in the United States
By Bookmasters